TRACK
RESEARCH
COMPENDIUM

Reprints of Articles
on Track Research, 1928-1980

TRANSPORTATION RESEARCH BOARD
NATIONAL RESEARCH COUNCIL

National Academy of Sciences
Washington, D.C. 1982

in cooperation with
AMERICAN RAILWAY ENGINEERING ASSOCIATION

TRACK RESEARCH COMPENDIUM
Price $45.00

Published by
Transportation Research Board
2101 Constitution Avenue, N.W.
Washington, DC 20418

Library of Congress Cataloging
    in Publication Data
Track Research Compendium
    1. Railroads—Track—Addresses, essays, lectures.
I. National Research Council (U.S.). Transportation
Research Board. II. American Railway Engineering
Association.
TF240.T67   1982   625.1'4   82-18961
ISBN 0-309-03366-7

Notice

This project was approved by the Governing Board of the National Research Council, whose members are drawn from the councils of the National Academy of Sciences, the National Academy of Engineering, and the Institute of Medicine. The members of the committee were chosen for their special competence and with regard for appropriate balance.

The **Transportation Research Board** is an agency of the National Research Council, which serves the National Academy of Sciences and the National Academy of Engineering. The Board's purpose is to stimulate research concerning the nature and performance of transportation systems, to disseminate information that the research produces, and to encourage the application of appropriate research findings. The Board's program is carried out by more than 270 committees, task forces, and panels composed of more than 3300 administrators, engineers, social scientists, attorneys, educators, and others concerned with transportation; they serve without compensation. The program is supported by state transportation and highway departments, the modal administrations of the U.S. Department of Transportation, the Association of American Railroads, the National Highway Traffic Safety Administration, and other organizations and individuals interested in the development of transportation.

The National Research Council was established by the National Academy of Sciences in 1916 to associate the broad community of science and technology with the Academy's purpose of furthering knowledge and of advising the federal government. The Council operates in accordance with general policies determined by the Academy under the authority of its Congressional charter, which establishes the Academy as a private, nonprofit, self-governing membership corporation. The Council has been the principal operating agency of both the National Academy of Sciences and the National Academy of Engineering in the conduct of their services to the government, the public, and the scientific and engineering communities. It is administered jointly by both Academies and the Institute of Medicine.

The National Academy of Sciences was established in 1863 by Act of Congress as a private, nonprofit, self-governing membership corporation for the furtherance of science and technology, required to advise the federal government upon request within its fields of competence. Under its corporate charter, the Academy established the National Research Council in 1916, the National Academy of Engineering in 1964, and the Institute of Medicine in 1970.

TRANSPORTATION RESEARCH BOARD

Steering Committee to Develop a
Railroad Track Engineering Compendium

Chairman
Mike Rougas, *Chief Engineer, Bessemer and Lake Erie Railroad Company, Greenville, Pennsylvania*

Members
Louis T. Cerny, *Executive Director, American Railway Engineering Association, Washington, D.C.*
William W. Hay, *Professor (Emeritus) of Civil Engineering, University of Illinois, Urbana*
Thomas B. Hutcheson, *Jacksonville, Florida*
Arnold D. Kerr, *Professor of Civil Engineering, University of Delaware, Newark*
W. Scott Lovelace, *Assistant Vice President, Engineering and Research, Southern Railway System, Washington, D.C.*
William B. O'Sullivan, *Senior Technical Advisor, Office of Research & Development, Federal Railroad Administration*
Gerald P. Raymond, *Professor of Civil Engineering, Queen's University, Kingston, Ontario, Canada*
Albert J. Reinschmidt, *Manager, Track Research, Technical Research Center, Association of American Railroads, Chicago, Illinois*
J. Frank Scott, *Research Engineer, CN Rail Research Centre, Montreal, Canada*
Marshall R. Thompson, *Professor of Civil Engineering, University of Illinois, Urbana*
George H. Way, Jr., *Assistant Vice President, Research and Test Department, Association of American Railroads, Washington, D.C.*

TRB representative
Edward J. Ward

CONTENTS

Preface

Since railroading began, the provision of safe track at minimum cost for the expected level of service has been a major engineering research priority. Research on ever-changing materials, methods, and analytical tools has been an ongoing process—as important today as it was decades ago in meeting the needs of track engineers.

The findings generated by researchers in fields related to track engineering have appeared over the years in a wide variety of publications. Some are now out of print, and others are no longer easily accessible.

One of the first attempts to fill this information void involved the reprinting of the seven reports (1304 pages) of the Special Committee on Stresses in Railroad Track that were published under the chairmanship of A.N. Talbot. Considered the most important collection of material on track, *Stresses in Railroad Track—The Talbot Reports (1918-1940)* was published by the American Railway Engineering Association (AREA) in 1980. Although the AREA volume represents a massive undertaking and an important contribution to the literature, it was recognized that many more works related to track engineering were worthy of reprinting in like manner.

With this in mind, the Transportation Research Board (TRB) of the National Research Council, in cooperation with AREA and with the support of the Federal Railroad Administration, has collected other classic track-related materials and has included them in this *Track Research Compendium.*

Due to time and space constraints, preference was given to papers that pertain to North American track maintenance and construction practice. In addition, several more recent works from the 1978 Australian Heavy Haul Conference are included because they are not generally available.

The Steering Committee responsible for the selection of the materials included in this *Compendium* also recommends the following publications in addition to those reprinted here. They are *Rail Steels, Development Processing and Use* (D.H. Stone and G.G. Knupp, eds. ASTM STP 644, Philadelphia, 1976) and *Railroad Track* (F. Fasenrath, ed. Frederich Unger, New York, 1981).

The *Track Research Compendium* is an effort to compile in a single volume those old and rare publications that have become classic and that are as pertinent to engineering needs today as when they were first written. In this spirit, the *Compendium* is offered by TRB and AREA to the practicing track engineer as a convenient reference to some of the classic "tools of the trade" and as a means to enhance the work of making and maintaining railroads as an efficient and important mode of transportation.

In using this document, readers are reminded that the older test projects dealt with in some of the articles reprinted here used instruments considered crude by today's standards. Therefore, absolute values of stresses and deformations should be viewed cautiously.

All of the texts incorporated within this compendium have been reprinted with the permission of the respective publishers. In a few cases, the reproductive quality of the original source material was inadequate and is reflected in the reprint used in this volume.

Special acknowledgment is given to the American Railway Engineering Association for its assistance and cooperation.

Special thanks also go to G. Magee, Association of American Railroads (AAR) retired, and D.H. Stone, also of AAR, for their assistance in identifying and locating papers for this project. Also acknowledged are W.S. Autrey, Sante Fe Railway; A.M. Zarembski, Speno Rail Services, formerly with AAR; and R.K. Steele, AAR, formerly with the Transportation Test Center.

Chapter I

Rail
and Rail Materials

TEXT I

AREA Proceedings, Vol. 43, 1942

III Metallurgical Tests

By R. E. CRAMER

4. Proposed Recommended Practice for the Control Cooling of Rails.—At the 1941 March meeting of the Contact committee of the Rails Investigation the following Revised Recommended Practice for Control Cooling of Rails was drawn up for consideration by the mills and railroads during the coming year.

PROPOSED RECOMMENDED PRACTICE FOR THE CONTROL COOLING OF RAILROAD RAILS

1. All rails shall be cooled in the regular way on hot beds or runways until the temperature is between 725 deg. F. and 1,000 deg. F., then charged immediately into the containers.

2. The temperature of the rails before charging shall be determined with a reliable pyrometer at the top of the rail head at least 12 in. from the end.

3. The handling of rails between the hot bed and the container and their subsequent removal shall be carefully conducted to avoid bending and to minimize cold straightening.

4. The cover shall be placed on the container immediately after completion of the charge and shall remain in place for at least 10 hours. After the removal or raising of the lid of the container no rails shall be removed until the temperature of the top layer of rails has fallen to 300 deg. F., or lower.

5. The temperature between an outside rail and the adjacent rail in the bottom tier of the container, at a point not less than 12 in., or more than 36 in., from the rail end, shall be recorded with reliable equipment. This temperature shall be the control for judging rate of cooling.

6. The container shall be so protected or insulated that the control temperature shall not drop below 300 deg. F. in 7 hours from the time that the bottom tier is placed in the container.

7. All control-cooled rails shall be hot-stamped "CC", except that control-cooled rails which are also end hardened shall be hot-stamped "CH".

Tests carried out during the past two winters on rails in mill cooling containers indicated the desirability of paying more attention to the cooling of the rails in the bottom tiers of the containers. The revised recommended practice places the control thermocouple between an outside rail and the adjacent rail, or against either rail, in the bottom tier of the container and specifies that the temperature in this location shall not drop below 300 deg. F. in 7 hours from the time the bottom tier is placed in the container.

It is recognized that this is a drastic change from the recommended practice adopted in 1937 which placed the control couple in the middle of the pile of rails in the container and specified that the temperature in this location should not drop below 300 deg. F. in 15 hours time. The representatives of the rail mills could not be expected to agree to meet this requirement until they have had time to experiment with methods of insulating their containers and of elimination of free air space at the ends of the containers and underneath the bottom tier of rails. These experiments may require nearly all of the winter of 1941–42, because the fastest cooling conditions will be encountered only during cold weather.

This situation was reported to the members of the AREA Rail Committee at their March 1941 meeting and it was explained that whatever changes the mills made should result in an improvement in the uniformity of rate of cooling of the rails in the containers. It was recommended that the railroads cooperate with the rail mills and accept rails meeting either the old recommended practice or the revised recommended practice during the winter of 1941–42. It is the plan of the members of the test party to make cooling tests of rails in the containers of several mills during the cold weather of the winter of 1941–42.

5. Mill Tests of Control Cooling of Rails Using Hydrogen-Treated Ingots.—Further experiments were made at two rail mills to gather information on the effect of control cooling on the development of shatter cracks in rails. In both cases all the tests of specimens were made in the steel mill laboratories and the members of the Rails Investigation were only observers of the tests, as this investigation no longer employs sufficient shop help to permit the slicing and etching of large numbers of test specimens at the laboratory.

6. Tests to Determine the Temperature and Manner of Growth of Shatter Cracks in Steel Rails.—The members of the test party of the Rails Investigation were invited to help plan and observe part of a series of tests made in 1940 and early in 1941 at the Gary rail mill by Mr. H. B. Wishart and Mr. E. P. Epler. The results of these tests were presented as a paper (Preprint No. 52) at the 1941 convention of the American Society for Metals. The following paragraphs are taken from this paper by permission of that society.

Tests 1 and 2.—Rails from Heat Numbers 85128 and 83263 were used in these tests. The ingots from both heats were treated with 20 cu. ft. of hydrogen. Only 10 specimens were used from each heat. After cutting at the hot saws the specimens were cooled in still air to temperatures of 500, 400, 300, 200, 100 and 70 deg. F. Upon reaching these temperatures, the specimens were immediately placed in a furnace at 700 deg. F. for at least 7 hours, then slow-cooled over a period of 10 hours. This temperature of 700 deg. F. and the method of cooling have been found in previous tests to completely prevent any further formation of shatter cracks in rails. Also specimens from each heat were held at 70 deg. F. for 2, 4, and 6 hours before being placed in the 700 deg. F. furnace. In each test a control specimen which was a crop end from the rails was

TABLE 4
TESTS 1 AND 2—COOLING TEMPERATURES, HOLDING TIMES AND ETCH TEST RESULTS OF RAIL SPECIMENS

Rail Specimen No.	Temperature Deg. F. Rail Specimen Cooled in Still Air	Time Held Before Placing in Furnace at 700 Deg. F. Hours	Shatter Cracks on 6-in. Specimen			
			Heat 85128		Heat 83263	
			Long.*	Trans.**	Long.*	Trans.**
500	500	0	0	0	0	0
400	400	0	0	0	0	0
300	300	0	0	0	0	0
200	200	0	0	0	0	0
100	100	0	7	1	5	0
70–0	70	0	30	8	25	6
70–2	70	2	50	9	43	7
70–4	70	4	56	8	48	5
70–6	70	6	67	14	55	12
Crop End	Cooled in Air	72 hours	78	27	69	18

* Longitudinal.
** Transverse.

cooled on the mill floor for 72 hours to represent the sensitivity of the steel to the development of shatter cracks.

To determine the presence of shatter cracks, a longitudinal slice 6 in. long and ⅞ in. below the top of the rail head was cut from each specimen. These slices were ground smooth, etched in hot 1–1 hydrochloric acid and examined for shatter cracks with low-power magnifying glasses. The number of longitudinal and transverse cracks found in each specimen is recorded in Table 4, while photographs of representative specimens are shown in Figs. 9 and 10, at approximately half natural size. The photographs are especially interesting because they show the increase in size of the shatter cracks as the specimens cooled to lower temperatures or remained at room temperature for increased periods of time before being placed in the 700 deg. F. furnace. This series of pictures furnishes very good evidence that the cracks gradually increase both in number and size with time. In the past there has been considerable discussion whether such cracks formed suddenly or grew gradually. This experiment also shows that for the particular steel used in these tests the shatter cracks began to develop in the rails while they were cooling between 200 and 100 deg. F.

Tests 3 and 4.—These experiments were designed to determine more completely the effect of holding specimens for varying lengths of time at temperatures between 400 and 100 deg. F. to ascertain if increased holding time at relatively low temperatures would allow the formation of shatter cracks. Further information was gained by using steels of different sensitivity to cracking, by varying the amount of hydrogen used in treating the ingots.

About 60 rail specimens, one foot in length, from Heats 51106 and 54007 were used. These were trucked while still at temperatures above 700 deg. F. to the mill heat treating department. In working with steel which may develop shatter cracks all experiments must be made while the specimens are cooling after rolling. Two electric furnaces and three steam heated water tanks were previously heated to the holding temperatures

(text continued on page 623)

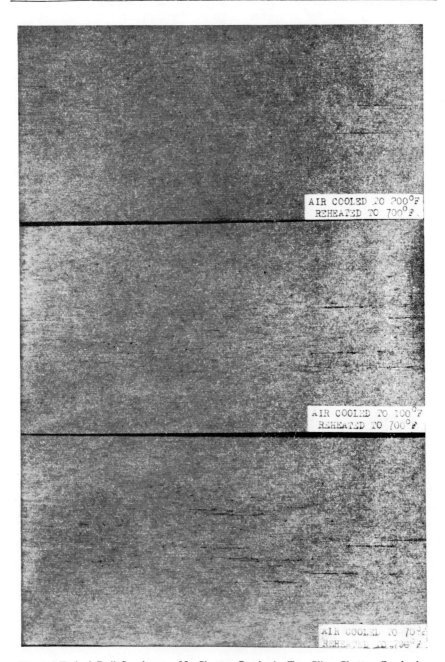

Fig. 9.—Etched Rail Specimens—No Shatter Cracks in Top Slice, Shatter Cracks in
Bottom Two Slices.
Etched in hot 1–1 hydrochloric acid.

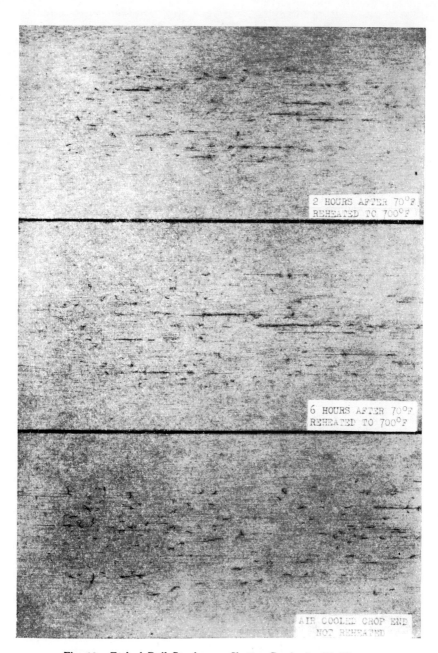

Fig. 10.—Etched Rail Specimens—Shatter Cracks in All Slices.
Etched in hot 1–1 hydrochloric acid.

TABLE 5

TEST 3—NUMBER OF SHATTER CRACKS IN SIX-INCH SLICE FROM RAIL HEADS

Heat 54007, Ingot 7—40 Cu. Ft. Hydrogen

Time in Hours Rail Specimen Held at Temp.	Method of Cooling	Holding Temperatures									
		100 deg. F.		150 deg. F.		200 deg. F.		250 deg. F.		300 deg. F.	
		L*	T**	L*	T**	L*	T**	L*	T**	L*	T**
0	Furnace†	113	9	18	3	8	0	0	0	0	0
2	Furnace†	80	7	96	7	58	3	28	0	4	0
4	Furnace†	92	5	74	6	45	1	24	0	9	0
6	Furnace†	97	4	68	5	74	3	25	0	13	0
8	Furnace†	120	13	72	6	70	0	22	0	22	0
10	Furnace†	103	9	83	6	65	3	25	0	20	0
0	Air‡	210	10	210	10	210	10	210	10	210	10
2	Air‡	52	3	70	6	62	0	25	0	24	0
4	Air‡	95	3	75	6	60	2	10	0	36	0
6	Air‡	73	7	90	8	80	7	9	0	26	0
8	Air‡	104	9	90	5	50	3	21	0	10	0
10	Air‡	72	7	60	8	60	6	20	1	15	0

* Longitudinal cracks.
** Transverse cracks.
† Specimens reheated to 700 deg. F. after holding at given temperature.
‡ Specimens air cooled after holding at given temperature.

(text continued from page 619)

shown in Tables 5 and 6. The rail specimens were spread out evenly over the shop floor to cool to the holding temperatures. When a group of 11 specimens reached each holding temperature, 10 of them were put in a furnace or water tank at that temperature and one was placed in a reheating furnace operating at 700 deg. F. At two-hour intervals, up to 10 hours, two specimens were removed from each furnace or tank and one specimen cooled in air while the other was placed in the 700 deg. F. reheating furnace. This furnace was operated at temperatures for 7 hours after the last specimen was placed in it and then slow-cooled over a period of 10 hours.

Tables 5 and 6 give the holding temperatures and time of holding for each specimen together with the number of longitudinal and transverse shatter cracks found in a 6-in. slice from each specimen. It will be noted that the control specimen for each test is the specimen held zero hours and cooled in air. The ingot of Heat No. 54007 was treated with 40 cu. ft. of hydrogen which produced 210 longitudinal and 10 transverse shatter cracks in the control specimen, while only 25 cu. ft. of hydrogen was used in the ingot of Heat No. 51106, producing 82 longitudinal and 14 transverse shatter cracks in the control specimen. This difference in the crack sensitivity of the two heats of steel explains why all the furnace cooled specimens of Heat No. 54007 held 2 hours or longer at 300 deg. F. developed shatter cracks while no shatter cracks developed in the specimens from Heat No. 51106, held at this same temperature up to 10 hours and furnace cooled.

It will be further observed from Table 5 that the specimen treated with 40 cu. ft. of hydrogen developed a few shatter cracks when cooled to 200 deg. F. and immediately reheated, and another specimen held at 300 deg. F. for only 2 hours developed a few cracks. The tests also show in Table 6 that holding rails treated with 25 cu. ft. of hydrogen at either 400 deg. F. or 300 deg. F. for 6 hours, followed by cooling in air was sufficient treatment to prevent the formation of shatter cracks.

Conclusions.—The following general conclusions can be drawn from these experiments:

1. Shatter cracks develop gradually both in size and number in shatter-sensitive carbon steel rails as they are allowed to cool between the range of 400 and 70 deg. F. The temperature at which shatter cracks were initially observed depended upon the sensitivity of the steel and the manner in which the rails were cooled through this temperature range.

2. Shatter crack development continues after the rails reach room temperature and are held at this temperature for increasing periods of time.

3. Conclusions 1 and 2 apply only to shatter-sensitive air-cooled rails which are not control-cooled or held between temperatures of 1,200 deg. F. to 400 deg. F. for lengths of time sufficient to properly eliminate shatter sensitivity.

4. The temperature at which shatter cracks begin to form and the amount of retarded cooling required to prevent their formation depend on the sensitivity of the steel to the development of shatter cracks.

All these tests give further confidence in the revised recommended practice for control cooling of rails and indicate that the requirements seem adequate to prevent the formation of shatter cracks in all regular production rails.

7. Failed Rails Sent to the Laboratory for Examination.—Special reports have been written on a considerable number of failed rails, and sent to Mr. W. C. Barnes for the rail failure statistics and to the railroads supplying the rails.

A

TABLE 6

TEST 4—NUMBER OF SHATTER CRACKS IN SIX-INCH SLICE FROM RAIL HEADS

Heat 51105, Ingot 4—25 Cu. Ft. Hydrogen

Time in Hours Rail Specimen Held at Temp.	Method of Cooling	Holding Temperature									
		100 deg. F.		*150 deg. F.*		*200 deg. F.*		*300 deg. F.*		*400 deg. F.*	
		L*	T**	L*	T**	L*	T**	L*	T**	L*	T**
0	Furnace†	8	1	1	0	0	0	0	0	0	0
2	Furnace†	45	4	2	0	3	0	0	0	0	0
4	Furnace†	43	2	40	0	8	0	0	0	0	0
6	Furnace†	50	2	15	0	14	0	0	0	0	0
8	Furnace†	27	1	12	0	20	0	0	0	0	0
10	Furnace†	25	0	23	0	27	0	0	0	0	0
0	Air‡	82	14	82	14	82	14	82	14	82	14
2	Air‡	30	0	28	2	40	4	40	6	29	1
4	Air‡	15	0	28	3	30	3	24	0	4	0
6	Air‡	55	7	19	0	20	2	0	0	0	0
8	Air‡	25	2	15	1	25	1	0	0	0	0
10	Air‡	20	0	10	0	15	0	0	0	0	0

* Longitudinal cracks.
** Transverse cracks.
† Specimens reheated to 700 deg. F. after holding at given temperature.
‡ Specimens air cooled after holding at given temperature.

Several rails examined had failed by gage corner shelling, being the high rails of sharp curves. It was found that fatigue cracks causing the shelling had started inside the rail heads and spread to the gage sides on many different levels. This loosened pieces of the head on the gage side which subsequently dropped out causing a rough surface on the tread. Hardness tests indicated that severe cold working by car wheels had exhausted the ductility of the rail steel, causing internal fatigue cracks. These cracks started about ⅛ in. below the surface and from ½ to 1 in. from the gage side of the head and progressed mostly toward the gage side. The contact of wheels and rail on sharp curves apparently produces conditions of stress much more severe than on tangent track, and these severe conditions produce internal fatigue cracks. This type of rail failure would require considerable study to find the best solution. This may involve consideration of the radius of the gage corners of rails, the radius between flange and tread of wheels, the canting and superelevation of the rails on the curves, or the composition of the rail steel.

Other failed rails examined included the transverse and compound fissures developed from blow holes in control-cooled rails and one transverse fissure which started at a spot where the rail had been built up by welding, as described in the following section.

IV Control-Cooled and Brunorized Rails in Service

By R. E. CRAMER

8. Service Record of Control-Cooled Rails.—Six years have elapsed since the first control-cooled rails for use on railroads in the United States were made and sold under contract. Mr. W. C. Barnes, engineer of tests for the AREA Rail Committee reports that up to June 30, 1941, 3,863,372 tons of control-cooled rails had been purchased by railroads in the United States.

At the time this report is being written, November 15, 1941, only seven transverse fissures and four compound fissures have been reported and verified in this tonnage of control-cooled rails. Only two of the transverse-fissured rails showed any shatter cracks on etch testing, and none of the compound-fissured rails showed shatter cracks.

Both of the control-cooled rails which developed transverse fissures and showed shatter cracks on etching were from the same mill and were rolled during December 1936 and March 1937, respectively. This was during the first year when that mill made control-cooled rails under contract. At that time the control-cooled practice at that mill was not the best, but was greatly improved during the second year of production by the use of tight fitting lids on the cooling containers in place of a cover merely resting on the container; and it is significant that these rails were placed, one in the top layer in the container and the other in the next to the top layer. Since 1936 all the rail mills in the United States have improved the insulation of their control-cooling containers.

Of the other five transverse fissures which have developed in control-cooled rails, two developed from blow holes, two from slag inclusions near the tread of the rail, and the remaining fissure developed from a welded area where a worn spot, probably a wheel burn, had been built up by welding. The compound fissures both started from blow holes near the tread of the rail.

It seems probable that other control-cooled rails produced during the first year of manufacture under contract may develop transverse or compound fissures in service, nevertheless the six-year record of control-cooled rails seems distinctly good. It is believed that the improvements being made by the mills to prepare their cooling container to meet the new "Recommended Practice for Control Cooling of Rails" now being considered for adoption will offer an even greater degree of security against the presence of shatter cracks in control-cooled rails.

Summing up the performance of control-cooled rails it is evident that control cooling has very greatly reduced fissures which can be charged against shatter cracks. Probably a few control-cooled rails will develop fissures, compound and transverse from blow holes, large slag inclusions, etc., near the tread of the rail and, perhaps, from built-up welded spots on the surface of the head of the rail. At least one faulty method of control cooling has been corrected, and insulation practice has been improved by all rail mills.

9. **Service Record of Brunorized Rails.**—In September 1941 Mr. Barnes' records showed that there were 140,251 tons of Brunorized (normalized) rail in service. During the past 11 months only 2 further fissures have been reported in the Old Process Brunorized rails. The improved Brunorizing process was put into use in April 1938, and no fissures have been reported in rails made under the improved Brunorizing process, which includes holding rails for several hours at a temperature above that at which shatter cracks will develop, after they have been rolled, and before entering the Brunorizing furnace.

Zur Wirkung von Wasserstoff in Schienenstahl und Möglichkeiten einer wasserstoffarmen Erschmelzung

Von Wilhelm Heller, Lutz Weber, Peter Hammerschmid und Reinhard Schweitzer in Rheinhausen

Mitteilung aus dem Qualitätswesen der Fried. Krupp Hüttenwerke AG, Werk Rheinhausen

Erzeugung einzelner Blöcke aus Schienenstahl mit unterschiedlichen Wasserstoffgehalten. Metallographisch geführter Nachweis der Flockenbildung an Seigerungsstreifen und nichtmetallischen Einschlüssen. Abhängigkeit des für die Flockenbildung kritischen Wasserstoffgehaltes vom Mangangehalt. Kritische Wasserstoffgehalte der verschiedenen Schienenstahlsorten. Einfluß des Schwefelgehaltes auf die Flockenanfälligkeit. Ermittlung der Flockenempfindlichkeit durch Auslagerungsversuche. Beeinflussung der mechanischen Eigenschaften durch die Wasserstoffversprödung. Maßnahmen zur wasserstoffarmen Erschmelzung von Schienenstählen.

On the effect of hydrogen in rail steel and the possibilities of hydrogen-depressing melting operations

Production of some ingots of rail steel having different water contents. Metallographical evidence of flake formation at segregation lines and non-metallic inclusions. Dependence of the water content critical for flake formation on the manganese content. Critical hydrogen contents of the different rail steel grades. Effect of the sulphur content on the susceptibility to flake formation. Determination of the susceptibility to flake formation by holding tests. The effect of hydrogen embrittlement on the mechanical properties. Measures for the low-hydrogen melting of rail steels.

Les effets de l'hydrogène dans l'acier pour rails. Possibilités d'élaboration d'aciers pauvres en hydrogène. Production de quelques lingots d'aciers pour rails à différentes teneurs en hydrogène. Vérification métallographique de la formation de flocons sur les lignes de ségrégations et les inclusions non métalliques. Relation entre la teneur en manganèse et la teneur critique en hydrogène pour l'apparition des flocons. Teneurs critiques en hydrogène des différentes sortes d'aciers pour rails. Influence de la teneur en soufre sur la tendance aux flocons. Détermination de la susceptibilité à la formation de flocons par essais de stockage. Influence de la fragilisation par l'hydrogène sur les caractéristiques mécaniques. Mesures à prendre pour l'élaboration d'aciers pour rails pauvres en hydrogène.

In Europa kommt den in den Technischen Lieferbedingungen 860 des Internationalen Eisenbahnverbandes (UIC) vorgesehenen naturharten Schienengüten wegen der großen Erzeugungsmengen besondere Bedeutung zu. Wie *Tafel 1* zu entnehmen ist, gibt es eine Regelgüte mit 690 N/mm² und drei verschleißfeste Güten mit 880 N/mm² Mindestzugfestigkeit. Die Schienen der Regelgüte sind perlitisch mit geringen Ferritanteilen, die verschleißfesten Güten haben

In Europe, the rail steel grades in the as-rolled condition as covered by Technical Supply Specification 860 of the International Railway Association (UIC) are of special significance in view of the high production tonnages involved. As *table 1* shows, there is a standard grade with 690 N/mm² and three wear-resisting grades with 880 N/mm² minimum tensile strength. The standard-grade rails are pearlitic with small amounts of ferrite, and the wear-resisting grades

Tafel 1. Chemische Zusammensetzung und Mindestzugfestigkeit von naturharten Schienenstählen
Table 1. Chemical composition and minimum tensile strength of rail steels in the as-rolled condition

Stahlsorte Steel grade	Chemische Zusammensetzung Chemical composition						Mindestzugfestigkeit Minimum tensile strength
	% C	% Si	% Mn	% P	% S	% Cr	N/mm²
Regelgüte	0,40 — 0.60	≦0,35	0,80 — 1,20	≦0,05	≦0,05	—	690
Verschleißfeste Güten Wear-resisting grades							
A	0,60 — 0,75	≦0,50	0,80 — 1,30	≦0,05	≦0,05	—	880
B	0,50 — 0,70	≦0,50	1,30 — 1,70	≦0,05	≦0,05	—	880
C	0,45 — 0,65	≦0,40	1,70 — 2,10	≦0,03	≦0,03	—	880
Sondergüte Chrom-Mangan-Stahl Special grade chromium-manganese steel	0,65 — 0,80	0,50 — 0,90	0,80 — 1,20	≦0,03	≦0,03	0,70 — 1,10	1 080

im allgemeinen ein rein perlitisches Gefüge. Für besondere Anwendungsfälle wird in Rheinhausen noch eine Sondergüte aus Chrom-Mangan-Stahl mit einer erhöhten Mindestzugfestigkeit von 1080 N/mm² erzeugt, die ebenfalls ein eutektoides Gefüge aufweist, das gegenüber verschleißfesten Güten jedoch feinkörniger und feinlamellarer ausgebildet ist.

Während die Erzeugung von Schienen der Regelgüte bezüglich des Wasserstoffs im allgemeinen keine Probleme aufwirft, lassen frühere amerikanische Erfahrungen an Schienen, mit höherem Kohlenstoffgehalt und einer um etwa 100 N/mm² höheren Festigkeit erwarten, daß bei der Erzeugung verschleißfester Schienengüten nach UIC 860 und

generally have a purely pearlitic structure. For special applications, a further special grade is produced in Rheinhausen using chrome-manganese steel. This grade has an increased minimum tensile strength of 1080 N/mm² and also has a eutectoid structure. Compared with the wear-resisting grades, however, this structure exhibits a finer grain and finer laminations.

Hydrogen normally poses no problems in the production of standard-grade rails. However, previous experience in America with rails having a higher carbon content and also a higher tensile strength (plus approx. 100 N/mm²) indicates that particular attention must be paid to the effect of hydrogen during the production of wear-resisting rail grades

von noch höherfesten Sondergüten der Einfluß des Wasserstoffes besonders zu beachten ist. Wasserstoff kann die Bildung von Flocken im Schienenkopf verursachen, aus denen sich im Laufe der Zeit unter der Betriebsbeanspruchung die wegen ihrer Form als Nierenbrüche bezeichneten Dauerbrüche entwickeln *(Bild 1)*.

Umfangreiche Untersuchungen in den USA[1] bestätigen den Zusammenhang zwischen Wasserstoff und Flocken[2] und zeigen, daß sich Flocken zwischen 200 und 20 °C bilden. Sie können jedoch durch eine verzögerte Abkühlung im Temperaturbereich von 370 bis 150 °C vermieden werden. Diese Erkenntnisse haben zur Vorschrift der verzögerten Abkühlung von Schienen in der Norm A 1-65 der American Society for Testing and Materials geführt.

In Europa hat die Frage des Wasserstoffgehaltes bei Schienen erst mit der Erzeugung der verschleißfesten Schienengüten Bedeutung erlangt. Zur Vermeidung von Flocken werden außer einem verzögerten Abkühlen auch die Verfahren der Vakuumentgasung des flüssigen Stahles[3] und einer wasserstoffarmen Erschmelzung[4] angewandt.

Bei der Erzeugung der verschleißfesten Schienen und der Sondergüte machten wir in Rheinhausen die Beobachtung, daß die verschiedenen Güten eine unterschiedliche Neigung zur Bildung von Flocken aufweisen. Durch die folgenden Untersuchungen sollen die bestehenden Zusammenhänge aufgezeigt werden. Abschließend wird über die neueren Erfahrungen bei der wasserstoffarmen Erschmelzung im Elektro-Lichtbogenofen und nach dem Sauerstoffblasverfahren berichtet.

Ermittlung der zur Flockenbildung führenden Wasserstoffgehalte

Die für die Flockenbildung bei den einzelnen Schienenstählen kritischen Wasserstoffgehalte wurden an Schienen ermittelt, die im normalen Erzeugungsgang gewalzt worden sind. Dazu wurden Einzelblöcke mit höheren Wasserstoffgehalten steigend vergossen, um größere Ausfälle durch Flocken zu vermeiden. Die Einstellung der höheren Wasserstoffgehalte erfolgte durch Zugabe von Calciumhydrid (CaH$_2$) in gekörnter Form über den Gießtrichter.

Die Proben aus dem Gießstrahl wurden in die Kupferkokille[5] gegossen und in Wasser abgeschreckt. Proben aus den Schienen wurden der Schienenkopfmitte entnommen. Sämtliche Proben wurden bis zur Ermittlung des Wasserstoffgehaltes unter flüssigem Stickstoff aufbewahrt.

Die Proben wurden 30 min bei 600 °C bei einem Druck von 10^{-4} Torr ausgelagert. Der effundierte Wasserstoff wurde anschließend durch chromatographische Gasanalyse ermittelt. Die angegebenen Wasserstoffgehalte sind Mittelwerte aus mindestens zwei Parallelproben. Alle Werte wurden auf das Volumen bei 0 °C bei Normaldruck umgerechnet; sie werden in dieser Arbeit in cm^3 H$_2$/100 g Stahl angegeben.

Zur Feststellung von Flocken wurde eine Ultraschallprüfung mit 4 MHz durchgeführt. Dabei werden zwei in einem Prüfroller eingebaute Prüfköpfe mit getrenntem Sender- und Empfängerteil über eine Schienenkopfseite geführt, weil auf diese Weise die Flocken wegen ihrer bevorzugten Orientierung (kleiner Winkel zwischen Rißfläche und Symmetrieebene) am besten zu erfassen sind. Die Empfindlichkeit des Prüfgerätes wird so eingestellt, daß Ungänzen mit einem Ersatzfehlerdurchmesser von 2 mm noch erfaßt werden. Die auf diese Weise angezeigten Fehler wurden metallographisch auf Flocken untersucht.

[1] Heller, W.: Stahl u. Eisen 81 (1961) S. 200/02.
[2] Bennek, H., H. Schenck u. H. Müller: Stahl u. Eisen 55 (1935) S. 321/31 u. 4 Taf.
[3] Siekbert, A., u. P. Schwarzfischer: Techn. Mitt. Krupp, Werksber., 23 (1965) S. 117/24.
[4] Reinders, F., u. W. Heller: Stahl u. Eisen 90 (1970) S. 1489/96.
[5] Stetter, A.: Arch. Eisenhüttenwes. 29 (1958) S. 401/10; s. bes. S. 408/09.

to UIC 860 and special grades with higher tensile strength values. Hydrogen can lead to the formation of flakes in the rail head. In the course of time and under the operational loads imposed on the rail, these flakes lead to the development of transverse fissure failures as shown in *figure 1*, designated because of their shape as nodular fractures.

Extensive investigations in the USA[1] confirmed the connection between hydrogen and flakes[2]. They revealed that flakes are formed between 200 and 20 °C, but also that

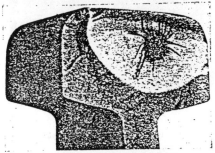

Bild 1. Nierenbruch durch Flocke verursacht
Figure 1. Shatter crack caused by a flake

they can be suppressed by delayed cooling in the 370 to 150 °C temperature range. These findings resulted in the regulation covering the delayed cooling of rail steels in Standard A 1-65 of the American Society for Testing and Materials.

In Europe, the question of the hydrogen content of rail steels did not attain significance until the production of wear-resisting rail grades was commenced. To prevent the formation of flakes, vacuum degassing[3] and hydrogen-depressing melting operations[4] are used in addition to delayed cooling.

During the production of wear-resisting rails and the special grades in Rheinhausen, we observed that the tendency to flake formation varies between the different grades. The investigations undertaken to determine the causes are described in this report, which then continues with an account of recent experience gained in hydrogen-depressing melting operations in the electric arc furnace and the top-blown oxygen converter.

Determination of the hydrogen content resulting in flake formation

The critical hydrogen contents for the formation of flakes in the various rail steels were established using rails rolled in conformity with standard practice. Single ingots with higher hydrogen contents were bottom-poured to restrict rejects through flakes. The higher hydrogen contents were adjusted by adding calcium hydride (CaH$_2$) in granular form via the pouring funnel.

The specimens taken from the pouring stream were cast into the copper mould[5] and quenched in water. Specimens from the rails were taken from the centre of the rail head. All specimens were kept under liquid nitrogen until the hydrogen content was determined.

The test specimens were held at 600 °C under a negative pressure of 10^{-4} Torr for a period of 30 min. The escaped hydrogen was then measured using chromatographic gas analysis. The stated hydrogen contents are average values based on at least two parallel specimens. All values were recalculated for normal pressure volume; they are indicated in this paper in cm^3 H$_2$/100 g steel.

Die kennzeichnende Lage der Flocken im Schienenquerschnitt zeigt *Bild 2*. Eine weitergehende metallographische Untersuchung ergab, daß die Flocken bei allen Güten in Seigerungsstreifen (Schattenstreifen) liegen oder von

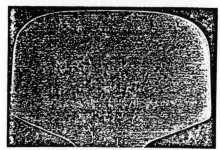

Bild 2. Flocken im Schienenkopf
Figure 2. Flakes in the rail head

ihnen ausgehen. In *Bild 3* sind an einem Querschliff aus dem Schienenkopf als kennzeichnende Beispiele zwei Flocken im ungeätzten Zustand und nach einer Primärgefügeätzung gezeigt. Die hellen Bereiche im unteren Bildteil sind die Durchstoßpunkte von Seigerungsstreifen. Treten nur vereinzelt Seigerungsstreifen auf, so sind die Flocken meist jeweils auf einen einzelnen Streifen beschränkt (*Bild 3*, rechts). Bei einer örtlichen Anhäufung von Seigerungsstreifen erstrecken sich die Flocken über einen größeren Bereich (*Bild 3*, links). Diese Aussage gilt für die kritischen Grenzwasserstoffgehalte. Bei höheren Wasserstoffgehalten kann die Flockenbildung auch in seigerungsfreien Bereichen erfolgen. Während bei den Güten A, B und dem Chrom-Mangan-Stahl die Seigerungsstreifen noch perlitisch umgewandelt waren, trat bei der Güte C in den Seigerungsstreifen vorwiegend Martensit auf.

Bei Vorliegen grober nichtmetallischer Einschlüsse können diese auch Ausgangspunkte von Flocken sein. *Bild 4* zeigt als Beispiel einen silicatischen Einschluß, von dem eine Flocke ausgeht. In solchen Fällen reichen geringere Wasserstoffgehalte als bei Schienen mit gutem Reinheitsgrad zur Bildung von Flocken aus.

Über Seigerungsstreifen oder gesigerte Bereiche und oxydische Einschlüsse sowie martensitisch umgewandelte Gefügeteile als bevorzugte Orte für die Flockenbildung ist oft berichtet worden [6] bis [10]). Die vorliegenden Ergebnisse stimmen mit dem Schrifttum überein.

In *Bild 5* sind die Ergebnisse der Wasserstoffuntersuchung an Schienen der laufenden Erzeugung und den mit Wasserstoff angereicherten Schienen für die drei verschleißfesten Güten in Abhängigkeit vom Mangangehalt zusammengestellt.

Der Ultraschallbefund ist mit angegeben. Offene Kreise kennzeichnen flockenfreie Schmelzen, ausgefüllte Kreise Schmelzen mit Flocken. Das schraffierte Feld beschreibt den Bereich, in dem mit der Bildung von Flocken zu rechnen ist. Die untere Begrenzung des Feldes gibt die kritischen Wasserstoffgehalte an, bei deren Überschreiten Flocken auftreten können. Dem Bild ist zu entnehmen, daß die

[6]) Cramer, R. E.: Trans. Amer. Soc. Metals 25 (1937) S. 923/34.
[7]) Houdremont, E., u. H. Schrader: Stahl u. Eisen 61 (1941) S. 619/53 u. 671/80. — Bennek, H., u. G. Klotzbach: Techn. Mitt. Krupp, A: Forsch.-Ber., 4 (1941) S. 47/66.
[8]) Houdremont, E.: Handbuch der Sonderstahlkunde. 3. Aufl. Bd. 2. Berlin/Göttingen/Heidelberg u. Düsseldorf 1956. S. 1375/90.
[9]) Scott, T. E., u. A. R. Troiano: J. Metals 11 (1959) S. 619/22.
[10]) Laizner, H.: Berg- u. hüttenm. Mh. 113 (1968) S. 93/104.

Flake detection was carried out by ultrasonic examination at 4 MHz. Here, two test heads built into a roller and featuring separate transmitter and receiver sections were guided along the side of the rail head, this being the best way to detect flakes in view of their preferred orientation (small angle between projection area and plane of symmetry). The sensitivity of the ultrasonic testing apparatus was adjusted to detect defects with diameters of down to 2 mm. The defects found in this way were examined metallographically for flakes.

Figure 2 shows the characteristic location of the flakes in the rail cross-section. A more detailed metallograhic examination showed that in all grades the flakes lie in segregation lines (ghost lines) or emanate from them. *Figure 3* shows as a characteristic example a cross-sectional

Bild 3. Flocken und Seigerungsstreifen
Figure 3. Flakes and segregation lines

micrograph of the rail head with two flakes before etching and after etching of the primary structure. The light areas in the lower section of the micrograph are the penetration points of segregation lines. Where segregation lines are isolated, the flakes are usually limited to a single segregation line, as shown on the right of *figure 3*. With a high local incidence of segregation lines, the flakes cover a wider area (*figure 3*, left). This applies to the critical hydrogen contents.

Bild 4. Flocke und grober nichtmetallischer Einschluß
Figure 4. Flake and coarse non-metallic inclusion

With higher hydrogen contents, flake formation can also take place in areas free from segregation. Whereas in Grades A and B and chrome-manganese steel the segregation lines were still pearlitic, martensite was predominant in the segregation lines of Grade C.

Where coarse non-metallic inclusions are present, these can form the points of origin of flakes. *Figure 4* shows by way of an example a silicate inclusion from which a flake starts. In such cases, lower contents of hydrogen suffice for flake formation than is true of rails with a high degree of cleanness.

Numerous reports have been published[6] to [10]) on segregation lines or segrated areas, oxide inclusions, and marten-

Stahl u. Eisen 92 1972)
Nr. 19. 14. September *On the effect of hydrogen in rail steel and the possibilities of hydrogen-depressing melting operations*

kritischen Wasserstoffgehalte mit steigendem Mangangehalt abnehmen.

Bei der in *Bild 5* nicht berücksichtigten Sondergüte wurden in 6 Versuchen Wasserstoffgehalte zwischen 2,9 und 3,1 cm³/100 g Stahl eingestellt, ohne daß Flocken auftraten. Diese Güte kann deshalb in ihrer Empfindlichkeit gegen

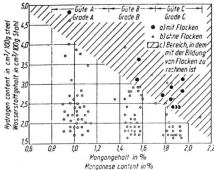

a) flake affected; b) flake free; c) area where flake formation is to be expected

Bild 5. Auftreten von Flocken in Abhängigkeit vom Mangangehalt bei verschleißfesten Schienenstählen

Figure 5. Occurrence of flakes as a function of Mn content in wear-resistant rail steels

sitic areas as preferred locations for flake formation. The results of these investigations coincide with the findings given in the above reports.

Figure 5 summarizes the results of the hydrogen investigations made on normal production rails and rails enriched with hydrogen in respect of the three grades as a function of the manganese contents.

The ultrasonic diagnosis is also given: the white circles denote heats free from flakes, the dark circles heats with flakes. The hatched area indicates the region in which flake formation is to be expected. The lower limit of the hatched area in the boundary limit for critical hydrogen contents; if these are exceeded, the formation of flakes can occur. The diagram shows that the critical hydrogen contents are reduced as the manganese content is increased.

In the case of the special grade not covered in *figure 5* hydrogen contents were adjusted between 2.9 and 3.1 cm³/100 g steel in 6 investigations without flakes forming. Thus, this grade can be considered at least the equal of Grade B as regards flake susceptibility. Accordingly, the critical hydrogen contents for the various grades are

Grade A: 3.6 cm³/100 g steel
Grade B: 2.8 cm³/100 g steel
Grade C: 2.0 cm³/100 g steel
Special-grade chrome-manganese steel: 3.0 cm³/100 g steel

Since the flakes are predominantly located in segregation lines, enrichment with accompanying and alloying elements

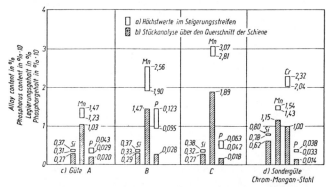

a) Maximum content in segregation line;   b) Random analysis over the cross-section of the rails
c) Grade A, B, C   d) Special grade chromium-manganese steel

Bild 6. Chemische Zusammensetzung nach der Stückanalyse über den Querschnitt sowie Anreicherungen von Legierungs- und Begleitelementen in Seigerungsstreifen an Schienen der verschiedenen Güten

Figure 6. Chemical analysis according to random analysis over the the cross-section and concentrations of alloying and accompanying elements in segregation lines in rails of various qualities

Flocken zumindest wie die Güte B eingeordnet werden. Die kritischen Wasserstoffgehalte betragen demnach für

Güte A: 3,6 cm³/100 g Stahl
Güte B: 2,8 cm³/100 g Stahl
Güte C: 2,0 cm³/100 g Stahl
Sondergüte Chrom-Mangan-Stahl: 3,0 cm³/100 g Stahl

Da die Flocken bevorzugt in Seigerungsstreifen liegen, wurde mit der Elektronenstrahl-Mikrosonde die Anreicherung der Begleit- und Legierungselemente im Bereich der Seigerungsstreifen bestimmt. *Bild 6* zeigt die Ergebnisse für die verschiedenen Schienengüten. Über den mittleren Gehalten über den Querschnitt der Schiene ist der Bereich der Höchstwerte aus mehreren Seigerungsstreifen angegeben. Erwartungsgemäß seigert Phosphor am stärksten. Die Chromseigerung ist größer als die von Mangan und Silicium. Wegen

on the segregation line area was determined using the electron-beam microprobe. *Figure 6* shows the results for the various rail steel grades. The range of the highest values in respect of several segregation lines is plotted above the mean contents over the cross-section of the rail. As to be expected, phosphorous segregates to the highest degree. Chromium segregation exceeds that of manganese and silicon. The high manganese content in the segregation lines of Grade C provides an explanation for the formation of martensite in rails of this grade as mentioned above.

In addition to the alloy content, the size of the segregation lines is also decisive as regards the possibility of flake formation. In two heats of Grade C with 1.9% Mn, flakes were formed with 2.4 cm³/H₂/100 g steel, but not with 3.0 cm³ H₂/100 g steel. In both instances, however, the

938   *Heller, Weber, Hammerschmid, Schweitzer: Möglichkeiten zur wasserstoffarmen Erschmelzung von Schienenstahl*   Stahl u. Eisen 92 (1972)
Nr. 19. 14. September

des hohen Mangangehaltes in Seigerungsstreifen der Güte C wird die beschriebene Martensitbildung in Schienen dieser Güte verständlich.

Neben dem Legierungsgehalt ist auch die Größe der Seigerungsstreifen für eine mögliche Flockenbildung entscheidend. Bei zwei Schmelzen der Güte C mit 1,9 % Mn traten bei einem Wasserstoffgehalt von 2,4 cm³/100 g Stahl Flocken auf, bei 3,0 cm³/100 g Stahl dagegen nicht. In beiden Fällen lagen jedoch martensitische Seigerungsstreifen vor, nur betrug die mittlere Fläche der Seigerungsstreifen je Durchstoßpunkt im Querschliff bei der Schmelze mit Flocken 0,060 mm², bei der ohne Flocken 0,008 mm².

Ultraschallprüfungen vor und nach dem Richten der Schienen zeigten, daß die Größe und Zahl der Flocken durch den Richtvorgang erhöht werden.

Eine statistische Auswertung von Schienen mit Flocken ergab, daß Schienen aus dem Bereich des unteren Blockviertels im allgemeinen keine Flocken aufweisen.

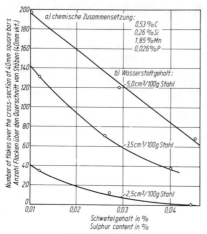

a) Chemical analysis;
b) Hydrogen content: 5,0 cm²/100 g steel; 3.5 cm²/100 g steel; 2.5 cm²/100 g steel

Bild 7. Flockenbildung in Abhängigkeit vom Schwefelgehalt bei unterschiedlichen Wasserstoffgehalten für einen Schienenstahl der Güte C

Figure 7. Flake formation as a function of S content with various hydrogen contents for a grade C rail steel

Der bekannte günstige Einfluß eines steigenden Schwefelgehaltes auf die Flockenanfälligkeit[11] wurde an Versuchsschmelzen überprüft. Dazu wurden im Vakuuminduktionsofen zur Einstellung unterschiedlicher Wasserstoffgehalte unter verschiedenen Argon/Wasserstoffgemischen 8-kg-Blöcke aus Schienenstahl der Güte C mit steigendem Schwefelgehalt erschmolzen und abgegossen. Nach Erstarrung und Temperaturausgleich im Schmiedeofen wurden die Blöcke zu Stäben 40 mm vkt. ausgeschmiedet und an Luft abgekühlt. Die Flockenzahl wurde an sechs Querschnittsscheiben aus jedem Stab ermittelt. Wie *Bild 7* zeigt, sinkt die Flockenzahl mit steigendem Schwefelgehalt ab und wird bei niedrigen Wasserstoffgehalten Null.

Ermittlung der Flockenempfindlichkeit durch Auslagerungsversuche

Durch Effusionsversuche sollte geprüft werden, ob die unterschiedliche Flockenempfindlichkeit der Stähle auf eine zeitlich unterschiedliche Wasserstoffabgabe zurückzuführen ist.

11) Hewitt, J.: In: Hydrogen in steel. London 1962. (Spec. Rep. Iron Steel Inst. Nr. 73.) S. 149/51.

segregation lines were martensitic, but the average area of the segregation lines per penetration point in the micrograph was 0.060 mm² in the heat with flakes, and 0.008 mm² in the heat without flakes.

Ultrasonic testing before and after straightening of the rails showed that both the size and the number of flakes are increased by the straightening operation.

A statistical evaluation of rails with flakes revealed that rails made from the bottom quarter of the ingot usually have no flakes.

The recognised favourable effect of increasing sulphur content on flake formation susceptibility[11] was checked using test heats. A vacuum induction furnace was employed in conjunction with various argon/hydrogen mixtures to adjust to different hydrogen contents, and rail steel or Grade C with increasing contents of sulphur melted and cast to produce ingots weighing 8 kg. Following solidification and temperature balancing in a forging furnace, the ingots were forged to bars 40 mm square and then coiled in air. The number of flakes was established using six cross-sectional slices from each bar. As *figure 7* shows, the number of flakes decreases as the sulphur content increases, no flakes being present at all where the hydrogen content is low.

Determination of flake susceptibility by holding tests

Effusion tests were carried out to ascertain whether the varying degrees of susceptibility to flake formation among the different steels can be traced back to varying degrees of hydrogen escape as related to time. First of all, the hydrogen contents of the products were established at certain steel production stages. In all the pearlitic grades it was established that there are no differences in the hydrogen content from pouring stream via the ingot to the finish-

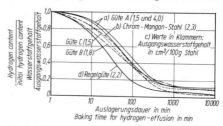

a) Grade A, B, C; b) Chromium-manganese steel; c) Values in parentheses: Initial hydrogen content in cm²/100 g steel; d) Standard grade

Bild 8. Wasserstoffeffusion bei 100 °C, gemessen an Rundproben (10 mm Dmr.) verschiedener Schienenstähle

Figure 8. Hydrogen effusion at 100 °C measured on round specimens (10 mm diameter) of various rail steels

rolled-rail at 950 °C. This applies to the central area of the rail head. Lower contents are found near the surface. Beyond the cooling bed, the hydrogen contents of all the pearlitic grades are about 10 % lower than the values for the samples taken from the pouring stream.

In addition, the effusion pattern was checked by holding 10 mm round specimens from the rail head centre at 100 °C. As shown in *figure 8*, all pearlitic grades have the same time/effusion curves for the ratio of the appropriate content to initial content, in spite of the differences in the initial hydrogen contents. In contrast, hydrogen effusion from the standard grade, the pearlite grains of which are surrounded by a ferrite network, is distinctly more rapid. This is evidently due to the ferrite supporting the diffusion of hydrogen to the surface[12].

Stahl u. Eisen 92 (1972)
Nr. 19. 14. September *On the effect of hydrogen in rail steel and the possibilities of hydrogen-depressing melting operations*

ist. Zunächst wurden im Fertigungsablauf die Wasserstoffgehalte an den Erzeugnissen in verschiedenen Fertigungsstufen ermittelt. Dabei wurde für alle perlitischen Güten festgestellt, daß sich vom Gießstrahl über den Vorblock bis zur gewalzten Schiene bei 950 °C keine Unterschiede im Wasserstoffgehalt ergeben. Dies gilt für die Schienenkopfmitte. In Oberflächennähe liegen geringere Gehalte vor. Die Wasserstoffgehalte nach der Kühlbettabkühlung liegen bei allen perlitischen Güten gleichermaßen um etwa 10% unter den Werten der aus dem Gießstrahl entnommenen Proben.

Zusätzlich wurde der Effusionsverlauf durch Auslagerung von Rundproben mit 10 mm Dmr. aus der Schienenkopfmitte bei 100 °C überprüft. Wie die in *Bild 8* dargestellten Ergebnisse zeigen, erhält man für die perlitischen Güten trotz unterschiedlicher Ausgangsgehalte für den Wasserstoff gleiche zeitliche Effusionskurven für das Verhältnis aus dem jeweiligen Gehalt zu dem Ausgangsgehalt. Dagegen effun-

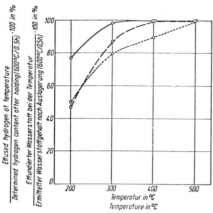

Wasserstoffgehalt (0,5 h/600 °C): 4,1 cm³/100 g Stahl
Hydrogen content (0.5 h/600 °C): 4,1 cm³/100 g steel
0,015 % S ———; 0,080 % S — — —; 0,170 % S - - - -
Auslagerungsdauer im Vakuum (10⁻⁴ Torr)
Holding time in vacuum (10⁻⁴ Torr)
bei/at 200 °C/1 h; bei/at 300 °C/1 h; bei/at 400 °C/1 h; bei/at 500 °C/0,5 h

Bild 9. Wasserstoffeffusion bei Schienenstahl der Güte C mit 0,53 % C, 0,26 % Si, 1,85 % Mn, 0,026 % P und mit unterschiedlichen Schwefelgehalten
Figure 9. Hydrogen effusion in rail steel of the grade C with 0.53 % C, 0.26 % Si, 1.85 % Mn, 0.026 % P and various S contents

diert der Wasserstoff aus der Regelgüte, deren Perlitkörner von einem Ferrit-Netz umgeben sind, deutlich schneller, offensichtlich deswegen, weil der Ferrit die Diffusion des Wasserstoffs zur Oberfläche begünstigt[12]).

In weiteren Versuchen wurden zur Erfassung des Einflusses von Schwefel auf die Effusion des Wasserstoffs Proben aus geschmiedeten Stäben mit steigendem Schwefelgehalt von drei Blöcken einer Versuchsschmelze bei verschiedenen Temperaturen bei einem Druck von 10⁻⁴ Torr ausgelagert. Der bei den jeweiligen Temperaturen effundierte Wasserstoff ist in *Bild 9* als Anteil des wie üblich nach halbstündiger Auslagerung bei 600 °C ermittelten Wasserstoffgehaltes dargestellt. Danach wird im Temperaturbereich unter 400 °C die Wasserstoffeffusion durch steigenden Schwefelgehalt verringert. Dieser Einfluß war bei den vorher geschilderten Effusionsversuchen bei 100 °C ausgeschaltet, da nur Stähle gleichen Schwefelgehaltes (0,016 bis 0,018 % S) verwendet worden waren.

¹⁴) Bhat, U. V., u. H. K. Lloyd: J. Iron Steel Inst. 165 (1950) S. 382/89.

During the course of further investigations, the effect of sulphur on the effusion of hydrogen was determined using specimens in the form of forged bars with increasing sulphur contents; these bars were taken from three ingots of a test heat, and held at various temperatures at a pressure of 10⁻⁴ Torr. The hydrogen escaping at various temperatures is shown in *figure 9* as a proportion of the hydrogen content found in the normal way after 30 minutes holding at 600°C. The results indicate that the effusion of hydrogen is reduced as the sulphur content increases in the temperature range below 400 °C. This effect was eliminated during the above-described effusion tests at 100 °C, since all steels used had the same sulphur contents (0.016 to 0.018 % S).

Investigation of hydrogen embrittlement by testing the mechanical properties of the steels

This varying degree of hydrogen embrittlement among the different grades of rails was investigated by means of tensile tests with uni-axial and multi-axial states of stress. Both plain and notched test bars were employed. The plain bars with a diameter of 10 mm were taken from the centre of the rail head. They had the same hydrogen contents as the rail in question, and were tested either immediately after being taken from the rails or following a hold at 100 °C for 48 h. The rate of loading during the tensile test was kept constant, the duration of the test being the usual approx. 1 min. Since the linear relationship between the material values obtained from the tensile test and the hydrogen content is known[13]), only two points were needed to establish the curve. However, these two points were each confirmed by 10 other specimens. As also to be expected on the basis of earlier tests[13]), no significant influence of hydrogen content on yield point and tensile strength was to be noted. In contrast, the rupture stress and thus the values for elongation at rupture and reduction of area at rupture are greatly reduced, as shown in *figure 10*. Uniform elongation is affected only when the specimen ruptures in the region of the maximum load. The curves showing the dependence of rupture stress, elongation at rupture, and reduction of area on the hydrogen content of the various rail grades still have a relatively restricted scatter range, but differences in the curve gradient are already noticeable and provide a measure for hydrogen embrittlement. If the curve gradient is plotted against the manganese content, as shown in *figure 11*, it can be seen that the pearlitic grades exhibit a linear relationship between hydrogen embrittlement and the manganese content. The special grade with 1% Mn and 1% Cr can be compared with Grade A with 1% Mn. Even though the standard grade also has only 1% Mn, the ferrite network produces something of an increase in embrittlement[14]).

The notched-bar tensile test specimens were taken from the rail head edge, held in the manner described for hydrogen effusion, and testing in this state or after electrolytic charging with hydrogen. The cylindrical portion of the specimens had a diameter of 7 mm, the notch cross-section having a diameter of 5 mm. The notch radius was 0.025 mm, and the notch angle 60 °C. Electrolytic charging took place in a solution of 0.1n H_2SO_4 with 10 ppm As using a current density of 0.0075 A/cm². The notched-bar tensile tests were carried out using a constant load application rate over times of 4 to 12 min. depending on the maximum load withstood. The governing hydrogen contents near the surface were then determined using cross-sectional and core specimens 5 mm in diameter. The results of three to four notched-bar tensile tests of material held for hydrogen effusion and of six to ten tensile tests made in the hydrogen-charged state are given

Untersuchung der Wasserstoffversprödung durch Prüfung der mechanischen Eigenschaften der Stähle

Die unterschiedliche Wasserstoffversprödung der verschiedenen Schienengüten wurde durch Zugversuche im ein- und mehrachsigen Spannungszustand an glatten und gekerbten Zugstäben untersucht. Die glatten Zugproben mit 10 mm Dmr. wurden aus der Mitte des Schienenkopfes entnommen; sie hatten die Wasserstoffgehalte der jeweiligen Schiene und wurden entweder sofort nach der Probenahme oder nach einer Auslagerung von 48 Stunden Dauer bei 100 °C geprüft. Die Belastungsgeschwindigkeit beim Zugversuch wurde konstant gehalten, die Versuchsdauer betrug wie

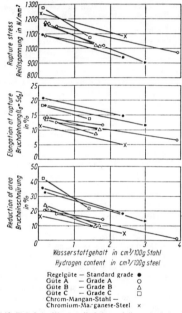

Regelgüte — Standard grade ●
Güte A — Grade A ○
Güte B — Grade B △
Güte C — Grade C □
Chrom-Mangan-Stahl —
Chromium-Manganese-Steel ×

Bild 10. Einfluß des Wasserstoffgehaltes auf die mechanischen Eigenschaften verschiedener Schienenstähle

Figure 10. Effect of hydrogen content on the mechanical properties of various rail steels

in *figure 12*. The notched-bar tensile strength values of the various rail grades, including the standard grade, as tested after being held for hydrogen effusion are of the same magnitude within the scatter range. Even low hydrogen contents lead to greatly reduced notched-bar tensile strength values. The embrittling effect of hydrogen is reduced as its

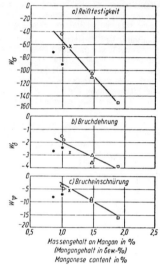

a) Rupture stress; b) Elongation at rupture; c) Reduction of area

Regelgüte — Standard grade ●
Güte A — Grade A ○
Güte B — Grade B △
Güte C — Grade C □
Chrom-Mangan-Stahl —
Chromium-Manganese-Steel ×

Bild 11. Wasserstoffversprödung, ausgedrückt als das Steigungsmaß der Kurven in *Bild 10*, in Abhängigkeit vom Mangangehalt, Es bedeuten:

Figure 11. Hydrogen embrittlement expressed as the degree of slope of the curves in *figure 10* as a function of Mn content, with:

$$W_\sigma = \Delta\sigma_R \text{ in } \frac{N}{mm^2} / \Delta H, \text{ in } \frac{cm^3}{100 \text{ g Stahl/Steel}}$$

$$W_\sigma = \Delta\sigma_t \text{ in } \%/\Delta H, \text{ in } \frac{cm^3}{100 \text{ g Stahl/Steel}}$$

$$W_\sigma = \Delta\psi \text{ in } \%/\Delta H, \text{ in } \frac{cm^3}{100 \text{ g Stahl/Steel}}$$

üblich etwa eine Minute. Da der lineare Zusammenhang zwischen den Werkstoffkennwerten des Zugversuches und dem Wasserstoffgehalt bekannt ist[13], genügten zwei Punkte, um den Verlauf der Kurve zu bestimmen. Diese Punkte waren jedoch mit jeweils 10 Proben belegt. Wie ebenfalls aus früheren Versuchen[13] zu erwarten, wurde kein nennenswerter Einfluß des Wasserstoffgehaltes auf die Streckgrenze und die Zugfestigkeit festgestellt. Dagegen werden, wie *Bild 10* zeigt, die Reißspannung und damit die Verformungskennwerte für die Bruchdehnung und Brucheinschnürung stark vermindert. Ein Einfluß auf die Gleichmaßdehnung zeigt sich nur dann, wenn die Probe im Bereich der Höchstkraft bricht. Die Kurven, die die Abhängigkeit der Reißspannung, Bruchdehnung und Brucheinschnürung vom Wasserstoffgehalt für die verschiedenen Schienengüten wiedergeben, liegen zwar in einem verhältnismäßig engen Streuband, jedoch sind bereits Unterschiede in der Steigung, die ein Maß für die Wasserstoffversprödung

[13] Heller, W., u. W. Jäniche: Stahl u. Eisen 83 (1963) S. 145/54.

content is increased. However, in this respect great differences were to be noted among the various grades. *Figure 12* shows the scatter ranges for notched-bar tensile strength and the scatter range for the subsequently established hydrogen contents. The standard grade and Grade A exhibit the lowest reductions in notched-bar tensile strength, Grade C and the chrome-manganese steel the highest; Grade B is in between. Plotting of the notched-bar tensile strength values of the material held for hydrogen effusion and the material charged with hydrogen over the sum total of the manganese + chromium content in *figure 13* reveals the influence of chemical composition. Chromium and manganese both result in hydrogen embrittlement, carbon remaining without influence in this respect.

Discussion of the test results

The results of the tests to determine flake formation susceptibility show that it increases from Grade A via Grade B to Grade C, i.e. with increasing manganese content

ist, erkennbar. Trägt man diese Steigung wie in *Bild 11* über dem Mangangehalt auf, so zeigt sich bei den perlitischen Güten eine lineare Abhängigkeit der Wasserstoffversprödung vom Mangangehalt. Die Sondergüte mit 1% Mn und 1% Cr verhält sich ähnlich wie die Güte A mit 1% Mn. Bei der Regelgüte, die zwar auch nur 1% Mn enthält, führt das Ferritnetz zu einer etwas stärkeren Versprödung[14]).

Die gekerbten Zugproben zur Ermittlung der **Kerbzugfestigkeit** wurden dem Schienenkopfrand entnommen, ausgelagert und dann entweder in diesem Zustand oder nach

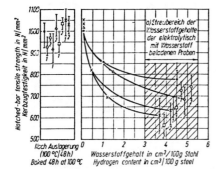

a) Scatter ranges of hydrogen content of specimens charged electrolytically with hydrogen

Regelgüte — Standard grade	●
Güte A — Grade A	○
Güte B — Grade B	△
Güte C — Grade C	□
Chrom-Mangan-Stahl — Chromium-Manganese-Steel	×

Bild 12. Einfluß des Wasserstoffgehaltes auf die Kerbzugfestigkeit bei verschiedenen Schienenstahlsorten

Figure 12. Effect of hydrogen content on the notch impact strength of various rail steel grades

elektrolytischer Wasserstoffbeladung geprüft. Der Durchmesser der Proben betrug 7 mm in ihrem zylindrischen Teil und 5 mm im Kerbquerschnitt. Der Kerbradius betrug 0,02 mm, der Kerbwinkel 60°. Die elektrolytische Beladung geschah in einer Lösung aus 0,1n H_2SO_4 mit 10 ppm Arsen bei einer Stromdichte von 0,0075 A/cm². Die Kerbzugproben wurden bei konstanter Belastungsgeschwindigkeit mit einer Versuchsdauer von 4 bis 12 min, je nach ertragener Höchstkraft, geprüft. Anschließend wurde der maßgebliche Randwasserstoffgehalt aus Querschnitt- und Kernanalysen (5 mm Dmr.) bestimmt. Die Ergebnisse von drei bis vier Kerbzugproben des ausgelagerten und von etwa sechs bis zehn Zugproben des wasserstoffbeladenen Zustandes zeigt *Bild 12*. Im ausgelagerten Zustand sind die Kerbzugfestigkeiten der verschiedenen Schienengüten einschließlich der Regelgüte innerhalb der Streuungen gleich groß. Bereits kleine Wasserstoffgehalte führen zu einer starken Verminderung der Kerbzugfestigkeit. Zu höheren Wasserstoffgehalten hin wird der Einfluß des Wasserstoffs auf die Kerbzugfestigkeit geringer. Es zeigt sich dabei jedoch eine starke Unterscheidung nach Güten. In *Bild 12* sind die Streubereiche der Kerbzugfestigkeiten und der Streubereich der anschließend ermittelten Wasserstoffgehalte angegeben. Die Regelgüte und die Güte A zeigen die geringste Abnahme der Kerbzugfestigkeit, die Güte C und der Chrom-Mangan-Stahl die größte; die Güte B ordnet sich dazwischen ein. Eine Auftragung der Kerbzugfestigkeiten im ausgelagerten und wasserstoffbeladenen Zustand über der Summe des Mangan- und Chromgehaltes in *Bild 13* läßt den Einfluß der chemischen Zusammensetzung erkennen. Chrom und Mangan

[14] Hobson, J. D., u. J. Hewitt: J. Iron Steel Inst. 173 (1953) S. 131/40 u. 1 Taf.

and decreasing carbon content. The special grade is no more susceptible than Grade B. The standard grade was not subjected to closer examination, but experience shows that its susceptibility to flake formation is lower than that of the pearlitic grades.

According to the present findings, tensile strength is not an influencing factor in pearlitic rail steels. Neither is there any difference in the hydrogen effusion rates. Only the standard grade exhibits a higher degree of hydrogen effusion. Measured against the hydrogen content of the pouring stream specimen, this would result in a lower degree of susceptibility to flake formation in this grade than Grade A.

The varying degree of hydrogen embrittlement of the different rail grades during the tensile test and particularly during the notched-bar tensile test also indicate that the chemical composition of the steel exerts an influence in this

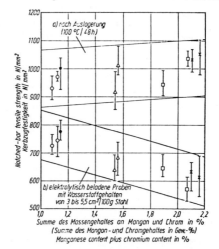

a) baked 48 h at 100 °C; b) electrolytically charged specimens with hydrogen contents of 3—5.5 cm²/100 g steel

Regelgüte — Standard grade	●
Güte A — Grade A	○
Güte B — Grade B	△
Güte C — Grade C	□
Chrom-Mangan-Stahl — Chromium-Manganese-Steel	×

Bild 13. Abhängigkeit der Kerbzugfestigkeit von der Summe des Mangan- und Chromgehaltes bei verschiedenen Schienenstählen

Figure 13. Dependence of notch impact strength on the total Mn and Cr content of various rail steels

regard. Embrittlement increases as the manganese and chromium contents rise. Long-time tests incorporating a multi-axial state of stress would in all probability help to clarify the relationship still further.

The flakes lie in segregation lines. The increasing degree of susceptibility to flake formation from Grade A via Grade B to Grade C is due to the higher manganese contents in the segregation lines. This coincides with an increasing depth of hydrogen embrittlement as revealed by the mechanical tests covering the pearlitic structure. With Grade C, the higher manganese content in the segregation lines results in an extent in a transformation in the martensite stage. The martensitic structure is particularly susceptible to flake formation[9] to [10]). In addition, transformation of the matrix takes place earlier than in the segregation lines; the latter thus remain austenitic for a longer period of time, and higher

führen in gleicher Weise zu einer Wasserstoffversprödung, der Kohlenstoffgehalt hat keinen Einfluß.

Erörterung der Versuchsergebnisse

Die Ergebnisse der Versuche zur Bestimmung der Flockenempfindlichkeit zeigen, daß die Empfindlichkeit von der Güte A über die Güte B zur Güte C, das heißt mit steigendem Mangan- und abnehmendem Kohlenstoffgehalt zunimmt. Die Sondergüte ist nicht empfindlicher als die Güte B. Die Regelgüte wurde zwar nicht näher untersucht, ihre Empfindlichkeit ist erfahrungsgemäß jedoch geringer als die der perlitischen Güten.

Nach den vorliegenden Ergebnissen scheidet die Festigkeit als Einflußgröße für die perlitischen Schienenstähle aus. Eine unterschiedliche Wasserstoffeffusion liegt ebenfalls nicht vor. Nur die Regelgüte zeigt eine größere Effusion. Gemessen am Wasserstoffgehalt der Gießprobe ergäbe sich damit für diese Güte gegenüber der Güte A eine geringere Flockenempfindlichkeit.

Die unterschiedliche Wasserstoffversprödung der verschiedenen Schienengüten im Zugversuch und vor allem im Kerbzugversuch weisen auch auf einen Einfluß der chemischen Zusammensetzung hin. Die Versprödung nimmt mit steigendem Mangan- und Chromgehalt zu. Langzeitversuche unter mehrachsigem Spannungszustand würden hier gegebenenfalls den Zusammenhang noch besser kennzeichnen können.

Die Flocken liegen in Seigerungsstreifen. Die von der Güte A über B nach C zunehmende Empfindlichkeit erklärt sich aus den jeweils größeren Mangangehalten in den Seigerungsstreifen. Diese Aussage steht in Übereinstimmung mit einer zunehmenden Wasserstoffversprödung nach den Ergebnissen der mechanischen Untersuchungen für das perlitische Gefüge. Bei der Güte C führt der höhere Mangangehalt in den Seigerungsstreifen teilweise zu einer Umwandlung in der Martensitstufe. Das martensitische Gefüge ist besonders flockenempfindlich[8] bis [10]). Zusätzlich ist wegen der verzögerten Umwandlung gegenüber der Matrix in dem längere Zeit austenitischen Seigerungsstreifen mit einem höheren Wasserstoffgehalt zu rechnen. Darüber hinaus treten wegen der verzögerten Umwandlung in diesen Bereichen Spannungen auf.

Die geringe Flockenempfindlichkeit der Sondergüte ist einmal darauf zurückzuführen, daß deren Seigerungsstreifen nicht in der Martensitstufe umwandeln; Chromanreicherungen und der höhere Kohlenstoffgehalt wirken sich vergleichsweise günstiger auf das Umwandlungsverhalten als Mangananreicherungen bei niedrigerem Kohlenstoffgehalt aus. In diese Richtung weisen auch die an Schienenstählen und an anderen Stählen mit höheren Legierungsgehalten aufgenommenen Umwandlungsschaubilder[15] [16]). Zum anderen dürfte sich der niedrige Phosphorgehalt der Sondergüte im Seigerungsstreifen günstig auf die Zähigkeit des perlitischen Gefüges auswirken.

Die Verteilung der Flocken über die Länge einer aus einem Block gewalzten Schiene läßt sich mit der Lage der Seigerungsstreifen im Rohblock *(Bild 14)* erklären. Der Fußteil des Blockes weist keine Seigerungsstreifen auf; die aus diesem Teil gewalzten Schienen sind auch noch bei kritischen Wasserstoffgehalten flockenfrei. Der Einfluß einer Wasserstoffseigerung scheidet als Ursache, da bei diesen Untersuchungen keine unterschiedlichen Wasserstoffgehalte über die Blocklänge festgestellt wurden.

Durch den Schienenrichtvorgang werden vorhandene Flocken vergrößert und zusätzlich Flocken erzeugt. Dies ist auf die hohen Spannungen während des Richtens zurück-

[15]) Heller, W.: Eisenbahntechn. Rdsch. 20 (1971) S. 71/78.
[16]) Bungardt, K., u. O. Mulders: Stahl u. Eisen 80 (1960) S. 1603/18.

hydrogen contents must therefore be expected in them. Furthermore, stresses are generated in these areas by the delayed transformation.

The lower degree of susceptibility to flake formation in the special grade can at once be traced back to the fact that its segregation lines do not undergo transformation in the martensite stage; chromium concentrations and the higher carbon content have a more favourable effect on transformation behaviour than is true of manganese concentrations with a lower carbon content. Transformation diagrams of rail steels and of other steels with higher alloying additions lead to the same conclusions[15] [16]). On the other hand, the low phosphorous content in the segregation lines of the special grade probably has a favourable influence on the toughness of the pearlitic structure.

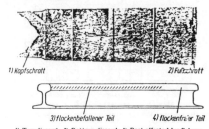

1) Top discard; 2) Bottom discard; 3) Part affected by flakes;
4) Flake-free part

Bild 14. Verteilung der Seigerungen im Rohblock und entsprechender Flockenabfall über die Länge einer aus diesem Block gewalzten Schiene
Figure 14. Distribution of segregations in the ingot and corresponding drop in flakes over the length of rails rolled from this ingot

The distribution of the flakes over the length of a rail rolled from a single ingot can be explained by the position of the segregation lines in the as-cast ingot *(figure 14)*. The foot of the ingot has no segregation lines; the rails rolled from this portion of the ingot are free from flakes even at critical hydrogen contents. Thus, the influence of hydrogen segregation can be discounted, since during these investigations no variable hydrogen contents were detected over the length of the ingot.

During straightening existing flakes are enlarged, and new flakes formed. This can be traced back to the high stresses generated during straightening. In addition, it may be taken that internal stresses in the rails also exert an influence on flake formation.

The effusion tests show that the reduced degree of susceptibility to flake formation with increasing sulphur content indicates that a proportion of the hydrogen is not available for flake formation at temperatures below 300 °C.

Low-hydrogen melting of rail steels

Low hydrogen melting, vacuum treatment of the melt and delayed cooling after rolling can be employed for the flake-free production of rail steels with a minimum tensile strength or more than 880 N/mm².

With delayed cooling of the rails after rolling using the so-called Sandberg furnace on the hot cooling bed or in cooling pits, the hydrogen content can be so reduced that no further flakes are formed. *Figure 15* shows the cooling curves and the reached hydrogen contents. With an initial hydrogen content of about 2.1 cm³/100 g steel, the slowest cooling rate can produce a hydrogen content of 0.5 cm³ 100 g

Stahl u. Eisen 92 /1972
Nr. 19. 14. September
On the effect of hydrogen in rail steel and the possibilities of hydrogen-depressing melting operations   **943**

zuführen. Es ist außerdem zu erwarten, daß die in den Schienen vorhandenen Eigenspannungen die Flockenbildung ebenfalls beeinflussen.

Die mit steigendem Schwefelgehalt verringerte Flockenempfindlichkeit läßt sich aufgrund der Effusionsversuche so deuten, daß bei Temperaturen unter 300 °C ein Teil des Wasserstoffs nicht zur Flockenbildung zur Verfügung steht.

Wasserstoffarmes Erschmelzen von Schienenstählen

Für die flockenfreie Erzeugung von Schienen über 880 N/mm² Mindestzugfestigkeit bieten sich die Möglichkeiten einer wasserstoffarmen Erschmelzung, einer Vakuumbehandlung der Schmelze und einer verzögerten Abkühlung nach dem Walzen an.

Beim verzögerten Abkühlen der Schienen nach dem Walzen durch den Sandbergofen, auf dem Warmbett oder in Abkühlgruben kann der Wasserstoffgehalt so abgesenkt werden, daß sich keine Flocken mehr bilden. In *Bild 15* sind Abkühlkurven und die jeweils erreichten Wasserstoffgehalte von Schienen wiedergegeben. Bei einem Ausgangswasserstoffgehalt von etwa 2.1 cm³/100 g Stahl kann auf diese Weise nach der langsamsten Abkühlung ein Wasserstoffgehalt von 0.5 cm³/100 g Stahl erreicht werden.

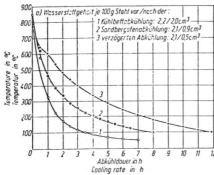

a) Hydrogen contents prior to subsequent to: 1 cooling bed cooling; 2 Sandberg furnace cooling; 3 delayed cooling
Bild 15. Wasserstoffgehalte in Schienenstahl nach unterschiedlichen Abkühlungsverläufen
Figure 15. Hydrogen contents in rail steel after different cooling cycles

Bei Ausgangsgehalten von 5 bis 6 cm³/100 g Stahl, wie sie bei normaler Erschmelzung vorliegen, sind Wasserstoffgehalte um 1 bis 1,5 cm³/100 g Stahl zu erwarten.

Durch die Vakuumbehandlung des flüssigen Stahls nach dem Abstich läßt sich der Wasserstoffgehalt auf Werte senken, die unter den für Flockenfreiheit geforderten liegen. So wurde beispielsweise durch die Gießstrahlentgasung[3] von Schienenstahlschmelzen ein Bereich der Wasserstoffgehalte im Gießstrahl zwischen 1 und 2 cm³/100 g Stahl erreicht (*Bild 16*).

Da die verzögerte Abkühlung keinen stetigen Fertigungsablauf zuläßt, die volle Wirksamkeit der Legierungselemente auf die Festigkeit verhindert und die Vakuumbehandlung mit zusätzlichen Kosten verbunden ist, wurde in Rheinhausen die wasserstoffarme Erschmelzung von Schienenstählen entwickelt. Dieses Verfahren wird in Rheinhausen seit 1961 für Schienen und andere wasserstoffempfindliche Stähle wie Spannbetonstahl im Elektrolichtbogenofen angewandt. Dabei wird mit hoher Entkohlungsgeschwindigkeit von 0,4 % C/h unter Verwendung von Kalkstein, geglühten Erzpellets und gasförmigem Sauerstoff der Wasserstoffgehalt

steel. With initial contents of 5 to 6 cm³/100 g steel, as with normal melting operations, contents of 1 to 1.5 cm³/100 g steel are to be expected.

Vacuum treatment of the molten steel after tapping reduces the hydrogen content to values below those specified for freedom from flakes. Thus, for example, stream degassing[3] of rail steel heats produced a hydrogen content scatter range in the pouring stream of between 1 and 2 cm³/100 g steel (*figure 16*).

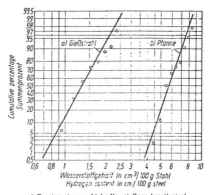

a) Pouring stream; b) Ladle; c) Open hearth-steel

Bild 16. Häufigkeitskurven für Wasserstoffgehalte in der Schmelze vor (Pfanne) und nach (Gießstrahl) der Gießstrahlentgasung

Figure 16. Frequency curves for hydrogen content in the melt before (ladle) and after (casting stream) ladle degassing

Since delayed cooling interrupts continuous production operations and reduces the full effect of the alloying elements on strength, and since vacuum treatment incurs additional costs, the low hydrogen melting of rail steels was developed at Rheinhausen. This process has been used at Rheinhausen since 1961 for rails and other steels sensitive to hydrogen, such as concrete prestressing steel, in conjunction with the electric arc furnace. A high decarburization rate of 0.4% C/h is employed with limestone, calcined ore pellets and gaseous oxygen to reduce the hydrogen content to values below 2 cm³/100 g steel (*figure 17*). A total oxidising loss of 1% C is required.

In the oxidation phase, the last 0.2% C must be eliminated within a period of max. 60 min, and the heat must continue to lose carbon during tapping. Since 1961 it has proved possible to reduce the average hydrogen content in the furnace before tapping to 1.7 cm³/100 g steel on average with a scatter range of 1.4 to 1.9 cm³/100 g steel, as compared with the initial results of 2.5 cm³/100 g steel on average. This reduction was attained by a strict elimination of the introduction of moisture by additions such as limestone and ore pellets and also by using good scrap.

The influence of air humidity cannot be eliminated. The values of the upper scatter range of the stated frequency distribution for hydrogen contents relate to periods with high absolute humidity values.

Hydrogen absorption during tapping and deoxidation can be restricted to an average of 0.4 cm³/100 g steel by employing low hydrogen nonmetallic additions in the ladle or calcined deoxidizing agent (*figure 17*). Other precautions are required during tapping to achieve the stated scatter range of 2.0 to 2.5 cm³ H_2/100 g steel in the pouring stream,

auf Werte unter 2 cm³/100 g Stahl abgesenkt *(Bild 17)*. Insgesamt ist ein Abbrand von 1 % Kohlenstoff erforderlich.

In der Abfangzeit müssen die letzten 0,2 % C in höchstens einer Stunde herausgefrischt werden, und die Schmelze muß auch beim Abstich noch Kohlenstoff verlieren. Seit 1961 ist es gelungen, den Wasserstoffgehalt im Ofen vor dem Abstich auf im Mittel 1,7 cm³/100 g Stahl bei einem Streubereich von 1,4 bis 1,9 cm³/100 g Stahl gegenüber anfänglichen Ergebnissen von im Mittel 2,5 cm³/100 g Stahl zu senken. Diese Erniedrigung konnte durch zielstrebige Vermeidung des Einbringens von Feuchtigkeit über Zusätze wie Erzpellets und Kalkstein und guten Schrott erreicht werden.

Der Einfluß der Luftfeuchtigkeit läßt sich nicht ausschalten. Die Werte des oberen Streubereichs der angegebenen Häufigkeitsverteilung für die Wasserstoffgehalte stammen aus Zeiträumen hoher absoluter Luftfeuchtigkeit.

Die Aufnahme von Wasserstoff beim Abstich und beim Desoxydieren kann durch Verwendung wasserstoffarmer nichtmetallischer Zusätze in der Pfanne oder geglühter Desoxydationsmittel auf im Mittel 0,4 cm³/100 g Stahl begrenzt werden *(Bild 17)*. Weitere Vorsichtsmaßnahmen beim Abstich, wie die Verwendung von Pfannen erst nach dem zweiten Abguß, und kurze Abstichlaufzeiten sind erforderlich, um den angegebenen Streubereich von 2,0 bis 2,5 cm³ H₂/100 g Stahl im Gießstrahl einzustellen.

Nach Einführung des Sauerstoffblasverfahrens gelang es uns vor einigen Jahren, Schienenstahl mit niedrigen Wasserstoffgehalten auch mit diesem Verfahren herzustellen *(Bild 17)*. Hierbei wurden die Schmelzen kurz unterhalb des angestrebten Kohlenstoffgehaltes abgefangen, um höhere Sauerstoffgehalte und eine stärkere Aufkohlung zu vermeiden.

Beim Abfangen der Schmelze ergeben sich dann zwar etwas höhere Wasserstoffgehalte als beim Herunterblasen auf niedrige Kohlenstoffgehalte. Anderseits würde ein Aufkohlen von niedrigen Kohlenstoffgehalten zu höheren Wasserstoffgehalten führen. Zur Einhaltung niedriger Wasserstoffgehalte ist weiterhin die Vermeidung höherer Temperaturen für die Schmelze von Bedeutung. Ein Temperaturanstieg um 100 °C verursacht eine Zunahme des Wasserstoffgehaltes um 0,6 bis 0,7 cm³/100 g Stahl.

Während der Wartezeit zwischen Probenahme und Abstich ändert sich im allgemeinen der Wasserstoffgehalt der Schmelze. Das kann durch den Verteilungsvorgang zwischen Bad und Schlacke erklärt werden. Als zeitabhängiger Vorgang wird sich die Verteilung dem Gleichgewicht um so mehr nähern, je länger die Wartezeit zwischen Probenahme und Abstich ist. Es sind deshalb möglichst kurze Wartezeiten einzuhalten. Unter Beachtung dieser Maßnahmen lassen sich beim Sauerstoffblasverfahren, wie *Bild 17* zeigt, ebenfalls Wasserstoffgehalte mit einem Streubereich von 1,8 bis 2,5 cm³/100 g Stahl im Gießstrahl einstellen.

Es sind bisher über 700000 t Schienen mit mehr als 880 N/mm² Mindestzugfestigkeit wasserstoffarm erschmolzen worden. Das Verfahren hat sich als zuverlässig und wirtschaftlich erwiesen. Mit der Ultraschallprüfung wurde die Flockenfreiheit nachgewiesen. Von Flocken ausgehende Nierenbrüche sind an entsprechend erzeugten Schienen nicht mehr aufgetreten.

Zusammenfassung

Von Flocken ausgehende Dauerbrüche ließen die Bedeutung des Wasserstoffes im Stahl für die Erzeugung und das Betriebsverhalten von Schienen erkennen.

Die verschiedenen Schienengüten haben eine unterschiedliche Flockenempfindlichkeit. Durch Betriebsversuche wurden die kritischen Wasserstoffgehalte, deren Überschreitung

e.g. the use of ladles only after the second teem and short tapping times.

Several years ago, following the introduction of the oxygen converter process, we succeeded in producing rail steel with a low hydrogen content by this method *(figure 17)*. The heats were caught just below the required carbon content in order to prevent high oxygen contents and heavier recarburization.

Catching the heats does produce rather higher hydrogen contents than blowing down to low carbon contents. On the other hand recarburization from low C contents would

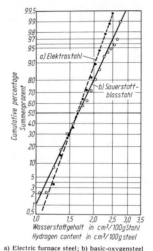

a) Electric furnace steel; b) basic-oxygensteel

Bild 17. Häufigkeitskurven für Wasserstoffgehalte bei wasserstoffarmer Erschmelzung

Figure 17. Frequency curves for hydrogen content with low-hydrogen melting

produce higher hydrogen contents. To attain low hydrogen contents, it is also important to avoid high melt temperatures. A temperature rise of about 100 °C causes an increase in hydrogen content of 0.6 to 0.7 cm³/100 g steel.

During the waiting period between sampling and tapping the hydrogen content of a melt generally alters. This can be explained by the distribution movement between slag and bath. This distribution is governed by time, and will therefore approach equilibrium more closely the longer the period between sampling and tapping. This waiting period must therefore be kept as short as possible. Provided these measures are adhered to, hydrogen contents in the scatter range of 1.8 to 2.5 cm³/100 g steel in the pouring stream can also be attained using the oxygen converter process, as shown in *figure 17*.

So far, more than 700,000 tonnes of rails with minimum tensile strength values of over 880 N/mm² have been produced using the low hydrogen melting process. The process has proved itself to be both dependable and economical. Freedom from falkes was demonstrated ultrasonically. Shatter cracks arising from flakes have not occurred on rails produced in the described way.

Summary

Fatigue cracks emanating from flakes indicated the significance of hydrogen in steel as regards the production and the service performance of rails.

Stahl u. Eisen 92 (1972)
Nr. 19. 14. September

Umschau – Technical review 945

zur Bildung von Flocken führt, ermittelt. Die Empfindlichkeit gegenüber Wasserstoff nimmt danach von der Güte A zur Güte C, also mit steigendem Verhältnis von Mangan zu Kohlenstoff zu. Höhere Schwefelgehalte vermindern die Flockenanfälligkeit. Die Sondergüte aus Chrom-Manganstahl ist trotz höherer Festigkeit weniger flockenempfindlich als die Güte C. Die Wasserstoffeffusion ist bei den perlitischen Güten nicht unterschiedlich.

Wenn höhere Wasserstoffgehalte zu Flocken führen, liegen sie vorwiegend in Seigerungsstreifen. Deshalb wird die Neigung der verschiedenen Schienenstähle zur Bildung von Flocken hauptsächlich durch den Gehalt von Legierungs- und Begleitelementen in den Seigerungsstreifen bestimmt. Mangan ist dabei von besonderer Bedeutung und führt vor allem bei Schienen der Güte C zu einer Umwandlung der Seigerungsstreifen in der Martensitstufe.

Festigkeitsuntersuchungen bestätigen den Einfluß der Legierungselemente auf die Wasserstoffversprödung für das perlitische Gefüge. Beim üblichen Zugversuch nimmt die Wasserstoffversprödung mit steigendem Mangangehalt, im mehrachsigen Spannungszustand des Kerbzugversuches mit steigendem Mangan- und Chromgehalt zu. Kohlenstoff ist ohne Einfluß auf die Wasserstoffversprödung.

Der Wasserstoffgehalt kann durch eine kontrollierte Abkühlung der Schienen oder durch eine Vakuumbehandlung des flüssigen Stahls auf einen hinreichend niedrigen Wert gesenkt werden. Noch vorteilhafter ist eine wasserstoffarme Erschmelzung.

Seit 10 Jahren wird diese Erschmelzung in Rheinhausen im Elektrolichtbogenofen durchgeführt. Dabei wird mit hoher Entkohlungsgeschwindigkeit gefrischt und noch kochend abgestochen. Auch beim Sauerstoffblasverfahren werden inzwischen niedrige Wasserstoffgehalte eingestellt. Dazu gelangen Stoffe mit geringsten Feuchtigkeitsgehalten zum Einsatz. Die Wartezeiten zwischen Probenahme und Abstich werden wegen des möglichen Wasserstoffausgleichs zwischen Schlacke und Bad kurz gehalten. Überhöhte Badtemperaturen werden vermieden.

Durch diese Arbeitsweisen und weitere Vorsichtsmaßnahmen beim Abstich, zum Beispiel die Verwendung geglühter Pfannenzusätze, ergeben sich Streubereiche für den Wasserstoffgehalt von 1,4 bis 2,1 cm³/100 g Stahl vor dem Abstich und 1,8 bis 2,5 cm³/100 g Stahl im Gießstrahl. Dadurch ist die Erzeugung flockenfreier Schienen sichergestellt.

The various rail grades have different degrees of susceptibility to flake formation. Investigations were made to establish the critical hydrogen contents, above which flakes are formed. These investigations revealed that sensitivity to hydrogen increases from Grade A to Grade C, i.e. with an increasing manganese-carbon ratio. Higher sulphur contents reduce susceptibility to the formation of flakes. The chromium-manganese special grade is less sensitive to flaking than Grade C, in spite of having a higher tensile strength. Hydrogen effusion does not differ between the pearlitic grades.

Where higher hydrogen contents lead to flaking, these occur predominantly in segregation lines. Accordingly, the tendency of the various rail steels to form flakes is governed mainly by the content of alloying and accompanying elements in the segregation lines. In this context, manganese is of particular significance and, particularly in rails of Grade C, leads to a transformation of the segregation lines to the martensitic stage.

Tensile strength tests confirmed the influence of the alloying elements on the hydrogen embrittlement of the pearlitic structure. In the standard tensile test, hydrogen embrittlement increases with increasing manganese contents, and in the multi-axial state of stress of the notched-bar tensile test it increases with higher manganese and chromium contents. Carbon has no effect on hydrogen embrittlement.

The hydrogen content can be reduced to a suitably low level by subjecting the rails to controlled cooling or by vacuum degassing of the molten steel. Low hydrogen melting is even more advantageous.

This latter process has been employed for the past ten years at Rheinhausen in conjunction with the electric arc furnace. Oxidation is effected with a high decarburization rate, and the melt tapped during the boil. In addition low hydrogen contents have also been achieved using the topblowing oxygen practice. Here, materials with minimum moisture contents are charged. The waiting times between sampling and tapping are kept short in view of the possible adjustment of hydrogen between slag and bath. Very high bath temperatures are avoided.

These methods and other precautions taken during tapping e.g. calcined additions to the ladle produce scatter ranges of 1.4 to 2.1 cm³ H_2/100 g steel before tapping and 1.8 to 2.5 cm³ H_2/100 g steel in the pouring stream. This guarantees the production of flake-free rails.

Umschau — Technical review

Aktuelle Aspekte der Energiewirtschaft in der Bundesrepublik Deutschland *)

Current aspects of the energy market in the Federal Republic of Germany

Voraussichtlich wird der Primärenergieverbrauch in der Bundesrepublik von 340 Mill. t Steinkohleeinheiten (SKE) — ohne Hochseebunker — im Jahr 1971 auf 508 Mill. t SKE im Jahr 1980 ansteigen. Der Anteil des Mineralöls wird sich von 54% im Jahr 1971 auf rd. 58 bis 59% bis 1980 erhöhen.

Innerhalb dieses skizzierten Rahmens der Gesamtentwicklung ist die Frage nach der langfristigen Verfügbarkeit und auch der Entwicklung des Preises von schwerem Heizöl für die Industrie im allgemeinen und für die Eisenhüttenindustrie im besonderen von grundlegendem Interesse.

Wenn nach der zukünftigen Entwicklung des Preises von schwerem Heizöl auf dem Energiemarkt der Bundesrepublik gefragt wird, müssen eine Reihe von Einflußfaktoren analysiert werden, die hinsichtlich ihrer langfristigen Wirkung und ihrer Bewegungstendenz weitgehend bekannt sind.

Auf der Angebotsseite sind zunächst die langfristig gesicherte Verfügbarkeit des Rohöls sowie die zu seiner Verarbeitung im Versorgungsgebiet der Bundesrepublik Deutschland bestehenden und geplanten Erweiterungen der Raffineriekapazitäten zu nennen.

It is anticipated that the primary energy consumption in the Federal Republic will increase from 340 million tons of coal units–not including fuel for high seas shipping–in 1971 to 508 million tons of coal units in 1980. The proportion of mineral oil will increase from 54% in 1971 to about 58 to 59% by 1980.

Within this outlined framework of overall development the question of long term availability as well as the price development of heavy fuel oil for industry in general and for the ferrous metallurgical industry in particular is of basic interest.

When a question is asked about the future development of heavy fuel oil prices on the energy market of the Federal Republic then a number of factors, which are largely known, must be analysed with respect to their long term effect and their movement trends.

On the supply side the long term guaranteed availability of crude oil as well as the existing and planned extensions to its refining capacity within the supply area of the German Federal Republic must be named first. The extension of the capacity from 125 million tons in 1971 to 230 million tons in 1980 exceeds even the estimated increase of the total mineral oil consumption

*) Auszug aus einem in der 207. Vollsitzung des Ausschusses für Energiewirtschaft und Wärmetechnik am 10. Dezember 1971 in Düsseldorf vorgetragenen Bericht.

The Role of Microstructure on the Strength and Toughness of Fully Pearlitic Steels

J. M. HYZAK AND I. M. BERNSTEIN

An experimental program was carried out to clarify the structure-property relationships in fully-pearlitic steels of moderately high strength levels, and to identify the critical microstructural features that control the deformation and fracture processes. Specifically, the yield strength was shown to be controlled primarily by the interlamellar pearlite spacing, which itself was a function of the isothermal transformation temperature and to a limited degree the prior-austenite grain size. Charpy tests on standard and fatigue precracked samples revealed that variations in the impact energy and dynamic fracture toughness were dependent primarily on the prior-austenite grain size, increasing with decreasing grain size, and to a lesser extent with decreasing pearlite colony size. These trends were substantiated by a statistical analysis of the data, that identified the relative contribution of each of the dependent variables on the value of the independent variable of interest. The results were examined in terms of the deformation behavior being controlled by the interaction of slip dislocations with the ferrite-cementite interface, and the fracture behavior being controlled by a structural subunit of constant ferrite orientation. Preliminary data suggests that the size of such units are controlled by, but are not identical to, the prior-austenite grain size. Possible origins of this fracture unit are considered.

THE relation of microstructure to mechanical properties in carbon steels has been the subject of considerable research. It is well known for example that increasing the carbon content increases a steel's strength, but usually only at the expense of fracture toughness. More specifically, however, there is considerable debate as to how microstructural variations affect mechanical properties. We intend to examine the origin of such variations for fully pearlitic eutectoid steels.

It is generally agreed that in high carbon near-eutectoid steels, it is the pearlite rather than proeutectoid ferrite that controls strength, and refining the pearlite interlamellar spacing results in an increase in yield strength.[1-3] However, the fracture process in pearlitic steels is less well understood. This is due, in part, to the difficulty in isolating different microstructural variables. There have been conflicting results reported in the literature as to the effects of pearlite interlamellar spacing,[4,5] pearlite colony size,[1] and prior-austenitic grain size[6] on the toughness of steel. Differences in carbon level, alloy content, and processing conditions among the steels examined make definitive evaluation of the literature results difficult.

The present work was undertaken, therefore, to clarify the structure-property relationships in fully-pearlitic steel, and to identify which of the above critical microstructural features control the deformation and fracture processes.

EXPERIMENTAL

Material

The material used for this investigation was supplied by the Association of American Railroads as hot

rolled rail steel stock. The chemical composition was analyzed to be: C-0.81 wt pct, Mn-0.87 wt pct, P-0.018 wt pct, S-0.013 wt pct, Si-0.17 wt pct and Fe-Balance.

Both standard ASTM Charpy and tensile blanks were cut from the stock so that the fracture plane of each specimen would be transverse to the rolling direction.

Heat Treatment

Specimens were heat treated over a range of temperatures for various times to produce a systematic variation in microstructure (Table I). Oversized blanks (12 mm sq.), were austenitized for 1 to 3 h in the temperature range from 1073 K (1472°F) to 1473 K (2192°F). The finest grain structure was developed by rapidly austenitizing the samples to a temperature of approximately 1103 K (1526°F), and subsequently

Table I. Heat Treatment Schedule for Eutectoid Steel

Heat Treatment	Austenization* Temperature		Salt Bath Temperature	
	K	°F	K	°F
1†	1103	(1526)	838	(1049)
2†	1103	(1526)	858	(1085)
3†	1103	(1526)	898	(1157)
4†	1073	(1472)	823	(1072)
5	1073	(1472)	838	(1049)
6	1073	(1472)	858	(1085)
7	1073	(1472)	898	(1157)
8	1073	(1472)	948	(1247)
9	1143	(1598)	.823	(1022)
10	1143	(1598)	838	(1049)
11	1143	(1598)	858	(1085)
12	1143	(1598)	898	(1157)
13	1273	(1832)	823	(1022)
14	1273	(1832)	858	(1085)
15	1473	(2192)	858	(1085)
16‡	1473	(2192)	858	(1085)
17	As Received Rail Structure			

*Austenization time–1 h.
†Thermal cycle treatment.
‡Austenization time–3 h.

J. M. HYZAK is Metallurgist, Air Force Materials Laboratory, (LLN), Wright Patterson Air Force Base, Dayton, OH 45433. I. M. BERNSTEIN is Associate Professor, Department of Metallurgy and Materials Science, Carnegie-Mellon University, Pittsburgh, PA 15213.
Manuscript submitted September 23, 1975.

transforming below the A₁ before there was time for substantial grain growth in the high temperature range.[7] After austenitizing, specimens were transformed to pearlite in salt pots held at various temperatures in the range 823 K (1022°F) to 948 K (1247°F). Transformation times were chosen sufficient to ensure complete transformations, without appreciable spheroidization. Specimens were then machined to final size; for the Charpy this was 10 mm sq, and for the tensiles this was to a gage diam of 6.35 mm. Although the actual transformation temperature was higher than the salt bath temperature (by as much as 40°C for the lowest temperature), the transformation was sensibly isothermal in nature. This was confirmed by pearlite spacing and hardness measurements taken on cross-sections of specimens machined to final size. Inasmuch as reaction kinetics were not of interest in this study, the transformation will be described by the bath rather than the reaction temperature.

Quantitative Metallographic Techniques

Quantitative analyses of the microstructure developed from each of the heat treatments included measurements of the prior-austenite grain diameter, the pearlite colony diameter, and the pearlite interlamellar spacing.

The random intercept method[8] was used to determine the austenite grain size. Measurements were taken from coupons that had been austenitized with the test specimens, quenched, and subsequently heat treated and etched to reveal the grain structure. Tempering these coupons at 783 K (950°F) for 16 h, followed by etching in boiling picric acid, successfully revealed the prior-austenite structure as dark grain boundaries on a white matrix.[7]

In order to better resolve the pearlite structure, electron transmission microscopy employing conventional two-stage carbon replica techniques was used. The colony size was determined from the same micrographs by the random intercept method.

After considerable preliminary study, it was decided to obtain the pearlite spacing by measuring the interlamellar distance in those colonies where the plates were oriented nearly perpendicular to the plane of observation. The pearlite in these colonies would thus be most likely to project the true spacing. This method was chosen in order to reduce the statistical counts needed, especially when using the random intercept technique. Measurements were made along secants drawn perpendicular to these colonies in similar fashion to the work of Brown and Ridley.[9] Results of this technique compared favorably with limited data obtained using the random intercept method, and, as mentioned, were not a function of location in the cross-section.

Mechanical Testing

The testing program included both tensile and instrumented impact tests. Room temperature tensile tests were performed at a strain rate of 0.01 per min. Both the yield strength (0.2 pct offset) and the reduction in area were calculated and correlated with microstructure variations due to heat treatment.

Dynamic instrumented impact tests, on precracked Charpy specimens, were chosen to evaluate the impact fracture toughness as a function of heat treatment.[10] An instrumented impact system utilizes strain gages mounted in the striking tup to sense and record the load-time history of the fracture process. In addition, the more conventional measure of toughness, energy absorbed, is also recorded. From these data, both W/A (absorbed energy per fractured area) and dynamic fracture toughness, K_{ID}, values were determined for each test condition.

K_{ID} is the fracture toughness of a material as measured under dynamic or impact conditions. For these experiments the stress intensity rate, $(\dot{K})$, was 3.3 to $4.4 \times 10^5 \, \dfrac{N}{m^{3/2} \, s}$. Since there is as yet no standardized procedure for this type of testing and data reduction, calculation of K_{ID} values from test data is discussed in Appendix 1, for both the elastic and plastic types of fracture. While the physical significance of K_{ID} values may be a source of disagreement due to nonstandardized test methods, they are none the less important as an additional means of evaluating relative changes in impact toughness levels. It should be noted that changes in dynamic fracture toughness correlated well with variations in impact energy for this series of experiments.

The results of the impact toughness tests will be represented primarily as Charpy transition curves, and only the Charpy transition will be correlated with microstructure. The Charpy transition temperature reported herein will be the temperature corresponding to a W/A ratio of $13.5 \times 10^4 \, \dfrac{N}{m}$ (71 ft lb/in.²). This value is roughly equal to one-half the difference between the lower and upper shelf energy, a value frequently used in the past as a measure of transition temperature.[11]

Statistical Analysis

Multiple-linear regression analyses were performed to determine statistically the dependence of the variables, yield strength, Charpy transition temperature, and reduction in area, on the three microstructural parameters of interest, viz, austenite grain size, pearlite colony size, and pearlite interlamellar spacing. A basic linear multiple regression computer subprogram was used. Because the program did not have the capability of determining the functional dependence of each dependent variable, the functional relationships had to be assumed. The final analysis was based on the relationships of $d^{-1/2}$ (grain size $^{-1/2}$), $P^{-1/2}$ (colony size $^{-1/2}$), and $S^{-1/2}$ (pearlite spacing $^{-1/2}$). In preliminary analyses, these relationships gave the best correlation with the experimental data. Functional relationships of this type have been previously described in the literature[1-3] for similar types of steels. A complete description of the analyses is contained in Appendix 2. The units for the three structural parameters, grain and colony size and pearlite spacing are in centimeters.

EXPERIMENTAL RESULTS

Microstructure

Results of the quantitative microscopy aspect of the study are presented in Table II. Examination of the microstructure for each heat treatment revealed a

Table II. The Effect of Heat Treatment on Microstructure of Eutectoid Steel

Heat Treatment	Austenitic Grain Size, 10^{-3} cm	Pearlite Colony Size, 10^{-4} cm	Pearlite Spacing, 10^{-6} cm
1	1.43	4.78	14.10
2	1.43	4.57	15.35
3	1.43	5.26	19.50
4	2.52	5.38	13.00
5	2.52	4.75	13.75
6	2.52	6.58	15.16
7	2.52	6.09	17.50
8	2.52	6.34	27.00
9	3.51	6.04	12.10
10	3.51	5.33	14.00
11	3.51	4.29	14.10
12	3.51	5.15	16.35
13	4.02	5.56	11.93
14	4.02	5.76	13.75
15	14.73	5.67	13.62
16	16.65	5.70	11.57
17	13.0*	7.12	15.67

*Estimated.
(The uncertainty in the values for grain size, colony size and pearlite spacing is of the order of 10 pct.)

Table III. Effect of Heat Treatment on Mechanical Properties of Eutectoid Steel

Heat Treatment	Charpy Transition Temperature, °F		Yield Strength, ksi		Reduction in Area, Pct	Hardness, R_c
	K	°F	(MN/m²)	ksi		
1	397	220	544.0	78.9	47.9	23.7
2	369	205	509.5	73.9	44.5	22.8
3	369	205	437.1	63.4	43.5	16.0
4	395	252	570.2	82.7	32.1	27.7
5	390	243	568.8	82.5	33.2	27.3
6	397	255	546.1	79.2	28.8	26.3
7	405	270	479.9	69.6	22.5	22.1
8	400	260	422.0	61.2	26.8	17.3
9	402	265	633.6	91.9	36.1	28.6
10	405	270	580.5	84.2	30.0	28.3
11	401	263	559.9	81.2	29.9	26.1
12	405	270	467.5	67.8	24.5	21.7
13	406	272	621.2	90.1	32.5	30.8
14	402	265	610.9	88.6	31.0	29.0
15	433	320	620.5	90.0	15.2	28.8
16	433	420	620.5	90.0	9.6	30.6
17	430	315	505.4	73.3	14.0	24.0

fully pearlitic structure. As expected, austenite grain size increased with increasing austenization time and temperature, from 1.43×10^{-3} cm to 16.65×10^{-3} cm. As noted previously, the finest austenite grain structure was produced by a rapid thermal cycle technique.[7]

The pearlite interlamellar spacing was a strong function of the isothermal transformation temperature: the pearlite spacing also increased as the prior austenite grain diameter decreased. This rather interesting result, substantiated by statistical analysis (see Appendix 2.13), has also been observed by Gladman *et al*[1] in a recent paper on continuously cooled steels, and by others.[12] The reason for this behavior is not clear, but it does not appear to be related to variations in austenitizing temperature and subsequent changes in cooling rate. To demonstrate this, specimens step-quenched from a higher austenitizing temperature (*e.g.*, 1273 K) to a lower one (*e.g.*, 1073 K) had a finer pearlite spacing than specimens austenitized only at 1073 K. This is an intriguing result which clearly deserves further study.

For the heat treatments performed, the pearlite colony diameter was relatively constant, in the range 4.5 to 6.0×10^{-4} cm. Gladman[1] has reported a much larger range of colony size than reported herein, for steels continuously cooled, but of variable composition. Because of the small variation in colony size in this study, it will be difficult to determine conclusively to what extent pearlite colony structure affects mechanical properties. The large variations in properties that are observed however, tends to negate any critical role of colony size in controlling resultant properties.

Strength and Hardness

As expected, both the room temperature yield stress and hardness were found to be a strong function of the pearlite interlamellar spacing. For a given prior austenitic grain size, there is typically a 20 to 30 pct increase in the 0.2 pct offset yield stress going from the coarsest pearlite spacing developed in this program

to the finest (Table III). A larger pearlite range was not studied because of our interest in this steel's behavior at high strength levels.

The regression equation found to best describe the relationship between yield stress and the three microstructural features is:

$$\sigma_{ys} \, (\text{Ksi})^* = 3.16 \times 10^{-1} \, (S^{-1/2}) - 5.79 \times 10^{-2} \, (P^{-1/2}) - 4.17 \times 10^{-1} \, (d^{-1/2}), + 7.58,$$

---

*1 ksi = 6.89 MPa. $K = (5/9)(°F + 459.67)$.

with standard errors of the coefficients of 4.61×10^{-2}, 4.19×10^{-1} and 2.25×10^{-1}, respectively. According to the statistical treatment, comparison of the standard error of the coefficient to its corresponding regression coefficient gives a measure of the correlation between variables. A relatively large error would indicate that the two variables are not significantly related. The computed T value which is simply the regression coefficient divided by the standard error of the coefficient is presented in Appendix 2 for the purpose of comparison; the greater the absolute value of T the better the correlation between variables.

Thus, the previous equation shows that increases in yield strength correlate best with decreases in pearlite spacing, and although the prior austenite grain size also has an effect on strength, the correlation is not as great. Indeed, further analyses (Appendix 2.8, 2.9, 2.10) indicate that pearlite spacing alone can account for 84 pct of the variation in strength, while grain size can only account for 37 pct. Variations in pearlite colony size have minimal effect on strength for the limited range available in this study, as shown by the standard error of the coefficient being larger than the regression coefficient.

The analyses indicate that yield stress does increase somewhat as prior austenite grain size increases. However, this is probably not a direct effect of grain size on the deformation process, but instead is attributable to the relationship between grain size and pearlite spacing. As mentioned above, for a given isothermal transformation temperature, pearlite spacing decreases as the grain size increases. Therefore, the beneficial effect of a large grain size on strength is not a direct effect, but results from a refinement of the pearlite spacing.

The complete range of data is summarized in Fig. 1. The graph bears out the conclusion that strength is primarily a function of the pearlite interlamellar spacing, and also that the relationship is satisfactorily represented by an inverse squared power law.

Toughness

Impact toughness, as measured by the Charpy transition temperature, ranged from 205°F (368 K) for two fine-grained microstructures to 315°F (430 K) for the coarsest grained steel (Table III). The best fit regression equation, containing terms for each of the three microstructural variables was determined to be: T.T. (°F) = -8.25×10^{-2} $(S^{-1/2}) - 1.22$ $(P^{-1/2}) - 5.55$ $(d^{-1/2})$ $+ 4.35 \times 10^2$ with standard errors of the coefficients of $\overline{8.74 \times 10^{-2}}$, 7.94×10^{-1} and 4.27×10^{-1}, respectively.

The large standard error of the coefficient for the pearlite spacing factor indicates that there is no significant correlation between toughness and pearlite spacing. Prior-austenite grain size, however, correlated well with transition temperature. In fact in a separate analysis (Appendix 2.3), grain size was able to account for 94 pct of the variation in toughness. The statistical fit is increased at the 10 pct significance

level by retaining the term for pearlite colony size, suggesting that this factor can contribute.

The resultant regression equation incorporating only these two terms is: T.T. (°F) $- 1.49$ $(P^{-1/2}) - 5.33$ $(d^{-1/2}) + 4.21 \times 10^2$ with standard errors of the coefficients of $\overline{7.49 \times 10^{-1}}$ and 3.57×10^{-1}, respectively. Note that the prior austenite grain term has a regression coefficient larger than that for colony size by a factor of approximately 4 to 1. This supports the graphical results, plotted in Fig. 2, and indicates that grain size is the effective means of influencing the toughness of eutectoid steel.

Fig. 2 shows that the Charpy transition temperature is shifted down the temperature scale as the grain size is decreased, with the pearlite spacing maintained at a constant value. The conjugate case is represented in Fig. 3; here the prior-austenitic grain size is kept constant and the pearlite spacing is varied, with no apparent effect on the transition temperature. The complete range of data is summarized in Fig. 4 by plotting Charpy transition temperature vs $(d^{-1/2})$. These data support the previous conclusion that toughness is primarily a function of prior-austenite grain size.

The corresponding values of dynamic fracture toughness, (K_{ID}), associated with the data of Fig. 2 are illustrated in Fig. 5. At a temperature of 0°F, the dynamic fracture toughness, K_{ID}, increased from approximately 20 ksi $\sqrt{\text{in}}$. (22 MN/m$^{3/2}$) to 38 ksi $\sqrt{\text{in}}$. (41.7 MN/m$^{3/2}$) by refining the grain size an order of

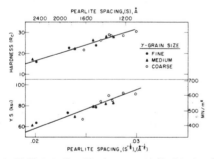

Fig. 1—Yield strength and hardness vs pearlite interlamellar spacing.

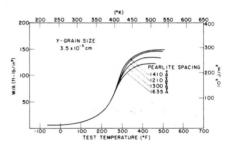

Fig. 3—Charpy transition curves as a function of pearlite interlamellar spacing.

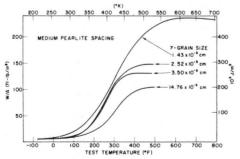

Fig. 2—Charpy transition curves as a function of prior austenitic grain size.

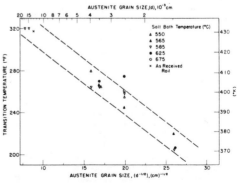

Fig. 4—Charpy transition temperature vs prior austenitic grain size.

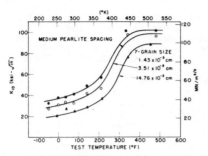

Fig. 5—Dynamic fracture toughness, K_{ID}, curves as a function of prior austenitic grain size.

magnitude. This corresponds to an increase in critical flaw size of almost a factor of four. The above illustration shows that for dynamic service application, microstructural manipulations can affect a large change in the critical crack size, putting it for some loading situations into the detectable size range for nondestructive testing.

Finally, it is of interest to examine the role of microstructure on the upper shelf energy (Figs. 2 and 3). A refined austenite grain size greatly increases the energy absorbed during the plastic tearing processes normally associated with the upper shelf. The pearlite spacing has a nonsystematic effect; if anything, the upper shelf energy shows a tendency to increase with decreasing pearlite spacing. It seems clear that for eutectoid steels, the critical structural parameter controlling toughness is the austenite grain size. This behavior extends to the case of tensile ductility as discussed in the next section.

Ductility

Ductility, as measured by the reduction in area, varied with microstructure from approximately 10 pct to 50 pct. The regression equation correlating reduction in area to microstructure was: R_A (pct) = 1.24 $\times 10^{-1}$ $(S^{-1/2})$ + 2.66 $\times 10^{-1}$ $(P^{-1/2})$ + 1.85 $\overline{(d^{-1/2})}$ − 4.71 $\times 10^1$ with standard errors of the coefficients of 4.95 $\times 10^{-2}$, 4.50 $\times 10^{-1}$ and 2.42 $\times 10^{-1}$, respectively.

Examination of the regression coefficients indicates that the prior austenite grain diameter has the greatest influence on ductility, with pearlite spacing having a more modest effect and colony size (for the range available in this study) having little effect.

DISCUSSION

It has been shown that the strength of fully pearlitic eutectoid steel is controlled microstructurally by the pearlite interlamellar spacing, while fracture toughness and tensile ductility vary inversely with prior austenite grain size. The results also suggest, based on a limited range of data, that pearlite colony size does not significantly affect strength, and has, at most, a secondary influence on toughness. A major significance of these results is that strength and toughness are controlled by different microstructural parameters, and thus, an increase in either property need not be compromised, as in the more common case when the two properties are inversely related.

The dependence of the yield strength of high carbon steels on pearlite spacing has been previously reported in the literature.[1,3] These studies concluded that the flow stress of pearlite follows a Hall-Petch relationship:

$$\sigma_y = \sigma_i + k_y \, (S)^{-1/2}$$

which also fits the data reported herein. Karlsson et al[13] have recently summarized existing data for eutectoid steels and have stated that a best mean value of the Hall-Petch slope (k_y) for the yield stress is 0.25 $MN/m^{3/2}$ which is in excellent agreement with the value of 0.246 $MN/m^{3/2}$ obtained in this study. It should be noted that the regression analysis for the results of this study resulted in a negative intercept which although clearly inconsistent with the definition of friction stress as the stress for dislocation movement in the lattice, has also been reported in two of the three studies on eutectoid steel.[2,3] A statistically satisfactory correlation can also be obtained with S^{-1}, and a positive friction stress is obtained. The lack of a rigorous model for either function makes further analysis unnecessary. The Petch slope value obtained from the former relationship is in good agreement with a variety of iron alloys, implying that carbide-ferrite interfaces and ferrite-ferrite interfaces are equally effective dislocation barriers.

The explanation generally advanced as to why the flow strength should be controlled by the pearlite spacing is that the available slip distance, in this case the distance between pearlite lamellae, is the most important variable in determining strength. This explanation is quite reasonable since it has been shown that carbide lamellae are effective barriers to dislocation motion.[14] In fact, this argument is essential to several theories of microcrack initiation in pearlite which require the stress buildup at the carbide-ferrite interface to be large enough to cleave the carbide lamella.[15]

The fracture process in eutectoid steels, however, is less well understood. Austenitic grain size,[6] pearlite colony size,[1] and pearlite spacing[4,5] have all previously been correlated with toughness in the literature. The present research has demonstrated that varying the prior-austenitic grain size has a much greater effect on the subsequent fracture toughness than varying the pearlite spacing or colony size.

The effect of pearlite interlamellar spacing on toughness has been a matter of controversy in the literature. We believe that this uncertainty may be due, in part, to the varied carbon and alloy contents of the previously studied steels, since the present data indicates little or no effect of pearlite spacing on impact fracture toughness of precracked specimens. An explanation proposed by Gladman et al, who found similar results using V-notch specimens, is that the effect of cementite plate thickness and ferrite spacing tend to cancel one another out, with the advantages of a reduction in cementite plate thickness being offset by the harmful effects of refining the interlamellar ferrite spacing. Although this rationalization accounts for the data, we believe it more likely that running cleavage cracks are for all practical purposes insensitive to interpearlite structure, so long as the pearlitic ferrite orientation is continuous. We shall return to this point.

It may also be worthwhile to mention that in preliminary testing using unprecracked V-notch specimens, the V-notch transition temperature was affected to a greater extent by variations in pearlite spacing than was the value obtained with dynamic fracture toughness specimens. This would indicate that the initiation process in these steels is more sensitive to pearlite structure than the propagation phase, a result consistent with cracks being initiated at stress concentrations at the ferrite-carbide interface.

The remaining parameter that has not been considered, and that can be controlled by the prior-austenitic grain size, is the relative crystallographic orientations of the various microstructural units. Previous researchers[6,16] who have studied the fracture process in pearlitic steels, have noted that the cleavage cracks apparently follow certain cleavage planes in the ferrite laths. Thus, if the prior-austenite grain structure can control the resultant ferrite orientations in pearlite, it may explain the influence of grain size on toughness.

To model the situation, consider that toughness is related to the number of mismatch boundaries in a microstructure at which a running crystallographic cleavage crack must alter direction, possibly by renucleation or by some other energy absorbing process. For pearlitic steels, Turkalo[6] has observed that the fracture path often continued as a single cleavage facet across a number of pearlitic colonies, extending over part of, or in some cases, the whole of one former austenite grain. This would seem to imply that the ferrite from a single austenite grain has a preferred orientation, such that cleavage planes in adjacent pearlite colonies are continuous or closely aligned. In line with this thinking, a finer prior austenitic grain size would lead to smaller units of preferred ferrite orientation and, therefore, a higher fracture toughness.

An alternative explanation, based on Smith's[17] results on pearlite growth in eutectoid steel is that for a given transformed austenite grain, the ferrite laths in pearlite should bear a specific orientation relationship to a neighboring grain of austenite; this adjacent grain being the true parent crystal for the crystal of ferrite. This, of course, differs from the explanation proposed above, which required the pearlitic ferrite of each colony be related to the prior-austenite grain in which it is contained. In this model, the effect of prior-austenite grain size on toughness is explainable by relating austenite grain diameter to the number and size of orientation "units" in the pearlite. Each "unit" is made up of adjacent pearlite colonies of common parentage and therefore common ferrite orientation. In a structure that has a large prior-austenitic grain size, there may be several colonies nucleated on a given grain side and therefore of the same 'unit' parentage. In a fine grained structure far fewer colonies would have common parentage, so each "unit" may be comprised of as few as one colony. For an equal pearlite colony size, the fine-grained structure would thus have considerably more orientation "units" and, therefore, would present more resistance to crack propagation. In support of this approach, Dippenaar and Honeycombe[18] recently found, in a high manganese steel, that the pearlitic ferrite and cementite are related to the austenite grain into which they are not growing.

To ascertain which of the two proposed models is operative requires being able to differentiate between prior-austenite and colony boundaries in fully eutectoid steels, in order, for example, to show if there is a one-to-one correspondence between a fracture facet and a prior-austenite grain. Such studies are underway, as are orientation determinations of the ferrite within adjacent colonies. As part of this more comprehensive study, Park[19] has measured the facet size in more than one hundred fractured precracked Charpy specimens. He finds that while the average facet size is a strong function of the prior-austenitic grain size, it is always somewhat less, particularly for larger grain sizes. As expected from our results, he finds little systematic variation between pearlite spacing and facet size. The lack of direct correspondence between prior-austenitic grain size and facet size tends to support the approach of Smith[17] and Dippenaar and Honeycombe,[18] although considerably more work is needed to establish the origin of these pearlite colony units.

CONCLUSIONS

1) The strength and toughness of fully pearlitic steel are controlled by different microstructural parameters, and can be varied independently of one other to optimize service performance in such materials as rail steel.

2) Strength is dependent on the pearlite interlamellar spacing; decreasing the spacing results in an increase in strength. Pearlite spacing can be refined by decreasing the transformation temperature and to a lesser extent by increasing the austenitic grain size. The reason for this latter effect is not known.

3) Fracture toughness is more strongly a function of the prior-austenitic grain size. The finer the grain size, the greater the toughness. Pearlite colony size for the range studied has a minor influence at best on toughness. The fact that large variations in toughness are possible with little change in colony size, suggests that this is not a useful microstructural parameter to control toughness.

4) The results of this study suggest that the fracture process is controlled by a structural unit made up of a number of colonies, within which the ferrite should have the same crystallographic orientation. The size of this unit is controlled by, but is not identical to, the prior austenitic grain size.

APPENDIX 1

Dynamic fracture toughness values were calculated using instrumented impact data for both the linear elastic type of fracture, and the case of yielding before fracture. For the linear elastic case, a "valid" toughness value may be obtained for dynamic testing by applying linear elastic fracture mechanics, Ref. 1a:

$$K_{ID} = \frac{1.5 \, Y \, L \, (P_F) \, a^{1/2}}{B W^2} \qquad \text{Eq. [1A]}$$

where

$$Y = \text{function of } (a/W)$$

L = support span width
P_F = load at fracture
a = total crack depth
B = thickness
W = width.

When the appropriate Charpy and load dimensions (in inches and pounds are considered), Eq. [1] reduces to:

$$K_{ID} = 38.7 \, Y(P_F) \, a^{1/2}. \qquad \text{Eq. [2A]}$$

There is considerable controversy regarding the calculation of a meaningful fracture toughness value based on data derived from a specimen which fractures after general yielding. Several methods have been developed, however, for estimating the material's toughness, had the test sample been large enough for linear elastic fracture to occur. The lower-bound equivalent-energy approach was used for this study.[2a,3a] This method assumes that for a valid size specimen, fracture would have occurred at an energy equivalent to the initiation energy (energy at maximum load) measured for the Charpy size specimen. From this method, extrapolated values of P_F, corrected for machine compliance, are used in Eq. [2A] to obtain K_{ID}.[4a]

APPENDIX 2

Multiple linear regression analyses were performed in order to determine which microstructural parameters are related to each mechanical property, and, if possible, to rate the variables in order of their importance. As previously mentioned, the Computer Science Corporation (CSCX) commercial basic multiple linear regression analyses program was used. The results of each analyses are contained in this section.

For each analysis, the independent and dependent variables are identified as numbers. The data matrix contained the following parameters:

1 pearlite spacing $S^{-1/2}$
2 pearlite colony size $P^{-1/2}$
3 austenite grain size $d^{-1/2}$
4 transformation temperature   (°C)
5 austenite grain size d
6 Charpy transition temperature   (°F)
7 yield strength   (Ksi)
8 reduction in area   (pct)
9 hardness (R_c)

The units for 1 to 3 have been given in the text.

2.1) Dependent Variable—6
Independent Variables—1, 2, 3

Variable	Regression Coefficient	Standard Error Coefficient	Computed T
1	− 8.25 E−02	8.74 E−02	− 9.44 E−01
2	− 1.22 E+00	7.94 E−01	− 1.54 E+00
3	− 5.55 E+00	4.27 E−01	− 1.29 E+01

R-squared = 0.957 (gives the confidence to which the dependent variable can be accounted for in terms of the independent variables).

2.2) Dependent Variable—6
Independent Variables—2, 3

Variable	Regression Coefficient	Standard Error Coefficient	Computed T
2	−1.49 E+00	7.43 E−01	− 2.00 E+00
3	−5.33 E+00	3.57 E−01	−1.49 E+01

R-squared = 0.954.

2.3) Dependent Variable—6
Independent Variable—3

Variable	Regression Coefficient	Standard Error Coefficient	Computed T
3	− 5.55 E+00	3.75 E−01	−1.48 E+01

R-squared = 0.939.

2.4) Dependent Variable—6
Independent Variable—2

Variable	Regression Coefficient	Standard Error Coefficient	Computed T
2	− 4.85 E+00	2.90 E+00	− 1.67 E+00

R-squared = 0.166.

2.5) Dependent Variable—6
Independent Variable—1

Variable	Regression Coefficient	Standard Error Coefficient	Computed T
1	4.49 E−01	3.02 E−01	1.49 E+00

R-squared = 0.136.

2.6) Dependent Variable—7
Independent Variables—1, 2, 3

Variable	Regression Coefficient	Standard Error Coefficient	Computed T
1	3.16 E−01	4.61 E−02	6.85 E+00
2	−5.79 E−02	4.19 E−01	−1.38 E−01
3	−4.17 E−01	2.25 E−01	−1.85 E+00

R-squared = 0.883.

2.7) Dependent Variable—7
Independent Variables—1, 3

Variable	Regression Coefficient	Standard Error Coefficient	Computed T
1	3.14 E−01	4.16 E−02	7.54 E+00
3	−4.31 E−01	1.96 E−01	−2.19 E+00

R-squared = 0.883.

2.8) Dependent Variable—7
Independent Variable—1

Variable	Regression Coefficient	Standard Error Coefficient	Computed T
1	3.57 E−01	4.16 E−02	8.58 E+00

R-squared = 0.840.

2.9) Dependent Variable—7
Independent Variable—3

Variable	Regression Coefficient	Standard Error Coefficient	Computed T
3	−1.12 E+00	3.88 E−01	−2.89 E+00

R-squared = 0.373.

2.10) Dependent Variable—7
Independent Variable—2

Variable	Regression Coefficient	Standard Error Coefficient	Computed T
2	1.37 E—01	1.02 E+00	1.34 E—01

R-squared = 0.001.

2.11) Dependent Variable—8
Independent Variables—1, 2, 3

Variable	Regression Coefficient	Standard Error Coefficient	Computed T
1	1.24 E—01	4.95 E—02	2.50 E+00
2	2.66 E—01	4.50 E—01	5.92 E—01
3	1.85 E+00	2.42 E—01	7.62 E+00

R-squared = 0.866.

2.12) Dependent Variable—9
Independent Variables—1, 2, 3

Variable	Regression Coefficient	Standard Error Coefficient	Computed T
1	1.39 E—01	1.89 E—02	7.36 E+00
2	—9.72 E—02	1.71 E—01	—5.67 E—01
3	—2.15 E—01	9.22 E—02	—2.33 E—00

R-squared = 0.902.

2.13) Dependent Variable—1
Independent Variables—4, 5

Variable	Regression Coefficient	Standard Error Coefficient	Computed T
4	—6.33 E—04	6.42 E—05	—9.85 E+00
5	—2.08 E+00	4.95 E—01	—4.20 E+00

R-squared = 0.901.

ACKNOWLEDGMENTS

The authors would like to acknowledge the generous support of the Association of American Railroads, the Processing Research Institute of Carnegie-Mellon University, and the National Science Foundation, who sponsored this research. The authors wish to thank D. H. Stone, of the Association of American Railroads Research Center, who served as technical liaison for the project, W. Server and D. Ireland of Dynatup for their valuable discussions concerning instrumented impact testing, and Professor J. R. Low, Jr. for valuable and fruitful discussions on the fracture of pearlite. Special thanks are due to Y. J. Park and G. K. Bouse, graduate students in the Department of Metallurgy and Materials Science at Carnegie-Mellon University, for experimental assistance, valuable discussions, and for permitting us to use some of their preliminary results. The findings presented herein were part of a final report submitted by J. M. Hyzak in partial fulfillment of the requirements for the degree of Master of Engineering at Carnegie-Mellon University.

REFERENCES

1. T. Gladman, I. McIvor, and F. Pickering: *J. Iron Steel Inst.*, 1972, vol. 210, p. 916.
2. M. Gensamer, E. B. Pearsall, W. S. Pellini, and J. R. Low, Jr.: *Trans. ASM*, 1942, vol. 30, p. 983.
3. T. Takahashi and M. Nagumo: *Trans. Jap. Inst. Metals*, 1970, vol. 11, p. 113.
4. J. Gross and D. Stout: *Weld. J.*, 1955, vol. 34, p. 117S.
5. G. Burns and C. Judge: *J. Iron Steel Inst.*, 1956, vol. 182, p. 292.
6. A. Turkalo: *Trans. TMS-AIME*, 1960, vol. 218, p. 24.
7. R. Grange: *Met. Trans.*, 1971, vol. 2, p. 65.
8. American Society for Testing Materials, 1974 Standard Designation E-112.
9. D. Brown and R. Ridley: *J. Iron Steel Inst.*, 1966, vol. 204, p. 812.
10. R. A. Wullaert: ASTM STP 466, p. 148, 1970.
11. G. E. Dieter: *Mechanical Metallurgy*, p. 370, McGraw-Hill, N.Y., 1961.
12. J. R. Vilella, G. E. Guellich, and E. C. Bain: *Trans. ASM*, 1936, vol. 24, p. 225.
13. B. Karlsson and G. Linden: *Mater. Sci. Eng.*, 1975, vol. 17, p. 153.
14. A. Rosenfield, E. Votava, and G. Hahn: *Trans. ASM*, 1968, vol. 61, p. 807.
15. A. Rosenfield, G. Hahn, and J. Embury: *Met. Trans.*, 1972, vol. 3, p. 2797.
16. U. Lindborg: *Trans. ASM*, 1968, vol. 61, p. 500.
17. C. S. Smith: *Trans. ASM*, 1953, vol. 45, p. 533.
18. R. J. Dippenaar and R. W. K. Honeycombe: *Proc. Roy. Soc., London*, 1973, vol. A333, p. 455.
19. Y. J. Park: Unpublished research, Department of Metallurgy and Materials Science, Carnegie-Mellon University, Pittsburgh, Pa., 1974.

APPENDIX REFERENCES

1a. W. Brown and J. Srawley: *Plane Strain Fracture Toughness Testing of High Strength Materials*, ASTM STP 410, 1966.
2a. F. J. Witt: *Equivalent Energy Procedures for Predicting Gross Plastic Fracture*, USAEC Report ORNL-TM3172, Oak Ridge National Laboratories, 1970.
3a. J. A. Begley and J. Landes: *Progress in Flaw Growth and Fracture Toughness Testing*, ASTM STP 536, p. 246, 1973.
4a. W. Server, D. Ireland, and R. Wullaert: *Strength and Toughness Evaluations from an Instrumented Impact Test*, Dynatup Report TR74-29R, 1974.

The Process of Crack Initiation and Effective Grain Size for Cleavage Fracture in Pearlitic Eutectoid Steel

Y. J. PARK AND I. M. BERNSTEIN

The process of cleavage crack initiation and the character of the effective grain size which controls the fracture toughness of pearlitic eutectoid steel has been investigated using smooth tensile and precracked Charpy impact specimens. The results demonstrated that initial cracking in both specimens was largely the result of shear cracking of pearlite; *i.e.*, localized slip bands in ferrite promoted cracking of the cementite plates, which was then followed by tearing of the adjacent ferrite laths. Such behavior initially results in a fibrous crack. In the tensile specimen, the initiation site was identified as a fibrous region which grew under the applied stress, eventually initiating an unstable cleavage crack. In precracked impact specimens, this critical crack size was much smaller due to the high state of stress near the precrack tip. Fracture mechanics analysis showed that the first one or two dimples formed by the shear cracking process can initiate a cleavage crack. Using thin foil transmission electron microscopy, a cleavage facet was found to be an orientation unit where the ferrites (and the cementites) of contiguous colonies share a common orientation. The size of this orientation unit, which is equal to the cleavage facet size, is controlled by the prior austenite grain size. The influence of austenite grain size on toughness is thus explained by the fact that the austenite grain structure can control the resultant orientation of ferrite and cementite in pearlitic structures.

PEARLITE plays an important role in the ductile to brittle transition behavior of ferrite/pearlite steels.[1,2] In particular, pearlite tends to promote brittle fracture, and because of this it has been studied extensively for a number of years,[2-7] with some aspects of the process now well established and documented.[8] For example, it has been observed that in tensile specimens of ferrite/pearlite steels, pearlite cracks lie predominantly at 45 deg to the tensile axis, in pearlite colonies whose lamellae lie parallel to the tensile axis.[3,5,7] In other words, the fracture process is initiated by the concentration of stress on the plane of maximum resolved shear stress, which in turn promotes cracking of that cementite which lies in the direction of maximum tensile stress. When the shear stress becomes large enough, the small cracks or holes in adjoining cementite lamellae can link up to form a macroscopic crack. This mechanism is known as a shear cracking process in pearlite, after Miller and Smith.[7]

However, confusion has arisen in attempting to correlate this shear cracking process to the subsequent process of brittle cleavage fracture. Rosenfield *et al*[5] and Ohmori and Terasaki[9] have claimed that cleavage fracture in ferrite/pearlite steels was initiated from this type of pearlite cracks, which they thought to be cleavage cracks. On the other hand, Tetelman and McEvily[10] concluded, from the early work of Bruckner,[3] that the initial holes in cementites would link up to form fibrous cracks, rather than cleavage

cracks, with these cracks subsequently developing into fast running cleavage cracks. Because of limited fractographic studies performed to date, it was impossible to resolve this conflict without further experimentation.

Another interesting subject related to the process of cleavage fracture in pearlitic steels is the role of prior austenite grain structure. It has been established for a considerable time that prior austenite grain size is the dominant microstructural factor controlling the fracture toughness of pearlitic steels; the finer the grain size, the greater the toughness.[11-13] This is intriguing since the austenite grain structure, which is a high temperature phase and which does not exist at the test temperature, controls the fracture process of these steels.

The effect of pearlite colony boundaries, which do exist at the test temperature, on the fracture toughness of these steels is also controversial. While Gladman *et al*[14] found the pearlite colony size to be an important parameter in controlling the fracture toughness of pearlitic steels, Hyzak and Bernstein[13] suggested that the colony size is not a useful parameter. The latter study is supported by an early electron microscopy observation of Turkalo.[15] She observed, in a high carbon pearlitic steel, that while the fracture path often changed direction at a colony boundary, the crack more often continued as a single cleavage facet across a number of pearlite colonies. This observation was recently confirmed by a direct correlation study between fracture surface and pearlitic microstructure.[16]

The fact that a crack can propagate across a number of pearlite colonies requires that {100} cleavage planes of the ferrite lamellae in these colonies be essentially continuous, if indeed the cracking is cleavage in nature. The size of such an orientation unit can then be related to the fracture toughness, because most of the energy

Y. J. PARK, formerly with Carnegie-Mellon University, Pittsburgh, PA, is now with Technical Center, Association of American Railroads, Chicago, IL 60616. I. M. BERNSTEIN is Professor, Department of Metallurgy and Materials Science, Carnegie-Mellon University, Pittsburgh, PA 15213.
Manuscript submitted February 2, 1979.

absorbing processes for a propagating crack are associated with mismatch boundaries.[17] This orientation unit can thus be considered as an effective grain size which controls the fracture toughness of these steels. In order to demonstrate the validity of this hypothesis, a crystallographic orientation study of adjoining colonies was necessary.

It is the purpose of this investigation to study in detail the specific roles of the pearlitic microstructure in the process of cleavage crack initiation, and the prior austenite grain size on the fracture toughness of pearlitic eutectoid steel. By understanding these detailed aspects of the fracture process, it is hoped that means of improving the resistance of this steel to cleavage fracture can be suggested.

EXPERIMENTAL

Material

Specimens used for the present study were selected from fractured specimens obtained from a previous study on rail steel.[13] The history of the selected specimens are briefly described below.

The material used in the investigation was hot-rolled plain-carbon rail steel, having the following composition (wt pct):

C	Mn	Si	P	S	Fe
0.81	0.87	0.17	0.018	0.013	Balance

Oversized blanks ($12 \times 12 \times 68$ mm) were cut from a rail head such that the longitudinal direction of the blanks was parallel to the rolling direction of the rail. One set of the blanks was austenitized for 3 h at 1200°C, and two other sets for 1 h at 800 and 1200°C, respectively. After austenitizing, they were isothermally transformed to pearlite in salt baths held at a constant temperature of either 585 or 675°C. Transformation times were chosen to ensure complete transformations, without the complication of appreciable spheroidization. The heat treatment schedule is summarized in Table I, and the resulting microstructure and yield strength for each heat treatment are listed in Table II.

After heat treatment, the blanks were machined to final size; for the tensile test this was to a gage diameter of 6.35 mm with a gage length of 25.4 mm, and for the

impact tests this was $10 \times 10 \times 55$ mm. Room temperature tensile tests were performed at a strain-rate of 0.01/min. Dynamic instrumented impact tests, on fatigue precracked standard Charpy V-notch specimens, were used to evaluate the impact fracture toughness. More experimental details on this aspect of the study are described elsewhere.[13]

Charpy bars broken at or below room temperature (service temperature range of rails) and the tensile specimens of heat treatment no. 1, were used to examine the process of crack initiation. Charpy bars of heat treatments no. 2 and 3, which were also broken at or below room temperature, were selected to study the effective grain size for cleavage fracture. These specimens were selected because they apparently exhibited a complete cleavage fracture mode.

Electron Microscopy

In order to investigate the process of crack initiation, microcracks near the fracture surface were examined by both scanning electron microscopy and thin foil transmission electron microscopy. Thin foils were prepared from some of the fractured specimens by the following technique: nickel was electroplated onto the fracture surface from an aqueous solution of 330 g $NiSO_4 \cdot 6H_2O$ + 45 g $NiCl_2 \cdot 6H_2O$ + 37 g H_3BO_3 + 0.3 g of sodium lauryl sulfate per liter at 60°C, at a current density of 50 mA/cm^2 for 72 h, to give a deposit about 1.5 mm thick. Following plating, 0.2 mm thick slices were cut from the specimen so as to include the fracture surface. These slices were mechanically ground to 50 μm and then discs of 3 mm diam were cut out such that the fracture surface was located across the center of the disc (Fig. 1). The discs of half nickel and half steel were thinned by argon ion bombardment in an ion miller. The thinning was performed until a perforation crossed the fracture surface. It was then possible to examine the fracture surface and the region directly adjacent to it by transmission electron microscopy, yielding information on both crack initiation and propagation.

In order to establish the effective grain size for cleavage fracture, the crystallographic orientation relationships among adjacent pearlite colonies were studied by thin foil transmission electron microscopy. For this study, two specimens were selected to compare the effect of different prior austenite grain sizes. One (heat treatment no. 2) has a large austenite grain size of 147 μm, and the other (heat treatment no. 3) a small austenite grain size of 25 μm. In both cases, the pearlite colony sizes were similar and about 6 μm.

The ferrite-ferrite orientation relationships in adjacent pearlite colonies were studied by selected area electron diffraction techniques to determine whether or not {100} ferrite cleavage planes in these

Table I. Heat Treatment Schedule for Eutectoid Steel

Heat Treatment	Austenitization Temperature, °C	Austenitization Time, h	Salt Bath Temperature, °C
1	1200	3	585
2	1200	1	585
3	800	1	675

Table II. Effect of Heat Treatment on Microstructure and Yield Strength of Eutectoid Steel

Heat Treatment	Austenite Grain Size, μm	Pearlite Colony Size, μm	Pearlite Spacing, nm	0.2 Pct Offset Yield Strength, MPa
1	166.5	5.70	115.7	621
2	147.3	5.67	136.2	621
3	25.2	6.34	270.0	422

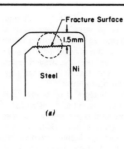

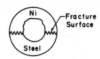

Fig. 1—Thin foil preparation method for an ion miller: (a) A specimen half nickel and half steel containing the fracture surface was cut from a nickel plated specimen, (b) The final form of the specimen after a perforation crossed the fracture surface.

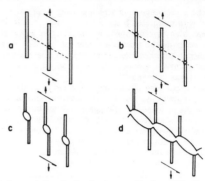

Fig. 3—A suggested mechanism for shear cracking in pearlite, after Miller and Smith.[7]

colonies are closely aligned. Three diffraction patterns were usually taken for a given pair of pearlite colonies; one from each colony and one encompassing both regions and the colony boundary. The diffraction patterns obtained were often quite complicated, mainly due to numerous diffraction spots from the cementite. In such cases, the microdiffraction capability of the scanning transmission electron microscope permitted the unique and simple determination of individual ferrite laths. This technique has the advantage of allowing orientations to be obtained from very small areas, on the order of 3 nm in diam.[18] Since the widths of ferrite lamellae are on the order of 100 nm, such widths are well within the resolution of microdiffraction.

In several cases, the orientation relationships of cementite were also studied to establish whether the cementite lamellae in adjacent colonies have a similar crystallographic orientation when such colonies have a similar ferrite orientation.

RESULTS

Process of Crack Initiation

In the necked region of the tensile specimen of heat treatment no. 1, a number of microcracks were observed. These microcracks had a tendency to align at 45 deg to the tensile axis when the lamellae were approximately parallel to the tensile axis (Fig. 2), in agreement with previous studies.[3,5,7] This suggests that the microcracks were formed by the so-called 'shear cracking process' (Fig. 3) described by Miller and Smith.[7] Sequentially, this entails slip occurring in ferrite when the specimen is stressed. Then, due to the stress concentration at the ferrite/cementite interfaces along the ferrite slip plane, the initial cracking occurs in the cementite plates. The cracked cementites promote shear of the ferrite on the slip plane. Finally, when the shear becomes large enough, the initial holes in cementite link up to form a macroscopic microcrack.

This type of initial cracking of cementite was abundantly observed on thin foils of the tensile specimen. An example showing the cementite cracks is shown in

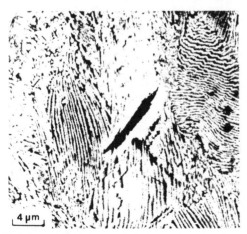

Fig. 2—Scanning electron micrograph showing nonpropagating microcracks in a sectioned tensile specimen. The arrows indicate the direction of tensile axis.

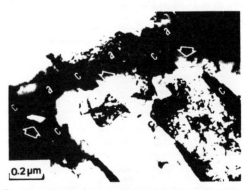

Fig. 4—Ion milled thin foil transmission electron micrograph showing the early stage of shear cracking process in a tensile specimen. The arrows, a and c indicate microcracks, ferrite, and cementite, respectively.

Fig. 4. Even though we could not identify the direction of the tensile axis on a thin foil, the inclined micro-cracks in Fig. 4 imply that the lamellae probably lie parallel to the tensile axis. In this case, we hoped to observe localized slip bands in ferrite near the cementite cracks, but no such evidence has been found. Rather, Fig. 4 shows an apparently fine recrys-tallized microstructure near some of the cracks. The explanation for these observations is not presently at hand, but one possible suggestion is that heavily de-formed regions in the ferrite may recover or recrys-tallize during the 20 h exposure at the relatively high temperatures developed in the presently used ion miller.

In the precracked impact specimens of the same heat treatment, far fewer nonpropagating microcracks were observed, and only very near the fracture surfaces. This is believed due to the higher intrinsic brittleness of the impact specimens, as compared to the tensile specimen. However, in the impact specimens as well, thin foil transmission electron microscopy also showed the same type of cementite cracks as in the tensile specimen. An example is illustrated in Fig. 5. These results suggest that the shear cracking process is responsible for the formation of the microcracks in both tensile and impact specimens. A problem in extending the shear cracking process to impact frac-ture is that the process should result in a fibrous crack surface (Fig. 3), and not the observed cleavage mode, suggesting that the two crack stages have different origins.

To further investigate the origin of crack initiation, the fracture surfaces for both specimen types were carefully examined by scanning electron microscopy. Because of the nature of river patterns in cleavage fracture, it was possible to locate the points of origin of each crack by following the river patterns back to their sources. In the tensile specimen, initiation sites with associated plastic deformation were observed (Fig. 6(a)). Thus in this case, while a crack was ini-tiated from the center of the cleavage facet, the initia-tion site itself was revealed to consist of a number of dimples (Fig. 6(b)). This fibrous crack appears to be formed by the shear cracking of pearlite, the same mechanism for the nonpropagating microcracks dis-cussed above. In the impact specimens, however,

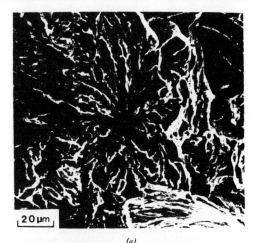

(a)

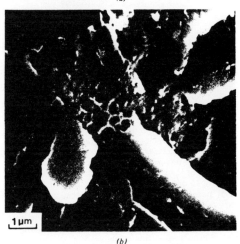

(b)

Fig. 6—Scanning electron fractographs showing an initiation site in a tensile specimen.

initiation sites, found very near the tip of the fatigue precrack, were almost featureless. An example is shown in Fig. 7. Even at the highest magnifications obtain-able, this type of initiation site showed only fine river patterns, and little could be learned from detailed studies of their morphology. It appears that in such instances the first microcrack formed was capable of propagating catastrophically as a cleavage crack. In other words, the critical crack size for cleavage crack propagation is very small, most likely due to the high stress concentration near the precrack tip of the impact specimen. More detailed discussions of these points are made later.

Orientation Relationships in Adjacent Colonies

The orientation studies, as reported in a previous paper,[19] demonstrated that many adjoining pearlite

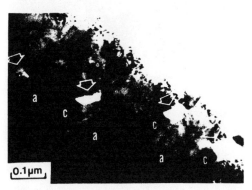

Fig. 5—Ion milled thin foil transmission electron micrograph showing the early stage of shear cracking process in an impact specimen.

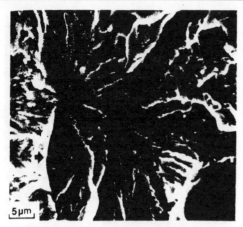

Fig. 7—Scanning electron fractograph of a crack initiation site near fatigue precrack tip in an impact specimen. The arrows indicate the precrack tip. The left side of the tip is the fatigue zone.

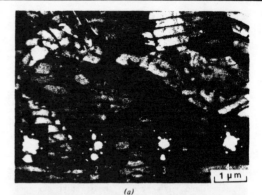

(a)

(b)

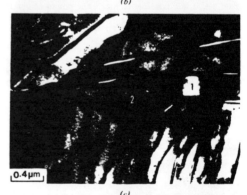

(c)

Fig. 8—Four pearlite colonies with a common [100] ferrite zone axis: (a) bright-field electron micrograph, and corresponding micro-diffraction patterns; misorientation between colony 1 and 2 is 6 deg; colony 2 and 3, 3 deg; colony 3 and 4, 19 deg; colony 1 and 4, 10 deg; colony 2 and 4, 16 deg, (b) selected area diffraction patterns from colony 1 and 2, and (c) the corresponding bright field electron micrograph.

colonies have a similar crystallographic orientation of ferrite, especially in the large grain size material. Figure 8 shows an example of this, where four pearlite colonies share a common <100> ferrite zone axis. Microdiffraction patterns 1 to 4 were taken from ferrite lamellae 1 to 4, respectively. Selected area diffraction patterns were also obtained from each combination of pearlite colony pairs. The selected area diffraction patterns from a pair of pearlite colonies 1 and 2 are illustrated in Fig. 8(b) with the corresponding bright-field electron micrograph (Fig. 8(c)). The misorientations, determined from both the selected area and microdiffraction patterns, varied from 3 to 19 deg. Although the misorientation between colonies 3 and 4 along two of the three cube directions (say [010] and [001]) is 19 deg, the misorientation along the other [100] direction will be very small, because the colonies have essentially the same [100] ferrite zone axis. In the present study, it is assumed that a cleavage crack propagates on the planes of least misorientation; i.e., (100) planes in this case.

When diffraction pairs yielded nonequivalent zone axes, standard stereographic projections for cubic crystals were used to ascertain the smallest angle between the {100} ferrite planes in the adjoining pearlite colonies. An example is illustrated in Figs. 9 and 10. In Fig. 9, the selected area diffraction patterns (b) and (c) were obtained from pearlite colonies, b and c, respectively. The dark-field technique was always utilized in identifying reflections from different colonies. The analysis of the selected area diffraction pattern (b) shows a <133> ferrite zone axis, while (c) shows a <011> zone axis. A selected area diffraction pattern which contained the superimposed patterns from the two colonies was also obtained by monitoring the area encompassing both colonies and the colony boundary (Fig. 9(d)). Figure 9(e) illustrates the indexing diagram of the diffraction pattern. The stereographic projection (Fig. 10) was constructed using the indexed diffraction pattern, and the angle between {100} ferrite planes was measured from the superimposed stereograms with the use of a Wulff net. An 18 cm

diam Wulff net has been used on which the lines of longitude and latitude are separated by 2 deg. Because of this fairly coarse net and since the diffraction patterns are not exactly symmetrical, the result is only approximate to within several degrees. In this particu-

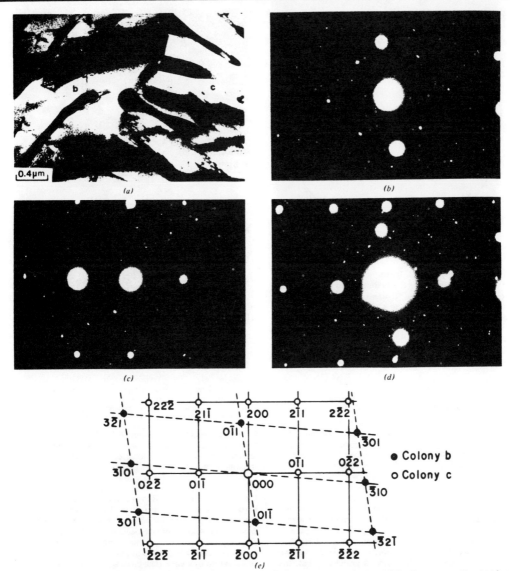

Fig. 9—Two pearlite colonies with nonequivalent zone axes of ferrite: (a) bright-field electron micrograph and diffraction patterns, (b) and (c) from colony b and c, respectively, (d) Superimposed diffraction patterns from the two colonies, and (e) a line diagram corresponding to the above patterns.

lar case, the smallest angle between any of the {100} planes in the two colonies was determined to be about 33 deg.

Nineteen individual pairs of pearlite colonies were analyzed for each of the two specimens, and the results are summarized in Table III. For the larger grain sized materials, misorientation between {100} ferrite planes is less than 5 deg in 12 of 19 random colony pairs examined, while for the smaller grain sized ones, this is true for only 5 of the 19 cases studied. This result suggests that when colonies are closely

enough aligned such that a running crack will not deviate at a colony boundary, a single cleavage facet will be produced.

This is further confirmed by direct observation of ion milled thin foils containing the fracture surface. Figure 11 illustrates an example where three pearlite colonies lie within a single cleavage facet. In Fig. 11(b), a dark-field micrograph using a (110) ferrite spot shows that the three colonies have a similar ferrite orientation. Thus, it is concluded that pearlite colonies with a similar ferrite orientation are neces-

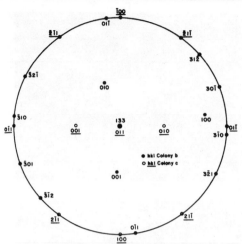

Fig. 10—Stereographic projection showing the orientation relationship of Fig. 9(d).

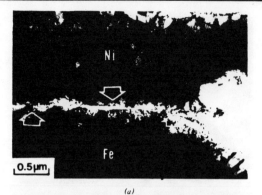

(a)

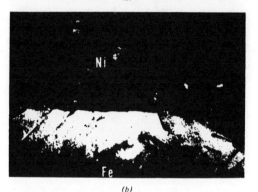

(b)

Fig. 11—Transmission electron micrographs showing pearlite colonies with a similar ferrite orientation under a single cleavage facet: (a) bright-field micrograph and (b) dark-field micrograph using (110) ferrite spot. The arrows indicate the fracture surface.

sary to produce a single cleavage facet.

In several cases where the orientation relationships of cementite were studied, it was observed that cementite lamellae also have similar orientation in adjacent pearlite colonies with similar ferrite orientations. A demonstration of this is shown in Fig. 12, where the ferrite lamellae have almost the same orientation, while the misorientation in cementite between two colonies was measured to be about 5 deg.

DISCUSSION

Process of Crack Initiation

Fractographic Analysis. The results of the investigation of nonpropagating microcracks near the fracture surfaces in both tensile and impact specimens are consistent with the suggestion that they are formed by the shear cracking of pearlite. Rosenfield et al[5] described the first step of cleavage crack initiation in a ferrite/pearlite steel as the formation of this type of pearlitic crack. Ohmori and Terasaki[9] have also claimed that cleavage fracture in ferrite/pearlite steels was initiated from pearlitic cracks formed by shear cracking. They thought that this type of microcrack, as illustrated in Fig. 2, directly becomes the subsequent observed cleavage crack. However, there are several reasons that such an occurrence is unlikely: first, the previous studies[5,9] were performed on specimens which exhibited appreciable macroscopic ductility, and very likely ductile regions on the fracture surfaces. Second, the process of shear cracking in pearlite (Fig. 3) shows

the typical sequence for ductile fracture of microvoid nucleation, growth, and coalescence. As observed previously in a coarse pearlitic steel,[16] initial cracks in cementite grow into the adjacent ferrite lamellae and eventually link up to form a microcrack. Therefore, this process should result in a dimpled rupture fracture mode, and not a cleavage mode. Finally, if the shear cracking of pearlite leads to a cleavage crack, the slip plane of ferrite should form the fracture surface. Since slip in ferrite occurs on {110}, {112}, or possibly {123} planes,[20] these planes should be the operative cleavage planes of pearlite. However, there is as yet no evidence that cleavage occurs on slip planes in pearlitic structure, while {100} ferrite planes have been determined as cleavage planes in a pearlitic high carbon steel.[21]

Therefore, it is more reasonable to assume that

Table III. Angles Between {100} Ferrite Planes in Neighboring Colony Pairs

Heat Treatment No.	Austenite Grain Size, μm	Cleavage Facet Size, μm	Pearlite Colony Size, μm	Number of Colony Pairs of a Given Misorientation		
				0–5 deg	5–10 deg	> 10 deg
2	147	96	5.7	12	5	2
3	25	25	6.3	5	7	7

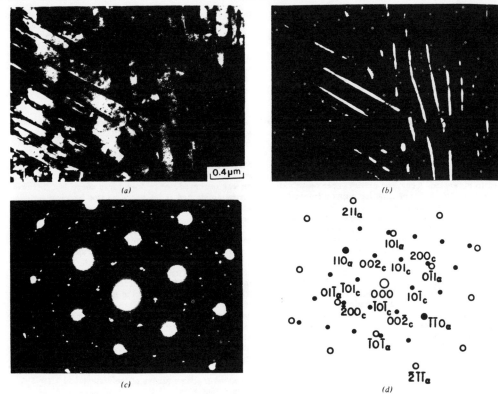

Fig. 12—Two pearlite colonies with a common < 111 > ferrite zone axis and < 010 > cementite zone axis: (a) bright-field micrograph, (b) dark-field micrograph from (101) spot of cementite, (c) selected area diffraction patterns, and (d) indexation showing the Bagaryatskii orientation relationship.

cracks in adjoining cementite lamellae initially link up to form a fibrous microcrack, as illustrated in Fig. 3. When the fibrous crack becomes large enough, it acts as a Griffith type crack in initiating unstable cleavage fracture. As shown in Fig. 6, this phenomenon was experimentally observed in the tensile specimen. Examining these figures, it is clear from the directions of river patterns that the cleavage crack was indeed initiated from the fibrous crack. Lindborg previously made a similar observation in tensile fractured pearlitic eutectoid steels.[4] He further found, from detailed studies of fracture topography using a replica technique, that the plane of a fibrous crack, which is probably a slip plane of ferrite, was different from the cleavage plane in pearlite.

Therefore, it appears that in the smooth tensile specimen fractured at room temperature, the formation of a fairly large fibrous crack is a prerequisite for initiating unstable cleavage fracture. In the present study, the smallest fibrous crack observed in the tensile specimen, which was broken at a tensile fracture stress of 1200 MPa, had a diameter of about 2 μ. However, this type of fibrous crack was only observed on the fracture surfaces of the tensile specimen. In the impact specimens, on the other hand, no indication of ductile fracture was found at initiation sites. This difference in the early stages of cracking can be explained by the different stress states between tensile and impact specimens. In impact specimens a much higher stress state exists as compared to the tensile specimens, due to the stress concentration at the precrack tip. Thus, the critical crack size for crack propagation could be on the order of the microstructural unit size, and the first microcrack formed is very likely to propagate catastrophically. To provide support for this explanation, a more detailed fracture mechanics analysis is necessary and is presented in the next section.

Fracture Mechanics Analysis. The critical crack size for cleavage crack propagation can be calculated from the following form of the Griffith relation:[22]

$$\sigma_F = \left[\frac{4E(\gamma_{eff})}{\pi(1 - \nu^2)c} \right]^{1/2} \qquad [1]$$

where σ_F is the fracture stress, E is Young's modulus, ν is Poisson's ratio, γ_{eff} is the effective surface energy, and c represents the critical crack size.*

---

*Although the fracture mechanics analysis used in the present study had been originally developed for slow bending tests, the analysis can be applied for the present impact study using impact strength properties instead of static values. This extension is justified based on the observations of Green and Hundy[23] that the patterns of stress distribution in Charpy impact tests are similar to those in slow bending tests.

In order to calculate the critical crack size for an impact specimen, the values of effective surface energy and fracture stress must first be obtained. The effective surface energy in this study was calculated using the experimental data from the tensile test described in the previous section, i.e., σ_F = 1200 MPa and c = 2 μm. Taking E = 2×10^5 MPa and ν = 0.3 for pearlitic eutectoid steel,[6] the effective surface energy was calculated to be about 10 J/m² from Eq. [1]. This value is comparable with that of 14 J/m² for a mild steel,[22,24] but both values are substantially greater than the elastic work to fracture (two times the true surface energy of iron), which is about 2 J/m².[24] This value also will be the upper limit of the effective surface energy for an impact test, since a crack is expected to propagate in a more brittle manner in impact as opposed to in tension. Thus, the critical crack size calculated from this value of γ_{eff}, for a given fracture stress, will also be an upper limit (see Eq. [1]).

The fracture stress in notched or precracked specimens depends on the plastic zone size and can be calculated if the plastic zone size is known.[25] However, since the experimental measurement of plastic zone sizes is extremely difficult and tedious,[25] the fracture stress is more usually estimated by measuring the load at the temperature T_{GY} for which cleavage fracture coincides with general yielding of a specimen. At this temperature, the plastic zone is large enough to eliminate any zone size effects, and the fracture stress can be obtained from plasticity theory. At T_{GY}, the fracture stress coincides with the maximum achievable tensile stress of the specimen predicted by plasticity theory.[22,26]

To determine T_{GY}, where fracture and general yield coincide, the values of general yield and fracture stresses are plotted as a function of test temperature (Fig. 13). Since the instrumented impact system used

to obtain data in the present study also recorded the load-time history of the fracture process, the values of general yield and fracture load could be directly obtained. In Fig. 13, the loads are expressed in terms of the nominal bending stress, σ_N. The nominal stress applied at the notch root (ignoring the stress concentration effect) is:[26,27]

$$\sigma_N = 6M/Ba^2 \qquad [2]$$

where M is the applied bending moment (half applied load × bending arm), a is the ligament depth, and B is the specimen thickness.

Figure 13 shows that the fracture and general yield stresses coincide at 160°C. At temperatures less than 160°C, fracture should occur before general yield, as was observed. At temperatures above 160°C fracture also started at the precrack tips by apparent cleavage, but changed to a fibrous mode during propagation.

At T_{GY} (160°C), the fracture stress is equal to the maximum tensile stress below the crack tip.[22,26] Then, the fracture stress can be calculated using Rice and Johnson's finite element analysis of the plane strain stress distributions in cracked specimens,[27] modeled in our case by fatigue precracked notched Charpies. Their analysis shows that the maximum achievable tensile stress for a material with a strain hardening exponent of 0.2, is 5.1 times the yield strength of the material. Since the value of strain hardening exponent only increases slightly with strain-rate and decreases slowly with temperature,[28] we have used this value for the impact test at 160°C. The dynamic yield stress at 160°C was found to be about 690 MPa (see Appendix); thus, the fracture stress of the material is 5.1 × 690 MPa = 3500 MPa.

Since the cleavage fracture stress is relatively independent of temperature,[25,29-32] the fracture stress at room temperature was also taken to be 3500 MPa. Then, taking the effective surface energy as 10 J/m² and the fracture stress as 3500 MPa, Eq. [1] gives a critical crack size of 230 nm. This magnitude of crack size is on the order of the pearlite spacing, and thus the first or first few dimples formed by the shear cracking of pearlite are capable of propagating in a lower energy cleavage mode at this high stress state before a large fibrous dimpled crack could develop. Thus, as found, little or no sign of ductile fracture should be observed on the initiation sites of impact specimens.

It is interesting to note here that fracture stresses for cementite have been measured to be between 3900 and 8000 MPa, assuming that it only deforms elastically up to its breaking point.[33] However, recent transmission electron microscopy studies[34-36] have shown that cementite can plastically deform prior to cracking, and thus the observed fracture stress of cementite will probably be lower than these values. Therefore, at the high tensile stress of 3500 MPa near the precrack tip of an impact specimen, cementite requires little aid from the stress concentration at the ferrite/cementite interface due to the slip in ferrite in order to fracture. Away from the precrack tip, however, the stress state is lower so that an enhancement of the stress, due to perhaps a dislocation pile-up at the interface, is necessary to reach the high fracture stress of cement-

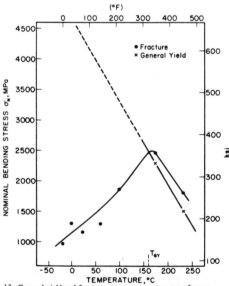

Fig. 13—General yield and fracture stresses vs temperature for precracked impact specimen of heat treatment no. 1.

ite. This is the reason why many microcracks formed by the shear cracking process could be observed in the region of the fracture surface of impact specimens of a coarse pearlitic steel.[16]

In conclusion, precracked Charpy impact tests accelerate cleavage fracture in two ways. First, high strain-rates increase the yield stress of the material. Second, high triaxialities near the precrack tip produce a high local tensile stress for a given applied stress. These combined effects lead to a much higher local tensile stress for impact specimens, as compared to tensile specimens. At these high stress states, not only can cementite break prior to gross yield of the specimen, but a crack nucleus as small as the order of the pearlite spacing can catastrophically propagate as a cleavage crack through adjacent ferrite and cementite.

Effective Grain Size

It has been observed previously that while a crack could change direction at pearlite colony boundaries, more often than not it traversed across several pearlite colonies as a single cleavage facet.[15,16] Since most investigators agree that a cleavage crack propagates along $\{100\}$ ferrite planes in pearlitic steels,[21] this observation implies that the cleavage planes in these adjoining colonies must be continuous.

In support of this hypothesis, thin foil transmission electron microscopy studies have shown that $\{100\}$ ferrite planes can be closely aligned across a number of pearlite colonies. The results summarized in Table III show that in almost 65 pct of the random colony pairs examined in the larger austenite grain size material, misorientations between $\{100\}$ ferrite planes in adjacent colonies are less than about 5 deg. If an orientation difference of about 10 deg (low angle boundary) is included and assumed to still produce a single cleavage facet, about 90 pct of colony pairs of the larger grain size sample, as opposed to only 65 pct of the smaller grain size sample, can generate a macroscopically flat fracture facet. Such large percentages are consistent with the fact that the cleavage facet sizes are many times larger than the colony sizes. Transmission electron microscopy, using ion milled thin foils containing fracture surfaces and underlying microstructures provided more direct evidence that pearlite colonies within a single cleavage facet indeed have similar ferrite orientations.

Since a running cleavage crack must alter direction at mismatch boundaries, the orientation unit made up of adjacent pearlite colonies of common orientation describes an individual facet. As we have discussed, toughness can then be directly related to the number of these mismatch boundaries in a microstructure. If the prior austenite grain structure controls the resultant ferrite orientations in pearlite, as is reasonable to believe, the influence of austenite grain size on toughness is explainable.

There have been two different approaches to account for the controlling effect of prior austenite grain structure on the ferrite orientations in pearlite. Mehl and his coworkers[37,38] proposed that the orientation of ferrite in pearlite is related to the prior austenite grain in which it is contained. In this model, the pearlitic ferrite from a single austenite grain has a preferred orientation, such that cleavage planes in adjacent pearlite colonies are continuous or closely aligned. However, this model has drawn considerable criticism,[39,40] and its validity is now in doubt. For example, since it is unlikely that the lattice orientation of ferrite (or cementite), which gives the correct orientation relationship to a particular grain of austenite, should also yield the correct orientation relationship to a twin of this grain, the lamellae should always change direction when pearlite grows across an austenite twin boundary. This is seldom observed.[40]

An alternative explanation, originally hypothesized by Smith,[39] is that the ferrite in pearlite of a given transformed austenite grain should bear a specific orientation relationship to a neighboring grain of austenite, thus resulting in a partially coherent interface at the boundary with this parent grain. An incoherent interface, on the other hand, will usually form with the matrix austenite grain into which the pearlite front is growing. Since the mobility of an incoherent interface is high, whereas a coherent interface is usually relatively immobile, growth will occur predominantly by the movement of the incoherent interface. Pearlite thus grows into the austenite grain to which it bears no specific orientation relationship. Therefore, twin or austenite grain boundaries cannot be barriers to pearlite growth, in agreement with experimental observations.[41,42]

In support of Smith's hypothesis, Dippenaar and Honeycombe[43] recently found in a high manganese eutectoid steel that, for many of the cases examined, the orientation of pearlitic ferrite was related to that of the austenite grain into which it was not growing. This orientation relationship between the two was close to the classical Kurdjumov-Sachs relationship.[44,45]

In such a model where the adjacent austenite grain is the true parent grain, the effect of prior austenite grain size on toughness can be explained by relating austenite grain size to the size of orientation units in the pearlitic structure. Each unit consists of adjacent pearlite colonies of common parentage and therefore common orientation. In a structure that has a large prior austenite grain size, there may be many colonies nucleated on a given grain side and therefore with the same parentage. These colonies would make up one unit. In a fine grained structure, however, far fewer colonies would have common parentage. This would also mean that for an equal pearlite colony size, the fine grained structure would have considerably more orientation units, and therefore would present more resistance to crack propagation. Thus, the size of these orientation units can be considered as an effective parameter to represent the fracture toughness of materials. As discussed above, an orientation unit will make up a cleavage facet, since a running crack must alter its direction at mismatch boundaries. Therefore the size of such orientation units can be obtained by measuring the cleavage facet sizes. In an earlier publication,[16] the cleavage facet sizes were found to be a strong function of the prior austenite grain sizes. This supports the results of previous studies[11-13] which showed that the fracture toughness in pearlitic steel is primarily dependent on the prior austenite grain sizes.

Up to now we have concentrated on the assumption that the orientation of the ferrite in pearlite is the critical parameter controlling the fracture process.

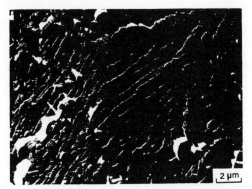

2 µm

Fig. 14—Replica showing the lamellar structure on the fracture surface.

The existence of the cementite has been neglected, partly because of its brittleness compared to the ferrite matrix. However, a lamellar pearlite structure was observable usually as a faint striated pattern in many areas of the fracture surface (Fig. 14) by transmission electron microscopy. This observation suggests that there are also potential discontinuities at the ferrite/cementite interfaces during crack propagation. Therefore it seems appropriate at this stage to briefly discuss the influence of cementite on the fracture mode, as well as the effect of the lamellar structure on the process of crack propagation.

The cementite in pearlite has also been observed to cleave.[4] The cleavage planes of cementite have been recently determined to be {110}, {100}, or {210} planes.[46] These planes are not usually aligned parallel to the {100} ferrite cleavage planes, considering either the Pitsch or the Bagaryatskii orientation relationship between ferrite and cementite. Thus the fracture surfaces of cementite will be inclined to those of ferrite, and there will be slight orientation changes at the ferrite/cementite interfaces during crack propagation. However, the scale of the discontinuities at the interfaces must be quite small, at least less than the 10 µm resolving power of our SEM, and the fracture surface studies showed that a crack usually propagated across the ferrite/cementite interfaces without much difficulty. Therefore it is concluded that the effect of the dual phase lamellar structure on the process of crack propagation is minor.

SUMMARY

We are now in a position to accurately describe the cleavage fracture process in pearlitic steels: Upon the imposition of a normal stress, localized plasticity is triggered at a discontinuity; in a tensile test this can be microstructural in origin, while in a precracked impact test, the mechanical notch is highly effective. Our study suggests that initiated slip is localized in a slip band, presumably because of the constraints of the composite structure. These shear bands promote cracking of the cementite plates, followed by tearing of the adjacent ferrite laths. Such behavior results, for tensile specimens, in a highly ductile crack initiation region, as manifested by dimpled fracture. For our test conditions a typical size for this region would be 2 µm. This shear crack subsequently initiates a brittle

cleavage crack. In precracked impact specimens, the same process is believed to occur, except that now the critical crack size is much smaller. We have calculated that the fracture of one (or two) cementite plates is of sufficient size to initiate cleavage crack growth. With a blunter precrack or a slower strain rate, this critical size increases.

Once initiated, cleavage cracks propagate through the lattice. How they interact with the microstructure will determine in large part the intrinsic toughness of such a material. The critical fracture unit has unequivocally been shown to be a region where the ferrites (and the cementites) of contiguous colonies share a common {100} orientation. The size of this orientation unit is controlled by the prior austenite grain structure. In practice, the size of such orientation units can be obtained by measuring the size of cleavage facets.

APPENDIX

Dynamic Yield Stress Calculation

In a dynamic, instrumented impact test, when general yielding occurs before fracture, the dynamic yield stress, σ_{yd}, is calculated from the measured general yield load P_{GY}. The equation for conversion is:[47]

$$\sigma_{yd} = P_{GY} \frac{L}{1.21 \, Ba^2} \quad [A.1]$$

Where L is the support span length for the test, B is the specimen thickness, and a is the ligament depth.

At 160°C, where fracture and general yield coincided (Fig. 13), the dynamic yield stress was calculated from the value of the nominal bending stress, which is given by elasticity theory as:[25-27]

$$\sigma_N = 6M/Ba^2 \quad [A.2]$$

where M is the applied bending moment expressed as:

$$M = 1/2 \, P_{GY} \cdot L \text{ at } T_{GY} \quad [A.3]$$

Then:

$$\sigma_N = 3P_{GY} \cdot \frac{L}{Ba^2} \quad [A.4]$$

For the given geometry of our specimen, the ratio of nominal bending stress to yield stress is obtained as 3.63, using Eqs. [A.1] and [A.4]. In Fig. 13, the nominal bending stress is about 2500 MPa at 160°C. Using the ratio of 3.63, the dynamic yield stress at this temperature is determined to be 690 MPa.

ACKNOWLEDGMENTS

The authors would like to thank D. H. Stone, Director of Metallurgy, Association of American Railroads, Technical Center, and J. M. Hyzak and G. K. Bouse, former graduate students at Carnegie-Mellon University, for their help, encouragement, and for valuable discussions throughout this study. This research has been supported by the Association of American Railroads and the Processing Research Institute of Carnegie-Mellon University.

REFERENCES

1. J. A. Rinebolt and W. J. Harris, Jr.: *Trans. ASM*, 1951, vol. 43, pp. 1175-1214.
2. K. W. Burns and F. B. Pickering: *J. Iron Steel Inst.*, 1964, vol. 202, pp. 889-906.
3. W. H. Bruckner: *Weld. J.*, 1950, vol. 29, pp. 467S-76S.
4. U. Lindborg: *Trans. ASM*, 1968, vol. 61, pp. 500-04.
5. A. R. Rosenfield, E. Votava, and G. T. Hahn: *Trans. ASM*, 1968, vol. 61, pp. 807-15.
6. J. T. Barnby and M. R. Johnson: *Met. Sci. J.*, 1969, vol. 3, pp. 155-59.
7. L. E. Miller and G. C. Smith: *J. Iron Steel Inst.*, 1970, vol. 208, pp. 998-1005.
8. A. R. Rosenfield, G. T. Hahn, and J. D. Embury: *Met. Trans.*, 1972, vol. 3, pp. 2797-04.
9. Y. Ohmori and F. Terasaki: *Trans. Iron Steel Inst. Jpn*, 1976, vol. 16, pp. 561-68.
10. A. S. Tetelman and A. J. McEvily, Jr.: *Fracture of Structural Materials*, pp. 518-20, John Wiley and Sons, NY, 1976.
11. J. H. Gross and R. D. Stout: *Weld. J.*, 1951, vol. 30, pp. 481S-85S.
12. J. Fluegge, W. Heller, E. Stolte, and W. Dahl: *Arch. Eisenhuettenwes.*, 1976, vol. 47, pp. 635-40.
13. J. M. Hyzak and I. M. Bernstein: *Met. Trans. A*, 1976, vol. 7A, pp. 1217-24.
14. T. Gladman, I. D. McIvor, and F. B. Pickering: *J. Iron Steel Inst.*, 1972, vol. 210, pp. 916-30.
15. A. M. Turkalo: *Trans. TMS-AIME*, 1960, vol. 218, pp. 24-30.
16. Y. J. Park and I. M. Bernstein: ASTM STP 644, pp. 287-02, 1978.
17. J. R. Low, Jr.: *Progr. Mater. Sci.*, 1963, vol. 12, pp. 1-96.
18. R. H. Geiss: *Appl. Phys. Lett.*, 1975, vol. 27, pp. 174-76.
19. J. F. Knott: *Proceedings of Fourth International Conference on Fracture*, D. M. R. Taplin, ed., vol. 2, pp 33-40, University of Waterloo Press, Waterloo, 1977.
20. G. E. Dieter: *Mechanical Metallurgy*, Second ed., p. 165, McGraw-Hill Book Co., NY, 1976.
21. H. Ohtani and F. Terasaki: *Tetsu-to-Hagane*, 1972, vol. 58, pp. 67-80.
22. J. D. G. Groom and J. F. Knott: *Met. Sci.*, 1975, vol. 9, pp. 390-400.
23. A. P. Green and B. B. Hundy: *J. Mech. Phys. Solids*, 1956, vol. 4, pp. 128-44.
24. J. F. Knott: *Proceedings of the Fourth International Conference on Fracture*, D. M. R. Taplin, ed., vol. 1, pp. 61-92, University of Waterloo Press, Waterloo, 1977.
25. T. R. Wilsaw, C. A. Rau, and A. S. Tetelman: *Eng. Fract. Mech.*, 1968, vol. 1, pp. 191-211.
26. R. O. Ritchie, J. F. Knott, and J. R. Rice: *J. Mech. Phys. Solids*, 1973, vol. 21, pp. 395-410.
27. J. R. Rice and M. A. Johnson: *Inelastic Behavior of Solids*, M. F. Kanninen *et al*, ed., pp. 641-72, McGraw-Hill Book Co., NY, 1970.
28. W. J. McGregor Tegart: *Elements of Mechanical Metallurgy*, pp. 1-44, Macmillan Co., New York, 1966.
29. J. R. Griffiths and D. R. J. Owen: *J. Mech. Phys. Solids*, 1971, vol. 19, pp. 419-31.
30. E. Orowan: *Rep. Progr. Phys.*, 1948, vol. 12, pp. 185-232.
31. J. F. Knott: *J. Iron Steel Inst.*, 1966, vol. 204, pp. 104-11.
32. G. Oates: *J. Iron Steel Inst.*, 1968, vol. 206, pp. 930-35.
33. W. W. Webb and W. D. Forgeng: *Acta Met.*, 1958, vol. 6, pp. 462-69.
34. K. Maurer and D. H. Warrington: *Phil. Mag.*, 1967, vol. 15, pp. 321-27.
35. J. Gil Sevillano: *Mater. Sci. Eng.*, 1975, vol. 21, pp. 221-25.
36. A. Inoue, T. Ogura, and T. Masumoto: *Trans. Jpn. Inst. Met.*, 1976, vol. 17, pp. 149-57.
37. R. F. Mehl and D. W. Smith: *Trans. AIME*, 1935, vol. 116, pp. 330-41.
38. G. V. Smith and R. F. Mehl: *Trans. AIME*, 1942, vol. 150, pp. 211-26.
39. C. S. Smith: *Trans. ASM*, 1953, vol. 45, pp. 533-75.
40. M. Hillert: *Decomposition of Austenite by Diffusional Processes*, V. F. Zackay and H. I. Aaronson, eds., pp 197-247, Interscience Co., NY, 1962.
41. F. C. Hull and R. F. Mehl: *Trans. ASM*, 1942, vol. 30, pp. 381-24.
42. G. W. Rathenau and G. Baas: *Acta Met.*, 1954, vol. 2, pp. 875-83.
43. R. J. Dippenaar and R. W. K. Honeycombe: *Proc. Roy. Soc. London*, 1973, vol. A333, pp. 455-67.
44. K. W. Andrews: *Acta Met.*, 1963, vol. 11, pp. 939-46.
45. G. Kurdjumov and G. Sachs: *Z. Phys.*, 1930, vol. 64, p. 325.
46. A. Inoue, T. Ogura, and T. Masumoto: *Trans. Jpn. Inst. Met.*, 1976, vol. 17, pp. 663-72.
47. W. L. Server, D. R. Ireland, and R. A. Wullaert: Dynatup Report TR74-29R, Effects Technology, Santa Barbara, CA, 1974.

TEXT 5

Development of improved rail and wheel materials

S. Marich

(BHP Melbourne Research Laboratories, Australia)

Recent developments in rail-steel technology are summarized in this paper. These developments have been motivated by the economic need to operate at higher axle loads and/or speeds. Various laboratory techniques used to assess new steel types and appropriate field trials are presented in detail. Based on these studies, fully pearlitic rail steels have been developed with yield strengths greater than 900 MPa (130 ksi) and good balance of other mechanical properties.

Concurrent with new rail developments, new wheel materials have been tested and commercially produced. Because of their improved fracture-toughness characteristics, these new wheel materials show a higher resistance to catastrophic brittle fracture.

INTRODUCTION

Among the numerous components used in the railroad industry for high axle load operations, wheels and rails give rise to a major source of running expenditure. Indeed the wheel/rail interaction is the main technical factor determining design procedures and maintenance and replacement schedules for both vehicles and track.

The degradation of rails in track is due to (a) wear, (b) fatigue and (c) plastic flow.

(a) Wear

Wear occurs primarily in the high rails of curves due to wheel/rail flange contact. Fig. 1(a) illustrates the extensive loss of material that can occur from the gauge corner of rails subjected to 30 tonne axle loads, unit train operations and situated in a relatively shallow curve of 873 m radius (2 degrees). The effect of curve radius on rail wear is shown in Fig. 1(b).

As mentioned in a previous report[1], the problem of rail wear can be reduced by the adoption of various approaches including: rail lubrication, the use of rail steels exhibiting higher hardness levels and modifications to wheel and rail profiles to improve the bogie tracking characteristics and therefore reduce the occurrence and the magnitude of flanging.

(b) Fatigue

Fatigue occurs in the form of transverse defects, shells and horizontal split heads (see Figs. 2(a), (b) and (c), respectively). All of these defects, if not detected in time, can result in rail failures and therefore derailments.

(c) Plastic flow

Plastic flow leads to mushrooming of the head of low rails in curves (Fig. 3(a)) and, more importantly, to corrugations on the running surface (Fig. 3(b)). Work previously reported[2-4] has shown that the corrugation problem can be minimised by the development and use of rail steels which

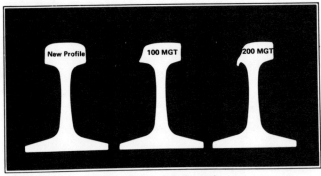

Fig.1(a)   Standard rail profiles in 2 degree (873 m radius) curve

Vanadium in Rail Steels

Table I. Typical chemical compositions and mechanical properties of standard and high strength rail steels

Manufacturer	Rail Type	Chemical Composition						
		C, %	Mn, %	Si, %	Cr, %	V, %	Cb, %	Mo, %
Standard AREA		0.80	0.90	0.20	—	—	—	—
C.F. & I.	Hi–Si	0.75	0.80	0.65	—	—	—	—
	Cr–Mo	0.78	0.84	0.21	0.74	—	—	0.18
Algoma	Cr	0.75	0.65	0.25	1.15	—	—	—
British Steel	Cr	0.75	1.25	0.35	1.15	—	—	—
Krupp	Cr–Si	0.70	1.05	0.75	1.00	—	--	--
Thyssen	Cr–Si–V	0.65	1.05	0.60	1.15	0.20	--	--
Klockner	Cr–Mo–V	0.65	0.80	0.30	1.00	0.10	—	0.10
Sydney	Mn–Cr–V	0.70	1.65	0.20	0.30	0.10	—	--
	Cr–Si–Cb	0.70	1.10	0.55	0.80	—	0.06	--
Brazil Steel	Si–Cb	0.74	1.30	0.80	—	—	0.03	—
Bethlehem	Through Hardened	0.80	0.90	0.20	—	—	—	—
U.S. Steel*	Head Hardened	0.80	0.90	0.20	—	—	--	—
Russia	Through Hardened	0.75	0.90	0.30	—	—	—	—
Nippon Steel*	Head Hardened	0.75	0.80	0.22	—	—	—	—
Nippon Kokan*	Head Hardened	0.75	0.83	0.22	—	--	—	—

Manufacturer	Rail Type	Mechanical Properties						
		0.2% Proof Stress		Ultimate Tensile Strength		Elong., %	Redn. of Area, %	Brinell Hardness Number
		N/mm²	ksi	N/mm²	ksi			
Standard AREA		510	73.9	920	133.4	11	18	255
C.F. & I.	Hi Si	520	75.4	980	142.1	11	14	285
	Cr–Mo	807	117.0	1228	178.1	9	17	352
Algoma	Cr	650	94.3	1100	159.5	9	17	320
British Steel	Cr	690	100.1	1130	163.9	11	17	325
Krupp	Cr–Si	675	97.9	1140	165.3	12	20	315
Thyssen	Cr–Si–V	680	98.6	1130	163.9	12	20	320
Klockner	Cr–Mo–V	705	102.3	1145	166.1	12	20	325
Sydney	Mn–Cr–V	705	102.3	1035	150.1	12	18	325
	Cr–Si–Cb	705	102.3	1040	150.8	10	16	340
Brazil Steel	Si–Cb	645	93.5	1070	155.2	10	15	320
Bethlehem	Through Hardened	870	126.2	1220	176.9	13	30	365
U.S. Steel*	Head Hardened	910	132.0	1260	182.8	12	33	380
Russia	Through Hardened	820	118.9	1250	181.3	14	40	380
Nippon Steel*	Head Hardened	857	124.3	1231	178.5	12	34	370
Nippon Kokan*	Head Hardened	817	118.5	1192	172.9	14	37	365

* Tensile and hardness properties measured at 10 mm (0.39 in) and 5 mm (0.2 in) respectively from the top corners of the rail head

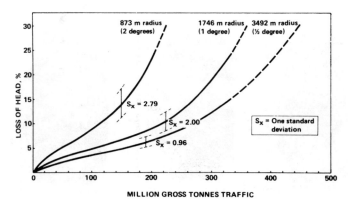

Fig.1(b) Wear of standard carbon rail in curves of various radii

Development of improved rail and wheel materials

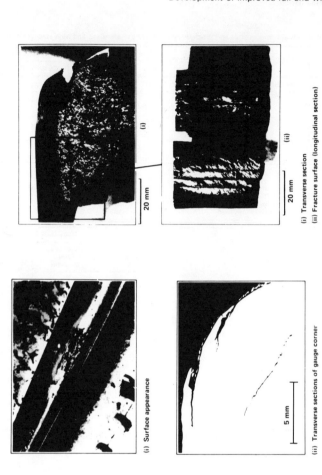

(i)

20 mm

(ii)

20 mm

(i) Transverse section
(ii) Fracture surface (longitudinal section)

Fig.2(c) Horizontal split head from the outer rail of a 3 degree (582 m radius) curve

(i) Surface appearance

5 mm

(ii) Transverse sections of gauge corner

Fig.2(b) Shelling

(i) Outer rail in ½ degree (3492 m radius) curve

(ii) Inner rail in 2 degree (873 m radius) curve

(iii) Tangent rail

Fig.2(a) Transverse defects

Vanadium in Rail Steels

exhibit yield or proof strength values that are appropriate for the particular wheel loadings applied.

Rail manufacturers throughout the world are now marketing "improved" materials which generally exhibit higher strength and hardness properties than the standard rails used in the respective countries. Table I summarises the characteristics of some of these materials. The improvements are generally achieved either by heat treatment of the steel, partial or throughout the rail sections, or by the addition of alloying elements. In both cases the primary objective is to produce a product containing a fully pearlitic microstructure since, in practice, this has been found to exhibit advantages over other microstructural types.

From Table I it is evident that the mechanical properties of the heat treated products are generally better than those of the alloyed varieties. However, previous work conducted at BHP Melbourne Research Laboratories[5] has shown that by optimising the additions of alloying elements such as chromium, columbium, molybdenum and vanadium, it is technically feasible to manufacture fully pearlitic rail steels exhibiting a range of yield strengths up to 1000 MPa (145 ksi) without adversely influencing, and frequently improving, other mechanical properties.

As a result of the materials development programme, a number of the alloy rail steels have been produced commercially and are now undergoing extensive in-track trials at the Mt. Newman Mining Company and Hamersley Iron. Both of these companies operate 30 tonne mean axle loads, unit train operations for the haulage of iron ore. As detailed in a previous publication[5], these trials also cover the

assessment of various heat treated rail types produced commercially in Japan, U.S.A. and Russia. Table II gives a summary of the basic chemistries and mechanical properties of some of the alloy rails being studied, together with those of the equivalent alloys developed in the experimental programme. Similar data for the heat treated rails is shown in Table I.

Although both railroads mentioned above average a yearly traffic of 50 to 60 MGT (million gross tonnes), the assessment of rails is still a long term project. Furthermore, there are certain aspects of such a programme that cannot be covered by field trials because of the inherent variability of the true life situation. Because of these factors it becomes necessary to use laboratory tests as an aid to the overall assessment programme.

The following sections cover the work conducted at BHP Melbourne Research Laboratories aimed at assessing various rail steel types in terms of:

> (a) Their wear resistance and in particular the influence which the different rail types will have on the wear of wheels. The latter aspect is of major importance since it has been shown that wheel wear rather than rail wear, could have the overriding influence on the final selection of a cost optimum rail type. Furthermore, unless use is made of a captive experimental track, the quantitative influence of rail type on wheel wear is extremely difficult to obtain under actual operating conditions due to the numerous other track and vehicle parameters that also influence wheel wear.

> (b) Their fatigue characteristics in terms of all stages of fatigue deterioration, i.e. nucleation, growth and catastrophic failure. The fatigue data obtained in the laboratory tests have been used as input to a model which simulates the growth of transverse defects in rails so that the work would have meaningful implications in terms of in-track performance.

The last section of this paper deals with the recent developments in wrought wheel materials that have occurred

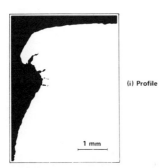

(i) Profile

1 mm

Field corner

200 MGT

(ii) Field corner

Fig.3(a) Inner rail from 2 degree (873 m radius) curve

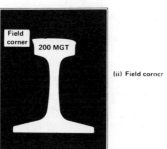

Fig.3(b) Corrugations

at the Commonwealth Steel Company. As for rails, the degradation of wheels is due to wear and fatigue mechanisms (gross plastic flow of the material plays only a minor role in determining wheel life). The experimental programme has shown that by the appropriate usage of alloying elements and heat treatment procedure, considerable improvements can be made to the mechanical properties which influence the above degradation mechanisms.

EXPERIMENTAL DETAILS

1. Rail and wheel wear

Various laboratory techniques have been used to determine the wear behaviour of wheel and rail materials under rolling contact conditions. Generally use is made of small cylindrical specimens, machined from actual rails and wheels, which are independently driven to induce a certain slip between the contact surfaces[5-9] to simulate the flanging condition at the wheel/rail interface. Using this technique, and for slip values of 19 to 25%, it has been found that a reduction in the wear rate of one of the components will also lead to reduction in the wear rate of the mating component[5-7]. However, other researchers using considerably lower slip conditions have reported contradictory results[10-12]. More sophisticated tests have been quoted in the literature. and indeed Russian workers have used small diameter (approximately 40 mm (1.57 in)) samples exhibiting scaled wheel and rail profiles so that both vertical and lateral forces could be applied to simulate flanging conditions in

curved track[13]. The limited results quoted showed a similar trend to those obtained in cylindrical specimens tested at high slip values.

In the current work, since the data would have a major influence on the selection of rail materials, it was felt that the technique used should closely simulate the real life situation. In particular the wear process which occurs over the whole of the wheel/rail flange area and therefore over a wide range of slip conditions that are determined by the geometry of the components. The test rig illustrated in Fig. 4 was designed and manufactured to achieve this objective.

Figures 5(a) and 5(b) show the samples used in the wear experiments. The larger sample (300 mm (11.8 in) diameter) represents the rail and the smaller sample (100 mm (3.94 in) diameter) the wheel, although specimens up to 1 m (39.4 in) in diameter can be tested. It is evident that both rail and wheel specimens have machined profiles equivalent to those of commercial products, which for this case were AAR 66 kg/m (132 lb/yd) rails and wide flange wheels.

The specimen configuration allows the simultaneous application of both vertical and lateral loads equivalent to those obtained under in-track conditions. Therefore, surface slip at the wheel/rail flange is obtained, similar to service conditions, by the interactiion of differing profiles.

The loads are monitored continuously through a test period by means of calibrated load cells to allow changes to be made and thus maintain constant loading conditions.

To compensate for the effect of specimen dimensions on contact pressure, the equations set out by Timoshenko and

Table II. Chemical compositions and mechanical properties of experimental alloy rails

Rail Type	Chemical Composition						
	C, %	Mn, %	Si, %	Cr, %	V, %	Cb, %	Mo, %
V1215	0.53	1.38	0.20	0.62	0.07	0.05	—
V1226	0.55	1.42	0.20	0.61	0.07	0.06	—
1/Cr—Cb—V	0.54	1.38	0.11	0.58	0.05	0.04	—
V1070	0.72	1.30	0.18	0.80	0.11	—	—
2/Cr—V	0.76	1.29	0.36	0.82	0.12	—	—
V1128	0.72	1.07	0.55	0.86	—	0.05	—
4/Cr—Cb	0.80	1.10	0.52	0.87	—	0.04	—
V1057	0.75	0.88	0.17	0.75	—	—	0.22
5/Cr—Mo	0.73	0.83	0.28	0.74	—	—	0.21
V1657	0.70	0.95	0.20	0.84	0.06	—	0.18
V1448	0.70	0.93	0.19	0.81	0.05	—	0.16
6/Cr—Mo—V	0.68	0.92	0.21	0.78	0.07	—	0.17

Rail Type	Mechanical Properties						
	0.2% Proof Stress		Ultimate Tensile Strength		Elong., %	Redn. of Area %	Brinell Hardness Number
	N/mm²	ksi	N/mm²	ksi			
V1215	730	105.9	1105	160.3	10.5	29	320
V1226	710	103.0	1090	158.1	13	33.5	310
1/Cr—Cb—V	704	102.1	1080	156.6	15	33	315
V1070	740	107.3	1225	177.7	11	15	365
2/Cr—V	747	108.3	1235	179.1	10	15	375
V1128	673	97.6	1115	161.7	11.5	22	325
4/Cr—Cb	705	102.2	1190	172.6	11	16	340
V1057	905	131.3	1290	187.1	8.5	13	390
5/Cr—Mo	897	130.1	1300	188.6	10	19	390
V1657	1030	149.4	1393	202.0	10.5	30	400
V1448	938	136.0	1312	190.3	12	31.5	395
6/Cr—Mo—V	953	138.2	1283	186.1	13	38	375

NOTE: V precedes experimental alloy heat numbers

Vanadium in Rail Steels

Goodier[14], which are based on Hertzian elastic contact theory, were used to determine the loading conditions in the test rig which would result in contact stresses equivalent to those expected to occur in track. The range of equivalent wheel loads that can be applied to the samples are:

Vertical load (V), 0 to 250 kN (0 to 56,200 lb)
Lateral load (L), 0 to 200 kN (0 to 44,960 lb)
i.e. L/V ratio, 0.8 maximum

By rotation of the wheel specimens about their vertical axis, the machine is capable of imposing wheel/rail angles of attack of up to 2 degrees (lateral creep).

In the series of tests reported herein the wheel specimens were run at a peripheral speed of about 60 km/h (37.5 miles/h), i.e. similar to high axle load, unit train speeds. However, facilities for testing speed effects can be readily incorporated in the rig together with facilities for introducing slip conditions on the running surfaces of the specimens (longitudinal creep).

The specimens used in the tests are manufactured and heat treated under laboratory conditions to ensure consistency in product quality and mechanical properties. All wheel specimens were manufactured according to AAR Class C specifications while the rail steels tested were representative of the following:

AREA Standard Carbon (Table I)
Through Hardened (Table I)
Type 2/Chromium-Vanadium (Table II)
Type 6/Chromium-Molybdenum-
Vanadium (Table II)

Wear measurements are obtained by weighing the specimens using an electronic balance with an accuracy of within 0.1 gm.

Fig.4   Wear rig

Fig.5(a) and (b)   Wear specimens

2. Rail fatigue characteristics

As mentioned previously[15], due to the current trends towards higher axle loads, it is now frequently observed that rails do not achieve their expected wear life, having to be replaced prematurely due to the development of fatigue defects which, if not detected in time, can be the cause of rail failures and therefore derailments. Because of this trend, in recent years increased emphasis has been placed on determining the fracture behaviour and fatigue characteristics of rail steels and a number of papers have been published on the subject, e.g.[16-22].

However, most investigators have employed test materials, experimental techniques, including stress conditions, and testing machinery which would satisfy their respective particular immediate objectives. As a consequence, the results of independent investigations can rarely be correlated directly to establish general parameters involved in fatigue.

To determine the relative fatigue crack nucleation characteristics of the steels, specimen blanks were cut from the head of the rails, as shown schematically in Fig. 6(a). Cylindrical fatigue specimens with uniform gauge and with dimensions given in Fig. 6(b) were machined from the blanks (all dimensions are in mm). The smaller thread diameter indicated in Fig. 6(b) was used in the initial set of experiments. However, it was found that the specimens tended to fail in the thread region rather than in the gauge length, particularly at the lower stress levels. This problem was rectified by using the larger diameter thread. To ensure that the specimen surface had a minimum effect on fatigue nucleation, the reduced section of all test specimens was final machined in 20 passes of not more than 0.025 mm (0.001 in) per pass. Samples were subsequently polished longitudinally with silicon carbide papers lubricated with kerosene to a surface roughness of about 15 μm (590 μin). The specimens were finally polished using diamond compounds to a mirror finish of about 3 μm (118 μin).

Specimen blanks
26 mm x 26 mm and
32 mm x 32 mm

(a)

(b)

24 mm thread x 3.0 mm pitch and
30 mm thread x 3.5 mm pitch

Fig.6 Details of cylindrical fatigue specimens (dimensions in millimetres)

Furthermore, a considerable amount of controversy still exists on the influence, or lack thereof, of microstructure and mechanical properties on the rate of crack propagation of fatigue defects[21-25].

Indeed, Nisida et al[26] have shown that by relieving residual stresses in specimens negligible differences in fatigue crack growth rates are observed in rail steels of different chemistries. Nevertheless residual stresses are an inherent characteristic of rails in service. It was therefore felt that the fatigue characteristics of the various rail steels undergoing in-track trials should be determined as part of the overall rail assessment programme.

Fatigue tests were conducted on numerous rail steel types. The results reported in detail below were obtained in the following steel types:

AREA Standard Carbon	(Table I)
Russian Through Hardened	(Table I)
Type 2/Chromium-Vanadium	(Table II)
Type 4/Chromium-Columbium-Vanadium	(Table II)
Type 6/Chromium-Molybdenum-Vanadium	(Table II)

(a)

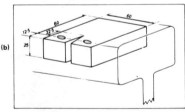

(b)

**Fig.7(a) Compact tension specimen in fatigue machine
(b) Dimensions of specimen (in millimetres)**

Testing of the specimens was conducted in a Tinius Olsen servo hydraulic test system under uniaxial tension compression fatigue loading conditions. All testing was performed in load control at a cyclic frequency of 15 Hz and with a mean stress of +25.5 MPa (+3.7 ksi). Each steel type was tested at various stress range levels to determine the number of stress cycles required to cause specimen failure at the respective stress levels. Failure was defined as fracture of the specimen into two parts at some location within the gauge length. For fractures which occurred outside the gauge length the results were considered invalid.

To determine the fatigue crack growth characteristics of the various rail steels, compact tension specimens were machined from the head of the rails as illustrated schematically in Fig. 7(b), which also shows the main dimensions of the specimens.

Testing of the compact tension specimens was also conducted in a Tinius Olsen servocontrolled hydraulic test system. To eliminate the effects of the machined notch, each specimen was pre-cracked using a force range of 1 to 19 kN (225 to 4271 lb), until a fatigue crack had extended a distance of $\frac{1}{2}$ to $2\frac{1}{2}$ mm (0.02 to 0.1 in) from the chevron notch. The specimens were subsequently subjected to constant amplitude cyclic loading applied at a frequency of 10 Hz. The Standard Carbon specimens were tested at various force range levels varying from 1 to 13 kN (225 to 2922 lb) to 1 to 25 kN (225 to 5620 lb). All other specimens were tested at a force range of 1 to 15 kN (225 to 3372 lb) until failure occurred.

Crack growth was measured visually, as illustrated in Fig. 7(a), using a ×30 travelling microscope which was accurate to ±0.01 mm. Crack length a was recorded as a function of the number of load cycles N. Note was also made of the final crack size prior to fracture. Each crack growth run was duplicated. The crack growth rate, da/dN, was then calculated at various values of crack size together with the stress intensity factor range, ΔK, obtained at the respective crack sizes. The parameter ΔK is representative of the mechanical driving force for the crack and incorporates the effect of changing crack length, cyclic load magnitude and crack geometry. For the compact tension specimens used in this investigation, ΔK is given by:

$$\Delta K = \left[\frac{\Delta P}{BW^{\frac{1}{2}}} 29.6\left(\frac{a}{W}\right)^{\frac{1}{2}} - 185.5\left(\frac{a}{W}\right)^{\frac{3}{2}} + 655.7\left(\frac{a}{W}\right)^{\frac{5}{2}} - \right.$$
$$\left. 1017\left(\frac{a}{W}\right)^{\frac{7}{2}} + 638.9\left(\frac{a}{W}\right)^{\frac{9}{2}} \right]$$

Equation (1)

where ΔP = load range, i.e. 14 kN (3147 lb) for most of the present tests

B = specimen thickness (25 mm (0.98 in))
W = specimen width (60 mm (2.36 in))
a = crack length measured from the load line

The rate of crack growth is related to ΔK through:

$$da/dN = f(\Delta K, R) \qquad \text{Equation (2)}$$

where R is the ratio between minimum and maximum applied load, i.e. 0.07 in most of the present tests.

Various investigators[9–11,16–19,23–25] have shown that for Standard Carbon rail steels, and indeed for any steel, over a wide range of growth rates and for fixed R, equation (2) can be approximated by:

$$da/dN = C(\Delta K)^m \qquad \text{Equation (3)}$$

where C and m are constants for a given material.

Equation (3) implies that a straight line of slope m and intercept C will be obtained by plotting da/dN versus ΔK on double log paper. In reality it has been shown that the relation $da/dN - \Delta K$ has two asymptotes, with da/dN becoming infinite and approaching zero as the stress intensity factor approaches a critical value, K_{Ic} and a threshold value, K_{th} respectively. An equation that accounts for both K_{Ic} and K_{th} has been given[19] as:

$$\frac{da}{dN} = C(1 - R)^2 (K_{max}^2 - K_{th}^2) \frac{K_{max}^{m-1}}{K_{Ic} - K_{max}}$$

Equation (4)

In the current work use has been made of the simpler equation (3) since the K_{th} values of the various steels were not

determined. Furthermore it was felt that equation (3) was a reasonable approximation since the range of defect sizes analysed in this study exhibited ΔK values that were within the linear portion of the $da/dN - \Delta K$ relationship.

The values of m and C for the various rail steels were used as inputs to the analytical model of transverse defect growth developed at BHP Melbourne Research Laboratories to determine the number of cycles required to grow transverse defects in the steels from a detectable size, assumed to be 10 mm (0.39 in) diameter, to a critical size which would cause rail failure. All of the computer runs were conducted using the following load input values:

Wheel load,	150 kN (33,720 lb)
Thermal load,	−25°C (−13°F)
Lateral load,	30 kN (6744 lb)

It must be emphasised that the results obtained from the analysis should be regarded as approximate since it was necessary to assume that the residual stress pattern which develops in the high strength rails during service are equivalent to that in Standard Carbon rails. A more detailed analysis will be the subject of a future publication.

The fracture surfaces of some of the cylindrical fatigue and compact tension specimens were examined in a scanning electron microscope to determine whether any microstructural features could be associated with the observed difference in fatigue behaviour of the steels.

3. Wheel development

The development work conducted at the Commonwealth Steel Company on wheel steels was aimed at improving the overall mechanical properties of a wide range of wheel types commonly used in the railroad industry. This was achieved by additions of vanadium (up to 0.1%) to the steel and modifying the heat treatment process which follows the rolling of the wheel blank.

The assessment programme entailed the measurement in full scale wheels, of the following parameters:

(a) Brinell hardness traverses conducted on radial sections.

(b) Strength and ductility obtained using standard tensile specimens machined with their axis parallel to the wheel tread at various locations.

(c) Charpy V-notch.

(d) Plane strain fracture toughness (K_{Ic}) obtained by testing pre-cracked specimens in 3 point bending according to British Standard 5477:1977. The specimens were machined such that the pre-cracking and final cracking occurred in a radial plane. The dimensions of the specimens were:

Thickness,	25 mm (0.984 in)
Width,	50 mm (1.968 in)
Half loading span,	100 mm (3.937 in)

All tests were conducted in an MTS servocontrolled hydraulic test system.

(e) Fatigue crack growth rate was also obtained using the specimens described above tested at a force ratio R of 0.05. As for the rail steels were expressed in terms of the crack growth rate, da/dN, as a function of the stress intensity factor range, ΔK, determined at various crack lengths using the formula:

$$\Delta K = \frac{3\Delta PS}{BW^{\frac{3}{2}}} \left[1.93\left(\frac{a}{W}\right)^{\frac{1}{2}} - 3.07\left(\frac{a}{W}\right)^{\frac{3}{2}} + 14.53\left(\frac{a}{W}\right)^{\frac{5}{2}} - \right.$$
$$\left. 25.11\left(\frac{a}{W}\right)^{\frac{7}{2}} + 25.80\left(\frac{a}{W}\right)^{\frac{9}{2}} \right]$$

Equation (5)

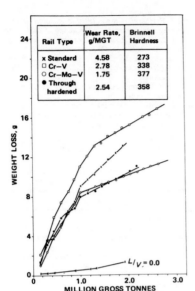

Rail Type	Wear Rate, g/MGT	Brinnell Hardness
x Standard	4.58	273
□ Cr–V	2.78	338
○ Cr–Mo–V	1.75	377
● Through hardened	2.54	358

Fig.8 Rail wear. 150 kN (33,720 lb) wheel load (L/V = 0.2)

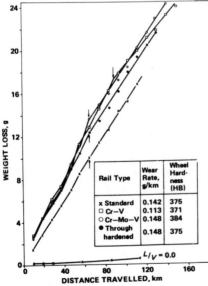

Rail Type	Wear Rate, g/km	Wheel Hardness (HB)
x Standard	0.142	375
□ Cr–V	0.113	371
○ Cr–Mo–V	0.148	384
● Through hardened	0.148	375

Fig.9 Wheel wear. 150 kN (33,720 lb) wheel load (L/V = 0.2)

where S = half loading span (100 mm (3.937 in))
B = thickness (25 mm (0.984 in))
W = width (50 mm (1.968 in))
ΔP = load range
a = crack length

The results given in the following section apply to AAR Class C wheel steels. Similar trends were also observed in other wheel grades.

RESULTS AND DISCUSSION

1. Rail and wheel wear

Although the rail and wheel wear testing programme is still in its initial stages, several important aspects have already been observed.

The wear data obtained from the runs have been presented graphically in Figs. 8 and 9 for the various rail and AAR Class C wheel samples, respectively. Rail wear is shown as weight loss as a function of million gross tonnes imposed by the wheel, while wheel wear is expressed as weight loss as a function of distance travelled over the rail sample.

Most of the data shown in the Figures were obtained at a wheel vertical load of 150 kN (33,720 lb) and a lateral load of 30 kN (6744 lb), i.e. an L/V ratio of 0.2. In 30 tonne axle load, unit train operations, this load condition approximates curves 700 to 800 m in radius (2.2 to 2.5 degree curves).

A set of data obtained without lateral loading, i.e. with no flanging, for standard carbon rails is also shown. The marked effect of flanging on wear of components is evident.

For the l/V ratio of 0.2, the rail wear rate becomes linear after a certain "bedding in" period, the transition point occurring at 1.0 to 1.3 MGT. A similar behaviour has been observed in the in-track rail assessment programme except that under actual operating conditions the transition occurs after 50 to 70 MGT of traffic[4].

The wear rates for the various rail steels obtained in the linear section of graphs have been summarised in the table in Fig. 8 together with the respective hardness values of the rail samples.

Using a procedure described previously[4] the predicted rail wear life of the rail steels would be as follows:

AREA Standard Carbon,	1.0
Through Hardened,	1.8
Type 2/Chromium-Vanadium	1.6
Type 6/Chromium-Molybdenum-Vanadium	2.6

The values of predicted rail life obtained from the in-track trials for Through Hardened and Type 2 rails are 1.9 to 2.0 and 1.5 to 1.6, respectively. Considering that the hardness of the standard rail sample (273 HB) is slightly higher than the mean hardness of commercial rails, it is apparent that the laboratory wear tests simulate successfully rail wear behaviour and can therefore be used to make quantitative predictions. This is a marked improvement over results that were obtained previously from cylindrical type specimens which could only be used to give a qualitative grading of rail steel materials.

By plotting the wear rate of the various rail steels tested, as a function of their respective hardness (Fig. 10), it can be seen that the following inverse linear relationship applies:

$$\text{Wear Rate, (g/MGT)} = 11.40 - 0.025 \text{ HB}$$

The arrows shown in the wheel wear plots (Fig. 9) indicate the transition points observed in the rail samples. From the Figures it is apparent that the transition was not as marked in the wheel materials. Beyond the transition, the wheel wear rates are also linear. However, more importantly, it was found that the Standard Carbon, Type 6 and Through Hardened rails all led to the same wheel wear rates. The Type

Vanadium in Rail Steels

2 rail on the other hand, resulted in a slight reduction in the wear rate. Therefore although a more detailed examination is required, it does appear that the rail type may have only a small influence on the wheel wear characteristics, unlike findings quoted in previous literature.

2. Rail fatigue characteristics

2.1 Crack nucleation

The data obtained from the cylindrical specimens tested under uniaxial tension/compression fatigue conditions have been summarised in Fig. 11 in the form of S/N diagrams, i.e. the number of stress cycles required to cause failure of the specimen at various stress range values.

In specimens of the size used, the fatigue life is primarily determined by the time taken to initiate a crack whose diameter is 2 to 4 mm (0.079 to 0.157 in) and whose surface covers an area of 3 to 12 sq mm (0.005 to 0.019 sq in), the size and area typically observed in this test specimen configuration. As pointed out by Leis[27], such cracks develop in the last 5% of the total specimen life. Thus, crack separation can be taken as a reasonable measure of crack initiation life. However, it should be emphasised that this test procedure gives an indication of the resistance to crack nucleation of the bulk material. It does not account for the possible presence of large but isolated inhomogeneities which generally lead to a

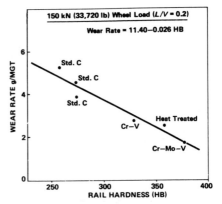

Fig.10 Rail wear/rail hardness

marked reduction in the number of stress cycles required for crack nucleation.

As illustrated in Fig. 11, all of the high strength rail steels exhibited a greater resistance to fatigue crack nucleation than

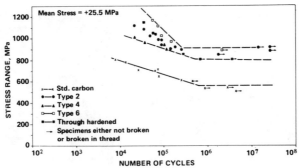

Fig.11 Summary of S/N fatigue data

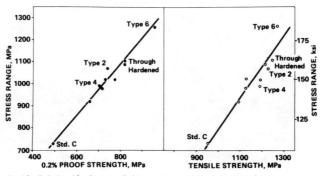

Fig.12 Relationships between fatigue resistance and tensile strength

the Standard Carbon steel. From Fig. 11 it should be noted that the Type 6 steel exhibits the highest values while the Type 4 steel exhibits the lowest values.

The results indicate that the resistance to fatigue of the steel is primarily a function of their proof and tensile strengths. This relationship is evident in Fig. 12, in which the proof and tensile strengths of the various steels have been plotted as a function of the stress range required to cause failure of the specimen in 5×10^4 stress cycles. Fig. 12 also shows data obtained in other steel types not covered in this discussion.

In summary, the rail steel types can be listed in terms of increasing resistance to fatigue crack nucleation as follows:

Standard Carbon
Type 4
Type 2
Through Hardened
Type 6

Examination of the fractured specimens showed that crack nucleation had occurred at or very close to the surface of the specimens.

Figure 13 illustrates the fracture morphologies observed in various steel types within 0.1 mm (0.004 in) of the nucleation point. All of the high strength steels shown in the Fig. were tested at a stress range level of 910 to 960 MPa (132 to 140 ksi), while the Standard Carbon steel was tested at 800 MPa (116 ksi).

It is evident that all of the fracture surfaces appear to be very similar. Inclusions were observed on all fracture surfaces. The Standard Carbon rail exhibits the greatest number of inclusions, as would be expected from a product manufactured in the semi-killed condition.

2.2 Crack growth

The crack growth data obtained for the Standard Carbon and the high strength rail steels are presented in Figs. 14–18 as crack growth rates v stress intensity factor ranges. The Figs. also show the calculated values of the material's constants m and C for the various steel types.

The Standard Carbon steel was tested at four different maximum load levels to determine the most suitable conditions for the other steels. The optimum maximum load level was found to be 15 kN (3373 lb) since, as shown in Fig. 14, the higher load levels resulted in an insufficient number of data points and deviations from the linear growth rate at relatively low ΔK values, while at the lower load level the testing of each specimen took too much time.

The values of the constants m and C obtained at a maximum load of 13 kN (2922 lb) i.e. 3.43 and 9.62×10^{-10} respectively, are very similar to values reported previously by Barsom and Imhof[24] for tests conducted at a maximum load of 9 kN (2023 lb), i.e. 3.33 and 1.2 to 3.0×10^{-9}. However, from Fig. 14 it is evident that the results obtained at the higher load levels were consistently different from the 13 kN

Standard Carbon

Type 2

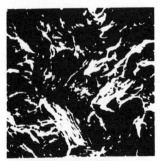
Type 4

Type 6

Fig.13　Fracture morphologies of cylindrical fatigue specimens　x570

Vanadium in Rail Steels

(2922 lb) condition. An explanation for this difference is not known and the results contradict a previous statement that R ratios of less than 0.2 do not influence the linear portion of the da/dN versus ΔK relationship[23]. The need for further research in this area is emphasised by the fact that the data reported in the literature on rail steels have been obtained for widely varying R ratios[17,19,23,25], for example: 0, 0.2, 0.5 and -1.0. There has been a negligible amount of work similar to the current study where the R ratios examined have all been less than 0.1, while the maximum stress levels used have been varied by up to a factor of 2.

From Figs. 14 to 18, it is evident that the reproducibility of the results obtained on each of the rail types was excellent. The Through Hardened (Fig. 18) material was the only rail type in which the growth rate data points from the duplicate runs could not be described by a single graph. In this material two sets of m and C values were determined.

The values of the final crack size just prior to fracture measured in the various rail steels have been summarised in Table III in the form of a/W ratios. The values of a/W were used in equation (1) to determine the stress intensity factors of the steels which correspond to conservative values of critical stress intensity factors.

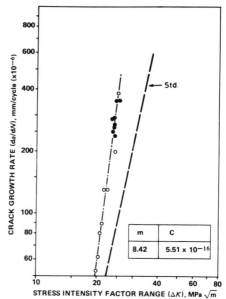

Fig.15   Type 2, chromium-vanadium rails

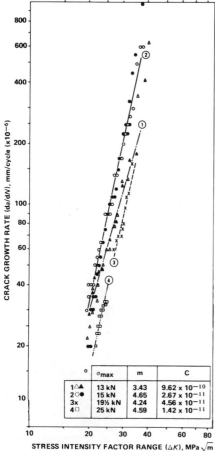

Fig.14   Standard carbon rails

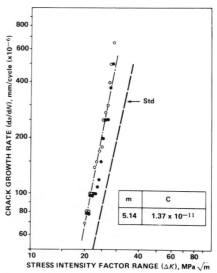

Fig.16   Type 4, chromium rails

Table III. Fracture characteristics of rail steels

Rail Type	Final a/W	Final K_L MPa $\sqrt{m}$	Calculated d_c, mm
Type 2	0.58	28.7	17.3
Type 4	0.58	31.5	20.8
Type 6	0.65	41.5	36.1
Standard	0.66	43.7	40.0
Through Hardened	0.72	54.6	62.4

Table IV. Crack growth characteristics of rail steels

Rail Type	Calculated d_c, mm	Relative Growth Times 10 mm $\rightarrow d_c$, days
Type 4	20.8	34
Type 6	36.1	66
Standard	40.0	100
Through Hardened	62.4	122–156
Type 2	17.3	189

As described previously[5,28], for an elliptical crack of the transverse defect type, the critical crack diameter, d_c, can be calculated by the following function:

$$d_c = A \frac{K_{Ic}^2}{\sigma} \qquad \text{Equation (6)}$$

where A = constant (independent of steel type)
K_{Ic} = critical stress intensity factor
σ = applied uniaxial tensile stress

Therefore, assuming that the critical crack diameter in Standard Carbon rails is 40 mm (1.57 in), that is about 80% of the rail head, under equivalent and uniform stress conditions the critical crack diameter for any rail type (x) is given by:

$$d_c \text{ (rail x)} = \frac{K_{Ic}^2 \text{(rail x)} \times 40}{K_{Ic}^2 \text{(std)}} \qquad \text{Equation (7)}$$

Equation (7) is to be regarded as approximate since different residual stresses and stress gradients are known to exist near the running surface of rails of different types. However, since the equation is being used for cracks in an advanced stage of development, the crack front is in a reducing stress gradient field well below the compressive residual stress layer. Therefore, it is believed that the application of the equation will give valid ratings and will result in conservative critical crack size values.

The values of the final stress intensity factors obtained from the compact tension fatigue tests have been used in equation (7) to determine the expected critical crack sizes, for cracks of the transverse defect type, in the various rail steels. The calculated values of d_c have been summarised in Table III.

Figure 14 shows the crack growth curves obtained by using the m and C values of the rail steels in the analytical model of transverse defect growth. The calculated critical crack diameters are indicated on the growth curves by the arrows.

Assuming that in Standard Carbon rail it would take 100 days of operations to grow a transverse defect from 10

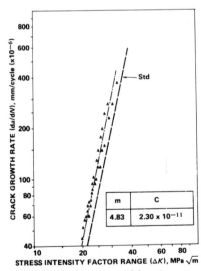

	m	C
	4.83	2.30×10^{-11}

Fig.17 Type 6, chromium-molybdenum-vanadium rails

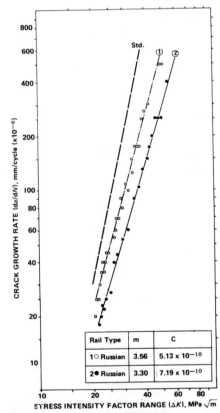

Rail Type	m	C
1 ○ Russian	3.56	5.13×10^{-10}
2 ● Russian	3.30	7.19×10^{-10}

Fig.18 Through Hardened rail

Vanadium in Rail Steels

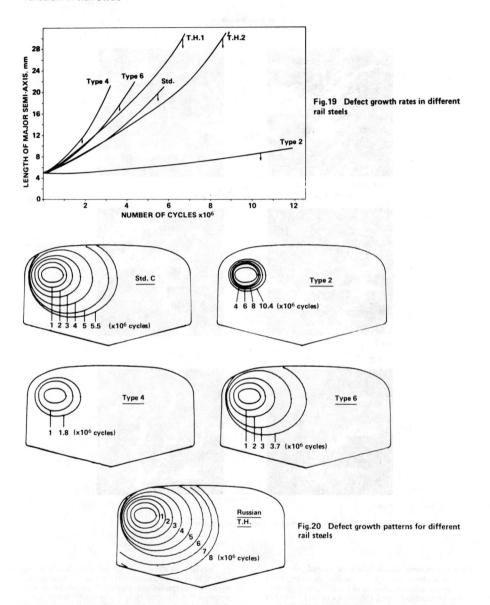

Fig.19 Defect growth rates in different rail steels

Fig.20 Defect growth patterns for different rail steels

mm (0.39 in) diameter to critical crack size (40 mm (1.57 in)), the crack growth data shown in Fig. 19 have been used to determine the relative times, t, required to grow defects in the high strength rails from the same initial size to the respective critical crack sizes under similar operating conditions. The results are given in Table IV which lists the rail types in terms of increasing crack growth times together with the calculated critical crack diameters, d_c, of the respective steels.

From Table IV it can be seen that Type 4 rails exhibit the shortest crack growth times, while Through Hardened and Type 2 rails exhibit times longer than Standard Carbon rails.

The results obtained for the Type 2 rails are of particular interest since, as shown in Fig. 15, they exhibited high m values in the da/dN versus ΔK relationship. Therefore, high crack growth rates would be expected. The opposite has been observed because of the retarding influence of the very low C value on the initial stages of crack growth.

The growth data shown in Fig. 19 have been used to

58

Crack growth direction →

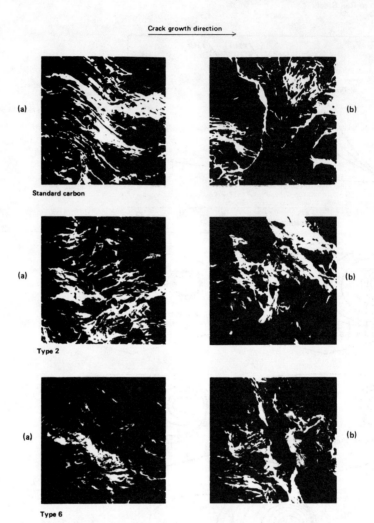

Fig.21 Fracture morphologies of compact tension specimens   x300

depict growth patterns on defects in the head of some of the rail types, as illustrated in Fig. 20. The Figs. show the growth of transverse defects at intervals of 1 million stress cycles (2 million for the case of Type 2 rails) from a size of 10 mm (0.39 in) (major axis) to critical size as given in Table III. The Figs. emphasise the relatively small critical crack sizes that are predicted in the Type 2 and Type 4 rails, while in the Through Hardened rails the cracks are expected to extend almost throughout the rail head before catastrophic failure of the rail occurs. Thus, although the Type 2 rails exhibit the longest crack growth times, the detection of transverse defects approaching critical size may be difficult using current ultrasonic inspection techniques.

Similar testing and analytical techniques could not be applied to Head Hardened rails because of their varying mechanical properties and microstructure. However, it is proposed that these rail types would exhibit fatigue crack growth and fracture characteristics that are between those of Standard Carbon and Russian Through Hardened rails.

The fracture morphologies of some of the samples are shown in Fig. 21. The fields shown in the micrographs identified by (a) are typical of "normal" fatigue crack growth. As pointed out previously[23], what appear to be fatigue striations actually consist of the underlying pearlite microstructure and, as is evident from the Figs., bear no relationship to the crack growth direction. The high strength rails all

37

Vanadium in Rail Steels

exhibit a much finer fracture morphology than the Standard Carbon steel as would be expected from the finer microstructure observed in these steels. The micrographs identified by (b) show the cleavage facets that are observed as the stress intensity factor of the crack approached critical value, i.e. as the crack growth departs from linearity in the da/dN versus ΔK relationship. Growth of the crack by stable cleavage bursts may occur for a limited number of stress cycles after which catastrophic failure of the sample will occur.

The examination of the fracture surfaces and the crack growth data have supported previous observations[23] that indigenous inclusions have a negligible effect on crack propagation. Indeed, inclusions were rarely observed on the fatigue fracture surface of the specimens.

In the extensive work conducted by Battelle on fatigue crack growth characteristics of Standard Carbon rails[19,25], it was concluded that crack growth properties do not show obvious correlations with any other material parameters such as tensile strength, hardness, ductility, toughness, etc. However, the results obtained in the current study have shown that such a correlation exists. Fig. 22 shows the variation of crack growth rate (da/dN) of the steel types with the final stress intensity factor (K) summarised in Table III. The da/dN values were obtained by using the respective m and C values (Figs. 14 to 18) in equation (3) at a stress intensity factor range (ΔK) value of 30 MPa $\sqrt{m}$. Data obtained for various other rail types have also been included. From the Fig. it is evident that materials with higher final or critical stress intensity factors generally exhibit lower fatigue crack growth rates. Deroche[29] in a private communication with the author, indicated observing a similar relationship in some rail steels different from those examined in this study. It is felt that the work does merit a more detailed examination particularly since Ritchie and Knott[30], in summarising the results obtained by several authors for medium and high strength alloy steels, have shown that the exponent m in the Paris equation (equation 3) is increased in materials of low static fracture toughness.

3. Wheel development

Representative mechanical properties of the Standard AAR Class C and the improved wheel steels are given in Figs. 23, 24 and 25.

From Fig. 23 it can be seen that the additions of vanadium, which result in a refinement of the grain size, together with the modification of the heat treatment procedure have led to a general improvement of all tensile and Charpy properties.

However, the most important improvements associated with the new wheels are summarised in Fig. 23, i.e. (a) a considerably flatter rim hardness profile and (b) a marked improvement in the fracture toughness of the material.

The major advantages of the new hardness profile are:
(i) Greater depth of hardness in the flange and flange throat area, giving rise to a better flange wear resistance.
(ii) A higher hardness level and a higher compressive residual stress level on the back face of the rim which, in turn, result in a greater resistance to fatigue crack initiation by, for example, ore car retarder scoring marks. As for the case of rail steels, detailed in the previous section, higher hardness and strength values would also lead to an improved fatigue strength of the bulk material.

Equation (6) may also be applied to wheel materials to describe the relationship between the critical crack size of a radial crack, the applied stress and the fracture toughness of the material. Therefore, the improvement of up to 50% in the fracture toughness of the steel means that defects or cracks up

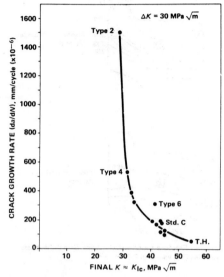

Fig.22 Variation of crack growth rate with final stress intensity factor

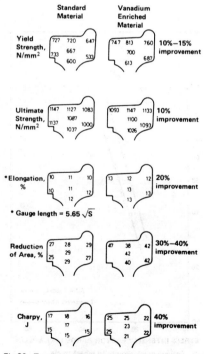

Fig.23 Tensile and Charpy properties

60

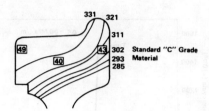

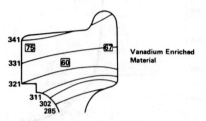

Fig.24 Fracture toughness (K_{Ic}) and Brinell hardness profiles (K_{Ic} values in MN m$^{-3/2}$)

to $2\frac{1}{4}$ times the size of the current critical defect size may be tolerated before catastrophic failure of the wheel occurs. The major advantages associated with this increase are:

(i) A critical defect will take longer to form.

(ii) A critical defect will be larger and therefore more easily detected by on-site personnel.

(iii) The probability of a wheel failure will be decreased.

Finally, from Fig. 25 it can be seen that the fatigue crack growth rates of both standard and improved wheel steels are very similar. Crack growth, therefore, has not been adversely influenced by the improvements achieved in the other mechanical properties.

The new wheel materials are currently undergoing in-track assessment at both Hamersley Iron and Mt. Newman Mining.

CONCLUSIONS

1. A laboratory technique for assessing wheel/rail wear characteristics has been developed. Results obtained for rail steels show excellent agreement with data from in-track trials. The data have shown an inverse linear relationship between rail wear rate and rail steel hardness. Furthermore rail type has only a minor influence on wheel wear characteristics.

2. The examination of the fatigue nucleation, crack growth and catastrophic failure characteristics of several rail steel types has shown that:

(a) Fatigue crack nucleation of the bulk material is a function of material strength.

(b) Materials with higher critical stress intensity factors generally exhibit lower fatigue crack growth rates. Both factors must be taken into account when assessing the fatigue performance of rails in track.

3. By alloy additions and modifications to the heat treatment procedure it is possible to manufacture wrought wheels which exhibit considerable improvements in both fatigue crack nucleation and critical crack size characteristics.

REFERENCES

1. P. H. Townend, C. J. Epp and P. J. Clark: "Bogie Curving Trials, Rail Profiling and Theoretical Modelling to Reduce Rail Deterioration and Wheel Wear on Curves", Proceedings Heavy Haul Railways Conference, Perth, Western Australia, September, 1978, Session 203.

2. R. I. Mair and R. Groenhout: "A Prediction of Rail Strength Requirements — a Reliability Analysis", ASTM Symposium Rail Steels — Developments, Processing and Use, ASTM Special Technical Publication, No. 644, 1978, pp. 342–360.

3. R. I. Mair, R. A. Jupp and R. Groenhout: "The Characteristics and Control of Long Pitch Corrugation at Heavy Axle Loads", Proceedings Heavy Haul Railways Conference, Perth, Western Australia, September 1978, Session 417.

4. P. Curcio, S. Marich and G. Nisich: "Performance of High Strength Rails in Track", Ibid, Session 313.

5. S. Marich and P. Curcio: "Development of High Strength Alloyed Rails Suitable for Heavy Duty Applications", ASTM Symposium Rail Steels — Developments, Processing and Use, ASTM Special Technical Publication, No. 644, 1978, pp. 167–211.

6. A. S. Babb and J. Lee: "The Laboratory Wear Testing of Tyre Wheel Steels", 4th International Wheelset Congress, Paris, July 1972, pp. 16–30.

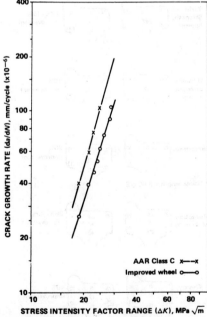

Fig.25 Fatigue crack growth in wheel steels

7. A. S. Babb: "Testing Techniques for Railway Materials", British Steel Corporation Research Report Prod/Eng/7063/73/A.

8. H. Masumoto, K. Sugino and H. Hayashida: "Development of Wear Resistant and Anti-Shelling High Strength Rails in Japan", Proceedings Heavy Haul Railways Conference, Perth, Western Australia, September 1978, Session 212.

9. H. Ichinose, et al: "An Investigation of Contact Fatigue and Wear Resistance Behaviour in Rail Steels", Ibid, Session 307.

10. W. Heller, E. Koerfer and H. Schmedders: "Naturally Hard Special-Grade Rails for Heavy Duty Application", Ibid, Discussion Session 216.

11. S. Kumar and R. Margasahayem: "Quantitative Wear Analysis of a Simulated Steel Wheel and Rail", Illinois Institute of Technology Report No. I.I.T. — Trans-77-, 3rd July, 1977.

12. W. E. Jamison: "Final Summary Report on Mechanical Wear of Railroad Components", Colorado School of Mines, prepared for Association American Railroads, March, 1978.

13. N. A. Veckser, D. S. Kazarnovskii and L. S. Khurgin: "Method of Testing Wheel and Rail Steels for Wear and Contact-Fatigue Galling", Industrial Laboratory, Vol. 36, 1970, pp. 760–761.

14. S. Timoshenko and J. N. Goodier: "Theory of Elasticity", McGraw-Hill Book Co. Inc., 2nd Ed., New York, 1951, pp. 377–380.

15. S. Marich: "Research on Rail Metallurgy", AREA Bulletin No. 663, Vol. 78, 1977, pp. 594–610.

16. P. R. V. Evans, N. B. Owen and B. E. Hopkins: "Fatigue Crack Growth and Sudden Fast Fracture in a Rail Steel", J.I.S.I., Vol. 208, 1970, pp. 560–567.

17. P. R. V. Evans, N. B. Owen and L. N. McCartney: "Mean Stress Effects on Fatigue Crack Growth and Failure in a Rail Steel", Eng. Fracture Mech., Vol. 6, 1974, pp. 183–193.

18. R. J. Cooke and C. J. Beevers: "Slow Fatigue Crack Propagation in Pearlitic Steels", Mat. Sc. Eng., Vol. 13, 1974, pp. 201–210.

19. D. Broek and R. C. Rice: "Fatigue Crack Growth Properties of Rail Steels", Battelle Columbus Labs. Report DOT-TSC-1076, July, 1977.

20. D. Griffiths: "Fatigue Life of Rails. A Literature Survey", BHP Melb. Res. Lab. Rep. BHP/MNM/HI/RPC/77/048, July, 1977.

21. D. H. Stone and G. G. Knupp (editors): ASTM Symposium "Rail Steels — Developments, Processing and Use", ASTM Special Technical Publication No. 644, May, 1978.

22. H. Masumoto et al: Ibid, pp. 233–255.

23. G. J. Fowler and A. S. Tetelman: Ibid, pp. 363–386.

24. J. M. Barsom and E. J. Imhof: Ibid, pp. 387–413.

25. C. E. Fedderson and D. Broek: Ibid, pp. 414–429.

26. S. Nisida et al: "A Study on Fatigue Crack Propagation of Rail Steels", Presented at 5th International Conference on the Strength of Metals and Alloys, Aachen, W. Germany, August, 1979.

27. B. N. Leis: "Cyclic Inelastic Deformation and Fatigue Resistance Characteristics of a Rail Steel", ASTM Symposium Rail Steels — Developments, Processing and Use, ASTM Special Technical Publication, No. 644, 1978, pp. 499–468.

28. D. P. Rooke and D. J. Cartwright: "Compendium of Stress Intensity Factors", Her Majesty's Stationery Office, London, 1976.

29. R. Y. Deroche: "Mechanical Properties of Rail Steels", Internal Publication, Sacilor, France, 1978 (Private Communication).

30. R. O. Ritchie and J. F. Knott: "Mechanisms of Fatigue Crack Growth in Low Alloy Steels", Acta Met., Vol. 21, 1973, pp. 639–648.

ACKNOWLEDGEMENTS

The work on rail steels was part of a joint railroad research programme between the Mt. Newman Mining Co., Hamersley Iron Pty. Ltd., and The Broken Hill Proprietary Co. Ltd., while the study on wheels was part of a development programme at the Commonwealth Steel Co. The author is grateful to all four companies for permission to publish these results. The author also acknowledges the contributions to all of the experimental work made by Messrs. P. Mutton, R. Cornish, G. Long and R. Groenhout.

DISCUSSION ON

Development of improved rail and wheel materials

S. Marich

P. M. GARDNER (Canadian National Railroad) Your work has shown that the wear rates of the wheels was not influenced by the hardness or wear rate of the alloy rail. Would you expect that this would also be valid for other classes of AREA wheels?

S. MARICH It depends on the relative hardnesses, and we find that it's actually a U-shaped curve. That is, for the AREA Class C wheel against standard carbon rail or against the very hard alloy rail, there is no effect. However, where we suspect there is an effect it is in material types that have an intermediate hardness to the ones we tested. If that is the case, then we are dealing with a case of matching wheel and rail properties.

D. J. OULTON (Algoma Steel Corp.) Why did you specify the high silicon content in your Type 4 steel?

S. MARICH Silicon has quite an effect, we find, on the work hardening characteristics of the steel. In track, this could pay off in terms of improved plastic flow behavior, for example, and this was the main reason we added silicon at that level. Unfortunately, this particular alloy did not behave too well at all in terms of crack growth characteristics. Since I can see no explanation for this other than the high silicon content, I would not recommend silicon at this level in rail steels. It has nothing to do with silicates though, since we found there was very little influence of inclusion content on crack growth rates.

Session 313
Paper I.10

PERFORMANCE OF HIGH STRENGTH RAILS IN TRACK

P. CURCIO

S. MARICH

G. NISICH

1   INTRODUCTION

The rails used for transportation of iron ore at Mt Newman Mining Company Pty Ltd, in Western Australia, are subjected to service conditions which are among the most severe in the world. The open pit mining operation is centred on Mt Whaleback and its link with the port is provided by 426 km of continuously welded rail weighing 65.5 kg/m. At the present time nine to ten trains leave the mine daily each consisting of 138 cars drawn by three 2680 kw Alco-Goodwin diesel-electric locomotives. The whole unit weighs approximately 17,500 tonnes, of which 13,400 is payload, and operates to a maximum speed of 65 kph. The action of these unit trains with mean axle loads of 300 kN and peak loads reaching 400 kN has been found to cause rapid deterioration of the standard AREA carbon rails and has necessitated very costly inspection, maintenance and rerailing programmes.

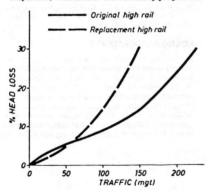

Figure 1   Wear of original and replacement
high rail in a 2° curve.

One of the factors contributing to this rail deterioration has been the increase in wear rate which has occurred since the rerailing of the track - the main problem being the rapid erosion of the gauge face, especially on the high rails of the curves. This is illustrated in Figure 1 where percentage head loss is given as a function of traffic in million gross tonnes (mgt) for the original and replacement high rails on a 2° (875 m radius) curve. The difference in performance of these rails was found to be quite considerable. The original rails suffered a 20-25% head loss after approximately 200 mgt of traffic whereas the

replacement rails achieved the same amount of wear after only 130 mgt. A similar behaviour was found with the wheels. As Figure 2 shows, wheels placed in service at the beginning of operations (May 1969) travelled in excess of 20,000 km (loaded) before reaching a flange thickness number of 9, at which point they are discarded. However, the life of the wheels which came into service in March and December 1975 was reduced to 8,000 and 4,000 loaded kilometers respectively.

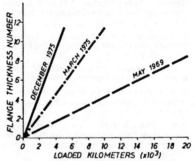

Figure 2   Wheel flange wear rates.

The other factors encountered in rail deterioration were gross plastic deformation of the rail head particularly in the low legs of curves and short pitched corrugations of wavelengths in the ranges 270 to 320 mm and 180 to 215 mm primarily in the high rails (Marich and Curcio, 1976). Furthermore the deterioration of standard carbon rails had manifested itself through the development of various fatigue type defects such as shells and transverse defects.

This problem of accelerating rail wear has been found in other railroads operating heavily loaded unit trains. King and Kalousek report similar findings from studies of rail wear occurring on two Canadian railways' main lines (King and Kalousek, 1976). These indicated that rail wear was much greater than would be anticipated based only on increased annual traffic. It is also interesting to compare the results shown in Figure 1 with those reported by Rougas on wear data obtained from the Bessemer and Lake Erie Railroad (Rougas, 1977). The latter results indicate a 65 mm^2 head loss per 100 mgt of traffic for the high rails of a 2° curve whereas, on the Mt Newman track, average head losses of 320 and 490 mm^2 per 100 mgt of

Session 313
Paper I.10

TABLE I
MEAN COMPOSITIONS AND PROPERTIES OF ALLOY RAILS IN TRACK

RAIL TYPE	MANUFACTURER/ HEAT No.	COMPOSITION									PROPERTIES				
		C	Mn	Si	P	S	Cr	Nb	Mo	V	0.2%PS MPa	U.T.S. MPa	El%	RA%	B.H.N.
Standard C.		0.82	0.87	0.16	0.02	0.04					493	952	11	14	256
TYPE 1A	AIS/265847	0.59	1.33	0.08	0.03	0.02	0.33	0.04		0.06	673	1070	14	25	308
	AIS/265848	0.59	1.34	0.09	0.03	0.02	0.52	0.04		0.06	641	1057	15	30	302
	AIS/265849	0.50	1.32	0.10	0.01	0.01	0.36	0.05		0.05	632	996	17	31	290
	AIS/265850	0.56	1.34	0.11	0.01	0.01	0.59	0.04		0.06	697	1077	15	33	315
	AIS/265853	0.57	1.74	0.12	0.02	0.04	0.47	0.05		0.07	705	1105	17	37	311
	AIS/265854	0.61	1.74	0.13	0.02	0.03	0.69	0.04		0.06	767	1218	12	22	334
TYPE 2	AIS	0.75	1.30	0.30	0.02	0.02	0.80			0.12	740	1230	10	15	365
Hi-Si	C.F.& I.	0.72	0.84	0.64	0.02	0.05					520	981	12	16	270
TYPE 4	AIS	0.82	1.11	0.52	0.02	0.03	0.87	0.04			702	1195	11	16	342
TYPE 5	AIS/2K8713	0.75	0.83	0.28	0.02	0.03	0.74		0.21		828	1295	11	24	360
	C.F.& I/11406	0.78	0.84	0.21	0.03	0.02	0.74		0.18		807	1128	9	17	352
	C.F.& I/12547	0.77	0.89	0.20	0.01	0.03	0.76		0.16		804	1217	11	25	352

traffic were suffered by the original and replacement high rail respectively in a similar curve (Fig. 1). Even though such a comparison may not be strictly correct in view of the smaller rail section used on the Mt Newman track (65.5 kg/m compared to 70 kg/m), it nevertheless gives an indication of the severe rail wear problem which exists on this railroad.

Theoretically such rapid gauge corner wear would not be expected to occur since the geometry of the track and the conicity of the wheel tread are intended to ensure a self-steering action. However, in practice this was found not to be the case. Indeed, the amount of wear may vary considerably from one wheel set to another and from curve to curve. Although this emphasises the importance of bogie tracking behaviour and alignment of the track, it also points to the need for developing more effective wear-resistant materials for economic operations.

2 MATERIALS

A research programme was undertaken by BHP Melbourne Research Laboratories (MRL) on behalf of the Mt Newman Mining Company, to determine on a cost/performance basis the rail material most suited to their operations. Preliminary studies indicated that a prerequisite for such a material would have to be an increase in yield strength and hardness without adversely affecting other properties required for successful application such as weldability, impact resistance and fatigue characteristics. This can be achieved by:
(i) additions of alloying elements and (ii) heat treatment.

2.1 Alloy Rail Steels

An extensive programme was established at MRL and Australian Iron and Steel Works at Port Kembla to study the effects of individual and combinations of various alloying elements, such as chromium, molybdenum, niobium, and vanadium, on material properties of rail steels. A number of alloys of

widely different composition were manufactured in the laboratory and their mechanical properties were evaluated. These materials were divided into four main classes, viz: chromium-niobium-vanadium steels, chromium-vanadium, chromium-niobium and chromium-molybdenum steels. Rails were produced from the steel in each class which was found to have the optimum combination of properties. The reason for producing such a wide variety of materials was to enable a final assessment to be made on an economic basis. For example, it could be that the added cost associated with the use of high strength rail in terms of its production and complex welding procedures may not justify the extra performance obtained over a medium strength type which would be less expensive to manufacture and easier to weld.

Two manufacturers were involved in the production of the various rails mentioned. The chromium-niobium-vanadium (Cr-Nb-V), chromium-vanadium (Cr-V) and chromium-niobium (Cr-Nb) which will be referred to as Type 1A, Type 2 and Type 4 rails respectively in this text were produced by Australian Iron and Steel Pty Ltd (A.I. & S.) Hoskins Kembla Works at Port Kembla. Rails from three heats of chromium-molybdenum (Cr-Mo) material, referred to as Type 5, were also produced. Two of the heats, designated 11406 and 12547, were manufactured by Colorado Fuel and Iron Steel Corporation in the United States. Rails from the other heat, 2K8713, were produced by A.I. & S. The mean compositions and mechanical properties of these various rail types are summarized in Table 1; the standard carbon material has also been included in the table as a basis for comparison.

The development and properties of these steels have been covered in a previous publication (Marich and Curcio, 1976). However, further comments are necessary to place the materials in their proper perspective. The Type 1A (Cr-Nb-V) material was produced in the semi-killed condition from six heats each varying in composition as shown in Table 1. This provided a group of rails

64

TABLE II
MEAN COMPOSITION AND PROPERTIES OF HEAT TREATED RAILS IN TRACK

RAIL TYPE	MANUFACTURE	C	Mn	Si	P	S	Al	Ti	HARDNESS* B.H.N.	0.2%P.S. MPa	U.T.S. MPa	El%	RA%
HEAD HARDENED	N.S.C.	0.63	0.85	0.23	0.01	0.02	0.02	0.01	360	797	1108	18	54
CURVEMASTER	U.S. Steel	0.76	0.80	0.17	0.02	0.03	0.01	-	370	867	1207	15	38
RUSSIAN P65 TROUGH HARDENED	Nyzhni-Tagil	0.75	0.87	0.28	0.01	0.04	0.02	-	363	820	1256	14	20
IMPROVED HEAD HARDENED	N.S.C.	0.75	0.80	0.22	0.03	0.019	-	0.003	369	828	1210	14	35

* Hardnesses quoted are peak values.

with the desired range of properties at minimum cost. By varying the chromium and manganese levels in the steels, a wide range in mechanical properties was achieved for the various heats, thus enabling a correlation between performance and strength to be made in the final assessment of these rails. Varying these alloying elements also produced rails of different hardenability which, as will be discussed in a later section, greatly influences the weldability of the material. With the exception of heats 265847 and 265849 which showed some grain boundary ferrite, the Type 1A materials exhibited a fully pearlitic microstructure.

All the other rail types were produced in the fully-killed condition and their microstructure was found to be fully pearlitic. However, rails from heat 2K8713 of Type 5 (Cr-Mo) material showed traces of bainite which was probably associated with the higher molybdenum level present in the steel (compared to the C.F. & I. heats). The higher levels of alloying elements and the production of the material in the fully-killed condition would make the manufacturing of rail Types 2, 4 and 5 more costly than the Type 1A (Cr-Nb-V) and, as mentioned before, this would have to be considered in the final assessment of the various material types.

2.2   Heat Treated Rails

Heat treatment of standard carbon rails is a practice adopted by several manufacturers in overseas countries such as Japan, the United States and Russia. Two types of heat treated rails are produced: a "head-hardened" rail in which part of the rail head is heated to austenitising temperature, usually by electromagnetic induction, and subsequently air quenched (United States Steel, 1975). The other type is a "through-hardened" or fully heat treated rail in which the entire section is heated and quenched in oil (Stone, 1976). Both processes produce a very fine pearlitic microstructure in the heat affected zone with a resultant improvement in all mechanical properties, particularly strength and hardness. Both head-hardened and through-hardened rails were included in the assessment programme to enable their performance characteristics to be compared with those of alloy rails.

NSC Head Hardened and USS Curvemaster rails were purchased by the Mt Newman Mining Co from Nippon Steel Corporation and United States Steel respectively. Although both of these rail types could be regarded as being similar, laboratory examination conducted at MRL showed that their respective heat treatment processes led to significant differences in the microstructure of the rail head. The NSC rails exhibited a quench and tempered martensitic structure to a depth of approximately 4mm from the running surface thereafter changing to pearlite, whereas the Curvemaster was found to be fully pearlitic. An additional head-hardened rail type, referred to as "Improved Head Hardened" (IHH), was obtained from Japan. It has been shown that this material is very similar to Curvemaster with respect to composition, microstructure and tensile properties.

Russian P65 fully heat treated rails, produced at the Nyzhni-Tagil steel works, were also purchased by Mt Newman Mining Co. Detailed metallographic examination carried out on some rail samples revealed a region of heavily tempered upper bainite to a depth of approximately 1 mm from the rail surface and thereafter fine pearlite with some grain boundary ferrite (~5%). The mean composition and mechanical properties of the P65 rail sections examined at MRL, together with those obtained from the head-hardened rails, are shown in Table II.

3.   IN-TRACK TEST PROGRAMME

3.1   11.7 km Trial Curve

The first evaluation of some of these high strength rails under the actual operating conditions on the Mt Newman track was conducted on a 2° curve located 11.7 km from the port. A major factor which had contributed to the deterioration of the standard carbon rails on the high leg of this curve was the development of corrugations and the main objective of this trial was to assess the resistance of the higher strength rails to corrugation formation.

Approximately half of the original high rails in the curve were replaced in October 1973 with a string of 43 rails flash butt welded using standard procedures. The string was comprised mainly of rails from the six heats of Type 1A (Cr-Nb-V) material but also included a high silicon alloy type, designated as Hi-Si, which was manufactured by C.F. & I. This latter alloy rail was offered to the Mt Newman Mining Company as a high wear resis-

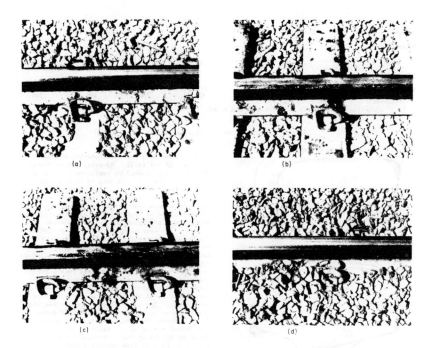

Figure 3 Surface condition of rails in 11.7 km curve after 90 mgt

(a)   Type 1A, heat 265848
(b)   Standard carbon
(c)   Standard carbon
(d)   Type 1A, heat 265847

tant material; its composition and mechanical properties are given in Table 1. The rails were laid in groups of three according to type and class. However, in the case of the Type 1A alloys they were grouped according to yield strength rather than heat number. This enabled a correlation to be made between resistance to corrugation formation and the proof strength of the material. Standard carbon rails were laid adjacent to the other types in several parts of the curve as a basis for comparison.

Corrugation measurements were recorded after the rails had been subjected to approximately 90 mgt of traffic. Visual observations indicated that most of the standard rails were corrugated whereas corrugations on the experimental rails were isolated to areas near the welds joining the standard and higher strength rails. Figure 3 shows the surface condition of two standard rails and two Type 1A rails (heats 265847 and 265848) laid on either side of a standard carbon rail. It is evident that the alloy rails exhibited no visible indication of the corrugation pattern observed in the respective adjoining standard rails. The effect of corrugations on ballast displacement is

also illustrated in Figure 3. In the corrugated standard rails the sleepers have become considerably exposed whereas in both alloy rails little displacement of ballast has taken place. The analysis of the data obtained over a distance of 6m on either side of a thermit weld joining a Type 1A (heat 265848) alloy rail to a standard carbon is illustrated in Figure 4 and substantiates the visual observations. There is also no evidence of corrugations having developed on the alloy rail up to the thermit weld whereas the standard carbon material had severely corrugated. This was found to be the general behaviour throughout the test section and it seemed that under the track conditions associated with the string of rails examined, steel with a proof strength of above 630 MPa will suppress the formation of corrugationsat least up to 90 mgt. It has been determined by Mair and Groenhout (1976) that a rail steel with a minimum 0.2% proof stress level of 670 MPa will prevent continued corrugation development and this is in good agreement with the results of this study.

In addition to evaluating the merits of the alloy rails with respect to their resistance to corrug-

4

Session 313
Paper I.10

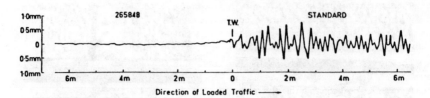

Figure 4 Corrugations in 11.7 km curve

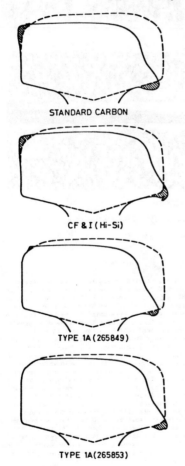

STANDARD CARBON

CF & I (Hi-Si)

TYPE 1A (265849)

TYPE 1A (265853)

Figure 5 Head profiles of worn rails from 11.7 km curve after 140 mgt.

ations, some data was also obtained on the wear suffered by the rails. However, before discussing the results it should be mentioned that since the rails were grouped according to their respective proof strength rather than heats, it was not possible to conduct an accurate assessment of performance on an economic basis. As it will be shown in the following section, the rerailing sequence was changed significantly in all the other trial curves which were used to study rail performance. The final assessment of the high rails on the 11.7 km curve was conducted in November 1976 after the rails had been subjected to approximately 140 mgt of traffic. The trial section had to be rerailed as a result of the extensive head loss suffered by the rails, especially the lower strength ones. This is illustrated in Figure 5 which shows typical head profiles of the various worn rails prior to rerailment. The original rail profile has been superimposed in each case for a better comparison. It is evident that the main contributing factor to the deterioration of the rails is the loss of material at the gauge corner region of the rail head with some plastic flow occurring down the gauge face of the rails and to some extent towards the field side as the shaded areas of the profiles indicate. With the exception of heat 265849, the Type 1A (Cr-Nb-V) rails showed a higher resistance to gauge corner wear than either standard carbon or the Hi-Si rails. The superiority of the Type 1A rails is more evident from their resistance to flow of the metal on the field side of the head. This region remained virtually undeformed after 140 mgt. However, the Hi-Si and particularly the standard carbon rails exhibited considerable plastic flow on the field corner which is indicative of the lower proof strength of these materials. Final substantiation of these observations is given by the average percentage head loss calculated for each rail type from the profiles taken prior to rerailment, as shown in Table III. The results also illustrate the range in performance observed in the different heats of Type 1A rails.

TABLE III

Rail Type (Heat Number)	Head Loss (140 mgt)
Standard Carbon	21½
C.F. & I. Hi-Si	19
Type 1A (265849)	21
" (265847)	17½
" (265850)	15½
" (265848)	14½
" (265853)	14
" (265854)	13

TABLE IV

CHARACTERISTICS OF TRIAL CURVES

CURVE No.	CURVATURE (RADIUS m)	SUPERELEVATION (mm)	GRADE (%)	RAIL TYPE IN CURVE
1	3° (582)	12	+0.08	Alloy
2	3° (")	12	-0.44	"
3	2° (873)	12	-0.48	"
4	2½° (699)	12	-0.45	Heat Treated
5	2° (873)	46	+1.50	Alloy
6	2½° (699)	58	+1.50	Alloy + Heat Treated
7	2° (873)	26	+0.13	Alloy + Heat Treated
8	3° (582)	14	+0.02	Alloy + Heat Treated
9	2° (873)	43	+0.06	Alloy + Heat Treated
10	1½° (1164)	21	+0.46	Heat Treated
11	3° (582)	13	-0.44	Alloy + Heat Treated
12	2½° (699)	13	-0.46	Alloy + Heat Treated

3.2 CURRENT TRIALS

The current in-track assessment at Mt Newman utilizes twelve curves and a section of tangent track. The latter is being used to study the behaviour of higher strength rails on a section of track prone to hunting. Since this has been a recent addition to the programme, insufficient results have so far been obtained and consequently they will not be included in this publication. The "trial" or "experimental" curves selected for this study have different physical characteristics such as degree of curvature, superelevation and gradient as shown in Table IV. All curves have timber sleepers with the exception of curve 9 which was rerailed on concrete sleepers in order to determine their effect on rail performance. Each curve is grease lubricated by a single automatic lubricator which is activated by the passage of the wheels from each loaded train. The grease is directed on the wheel flanges which in turn transfer it on the gauge face of the rails in the curve. Each curve contains a variety of rail types which have been laid in strings of at least five lengths on both high and low sides of the curve. The rails were numbered and grouped according to their respective heats rather than proof strength as was the case for the 11.7 km curve described in the previous section (3.1). The numbering sequence started from the port end of each curve. Several factors had to be considered in establishing the rerailing sequence for each curve. It was felt that a better assessment of performance of the various rail types could be made if rails of standard composition were included in each curve as a basis for comparison. However, the problems associated with having such a mixture of rail types in the same curve had to be also considered. For example, although it would be desirable to place standard carbon rails in various sections of the curve, it might be impracticable in view of the maintenance required on these rails and their relatively short replacement time. Consequently it was decided that the use of the standard rails should be restricted to the beginning and end of the curve.

Other problems which had to be considered were associated with the welding of the various rail types. Although it is not the aim here to deal with the welding aspects of the various materials since this work is detailed in another publication (Vines et al, 1978), some comments are felt to be necessary. Increasing the strength of a steel by additions of alloying elements also increases its hardenability which can influence considerably the weldability of the material. Consequently there was a need to determine which alloy steels could be welded by using the same procedure normally adopted to weld rails of standard composition. Extensive use was made of transformation data obtained in the laboratory for the different rail materials and the results indicated that the standard welding cycle would not be suited to the Type 2 (Cr-V) and Type 5 (Cr-Mo) rails because the cooling rate associated with such a cycle would lead to the formation of martensite in the heat affected zone of the weld. Special welding procedures had to be applied to these two alloy rail types in order to minimize the occurrence of the hard martensitic phase in the weld region.

At the time of rerailing the trial curves, very little information was available on welding of heat treated rails. It was the general practice overseas to weld this rail type similarly to the standard carbon material and consequently the same method was adopted for these trials. However, it was soon realized that welding of the heat treated rails would become a major problem. Soft regions were detected in flash butt and particularly thermit welds of some head-hardened rails after only 25 mgt of traffic.

The presence of hard or soft regions in the heat affected zone of the welds is detrimental to rail performance, since these may act as initiators for development of corrugations which eventually would have to be removed by grinding. Such an operation would not only reduce the life of the rails, but it would also lead to inaccurate assessments of performance. Therefore it became evident that special welding techniques would also have to be developed for the heat treated rails.

3.3 IN-TRACK MEASUREMENTS

The first assessment of performance of the rails in the trial curves was conducted after approximately 50 mgt of traffic. It was felt unnecessary to record measurements prior to this tonnage because the amount of information obtained on the initial wear behaviour of the rails would not have justified the extra cost. However, in subsequent assessments, the monitoring of rail wear in the trial curves was conducted at intervals of approximately every six months or 25 mgt of traffic.

Figure 6   Seiki rail profile gauge

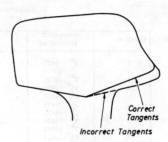

Figure 7   Skew rail head profile

Rail head profiles are recorded at mid-rail length with a Seiki profile gauge, illustrated in Figure 6, and the areas are measured by means of a planimeter. The gauge is calibrated to reproduce a 1:1 profile (within 10mm^2) on a standard AREA 65.5 kg/m new rail section and its calibration is checked periodically to ensure that it remains constant. The percentage head loss for each rail is derived as follows:

$$\text{\% Head Loss} = \frac{a_o - a_w}{a_o} \times 100 \qquad (1)$$

where a_o is the original area of the worn rail a_w.

One of the major sources of error in determining percentage head loss particularly in the early stages of rail wear is associated with the value given to a_o. It would be incorrect to regard this parameter to be a constant because of the variations which can occur in original rail head size due to rolling tolerances. Since the head loss is represented as a small difference between relatively large worn and unworn rail head areas, these size variations could cause quite large errors. However, these can be eliminated by recording the profiles of the rails prior to being subjected to any traffic and using them as original areas for calculating percentage head losses. For rails already in service for which the original head profiles cannot be obtained, it is usually possible to reduce these errors to acceptable limits by using the unworn rail head edge on the gauge side to reconstruct the original rail head profile and substituting its area for a_o in equation (1).

Another common source of error stems from measuring the area of the profile taken from a high rail which has developed a large lip as a result of plastic flow down the gauge face. Under these circumstances the Seiki gauge pin cannot make contact with the rail head surface in the region under the lip and consequently an asymmetrical profile results. If the tangents are not drawn in correctly, a substantial error will be introduced in calculating percentage head loss, i.e. the worn rail head will appear to have lost less material as illustrated in Figure 7.

With respect to head loss on the 68 kg/m rails such as the NSC Head Hardened, because of the larger head size of this rail (cf the 65.5 kg/m) the same amount of head loss would represent a smaller percentage on the larger rails and would give them an apparent superiority. Since the 68 kg/m rail head section is 10% greater than that of the 65.5

kg/m, a given head area loss "A" would give values $\frac{100A}{a_o}$ and $\frac{100A}{1.1a}$ as percentage head losses for the respective rails (a = area of the 65.5 kg/m rail). Increasing the latter by 10% gives:

$$\frac{100A}{1.1a} \times 1.1 = \frac{100A}{a} = \text{value for the 65.5kg/m rail.}$$

Therefore the values of head losses given in this text for 68 kg/m rails have been increased by 10% to make them comparable to the 65.5 kg/m rails.

It should be noted that "head loss" in this text refers to material removed from the rail head as a result of wear and also any metal flow due to plastic deformation. Furthermore, the results presented are those from the high legs of the curves. Due to the small amount of wear suffered by the low rails in the trial curves, insufficient data have been available so far to enable a quantitative assessment to be made on the performance of the various rail types.

4.   RESULTS AND DISCUSSION

4.1   Effect of Rail Wear on Performance

Measuring rail wear at specified intervals has enabled a percentage head loss to be calculated at specific tonnages and consequently the performance of the different rail types can be monitored at various stages of curve life.

The methods originally adopted in assessing performance was to measure two or three rails on either side of the weld adjoining the respective rail strings. The first set of results obtained by this method showed that considerable variation existed in the head losses suffered by similar rails. This variability is shown by the results from the assessment conducted on curve 1 (3°D of C) after 60½ mgt of traffic (Figure 8). For example, the percentage head loss suffered by the standard carbon string (rail Nos 7-11) varied between 7 and 15½%. Similar differences, although to varying degrees, can be observed in all the other rail strings in the curve. This variability in performance was also found in the other trial curves and was at first attributed to scatter resulting from measurement errors. It was felt, therefore, that this method of measuring a limited number of rails was inadequate in assessing accurately the performance of the rail types in the curves and consequently in subsequent assessments head profiles from every rail in each curve

Session 313
Paper I.10

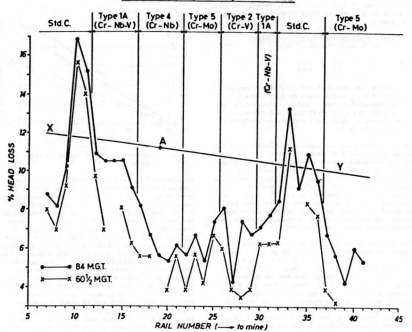

CURVE Nº 1 – (3° DofC) HIGH RAIL

Figure 8   Differential wear of rails in curve 1

were recorded. Analysis of these data showed variations in percentage head loss consistent with those from the previous results which therefore could no longer be explained in terms of measurement errors.

Plotting percentage head loss, from the two assessments conducted on curve 1 at the specified tonnages as a function of rail type and position in the curve as shown in Figure 8 revealed that a particular rail wear pattern was developing for the curve and that rail types located at the port end of the curve suffered more wear than similar ones railed at the mine end. Typical examples of the latter behaviour are the standard carbon and the Type 1A (Cr-Nb-V) strings after 84 mgt. Those railed at the beginning of the curve have suffered average percentage head losses of 11.8 (rails 7-11) and 10.3 respectively whereas the corresponding ones located towards the end of the curve have been subjected to less wear (10.2 and 7.4%) head loss. Similar findings were observed in the other trial curves.

As a result of this differential wear of the rails with position in the curve it was felt that an accurate comparison in performance could not be made by simply averaging the percentage head losses of all similar rail types. There was a need, therefore, to develop a method which could compensate for the variation in wear rate for different parts of the curve.

As shown in Figure 8 a line XY, joining points representing the average percentage head loss of the standard carbon strings (84 mgt) at both ends of the curve, has been drawn. The slope of this line is assumed to represent the wear which the standard carbon rail would suffer on any given position in the curve and this provides a new basis for comparing the performance of the other rail types. The standard carbon rail is given an arbitrary "performance rating" value of 100 and figures representing percentage wear relative to the standard carbon material can be calculated for each rail type. For example:

Average % head loss of the Type 4 (Cr-Nb) string at 84 mgt = 6.3

Assumed % head loss of Standard Carbon in similar position in the curve (point A on line XY) = 11.1

Therefore performance of Type 4 cf Standard Carbon is given by: $\frac{6.3}{11.1} \times 100 = 57\%$

i.e. The Type 4 (Cr-Nb) rails in this curve have a performance rating value of 57 (cf 100 for Standard Carbon).

Repeating this procedure for the other rail types in the curve, their respective performance rating values can be obtained. Furthermore, if it can be assumed that the current wear rate of the experimental rails relative to standard carbon remains constant, these performance rating values can be used to predict rail life. Again, taking the type 4 rails as an example, their predicted rail life is given by:

$$\frac{\text{Performance Rating of Standard Carbon}}{\text{Performance Rating of Type 4}}$$

i.e. $\frac{100}{57} = \underline{1.75}$

This would indicate that the life expectancy of the Type 4 alloy rails would be 1.75 times that of the standard carbon. Similar calculations can be made for the other rail types and these are given, together with their respective performance ratings in Table V.

These results show the superior performance of the alloy rails over the standard carbon material and in this respect the higher strength rails have been successful in exhibiting a higher resistance to wear. Rail Types 4 (Cr-Nb) and 5 (Cr-Mo) show the best performance with a life expectancy of 1.75 times that of the standard material. However, it should be emphasised that these values have been obtained after only 84 mgt of traffic and consequently assessments at higher tonnages would be required to validate these predictions.

The difference in performance of the various rail types can also be demonstrated by plotting the average percentage head loss of each rail type as a function of gross traffic (mgt) as illustrated in Figure 9. Even though this method of presentation does not take into consideration the effect of rail position in the curve, the results nevertheless are in good agreement with the rail life expectancy values. Some improvement in wear rate has been achieved by the Type 1A (Cr-Nb-V) rails compared to the standard carbon material, but the best performance is exhibited by the Type 2 (Cr-V), Type 4 (Cr-Nb) and Type 5 (Cr-Mo) rails. The difference in the average percentage head loss suffered by the latter three rail types is less than 1% and consequently future assessments will be necessary to determine whether any significant changes in wear rate from the present trend will occur during the later stages of rail life.

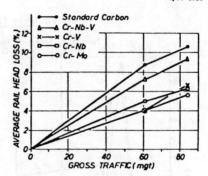

Figure 9   Comparative performance of rails in curve 1

As mentioned in section 2, heat treated rails were obtained by the Mt Newman Mining Co so that their performance could be directly compared with that of the alloy rails. Curve 7 (2^OD of C), situated at 216 km from the port, is one of the curves which has been utilized for such a comparison. It was rerailed in October 1975 with the six heats of Type 1A (Cr-Nb-V) material, Type 5 (Cr-Mo) and U.S.S. Curvemaster (USCM) rails. Three assessments have been conducted to date at 42½, 66½ and 93 mgt of traffic. Similarly to curve 1, the percentage head loss at the specified tonnages have been plotted as a function of rail type and position in the curve as illustrated in Figure 10. The results show that the rails in this curve have developed a specific wear pattern and by using the method described previously, two lines have been drawn representing the different wear of the standard carbon rails along the curve at the two specified tonnages (66½ and 93 mgt). Calculating the performance rating values and life expectancies for the various rail types compared to standard carbon, gives the results shown in Table VI.

TABLE VI

PERFORMANCE ASSESSMENT OF RAILS FROM CURVE No. 7

Rail Type	Performance Rating		Predicted Rail Life	
	66½ mgt	93 mgt	66½ mgt	93 mgt
Standard Carbon	100	100	1	1
Type 1A				
(265849)	105	105	0.95	0.95
(265847)	105	110	0.95	0.90
(265853)	89	96	1.1	1.0
(265850)	81	88	1.2	1.1
(265848)	69	80	1.4	1.3
(265854)	75	77	1.3	1.3
Type 5				
(Cr-Mo)	56	69	1.8	1.4
USCM	51	52	2.0	1.9

These results indicate that little or no improvement in performance has been achieved by the first four heats of Type 1A (Cr-Nb-V) material shown in Table VI whereas a significant increase in rail life has been shown by the rails from heats 265848

TABLE V

ASSESSMENT OF RAILS FROM CURVE No. 1

Rail Type	Performance Rating	Predicted Rail Life
Standard Carbon	100	1
Type 1A (Cr-Nb-V)	81	1.2
Type 2 (Cr-V)	62	1.5
Type 4 (Cr-Nb)	57	1.75
Type 5 (Cr-Mo)	56	1.75

Session 313
Paper 1.10

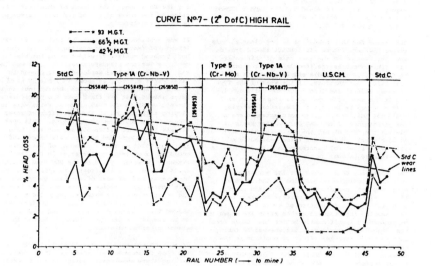

Figure 10   Differential wear of rails in curve 7

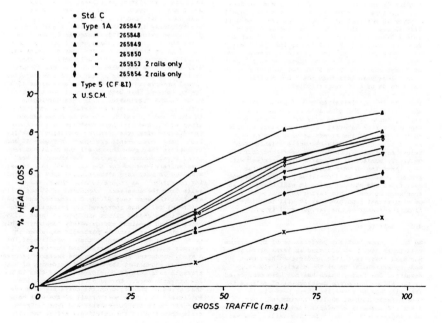

Figure 11   Comparative performance of rails in curve 7

and 265854 - both with approximately 1.3 times that of the standard carbon material. The life expectancy values obtained for the Type 5 (Cr-Mo) rails differ considerably at the two tonnages - 1.8 at 66½ mgt cf 1.4 at 93 mgt.

The reason for this behaviour is not clear at this stage; however, future assessments should provide more information on the wear rate of this material. This stresses the importance of monitoring performance at the middle and later stages of rail life. For instance, if the wear of the Type 1A (heat 265848) and Type 5 (Cr-Mo) rails continued at the same rate, the small increase in rail life achieved by the use of the latter material would not justify its extra manufacturing costs. The performance of the USS Curvemaster rails is clearly the best of all the rails in this curve. At both specified tonnages these head hardened rails show a two fold increase in life compared to the standard carbon.

The importance of allowing for the variation in wear rate according to position in the curve when assessing rail performance is emphasised in Figure 11 which shows average percentage head loss of each rail type as a function of gross traffic (mgt). For example, the standard carbon rails are shown to be performing significantly better than those from heat 265849 of Type 1A material whereas by taking into consideration the effect of position in the curve very little difference was found between these two rail types (Table VI). This apparent better performance of the standard material is mainly due to its percentage head loss value being the average of strings placed at both ends of the curve. The value quoted for the 265849 rails is only the average of the string situated at the port end of the curve which is more prone to rail wear. Similar differences in performance are shown between the Type 5 (Cr-Mo) and rails from heat 265848 of Type 1A material at 93 mgt. The predicted rail life values calculated for these two rail types were 1.3 and 1.4 respectively (Table VI) which indicate an 8% longer rail life for the Type 5 material. However, a comparison of the average percentage head losses suffered by these two rail types at 93 mgt shows the Type 5 (Cr-Mo) to have suffered 23% less head loss than the Type 1A (265848) rails (5.3% of 6.9% respectively).

Even though this latter method of presentation of the results may not give an accurate assessment of rail performance particularly with respect to the standard carbon material, it nevertheless provides an indication of the trends in wear rate of each rail type. As more data becomes available from future assessments, changes in wear behaviour can be easily monitored. Of particular interest will be determining to what stage of rail life the present wear rate will continue for the different rail types and at what point it will change to an accelerating one. This factor is considered to be of significant importance as it will influence the final assessment of the various rail types.

4.2 Rail Defects

So far in this text the performance of the various rail types have been assessed in terms of percentage head loss; rail life predictions have been made by extrapolation of these relatively early results. One factor which has not been considered is the effect which the development of defects in the rails has in assessing their performance. Some defects such as shells, horizontally split heads and transverse defects lead to almost immediate replacement of the defective rails. However,

running surface or gauge corner checking, corrugations and wheel burns are usually removed by grinding the rail head. The effect of this latter operation on the rails of two of the trial curves will be discussed firstly.

It was mentioned in section 3.2 that due to insufficient information being available at the time, heat treated rails were welded using the similar cycle as for the standard material. This was the case for the NSC Head Hardened rails placed in trial curve 6 which, as shown in Table IV is of 24° with a +1.50% grade. In-track observations on this curve showed that the flash butt and particularly thermit welds in the head hardened rails were developing soft regions in the heat affected zones and consequently would require grinding. This operation was conducted after 56½ mgt and rail head profiles were recorded on each rail before and after grinding so that the amount of head loss could be taken into consideration in the final assessment. However, grinding the NSC Head Hardened rails proved to be detrimental to their performance because it removed most of the hard quench and tempered martensitic region in the rail head leaving the relatively softer material which led to a marked increase in wear rate. Subsequent assessments showed the performance of these head hardened rails to be similar or perhaps marginally better than the standard carbon material.

Other problems associated with rail grinding are the changes in wear rate which result from establishing a new wheel/rail contact region by profiling the worn rail head. The problem becomes more complex if only selected sections of curves are ground. This has the added effect of changing the existing differences in the relative performances of the various rail types and consequently an accurate quantitative assessment of performance would not be possible until a later stage of rail wear when this head loss due to grinding will not significantly affect the results. A good example of this behaviour is illustrated in Figure 12 which shows the average percentage head loss as a function of gross traffic (mgt) for four different rail types in curve 9. As previously mentioned (Section 3.2) this curve was rerailed on concrete sleepers in order to study their effect on rail performance. Visual observations made on this curve after 15 and 38½ mgt showed that both flash butt and thermit welds in the Curvemaster rails were developing soft regions which were initiating corrugations on the high and low rails. The whole curve was ground after 44 mgt and rail head profiles were recorded immediately after the grinding operation. Results from these measurements are shown in Figure 12 and it appears that even though all the rails had received equal number of passes, the amount of head loss suffered varied for the different rail types. A change in wear rate also resulted from the grinding operation. As Figure 12 also shows, the results from the assessment conducted at 65 mgt indicate that the wear rate of the Curvemaster and Type 5 (Cr-Mo) rails had increased significantly whereas for the standard carbon and Type 1A (heat 265850) rails it had remained approximately constant. This behaviour may at least be partially explained in terms of the work hardening characteristics of the various material types (Marich and Curcio, 1978). A study conducted at the Melbourne Research Laboratories has shown that the depth of hardening of high strength materials is considerably less than in the low strength ones. Consequently it is possible that grinding conducted on the curve may have been sufficient to remove most or all of the work hardened region in the Curvemaster and Type 5 (Cr-Mo) rails thus leaving the relatively softer material which would lead to an increase in wear rate. In the case of the Type 1A and standard rails the work hardening region would extend well beyond the depth of material removed by grinding thus subsequently resulting in a fairly constant wear rate. It should be noted that the accuracy suggested by the scale on the vertical axis of Figure 12 is not realistic; it has been extended only to emphasise the difference in behaviour of the various rail types.

It is felt that insufficient information is available at this stage to fully explain the observed changes in wear rate resulting from rail grinding. Perhaps as more data are obtained from future assessments of this curve, they will lead to a better understanding of this behaviour.

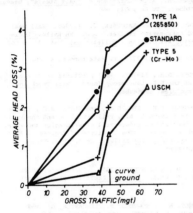

Figure 12   Effect of grinding on wear rate

Figure 13   Typical shells observed in USS Curve-master and Type 5 (Cr-Mo) rails

Apart from the development of corrugations initiating at the welds, the only other major type of defects so far detected in some of the high strength rails have been shells. These were observed in rails from curve 7 after 93 mgt of traffic (section 4.1) and curve 8 (3°D of C) after 61½ mgt. The defective rails in both curves were USS Curve-master head hardened manufactured by United States

Steel and those from one heat of Type 5 (Cr-Mo) material produced by C.F. & I. as illustrated in figure 13. It cannot be said at this stage whether the occurrence of these shells is a characteristic of material properties or whether they may be associated with manufacturing practices. Sections of rails containing shells at an early stage of development will be sent to the Melbourne Research Laboratories for a detailed metallurgical examination. The occurrence of shells in these high strength rails particularly at such an early stage of rail life is of major concern since the main objectives in developing such materials were not only to produce a rail which offered a high resistance to wear and deformation but also one which minimised the development of these defects.

4.3   Effects of Changes in Track Maintenance Procedures

It has become evident from this work that even though the relative performance of the various experimental rail types in the trial curves can be determined at the early stages of rail life, and predictions can be made by extrapolation of these early results, more data are required to validate these predictions. Because of the long term trials involved in obtaining such data, programmes of this nature need the flexibility to incorporate any changes in track maintenance procedures which may be introduced during their life.

The Mt Newman Mining Co has adopted two techniques aimed at increasing rail life: transposition and asymmetrical rail head profiling. In the former operation the rails in the curves are transposed when the percentage head loss of the high rails reaches a maximum of 10%. Reprofiling the rail head is a recently developed method aimed at reducing gauge corner wear on the high rails in curves (Townend et al, 1978). Special grinding techniques may be used to produce asymmetrical rail head profiles on both legs of the curve. This results in a shift of the wheel/rail contact region towards the low leg thus minimising gauge corner contact by the wheel flange on the high rails. Even though these two operations have indicated to be beneficial to rail life, the results so far obtained have been qualitative or at best, semi-quantitative. There seemed a need, therefore, to obtain more accurate data and consequently some of the trial curves have been utilized to incorporate such a programme.

Five trial curves have been transposed and asymmetrically reprofiled. Monitoring the performance of these rails will be conducted in a similar manner described for the other curves and the results from these assessments should provide an accurate determination of the effect of these operations on rail life. Furthermore, by reprofiling some of the other trial curves without transposing the rails it will enable the effect of the former operation on rail performance to be determined. These changes which have been introduced into the in-track assessment have given a broader scope to the programme without affecting its original objective.

5.   CONCLUSIONS

The performance of the various experimental rails placed in selected trial curves on the Mt Newman line has been found to vary significantly not only for the different rail types, but also between similar ones railed in the same curve. This variation has been shown to be associated with the differential wear which has been found to occur with position in the curve. Therefore a method of assessing

74

rail performance which also took into consideration this differential wear behaviour was developed. Life expectancies of the various rail types compared to the standard carbon material have been predicted from the results obtained at relatively early stages of rail wear and consequently data from assessments at higher tonnages will be required to validate these predictions. Nevertheless, a clear indication has been given on the superior performance of the alloy and heat treated rails over the standard carbon material in terms of a higher resistance to wear, plastic deformation and corrugation development.

The performance of the alloy rails varied considerably with the different types. Alloy types 4 (Cr-Nb) and 5 (Cr-Mo) showed similar performances up to about 83 mgt of traffic and indicated a 75% increase in rail life over that of the standard carbon material. However, the development of shells observed in one heat (11406) of Cr-Mo rails must place some doubt on the validity of life expectancy predictions based on material loss measurements alone. The same applies to the USS Curvemaster rails. These have so far exhibited the highest resistance to wear than any other rail type in track, indicating at least 100% improvement in rail life over the standard carbon. However, similarly to some of the Type 5 (Cr-Mo) rails, the USS Curvemaster have developed shell defects after only 87 mgt of traffic. This also emphasises the need for longer term trials to study any possible future development of these defects. Other heat treated rail types and those from the other two heats of Type 5 material (12547 and 2K8713) railed in track will be kept under close observation in all future assessments for any possible indications which could suggest further development of these or any other types of defects.

The in-track assessment programme on the Mt Newman line has so far shown that it has the flexibility to cope with changes introduced by routine and new track maintenance procedures such as rail grinding, transposition and asymmetrical reprofiling. Although these factors make rail evaluation on a cost/performance basis more complex, they have enabled this study to combine the experimental as well as the practical aspects of railroad operations.

6. ACKNOWLEDGEMENTS

The work was conducted as part of a joint railroad research programme between the Mt Newman Mining Co., Hamersley Iron Pty. Ltd., and The Broken Hill Proprietary Co. Ltd. The authors are grateful to all three companies for permission to publish this work.

7. REFERENCES

MARICH, S., and CURCIO, P., (1976). Development of high strength alloyed rails suitable for heavy duty applications. ASTM Conference on "Rail Steels", Denver, October. To be published.

MAIR, R.I., and GROENHOUT, R., (1976). Prediction of rail steel strength requirements - a reliability approach. ASTM Conference on "Rail Steels", Denver, October. To be published.

KING, F.E., and KALOUSEK, J., (1976). Rail wear and corrugation studies. American Railway Engineering Association - Bulletin 658, Vol. 77, p 601.

ROUGAS, M., (1977). Private communication.

STONE, D.H., (1976). Rail practices in Russia: what the U.S. tour group found. Rail Track and Structures, September.

TOWNEND, P.H., EPP, C.J., and CLARK, P.J., (1978). Bogie curving trials, rail profiling and theoretical modeling to reduce rail deterioration and wheel wear on curves. The Institute of Engineers, Australia, Heavy Haul Railways Conference, Perth, September.

UNITED STATES STEEL (1975). Curvemaster an extended life rail. Railroad Facts Technical Report No. 3.

VINES, M.J., TOWNEND, P., LANCASTER, G., and MARICH, S., (1978). The flash butt welding of high strength rail. The Institution of Engineers, Australia Heavy Haul Railways Conference, Perth, September.

Review of Rail Research on British Rail

C. O. Frederick and E. G. Jones

The rail research program of British Railways, which is aimed at understanding and reducing the severity of various mechanisms of rail failure,
is described. An important part of the work is the measurement and
prediction of rail stresses and the study of force-free temperature for
continuous welded rail. To reduce failure problems, it is necessary to
develop laboratory-based techniques to assess the performance of rail
steels and welds. This requires a knowledge of the dynamic and static
stress environment of the rails and computer programs to calculate these
stresses. The study of failures includes the study of Thermit and flash-
butt weld failures, tache ovale defects, star cracks at bolt holes, and
squat defects. It has been found that the majority of Thermit weld
failures can be attributed to poor welding practice. Flash-butt weld
failures are much less frequent but may become more of a problem
as the more wear-resistant rail steels are introduced into welded track.
The need to develop better steels for switch and crossing work has provided an impetus to develop a weldable austenitic manganese steel
and also bainitic steels of high strength and toughness. These developments are reviewed.

Rail research should reflect the future objectives and
problems of the railways concerned. British Railways
(BR) is a high-speed railway, and this has tended to
cause rather special problems. In addition, the move
to continuously welded rail (CWR), while solving some
problems, has created new ones—all of which has provided the impetus for research.

The thermal stresses in long, welded rails are, of
course, invisible and are commonly overlooked; nevertheless, they are large and very significant in controlling
the modes of failure. In designing a railway with CWR,
it is always necessary to choose the force-free temperature with care. Too high a force-free temperature will
assist the rapid growth of transverse fatigue cracks and
brittle fracture of the rail in winter, whereas too low a
force-free temperature will create a buckling problem
in the hot weather of summer. After a spate of buckling
incidents in 1969, BR raised the force-free rail temperature by 5.5°C to improve track stability. Subsequently,
an investigation was conducted into the factors that affect
track buckling with a view toward improving track design. The rise in force-free rail temperature may explain why there has been an increase in transverse rail
defects in recent years. There have, however, been
other problems, two of which are closely associated
with high-speed lines: squats and short pitch corrugations.

The current maximum strict axle load on BR is 250
kN. This is higher than on most European railways and
lower than U.S. values, which can exceed 298 kN. Rail-
crushing and side-wear problems are much less severe
in the United Kingdom than in the United States. Nevertheless, rail side wear still limits rail life on curves.
For large-radius, high-speed curves, where use of the
correct transverse rail profile is important to good riding, it has been necessary to prohibit the practice of
transposing side-worn rails. Thus, there are incentives
to use more wear-resistant rail. The standard BR rail
steel [710-MPa ultimate tensile strength (UTS)] is somewhat less wear resistant than the standard U.S. compositions. However, BR is using an increasing quantity
of wear-resistant Union Internationale des Chemins de
Fer (UIC) grades (880-MPa UTS) and 1 percent chromium rails (1080-MPa UTS) in sharply curved situations.
These rail steels bring with them some welding problems and slightly less toughness. There is a need for
simultaneous improvements in wear resistance, toughness, and weldability.

The BR rail research program has sought to establish an understanding of and to lessen the existing problems and also to look to the future to see what might be
achieved by new rail steels. This paper is an account
of some of the main lines of investigation.

FORCE-FREE RAIL TEMPERATURE

Track Buckling

The force-free rail temperature is defined as the rail
temperature at which long welded rail experiences zero
resultant longitudinal force. This temperature is determined by the procedures used to install the welded
rail. In deciding this temperature, it is desirable to
have an understanding of track-buckling behavior. Some
early experiments in track buckling were done in Mousehole Tunnel between 1956 and 1959 (1). At first, the
buckling theories could only account for the behavior of
an infinite sinusoidal irregularity in straight track (2).
More recently, a more advanced theory has been developed that allows for an individual irregularity on
straight and curved track (3). This is an important advance because it shows for the first time the importance
of the longitudinal restraint between the rails and the
sleepers. If this restraint is large, it helps to prevent
feeding of rail compression into the buckling zone as a
misalignment develops. The new theory also shows that
there is a fairly clearly defined value of the maximum
rise in rail temperature at which thermal buckling will
not occur despite the presence of misalignments. This
"safe" maximum increase in rail temperature is shown
in Figure 1, where it can be seen that, in the curve for
temperature increase versus deflection, there is first a
peak followed by a trough. The height of the peak is
very sensitive to misalignments, but the height of the
trough is insensitive to these and provides a better design limit.

The calculated variation in the safe temperature increase with lateral and longitudinal resistance for
standard BR track components is shown in Figure 2.
Buckling experiments have recently been under way at
Old Dalby to check these predictions. The value at
which buckling took place was always above the calculated safe temperature increase and was sensitive to
rail straightness. After the first experiment, the rail
developed a permanent lateral set. Even when the track
and rails were laid apparently straight, the built-in set
in the rail strongly influenced the buckling behavior.

Rolling Out

There have been many observations of BR in-service
rails experiencing a general drop in force-free rail
temperature, a phenomenon referred to as "rolling out".
This should be distinguished from changes in the distribution of force-free temperature along the track, which
is caused by creep of the rail along the track associated
with movement through the fastenings or movement of
the sleepers in the ballast. The rolling-out effect is
caused by the rails becoming longer. The magnitude of
this effect has been measured by taking out 240-m
lengths of rail, measuring their length, and then replacing them. Reductions in force-free temperature of
approximately 6°C in a year have been measured for new
rails. It is thought that this effect will stabilize and
considerably lessen over the years. Nevertheless, it
means that a higher initial rail tension is required to

Figure 1. Typical buckling response.

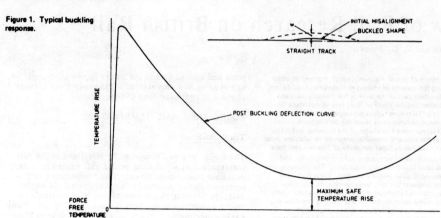

Figure 2. Maximum safe temperature rise for standard BR components.

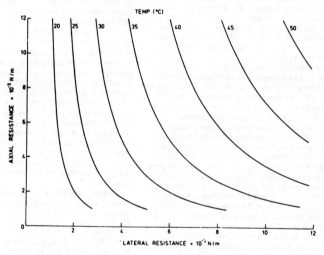

prevent track buckling (1°C is equivalent to 1.7 Mg for 56-kg/m rail).

RAIL STRESSES

Wheel-Rail Contact

It is fitting to start an investigation of rail behavior by considering the stress environment of the rail steel. Clearly, the highest stresses come from wheel-rail contact force. These stresses, however, are very dependent on the precise profiles of wheel and rail. Iterative computer programs have been written to calculate the shape of the contact area for different wheel-rail-profile contact arrangements. Contact at the gauge corner will tend to produce an elliptical contact patch that is long and thin, whereas contact of worn wheel and rail near the rail center line tends to produce a wide and short contact patch. These programs must be iterative, since the dimensions of the contact patch depend on the out-of-plane surface deflections. It is customary to assume elastic material behavior and to assume that the

surface deflections are those of a semi-infinite half-plane. The latter assumption is somewhat dubious for gauge-corner contact. Since it is well known that rails plastically deform, it may be thought that the assumption of elastic behavior is also dubious. However, the plastic deformation of rails is something that occurs slowly under many thousands of cycles, and the plastic deformation that occurs under one cycle is almost certainly negligible compared with the elastic strains.

Calculations of the Hertzian stresses caused by wheel-rail contact do not usually allow for flexure of the rail as a beam, nor do they allow for phenomena such as bending of the railhead as a beam supported by the rail web. To investigate these effects, it is usually necessary to resort to finite-element analyses of some sort. These analyses allow the true shape of the rail to be included but make crude assumptions for stresses and strains that occur in the immediate contact zone. When conventional three-dimensional finite elements are used, the computation rapidly becomes very large because of the large number of unknowns. The Research and Development Division of the British Railways Board has

Figure 3. Calculated rail stresses for off-center vertical load: vertical stresses on the rail web.

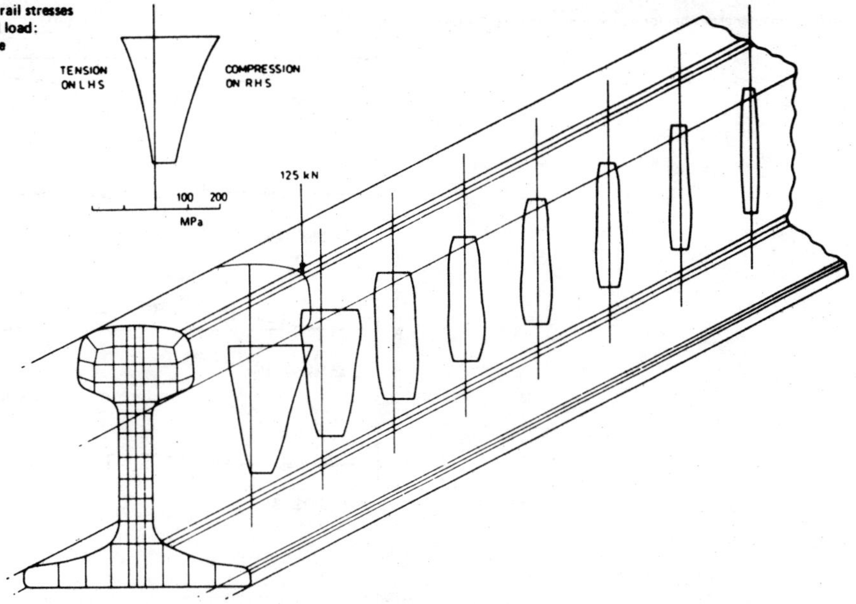

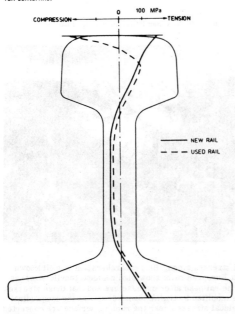

Figure 4. Longitudinal residual stresses in new and used rail on rail centerline.

found the most promising analysis method to be one that combines finite elements and Fourier techniques (4). This analysis divides the rail up into longitudinal prisms of quadrilateral cross section. Although the loading must itself be expressed in Fourier harmonics along the

rail, a good representation of a localized load is possible. This program has been used successfully to analyze the effect of off-center vertical loads on strains in the rail web (see Figure 3).

In the past, lateral forces have been measured for experimental purposes by measuring the bending of the rail web at two positions that are vertically one above the other. This arrangement is, however, affected by off-center vertical loads (5), and this can be demonstrated by using the computer program. In the future, it should be possible to design improved load-measuring systems by using an array of gauges and a small on-line computer.

Dynamic Load Variations

In calculating stresses in rails, it is usually necessary to consider dynamic wheel loads. Dynamic variations in load are especially important at high speeds or when the wheels have formed flats. There are very few data on wheel and rail roughness, but it is clear from calculations that contact forces can vary substantially with very small levels of roughness (6). These variations are so large because the wheel-rail contact spring is so stiff and because the rail inertia is significant at high frequencies of oscillation. When longitudinal profiles have been measured by using an inertial trolley, it has been found that rail roughness usually decreases under the influence of traffic unless some phenomenon such as corrugation is at work. It is worth noting that, at high speeds, wheel-rail contact forces can be expected to increase if rail weight is increased; thus, mechanisms of rail surface damage are likely to get worse with heavier rails.

Tensile Stresses in Railhead

In considering rail fracture, it is especially important to consider the extreme values of tensile stress in the railhead, since failures rarely initiate in the rail foot

Figure 5. Computer algorithm for correction of an irregular weld.

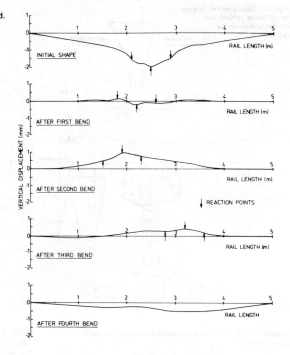

Table 1. Physical properties of rail steels.

Material	Coefficient of Linear Expansion ($°C^{-1} \times 10^6$)	Young's Modulus (GPa)		
		$-15°C$	$20°C$	$50°C$
BS 11 normal quality	11.25	216	213	211
UIC grade B	11.4	211	208	206
1 percent chromium	11.8	216	213	212
Cast LCAMS	17.0	181	180	178
Rolled LCAMS	17.1	201	200	197
Bainitic[a]	11.6	211	209	207

[a]Composition (percentage by weight) = 0.16 carbon, 0.19 silicon, 1.01 manganese, 0.23 sulfur, 0.025 phosphorus, 1.40 chromium, and 0.53 molybdenum.

Figure 6. White phase embedded in rail running surface.

(the exceptions in the United Kingdom being defective welds or cracking from corrosion pitting or chair gall). The highest tensile stresses are attributable to a combination of the effects of cold-weather contraction and wheel-flat impact. Thus, the tensile stresses caused by hogging of the rail at either side of the point of impact are more important than the stresses immediately under the point of impact. There has been a substantial program of research to study wheel-flat impact (7), and it has been found that the resultant hogging bending waves propagate very rapidly along the rail and lessen only slowly with distance. As a result, all of the rail will experience to some extent the hogging stresses caused by a wheel flat, although the maximum stresses occur where the quasistatic procession wave is combined with the dynamic effect.

The dynamic testing of rails reflects the importance of tensile stresses in the railhead and is described later in this paper.

Residual Stresses

Recently, there has been an increased interest in resid-

ual stresses among BR researchers. It is well known that European rails show high residual tensile stresses in the railhead after manufacture and that these stresses are modified by traffic loads (8) so that the longitudinal residual stresses near the running surface are converted from tensile to compressive stresses (see Figure 4). According to German researchers (9), the original residual tensile stresses are caused by the roller straightening process. These residual stresses in the railhead are undesirable because (a) they must increase the magnitude of the rolling-out process and (b) they will probably increase the tendency of cracks to propagate downward across the rail section rather than parallel to the rail surface.

Alternative systems of rail straightening are being examined, and the possibility of a computer-controlled gag press is being considered. Such a device would require a preliminary measurement of longitudinal rail profiles (vertical or lateral) followed by a traverse of one or more automatically controlled presses that obey pressing instructions worked out according to a computer algorithm. Such a system would not produce large residual tensile stresses in the head of the rail.

Work is proceeding to identify suitable computer algorithms. Figure 5 shows the effect of one computer algorithm in correcting an irregular vertical weld profile.

Physical Properties

Thermal stresses in CWR are, of course, dependent on the temperature change from the force-free condition, but they are also dependent on the product of Young's modulus and the coefficient of expansion. There are slight differences (±5 percent) in the values used in different countries for the coefficients of expansion of pearlitic rail steels. These differences could be very significant when it comes to selecting a rail steel. We decided, therefore, to obtain some reliable comparative data. The results, which are given in Table 1, seem to show that any variations between pearlitic and bainitic steels are unimportant, although these two steels are very different from austenitic steels.

LIMITS ON RAIL LIFE

Sleeper Condition

The bulk of rails withdrawn from BR service are withdrawn as a consequence of the normal track relaying pattern. The commonest determinant of relaying priority is poor sleeper condition, since there are still many lines with timber sleepers. It has been found that rails removed from straight or slightly curved track for this reason are no longer suitable for use in high-speed lines because of rail-end batter, corrosion, galling of the rail seating area, or localized loss of railhead profile. Nevertheless, the 710-MPa UTS rail steel in current use performs adequately with long-lived sleepers and gives a life of more than 20 years in most lines. More sharply curved track, however, presents a very different picture, and the life of 710-MPa UTS rail can be much less than 2 years. This has led to some use of 900-MPa UTS rail steels. The use of these steels is currently restricted by welding problems and to some extent by availability. Chromium rail steel with 1080-MPa UTS has so far been used on a very restricted experimental basis.

Corrugation

Corrugatory wear on both straight and curved track leads to a shortening of service life and, although its appearance has been reported since the 19th century, the causes are still not understood. The incidence of this phenomenon on BR is increasing, and at present the only remedy is periodic grinding, which obviously will lead to a shortening of rail life. The effect of corrugations on general track deterioration is slowly emerging and is giving cause for concern.

The loosening of iron shoulders cast into concrete sleepers has been observed where rails are severely corrugated, and it is also thought that the corrugations may shorten the fatigue life of the rail. The steel at the crests of corrugations is often severely deformed plas-

tically, and small cracks have been observed that follow the same direction as the plastically deformed grain boundaries. In a joint exercise with Speno International SA to study the effectiveness of rail grinding, it was found that ground rails subsequently developed squat defects, which may well have initiated from cracks that were not completely removed in grinding (10).

Corrugations on high-speed lines usually exhibit patches of "white phase" on the crests. This is very similar in appearance to martensite and is very hard. The possibility that corrugations worsen because of differential rates of wear or corrosion is currently being examined. In this context, the presence of white phase could be important, since it is frequently observed on BR rails. White phase could also play a role in surface-initiated fatigue mechanisms since, as Figure 6 shows, hard pieces of white phase can become embedded in the surface and cause severe plastic deformation (11). These investigations are still exploratory, and the importance of white phase in surface damage mechanisms has still to be ascertained.

Rail Fracture

Sometimes rail fracture causes premature withdrawal of rails from service. In a passenger-carrying system, safety is of the greatest concern, and so some forms of fracture are regarded as more serious than others. The most dangerous forms are those in which a piece of the running surface is removed. In general, a single transverse fracture in CWR is not so dangerous and is usually detected promptly by its effect on track circuits.

In plain track, the following fracture types are of prime interest:

1. Squat fractures—surface defects initiated by rolling-contact fatigue that propagate at a shallow angle and then turn down to form transverse fractures (see Figure 7);
2. Tache ovales—in the United Kingdom, hydrogen-flake-initiated fatigue fractures in the center of the railhead;
3. Star cracks—fatigue-initiated cracks that start in the bore of fish bolt holes;
4. Wheel burns—isolated depressions in the running surface of the rail that lead to (a) high dynamic stresses and subsequent fatigue cracking or (b) continuous transformation of the running surface of the rail, causing hardened microstructures with subsequent fatigue or brittle fracture; and
5. Weld fractures—Thermit weld failures, which generally initiate from a lack-of-fusion defect, and flash-butt failures, which initiate from "flat spots" (entrapped oxide plates on the weld center line).

In all of these fracture types, final fracture is always by brittle cleavage and causes either a complete transverse fracture through the rail or detachment of a portion of the railhead. A star-crack fracture often removes part of the running surface. Tache ovales and wheel burns are particularly dangerous when they initiate at multiple sites at short intervals along the rail.

TESTING OF RAIL STEELS

As demonstrated above, the service life of rail is reduced by wear, rolling-contact fatigue, fatigue, and brittle fracture. To improve service performance, it first becomes necessary to understand how these mechanisms are induced and how rail steels respond.

The assessment techniques used by BR in the evaluation of rail steels have been described in detail elsewhere (12). The basic approach adopted has been to quantify the environment that the rail is subjected to and then use the data so obtained to define a suitable laboratory test. This allows quicker and cheaper evaluation of possible improved materials. This approach also lends itself to gaining an understanding of how the metallurgical structures of rail steels are affected by the various detrimental environmental mechanisms and leads to a materials design concept.

Laboratory Assessment of Fatigue Life

The occurrence of the squat type of defect in BR track has required the development of laboratory assessment methods for failure under rolling-contact fatigue. Preliminary work to date has been carried out on Amsler twin-disc-type machines and small-diameter specimens. Initial experiments indicated that a liquid contaminant (water in this case) was necessary to induce failures. The work to date has been concerned with studying the effect of different creepages—i.e., the percentage of sliding between the two rollers—and contact stresses on the failure rates of a range of rail steels.

In the Amsler tests, it is customary to fix the load and creepage γ, thereby generating in the test certain levels of contact stress σ_c and traction force T. For normal-grade BR rail steel (710 MPa), it was found that cycles to failure N depended approximately on the square of the contact stress. When the creep rate was varied with a range of steels, it was found that the shortest lives occurred at a creep rate of 0.3 percent for all steels. It is thought that this minimum is associated with zero traction at zero creep and, when creep is plotted against the parameter NT for a given contact stress, the minimum disappears. Figure 8 shows a plot of $NT\sigma_c^2$ versus creep for a range of steels. These results tend to indicate a relationship of the following form:

$$N = (1 \, T\sigma_c^2) f(\gamma) \tag{1}$$

where the function f depends on the steel. Since the work is at an early stage, this result can only be viewed as provisional; it may be a function of the test machine and the limited variation in possible specimen geometries. Specimens of narrow width deform plastically at the loads used so that the original geometry and contact stress are lost. Work is continuing to determine the effect of geometry on contact stress and may lead to a requirement for a larger-scale test rig.

Research on rail wear has continued, but a change of direction has taken place. Previous work was aimed at producing semiquantitative relations between laboratory-generated wear data and service experience and attempting to relate wear performance over a wide range of test conditions to a single property parameter. More recent work has been aimed at relating wear to the conditions that exist in the wheel-rail contact zone. A nonlinear curving theory that predicts the forces, creep rates, and contact-zone sizes for a given set of conditions has been developed (13). Current work is aimed at developing an extension to this theory that will lead to wear-rate predictions. Several hypotheses that relate wear rate to traction force T, creep rate γ, and either the contact-zone width 2b or the contact-zone area are under investigation.

A series of laboratory tests performed by using a small-scale Amsler wear-testing machine and a range of creep conditions (1-10 percent) and contact stresses (500-1300 MPa) indicated that two regimes of wear were operating. These regimes were termed mild and severe and were characterized by the debris. Wear rates in the

severe regime were found to be dependent on both contact stress and creep rate, whereas in the mild regime wear rate could be independent of creep rate. Correlations were then attempted between wear rates and expressions such as $(T\gamma^n/2b)$. In the mild-wear regime, where there was no interdependence on creep rate, no correlation was obtained. In the severe-wear regime,

Figure 7. Longitudinal vertical section through a typical squat defect.

Figure 8. Rolling-contact fatigue results for a range of steels.

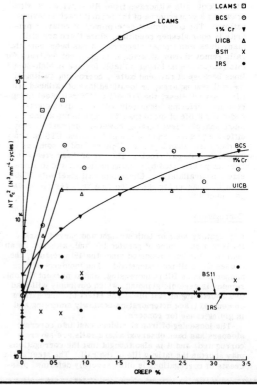

81

Figure 9. Wear rate versus ($T\gamma^{3/2}/2b$).

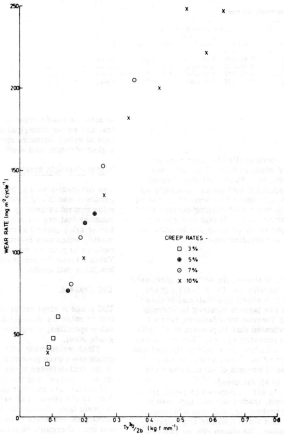

CREEP RATES -

□ 3%
⊕ 5%
○ 7%
X 10%

WEAR RATE (mg m⁻² cycle⁻¹) — vertical axis, values 50, 100, 150, 200, 250

$T\gamma^{3/2}/2b$ (kg f mm⁻¹) — horizontal axis, values 0.1, 0.2, 0.3, 0.4, 0.5, 0.6, 0.7, 0.8

when combined wear rates (the total wear rate of both rollers) were considered, it was found that neither of the two parameters—($T\gamma/2b$) or ($T\gamma^2/2b$)—gave a satisfactory relationship. However, when the value of $n = 1.5$ was substituted, a better relationship was obtained (see Figure 9).

Currently, the effect of contact-zone geometries on wear for given contact stresses is unknown, and therefore the general validity of the wear parameters cannot be established. Further work will investigate this geometry effect and also explore whether the relations apply to other rail steels.

Toughness of Rail Steels

The toughness of steels depends on ambient temperature and rate of load application and, to a large extent, the effects of these two parameters are interchangeable. The lowest toughness can be expected at the highest rate of loading and the lowest ambient temperature. It has been estimated that for BR these are 100 GPa/s and -15°C, although clearly there will be rare occasions when these values will be surpassed. The rate of load application corresponds to the impact of a wheel flat.

Most steels show a transition in toughness from a lower to an upper plateau as the temperature rises.

Most pearlitic rail steels, including the UIC grades and 1 percent chromium steel, are on the lower plateau at normal ambient temperatures and slow rates of loading so that the reductions in toughness caused by higher loading rates and lower temperatures are not very large, although they can be significant. When a new, tougher rail steel is produced, however, it is usually found to be in the transition region so that loading rate and temperature are significant. The fracture-tough rail steel developed jointly by BR and the British Steel Corporation is in this category (12).

The effective toughness of rails is affected by residual stresses and also by the size of the specimen. As a result, to measure toughness it is now the practice to test both small specimens and full-section rails. To generate the necessary high loading rates for full-sized specimens, a drop-weight test facility is used. Before testing, a notch and a fatigue crack are formed 6 mm deep across the head of the rail. The rail is tested in bending with the head in tension to simulate wheel-flat loading on a rail with a head defect. Strain gauges are used to identify the load at which the crack begins to run. The drop-weight test facility has also been used in the laboratory to simulate the dynamic loads caused by a wheel flat.

Table 2. Composition of commercial rail steels.

Grade	Minimum UTS (MPa)	Composition (percentage by weight)					
		Carbon	Silicon	Manganese	Sulfur	Phosphorus	Chromium
Normal-quality BS 11	710	0.45-0.60	0.05-0.35	0.95-1.25	0.050 max	0.050 max	-
UIC grade A	880	0.60-0.75	0.50 max	0.80-1.30	0.050 max	0.050 max	-
UIC grade B	880	0.50-0.70	0.50 max	1.30-1.70	0.050 max	0.050 max	-
One percent chromium	1080	0.68-0.78	0.35 max	1.10-1.40	0.04 max	0.03 max	1.00-1.30

WELDING OF RAILS

Procedures

Considerable effort has been applied to improving the service performance of welds in rails (14). BR uses three basic weld procedures. Flash-butt and Thermit welding are used for producing butt joints, and build-up repair is being increasingly applied because of increases in the number of defects in the rail running surface and the rising cost of replacing rails. In this method, the defects are usually repaired by grinding and building up the surface with metal arc-welding deposit.

Causes of Defects

Until comparatively recent times, the only rail steel used on BR in considerable quantity was the 710-MPa grade. In the two butt-welding processes this material presents few problems; failures are largely confined to Thermit welds. A survey of all Thermit weld failures carried out in 1971 and 1972 indicated that 80 percent of all failures were attributed to operator errors. These failures resulted from (a) lack of fusion, generally in the foot and lower web area (50 percent of all failures); (b) hot tears, usually in the head area (7 percent of all failures); and (c) porosity (6 percent of all failures).

Lack-of-fusion defects are considered to result from poor rail-end preparation, inadequate rail gap, use of oxidizing flame during preheating, and cold additions to the Thermit reaction. Hot tears emanate from premature release of rail tensors, or clamp slip on rail tensors, and porosity results from the use of damp or contaminated molds or luting sand. All of these can be attributed to operator deficiency. As a result of the investigation, a major change in the Thermit process was introduced on BR. From an aluminothermic quick-welding process referred to as the SmW process, which requires 6-7 min of preheating, BR went to a quick-welding process called the SkV process, which requires 1-2 min of preheating, thus reducing the operator dependency involved in preheating [these processes are derived from a German company and marketed by Thermit Welding (GB), Ltd.] The other aspects of operator deficiencies were covered by retraining and adequate supervision of welders in the field. The performance of the SkV weld is currently being evaluated by a further survey of weld failures. Supplies of Thermit consumables are rigidly inspected under a BR specification that ensures a regular supply of consistent consumables.

The failure rate of flash-butt welds is much lower than that of Thermit welds: 0.1/1000 compared to 1.0/1000 for 710-MPa steel. However, investigation of flash-butt-weld failures indicates that 80 percent can be attributed to welding machine and post-weld-treatment deficiencies (40 percent of failures result from incomplete fusion and 40 percent from postweld treatments such as weld trimming and arc spots). Some of the faults can be remedied by good housekeeping; incomplete-fusion defects, however, arise because of machine malfunction or incorrect machine settings that are either electrical or mechanical in action. This type of defect becomes more evident in the welding of higher-strength rail steel.

Higher-Strength Steels

The non-heat-treated, higher-strength rail steels—UIC grades A and B and 1 percent chromium—rely on higher alloy content to develop the higher strength and wear resistance that are their desirable features. However, the higher alloy content also reduces the weldability of these steels, which may require special processes and procedures to produce satisfactory butt and repair welds. Table 2 gives the composition ranges of commercially available rail steels.

UIC Grade A

UIC grade A steel relies on an increase in carbon content to raise its strength level to the 880-MPa minimum value specified, compared with the 710 MPa for normal-grade steel.

Flash welds made with the settings used for normal-grade steel gave good results. Metallographic sections of the heat-affected zones (HAZs) were fully pearlitic in microstructure, and the mechanical properties were satisfactory. Some flat spots—i.e., small oxidized areas that are the remains of arc craters—have been found on the weld line. These can initiate fatigue cracking and subsequent complete transverse fracture of the welds and must therefore be minimized by optimization of the machine controls.

Thermit welds were also found to be satisfactory with fully pearlitic HAZ microstructure and good mechanical properties. Samples put in track showed some "cupping" (local wear) in the weld zone, but this was attributable to the use of a Z80 Thermit portion—i.e., one with 795-MPa tensile strength—whereas a Z90 (880-MPa) strength would now be recommended as matching the rail steel properties.

UIC Grade B

UIC grade B steel derives its extra strength from a 0.1 percent increase in carbon content and an increase of 0.45 percent in manganese content compared with the normal-grade steel. The manganese has a considerable effect on the transformation time, which has to be allowed for during welding. Segregation of manganese aggravates this problem and can lead to the formation of small bands of hard microstructures in HAZs.

In flash welding this steel, difficulties were encountered in optimizing the flash-welder control settings to (a) reduce the flat spots on the weld center line and (b) obtain consistent mechanical properties in commercial production. Flash welding in FB 113A section rail with the optimized machine settings gave cooling rates that were generally slow enough to avoid the formation of hard microstructural phases, although isolated cases of these phases were observed. To minimize the occurrence of flat spots and to maintain good mechanical properties, it was necessary to set machine controls to give (a) an adequate power to flash off the rail, (b) a low enough voltage to avoid deep craters, (c) a high acceleration to avoid oxidation, and (d) a correct flashing distance.

It was also found to be necessary to carry out the investigation on full 18-m-length rails since a considerable variation in results was obtained when welds were made with "shorts", apparently because of power losses through earth leakage. It was concluded that with adequate care and supervision satisfactory welds could be produced in this grade of steel with the current flash-welding machines but that future machines should incorporate feedback control systems.

For the Thermit welding of UIC grade B steel, it was necessary to ensure that a good sound weld with a matched weld metal and nonhardened HAZ was produced. The soundness of welds was attained by use of the SkV short-preheat Thermit process (15), and a Z90 (880-MPa tensile strength) portion was used to give a weld metal that matched the rail in tensile strength and wear resistance. Cooling rates of welds made in FB 113A section rail by using this process were measured at about 20°C/min between 800°C and 400°C. Considered in relation to the continuous cooling transformation diagram for this steel, this would appear to give adequate protection against undesirable hard phases in weld HAZs. However, since these cooling rates were determined under ideal laboratory conditions whereas in-service ambient rail temperatures could be much lower, the effect of muffle cooling was determined. An insulated muffle placed over the welded joint after weld trimming (completed 6 min after weld tapping) reduced the cooling rate from 20°C/min to about 10°C/min in the 800°C-400°C range. Welds produced by using this process and proportion and muffle cooling were free from defects and had good mechanical properties. Further work must be done on the effect of adverse weather conditions and the use of muffle cooling.

One Percent Chromium Steel

The high tensile strength (1080 MPa) of 1 percent chromium steel is generated by the use of as much as 0.78 percent carbon and the addition of as much as 1.4 percent chromium; the alloy additions again had to be allowed for in welding such a steel.

Flash welding was carried out, and machine control settings similar to those used for UIC grade B steel were found to produce welds of good quality. However, the normal cooling rate for flash welds (46°C/min in FB 113A section) produce hardened microstructures in the weld HAZ. Several procedures for retarding the cooling rate were investigated. Direct postheating in the welding machine reduced the cooling rate; about 4 min of postheating was required to produce a satisfactory cooling rate. Muffle cooling was found to be inadequate, but a special flame heating rig in which the joint was heated for 5 min retarded the cooling rate to about 28°C/min. This last treatment gave fully pearlitic microstructures in the HAZs and gave the best and most satisfactory mechanical properties. This procedure reduces delay time in production by not occupying the welder as in direct postheating.

For the Thermit welding of this steel, the SkV short-preheat process is used, and a special high-strength portion has been developed by Thermit Welding (GB), Ltd., to produce matched weld properties. Metallographic examination and mechanical testing indicated that fully pearlitic HAZ microstructures were obtained. However, as with the UIC grade B steel, the recom-

mended practice in service is to use muffle cooling to counter possible effects from adverse weather conditions.

Repair Welding of Rails

Normal-quality rails that have isolated defects in the railhead are often repaired on BR by using the metal arc process, and codes of practice have been issued for the repair of defects such as isolated wheel burns and squats. Work is continuing to extend the procedures to cover the higher-strength rail steels and is aimed at determining preheat levels, the suitability of consumables, preparation geometry, welding techniques, and finishing methods.

Work is also being carried out to explore the use of semiautomatic processes for rail repair, and an evaluation of welding machines and consumables is currently under way. A longer-term objective in this area is the development of fully automatic machines for the repair of railhead defects.

NEW DEVELOPMENTS IN RAIL STEELS

The higher-strength pearlitic steels discussed previously are likely to be sufficiently resistant to wear and fatigue to satisfy BR needs for plain line rails in the foreseeable future. However, the loading environment is more severe in switch and crossing work, and further improvements in rail steels are needed.

BR currently uses a range of crossing types. For the severest locations, cast austenitic manganese steel (AMS) crossings are used. For the less severe locations, the crossing types listed below are used:

1. Bolted AMS crossings (machined from FB 113A section AMS rails),
2. Bolted BS 11 normal-grade crossings (machined from FB 113A section rail), and
3. Semiwelded BS 11 normal-grade crossings (the vees are produced by electroslag welding FB 113A section rail, and wings are attached by bolting).

These various types of crossings generally perform adequately in service but have deficiencies of various kinds that could be overcome or minimized by material or fabrication changes. Cast AMS crossings are difficult to produce without casting defects, which lead to structural failure, and the alloy in current use is virtually unweldable. Furthermore, rolled AMS crossings are prone to fatigue cracking that results from the damage produced when the bolt holes are drilled. BS 11 normal-grade crossings deform quickly in heavy-traffic locations because of inadequacies in material strength. There is a need, therefore, for crossing materials that can be produced without defects and are weldable and of adequate strength. Two material developments have led to new fabrication procedures and modifications to existing fabrication procedures.

The problems of casting defects and poor weldability with AMS arise from the high coefficient of expansion and the thermal instability of the conventional Hadfield alloy. The coefficient of expansion of the alloy is much higher than that for the pearlitic rail steels; this, coupled with the narrow range of freezing and the long, narrow castings needed for crossings, results in gross shrinkage cavities and hot tears in the finished product.

The original Hadfield alloy has a carbon range of 1.1-1.4 percent and is used in the water-quenched condition. Subsequent heating above 300°C in welding processes results in carbide precipitation and severe embrittlement of the otherwise high-toughness alloy.

The testing of an experimental series of alloys of varying carbon and manganese levels (16) has shown that

Figure 10. Charpy impact curves for bainitic steels.

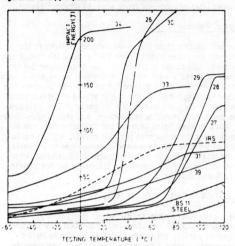

they are thermally stable—i.e., there is very little carbide precipitation and resultant embrittlement, providing the carbon level is below 0.9 percent. The decrease in tensile strength properties that results from this reduced carbon content can be offset by increasing the level of manganese. The work has indicated that good mechanical properties and thermal stability can be achieved within the composition ranges 0.7-0.8 percent carbon and 14-17 percent manganese. This composition is now referred to as low-carbon austenitic manganese steel (LCAMS). Commercial quantities of rails have been produced in this alloy, and flash and Thermit welding procedures and consumables have been developed for butt welding of rails in CWR. The high coefficient of expansion of this alloy still limits the use of long, welded rails to locations that have small variations in rail temperature, such as tunnels. However, in the manufacture of crossings, the improved weldability of the alloy lends itself to the production of (a) semiwelded crossing vees and (b) shorter-cast crossing centers with welded-on legs. The development work on semiwelded vees, which is being pursued jointly with Thomas Ward (Railway Engineers), Ltd., is nearing completion, and crossings that incorporate such vees will shortly be installed in track for service evaluation. The production of short-cast crossing centers will relieve the casting defect problem considerably, and welding techniques for the attachment of legs have been developed. Trial track installations will be made for service evaluation.

The remaining problem in the use of LCAMS is the need to weld it to pearlitic rail steels. The alloy contents of the two steels result in the formation of very brittle phases when fusion welding is attempted. Practical solutions are still being sought.

The limitations of LCAMS prompted a search for alternative materials with the desirable properties of LCAMS, such as high strength, impact resistance, and fracture toughness, but without the undesirable properties (the material would have an acceptable coefficient of expansion and could be welded to pearlitic rail steels). The work of Irvine and Pickering (17, p. 292) indicated that such properties could be obtained in the as-rolled condition by an air-cooled, low-carbon bainitic steel. These structures are achieved by the suppression of the ferrite-pearlite transformation, which is best achieved by additions of molybdenum and boron.

Although some data were available on the mechanical properties of some low-carbon molybdenum-boron steels, no systematic study of the effect of carbon, manganese, and chromium on mechanical properties had been carried out. These alloy additions depress the bainitic transformation temperature and thereby improve the tensile properties. An experimental molybdenum-boron alloy series with suitably varying levels of carbon, manganese, and chromium has been produced and tested (18). Tensile strengths as high as 1525 MPa have been achieved, and the fatigue limits were all higher than those of normal-grade steel. The Charpy impact curves were generally much higher than those for normal-grade steels and, in some cases, higher than those previously developed for fracture-tough rail steel (see Figure 10). Work is currently proceeding to evaluate the extent to which these properties can be maintained in commercial production.

CONCLUSIONS

Although the main trend of rail research must be toward improved steels and a better choice of steels and operating practices, it is clear that many problems are still inadequately understood and as such difficult to quantify. It is clear that in the future greater priority must be given to understanding the wear and fatigue mechanisms that act at the surface of rails and how these mechanisms interact. Until this is done, the practicality of defining an optimum steel for a particular set of circumstances must be questionable.

ACKNOWLEDGMENT

We wish to acknowledge the British Railways Board for permission to present and publish this paper and to acknowledge the many contributions made by our colleagues in the Metallurgy, Track, and Structures Section and Strength of Materials Section of the Research and Development Division. We would also like to acknowledge the contribution to the research program that is being made by several companies involved in track component manufacture and maintenance, namely, the British Steel Corporation, Thermit Welding (GB), Ltd., Thomas W. Ward (Railway Engineers), Ltd., Edgar Allen Engineering, Ltd., and Speno International SA.

REFERENCES

1. D. L. Bartlett. Experiments on the Stability of Long Welded Rails. British Transport Commission, London, 1961.
2. C. O. Frederick. The Lateral Strength of CWR. Proc., Symposium on Railroad Track Mechanics and Technology, Princeton Univ., Princeton, NJ, April 1975.
3. G. Samavedam. Buckling and Post-Buckling Analysis of CWR in the Lateral Plane. British Railways Board, Wilmorton, Derby, England, R&D Tech. Note TS 34, Jan. 1979.
4. G. Samavedam and G. Hunt. A Three-Dimensional Analysis of Elastic Stresses in Rails. British Railways Board, Wilmorton, Derby, England, R&D Tech. Note (in preparation).
5. E. I. Danilenko and E. Moras. Measurement of Horizontal Forces on Rails. Die Eisenbahntechnik, Vol. 27, No. 6, 1979, pp. 228-231; British Railways Board, Wilmorton, Derby, England, Translation 79/07/13, 1979.
6. C. O. Frederick. Effect of Wheel and Rail Irregularities on Track. Heavy-Haul Railways Confer-

ence, Perth, Australia, Sept. 1978.
7. S. G. Newton and R. A. Clark. An Investigation into the Dynamic Effects on the Track of Wheel Flats on Railway Vehicles. Journal of Mechanical Engineering Science, Vol. 21, No. 4, Aug. 1979, pp. 287-297.
8. Behaviour of the Metal of Rails and Wheels in the Contact Zone: Composition of the Different Stress Conditions in the Wheel/Rail Contact Zone. Office de Recherches et d'Essais, Utrecht, Netherlands, C53, Rept. 7, April 1972.
9. H. O. Asbeck and M. Heyder. Residual and Straightening Stress in New Rolled Rails. Eisenbahntechnische Rundschau, Vol. 25, No. 4, 1977, pp. 217-222; British Railways Board, Wilmorton, Derby, England, Translation D/77/11/15, 1977.
10. P. Clayton. Rail-Grinding Experiments at Rugby. R&D Division, British Railways Board, Wilmorton, Derby, England, Tech. Rept. Met 5, Dec. 1978.
11. P. Clayton. Vertical Wear of Rails. R&D Division, British Railways Board, Wilmorton, Derby, England, Tech. Note FM 55, Jan. 1976.
12. K. Morton and others. Rail Steels. ASTM, Philadelphia, Special Tech. Publ. 644, Nov. 1976.
13. J. A. Elkins and R. J. Gostling. General Quasi-Static Curving Theory for Railway Vehicles. International Union of Theoretical and Applied Mechanics Symposium, Vienna, Austria, Sept. 1977.

14. M. E. Ashton. Thermit Welding of Rail Steels. Railway Engineer, Vol. 2, No. 3, May-June 1977.
15. J. T. Dyke and M. E. Ashton. Evaluation of the SkV.F Thermit Welding Process for the Welding of U.I.C. Wear-Resistant Rail Grade B. R&D Division, British Railways Board, Wilmorton, Derby, England, Tech. Memorandum Met 31, May 1978.
16. A. Faley and D. S. Hoddinott. The Development of a Weldable High-Manganese Steel. R&D Division, British Railways Board, Wilmorton, Derby, England, Tech. Note FM 67, Aug. 1975.
17. K. J. Irvine and F. B. Pickering. Low-Carbon Bainitic Steels. Journal of Iron and Steel Institute, Vol. 187, 1952.
18. G. M. Pell. The Initial Development of a Bainitic Steel for Crossings. R&D Division, British Railways Board, Wilmorton, Derby, England, Tech. Note Met 13, Dec. 1977.

Publication of this paper sponsored by Committee on Track Structure System Design.

Note: The Transportation Research Board does not endorse products or manufacturers. Trade and manufacturers' names appear in this paper because they are considered essential to its object.

TEXT 8

Session 312
Paper I.9

A RESEARCH TRIP FOR THE STUDY OF AXLE LOAD

LUIZ DE LUCCA SILVA

MARCELO LEBRE NOBREGA

1 INTRODUCTION

The economical transportation of iron ore depends in large measure on the characteristics and performance of the railroad joining the mine and the port. Naturally, the longer the railroad is, the greater its influence will be on the overall profit position of the project. In the design stage, almost all variables are control variables (in the sence that they can be controlled by the designer). Thus, a reasonable objective would be to find a combination of physical and operational variables that will contribute most to a favourable outcome. Decisions made during the initial design and construction stages can have a significant bearing on longer term operating costs.

Being aware of the problems faced by iron ore railways, the parties responsible for the Carajás Project railroad design concentrated on rail life as a fundamental task.

The subject was focussed following three stages:

(a) Theoretical studies.
    The available literature was duly analysed.

(b) Field observations.
    A group was formed with the objective of gathering field elements and develop their interpretation.
    The components of this group were:
    - L. de Lucca Silva - from AMZA
    - W.R. Fahey - from CANAC (Consultants)
    - C.A. Fraser - from CANAC (Consultants)

(c) Conclusions and recommendations.
    Based on the two items above, the authors developed the technical and economic considerations and came to some conclusions and recommendations, as will follow.

2 BASIC CONSIDERATIONS

The magnitude of the axle load is paramount in an iron ore railway. It effects investment, maintenance and operation.

Rail life is important not only because of the cost of the rails itself, but also because of traffic interruptions for replacement.

The problem becomes quite serious when it turns out to be epidemic.

It is normal to expect that additional capital expenditures for achieving higher initial track standards will result in reduced operating costs and higher reliability of the system. Nevertheless budget constraints may lead to solutions that will entail an operating cost higher than the minimum possible.

There are times when financial possibilities and economic considerations, if taken separately, do not lead to the same scheme. However, fast degradation of relevant elements should not be accepted.

An enterprise must be financially possible, but it also must be safe, reliable and economically feasible.

3 INVESTIGATIONS

After the analysis of the teoretical and practical data available, the conclusion was reached that more detailed data should be collected. Gathering field elements was mandatory to enable designers to specify axle load, wheel diameter, rail weight, fastening, etc.

Thus, a group of AMZA and consulting engineers visited Africa, Australia, South America and Canada for a more accurate assessment of the matter.

The following iron ore railroads were visited:

CVRD	MIFERMA
LAMCO	HAMERSLEY
MOUNT NEWMAN	ORINOCO
QUEBEC CARTIER MINING	
QUEBEC NORTH SHORE AND LABRADOR	

The first two had 25 ton axle loads and the others approximately 30 tons. It should be emphasized that, the nominal axle load is frequently surpassed.

It was off-hand confirmed that rail life is indeed a function of axle load. Within the load range investigated it is apparent that, insofar as can be judged from the one case of CVRD, rail life is considerably higher under an axle load of 25 tons than it is under a nominal 30 tons. This difference exceeds 50 million gross tons over the relevant range of curvature (Fig. 1), though the statistics available from CVRD at the time were related to 115 RE rail as opposed to 132 RE.

4 GENERAL OBSERVATIONS

Operating experience of railways using heavy axle loads has indicated that annual costs of track maintenance have been sufficient to warrant a re-examination of the assumption that economics favoured specification of the largest capacity equipment available.

For a given train speed and static loading, wheel-rail contact forces are a function of dynamic loading, which is related to the construction and the

87

Session 312
Paper I.9

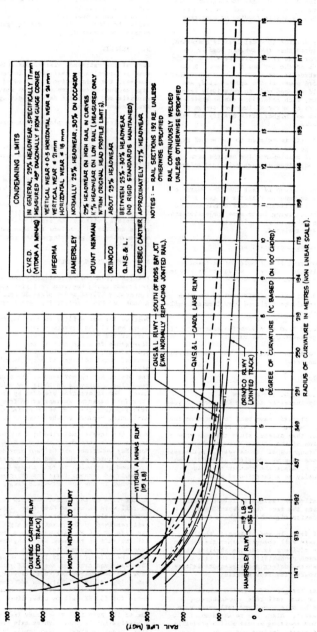

FIGURE 1

maintenance standards. Dynamic loading can therefore be reduced by improving track standards as well as by reducing static loading or operating speed.

Insofar as a reduction in wheel load is concerned, it should be noted that the dynamic load is the governing factor, and it is quite sensitive to the characteristics of the car and the track. Hence, though shear stresses are shown to be proportional to the one-third power of the applied load, and therefore would respond only to relatively large load reductions, such reductions can be achieved in dynamic loads by means of improved design of cars and trucks and higher track quality and maintenance standards.

In short, rail life is related to the actual axle load, the tonnage and the quality of design, construction and maintenance (we use the term actual axle load, since nominal axle load seldom occurs).

It is a generally accepted fact that the degree of maintenance is an important factor on raol life. Of course, it is difficult to make comparisons on that area without giving in to some subjectiveness. That should be taken into consideration, when railway data are analyzed.

Other points to be considered are:

- Statistics on rail life should not be taken as entirely reliable. There is no way to determine the accuracy of the weights shown.

- The criteria for the determination of the time when rails should be replaced vary from one railroad to another.

These facts could lead to a doubtful conclusion if statistics were taken at face value.

Iron ore railroads generally have the same operatio operation parameters:

- Heavy axle load
- Large trains
- Speeds not too high, nor too low
- Progressively increased tonnage from year to year

Some of these railroads have been in operation for a fairly long time and their rail life statistics are more useful than others, since they can show a real integration of the effects brought about by the traffic throughout all those years. A theoretical model based on a steady rithm of traffic would not be realistic, since the tonnage tends to increase gradually as a function of market conditions.

In iron ore railroads fatigue is indeed a main concern, despite the fact that, depending on curvature, abrasion might be a problem too.

As a matter of fact, in and of itself, shelling does not motivate rail change; rather the concern of maintenance officers is not the shelling itself but the increased probability that the rail will suffer a transverse defect and subsequent failure arising and progressing from shelling.

It appears that fatigue and abrasion combine with each other to reduce rail life. Undoubtedly, abrasion tends to make wheel and rail match each other more closely. Also, due to abrasion, the point of maximum shearing stress shifts gradually downward. Therefore, fatigue may be delayed by

abrasion. Nevertheless, it seems that, since some surface material has been lost from fatigue, abrasio abrasion takes over fiercely the task of eating the rail. In other words, surface fatigue would accelerate abrasion.

5. RESULTS

Each of the railroads visited was able to supply some information on rail life. In certain cases, however, the information consisted of average figures summarized from their own statistical analysis and not basic data reflecting actual rail replacement figures.

The results have been plotted comparatively and are shown on Fig. 1.

The vertical and horizontal axes show rail life in millions of gross metric tons and degree of curvature, respectively.

It is clear in the minds of the group members that the figures on which the curves are based require considerable qualification for proper interpretation. It goes almost without saying, therefore, that such interpretation would have been difficult, if not impossible, without the actual visit to the railroads and the discussions and observations that accompanied the gathering of the statistical information.

6 COMMENTS ON RESULTS

Results appear to be reasonably consistent, with the railroads using the same rail size and axle load (generally 132 RE and nominal 30 tons respectively) grouped within a relatively narrow range.

Most of the variability in the results occurs on the lower end of the curvature sacle, with Quebec Cartier and Mount Newman showing the greatest divergence from the central tendency. It should be pointed out, however, that these two railroads had handled total tonnages of only 134 million and 91 million net tons respectively up to the occasion of the visit, having not reached the total tonnages requiring changeouts in these low values of curvature. The information provided by the companies is therefore based on extrapolation from present rail wear figures; they can be so optimistic as to be misleading because of the possible intervention of fatigue effects and the shortening of rail life below the levels indicated by the projections. It is therefore considered that Q.N.S. & L. (South of Ross Bay Junction) and Orinoco provide a more reliable guide at this end of the scale since both provided statistics on rail change based on an accumulated tonnage large enough to require rail changeout in the low curvature range.

At the time of the visit, both 119 lb. and 136 lb. RE rail were in use at Hamersley, though the transition was almost complete and very little 119 lb. rail remained in the track. As might be expected, the life of 136 RE rail was longer than that of 119 lb. rail in the same operating environment. Hamersley had accumulated enough tonnage to document well the life of the 119 lb. rail in particular. This was less true for the 136 RE rail; yet, at the level of 36 million net tons per year, experience was being gained quickly. In addition, the results for the heavier rail appear to be consistent with those for 132 RE rail on other lines.

One of the principal hypotheses leading to this investigation is that lighter axle loads result in less intensive shear stress levels in the rail head,

Session 312
Paper 1.9

thus lessening wheel-rail contact damage and pro-
longing the fatigue life of the rail. This
hypothesis appears to be well supported by the
position of the C.V.R.D. - Victória-a-Minas curve
in relation to the group already mentioned. Significantly, C.V.R.D. is using a 25 ton axle load while
while the members of the other group are using a
nominal 30 ton value.

It is felt that not too much importance need be
attached to the fact that certain other curves cro
cross C.V.R.D. at the low end of the scale, for the
reasons already mentioned, i.e., lack of accumulated tonnage sufficient to provide a sound statistical data base for replacement of rail in curves of
less than 3° (or equivalent radius of approximately
600 meters).

As already mentioned, over the relevant range of
curvature, it would appear that C.V.R.D. is
achieving a rail life over 50 million tons longer
than the main group, despite the fact that lighter
rail - 57 kg vs. 65,5 kg - was in use. Insofar as
judgments can be made from this one example,
experience seems to be in agreement with theoretical analysis, at least qualitatively.

7   QUALIFICATION AND INTERPRETATION OF RESULTS

The rail life obtained from each railroad are not
necessarily directly comparable because of the many
influencing factors which can be peculiar to each.
Before assessing the principal determinants of rail
life, however, it is appropriate to comment on the
quality of the statistics themselves. In particular, it is important to note that they refer to
rail life in terms of wear, rather than a purely
statistical life resulting from replacement due to
all causes, i.e., including mill defects, service
defects, damage due to derailment, etc. In
general, however, the number of replacements of
isolated rails, or restricted lenghts of rail, due
to defects will be small and, in the long run, may
amount to something less than 5% of the rails
replaced due to wear.

One of the main purposes of the visits was to
identify conditions or practices at each railroad
which could have a bearing on rail life. To the
group members, the following appeared to be significant influences:

(a) Loading Practices

Facilities and methods used for loading are
generally volumetric and range from a precise
degree of control with sophisticated metering equipment to the simple practice of dumping from large
trucks directly onto cars, with no measurement or
control. Even where facilities exist, weighing did
not appear to be done as a normal routine practice,
though track people seem to be convinced that many
cars exceed the nominal maximum load. Indeed, in
one instance where records of car weights had been
kept, it was apparent that there was great
inconsistency in gross weights.

Apart from the question of total load, it appeared
to the observers that the distribution of load in
the car could be of significant influence in the
dynamics of wheel on rail. Considerable variation
was also noted in this respect among the various
companies and is a direct outcome of the general
precision of the loading process, which receives
more emphasis from some companies than it does from
others. In some instances the distribution of
material in the cars appeared to be very uneven,
both longitudinally and laterally, so that, apart

from an unknown total, there would have been
considerable differences in the proportions between
the trucks and even among the wheels of one truck.

In summary, some railroads seemed to be carrying
loads about which they had little day-to-day knowledge. Concern was often expressed about a probable
relationship between load magnitude and distribution
on the one hand, and accelerated rail deterioration
on the other.

(b) Wheel Wear

Wheels wear rails, and vice versa. In the crucial
matter of wheel-rail contact, the shape of both
wheel and rail obviously exert considerable
influence on the ultimate life of both elements.
Upon prolonged contact in service, each tends to
wear to a characteristic shape, and the longer the
exposure, the more pronounced this configuration
becomes. In general, it is logical to assume that
there will be some mutual accommodation of the
shapes, so that contact pressures are minimized.
The extent of wheel wear, with respect to both final
diameter and shape assumed, is therefore an importan
important determinant of rail life.

Though standards are nominally quite similar among
the railroads, there are variations due to the fact
that wheels are examined visually in the normal
course of routine train inspection at terminals.
Consequently, the point at which wheels are called
in for machining, or even gauged, depends on the
competence and judgment of individual inspectors.

(c) Track and Maintenance Standards

The following factors, which differ from one railroad to another, may have a considerable influence:

- Size and type of rail
- Condition of rail with respect to straightness,
  surface smoothness and freedom from corrugations,
  engine burns, crushed areas, etc.
- Discontinuities, such as joints, hard or soft
  welds, etc.
- Type and size of tie plate and rail fastening
- Size, type and spacing of ties.
- Type and depth of ballast and subgrade (including
  elasticity).

It is recognized by railroad maintenance people
everywhere that line and level are difficult to
maintain even in general cargo systems. It is
evident to officers with experience in these systems
who turned to the maintenance of iron ore tracks
that the difficulties are increased considerably not
just by the high tonnages, but by the heavy axle
loads. Both of these factors tend to cause very
rapid deterioration of any weaknesses in the track.
Consequently, maintenance forces must be alert to
the need to remedy any deficiency so identified,
since the heavy wheels may quickly accelerate
weaknesses to the point where they become dangerous.

Superelevation in curves is a good example of the
damage to rail which can occur when track conditions
are not matched to traffic requirements. In a
number of cases rapid rail wear in curves had been
traced to a superelevation found to be unsuited to
train speeds, either because the latter had been
changed from original design values or because the
superelevation itself changed over time. It is
interesting to note that a number of railroads
identified inappropriate superelevation as an
important factor. While design values may have been
based on some criterion such as the expected average
speed of loaded and empty trains, the conclusion is

4

Session 312
Paper I.9

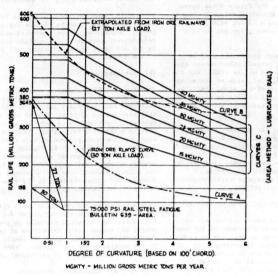

FIGURE 2

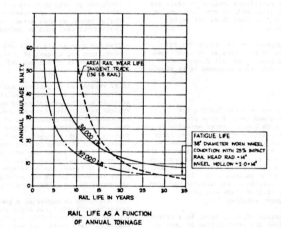

RAIL LIFE AS A FUNCTION
OF ANNUAL TONNAGE

FIGURE 3

now common that the superelevation in a particular curve should match the actual speed of the loaded train on that curve.

(d) The Decision to Change Rail

Despite the nominal wear limits which most railroads ostensibly follow, it is obvious that the decision to change is not based on so simple a criterion and is indeed much more subjective - and more complex - than that. For one thing, wear, as determined by measurement, is very often accompanied by a considerable amount of damage to the rail head in the form of checking, spalling, head flow, shelling, etc., all evidencing excessive contact pressures and fatigue effects. Corrugation is another aspect which certainly cannot be ignored. Obviously, all these factors must play some role in the judgment of the decision maker. In many cases, the wear limits may be nothing more than a guide and, in the presence of heavy rail head degradation, may become inoperative.

In addition, the decision to change the rail is subject to many factors of a more pragmatic nature, such as short term constraints. In any given year, decisions on rail change may be influenced by such factors as:

- budget constraints, arising from the decreed necessity to effect operating economies in the face of unfavourable market or performance outlook. The effect might well be to reduce rail purchases and defer replacement;

- material availability, which, of course is a function of market demand and supply. Although funds are available for purchase, it may happen that demand is extremely heavy and the mills are forced to allocate supply on some basis;

- resource limitations, such as a shortage of available labour or the inability to purchase or mobilize sufficient machinery to carry out an extensive rail program;

- market factors which, in the case of a particularly favourable outlook, may lead to the desire of maximizing tonnage in the short term, with the result that traffic interruptions are unacceptable and must be deferred to the greatest extent possible.

8   TECHNICAL CONSIDERATIONS

Figure 2 shows a comparison of the rail life curves established on general cargo systems (AREA formula) with that based on the information provided by the iron ore railways (the latter being represented by the average relevant curve obtained from Figure 1. The curves from AREA formula were plotted for some specific annual haulages.

Although the magnitude of axle load in use is not specifically recognized in the AREA wear formula, the marked difference in rail life on iron ore railways indicates that indeed this is a very significant variable. It is readily apparent that the AREA formula is not suitable for predicting rail life as experienced by iron ore railroads.

On the other hand, surface fatigue is not an immediate cause for replacement. It may turn out to be a further cause when it propagates to a dangerous defect or, indirectly, because of the resulting acceleration of abrasion.

These seem to be the reasons why the actual rail

lives from Figure 1 appear to be longer than the fatigue life of the rail steel under the stresses obtained from Thomas and Hoersch formula (see Bulletin 639 AREA) and shorter than the wear life obtained from the AREA formula. That may be gathered from Figure 2.

Certainly, fatigue depends on axle load and tonnage. Yet it appears that heavy axle load is a "conditio sine qua non" for the phenomenon. Severe shelling was observed on railroads using nominal 30 ton axle loads, and was not observed on the two railroads using 25 tons.

From the analysis of Figure 3 (Figure 6 of Mr. Read's paper published on the Bulletin 639 AREA), it can be seen that rail steel fatigue life in years varies with annual haulage along equilateral hyperboles. For each axle load there is a different curve. For each axle load the fatigue life in millions of tons is constant. Thus, rail steel fatigue life in millions of tons is independent from annual haulage, unlike what would happen if the AREA wear formula were valid in this case.

Yet rail steel fatigue life in years depends on annual haulage and fatigue life in millions of tons. The latter depends on the axle load, and is constant for the same axle load.

Thus, rail steel fatigue life in millions of tons is constant if the axle load, the wheel diameter, the wheel profile and the rail profile are kept constant.

As already mentioned, according to the AREA formula, rail wear life in millions of tons depends on the annual haulage and not on axle load.

At any rate, field observations are consistent with Mr. Read's paper (Bulletin 639 AREA) as regards the influence on rail life when the wheel load varies from 30,000 lbs to 32,000 lbs. Despite the difference between actual rail life and rail steel fatigue life, and despite the fact that fatigue is not normally a cause for immediate replacement, fatigue is indeed the primary condition for fast degradation.

It seems, therefore, that 30,000 lbs is a wheel load limit not to be surpassed on a 38" wheel and a 136 lb carbon steel rail.

From 30,000 lbs to 32,000 lbs, the maximum shearing stress varies very rapidly. Thus, rail steel fatigue life is significantly reduced, and so is the actual rail life.

8.1 Technical Conclusions.

Almost every iron ore railroad visited specifies a 30 ton axle load or thereabouts, with the exception of C.V.R.D., where a 25 ton axle load is adopted in practice.

Miferma also uses a 25 ton axle load, yet its operating conditions are quite particular, because of intense abrasion of rails and wheels (due to the Sahara sands) and of heavy metal flow and corrugation (due to the exceptional rigidity of the track - the sand is blown into the ballast and the mixture of differently graded granular elements is strongly compacted by the vibration of the trains as they pass, thus making the track extremely rigid).

Despite the information gap between 25 and 30 ton

axle loads, it appears, when field data are combined with theoretical studies, that a 27 ton axle load is the best solution for a new project such as Carajás Project. The critical point would not be surpassed and the number of wagons needed for the programmed annual haulage would be kept within a reasonable range.

It is worthwhile seeing how the maximum shearing stress varies for each nominal wheel diameter and axle load. For a 14" rail head radius and an impact of 25%, the following values of the maximum shearing stress in p.s.i. are obtained (worn wheel condition):

TABLE 1

Axle Load	Wheel Diameter (nominal)		
(metric tons)	33"	36"	38"
25	50 868	49 086	48 015
27	52 187	50 358	49 260
30	54 055	52 161	51 024

The combination of 38" wheel and a 27 ton axle load appears indeed to be a good solution, since the maximum shearing stress would be kept immediately below the critical level (50,000 p.s.i.).

Despite the impression that an impact of 25% would be too optimistic an assumption, it is expected that - if the track is adequately designed, if construction is performed according to specifications, and if the highest quality maintenance is guaranteed - a 25% impact could even be considered somewhat conservative.

9   ECONOMIC CONSIDERATIONS

Considering the Carajás Project conditions, the 27 ton axle load and the 30 ton axle load were compared with each other for train sets of 3 locomotives and 160 wagons, both for electric traction and diesel-electric traction. Various annual haulages were analyzed.

For the evaluation of the cash flow for each alternative the rolling stock capital costs, as well as the annual costs related to energy consumption, train crews and rail replacement (including manpower, transport, welding and materials), were considered.

The comparison was based on the "present worth" and "equivalent annual cost" methods. The "Financial Equivalence" of the cash flows was based on the following parameters:

- interest rate (15% p/year)
- horizontal analyses of the project (30 years)
- electric locomotive life (30 years)
- diesel electric locomotive life (15 years)
- wagon life (15 years)
- rolling stock salvage value (10% of capital cost)
- price of scrapped rail (estimated according to the Brazilian market).

An analytic model, developed by J. Elbrond, on the basis of the "queueing theory", was used to estimate the rolling stock needed for each annual haulage.

Deceleration, signal and acceleration delays, train waiting times in meetings, delays due to incidents on track and on trains, delays due to planned closures of section of track for maintenance (kept

constant), departure delays, stay at loading and unloading terminals, priority, rolling stock maintenance and net travel time (at permitted and obtainable speeds without stops) were considered in the model. The next travel time was calculated by T.P.O. (Train Performance Optimizer), a program owned by C.V.R.D.

Figure 2 shows the rail lives under various conditions as a function of curvature.

Curve A is based on the information delivered by the iron ore railways using a 30 ton axle load. This curve was interpolated within the range of the relevant curves shown on Figure 1, and is an avera average of these curves.

Curve B corresponds to the 27 ton axle load and was inferred from curve A. To plot this curve, it was assumed that the rail lives would vary from one axle load to the other as if the only factor were the surface. The method used was based on the concept that surface fatigue is at least the starting point of rail degradation. In other words, it was assumed that, as the axle load increases, only the fatigue life is affected, and rail life is reduced as much as the rail steel fatigue life. Therefore the difference between the 27 ton axle load and the 30 ton axle load rail steel fatigue lives was added to the lives related to curve A in order to obtain the lives based on which curve B was plotted.

Assuming some annual haulages, the average rail lives for Carajas Project were estimated on basis of the curves of Figure 2, for 30 and 27 ton axle loads respectively (see Table II below).

TABLE II

MNMT/Y	MGMT/Y		RAIL LIFE (MGMT)		RAIL LIFE (YEARS)	
	30	27	30	27	30	27
10	14.39	15.00	306.00	324.56	21.27	21.64
20	28.78	30.00	345.00	479.34	11.99	15.98
30	43.16	45.00	345.00	572.35	7.99	12.72
40	57.55	60.00	345.00	572.35	5.99	9.54
50	71.94	75.00	345.00	572.35	4.80	7.63
60	86.33	90.00	345.00	572.35	4.00	6.36

MNMT/Y - Million Net Metric Tons p/year
MGMT/Y - Million Gross Metric Tons p/year

Welding, insulated joints, transport, manpower and material costs were calculated on the basis of rail life and of the price estimated for each item.

Energy consumption figures were obtained from the TPO simulation.

For diesel-electric traction the fuel consumption during meetings were added to the consumption obtained from the TPO, the waiting time being evaluated by the Elbrond model.

For electric-traction the cost of the KWH was estimated for each annual haulage according to consumption and available power.

The manpower cost, related to train crews, was calculated in accordance with the Brazilian laws.

9.1   Economic Conclusions

Exhibits 1 (a and b) and 2 (a and b) show the costs of the relevant items for each alternative of axle

Session 312
Paper 1.9

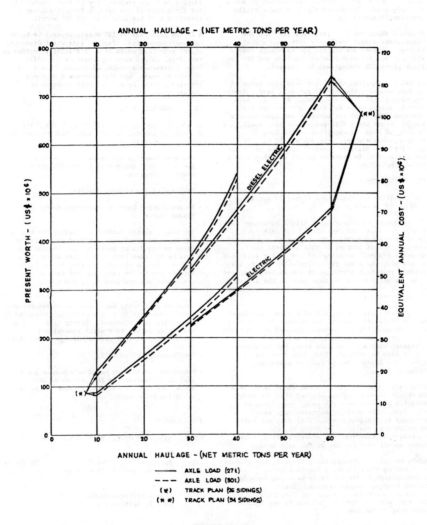

ANNUAL HAULAGE - (NET METRIC TONS PER YEAR)

PRESENT WORTH - (US$ × 10⁶)

EQUIVALENT ANNUAL COST - (US$ × 10⁶).

ANNUAL HAULAGE - (NET METRIC TONS PER YEAR)

————— AXLE LOAD (27t)
- - - - AXLE LOAD (30t)
(*) TRACK PLAN (26 SIDINGS)
(* *) TRACK PLAN (54 SIDINGS)

FIGURE 4

load at each annual haulage, for diesel-electric and electric traction, respectively, and two track plans (26 and 54 sidings, respectively).

Exhibits 1c and 2c show the annual costs and "present worth" for both axle loads, as well as the absolute and relative differences between 30 and 27 ton axle loads, for diesel-electric and electric traction, respectively.

Figure 4 shows how the "present worth" and the "equivalent annual cost" vary with each annual haulage. Curves are plotted for each axle load alternative, for each type of traction and for two track plans (26 sidings and 54 sidings).

It can be seen that the 30 ton axle load seems to be more economic than the 27 ton axle load. Nevertheless, the difference in favour of 30 ton axle load is always below 6.16% for diesel-electric traction, and 8.39% for electric traction respectively. Since these differences are very small, and bearing in mind the magnitude of the Carajás Project, this economic approach should be duly qualified and analyzed together with the technical considerations, in order to permit reaching a well based conclusion.

10   FINAL CONCLUSION

The technical considerations favour 27 ton axle load on 38" wheels.

The economic analysis shows a slight advantage for the 30 ton axle load over the 27 ton axle load. Taken into consideration the degree of accuracy of the assumptions adopted in this analysis the apparent economic advantage of the 30 ton axle load is not only small but quite irrelevant due to the evident technical advantage of the 27 ton axle load - not to mention observations made on the field, where the consequences of using a 30 ton axle load could be verified.

The extrapolation of curve B of Figure 2 was based on the estimated delay of the surface fatigue when a 27 ton axle load is assumed, instead of the basic 30 ton axle load. In fact, not only fatigue is mitigated with a 27 ton axle load, but abrasion should also be reduced. Such reduction was not taken into account due to lack of reasonably reliable data.

When rail steel fatigue life was added to curve A to obtain curve B, it was assumed that the maximum shearing stresses were the same, regardless of curvature. The shearing stresses used were obtained for tangent track. This does not quite correspond to reality. By doing so, the relevancy of rail cost was underestimated, which again unduly favoured the 30 ton axle load.

Again because of insufficiency of data, the effects of reducing track capacity due to traffic interruptions to replace rails were not considered in the economic considerations. These interruptions reduce operational flexibility, and the economic consequences may not be negligible, depending on haulage.

Another relevant point to be considered is price variations, particularly as concerns the rail. The rail price used on the economic considerations was estimated on the basis of information obtained from would-be-suppliers, which were delivered at a time of abnormal steel market conditions. This price may turn out to be too optimistic.

Neither the cost of rail storage nor the capital immobilization on rails were considered in the economic analysis.

Consistent with the foregoing, and bearing in mind that only proved and successful solutions should be adopted in a new project, the parties responsible for the design of the Carajás Project railway specified a 27 ton axle load and 38" wheels.

A 27 ton axle load on 38" wheels appears to be an optimal combination. For the same wheel diameter, higher axle load would lead to drastic reduction in rail life, unless some improvements are added. These improvements would, of course, entail additional costs, and the assessment of their benefits may not be sufficiently accurate to justify them.

11   RECOMMENDATIONS

In addition to the axle load itself, the following general recommendations are suggested for consideration in new projects:

- The best possible standards of track construction, specially with respect to compaction and top width of subgrade.

- Drainage of the highest quality.

- Superelevation based on operating speeds of loaded trains.

- The best possible control of loading, in such a way that the specified axle load is not surpassed. Cargo on board must be even. The loading system must be provided with such scales and devices as will enable the operator to control easily the flow of ore to the cars, so that cars are never overloaded and the load is spread evenly on board.

- Adoption of elastic fastening (it is evident that track components life is considerably enhanced if elasticity is guaranteed. Spring type fittings would also permit easy quick removal and installation of rail without damage to the ties).

- Continuously welded rail.

- Provision for section based maintenance gangs (for quick reaction to indications of deterioration) and for special moving teams (to perform scheduled heavy work).

BIBLIOGRAPHY

CANAC   "Axle Load Study" (W.R. FAHEY)

AREA   Bulletin 639 - "The Rail for High Intensity Mineral Traffic" (R.G. READ)

CVRD   "Train Performance Optimizer" (M.A.F. ALBERNAZ)

ELBROND "Transit and Cycle Times of Trains and Required Number of Trains Sets at Certain Production Levels at the Carajás Railroad" (J. ELBROND)

Session 312
Paper I.9

EXHIBIT 1a – DIESEL ELECTRIC TRACTION

MNMT/Y	MGMT/Y	AXLE LOAD	CAR CAPACITY	INVESTMENT (US$ X 1000)	
				CARS	LOCOS
10*	14.388	30 t	98 t	31.675	20.070
	15.000	27 t	86 t	33.390	21.185
20*	28.776	30 t	98 t	63.490	40.140
	30.000	27 t	86 t	66.745	41.255
30*	43.163	30 t	98 t	95.165	59.095
	45.000	27 t	86 t	100.100	61.325
40*	57.551	30 t	98 t	152.460	93.660
	60.000	27 t	86 t	158.655	97.005
30**	43.163	30 t	98 t	82.705	51.290
	45.000	27 t	96 t	87.220	53.520
40**	57.551	30 t	98 t	114.485	69.130
	60.000	27 t	86 t	120.190	72.475
50**	71.939	30 t	98 t	152.005	91.430
	75.000	27 t	86 t	158.515	94.775
60**	83.327	30 t	98 t	199.290	120.420
	90.000	27 t	86 t	205.100	123.765

    *   Track plan with 26 sidings
    **   Track plan with 54 sidings

EXHIBIT 1b – DIESEL ELECTRIC TRACTION

MNMT/Y	MGMT/Y	AXLE LOAD	CAR CAPACITY	ANNUAL COST (US$ X 1000)							
				FUEL	CREWS	RAILS	TRANSPORT	WELDING IN THE FIELD	WELDING IN THE PLANT	INSULATED JOINT	TRACK EQ. AND M.P.W.
10*	14.388	30 t	98 t	7164.980	617.006	1546.074	68.064	38.700	96.639	5.500	250.236
	15.000	27 t	86 t	7765.568	714.428	1519.634	66.900	38.000	94.981	5.550	245.958
20*	28.776	30 t	98 t	14365.687	1234.012	2742.700	120.744	68.600	171.443	9.900	443.910
	30.000	27 t	86 t	15530.924	1428.856	2057.979	90.600	51.500	128.643	7.350	333.090
30*	43.163	30 t	98 t	21530.667	1851.018	4114.050	181.116	102.800	257.157	14.700	665.868
	45.000	27 t	86 t	23296.491	2110.810	2585.421	113.820	64.600	161.604	9.300	418.458
40*	57.551	30 t	98 t	29453.728	2468.024	5485.400	241.488	137.100	342.871	19.650	887.826
	60.000	27 t	86 t	31806.187	2825.238	3447.047	151.752	86.100	215.472	12.300	557.910
30**	43.163	30 t	98 t	21162.831	1851.018	4114.050	181.116	102.800	257.157	14.700	665.868
	45.000	27 t	86 t	22915.760	2110.810	2585.421	113.820	64.600	161.604	9.300	418.458
40**	57.551	30 t	98 t	28331.617	2468.024	5485.400	241.488	137.100	324.871	19.650	887.826
	60.000	27 t	86 t	30669.912	2825.238	3447.047	151.752	86.100	215.472	12.300	557.910
50**	71.939	30 t	98 t	35669.733	3085.030	6856.477	301.848	171.300	428.571	24.450	1109.735
	75.000	27 t	86 t	38611.787	3539.666	4308.672	189.684	107.700	269.326	15.450	697.365
60**	83.327	30 t	98 t	43295.988	3702.036	8227.827	362.220	205.600	514.285	29.400	1331.694
	90.000	27 t	86 t	46767.599	4221.620	5170.843	227.640	129.200	323.209	18.450	836.910

    *   Track plan with 26 sidings
    **   Track plan with 54 sidings

Session 312
Paper I.9

EXHIBIT 1c - DIESEL ELECTRIC TRACTION

MNMT/Y	MGMT/Y	AXLE LOAD	CAR CAPACITY	PRESENT WORTH (US$ x 1000)			EQUIVALENT ANNUAL COSTS (US$x1000)	EQUIVALENT ANNUAL COST DIFFERENCE (US$x1000)	PRESENT WORTH DIFFERENCE (US$x1000)	PRESENT WORTH DIFF. (%)
				INVESTMENT	ANNUAL COSTS	TOTAL				
10*	14.388	30 t	98 t	57390.107	64262.878	121652.985	18527.774	–	–	–
	15.000	27 t	86 t	60528.845	68621.178	129150.023	19669.574	1141.800	7497.038	6.16
20*	28.776	30 t	98 t	114935.487	125784.466	240719.933	36661.694	–	–	–
	30.000	27 t	86 t	119782.231	128883.233	248665.465	37871.800	1210.106	7945.532	3.30
30*	43.163	30 t	98 t	171088.953	188557.706	359646.659	54774.257	–	–	–
	45.000	27 t	86 t	179035.617	188840.884	367876.501	56027.664	1253.407	8229.842	2.29
40*	57.551	30 t	98 t	272970.395	256310.152	529280.548	80609.532	–	–	–
	60.000	27 t	86 t	283551.159	256742.975	540294.134	82286.904	1677.372	11013.586	2.08
30**	43.163	30 t	98 t	148613.149	186142.502	334755.651	50983.352	–	–	–
	45.000	27 t	86 t	156093.993	186341.012	342435.004	52152.919	1169.567	7679.353	2.30
40**	57.551	30 t	98 t	203646.429	248942.394	452588.824	68929.308	–	–	–
	60.000	27 t	86 t	213683.737	249282.215	462965.953	70509.806	1580.438	10377.129	2.29
50**	71.939	30 t	98 t	269992.476	312850.184	582842.660	88767.053	–	–	–
	75.000	27 t	86 t	280922.605	313457.589	594380.194	90524.221	1575.168	11537.534	1.98
60**	83.327	30 t	98 t	354588.677	378653.808	733242.485	111672.976	–	–	–
	90.000	27 t	86 t	364742.438	378827.288	743569.727	113245.817	1572.841	10327.242	1.41

* Track plan with 26 sidings
** Track plan with 54 sidings

EXHIBIT 2a - ELECTRIC TRACTION

MNMT/Y	MGMT/Y	AXLE LOAD (met.ton)	CAR CAPACITY	INVESTMENT (US$ x 1000)	
				CARS	LOCOS
10*	14.338	30 t	98 t	25.445	20.720
	15.000	27 t	86 t	28.280	23.680
20*	28.776	30 t	98 t	51.030	41.440
	30.000	27 t	86 t	56.525	45.880
30*	43.163	30 t	98 t	76.440	60.680
	45.000	27 t	86 t	84.770	68.080
40*	57.551	30 t	98 t	110.285	87.320
	60.000	27 t	86 t	123.550	97.680
30**	43.163	30 t	98 t	70.070	52.240
	45.000	27 t	86 t	77.070	62.160
40**	57.551	30 t	98 t	94.990	75.480
	60.000	27 t	86 t	104.580	82.880
50**	71.939	30 t	98 t	122.675	96.200
	75.000	27 t	86 t	135.170	105.080
60**	86.327	30 t	98 t	154.280	119.880
	90.000	27 t	86 t	169.785	131.720

* Track plan with 26 sidings
** Track plan with 54 sidings

11

Session 312
Paper 1.9

EXHIBIT 2b - ELECTRIC TRACTION

MNMT/Y	MGMT/Y	AXLE LOAD	CAR CAPACITY	ANNUAL COST (US$ X 1000)							
				POWER	CREWS	RAILS	TRANSPORT	WELDING IN THE FIELD	WELDING IN THE PLANT	INSULATED JOINT	TRACK EQ. AND M.PW.
10*	14.338	30 t	98 t	2313.734	454.636	1546.074	68.064	38.700	96.639	5.500	250.236
	15.000	27 t	86 t	2380.102	519.584	1519.634	66.900	38.000	94.981	5.550	245.958
20*	28.776	30 t	98 t	4639.096	909.272	2742.700	120.744	68.600	171.443	9.900	443.910
	30.000	27 t	86 t	4760.221	1006.694	2057.979	90.600	51.500	128.643	7.350	333.090
30*	43.163	30 t	98 t	6952.830	1331.434	4114.050	181.116	102.800	257.157	14.700	665.868
	45.000	27 t	86 t	7140.323	1526.278	2585.421	113.820	64.600	161.604	9.300	418.458
40*	57.551	30 t	98 t	8721.472	1786.070	5485.400	241.488	137.100	342.871	19.650	887.826
	60.000	27 t	86 t	8960.400	2013.388	3447.047	151.752	86.100	215.472	12.300	557.910
30**	43.163	30 t	98 t	6952.830	1331.434	4114.050	181.116	102.800	257.157	14.700	665.868
	45.000	27 t	86 t	7140.323	1526.278	2585.421	113.820	64.600	161.604	9.300	418.453
40**	57.551	30 t	98 t	8721.472	1786.070	5485.400	241.488	137.100	342.871	19.650	887.826
	60.000	27 t	86 t	8960.400	2013.388	3447.047	151.752	86.100	215.472	12.300	557.910
50**	71.939	30 t	98 t	10217.910	2208.232	6856.477	301.848	171.300	428.571	24.450	1109.736
	75.000	27 t	86 t	10509.720	2532.972	4308.672	189.684	107.700	269.326	15.450	
60**	86.327	30 t	98 t	12259.440	2662.868	8227.827	362.220	205.600	514.285	29.400	1331.694
	90.000	27 t	86 t	12609.825	3020.082	5170.843	227.640	129.200	323.209	18.450	836.910

* Track plan with 26 sidings
** Track plan with 54 sidings

EXHIBIT 2c - ELECTRIC TRACTION

MNMT/Y	MGMT/Y	AXLE LOAD	CAR CAPACITY	PRESENT WORTH (US$ x 1000)			EQUIVALENT ANNUAL COSTS (US$x1000)	EQUIVALENT ANNUAL COST DIFFERENCE (US$x1000)	PRESENT WORTH DIFFERENCE (US$x1000)	PRESENT WORTH DIFF. (%)
				INVESTMENT	ANNUAL COSTS	TOTAL				
10*	14.338	30 t	98 t	48909.622	31343.577	80253.199	12222.578	-	-	-
	15.000	27 t	86 t	55009.435	31980.976	86990.411	13248.657	1026.079	6737.212	8.39
20*	28.776	30 t	98 t	97974.517	59787.611	157762.128	24027.203	-	-	-
	30.000	27 t	86 t	108502.287	55391.110	163893.397	24960.997	933.794	6131.269	3.89
30*	43.163	30 t	98 t	145367.556	89428.347	234795.903	35759.463	-	-	-
	45.000	27 t	86 t	161995.139	78921.788	240916.927	36691.696	932.233	6121.024	2.61
40*	57.551	30 t	98 t	209504.886	115704.886	325209.518	49529.474	-	-	-
	60.000	27 t	86 t	234561.128	101407.412	335968.540	51168.075	1638.601	10759.022	3.31
30**	43.163	30 t	98 t	133869.328	89428.347	223297.676	34008.280	-	-	-
	45.000	27 t	86 t	147544.050	78921.788	226465.839	34490.792	482.512	3168.163	1.42
40**	57.551	30 t	98 t	180718.911	115704.886	296423.796	45145.403	-	-	-
	60.000	27 t	86 t	198743.953	101407.412	300151.365	45713.364	567.709	3727.569	1.26
50**	71.939	30 t	98 t	232112.905	139976.995	372089.893	56669.364	-	-	-
	75.000	27 t	86 t	254837.632	122330.058	377167.690	57442.714	773.350	5077.797	1.36
60**	86.327	30 t	98 t	290810.080	168045.310	458855.390	69883.767	-	-	-
	90.000	27 t	86 t	319828.765	146658.765	466487.477	71046.135	1162.368	7632.087	1.66

* Track plan with 26 sidings
** Track plan with 54 sidings

Deformation Behavior of Rail Steels

D. H. Stone, S. Marich, and C. M. Rimnac

The cyclic deformation behavior of three rail steels was determined under conditions of uniaxial plane-strain compression. Two loading programs were used: (a) one load (simple loading) for the entire test and (b) two loads (split loading) in which the load was increased at set intervals during the test. The results for simple loading showed that the steel softened under cyclic compression; i.e., for a constant stress, compressive cyclic loading caused an increase in strain. Increasing the applied stress increased both the rate and the amount of softening. Rails with higher hardness and yield strength showed an increase in deformation resistance. Split loading produced either increased or decreased resistance to deformation, depending on the type of steel. An equation is presented that can be used to predict the expected amount of plastic flow in rail in service.

The deformation behavior of rail steels has taken on great importance with the increasing severity of service conditions. The average weight of a carload has risen 20 percent in 10 years, and train speeds have also increased (1). Consequently, rails are wearing and failing at higher than expected rates. Research into this problem is being done by several agencies, including Battelle Memorial Institute and the Association of American Railroads (AAR).

Research at Battelle showed that fully reversed cyclic straining caused softening of standard rail steel at low strain levels and hardening at strain levels greater than 0.6. However, when the steel was cycled with a mean tensile or compressive strain, softening occurred over the entire strain range. In addition, the softening rate, or relaxation rate, was the same for both mean strains. The results of the Battelle studies indicated that tests made with fully reversed strain amplitudes may not accurately duplicate the straining of rail in service (2).

Because rails undergo compressive loading, Marich and Curcio (3) proposed that deformation tests on rails should be made in compression, thus eliminating the Bauschinger effect and approximating more closely actual service conditions. Their work on rails tested in monotonic plane strain compression showed that, as the yield strength of the rail increased, the depth of deformation in the railhead decreased, thus decreasing the occurrence of shelling and transverse defects. In addition, the work-hardening behavior of a hot-rolled pearlitic steel was related to dislocation processes occurring in the ferrite lamellae, a decrease in the interlamellar spacing, and dislocation tangles in the cementite.

As an initial part of this study, the deformation pattern and microstructure of rails that had undergone 468 million-662 million gross Mg (515 million-728 million gross tons) of traffic were evaluated to characterize service-induced deformation behavior. The resulting hardness profiles and microstructures serve as standard to ensure that laboratory experiments are reproducing service conditions.

This present investigation is part of the AAR's effort to increase research and development on the improvement of rail performance. The purpose of this project is to study the deformation behavior of several rail steels under cyclic uniaxial plane strain compression.

OBSERVED BEHAVIOR IN RAILS REMOVED FROM SERVICE

Three rails removed from service on the Union Pacific Railroad were used to characterize rail work hardening attributable to plastic flow and the change in microstructure that accompanies deformation. Two of the rails had undergone 468 million gross Mg (515 million gross tons) of traffic, and one of the rails had undergone 662 million gross Mg (728 million gross tons) of traffic. Figure 1 shows the results of two Vickers microhardness test surveys made at the gage corner of the rail. The rails typically had been work hardened to 85-95 Vickers hardness above the base hardness [Vickers microhardness numbers are approximately equivalent to Brinell hardness numbers (BHN)]. It is important to note that, between 6 and 8 mm (0.24 and 0.31 in) in depth, a zone of work-softened material exists. It has been shown, by Leis (2) for rail steel and Park and Stone (4) for wheel steels, that these pearlitic steels work soften under cyclic strains of less than 0.6 percent.

There are also dramatic changes in the microstructure that may be associated with work hardening. Figures 2-4 show scanning electron microscope photomicrographs of the same rail specimen, after 662 million gross Mg (728 million gross tons) of service, at depths of 2.25, 6.75, and 7.5 mm (0.09, 0.27, and 0.30 in), respectively. At 2.25 mm (Figure 2), the material has been work hardened to 320 BHN and exhibits a very heavily deformed microstructure within which the cementite plates either have become kinked (in a wavelike pattern) and cracked or have thinned out. The difference in deformation behavior could be associated with the orientation of the cementite plates within individual cells relative to the applied load. In the work-softened zone, the cementite is either straight with some cracking or slightly deformed in a sinusoidal pattern. In the base material at 7.5 mm (Figure 4), the cementite plates are in their normal straight and undeformed condition. Several investigators have observed the same microstructure as that shown in Figure 2 in cold-drawn, high-carbon steel wire (5, 6).

TESTING PROCEDURE

Materials

Three rail steels were tested: (a) hot-rolled carbon steel, (b) heat-treated carbon steel, and (c) pearlitic chromium-molybdenum (CrMo) alloy. Their compositions and mechanical properties are given in Table 1.

The hot-rolled carbon steel had a fully pearlitic microstructure. The heat-treated carbon steel was also pearlitic but had a smaller grain size. The alloyed pearlitic rail was also fine grained.

Samples were cut from the railhead with the deformation face parallel to the running surface (Figure 5). The samples were 6.35 mm (0.25 in) thick, and except for the heat-treated samples, which had a width of 23.8 mm (0.9375 in), were 25.4 mm (1 in) wide.

Because the hardness of rails varies with depth from the surface, the average hardness of each sample was determined and any sample that varied more than 2 points Rockwell C from the average was discarded. The hardness values given in Table 1 are thus the average of the samples tested.

Mechanical Testing

The compression test used in this project was designed by Watts and Ford (7) for testing steel sheet and strip. The test consists of applying a compressive load to the

Transportation Research Record 744

sample by means of two parallel indenting dies (see Figure 6). The width b of the dies was equal to the thickness t of the samples. It has been found that the true yield stress is achieved only when t is an integral multiple of b. By keeping b small in comparison with sample width w, the deformed region of the sample is constrained in the width dimension by the undeformed material on either side. Thus, the sample deformed under plane strain conditions. This test approximates the loading conditions experienced by rail in service, especially in tangent track and on the low rail of curves.

Figure 1. Hardness profiles of standard carbon steel rail in the high rail of a 1° curve after 468 million gross Mg (515 million gross tons) of service.

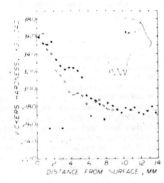

Figure 3. Microstructure of rail specimen 6.75 mm (0.27 in) below running surface (4900X etched in Nital).

Figure 2. Microstructure of rail specimen 2.25 mm (0.9 in) below running surface (4900X etched in Nital).

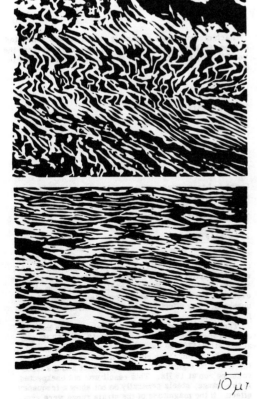

Figure 4. Microstructure of rail specimen 7.5 mm (0.3 in) below running surface (4900X etched in Nital).

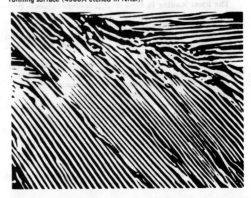

Table 1. Composition and mechanical properties of rail steels.

Type of Rail Steel	Composition (`)	Yield Strength (MPa)	Rockwell C Hardness
As-rolled carbon steel	0.69-0.82 carbon, 0.7-1.0 manganese, 0.04 max phosphorus, 0.05 max sulfur, 0.1-0.25 silicon		
Heat-treated carbon steel	0.69-0.82 carbon, 0.7-1.0 manganese, 0.04 max phosphorus, 0.05 max sulfur, 0.1-0.25 silicon	517	22-23
CrMo steel, pearlitic	0.78 carbon, 0.84 manganese, 0.22 silicon, 0.72 chromium, 0.19 molybdenum, 0.026 phosphorus, 0.022 sulfur	827	38-39
		752	35-36

Note: 1 MPa = 145 lbf/in².

Figure 5. Test sample as taken from the head of a rail.

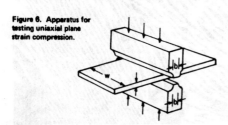

Figure 6. Apparatus for testing uniaxial plane strain compression.

Testing was done on a Material Testing System electrohydraulic close-loop machine in load control (cyclic deformation tests are usually run in strain control, but in this case load control was the simpler mode).

The ideal loading is zero to P_{max} (compressive). However, because of the instability of the samples at zero load, samples were loaded from -13 kN (-3000 lbf) to P_{max}. Loads were applied following a sine wave function at frequencies from 6 to 18 Hz. P_{max} varied from 110 to 200 kN (25 000-45 000 lbf).

To reduce friction effects, the contact surface of the specimens was covered with Teflon tape. In order to record the progressive deformation behavior, the reduction in sample thickness was measured by a micrometer to the nearest 0.002 54 mm (0.0001 in) after a set number of cycles. To facilitate plotting on logarithmic paper, thickness was measured after 1, 2, 5, 10, 20, 50, and 100 cycles, up to 100 000 cycles or 10 percent reduction in thickness, whichever came first. After each measurement, the surface was again covered with Teflon tape. In replacing the samples, care was taken to align the indentation with the dies. The load was then applied again for the next cyclic increment.

Two loading patterns were used. The first pattern (simple loading) consisted of cycling at the same load for the entire run. Simple loading was done for a range of loads to observe the effect of increasing stress on deformation behavior. The second loading pattern (split loading) consisted of cycling the sample at one load for 100, 1000, or 10 000 cycles and then finishing the run at a higher load. Split-loading tests were run after the simple-loading tests so that the low loads could be chosen for little or no cyclic deformation and the high loads for marked cyclic softening behavior. One split-loading set (three runs) was done for each rail type.

Calculations

The axial compressive stress for plane strain compression in this case is simply the applied load divided by the area being deformed:

$$\sigma = P/wb \tag{1}$$

Each measurement of sample reduction was converted to true strain by the following formulas (derived from the Von Mises yield criterion): For percentage reduction in thickness,

$$(t_0 - t)/t_0 = \epsilon_t \tag{2}$$

For plane strain,

$$\ln(1 - \epsilon_t) = \epsilon_p \tag{3}$$

For true strain,

$$(2/\sqrt{3})\epsilon_p = \epsilon_t \tag{4}$$

Graphs of true strain versus cycles were thus obtained for the rail steels for simple and split loading.

TESTING QUALIFICATIONS

Frequency Effect

The frequency of the wheels of a train going over a section of rail is about 3 Hz. Tests previously run at AAR were conducted at a low frequency (6 Hz) to approximate service conditions. Because of time limitations, however, the current tests were conducted at higher frequencies. The effect of frequency on strain was therefore examined.

The curves produced by progressive cyclic loading of hot-rolled carbon steel rail at 6, 12, and 18 Hz and at 827 MPa [120 000 lbf/in² (120 kips/in²)] are shown in Figure 7. From these curves, it was concluded that there was no significant frequency effect and the tests could be run at 18 Hz. This result was not unexpected. In this range, steels generally do not show a frequency effect. If the magnitude of the strain range were great,

Figure 7. Effect of frequency on compressive cyclic softening of rail steel.

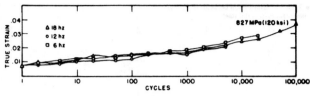

Figure 8. Schematic of hardness traverse (values in Rockwell C hardness numbers) across deformed region of standard rail steel specimen [σ = 1102 MPa (140 000 lbf/in²)].

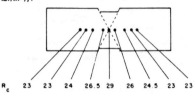

or if the tests were run in an aggressive environment, a frequency effect could be expected.

Extent of Deformation

Because more than one region of each sample was used for tests, it was desired to determine how much material on either side of a deformation region was affected. A hardness traverse was therefore made across the deformed area of a specimen (see Figure 8). The results showed that the hardening effect was well confined directly under the dies.

RESULTS AND DISCUSSION

Simple Loading

The results for the hot-rolled carbon steel rail are shown in Figure 9. At all stress levels, strain increased as the number of cycles increased, which indicated that the steel was softening. As the stress level increased, so did the rate of softening and the total amount of softening.

It appears that, at 896 MPa (130 000 lbf/in²) or less, the softening behavior would eventually stabilize if the cycling were continued beyond 100 000 cycles. However, above 896 MPa, the metal appeared to soften continuously. Cycling at the higher stresses was not continued to 100 000 because the sample thickness had been reduced 10 percent and cracks were forming. It was presumed that those samples would fail before the softening stabilized.

The other steel types also showed increased softening with increasing stress (see Figures 10 and 11). Note, however, that the effect is less severe for the heat-treated rail and the softening effect is even more damped for the pearlitic CrMo steel.

The increasing deformation resistance is probably partly a function of the increasing hardness and yield strength of the steels. However, the heat-treated carbon steel had slightly greater hardness and yield strength than the pearlitic CrMo steel but exhibited worse deformation behavior. Therefore, other factors must be considered in the deformation behavior. The alloying additions in the CrMo steels might increase deformation resistance by inhibiting dislocation movements.

Split Loading

The results of the split-loading tests are less clear than those for simple loading. In the case of the hot-rolled carbon steel, preloading at a lower stress caused an increase in the softening rate at the higher stress (see Figure 12). For the heat-treated rail (see Figure 13), preloading improved the deformation resistance at 100 and 10 000 cycles and decreased deformation resistance when the load was increased after 1000 cycles. Preloading the pearlitic CrMo steel improved its deformation resistance at the higher stress (see Figure 14).

The reasons for the variable effects of preloading on the different steels are not clear. Preloading of the plain carbon steel may promote dislocation movement in the pearlite, whereas the alloying additions in the other steels may inhibit dislocation movement and thus improve deformation resistance at the higher loads. The heat-treated rail, at 1000 cycles, must reach some critical dislocation arrangement that promotes the increased softening behavior. Further study is under way to explain this behavior more fully.

Microstructure of Deformed Specimens

The microstructure of a deformed specimen 0.5 mm (0.02 in) below the surface is shown to be comparable to that of service-deformed rail steel (see Figure 15).

Prediction of Plastic Flow

Deformation as a function of stress, number of cycles, and microstructure can be calculated by a modified form of an equation developed by Langford [8] for deformation caused by cold rolling. Langford's equation for axisymmetric compression of pearlite is

$$\sigma = \sigma_0 + (k/\sqrt{2d}) \exp(\epsilon_p/2) \qquad (5)$$

where

σ = compressive stress,
σ_0 = friction stress (76.4 MPa),
k = Hall Petch constant (0.5 to 0.68 MN/m$^{3/2}$),
d = pearlite spacing, and
ϵ_p = plane strain.

Rearranging terms,

$$\epsilon_p = 2\left\{\ln\left[(\sqrt{2d}/k)(\sigma - \sigma_0)\right]\right\} \qquad (6)$$

and, from Equation 4,

$$\epsilon_t = (4/\sqrt{3})\left\{\ln\left[(\sqrt{2d}/k)(\sigma - \sigma_0)\right]\right\} \qquad (7)$$

Figures 9-14 show that ϵ_t is made up of the strain after one cycle ϵ_1 and the cyclic strain ϵ_c if more than one cycle is considered. In addition, each increment of ϵ_c is accompanied by the log of a cycle of stress. Therefore, for more than one cycle of stress, Equation 7 can be modified as follows to fit the curves presented:

20   Transportation Research Record 744

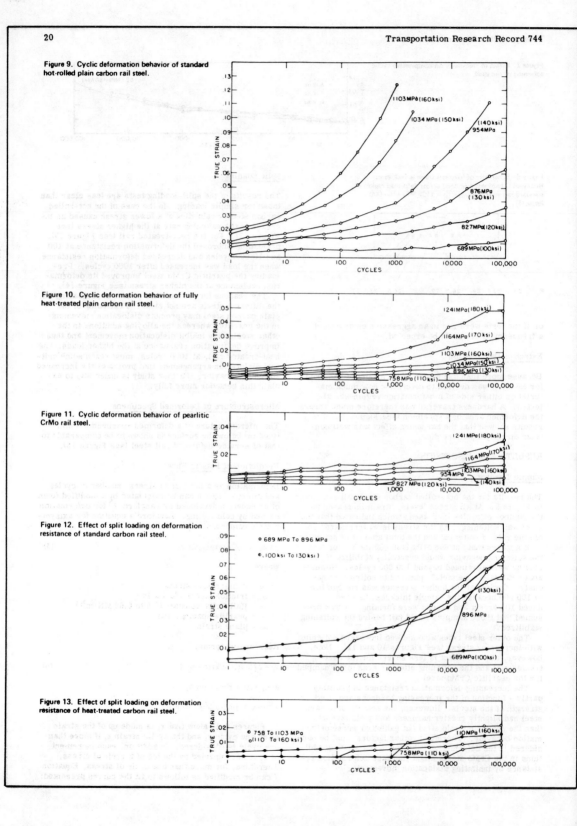

Figure 9. Cyclic deformation behavior of standard hot-rolled plain carbon rail steel.

Figure 10. Cyclic deformation behavior of fully heat-treated plain carbon rail steel.

Figure 11. Cyclic deformation behavior of pearlitic CrMo rail steel.

Figure 12. Effect of split loading on deformation resistance of standard carbon rail steel.

Figure 13. Effect of split loading on deformation resistance of heat-treated carbon rail steel.

Figure 14. Effect of split loading on deformation resistance of pearlitic CrMo rail steel.

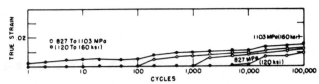

Figure 15. Microstructure of standard rail steel specimen 0.5 mm (0.02 in) below deformed surface (4900X etched in Nital).

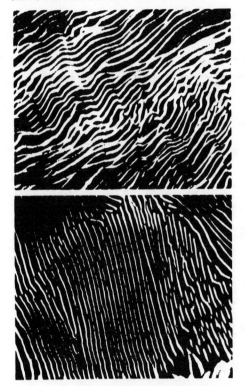

$$\epsilon_c + \epsilon_t = (4/\sqrt{3})\, A \ln N \left\{ \ln \left[(\sqrt{2d}/k)(\sigma - \sigma_0)\right] \right\} \qquad (8)$$

Evaluation of the curve, for 689 MPa (100 000 lbf/in²) in Figure 9, gives a mean value of 0.17 MN/m (11 680 lbf/ft) for A, and Equation 8 reduces to

$$\epsilon_c - \epsilon_t = 4.27 \times 10^{-3} \ln N \left\{ \ln \left[(\sqrt{2d}/k)(\sigma - \sigma_0)\right] \right\} \qquad (9)$$

A set of experiments was performed by Code (9) in which brass pins were inserted in railheads that were then placed in service. The rails were removed after varying amounts of traffic load and were sectioned, and the deformation of the pins was measured. For two pins, after 68 million gross Mg (75 million gross tons) of traffic, the average true strain can be calculated from Code's data as 0.023 and 0.017. In 1951, the average freight carload was 38 t (42 tons); adding 28 tons for the empty car weight gives a gross load of 63 Mg/car (70

tons/car). This provides an estimate of 4.3 million cycles for the duration of Code's test (number of cars times four axles). Substituting this value into Equation 9 gives a strain of 0.016. This value is in close agreement with the values measured in the field, which run from a maximum of 0.046 at the surface to 0 at a distance of 8 mm (0.34 in) below the surface.

CONCLUSIONS

1. When cycled in plane strain compression, plain carbon steels, heat-treated steels, and CrMo steels exhibit softening. The rate and the amount of softening increase with increasing stress.
2. Deformation resistance increases with increasing hardness and yield strength of the steel.
3. The behavior of steels under split loading varies depending on steel type. The reason for the difference is not clear.
4. The wavy pearlite microstructure developed in rails during service is duplicated in laboratory specimens.
5. The average flow in rails can be predicted if stress, microstructure, and number of cycles are known.

REFERENCES

1. Yearbook of Railroad Facts. Assn. of American Railroads, Washington, DC, 1979.
2. B. N. Leis. Cyclic Inelastic Deformation and Fatigue Resistance Characteristics of Rail Steels. In Rail Steels: Developments, Processing, and Use (D. H. Stone and G. G. Knupp, eds.), ASTM, Philadelphia, Special Tech. Publ. 644, 1978.
3. S. Marich and P. Curcio. Development of High-Strength Alloyed Rail Steels Suitable for Heavy-Duty Application. In Rail Steels: Developments, Processing, and Use (D. H. Stone and G. G. Knupp, eds.), ASTM, Philadelphia, Special Tech. Publ. 644, 1978.
4. Y. J. Park and D. H. Stone. Cyclic Behavior of Class U Wheel Steel. ASME, New York (in preparation).
5. M. A. P. Dewey and G. W. Briers. Structure of Heavily Cold Drawn Eutectoid Steel. Journal of Iron and Steel Institute, Vol. 204, 1966, p. 102.
6. G. Langford. A Study of the Deformation of Patented Steel Wire. Metallurgical Trans., Vol. 1, 1970, p. 465.
7. A. B. Watts and H. Ford. An Experimental Investigation of the Yielding of Strip Between Smooth Dies. Proc., Institute of Mechanical Engineers, Vol. 1B, 1952, pp. 448-453.
8. G. Langford. Deformation of Pearlite. Metallurgical Trans., Vol. 8A, 1977, p. 861.
9. C. J. Code. Determination of Plastic Flow in Rail Head. AREA Bull., Vol. 59, 1958, p. 962.

Publication of this paper sponsored by Committee on Track Structure System Design.

LABORATORY INVESTIGATION OF TRANSVERSE DEFECTS IN RAILS

S. MARICH

J. W. COTTAM

P. CURCIO

1   INTRODUCTION

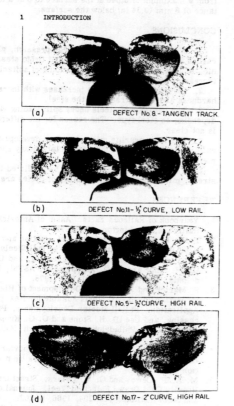

(a)   DEFECT No.8 - TANGENT TRACK

(b)   DEFECT No.11 - ½ CURVE, LOW RAIL

(c)   DEFECT No.5 - ½ CURVE, HIGH RAIL

(d)   DEFECT No.17 - 2° CURVE, HIGH RAIL

Figure 1

Fatigue of rails is a problem shared by railways throughout the world. The Mt. Newman Mining Company (MNM) railway is no exception, understand-ably so considering that the rails are subjected to average wheel loadings which are among the highest experienced anywhere. In particular, transverse defects (illustrated in Figure 1) or detail frac-tures from shelling, as classified in the Sperry Rail Defect Manual, have become a major cause of concern to track personnel because of three major reasons:

(a)   On reaching critical size, transverse defects lead to a complete break of the rail section across the head, web and base. Such a break thus becomes a potential site for a derail-ment.

(b)   Because of their growth characteristics, transverse defects may reach a critical size without becoming apparent on the surface of the rails. Prevention of failure, therefore, relies entirely on the timely detection of such defects by means of frequent and expen-sive ultrasonic inspection of the track.

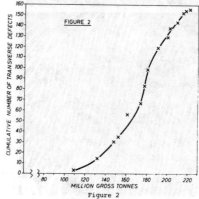

Figure 2

(c)   As shown in Figure 2 the first transverse defects at MNM were reported after the rails had experienced a traffic of 109 million gross tonnes (M.G.T.). Over the following 18 months (approximately 70 M.G.T. of traff-ic) data from ultrasonic track inspections indicated that the defects were developing at an almost exponential rate. Replacement of defective rails was thus leading to con-siderable maintenance costs and interference to operating schedules.

For the above reasons, the original BHP/Mt. Newman Mining Railroad Research Programme was extended to include:

(a)   A detailed metallographic study of the nucl-eation and growth characteristics of trans-verse defects;

Session 303
Paper I.1

(b) An examination of the growth of transverse
defects under various rolling load fatigue
conditions.

The latter study is being conducted in a rolling
load fatigue machine designed to simulate the
various stress conditions experienced by rails in
track during the passage of trains, i.e. the
Hertzian stresses due to the wheel/rail interaction, the shear stresses due to bending of the rail
and the tensile and compressive stresses also
caused by rail bending. The machine allows each
stress condition to be applied independently so
that its effect and relative importance on fatigue
growth may be established.

This report covers the metallographic study and
some of the preliminary results obtained on the
rolling load machine.

2 EXPERIMENTAL DETAILS

2.1 Metallographic Study

A total of 17 rail sections, in which transverse
defects had been detected by ultrasonic track inspection, were received for examination. The sections represented the following track geometry conditions: tangent track, high leg of curves with a
large radius (3493 metres, ¼° curvature), high leg
of curves with small radii (873 metres, 2° curvature, and 582 metres, 3° curvature) and low leg of
curves.

The first step in the examination procedure was to
break open the defects and thus reveal the fracture
surfaces. The samples were broken in a 500 tonne
hydraulic press, by fixing the ends of the rail
sections and applying the load on the foot of the
rails so that the transverse defects acted as a
notch.

Failure of the rails invariably occurred in a
brittle manner. The fatigue defects were thus
clearly delineated.

The metallographic examination was conducted on
sections cut from the rails in both longitudinal
and transverse planes. In each case both sides of
the defect were examined (in the following text
these are referred to as port and mine sides). The
transverse sections were cut at varying distances
from the fracture surface, while most of the longitudinal sections were cut through what appeared to
have been the nucleation point of the defects. The
sections were examined by means of both optical and
scanning electron (SE) microscopy. The latter was
also used to examine the fracture surfaces of the
defects in their "natural" state.

2.2 Fatigue Growth Study

2.2.1 The rolling load machine

Figure 3 shows a general view of the rolling load
machine. It consists of two wheel segments which
rock longitudinally over 300 mm of the two rail
samples which are tested simultaneously. The wheel
segments are driven by two connecting rods which
are horizontally opposed to maintain the machine
dynamically balanced during operation. Two large
flywheels absorb the peak energy demands during the
simple harmonic motion. cycle. This allows two
relatively small motors, 11.25 kw and 750 W to
drive the system. The motors are independently
driven to allow variable speed control. The small
motor drives the machine through a reduction gear
box, resulting in a speed of one cycle per minute.

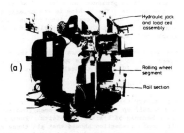

(a)

Hydraulic jack
and load cell
assembly

Rolling wheel
segment

Rail section

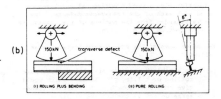

(b)

150kN   transverse defect   150kN   6°

(i) ROLLING PLUS BENDING   (ii) PURE ROLLING

Figure 3

This speed is suitable for setting up of the machine, measuring stress variation in the rail during
cycling and in the case of crack growth studies,
conducting ultrasonic inspection of the defects.
The larger motor drives the system through an infinitely variable belt drive enabling the machine
to be run between 2 Hz and 4 Hz.

The vertical forces required to simulate the wheel
/rail contact zone condition are applied with
hydraulic cylinders pressurised from an air operated pump. The forces are monitored by means of
electronic load cells and are variable between 1
and 200 kN on each wheel segment. Variations in
deflection of the rail specimen and to a lesser
extent the machine frame during the rocking action
of the wheel segment, cause corresponding variation in the vertical wheel force. This variation
has been minimised to approximately 5% of the
nominal during each cycle by applying the vertical
force through a spring assembly located between
the load cell and the roller on the wheel segment.
Incorporated in the spring assembly is a compression screw which when operated allows the vertical
wheel force to be maintained without the need for
the hydraulic pump to be continuously operated.

The rail specimens are assembled on a base plate
before they are fixed in the machine. Different
base plates can be used so that the head of the
rail can be laterally inclined beneath the wheel
segment at various angles. This adjustment allows
the wheel/rail contact zone to be located on any
position between the centre of the rail head and
the gauge corner. The base plates also allow the
rail specimens to be fully supported along the
foot or cantilevered to give tensile bending
stresses in the head of the samples. Combinations
of these rail positions produce contact conditions
consisting of pure rolling, rolling plus vertical
bending, rolling plus lateral bending or rolling
plus combined vertical and lateral bending.
Longitudinal loads simulating thermal stresses may

2

also be imposed on the rail samples by suitable connections to pressure jacks located at either end of the machine. The machine is not capable of reproducing impact forces or longitudinal and lateral sliding forces that are experienced under track conditions.

The machine running 16 hours daily at the maximum speed of 4 Hz can simulate one year's track experience (40 x 10^6 gross tonnes) in 3 days.

2.2.2 Preliminary tests

Preliminary tests were conducted on three standard carbon rail specimens which had been removed from track because of transverse defects. Further ultrasonic inspection showed that all three rails contained a transverse defect located at the gauge corner of the head and extending approximately 30 mm across the head of the rail. The ultrasonic inspection also showed a horizontal crack associated with each of the transverse defects. The cracks extended from the nucleus of the transverse defects towards the mine side.

The major aims of the preliminary tests were as follows:

(a)   to establish the mode of rolling, i.e. pure rolling or rolling plus bending which would give continued growth of the initial transverse defect in the transverse plane;

(b)   to establish an ultrasonic technique that would allow the growth of the transverse defects to be monitored in situ.

Specimens 1 and 3 were tested identically. They were assembled in the rolling load machine to provide rolling contact stresses and tensile bending stresses at the transverse defects. Specimen 2 was initially tested under a pure rolling contact mode. However, since after 700 000 cycles negligible growth of the transverse defect could be detected, the specimen was reassembled in the machine and tested as specimens 1 and 3. The two test methods are shown schematically in Figure 3(b).

In both test methods the vertical wheel segment/rail contact force was 150 kN, the nominal MNM ore car wheel load. This force produced a nominal tensile bending stress of 100 MPa at the centre of the defects. In order that the wheel/rail contact zone and the corresponding Hertzian stresses would act directly over the transverse defect, the rail samples were laterally inclined at 6° as shown in Figure 3(b).

During the test on specimen 3, the growth rate of the transverse defect was monitored using 45° transmitting and receiving probes of 4 MHz frequency and a near zone length of approximately 19 mm making contact with the field side of the rail head. Figure 4(a) shows the probe assembly. The probes were maintained at a constant skip distance by a connecting rod. As shown schematically in Figure 4(b) as the crack advanced across the rail head the beam was progressively cut off, reducing the signal.

After increments of 50 000 cycles the echo intensity was restored to its original value by moving the probes along the rail by means of a lead screw. The distance over which the probes are moved is equivalent to the growth of the defect across the rail head in the 50 000 cycle increment.

During the test on specimen 3 the wheel/rail force

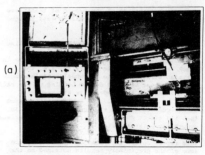

(a)

Figure 4(a)

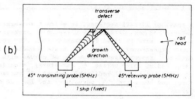

(b)

Figure 4(b)

was increased to 180 kN for 100 cycles at 100 000, 200 000 and 300 000 cycles in an attempt to mark the fracture surface and therefore provide a second method for estimating the defect growth rate.

3   RESULTS

3.1   General Characteristics of Transverse Defects

Figure 1 shows the general appearance of the transverse defects in rails sections representing all four track geometry conditions mentioned in Section 2.1. The first three defects (tangent, low rail of 2° curve and high rail of 4° curve) are very similar in appearance. The fourth defect (high rail of 2° curve) is of particular interest since it resulted in a rail failure in track and therefore it gives an indication of the critical crack size. The crack covers about 90% of the rail head and has a mean "diameter" of about 50 mm. In another rail section which had also failed in track (No. 14), the defect was found to cover about 80% of the rail head and have a mean diameter of 45 mm.

In each of the defects shown in Figure 1, nucleation appears to have taken place within the rail head below the gauge corner.

Throughout most of their growth the defects avoid joining the running surface and the gauge face of the rails.

As illustrated in Figure 5, growth of the defects occurs on a plane inclined at an angle of 65° to 90° to the running surface of the rails and in the direction of loaded traffic. This is indicative of a stress system in which one of the principal axes is not simply longitudinal. Figure 6(a) shows the cross section of defect No. 2. On taking a longitudinal section on the mine side of the defect in the plane AA, through what appeared to

Session 303
Paper I.1

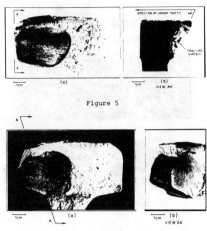

Figure 5

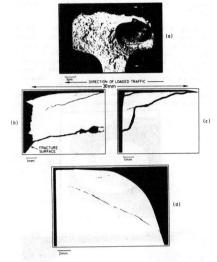

Figure 7

Figure 6

be the nucleation point, a section of the gauge (indicated by the shaded area) spalled off. As shown in Figure 6(b) this revealed a longitudinal crack (arrowed) joining the transverse defect.

The sectioning procedure was repeated in defect No. 1 and the specimens were mounted and polished. Transverse sections of the rails were also cut on both mine and port sides of the transverse defect at varying distances from the fracture surface.

Figure 7(a) shows the cross section on the mine side of defect No. 1 and the longitudinal plane of sectioning. The longitudinal crack which joins the transverse defect is shown in Figure 7(b). Away from the transverse defect, the longitudinal crack becomes progressively shallower and eventually joins the running surface of the rail at a distance of about 30 mm from the transverse separation, as shown in Figure 7(c). Figure 7(b) also shows a smaller crack running almost parallel to the longitudinal crack from the surface of the rail in the direction of the loaded traffic. As discussed previously by Marich and Curcio (1976), this smaller crack can be described as a gauge corner check crack.

The transverse section of the rail separating the two longitudinal sections, taken at 12 mm from the fracture surface, is shown in Figure 7(d). It can be seen that the longitudinal crack runs at an angle of about 30° to the horizontal and is considerably deeper than the gauge corner check crack which is also present. The longitudinal crack joins the gauge face of the rail but not the running surface.

Figure 8 shows transverse sections taken on the port side of the transverse defect at 5 mm and 10 mm from the fracture surface. On this side the longitudinal crack runs deeper into the rail head, decreases in width, no longer joins the gauge face of the rail and eventually disappears at a distance of about 13 mm from the fracture surface.

All of the defects examined exhibited a similar longitudinal crack pattern even though there were differences in the distance from the transverse

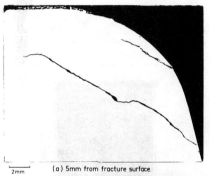

(a) 5mm from fracture surface.

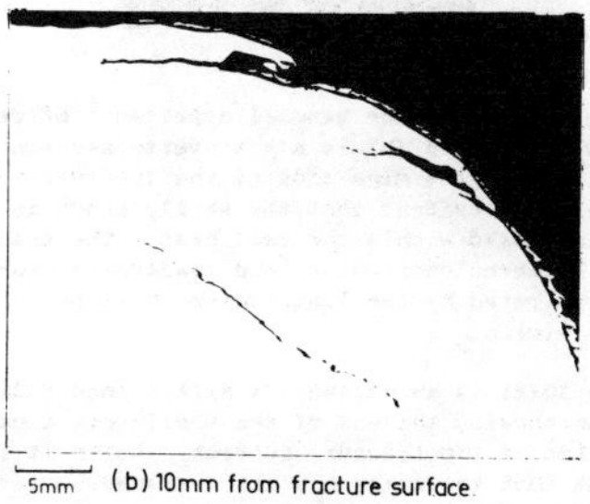

(b) 10mm from fracture surface.

Figure 8

fracture at which the longitudinal crack joined the running surface of the rail on the mine side of the defect and disappeared in the rail head on the port side. On the basis of their general appearance the

4

longitudinal cracks could be classified as shelly cracks.

In most of the samples examined, the shelly cracks had joined the surface of the rail and had become completely oxidised. In these samples, therefore, it was difficult to conclude whether the nucleation of the shelly cracks had occurred within the rail head or whether the cracks were simply extensions of the gauge corner check cracks. However, in two samples (Nos 10 and 13) the defects exhibitied shiny fracture surfaces, indicating no contact with the atmosphere.

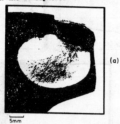

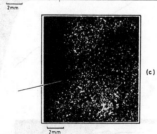

Figure 9(a) shows the general appearance of defect No. 10. Figure 9 (b) is a transverse section taken 5 mm on the mine side of the fracture surface. It is evident that the shelly crack is fully enclosed within the rail head. The transition between longitudinal and transverse cracks is illustrated by the longitudinal section in Figure 9(c).

Figure 10(a) is an etched (2% Nital) longitudinal section showing the end of the shelly crack on the mine side of the fracture surface. Again it is evident that the crack has not surfaced.

On closer examination of the longitudinal section, a white etching phase was found to outline the shelly crack. This phase is illustrated in more detail in the scanning electron micrograph, Figure 10(b), and the optical micrographs, Figures 10(d)

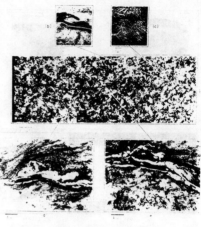

Figure 10

and (e). Microhardness measurements taken in the white etching regions showed hardness values in the range 1000 to 1200 Vickers.

The formation of a white phase in the vicinity of shelly cracks in rails was reported and discussed previously by Henry (1970) who concluded that the phase was a plastic deformation within the rail head which resulted from the rolling contact stress. Henry seemed to infer that the white etching phase could contribute to or indeed cause the growth of shelly cracks. A similar suggestion was presented by Ravitskoya (1974).

However, as shown in Figure 10(c) the white etching phase is not observed within a distance of 0.1 mm from the tip of the shelly crack. This indicates that the formation of the phase occurs some time after the formation of the shelly crack and therefore cannot act as a nucleation site for the crack.

The white etching phase was also observed on the fracture surface of the transverse defects (Nos 10 and 13). However, the phase was present only within an area of diameter 5 - 10 mm from the point of intersection of the transverse defect and the shelly crack.

It is proposed that the formation of the white etching phase is due to the very rapid and localised thermal cycling and deformation which result from friction at the rubbing surfaces of the shelly cracks and transverse defects in their early stages of growth. Bedford et al (1974) have presented an excellent review of the literature on the formation of white etching phases at rubbing surfaces.

Evidence of the brittleness of the white etching phase is illustrated in Figures 10(d) and (e), where it is evident that considerable cracking has occurred within the phase. It is therefore suggested that the phase does contribute to the formation of secondary cracks which, as shown in the figures, branch out from the main crack and on rejoining it lead to spalling of material. On sectioning samples such spalling gives the impression of cavities of considerable size associated with the shelly cracks.

Session 303
Paper I.1

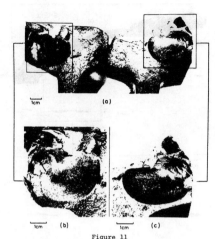

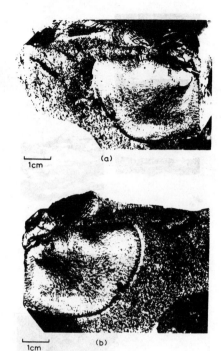

Figure 11

3.2 Nucleation and Growth

As mentioned previously, by careful sectioning of the rail specimens it was possible to break away the gauge corner section of the rail above the shelly crack, expose all fracture surfaces and thus determine the exact location of the nucleation point of the transverse defect and the associated shell. In the fully enclosed defects (Nos 10 and 13) two longitudinal cuts were necessary to expose the fracture surface. Figures 11 and 12 illustrate some of the defects that were examined in this manner.

From the figures, it can be seen that the nucleation site of the defects (N.S.) is readily detected macroscopically by the striations surrounding the site and/or by the beach marks radiating from the site.

In all samples examined, the nucleation of both shelly crack and transverse defect was found to occur at the same location. This is particularly noticeable in Figure 11 which shows the continuity of the growth striations in both longitudinal and transverse planes.

The majority of defects showed a gradual transition between the longitudinal and transverse cracks, as illustrated in Figure 11, with the initial propagation appearing to have occurred longitudinally. In some samples, however, it appeared that the shell and transverse defect had nucleated and propagated in both planes simultaneously (Figure 12).

Generally the depth at which crack initiation had occurred was found to be 5 to 7 mm below the gauge corner of the rails. Slightly lower values were measured in the high rails from 2° and 3° curves; however this may have been due to the considerable gauge corner wear which is characteristic of such rails.

As shown in Figure 12, a fine line was observed at the nucleation point of most of the defects. The line ran longitudinally and was up to 4 mm in length. This feature was studied in more detail by means of scanning electron microscopy in the two defects which exhibited no surface oxidation, viz.

Figure 12

Nos 10 and 13.

As shown in Figure 13, the line was actually found to be a step 0.1 to 0.2 mm in height. Elongated inclusions at least 400 μm in length were observed embedded along the surface of the step, as indicated by the arrows.

On examining transverse sections cut through the step (Figure 14), inclusions were again observed on the surface of the step. The diameter of the inclusions was at leat 30 μm, although accurate measurements were not possible because, as shown in Figure 14, the inclusions exhibited considerable cracking which could have led to loss of material on mounting and polishing the specimens.

Qualitative analysis of the inclusions in the scanning electron microscope showed them to contain calcium, aluminium, manganese and silicon. The inclusions were therefore assumed to be complex silicates.

On sectioning other rail samples through the nucleation point of the defects, inclusions similar to the above were invariably observed in the vicinity of the major cracks. For example, Figure 15 shows a longitudinal section containing a high concentration of the complex silicate inclusions adjoining the shelly crack near the nucleation point of defect No. 5. It is evident that the inclusions are in the form of long stringers. As such they are potential nucleation sites for longitudinal cracks such as shells.

Figure 16 shows a transverse section cut through

Session 303
Paper I.1

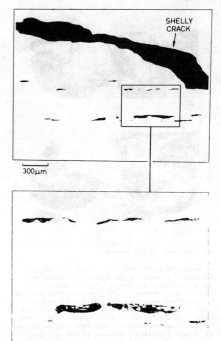

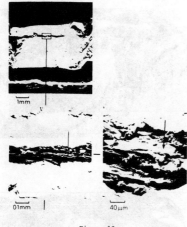

Figure 13

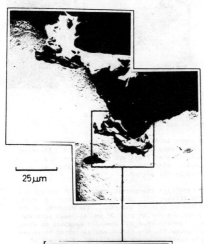

25μm

12·5μm

Figure 14

Figure 15

the nucleation point of defect No. 6. The very large inclusion is a complex silicate. It measures 200 μm across its largest dimension. The figure is of particular interest since it shows fine cracks (arrowed) at the tips of the inclusion extending into the steel matrix.

To determine whether such inclusions were present throughout the length of the defective rails, transverse sections were cut in the vicinity of the nucleation point of the defects and at various distances away from it, where the rails exhibited no ultrasonic indications of defects. The large complex silicates were only observed in the sections near the defects. Two such sections are compared in Figures 17(a) and (b). Figure 17(a) shows the concentration of large silicates present near the nucleation point while Figure 17(b) gives an indication of the size of the "typical" indigenous inclusions found in semi-killed rail steels. These inclusions are of two types: (a) manganese sulphides and (b) manganese silicates ($MnO - SiO_2$).

The composition of the complex silicate inclusions present in the various specimens was determined quantitatively by electron probe microanalysis and found to be as follows (in weight %):

CaO = 6 - 11%
Al_2O_3 = 20 - 24%
MnO = 17 - 25%
TiO_2 = 2 - 3%

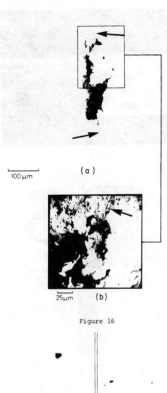

100 μm

(a)

25μm   (b)

Figure 16

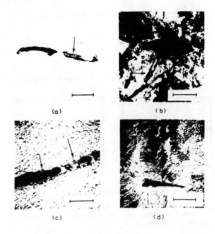

(a)   (b)

(c)   (d)

Figure 18

Figures 18 (b) and (d).

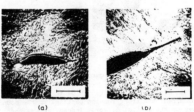

(a)   (b)

Figure 19

30μm   (a)   30μm   (b)

Figure 17

$$SiO_2 = 45 - 46\%$$

The composition is equivalent to that quoted by Kiessling and Lange (1966) for exogenous inclusions originating from ladle slags. It is therefore concluded that the complex silicate inclusions present in the rail sections in which defects had developed were exogenous slag inclusions which had become entrapped in the steel during steelmaking.

A more detailed microscopic examination of longitudinal sections near the nucleation point of defects revealed that the majority of exogenous inclusions were cracked in the transverse plane, as shown by the arrows in Figures 18(a) and (c). Some of the inclusions also gave rise to transverse cracks which extended into the steel matrix, as shown in

Longitudinal cracks were also found to nucleate from manganese sulphide inclusions, as shown in Figure 19, and indigenous manganese silicate inclusions. However, unlike the exogenous silicates, neither of the indigenous inclusion types were found to be cracked nor to nucleate transverse cracks in the steel matrix.

One of the longitudinal sections cut near the nucleation point of defect No. 9 is shown in Figure 20. It illustrates the usual concentration of exogenous silicate inclusions present near a secondary shelly crack. However, the section is of particular interest because it clearly shows the branching of the horizontal crack which has occurred at an exogenous inclusion (arrowed). One branch continues in a roughly horizontal plane while the second branch turns downward in a manner very similar to the transition between longitudinal and transverse crack components illustrated in Figure 11. It is thought that this section typifies the nucleation of a transverse defect which in this sample developed some time after the main defect.

3.3 Laboratory Growth Studies

Specimen 1 was tested for 244 000 cycles. At this stage the defect surfaced on the gauge face of the rail head. The specimen was removed from the mach-

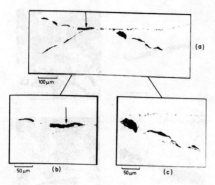

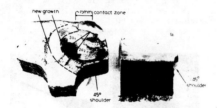

Figure 20

ine and broken open for inspection. The original
transverse defect and the new growth have been outlined in Figure 21.

Figure 21

It is evident that the growth of the induced crack
occurred on a front running parallel to the boundary of the initial defect. Indeed, across the
rail head, there was no marked transition between
original and new crack. The lower part of the
defect, on the other hand, did show some discontinuity which was associated with a 45° shoulder,
approximately 5 mm wide, that was present at the
lower edge of the original defect. The original
defect had grown a distance of 26 mm across the
rail head from the nucleation point and a further
14 mm in the rolling load machine. The average
growth rate of the induced growth region over the
244 000 cycles was thus 5.74×10^{-5} mm/cycle.

Specimen 2 was first tested in the pure rolling
mode for 710 000 cycles. During this period there
was no ultrasonic indication to suggest that crack
growth was taking place in the transverse plane.
Visual inspection of the specimen after testing
showed cracks on the surface of the gauge face of
the rail head adjacent to the transverse defect
location (Figure 22(a)). The specimen was then
tested under rolling plus bending for 825 000
cycles until failure occurred. The resulting fracture surface is shown in Figure 22(b) together with
the horizontal crack associated with the original
transverse defect. It can be seen that the induced
fracture surface shows no resemblance to the original crack. The crack front is irregular and extends into the web of the rail. Growth of the induced crack over the first 10 mm occurred over a
curved surface indicating an initial horizontal
crack component which could have been induced during the first test under a pure rolling load. A

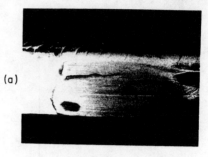

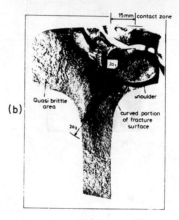

Figure 22

horizontal crack approximately 40 mm in length was
also present at the lower edge of the transverse
defect. Crack growth had occurred towards the port
side of the defect, i.e. in the opposite direction
to the crack present at the nucleation point of the
defect. The position of the crack is indicated by
the drawn line in Figure 23(a). The figure also
shows the crack in a transverse section cut 5 mm
away from the original transverse defect. Figure
23(b) shows the exposed crack surfaces. It is
possible that growth of this defect also occurred
during the first test.

Specimen 3 was tested for 466 000 cycles at which
time failure occurred. Figure 24(a) shows the
fracture surface of the sample, with the original
and new crack growth fronts having been outlined.
As in specimen 1, the only indication of a transition between the two regions was observed at the
lower edge of the original transverse defect and
was associated with the 45° shoulder mentioned
previously. The original defect had grown a distance of 26 mm across the rail head from the nucleation point and a further 22 mm in the rolling load
machine, i.e. at an average growth rate of 4.72×10^{-5} mm/cycle. The size of the defect at fracture
was an average of 47 mm from the nucleation point,
which is equivalent to the critical size of defects
in track as mentioned in Section 3.1.

For comparison, one of the defects which had

Session 303
Paper I.1

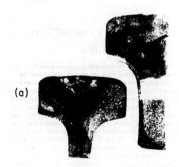

Figure 23

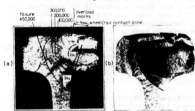

Figure 24

reached critical size in track (No. 14) is shown in Figure 24(b). It is evident that the general shape of the crack front of the two defects is very similar. In the simulated defect crack growth has extended into the web section of the rail slightly more than in the track defect, indicating that the ratio of lateral to normal stress obtained in the laboratory tests should be increased.

The fracture surface of the specimen showed signs of the overloads imposed on the specimen at 100 000, 200 000 and 300 000 cycles. The positions of the overload marks are shown in Figure 24(a). The distance between the first and last marks was 7½ mm, indicating an average crack growth rate of 3.75×10^{-5} mm/cycle. The distance between the last mark and the critical crack front was 8 mm indicating an average crack growth rate of 4.8×10^{-5} mm/cycle.

Figure 24(c) shows the lateral growth data obtained by ultrasonic testing and the position of the three overload marks. The growth rates measured from the curve in segments A, B and C were 3.2×10^{-5}, 6.1×10^{-5} and 6.7×10^{-5} mm/cycle respectively. These growth rates are slightly higher than those calculated from observation of marks on the fracture surface of the defect. However, they are in agreement with the average growth rate of the simulated crack, i.e. 4.72×10^{-5} mm/cycle.

4   DISCUSSION

4.1   Metallographic Study

The study has shown that the nucleation of transverse defects and associated shells in standard rails is a subsurface phenomenon, occurring at a common point situated at a depth of 5 - 7 mm below the gauge corner of the rails. Both crack types are therefore in no way related to gauge corner check cracks which initiate at the surface of the rails and which grow much closer to the surface.

Large (> 30μm in diameter), elongated, exogenous Al-Ca-Mn(SiO_2) inclusions were invariably present at the point of nucleation of the defects. Similar observations have been made by Sonon et al (1977) on examining equivalent fatigue defects in rails manufactured in U.S.A. These inclusions contain cracks in the transverse plane, presumably as a result of the subsurface microstructural deformation which, as mentioned by Marich and Curcio (1976), develops in the head of rails due to wheel/rail forces and extends to a depth of 10 mm from the gauge corner. These cracks are equivalent to notches and as such are potential nucleation sites for fatigue crack growth. Indeed it has been illustrated that in certain cases the cracks in the inclusions propagate into the surrounding steel matrix.

The current findings are in general agreement with those of Ito and Kurihara (1965), Heller (1971) and Zolatarsky and Rauzin (1971), all of whom have emphasised the adverse effect of inclusions on the fatigue damage in rails. Previous research work on the fatigue properties of bearing steels has also clearly shown that exogenous inclusions and calcium aluminates have the most deleterious effect on fatigue life.

By considering the various maximum stresses which are acting at the point of defect nucleation and the material properties, it is possible to use fracture mechanics formulae to give an indication of the minimum or threshold crack size in the material that will lead to fatigue crack propagation.

As discussed in detail by Johns and Davies (1975), rails in service are subjected to both longitudinal tensile and shear stresses. Therefore crack propagation, at least in the initial stages, occurs in Mode I (tension) and Mode II (in-plane shear) loading. Data reported by Shah (1974) indicates that under conditions of mixed loadings, the effective stress intensity factor (K_{ef}) for a crack is simply the sum of the stress intensity factors associated with each mode of loading, i.e.

$$K_{ef} = K_I + K_{II} \qquad (1)$$

The formulae for K_I and K_{II} are given by Rooke and Cartwright (1974). For the case of a circular crack of radius, a, in a solid under a uniform tensile stress (σ) and shear stress (τ):

$$K_I = 2\sigma \sqrt{\frac{a}{\pi}} \qquad (2)$$

$$\text{and} \qquad K_{II} = 0.8 \tau \sqrt{\pi a} \qquad (3)$$

Broek and Rice (1977) have determined the maximum threshold stress intensity factor (Kmax th) for rails of standard composition to be 14.8 MPa√m. Combining equations 1, 2 and 3 gives

$$K_{max\ th} = 14.8 = 2\sigma \sqrt{\frac{a_{th}}{\pi}} + 0.8 \tau \sqrt{\pi a_{th}} \qquad (4)$$

where a_{th} is the minimum radius of a crack which will lead to fatigue crack propagation.

Values for σ and τ, applicable to MNM railway, have been determined as follows;
σ is the sum of longitudinal tensile stresses obtained from
(a) lateral and vertical bending of the rails during the passage of wheels (σ_{LV}). In track measurements have shown that in some trains at least 1% of wheels give rise to σ_{LV} values of 80 to 100 MPa.

(b) thermal contraction of the rails on cooling below the stress free temperature of welding (σ_T). In-track data indicates temperature differences of up to 50°C leading to σ_T values of up to 110 MPa.

(c) residual stresses (σ_R). The ORE (1973) has shown that new rails exhibit tensile σ_R values of up to 210 MPa near the running surface. However, due to the microstructural deformation which occurs in the rail head, the residual stresses become compressive near the surface but remain tensile at a depth greater than 6 mm. The only data available on subsurface σ_R near the gauge corner of worn rails have been those of Mannin (1949) who quotes values of 140 MPa measured at a depth of 3 mm below the gauge corner. Without more accurate data, for this analysis σ_R is assumed to be 140 MPa.

Therefore $\sigma = \sigma_{LV} + \sigma_T + \sigma_R = 340$ MPa $\qquad (5)$

By applying the equations of Thomas and Hoersch, as presented by Timoshenko and Goodier (1970), for the contact case of new wheels on new rails and for measured maximum wheel loads of 200 kN, it was found that

$$\tau = 530 \text{ MPa} \qquad (6)$$

By combining equations 4, 5 and 6.

$$2 \times 340 \sqrt{\frac{a_{th}}{\pi}} + 0.8 \times 530 \sqrt{\pi a_{th}} = 14.8 \quad (6)$$

i.e. $\qquad a_{th} = 0.17$ mm

According to the above analysis, cracks with diameters less than about 0.3 mm would not lead to fatigue crack propagation. This value is considerably greater than the diameters of the majority of exogenous inclusions observed near the nucleation point of the defects. However, the dimension is similar to the height of the step observed at the nucleation site of most defects. As mentioned in Section 3, numerous exogenous inclusions were observed on the step. This indicates that the clustering of exogenous inclusions also plays a major role in the initiation of transverse defects. In this respect, the work of Brooksbank and Andrews (1972) on tessellated stress fields around inclusions has shown that the effective area of influence is within an area of radius 4r from the inclusion centre (for an inclusion of radius r) and therefore because of the possibility of overlapping stress fields, segregation and clustering of smaller inclusions can lead to detrimental effects on fatigue life. In the current work it was clearly shown that the inclusions present on the step were well within the sphere of influence mentioned above.

It is proposed that in a very few cases an exogenous inclusion is sufficiently large to nucleate transverse defects. In such cases simultaneous growth of the fatigue crack in both longitudinal and transverse planes will occur giving rise to a shelly crack and a transverse defect respectively.

The inclusions, however, are aligned and elongated in the rolling direction of the rail. Thus because of the effect of shape on stress intensity, a longitudinal crack would tend to nucleate first. Furthermore, Broek and Rice (1977) have shown that crack growth along the longitudinal plane occurs at a faster rate than on the transverse plane. Therefore, it is more likely that in the initial stages of crack development a shelly crack grows along a number of inclusion lengths until it reaches a cluster of inclusions which has developed a transverse crack component. At this point the crack will branch and give rise to a transverse defect.

As mentioned in Section 3, rail steels produced in the semi killed condition also contain indogenous manganese sulphide and manganese silicate inclusions. In the samples examined there was no indication that these inclusion types were associated with the nucleation of transverse defects, presumably because of their small size (generally considerably less than 30 µm in diameter) and deformation characteristics, i.e. their ability to deform without cracking. However, some of the indogenous inclusions were observed to nucleate longitudinal cracks. It is therefore suggested that such indogenous inclusions could be potential nucleation sites for shelly cracks, depending on the stresses developed in the rail head and the size and distribution of the inclusions present. A further study is in progress to determine the nucleation and growth characteristics of shelly cracks which are not associated with transverse defects.

The obvious conclusion which could be made from the current study is that to prevent the in-service initiation of transverse fatigue defects, clusters of exogenous stringer inclusions having diameters

Session 303
Paper I.1

greater than about 30 μm would have to be eliminated from the steel or at least detected in the rails after manufacture. However, as Barsom and Imhof (1977) have pointed out, the detection of such small discontinuities is beyond the capabilities of presently available non-destructive inspection procedures. The number of deleterious inclusions in the steel could be reduced by adopting more refined steel making practises such as producing the steel in the fully killed hot topped condition, bottom pouring and vacuum degassing. However, as yet there is no data which can be used to ecomonically assess the possible advantages associated with such processes.

Considerable laboratory and in-track evidence has been obtained showing the increase in resistance to shelling exhibited by high strength alloy or heat treated steels. It is proposed that the occurrence of transverse defects may also be reduced by improving the mechanical properties of rail steels and in particular : yield and tensile strengths, work hardening characteristics and wear resistance.

As mentioned previously, the initial cracking of exogenous inclusions is enhanced by the subsurface microstructural deformation which occurs in the rail head. The current in-track rail assessment programme at MNM has shown that in high strength rails the depth of deformation is reduced considerably. This is expected to lead to an equivalent reduction in the number of potential nucleation sites for transverse defects.

An increase in resistance to deformation would also delay the development of adverse residual stresses in the rail head. Indeed, O.R.E. data (1973) indicates that in worn high strength rails longitudinal residual stresses are compressive throughout the head. This would reduce considerably the value of σ in equation 5 and therefore increase the threshold crack size. A further reduction in the value of σ would be obtained by a reduction in the vertical and bending stresses associated with lower wear rates.

4.2 Rolling Load Tests

The preliminary tests showed that growth of relatively large (30 mm in diameter) transverse defects will not occur under a pure rolling stress mode. Thus, although contact stresses play a considerable role in the nucleation and initial crack propagation stages they have negligible influence during later growth. Pure rolling conditions, on the other hand, do enhance growth of horizontal or shelly type cracks.

Continued growth of transverse defects was successfully obtained with the introduction of tensile bending stresses. As mentioned in Section 3.3, there was no noticeable transition between original and simulated crack, with the growth front of the latter maintaining a shape similar to that of transverse defects which develop in-track.

The average lateral crack growth rate obtained in the two transverse defects grown in the rolling load machine was: 5.2×10^{-5} mm/cycle. Using this value growth of a transverse defect from a size which is readily detectable by ultrasonic inspection, for example 25 mm, to the critical size of about 45 mm would require 3.85×10^5 stress cycles. This is equivalent to 623 loaded trains or 62 days of operation, assuming that each wheel gives rise to tensile bending stresses of 100 MPa (actually an average of 8% of the wheels have been

found to cause bending stresses equal or greater than 100 Mpa). It is felt that this period could be reduced considerably by the affects of thermal and residual stresses which were not taken into account in this preliminary study.

To obtain an indication of the influence of maximum stress level on crack growth rate, the following expression may be used:

$$\int_{N_2}^{N_2} dN = N = \int_{a_1}^{a_2} \frac{da}{C\Delta K^m}$$

The formula is an extension of the general Paris equation for fatigue crack growth. The stress intensity factor range term, ΔK, has been calculated using an expression by Shah (1974) for an elliptical defect in a pure bending mode. The limits a_1 and a_2 are the initial and final semi major axes of the defect respectively and the term N is the number of cycles required to grow the crack between these limits. The material constants c and m were obtained by determining crack growth rates in compact tension specimens.

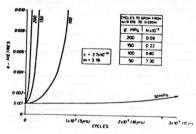

	CYCLES TO GROW FROM $a=0.016$ TO 0.020m
σ MPa	N x 10^3
200	0.09
150	0.22
100	0.80
50	7.30

$c = 2.7 \times 10^{-13}$
$m = 3.16$

Figure 25

The results obtained by successively integrating the above equation for $a_1 = 1$ mm and values of a_2 up to 20 mm for various maximum stress levels are shown in Figure 25. The effect of stress (indicated on each curve) is evident. For example: as shown in the table, at a stress of 100 MPa 80×10^4 cycles would be required to grow a crack from 1 mm to 20 mm while at 200 MPa only 9×10^4 cycles would be required.

Further testing in the rolling load machine is continuing and more details results will be reported in a future publication.

5 CONCLUSIONS

(a) Nucleation of transverse defects and associated shells in rails is a subsurface phenomenon.
(b) Single or more commonly clusters of complex exogenous silicate inclusions nucleate both crack types.
(c) Fracture mechanics formulae have been used together with stress conditions in the rails and material properties to show that the threshold crack size is about 0.3 mm.
(d) The development of transverse defects in rails may be reduced by adopting more refined steel making practices and/or improving the mechanical properties of rail steels.
(e) To obtain crack growth of large defects, tensile stresses due to bending have to be present. Stresses due to pure rolling do not contribute to defect growth.

6   ACKNOWLEDGEMENTS

The work was conducted as part of a joint railroad research programme between the Mt. Newman Mining Co., Hamersley Iron Pty. Ltd. and The Broken Hill Proprietary Co. Ltd. The authors are grateful to all three companies for permission to publish the work.

7   REFERENCES

BARSOM, J.M. and IMHOF, E.J. (1977). Fatigue and fracture behaviour of carbon - steel rails, technical report No. 2. Prepared for AISI-AAR-AREA Ad Hoc Committee on Rail Research.

BEDFORD, A.J., WINGROVE, A.L. and THOMPSON, K.R.L. (1974). The phenomenon of adiabatic shear deformation. J. Australian Inst. Met., Vol 19, pp 61-73

BROEK, D. and RICE, R.G. (1977). Fatigue crack growth properties of rail steels. Battelle's Columbus Labs.— Rep. No. DOT-TSC-1076. Prepared for U.S. Dept. of Transportation, Federal Railway Administration.

BROOKSBANK, D. and ANDREWS, K.W. (1972). Stress fileds around inclusions and their relation to mechanical properties. J.I.S.I., Vol. 210, pp 246 -253

HELLER, W. (1971). The development and further development of the quality and service properties of modern rail steels. ETR Eisenbanntechnishe Rundschau, Jan./Feb. pp 71-78.

HENRY, R.J. (1970). The cause of white etching material outlining shell type cracks in rail heads. A.R.E.A. Proc., Vol. 71, pp 682-688.

ITO, A. and KURIHARA, R. (1965). Shelling of rails experienced in Japanese Railways. Permanent Way Soc. of Japan, Vol. 8, pp 17-32.

JOHN, T.J. and DAVIES, K.B. (1975). Preliminary description of stresses in railroad rails. Battelle's Columbus Labs. Rep. No. G-6266-0101, Prepared fo U.S. Dept. of Transportation, Federal Railway Administration.

KIESSLING, R. and LANGE, N. (1966). Non-metallic inclusions in steel - part II. I.S.I. Special Pub. 100, pp 27-86.

MANNING, G.K. (1949). Summary report on the examination of shelled rails. A.R.E.A. Proc., Vol 50, p 542.

MARICH, S. and CURCIO, P. (1976). Development of high strength rail steels suitable for heavy duty applications. BHP Melbourne Research Labs. Rep. MRL/083/76/025.

O.R.E. (1973). Behaviour of the metal of rails and wheels in the contact zone. Question C53, Report No. 8. Oct.

RAVITSKOYA, T.M. (1974). Features of the intiation and development of internal fatigue cracks considered on the examples of rail failure. Strength of Materials, Vol. 6, pp 1374-1378.

ROOKE, D.P. and CARTWRIGHT, D.J. (1976). Compendium of stress intensity factors. London, Her Majesty's Stationary Office.

SHAH, R.G. (1974). Fracture under combined modes in 4340 steel. ASTM STP 560, pp 29-52.

SONNON, D.E., PELLEGRINO, J.V. and WANDRISCO, J.M. (1977). Metallurgical examination of carbon steel rails with service development defects, technical report No. 1. Prepared for AISI-AAR-AREA Ad Hoc Committee on Rail Research.

TIMOSHENKO, S. and GOODIER, J.N. (1970). Theory of elasticity, 3rd ed. New York, McGraw Hill.

ZOLATARSKY, A.F. and RAULIN, Ya, R. (1971). Increasin the strength of rails and their reliability in service on the railways of U.S.S.R. Rail Interational Dec. pp 908-915.

Session 308
Paper I.4

PROBABILITY ANALYSIS OF RAIL DEFECT DATA

P. M. BESUNER

D. H. STONE

K. W. SCHOENEBERG

M. A. DE HERRERA

SUMMARY   Rail defect data from six locations on American railroads are summarized and analyzed using cumulative probability techniques. Relations for defect occurrence as function of traffic and stress are developed.

1   INTRODUCTION

Six test sites were selected for an analysis of rail failure statistics. The six test sites carried average annual tonnages of 21 to 36 million gross tonnes (MGMT) (23 to 40 million gross tons (MGT) per year. Freight train speeds were as high as 127 Km/h (79 mph), and a significant percentage of axle loads were 30 tonnes (32.9 tons). Table I gives the details of each site.

The data comprise 1160 rail failures and defects rejected during inspection of the six test sites by detector cars at least annually (usually quarterly) and by weekly visual inspections. The objective of the analysis was to perform an engineering statistical analysis of the defect data in order to estimate the underlying time-to-occurrence probability distributions governing defect occurrence, and to compare the defect occurrence probability distributions for various rail locations, defect types and rail sections.

2   CUMULATIVE PROBABILITY DISTRIBUTION OF DEFECT OCCURRENCE--RAW DATA AND PLOTTING METHOD

Figure 1 shows the general format of reducing and interpreting the defect data provided by the Association of American Railroads (AAR). The independent variable plotted along the abscissa is the usage of the rail in MGT. The dependent variable plotted along the ordinate is the cumulative probability, PD(MGT), of a defect occurring at or before a given value of MGT usage.

2.1   Rail Usage Unit

In reference [1], definition of nominal rail life in terms of gross tonnage and wear, rather than an arbitrary 60-year life, is recommended. It is evident that the nominal rail life is more appropriately defined in terms of usage and wear rather than an arbitrary number of years; use of the MGT parameter is obviously a step in this direction. However, the MGT parameter does not differentiate between the cases of (1) a certain number (say m) of heavy wheel loads of magnitude P and (2) say twice this number (2m) of smaller wheel loads of magnitude P/2. It is well known that for most wear-out phenomenona, including fatigue crack initiation and propagation, the heavier wheel load of case (1) is far more damaging to the rail than the larger number of lighter loads of case (2). It was estimated in earlier work [1] that the crack propagation rate da/dN is proportional approximately to the fourth power of stress. This relationship suggests that an _effective_ usage parameter, $MGT_{effective}$ given by

$$MGT_{effective} = \left[\sum_{\substack{\text{all} \\ \text{wheel} \\ \text{loads}}} \left[MGT^4_{\substack{\text{each} \\ \text{wheel}}} \right] \right]^{\frac{1}{4}}$$

(1)

could provide a far better description of rail damage and usage than MGT alone. Obviously, the use of Equation (2.1) would require a somewhat detailed knowledge of the load spectra for the particular rail location being studied. Although significant load spectra data are being developed, these data are not available in time for development herein of a usage parameter, such as $MGT_{effective}$. Therefore, MGT has been chosen to characterize rail usage and wear, and it is recommended that a better usage parameter, such as given in Eq. (1), be applied to reanalyze these defect data in the future. The usage parameter would be a semi-empirical function of gross tonnage, speed, and curvature such that the damage level (wear, defect, and failure rate) can be expressed in terms of $MGT_{effective}$ alone. It is expected that an expression of usage in terms of $MGT_{effective}$ would minimize the railroad-to-railroad and location-to-location variation of the defect occurrence probability distribution and rates. However, for the six rail locations studied, the defect rate, when expressed in terms of MGT, varies only mildly as shown in Table I where the rates of six rail locations show a five-fold difference from a low 2.5 (SF1) to a high of 12.3 (UP2A) defects per track mile per MGT.

2.2   Structural Unit

Session 308
Paper 1.4

TABLE I

SUMMARY OF RAIL DEFECT TEST SITES

	Code	Site Length km	Site Length mi	Rail Age yrs	Total Traffic MGMT	Total Traffic MGT	Rail Weight Kg/m	Rail Weight lb/yd	Number of Defects	Defect Rate
Union Pacific Nebraska Division East Bound	UP1	94.9	59.0	19	529	583	66	133	237	6.9
Union Pacific Nebraska Division West Bound	UP2	100.9	62.7	18	369	407	66	133	210	8.2
Union Pacific Nebraska Division West Bound	UP2A	82.2	51.1	19	614	677	66	133	427	12.3
Union Pacific Wyoming Division East Bound	UP3	87.5	54.4	8-20	360	397	66	133	114	5.3
Santa Fe New Mexico Division	SF1	35.9	22.3	16	581	640	68	136	35	2.5
Santa Fe Los Angeles Division	SF2	46.8	29.1	16	467	515	59	119	133	8.9

As described in reference [1], the choice of a proper structural unit can be an important part of any structural proba- bility analysis. For interpretation of the defect occurrence data, the only important constraints on this choice are that (1), preferably, the structural unit be a natural one, such as one rail, and (2) the size of the unit should be small enough that the probability of more than one defect in this unit be negligible compared to the probability of no defects or one defect. To comply with these constraints, a 39-foot railroad rail has been chosen as the structural unit. Thus, in Figure 1, the ordinate should be interpreted as the probability of the first defect occurring in the 39-foot rail at or before a given MGT usage.

2.3 Plotting Position

The choice of the structural unit provides a basis for nomalizing the defect data and a simple method for calculating the cumula- tive probability plotting position. In this study, which deals with the first few percent of rail defect occurrences, the mean-rank plotting position is used for its scope and simplicity, as recommended by Gumbel in his book [2] on extreme value order statistics. The mean-rank, for data with no suspended items*, is given by

$$PD(MGT) = i/(n + 1) \qquad (2)^{**}$$

where i = the order number of the MGT value of the defect (that is whether the defect's MGT occurrence value is lowest, second lowest,..., ith lowest, etc.), and n is the total number of rails subject to a defect. Since the length of a U. S. rail is known to be 39 feet, the number of rails "n" in a given rail test location is computed easily

*Asterisks are in reference to footnotes

from, n = Number of track miles x 270.8 rails/track mile

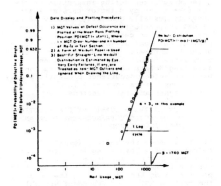

Fig. 1 - Schematic Description of Rail Defect Data Reduction and Disply

2.4 Raw Data

2.4.1 Summary Tables

Table I has been introduced previously to summarize the rail defect statistics of the Union Pacific and Santa Fe Railroads. The six rail test locations produced approxi- mately 1,160 rails which had either failed (broken or undergone severe plastic de- formation) or more frequently had been rejected by an inspector and replaced. Such failed and rejected rails are called "defects." Location SF1 had 35 defects, the lowest frequency of the six rail sections. This section also had the lowest defect rate (2.4×10^{-3} defects per track mile per MGT (mi^{-1} MGT^{-1})). Locations SF2, UP1, UP2 and UP3 had intermediate defect rates ranging from 5×10^{-3} to 9×10^{-3} mi^{-1} MGT^{-1}. Location UP2A has the largest defect rate of 12.3×10^{-3} mi^{-1} MGT^{-1}. Although several causes of the mild but statistically significant difference in defect rates could be speculated, one obvious consideration is the character of the stress spectrum as discussed previously in Section 2.1. Some evidence of this dependence on stress spectra is available if the almost four-fold difference in defect rate from SF1 to SF2 is noted. SF1 and SF2 have similar traffic patterns as shown in Table II, but different rail weights (136 lb/yd for SF1 and 119 lb/yd for SF2). In Section 3.1, the performance of the lower stress rail of SF1 is contrasted in more detail with the performance of the higher stress rail in location SF2.

In Table III the number of defects is given as a function of both rail test location

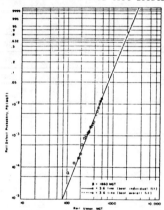

Fig. 2 - Cumulative Probability Distribution for Defects at the Union Pacific #1 Location

and defect type. Clearly, the most common defect by far in the rail test locations is the shell-initiated transverse defect, also known as the detail fracture shell (DFS). The DFS defect comprises at least 73% (850 of 1160) of all defects and occurs over eight times more frequently than either of the next two most frequent defects, the shell (9%) and the bolt hole break (8%).

3   CUMULATIVE PROBABILITY OF DEFECT
      OCCURRENCE--REDUCED PLOTS

3.1   Probability Distributions for the
        Six Rail Locations

The raw data summarized in Tables I through III have been plotted on two types of probability paper; one in which a straight line with positive slope indicates a Weibull life or usage distribution, and one in which the line represents a lognormal

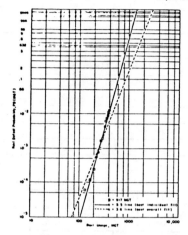

Fig. 3 - Cumulative Probability Distribution for Defects at the Union Pacific #2 Location

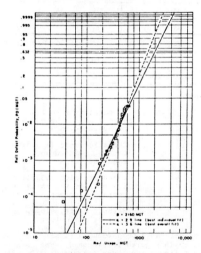

Fig. 4 - Cumulative Probability Distribution for Defects at the Union Pacific #2A Location

distribution. In general, the data are represented somewhat better by the Weibull distribution lines so that only the Weibull-type probability paper is used throughout the paper.

The two-parameter Weibull distribution is represented by the equation

$$PD(MGT) = 1 - \exp\left[-(MGT/\beta)^{\alpha}\right] \quad (3)$$
$$MGT, \beta, \alpha \geq 0$$

3

TABLE II

DISTRIBUTION OF CAR LOADS OVER SITES SF1 AND SF2 IN 1974

	Site SF1 Number	Percent	Site SF2 Number	Percent
No. of Cars > 119 Tonnes (131 Tons)	2,326	0.4	4,506	0.6
No. of Cars 100 to 119 Tonnes (110 to 131 Tons)	49,009	8.5	31,018	4.1
No. of Cars < 100 Tonnes (110 Tons)	527,217	91.1	721,757	95.3
Total	578,552	100.0	757,281	100.0
MGMT (MGT)	32.4	(35.7)	47.1	(51.9)
Average Car Weight, Tonnes (Tons)	56.0	(61.7)	62.1	(68.5)

TABLE III

NUMBER OF OCCURRENCES REPORTED OF DEFECT TYPES FOR SIX RAIL LOCATIONS

Rail Location Symbol (See Table I)	Defect Type Detailed Fracture Shell (DFS)	Bolt Hole Break (BHB)	Vertical Split Head (VSH)	Horizontal Split Head (HSH)	Compound Fissure (CF)	Shell (SH)	Others or Unclassified	Total Defects In Rail Location
UP1	197	25	12	2	1	4	0	241
UP1	177	4	0	0	0	11	18	210
UP2A	319	15	0	5	0	76	12	427
UP3	87	5	2	7	0	10	3	114
SF1	10	10	1	4	1	0	9	35
SF2	60	37	6	6	9	0	16	133
Total Number of	850	96	21	23	11	101	58	1160

where

PD(MGT) = Probability a rail will have a defect before undergoing usage, MGT

β = Characteristic (approximately, mean) usage required for a defect. β corresponds to the MGT value at which .632 (i.e., $1 - e^{-1}$) of the rails will contain a defect.

α = Weibull shape, slope, or scatter parameter.

The data have been reduced to six plots given in Figures 2 through 7. The data in each figure have been fit graphically with a straight line representing a best-fit Weibull distribution and another straight (broken) line of scatter parameter representing the best overall fit for slope for all six probability distributions taken as a group.

The defect occurrence or "failure" rate can be calculated from (3) as

$$\lambda(MGT) = \frac{1}{1-PD(MGT)} \frac{d(PD(MGT))}{d(MGT)} \quad (4)$$

so that

$$\lambda(MGT) = \frac{\alpha}{\beta^{\alpha}} MGT^{\alpha-1} \quad (5)$$

Thus, since $\alpha - 1 = 2.6$, the defect occurrence rate λ increases rapidly with usage, with λ proportional to $(MGT)^{2.6}$. Figure 8 illustrates this rapid increase for a rail location with average defect rate (Table I), the Union Pacific No. 1, for which $\alpha = 3.6$ and $\beta = 1860$ MGT.

A rapidly increasing defect rate and its attended low life scatter may be due to one or more of several possible causes.

.A life-limiting phenomenon in which damage is accumulated with time or usage such as fatigue initiation and growth, environmental attack, wear, and creep

.An increase in the number of rejectable defects due to tightening of inspection procedures at a given MGT level

.An increase in the number of rail failures due to running surface imperfections which "hide" subsurface defects [1]

.Progressive deterioration of track features such as ballast conditions

.Changes in tonnage, speed, and other relevant parameters that affect rail stress

Studies should concentrate on identifying

Session 308
Paper I.4

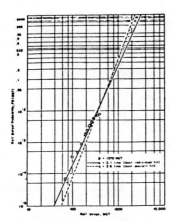

Fig. 5 – Cumulative Probability Distribution for Defects at the Union Pacific #3 Location

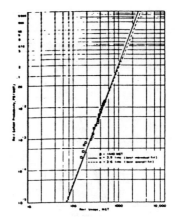

Fig. 7 – Cumulative Probability Distribution for Defects at the Santa Fe #2 Location

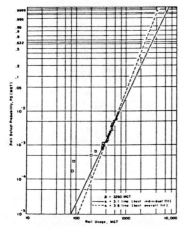

Fig. 6 – Cumulative Probability Distribution for Defects at the Santa Fe #1 Location

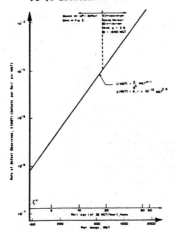

Fig. 8 – Relation Between Defect Occurrence Rate and Rail Usage for the Union Pacific #1 Site

the cause or causes of the increase in failure rate since extrapolations based on the Weibull distribution, as in Figure 8, indicate that rails in the six test locations studied will suffer an increase in the defect rate of more than ten-fold before they reach their initially projected useful life of 60 years. The most important task should be to analyze failed and rejected rail separately rather than in combination as herein. This should determine whether or not failure rate and rejection rate are increasing simultaneously.

In Figure 9, the best-fit probability distributions for the six rail test sections are replotted for comparison. Over the range of available data, only a 2:1 life variation for the six rail locations of maximum to minimum rail life is observed. All rail test sections show an increasing defect rate (α > unity) although the α value varies significantly from a low of 2.9 for rail location UP2A (indicating that the defect rate of UP2A, although currently highest of all six locations, will be surpassed eventually by those of other rail test locations), to a high value of 5.5 for

5

Session 308
Paper I.4

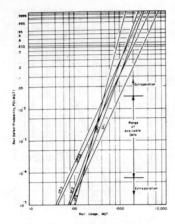

Fig. 9 - Best-Fit Cumulative Probability
Distribution for Defects at the
Six Rail Locations

rail location UP2. With reference to
Figure 9, and to Figures 4, 5, and 6, it
is of interest to note that the three rail
locations with the lowest values of slope
(and, hence, the most slowly increasing
defect rates) show a definite tendency of
further slope decrease in the last few
years (i.e., the probability distribution
curves deviate from a straight-line Weibull
and flatten out at the upper limit of the
data). This trend may indicate that more
than one population (i.e., high stress
rails versus low stress rails) occurs in
these three rail locations, as indicated
schematically in Figure 10. However, as
shown in Figures 2, 3, and 7, the three
rail test locations, UP1, UP2, and SF2,
are characterized by defect rates whose
large rates of increase have shown no
indication of slackening, in that straight
line Weibull distributions provide excellent fits of the data. It is believed
that much can be learned from comparing
the failure rate versus the usage characteristics of the six rail locations and

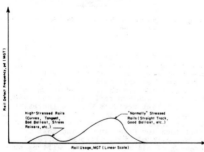

Fig. 10 - Schematic of a Possible Two-
Population Probability Density
Function of Rail Defects

correlating defect occurrence statistics
with known track features, usage, and
engineering facts about these locations.
In future studies, it would be helpful to
include rail locations showing greater life
differences than the six location reported
herein.

Although Weibull slopes vary significantly
for the rail locations, a single best-fit
slope of α = 3.6 was chosen to fit the data
in Figures 2 through 7. In Figure 11, all
six α = 3.6 lines are replotted for comparison. It may be seen that the lines
are fairly close together with the
characteristic lifetimes which vary over
the range,

$$1250 < \beta < 2350 \text{ MGT}, \qquad (6)$$

showing approximately a factor-of-two

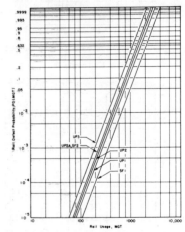

Fig. 11 - Cumulative Probability Distribution for Defects at the Six
Rail Locations (with α = 3.6)

difference in characteristic rail life, for
constant α, among all six rail test locations. It is of special interest to compare the Santa Fe #1 with the Santa Fe #2
defect probability distribution because,
as previously mentioned, the train make-up
and other relevant factors for the two rail
test sections are quite comparable with the
exception that the Santa Fe #2 section uses
rail of weight 119 lb/yd while the Santa Fe
#1 section uses a rail of weight 136 lb/yd.
In references [1, 5], it is hypothesized
that the life (in years) required for
defect occurrence should be inversely proportional to the stress level to the power
p where p = 4. This concept is also given
in [6] which used a model which is
analogous to roller bearing data to derive
a similar inverse proportionality between
life usage and stress with the exception
that p = 3.33 rather than 4.0.

Since the section modulus and moment of
inertia of the 119-lb/yd rail are 86% and

82% of the corresponding properties of the 136-lb/yd rail [8], it follows that, on average, the bending stresses in the 119-lb rail, determined from beam-on-elastic-foundation theory, should be approximately 110.5% of the 136-lb rail bending stresses. Thus, if bending stresses govern the growth of defects, the following life relationship should be true.

$$\frac{Life_{136}}{Life_{119}} = \frac{Life_{SF1}}{Life_{SF2}} = (1.105)^4 = 1.49 \qquad (7)$$

This ratio is in agreement with the 1.4-1.5 ratio of the SF1 and SF2 lives observed in Figures 6 and 7. This does not in itself imply that bending stress has more effect on rail performance than other stresses: The use of p = 4 may be in error, the assumption that SF1 and SF2 are equivalent except for rail weight may be wrong, and/or other stresses (e.g., contact) may vary with rail weight similarly to the bending component. Therefore, further work should be done to test the hypothesis in [5] that life is governed by contact and/or residual stresses rather than bending stresses using three-dimensional stress analysis as in [7], for the two rail weights.

3.2 Rail Life Variability

The standard deviation of log life (in time or MGT) may be calculated from the equation

$$s = \text{std. dev. } (\log_{10} MGT) = \qquad (8)$$
$$\frac{\pi}{6 \ln 10} \; \frac{1}{\alpha} = .557/\alpha$$

Recall that the "all defects" and dominant DFS defect probability distributions are described adequately by $\alpha = 3.6$. The standard deviation for $\alpha = 3.6$ is

$$s = .557/3.6 = 0.155 \qquad (9)$$

a value which is less than the typical value s = 0.196 derived in equation (5) and reference [8]. The 0.196 value is representative of material variability among carefully controlled laboratory tests on steel crack-initiation specimens tested under nominally identical constant amplitude cyclic loading. Consequently, it may be speculated that the life variation or scatter in the range of MGT values from 200-700 is due mostly to material variations from rail to rail for a given rail test location. Thus, the contribution of variable track features and other causes of stress variation under given MGT and usage spectrum may not have a dramatic influence on the defect rate for this range of MGT values. On the other hand, according to [9], the logarithmic standard deviation associated with crack propagation is of the order 0.105, a value significantly less than the above 0.196 value. Thus, if it can be shown that the majority of life is spent growing rather than initiating the crack (a subject of great debate in a recent rail conference [10]), then sources other than material variation would be responsible for approx-

imately S_0 life variation. S_0 may be estimated from

$$S_0^2 = S^2 - S_{mp}^2 = (0.155)^2 - (0.105)^2 \qquad (10)$$

or

$$S_0 = 0.114 \qquad (11)$$

where

S = Standard deviation of log life (total)

S_{mp} = Standard deviation of log life caused by material crack growth variation

S_0 = Standard deviation of log life caused by other causes

Thus, intrinsic material crack propagation variation would be responsible for half the scatter, leaving other causes responsible for the second half.

In summary, it is clear that the data show a rapidly increasing defect occurrence rate for MGT range of 200-700. This may indicate a fatigue or similar wear-out phenomenon is dominant. Further, if the current data are extrapolated, assuming no changes in railroad logistics or inspection procedures, the rate of defect occurrence is calculated to increase ten-fold before the 8-20 year old rails under study reach an age of 60 years.

The analysis of rail life variability or scatter given above does not separate failed from rejected rails. We recommend that the scatter analysis be repeated for failed rail only. The proposed failed-rail analysis will determine if the very interesting and important trends of low life scatter and rapidly increasing defect rate discussed above are (1) real manifestations of the rail fatigue life or (2) artifacts of the inspection procedures.

4 CONCLUSIONS

1. The probability distribution of occurrence of rail defect, as a function of rail usage measured in millions of gross tons (MGT) of traffic is well fit by the untruncated two-parameter Weibull distribution, except for occasional early (first of ten thousand rails) defects.

2. For the six Union Pacific and Santa Fe Railroad rail locations investigated, there is a five-fold or less difference in cumulative percent of defective rails at a given value of MGT (200 < MGT < 650).

3. Similarly, there is a two-fold or less difference in life (MGT) required for a given cumulative percent of defective rails among the six rail locations.

4. The above differences in rail defect rates and lives among the six rail locations are statistically and economically significant, but are not extremely large.

Session 308
Paper I.4

5. The rail-to-rail life variation within any of the six rail locations is surprisingly small. The estimated average value of Weibull slope or scatter parameter of $\alpha = 3.6$ corresponds to a standard deviation of life ($\log_{10}$ MGT) of $S = 0.16$. The 0.16 value lies between typical values for steel specimens (under constant amplitude and carefully controlled laboratory loads) of $S = 0.11$, for crack propagation, and $S = 0.02$, for crack initiation life variations.

6. Since failed (i.e., ruptured) rails and rejected rails could not be analyzed separately, it cannot be determined whether the trends of low life scatter and rapidly increasing defect rate are (1) real manifestations of the rail fatigue life phenomena or (2) artifacts of the inspection procedures. Therefore, a separate analysis of failed and rejected rails is recommended to determine whether or not failure and rejection rates are increasing simultaneously.

7. The trend of low rail-to-rail life scatter, if extrapolated to future performance indicates that the defect rate will increase at least ten-fold before the rails reach a projected useful life of 60 years.

8. More detailed load and stress data should be obtained in future studies since such data may explain most differences in rail location performance observed.

9. The dependence of the rate of derailments per rail failure on such parameters as defect type, defect proximity, and train/track features is not well understood and should be studied in future analyses of rail performance.

10. Future studies should include rail locations with greater differences than the six studied herein.

11. Shell-initiated transverse defects, also called detailed fracture shells (DFS), make up nearly three-quarters of the total defects observed for the six rail locations. The six rail locations considered consist of post-1956 rails only and apparently are not typical of older rails in which defects other than DFS occur most frequently.

12. Based on Conclusion 10, different models for different rail types and rail vintages will be required to perform optimized reliability analysis.

13. It is possible to apply the risk analysis and crack growth models developed in [1] to produce simulated rail defect data which is a close match of the actual data analyzed in this paper. This is accomplished by reducing preliminary estimates of initial defect size (by a factor of 2.5) or by including an estimate of the usage required to initiate fatigue cracks from metallurgical defects in

the model.

5   REFERENCES

1   D. P. Johnson and P. M. Besuner, "Engineering Cost Risk Analysis of Defective Rail", Association of American Railroads Report, R-2, January, 1977.

2   E. J. Gumbel, Statistics of Extremes, Columbia University Press, (New York, 1958).

3   C. Lipson and N. J. Sheath, Statistical Design and Analysis of Engineering Experiments, McGraw-Hill, (New York, 1973)

4   A. C. Cohen, "Maximum Likelihood Estimation in the Weibull Distribution Based on Complete and Censored Samples", Technometrics, 7, 1965, pp. 578-88.

5   P. M. Besuner, "Fracture Mechanics Analysis of Rails with Shell Initiated Defects" in Rail Steels-Processing, Development, and Use, D. H. Stone and G. G. Knupp, Editors, ASTM Special Technical Publication 644 (Philadelphia, 1978).

6   S. G. Guins, "Estimating the Effects of Heavy Wheel Loads: A Roller Bearing Analogy" ASME Paper 77-RT-9, March, 1977.

7   G. C. Martin and W. W. Hay, "The Influence of Wheel-Rail Contact Forces on the Formation of Rail Shells" ASME Paper 72-WA-RT-8, November, 1972.

8   C. C. Osgood, Fatigue Design, John Wiley & Sons (New York, 1970) p. 395.

9   P. M. Besuner, Unpublished Results from Statistical Analysis of Gas Turbine Aircraft Engine Rotor Crack Growth Rates, Pratt & Whitney Aircraft Division, United Technology Corporation, 1973-1974.

10   D. H. Stone and G. G. Knupp, Editors Rail Steels-Processing, Development, and Use, ASTM Special Technical Publication 644, (Philadelphia, 1978).

6   FOOTNOTES

*   If the usage of each of the n rails considered is equal to or greater than the MGT value at which the last defect was observed, then none of the rails are said to be suspended items. If only a few rails (i.e., new replacements) have MGT usage values less than the largest MGT value at which a defect was observed, then these suspended items (i.e., undefected rails) can be ignored with little or no error. However, if a substantial percentage (more than 10-20%) of the population are suspended items, care must be taken for parameter estimations and plotting position calculations must use either reasonable heuristic

procedures as given in [3] or rigorous
statistical estimation procedures as
given by [4].

** If there is no spatial correlation
of defects, the probable number of
defects in a rail is i/n and the
plotting position is PD(MGT) = 1 -
exp(-i/n) (Poisson distribution),
rather than PD(MGT) = i/(n+1). However for i<<n, as is true in this
study, the two formulas for PD(MGT)
give no significant numerical
differences.

Session 417
Paper I.8

THE CHARACTERISTICS AND CONTROL OF LONG PITCH RAIL CORRUGATION
AT HEAVY AXLE LOADS

R. I. MAIR

R. A. JUPP

R. GROENHOUT

SUMMARY   A study has been undertaken on the formation of long pitch rail corrugation at heavy axle loads. From spectral analyses of corrugation profiles and track vibrations a correlation has been noted between track/vehicle resonance and the dominant corrugation pitch.   It is concluded that corrugation development is best controlled by the use of high strength rails and recommendations are given on the strength level required for different wheel load/wheel diameter combinations.

1   INTRODUCTION

Periodic - or apparently periodic - undulations along the running surface of railway rails are well known to railway engineers.   In their shorter pitch form, 25-50 mm, they have been termed corrugations and contribute to the familiar title of "roaring rail".   As the name implies these corrugations are primarily considered to be a source of noise pollution, disturbing both passengers and residents living near the track, whilst not constituting a serious operating hazard.   It might broadly be said that these shorter pitch corrugations occur in systems operating with axle loads below 20 tonnes.   The traffic is frequently mixed freight and passenger, although severe cases of corrugation have been noted with tram car and underground passenger services.

Another class of undulation with pitches in the region of 200-300 mm has also adopted the term corrugation.   Their occurrence has been noted on light axle load passenger lines (Ref. 1), generally in areas immediately following a rail joint, but more commonly on heavier axle load services. Of the latter, high axle load unit train operations have shown a relatively high incidence of this form of deterioration.   Unlike the shorter pitch variety with light axle loads, the longer pitch type are considered by unit train operators to constitute a definite operating hazard.

The repeated dynamic loads which occur as each wheel traverses a region of corrugation (Ref. 2) promotes the accelerated growth in corrugation amplitude.   During the corrugation formation the increased wheel impact loads contribute to ballast deterioration and further, grinding of the rail head, which at present is the principal method of controlling corrugations, is both expensive and disruptive to operating schedules. Eventually, as the depth increases, the corrugations present a derailment possibility as a result of rail failure.

Several common features have been noted with unit train operations experiencing the longer corrugation type, namely;

(a)   heavy axle loads (generally above 25 tonne),

(b)   uniformly designed and equipped wagons with rigid bogies and snubbed spring systems, and

(c)   rail steel ultimate tensile strengths around 700 MPa.

Although these factors may indicate points to be wary of if corrugations are to be avoided, they do not completely specify the problem or suggest economical remedies.   The following sections of this paper cover field measurements and analyses conducted between 1972 and 1975 to identify the problem on the track of the Mt. Newman Mining Co. and outline the successful control of corrugation through the use of high strength rails for the particular operating conditions of that company.   The mechanism of corrugation development outlined and the procedure of control adopted are applicable to similar operations with unit train traffic.

2   FREQUENCY COMPONENTS OF RAIL CORRUGATION PROFILE

Long pitch rail corrugations are associated with gross plastic deformation of the rail head (Refs. 3, 4) and may occur on the high (Refs. 5, 6, 7) or low (Ref. 8) rail of curves and even tangent track, (Ref. 9) although infrequently.   Australian experience shows a predominance on the high rail irrespective of track superelevation or operating speed.   Cursory examination of the rail profile indicates a range of pitch lengths of apparently random occurrence (Fig. 1).   But, spectral analyses of lengths of rail head profile reveal that the deformation actually consists of a periodic wavelike pattern composed of several superimposed frequencies.

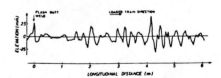

Fig.   1.   Corrugated Rail Head Profile

Detailed measurements have been made of the vertical rail head profile at four track locations (Table I).   The measuring apparatus consisted of a long straight edge clamped to the rail head and set horizontal with a precision spirit level.

Session 417
Paper I.8

TABLE I

TRACK PARAMETERS AT LOCATIONS OF CORRUGATION PROFILE MEASUREMENT

	Measurement Location			
	217.1 km	51.8 km	218.0 km	11.6 km
Degree of curvature	2°30'	Tangent	2°30'	2°
Curve length	966.5 m	N.A.	867.3 m	1273.8 m
Superelevation (Nominal)	70 mm	N.A.	70 mm	57 mm
AREA Theoretical Superelevation for 40 km/h	26 mm	N.A.	26 mm	20 mm
Gradient (%)	+0.13 215.1 km- 216.6 km . -0.03 216.6 km	+0.17 49.8 km- 51.1 km -0.20 51.2 km-	+0.13 215.1 km- 216.6 km -0.03 216.6 km-	+0.16 9.5 km- 11.3 km +0.09 11.3 km-
Ballast Depth (Minimum)	205 mm	205 mm	205 mm	205 mm
Ballast size	AREA No. 4	AREA No. 4	AREA No. 4	AREA No. 4
Sleeper Spacing centre-centre	533 mm	533 mm	533 mm	533 mm
Sleeper size	230x150x2590 mm	230x150x2590 mm	230x150x2590 mm	250x200x2515 mm
Sleeper type	Jarrah	Jarrah	Jarrah	Concrete
Rail size (AREA Profile)	66 kg/m	66 kg/m	66 kg/m	66 kg/m
Fastening Type	Spike	Spike	Spike	Pandrol
Track Gauge (Nominal)	1435 mm	1435 mm	1435 mm	1435 mm

TABLE II

OBSERVED CORRUGATION PITCH LENGTHS AND CORRESPONDING FREQUENCIES OF VIBRATION

Recording Location (km)	217.1	51.8	217.9	11.6	217.1	51.8	217.9	11.6
Length of Measured Profile (m)	96.1	40.7	11.6	107.0	96.1	40.7	111.6	107.0
Train Speed (km/h)	LOADED				EMPTY			
	40	56	43	40	48	64	64	50
Dominant Pitches Observed (mm) (Frequency at Designated Speed (Hz))	476-500 (23-22)	590-710 (26-22)	556 (22)	555 (20)				
					476-500 (28-27)	590-710 (30-25)	556 (32)	555 (25)
	313-323 (36-34)	420-430 (37-36)	319 (37)	322 (34)				
	250 (44)		275 (43)	270 (41)	313-323 (43-41)	420-430 (42-41)	385-429 (43-41)	322 (43)
		320-330 (49-47)	240 (49)					
	210 (53)		214 (55)	208 (53)	250 (53)	320-330 (56-54)	319 (56)	270 (51)
			195 (61)	181 (61)				
					210 (64)		275 (65)	208 (67)
							240 (74)	181 (76)

2

Readings were taken at 25 mm intervals with a dial gauge graduated to 0.01 mm overlapped to give a continuous record.

Data analysis consisted of computing power spectral density and auto-correlation functions; the former were calculated using both the Direct and Blackman-Tukey methods. To remove low frequency effects (for example due to the gradient of the track) the data were digitally filtered using a high-pass filter. All data were initially analysed at the sampling interval providing a maximum frequency of 20 cs/m (50 mm pitch). Since most of the spectral power is concentrated below 5 cs/m the data were generally decimated by discarding every second point. This effectively doubled the sampling interval to 50 mm and the maximum frequency reduced to 10 cs/m but the low frequency cut-off could be lowered to 1 cs/m and, by averaging the results for odd-numbered and even-numbered readings, the random error kept to a minimum. The power spectral density plots for each of the four locations are shown in Fig. 2 and a summary of the dominant frequency peaks given in Tables II for

the relevant loaded and empty train speeds.

It is apparent that the corrugation profiles consist of a limited number of superimposed frequencies which are not speed dependent and are common to both tangent and curved track. As a consequence it is reasonable to surmise that the component frequencies relate to track/vehicle resonant frequencies (Ref. 11) and that the mechanism of corrugation development is the same for both curved and tangent track. At this stage it should be recalled that a necessary (but not sufficient) condition for long pitch corrugation development is the presence of gross plastic flow. The predominance of corrugation in curves is due to the more severe contact stresses which exist to cause plastic flow (Ref. 3) and tangent track corrugations usually only arise when a soft rail is present. It is also observed that the corrugations are more pronounced near rail joints and progress along the track in the loaded train direction (Ref. 5).

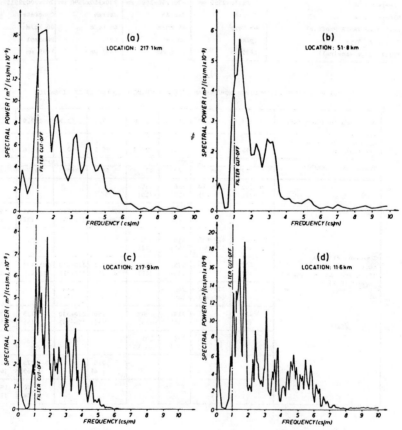

Fig. 2   Power Spectral Density Plots of Rail Corrugation Profile Data

Session 417
Paper I.8

3   OBSERVATIONS OF SYSTEM VIBRATIONS

An implication from the rail profile spectral
analyses is the excitation of track and vehicle
resonance which moulds the gross plastic flow,
from contact stress overload, into the characteristic corrugation pitch lengths (Ref. 12).   Confirmation of the occurrence of resonance has been
accomplished from spectral density plots of dynamic
records of rail and sleeper accelerations generated
by both loaded and empty unit ore trains over a
range of operating speeds on corrugated and uncorrugated track.   The track response data have been
compared with spectral density plots of axle box
lateral and vertical accelerations recorded from
instrumentation mounted on an operational ore car.

Loaded trains at standard speed on sections of well
maintained and corrugation free track generate a
broad spectrum of vibration frequencies when
analysed up to 400 Hz (Fig. 3).   There is, however,
evidence of bands of above average power particularly around 40 Hz, 230 Hz and 300 Hz, but
not sufficient to indicate resonance in the
frequency range of the corrugation pitch measurements.   On the other hand records taken on
corrugated track at the normal loaded train operating speed exhibit a very pronounced peak in the
spectral power density in the corrugation frequency range with sharp, but less dominant, peaks
in the same vicinity.   The record shown in Fig. 4
for the 217.9 km location indicates strong
vibrations at 53 Hz.   (Note carefully scales on
PSD axes).

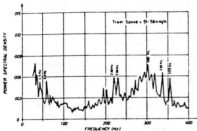

Fig. 3   Frequency Response of Uncorrugated
           Rail at Normal Operating Speed (16.1 km)

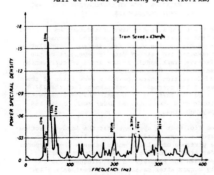

Fig. 4   Frequency Response of Corrugated Rail
           at Normal Operating Speed (217.9 km)

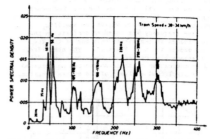

Fig. 5   Frequency Response of Corrugated Rail
           Below Normal Operating Speed (217.9 km)

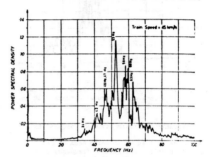

Fig. 6.   Frequency Response of Axle-Box Vertical
           Vibrations on Corrugated Track
           (217.9 km)

A similar record (Fig. 5) for the same location,
but at a speed below the normal operating speed,
does not display the same dominant vibration
frequency.   However, there is a correspondence
between the frequency peaks present in each case
indicating that the corrugation profiles are acting
as a forced vibration input.   An increase in
spectral power is generally evident at the higher
speed with the peak frequencies doubling in power.
The exception is the 53 Hz value which has a ten
fold increase over the related forced frequency of
46 Hz at the lower speed.   Simultaneous measurements on the sleepers also show the dominant frequency at 53 Hz but with little response above 80 Hz
(Ref. 17).

Spectral analysis of axle box vertical acceleration
in the range 0-100 Hz (Fig. 6) reveals a near
correspondence to the track spectra at close to the
same operating speed indicating that the track and
wheelset are vibrating together.   Indeed, the power
levels, which relate to acceleration amplitude, are
of similar level with the 53 Hz value again domina-
ting.

A further comparison of vibration response is also
given in Fig. 7 for the axle box vibration spectrum
on uncorrugated track at the 219 km location.   Of
note here is the reduction in vibration power ($^1/3$)
and the more pronounced drop in the nominal resonance power level at 53 Hz (a reduction to $^1/7$) again
illustrating the importance of corrugation presence
in promoting forced resonance.

Thus the rail head deformation occurs at a pitch

which corresponds to a system resonance which involves the total track and ore car components and acts as a forcing input for further corrugation development. However, whilst one specific resonant frequency was noted to dominate in the above traces it represents only one of the frequency groups shown in Table II. The other frequencies are also present in the vibration modes and an indication of their source can be obtained from a simplified analysis of the system dynamics.

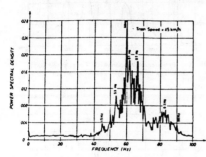

Fig. 7. Frequency Response of Axle-Box Vertical Vibrations on Uncorrugated Track (219 km)

4 THEORETICAL SYSTEM RESONANT FREQUENCIES

Treating the rail as an infinite beam on an elastic foundation, the natural frequency of the track may be calculated as (Ref. 11);

$$f_1 = \frac{1}{2\pi} \sqrt{k_1/m} \qquad (1)$$

where m is the effective track mass per rail and k_1 the spring stiffness of the track per rail. Within the range of practical track properties the resonant frequency is unaffected by axial load and has less than a 4 percent shift due to damping.

A simplified expression for the effective mass may be obtained from (Ref. 13) as;

$$m = m_1 + \frac{m_2}{1.89} \left[\frac{k_1}{4EI}\right]^{\frac{1}{4}} \qquad (2)$$

where m_1 = mass of vibrating track components per rail,
m_2 = unsprung vehicle mass per rail, and
EI = rail flexural stiffness,

which leads to a value of the single mass resonant frequency of;

$$f_1 = \frac{1}{2\pi} \left[\frac{k_1}{m_1 + \frac{m_2}{1.89}\left[\frac{k_1}{4EI}\right]^{\frac{1}{4}}}\right]^{\frac{1}{2}} \qquad (3)$$

An alternative analysis (Ref. 14) which allows for the linearized "contact spring" stiffness, k_2, between the wheel and rail results in the relationship;

$$f_1 = \frac{1}{2\pi} \left[\frac{1}{2}\left(\frac{k_1}{m_1} + \frac{2k_2\beta}{3m_1} + \frac{k_2}{m_2}\right) - \frac{1}{2}\sqrt{\left(\frac{k_1}{m_1} + \frac{2k_2\beta}{3m_1} + \frac{k_2}{m_2}\right)^2 - \frac{4k_2k_1}{m_1m_2}}\right]^{\frac{1}{2}}$$

$$\text{where } \beta = \left[\frac{k_1}{4EI}\right]^{\frac{1}{4}} \qquad (4)$$

Both functions give similar values for the single mass resonance (Fig. 8) and show the dependence on track modulus. In practice, however, the track is loaded by adjacent bogie wheels which vibrate in phase (bounce mode) or out of phase (pitch mode) to give two resonant frequencies. Modelling the system as two disconnected "unsprung" masses supported through the wheel/rail contact stiffness, on a damped beam on an elastic foundation Mair (Ref. 14) has computed the natural frequencies of rail vibration and these are compared with the single mass solutions in Fig. 8.

To complement the loaded track conditions the theoretical resonant frequencies for the unloaded track vibrations (allowing for sleeper and ballast mass) and the unloaded rail vibration are also plotted in Fig. 8.

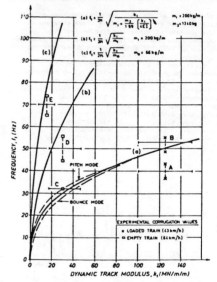

Fig. 8. Theoretical System Resonant Frequencies and Field Measured Values

5 CORRELATION BETWEEN CORRUGATION PITCH AND RESONANT FREQUENCIES

The preceding sections have considered the spectral content of rail corrugations and the resonant frequencies of the wheel/rail system. Correlation between the two sets of data is dependent on the effective track moduli in the areas of corrugation development. Measurements of the track static load-deflection characteristics were taken at the time of the corrugation measurements at the 217.9 km location (Ref. 7). Dynamic load and deflection records were also obtained under both loaded and empty vehicles.

From Fig. 9 it is apparent that the load-deflection response under static load is non-linear due to the presence of ballast voids beneath the sleepers. Under traffic loading the rail is permanently depressed and recovery to the unloaded position only occurs after passage of the rear axle (Fig. 10). The lack of displacement recovery between axles is a result of the increased wavelength of track deflection resulting from the lowered effective modulus due to the presence of voids

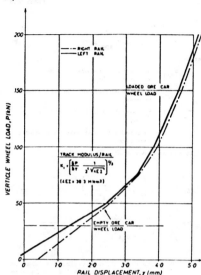

Fig. 9   Static Load-Deflection Plot of Corrugated
         Track (217.9 km)

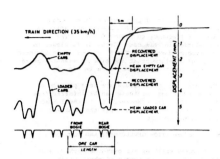

Fig. 10.   Track Deflection During Train
            Passage (217.9 km)

TABLE III

VALUES OF TRACK MODULUS CORRESPONDING TO
TRACK DISPLACEMENT (217.9 km)

Track Displacement Status	Static Track Modulus k_1
Mean Gross Wheel Load Displacement	40-60 MN/m/m
Recovered Displacement between Loaded Train Bogies	15-30 MN/m/m
Mean Tare Wheel Load Displacement	10-25 MN/m/m
Recovered Displacement between Unloaded Train Bogies	5-15 MN/m/m

(Ref. 15).   An estimate of the effective static
track modulus values can be obtained from Fig. 9
over the range of displacement under traffic
(Fig. 10) using;

$$k_1 = \left[\frac{\delta P}{\delta y} \cdot \frac{1}{2 \sqrt[4]{4EI}} \right]^{4}/3 \qquad (5)$$

derived from beam-on-elastic foundation analysis
where $\delta P/\delta y$ denotes the gradient over the load
increment δP.   Values of k_1 for the 217.9 km
location are listed in Table III.   Application
of the static values cannot be used directly in
in the analysis of track vibrations under dynamic
load as they have to be adjusted to give the
dynamic modulus values   (Ref. 16, 17) (Fig. 11).
It is observed that the dynamic modulus value can
be up to 2.5 times the static value at a wheel
load at 150 kN in the frequency range of 35-55 Hz
with lower ratios at lighter wheel loads or at
frequencies outside this range.

Adjusting the modulus values of Table III appropriately, the frequency data from Table II have
been superimposed on Fig. 8.   Corrugation pitches
around 320 mm (Group A) and 210 mm (Group B) are
evidently associated with loaded track resonances.
The Group A values, 35-45 Hz, are generally noted
to be more pronounced than the 45-55 Hz values in
the early stages of corrugation formation, at
which stage the track roughness is relatively low
and there is only slight bogie spring nest movement (Ref. 18).   Attenuation of vibrations
through the bogie friction wedge damping system is
not complete due to lack of activation and the
effective unsprung mass probably contains a
contribution from the body giving a lower than
predicted resonant frequency.   It is also possible that the full dynamic modulus is not developed at this stage, both factors accounting for the
variation between theory and observation.

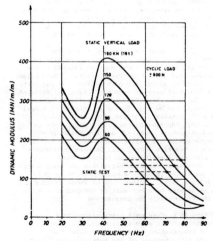

Fig. 11.   Variation of Dynamic Modulus with
            Frequency for Circular Plate (Ref. 16)

With development of corrugations the surface roughness increases with a consequent shift in dominant frequency to around 53 Hz. The correlation in this case (Group B) is closer to the predicted value. The 53 Hz was in an advanced stage of development at the time of measurement as evident from the frequency data in Fig. 4.

The remaining pitch values are less pronounced and correlations for these can be inferred from Fig. 8 (Ref. 7). However, it is the loaded train condition which controls the dominant corrugation profile.

6   CORRUGATION DEVELOPMENT AND CONTROL

Controversy still exists over the mechanism of initiation and development of short pitch corrugations. The situation is no more clear for the initiation of long pitch corrugations, although the observations noted above strongly support a mechanism of development by track resonance (Ref. 11). The development stage is reached once an adequate surface roughness exists and the formation of short pitch corrugations could be a transition stage arising from the excitation of contact vibrations (Ref. 19, 20). Indeed, close examination of rolling disc results in Ref. 20 shows an increase in pitch length with corrugation development towards a pitch corresponding to the support system resonance, which is analogous to track resonance in the field.

The necessary conditions for the development of long pitch corrugations involve both gross plastic deformation and the excitation of system resonance. Conversely, a sufficient condition exists for the control of corrugations by the avoidance of resonance or the prevention of plastic flow. In practical terms the rail track system is heavily damped with a value between 8 to 18 per cent of critical damping (Ref. 11) and it is not possible to damp out or remove all sources of vibration initiation e.g. rail joint impact. Consequently, the most acceptable approach to control of corrugations is to bring the wheel/rail stress levels and the rail steel flow resistance into balance. This can be achieved by reducing wheel loads (Ref. 21) or increasing the rail strength level (Ref. 3,12).

Within the terms of the above mechanism the formation of corrugations on either the high rail or the low rail of a curve must be related to the relative ease with which yield occurs. More severe conditions on either the high or low rail can occur as a result of several factors. King and Kalousek (Ref. 22) have identified a 'false flange' condition which can be significant in increasing normal low rail stresses. On the other hand, since wheel/rail tractive forces play a major role in yield initiation (Ref. 10) and the build up of deformation at the rail surface (Ref. 23) any variation in tractive forces will be more pronounced. An important contributor to tractive force differential arises from variations in bogie tracking due either to vehicle variations or track geometry effects. Discussion of these factors will not be covered here but will be treated in a related report currently in preparation.

Yielding to produce rail corrugations is a cumulative effect arising from multiple overloads and is dependent on both the mean axle load and the distributions of the vertical wheel loads with the associated creep and slip forces. The probability of yield can be expressed as (Ref.10);

$$Q = \text{Prob}(\sigma_{all} < \sigma_{app}) \qquad (6)$$

$$= \int_{-\infty}^{\infty} F_{all}(z) \, f_{app}(z) \, dz \qquad (7)$$

where,

σ_{all} = allowable wheel/rail normal contact stress,

σ_{app} = applied wheel/rail normal contact stress,

$F_{all}(z)$ = allowable stress probability function,

$f_{app}(z)$ = applied stress probability density function,

and it can be shown that;

$$F_{all}(z) = F_u \left(\frac{zm_{\mu'} - m_{\gamma'}}{\sqrt{s_{\gamma'}^2 + z^2 s_{\mu'}^2}} \right) \qquad (8)$$

$$f_{app}(z) = \frac{2z(\lambda^2 m_w s_p^2 + \lambda m p s_w^2 z^2)}{\sqrt{2\pi(\lambda^2 s_p^2 + s_w^2 z^2)^3}} \exp\left\{ \frac{-(\lambda m_p - m_w z^2)^2}{2(\lambda^2 s_p^2 + s_w^2 z^4)} \right\} \qquad (9)$$

in which F_u = the cumulative distribution function of the standard normal variable with mean zero and unit standard deviation,

m = mean of subscripted variable,

s = standard deviation of subscripted variable,

$Y' = 2.31 Y$,

$\mu' = 1/(1-\mu)$,

Y = material yield stress,

μ = wheel/rail coefficient of contact friction,

P = vertical, wheel load,

w = wheel/rail contact width,

$\lambda = 0.16E/(1-v^2)R$,

R = wheel radius,

v, E = Poisson's ratio and Young's modulus.

A critical factor in the application of equation (6) is the establishment of an acceptable probability of yield. For the Mt. Newman Mining Co. operations this was set at 0.08 based on observations from tangent track where corrugation was not a problem. Application of the above procedure then established for curved track a mean 0.2% proof stress of 745 MPa (670 MPa minimum proof stress) after allowing for work hardening effects in the rail steel. A number of rails with properties in this strength range have been under test by the Mt. Newman Mining Co. and have supported the analysis.

In most railway applications the operating parameters have been set and the available means of adjustment are usually limited to the replacement of the rail steel. On this basis Fig. 12 draws on the experience of the Mt. Newman Mining Co. to establish recommended mean 0.2% stress levels for systems having alternative combinations of mean wheel load, wheel load distribution and wheel diameter. The data presented can be used to prevent gross plastic flow leading to corrugation. However, it cannot be presumed that adoption of

Session 417
Paper I.8

the above strength levels will compensate for poor standards of track maintenance nor the presence of excessive vertical joint misalignment, both of which will contribute to more severe conditions than those present on the Mt. Newman System.

The data of Fig.12 can be used as a guide to the selection of required strength levels, however, for an accurate estimate the full reliability analysis should be used with the actual operating conditions.

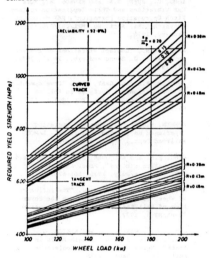

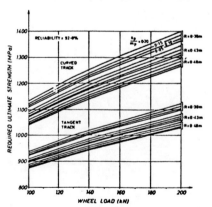

Fig. 12   Rail Strength Requirements to Avoid
           Corrugation (a) Yield
                        (b) Ultimate Tensile

7   SERVICE OBSERVATIONS WITH HIGH STRENGTH RAIL

Corrugations were first noticed on the Mt. Newman track on the high rail of a 600 metres radius curve, after a service tonnage of approximately 50 million gross tonnes. This curve was finally replaced

after 133 million gross tonnes of traffic at which time corrugations were also apparent on the low rail. Considerable grinding was necessary during the interim period.

Service experience with standard carbon rails shows that, depending on degree of curvature and service conditions, the rails need grinding at intervals of between 20 and 30 million gross tonnes to avoid serious track damage due to corrugations.

High strength rail steels installed in track for service evaluation in 1974 showed a marked resistance to corrugation. However, adjacent standard carbon rails laid at the same time in the same curve were seriously affected. Over longer periods of time minor undulations have been observed to form in high strength rails with a 0.2 per cent proof stress of up to 670 MPa, but in no instance have these developed into a defined corrugation profile. (These comments must, however, be qualified by pointing out that grinding of rail is currently undertaken in service on some rails to control head profile and to remove irregularities associated with hardness variations at thermit welds).

Additional trials (Ref. 24) of high strength rails with 0.2 per cent proof stress values of up to 1000 MPa introduced to control serious curve wear have shown increased resistance to deformation and on current evidence it can be said that such rails are completely effective in limiting the formation of serious corrugations. Rails of this strength level are now being introduced on all curves in the Mt. Newman mainline of 1000 metres radius and below

8   ACKNOWLEDGEMENTS

The authors acknowledge contributions of Mr. P. Townend to the identification of the corrugation problem and thank both the Mt. Newman Mining Co. and BHP for permission to report the above observations.

9   REFERENCES

1.   SMITH, T., "Rail and Road Corrugations", Public Transport Commission, Dept. of Railways, N.S.W., 1967.

2.   MEACHAM, H.C. and AHLBECK, D.R., "A Computer Study of Dynamic Loads Caused by Vehicle - Track Interaction", ASME Paper No. 69-RR-1, 1969.

3.   MARICH, S., "An Investigation of Worn Rails", BHP Melbourne Research Laboratories Report No. MRL 83/2, December, 1973.

4.   MEACHAM, H.C. and ELACO, A.R., "Summary Report on Sections of Corrugated Rail", Battelle Memorial Inst., Columbus Labs., September, 1968.

5.   GROENHOUT, R. and MAIR, R.I., "Spectral Analysis of Rail Corrugations", BHP Melbourne Research Laboratories Report No. MRL 81/2, January, 1974.

6.   GROENHOUT, R. and MAIR, R.I., "Spectral Analysis of Rail Corrugations at 217.9 km", BHP Melbourne Research Laboratories Report No. MRL/081/75/012, December, 1975.

7.   GROENHOUT, R. and CURCIO, P., "Rail Corrugation Profile Data from Standard Carbon and Alloy High Strength Rails at 11.6 km", BHP Melbourne Research Laboratories, Report No.

MRL/081/76/014, February, 1976.

8. KALOUSEK, J., "Rail Corrugations", Dept. of Research, Canadian Pacific Ltd., Report No. 5488-75, February, 1975.

9. GROENHOUT, R., "Corrugation Profile and Head Hardness Correlations in Tangent Track", BHP Melbourne Research Laboratories Report No. MRL 81/6, October,1974.

10. MAIR, R.I. and GROENHOUT, R., "Prediction of Rail Steel Strength Requirements - A Reliability Analysis", ASTM Symposium, Rail Steels - Developments, Processing & Use, ASTM Special Technical Publication, No. 644, 1978.

11. MAIR, R.I., "Natural Frequency of Rail Track and its Relationship to Rail Corrugation", I.E. Aust., Civil Eng. Trans., CE19(1), 6-11, 1977.

12. BJORK, J., "Dynamic Loading at Rail Joints - Effect of Resilient Wheels", Railway Gazette, June 5, 1970, 430-434.

13. MAIR, R.I., "Aspects of Railroad Track Dynamics - Vertical Response", BHP Melbourne Research Labs. Report No. MRL 81/3, February, 1974.

14. MAIR, R.I., "The Rail as a Beam on a Stiffening Elastic Foundation", Rail International, August, 1976, 443-450.

15. MAIR, R.I. and JUPP, R.A., "Rail Track for Heavy Unit Train Operations", Annual Eng. Conf., I.E. Aust., Townsville, May, 1976.

16. BIRMANN, F., "Recent Investigations of the Dynamic Modulus of Elasticity of the Track in Ballast with Regard to High Speeds", Princeton University Symp. on Railroad Track Mechanics, 1975.

17. MAIR, R.I., "Dynamic Response of Ballasted Rail Track", Proc. 2nd International Rail Sleeper Conf., Perth, Australia, August, 1976.

18. LONG, G., JUPP, R.A. AND KENYON, M., "Ore Car Vibrations and Their Implication to Long Pitch Corrugation Formation", BHP Melbourne Research Labs. Rept. No. MRL/081/076/13, January, 1976.

19. NAYAK, P.R., "Contact Vibrations of a Wheel on a Rail", J. Sound and Vib., 28(2), 1973, 277-293.

20. JOHNSON, K.L. and GRAY, G.G., "Development of Corrugations on Surfaces in Rolling Contact", Proc. I. Mech. E., 189(3), 1975, 45-58.

21 KOENEN, B.H.N., "10 Years of Operating Experience on the LAMCO Railroad", LAMCO Railroad Dept., Rept., May, 1973.

22. KING, F.E. and KALOUSEK, J., "Rail Wear and Corrugation Studies", Proc. AREA Bulletin 658, 77, June/July, 1976, 601-620.

23. MARTIN, G.C. and HAY, W.W., "The Influence of Wheel-Rail Contact Forces on the Formation of Rail Shells", Tran. ASME, Paper No. 72-WA/RT-8, 1972.

24. CURCIO, P., MARICH, S. and NISICH, G., "Performance of High Strength Rails in Track", Heavy Haul Railroad Conference, I.E. Aust., Perth, Sept., 1978.

FIRST PROGRESS REPORT—JOINT INVESTIGATION OF CONTINUOUS WELDED RAIL

By Herbert F. Moore

Research Professor of Engineering Materials, University of Illinois, In Charge, Joint Investigation of Continuous Welded Rail

Howard R. Thomas

Special Research Professor of Engineering Materials, University of Illinois, Engineer of Tests, Joint Investigation of Continuous Welded Rail

and

Ralph E. Cramer

Special Research Assistant Professor of Engineering Materials, University of Illinois, Metallurgist, Joint Investigation of Continuous Welded Rail

I. INTRODUCTION

Foreword:—In putting out this progress report especial emphasis is laid on the fact that it is a progress report and not a final report. It has been necessary to report tentative values of fatigue strength, drop-test values and bend-test values for continuous welded rail on the basis of very few tests. This necessity in the case of fatigue tests is one faced by all investigators of fatigue properties of full-sized members. It is most strongly urged that these results be regarded as tentative, and if they are so regarded, it is believed that the publication of them at this time will be of value.

1. **Beginning of Investigation:**—In September 1937 arrangements were completed for a co-operative investigation of continuous welded rail. The investigation is under the joint auspices of the Association of American Railroads and the Engineering Experiment Station, University of Illinois. The Association of American Railroads through the American Railway Engineering Association Committee on Rail appointed the following Advisory committee for the investigation:

J. C. Patterson, Chief Engineer Maintenance of Way, Erie Railroad (Chairman)

G. M. Magee, Research Engineer, Engineering Division, Association of American Railroads

C. E. Morgan, Superintendent Work Equipment and Track Welding, Chicago, Milwaukee, St. Paul & Pacific Railroad

G. R. Smiley, Chief Engineer, Louisville & Nashville Railroad

H. S. Clarke, Engineer Maintenance, Delaware & Hudson Railroad

Mr. Clarke has died since the beginning of the investigation, and the members of the test party of the investigation wish to record here their appreciation of his help in the early testing work of the investigation, and their deep sorrow at his loss. Mr. P. O. Ferris, Engineer of Maintenance of Way, Delaware & Hudson Railroad has been appointed in Mr. Clarke's place.

At the University of Illinois the work was placed under the general direction of Professor H. F. Moore. Close contact is maintained with Professor A. N. Talbot and the Special Committee on Stresses in Railroad Track. One-quarter of the time of Professor H. R. Thomas, engineer of tests, and of Professor R. E. Cramer, metallurgist, is given to this investigation. The assistance of Messrs. S. W. Lyon, J. L. Bisesi, E. C. Bast, and N. J. Alleman is gratefully acknowledged. Acknowledgment is also made of the co-operation of the following representatives of welding companies in preparing specimens and offering constructive criticisms of test methods and form of presentation of results:

Lem Adams, Vice-President, Oxweld Railroad Service Company
C. A. Daley, Maintenance of Way Engineer, Air Reduction Sales Company
J. H. Deppeler, Chief Engineer, Metal & Thermit Corporation
H. C. Drake, Director of Research, Sperry Products, Incorporated

2. General Outline of Work:—Eventually a considerable amount of field study of welded joints will have to be done, and some is in progress already. The general lines of laboratory investigation in progress are:

1. Etch tests of the metal in specimens of welded rail joints made by various processes, to see whether any "flakes," laps, holes, burns, inclusions, cracks, or any other type of defect, have formed during the process of welding and subsequent cooling, and, if so, where these defects are located in the joint.
2. Hardness surveys of the metal in the weld, in the adjacent rail and in the transition zone between weld metal and rail metal.
3. Survey of typical crystalline structure in weld, rail and transition zone by means of the metallographic microscope.
4. Chemical analyses of steel in rail, in weld and in the transition zone.
5. Mechanical tests of specimens cut from weld metal, rail metal, and transition zone. These tests include tension tests, impact tests and fatigue tests.
6. Rolling-load fatigue tests of full-size specimens of welded rail to determine: (a) Whether internal fissures can be developed in welded joints, (b) to determine the fatigue strength in flexure of welded joints, and (c) to determine likelihood of damage to the web of the rail near the weld.
7. Drop tests and bend tests of full-size rail joints.

In planning tests and considering test results two bases of comparison must always be kept in mind: (1) A comparison between the welded joint and the ordinary joint-bar joint as to strength and toughness and wearing qualities, and (2) a comparison between the welded joint and the rail. In comparing the strength and other properties of welded joints with those of ordinary joint-bar joints close contact is maintained with the work of Professor A. N. Talbot's Committee on Stresses in Railroad Track.

3. Types of Welded Joint Studied:—Up to the present time 104 test rails welded by five different processes have been supplied.

Process A. Twelve 112-lb. rails and twelve 131-lb. rails. This process is a gas welding process. The rails were first beveled with a torch and the joint welded by two welders, one on each side of the weld. A special welding rod was used. The base was welded first, starting at the web; next the web was welded from base to head, then the head was welded. When completed the top surface was peened by hammering. It took about one and one-half hours to complete a weld. After the head had cooled to black heat the entire rail was heated with a large acetylene torch to a normalizing temperature (about 1,600 deg. F.) for a distance of about 3½ in. on each side of the weld. Then a strip of sheet metal was placed around the weld and filled with ground magnesia insulating material, covering a distance of about eight inches on each side of the weld. This material allowed the heated head of the rail to cool to about 200 deg. F. in about three hours.

Process B. Twelve 112-lb. rails and twelve 131-lb. rails. This was also a gas welding process. The rail ends were beveled with a cutting torch. The surface of the bevel was ground clear of oxide. One welder made each joint. First the web of the rail was welded, starting from the junction of web and base and welding up to the head. The second step was to weld the base on both sides from the web out. The head was welded last. The weld metal was deposited in layers across the extent of the head and peened several times with the hammer during welding. The weld took about three hours to complete.

After the welding was complete, a special furnace was put around the weld and the weld was heated to about 1,200 deg. F.—a stress-relieving treatment. The holes in the furnaces used for burners were then covered and the rail allowed to cool in the furnace. It required approximately three hours for the rail to cool to 300 deg. F.

Process C. Twelve 112-lb. and twelve 131-lb. rails. This was the Thermit process using the intense heat generated by the transformation of aluminum to aluminum oxide. The welding of the rails by this process consists of three main steps: (1) The preparation of the rails for welding—including cutting of the gap, end-facing and alinement; (2) the actual welding of the rail—which includes preheating, pouring of the molten products of the reaction into the molds, and pressing together the rails in order to effect the pressure weld; and (3) the finishing operation—knocking off the catch basins and steel nubs on the sides of the head, post-heating to relieve strain, grinding and finishing the gage and tread surfaces.

The extensive details of this process and further details of the other processes are not given here in this summary but are on file at the office of the investigation at the University of Illinois.

Process D. Electric Flash Pressure Butt Welds. Twelve 131-lb. rails. The detailed description of this process involving, as it does, very elaborate equipment and the welding together of as much as 1,400 ft. of rail before placing it in the track will not be given here. A quite complete description may be found in the Railway Age for September 4, 1937, page 300.

Process E. Gas-heated Pressure Butt Welds. Twelve 112-lb. rails. The rail ends to be joined were ground square. A special oil-pressure cylinder was used to force the rail ends together under longitudinal pressure. While pressure was being applied the metal on both sides of the joint was heated by a large number of small oxy-acetylene flames, completely surrounding the rail joint. These flames were on a movable frame which oscillated back and forth along the rail through about 1½ in. on each side of the abutting rail ends. As the rail steel softened under the heat of the gas flames, the steady pressure of the oil-pressure cylinder forced the rail ends together about ⅞ in., forming an upset bead of deformed metal at the joint. After the flames had been shut off, and the rails had cooled below the critical temperature of the rail steel, they were reheated in another oxy-acetylene heating rig slightly above the critical temperature to refine the grain of the joint metal and relieve internal stresses in the steel.

II. ETCH TESTS, METALLOGRAPHIC TESTS AND HARDNESS SURVEYS

By R. E. Cramer, assisted by E. C. Bast

4. Etch Tests of Metal at Welded Joint:—Fig. 1 shows typical etch test results for test joints welded by the five processes studied. The etch tests shown in Fig. 1 were on horizontal slices from rail heads, approximately $\frac{1}{16}$ in. below the tread. The slices were rough polished and then etched in a 50 percent solution of hot hydrochloric acid for 20 to 40 min. In Fig. 1 (a) and (b) the regularly spaced dots are the marks of the Rockwell "C" diamond cone, used in the hardness surveys.

Evaluating etch-test results is very difficult. Evidences of inclusions, laps, bending of the "fiber" of the metal and some crack-like markings are shown. How much damage these do is rather uncertain, although actual cracks may do very considerable structural damage by acting as nuclei for the spread of fissures, or other fatigue cracks. Obviously the macro-structure of the steel in and near the weld has been changed from that in the rail itself. The macro-structure of the joint metal is further discussed after the results of tests of joints to fracture under repeated wheel loads have been presented.

138

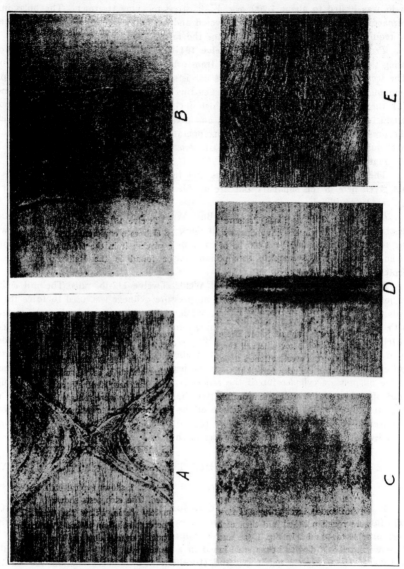

Fig. 1. Horizontal Etched Sections of Welds $\frac{3}{16}$ in. Below the Tread.

Etched with hot hydrochloric acid. Approx. 0.6 natural size.
A. Fusion gas weld, Specimen W 8, Process A.
B. Fusion gas weld, Specimen W 101, Process B.
C. Thermit weld, Specimen W 252, Process C.
D. Electric flash pressure weld, Specimen W 303, Process D.
E. Gas-heated pressure weld, Specimen W 406, Process E.
Note, the regularly spaced dots on A and B are the marks of the Rockwell "C"
diamond cone point used in the hardness surveys.

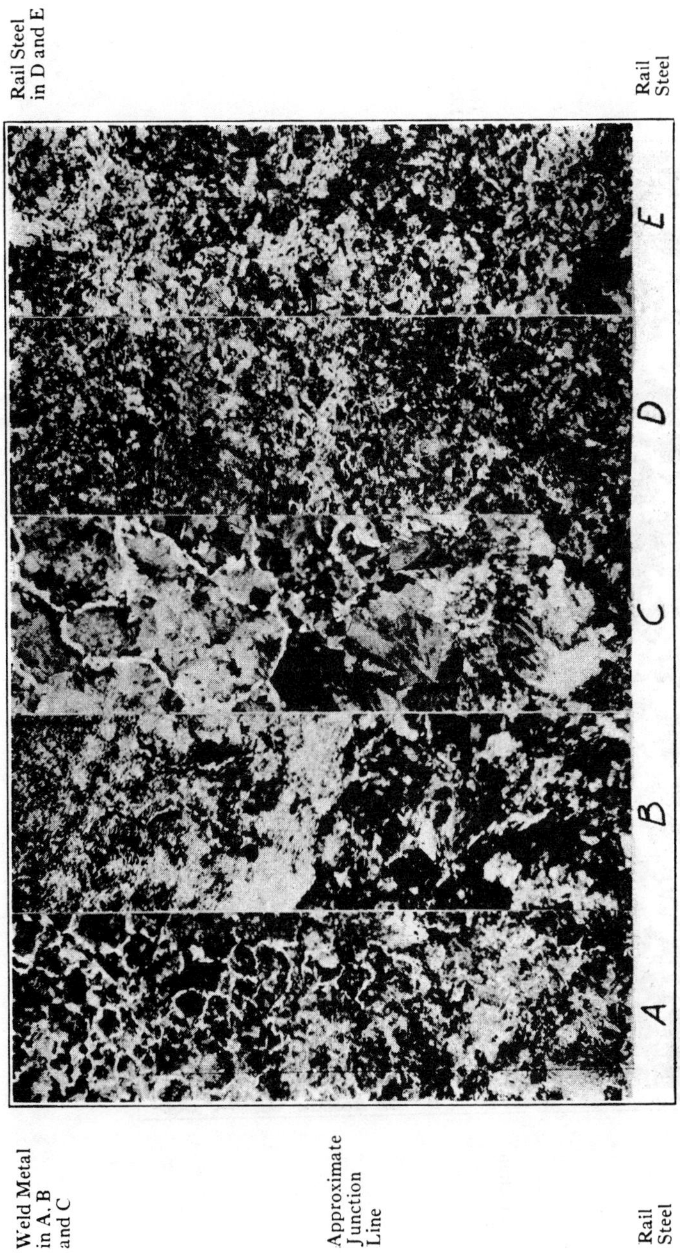

139

Fig. 2. Micrographs of Crystalline Structure at Junction of Weld Metal and Rail Steel.

Magnification 56 X.
Etch 2 percent nital.

A. Fusion gas weld. Process A.
B. Fusion gas weld. Process B.

C. Thermit weld. Process C.
D. Electric flash pressure weld. Process D.
E. Gas-heated pressure weld, Process E.

Rail Steel in D and E

Rail Steel

Weld Metal in A, B and C

Approximate Junction Line

Rail Steel

Junction
Line

Junction
Line

Fig. 3. Micrograph Showing Junction Line Outlined by Break in Crystalline Structure of Steel in
Butt Weld. Process E.

Magnification 320 X.
Etch 2 percent nital.

One method of locating the junction line of butt
welded rails is to examine the surface of the rails, espe-

cially if it is decarburized as was the case in the joint
shown above. In this decarburized metal the pattern of
the ferrite network in one rail does not match that of
the other, thus making the junction line quite distinct.

5. **Micrographs of Steel in Welded Joints:**—Fig. 2 shows micrographs of the metal at the weld and on each side of it for the five types of welded joints tested. It will be noted that the specimens for Processes A, B and C show more ferrite and larger grain sizes than do the specimens for Processes D and E. Fig. 3 shows a method for locating the junction line of butt-welded rails by examining the decarburized surface of the rails. In this metal the ferrite and pearlite grains of the two rails do not "match" and thus the junction line is made quite distinct.

6. **Hardness Surveys of Welded Joints:**—The Rockwell "C" hardness test was selected as the most suitable for hardness surveys of areas of rail steel, weld metal, and the fairly well-defined "heat affected area" adjacent to the weld metal. This test measures the net penetration of a diamond cone point under a load of 150 kg. after an initial load of 10 kg. has been applied. Hardness tests were made over the area of the weld region cut by various planes, horizontal and vertical. Indentations were made ½ in. apart along the rail, and, usually, ¼ in. apart across the rail. The results on a horizontal plane ⅜ in. below the tread of the rail are given in Table 1. These results give some idea of the relative hardness of rail, heat-affected zone and weld metal, and also some idea of the "scatter" of hardness values. With the small indentation made by the Rockwell "C" diamond brale (cone point) more localized spots of hard or soft metal are detected than with the relatively large indentation of a Brinell ball. It is rather doubtful

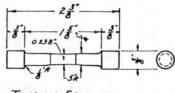

TENSION SPECIMEN

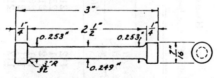

IMPACT TENSION SPECIMEN

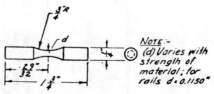

HIGH SPEED FATIGUE SPECIMEN

Fig. 4. Types of Specimens for Mechanical Tests
of Welded Joints.

TABLE 1

HARDNESS SURVEYS OF WELDED RAIL JOINTS

Rockwell "C" numbers along horizontal section $\frac{3}{16}$ in. below tread of rail

Type of Joint	Weight of Rail lb. per yd.	Rockwell "C" Numbers								
		Rail			Heat affected zone			Weld metal or junction line		
		Min.	Av.	Max.	Min.	Av.	Max.	Min.	Av.	Max.
Fusion weld A (gas)	112	21	22	24	13	21	25	13	22	30
Fusion weld B (gas)	131	22	23	24	17	26	29	28	31	37
Thermit weld C	112	21	23	24	19	24	26	16	22	26
Thermit weld C	131	20	22	24	23	27	29	10	25	28
Electric flash butt weld D	131	21	23	24	27	28	30	27	30	32
Gas heated pressure weld E	112	21	23	24	16	20	24	17	25	28

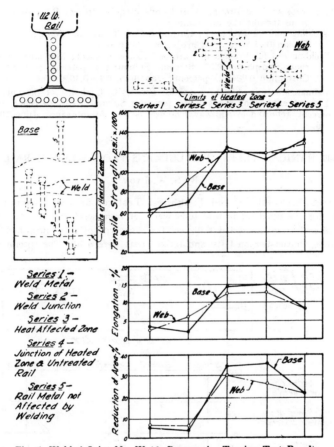

Fig. 5. Welded Joint No. W-12, Process A—Tension Test Results.

whether the low Rockwell numbers reported are as significant as an index of general hardness of the metal as Brinell readings, but Rockwell readings are more sensitive to localized variation of hardness in the metal. It will be noted that for Fusion gas weld B the weld metal was distinctly harder than the rail steel. This is probably due to the welding rod used. In general, it would seem to be of advantage to have the weld about as hard as the rail steel, to even up the wear along the track.

7. **Chemical Analyses of Rail Steel and of Welding Rods:**—The following analyses were reported for rail steel and welding rods.

Rail steel for joints made by Processes A, B, C and D, reported by Robert W. Hunt Company;
131-lb. rail, Carbon 0.71 percent; Manganese 0.81 percent; Phosphorus 0.023 percent; Sulphur 0.037 percent; Silicon 0.15 percent.
112-lb. rail, Carbon 0.70 percent; Manganese 0.76 percent; Phosphorus 0.020 percent; Sulphur 0.024 percent; Silicon 0.19 percent.
Rail steel for joints made by Process E, reported by firm making the test joints.
112-lb. rail, Carbon 0.73 percent; Manganese 0.80 percent; Phosphorus 0.020 percent; Sulphur 0.022 percent; Silicon 0.20 percent.

Welding rods used in Process A and rods used in Process B, analyses reported
firms making the test joints.
Welding rod for Process A, Carbon 0.45–0.50 percent; Manganese 1.00 perce
Silicon 0.45 percent; Chromium 1.00 percent.
Welding rod for Process B, Carbon 0.20–0.40 percent; Manganese 0.85–1.15 p
cent; Phosphorus 0.035 percent; Sulphur 0.04 percent; Silicon 0.15 perce
Chromium 0.90–1.25 percent; Vanadium 0.10–0.30 percent.
Approximate analysis of weld metal for Process C, Carbon 0.41 percent; Mangar
0.74 percent; Phosphorus 0.036 percent; Sulphur 0.058 percent; Silicon 0.
percent, reported in Railway Engineering and Maintenance, June 1936, p. 3
356.

III. MECHANICAL TESTS OF SPECIMENS FROM WELDED RAIL JOIN1

By S. W. Lyon

8. **Strength, Ductility and Toughness Tests of Specimens from Weld**
Specimens for the usual mechanical tests were cut from weld metal, from heat-affe
zone metal and from unaffected rail steel for each type of joint furnished for tes
Tension tests, impact-tension tests, and fatigue tests were made. The specimens used

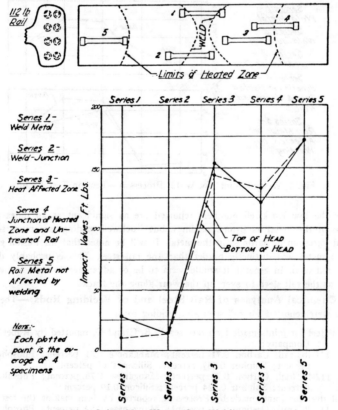

Fig. 6. Welded Joint No. W-12, Gas Welding Process A—
Impact Tension Results.

shown in Fig. 4. Tension tests were made in an Olsen screw-power testing machine using Robertson shackles to hold the specimens; impact-tension tests were made in a Charpy impact machine, fitted with a Lyon tension attachment, and fatigue tests were made in small rotating-cantilever machines which subjected the specimen to a complete reversal of flexural stress during a cycle of stress (one revolution of the machine).

Figures 5, 6 and 7 show graphically typical results for tension, tension-impact, and fatigue tests. As will be noted from these figures, specimens were cut from various portions of the welded joint and from the rail steel which is unaffected by the welding treatment. There have been made approximately 550 tension tests, 520 tension-impact tests, and 1,050 fatigue tests, a total of approximately 2,120 specimens tested. Table 2 summarizes the results of these tests. Table 2 is divided into two parts, in one of which (a) the actual test values are tabulated, and in the other of which (b) the values are tabulated in terms of percentage of the figures obtained from the rail steel.

9. Conclusions From the Tests of Specimens:—These tests of specimens cut from welded joints give an indication of the variation of strength of material in different parts of the joint. They do not give any indication on the effect of imperfections such as laps, blow holes, small cracks, inclusions, and sharp changes of outline upon the

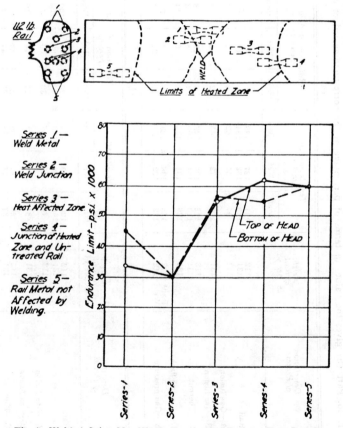

Fig. 7. Welded Joint No. W-15, Process A—Fatigue Test Results.

TABLE 2

TEST RESULTS FOR SPECIMENS CUT FROM WELDED RAIL JOINTS

The values given for rail steel are the average values for the specimens cut from a location in the joint specimen outside the heat-affected zone of metal. The values given for weld metal are the lowest values observed along the length of the weld and in its immediate vicinity. Most of these values are for weld metal, but a few are for the metal at the junction of weld and rail steel.

Part (a) of this table gives the results in terms of the units commonly used in reporting test results, lb. per sq. in., percent and ft.-lb. Part (b) gives the values in terms of percentage of the corresponding values obtained for rail steel.

(a)

Description of Process	Weight of Rail lb. per yd.	Tensile Strength 1,000 lb. per sq. in.			Reduction of Area percent			Impact Tension ft.-lb.			Endurance Limit 1,000 lb. per sq. in.		
		Head	Web	Base	Head	Web	Base	Head	Web	Base	Head	Web	Base
Rail	112 / 131	131 / 130	127 / 132	133 / 134	20 / 19	21 / 17	22 / 21	170 / 126	167 / 141	167 / 147	60 / 62	59 / 60	62 / 60
A—Gas fusion	112	97	57	62	6	7	4	14	6	24	30	35	33
B—Gas fusion	131	105	72	85	2	3	2	5	11	8	55	50	44
C—Thermit	112 / 131	113 / 113	106 / 101	122 / 100	4 / 4	12 / 8	8 / 2	28 / 37	50 / 52	9 / 15	29 / 34	44 / 46	45 / 44
D—Electric flash	131	126	131	133	4	6	14	160	85	112	54	44	54
E—Gas pressure	Rail* 112 / Weld 112	135 / 122	136 / 122	139 / 124	18 / 16	19 / 21	21 / 17	134 / 92	145 / 107	141 / 108	61 / 48	62 / 47	62 / 54

(b)

Description of Process	Weight of Rail lb. per yd.	Tensile Strength			Reduction of Area percent			Impact Tension Values			Endurance Limit		
		Head	Web	Base	Head	Web	Base	Head	Web	Base	Head	Web	Base
Rail	112 / 131	100 / 100	100 / 100	100 / 100	100 / 100	100 / 100	100 / 100	100 / 100	100 / 100	100 / 100	100 / 100	100 / 100	100 / 100
A—Gas fusion	112	74	45	47	30	33	18	8	4	14	50	59	53
B—Gas fusion	131	81	55	63	11	18	10	4	8	5	89	83	73
C—Thermit	112 / 131	86 / 87	84 / 77	92 / 75	20 / 21	57 / 47	36 / 10	16 / 29	30 / 37	5 / 10	48 / 55	75 / 77	73 / 73
D—Electric flash	131	97	99	99	21	35	67	127	60	76	87	73	90
E *—Gas pressure	112	90	90	89	89	110	81	69	74	77	79	76	87

* Rail for Process E not the same as for other processes. Percentage strength for Process E welds computed on basis of rail used for Process E joints.

fatigue strength of a joint as a whole. For judging this effect, the rolling-load tests, which are discussed in the next section, seem distinctly more significant.

However, the tests of these specimens do indicate for all the welded joints a rather wide variation in the quality of material in the joint as welded. None of the material in the welded joint reaches 100 percent of the values for the rail steel with the exception of the impact-tension values for steel from the head of the rail joints welded by Process D, and the reduction of area values for the web of the rail joints welded by Process E. The tensile strength for head, web and base of joints welded by Process D very nearly reached the tensile strength of the rail steel.

IV. TESTS OF WELDED JOINTS UNDER REPEATED WHEEL LOAD

By H. F. Moore, H. R. Thomas and N. J. Alleman

10. Rolling-Load Tests of Welded Joints:—The testing machine used for rolling-load tests of welded rail joints is similar to those used in the Investigation of Fissures in Railroad Rails except that the stroke of the machine is 12 in. instead of 7 in. Fig. 8 (a) shows this machine with a welded specimen after fracture.

The specimen to be tested is placed as shown in Fig. 8 (b). The moment arm at the weld is ten inches and at the weld the bending moment (inch-pounds) is ten times the wheel load.

The following routine has been used in the test: A specimen was put in the machine under a load of 75,000 lb. If the specimen broke before 2,000,000 cycles had been reached a second specimen was put in under a lower wheel load, usually a load of 60,000 lb. If this one broke, a specimen was put in at a still lower load, and the test continued to fracture or to 2,000,000 cycles of load.

The selection of 2,000,000 cycles as the limiting number of cycles for the rolling-load test was based on the following line of reasoning. During the passage of 300,000,000 tons of traffic, a location at any point in the rail would be subjected to approximately 30,000,000 wheel loads, allowing 5 tons as the average wheel load and remembering that the total tonnage is divided between the two rails. From the reports of the Investigation of Fissures in Railroad Rails it may be seen that, judged by records of about one-half a million wheel loads at four characteristic locations, about one wheel load out of one thousand has a magnitude of 40,000 lb. or greater. In rolling-load tests of rail, 40,000 lb. was the lowest wheel load which developed a fissure. Recent experiments at the University of Illinois by Dr. R. N. Arnold* indicate that, owing to inertia effects of the rails, this ratio of one in one thousand might be increased considerably, possibly to a point where one wheel load out of 300 may be expected to reach the value of 40,000 lb. or greater. This would mean that when 300,000,000 tons of traffic had passed over a location—a fair length of service for rail—about 100,000 wheel loads of 40,000 lb. or greater might be developed. Now in fatigue tests in the laboratory it is desirable to make tests under a much greater number of cycles of stress than will probably occur in practice. The reason for this is that above the fatigue limit a small increase in stress causes a great shortening of life. It is well then to make tests to ten times the number of cycles of stress expected in service. In these rolling-load tests the limiting number of cycles chosen was 2,000,000—twenty times the expected number of cycles of the load of 40,000 lb. which may be expected after 300,000,000 tons of traffic has passed over the track.

This maximum number of cycles, 2,000,000, is the same as that used by Professor W. M. Wilson in his studies in fatigue in structural members. The identity of these two figures for number of cycles is an interesting coincidence, nothing more.

* Proc., (British) Inst. Mech. Engr's., Vol. 137, p. 217 (1937).

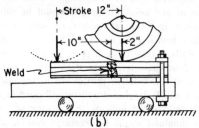

Fig. 8. Rolling-Load Testing Machine for Tests Under Repeated Wheel Load.

(a) General view of machine. Stroke 12 in., speed 60 r.p.m. Note fractured specimen.
(b) Wheel positions on specimen at ends of stroke. During a stroke the bending moment at the weld ranges from zero to ten times the wheel load.

11. Stresses Developed in Rolling-Load Tests:—Failure of a rail or a welded rail joint under repeated wheel loads may arise from several causes. Failure may take place as the result of repeated flexural stresses, and in this case it is usually the tensile stress that causes failure. Failure may take place due to repeated shearing stress in the web of the rail, and this depends upon wheel load rather than bending moment. Failure may take place by the development of internal fissures starting at minute imperfections and caused by the heavy stresses directly under the wheel load. All three of these causes of failure have occurred in the tests of welded joints so far carried out and Fig. 10 shows all three types of fracture.

The shearing stresses in the web and the flexural stresses in the head were computed by the common formulas of mechanics of materials. Their distribution is shown in **Fig. 9** for a wheel load of 75,000 lb. on a 131-lb. rail and for a 112-lb. rail.

The specimen is so placed in the rolling-load machine that the head of the specimen is subjected directly to wheel load, and, during a cycle of load, to tensile stress. This is probably a somewhat more severe condition than is met with in rails in track where the compressive stresses are larger than the tensile stresses, although as the train moves over the track there occurs a *partial* reversal of stress in the rail. The maximum flexural stress in the rolling-load test occurs when the wheel is 10 in. from the center line of the welded joint. The maximum wheel load at the weld occurs when the wheel is directly over the joint and the flexural stress is therefore zero. The shearing stresses in the web near the weld remain approximately constant throughout 10 in. of the 12-in. stroke. This arrangement of stress was chosen, not with the idea of reproducing conditions in service pre-

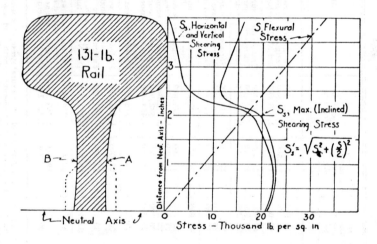

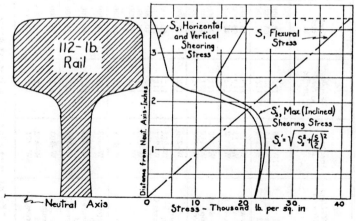

Fig. 9. Shearing and Flexural Stresses in Test Rail Joint under 75,000 lb. Wheel Load (750,000 In.-Lb. Bending Moment in Rolling-Load Test).

TABLE 3

RESULTS OF ROLLING-LOAD FATIGUE TESTS OF SPECIMENS OF WELDED RAIL

Welding Process	Specimen No.	Weight of Rail lb. per yd.	Wheel Load lb.	Maximum Flexural Stress* (S) lb. per sq. in.	Maximum Shearing Stress* (Ss) lb. per sq. in.	Cycles for Fracture	Manner of Failure and Remarks
Rail without weld	NW–406	112	75,000	49,900	24,800	511,200	Fatigue crack corner of head, edge of cold-rolled path.
	NW–410	112	65,000	43,300	21,500	1,650,900	Fatigue crack corner of head, edge of cold-rolled path.
	NW–408	112	60,000	40,000	19,900	2,038,800	Did NOT fracture.
Gas weld fusion Process A	W– 17	112	75,000	41,600	24,400	67,900	Transverse fissure in head.
	W– 13	112	60,000	33,300	19,500	107,300	Transverse fissure in head.
	W– 2	112	40,000	22,200	13,000	1,261,300	Compound fissure in head.
Gas weld fusion Process B	W–109	131	75,000	33,100	23,000	59,500	Horizontal fissure and failure at junction head and web.
	W–110	131	60,000	26,500	18,400	190,800	Transverse fissure in head.
	W–106	131	40,000	17,700	12,300	532,800	Failure started in weld at lap at junction head and web.
Thermit weld Process C	W–256	112	75,000	41,600	24,400	307,400	Transverse fissure in head. Previously tested for 2,000,000 cycles of 40,000-lb. wheel load without fracture.
	W–261	112	60,000	33,300	19,500	275,000	Fatigue crack corner of head, edge of cold-rolled path.
	W–257	112	50,000	27,800	16,200	1,004,100	Fissure near tread, apparently burnt metal.
	W–256	112	40,000	22,200	13,000	2,002,900	Did NOT fracture.
	W–205	131	75,000	33,100	23,000	582,900	Transverse fissure in head.
	W–211	131	60,000	26,500	18,400	1,484,700	Transverse fissure in head and also failure at junction head and web.
	W–208	131	55,000	24,300	16,900	1,378,100	Failed in web at "collar" of weld.
Electric flash pressure weld Process D	W–308	131	75,000	33,100	23,000	1,769,400	Failed in web where metal has been ground off so as to form a re-entrant angle. See "A" Fig. 10 and (b) Fig. 12.
	W–305	131	75,000	33,100	23,000	942,300	Fatigue failure in web outside of weld, starting at a stamped letter on web. See Fig. 12 (a).
	W–309	131	75,000	33,100	23,000	2,001,600	Did NOT fracture.
Gas pressure weld Process E	W–403	112	75,000	41,600	24,400	650,600	Fatigue crack at corner of head, edge of cold-rolled path, also crack started at a stamped letter on web.
	W–402	112	60,000	33,300	19,500	1,269,900	Fatigue crack at side of head.
	W–401	112	55,000	30,600	17,900	2,046,500	Did NOT fracture.

* For specimens with welds Fig. 10 shows variation from tread of rail to neutral axis of: (1) Flexural stress, (2) horizontal and vertical shearing stress and (3) maximum shearing stress (inclined). For specimens of rail without weld the values of S for specimens with weld are multiplied by 1.2, since the maximum moment arm to the center of the weld is 10 in., while the maximum moment arm for specimen without weld is 12 in.

cisely, but with the idea of producing measurable stresses of the same kind which occur in practice and studying their effect.

12. **Results of Rolling-Load Tests to Date:**—Table 3 gives the results of rolling-load tests so far run. It will be noted that the two gas weld joints failed to withstand 2,000,000 cycles of load of even 40,000 lb. The Thermit 112-lb. specimen under

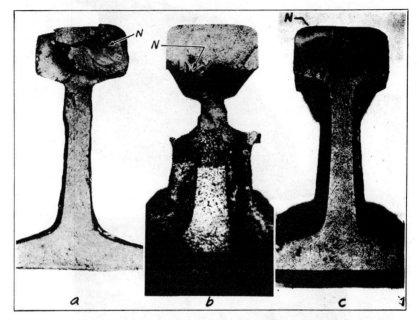

Fig. 10. Typical Fractures of Welded Joint Specimens in Rolling-Load Test.

a. Transverse fissure in head. Fissure started at N, and fracture occurred after 1,216,300 cycles of a 40,000-lb. wheel load.
b. Fissure started at N near junction of web and head, just outside the weld. Fracture occurred after 1,378,100 cycles of a 55,000. wheel load.
c. "Fatigue" failure by spreading crack starting at N near corner of tread of rail. Crack started in coarse transverse grinding marks left on head of rail. Failure occurred after 650,600 cycles of a 75,000-lb. wheel load.

40,000-lb. load did withstand 2,000,000 cycles, but the specimens under 50,000 lb., 60,000 lb. and 75,000 lb. did not. The test of the Thermit 112-lb. welded joint under 75,000-lb. wheel load is of interest in that it withstood more cycles of load than did the joint under 60,000 lb. This may be due to the fact that it had previously been subjected to 2,000,000 cycles of a 40,000-lb. load without fracture. This seems to indicate that welded joints may be strengthened by being subjected to many cycles of stress below the fatigue limit of the original material. This phenomenon of strengthening of metals by repeated understress has been known for several years, and repeated understress is just what rail joints receive in service—together with a rather rare overstress.

Three electric flash welded joints have so far been put into the machine and all tested under 75,000-lb. wheel load. In the first one the excess metal was ground off over about as much of the perimeter of cross-section as is common in practice. The shape of metal left is shown at "A" in Fig. 9. This left a sharp re-entrant corner across the line

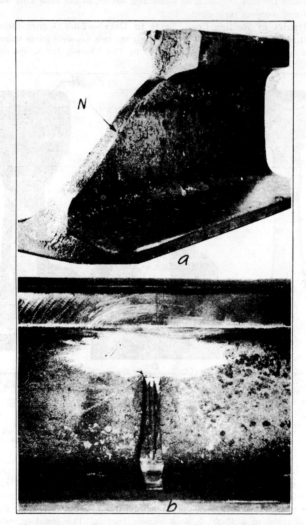

Fig. 11. Welded Joint Fractures Starting at "Stress Raisers"
in the Web.

a. Fracture started at N on a line tangent to the curved part of the letter "C"
which was stamped on the web of the rail. Fracture was outside the weld
zone.

b. Fracture started at N where there was a sharp re-entrant angle (shown at
A in upper half of Fig. 9) left after grinding off excess weld metal. After
this rail failed the excess metal was ground off as shown at B in Fig. 9,
avoiding a sharp re-entrant angle.

of vertical shearing stress,—a "stress raiser." The second specimen had the metal ground off as shown at "B" in Fig. 9, in an attempt to avoid this stress raiser. The first specimen failed by a crack starting at point "A", and this crack is shown in Fig. 11 (b).

The second specimen failed after 942,300 cycles of a 75,000-lb. wheel load. The failure was not through the weld, not in the heat-affected metal, but it started from a stamped letter on the web of the rail. (See Fig. 11 (a)).

The third specimen, which had no stamped letter on the web of the test specimen and in which the excess weld metal had been ground off so as to avoid a sharp re-entrant corner, ran out for 2,000,000 cycles of a 75,000-lb. wheel load without failure.

Three specimens of welded joints in 112-lb. rail have been tested in the rolling-load machine in which specimens the weld was a pressure butt weld with the heat furnished by gas, (Process E). In ·these welds the temperature used was less than in the fusion processes A and B. Under 75,000-lb. wheel load 650,600 cycles were required to produce

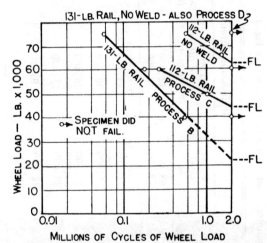

Fig. 12. Typical Load-Cycle Diagrams for Estimating the Endurance Limit Under 2,000,000 Cycles of Wheel Load on Specimens of Continuous Welded Rail.

FL denotes the endurance (fatigue) limit.

fracture. The fracture started at the edge of the path cold rolled on the tread by the wheel, but at the same time another spreading fracture had started at a stamped letter on the web. The second specimen fractured after 1,269,900 cycles of a 60,000-lb. wheel load. The fracture started in the fillet between head and web. The third specimen withstood without fracture 2,046.500 cycles of a 55,000-lb. wheel load.

13. Tentative Endurance Limits for Welded Joint Specimens:—As has been previously noted, it seems suitable to determine endurance limits of welded rail joints for 2,000,000 cycles of wheel load. Fig. 12 shows how this limit was determined for specimens of 112-lb. rail without welds, for 112-lb. rail with Thermit welds, and for specimens of 131-lb. rail gas-welded by Process B. The endurance limits for the other types of weld were determined in a similar manner. The results of three or more tests of each type of joint were plotted on load-cycle diagrams, in which wheel load was plotted as ordinates and number of cycles of load were plotted (to a logarithmic scale) as abscissas. For each type of joint the straight line which seemed best to fit the three

A

TABLE 4

TENTATIVE ENDURANCE LIMITS OF WELDED JOINTS FOR 2,000,000 CYCLES OF WHEEL LOAD

Wheel load at endurance limit is estimated as shown in Fig. 12

Type of Weld	Weight of Rail lb. per yd.	At Endurance Limit			Approximate Ratio of Fatigue Strength of Weld to that of Rail
		Wheel Load lb.	Maximum Flexural Stress lb. per sq. in.	Maximum Shearing Stress lb. per sq. in.	
Rail without weld	112	63,000	42,000	25,600	1.00
Rail without weld	131	79,000*	42,000*	24,200	1.00
Pressure butt weld (electric) Process D	131	more than 75,000	more than 33,100	more than 19,500	more than 0.79**
Pressure butt weld (gas) Process E	112	55,000	30,600	17,900	0.73**
Thermit weld Process C	112	46,000	25,400	15,100	0.61**
	131	52,000	23,000	16,000	0.66***
Fusion weld (gas) Process A	112	32,000	17,800	10,400	0.51†
Fusion weld (gas) Process B	131	22,000	9,700	6,700	0.28†

* Estimated on assumption that 131-lb. rail will develop as high flexural stress at endurance limit as 112-lb. rail. Maximum load which can be applied by machine 75,000 lb.
** Based on flexural stress at endurance limit. Failures by fatigue crack from surface.
*** Based on shearing stress at endurance limit. Fatigue failures were in web.
† Based on wheel load. Failures started from internal fissures.

or more test results was drawn, remembering that for a test in which 2,000,000 cycles of stress were withstood without fracture the plotted point cannot be *above* the load-cycle line. If none of the tests showed a "life" of 2,000,000 cycles the straight line for the three tests was extended until it intersected the ordinate for 2,000,000 cycles. This is shown in Fig. 12 for the tests of 131-lb. rail welded by Process B. Where one of the specimens ran to 2,000,000 cycles or over without fracture the straight line was drawn through the points for the two specimens which did fail. This is shown in Fig. 12 for the 112-lb. rail without weld and 112-lb. rail specimens welded by Process C. These endurance limits are distinctly more uncertain than the endurance limits of small polished specimens tested at high speeds, and determined from six or more specimens. However, the differences which they show are believed to be significant. Table 4 shows the tentative endurance limits determined in this manner. In determining the probable endurance limit for 131-lb. rail without weld it is evidently more than 39,600 lb. per sq. in. maximum flexural stress, since in the tests of the Process D welds the rail itself adjacent to the weld and directly over the supporting block was subjected to 1.2 times the stress in the center of the weld which was 33,100 lb. per sq. in. and failure occurred neither in the weld nor in the rail. It was then assumed that the 131-lb. rail did develop a maximum flexural stress as high as 112-lb. rail, that is, 42,000 lb. per sq. in. and the wheel load and maximum shearing stress accompanying this flexural stress were computed. The right hand column in Table 4 gives the approximate ratios of the fatigue strengths of the welds to that of the rail which were developed in these tests.

Again it is noted that welded rails should *not* be judged by the results of rolling-load tests alone. Lack of homogeneity shown by etch tests and microscopic examination, variation of strength, ductility and toughness qualities as shown by the tests of specimens cut from the joints—these factors must be given consideration. It must also be remembered that all the welded joints tested in the rolling-load machine were made with the knowledge that they were test joints, and this might make them either better or poorer than the average joint welded under service conditions. It is inevitable that joints made by the firm regularly doing rail welding and known to be used for tests of their product would be made with somewhat more care and closer inspection than is the case in

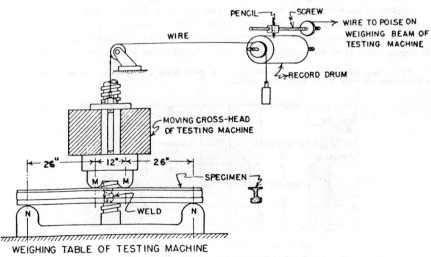

Fig. 13. Bend Test Rig with Specimen.

156

routine welding. This is in no sense a reflection on the honesty of the producers, it is merely the inevitable increase of carefulness which is present when a man knows he, or the product of his firm, is under examination. Now this very increase of carefulness may defeat its own object. Conditions accompanying the making of test joints are somewhat different from those accompanying the making of service welds, and the very additional care used, and the slowing down of the welding process which often happens may tend to make the test joints poorer than the average joint turned out.

In all consideration of welds the occasional occurrence of a poor weld must be recognized. There is at present no reliable non-destructive test for poor welds, and there are very few, if any, data on the probable frequency of occurrence of poor welds in rail joints. These considerations, together with considerations of the relative seriousness of failure of joint bars and of welded joints in rails must be factors in deciding whether or not to use welded rail joints in track.

V. BEND TESTS AND DROP TESTS OF WELDED JOINTS

By N. J. ALLEMAN and H. F. MOORE

14. A Comparison of Bend Tests and Drop Tests for Rails:—The standard drop test for rails consists of striking the rail, which is mounted over a span of three or four feet on a spring-supported anvil, with a falling weight, or "tup". The tup weighs 2,000 lb. and falls from a distance of from 18 to 22 ft., depending on the weight per yard of the rail. It strikes the test specimen at mid-span. This is a "pass or fail" test and gives very little information about the strength of the rail. Force is not measured at all and, if repeated blows are used until the rail breaks, only the energy required to fracture the rail and to compress the springs is indicated, and that only in "steps" of about 40,000 ft.-lb. Moreover, the distribution of energy between rail and springs is variable for different sections of rail, and for rail steels of different elastic strength.

In a cross-bending test of a rail, if a load-deflection diagram is plotted up to fracture the area under that diagram is a measure of the energy required to fracture the rail. A number of investigations* have shown that up to a certain critical speed,—a speed higher than that acquired by a weight falling 22 ft.—the energy absorbed is about the same for a given specimen of a given steel whether the load be applied slowly or rapidly. Moreover, in a bend test strength values are determined as well as energy values.

* For these references and a fuller discussion of the relative advantages of the bend test, see the Fifth Progress Report of the Rails Investigation.

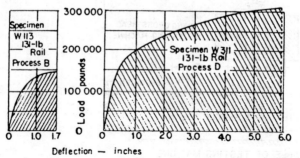

Fig. 14. Typical Bend-Test Load-Deflection Diagrams.

TABLE 5

RESULTS OF DROP TESTS OF WELDED RAIL SPECIMENS

Standard MCB testing machine and recommended AREA testing procedure used. Specimens tested head-up

Specimen No.	Weight of Rail lb. per yd.	Welding Process	Height of Drop of 1-ton tub, ft.	Number of Blows for Fracture	Elongation in each inch of gage length on tension side, in.
W 3	112	A	20	1	0-1-3*-2-0-0
W 23	131	A	22	1	0-0-1*-0-0-0
W 124	112	B	20	1	0-1-3*-0-0-0
W 102	131	B	22	1	----------
W 259	112	C	20	1	----------
W 210	131	C	22	1	3-3-7*-3-4-3
W 304	131	D	22	2	3-4-2*-0-4-4
W U4	112	E	20	1	

* Measurement across fracture.

Table 6

Results of Bend Tests of Welded Rail Specimens

Specimens tested head-down

Specimen No.	Weight of Rail lb. per yd.	Welding Process	Maximum Load before Fracture lb.	Energy for Fracture ft. lb.	Deflection at Fracture in.	Elongation in each inch of gage length on tension side in.	Remarks
Rail**	112	None	225,000	75,000	4.0	-----	
Rail**	131	None	300,000	100,000	5.0	-----	
W 4	112	A	124,200	4,200	0.71	0-0-0-2*-0-0	Lap side of head
W 22	131	A	168,500	7,360	0.53	0-0-0-1*-0-0	Lap side of head
W 113	112	B	140,500	6,900	0.92	0-0-0-0-0-0	Lap web & base
W 105	131	B	79,400	867	0.21	0-0-0-0-0-0	Lap at junction, head and web
W 253	112	C	193,900	23,370	1.33	1-1-1-1*-1-2	
W 203	131	C	231,500	22,200	1.65	1-1-1-2*-1-1	
W 311	131	D	315,100	121,500	5.98	7-6-10*-9-7-7	
W 404	112	E	217,600	42,600	3.16		
W 405	112	E	239,200	72,100	4.70	3*-3-4-6-6-6	

* Measurement across fracture.
** Values for rails without welds taken from records of bend tests made by the Rails Investigation. Minimum values for crack-free rails recorded here.

15. Drop Test Results:—Both drop tests and bend tests have been made on specimens of welded rail. The drop tests were the standard drop tests for rails. The rails were tested "head up" (base in tension), and test results for rails welded by Processes A, B, C, D, and E are given in Table 5. It will be noted that only the joints welded by Process D passed the requirement of one blow without fracture.

16. Bend Test Apparatus and Test Results:—Fig. 13 shows in diagram the testing apparatus and the specimens used for the bend tests of welded joints. It is believed that this figure is self explanatory. Fig. 14 shows (reduced) two typical load-deflection diagrams. The ordinates of these diagrams measure strength values, the abscissas measure ductility values, and the area under the entire diagram measures energy absorption up to fracture which is here designated as "toughness."

Table 6 gives the results of the bend tests so far performed on welded rail joints. All specimens were tested "head down" (head in tension). The specimens for Process D welds gave results, both for bend tests and for drop tests, which would be regarded as satisfactory for rail without welds.

Appendix

BIBLIOGRAPHY ON WELDED RAILS TO MARCH, 1939

By R. E. Cramer

1. Ahledt. Wm.—"A New Welding Method for Rails of High Wear Resistance," Organ Fortschr. Eisenbahnw., Vol. 92, June 15. 1937, pp. 222–225.
   Abstracted in Metals and Alloys. March 1938, p. M.A. 168 L/7
2. Benesch, F.—"Irregularities in the Welding of Rails." Preprint of paper 2 of Technical Session 6, Fourth International Rail Assembly 1938.
3. Bronson, C. B.—"Arc-Welding Rail Ends—Some Pertinent Considerations," Railway Engineering and Maintenance, Feb. 1938, p. 96.
4. Bronson, C. B.—"Rail Maintenance the Roadmaster's Problem," Railway Engineering and Maintenance. Nov. 1936, pp. 697–700.
5. Campus, F.—"Fatigue Tests of Welded Rail Joints," Rev. Universelle Mines, Vol. 14, June 1938, pp. 493–499.
   Abstracted in Metals and Alloys, Nov. 1938, p. M.A. 664 R/2
6. Clarke, H. S.—"Welded Rail Discussion—Progress in Track Maintenance Must Continue," Railway Age, Vol. 97, Dec. 1934, p. 853.
7. Clarke, H. S.—"Welded Rail Joints in Main Track Steam Railroads," The Welding Journal, Sept. 1934, pp. 21–22.
8. Clarke, H. S.—"Maintenance of Way Men Cannot Rest in An Established Practice," New England Railroad Club, Nov. 13, 1934.
9. Clarke. H. S.—"Building a Railroad for Today's Traffic," Railway Age, Vol. 103, Nov. 14, 1937, p. 450.
10. Clarke, H. S.—"Building for Today's Traffic", Railway Engineering and Maintenance, Vol. 33, Nov. 1937, p. 794.
11. Csillery, D. and Peter, L.—"Comparative Investigation of Hard Rail Steels Welded Electrically by Hand or Automatically," Preprint of Paper No. 5 of Technical Session 6, Fourth International Rail Assembly 1938.
12. Drake, H. C.—"Flash Welding of Rails," Welding Journal, N.Y., Vol. 17, Oct. 1938, pp. 17–21.
    Abstracted in Metals & Alloys, Feb. 1939, Vol. 10, No. 2, p. M.A. 109 L/7
13. Dumpelmann, R.—"Metallurgy of Autogenous Welding of Rails," Autogene Metallbearbeit, Vol. 31, Feb. 1938. pp. 33–40.
    Abstracted in Metals & Alloys, Aug. 1938, p. M.A. 494 L/2
14. Dumpelmann, R.—"The Development of the Oxy-acetylene Welding of Rail Joints." Preprint of Paper 6 of Technical Session 6, Fourth International Rail Assembly 1938.

15. Frankenbusch, H.—"Modern Rail Welding," Tech. Blatter, Sept. 18, 1938, pp. 547–550.
    Abstracted in Metals & Alloys, March 1939, p. M.A. 160 R/7
16. Graf, O.—"Bending Fatigue Strength of Welded Rails," Autogene Metallbearbeit, Vol. 31, Aug. 15, 1938, pp. 255–266 and Sept. 1, 1938, pp. 271–279.
    Abstracted in Metals & Alloys, Jan. 1939, Vol. 10, No. 1, p. M.A. 47 L/5
17. Harding, C. R.—"Welding of Rail Ends," AREA Report on Track, Railway Age, Vol. 95, March 1933, p. 417.
18. Jones, W. C.—"Fighting Rail Corrosion in the 6.21 Mile Moffat Tunnel," Railway Age, Vol. 105, No. 16, Oct. 1938, pp. 545-549.
19. Knowles, C. R.—"Report on Maintenance of Way Work Equipment," AREA Report, Railway Age, Vol. 96, March 1934, p. 404.
20. Lanquepin, M. J. E.—"Researches on Resistance-Welded Rails," Preprint No. 4 of Technical Session 6, Fourth International Rail Assembly 1938.
21. McCutcheon, E. M., Jr. and Kingsley, D. M., Jr.—"Peening and Its Effects on Arc Welds," Welding Journal, N.Y., Vol. 16, July 1937, Supplement, pp. 22–28.
22. Moe, M.—"Welded Rail Joints of the Norwegian State Railway," Arcos Z., Vol. 14, Dec. 1937, pp. 1741–1743.
    Abstracted in Metals & Alloys, Oct. 1938, p. M.A. 606 L/2
23. Nemesdy, Nencsek J.—"On Uniform Conditions for Examination and Acceptance of Welded Rail Joints," Preprint of Paper No. 1, Technical Session 6, Fourth International Rail Assembly 1938.
24. O'Rourke, G. M.—"Flatter vs. Grinder in Gas Rail Welding," Railway Engineering and Maintenance, Vol. 31, April 1935, pp. 221–223.
25. Sitton, G. L.—"The Maintenance of Rail Joints," The report of a committee of the Roadmasters Association, Railway Engineering and Maintenance, Vol. 33, Oct. 1937, p. 724.
26. Stimson, Earl—"Where Do We Stand," Railway Engineering and Maintenance, Vol. 30, Nov. 1934, pp. 627–629.
27. Swinnerton, N. W.—"Notes on Welding as Applied to Trackwork," Welding Industry, London, Vol. 4, Aug. 1936, p. 284–288.
    Abstracted in Metals & Alloys, July 1937, p. M.A. 424 L/9
28. Swinnerton, N. W.—"Oxy-acetylene Welding and Cutting as Applied to Trackwork," Welding Industry, London, Vol. 5, June 1937, pp. 180–188.
    Abstracted in Metals & Alloys, March 1938, p. M.A. 166 R/9
29. Tracy, S. E.—"Welding Special Trackwork—How the Burlington Does It," Railway Engineering and Maintenance, Vol. 33, Aug. 1937, p. 543.
30. Walzel, Richard—"Advances in the Metallurgy of Steels for Permanent Way Material in Austria," Preprint of Paper No. 4 of Technical Session 5, Fourth International Rail Assembly 1938.
31. Wattmann, John—"The Alumino-Thermic Welding in the Construction of Long Rails in Jointless Track," Preprint of Paper No. 3 of Technical Session 6, Fourth International Rail Assembly 1938.
32. Wise, C.—"Your Welding—Are You Getting the Most From It," Railway Engineering and Maintenance, Vol. 30, Aug. 1934, p. 429.
33. An Editorial—"Delaware & Hudson Installs More Welded Track," Railway Age, Vol. 103, No. 10, 1937, p. 300.
34. Editorial—"International Railway Congress," Engineer, Vol. 163, June 25, 1937, pp. 722–725. Engineering, Vol. 143, June 18, 1937, pp. 698–701.
35. Editorial—"Extending Life of Rail by Gas Welding," Railway Engineering and Maintenance, Vol. 29, Feb. 1933, p. 66.
36. Editorial—"Manganese Trackwork Can Be Repaired by Welding," Railway Engineering and Maintenance, Vol. 29, Feb. 1933, p. 68.
37. Editorial—"Pennsylvania Arc-Welds Crossings by Contract," Railway Engineering and Maintenance, Vol. 29, Feb. 1933, p. 72.
38. Editorial—"Building Up Rail Ends With the Electric Arc," Railway Engineering and Maintenance, Vol. 29, Feb. 1933, p. 74.
39. Editorial—"Welded Joints Improve Tunnel Track Conditions," Railway Engineering and Maintenance, Vol. 29, Feb. 1933, p. 85.
40. Editorial—"Rail End Welding Reaches High Peak," Railway Engineering and Maintenance, Vol. 30, June 1934, p. 318.

41. Editorial—"How Long Rails?", Railway Engineering and Maintenance, Vol. 31, Jan. 1935, pp. 20-23.
42. Editorial—"Three-Flame Welding Tip for End-Hardening and Building Up Rail Ends," Railway Engineering and Maintenance, Vol. 31, June 1935, pp. 360-361.
43. Editorial—"How Flexible Are Long Rails?", Railway Engineering and Maintenance, Vol. 32, Feb. 1936, pp. 82-85.
44. Editorial—"Mile Long Rails Installed in GEO Test Track," Railway Engineering and Maintenance, Vol. 32, June 1936, pp. 352-356.
45. Editorial—"Welding Frogs in Track or Shop?", Railway Engineering and Maintenance, Vol. 32, Dec. 1936, pp. 797-798.
46. Editorial—"Butt Welded Rails in 4000 Ft. Lengths," Railway Engineering and Maintenance, Vol. 33, April 1937, p. 264.
47. Editorial—"Making Rails Last Longer on the Missouri Pacific," Railway Engineering and Maintenance, Vol. 33, Aug. 1937, pp. 532-36.
48. Editorial—"30 More Miles of Welded Track," Railway Engineering and Maintenance, Vol. 33, Sept. 1937, p. 596.
49. Editorial—"Getting the Most from Rail on the Chesapeake & Ohio," Railway Engineering and Maintenance, Vol. 33, Sept. 1937, p. 602.
50. Editorial—"Uses Oxy-Acetylene Process to Butt-Weld Rails in Open Track," Railway Engineering and Maintenance, Vol. 33, Dec. 1937, p. 894.
51. Editorial—"Building-Up Rail Ends with Multiple-Flame Torches," Railway Engineering and Maintenance, Vol. 34, No. 8, Aug. 1938, pp. 476-479 and 483.
52. Editorial—"New Oxy-Acetylene Process for Butt-Welding Rails," Railway Engineering and Maintenance, Vol. 35, Jan. 1939, pp. 28-31.

Second Progress Report—Joint Investigation of Continuous Welded Rail

By H. F. Moore

Research Professor of Engineering Materials, University of Illinois, In Charge, Joint
Investigation of Continuous Welded Rail

Howard R. Thomas

Special Research Professor of Engineering Materials, University of Illinois, Engineer of Tests,
Joint Investigation of Continuous Welded Rail

and

Ralph E. Cramer

Special Research Assistant Professor of Engineering Materials, University of Illinois, Metallurgist,
Joint Investigation of Continuous Welded Rail

I. Introduction

1. Organization of Investigation.—This investigation, begun in September 1937, is carried on under the joint auspices of the Association of American Railroads and the Engineering Experiment Station, University of Illinois. The Association of American Railroads, through the Committee on Rail of the American Railway Engineering Association, appointed the following advisory committee for the investigation:

J. C. Patterson, Chief Engineer Maintenance of Way, Erie Railroad (Chairman)

P. O. Ferris, Chief Engineer, Delaware & Hudson Railroad

G. M. Magee, Research Engineer, Engineering Division, Association of American Railroads

C. E. Morgan, Superintendent Work Equipment and Track Welding, Chicago, Milwaukee, St. Paul & Pacific Railroad

G. R. Smiley, Chief Engineer, Lousville & Nashville Railroad

At the University of Illinois the work was placed under the general direction of Professor H. F. Moore. Close contact is maintained with Professor A. N. Talbot and the Special Committee on Stresses in Railroad Track. One-quarter of the time of Professor H. R. Thomas, engineer of tests, and of Professor R. E. Cramer, metallurgist, is given to this investigation. The assistance of Messrs. S. W. Lyon, J. L. Bisesi, E. C. Bast, and N. J. Alleman is gratefully acknowledged. Acknowledgment is also made of the cooperation of the following representatives of welding companies in preparing specimens and offering constructive criticisms of test methods and the form of presentation of the results:

Lem Adams, Vice-President, Oxweld Railroad Service Company

C. A. Daley, Maintenance of Way Engineer, Air Reduction Sales Company

J. H. Deppeler, Chief Engineer, Metal & Thermit Corporation

H. C. Drake, Director of Research, Sperry Products, Inc.

2. Previous Work of the Investigation.—In the First Progress Report* of this investigation there were published data and preliminary results of (1) metallographic studies of welded joints in rails, (2) mechanical tests of specimens cut from rail metal, weld metal and metal in the junction zone between weld and rail, (3) tests of full-section welded-joint specimens under repeated wheel load and (4) drop tests and bend tests of full-section specimens of welded joints. The "rolling-load" testing machine for

---

* Proceedings of the American Railway Engineering Association, Vol. 40, pages 687–713 (1939).

subjecting rail-joint specimens to repeated wheel load was described, as was the testing rig for making bend tests of full-section rail joints. A bibliography on welded rails was printed as an appendix to the report. Attention was directed to the fact that all results obtained were preliminary and tentative.

3. General Outline of the Work Since March 1939.—In a general way the work reported in the First Progress Report has been continued. This is especially true in the case of rolling-load tests. Sixteen such tests have been completed, during which time 21,772,200 cycles of wheel load have been applied to specimens. This is equivalent to running the rolling-load machine continuously day and night for 252 days. A number of rolling-load tests of specimens with joint bars instead of welded joints have been tested. Further bend tests have been made and more micrographic study has been done. Plans have been made for the systematic reporting of welded rail failures in service.

4. Types of Welded Joints Studied.—Five different processes of welding rail have been studied. From all of these but one (Process D) joints with both 112-lb. rail and 131-lb. rail were furnished. Joints welded by Process D were furnished only with 131-lb. rails.

The detail of welding processes is covered rather fully in the First Progress Report. In general, the processes may be summed up as follows:

Process A. Rail joint welded by oxacetylene blow torch. A fusion weld made without pressure.

Process B. Similar to Process A but joints welded by a different company.

Process C. The Thermit process, using the intense heat generated by the transformation of aluminum to aluminum oxide. This process involves fusion, but after solidification of the molten metal has begun, pressure is applied.

Process D. An electric flash butt weld made with pressure. The weld is heated by striking an arc between the two rails to be joined and forcing the rails together at welding heat by pressure.

Process E. A gas butt weld with pressure. A special welding machine using oxacetylene gas is used and the rails are pressed together while welding.

In practically all the processes there is some heating for stress relieving or normalizing after the weld has been made and, of course, the grinding off of the excess metal over the tread and sides of the rail head.

II. Tests of Welded Joints Under Repeated Wheel Load

By N. J. Alleman and H. F. Moore

5. Rolling-Load Testing Machine.—The machine used for repeated-load tests of welded joints is called the "Rolling-load" machine. A halftone cut of the machine was shown in Fig. 8 of the First Progress Report. A diagrammatic sketch of the machine is shown in Fig. 1 of this second report for the benefit of those who may not have any other description available. The welded joint specimen S is pulled backward and forward under a wheel W, the load on which can be varied from zero to 75,000 lb. The load is applied through the lever L by means of a screw jack J, and is measured by the compression of the spring P. The maximum bending moment on the weld is equal to the load on the wheel times the distance from the center line of the weld to the point of contact of the wheel when the specimen is in its extreme left-hand position. A revolu-

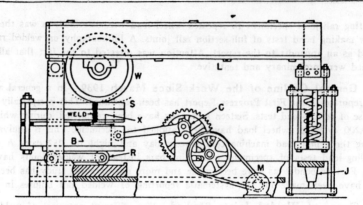

Fig. 1. Machine for Rolling Load Tests.

tion counter is attached to the crankshaft of the machine, and an automatic cut-off switch is operated by the drop of the lever *L* when a specimen breaks. The stroke of the machine is 12 in. and its speed is 60 strokes per minute.

6. Procedure of Rolling-Load Tests.—A number of specimens of each type of welded joint (not less than three) were tested for each of two weights of rail, 112-lb. and 131-lb.† The first specimen of each group was tested under a load of 75,000 lb. If the specimen broke before it had withstood 2,000,000 cycles of load a second specimen was put in under a lower load. If this specimen broke a third specimen was put in at a still smaller load and was tested to fracture, or until it had withstood 2,000,000 cycles of load. The selection of 2,000,000 cycles as the limiting number of cycles of stress is discussed in detail in the First Progress Report.

7. Endurance Limit for Welded-Joint Specimens.—The endurance limit for a given type of welded joint and given weight of rail is determined by drawing a stress-cycle (or S–N) diagram with wheel loads or bending moments as ordinates to an ordinary scale, and with number of cycles of stress for fracture as abscissas to a logarithmic scale. A line is drawn to fit the plotted points for specimens which break, and it is extended, if necessary, to intersect the vertical line for 2,000,000 cycles of load. The wheel load or bending moment represented by this intersection is taken as the endurance limit for 2,000,000 cycles of stress.

Figures 2 and 3 give S–N diagrams for the welds tested, and also S–N diagrams for rails without weld and rails with joint-bar joints. Whenever a specimen was removed from the machine without breaking, the plotted point for that specimen is marked with an arrow. Evidently an S–N diagram should not lie *below* such a plotted point. It is necessary in determining endurance limit for some of these S–N diagrams to estimate the endurance limit from rather unsatisfactory data. A few illustrations may be of service.

In the S–N diagram (Fig. 3) for gas fusion welds of 131-lb. rails the longest life of specimen was about 550,000 cycles. Three plotted points for the diagram fall closely on a straight line, and this line is extrapolated to 2,000,000 cycles. It is quite possible that the S–N diagram might flatten out like that in Fig. 2 for the gas pressure weld

† No specimens of the electric pressure butt-welded joints using 112-lb. rails have been supplied to the test party.

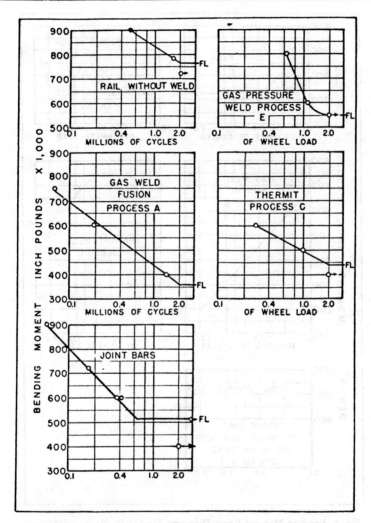

Fig. 2. Bending Moment-Cycle Diagrams for 112-lb. Rails, Joint Bars
and Welded Rails. FL Denotes the Fatigue (Endurance) Limit.

specimens with 112-lb. rail. Then in Fig. 2 consider the S–N diagram for specimens
with joint bars and 112-lb. rails. Evidently the S–N diagram should not pass below
the plotted point for the specimen which did not fail after 3,028,600 cycles at 510,000
in.-lb., yet if the straight line connecting the three points for specimens which failed
were extrapolated to 2,000,000 cycles, it would pass below the point for the unbroken
specimen. The endurance limit is evidently less than 600,000 in.-lb. and not less than
510,000. It is estimated at 510,000.

8. Types of Fracture of Welded Joints in Rolling-Load Tests.—Figure 4
shows the three types of fractures which were found in welded joints, namely (a)
failure by transverse fissure in head starting from some imperfection usually a minute

166

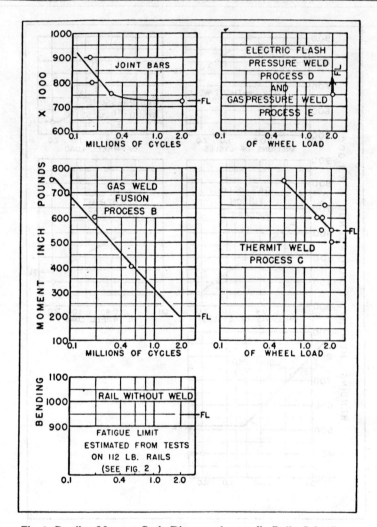

Fig. 3. Bending Moment-Cycle Diagrams for 131-lb. Rails, Joint Bars
and Welded Rails. FL Denotes the Fatigue (Endurance) Limit.

crack, (b) failure starting in the web or at the junction of web and head—usually
starting in some irregularity in welding surface which serves as a stress raiser, and
(c) a fatigue failure by spreading crack starting near the corner of the tread of the
rail—a conventional fatigue failure of the rail. Figure 4 (d) shows a typical rolling-load
failure of a joint bar.

9. **Rolling-Load Tests of Joints Connected by Joint Bars.**—To secure a
basis of comparison of the resistance of welded rail joints to repeated stress with that
of joint-bar joints, a series of rolling-load tests on rails connected by joint bars is in
progress. In this test the joint bars are carefully fitted and are tightened with a bolt
tension of 20,000 to 25,000 lb. which is maintained as the rolling-load test proceeds.

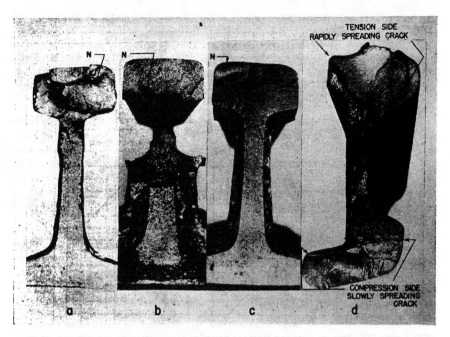

Fig. 4. Typical Fractures of Welded Joint Specimens in Rolling-Load Test.

a. Transverse fissure in head. Fissure started at N, and fracture occurred after 1,216,300 cycles of a 40,000-lb. wheel load.

b. Fissure started at N near junction of web and head, just outside the weld. Fractures occurred after 1,378,100 cycles of a 55,000-lb. wheel load.

c. "Fatigue" failure by spreading crack starting at N near corner of tread of rail. Crack started in coarse transverse grinding marks left on head of rail. Failure occurred after 650,000 cycles of a 75,000-lb. wheel load.

d. "Fatigue" failure of joint bar starting at upper and lower fishing surface after 56,100 cycles of a 75,000-lb. wheel load. Bending moment 900,000 in.-lb.

The specimen is so placed that the gap between the rails is at the edge of the block on which the rail rests and the path under the wheel load extends from this point to a point an inch or two from the free end of the specimen, which is mounted as a cantilever.

The rail joints with joint bars were placed in the machine the same way as the rail specimens. It is recognized that this throws tensile stress to the top of the joint bar and compressive stress to the bottom and that the cycle of the stress is quite different from that which has to be withstood by the joint bar in service. However, it was felt that the best comparison of strength under repeated load would be obtained by subjecting welded joints and joint-bar joints to the same testing conditions, namely, a cycle of bending moment varying from zero to maximum, with tension on the top side and compression on the bottom of the specimen.

The joint bars used in the test specimens were of heat-treated steel, and bars from the same lot were used for the 112-lb. joints. The joint bars for the 131-lb. rails were from two lots. It is recognized that there would be a wide difference between strength of different joint bars with different heat treatments and also that variations of bolt tension may produce wide differences in fatigue strength, as Professor Talbot's investigation has shown. These tests may be considered as representing test joints with a joint bar made of strong steel, carefully fitted to the rail and with a uniform bolt tension carefully maintained. (Note: The test results for the two lots of 131-lb. joint bars fall on the same curve in Fig. 3). This would seem to represent good practice in joint bars. Perhaps it might be considered that the joints with joint bars were made up with care corresponding to the care with which the welded joints were made. In any event the values from the few tests which it has been possible to make thus far should be regarded as indicative of general ranges of figures rather than a basis for sharp comparisons of strengths.

10. **Fatigue Failures in Joint Bars.**—In the joint-bar joints the final failure was always by a fatigue crack on the tension side. In one or two cases it was observed that fatigue cracks *started* on the compression side but progressed very slowly. In some cases the fatigue cracks on the compression side appeared first, and were followed by rapidly spreading cracks on the tension side. This is in agreement with the cracking observed in some joint bars in service. However, as is commonly assumed today, a fatigue crack starts under repeated shearing stress and tends to spread most rapidly under tensile stress. In view of this the behavior of joint-bar test joints is quite natural. Shearing stress is very nearly as severe on the compression side of the bar as on the tensile side. There is no reason why a crack could not be expected to *start* under either compression or tension. However, the rate of spread of the crack is distinctly diminished by the closing up of the crack on the compressive side while on the tension side there is a tendency for it to open. (See Fig. 4 (d)).

11. **Results of Rolling-Load Tests.**—As has been previously noted the number of rolling-load tests which have been carried out is relatively small. The endurance limits which have been determined must be regarded as at best only roughly approximate. In a general way it may be said that in the rolling-load tests so far carried out, the electric butt pressure welds seemed to develop strength almost, if not quite, up to that of the rail itself; the gas pressure welds were but little, if any, inferior to the electric butt pressure welds; the Thermit weld specimens and the joint-bar specimens had almost the same strength; and the gas fusion welds tested showed lower strength than the joint-bar tests. Table 1 shows results of rolling-load tests.

12. **Bend Tests on Rail Joints.**—Table 2 gives the results of bend tests on welded-rail specimens made up to date. The testing rig for bend test is shown in detail in the First Progress Report and all the specimens were tested under a 64-in. span with two equal loads spaced 6 in. either side of the center of length of the specimen. Thus the middle 12 in. of length of the specimen was under uniform bending. In Table 2 the maximum load before failure would be an indication of the strength of the joint, while the energy for fracture is taken as a measure of its toughness. The deflection at failure might be taken as a measure of its static ductility. It will be noted that the electric pressure weld and the gas pressure weld actually developed a higher load than a minimum value for crack-free rails tested for the Rails Investigation. They also developed higher energy for fracture in 131-lb. specimens. It is noted that the joints with joint bars developed a high amount of energy for fracture.

13. **Bend Tests and Rolling-Load Tests as Criteria of Strength of Joint.** In the study of fatigue of metals it has been found by many investigators that for many methods there seems to be a correlation between tensile strength and fatigue strength. A study of the results of rolling-load tests and bend tests was made to see whether any such correlation can be traced in the joints tested. It was found that the data were not sufficient nor the results consistent enough to justify any precise quantitative correlation, but the relative order of results for the two tests is shown graphically

TABLE 1

ENDURANCE LIMITS FOR 2,000,000 CYCLES OF ROLLING WHEEL LOAD FOR WELDED RAIL SPECIMENS, RAIL SPECIMENS WITHOUT WELDS AND SPECIMEN JOINTS USING JOINT BARS

During test head of rail subjected to cycles of tensile stress varying from zero to a maximum

Type of Joint	At Endurance Limit				Rolling-load Strength Ratio*	Remarks
	Wheel Load, lb.	Maximum Moment, in.-lb.	Maximum Flexural Stress, lb. per sq. in.	Maximum Shearing Stress, lb. per sq. in.	percent	
Joints with 112-lb. Rails						
Rail without weld	63,000	756,000	42,000	25,600	100	Based on bending moment
Rail with joint bar	41,700	510,000	(1)	(1)	66	Based on bending moment
Gas fusion weld—Process A	36,000	360,000	20,000	11,700	51	Based on wheel load, failed by internal fissure
Thermit weld—Process C	44,000	440,000	24,300	14,400	58	Based on bending moment
Gas pressure weld—Process E	55,000	550,000	30,600	17,900	73	Based on bending moment
Joints with 131-lb. Rails						
Rail without weld	(2) 79,000	(2) 948,000	(2) 42,000	24,200	100	Based on bending moment
Rail with joint bar	60,400	725,000	(1)	(1)	76	Based on bending moment
Gas fusion weld—Process B	20,000	200,000	8,800	6,100	25	Based on wheel load; failed by internal fissure
Thermit weld—Process C	55,000	550,000	24,400	17,000	70	Based on shearing stress; Web failure.
Electric pressure weld—Process D	More than 75,000	More than 750,000	More than 33,100	More than 19,500	More than 77	Based on bending moment
Gas pressure weld—Process E	More than 75,000	More than 750,000	More than 33,100	More than 19,500	More than 77	Based on bending moment

* Ratio of (Endurance Limit for specimen) to (Endurance Limit for Rail without Weld).
(1) Flexural stress in joint bars not computed; joint bars and rails made of different strength stee
(2) Estimated on the assumption that 131-lb. rail will develop as high flexural stress at endurance limit as 112-lb. rail. Maximum load which can be applied to machine, 75,000 lb.

TABLE 2

RESULTS OF BEND TESTS OF WELDED RAIL SPECIMENS, RAIL SPECIMENS WITHOUT WELDS AND SPECIMEN JOINTS USING JOINT BARS

Specimens were tested head-down unless otherwise noted

Number	Specimen Classification	Maximum Load before Fracture, lb	Energy for Fracture, ft.-lb.	Deflection at Fracture, in.	Bend-Strength Ratio* percent	Remarks
	Joints With 112-lb. Rails					
	Rail without weld**	225,000	75,000	4.0	100	No head-up tests of rail without weld for comparison
	Joint with joint bar	151,100	193,500	20.0	67	
	do. (tested head-up)	154,400	69,300	6.8	----	
W 4	Gas fusion weld—Process A	124,200	4,300	0.7	55	
W113	Gas fusion weld—Process B	140,500	6,900	0.9	62	
W253	Thermit Weld—Process C	193,900	23,370	2.1	86	
W404 W405	Gas pressure weld—Process E	228,400	57,800	3.9	101	Average of two tests
	Joints With 131-lb. Rails					
	Rail without weld**	300,000	100,000	5.0	100	No head-up tests of rail without weld for comparison.
	Joint with joint bar	201,200	111,200	9.2	67	
	do. (tested head-up)	202,700	42,300	3.3	----	
W 22	Gas fusion weld—Process A	168,500	7,360	0.5	56	
W105	Gas fusion weld—Process B	79,400	867	0.2	26	
W203	Thermit weld—Process C Lot 1	231,500	22,200	1.65	77	
W223 W226	Thermit weld—Process C Lot 2	254,000	33,800	2.2	85	Average of two tests.
W311	Electric pressure weld—Process D	315,000	121,500	6.0	105	
W451 W452	Gas pressure weld—Process E	320,900	177,800	7.9	107	Average of two tests.

* Ratio of (Maximum load for specimen) to (Maximum load for rail without weld).
** Values for rails without welds taken from records of bend tests made by the Rails Investigation. Minimum values for crack-free rails recorded here.

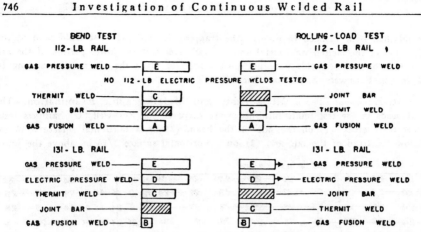

Fig. 5. Relative Strengths of Joints as Shown by Bend Test and Rolling-Load Test.
Letters on bars designate welding process.
Strength of Thermit weld joints in 131-lb. rails based on average for two lots of specimens.

in Fig. 5, in which the lengths of bars are proportional to the average strength ratios found. Attention is called to the fact that rolling-load tests for Processes D and E (131-lb. rail) merely indicated values greater than a certain amount. This is shown by arrows attached to the bars. An interesting fact in connection with this figure is that the bend tests and the rolling-load tests arranged the different types of weld in the same order of merit. It may be added here that taking both the bend tests and rolling-load tests into consideration it seems best to regard Processes D and E of so nearly equal value that a discrimination can not be made between them at present.

The correlation between order of merit as shown by the bend tests and that shown by the rolling-load tests is interesting. In view of the desirability of a reliable acceptance test for welded-rail joints further experimental study seems worth while. However, it would be unwise to conclude that such a correlation has been definitely established by these relatively few tests.

14. Proposed Study of Welded Rail Failures in Service.—A proposed questionnaire on the behavior of welded rails in service has been submitted to the Advisory Committee on Continuous Welded Rail with the request that some action may be taken so that this questionnaire or some other form may be sent to the railroads having welded rail in track. It would afford a source of systematic information on welded joint behavior in service, covering such items as first cost, maintenance cost, riding qualities, wear, and failures. At best, the laboratory tests of the strength of continuous welded rails indicate the order of magnitude of strength which may be expected as compared with the strength of rails without weld or with the strength of joint-bar joints in rails. Variations due to service conditions and variations in quality of the weld in joints made would have to be studied through service tests.

III. Metallographic Tests

By R. E. CRAMER, assisted by E. C. BAST

15. Second Lot of Thermit Welded Joints.—During the past year metallographic studies have been made on a group of Thermit rail joints welded in May 1939. These welds differed from previous Thermit welds studied in two respects. First, the

172

molds had been changed to prevent the trapping of slag and loose mold sand at the junction of the molten weld metal and the rail steel near the lower portion of the rail head. Second, these welds were not post heated or given the strain relief heating to 1,100 deg. F. as were the previous Thermit welds.

16. **Hardness Tests, Etch Tests and Metallographic Examination.**—The rail heads in the test joints furnished were prepared for Rockwell "C" hardness tests over three areas: (1) on the side of the head, (2) on a horizontal surface 3/16 in. below the tread of the rail, and (3) on a horizontal surface 3/16 in. above the junc-

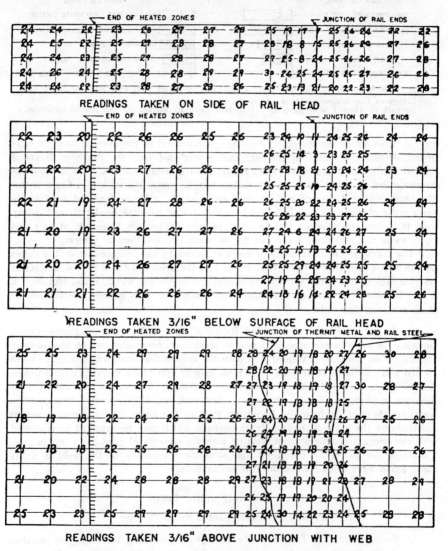

Fig. 6. Hardness Tests on Welded Rail Joint Made by Metal and Thermit Corporation New Type Weld No. W220. 131-lb. Section. Rockwell C Scale.

Fig. 7. Etched Horizontal Section of Weld ⅛ Inch Below the Tread.

Three-fourths natural size. Etched with hot Hydrocholoric Acid. The acid has brought out marks at both sides of the head at the junction of the rail ends. These marks are caused by oxide at the grain boundaries, as shown in Fig. 8.

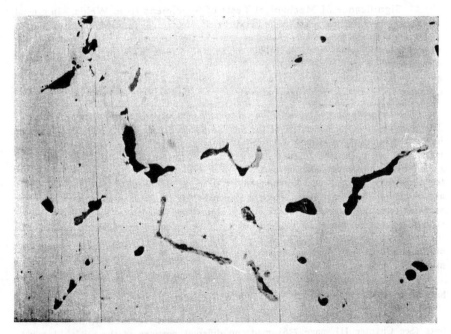

Fig. 8. Photomicrograph of Metal Showing Oxide Inclusions at Grain Boundaries. Magnification 80 X. No Etch.

Oxide inclusions appear as gray areas. The black areas are pits where the oxide has dropped out during polishing of the specimen.

tion of head and web. Typical Rockwell "C" readings are shown in Fig. 6. The hardness surveys show a few spots where the diamond brale of the Rockwell-tester hit either gas pockets or inclusions on the side of the head and also some spots where this same action occurred on the horizontal slice 3/16 in. below the tread of the rail. These spots are indicated in Fig. 6 by the Rockwell "C" numbers of 3, 6 and 8. In general, the hardness numbers near the junction of the rail ends approach in magnitude the hardness numbers of the steel outside the heated zone.

A six-inch section of the rail head, including the junction between the rails, was sliced into five horizontal slices and etched in 50 percent hydrochloric acid. Figure 7 shows the under side of the top slice, which was taken about ⅛ in. below the tread of the rail. Along both sides of the head at the weld region, the acid has brought out markings which look like cracks. However, microscopic examination shows that these markings were caused by the metal having been burned during the welding operation. This action deposited iron oxide at the grain boundaries. The oxide is dissolved by the etching acid. Figure 8 is a photomicrograph of the metal in this area, showing the gray inclusions of iron oxide along the grain boundaries. Some of the oxide dropped out during the polishing of the surface of the specimen, leaving pits which show black in the figure.

IV. Mechanical Tests of Specimens From Welded Joints

By S. W. LYON

17. Significance of Mechanical Tests of Specimens from Welds.—In general, mechanical tests of specimens from welded-rail joints give a measure of the quality of the metal in the joint rather than a measure of the strength or toughness of the joint as a whole. In some cases, doubtless, mechanical defects were present in the small specimens cut from various parts of welded rail. But in general these tests would give an idea of the quality of the material itself when undamaged by mechanical defects—cracks, notches and other "stress raisers."

18. Strength, Ductility and Toughness Tests of Specimens from Welds.— The tests used to give some idea of the mechanical properties of the metal in the welds included, tension tests, fatigue tests and tension-impact tests. The tension test gives a measure of the static strength and static ductility of the material; the fatigue test gives some idea of the strength of the specimen under repeated stress; and the tension-impact test gives some measure of a combination of strength and ductility which is designated as "toughness." The specimens used are shown in Fig. 9. Tension tests were made in an Olsen screw-power testing machine using Robertson shackles to hold the specimens; fatigue tests were made in small rotating-cantilever machines which subjected the specimen to a complete reversal of flexural stress during a cycle of stress (one revolution of the machine), and tension-impact tests were made in a Charpy impact machine, fitted with a Lyon tension attachment.

Approximately 725 tensions tests, 1,280 fatigue tests, and 650 tension-impact tests have been made. Figures 11, 12 and 13 show the results of these tests.

19. Quality of Metal in Different Parts of the Welded Joint.—The etch tests (See Chapter III, page 746) made on different portions of the rail yielded etch patterns which show in a general way areas of section occupied by weld metal, metal affected by the heat of welding, and unaffected rail steel, as shown in Fig. 10 a. Groups of specimens were cut from the head, the web, and the base of joints, and in each

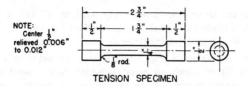

TENSION SPECIMEN

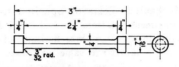

IMPACT TENSION SPECIMEN

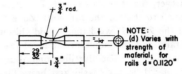

HIGH SPEED FATIGUE SPECIMEN

Fig. 9. Types of Specimens for Mechanical Tests
of Welded Joints.

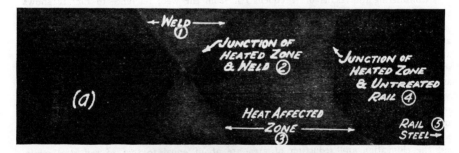

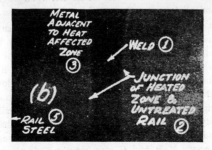

Fig. 10. Sections of Rails Welded by Processes A and D.

Etched to show extent of heated zone and location of various zones from which mechanical test
specimens were machined. Approximately half natural size. Etched with Ammonium Persulphate.
(a) Gas Fusion Weld—Process A
(b) Electric Pressure Weld—Process D.

group specimens were cut from five "zones": (1) weld metal, (2) junction metal between weld metal and heat-affected metal, (3) heat-affected metal, (4) junction between heat-affected metal and rail steel, and (5) unaffected rail steel.

In this connection, as shown in Fig. 10 b, it may be noted that for the electric pressure weld (Process D) in which no metal is added during welding, and in which the heat-affected zone is very narrow, the system of zone designation as used eliminates specimens from Zone 4.

20. **Results of Mechanical Tests of Specimens.**—Figure 11 shows the results of mechanical tests of specimens cut from the rail head. In this series specimens were actually taken at each of either two or three horizontal layers in the head. The value reported is for that layer whose average value was lowest.

In the case of specimens from the web and from the base, only one layer of specimens was taken,—vertical in the web and horizontal in the base. In Fig. 11 the tensile strength seemed lowest in Zone 2, the junction metal between weld and heat-affected metal. However, for the 131-lb. rail, Processes C and D, the tensile strengths seem to be about equal to that of the rail steel, Zone 5. The endurance limit seemed to be slightly lower in the Zone 1, weld metal, and this was in general true both for the 112-lb. and 131-lb. rails, and the endurance limit of the rail steel, in general, was higher than that for the weld metal. The ductility and toughness were in general lowest in Zone 2, the junction metal between weld and heat-affected metal. Values of elongation, reduction of area, and energy for fracture (impact-tension values) were lower for weld metal than for rail steel, except for Process D, in which weld metal and rail steel showed nearly equal values for ductility and toughness.

Considering the results of specimens cut from the web, reference to Fig. 12 shows that the tensile strength in general is about equal in Zone 1, weld metal, and Zone 2, junction metal between weld metal and heat-affected metal. These values for Processes A and B are distinctly below those for rail steel. For Processes C and D the values are about the same as those for rail steel. For Process E, 131-lb. rail, the figures seem to be somewhat lower than for rail steel. The endurance limit is also lowest in Zones 1 and 2, and in all cases seems somewhat lower than for rail steel. The values for elongation, reduction of area and toughness are lowest in Zones 1 and 2, and for Processes A, B and C they are distinctly below the values for the rail steel. For Process D the results are slightly below the values for rail steel except reduction of area, which is about equal to that for rail steel. For Process E the data are incomplete, but for the 112-lb. rail the elongation and reduction of area are about equal to that of rail steel while for the 131-lb. rail and all tension-impact values the toughness is distinctly less.

Figure 13 gives a summary of the values for specimens cut from the base of the rail. The values of tensile strength again seem in general to be smallest in Zones 1 and 2. For Processes D and E the tensile strength seems to be equal to, and in some cases slightly above, that for the rail steel. For Processes A, B and C it is distinctly lower than that for the rail steel. The endurance limit is also lowest at Zones 1 and 2. In general, none of the fatigue tests show results quite up to the fatigue strength of the rail steel, although Processes D and E and the 112-lb. rail, Process C, approach that value. The ductility and toughness tests of material in the base again give minimum values for Zones 1 and 2. And again Processes D and E approach or equal the value for rail steel, and Processes A, B and C give results distinctly below. For the tension-impact results for Zones 1 and 2 it is again noted that values for Processes D and E approach (but in this case do not equal) values for rail steel, while for Processes A, B and C, values are lower than for rail steel.

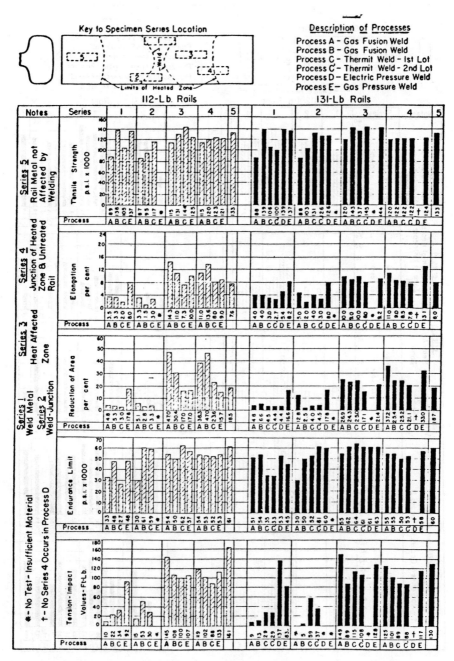

Fig. 11. Summary of Results of Mechanical Tests on Welded Rail Joints.
Specimens Cut from Head.

178

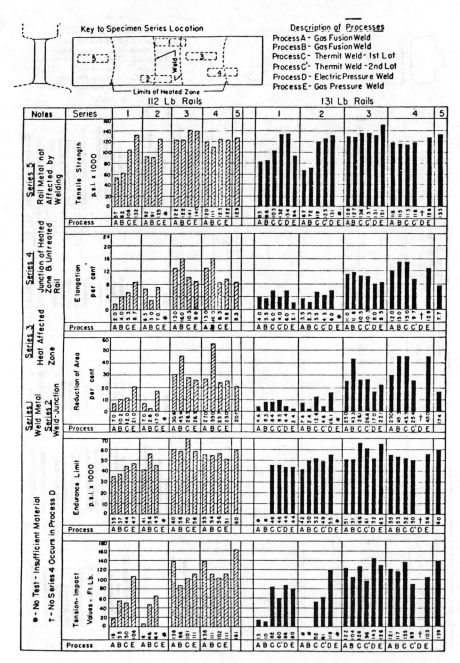

Fig. 12. Summary of Results of Mechanical Tests on Welded Rail Joints.
Specimens Cut from Web.

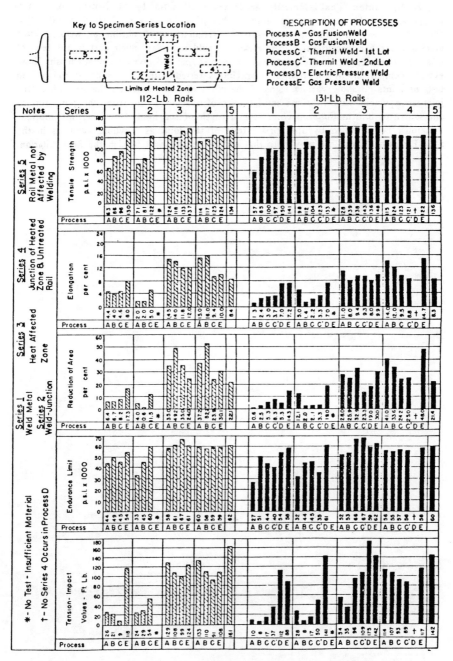

Fig. 13. Summary of Results of Mechanical Tests on Welded Rail Joints.
Specimens Cut from Base.

21. Specimen Tests Results as Indexes of Quality of Joints.—As pointed out previously, the specimens cut from welded joints indicate qualities of metal rather than of the welded joints. Such factors as irregularities of outline at welds, minute cracks, and other mechanical "stress raisers" would not play much part in the tests of small specimens cut from the joint, machined to shape, and given a smooth finish. However, a comparison of the results of specimens tested with the results of rolling-load tests of joints do show various signs of the effect of poor metal on the strength of the joint as a whole. Evidently mechanical tests of specimens cut from the joint furnish one source of information concerning the strength of the joint. However, this information must be amplified by appropriate tests of the joint as a whole,—and, as in the First Progress Report, we may note that service records will furnish the final criterion.

A

Session 411
Paper H.6

THE FLASH BUTT WELDING OF HIGH STRENGTH RAIL

M. J. VINES

P. H. TOWNEND

G. LANCASTER

S. MARICH

SUMMARY   The paper outlines problems associated with the flash butt welding of high strength materials and describes the modified procedures which are required for the various types of alloy and heat-treated rail.   In high hardenability alloy material fully pearlitic weld microstructures are achieved through an accurately controlled post-heating cycle while for medium hardenability materials a relatively strong pre-heat may be sufficient. For heat-treated rail some increase in weld zone hardness and reduction in weld zone width are necessary and a number of experimental techniques to achieve this are described.   Emphasis is placed on the need for strict machine control and cycle consistency in all high strength rail welding.

1   INTRODUCTION

The flash butt welding of standard carbon rail has been regarded in the Pilbara as a relatively straight-forward process.   Once appropriate machine settings for a satisfactory weld micro-structure and sound joint were established there was found to be little need for regular, detailed examination of welds produced or for stricter con-trol over welding conditions.   In early production programmes all welds were ultrasonically checked but this practice was considered unnecessary when few defects were found.   Provided there were no visible faults, the welds could be safely deemed satisfactory and expected to perform well in-track.

The main reason for this situation has been the relatively low strength and simple metallurgy of the plain carbon, A.R.E.A. standard rail where a variety of machine settings and energy output will all give a weld zone sufficiently similar to the base material in terms of microstructure and mechanical properties.

This is not the case with high strength alloy or heat treated rail as the weld zone may be markedly different from the base material.   Hard welds in alloy rail will form high spots in-track which can lead to corrugations after only 50 million gross tonnes (mgt) of traffic (Mair, 1976) and which pro-mote cyclical gauge face wear on tangent track after roughly 200 mgt (Jupp, 1978): in the extreme case hard welds can be dangerously brittle. On the other hand, standard butt welds in heat treated rail will be relatively soft, will dip in service under high axle load conditions and serious-ly affect vehicle tracking characteristics.   The resulting high dynamic stresses adjacent to the weld can also induce fatigue defects which have been observed after 250 mgt.

It is the purpose of this paper to outline the various techniques developed as part of a joint research programme between the Mt. Newman Mining Co., Hamersley Iron Pty. Ltd. and BHP to avoid these problems and ensure that inappropriate weld-ing procedures do not detract from the improved performance of these high strength materials. The need for much greater attention to the welding process will be demonstrated and the requirements of greatly improved machine control will be emphasized.

2   GENERAL

Almost all rail steels consist of a lamellar pearlite microstructure. In flash butt welds pearlite forms on cooling through 700° – 500°C and this can be conveniently simulated in the laborat-ory by vacuum dilatometry.   Samples are given a heating cycle approximately equivalent to that of welding and then cooled at various rates.   Phase transformations are shown by changes in sample length.

The resulting continuous cooling transformation (CCT) diagram of Temperature vs. Time is shown in Figure 1 for standard carbon rail.   In this material pearlite forms at all cooling rates up to approximately $33C^{\circ}$/sec.   As flash butt welding machines produce cooling rates of around $0.7 - 2C^{\circ}$/sec it is apparent that welds in this material will always be pearlitic as in the base material.   Weld zone hardnesses of 300 HV have been observed compared with 280 HV for the as-rolled material. In head-hardened and through-hardened rails, both of which have similar chemistries to standard material, similar weld hardnesses and microstruct-ures will result.   However, the base material is now harder at 380 HV through prior heat-treatment, and the weld zone thus becomes a soft patch in-track.

In alloy material the effect of elements such as chromium, molybdenum and vanadium is to increase hardenability, thereby reducing the maximum cooling rate at which pearlite can form.   In most alloy rails this has a marked effect with pearlite unable to form at cooling rates in excess of approximately

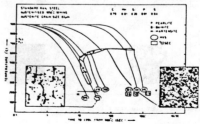

Figure 1   CCT diagram - standard carbon rail

TABLE I

TYPICAL ANALYSES OF STANDARD AND HIGH STRENGTH RAILS

Steel	Composition (%)								
	C	Mn	Si	S	P	Cr	Mo	V	Nb
Standard	0.79	0.81	0.20	0.04	0.01	–	–	–	–
Head Hardened (pearlitic)	0.75	0.80	0.22	0.02	0.03	–	–	–	–
Cr-V	0.76	1.27	0.21	0.02	0.02	0.86	–	0.12	–
Cr-Nb	0.82	1.11	0.52	0.03	0.02	0.87	–	–	0.04
Cr-Mo	0.76	0.90	0.22	0.03	0.02	0.77	0.17	–	–
Cr-Mo-V	0.71	0.92	0.19	0.03	0.02	0.78	0.17	0.06	–

$1C^o$/sec. at 650^oC and even as low as $0.3C^o$/sec. depending on rail chemistry. If these cooling rates are exceeded then martensite and bainite are formed. Bainite formation occurs at 400-500°C and is of moderate hardness, (approximately 350 HV), while martensite is formed at 200°C, is extremely hard (approximately 800 HV), and brittle. It is possible, of course, to have intermediate cooling rates with microstructures composed of all three constituents. Little is known as yet of the effects of various levels of bainite and martensite in flash butt welds but our approach has been to develop procedures which promote the formation of pearlite and reduce or eliminate completely these other constituents. As this may not always be successful, an estimate of acceptable martensite and bainite levels is then necessary and this is discussed later in the paper. The alternative approach is to temper any as-welded high-martensite structures. This was not seriously attempted for two reasons: fear of quench cracking and because the tempering operation cannot be performed in the machine itself but needs to be performed at a considerable distance downstream to cool the weld below 200°C and thus allow the formation of martensite.

In the development of these procedures it is important to realise that there can be considerable differences in the welding behaviour of the various types of alloy rail. For the purpose of this discussion it is convenient therefore to divide the alloys, on the basis of hardenability, into two groups.

3   MEDIUM HARDENABILITY ALLOY RAIL (MHAR)

This refers to rail of higher hardenability than standard carbon material but rail which may still be welded to form pearlitic microstructures with no post-weld heat treatment, i.e. little or no interference to the natural cooling rate. In

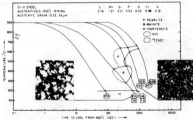

Figure 2   CCT diagram - Cr-V high strength rail

practice, this means that the material must be able to transform to pearlite at cooling rates in excess of 0.7-0.8C^o/sec. at 650°C as this seems to be the minimum which can be achieved naturally on flash butt welding machines. As shown in Figure 2 the Cr-V composition of Table I falls into this category and martensite and bainite are formed at cooling rates in excess of 0.7-0.8C^o/sec. The Cr-Nb steel is similar.

With regard to welding, these steels are attractive as there is little or no time loss compared with welding standard carbon rail. However, difficulties will arise if there is insufficient machine control to guarantee the same cycle consistently. Cooling rate is largely a function of total energy or heat input and if this varies, as has been observed with individual machines, then variable results are inevitable. Total martensite and bainite levels have been observed to range during a production programme in MHAR from 0-40% for this reason. It is therefore essential for modern flash butt welding machines to provide strict control of each welding cycle so that satisfactory welds obtained in procedure trials can be consistently repeated in full production. Perhaps in recognition of this, modern machines now boast electronic control systems based on feedback loops for improved welder control.

The rails themselves will vary in composition, and therefore hardenability, and this must also be considered in preparing a welding programme. Procedures developed on rail at the lean end of the chemical specification may not be adequate for material at the upper limits of the specification.

It is important to realise too that there are significant differences between individual makes of machine and that welding procedures must be developed for particular machines. Not all welders, for instance, can attain natural cooling rates as low as 0.7-0.8C^o/sec. In this case an insulating box can be applied to the completed weld immediately after shearing and straightening to reduce the cooling rate through the critical transformation range. Trials conducted with thermit welds have demonstrated the effectiveness of this technique. It would appear to be most appropriate where only moderate reductions in cooling rate are required or where the effects of variability in cooling rate need to be nullified.

4   HIGH HARDENABILITY ALLOY RAIL (HHAR)

High hardenability rail is defined here as material which on welding requires cooling rates of less than approximately 0.7C^o/sec. at 650°C for pearlite

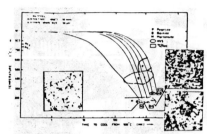

Figure 3   CCT diagram – Cr-Mo high strength rail

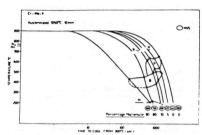

Figure 4   CCT diagram – Cr-Mo-V high strength rail

formation. To achieve these rates, or their equivalent effect, some form of post-weld heat treatment
is clearly necessary. Examples are the Cr-Mo and
Cr-Mo-V compositions of Table I; CCT diagrams are
shown in Figures 3 and 4.

It is possible to form a pearlitic microstructure
using a number of different post-heating techniques.
Post-heat can be used to either reduce the cooling
rate, stop it entirely, or even to raise the temperature of the weld zone. Hence a number of alter-
natives are available in seeking the most reliable,
effective and also the shortest post-heat cycle. It
should be noted here that the post-heating cycles
described have been carried out in the welder itself and not by a separate heating unit.

Procedure 1

As mentioned above, pearlite will form on continuous cooling if the cooling rate is sufficiently
slow. Some reduction in cooling rate may be obtained by applying post-heat almost immediately
after welding, when the weld zone temperature has
fallen to 750-800°C. Sufficient current pulses are
applied to arrest the cooling curve, as shown in
Figure 5 – Cycle A, for a period of 1-2 minutes,
after which the weld is allowed to cool naturally
at its reduced cooling rate. Heat losses by con-
vection and radiation mean that only cooling rates
of the order of 0.5-0.6C°/sec. are feasible. Martensite levels are therefore reduced in HHAR (<10%
in Cr-Mo-V) but not eliminated and the material is
largely bainitic. Some increase in soft zone width
will occur because of the hold time at high temperature. However, the technique is simple, strict
temperature control is unnecessary and there is
minimum delay between the welding and post-heating
operations.

It is also an appropriate technique for welding
medium hardenability materials on machines with

relatively fast natural cooling rates where other
factors may prevent the use of insulating boxes.
Its suitability for high hardenability materials
may be better judged when more is known of the influence of mixed microstructures on weld performance.

Procedure 2

A similar technique uses post-heating to reheat the
weld zones, as shown in Figure 5, Cycle B. Subsequent cooling rates are of the order of 0.4-
0.5C°/sec. but the reheat is not applied until the
weldment cools to a temperature below that mentioned in Procedure 1. This means, of course, a greater delay, 4-5 minutes, between welding and post-
heating and therefore a lower production rate.
Microstructures are similar to those of Cycle A,
with low levels of martensite in a largely bainitic
matrix but there is less softening of the thermally
-affected zone because of the lower post-heating
temperatures.

Procedure 3

Pearlite will also form isothermally, i.e. by allowing the weld to cool to the optimum temperature for
transformation and employing post-heat to maintain
it at this temperature until transformation is complete (Figure 5, Cycle C). Limited trials using
this technique have produced mixed results, with
fully pearlitic microstructures sometimes forming
in Cr-Mo-V welds after 2-5 minutes of hold time but
only consistently forming after 6 minutes. As there
is already a 4-5 minute delay to cool to the transformation temperature this is unacceptably slow.
The reason for the variable results is not yet
clear but it is apparently not due to poor temperature control.

Procedure 4

To avoid the above problem and ensure pearlitic
welds consistently, a more reliable technique was
developed. This is a two-stage post-heating cycle
comprising an initial temperature arrest followed
by a re-heating phase. The resultant cooling curve
is shown schematically in Figure 5, Cycle D. Actual
times and temperatures for each stage depend critic-
ally on the transformation characteristics of the
steel. However, the method has proved effective
and reliable in producing fully pearlitic weld
microstructures in the high hardenability Cr-Mo and
Cr-Mo-V compositions (Table I). This has been

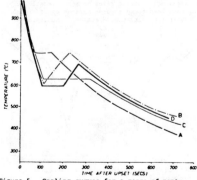

Figure 5   Cooling curves for a range of post-
heating cycles

3

Session 411
Paper H.6

achieved and yet reasonable production rates maintained by restricting the actual duration of the
post-heating cycle to the absolute minimum.

For the technique to be successful it is essential
that weld temperature be continuously monitored,
as variability in weld cooling rates means that
post-heat cannot be accurately applied at a single
fixed time interval after welding. An infra-red
pyrometer can monitor the surface temperature of
the rail head and this is then easily related experimentally to its core temperature. The main
feature of the technique is that consistent microstructures can be virtually guaranteed as welder
variability is nullified.

5 HEAT-TREATED RAIL

Heat-treated rail is generally less expensive
than alloy rail and could well emerge as the dominant high strength material. However, while its
performance compared to alloy rail is still under
study there is some controversy as to its weldability and particularly its behaviour under high
axle load conditions.

Unlike alloy rail it is felt that weld zones in
heat treated rail, head-hardened or through-
hardened, are too soft relative to the base material. A hardness transverse across a flash butt
weld is shown schematically in Figure 6. The hardness of the central weld zone, 300-320 HV, is
considerably less than that of the base material
at around 380 HV. In the spheroidized regions
each side of the weld zone the hardness drops to
around 250 HV.

The tempered martensite material initially used in
the Pilbara showed severe plastic flow in the soft
zones after only 25 mgt of traffic and this led to
the belief that they would have to be narrowed.
Later observation of pearlitic material (Table I)
showed similar results but in some areas there was
a general dipping of the whole weld region. Both
phenomena can seriously affect vehicle tracking
and lead to corrugation formation.

To prevent this it is therefore necessary to harden
and/or narrow as much of the weld as possible. A
number of techniques have been developed to achieve
these aims, but to date we have insufficient
results for any firm judgement. Weld cooling rates
have been increased by application of an air cooling treatment (Figure 7) immediately after welding
and shearing. Cooling rates of approximately 8C°/
sec. have been found to give hardnesses of around
380 HV in the central weld region. The improve-

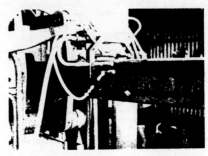

Figure 7   Experimental air-quenching rig for heat-
treated rail

ment obtained in hardness transverse is shown
schematically in Figure 6. Unfortunately the few
results obtained to date have not clarified the
effect of air cooling on soft zone width, although
some improvement might be expected.

Other techniques still to be thoroughly investigated include the inducement of changes in current
path through the rail head and modifications to
the rail head electrodes to harden and narrow the
weld zone.

A further proposal currently being evaluated is
flame or induction hardening of the completed weld.
Hardening to sufficient depth appears feasible,
the major concern being the width of the soft
zones adjacent to the heat-treated region.

Because of lack of field data on the performance
of welds in heat treated rail it is not yet possible to rely solely on simple techniques such as
hardness transverses for weld evaluation. For
this reason the most promising of the welding techniques for heat-treated rail will be used to produce test welds for the rolling-load machine at
BHP-MRL. This machine, described elsewhere at this
Conference (Marich, 1978), will enable the long
term performance of the welds to be assessed more
quickly.

Welder variability is also a problem for heat-
treated material by its effect on total weld width.
Welds taken from a recent programme showed widths
ranging from 30-70 mm. Clearly, the narrower
welds are preferable and indeed, if they could be
produced consistently, may even prove adequate
without the use of special welding techniques.

6 DISCUSSION

From the foregoing text it may appear that to weld
alloy rail requires a general degree of sophistic-
ation in procedure that could not be consistently
maintained at the welding station under normal
production conditions. However, if there is sufficient forethought and proper planning these materials can be welded to give optimum microstructures at good production rates, and with a minimum
of extra demands on the operator. With some
medium hardenability materials a relatively "hot"
welding procedure is sufficient while for others,
or for a "cooler" machine, the simple application
of an insulating box may be necessary. For higher
hardenability rail post-heating can be fully and
accurately automated; by means of continuous monitoring of temperature and the appropriate electronics, the machine can be made to follow any pre-
set temperature cycle.

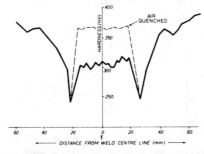

Figure 6   Flash butt weld in head-hardened rail

Session 411
Paper H.6

The procedures for welding alloy rail are therefore not difficult but it is essential that the welding machine itself be more consistent in heat input and general operation than is necessary for standard carbon rail. Most Australian experience has been gained on older and presumably more variable machines as the new generation of welders are just beginning to arrive here. It will be interesting to compare them with their predecessors in this respect.

The fundamental aim of the procedures outlined has been to reduce martensite levels and ultimately promote formation of fully pearlitic microstructures since these have proven satisfactory in service, while little is known as yet of the performance of welds containing significant levels of martensite and/or bainite. As alloy rail welding would be easier if these constituents could be tolerated, the question of maximum acceptable levels is of considerable interest.

A programme of work has therefore been started with the main areas of concern being the resistance of such welds to brittle fracture, wear and fatigue. It is hoped that a series of small and large-scale bend tests will relate fracture resistance to martensite level and also allow comparison with standard thermit welds, as these are generally considered to be inferior to good flash butt welds. A series of small-scale fatigue tests will show if premature crack initiation in martensite bands is likely or whether the soft thermally-affected region, over which there is little control, will be the eventual failure site. There are a number of high martensite welds in-track and their performance is being continually assessed. After 90 mgt there are no indications of serious deterioration. Once the results of all of these tests are known it should be possible to decide safe levels of martensite and bainite in flash butt welds.

With a knowledge of machine characteristics, rail materials and influence of weld microstructures, welding engineers will then be able to choose welding conditions most appropriate to operating conditions.

7   CONCLUSIONS

1. (a) For a number of high strength alloy rail materials a "hot" welding cycle is sufficient to ensure fully pearlitic weld microstructures.

    (b) On machines with "cooler" cycles similar results can only be achieved by using insulating boxes or a short post-heat.

2. For higher hardenability materials some form of post-heat is essential to avoid excessive levels of martensite. Fully pearlitic weld structures can be achieved by means of a two-stage post-heating cycle.

3. To improve weld performance in heat-treated rail some increase in weld hardness and reduction in weld zone width are necessary. This may be achieved by modifications to the welding cycle or re-hardening of the completed weld.

4. For successful welding of all high strength rail strict machine control and cycle consistency are essential.

8   REFERENCES

JUPP, R.A., and BAXTER, G.L. (1978). Practical and analytical studies into tangent track rail wear. Proc. Heavy Haul Railways Conf., Perth, Western Australia, Sept. 1978.

MAIR, R.I., and MURPHY, R.S. (1976). Rail wear and corrugation studies. American Railway Engineering Association, Bulletin 660, November-December, 1976.

MARICH, S., COTTAM, W.J., and CURCIO, P. (1978). Laboratory investigation of transverse defects in rails. The Institution of Engineers, Austalia Heavy Haul Railways Conference, Perth, September, 1978.

Chapter 2

Track Strength and Design

Final Report on a Three-Dimensional Photoelastic Investigation
of the Principal Stresses and Maximum Shears in the
Head of a Model of a Railroad Rail*

By M. M. Frocht†

June 26, 1953

Introduction

This report deals with a photoelastic study of the stresses in a model of the head
of a railroad rail, utilizing for this purpose the most recent developments in three-
dimensional photoelasticity. The study was undertaken in the expectation that the results
would lead to a better understanding of the phenomenon of shelling in rails.

The photoelastic procedure which makes the solution of a problem such as the rail
possible is rather complicated and a full description of this procedure is beyond the scope
of this report. Briefly it consists of: freezing, or fixing, stresses into plastic models of the
prototype; removing thin suitably oriented slices from these models; obtaining precision
data from these slices placed in the field of polarized light of a polariscope; and processing
the photoelastic data by the shear difference method. (See Studies in Three-Dimensional
Photoelasticity, by Max M. Frocht and Roscoe Guernsey, Jr., Proceedings of the First
National Congress of Applied Mechanics—1952.)

In order to freeze, or fix, elastic stresses into a photoelastic model the model is placed
in a furnace, the loads are applied, and the temperature is slowly raised to a certain
value, called the critical value, which depends on the model material. For Fosterite,
which is the material used in this investigation, the critical temperature is 188 deg F.
The loaded model is soaked at this temperature for several hours and then, still under
load, it is gradually cooled to room temperature.

---

* Submitted to the Joint Contact Committee of the AISI Technical Committee on Rails and
Joint Bars and the AREA Committee on Rail.
    † Research professor of mechanics, director of experimental stress analysis, Illinois Institute of
Technology, Chicago 16, Ill.

Upon removal of the load the model exhibits a photoelastic pattern which is geometrically similar to the patterns which are developed in that model at room temperature in the elastic state. The difference between frozen patterns and those at room temperature is the same as between room temperature patterns at different loads. Frozen patterns can be reproduced at room temperature by a suitable increase of the load. The stress distributions obtained from the frozen patterns are identical with those obtained at room temperature.

A body with frozen stresses differs from a body with ordinary stresses in two rather remarkable ways. First, the frozen stresses remain in the body after the loads are removed. Second, the frozen stresses are not affected by changes in the geometry of the body made after freezing. Thus, if a slice be carefully cut out from a body containing frozen stresses, the slice retains the frozen stresses after the cutting. Moreover, if a hole or groove be carefully machined in the slice that hole or groove will not affect the stress pattern of the slice. The slice may be cut in two or more parts without disturbing the locked-in stresses.

The process of freezing and slicing is the only practical approach to three-dimensional photoelasticity available today. Until 1951 only the principal stresses on the surface could be determined. No practical method was available to determine the principal stresses in the interior. In 1951 a new method was developed in our laboratory, at the Illinois Institute of Technology, by Dr. Guernsey and the writer, which makes it possible to determine the actual principal stresses at any interior point of an arbitrarily loaded body. From these it is relatively simple to find the principal shears.

Several problems have already been solved by this method which showed results of a high degree of accuracy. Among these is the sphere under diametral loads and struts compressed by flat dies.

This method has now been applied to a study of the principal stresses and of the maximum shears in a rail head. The present investigation is the first application of this new technique to a major practical problem. To the best of our knowledge no method exists, either mathematical or experimental, of equal power and scope.

Statement of Problem

Upon consultation with G. M. Magee and K. H. Kannowski of the AAR it was decided to use as prototypes a 132-lb RE rail and the average contour of 33-in diameter worn wheel treads. Stresses were to be determined for a vertical load and for a combination of vertical and horizontal loads transverse to the rail. The rails were to be set at a 40:1 cant and the loads were to be applied in such a manner as to pass through the gage corner.

Principal stresses and maximum shears were to be found in the transverse section of the rail under the center of the wheel, i.e., in the plane of symmetry of the rail. The study was confined to the elastic state.

Models

The models were machined from one block of Fosterite 6 in wide by 2½ in thick. The cross section of the rail head and the thickness of the web were made to two-thirds scale. However, the height of the web and the base of the rail were reduced in order to accommodate the available material (Fig. 1). It was felt that the modified web and base would have little, if any, effect on the stresses in the head, which were our primary point of interest. The length of the rail models was 6 in and the ends were left solid, i.e., the webs were not continued to the end (Fig. 2). The scale used for the head and web could not be applied to the length for that would have required a model about 20 ft long. The best that could be done with the available material was to make the model 6 in long. The solid ends tend in a measure to compensate for the loss of bending resistance about the axis of the web which a longer rail would have provided. The differences in the resistance between the short model and the longer one are not likely to affect seriously the stresses in the head in the region of interest.

As already stated the cross section of the wheel (Fig. 2) had the average contour of 33-in diameter worn wheel treads. Due to size limitations of available material only a small segment of the wheel, 3½ in long, was used. It was felt that the stresses in the head of the rail would not be appreciably affected by a longer or thicker wheel model.

The rail models were machined in two stages. First, an approximate stepped profile was formed by milling lengthwise with an end mill following a carefully calculated coordinate system so that the roots of the steps were on the true contour. Next, the steps were removed and a smooth surface formed by using a specially prepared profile cutter as a planing tool.

The wheel models were machined from blocks of Fosterite. These were mounted on an arm which was fixed to the compound of a lathe so that it could be swung in an arc of the proper radius. The contour was formed by end milling and finished by a form cutter as in the rail.

Loading Jigs

Fig. 3 shows a photograph of a pair of Fosterite models symmetrically mounted in the loading jig and subjected to a total central vertical load of 100.8 lb, which is equally distributed between the models making the net load on each model 50.4 lb. A sketch of the jig is shown in Fig. 4.

Fig. 5 shows a pair of Fosterite models and the loading jig used for combined loads. A sketch of the jig is shown in Fig. 6. Mr. Magee advised that, based on actual stress measurements in track, the ratio of the vertical to the horizontal component should be 3:1. Also, the horizontal component was made to pass through the gage corner (Fig. 6). The vertical load on each model was 51.0 lb. This load was applied in such a manner as to leave the axle essentially straight, which is equivalent to treating the axle as a rigid body. The wheels were carefully alined to rest on the gage corners.

The horizontal load was applied first and the vertical component later. In order to eliminate friction between the plates, rows of ball bearings were interposed as shown in Fig. 6.

Determination of Proper Load. Preliminary Test

After the models were made and the loading jigs built it became necessary to determine the magnitude of the loads to be applied. The load had to be large enough to produce measurable photoelastic effects, but not so large as to produce excessive deformations. This load could be determined only by experiment. In order not to run the risk of wasting the rather expensive Fosterite specimens a pair of rail models was made of Bakelite. The scale and the machining procedure were the same as for the Fosterite models.

Each Bakelite model was subjected to a load of 34.1 lb and the resulting stresses were frozen into it. Observations of the critical slice removed from this model showed that the applied load was approximately right for Bakelite.

Stress Patterns and Isoclinics

The load determined from the preliminary test with Bakelite was then increased to 50.4 lb to suit the Fosterite models and the resulting stresses were frozen into them. Transverse slices of symmetry were then removed and stress patterns obtained. Figs. 7 and 8 show a typical stress pattern and isoclinic from vertical loads. Figs. 9 and 10 show a typical stress pattern and isoclinic from combined loading.*

Photometric Methods for Isoclinics and Bi-refringence

In two-dimensional photoelastic work the standard procedure is to determine the fringe order and the isoclinic parameters from patterns such as shown in Figs. 7 and 9. However, the extension of the shear difference method to three dimensions involves more complicated equations than in two dimensions and depends more sensitively on the accuracy of the isoclinics and the bi-refringence. Of these the isoclinics are more difficult to determine accurately.

In the present investigation the isoclinic parameters and the corresponding bi-refringence were determined not from overall stress patterns but by point-by-point explorations using photometric devices which yield a much higher accuracy. The basic element in this method is a sensitive photometric cell. This procedure is more time consuming than the method which rests on the overall stress patterns, but, as stated above, it is also much more accurate. For example, with normal procedures, isoclinics are often ill defined and the error in the parameters may at times be as much as 2 deg. With the photometric technique, the error is seldom greater than 0.5 deg, and usually smaller. Similarly, the error in the bi-refringence, even when determined from a Babinet–Soleil compensator, is of the order of ±0.02 fringes. With photometric methods this error can be reduced to 0.005 fringes.

Lines Studied

After careful consideration it was decided to determine the stresses in the rail head along the 5 lines O'A, O'B, O'C, O'D, and O'E, shown in Fig. 11. It should be noted that O'Y'–O'Z' is a moving set of coordinate axes parallel to the fixed axes OY–OZ, with origin O at the top of the rail. The three vertical lines O'A, O'B, and O'C cover the most highly stressed region, the line O'B being chosen to pass through the highest fringe order.

It should also be noted that in integrating the differential equations of equilibrium the starting points were chosen on the free boundary. Thus, on the vertical lines the starting points were A, B, and C. On the horizontal lines they were at the origins O'. This was done in order to take advantage of the stress at the free boundary which can be determined directly from the local fringe order and isoclinics.

RESULTS AND DISCUSSION

Vertical Loads

Principal Stresses Along O'A, O'B, and O'C

The three curves in Fig. 12 show the principal stresses in fringes along line O'A. (In order to transform fringes into psi multiply by 17.65.) In this, as in all subsequent figures, σ_1 denotes the principal stress perpendicular to the plane of the paper, i.e., $\sigma_1 = \sigma_x$. The circles on σ_1 denote points where isoclinics and bi-refringence were measured.

---

* In the stress patterns, Figs. 7–10, the gage corner is on the left. In the subsequent figures the gage corner is on the right.

The other two principal stresses σ_2 and σ_3 lie in the plane of the paper, i.e., in the transverse section of symmetry of the rail. The directions of these stresses vary from point to point, as shown on the left side of the drawing. The full segments represent the directions of σ_2 and the dashed segments of σ_3. At the starting point A, σ_2 is tangent to the boundary and σ_3 is normal to it. Also, at point A, $\sigma_3 = 0$ since this point lies on a free boundary. We also note that along the line O'A, σ_2 is nearly horizontal and σ_3 is nearly vertical.

Inspection of the curve giving σ_1 shows that the upper fibers in the head are in compression and the lower fibers are in tension, indicating that the head of the model suffers bending. The stress σ_1 vanishes at a point for which $y'/O'A = 0.43$ approximately. Also, the maximum tension equals approximately the maximum compression.

On the line O'A there was a slight irregularity on the boundary at point O' and the isoclinics in that region could not be determined accurately. The dashed portions of the curves were obtained by extrapolation. This did not happen on O'B or O'C.

Turning now to σ_2 we note that this is the smallest of the three principal stresses and that it is compressive everywhere except in the immediate vicinity of A where it is tensile. The stress σ_3 is compressive all along the line O'A and varies from zero at A to 1.6 at O'.

The curves in Fig. 13 show the principal stresses along the line O'B. As already mentioned this line was chosen to pass through the zone of maximum fringe order in the region of contact. In this case the boundary was clear and undisturbed so that isoclinics and bi-refringence could be measured well nigh to O' and no extrapolation was needed. The curve of σ_1 again shows the presence of bending with the maximum compression at the top of the rail. Here, however, the maximum compression is considerably greater than the maximum tension, the ratio being about 22:13 approximately.

We also note that the directions of σ_2 and σ_3 vary considerably along O'B. The principal stress σ_2, which is compressive at the top, rapidly drops to zero and becomes tensile all the way to B, where both σ_2 and σ_3 vanish. The stress σ_3 is compressive all along O'B and has considerably higher values than along O'A.

Fig. 14 shows the principal stresses along O'C.

Fig. 15 is a composite of the curves of the principal stresses along O'A, O'B, and O'C.

Maximum Shears Along O'A, O'B, and O'C

Since in the region of contact the principal stresses are all compressive, the maximum shearing stresses assume particular significance in the phenomenon of failure and may be connected with the cause of shelling.

Inspection of the curves in Fig. 15 shows that in the region of contact σ_2 is the algebraic maximum and σ_3 the minimum in all cases. Consequently, the maximum shear, τ_{max}, in the region of contact is given by

$$\tau_{max} = \frac{\sigma_2 - \sigma_3}{2}$$

Moreover, σ_2 and σ_3 are the stresses in the YZ plane, i.e., in the transverse plane of symmetry. Therefore, vectors of the maximum shears lie in that plane and the stresses act on planes perpendicular to the plane YZ.

The maximum shear on O'A is 0.54 fringes and this stress is located at a point below O' for which $y'/O'A = 0.19$ approximately. It makes an angle of 45 deg with σ_2 and σ_3 and acts as shown in Fig. 12.

On O'B the maximum shear is 0.9 fringes. Its position below the surface of contact is approximately the same as on O'A. On O'C the shear progressively increases downward. In the vicinity of contact its values are between those on O'A and O'B.

Principal Stresses Along O'D and O'E

Figs. 16, 17 and 18 show the principal stresses along the horizontal lines O'D and O'E. These are seen to be tensile for approximately 0.4 of O'D and O'E, and numerically much smaller than in the region of contact.

Combined or Inclined Load

Principal Stresses and Maximum Shears on Lines O'A, O'B, and O'C

The principal stresses produced by the combined load are shown by the full curves in Figs. 19, 20, and 21. The dashed curves represent the principal stresses for the vertical load.

Again, the principal stresses are all compressive in the region of contact.

As in the case of the vertical load the maximum shear in the region of contact is due to σ_2 and σ_3 in the transverse section of symmetry, i.e.,

$$\tau_{max} = \frac{\sigma_2 - \sigma_3}{2}$$

On the line O'A, Fig. 19, the effect of the horizontal load is a measurable increase in σ_1, σ_3, and τ_{max}. Also, there is a slight shift in the position of the maximum shear toward the surface of contact. The shear adjacent to the surface of contact is slightly increased.

On line O'B, Fig. 20, the significant change seems to be in the shear adjacent to the surface of contact, which changes from 0.5 fringes to 0.65 fringes, approximately. The maximum shear remains essentially the same as for the vertical load.

The effects of the combined loading on the shears are more clearly shown in Fig. 21. It is seen that on line O'B the maximum shear is less localized for the combined loading than it is for the vertical load.

Fig. 22 shows the principal stresses for the line O'C. It is seen that numerically all stresses have been substantially increased.

Fig. 23 is a composite of all the curves of the principal stresses on lines O'A, O'B, and O'C for the inclined load.

The stresses along lines O'D and O'E are shown in Figs. 24 and 25. As in the case of the vertical load these stresses are predominantly tensile. The stresses produced by the combined load are also considerably greater than those produced by the vertical load.

Fig. 26 shows a composite for the principal stresses along O'D and O'E due to the combined load alone.

Checks

The most precise equipment and technique were employed in this investigation and every precaution was taken to assure accurate results. The similarity between the curves giving the stresses on the vertical lines O'A and O'B for vertical and combined loading reflects the precision methods employed.

A more direct index of the reliability of the results can be obtained from a static check. This is shown by the curves in Fig. 27 which give the values of the σ_y components along the horizontal sections O'D and O'E extended to the loaded side. The full portions of these curves represent the stresses along the lines O'D and O'E, respectively. The dashed portions are based on the stresses at the points of intersection of O'D and O'E with vertical lines O'A, O'B, and O'C. The areas under these curves represent the resultant normal forces R_1 and R_3, acting on the horizontal sections of the slice through O'D and O'E, respectively.

Taking as a free body the portion of the transverse slice lying between these horizontal planes, equilibrium must exist between R_1, R_2, and the vertical shears on the side faces. Since the slice is thin and the central plane of the slice is a plane of symmetry, these shears are negligible so that for equilibrium R_1 must equal R_2, approximately. Measurement of the areas under the curves shows that R_1 is greater than R_2 by less than 5 percent. Actual measurements of the shears show that they are very small and go in the right direction, i.e., upward. We thus have a satisfactory static check.

The curves for the stresses on the line containing O'E indicate that the results are independent of the path of integration. This follows from the smooth continuous merging of the dashed and the full curves.

Conclusions

1. Near the region of contact the principal stresses in the model are all compressive, both for the vertical load and for the combined loads used.

2. Below the region of contact the longitudinal stresses become tensile for both types of loading.

3. The maximum shear lies in the transverse section of symmetry for both types of loading.

4. For the vertical loads used the maximum shear is located on the line O'B, 0.2-in, approximately, below the contact area.

5. The effect of the horizontal thrust is primarily to increase the shear on O'B in the immediate vicinity of the area of contact by 30 percent, approximately. It also tends to move the position of the maximum shear closer to the surface of contact but does not alter its magnitude.

We note that wheel traction would produce longitudinal tensions in the rail which would sharply increase the maximum shear and bring it closer to the surface.

6. On the side of the rail away from the load the stresses are predominantly tensile and are much smaller than on the loaded side for both types of loading.

Note: All the figures referred to in this report are presented on the immediately following pages.

194

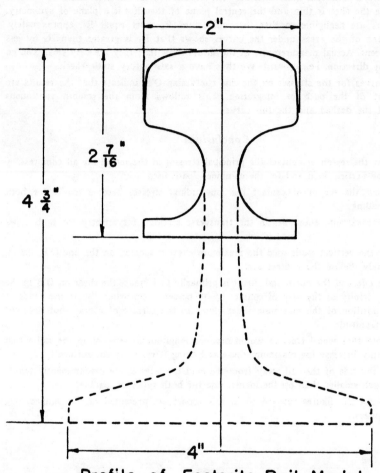

Profile of Fosterite Rail Model
Dotted lines show profile of web and base
of prototype drawn to same scale as model.

Fig. 1

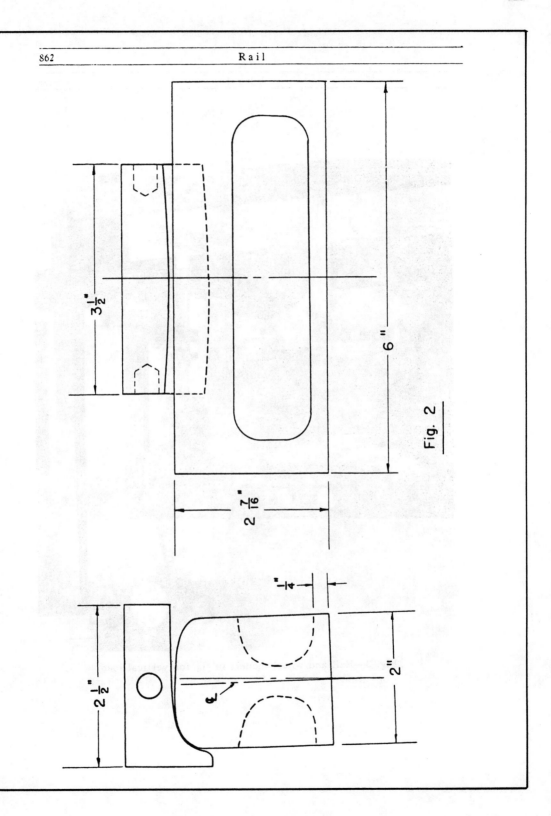

Fig. 2

196

Fig. 3—Rail and wheel models in jig for vertical load.

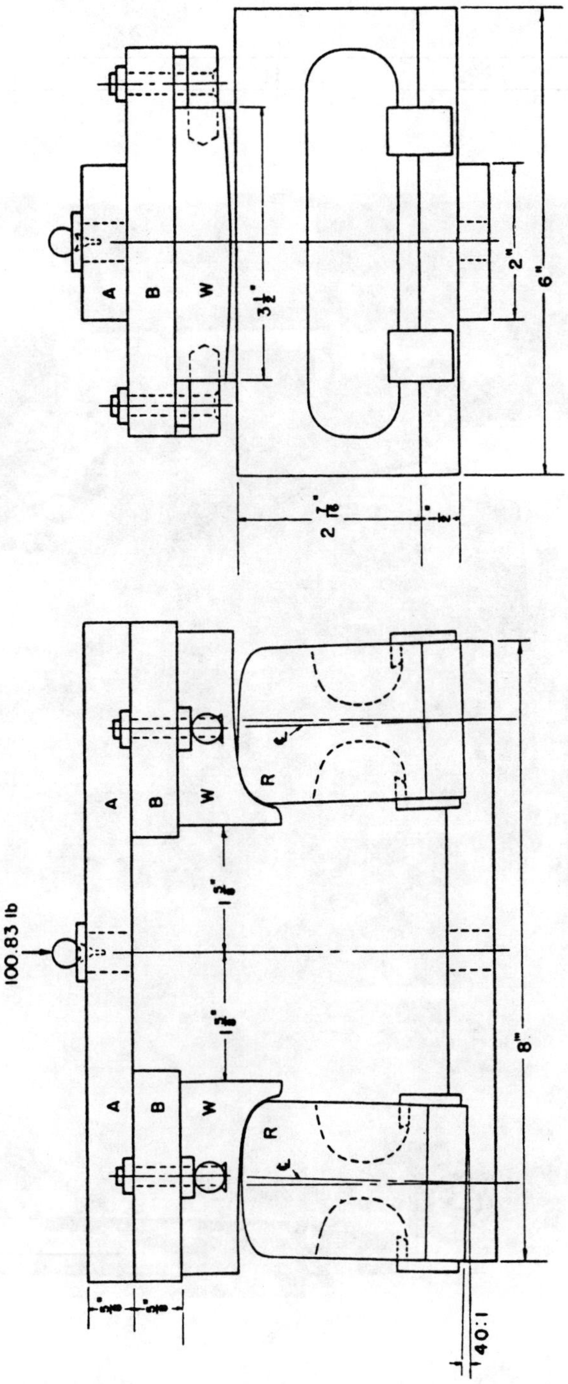

Fig. 4

198

Fig. 5—Rail and wheel models in jig for combined load.

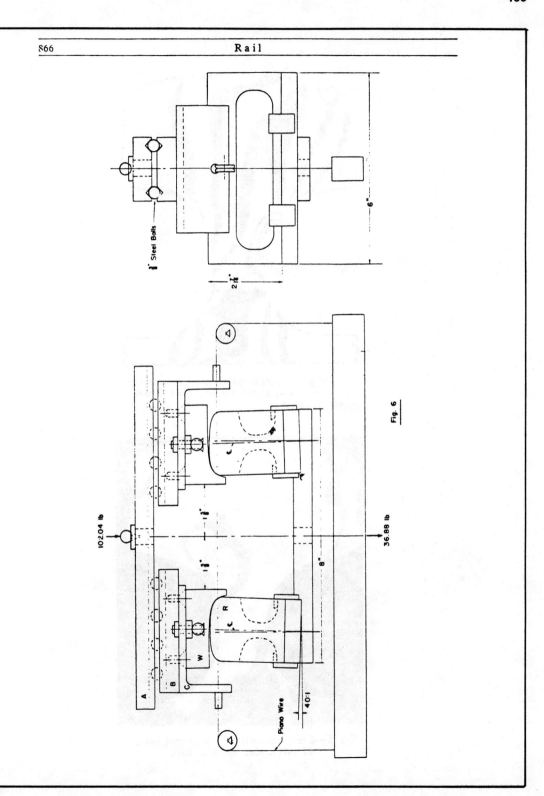

Fig. 6

Fig. 7—Stress pattern of transverse section of rail under vertical load. Thickness, 0.234 in.

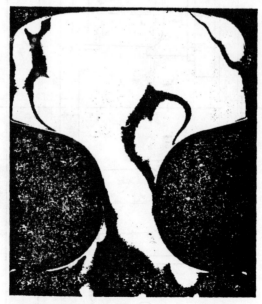

Fig. 8—Zero isoclinic of transverse section of rail under vertical load.

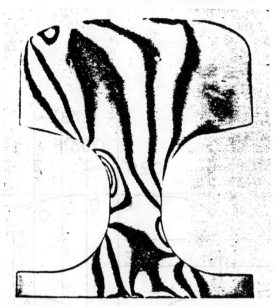

Fig. 9—Stress pattern of transverse section of
rail under combined load. Thickness, 0.234 in.

Fig. 10—Zero isoclinic of transverse section
of rail under combined load.

202

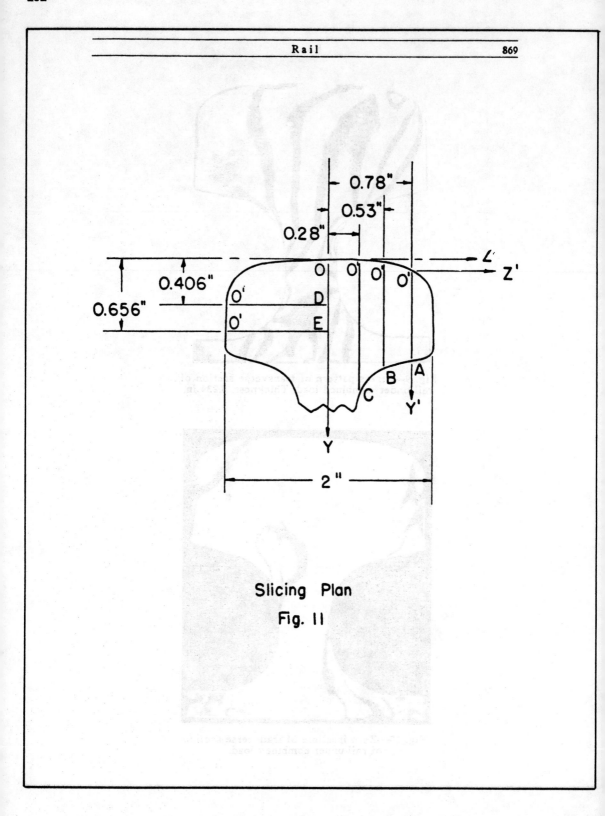

Slicing Plan

Fig. 11

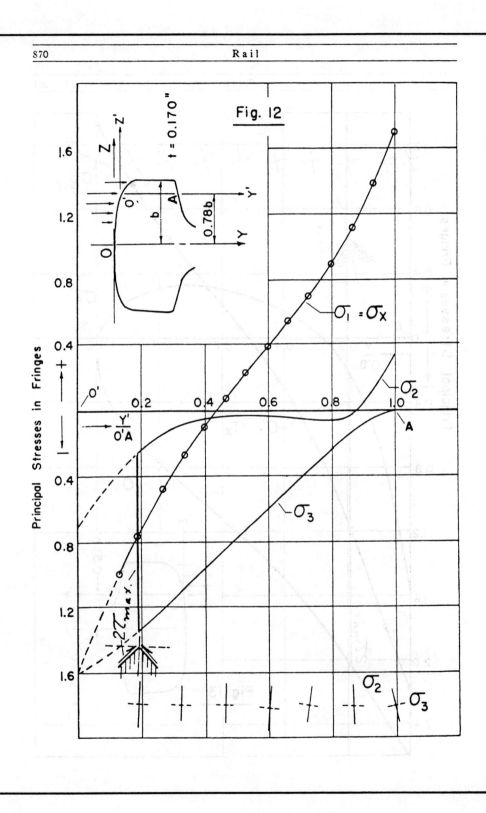

Fig. 12

204

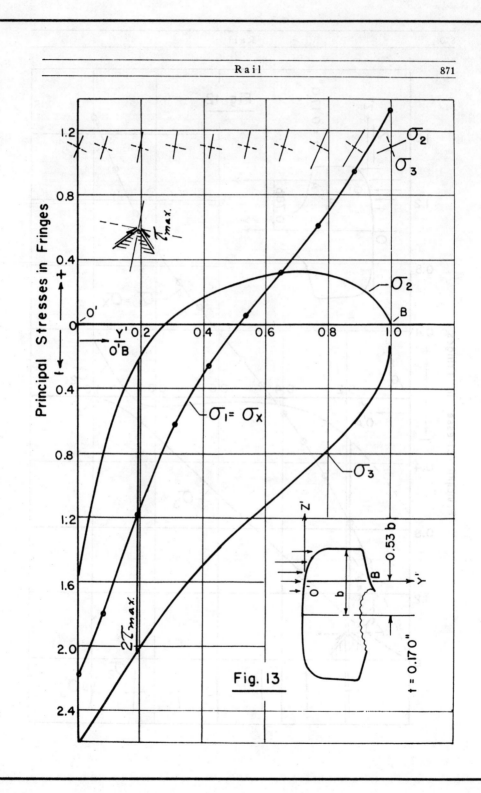

Fig. 13

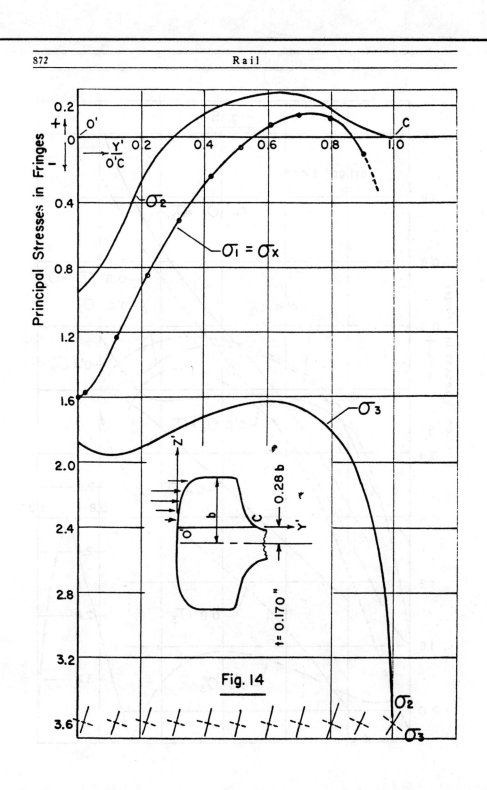

Fig. 14

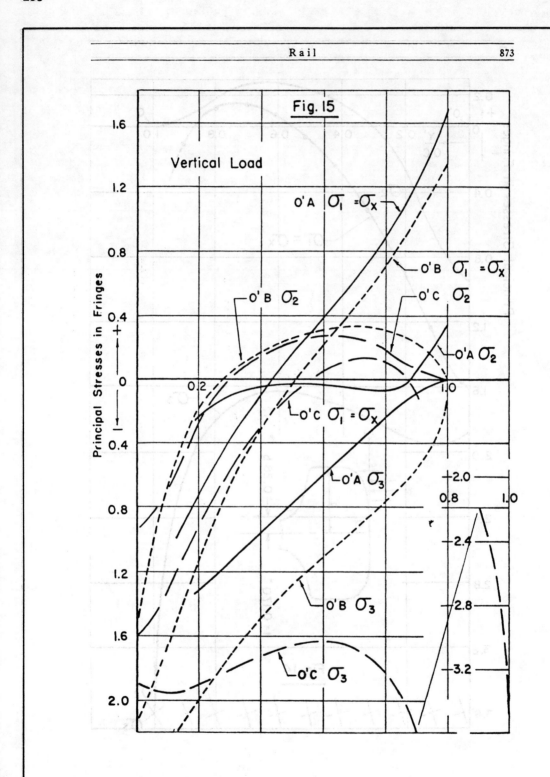

Fig. 15

Vertical Load

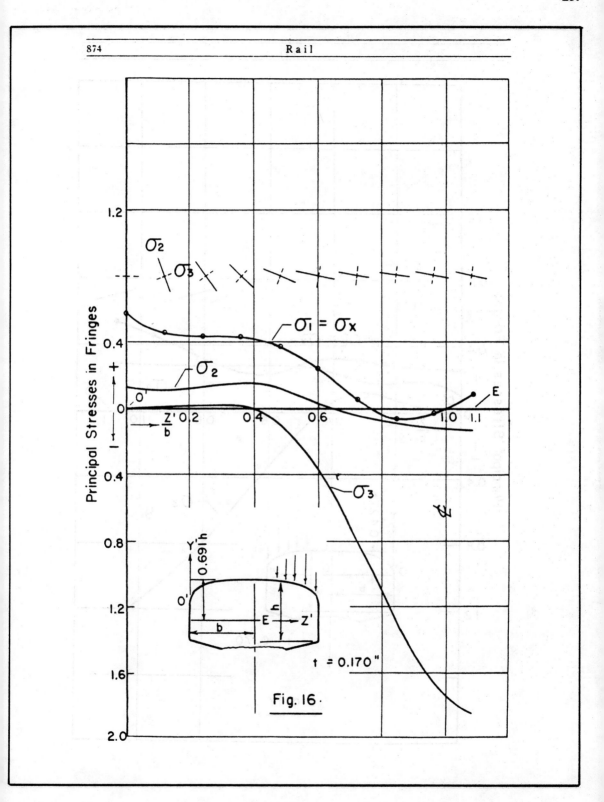

Fig. 16.

208

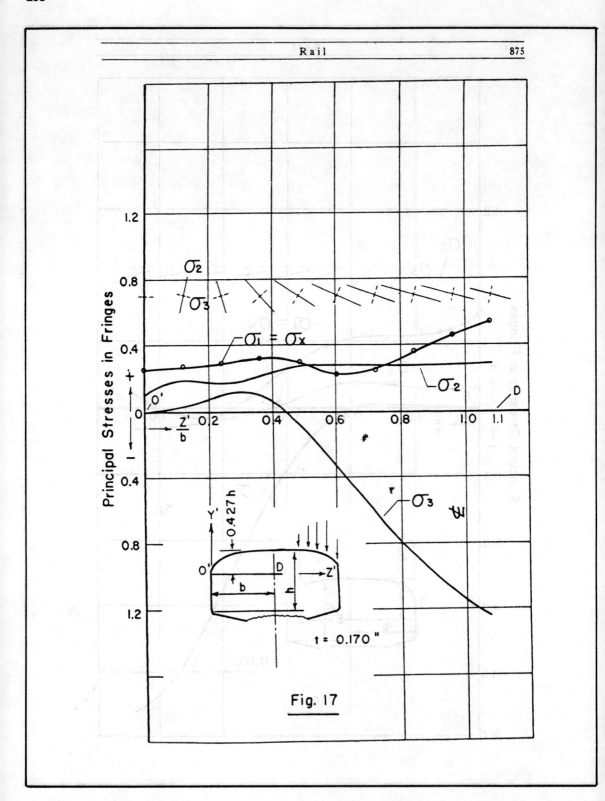

Fig. 17

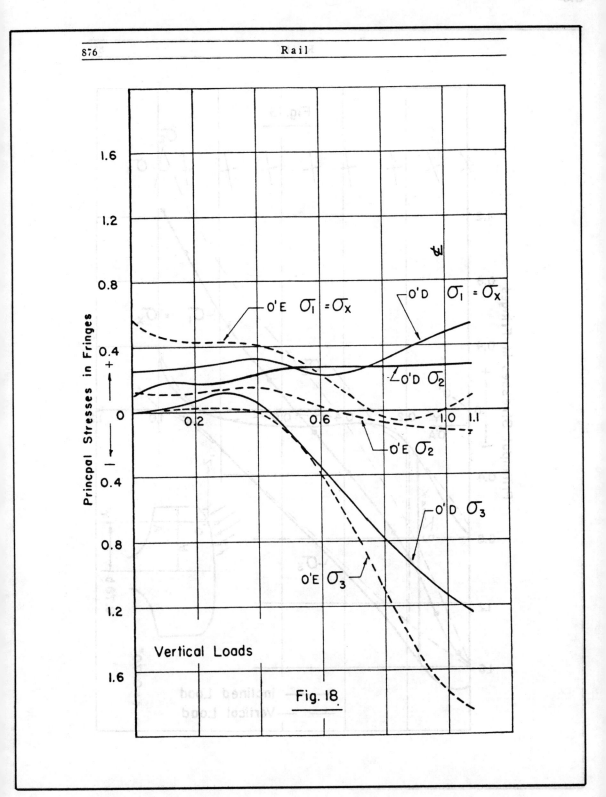

Fig. 18.

210

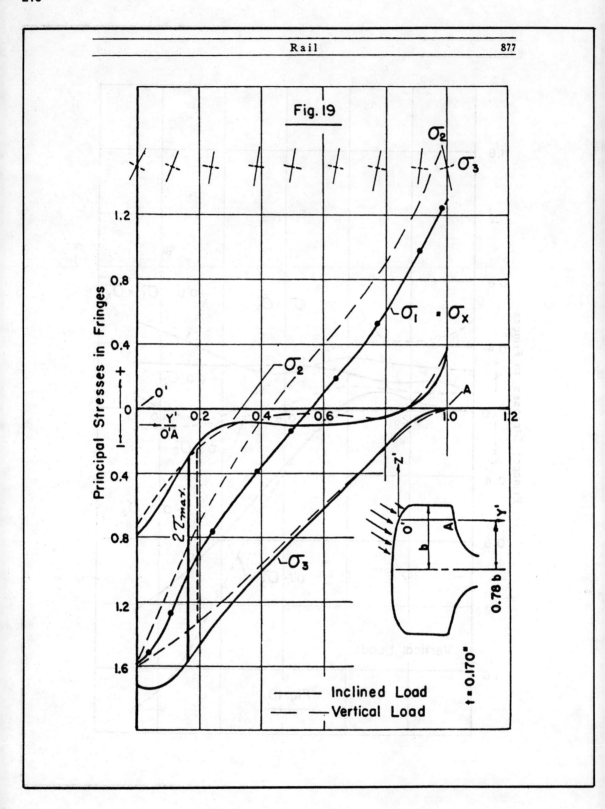

Fig. 19

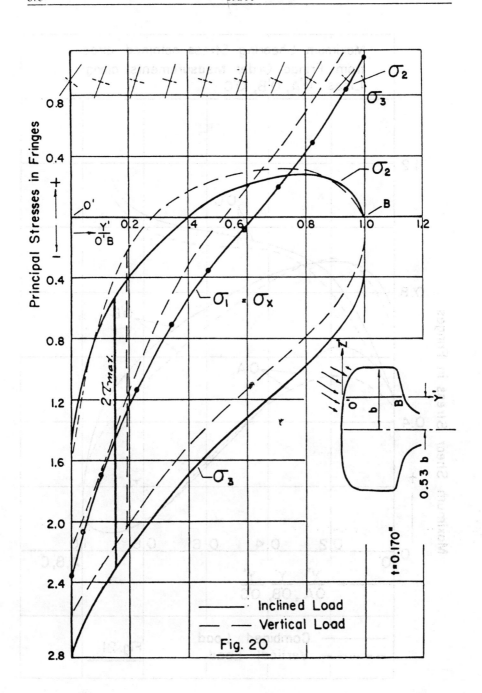

Fig. 20

212

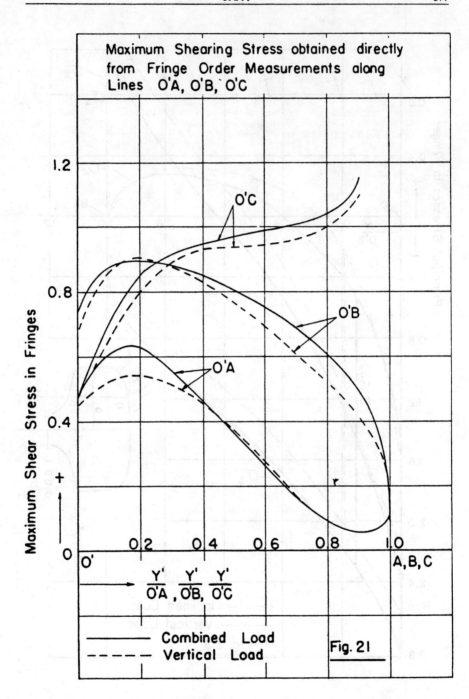

Maximum Shearing Stress obtained directly from Fringe Order Measurements along Lines O'A, O'B, O'C

Maximum Shear Stress in Fringes

O'C

O'B

O'A

$\dfrac{Y'}{O'A}, \dfrac{Y'}{O'B}, \dfrac{Y'}{O'C}$

——— Combined Load
– – – – Vertical Load

Fig. 21

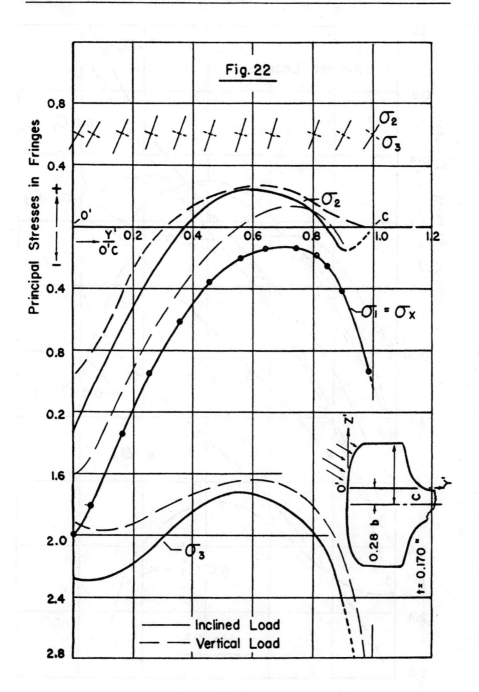

Fig. 22

214

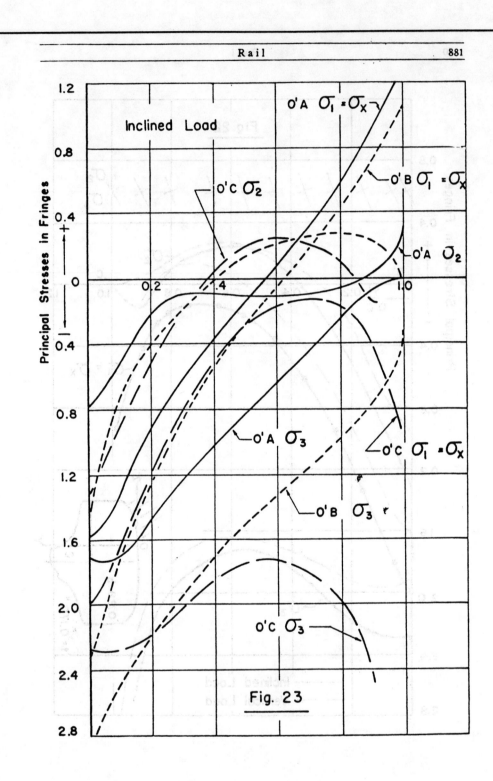

Fig. 23

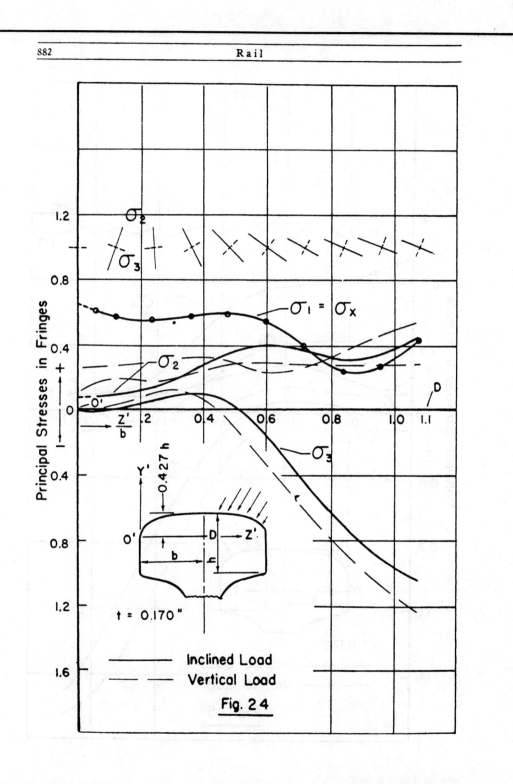

Fig. 24

216

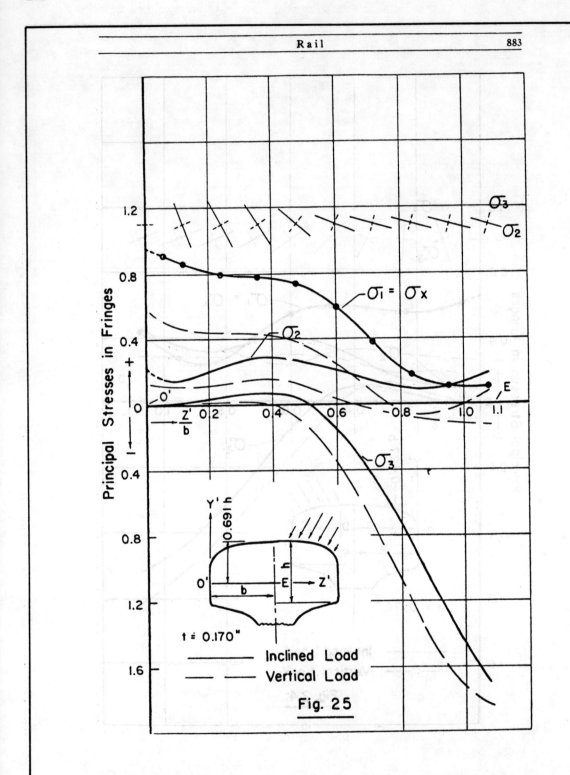

Fig. 25

Rail

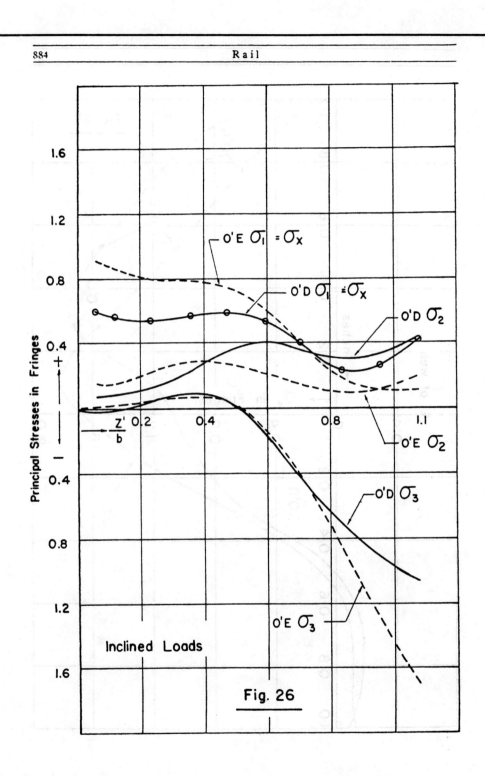

Fig. 26

218

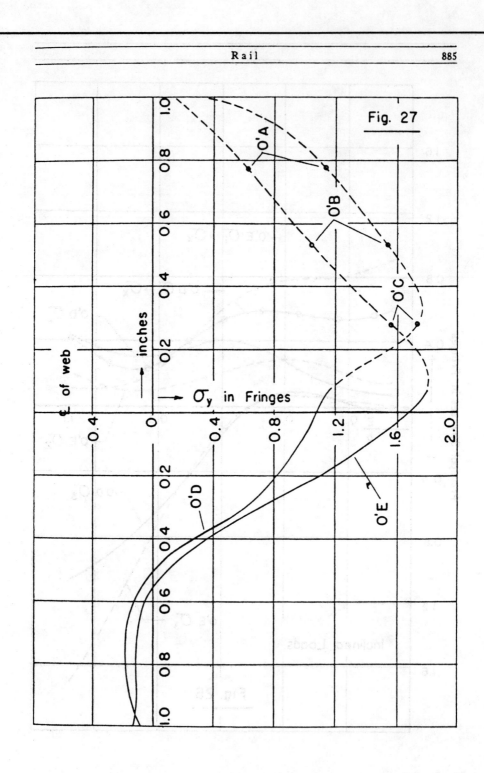

Fig. 27

Appendix 8-e

Final Report on a Three-Dimensional Photoelastic Investigation of the Stress Distribution in the Head of a Model of a Railroad Rail Along Lines Parallel to the Axis of the Rail

By M. M. Frocht

Research Professor of Mechanics; Director of Experimental Stress Analysis,
Illinois Institute of Technology

Introduction

This report may be viewed as an extension or supplement to the report (1)* of June 26, 1953, on a "Three-Dimensional Investigation of the Principal Stresses and Maximum Shear in the Head of a Railroad Rail." The above report was confined to stress determinations along lines in the plane of symmetry of the rail, which is transverse to the axis of the rail and passes through the center of the wheel. In the present report we deal with the stresses in the rail in the region of contact along interior lines parallel to the axis of the rail, such as line F–F, Fig. 1. The study was undertaken in order to see whether the interior stresses along the length of the rail may not throw some light on the possible cause of shelly failures.

The photoelastic models and loading jigs were of the same material and dimensions as those described in the first report. The general method of procedure was also the same. Specifically, the rectangular stress components were determined by the shear-difference method (2), (3), (4) from sub-slices containing frozen stresses. Typical stress patterns of a transverse and longitudinal slice, from which the sub-slices were taken, are shown in Figs. 2 and 3.

The stresses were determined in two different models under two different loads. In one model the load was 51 lb, which is the same as that used in the first study. The results from this model showed that while in the vicinity of the load the normal stress components σ_x, σ_y, and σ_z were all compressive, they changed into tensions at points approximately 1 in to either side of the wheel center.

In order to bring out more accurately this state of triaxial tension the tests were repeated with another model and a vertical load of 78.4 lb, which is roughly 50 percent greater than the first load.

It was found that the stress distribution is essentially the same for the higher and lower loads, thus showing that the stress distribution on the lines studied is little affected by the substantial increase in the contact area produced by the larger load.

Lines Studied

(a) *Vertical Load 51 Lb*—In the first model carrying 51 lb the stresses were determined along the two lines parallel to the axis of the rail passing through points F, G, in the plane of symmetry, Fig. 4. In this determination the initial values of σ_x were taken from the stress curves for lines AO′ and BO′ in the plane of symmetry, which were available from the first report for the same load. The line BO′ passes through the region of the maximum shear close to the region of contact. (See Figs. 12 and 13 in the first report).

(b) *Vertical Load 78.4 Lb*—The stresses were first determined along lines AO′ and BO′ in the plane of symmetry. Using the initial values from the curves for AO′

---

* Numbers in parenthesis pertain to references listed at the end of the report.

and BO' the stresses σ_x were next determined along the longitudinal lines F–F, G–G, and H–H passing through the points F, G, and H, Fig. 4. Lines F–F, and G–G were the same as those used for the smaller load.

RESULTS

(a) Vertical Load 51 Lb

Line F–F—Fig. 5 shows the six rectangular stress components along the longitudinal line F–F. It is seen that the normal stresses σ_x, σ_y and σ_z are all compressive in the region near the load and that their maximum numerical values occur under the center of the wheel. Also, as would be expected, σ_y is the greatest of these stresses. The curves further show that all three normal stresses change into tension at $X/L = 0.4$, approximately. Inspection of Fig. 5 further shows that τ_{xy} reaches a maximum at $X/L = 0.27$, where it attains a value approximately equal to 35 percent of the maximum σ_y. The shear component τ_{yz} remains fairly constant in the interval $X/L = 0$ to $X/L = 0.24$. In this interval the magnitude of τ_{yz} is about 20 percent of the maximum σ_y. The shear τ_{xz} was found to be extremely small.

Line G–G—The stresses along line G–G, Fig. 6, shows a similar distribution to that found on line F–F. The magnitudes of the normal stresses, however, were found to be higher than those on line F–F. For example, the stress σ_y at the center of the wheel is about 50 percent greater. The normal stresses along G–G, like those along line F–F, also change from compression to tension as the distance from the wheel center increases. The magnitude and position of the maximum τ_{xy} remain essentially the same as on line F–F. The shearing stress τ_{yz} near the region of contact was found slightly higher on line G–G than that on line F–F.

From the rectangular stress components the principal stresses σ_1, σ_2, and σ_3 were calculated (see Appendix A). These stresses are shown in Fig. 7. As in the case of the normal stresses the principal stresses also change from compression into tension.

(b) Vertical Load 78.4 Lb

Line AO'—The curves in Fig. 8 represent the stress distribution along line AO' in the plane of symmetry. Because of symmetry the shearing stresses τ_{xy}, and τ_{xz} are identically zero.

The stresses σ_x are tensile in the lower half of the head and compressive in the upper half. Except for a small region at point A the stresses σ_y are compressive all along the line AO'. The stresses σ_z have a small tensile value at the lower fiber, a small compressive value at the top and are practically zero in the middle of the line AO'. The vertical shearing stresses τ_{zy} are small and remain fairly constant across this line. In general, these stress distributions are similar to those produced by the smaller load.

Line BO'—The curves in Fig. 9 show the stresses along line BO'. As already mentioned, this line was chosen to pass through the point of maximum shear which occurs close to the contact surface. The stresses σ_x, σ_y, and σ_z are similar in shape to those for line AO', but the numerical values in the contact region are much higher on line BO'. For example, at contact σ_y equals -44 psi approximately on line BO' and only -25 psi on line AO'. Similarly, σ_x is -38 psi on BO' and only -20 psi approximately on line AO'. The stresses σ_z at the lower fiber of the head becomes compressive, whereas on AO' it was tensile.

Line F–F—The curves in Fig. 10 show the rectangular stress components along the longitudinal line F–F, Figs. 1 and 4. These curves are very much similar in shape to those on the same line for the smaller load, Fig. 5, except for τ_{xz}, which is no longer small. The stress σ_x in Fig. 10 obtained from numerical integration vanishes at the free end where $X/L = 1$, and thus satisfies the boundary condition. As in the case of the smaller load, the state of stress changes from large triaxial compression into small triaxial tension as the distance from the wheel center increases. The greatest of the three shearing stresses is τ_{xy}, which reaches a maximum value of 50 percent of the maximum σ_y at $X/L = 0.3$.

Fig. 11 shows the principal stresses σ_1, σ_2, and σ_3. The normal stress components σ_x, σ_y, and σ_z were also plotted for purpose of comparison. As would be expected, these components lie between the maximum and minimum principal stresses σ_1, and σ_3.

It will be noted that at point M, where $X/L = 0.35$, approximately, the principal stress σ_1 assumes a value almost equal to 50 percent of the maximum σ_y. Inspection of the curves further shows that the maximum compression, σ_3, does not occur at wheel center, but at $X/L = 0.2$ approximately.

The principal stress directions were also calculated (see Appendix B). The direction of each principal stress is given by the three angles θ_x, θ_y, and θ_z which the stress makes with the X, Y, and Z axes, respectively. The following table gives the principal stress directions at point M, where the maximum tension occurs:

	θ_x	θ_y	θ_z
σ_1	55.2°	54°	55°
σ_2	102.1°	124.7°	37.4°
σ_3	98.1°	54.9°	78.4°

The plane at point M, Fig. 11, on which the maximum σ_1 acts will be called the P-plane and the normal stress on planes parallel to plane P will be denoted by σ_p. The values of σ_p at $X/L = 0$ and $X/L = -0.35$ were also calculated (see Appendix C), and are given in the table below:

X/L	σ_p
0.35	11 psi
0	— 13 psi
— 0.35	— 10 psi

Line G–G—The stress distribution along line G–G is shown in Fig. 12. The curves for the rectangular stress components have characteristics similar to those observed along line F–F. The numerical values of the stresses in the loaded region are higher. The maximum compression σ_y at the wheel center is about 70 percent greater than that on line F–F. The normal stresses also change from large triaxial compression to small triaxial tension. The maximum τ_{xy} takes place at point N where $X/L = 0.3$ and is slightly lower than that on line F–F. The principal stresses are shown in Fig. 13. The results are also similar to those for line F–F. Of particular importance is point M at $X/L = 0.38$, where the maximum σ_1 occurs. The numerical value of maximum σ_1 is about the same as that on line F–F. The directions of the principal stresses at point M were again evaluated and are given in the table below:

	θ_x	θ_y	θ_z
σ_1	64.4°	70.8°	32.9°
σ_2	101.1°	151.2°	63.8°
σ_3	151.7°	69.2°	71.7°

The normal stresses σ_p at $X/L = 0$ and -0.38 were also determined, and their values at these positions are shown in the table below:

X/L	σ_p
0.38	12 psi
0	-14.8 psi
-0.38	1.6 psi

Line H–H—Fig. 14 shows the rectangular stress components on line H–H. The curves are similar to those along line F–F, and G–G. The maximum τ_{zy} at N is slightly higher than that on line G–G, but the position of N remains essentially the same. Small triaxial tensions were also found. The principal stresses, σ_1, σ_2, σ_3 are shown in Fig. 15. The maximum σ_1 at M where $X/L = 0.36$ is about 36 percent 'smaller than the maximum value on line G–G. The principal stress directions at M are tabulated below:

	θ_x	θ_y	θ_z
σ_1	61.6°	58.5°	44.9°
σ_2	118.6°	124.4°	47.8°
σ_3	44.1°	134.1°	88.5°

The values of the normal stresses σ_p at three significant positions are shown in the table below:

X/L	σ_p
0.36	7.7 psi
0	-10.8 psi
-0.36	-7.3 psi

Checks—The results were checked in two ways. The first check is provided by the fact that the integrated value of σ_x along the longitudinal lines F–F, G–G, and H–H satisfy the boundary conditions, i.e., σ_x vanishes at the free end, where $X/L = 1$.

The second check is provided by the fact that the values of σ_y and σ_z determined from the longitudinal sub-slices containing lines F–F, G–G, and H–H agree with the values of σ_y and σ_z determined from the sub-slices in the transverse section of symmetry.

Table 1 gives the stresses in pounds per square inch for the steel rail for a load of 30,000 lb. These were calculated from the stresses in the model by means of the same transition formulas as those used in the first report. (Eq's (1), (2), Appendix D).

Chief Sources of Error—The photoelastic models were carefully prepared and the loads were accurately measured. The photoelastic data, i.e., the birefringence and isoclinic parameters, were determined by precision methods and the calculations carefully checked. The only major source of error in the photoelastic work would come from the rather large area of contact, which in all probability modifies somewhat the true distribution of the contact pressures in the rail. However, the results from the two different loads show essentially the same characteristics so that no serious errors have been introduced by the higher load.

It would appear that the more concentrated contact pressure in the steel rail would tend to produce a more severe state of stress than that in the photoelastic model. The main source of error probably lies in the transition formulas.

TABLE 1

	Rail Load—30,000 lb		Model Load—78.4 lb

	Line F-F	*Line G-G*	*Line H-H*
Position of line below contact	0.05 in	0.04 in	0.11–0.2 in
Range of σ_x	12,000 psi to —45,000 psi	18,000 psi to —96,000 psi	7,500 psi to —52,000 psi
Range of σ_y	9,000 psi to —75,000 psi	6,000 psi to —126,000 psi	6,000 psi to —110,000 psi
Range of σ_z	9,000 psi to —13,500 psi	24,000 psi to —36,000 psi	9,000 psi to —10,800 psi
Range of τ_{xy}	±35,000 psi	±30,000 psi	±37,500 psi
Range of σ_p	33,000 psi to —39,000 psi	36,000 psi to —44,000 psi	23,400 psi to —32,400 psi
Range of τ_{max} from zero to	42,000 psi	51,000 psi	54,000 psi

DISCUSSION AND CONCLUSIONS

The complete state of interior principal stresses along critical lines parallel to the axis of the rail have been determined photoelastically in the head of a model of a railroad rail.

From the nature of the moving load it is apparent that each point in the rail is subjected to a fluctuating state of stress. The stress distributions which we have obtained from static conditions represent the stress history at a point on the lines studied as a function of the instaneous position of the wheel relative to the point. The curves of the stress distributions are, in effect, influence curves for the stresses for a moving load.

The study revealed several dangerous states of stress, which in themselves or in combination may contribute to, or produce, the shelly failure:

(1) The results show that the normal stress components σ_x, σ_y, and σ_z alternate between large compressions and relatively small tensions. The tensile triaxiality, which was rather unexpected, is known to produce embrittlement and may be a significant factor in failure.

(2) There exist oblique planes, the P-planes, which are subjected to completely reversed large normal stresses. The range of these stresses exceeds the endurance limit of 33,000 psi for completely reversed normal stresses (6) on lines F–F and G–G, and comes close to it in the region H–H of shelly failure.

(3) The range of the alternating shears τ_{xy} is ± 35,000 psi approximately, and the endurance limit for completely reversed shear is 37,000 psi (7).

(4) The planes on which the maximum shears during each loading cycle act, which we shall denote as Q-planes, are subjected to fluctuating shears and normal stresses. The range on line H–H of the variable shear on these planes is at least from 0 to 54,000 psi, which comes dangerously close to the endurance limit of 59,000 psi (5). A possibility exists that these shears may also reverse direction, which would certainly aggravate matters.

No definite conclusions regarding the possible cause of failure can be drawn, largely because no factual information is available on the behavior of materials under such complicated states of stress as encountered in this problem.

The most likely cause of failure lies either in the fluctuating shears on the Q-planes or in the reversal of the shears τ_{xy} which are approximately equal to their respective endurance limits. The decisive factor may, perhaps, lie in the effects of the associated stresses.

Whether the maximum shear in the region H–H produces yielding is uncertain because of the severe strain hardening, and also because the transient nature of the high stress may not allow sufficient time to develop yielding.

If failure is due to either one of these causes, and the transition formulas are approximately correct, then a wheel load of 30,000 lb would seem sufficient to put the rail in a state of incipient failure. A larger load would be required to produce failure by alternating normal stresses.

The reason why fractures do not occur in the regions F–F and G–G probably lies in the complicated effects which the combination of strain hardening, fatigue, and residual stresses may have on the strength of steel. It is known that fatigue may under certain conditions actually increase the strength of a metal before it weakens it (8).

Fatigue tests on actual rails may throw light on the cause of failure. Failure due to τ_{max} is likely to produce a jagged surface, more or less horizontal, whereas failure due to τ_{xy} is likely to produce a relatively even surface.

APPENDIX A—MAGNITUDE OF THE PRINCIPAL STRESSES

Given the six rectangular stress components at a point, the values of the three principal stresses can be determined from the cubic equation (9):

$$\sigma^3 - I_1\sigma^2 + I_2\sigma - I_3 = 0 \dots\dots(1)$$

where I_1, I_2, and I_3 are the stress invariants at the point

$$I_1 = \sigma_x + \sigma_y + \sigma_z$$
$$I_2 = \sigma_x\sigma_y + \sigma_y\sigma_z + \sigma_z\sigma_x - \tau_{xy}^2 - \tau_{yz}^2 - \tau_{xz}^2$$
$$I_3 = \sigma_x\sigma_y\sigma_z + 2\tau_{xy}\tau_{yz}\tau_{xz} - \sigma_x\tau_{yz}^2 - \sigma_y\tau_{xz}^2 - \sigma_z\tau_{xy}^2$$

The roots of the cubic equation are found by Cardan's method (10). This method yields directly the three roots without applying a trial-and-error procedure. By letting $\sigma = y + \dfrac{I_1}{3}$ the above equation is transformed into the following form:

$$y^3 + ay + b = 0 \dots\dots(2)$$

where the constants a and b are given by

$$a = I_2 - I^2_1/3$$
$$b = -I_3 + I_1I_2/3 - 2I^3_1/27$$

The three roots of Eq. (2) are

$$y_1 = 2\sqrt{\frac{-a}{3}}\cos\frac{\phi}{3}; \; y_2 = -2\sqrt{\frac{-a}{3}}\cos\left(60 - \frac{\phi}{3}\right);$$

$$y_3 = -2\sqrt{\frac{-a}{3}}\cos\left(60 + \frac{\phi}{3}\right)$$

where,

$$Cos\,\phi = 27\,b/2a\,\sqrt{-a}$$

The three principal stresses are then given by

$$\sigma_1 = y_1 + I_1/3$$
$$\sigma_2 = y_2 + I_1/3$$
$$\sigma_3 = y_3 + I_1/3$$

APPENDIX B—DIRECTIONS OF THE PRINCIPAL STRESSES

Let n_x, n_y, and n_z be the direction cosines of a principal plane, and σ the magnitude of the principal stress acting on this plane. It is shown in the theory of elasticity (9) that the following relations must be satisfied:

$$(\sigma_x - \sigma)n_x + \tau_{xy}n_y + \tau_{xz}n_z = 0 \quad\dotfill(1)$$
$$\tau_{yx}n_x + (\sigma_y - \sigma)n_y + \tau_{zy}n_z = 0 \quad\dotfill(2)$$
$$\tau_{zx}n_x + \tau_{zy}n_y + (\sigma_z - \sigma)n_z = 0 \quad\dotfill(3)$$

In addition, the direction cosines have to meet the condition

$$n^2_x + n^2_y + n^2_z = 1 \quad\dotfill(4)$$

The above equations can be solved for n_x, n_y, and n_z. The results are

$$n_z = \frac{1}{\sqrt{1 + \alpha^2 + \beta^2}} \quad\dotfill(5)$$
$$n_y = \alpha n_z \quad\dotfill(6)$$
$$n_x = \beta n_z \quad\dotfill(7)$$

where,

$$\alpha = \frac{\tau_{yx}(\sigma_z - \sigma) - \tau_{zx}\tau_{yz}}{\tau_{zx}(\sigma_y - \sigma) - \tau_{yx}\tau_{zy}}$$

$$\beta = -\frac{\alpha \tau_{xy} + (\sigma_z - \sigma)}{\tau_{zz}}$$

APPENDIX C—DETERMINATION OF NORMAL STRESS ON ANY ARBITRARY PLANE

Given the state of stress at a point, the normal stress acting on any arbitrary plane can be determined from the equation (9):

$$\sigma_n = n^2_x\sigma_x + n^2_y\sigma_y + n^2_z\sigma_z + 2n_xn_y\tau_{xy} + 2n_xn_z\tau_{xz} + 2n_yn_z\tau_{yz}$$

where n_x, n_y, and n_z are the direction cosiness of σ_n, or of the normal to the plane.
B-5075—AREA Feb.) Galley 62

APPENDIX D—TRANSITION FORMULAS

The transition formulas are taken from the supplementary report of October 1953 (1):

$$(\sigma_x, \sigma_y, \sigma_z, \tau_{max})_p = (\sigma_x, \sigma_y, \sigma_z, \tau_{max})_m \sqrt[3]{\left(\frac{1}{\lambda_p}\right)\left(\frac{\lambda_L}{\lambda_E}\right)^2\left(\frac{1 - \lambda^2 u \mu_p^2}{1 - \mu_p^2}\right)^2} \dotfill(1)$$

$$(Z)_p = (Z)_m \sqrt[3]{\frac{\lambda_E}{\lambda_L \lambda_p}\left(\frac{1 - \mu_p^2}{1 - \lambda^2 \mu \mu_p^2}\right)} \dotfill(2)$$

where $(Z)_p$ and $(Z)_m$ are distances from the contact area to points at which the stresses are related by Eq. (1).

Although the above equations are valid only along the load line in the immediate region of contact, they are also used to translate maximum τ_{xy}, maximum σ_p, triaxial tensions, and their corresponding positions in the region not directly under the load.

The essential data for the transition from the Fosterite model to a steel prototype rail are tabulated below:

Notation

$P =$ load between wheel and rail
$E =$ modulus of elasticity
$\mu =$ Poisson's ratio
$L =$ characteristic length

Subscripts m and p refer to the model and prototype, respectively.

Fosterite Model	*Steel Prototype*
$L_m = 2/3$	$L_p = 1$
$P_m = 78.4$ lb.	$P_p = 30,000$ lb.
$E_m = 2010$ psi	$E_p = 30 \times 10^6$ psi
$\mu_m = \frac{1}{2}$	$\mu_p = \frac{1}{3}$

Scale Factors

$\lambda_L = L_m/L_p = \frac{2}{3}$
$\lambda_P = P_m/P_p = 78.4/30,000 = 2.61 \times 10^{-3}$
$\lambda_E = E_m/E_p = 2010/30 \times 10^6 = 6.7 \times 10^{-6}$
$\lambda_\mu = \mu_m/\mu_p = 3/2$

Substituting these values into Eqs. (1) and (2) respectively, we obtain:

$$(\sigma_x, \sigma_y, \sigma_z, \tau_{max})_p = (\sigma_x, \sigma_y, \sigma_z, \tau_{max})_m \sqrt[3]{\left(\frac{10^3}{2.61}\right)\left(\frac{2 \times 10^6}{3 \times 6.70}\right)^2} \left[\frac{1 - \left(\frac{B}{2} \times \frac{1}{3}\right)^2}{1 - \left(\frac{1}{3}\right)^2}\right]^2$$

$$= 3000 \, (\sigma_x, \sigma_y, \sigma_z, \tau_{max})_m$$

$$(Z)_p = (Z)_m \sqrt[3]{\frac{6.7 \times 10^{-6}}{\left(\frac{2}{3}\right)(2.61 \times 10^{-3})} \times \frac{1 - \left(\frac{1}{3}\right)^2}{1 - \left(\frac{3}{2} \times \frac{1}{3}\right)^2}}$$

$$= 0.36 \, (Z)_m$$

As already mentioned above, and in the supplementary report of October 1953, these equations would at best be valid in a small region near the contact surface. For points below the surface the transition factors become a function of distance from the contact surface; the stress factor decreasing and the position factor increasing. For example, for a 30,000-lb load on the steel rail and 78.4 lb on the model the transition factor for stress varies from 3,000 at the contact surface to 170 approximately at points A and B in Fig. 4, where the contact effects disappear. The value of 170 was arrived at from the consideration that in geometrically similar bodies, neglecting the effect of Poisson's ratio, the stresses are directly proportional to the load and inversely proportional to the square of the scale ratio. Similarly near the surface of contact the transition factor for position calculated from Eq. (2) is 0.36. At the lower free surface of the head, points A and B in Fig. 4, where the contact effects disappear, the factor becomes 1.5, which is the scale ratio of prototype to model. A consideration of these possible variations shows that the transition factor for line H-H drops to 2900 or 2800, thereby reducing the stresses by about 7 percent. It would also appear that the weaknesses in the transition formulas are likely to produce greater errors in the triaxial tensions than in the triaxial compressions, because the compression regions are closer to the contact surface than the tensile regions. Specifically, the error tends to yield higher tensile values. The effect of variation of the position factor would be to lower the position of line H–H from 0.11 in to nearly 0.2 in below the contact surface, thus bringing the line H–H closer to the region of the shelly failures.

REFERENCES·

(1) Frocht, M. M., "Final Report on a Three-Dimensional Photoelastic Investigation of the Principal Stresses and Maximum Shears in the Head of a Model of a Railroad Rail", and Supplementary Report on "A Three-Dimensional Photoelastic Investigation of the Principal Stresses and Maximum Shears in the Head of a Model of a Railroad Rail", AREA Proceedings, Vol. 55, page 854.

(2) Frocht, M. M. and Guernsey, R. Jr., "Studies in Three-Dimensional Photoelasticity —The Application of the Shear Difference Method to the General Space Problem" Proceedings, 1st U. S. Nat. Congr. Appl. Mech., December 1952.

(3) Frocht, M. M. and Guernsey, R. Jr., "Further Work on the General Three-Dimensional Photoelastic Problem", Journal Applied Mechanics, Volume 22, No. 2, June 1955.

(4) Frocht, M. M., Pih, H., and Landsberg, D., "The Use of Photometric Devices in the Solution of the General Three-Dimensional Photoelastic Problem", Proceedings, Society Experimental Stress Analysis, Volume XII, No. 1, 1954.

(5) Jensen, R. S., "Effect of Wheel Diameter and Wheel Load on Extent of Rail Damage", AAR Research Center Files.

(6) AREA Proceedings, Vol. 51.

(7) AREA Proceedings, Vol. 58, page 971.

(8) Cazaud, R., "Fatigue of Metals", Philosophical Library, Incorporated, New York, 1953.

(9) Timoshenko, S., Goddier, J. N., "Theory of Elasticity", McGraw–Hill, New York, 1951.

(10) Uspensky, J. V., "Theory of Equations", McGraw–Hill, New York, 1948.

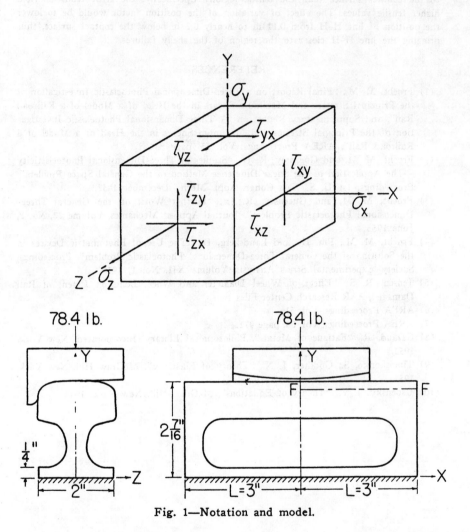

Fig. 1—Notation and model.

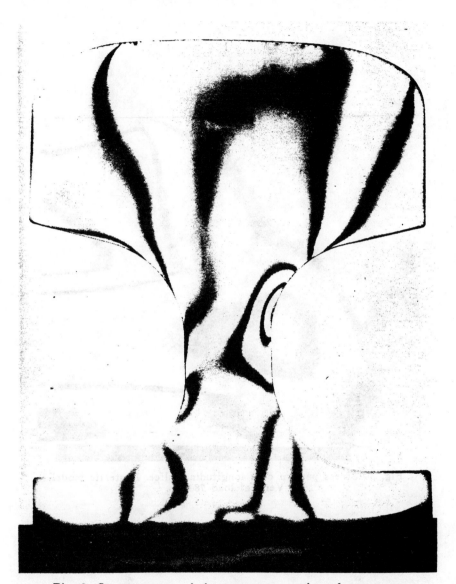

Fig. 2—Stress pattern of the transverse section of symmetry.
Fosterite model. Vertical load 78.4 lb.

Fig. 3—Stress pattern of a longitudinal slice. Fosterite model.
Vertical load 78.4 lb.

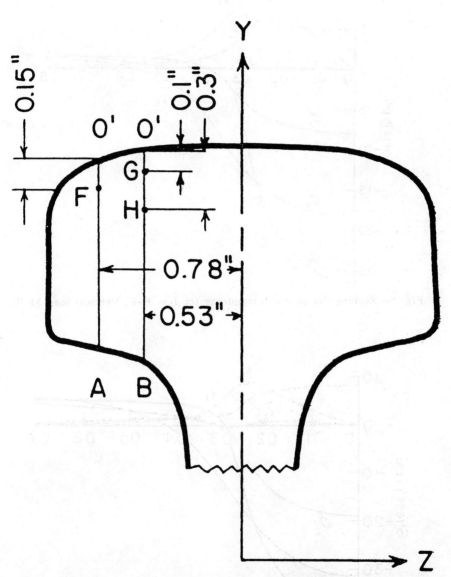

Fig. 4—Sketch showing locations of lines AO', BO', and of longitudinal sub-slices through F, G, and H.

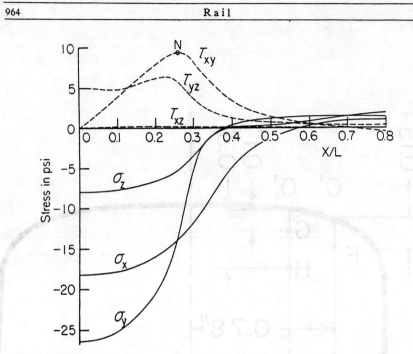

Fig. 5—Rectangular stress components for line F–F. Vertical load 51 lb.

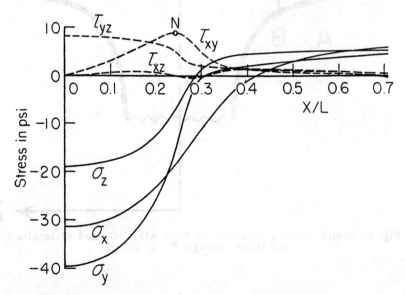

Fig. 6—Rectangular stress components for line G–G. Vertical load 51 lb.

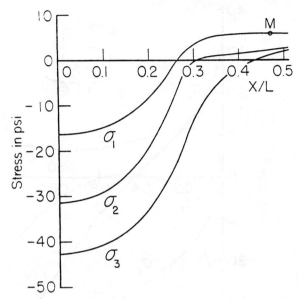

Fig. 7—Principal stresses for line G–G. Vertical load 51 lb.

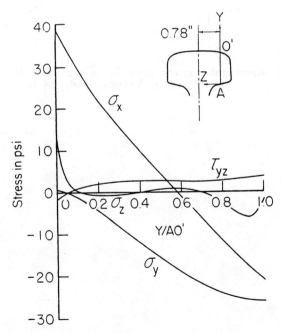

Fig. 8—Rectangular stress components for line AO' in the phane symmetry. Vertical load 78.4 lb.

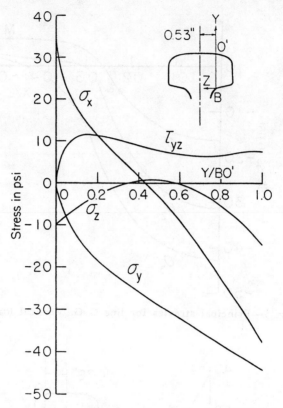

Fig. 9—Rectangular stress components for line BO′ in the plane of symmetry. Vertical load 78.4 lb.

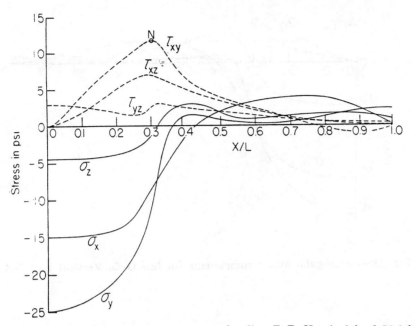

Fig. 10—Rectangular stress components for line F–F. Vertical load 78.4 lb.

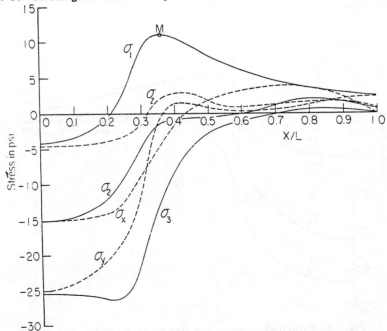

Fig. 11—Comparison of principal stresses with rectangular stress components on line F–F. Vertical load 78.4 lb.

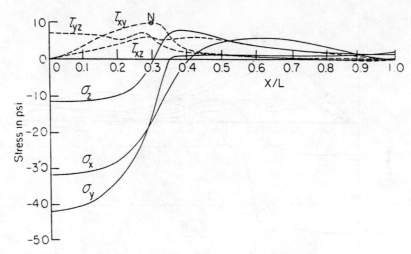

Fig. 12—Rectangular stress components for line G–G. Vertical load 78.4 lb.

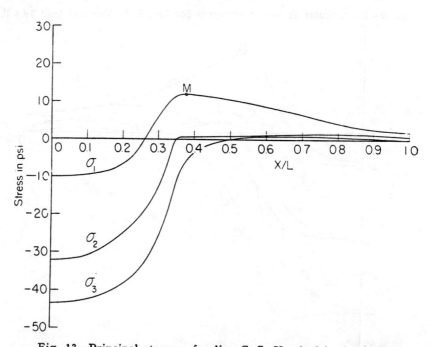

Fig. 13—Principal stresses for line G–G. Vertical load 78.4 lb.

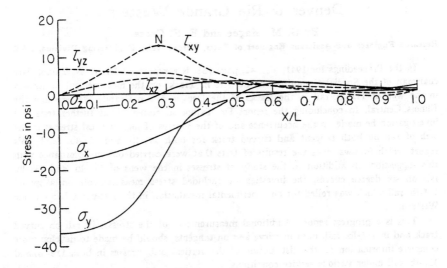

Fig. 14—Rectangular stress components for line H–H. Vertical load 78.4 lb.

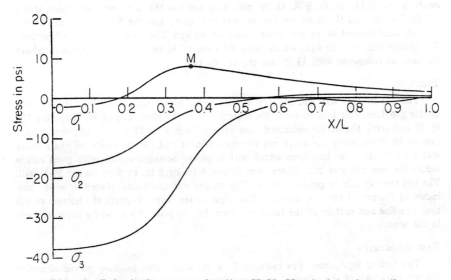

Fig. 15—Principal stresses for line H–H. Vertical load 78.4 lb.

Stress Measurements in the Web of Rail on the Denver & Rio Grande Western

By G. M. Magee and E. E. Cress

Research Engineer and Assistant Engineer of Tests, Respectively, Engineering Division, AAR

In the Proceedings for 1941, Vol. 42, page 758, is a report by Dr. A. N. Talbot, late chairman of the Special Committee on Stresses in Track, on the measurement of stresses in the web of 112-lb. rail in the tracks of the Denver & Rio Grande Western and the Illinois Central. In concluding the report Dr. Talbot suggested "That further tests and investigation be made on the occurrence and of the sources of high vertical stresses in the web of rail on both tangent and curved track for both 112-lb. and 131-lb. rail." This report which follows gives the results of tests that were carried out in accordance with this suggestion. In addition to the study of stresses in the webs of 112-lb. and 131-lb. rail on six degree curves, the investigation included stress measurements on a special 115-lb. rail which was rolled for an experimental installation in the Denver & Rio Grande Western.

This is a progress report. Additional measurements of the stresses in rail on curved track and in 131-lb. rail, both in curve and on tangents, should be made to develop more complete information on the distribution of the vertical web stresses in both 112-lb. and 131-lb. rail under various service conditions.

Tests of Vertical Stresses in Web of 115-lb. Rail

In July 1941, vertical web stress measurements were made on tangent track of the D. & R. G. W. two miles east of Price, Utah. The track was laid in May 1941, with the newly designed 115-lb. D. & R. G. W. rail. This rail has the same head and base as the 112-lb. RE rail and the same top and bottom web fillets, but the fillets are connected by straight lines instead of by the combination of 10 and 23-in. radii for the RE section. The change thickens the web, which has a thickness of $\frac{3}{4}$ in. at a height of $3\frac{3}{4}$ in. above the base, as compared with $\frac{19}{32}$ in. for the 112-lb. rail.

Track

The 115-lb. rail was laid in May 1941. The tie plates were 8 in. by $11\frac{1}{2}$ in. with double shoulders and 1 in 40 cant; the eccentricity of the plate was $\frac{1}{4}$ in. Along the 200 ft. of test track the actual measured cant ranged from 1 in 37 to 1 in 60; the average cant at 10 places along the north rail averaged 1 in 44 and for the south rail the average was 1 in 50. The ties had been adzed with a power adzing machine with good results before the new rail was laid. There were 23 ties, 6 in. by 8 in. by 8 ft., to the 39-ft. rail. The ties were in fair to good condition. The ballast was black slag, placed to within two inches of the top of the ties and extending eight or ten inches beneath the bottom of the ties. The line and surface of the track was from fair to good. There was a slight upgrade to the west.

Test Apparatus

The testing equipment was installed in a small portable building placed alongside the test track. All of the principal stress measurements were made with carbon strip gages of $\frac{1}{2}$-in. effective length cemented to the rail surface. As the gages are quite thin the point of effective measurement is not more than 0.01 or 0.02 in. beyond the rail surface.

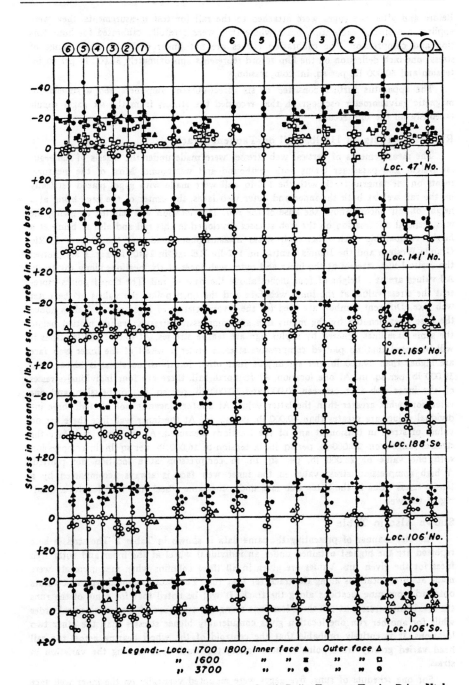

Fig. 1.—Vertical Web Stresses—115-lb. D. & R. G. W. Rail—Tangent Track—Price, Utah.

Before and after the gages were attached to the rail for test measurements, they were applied to a special calibration beam where they were carefully calibrated for both tension and compression. The calibration curves are not linear over the whole range of stress; one inch deflection on the film record represents approximately 30,000 lb. per sq. in. tension and 50,000 lb. per sq. in. compression.

The apparatus further consisted of six direct-current amplifiers and a six-element magnetic galvanometer oscillograph that recorded the strains from the six gages simultaneously on the film record.

Results of Tests on 115-lb. Rail on Tangent Track

The measurements of vertical web stresses were made under the wheels of the regular freight and passenger trains both eastbound and westbound. Most of the measurements on the tangent track with the 115-lb. rail were made with gages placed vertically on the rail web at both the inner and outer web faces, the center of the gage being at a height of four inches above the base of the rail. This location was selected as giving the most general information on the web stresses developed in this rail and also as being at a height comparable with other web stress measurements made on the Denver & Rio Grande Western and the Illinois Central on 112-lb. RE rail in 1940. In Fig. 1 are plotted the vertical web stresses at the inner and outer web faces at six locations along the track. All values are at a height of four inches above the base of rail. The closed points represent the stress values at the inner web face and the open points the values at the outer web face. Different symbols are used for the several classes of locomotives. Values above the base lines denoted by the minus sign are compressive stresses; values plotted below the same base lines denoted by a plus sign are tensile stresses. At one of the locations it will be noted that no plotted compressive stresses under a wheel at the inner web face are higher than 29,000 lb. per sq. in.; at four other locations, no stress is higher than 39,000 lb. per sq. in. At one location, 47 ft. north rail, there are four individual stresses on the inner web face between 40,000 and 50,000 lb. per sq. in. compression, and one value somewhat greater than the latter value. At another location not plotted, three individual values are greater than 40,000 lb. per sq. in. At the inner web face there are no values of stress in tension at any of the locations measured. At the outer web face the stresses range from 16,000 lb. per sq. in. in tension to 16,000 lb. per sq in in compression with one value of 26,000 lb. per sq. in. in compression at a location not plotted. A high compression stress value in the inner web face is always accompanied by a tensile stress value in the outer web face under the same wheel, and this denotes a bending of the web.

Shown Also in Table 1

Another manner of presenting the same data is shown in Table 1. The stresses here reported are the highest obtained under an individual wheel at the inner and outer web faces for the given run. Values are given in all three columns when measurements were made at three locations along the track for that run. The data presented represent values obtained from nine locations along the track. It will be noted that for some of the runs the maximum stresses at the three locations along the track are of the same general order while for another run one location gives considerably higher stresses than the other two locations. It is entirely probable that the centroid of the wheel bearing across the rail head varied greatly from point to point along the track thus causing the variation in stress.

For one schedule of runs, five gages were mounted vertically on the inner web face and one gage opposite on the outer web face so that the simultaneous distribution of the

TABLE 1.

MAXIMUM VERTICAL WEB STRESSES MEASURED UNDER A WHEEL
OF LOCOMOTIVES (AND TENDERS) PASSING THE TEST LOCA-
TIONS - 115-LB. D. & R. G. W. RAIL - TANGENT TRACK

Stresses are at 4.0 in. above base at nine locations along the track. Stresses are in thousands
of lb. per sq. in., + is tension; - compression.

3700 Class locomotive 4-6-6-4
1700, 1800 Class " 4-8-4
1600 Class locomotive 4-8-2 (3 cylin.)

Loco.	Run	Speed M.P.H.	Direc-tion	Sched-ule	STRESS		STRESS		STRESS	
					Outer Face	Inner Face	Outer Face	Inner Face	Outer Face	Inner Face
3700	206	42	W	O	+ 9.5	-22.2	+ 9.3	-24.4	+ 6.0	-23.4
3701	205	50	E	O	+ 6.5	-23.4	- 2.9	-25.3	+ 6.7	-34.8
3701	229	44	W	S					---	-42.0
3703	202	48	E	O	+ 7.8	-21.2	+14.6	-30.7	+ 9.8	-37.7
3704	204	46	W	O	+ 9.3	-25.8	+ 9.9	-23.3	+ 5.7	-23.8
3704	226	47	E	S					---	-37.5
3705	227	46	E	S					---	-44.0
3705	224	42	W	R					+11.7	-38.0
3706	212	44	E	P.	+ 8.9	-22.9	+ 8.0	-27.3	+ 7.8	-57.0
3706	217	45	W	Q	+15.3	-38.1			+11.2	-38.3
3707	207	46	W	O	+ 9.8	-21.7	+ 7.0	-38.2	+ 2.8	-21.2
3707	218	45	W	Q	+10.7	-26.8			+ 7.7	-32.8
3708	201	33	W	O	+ 8.3	-17.8	+10.7	-30.3	+ 7.9	-28.4
3709	209	35	E	P	+ 8.0	-28.5	+10.0	-26.3	+ 5.9	-31.3
3709	215	45	W	Q	+11.8	-33.7			+ 6.2	-33.0
3709	216	42	E	Q	+ 8.2	-23.4			+ 9.1	-32.8
3709	223	45	E	R					+ 7.0	-32.0
1710	225	53	W	R					+ 3.8	-20.5
1800	228	62	W	S					---	-35.5
1804	203	67	W	O	+ 6.3	-26.6	-4.0	-23.8	+ 8.0	-23.4
1600	210	53	E	P	+ 5.8	-23.4	-16.3	-31.7	+ 2.0	-32.2
1600	211	25	W	P	+12.7	-33.1	+ 2.7	-19.4	+ 8.9	-49.2
1602	213	37	E	P	+ 4.9	-18.1	+ 3.9	-22.2	+ 7.9	-36.0
1602	208	29	W	P	+ 5.8	-28.1	+15.3	-34.0	-1.1	-30.2
1605	219	30	W	Q	+ 2.8	-24.5			+ 3.7	-19.1
1606	220	35	W	R					+ 3.6	-17.3
1606	222	17	W	R					+ 9.8	-37.2

vertical web stresses at different heights on the inner web face could be obtained as indicated in Fig. 2. Stresses under individual wheels were selected to cover the total range of stress for all the wheels passing the location. In the inner web face the highest compressive stresses decrease rapidly from the upper gage (located at $4\frac{17}{32}$ in. above the base) to the lower gages. In most of the tests the gages were located at 4 in. above the base of rail; it is realized that for the inner web face the vertical compressive stresses above this height may be considerably larger than at the 4 in. To obtain the stress at the $4\frac{17}{32}$ in. height a gage of only ¼ in. effective length had to be used. As the distribution of stress down the inner web face in this figure is relatively similar to that down the inner face shown in Fig. 3 on page 765 of the Proceedings for 1941, Vol. 42, it can be reasoned that the stresses down the outer web face would have been of a magnitude somewhat comparable to the stresses shown in the outer face of that figure.

Table 2 is presented to show the range of vertical web stresses measured in the 115-lb. rail on tangent track. The values given in the top line cover the total range for

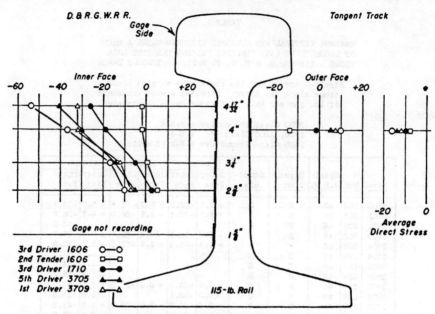

Fig. 2.—Range of Measured Vertical Web Stresses.

stresses at a web height of four inches at the nine locations along the track. The values given in the lower lines are for one track location only at four different web heights.

Comparison of the Measured Web Stresses in 112-lb. and 115-lb. Rail in Tangent Track

Fig. 3 is presented to give a résumé of the frequency of occurrence of high vertical web stresses in the several groups of tests made to date. The values given are for locomotive drivers only and represent a summation of all the data available from a given set of tests. From the figure it is seen that on the inner web face of the 115-lb. rail (at 4 in. above the base) 7.6, 1.0 and 0.3 percent of the compressive stresses under drivers were in excess of 35,000, 45,000 and 55,000 lb. per sq. in., respectively, while for the 112-lb. rail tests on the D. & R. G. W. made in 1940 the corresponding percentages of occurrence were, respectively, 11.4, 5.5, and 1.6 percent for the same stresses. This represents a considerable reduction in the frequency of the higher compressive stresses. At the location on the 115-lb. rail test the wheel bearing appeared to be largely towards the gage side of the head. The gage corner of the rails was quite bright with a semi-bright streak extending almost to the middle of the rail head; outside of the middle there was a dull streak about ½ in. wide and beyond that there had been no bearing between wheel and rail. This eccentricity of wheel bearing was greater than at the locations where the 1940 tests were made on the 112-lb. rail on the D. & R. G. W. Because of the highly eccentric general bearing at the 115-lb. rail test locations on tangent track it is reasonable to assume that there will be few places in ordinary tangent track laid with this rail where the vertical web stresses will be higher than those measured. Furthermore, it is to be expected that as this rail head wears more nearly to the average wheel contours the eccentricity of wheel bearing will be reduced with a corresponding decrease in the bending stresses in the rail web.

A

In the report on "Tests of Vertical Stresses in Web of Rail" page 758, Vol. 42 of the Proceedings, a preliminary analysis is presented of the distribution of the direct compressive stresses in the rail web under the wheel load and of the bending stresses in the web due to eccentric loading or an accompanying lateral force.

At a height of 4 in., the rail web of the 115-lb. rail is 0.75 in. thick as compared with about 0.60 in. for the 112-lb. section. For direct compressive stresses the heavier

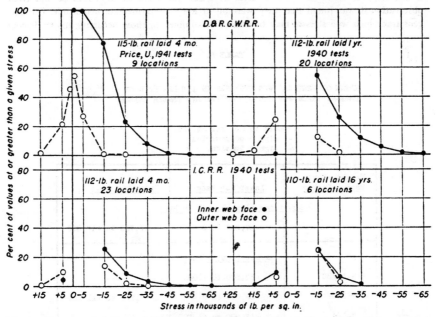

Fig 3.—Frequency of Vertical Web Stresses on Tangent Track (Locomotive Drivers Only).
Stresses below 15,000 lb. per sq. in. compression and 5,000 lb. per sq. in. tension
not tabulated in 1940 tests.

web under a comparable equal load should give a reduction of about 20 percent in stress, but for bending stresses due to eccentric wheel loads or to a lateral force on the rail head or a combination of the two, the reduction in stress would be more nearly as the squares of the thickness, or about 36 percent. As the higher web stresses are due to bending brought about by a combination of the above factors, it may be expected that the thicker web will have a considerable effect in reducing the magnitude of the web stresses existing under similar conditions.

Under most of the driving wheels the direct stress in the rail web ranged from 8,000 to 14,000 lb. per sq. in. in compression at a height of 3¾ or 4 in. above the base. The direct stress may be considered to be one-half the algebraic sum of the simultaneously measured stresses on the two opposite web faces. It has been found that the length of rail section resisting the direct load is relatively short, averaging perhaps 5 in. in front and behind the wheel, as compared with 15 in. or more each way for the bending stress. The bending stress is the algebraic difference between the measured stress in one face of the web and the direct stress. Bending of the web is due either to eccentricity of wheel loading or to a lateral force on the rail head or a combination of the two; combined they may be additive or they may counteract each other.

Measured stresses under the drivers have been used in determining the frequency of high stresses because the highest stresses obtained on tangent track were under the driving wheels. On the 115-lb. rail under the front truck, trailer, and tender wheels there was only one compressive stress higher than 35,000 lb. per sq. in., and only 7 percent of the stresses on the inner web face were greater than 25,000 lb. per sq. in. The stresses under the first two or three cars behind the tender were often recorded on the film before it was stopped. These car wheel stresses were not read from the film records, but from observation it was found that they were all of low or intermediate magnitude. On tangent track high web stresses may be said to be confined to those occurring under driving

TABLE 2.

RANGE OF VERTICAL WEB STRESSES IN 115 LB. RAIL ON
TANGENT TRACK FOR ALL LOCOMOTIVE AND TENDER WHEELS

Stresses in Lb. per Sq. In.
- sign = compression.
+ sign = tension.

Height above Base - Inches	Inner Web Face	Outer Web Face
9 Locations along Track, 29 Runs		
4	-57,000 to 0	-25,700 to +16,300
	1 Location, 5 Runs	
4-17/32	-53.500 to -500	---
4	-38,000 to 0	-15,300 to +11,700
3-1/4	-16,800 to +1,800	---
2-5/8	- 9,800 to +5,300	---

wheels of locomotives, as the other wheels of a train do not produce web stresses high enough to be of serious consequence.

As most of the records on the 115-lb. rail were made under freight trains the predominant speeds were about 45 miles per hour, but the range included speeds from 20 to 67 miles per hour. The speed of the train did not seem to have an effect on the frequency of the higher stresses. The data failed to disclose any particular distinction between the effect produced by particular locomotives or classes of them. Neither could a distinction be made between the stresses under eastbound and westbound runs. Higher stresses were well divided between the locations on the north and south rail. It is probable that with a considerably greater number of runs some of the above factors could have been segregated and more definite conclusions drawn.

Four of the locations of the measurements of web stresses were directly over the middle of the tie plates and five locations were between ties. Two of the locations directly over the tie plates gave the highest readings and the other two locations gave as high stresses as any of the locations between ties. It is possible that web stresses may be influenced to some extent by the proximity of the upward reaction at a tie, even though this upward reaction is only a third or a fourth of the load of an individual wheel in a group of normally spaced wheels. Further tests would have to be made and laid out with this matter in mind before any definite knowledge on these phenomena can be determined.

In the 1941 tests on the 115-lb. D. & R. G. W. rail on tangent track near Price, Utah, the principal source of the high web stresses was the eccentricity of wheel bearing on the rail head. There was a considerable decrease in both the magnitude and frequency of the higher web stresses compared with the measurements made on the 112-lb. rail on the same railroad in 1940, even though the wheel bearing can be considered to have been more eccentric on the 115-lb. rail tests. It is more than probable that the thicker web of the 115-lb. rail materially reduced the magnitude of the vertical web stresses.

Tests of Vertical Stresses in Web of 112-lb. and 131-lb. Rails on 6-deg. Curves

Track

The 6-deg. curve at Farnham, Utah, had 112-lb. rail laid in 1937, of intermediate manganese composition and not control cooled. There was a relatively small amount of head wear. The 8 in. by 11½ in. double shoulder tie plates had a cant of 1 in 40 and an eccentricity of ¼ in. The outer end of the tie plates under both rails had cut into the machine adzed ties from ⅛ to ⅜ in. more than the inner end, thus making the actual cant of each rail near zero. The track gage was wide by about 7/8 in. The superelevation of 4¾ in. corresponded to an equilibrium speed of about 35 miles per hour. The line and surface of the curve was good; the rail joints on the inner rail were slightly low.

The 6-deg. curve at Shoshone, Colo., had 131-lb. rail of intermediate manganese, not control cooled, that was originally laid in 1936. The rails had been transposed and re-laid in December 1940. The rail was not badly worn when the transfer was made. The tests were made seven months after the transfer, and at that time the flanges against the gage side of the outer rail had not worn off all of the lateral head flow produced on these rails when they were on the low rail of the curve. The 8 in. by 12 in. double-shoulder tie plates had a cant of 1 in 40 and an eccentricity of ¼ in. The outside ends of the tie-plates along the outer rail had cut into the machine-adzed ties from ⅛ to ¼ in., causing an actual rail cant of about 1 in 60. The outside ends of the tie plates along the inner rail had cut into the ties from ⅛ to ½ in., causing an actual rail cant of about 1 in 75 at two of the test locations, and a negative cant of 1 in 43 at the third test location (Schedule AA). The gage was wide by ⅛ in. and the elevation of the curve was 5 in. The line and surface of the curve were fair to good. The single track was down grade to the west in mountainous territory.

Results of Tests on 6-deg. Curves with 112-lb. Rail

Carbon strip gages were placed vertically on inner and outer web faces at three locations along both the inner and outer 112-lb. rails of a 6-deg. curve at Farnham, Utah. In the upper part of Fig. 4 are plotted the stresses measured under the individual wheels of the locomotives and tenders, in all cases where the stress was greater than 10,000 lb. per sq. in. either in tension or compression. The plottings are the composite of the records at three locations along each rail; at two locations the gages were placed on both web faces at heights above the base of rail of 4¼ and 2 in., and at the third location at heights of 4¼, 3½ and 2¾ in. About six runs were recorded at each of the three loca-

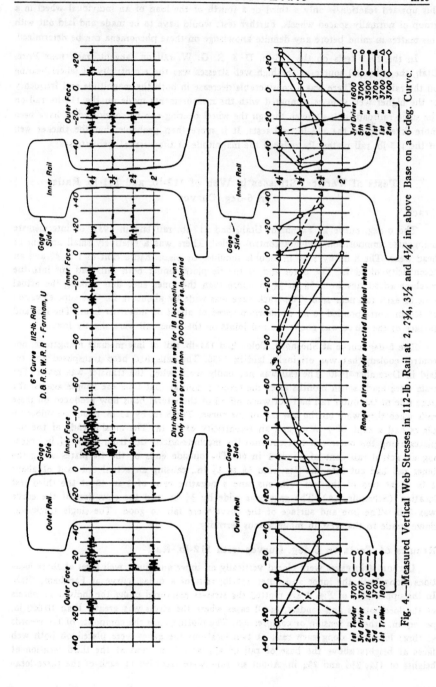

Fig. 4.—Measured Vertical Web Stresses in 112-lb. Rail at 2, 2¾, 3½ and 4¼ in. above Base on a 6-deg. Curve.

tions on each rail. In the top part of Table 3 is given the total range of stresses recorded at the several gage heights on the same curve.

For the inner face of the outer rail at a height of 4¼ in. it is seen that there were nine wheels that produced compressive stresses above 50,000 and up to over 70,000 lb. per sq. in. These high stresses were found to be under the wheels of four 3700 class locomotives (4–6–6–4) all running at speeds of from 41 to 46 miles per hour. There were

TABLE 3.

RANGE OF VERTICAL WEB STRESSES IN 6° CURVES.

Stress in lb. per sq. in; - sign is compression;
+ sign is tension. Locomotive and tender wheels.
Three locations each rail.

Height above Base - Inches	Inner Web Face	Outer Web Face
6° Curve - 112-Lb. Rail - Outer Rail		
4-1/4"	-72,000 to +10,000	-38,500 to +38,800
3-1/2"	-30,500 to + 1,800	--- ---
2-3/4"	-25,000 to +20,000	-34,600 to + 8,800
2	-16,000 to +18,500	-27,500 to +20,000
6° Curve - 112-Lb. Rail - Inner Rail		
4-1/4"	-67,000 to +20,600	-41,000 to +29,500
3-1/2"	-26,300 to +27,000	-55,000 to + 6,300
2-3/4"	-16,000 to +45,000	-50,000 to + 4,000
2	-10,000 to +10,000	-17,500 to + 5,500
6° Curve - 131-Lb. Rail - Outer Rail		
4-3/4"	-33,200 to + 3,900	-19,500 to +20,700
3-3/4"	-16,400 to + 4,200	-20,200 to + 6,500
2-3/4"	-12,000 to + 4,300	- 8,400 to + 7,800
2	-13,400 to +19,000	-19,400 to +13,000
6° Curve - 131-Lb. Rail - Inner Rail		
4-3/4"	-63,500 to 0	-15,700 to +26,000
3-3/4"	-20,000 to + 4,700	-18,300 to + 4,300
2-3/4"	-15,800 to + 5,300	-14,500 to + 6,200
2	- 6,600 to +16,800	-24,300 to 0

three 1600 class (4–8–2) and three 1800 (4–8–4) locomotives running at speeds of from 40 to 49 miles per hour that did not produce any stresses as high as those mentioned above. These high compressive stresses were accompanied by tensile stresses up to about 30,000 lb. per sq. in. at the same height on the outer web face. At the gage heights of 3½, 2¾ and 2 in. in the outer rail none of the stresses was very high. In the outer rail some of the higher stresses were found under the front truck and heavy tender wheels as well as under the locomotive driving wheels.

Some of the vertical web stresses measured in the inner rail of this 6-deg. curve were high. At the inner web face at a height of 4¼ in. there were eight individual values well above 50,000 lb. per sq. in. On the inner web face at a height of 2¾ inches there were a number of tensile stresses from 20,000 to 45,000 lb. per sq. in. Bending of the rail web in the direction indicated by such a disposition of the stresses would have to be explained either by the wheel bearing on the rail at or near the outside edge of the head or, more likely, by an outward lateral force on the rail head toward the center of the curve, or by a combination of both. In the outer web face the high values of stress are compressive and are greater at the 2¾ in. and 3½ in. heights than at the 4¼ in. height. These compressive values of stress in the outer face also denote an outward lateral force on the rail head under the individual wheels producing these values. The distribution of stress in the web of the inner rail was distinctly different from that found in any of the tangent track tests where only low stress values were recorded in the lower portion of the rail web. The measurements at the 2 in. height were not at the same location along the track as those at the height of 2¾ and 3½ in., so the variation in locations may account in part for the large difference in stresses at the lowest point. While the gages were on the inner rail, five of the freight trains were slowed to speeds of from 3 to 8 miles per hour as they passed over the gages. These slow speed runs produced some high stresses in the inner rail but high stresses were also produced by other trains running at speeds from 35 to 45 miles per hour.

Web Stresses for Individual Wheels

In the lower part of Fig. 4 are plotted the web stresses for a few individual wheels, the records for these few wheels being selected to give as nearly as possible the total range in stress at the several gages. At the inner face of both rails it will be noted that where there is a high compressive stress at the top gage, the stress decreases rapidly at the lower gages and also that the stresses may reverse in sign from the upper to the lower portion of the inner web face. In this same figure the record for two wheels shows progressively increasing compressive stresses down the webs at three gage heights on the outer side of the inner rail. These same two wheels produced tensile stresses in the opposite web face that increased in magnitude at the lower gages.

It can be said that where any stress is quite high in either compression or tension in one web face, the stress in the opposite web face will be of the opposite sign, and the two stresses will sum up algebraically to produce a direct stress always in compression. Under wheels that produce a high value of stress in one web face of either rail at the height of 4¼ in. the direct stress usually ranges from 10,000 to 20,000 lb. per sq. in. compression. At the height of 3½ in. the direct stress is somewhat lower; and at the heights of 2¾ and 2 in. the direct stress is usually from 4,000 to 10,000 lb. compression. At the locations toward the lower part of the web the direct stress decreases more rapidly than the web thickness increases, indicating that the length of the rail section resisting the direct load is somewhat longer toward the bottom of the web than toward the top. This conclusion is borne out by photo-elastic studies of the stresses produced in rail webs.

Results of Measurements on 6-deg. Curve with 131-lb. Rail

In the upper part of Fig. 5 are plotted the vertical web stresses under the individual wheels of the locomotives and tenders of trains in regular traffic in the outer and inner rails of a 6-deg. curve laid with 131-lb. RE rail. The diagrams are composites of the records at three locations along each rail. At two locations along each rail there were gages on both web faces at heights above the base of 4¾ and 2¾ in., and at one location gages were placed at heights of 4¾, 3¾ and 2 in. Usually the lowest stresses are not plotted. The range in vertical web stresses measured on this curve is given in the lower part of Table 3.

It will be seen at once that the stresses in the outer rail are materially lower than the stresses produced in the outer rail of the other 6-deg. curve laid with 112-lb. rail.

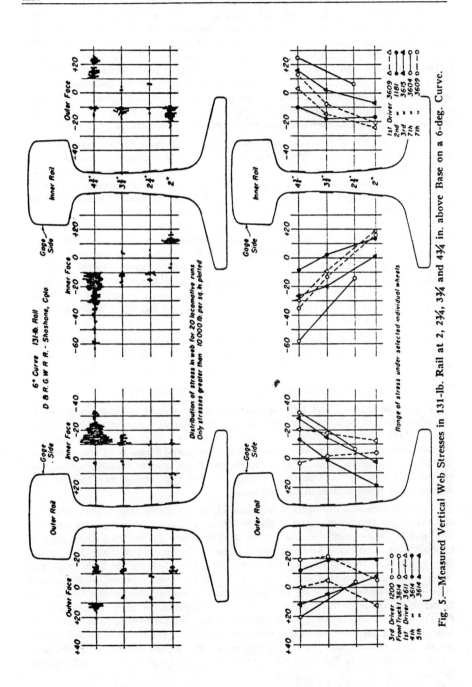

Fig. 5.—Measured Vertical Web Stresses in 131-lb. Rail at 2, 2¾, 3¾ and 4¾ in. above Base on a 6-deg. Curve.

At the highest gage on the inner web face there are no stresses as high as 35,000 lb. per sq. in. in compression. At this height there may be some tendency for an outward lateral force on the rail head to counteract the bending moment in the web caused by the presence of the centroid of the wheel bearing at or near the gage corner of the rail, for wheels whose flanges are against the rail. The stresses at the two-inch height are somewhat higher than at the intermediate heights and are so disposed as to denote some outward bending of the web. As this curve was in mountainous territory the train speeds were restricted which would not be conducive to the development of high stresses in the outer rail. Only two passenger trains were running at the speed of superelevation of 35 miles per hour; most other trains were traveling at speeds of from 20 to 32 miles per hour.

On the inner rail of the curve very high vertical compressive stresses were produced in the inner web face at a height of 4¾ in. There were 12 individual wheels that produced stresses greater than 50,000 lb. per sq. in. even in this heavy rail. Of the three locations along the inner rail of the track, one location produced no stresses as high as 40,000 lb. per sq. in.; the second location had only three individual stresses as high as this value, and the third location, where the rail was canted outward 1 in 43, produced almost all of the high stresses. The track was not out of line at the latter location, but it is probable that the outer ends of the tie plates at that point had cut into the ties to a greater extent than at most other places along the track. The stresses are slightly higher at the two-inch gage height than for the intermediate heights. For the 19 trains recorded at the inner rail, only three were running at slow speeds and the others were running at from 22 to 34 miles per hour. Some high stresses were recorded at the higher speeds but a much larger proportion of high stresses under individual wheels were recorded in the three low speed runs.

In the lower half of Fig 5, the records for five individual wheels have been selected for each rail to show the variation in stress at the various web heights. These records were selected also to cover the total range of stress recorded at the several gages.

Comments on the Web Stresses in the Rails of Curved Track

It is to be expected that high vertical web stresses will be produced in the upper part of the web of both the inner and outer rails of sharply curved track under those driving wheels where the centroid of the wheel bearing is well away from the middle of the rail head. It is to be further expected that large lateral forces at certain wheels on the rail head, either in turning the locomotive on the curve or in resisting turning, will produce high bending stress in the rail web and that this bending may produce high stresses in the lower portion of the rail web.

Fig. 6 is presented to show the frequency of stresses higher than a given stress for each rail of the two 6-deg. curves. Only the stresses at the top web gages are included. The black circles represent the values at the inner web faces and the open circles those at the outer faces. The heavy lines and circles represent the summation of the data for the driving wheels of locomotives, and the lighter lines show those for the front truck and trailer wheels of locomotives and the wheels of tenders. Twenty percent of the stresses under driver loading in the inner web faces of both inner rails were greater than 35,000 lb. per sq. in. compression, while the percentages of values at the higher stresses is large. For the outer rail of the 6-deg. curve laid with 112-lb. rail the percentage of high values is large, but for the outer rail of the curve laid with 131-lb. rail there are no high values. It will be remembered that the train speeds were higher on the first curve but the large difference in stresses in the outer rails cannot be explained entirely by the difference in speeds.

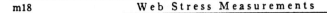

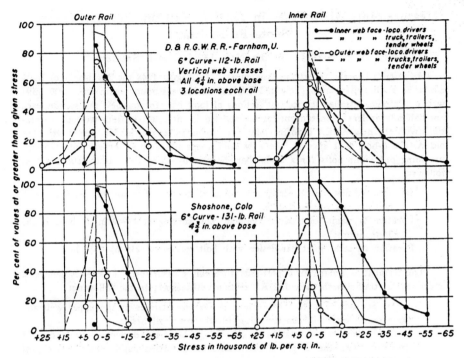

Fig. 6.—Frequency of Vertical Web Stresses on 6-deg. Curve.

For both inner rails the front truck, trailer and tender wheels produced much lower stresses than did the driving wheels, but in both outer rails the tender wheels produced a greater percentage of moderately high stresses than did the driving wheels.

Stresses were measured in both edges of the base of the inner and outer rails of both curves at two locations per rail. Only moderate longitudinal lateral bending stresses were developed in the rail bases and from this fact it can be reasoned that for curves producing higher lateral bending in the base of the rails, higher lateral bending stresses in a vertical direction would be produced in the lower portion of the webs than the stresses reported.

TEXT 19

Appendix 11–a

Measurements of Stresses in 132 RE Rail on Tangent Track—Santa Fe Railway

Web Stresses in the New 132 RE Rail Section

As described in the report on Assignment 7, in August 1948 the Atchison, Topeka & Santa Fe Railway, in laying new 132 RE rail in the eastbound main track 100 miles west of Chicago, installed service test sections of joint bars for the new rail section, each one-half mile in length on tangent track. Included in these test sections were three locations with the new AREA headfree joint bars 36 in. in length, having, respectively, the old AREA 6-hole bolt spacing, the new AREA spacing and an experimental spacing providing only four bolts for a 36-in. bar. Specifically these three test sections are as follows:

> Location V, new AREA design, headfree 36-in. joint bar for 132 RE rail, with bolt spacing of 3½–6–6 in.
> Location W, same joint bar design with bolt spacing of 4½–9 in. (4 bolts in the 36-in. joints.)
> Location X, same joint bar design with bolt spacing of 2½–6½–6½ in.

This installation offered an opportunity to obtain measurements of stresses developed under regular traffic in the new 132 RE section with respect to the following:

> A. To determine to what extent the service stresses in the upper web and upper rail fillets had been reduced with the new rail design.
> B. To obtain information on the range of stress developed by traffic for correlation with the fatigue strength tests being carried out in the laboratory of the University of Illinois.
> C. To obtain information on the effect of bolt hole spacing on the range of web stresses developed in service.

The measurements, analysis of data, and preparation of the report for these tests were made by the Engineering Division research staff of the Association of American Railroads, under the general direction of G. M. Magee, research engineer, by M. F. Smucker, assistant electrical engineer, and Olaf Froseth, assistant track engineer, assisted by other staff members.

Previous reports of the committee have described the high stresses that were found in the old 112 RE and 131 RE rail sections in the upper portion of the rail web and in the upper rail fillets. It was pointed out that these were due to stress concentration effects from the wheel-bearing pressure and were aggravated by the bending of the head on the web because the wheel load was frequently applied eccentrically, generally toward the gage corner. In the design of the new 115 and 132 rail sections the upper part of the web was thickened and longer fillet radii were used. Laboratory tests indicated this modification would effect a stress reduction of approximately 25 percent. In addition, the top of the rail was rounded to relieve the gage corner from excessive bearing pressure and bring the point of contact between wheel and rail more nearly to the center of the head.

The stress measurements were conducted at three different locations in the track. At Location 1 the stress gages were placed half way between ties and at the other two locations the gages were positioned directly over the same tie on opposite rails. Stresses

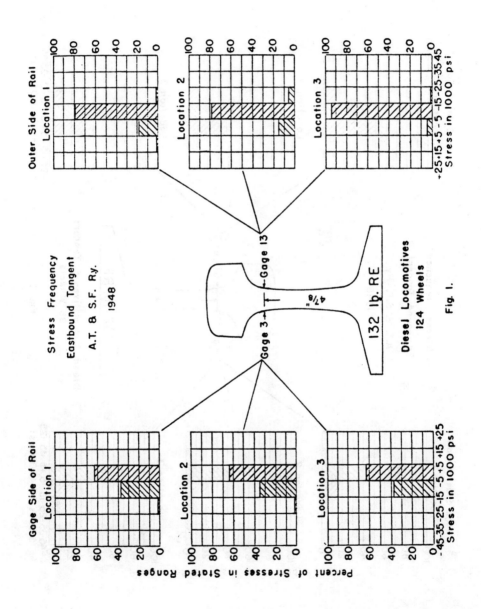

Fig. I.

Stress Frequency
Eastbound Tangent
A.T. & S.F. Ry.
1948

132 lb. RE
Diesel Locomotives
124 Wheels

254

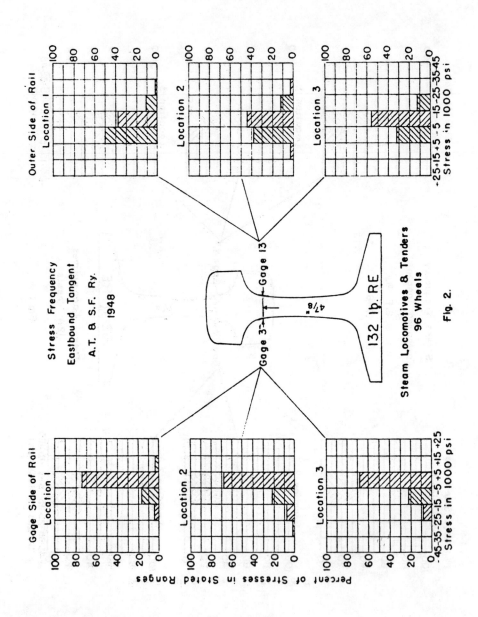

Fig. 2.

255

Rail   629

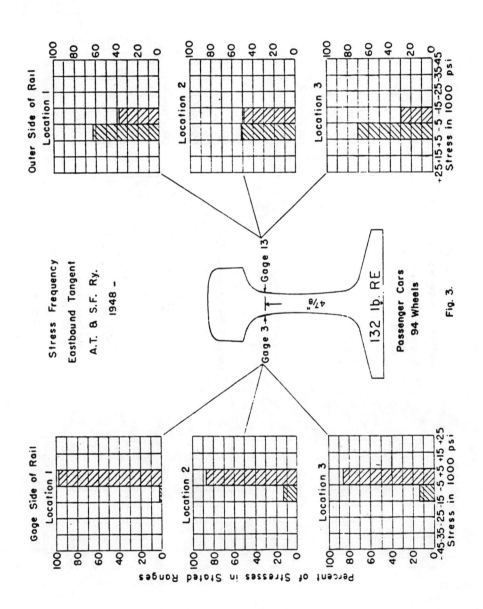

Fig. 3.

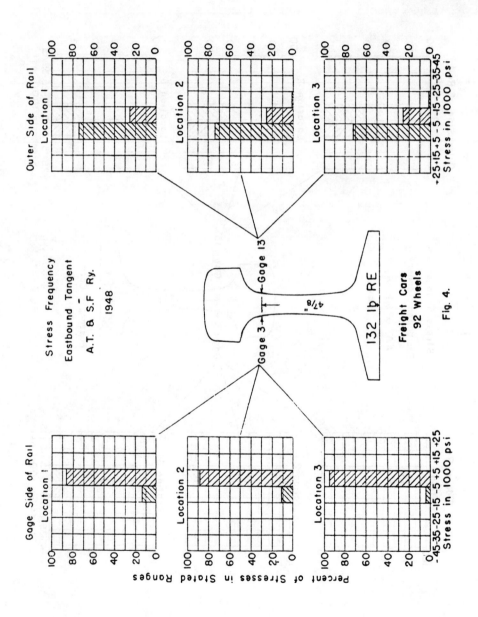

Stress Frequency
Eastbound Tangent
A.T. & S.F. Ry.
1948

Freight Cars
92 Wheels

Fig. 4.

were measured only near the upper web fillets on the gage and field sides of the rail, as previous tests had shown these to be the areas of highest stress. (See Fig. 1.) Fortunately, regular train operation over this track included both steam and diesel locomotives and passenger and freight trains, covering a speed range to almost 100 mph.

Figs. 1 to 4, incl., show the results obtained from the measurements. These charts were prepared to show the percentage of stresses occurring within a given stress range for diesel and steam locomotives separately and for passenger and freight cars separately. The diagrams were prepared in this manner so that the stress frequency to be anticipated for any traffic conditions could be estimated from these data. As the wheel loads experienced in these tests are representative of those normally encountered on almost any main line railroad, the results obtained in these tests provide a reasonably accurate picture of prevailing stress frequency.

It will be observed that with this improved rail section on tangent track the stress range is well balanced on both the gage and field sides, and for diesel locomotives and both passenger and freight cars the stress range lies mostly between 5000 psi. tension and 15,000 psi. compression. For steam locomotives the stress range is also well balanced on both field and gage sides, but is somewhat larger, lying mostly between 5000 psi. tension and 25,000 psi. compression. Measurements at the same position on the rail web on the old 131 RE section on tangent track on the Norfolk & Western Railway showed a stress range on the gage side from 35,000 psi. compression to 5000 psi. tension. with occasional stresses going as high as 55,000 psi. compression. On the field side the stress range was principally from 25,000 psi. compression to 15,000 psi. tension, with some stress values going as high as 45,000 psi. compression and 25,000 psi. tension. These stresses were measured under steam locomotives and were reported in AREA Proceedings Vol. 48, 1947, page 777. Comparison of the stress range obtained with the 132 RE section relative to that of the 131 RE indicates that a very substantial improvement has been effected in the range of fillet stress with the revised design on tangent track. Stress measurements have not as yet been made on the 132 RE section on curved track, but this is planned for 1950.

Web Stresses within Joint Bar Limits

In AREA Proceedings Vol. 49, 1948, page 464, a complete report was given of laboratory tests conducted at the University of Illinois by the research staff with three different bolt spacings for the new 115 RE rail section. As a result of the data obtained in these tests, the Association adopted a revised bolt hole spacing of 3½–6–6 in. in lieu of the old spacing of 2½–6½–6½ in. Laboratory tests indicated that the new spacing effected substantial reductions in the rail web stress in the upper fillet at the rail end and at the first bolt hole. It was also shown in these laboratory studies that the applied bolt tension alone is responsible for a substantial web stress, which is referred to as the static web stress. Dynamic stresses result from passing wheel loads and the flexure of the joint.

The installation on the Santa Fe afforded an opportunity to obtain measurements in the field with the new and old bolt spacings for the new 132 RE section. Also, because of the interest expressed by various railways in the possibility of using a 36-in. joint with only four bolts and the inclusion of this type of spacing in the test installation, an opportunity was afforded to obtain stress measurements with 4½–9 in. bolt spacing. Accordingly, rail web stress measurements were made in November 1948 at two joints with the AREA headfree design bars for each of the three different bolt spacings. These measurements included the dynamic stresses developed in the rail web under regular service trains. Measurements were made near the upper and lower fillets and at the first and last bolt holes on each rail end at the joint and on both the field and gage sides. In September 1949 the static stresses due to the applied bolt tension only and not including dynamic stresses were made at six joints for each bolt spacing in the upper fillet and at the first bolt hole for each rail end at the joint on both the field and gage sides.

Discussion of Dynamic Stresses

Figs. 5 to 7, incl., show the maximum tension and compression stress during each test run obtained at one joint with the new spacing (3½–6–6 in.) on the north rail. The chart shows the stresses for diesel and steam locomotives separately and also those developed under the cars. Values are plotted with respect to the speed of the train and the diagram shows the location at the rail end for each numbered gage, providing a convenient means of identification. It will be observed from these figures that there is no definite trend for change in stress range or increase in stress with increase in speed. In fact there appears to be no apparent relation between stress and train speed within the speed range covered—from 40 to almost 100 mph. In general, the range of stress does not appear to be high relative to the fatigue strength that may be expected of the rail steel. Some tests were made in which the bolts were intentionally left loose and for these runs, in general, considerably higher stresses were obtained, as shown in the diagrams. Similar diagrams were prepared for each of the six joints included in these dynamic tests, but are not reproduced, inasmuch as the general pattern of stresses obtained corresponds to those shown in these three diagrams.

A better visual comparison of the dynamic stresses is afforded by Fig. 8, in which the average maximum for each run and the single maximum stress obtained are shown for the two joints of each different rail drilling. It is interesting to note that the range of stress at the receiving rail end is somewhat higher than for the leaving end, particularly in the upper and lower fillets and at the first bolt hole. There does not seem to be a very pronounced difference in range of stress with respect to the three different bolt spacings included, but what difference there is, is in favor of the new spacing of 3½–6–6 in.

Correlation of Measured Stresses with Laboratory Fatigue Data

From the standpoint of the development of fatigue failures, the actual stress, or the combination of stresses due to bolt tension and passing wheel loads, is most significant. The measurements of static stress have shown that the static or initial stress applied in the rail web due to the bolt tension is quite variable. A bending may be set up in the rail web due to the manner in which the joint bars fit into the fishing surfaces and as a result the stress at any individual gage location may vary from a low to a very high tension. This means, therefore, that for any specific location within the joint bar, the actual dynamic stress range may be from a high tension to a low compression, equal tension to equal compression, high compression to low tension or any value in between.

In Appendix 11–b are presented the results of fatigue tests conducted by Professor R. S. Jensen in the laboratory at the University of Illinois. In these tests, specimens of rail steel taken from the rail web were tested and the fatigue strength determined for various ranges of applied stress. The results of these tests are shown in Fig. 9 in the form of a Goodman diagram. From this diagram it is then possible to determine what range of dynamic stress may be tolerated for any initial static stress developed by the applied bolt tension.

Table 1 shows for both the upper fillets and the first bolt holes the maximum static stress that was measured in any of the six joints tested at each location (V, W or X)

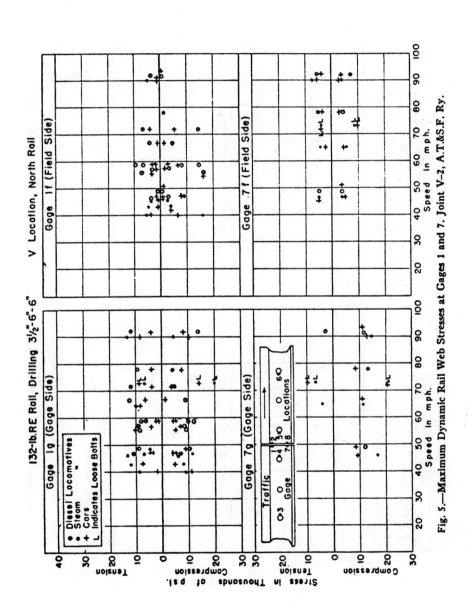

Fig. 5.—Maximum Dynamic Rail Web Stresses at Gages 1 and 7. Joint V–2, A.T.&S.F. Ry.

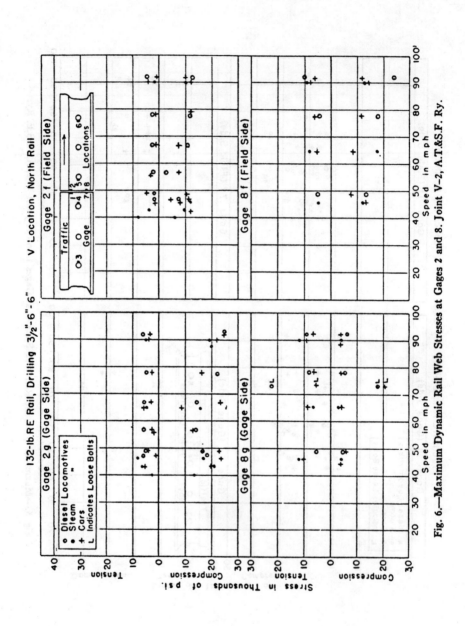

Fig. 6.—Maximum Dynamic Rail Web Stresses at Gages 2 and 8. Joint V–2, A.T.&S.F. Ry.

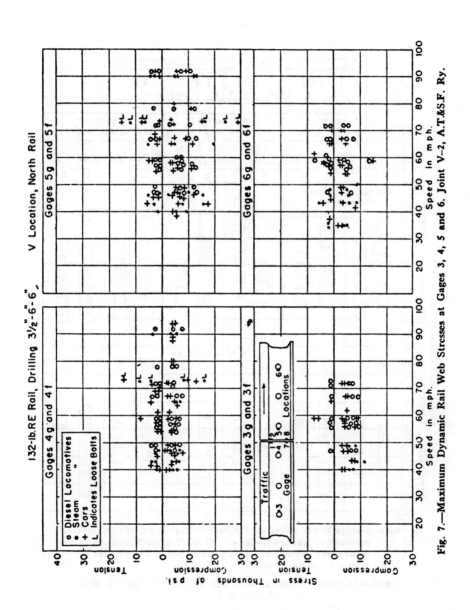

Fig. 7.—Maximum Dynamic Rail Web Stresses at Gages 3, 4, 5 and 6. Joint V–2, A.T.&S.F. Ry.

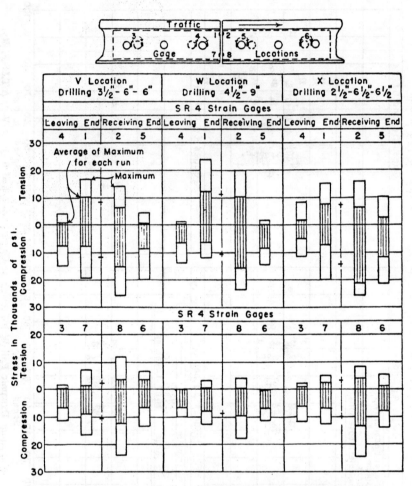

Note: Average stress values are the mean of gage and field side stresses
produced by locomotives in two rail joints at each location.
+ Indicates average of Leaving and Receiving end stresses in
gages 1 and 2, 7 and 8.

Fig. 8.—Dynamic Stresses in Rail Web at Joints of 132 RE Rail,
A. T. & S. F. Ry.

TABLE 1.—RAIL WEB STRESS IN THE VERTICAL DIRECTION WITHIN JOINT BAR LIMITS
Santa Fe Railway Tests of 132 RE Rail Section—Tangent Track
(Stresses are given in pounds per square inch)

| | Upper Fillets | | | First Bolt Hole | | |
Location	Max. Static Stress	Range of Dynamic Stress	Range of Fatigue Strength	Max. Static Stress	Range of Dynamic Stress	Range of Fatigue Strength
V	+12,000	28,000	61,000	+29,000	17,000	50,000
W	+ 9,000	28,000	62,000	+28,000	12,000	51,000
X	+18,000	32,000	57,000	+40,000	24,000	45,000

with the different bolt spacings. In the adjoining column is shown the maximum range of dynamic stress that was found at this particular gage location. This range was taken as the average of the maximum stresses obtained in each run rather than the single maximum for the reason, as previously explained, that the single maximum stress values would not be expected to occur with sufficient frequency to occasion a fatigue failure.

For comparison with the values of dynamic stress as they were measured in the field, are shown the values for the fatigue strength of the steel as obtained in the laboratory tests and shown in Fig. 9. It will be observed that for the new 132 RE rail section

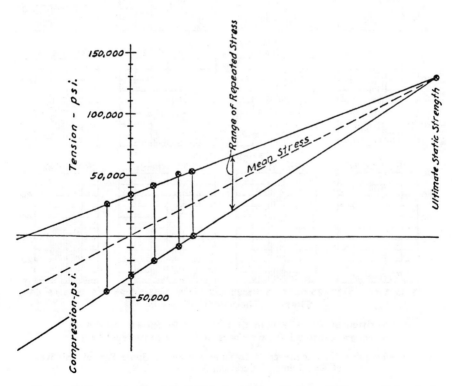

Fig. 9.—Fatigue Strength of Rail Web for Various Ranges of Stress as Determined by Laboratory Tests (As Rolled Surface without Corrosion).

A

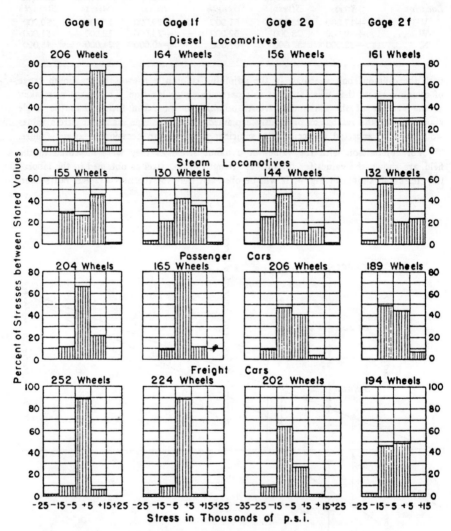

Note: Position of SR 4 Strain Gages 1 and 2 shown on Fig. 11.
Stresses measured from records of runs over two rail joints.

Fig. 10.—Frequency of Occurrence of Dynamic Stresses in Upper Part of Rail Web of Rail Joints. V Location, A. T. & S. F. Ry.

and the area ABkA will govern the form of the stress in a point located about one-third of the length therefrom of the rail section or so. As further information rail 40 which says are measured at the bottom at base at diametrically the hole area erators. The stress in the upper filler holes midward and at the first bolt holes sections.

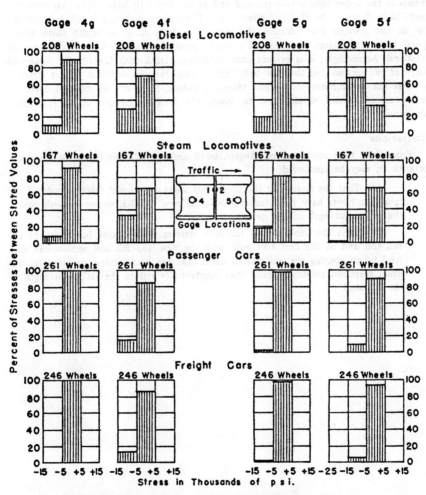

Note: Stresses measured from records of runs over two rail joints.

Fig. 11.—Frequency of Occurrence of Dynamic Stresses in Rail Web at First Bolt Holes from Rail Ends. V Location, A. T. & S. F. Ry.

and the new AREA bolt spacing (Location V) the range of dynamic stresses is only about one-third of the fatigue strength of the steel as determined from the laboratory tests. As further information, Figs. 10 and 11 show the frequency of occurrence of dynamic stresses as determined in the field measurements. These diagrams show the stresses in the upper fillet at the rail end and at the first bolt hole which past measurements have shown to be the high stress areas. From these diagrams it will be observed that at any specific gage location the maximum stress range at which there would appear to be a sufficient frequency of stress to produce fatigue failure does not exceed 30,000 psi. Accordingly, it is evident that on tangent track with the 132 RE improved design of rail section and the new bolt hole spacing, there is sufficient fatigue strength to resist the development of fatigue cracks, provided there are no unusual corrosive factors present which would tend to lower the fatigue strength of the rail steel substantially.

Conclusions

From these tests conducted on tangent track under conditions typical of main line operation, it may be concluded:

(a) That the stresses in the upper rail fillets on tangent track outside of the joint bar limits have been reduced with the new 132 RE section to well within the fatigue strength of rail steel, and

(b) That the concentrated rail web stresses within joint bar limits at the rail end and at the first bolt hole with the new 132 RE rail section and new AREA bolt spacing are well within limits that can be tolerated, provided no unusual corrosion conditions exist that substantially reduce the fatigue strength of the rail steel.

Appendix 11–b

Measurement of Stresses in 115 RE Rail on Tangent Track—North Western Railway

Web Stresses in the New 115 RE Rail Section

The report on Assignment 7 describes the test sections for the new 115 RE rail which was installed on the westbound main track of the Chicago & North Western Railway near Sterling, Ill., 106 miles west of Chicago on the Omaha Line. Each test section includes 100 joints and is approximately 2000 ft. long. The test section was installed for the purpose of testing various joint bar designs. Included in these designs were two AREA design bars on the following locations:

> Location AA—New AREA design, headfree 36-in. joint bar for 115 RE rail, with bolt spacing of 4½–9 in. (4 bolts in 36-in. bars).

> Location BB—Same joint bar design with new AREA bolt spacing of 3½–6–6 in.

This installation offered an opportunity to obtain measurements of stresses developed under regular traffic in the new 115 RE rail section. The measurements are thought to be informative, because they determine to what extent the service stresses in the upper web and upper rail fillets had been reduced with the new rail design, and indicate the effect of the number of bolt holes and their spacing on the range of web stresses developed in service.

The measurements, analysis of data, and preparation of the report for these tests were made by the Engineering Division research staff of the Association of American Railroads, under the direction of G. M. Magee, research engineer, M. F. Smucker, assistant electrical engineer, and Olaf Froseth, assistant track engineer, assisted by other staff members. The results of a similar investigation with the 132 RE rail section were reported in the AREA Proceedings, Vol. 51, 1950, page 626, Appendix 11–a.

Previous reports of the committee have described the high stresses that were found in the old 112 RE and 131 RE rail sections in the upper portion of the rail web and in the upper rail fillets. It was pointed out that these were due to stress concentration effects from the wheel-bearing pressure, and were aggravated by the bending of the head on the web because the wheel load was frequently applied eccentrically, generally toward the gage corner. In the design of the new 115 RE and the 132 RE rail sections, the upper part of the web was thickened and longer fillet radii were used. Laboratory tests indicated that this modification would effect a stress reduction of approximately 25 percent. In addition, the top of the rail was rounded to relieve the gage corner from excessive bearing pressure and to bring the point of contact between wheel and rail more nearly to the center of the head.

The stress measurements were conducted at four different locations in the track. At track Locations 1 and 2, the stress gages were placed directly over the same tie on opposite rails, and at Locations 3 and 4 the gages were placed halfway between ties on opposite rails. The stresses were measured only near the upper web fillets on the gage and field sides of the rail (at gages 3 and 13 located 4½ in. above the rail base), because previous tests had shown these to be the areas of highest stress. Regular train operation over this track included both steam and diesel locomotives and passenger and freight trains, covering a speed range to 80 mph. Figs. 1 to 4, inclusive, show the results obtained from the measurements. These charts were prepared to show the percentage of stresses occurring within a given stress range for diesel and steam locomotives separately and for passenger and freight cars separately. From this presentation of the data anticipated stress frequencies for any traffic condition can be estimated. As the wheel loads experienced in these tests are representative of those normally encountered on almost any main line railroad, the results obtained in these tests provide a reasonably accurate picture of prevailing stress frequency for tangent track.

It will be observed that with this improved rail section on tangent track the stress range is as well balanced as can be expected on both the gage and field sides. For diesel locomotives and passenger cars the stress range lies between 5000 psi. tension and 25,000 psi. compression on the gage side of the web and between 15,000 psi. tension and 15,000 psi. compression on the field side. For steam locomotives the stresses are somewhat larger, but still balanced with a stress range of 5000 psi. tension to 35,000 psi. compression on the gage side and a stress range of 15,000 psi. tension to 25,000 psi. compression on the field side. The freight cars show the best balanced stress range, with 5000 psi. tension to 25,000 psi. compression on the gage side and 5000 psi. tension to 15,000 psi. compression on the field side. These stress ranges are larger than those of the 132 RE rail of the same design, as reported in the AREA Proceedings, Vol. 51, 1950, due to difference in weight in the two rail designs.

Rail Web Stresses within Joint Bar Limits

In AREA Proceedings, Vol. 49, 1948, page 464, a complete report was given of laboratory tests conducted at the University of Illinois by the research staff with three different bolt spacings for the new 115 RE rail section. As a result of the data obtained in these tests, the Association adopted a revised bolt hole spacing of 3½–6–6 in. in lieu of the old spacing of 2½–6½–6½ in. Laboratory tests indicated that the new spacing effected substantial reductions in the rail web stress in the upper fillet at the rail end and at the first bolt hole. It was also shown in these laboratory studies that the applied bolt tension alone is responsible for a substantial web stress, which is referred to as the static web stress. Dynamic stresses result from passing wheel loads and the flexure on the joint.

The installation on the North Western Railway afforded an opportunity to obtain measurements in the field on the new bolt spacing for the new 115 RE section, as well as 4½–9 in. spacing, for which an interest had been expressed by several railways. Accordingly, rail web stress measurements were made in 1949 at two joints with the AREA headfree design bars for each of the two above bolt spacings. These measurements included the dynamic stresses developed in the rail web under regular service trains. Measurements were made at the rail end on the rail web 4½ in. above the rail base near the upper fillets at gage lines 1g, 1f, 2g and 2f. Other measurements were made as near to the edge of the first bolt hole as the gages permitted on each rail end at the joint and on both field and gage web faces at gage lines 4g, 4f, 5g and 5f.

Discussion of Dynamic Stresses

Figs. 5 to 8, inclusive, show the maximum tension and compression stress during each test run obtained at one joint with the new spacing (3½–6–6 in.) and another joint with the two hole spacing (4½–9 in.) on the north rail. The chart shows the stresses for diesel and steam locomotives separately, and also those developed under the cars. Values are plotted with respect to the speed of the train. The diagrams show the location for each numbered gage at the rail end, providing a convenient means of identification. It will be observed from these that there is no definite trend for change in stress range or increase in stress with increase in speed. In fact, there appears no apparent relation between stress and train speed within the speed range of 10 and 80 mph. The stresses in the upper webs at the rail ends of 2-hole drillings 4½–9 in.) compared to those of the 3-hole drillings (3½–6–6 in.) are less in the case of the 2-hole drillings. Practically all of the web stresses for the 2-hole drillings fell within a stress range of 20,000 psi. tension to 25,000 psi. compression, compared to the stress range of the 3-hole drillings of 15,000 psi. tension to 35,000 psi. compression. The stress range at the edge of the first bolt hole for the 2-hole drillings is 5000 psi. tension to 15,000 psi. compression, compared to the stress range of the 3-hole drilling of 10.000 psi. tension to 25,000 psi. compression.

A better visual comparison of the dynamic stresses is afforded by Fig. 9, in which the average maximum for each run and the single maximum stress obtained are shown for the joints of the two different rail drillings. It is interesting to note that the range of stress at the receiving rail end is somewhat higher than for the leaving end. Here again a difference in the stress range at the edge of the first bolt hole for the two different drillings can be noted.

(text continued on page 704)

270

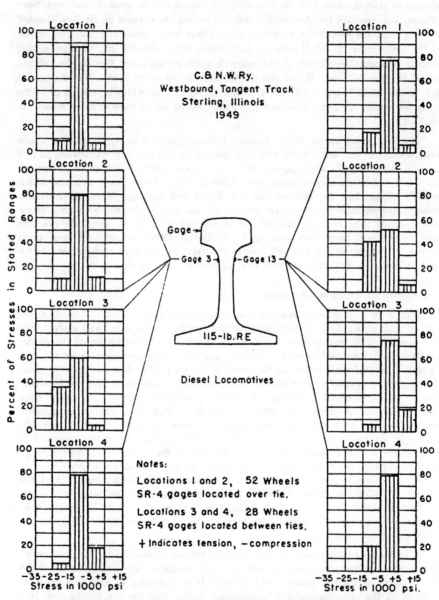

C. & N.W. Ry.
Westbound, Tangent Track
Sterling, Illinois
1949

Gage →

Gage 3 — Gage 13

115-lb. RE

Diesel Locomotives

Notes:

Locations 1 and 2, 52 Wheels
SR-4 gages located over tie.

Locations 3 and 4, 28 Wheels
SR-4 gages located between ties.

+ Indicates tension, − compression

Fig. 1. Frequency of occurrence of stresses in rail web at quarter points between rail joints. Stresses produced by diesel locomotives.

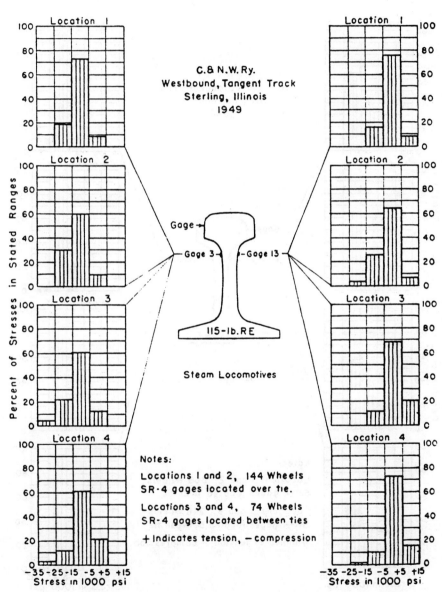

Fig. 2. Frequency of occurrence of stresses in rail web at quarter points between rail joints. Stresses produced by steam locomotives.

272

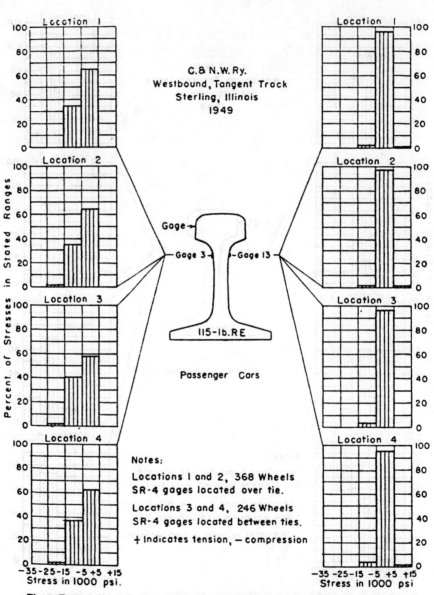

Fig. 3. Frequency of occurrence of stresses in rail web at quarter points between rail joints. Stresses produced by passenger cars.

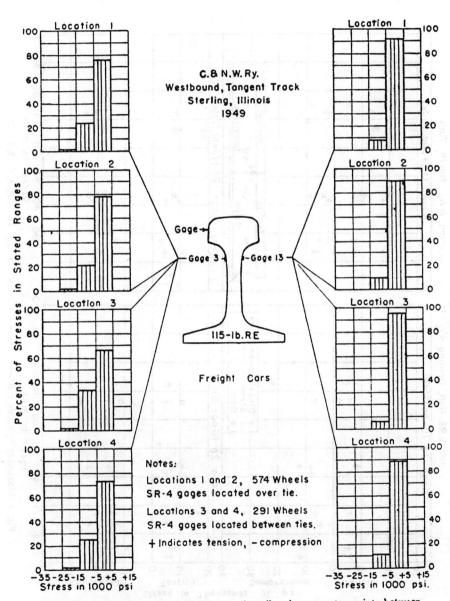

Fig. 4. Frequency of occurrence of stresses in rail web at quarter points between rail joints. Stresses produced by freight cars.

274

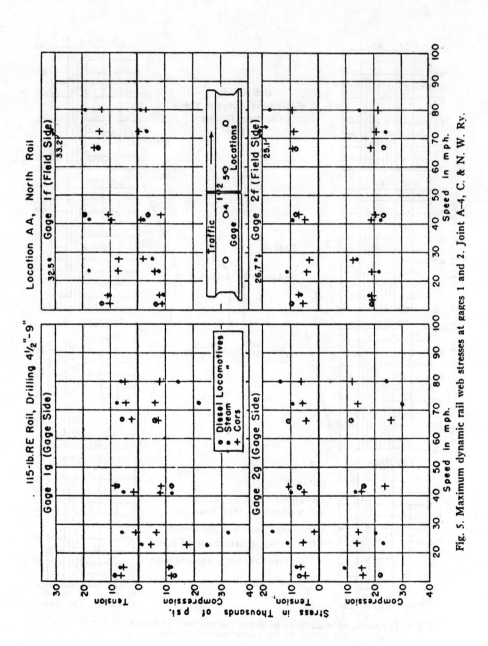

Fig. 5. Maximum dynamic rail web stresses at gages 1 and 2. Joint A–4, C. & N. W. Ry.

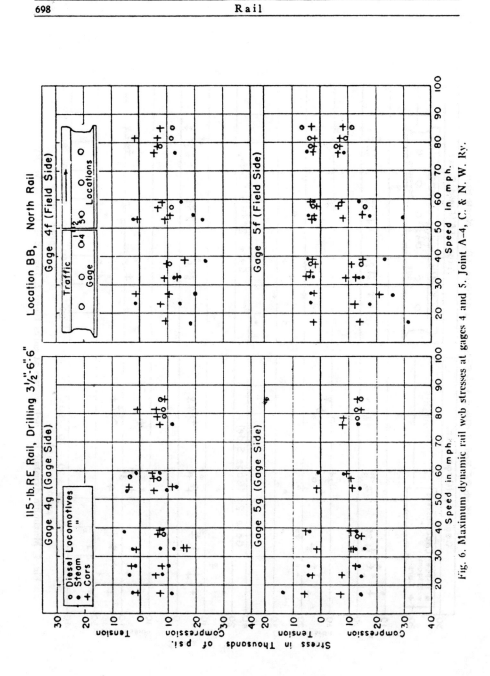

Fig. 6. Maximum dynamic rail web stresses at gages 4 and 5. Joint A-4, C. & N. W. Ry.

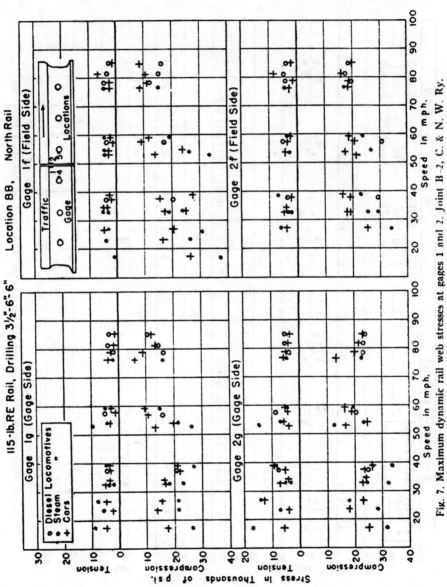

Fig. 7. Maximum dynamic rail web stresses at gages 1 and 2. Joint B-2, C. & N. W. Ry.

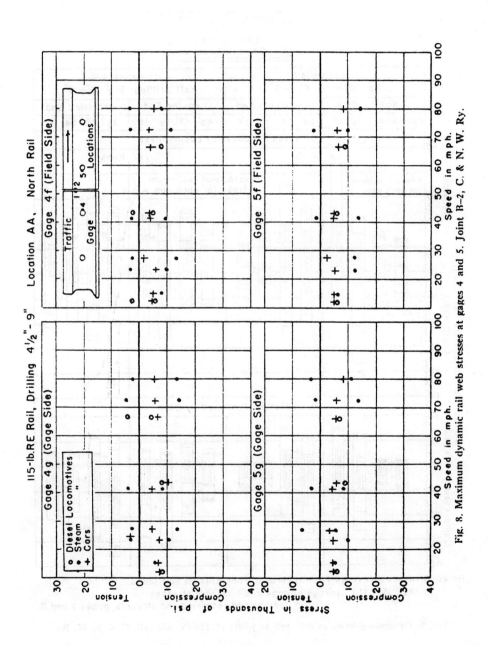

Fig. 8. Maximum dynamic rail web stresses at gages 4 and 5. Joint B-2, C. & N. W. Ry.

278

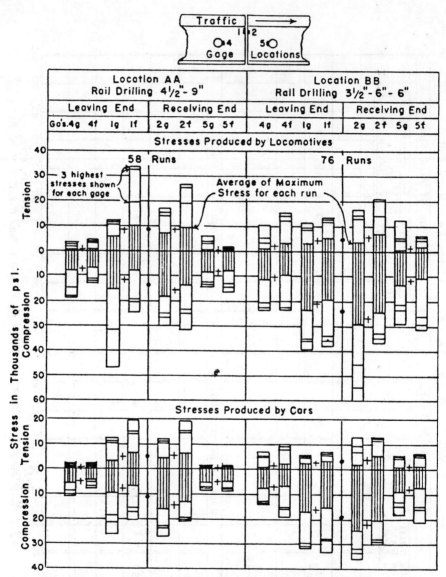

Fig. 9. Dynamic stresses in rail web at joints of 115-lb. RE rail. C. & N. W. Ry.

R a i l

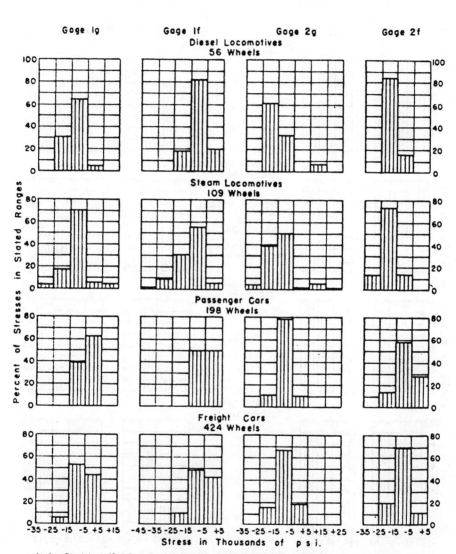

Note: Position of S R·4 Strain Gages shown on Fig.II.

Fig. 10. Frequency of occurrence of dynamic stresses in upper part of rail web at joint B–2, location BB, C. & N. W. Ry.

280

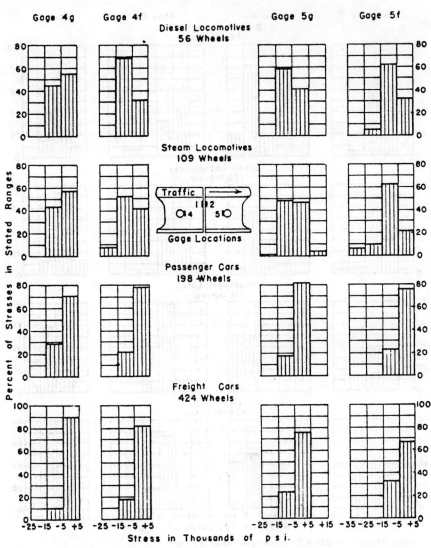

Fig. 11. Frequency of occurrence of dynamic stresses in rail web at first bolt holes
from rail ends, Joint B-2, Location BB, C. & N. W. Ry.

(text continued from page 692)

Correlation of Measured Stresses with Laboratory Fatigue Data

In the report on stresses in 132 RE rail on tangent track in the AREA Proceedings, Vol. 51, 1950, a comparison between measured stresses and laboratory fatigue data has been made. It was found in that investigation that the range of dynamic stresses is only one-third of the fatigue strength of the steel as determined from the laboratory tests. In view of the fact that Figs. 10 and 11 of the above named report, showing the frequency of occurrence of dynamic stresses, are comparable to Figs. 10 and 11 of the data pertaining to the 115 RE rail, it may be stated that the range of dynamic stresses is less than one-half of the fatigue strength of the steel. From the diagrams on Figs. 10 and 11 it can be noted that at any specific gage location the maximum stress range at which there would appear to be sufficient frequency of stress to produce fatigue failure does not exceed 30,000 psi. From this it is evident that the new 115 RE rail design on tangent track with either of the bolt hole spacings has sufficient fatigue strength to resist development of fatigue cracks, provided no unusual corrosion conditions exist.

Conclusions

From these tests conducted on tangent track under conditions typical of main line operation, it may be concluded:

(a) That the stresses in the upper rail fillets on tangent track outside of the joint bar limits have been reduced with the new 115 RE section to well within the fatigue strength of rail steel, and

(b) That the concentrated rail web stresses within joint bar limits at the rail end and at the first bolt hole with the new 115 RE rail section and new AREA bolt spacing are well within limits that can be tolerated, provided no unusual corrosion conditions exist that substantially reduce the fatigue strength of the rail steel.

TEXT 21

ASSOCIATION OF AMERICAN RAILROADS
OPERATIONS AND MAINTENANCE DEPARTMENT
ENGINEERING DIVISION
CENTRAL RESEARCH LABORATORY
3140 SOUTH FEDERAL STREET
CHICAGO 16, ILLINOIS
CALUMET 5-9600

G. M. MAGEE, RESEARCH ENGINEER

September 7, 1951

Mr. H. R. Clarke
Chief Engineer
Chicago, Burlington & Quincy Railroad
547 W. Jackson Blvd.
Chicago 6, Illinois

Dear Mr. Clarke:

We have your letter of July 9, file HRC-500, in reference to the report prepared by Electro-Motive Division, G.M.C., covering the stresses measured in 60-lb. and 72-lb. (rerolled) rails on the C. & N.W. Ry. branch track at McGirr, Ill.

After receiving their original report we recommended several changes, and their revised report was received last year. While the latest report is not exactly in the form we would have preferred, it does contain sufficient data to help establish a basis for determining the maximum speed at which locomotives can be permitted to operate on light rail sections used in branch lines. During the past few years several railroads have written regarding diesel operation on light rail, indicating this as a subject of considerable general interest.

Generally, speed restrictions as far as rail stresses are concerned are based on the primary flexural stresses at the centerline of the rail base. Table 1 is attached to show information obtained in the McGirr tests concerning the measured and calculated rail stresses which we consider pertinent in determining the maximum speed of operation. Computed stresses in the table are based on the Talbot formula for static rail stresses plus impact or speed effect from the following formula: Percent Impact = 33/D x mph. where D = diameter of the wheel in inches.

It will be noted that the average 5 mph. coasting stress was appreciably higher for the E.M.D. diesel than for the other two units of power, and also for the loaded coal car, the latter three values being of comparable magnitude. It will also be observed that for E.M.D. unit and the loaded gondola there was good agreement between the mean measured 5 mph. coasting rail stresses and the computed static stresses (column 7). The ratios for the steam locomotive and the 6-wheel truck diesel No. 1504 were not in quite as good agreement probably because of (1), effect of the equalizers (2), all wheels were not considered and (3), the rail stresses were only measured in one rail. In other tests we have found that the ratios similar to those in column 8 of the table varied several percent each way from a perfect ratio of 1.00. In general, we consider the agreement good between the calculated and measured values.

We have reviewed the subject of establishing a maximum allowable computed stress at the centerline of the rail base for limiting the speed of operation on branch lines laid with light rail where generally the speed is not over 35 mph., and there is little or no passenger traffic involved. In our opinion, which is based on available data and experience, we believe the maximum computed rail stress including impact or speed effect should be limited to 35,000 psi. for speeds of 35 mph. and less. Over 35 mph., the stress should be limited to 30,000 psi., the same as in main track. The 35,000 psi. limit has been determined in the following manner, using 70,000 psi. as the yield point of rail steel, which physical tests showed would be satisfactory for old rails as tested at McGirr.

Track or locomotive conditions that increase rail stress, but are not included in the usual computations and should be included in the factor of safety are:

1).	Lateral bending of rail	20%
2).	Track condition	35%
3).	Locomotive load factor	10%
4).	Temperature stresses	3,000 psi.
5).	Rail wear and corrosion	15%
6).	Unbalanced elevation	10%
		90%

$$\frac{70,000 - 3,000}{1.90} = 35,000 \text{ psi.} \quad (35 \text{ mph. max.})$$

At McGirr the test was made in tangent track and the measured stresses will only include the effects of the above items 2 and 3. Item 5 was eliminated by computing the rail stresses from the physical properties of the "as worn" rail sections. Therefore in that test we may expect the maximum measured values at the centerline of base to reach a magnitude of 46,000 psi. (67,000 ÷ 1.45 = 46,000 psi.). For steam locomotives, rail stress due to unbalance in the drivers should be added to the computed static stress before applying the impact or speed effect factor. Because of lack of information on the counterbalancing of the C. & N.W. steam locomotive used in the McGirr tests, we have not computed the rail stresses at speeds above 5 mph. for this locomotive.

From the stress limitations above described, as well as the stresses measured at McGirr, we would consider the following maximum operating speeds to be satisfactory, insofar as rail stress is concerned:

72-lb. Rerolled Rail		60-lb. Rail
10 mph.	E.M.D. Diesel 930	See Note
*25 mph.	C.&N.W. Steam 345	*25 mph.
35 mph.	C.&N.W. Diesel 1504	35 mph.

Note: Not considered advisable to operate this locomotive on 60-lb. rail.

*Based on measured stresses

Restrictions on 72-lb. rerolled rail

For the EMD diesel No. 930 the computed rail stress is 35,000 psi. at 4 mph., so it would not seem advisable to operate this locomotive at more than 10 mph. For C. &N. W. diesel No. 1504 the maximum speed of 35 mph. is the limiting speed for the allowable stress of 35,000 psi. The 35 mph. limit is also applicable to the loaded coal car.

Restrictions on 60-lb. rail

We do not believe the EMD diesel should be operated on rail section 6001. C.&N.W. diesel No. 1504 has a computed rail stress of 35,000 psi. at 34 mph. For the loaded coal car the computed stress of 35,000 psi is obtained at $19\frac{1}{2}$ mph. It seems reasonable to permit those loads to operate 25 mph, as all of the measured rail stresses were below 40,000 psi.

We believe consideration should also be given to keeping shear stresses in the rail below the wheel-rail contact area below 50,000 psi. From the attached graph dated December 1944, it will be observed that this permissible shear limit will not be exceeded.

If you desire a copy of the E.M.D. report (their No. 8052-1), it is possible you may obtain one from Mr. L. Petersen, Structural Engineer, Electro-Motive Division, G.M.C., La Grange, Ill., as he was in charge of test and gave us our copy.

Yours very truly,

/s/G. M. Magee

Encl.

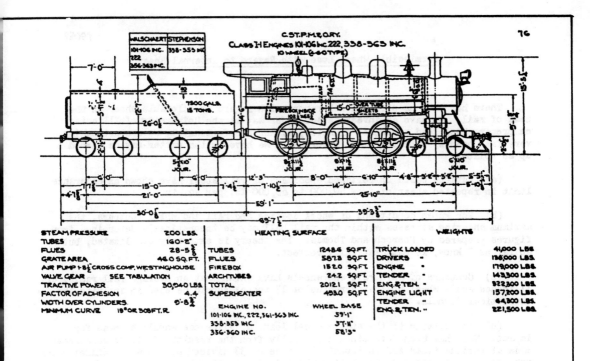

C.ST.P.M.&O.RY.
Class H Engines 101-106 inc. 222, 338-363 inc.
10 Wheel (4-6-0 Type)

76

STEAM PRESSURE	200 LBS.
TUBES	160-2"
FLUES	28-5½"
GRATE AREA	46.0 SQ.FT.
AIR PUMP 1-8½" CROSS COMP. WESTINGHOUSE	
VALVE GEAR	SEE TABULATION
TRACTIVE POWER	30,540 LBS
FACTOR OF ADHESION	4.4
WIDTH OVER CYLINDERS	9'-8½"
MINIMUM CURVE	18° OR 308FT. R.

HEATING SURFACE

TUBES	1248.6 SQ.FT.
FLUES	587.3 SQ.FT.
FIREBOX	152.0 SQ.FT.
ARCH TUBES	24.2 SQ.FT.
TOTAL	2012.1 SQ.FT.
SUPERHEATER	453.0 SQ.FT.

ENGINE NO.	WHEEL BASE
101-106 INC., 222, 361-363 INC.	59'-1"
338-353 INC.	57'-11"
356-360 INC.	58'-3"

WEIGHTS

TRUCK LOADED	41,000 LBS
DRIVERS "	138,000 LBS.
ENGINE "	179,000 LBS.
TENDER "	143,300 LBS.
ENG. & TEN. "	322,300 LBS.
ENGINE LIGHT	157,200 LBS.
TENDER "	64,300 LBS.
ENG. & TEN. "	221,500 LBS.

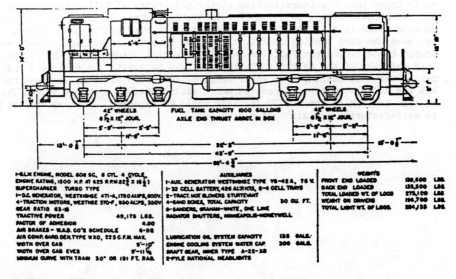

DIESEL ELECTRIC LOCOMOTIVE NO. 1504

175

A1A-A1A TYPE 1500 HORSE POWER

1-8LX ENGINE, MODEL 608 SC, 8 CYL. 4 CYCLE		AUXILIARIES		WEIGHTS	
ENGINE RATING, 1500 H.P. AT 625 R.P.M.8½ X 10½		1-AUX. GENERATOR WESTINGHS. TYPE YG-42A, 75 K.		FRONT END LOADED	139,500 LBS.
SUPERCHARGER TURBO TYPE		1- 32 CELL BATTERY, 426 ALT.R.K.S, 8-4 CELL TRAYS		BACK END LOADED	135,500 LBS.
1-D.C. GENERATOR, WESTINGHS. 471-A, 1780 AMPS, 600V.		2-TRACT MOT. BLOWERS STURTEVANT		TOTAL LOADED WT. OF LOCO.	275,100 LBS.
4-TRACTION MOTORS, WESTINGHS. 370-F, 930 AMPS, 350V		4-SAND BOXES, TOTAL CAPACITY 30 CU. FT.		WEIGHT ON DRIVERS	196,700 LBS.
GEAR RATIO 63-18		8-SANDERS, GRAHAM-WHITE, ONE LINE		TOTAL LIGHT WT. OF LOCO.	254,135 LBS.
TRACTIVE POWER 49,175 LBS.		RADIATOR SHUTTERS, MINNEAPOLIS-HONEYWELL			
FACTOR OF ADHESION 4.00					
AIR BRAKES - W.A.B. CO'S SCHEDULE 8-DB					
AIR COMP. GARD. DEN. TYPE WXO, 225 C.F.M. MAX.		LUBRICATION OIL SYSTEM CAPACITY 135 GALS.			
WIDTH OVER CAB 9'-10"		ENGINE COOLING SYSTEM WATER CAP. 300 GALS.			
WIDTH OVER CAB EVES 9'-11½"		DRAFT GEAR, MINER TYPE A-22-XB			
MINIMUM CURVE WITH TRAIN 30° OR 191 FT. RAD.		2-PYLE NATIONAL HEADLIGHTS			

Permissible Wheel Load with Regard to Internal Shear

There has been no official AAR report with regard to allowable shear on the head of rail. We have an investigation under way at the University of Illinois on proper wheel load and wheel diameter, although unfortunately we are not making very fast headway with it. What information we have on the matter may be summed up as follows:

(a) Fatigue tests on polished specimens of rail steel have shown an endurance limit in repeated shear of from 50,000 to 65,000 lb: per sq. in.

(b) For known conditions of wheel loading and rail and wheel contours, the maximum shearing stresses within the rail ball may be theoretically determined from figures prepared by Hoersch and Thomas. The theory is extremely complicated, but so far as I know, is mathematically correct.

(c) Contours of worn rail and wheels have shown that an average rail radius of 11 inches and a wheel hollowing radius of 17 inches should be used in applying the theoretical formula.

(d) In addition to the static wheel load, an allowance should be made for impact: This has been determined empirically from the results of stress measurements made at various times and an impact allowance of 33 divided by the wheel diameter per mph. of speed is added to the static wheel load. On the above basis, and figuring an allowable shear of 50,000 lb. per sq. in., the attached table, showing the permissible static wheel loads for different wheel diameters and different maximum allowable speeds, has been prepared. Frankly, I am not sure just how good this information is; I am sure it is safe, but it may be ultra-conservative. Limiting the load on a 33-inch wheel to 16,000 lb. at 120 mph, for example, appears rather conservative. On the other hand, at this same speed the allowance for a 50-inch diameter wheel is not out of line:

This is the best information we have on this matter at the present time. I am in hopes that the investigation at the University of Illinois may eventually develop a satisfactory solution of this problem. One difficulty in the rolling-load machine tests is that the rail and wheel tend to wear to fit each other and we do not have the same bearing conditions that we have in track. As a result we have been unable to develop shear failures in full size rail heads within the 75,000 lb: wheel load capacity of the machine. Tests have been made with the rail head reduced to 1-inch width of bearing, and shear failures have been produced in these specimens, but the calculated shear stress at which failure occurs is about 35,000 lb. per sq. in. instead of the 50,000 lb. that would be expected. We have not yet been able to satisfactorily explain this discrepancy.

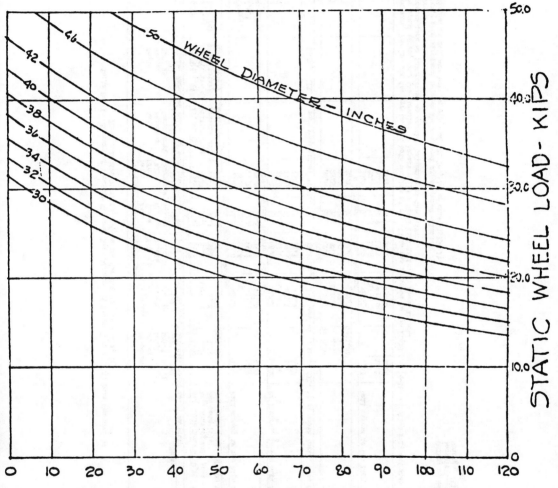

MAXIMUM SPEED-STATIC WHEEL LOAD CURVES
WORN WHEELS
12945.
ALLOWABLE SHEAR = 50,000 $^{\#}/\square$"

STATIC WHEEL LOAD - KIPS

MAXIMUM ALLOWABLE SPEED
MILES PER HOUR

ASSOCIATION OF
AMERICAN RAILROADS
OFFICE OF RESEARCH ENGINEER
CHICAGO, ILL.   DEC. 1944

.13364.

Table No. 1 - Summary of Vertical Flexural Rail Stresses at Center Line of Rail Base Measured by Electro-Motive Division, GMC on the C.& N.W. Ry. at McGirr, Ill.

Equipment (1)	Scale Weight, 1000 lb. (2)	Rail Stresses Considered (3)	Measured Stresses in 1000 psi.			(7) Calculated Rail Stress 1000 psi.	Ratio Measured Computed		Results
			Avg. for All Stresses (4)	Avg. of Three Highest Values (5)	Highest Single Value (6)		Col.4 Col.7 (8)	Col.6 Col.7 (9)	
Part I			**72-lb. Rerolled Rail. As worn properties: Wt., 60.9 lb., I=15.91 in., A c/I(base)=7.50 in.³ to tread**						
			5 mph. Coasting						
E.M.D. Diesel No. 930 (1-4)	232.3(total)	All wheels	33.9	43.5	44.5	33.8	1.00	1.20	Avg. axle load – 58,100 lb.
C.& N.W. No.345(1-4-0) steam	136.5(drivers)	Drivers only	26.0	33.8	34.2	28.3	1.17	(d)22.3	Avg. driving axle load – 45,500 lb.
C.& N.W. Diesel No.1504(6-6)(c)	270.0(total)	Drivers only	26.3	36.3	38.1	23.8	1.10	(d)26.3	See note (c)
Gondola loaded	202.8(total)	4-wheel(truck)	25.5	32.6	32.9	25.4	1.00	(e)30.0	Avg. axle load – 50,700 lb.
			0 – 25 mph. Working						
E.M.D. No. 930			33.4	44.8	46.0	*46.8	1.10	(e)46.8	Rail stress is too high for regular operation.
C.& N.W. No. 345 (steam)			28.0	40.8	40.8	–	–	(b) –	• • • •
C.& N.W. No. 1504 (c)			27.1	42.1	45.7	*28.5	1.40	(b)*28.5	• • • •
Gondola loaded 33"Wheels			25.0	33.6	35.5	*31.8	1.06	(b)*31.8	• • • •
			25 – 45 mph. Working						
E.M.D. No. 930			33.2	43.7	48.0	*62.4	0.94	(e)62.4	Rail stress is too high for regular operation.
C.& N.W. No. 345 (steam)			28.5	43.1	47.4	–	1.19	(b) –	• • • •
C.& N.W. No. 1504 (c)			27.4	38.2	39.3	*32.2	0.96	(b)*32.2	• • • •
Gondola loaded			25.5	35.5	37.7	*36.8		*36.8	• • • •
Part II			**60-lb. Rail. As worn properties: Wt., 60.5 lb., I=13.27 in., 4 I/C(base)=6.33 in., 3 Ill. Steel South Works, Sec. 6001-1905**						
			5 mph. Coasting						
E.M.D. No. 930			38.5	49.4	49.4	39.2	(e)0.99		Rail stress is too high for regular operation.
C.& N.W. No. 345 (steam)			29.5	35.8	38.2	(d)26.3	1.12		
C.& N.W. No. 1504 (c)			29.9	38.8	40.5	27.6	1.08		
Gondola loaded			30.1	37.2	41.0	29.3	(e)1.02		
			0 – 25 mph. Working						
E.M.D. No. 930			38.2	50.5	53.0	*47.3	(e)1.07		Rail stress is too high for regular operation.
C.& N.W. No. 345 (steam)			30.0	41.5	42.5	–	–		
C.& N.W. No. 1504 (c)			30.6	40.9	43.1	*33.0	1.24		
Gondola loaded			29.7	38.8	39.5	*36.6	1.05		

(a) Modulus of rail support, 930 lb. per in. per in. for both weights of rail.(This was measured in the field for 72-lb. rerolled rail and also applies to the 60-lb. rail).

(b) Includes impact or speed effect from the formula: % Impact = (33)° Wheel dia. in in.; x speed in mph.

(c) Stress omitted account lack of information on counter balancing of the drivers.

(d) Average for all drivers.

(e) These values indicate good agreement between the measured and computed values.

(f) Scale weight is divided as follows: Driving axle, 46,625 lb, idler axle 14,750 lb

Office of Research Engineer
Association of American Railroads
Chicago, Ill.   August 20, 1951
Dwg. No. (16-00) 4

Appendix 10–a

Measurements of Stresses in 115 RE and 132 RE Rail in Curved Track, Outside Joint Bar Limits

Purpose of Tests

One of the studies being pursued under the assignment of this subcommittee is (a) Field Measurements of Stresses (Outside the Joint) in the New Rail Sections. In AREA Proceedings, Vol. 51, 1950, page 626, is a report on Measurements of Stresses in 132 RE Rail in Tangent Track—Santa Fe Railway, and in AREA Proceedings, Vol. 52, 1951, page 690, is a report on Measurements of Stresses in 115 RE Rail in Tangent Track—North Western Railway. This present report describes the tests conducted on 115 RE rail on curves of 6 deg. and 4 deg., and on 132 RE rail on curves of 6 deg. and 4½ deg.

Previous reports of the committee have described the high localized stresses found in the old 112 RE and 131 RE rail sections in the upper web fillets and in the upper portion of the rail web. It has been pointed out that localized stress concentrations must be expected in any rail due to the effect of wheel bearing pressure, and are aggravated by the bending of the head on the web because the wheel load is often applied eccentrically, especially toward the gage corner of the inner rail of curves when steam locomotives are traveling at low speed. In the design of the new rail sections the upper part of the web was thickened and combined with longer fillet radii. Laboratory tests had indicated that these modifications would effect a stress reduction of approximately 25 percent. The tops of the new rails were also further rounded to relieve the gage corner from excessive bearing pressures and to bring the centroid of bearing between wheel and rail more nearly to the middle of the rail head.

The stresses reported here can be compared with stresses reported in earlier tests of 112 and 131 RE rails on curves. This report completes the series of field stress studies planned on 115 and 132 RE rails.

The measurements, analysis of data and preparation of the report in connection with these tests were made by the Engineering Division research staff of the Association of American Railroads, under the direction of G. M. Magee, research engineer, by M. F. Smucker, assistant electrical engineer, and E. E. Cress, assistant research engineer, assisted by other staff members. The committee and the Association are indebted to the engineering officers of the Illinois Central Railroad and the Louisville & Nashville Railroad for their cooperation and assistance in conducting these tests.

Measurements of Stresses in 115 RE Rail in Curved Track— Illinois Central Railroad

The Test Locations and Track

The 6-deg. curve selected for the tests on the 115 RE rail is located on the single-track main line of the Illinois Central at mile 187.8, 4½ miles west of Dubuque, Ia. The rail was laid in 1949 and the track was in good condition. The curve was elevated 4¼ in., which corresponds to a balanced speed of 33 mph. and a speed of 43 mph. for 3 in. unbalanced elevation. The tests were made in September 1950. SR–4, ¼-in. wire-resistance stress gages were located on both the inner and outer rails at gage positions 3 and 13 on the upper web of the rail (4½ in. above the base), and at gage position 17 in the lower outer web fillet, as shown in Fig. 1*. It had been found in former tests that these three positions on the rail are the critical stress areas. Four groups of these gages were located on both the inner and outer rails, each group about a rail length apart. The gage groups were located near the quarter points of the rails, over a tie and a double-shoulder tie plate, and the ties in the vicinity were good and had only a small amount of play. The group locations were designated K, J, L and M on the inner rail, and k, j, l and m on the outer rail, similar letters always being directly opposite each other on the two rails.

Tests were next made, during the same month, on a 4-deg. curve, also on single-track main line, located at mile 156.8, which is 8½ miles east of Galena, Ill. The rail was 115 RE, laid in 1949, and the track was in good condition. The curve was elevated $3\frac{7}{8}$ in., which corresponds to a balanced speed of 36 mph., and a speed of 49 mph. for 3 in. unbalanced elevation. The track gage was $56\frac{11}{16}$ in. Four groups of stress gages were located on the inner rails at locations N, P, R and S, and on the outer rails at n, p, r and s, with the spacing and conditions similar to those described above for the 6-deg. curve.

Measurements Made Under Regular Traffic

Stress measurements were recorded under the wheels of regular steam freight and diesel passenger locomotives, under the wheels of all passenger cars, and under a portion of representative freight car wheels. The records were read and the data recorded under all the engine wheels of the I.C. steam freight locomotives, Class 2800 19, which is a 2–10–2 type engine with 64½-in. drivers and a rigid wheelbase of 22 ft. 4 in. All drivers have flanged tires. The total engine weight is 416,000 lb., with 332,500 lb. on the drivers. The average driver axle load is 66,500 lb. Records were also read under all wheels of the 4000 class passenger EM diesels, which have 2 trucks of 3 axles each per unit with rigid wheelbases of 14 ft. 1 in. Wheel diameters are 36 in. Average driver axle loads are 52,600 lb.

For each train the maximum stress only was read under the freight or passenger car wheels for each stress gage. The range of these car wheel stresses is given in Table 1.

Range of Stresses with 115 RE Rail

In Fig. 1 is plotted the range of measured stresses in the outer and inner 115 RE rails at the 4 track locations on the 6-deg. curve under the 2800–19 class steam freight locomotive wheels, not including the tenders. For any gage only the few highest and lowest stresses under the 315 individual wheels of the engines are plotted to show the range of stress that occurs at a given gage location. Separate symbols are used for each of the four locations along the track to show differences in the range of stress at the various locations. For the data recorded on this curve, 1 freight engine was traveling at 7 mph., 11 engines were traveling at 22–29 mph., and 11 engines were traveling 30–37 mph. Had a greater number of engines been traveling at slow speed there would have been more high stresses recorded on the inner rail and correspondingly lower stresses on the outer rail. In Fig. 3 is given the similar range of stresses on the rails of the 4-deg. curve for the same class freight engines. For the data recorded on this curve, 8 of the steam engines were running from 14–19 mph., 11 engines from 23–29 mph., and 9 engines from 30–42 mph. Because a number of the engines were running at low speed, it would be expected that there would be a larger number of high stresses recorded at the inner rail than if the engines had been traveling at a higher speed.

---

* The Figures and Table referred to in this report begin on page 927.

It will be observed that in the upper gage fillet of the outer rail of both curves the stress range is from 40,000 psi. compression to a low tension. In the upper field fillet, the stress range is from about 30,000 psi. compression to about 20,000 psi. tension. In the lower field fillet the stress range is from about 40,000 psi. compression to practically 0.0 tension.

For the inner rail on both curves, the stress range in the upper gage fillet is about the same as for the outer rail, except for a very few higher compression values. For the upper field fillet the stress range is a little higher on the compression side, approximating 40,000 psi., and perhaps a little less, about 15,000 psi. on the tension side. The stress range at the lower field fillet is the same as on the outer rail for the 6-deg. curve, but somewhat greater, 60,000 psi. compression to 0.0 tension, on the 4-deg. curve.

The few measured stresses outside the above ranges would not be expected to occur with sufficient frequency to be a factor in causing fatigue failure. Therefore, the stress ranges to be considered are 40,000 psi. compression to 15,000 psi. tension, and 60,000 psi. compression to 0.0 tension for the 115 RE section for these two curves. It is believed the characteristics of the track and the long rigid wheelbase and heavy axle loads of the power tested were sufficiently typical of most service conditions to be considered representative of the maximum stress ranges which will be devloped in this rail section in service.

The endurance limit of rail steel as determined in the laboratory tests made at the University of Illinois, and previously reported, are shown in the Proceedings, Vol. 51, 1950, page 637, Fig. 9, and page 645, Fig. 7. The measured stress range at the upper and lower fillets is approximately 70 percent of this endurance limit for the 115 RE section, whereas for the tests previously reported on the 112 RE section this ratio was 90 percent.

In Figs. 2 and 4 are plotted the range of measured stresses in the outer and inner 115 RE rails of the 6-deg. and 4-deg. curves under the diesel passenger locomotives. All of these locomotives were running from 33 to 49 mph., which is at or above the balanced speed. The significant fillet stress range for diesel locomotives was found to be from about 30,000 psi. compression to 5000 psi. tension, or only about 40 percent of the endurance limit.

A further comparison of the range of measured stresses is afforded in Table 1 for the inner and outer rails of both curves with 115 RE rail for the steam freight engine wheels, for the diesel passenger engine wheels, and for the freight and passenger car wheels. The average of the three highest stresses recorded at each gage position, as in past tests, is considered as the upper maximum range of stress, and this value is used in the discussion and table rather than the one maximum stress value. In the table the stress range for the 115 RE rail with the steam engine may be compared with the range of stress for 112 RE rail on a 4-deg. curve on the Burlington, which is shown in Tables 5 and 6, pages 718 and 719, AREA Proceedings, Vol. 46, 1945. Previous tests have shown that gage 2 and 2a locations are the areas of maximum fillet stress for the 112 RE rail, and the gage 3 location practically so for the 115 RE rail. In the current tests, stresses in gages 2 and 2a were not measured for this reason. From the tables it can be seen that there is a considerable reduction in the range of maximum fillet stress for the 115 RE rail on curved track compared to the 112 RE rail, which is of value in preventing bending of the rail head on the web from an occasional heavy wheel load.

As shown in Table 1, the range of stresses in the 115 RE rail on the curves under the diesel locomotive wheels is quite low. All of these locomotives were running at or above the balanced speed so the reported stresses in the outer rails are as high as would be expected under any operating conditions. As none of the runs were at low speed, reported stresses in the inner rails are somewhat less than if some of the locomotives had been running at low speed. One of the most significant features of the table is that the range of stresses for both curves for the diesel locomotives is only slightly more than for the freight cars. Without exception, the range of stresses for both curves for the passenger car wheels is very low.

Frequency of Occurrence of Stresses

In the top half of Figs. 5 and 6 the range of measured stresses and frequency of occurrence are shown for the 6-deg. and 4-deg. curves for the steam engine wheels. Individual stresses at each gage line under all the engine wheels are grouped into brackets of 10,000-psi. variation. The percentage of the stresses falling into these several brackets of stated values is plotted in the figures for each gage location.

For the gage 3 position on the inner rail of curves where most of the difficulty with fillet cracks has been experienced, an interesting comparison can be made of the data shown in Figs. 5 and 6 with the laboratory tests of the fatigue strength of rail steel. For example, in Fig. 5 for the 6-deg. curve, only 3 percent of the measured stresses were above 45,000 psi. compression.

Assuming the maximum life of 115 RE rail on a 6-deg. curve at 150,000,000 gross tons of traffic carried, and an average train load of 3000 gross tons, there would be 50,000 train passages during the life of the rail. With the 2–10–2 type of locomotive tested, there would be 7 loads per train, or 350,000 wheel loads total. Applying the 3 percent to this figure indicates that during the rail life only 10,500 stresses above 45,000 psi. compression would be developed. According to the laboratory results, as shown in Fig. 2, page 806, Vol. 48, 1947, AREA Proceedings, the fatigue strength at this number of cycles for uncorroded rail steel is well over 100,000 psi., and for acid corrosion over 90,000 psi. It is evident, therefore, that considerable leeway exists between the measured stresses and the strength to be expected of rail steel, based on the laboratory tests. This leeway should serve to withstand usual service corrosion conditions and a reasonable amount of wear or flattening of the rail head.

In the bottom half of Figs. 5 and 6 the range and frequency of occurrence are shown for the two curves for the diesel locomotive wheels. The highest range of stress for any gage on either the outer or inner rails is from 35,000 psi. compression to 15,000 psi. tension.

Measurements of Stresses in 132 RE Rail on Curved Track— Louisville & Nashville Railroad

The Test Locations and Track

The 6-deg. curve on the northbound double-track main line, on which tests were made in August 1950, is located at mile 110½, which is about 8 miles north of Richmond, Ky. The 132 RE rail had been laid over a year before the test and the track was in good condition. The inner rail had a slight amount of lateral flow and the outer rail had a very slight amount of gage wear. There were gage rods on the curve, but before the tests were started the gage rods near the test locations were loosened so they would have no effect on the measured rail stresses. The track gage was 56⅜ in. The grade was 0.61 percent downgrade in the direction of traffic. The curve was elevated 6 in., which corresponds to a balanced speed of 39 mph. and a speed of 47 mph. for 3 in. unbalanced elevation. Wire resistance gages (SR-4 type of ¼-in. length) were located on both the inner and outer rails of the curve at gage positions 3 and 13 on the upper web of the rail (4⅞ in. above base), and at gage position 17 in the middle of the lower outer web fillet, as shown in Fig. 7. Four groups of these gages were located on both the inner and outer rails, each group about a rail length apart. The gage groups were located near the quarter points of the rails, directly over a tie and a double-shoulder tie plate, and the ties in the vicinity were good and had only a small amount of play. The group locations were named A, B, C and D on the inner rail, and a, b, c and d on the outer rail, similar letters always being directly opposite each other on the two rails.

The 4-deg. 34-min. curve, on which the tests were made in August 1950, was also on the northbound track, and is located at mile 112¼. Track conditions were similar to the above curve. The curve was elevated 5 in., which corresponds to a balanced speed of 41 mph. and a speed of 52 mph. for 3 in. unbalanced elevation. Four groups of stress gages were located on the inner and outer rails at location Ee, Ff, Gg and Hh, with the spacings and conditions similar to those described above for the 6-deg. curve.

Measurements Made Under Regular Traffic

Stress measurements were recorded under the wheels of steam freight, steam passenger, and diesel passenger locomotives, under the wheels of all passenger cars, and under a portion of representative freight car wheels. The records were read and the data recorded under all the engine wheels of L.&N. modern steam freight locomotive Class 1950–91, which is a 2–8–4 type engine with 69-in. drivers and a rigid wheelbase of 18 ft. 3 in. All drivers have flanged tires. There are Timken roller bearings on all journals, and there is a booster on the double trailer. The total engine weight is 447,200 lb., with an average driver axle load of 67,100 lb. Records were read under a few 400–15 class steam passenger engines of type 4–8–2. Records were also read under the 750–793 class passenger EM Model E diesel locomotives, which have 2 trucks of 3 axles per unit, with a rigid wheelbase of 14 ft. 1 in. Wheel diameters are 36 in. Average driver axle loads are 52,400 lb.

Under each train the maximum stress only was read under the freight or passenger car wheels for each stress gage. The range of these car wheel stresses is given in Table 1.

Range of Stresses With 132 RE Rail

The range of measured stresses in the outer and inner 132 RE rails at the 4 track locations on the 6-deg. curve under the 1950–91 class steam freight locomotive wheels is shown in Fig. 7. Only the few highest and lowest stresses of the 434 recorded values of the engine wheels for any gage line are plotted to show the range of stress that occurs at a given gage location. Separate symbols are used for each of the four test locations along the track so that any differences in the range of stress as related to track location can be seen.

For the data recorded on this 6-deg. curve, 4 freight engines were running below 19 mph., 10 engines were running from 20–39 mph., and 16 engines were running from 40–45 mph. If more engines had been running at slow speed there would have been more high stresses recorded at the inner rail. The similar range of stresses on the rails of the 4½-deg. curve is shown in Fig. 9 for the same class freight locomotives. For the data recorded on this curve, 9 of the engines were running below 19 mph., 6 engines were running from 30–39 mph., and 16 engines were running from 40–47 mph.

It will be noted that the general pattern of stress range for the upper fillets on both the field and gage sides, and for the lower fillet on the field side, for both inner and outer rails is similar to that for the 115 RE rail previously discussed. The maximum stress range insofar as fatigue failure is concerned occurs at the inner rail. This range in relation to the fatigue strength will be discussed later.

In Figs. 8 and 10 are plotted the range of measured stresses in the outer and inner 132 RE rails of the 6-deg. and 4½-deg. curves under the diesel passenger locomotives. All of these locomotives were running from 40 to 51 mph., which is at or above the balanced speed for the curves. As shown in the figures, only 1 stress is above 30,000 psi. compression in the outer and inner rails of both curves.

In Table 1 is recorded the range of measured stresses in the 132 RE rails of both curves for the steam freight engine wheels, the diesel passenger engine wheels, and the freight and passenger car wheels. The average of the three highest stresses recorded at each gage location is considered as the upper range of stress and this value is used in the table. In the table the stress ranges for the 132 RE rail with the steam engine and freight car wheels may be compared with the range of stress for the 131 RE rail on a 6-deg. curve of the Norfolk & Western Railroad, shown in Table 1, pages 780–781, AREA Proceedings, Vol. 48, 1947. The stresses under the steam engine wheels are also comparable to the range of stress in the 131 RE rail on a Pennsylvania Railroad 6½-deg. curve reported in Appendix 12–b, page 558, AREA Proceedings, Vol. 50, 1949. It is known from former tests that the stresses in gages 2 and 2a in the upper small fillets of the 131 RE rail are generally greater than in gage 3, while for the 132 RE rail stresses in gage 2, in the larger fillet, are somewhat less than in gage 3. In the current tests, therefore, stresses were only measured at the gage 3 location. From the tables and figures it can be seen there is a considerable reduction in the range of stresses under the steam engine wheels for the 132 RE rail on curved track, compared to the 131 RE rail.

Table 1 shows that the range of stresses found in the 132 RE rails on the curves under the diesel passenger locomotive wheels is quite low. All the diesel locomotives were running at or above the balanced speed so the reported stresses in the outer rails are as high as would be expected under any operating conditions. Even if some of the diesels had been running at slow speeds, it is judged that the inner rail stresses would have been increased by only a small amount. It will probably be of interest to railroad operating and maintenance officers to note from the table that the range of measured stresses on both rails of both curves under the passenger diesels is no higher than und r the freight car wheels. The range of stress for both curves for the passenger car wheels is, without exception, very low.

Frequency of Occurrence of Stresses

In the upper halves of Figs. 11 and 12 the range of measured stresses and frequency of occurrence are given for the 6-deg. and 4½-deg. curves for the steam engine wheels. Individual stresses at each gage line under all the wheels are grouped into brackets of 10,000 psi. variation, and the percentage falling into the several brackets is plotted in the figures.

A comparison of measured stresses with the expected fatigue strength for the 132 RE rail can be made from these figures in the same manner as was made above for the 115 RE rail. Using the same assumptions for rail life and average train load, the number of total wheel passages would also be 350,000 for the 2-8-4 type of locomotives. The number of measured stresses at gage 3 above 45,000 psi. compression is 4 percent of the total number of engine wheel loads, or 14,000 for the 6-deg. curve, and 8 percent, or

(Text continued on page 940)

TABLE I – Range of Measured Vertical Web and Lower Fillet Stresses under Locomotive and Car Wheels at Four Locations on the Inner and Outer Rails of Curves of the I.C. RR. and the L.&N. RR. – 1950.

Values are the average of the 3 highest stresses measured at each gage location; Stresses in 1000 psi.;
– sign = compression; + sign = tension.

Curve	Type of Wheels	Number of Trains	INNER RAIL OF CURVE			OUTER RAIL OF CURVE		
			Gage 3	Gage 13	Gage 17	Gage 3	Gage 13	Gage 17
I.C. RR.-115 RE Rail								
6°	Steam Loco.	23	-57 to +16	-48 to +17	-46 to 0	-39 to +9	-36 to +18	-47 to +2
	Diesel Loco.	5	-20 to +8	-19 to +4	-19 to 0	-33 to +5	-19 to +10	-30 to 0
	Freight Car	23	-16 to +8	-22 to +2	-27 to 0	-30 to +3	-14 to +8	-16 to 0
	Pass. Car	5	-12 to +5	-14 to +2	-10 to 0	-18 to +3	-12 to +6	-12 to 0
4°	Steam Loco.	28	-49 to +14	-51 to +19	-76 to +5	-44 to +6	-31 to +18	-37 to +2
	Diesel Loco.	11	-21 to +5	-26 to +5	-29 to 0	-34 to +7	-26 to +12	-21 to 0
	Freight Car	28	-14 to +7	-22 to +1	-28 to 0	-22 to 0	-12 to +6	-14 to 0
	Pass. Car	11	-12 to +4	-15 to +3	-16 to 0	-16 to +2	-12 to +6	-12 to 0
L.&N. RR.-132 RE Rail								
6°	Steam Loco.	19	-60 to +8	-29 to +27	-50 to 0	-43 to +6	-27 to +14	-41 to +1
	Diesel Loco.	4	-18 to +6	-20 to +5	-19 to 0	-28 to +2	-18 to +10	-20 to +3
	Freight Car	18	-25 to +10	-25 to +8	-26 to 0	-25 to +3	-15 to +9	-23 to 0
	Pass. Car	7	-12 to +7	-10 to +4	-12 to 0	-20 to 0	-11 to +7	-16 to +2
4½°	Steam Loco.	21	-61 to +6	-30 to +20	-51 to 0	-35 to +8	-30 to +9	-37 to 0
	Diesel Loco.	4	-19 to +6	-20 to +4	-29 to 0	-25 to +2	-19 to +10	-25 to 0
	Freight Car	19	-22 to +5	-20 to +7	-26 to 0	-26 to +1	-14 to +7	-22 to 0
	Pass. Car	8	-12 to +4	-13 to +4	-19 to 0	-16 to +1	-10 to +9	-17 to 0

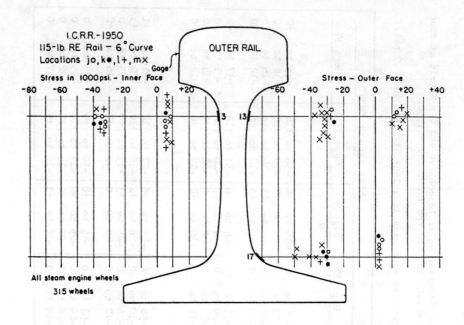

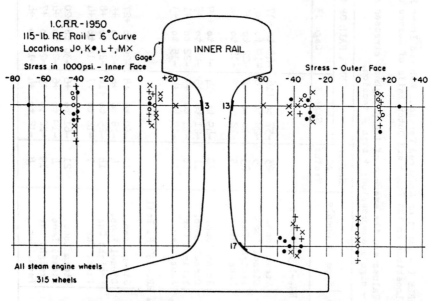

Fig. 1—Range of measured stresses in 115 RE rail on 6-deg. curve under steam engine wheels. Elevation 4¼ in., balanced speed 33 mph.— Illinois Central.

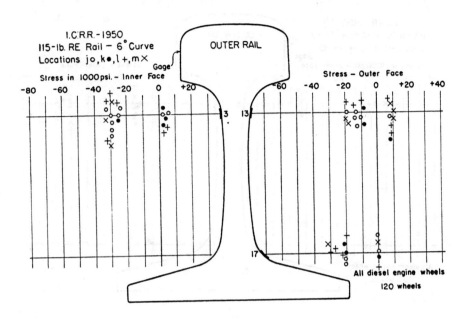

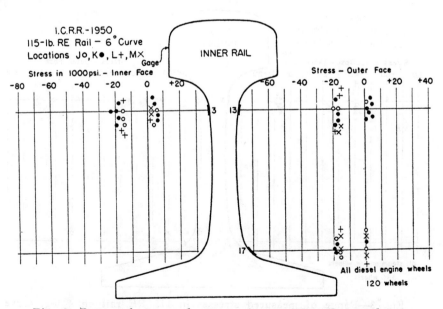

Fig. 2—Range of measured stresses in 115 RE rail on 6-deg. curve under diesel engine wheels. Elevation 4¼ in. balanced speed 33 mph.——Illinois Central.

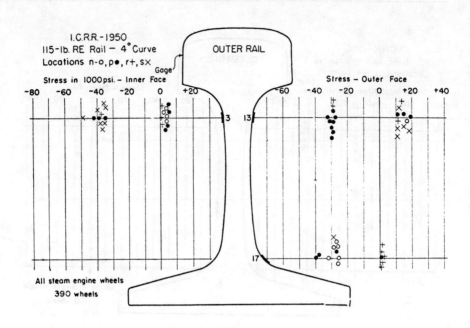

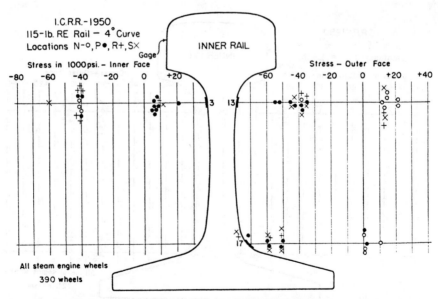

Fig. 3—Range of measured stresses in 115 RE rail on 4-deg. curve under steam engine wheels. Elevation 3-7/16 in., balanced speed 36 mph.— Illinois Central.

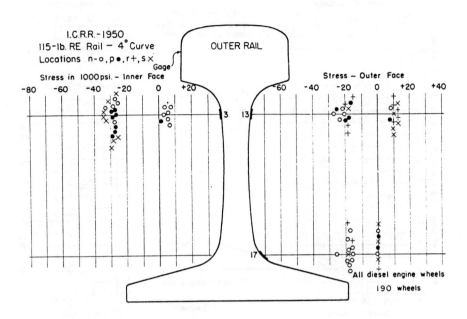

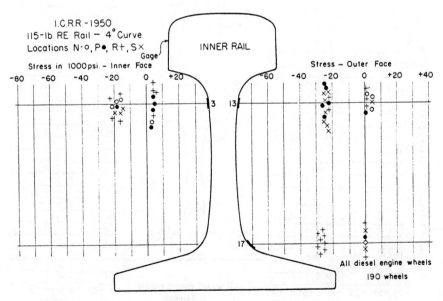

Fig. 4—Range of measured stresses in 115 RE rail on 4-deg. curve under diesel engine wheels. Elevation 3-7/16 in., balanced speed 36 mph.—Illinois Central.

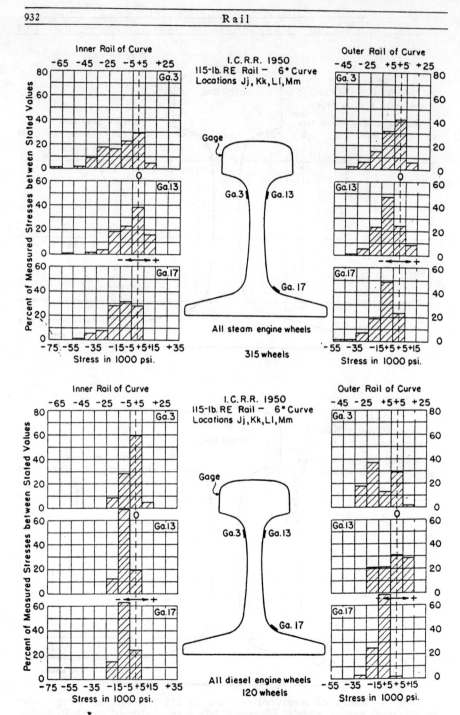

Fig. 5—Frequency of measured stresses in 115 RE rail on 6-deg. curve under steam and diesel engine wheels.—Illinois Central.

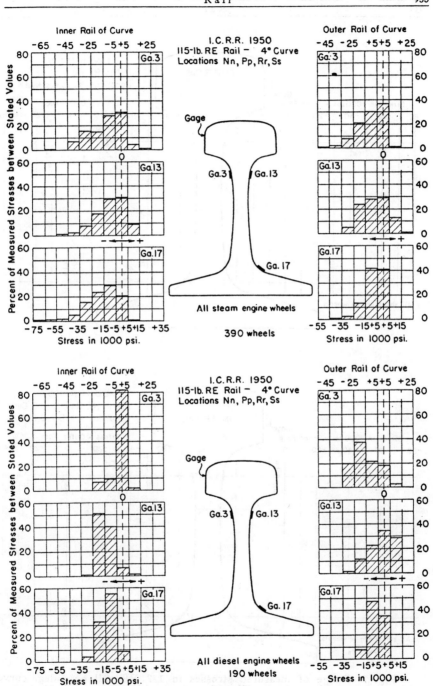

Fig. 6—Frequency of measured stresses in 115 RE rail on 4-deg. curve under steam and diesel engine wheels.—Illinois Central.

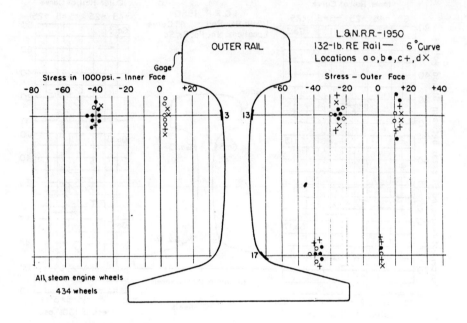

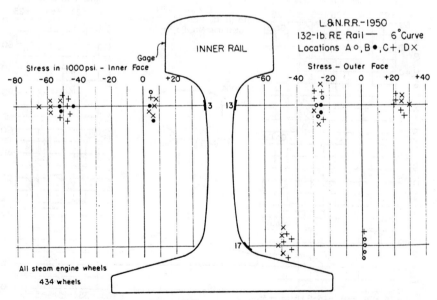

Fig. 7—Range of measured stresses in 132 RE rail on 6-deg. curve under steam engine wheels. Elevation 6 in., balanced speed 39 mph.— Louisville & Nashville.

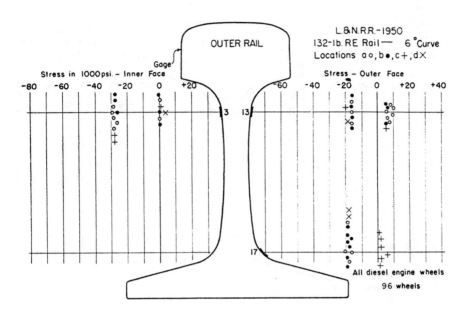

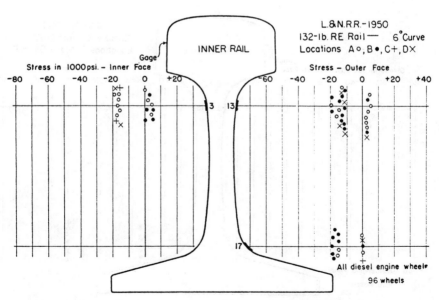

Fig. 8—Range of measured stresses in 132 RE rail on 6-deg. curve under diesel engine wheels. Elevation 6 in., balanced speed 39 mph.— Louisville & Nashville.

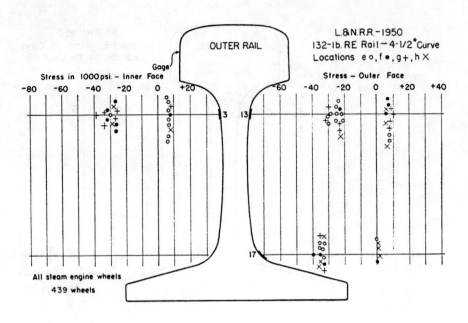

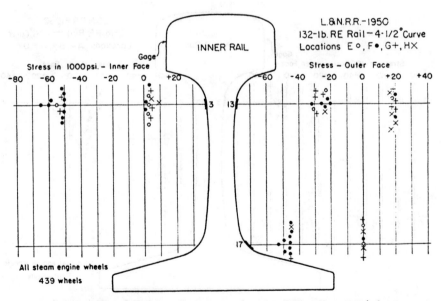

Fig. 9—Range of measured stresses in 132 RE rail on 4½-deg. curve under steam engine wheels. Elevation 5 in., balanced speed 41 mph.— Louisville & Nashville.

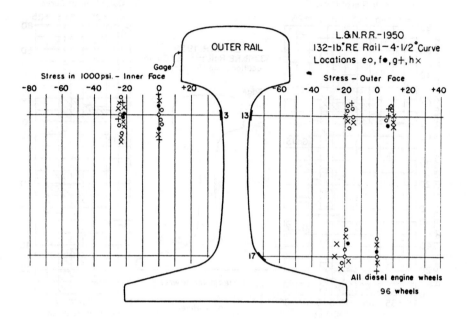

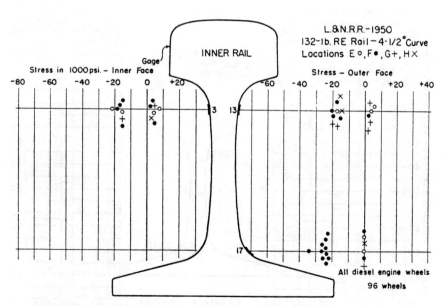

Fig. 10—Range of measured stresses in 132 RE rail on 4½-deg. curve under diesel engine wheels. Elevation 5 in., balanced speed 41 mph.— Louisville & Nashville.

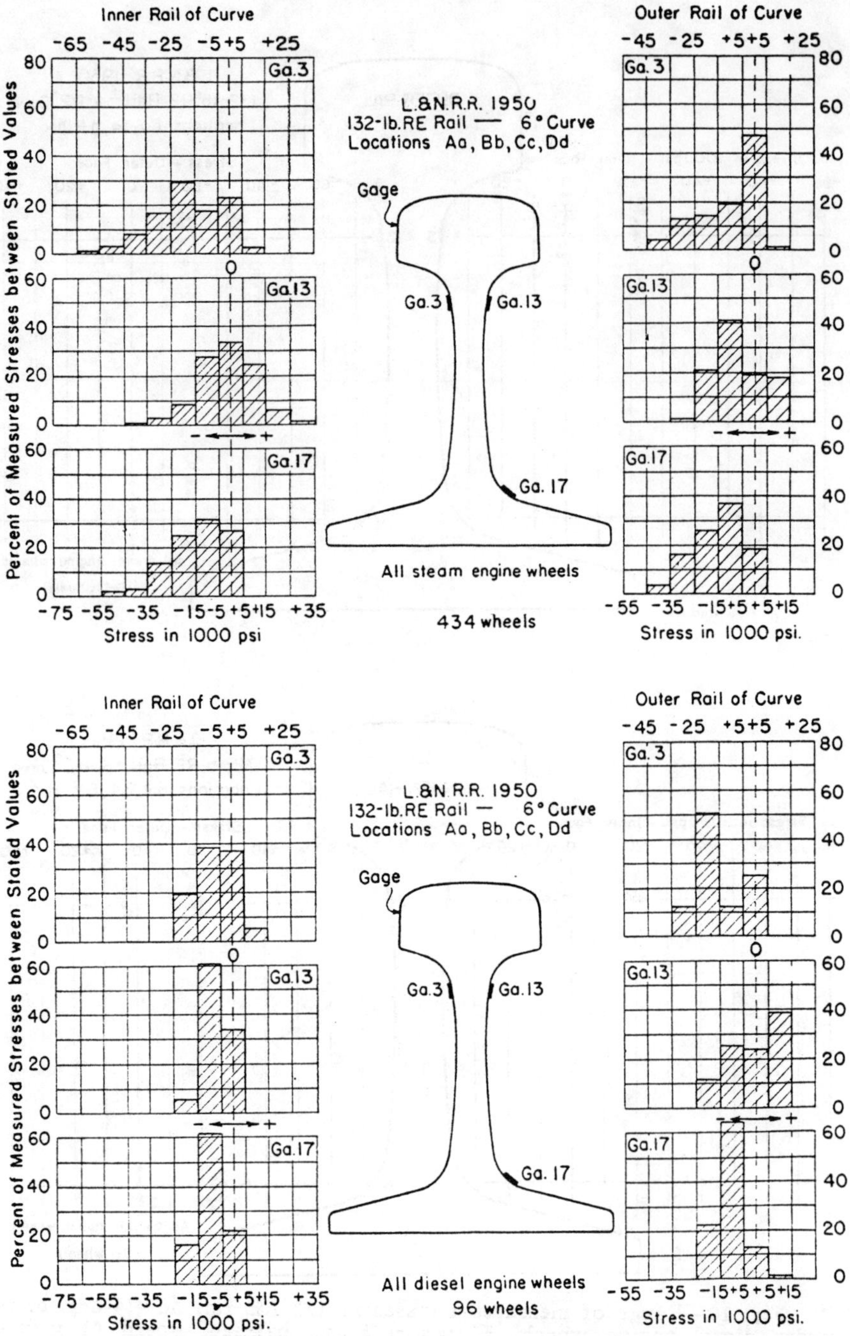

Fig. 11—Frequency of measured stresses in 132 RE rail on 6-deg. curve under steam and diesel engine wheels—Louisville & Nashville.

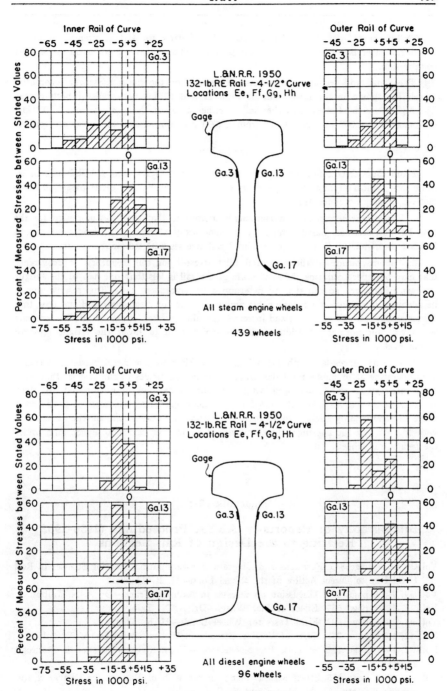

Fig. 12—Frequency of measured stresses in 132 RE rail on 4½ deg. curve under steam and diesel engine wheels—Louisville & Nashville.

28,000, for the 4½-deg. curve. For 28,000 cycles of stress the fatigue strength of uncorroded rail steel is over 100,000 psi. compression, and with acid corrosion 84,000 psi. compression.

The range and frequency of stress occurrence for the diesel passenger locomotive wheels are shown in the lower half of Figs. 11 and 12 for both rails of both curves. The highest range of stress on either rail of either curve at the gages is from 35,000 psi. compression to 5,000 psi. tension, or from 25,000 psi. compression to 15,000 psi. tension.

Conclusions

From these tests conducted on curved track with 115 RE and 132 RE rails under conditions typical of main-line operation with steam freight and diesel passenger locomotives, it may be concluded:

1. From these service test measurements it appears that the basis of design for the new RE rail sections, based principally on laboratory studies, was sound, and that it forecast the reduction in service of localized rail stresses with reasonable accuracy.

2. The magnitude of the measured fillet stresses for the frequency of occurrence that may be expected during the service life of the rail is less than one-half of the fatigue strength of uncorroded rail steel as determined by laboratory tests. This reserve should be adequate to provide for a reasonable amount of the top head wear and the flow that occurs on the low rail of curves and increases the fillet stresses. It should also be adequate to provide for normal corrosion conditions which tend to lower the fatigue strength of the steel.

3. For the curves laid with 115 RE and 132 RE rails, the diesel passenger locomotives operating at or above the balanced speed produced ranges of rail stresses that were quite moderate in value, and well within the endurance limit of uncorroded rail steel. In fact, on the curves laid with 115 RE rail, diesel passenger locomotives produced a range of stresses only slightly more than for freight car wheels, and on the curves laid with 132 RE rail the passenger diesels produced a range of stress no higher than under the freight car wheels.

Appendix 10–b

Bibliography of Reports in AREA Proceedings (1938–1952) Relating to the Design of Rail Sections

Vol. 39, 1938, page 835. Formulas and Diagrams for Computing Shearing Stresses in Rail Head Due to Direct Action of the Wheel Load—H. R. Thomas.

Vol. 39, 1938, page 857. Discussion on Stresses in Railroad Track—Dr. A. N. Talbot.

Vol. 41, 1940, page 669. Effect of Flat Wheel—Dr. A. N. Talbot.

Vol. 42, 1941, page 692. Field Tests for Wheel Loads—H. R. Thomas.

Vol. 42, 1941, page 758. Tests of Vertical Stresses in Web of Rail—Dr. A. N. Talbot.

Vol. 42, 1941, page 139. Seventh Progress Report—Committee on Stresses in Railroad Track.

Vol. 44, 1943, page M5. Stress Measurements in the Web of Rail on the Denver & Rio Grande Western—G. M. Magee and E. E. Cress.

Vol. 45, 1944 page 449. Rail Contours.

Vol. 45, 1944, page 470. Investigate Recent Developments Affecting Rail Sections.

Vol. 45, 1944, page 9. Investigation of the Impact Effect of Flat Wheels—G. M. Magee and E. E. Cress.

Vol. 46, 1945, page 660. Static Stress Measurements on Five Test Rails in Special Tangent Track Under Controlled Loading Conditions.

Vol. 46, 1945, page 692. Stress Measurements on Four 112–115-lb. Test Rails in Tangent Track and in a 4-Deg. Curve Under Regular Train Traffic.

Vol. 46, 1945, page 733. Shearing Stresses in Rail—G. A. Maney.

Vol. 46, 1945, page 744. Progress Report on Web Failures of Rails—H. F. Moore and R. S. Jensen.

Vol. 46, 1945, page 749. Effect of Spike Maul Blows on Rail Webs at Low Temperatures.

Vol. 46, 1945, page 761. Reported Web Failures in Service.

Vol. 47, 1946, page 438. Strains Produced on End of Outer Rail Head of 6-Deg. Curve.

Vol. 47, 1946, page 449. Rail Design Study and Tests on Modified Rail Sections—1945.

Vol. 47, 1946, page 464. Fatigue Tests of Rail Webs—R. S. Jensen.

Vol. 47, 1946, page 671. Determination of Lateral Outward Forces on Each Rail of a Turnout.

Vol. 48, 1947, page 660. Recommended Sections of 115, 132 and 133 RE Rail.

Vol. 48, 1947, page 768. Stress Measurements on 131 RE Rail in Tangent and in a 6-Deg. Curve Under Regular Traffic—N.&W. Ry.—1945.

Vol. 48, 1947, page 794. Summary of Report on Fillet and Web Stress Measurements on 90 ASCE and 112 RE Rail in 18-deg. Curves—D.T.&I. RR—1946.

Vol. 48, 1947, page 804. Fatigue Tests of Rail Webs—R. S. Jensen.

Vol. 48, 1947, page 987. A Method of Calculating the Maximum Stress in the Web of Rail due to an Eccentric Vertical Load—C. J. Code.

Vol. 49, 1948, page 414. End-Hardened Rails.

Vol. 49, 1948, page 464. Effect of Bolt Spacing on Rail Web Stresses Within the Rail Joint.

Vol. 49, 1948, page 485. Fatigue Tests of Rail Webs—R. S. Jensen.

Vol. 49, 1948, page 735. Effect of Weight Redistribution on the Magnitude of Lateral Forces Exerted by a Locomotive.

Vol. 50, 1949, page 558. Comparison of Web Stresses in 131 RE and 140 PS (Pennsylvania) Sections.

Vol. 51, 1950, page 626. Measurements of Stresses in 132 RE Rail on Tangent Track—Santa Fe Railway.

Vol. 51, 1950, page 640. Fatigue Tests of Rail Webs—R. S. Jensen.

Vol. 52, 1951, page 93. Lateral Forces Exerted by Locomotives on Curved Track.

Vol. 52, 1951, page 680. Fatigue Tests of Rail Webs.

Vol. 52, 1951, page 690. Measurement of Stresses in 115 RE Rail on Tangent Track—North Western Railway.

Vol. 53, 1952, page 921. Measurements of Stresses in 115 RE and 132 RE Rail on Curved Track, Outside Joint Bar Limits.

Vol. 53, 1952, page 423. Effect of Flat Wheels on Track and Equipment.

TEXT 23

DISCUSSION ON STRESSES IN RAILROAD TRACK

(For Report, see pp. 101–102)

Dr. A. N. Talbot (University of Illinois):—The report of the Committee is found on page 101 of Bulletin 381. That report concerns the general work of the year.

Instead of reading it I wish to present a report of observations and tests made on the stretches of welded rail in the track of the Delaware and Hudson Railroad at Albany and Schenectady, the last of the measurements and observations having been made in colder weather in January.

Tests on Delaware and Hudson Track made with Welded Rail: Tests and observations of the welded rail were made on one stretch at Albany and two stretches at Schenectady. The length of the welded stretch tested at Albany was 2660 ft. (0.5 mile) and at Schenectady 4460 ft. (0.85 mile) and 6980 ft. (1.32 miles).

It should be stated that all this track was high grade, well built and substantial, with 130- and 131-lb. rail fastened to the tie-plate by clips and the tie-plate screw-spiked to the tie and with the best of ballast and shoulders.

To begin with, something should be said as to the purpose and methods of the tests. Perhaps the word observations may better indicate the nature of the work.

The purpose of the tests: To learn the amount and distribution of changes in length in the rail itself all along a stretch of welded rail and particularly at places near the two ends of the stretch, and thus to find something of the magnitude of the anchorage forces (or restraining forces) provided by the track structure at and near the ends and possibly at various points along the stretch, and likewise to learn something of the values of the temperature stresses set up in the rail—all due to the effect of changes in temperature such as occurs from morning to afternoon or from summer to winter. In other words, to find (1) changes in length in the rail at any place along the stretch, (2) anchorage or restraint at any place along the length, (3) temperature stresses set up in the rail at any place.

The method: Gage lines on the web of rail (gage length of 8 in.) at various places along the stretch—relatively close together at the end portions of the stretch over a distance of five rail lengths; farther apart through the intermediate portion—every 4 or 5 rail lengths. Readings with a strain gage taken continuously over the stretch as expeditiously as possible and repeated at different times. Coincidentally with taking the strain gage measurements, the temperature of the rail was taken by two men by means of an open-ended thermocouple and portable potentiometer, which quickly gave the rail temperature at the points along the rail. Strain gage readings and temperature readings were also taken on a standard bar or comparator, and likewise on short pieces of rail. In the tests in summer weather, readings were taken on a cool cloudy day (rail temperature say 58 deg.) and in the hotter part of a day (rail temperature say 90 deg. to 105 deg.). In the test in winter weather, readings were taken at a rail temperature of about 16 deg., with air temperature as much as 13 deg. colder.

It should be said that this test work was attended with many difficulties, caused by cold, snow, wind, etc., and that many precautions were taken in regard to gage holes, instrumental manipulation, temperature calibrations and corrections, and checks in the work. Likewise the reduction of data and comparison of results involved careful study and consideration. It is believed that the results obtained are trustworthy and definite in telling a story of the change in length of the rail and of the temperature stresses set up.

Tests and observations were made on one stretch of track at Albany (a half-mile in length) and two stretches at Schenectady (one 0.85 mile and one 1.32 mile). The data of the tests on the 0.85 mile stretch at Schenectady have been chosen for presentation this morning. The tests of this stretch of track have less variable conditions of temperature and support than were found on the other stretches of track.

It should be said that on this stretch of welded rail there is a long 4 deg. curve at the north end, a 4 deg. curve north of the central portion, a 2 deg. curve at the central portion and a long 30 ft. curve towards the south end of the stretch. The grade was 0.75 per cent up-grade southward and in the direction of traffic.

The discussion will take up (a) Changes in length in the rail at the various points along the track, (b) Temperature stresses in rail, and (c) Various results and observations found by the tests.

In the view in Fig. 1, one man (the recorder) is holding the ends of the wires of the thermocouple to touch the head of the rail (or it may be another part of its surface) and the other is reading the potentiometer. Only a brief time is required to get the temperature of the rail. The fastening of the rail to the tie-plate is also shown in this view.

Fig. 1.—Measurement of Rail Temperature on D. & H. Welded Track.

Fig. 2 represents changes in length in the rail along this 0.85 mile stretch of welded rail for changes in rail temperature from a base temperature of 58 deg., which was the rail temperature on a cool, cloudy day in the summer test. Distances from the north end are given in rail lengths at the top of the diagram, 120 in all. Alinement is also indicated at the top of the figure. The change in length (increase or decrease) of course was found from the difference in strain gage readings at the different times and was converted into unit strains (inches per inch). However, as an aid to simplicity of comprehension, these unit strains have been expressed as equivalent stress, pounds per square inch, such as would occur under the application of tension or compression without change in temperature. Please remember, however, that on this slide pounds per square inch refers to the equivalent change in length; it does not give the stress put into the rail by the temperature change—that will be shown on another slide.

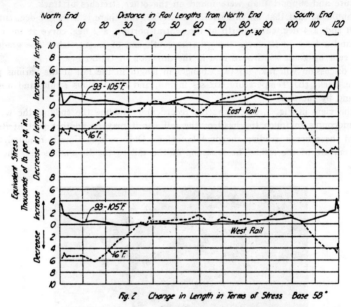

Fig. 2   Change in Length in Terms of Stress   Base 58°

In this slide, then, the ordinates (vertical distances) represent the change in length in the rail expressed as equivalent stress in thousands of pounds per square inch. If there is little or no change in length, regardless of the change in temperature, the rail has been held rigidly to prevent the natural expansion or contraction, as occurs throughout the larger part of the length. If at a given point there is some change in length though not as great as that due to the given change in temperature, as occurs in the end portions, there must exist a corresponding suitable holding or restraint.

The plotted lines in the upper part of the slide are for the east rail, those in the lower part for the west rail. The rail temperatures for the full line curves (late summer tests) varied along the track from 93 deg. to 105 deg., but were fairly uniform at about 100 deg. over all the track except for 10 rail lengths at the left portion where there was shade. The broken lines (winter tests) are for a rail temperature of 16 deg., which was very uniform over the whole stretch. Let me repeat that both summer and winter values are related to the cloudy day temperature of 58 deg. in the summer tests as a base value. Upward values represent increases in length and downward values decreases.

It is at once apparent from the slide that a characteristic of this track is that throughout all the intermediate portion of this 0.85 mile stretch the rail is held with sufficient restraint such that practically all change of length is eliminated for the entire range of temperature of the summer and winter tests, except for minor changes at different local points. The change of length in the rail in the high temperature run with respect to the 58 deg. run was a slight increase equivalent generally to less than 1000 lb. per sq. in. over most of the length, as shown by the full line curve. The low temperature run shows the same characteristics for a temperature change from 58 deg. to 16 deg. over almost as long a distance.

The principal changes in length of rail were observed at the end portions of the stretch as shown at the left and right portions of the diagram. The results for the high temperature run are complicated at the left end by a markedly lower temperature due to shade from a high bank and trees, so the right end portion is probably a more representative condition, or at least a better illustration of the action of the track under uniform conditions. Here at the right end the rail under the high temperature as compared with the measurements at 58 deg. increases in length over a distance of about 5 and 15 rail lengths on the two rails. Before the time of the winter observation a repair and readjustment of the track at the right end of the stretch had changed the end conditions, and under the low temperature the decrease in length extended over about 15 and 20 rail lengths as compared with the 58 deg. run taken in the previous summer. In the summer tests, the rate of change of length increased considerably over the end rail lengths for this and other stretches tested, the greater part of the change occurring in as little as 5 rail lengths. It should be borne in mind (to repeat again) that these values are unit changes in length determined directly from strain gage readings and for convenience expressed in terms of stress, but they are not the temperature stresses.

It will be well before going on to the next slide to state the significance of these changes in length with respect to their effect on the actual temperature stress in the rail. Wherever we observe a change of length in the same direction as the change that would be due to the change of temperature without restraining action, there is present also a lessening of the temperature stress in the rail. Thus, for example, in the end portions of a stretch where there is only partial restraint a temperature increase lengthens the rail as shown in Fig. 2 and results in a decrease from the full temperature stress present elsewhere in the rail. A decrease in length that accompanies a decrease in temperature also decreases the stress from that which would be present under conditions of full restraint; the actual stress in this case is of opposite nature. At the middle portion where little or no change in length is observed, approximately the full temperature stress is present that corresponds to the temperature range.

From the values of the changes in length given in Fig. 2 and the rail temperature measured at a particular point, the stress in the rail due to the change in temperature from 58 deg. was calculated. Fig. 3 shows these temperature stresses for the summer test at 93 deg. to 105 deg. and the winter test at 16 deg.

It will be seen from the slide (Fig. 3) that throughout all the intermediate portions of the stretch the compression in the rail for the summer test ranged from say

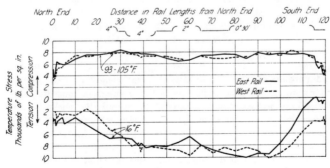

Fig 3 Temperature Stresses in Rail. Base 58°

7,000 to 8,000 lb. per sq. in., and for the winter test the tension ranged from 8,000 to 10,000 lb. per sq. in., if taken on the basis of a temperature of 58 deg. The total range in temperature thus was nearly 90 deg. and the total change in temperature stress from compression to tension was say 17,000 lb. per sq. in. This stress corresponds approximately to the stress equivalent calculated from the range in temperature, which indicates that, except for local conditions along the length, the rail over the main portion of the stretch on the average is held rigidly from changes in length through all this range of temperature.

It has been noted that the stresses given for both the summer and the winter tests have been based upon the readings taken at 58 deg. rail temperature. Having this set of readings an opportunity is given to learn the general uniformity and variations of both the summer and the winter tests. It is evident that the use of this medium temperature as a base is equivalent to assuming that the temperature stress is zero at 58 deg. This assumption will not affect the relative position of the upper curves and the lower curves with respect to each other. For any other base temperature than 58 deg., the corresponding values of the temperature stresses may be seen by raising or lowering the zero axis by a stress equivalent to the change in reference temperature desired, if the rail is assumed to return to its earlier position at a given temperature. Thus, if the temperature when the rail was free from temperature stress was 25 deg. higher than 58 deg., the axis would be raised 5,000 lb. per sq. in. and a compression value of 8,000 lb. per sq. in. would become 3,000 lb. per sq. in., while a tension value of 10,000 lb. per sq. in. would become 15,000 lb. per sq. in. As the rail was laid at a fairly high temperature it may be expected that a change of axis such as 5,000 lb. per sq. in. more nearly represents the actual temperature stresses developed in the rail at the time of the two tests.

A word as to the anchorage of the end portion of a stretch of welded rail to give fixity to the intermediate portion: Considering a range of stress of 90 deg. and a change in temperature stress of 17,000 lb. per sq. in., the total anchorage force required at the end portion of 131-lb. rail for this change in temperature would be about 220,000 lb. for each rail. This force is required at each end of the fixed portion comprising the main middle part of the welded stretch. It is apparent that except for some possible fixity at the extreme end this anchorage is gained in the length of track that shows increasing temperature stresses toward the fixed portion, giving a sloping line in the diagrams. If the rate of increase along this length is uniform (a straight line in the diagram, the anchorage force given by the ties may be considered to be applied to the rail rather uniformly from tie to tie. At various places along the anchoring portion, the rate of application of the anchorage force may be considerably greater or less than the average. It is perhaps true that the individual tie anchorage force may vary in amount in some way from the beginning of the anchorage to the intermediate portion. It should be said also that it has not been fully established whether a large range of temperature involves a longer length of anchorage than a smaller range, and if so how this length varies.

The end portions of the stretch have different conditions from the intermediate portion and require further discussion. As is to be expected, some distance along the end portions of the welded stretch is needed to acquire the anchorage and to give fixity for developing the greater compressive or tensile stresses found in the intermediate portion of the stretch. For the summer test (cool and cloudy day and bright and warm day) nearly the full temperature stress was acquired in 5 rail lengths from the ends of the stretch. The apparent compressive stress shown at and near the ends of the stretch is due partly to taking 58 deg. as the base, and the higher temperature existing at laying time would probably reduce the actual value of this compressive stress at 105 deg., by say, 4,000 or 5,000 lb. per sq. in. Besides, the joint bars at the ends of the stretch perhaps carried stress to the next stretch of rail and, too, the ends moved $\frac{1}{4}$ in. or so in the change of temperature from 58 deg. to 105 deg.

In the winter tests, the greater part of the tension found in the intermediate portion is acquired between a point a few rail lengths away from the end and another point 15 or 20 rail lengths farther on. Through the first 10 or 15 lengths of the north portion and the first 5 lengths of the south portion the tensile stress is fairly uniform, amounting to 3000 or 4000 lb. per sq. in. if counted from the 58 deg. temperature, and to about 8000 lb. per sq. in. if counted from a probable laying temperature, though the actual stress at the ends is not known because of changes made in track in November, as referred to in the following paragraph. Most of this stress is doubtless applied at the ends of the stretch from the rails beyond through the joint bars there.

As to this uniformity of stress over the 5 and 15 rail lengths of the two end portions: At the north end the data and the condition of the track gave evidence that final work on this portion of the track had been made after the date of the summer test (including the insertion of a second rail joint and a short piece of rail), which resulted in readjustments affecting the relations of the basic measurements from other causes than temperature. The measurements indicate a longitudinal rail movement here of an inch or more during this final work. At the south end, the east rail at the insulated joint, connected to the adjoining welded stretch of rail by joint

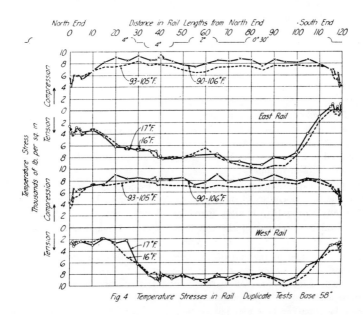

Fig 4   Temperature Stresses in Rail   Duplicate Tests   Base 58°

bars, broke through the bolt holes with a temperature drop in November. The insertion of a new piece of rail next to the insulated joint and also of a second rail-joint changed the amount and distribution of stress over some unknown distance. In the adjustment of this part of the track the conditions of stress in the west rail were also changed. It may be said then that the presence of uniform stress through this distance of 10 and 5 rail lengths at the two ends of the stretch is probably largely due to changes made in the track after the summer test was completed.

In Fig. 4, the temperature stresses found in a duplicate test are shown by the full lines, while the dotted lines give the results of the test already shown in Fig. 3. The slide indicates that the two sets of tests give results quite consistent with each other.

It may be of interest to see what forces this tie anchorage involves. An examination of the sloping parts of the diagram to learn the rate of change of stress in the rail seems a promising way of getting at the anchorage developed at the tie. See the sloping portions in Fig. 3 and 4. An examination shows considerable variation in the tie anchorage. Computing average anchorage per tie over different lengths (taken from the increases in stress in rail from point to point), it is found that sometimes the greater part of the anchorage is attained in 15 or 20 rail lengths and sometimes a considerable amount in 2 and 4 rail lengths. A study of all the eight series of the summer and winter tests on the 0.85 mile stretch at Schenectady and the eight series of tests on the one-half mile stretch of the northbound track at Albany, using an assumed laying temperature and assuming that changes in length are proportional to changes in temperature, gave values of average tie anchorage developed at certain places of varying lengths ranging from 100 lb. to 270 lb. per tie per rail for the summer tests (calculated between an assumed laying temperature and a cloudy day temperature), and from 165 lb. to 470 lb. for the winter tests when compared with the cloudy day observations of the summer test (58 deg.). A combination of high and low temperature tests gave values ranging from 270 lb. to 740 lb. per tie per rail. It is apparent that the values of the anchorage vary considerably at different places and that the distribution of the anchorage varies from place to place and from time to time. Besides, little is known of the relation of the tie resistance to the "give" of the tie longitudinally of the track.

From the strain data at and near the end of the stretches, it is thought that the rail-joints of three of the ends of the welded stretches at Schenectady transmitted as much as 6,000 lb. per sq. in. of rail section to the adjoining rails.

In closing, a few general observations on various aspects and actions of the stretches of welded track may be made:

All the welded stretches tested had kept their alinement well even on the curves including the 7° 30′ curve at Albany, so far as could be seen from the test and the general inspection and from the lateral measurements made by the Engineers of the Delaware and Hudson Company.

The longitudinal movement at the ends of the welded stretches and at points along the length, due to temperature changes, was small, say from 0 to ½ in. or a little more, and little if any greater than is often found in ordinary track.

No noticeable movement of the ties in a direction longitudinal of the track was seen.

It is apparent that at the end of a welded stretch of rail, a tensile or compressive force of considerable magnitude may be transmitted to the adjoining rail (whether welded or not)—a condition that warrants consideration and which may be beneficial or otherwise according to circumstances.

It may be remarked here that observations at various times and places on ordinary track with tight well-fitting joints have shown small movements at joints over a wide temperature range, indicating that large temperature stresses may be present in ordinary track.

The deep snow at the time of the winter tests, coming up on the head of the rail, kept the rail temperature quite above that of the air temperature in the cold weather.

On a bright, clear day in summer (not a hot day), the rail temperature was found to be 38 deg. higher than the air temperature of 68 deg. In another observation the rail temperature was 35 deg. higher than an air temperature of 90 deg.

The few breaks in rail on the welded stretches have left only small gaps, so that they were not troublesome and replacements were easily made.

In the welded stretch tested at Albany the anchorage at the end portions was of a character similar to that found at Schenectady and was acquired in from 5 to 10 rail lengths. Due to the presence of under-crossings and viaducts and other variable conditions, the summer rail temperatures and temperature changes were quite variable along the stretch, resulting in the development of variable anchorage forces at points along the length, as is to be expected.

It is recognized of course that the flexural stresses developed in the rail by the loads of traffic will be superimposed on the temperature stresses and the two sets of stresses at any point in the height of the rail must be added or subtracted according to their nature. To what extent the presence of high tension temperature stress will affect the growth of transverse fissures may be an interesting question.

It is planned to continue tests on this track and on other welded track. In such a departure from usual practice, a year or two of time may bring out all the characteristics of the action of such track (Applause).

The President:—Professor Talbot, I wish to thank you in the name of the Association for your splendid report, which well merits careful study by every Engineer interested in the advances in track construction and maintenance which must ultimately result from the explorations of your Committee. May I again assure you and the Committee that the Board of Direction is mindful of the increasing interest of this Association in the value of the work which has been so well pioneered by the Committee under your leadership. I am hopeful that added facilities and funds may soon be made available for a more extensive experimentation and research studies along the lines which are being developed. The Committee is now dismissed with the thanks of the convention (Applause).

A

DISCUSSION ON STRESSES IN RAILROAD TRACK

(For Report, see pp. 455–456)

Dr. A. N. Talbot (University of Illinois):—The report of the Committee is found on page 455 of Bulletin 392. That report concerns the general work of the year.

This seems an opportune time to make a brief report on the tests on the stretches of welded track under observation. As has been said before, one purpose of the observations is to learn something of the magnitude and distribution of the anchorage given between ties and ballast at the ends of the welded stretch and along its length to resist the forces set up by changes in the temperature of the rail, and to learn how the influences tending to change the length and alinement are met in the track, both in the early life of the track and at later dates when time and traffic may have had opportunity to show their effects. In these observational tests, stress measurements have been made

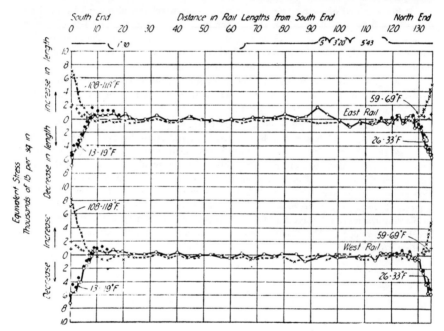

FIG. 1. Change in Length in Terms of Stress Base 53° Fahr. Welded Length 1.0 Mile— Bessemer & Lake Erie Railroad.

on the web of the rail in July and in February, at an early morning hour or in a cloudy time, and at the warmest part of the day. Accurate measurements of the temperature of the rail along the track have been taken at the same time by means of an open-ended thermocouple and portable potentiometer. The accuracy of the stress and strain deductions from the observed measurements has been guarded by the use of a compensating reference bar or comparator as well as by comparison with an invar bar and unstressed pieces of rail. The observations have been reduced by temperature corrections of gage readings and made comparable for both strains and stresses.

In Fig. 1 are plotted the changes in length observed along the mile stretch of the welded GEO track of the Bessemer and Lake Erie Railroad near Pittsburgh, Pennsylvania, for two representative series in summer and two in winter. Position along the stretch is shown in terms of rail lengths of 39 feet each. The rail temperatures along the track for the series were 108° to 118°, 59° to 60°, 26° to 33°, and 13° to 19° Fahr. As the changes in length in the rail from one temperature to another are quite minute, the unit changes (inches per inch) have been translated into equivalent stress per square inch in steel—that is, the stress which would be developed in the rail if an external force had produced the change in length without any change in temperature. The observations before sunrise on a day in July with a rail temperature of 53° Fahr. were taken as the base or zero line for the diagram. It will be seen that throughout the intermediate part of the welded stretch (about nine-tenths of the mile) very little change occurred—only small local changes—the rail has been held closely to one length through all these varia-

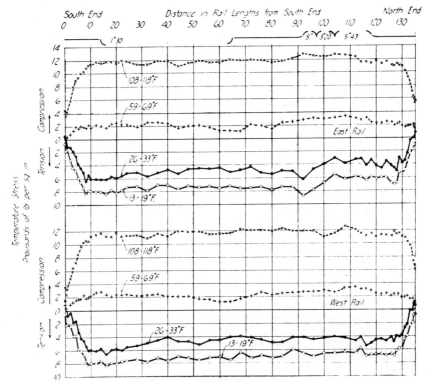

Fig. 2.—Temperature Stresses in Rail Base 53° Fahr. Welded Length 1.0 Mile—Bessemer & Lake Erie Railroad.

tions in temperature. As the differences are generally small, not all the points for the four series are plotted on the diagram. For the end portions of both rails and for both the summer and the winter tests the rails have changed length through an average distance of about seven rail lengths. This change in length increases rather regularly from the points at the end of the intermediate portion (which may be thought of as the point of fixation) to the end of the welded stretch, showing lengthening in summer and shortening in winter. The data indicate that the magnitude of the winter and summer temperatures has not affected the length of track over which expansion or contraction takes place in each end portion, and that the long intermediate portion remained practically fixed in position with the various changes in temperature at the time the observations were made.

In Fig. 2 are recorded the stresses developed in the rail throughout its length based on the rail temperature and strain gauge reading at time of observation as compared with strain gage readings at a base temperature of 53° Fahr., which were taken before sunrise last summer with temperature conditions very uniform over the whole stretch. For the summer observations, at a temperature averaging say 113° Fahr., the relative stresses along the intermediate nine-tenths of a mile average about 12,000 lb. per sq. in. compression, and for the winter observation at a temperature of about 16° Fahr. the relative stresses averaged somewhat less than 8,000 lb. per sq. in. tension, both values being compared with the readings at 53° Fahr. referred to above. If the reference line were placed at 63° Fahr. (the temperature at which the rails were originally fastened in the track), the corresponding compressive stress for the summer test would be approximately 10,000 lb. per sq. in. and for the winter test a tensile stress of approximately 10,000 lb. per sq. in. For the higher summer temperatures and the lower winter temperatures (relative to those observed), the stresses may be expected to increase in proportion to the increase in change of temperature from the 63° Fahr. base. The end portions show a tapering off of stress over the distance of say seven rail lengths to nothing at the end for the winter tests, and for the summer tests tapering off in seven rail lengths to 2,000 to 6,000 lb. per sq. in. at the joint connecting the welded stretch to the regular track beyond, a compression probably transmitted through the joint.

The data given in Fig. 1 and 2 indicate that the magnitude of the winter and summer temperatures does not particularly affect the length of track over which expansion or contraction takes place at each of the end portions. The central part of the track has remained practically fixed in position since the summer readings. The changes in length and in stress over the end portions of about seven rail lengths are fairly regular, though of course there are changes in position from time to time at the extreme ends of the welded rail. The length of these end portions giving anchorage to the intermediate portions and the stresses set up in the intermediate portions correspond to an average anchorage or restraint of about 600 lb. per tie per rail for the temperatures of 113° Fahr. and 16° Fahr., as counted from a laying temperature of 63° Fahr. If the anchoring length remains fairly constant for temperatures outside the range observed, the corresponding anchorage force would be proportionally greater than 600 lb. It may be added that no indication was observable of any movement between the ballast and ties one way or the other at the times of the tests, nor of any particular change in length of the anchorage developed. It is not known, of course, what the ultimate shearing strength of the ballast bed may be. The track seems to have kept close to an elastic condition of restraint.

The welded rail of the Delaware and Hudson Railroad at Schenectady, New York, under observation (.85 mile in length) was found to have held approximately to the positions assumed after the readjustment in the fall of 1935 except for the usual temperature expansion or contraction at the end portions that occurs with every change of temperature. The readjustment referred to took place after a break occurred in the insulated joint at one rail end in November 1935. At that time the three remaining joints at the two ends were also loosened and slightly longer rails inserted at those places. Probably the readjustment, which was a contraction of about 1½ or 2 inches at the ends, diminishing to zero at about 20 rail lengths, has put this track in a stable condition.

The Albany tests of this winter have not been worked up, but this track has been found to be quite stable and fixed, especially after the two breaks were welded soon after the summer tests of 1935. The periodical movements at the south end are somewhat larger than have been found in other stretches, due probably to the large temperature variations caused by the shade from the overhead bridges near that end.

The correctness of the comparisons that may be made between various series of tests on the welded track taken at different times with a wide range of temperature is dependent upon the accuracy of the comparisons which have to be made with standard reference bars during the time of the tests, for even the strain gage with parts made of invar changes length with change in temperature. For this use a compensating reference bar or comparator was devised, which has proved to be practically invariable in length over the atmospheric ranges of temperature. In Fig. 3 the points along the original zero line show the observed changes in the compensating reference bar with a 10 inch reference length over a range of temperature from —20° to 132° Fahr. The points

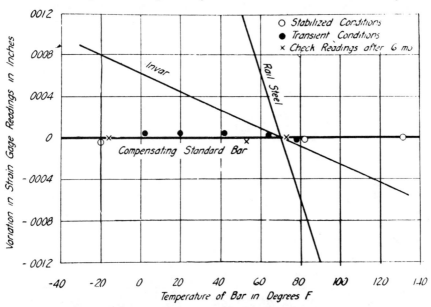

FIG. 3.—Change in Length of 10 inches Compensated Standard Bar, Rail Steel and Invar with Temperature Change.

plotted as open circles represent readings taken under stable or constant conditions; the closed circles represent readings taken as the temperature was rising from —20° Fahr. to room temperature; and the crosses are from the calibration taken after six months use of the bar. The variations from constant length in this compensating reference bar are less than the errors of reading. By contrast the steeply sloping line represents the changes that would have taken place in a piece of rail steel for the same temperatures, and the less steeply sloping line represents changes in a piece of invar of the same constant as the invar used in the construction of the compensating reference bar. This compensating reference bar has been a great convenience in decreasing labor in the reduction of test values and has contributed materially to the accuracy of the results.

From time to time work has been done in developing methods and instruments for the study of the amount and location of the wear and other irregularities in worn rail joints. Preliminary laboratory and field tests and observations have been made at va-

322

rious times when opportunity offered. One aspect of these tests was the selection of worn joints in the track and measurement of various stresses and deflections and movements as the inner bolts were tightened and loosened.

An annoying problem of maintenance of worn joints is caused by the dipping of the rail ends as wear occurs and bolts are tightened. The track may be raised and tamped but the dip at the rail ends increases; it seems probable that tightening the bolts moves the lower fishing surface of the bar upward on the sloping surface of the rail base and thus pulls the rail ends down. In Fig. 4 the dipping of the rail ends of 14 worn angle bar joints in track as measured when the inner bolts were tightened are plotted against the inward lateral deflection of the bar occurring at the same time (average deflection of two bars of a joint). This lateral deflection of the bars would be approximately proportional to the pull of the bolts. The bars are 24 inches long and their deflection was taken at the mid-point of a 24-inch chord. The trend of the magnitude of the dip is proportional to the amount of the lateral deflection of the bars and thus roughly pro-

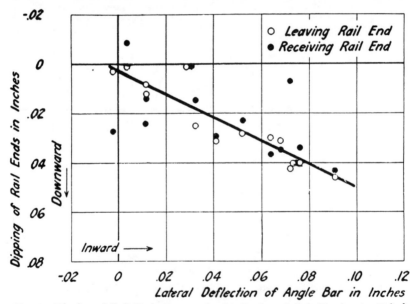

FIG. 4.—Dipping of Rail Ends Due to the Application of Bolt Tension to 24-inch Worn Angle Bars. Deflections are for the Mid-point of 24-inch Chord.

portional to the magnitude of the bolt pull. The lateral deflections referred to are measured from the loosened and unstressed position of the bars. It will be seen that the rail ends deflected downward as much as .04 inch in a 24-inch chord. Tamping of track will not maintain the surface of the joint under such circumstances.

Tightening the inner bolts in worn bars also develops lateral bending stresses in the bars. In Fig. 5 are plotted the stresses developed in the flange of the angle bar at midlength in the same 14 joints in track, as measured when the bolts were tightened, plotted against the inward deflection of the bar measured at the mid-point of a 24-inch chord located about the mid-height of the bar. The lateral deflection used is the total deflection from the position of the chord on the loosened bar. The upper group of points on the diagram are for bars worn each way from the rail ends as shown by the

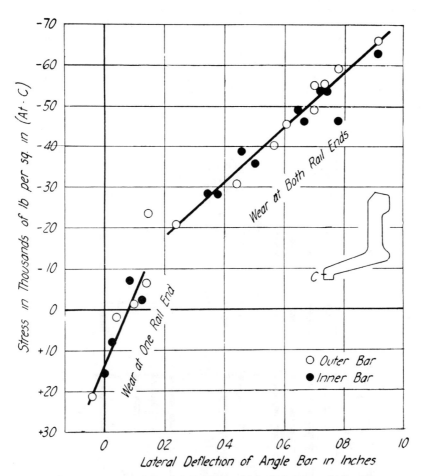

Fig. 5.—Stress and Lateral Deflection of 24-inch Worn Angle Bars
Due to Bolt Tension Chord Length 23 inches.

324

insertion of thickness gauges; the lower group have wear only one way from a rail end and thus the bar can be deflected but little by tightening bolts. These stresses are generally compressive and range up to more than 60,000 lb. per sq. in. for a lateral deflection of .09 in. Plotted separately in Fig. 6 are the stresses at three points of the section, A and B on the head of the bar and C on the edge of the flange for the same 14 joints. The solid black denotes the stress in the bar as the joint was found in track, and the open part denotes the additional stress produced by tightening the inner bolts; the bars were finally loosened and strain readings taken as a base for determining stresses for both original condition in track and tightened condition. It will be seen that for the highly stressed bars the tightening added 30 to 50 per cent to the original or initial stress. In Fig. 6 there is also given beside the stress line for point C a diagonally shaded line which represents the inward lateral deflection of the bar for tightened condition of the joint. The values of stresses and deflections given in Fig. 6 are averages for the two bars of a joint. As the stresses measured are generally compressive, the bar probably bends about an axis approaching the vertical, and evidently high tensile stresses occur on the inner flanges of a bar and these will add to whatever tensile bending stresses are produced by the wheel loads.

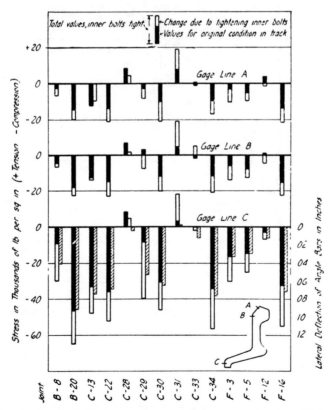

Fig. 6.—Stresses in Worn 24-inch Angle Bars Due to Tightening of Bolts— Original Condition and Inner Bolts Wrenched Very Tight.

These joints were on 100-lb. rail of substantial double track in good condition of maintenance, carrying heavy and fast trains. Although the angle bars were heat treated, many of the joints would be called badly worn, as is indicated by the fact that some of them were deflected inwardly nearly .10 inch from their loosened condition. Longitudinal profiles of the top fishing surface in some cases showed wear at the middle of the top fishing surface as much as .05 and .06 in., besides the wear of the fishing surface of the rail. Such wear is a source of large stresses and deflections in the joint bars when the bolts are tightened in an endeavor to bring the track to surface and eliminate looseness in the joints, and tightening bolts in obviously not effective in producing a smooth joint.

This is all the incidental information that is ready for presentation. Plans for the work of the coming year are progressing satisfactorily.

Appendix 12-a

Rail Web Stresses within Joint Bar Limits

As described in Assignment 7, in August 1948, the Atchison, Topeka & Santa Fe Railway in laying new 132-lb. RE rail in the eastbound main track 100 miles west of Chicago, installed four service test sections of various types of joint bars, each one-half mile in length on tangent track. Three locations include RE, headfree, 36-in. length bars. At Locations V and X, the new AREA and old AREA 6-hole bolt spacings were used. At Location W, the 36-in. length bars have four bolt holes spaced 9 in.—9⅛ in.—9 in. Location V is equipped with Rail Joint Company B-42, headfree 36-in. length bars with the old AREA 6-hole bolt spacing.

During November 1948, stresses within the joint bar limits were measured at two rail joints at each of the four locations under traffic. Rail web stresses were measured in the upper and lower web fillets near the rail ends and also in the upper web fillets outside the limit of the rail joints. Stresses in the rail webs at the edge of the bolt holes were measured. The change in bolt tension under moving loads was recorded at a few bolts. High tensions, medium tensions and zero tensions were set in the bolts of some of the test joints to study the effect of bolt tension on the stresses developed within the rail joints under traffic.

It is expected that the experience gained from the results of this Santa Fe test will be of help in laying out a similar test program for next year on the four new service test of joint bar locations just established for 115-lb. RE rail and joint bars on the Chicago & North Western Railway.

Appendix 12-b

Comparison of Web Stresses in 131-lb. RE and 140 PS— (Pennsylvania) Sections

One of the topics under assignment of this subcommittee is field measurement of web stresses in the new rail sections. This refers, of course, primarily to the adopted sections 115 RE, 132 RE and 133 RE. However, since a few railroads other than the Pennsylvania are now using the 140 PS section, it is desired to report the results of field measurement of stresses made by the Pennsylvania Railroad on the 140 PS section.

Design of 140 PS Section

In 1944 it became apparent that the 131 RE rail section was inadequate as to web strength for many conditions of traffic and alinement on the Pennsylvania Railroad. Investigation of split web failures, (head and web separations) showed evidence of such severe stress, and such rapid breakdown under certain conditions, that it was concluded a radical change in the design of the head and web were necessary.

The 140 PS rail section was hence designed to give the lowest possible upper fillet stress, under conditions of eccentric loading, consistent with reasonable weight of the section, without sacrificing girder strength of the rail as compared with 131 RE, and without sacrificing the ability to use head-contact joint bars. It was sought to reduce the maximum service web stress in the new section to the endurance limit of rail web steel as shown by the first fatigue strength curves for rail web steel produced at the

University of Illinois. This goal was not quite reached, but later studies indicate that an adequate reduction was obtained, particularly in view of the relatively infrequent occurrence of the maximum stress in the field.

A comparison of the 131 RE and the 140 PS sections is shown in Fig. 7.

In the course of the design or development of the 140 PS section, an extended laboratory study was made of web stresses in existing and modified sections. Seventeen sections in all were subjected to laboratory stress analysis under controlled static loading.

Fig. 4 shows the distribution of web stress in the 131 RE and 140 PS sections under eccentric load, based on laboratory test. Fig. 5 is a chart showing a comparison of the maximum stress in the upper fillet for various degrees of rail head wear (vertical) and for various eccentricities of load. This chart is based primarily on laboratory tests but the lines are extrapolated beyond the limits of laboratory tests on a theoretical basis.

In these two charts, as well as in all other charts and tables presented the stress reported is the maximum stress in the web in a vertical plane occurring under a concentrated load. The location of this maximum stress is near the bottom of the upper web fillet. It is compressive and occurs on the side of the web toward which the eccentricity of loading exists. If the wheel load is concentrated near the gage side of the rail, the maximum stress occurs on the gage side of the web, and vice versa.

In the service tests, made under conditions under which rails were failing, the maximum stress was always found on the gage side of the low rail and that is where the fatigue cracks developed. Measurements were also made of stresses on the outside of the web of the low rail, and on both sides of the web of the high rail, but in no case were these stresses found to be of consequence. Under different conditions of curvature,

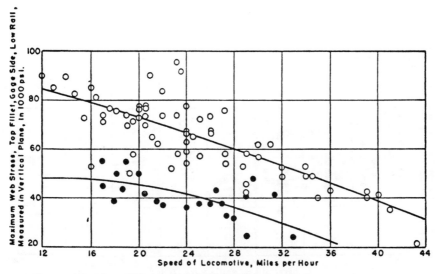

Fig. 1.—Maximum Web Stress vs. Speed of J 1 Locomotive on 6-deg. 30-min. Curve with 6-in. Elevation, 131-lb. and 140-lb. PS Rail.

○ 131-lb. RE Rail, Worn ⅛ in. on Standard Tie Plates:
Runs 551–606 (13 Runs); Runs 803–1030 (46 Runs);
Runs 1065–1128 (11 Runs); Total: 70 Runs.
● New 140-lb. PS Rail on Standard Tie Plates:
Runs 1205–1339 (23 Runs).

560   R a i l

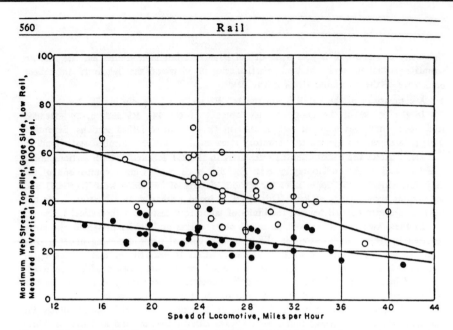

Fig. 2.—Maximum Web Stress vs. Speed of M 1 and M 1A Locomotives on 6-deg. 30-min.
Curve with 6-in. Elevation, 131-lb. RE and 140-lb. PS Rail.

○ 131-lb. RE Rail, Worn ⅛ in. on Standard Tie Plates;
Runs 551–606 (6 Runs); Runs 803–1128 (27 Runs); Total: 33 Runs.

● New 140-lb. PS Rail on Standard Tie Plates: Runs 1215–1340 (39 Runs).

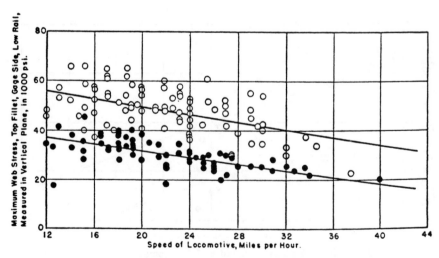

Fig. 3.—Maximum Web Stress vs. Speed of I 1 Locomotive on 6-deg. 30-min.
Curve with 6-in. Elevation; 131-lb. RE and 140-lb. PS Rail.

○ 131-lb. RE Rail, Worn ⅛ in., on Standard Tie Plates:
Runs 803–1067 (80 Runs); Runs 1096–1128 (15 Runs); Total: 95 Runs.

● New 140-lb. Rail on Standard Tie Plates: Runs 1200–1340 (78 Runs).

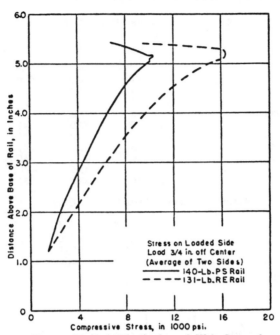

Fig. 4.—Vertical Distribution of Web Stress for
131-lb. RE and 140-lb. PS Rail under 20,000-lb.
Eccentric Load.

superelevation, speed, and character of traffic this situation would undoubtedly be different. The service stresses reported here are on the gage side of the low rail in all cases.

It is not proposed to go into detail of the methods of making the tests either laboratory or service, however, as an explanation of Fig. 4 it may be said that due to the
lack of perfect symmetry in rails as manufactured, and due to the difficulty of locating
the test load at the exact desired eccentricity, tests were made first with the load concentrated near the right hand side of the rail section (as you face it), then with the
load concentrated near the left hand side. The results reported on Fig. 4 are the
averages of the stresses for corresponding gages for the two tests for the side of the
rail web nearest the load. The stresses on the side of the rail web farthest from the load
are not reported and are relatively very small.

The purpose of this report is to present a comparison of the measured service
stresses in 140 PS rail and 131 RE rail under as near as possible identical conditions.
Other phases of the study of causes of failure of the 131 RE section and development
of the 140 PS section will not be reported here because of the space which would be
required.

Service Stress Measurement

Field measurement of stresses in 131 RE rail were made under the most severe
service conditions which could be found. A location was chosen in No. 2 westward track,
Panhandle division, west of Carnegie, Pa., where it had been necessary to renew 131 RE
rail after two years' service due to web failure. The location is known as Slag Dump
Curve. This is a 6-deg. 30-min. curve with 6-in. superelevation on a 0.7 percent ascend-

TABLE 1.—COMPARISON OF RECORDED STRESSES IN 131 RE WORN ⅛ IN. AND 140 PS NEW
—VARIOUS CLASSES OF LOCOMOTIVES

Stresses at Various Speeds Taken from Charted Curves of Stress

Class of Locomotive		15 mph	Stress in 1000 psi. 20 mph.	25 mph.	30 mph.
I1	131 RE	53,5	49.0	45.5	41.5
	140 PS	35.0	31.5	28.0	25.0
	Percent reduction	34.5	35.8	38.5	39.8
M1	131 RE	60.0	53.0	46.0	38.5
	140 PS	31.0	28.0	25.5	23.0
	Percent reduction	48.3	47.2	44.5	40.3
J1	131 RE	80.0	73.0	65.0	57.0
	140 PS	47.5	45.0	40.5	33.5
	Percent reduction	40.6	38.3	37.8	41.2

Maximum Recorded Stress for each Class

	131 RE*	140 PS	Percent Reduction
I1	66,000	45,000	32
M1	70,000	37,000	47
J1	96,000	56,000	42

* Runs 551 to 1128.

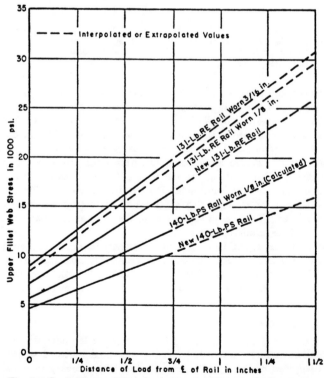

Fig. 5.—Comparison of Stresses in 131-lb. RE and 140-lb. PS Rail
under 20,000 lb. Vertical Load at Various Eccentricities.

TABLE 2.—PANHANDLE DIVISION—WESTWARD TRACK—SLAG DUMP CURVE ESTIMATED NUMBER OF CYCLES OF STRESS IN ONE YEAR

Top Web Fillet—Gage Side—Low Rail—6-deg. 30-min. Curve—6-in. Elevation
After Adzing of Ties and Resurfacing Track Locomotives and Tenders Only

Compression Stress—1000 psi.	Classification of Locomotives							Total
	J1 (3515)	I1 (4933)	M1 (2610)	L1 (512)	H10 (454)	K4 (9232)	C5 (2018)	
100								
95								
90	59							59
85	176							176
80	469							469
75	644							644
70	469		93					562
65	410	153	93					656
60	410	458	280					1,148
55	1,113	1,119	93		45		144	2,514
50	1,054	1,322	559		45			2,980
45	1,933	2,492	746	73	45		432	5,721
40	2,402	3,356	932	183	136	115	144	7,268
35	1,582	1,526	1,212	293	318	1,385	288	6,604
30	1,816	1,170	1,305	146	318	808	1,009	6,572
25	2,285	1,424	1,678	73	91	2,193	432	8,176
20	4,101	1,627	2,424	293	91	4,501	144	13,181
15	3,749	2,543	2,424	768	136	5,193	288	15,101
10	4,042	4,780	2,331	805	1,044	7,501	2,449	22,952
5	3,749	5,644	1,398	878	409	9,001	3,744	24,823
Tension Stress—1000 psi.								
5	12,595	12,611	8,856	805	590	22,272	3,889	61,618
10	6,209	3,711	3,915	329	136	12,002	576	26,879
15	2,285	254	653		4,962			8,154
20	410	51	93			923		1,477
25						115		115
								217,849

Notes—
Based on test runs 803 to 1128 (excluding special runs) August 12 to October 24, 1946.
Rail has head wear of approximately ⅛ in. (131-lb. RE rail).
Rail laid new in 1943 in this curve was removed because of web failure in 1945 (131-lb. RE rail).
SR-4 wire resistance strain gage mounted 5.19 in. above base of rail at point of maximum stress in fillet.
Number of cycles of stress shown expanded from 303 test runs to a basis of one year, based on a train sheet study of one week's traffic and an additional factor based on comparison of this week's traffic with the year's traffic.

ing grade. The maximum authorized speed is 40 mph., but the curve is so located that many freight trains pass around the curve at 15 to 20 mph.

The rail was supported on Pennsylvania standard heavy-duty tie plates, 7½ in. by 14¾ in., 1 in 40 cant, flat bottom, rolled crown. The ties had been adzed to give a uniform support to the tie plates. The track was ballasted with crushed stone.

The work was done by employees of the Pennsylvania Railroad engineering department. The equipment used for the field work consisted of SR-4 wire resistance strain gages and General Electric oscillograph and amplifiers. The test equipment was mounted in an automotive trailer hauled to, or near to, the site of the work over the highway. The trailer serves as a field office during progress of the work. The instruments and methods are very similar to, and in many cases identical with, those used by the research engineer, AAR, for similar work and the Pennsylvania Railroad is indebted to him and his staff for much information and guidance in planning and carrying out the work.

Extensive measurements of web stress on 131 RE rail were made on this curve in the summer and early fall of 1946.

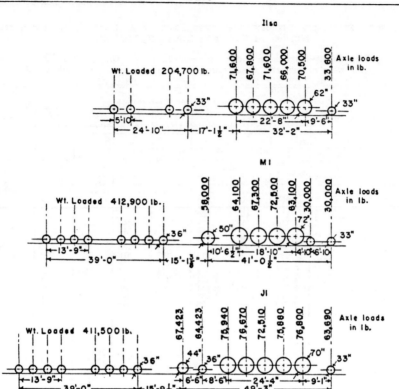

Fig. 6.—Wheel Arrangement and Loading for I 1sa, M 1 and J 1 Locomotives.

The first 140 PS rail was rolled in October 1946. Upon completion of the tests on 131 RE rail, 140 PS rail of one of the first rollings was laid, and stress measurements on the new section were immediately begun. No surfacing was done, and measurements were made under conditions as nearly as possible identical with those under which like stresses in the 131 RE were measured.

Comparison of Stresses 140 PS and 131 RE Rail

Table 1 gives a summary of the comparative stresses, and the percent of reduction in the average stress at various speeds for various classes of locomotives. A comparison is also shown of the maximum stress for each of these classes of locomotives. The theoretical improvement as based on laboratory tests is 45 to 46 percent for new 140 PS, compared with 131 RE worn ⅛ in.

It will be observed that in some cases the theoretical improvement was fully realized in the service stresses, while in others the improvement is somewhat less than anticipated. The over-all picture is however very encouraging as the very high maximum stress with the Class J1 locomotive is reduced 42 percent.

It should be understood that the service tests were not made under controlled conditions, as far as traffic is concerned, the stress measurements being made under regular traffic with a great variety of individual locomotives of each class, and with a variety of speeds and conditions as to weight of train hauled, etc.

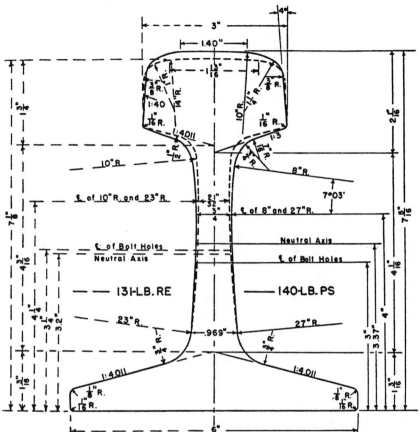

Fig. 7.—Comparison of 131-lb. RE and 140-lb. PS Rail Sections.

	131 RE	140 PS
Weight per yard, lb.	131.2	140.6
Area, sq. in.	12.9	13.8
Height, in.	7 ⅛	7 $\frac{7}{16}$
Width of base, in.	6	6
Moment of inertia, in.⁴	89	97
Section modulus above N. A., in.³	23	25
Section modulus below N. A., in.³	27	29
Head torsional rigidity*	32.6	44.3

* Note: In millions of in.-lb. per radian per inch.

The figures shown in Table 1 were taken from charts of stress versus speed for the three classes of freight locomotives shown. Fig. 1 shows stress versus speed for the J1 locomotive, comparing results obtained on 140 PS new rail with those obtained on 131 RE rail worn ⅛ in. Figs. 2 and 3 show the same information for the M–1 locomotive and the I–1 locomotive, respectively.

As of interest in this connection Fig. 6 is a chart showing the axle spacing and loading for the I–1, M–1, and J–1 locomotives.

TABLE 3.—PANHANDLE DIVISION—WESTWARD TRACK—SLAG DUMP CURVE ESTIMATED NUMBER OF CYCLES OF STRESS IN ONE YEAR

Top Web Fillet—Gage Side—Low Rail—6-deg. 30-min.—6-in. Elevation
Locomotives and Tenders Only

Compression Stress—1000 psi.	Classification of Locomotives							Total
	J1 (3515)	I1 (4933)	M1 (2610)	L1 (512)	H10 (454)	K4 (9232)	G5 (2018)	
100								
95								
90								
85								
80								
75								
70								
65								
60								
55	459							459
50	306							306
45	765	124						889
40	1,683	992	142					2,817
35	1,071	1,426	213			512		3,222
30	1,836	2,542	923	171	454	256		6,182
25	3,978	3,906	1,988	342	454	2,048	1,008	13,724
20	4,131	3,348	3,621	399		3,584	1,008	16,091
15	7,650	2,790	4,118	399	454	4,608	336	20,355
10	8,109	5,022	4,826	285		11,264	2,016	31,522
5	7,650	10,540	5,254	1,191		16,128	3,860	44,123
Tension Stress—1000 psi.								
5	11,016	12,152	7,100	1,767	454	29,184	5,712	67,385
10	153	124	142			512		931
								208,006

Notes—
Based on test runs 1200 to 1340 November 19 to December 6, 1946.
Rail is new 140-lb. PS rail.
SR-4 wire resistance strain gage mounted 5.11 in. above base of rail at point of maximum stress in fillet.
Number of cycles of stress shown expanded from 141 test runs to a basis of one year, based on a train sheet study of one week's traffic and an additional factor based on comparison of this week's traffic with the year's traffic.

Another comparison is presented in the form of a tabulation of the number of cycles of stress of each magnitude for the 131 RE rail, Table 2, and for the 140 PS rail, Table 3. The method of preparing these tables is explained in some detail in the footnotes. The elimination of stresses over 55,000 psi., and the general lowering of the over-all level of stress is readily seen from a comparison of these tables.

Conclusions

It was concluded from these service measurements that the laboratory basis of design of the new section was sound and that the laboratory stress measurements forecast the reduction in service stress with satisfactory accuracy.

The reduction in stress which it was sought to make has been realized in track, as shown by service stress measurements. Service experience will, of course, ultimately determine the value of the new section.

APM-54-26

Stresses in Railroad Track

By S. TIMOSHENKO[1] AND B. F. LANGER[2]

With the constant tendency in railroad practice to increase the axle loading and the speed of locomotives, the problem of stresses produced in rails by moving loads becomes more and more important. In a study recently made by engineers of the Westinghouse Electric and Manufacturing Company, principally in connection with the study of the tracking characteristics of electric locomotives, there has been developed a method for experimental determination, not only of vertical but also of lateral forces produced on the rails by a moving locomotive, and it is shown that these lateral forces produce in rails very high stresses. In this paper the authors briefly discuss the theory which has been used as a guide in this experimental research work, and describe some recent experiments in the laboratory and in the field.

WITH the constant tendency in railroad practice to increase the axle loading and the speed of locomotives, the problem of stresses produced in rails by moving loads becomes more and more important. During the last fifteen years an important piece of work in this field has been done by the Special Committee on Stresses in Railroad Track[3] under the direction of Prof. A. N. Talbot. In this work a complete theory for the bending of rails produced by vertical loads has been given, and also an experimental method for determining these loads has been developed.

Further progress in determination of track stresses has been made by engineers of the Westinghouse Electric & Manufacturing Company,[4] principally in connection with the study of the tracking characteristics of electric locomotives. There has been developed in this study a method for experimental determination not only of vertical, but also of lateral forces produced on the rails by a moving locomotive, and it has been shown that these lateral forces produce in rails very high stresses.

In this paper a brief discussion of the theory which has been used as a guide in this experimental research work is given, and some recent experiments in the laboratory and in the field are described. Special attention is given to the local stresses in rails produced by vertical and lateral forces. It seems that this is the first time that these stresses have been studied. The importance of knowledge of these stresses for a logical design of rail profiles cannot be overestimated.

I—RAIL AS A LONG BAR ON ELASTIC FOUNDATION

1 VERTICAL BENDING OF RAILS

The following theory of vertical bending of rails is based upon the assumption that the rail can be considered as a long bar continuously supported by an elastic foundation.[5] The rigidity of this foundation is defined by the magnitude k of the *modulus of foundation*, which is the load per unit length of the rail necessary to produce a deflection of the foundation equal to unity. The experiments show that the magnitude of the modulus can be always determined in such a manner that the deflection of the rail calculated on the assumption of the continuous foundation is in good agreement with the deflection of the actual rail supported by ties. Using the notations

EI = flexural rigidity of the rail

$$\beta = \sqrt[4]{\frac{k}{4EI}} \dots\dots\dots\dots\dots [1]$$

and applying the equation for the deflection curve

[1] Professor of Mechanical Engineering, University of Michigan, Ann Arbor, Mich. Mem. A.S.M.E. Dr. Timoshenko was educated in Russia and was called to the Polytechnic Institute of Kiev to occupy the chair of applied mathematics. For five years he was professor of applied mechanics in various engineering schools of St. Petersburg, and professor of applied mechanics at the Polytechnic Institute in Zagreb, Jugoslavia. In 1923 he entered the research department of the Westinghouse Electric & Manufacturing Company, East Pittsburgh, Pa., leaving there in 1927 to assume his present position.

[2] Mechanics Division, Westinghouse Research Laboratories, East Pittsburgh, Pa. Mr. Langer is a graduate of Stanford University, where he received the degree of B.A. in 1926 and of Engineer in 1928. He has been employed by the Westinghouse Research Laboratories since 1928, where he has been working on mechanical problems relating to railway engineering.

[3] The reports of this committee may be found in the following publications:
1st Progress Report: Proc. A.R.E.A., vol. 19 (1918); Trans. A.S.C.E., vol. 82 (1918).
2nd Progress Report: Proc. A.R.E.A., vol. 21 (1920); Trans. A.S.C.E., vol. 83 (1920); Circular No. S-II-10 of the A.R.A.
3rd Progress Report: Proc. A.R.E.A., vol. 24 (1923); Trans. A.S.C.E., vol. 86 (1923); Circular No. IV-32 of the A.R.A.
4th Progress Report: Proc. A.R.E.A., vol. 26 (1925); Trans. A.S.C.E., vol. 88 (1925).
5th Progress Report: A.R.E.A. Bulletin, vol. 31, no. 319, Sept., 1929.

[4] S. Timoshenko, "Method of Analysis of Statical and Dynamical Stresses in Rail," Proc. 2nd International Congress for Applied Mechanics, Zurich, 1926.
J. P. Shamberger, "A Magnetic Strain Gage." Proc. A.S.T.M., vol. 30 (1930), p. 1041.
B. F. Langer, "An Instrument for Measuring Small Displacements," Review of Scientific Instruments, vol. 2, 1931.
B. F. Langer and J. P. Shamberger, "The Measurement of Locomotive Wheel Loading." Proc. 3rd International Congress for Applied Mechanics, Stockholm, 1930.

[5] Such an analysis was made for the first time by Winkler. See his book, "Die Lehre von der Elasticität und Festigkeit," Prag, 1867. See also Dr. H. Zimmermann's book, "Die Berechnung des Eisenbahnoberbaues," 2nd ed., Berlin, 1930.
Contributed by the Applied Mechanics Division and presented at the Annual Meeting, New York, N. Y., Nov. 30 to Dec. 4, 1931, of THE AMERICAN SOCIETY OF MECHANICAL ENGINEERS.
NOTE: Statements and opinions advanced in papers are to be understood as individual expressions of their authors, and not those of the Society.

$$EI \frac{d^4y}{dx^4} = -ky \dots \dots \dots \quad \text{[2]}$$

we find[6] for the simplest case of a single load P acting in the vertical plane of symmetry on an infinitely long rail (Fig. 1):

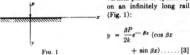

$$y = \frac{\beta P}{2k} e^{-\beta x} (\cos \beta x + \sin \beta x) \dots \quad \text{[3]}$$

Fig. 1

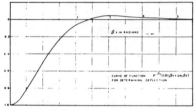

Fig. 2 Deflection Curve

The corresponding deflection curve is shown in Fig. 2. The maximum deflection is under the load P and is obtained from [3] by putting $x = 0$. Then

$$\delta = (y)_{x=0} = \frac{\beta P}{2k} \dots \dots \dots \quad \text{[4]}$$

This equation is usually employed in calculating the modulus of foundation k from the deflection of an actual rail. Measuring the deflection of the rail produced by a known vertical load P and using Equation [1], we can easily calculate from [4] the magnitude of k. (See description of the calibration of the track, Section III.)

From the solution [3] it is seen that the deflection curve is a wavy line, the amplitudes of which are damped out with the increase of the distance x from the point of the application of the load P. The length of the wave is

$$L = \frac{2\pi}{\beta} = 2\pi \sqrt[4]{\frac{4EI}{k}} \dots \dots \dots \quad \text{[5]}$$

Taking as an example a 130-lb. rail ($I = 72.8$ in.[4]) and assuming $k = 1500$ lb. per sq. in., we find from Equation [1] that $\beta = 0.020$ in.$^{-1}$ Then from Equation [5] we find that the length of a wave is more than 300 in. If instead of an infinitely long bar a bar of a finite length $2l$ is loaded at the middle, the equation for deflection can be put in the form

$$\delta = \alpha_1 \frac{\beta P}{2k}$$

In which α_1 is a numerical factor depending on the length of the bar. The values of this factor for various values of βl are given in the second line of the following table.[7]

[6] For derivation of formulas see S. Timoshenko, "Strength of Materials," vol. II, p. 401. Equation [3] is derived only for $x > 0$.
[7] See H. Zimmermann, "Die Berechnung des Eisenbahnober-baues," 2nd ed.

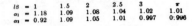

$l\beta$ =	1	1.5	2	2.5	3	π
α_1 =	1.18	1.09	1.08	1.04	1.02	1.01
α_2 =	0.92	1.09	1.05	1.01	0.997	0.996

It is seen that if a bar of a considerable length (say, $l\beta > 2.5$) is taken, the maximum deflection is about the same as in the case of an infinitely long bar.

Having the deflection curve, Equation [3], the bending moment is easily calculated from the equation

$$M = -EI \frac{d^2y}{dx^2} = \frac{P}{4\beta} e^{-\beta x} (\cos \beta x - \sin \beta x) \dots \quad \text{[6]}$$

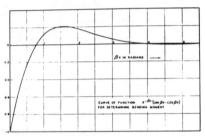

Fig. 3 Bending-Moment Curve

which moment is represented graphically in Fig. 3. The maximum bending moment is under the load. Substituting $x = 0$ in [6],

$$M_{max} = \frac{P}{4\beta} \dots \dots \dots \quad \text{[7]}$$

In the case of a bar of a finite length $2l$ loaded at the middle, the maximum bending moment is

$$M_{max} = \alpha_2 \frac{P}{4\beta}$$

The numerical values of the factor α_2 for various values of $l\beta$ are given in the table above. It is seen that for $l\beta > 2.5$, the maximum bending moment for a bar of finite length is practically the same as in the case of an infinitely long bar. In our laboratory tests (see Section II) $2l = 240$ in. and $\beta = 1/50$ in.$^{-1}$ Hence the stress conditions near the point of application of the load are practically the same as for an infinitely long bar.

By using Equation [1] the maximum bending moment is

$$M_{max} = \frac{P}{4} \sqrt[4]{\frac{4EI}{k}} \dots \dots \dots \quad \text{[7a]}$$

and using the notation S for the section modulus of the rail, the maximum bending stress is

$$\sigma_{max} = \frac{M_{max}}{S} = \frac{P}{4} \frac{\sqrt[4]{I}}{S} \sqrt[4]{\frac{4E}{k}} \dots \dots \dots \quad \text{[8]}$$

Since the right-hand member of [8] remains constant for geometrically similar cross-sections of rails, if E/k remains constant and P varies as the square of the linear dimensions of the cross-section, it can be concluded that σ_{max} remains unchanged if the weight of the rail per unit length increases in the same proportion as the load P. This conclusion gives a certain justification for increasing the weight of the rail in the same proportion as the axle load of the rolling stock that is to run over it.

The approximate value of the maximum pressure R_{max} on a tie is obtained by multiplying the maximum deflection, Equation [4], by the tie spacing a and by the modulus of foundation. Then

$$R_{max} = \frac{\beta P}{2k}\, ak = \frac{P}{2} \sqrt[4]{\frac{ka^4}{4EI}} \quad\dots\dots\dots [9]$$

It is seen from this that the pressure on the tie depends principally on the tie spacing a. It diminishes with a diminution of a and k, and with an increase in the flexural rigidity EI of the rail.

Having the solution for the vertical deflection produced by a single load P and using the principle of superposition, the deflection curve and the bending-moment diagram for any system of vertical loads can easily be obtained. For the purpose of illustrating the method of calculation, let us consider a 100-lb. rail with $I = 44$ in.^{4} and with $k = 1500$ lb. per sq. in. Then from [1], $\beta = 1/43.3$ in.$^{-1}$ Taking a system of four equal loads (Fig. 4) 66 in. apart, and fixing the origin of coordinates at the point of contact of the first wheel, the values of βx for four wheels are given in the following table.

Wheels	1	2	3	4
βx	0	1.52	3.05	4.57

By using now the curve in Fig. 3 and superposing the effects of all the loads acting on the rail, the bending moment under the first wheel is

$$M_1 = \frac{P}{4\beta}(1 - 0.207 + 0.051 + 0.008) = 0.75\,\frac{P}{4\beta}$$

i.e., the bending moment is 25 per cent less than that produced by a single load P. In the same manner, for the point of contact of the second wheel it is found that

$$M_2 = \frac{P}{4\beta}(1 - 2 \times 0.207 - 0.051) = 0.535\,\frac{P}{4\beta}$$

It is thus seen that, due to the action of the adjacent wheels, a considerable diminution of the bending moment under the second and the third wheels takes place.

In the same manner the bending moment at any other point can be calculated. For instance, at the point A, midway between the wheels 2 and 3, the bending moment is $-0.22\,P/4\beta$ and the rail is bent convex upward. From this we see that

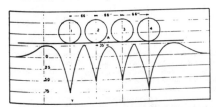

Fig. 4 Bending Moment Produced by Four Equal Wheel Loads
(Moment from one isolated load = unity.)

during the motion of such a system of loads as is shown in Fig. 4 the stresses change not only their magnitude but also their sign. Under the action of such cycles of stress, fatigue cracks in rails may occur. Many actual fractures in rails have a typical fatigue-crack appearance. The same kind of fracture occurs

also in splice bars (Fig. 5). The cracks usually begin at the points mm, which are the most remote points from the neutral axis nn. Sometimes cracks begin at the holes or at the re-entrant corners, where a high stress concentration takes place.

Fig. 5

By using the same method of superposition and the curve given in Fig. 2, the deflection produced by a system of vertical loads also can be easily calculated.

The inverse problem, i.e., of calculating the vertical pressures produced by locomotive wheels on the rail provided either the deflections or the stresses in the rail under the wheels have been determined by experiment, can also be solved without any difficulty. The application of such calculations to our experiments has always shown a good agreement between the sum of the calculated pressures and the actual weight of the locomotive used. This gives a certain justification to our assumption that the rail can be considered as a bar on a continuous elastic foundation.

2 Eccentric Vertical Load

If a vertical load P is applied with an eccentricity e, Fig. 6(a), it can be replaced by the load P centrally applied and by the torque Pe, Fig. 6(b). The central load produces vertical bending of the rail, discussed in the previous article, and the torque produces twisting of the rail.

If a rail with free ends is submitted to the action of two equal and opposite twisting couples M_t, the angle of twist may be roughly calculated from the known approximate equation of Saint-Venant, namely,

Fig. 6

$$\phi = \frac{M_t l}{C} \quad\dots\dots\dots\dots [10]$$

In which l = length of the rail, and

$$C = \frac{A^4 G}{40 I_p}$$

where
A = area of the cross-section
G = modulus of rigidity, and
I_p = polar moment of inertia.

To get a more accurate value for the torsional rigidity C, a direct torsion test is necessary. Such tests show that the actual value of the torsional rigidity is somewhat smaller than given by Saint-Venant's formula.

If the ends of the rail are fixed and a torque $2M_t$ is applied at the middle (Fig. 7), the twist of the rail is accompanied by a bending of the head and base of the rail.

Fig. 7

At any cross-section at a distance x from the middle, the torque M_t is transmitted partly in the form of simple twist and partly by bending of the head and of the base of the rail. Let M_1 and M_2 represent the first and second parts, respectively, and ϕ denote the angle of twist shown in Fig. 8. Then

$$M_1 = -C\,\frac{d\phi}{dx} \quad\dots\dots\dots\dots [11]$$

Fig. 8

The part M_2 is represented in Fig. 8 by the couple Qh, in which Q denotes the shearing force due to bending in the head and base of the rail, and h is the distance between the centroids of the head and base sections. Neglecting bending of the web[3] the position of the center of twist O is determined by the distances

$$h_1 = \frac{hI_2}{I_1 + I_2}, \qquad h_2 = \frac{hI_1}{I_1 + I_2} \dots\dots [12]$$

in which I_1 and I_2, respectively, denote the moments of inertia of the head and of the base sections with respect to the axis of symmetry of the rail cross-section. The shearing forces Q are then determined from the equation

$$Q = EI_1 \frac{d^2y}{dx^2} = EI_1 h_1 \frac{d^2\phi}{dx^2}$$

which gives

$$M_2 = Qh = Eh^2 \frac{I_1 I_2}{I_1 + I_2} \frac{d^3\phi}{dx^3} \dots\dots [13]$$

Using the notation

$$\frac{EI_1 I_2}{I_1 + I_2} = D$$

the differential equation of twist becomes

$$M_t = M_1 + M_2 = -C \frac{d\phi}{dx} + Dh^2 \frac{d^2\phi}{dx^2} \dots [14]$$

The solution of this equation for a long rail is

$$\frac{d\phi}{dx} = -\frac{M_t}{C}(1 - e^{-\gamma x}) \dots\dots [15]$$

in which

$$\gamma = \sqrt{\frac{C}{Dh^2}} \dots\dots [16]$$

It is seen that with an increase in the distance x from the middle cross-section of the rail, the second term in the parenthesis in the right-hand member of Equation [15] diminishes, and this equation approaches Equation [11] for simple torsion. The bending of the head and base of the rail have only a localized effect on the torsion of the rail. The results of the experiments made[9] are in very good agreement with Equation [15].

Imagine now that the rail shown in Fig. 7 is attached along its length to a continuous elastic foundation which resists the rotation of cross-sections of the rail during twist. Assuming that the resisting couple of the foundation per unit length of the rail is proportional at any cross-section to the corresponding value of the angle of twist ϕ and using for the factor of proportionality the symbol k_1, we find by differentiation of Equation [14],

$$\frac{dM_t}{dx} = -k_1\phi = -C \frac{d^2\phi}{dx^2} + Dh^2 \frac{d^4\phi}{dx^4}$$

and the equation for determining the angle of twist is

$$Dh^2 \frac{d^4\phi}{dx^4} - C \frac{d^2\phi}{dx^2} + k_1\phi = 0 \dots\dots [17]$$

---

[3] Further discussion regarding center of twist can be found in Timoshenko's "Strength of Materials," vol. 1.

[9] See paper by S. Timoshenko in Reports of Zürich Congress, loc. cit., footnote No. 4.

The solution of this equation shows that the twist of a rail affixed to an elastic foundation may be represented by a wavy line, and that the amplitude of the waves decreases with an increase in the distance from the loaded cross-section.

3 LATERAL LOAD

A single lateral force H applied to a rail produces lateral deflection and twist in the rail. Let us assume again that the rail is continuously supported by an elastic foundation which resists the lateral deflection and twist of the rail. Let k_1 be the modulus of foundation with respect to twist (see Art. 2) and k_2 the modulus of foundation with respect to lateral deflection. Denoting by y the lateral deflection of the center of twist of the rail and by ϕ the angle of twist, the deflection at the base of the rail is, from Fig. 9, $y - g\phi$, and the corresponding lateral reaction at the base per unit length is

$$q = k_2(y - g\phi) \dots\dots [18]$$

The reactive twisting moment per unit length is

$$m = k_1\phi \dots\dots [19]$$

Fig. 9

Now the differential equation of lateral bending of the rail is

$$EI_1 \frac{d^4y}{dx^4} = -k_2(y - g\phi) \dots\dots [20]$$

in which EI_1 is the flexural rigidity of the rail in a horizontal plane.

In discussing the twist of the rail we find from statics that the rate of change of torque is given by the equation:

$$\frac{dM_t}{dx} = qg - m$$

Using now the Equations [14], [18], and [19], we find

$$-C \frac{d^2\phi}{dx^2} + Dh^2 \frac{d^4\phi}{dx^4} = k_2(y - g\phi) - k_1\phi \dots\dots [21]$$

The two simultaneous Equations [20] and [21] determine the lateral bending and twisting of the rail under the action of the force H. In integrating these equations, the following conditions at the loaded cross-section must be satisfied:

$$\left.\begin{array}{l} \left(\dfrac{dy}{dx}\right)_{x=0} = 0; \quad EI_1\left(\dfrac{d^3y}{dx^3}\right) = \dfrac{1}{2} H; \quad \left(\dfrac{d\phi}{dx}\right)_{x=0} = 0 \\[2mm] -C\left(\dfrac{d\phi}{dx}\right)_{x=0} + Dh^2\left(\dfrac{d^3\phi}{dx^3}\right)_{x=0} = \dfrac{1}{2} Hf \end{array}\right\} \dots [22]$$

The other constants of integration must be chosen so as to make bending and twist of the rail disappear at infinity.

The application of this general theory in particular cases[9] shows that lateral bending and twist are of localized character; therefore if several lateral forces, such as lateral pressures produced by locomotive wheels, are acting on the rail, the maximum stress produced in the head of the rail by one of these forces is not substantially affected by the other forces.

4 EXPERIMENTAL DETERMINATION OF LATERAL FORCES, VERTICAL FORCES, AND THE ECCENTRICITY OF VERTICAL LOADS

In the most general case, the action of a force on the rail can be replaced by a vertical load P with a certain eccentricity e

and by a lateral load. In discussing stresses in rails and tracking characteristics of locomotives, it is of practical importance to know all three quantities: P, H, and e. There is no difficulty in finding experimentally the vertical load P. It is clear from

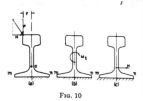

FIG. 10

Figs. 10(b) and 10(c) that at the two points m and n at the two opposite edges of the base of the rail the stresses produced by a torque M_t or by a lateral load H are numerically equal and of opposite sign. Hence by taking the strain-gage measurements at m and n, the average of these two readings can be used for determining the magnitude of the vertical load. This calculation can be made by using Equation [8] or, with a greater accuracy, by making a preliminary calibration of the track by applying a known vertical load and taking readings at m and n. The effect of the adjacent vertical loads on the readings at m and n can be determined by using the curve in Fig. 3.[10]

In our field experiments, a Westinghouse magnetic strain gage[11] was used and the strains produced at m and n by locomotive wheel pressures were recorded to a certain scale on an oscillograph film. Taking readings under all the wheels of the locomotive, the vertical pressures of these wheels on the rail can be calculated as it was explained in Art. 1. In order to obtain a higher accuracy, the curve obtained by calibration was usually applied instead of the theoretical curve, Fig. 3. Figs. 11, 12, and 13 show the strain gages attached to the base of the rail.

To determine the magnitude of lateral force H, Fig. 10(a), the longitudinal strain-gage measurements at the height of the center line of the rail were made as shown in Fig. 12 (strain gage B). The preliminary tests in the laboratory (see Section II) showed that this longitudinal strain depends principally on the magnitude of the lateral force H. The effect of the vertical force P, Fig. 10(a), is small and practically independent of the magnitude of the eccentricity e. Subtracting this small effect from the total reading of the strain gage B, the difference represents to a certain scale the lateral force H. The scale is usually established by making the preliminary calibration tests on the track.

For determining the eccentricity e of the vertical pressure P, the vertical strain gage C (Figs. 11 and 13) was used. This strain gage measures the change in the distance between the head and the base of the rail, which depends principally on the eccentricity e of the vertical load P. Thus having the readings on the strain gages A, B, and C, the quantities P, H, and e, determining completely the pressure of a wheel on the rail, can be calculated provided a preliminary calibration test on the track has been made. Several examples of such calculations will be given in discussing field measurements in Chapter III.

5 Dynamic Stresses in Rails

The dynamic deflection of the rail and the dynamic stresses under the action of the moving wheels of a locomotive may become much larger than those calculated on the basis of the static formulas discussed in Art. 1. There are various causes

---

[10] At the suggestion of J. P. Shamberger a method has been developed which will avoid the necessity of making corrections for the stress due to adjacent wheels when calculating vertical loads. Simultaneous measurements will be taken under each wheel of the locomotive.

[11] J. P. Shamberger, Proc. A.S.T.M., vol. 30 (1930), p. 1041.

FIG. 11 Strain Gages Mounted on Rail Model. End View

FIG. 12 Strain Gages Mounted on Rail Model. Gage Side of Rail

FIG. 13 Strain Gages Mounted on Rail Model. Outside of Rail

which may produce such an increase in deflection and stress, the principal ones being:

a Different kinds of irregularities in the shape of the wheel or rail, such as flat spots on the rim of the wheel, low spots on the rail, and discontinuities at the rail joints.

b Variation in the forces acting on the rail caused by variable spring forces on the wheel, the vertical component of the centrifugal force of the counterweights, and the vertical component of the forces in the connecting rods.

c Vibration of the rail under moving loads.

In discussing the dynamic stresses produced in a rail by the effect of a low spot (Fig. 14), let

FIG. 14

u = variable depth of the low spot, a given function of x

W/g = unsprung mass per wheel

$\alpha = 2k/\beta$, the vertical load necessary to produce a deflection equal to unity—see Equation [4]

y = additional deflection of the rail under the wheel due to the dynamic effect of the low spot.

Then the vertical displacement of the wheel due to the dynamic deflection of the rail and to the low spot is $y + u$, and the differential equation of motion of the wheel in the vertical direction is:

$$\frac{W}{g}\frac{d^2(y+u)}{dt^2} + \alpha y = 0 \dots\dots\dots\dots [23]$$

If v is the speed of the locomotive, then

$$\frac{du}{dt} = \frac{du}{dx}v; \qquad \frac{d^2u}{dt^2} = \frac{d^2u}{dx^2}v^2$$

and Equation [23] can be put in the form

$$\frac{W}{g}\frac{d^2y}{dt^2} + \alpha y = -\frac{W}{g}v^2\frac{d^2u}{dx^2} \dots\dots\dots [24]$$

If the shape of the low spot and the speed v are known, the right-hand member of [24] can easily be expressed as a function of the time and we arrive at the known equation of forced vibration of a system with one degree of freedom, the solution of which can be easily obtained in each particular case. Take, for instance, the low spot the shape of which is given by the equation

$$u = \frac{\delta}{2}\left(1 - \cos\frac{2\pi x}{l}\right) \dots\dots\dots\dots [25]$$

in which (see Fig. 14)

l = length of the low spot, and
δ = depth of the spot at the middle of its length.

Then the right-hand member of [24] becomes

$$-\frac{W}{g}v^2\frac{\delta}{2}\frac{4\pi^2}{l^2}\cos\frac{2\pi x}{l}$$

Measuring the time from the moment when the point of contact of the wheel coincides with the beginning of the low spot (Fig. 14), $x = vt$ and [24] becomes

$$\frac{W}{g}\frac{d^2y}{dt^2} + \alpha y = -\frac{W}{g}v^2\frac{\delta}{2}\frac{4\pi^2}{l^2}\cos\frac{2\pi vt}{l} \dots\dots [26]$$

Using the notations

T = period of vibration of the wheel on the rail[13]

$T_1 = l/v$ = time it takes the wheel to cross the low spot, we obtain a solution of Equation [26] satisfying the initial conditions

$$(y)_{t=0} = \left(\frac{dy}{dt}\right)_{t=0} = 0$$

in the following form:

$$y = \frac{\delta}{2}\frac{1}{1-\left(\frac{T_1}{T}\right)^2}\left(\cos\frac{2\pi t}{T_1} - \cos\frac{2\pi t}{T}\right) \dots\dots [27]$$

It is seen that the additional dynamic deflection is proportional to the depth of the spot δ and depends on the magnitude of the ratio T_1/T and on the position of the wheel. The variation of this deflection when the wheel is moving along the spot, i.e., in the interval $0 < t < T_1$ for different values of the ratio T_1/T, is shown in Fig. 15. At the beginning y is zero, and then becomes

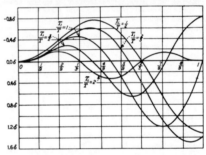

FIG. 15 ADDITIONAL (DYNAMIC) DEFLECTION PRODUCED BY FLAT SPOT ON WHEEL OR LOW SPOT ON RAIL
(δ = depth of flat spot; l = length of flat spot; T = period of free vibrations of wheel on rail; T_1 = time for wheel to cross flat spot.)

negative. This means that at the instant the wheel reaches the edge of the low spot the pressure on the rail and the deflection begin to diminish. This happens because the wheel, due to the low spot, begins to accelerate downward. When the wheel advances along the spot, the retardation of the vertical downward movement begins, and with it an increase in pressure and deflection, as seen from the figure. The values of the ratio of the maximum deflection y_{max} to the depth δ of the low spot, calculated from Equation [27] for different values of the ratio T_1/T, are given in the following table.

T_1/T	2	3/2	1	4/5	2/3	3/5	1/2
y_{max}/δ	0.33	0.65	1.21	1.41	1.47	1.45	1.33

A maximum additional deflection, equal to 1.47 δ, occurs at the speed corresponding to the ratio $T_1/T = 2/3$, i.e., when the time it takes the wheel to cross the low spot is equal to two-thirds of the period of natural vibration of the wheel on the rail. It can be concluded that the additional (dynamic) pressure due to

---

[13] The mass of the rail is neglected in this calculation. W/α is the static deflection of the rail under the action of the weight W of the wheel, then the formula for T coincides with the usual formula for the period of free vibration. See S. Timoshenko, "Vibration Problems in Engineering," p. 17.

the low spot is about equal to the load which produces a static deflection equal to 1.5 δ. Thus a comparatively small low spot produces, at certain speeds, a very appreciable dynamic effect, which must be added to the deflection calculated from the static Equation [4].

Similar results can be obtained for low spots of different contours. In the general case, Equation [26] becomes

$$\frac{W}{g}\frac{d^2y}{dt^2} + \alpha y = F(t)$$

and its general solution is[13]

$$y = \frac{g}{W}\frac{T}{2\pi}\int_0^{t_1} F(t) \sin \frac{2\pi(t_1 - t)dt}{T} \dots\dots[28]$$

Calculations made[14] for low spots of several different contours show that the ratio y_{max}/δ does not depend substantially on the contour of the low spot provided it is represented by a continuous curve. Hence we can state that the maximum additional dynamic pressure on the rail due to a low spot is about 50 per cent larger than the load which produces static deflection equal to the depth δ of the low spot.

The calculation made above for the case of a low spot can be applied also to the case of a flat spot on the rim of the wheel, because such a flat spot produces exactly the same vertical movements of the wheel as a low spot of the same shape on the rail.

The question of the dynamic effect of clearances between the rail and the tie and the dynamic effect of rail joints can also be treated in a similar manner.

In considering the additional wheel pressure of a locomotive due to the centrifugal force Q of a counterweight, we can use the theory of forced vibration. In calculating this pressure, we take the centrifugal force and multiply it by the magnification factor.[15] Then the additional pressure on the rail is

$$Q \frac{1}{1 - \left(\dfrac{T}{T_2}\right)^2}$$

in which T, as before, is the period of vibration of the wheel on the rail and T_2 is the time of one revolution of the wheel.

In this calculation the mass of the rail is neglected, which is justified because the time T_2 is usually large in comparison with the period of natural vibration of the rail.

To determine the period of lowest type of vibration, we note that this type of vibration consists of an oscillation of the rail in a vertical direction as an absolutely rigid body. Let q be the weight of the rail per unit length and k, as before, the modulus of foundation. The static deflection of the rail due to its own weight is q/k, and the period T_3 of the fundamental type of vibration is

$$T_3 = 2\pi \sqrt{\frac{q}{kg}}$$

Taking, for instance, a 130-lb. rail and $k = 1500$ lb. per sq. in.,

$$T_3 = 2\pi \sqrt{\frac{130}{36 \times 386 \times 1500}} = 0.0157 \text{ sec.}$$

This can be always considered as small in comparison with the time T_2 of one revolution of the wheels, and the magnification factor differs but little from unity.

II—LOCAL STRESSES IN RAILS

1 INTRODUCTION

In the previous section the rail was discussed as a beam on an elastic foundation, and it was shown that the usual theory for

FIG. 16 EQUIPMENT FOR STATIC FIELD TESTS

such bending can be applied to the rail as a whole. However, in the region near the point of application of the load the stresses deviate considerably from those that can be calculated from simple bending theory. In this section these local stresses near the load point will be discussed, and the results of some tests will be given.

The tests that will be mentioned were made partly on actual track and partly in the laboratory. The apparatus used for the static tests on actual track is shown in Fig. 16. A loaded flat car was supported from points outside the rail-tie structure. Hydraulic jacks were attached to the under side of the car directly over the rails in order to exert vertical loads. Lateral loads were produced by another hydraulic jack acting in such a way as to spread the rails apart. The magnitudes of the loads were read with hydraulic gages tapped into the high-pressure sides of the oil systems of the jacks. Deflections were measured with dial gages supported from outside the track, and stresses were measured with Huggenberger tensometers.

In the laboratory a 20-ft. length of rail was supported on cantilever springs spaced 21 in. apart to simulate track conditions. Fig. 17 shows the arrangement, and Fig. 18 details of one of the

[13] See S. Timoshenko, "Vibration Problems in Engineering," 1928, p. 20.

[14] See paper by S. Timoshenko in *Bulletin of Engineers*, St. Petersburg, 1915.

[15] See "Vibration Problems in Engineering," p. 18.

springs. The tests showed that the elasticity of these springs and the clamps holding the rail to them had a vertical modulus of foundation of 1500 lb. per sq. in. and a lateral modulus of 3000 lb. per sq. in. Lateral load was applied after turning the

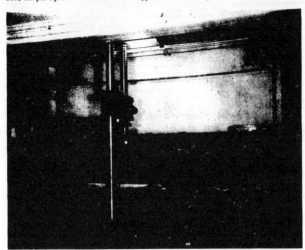

FIG. 17 EQUIPMENT FOR LABORATORY TESTS

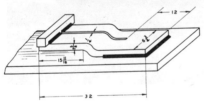

FIG. 18 SPRING USED IN LABORATORY TESTS

rail, springs, and base plate over on their sides so that the structure rested on the angles which were welded to the base plate.

2 WEB AND FILLET STRESSES

General. The tendency of American rail design has been toward the increase of vertical rail stiffness, and a thin, high section has resulted. Considering the rail as a beam, it seems justifiable to remove material from the web and place it in the head or base in order to reduce the longitudinal stresses produced by vertical bending of the rail as a whole. However, if the web is made too thin it will compress vertically or else bend, as a narrow plate, away from the longitudinal vertical plane of the rail, and vertical stress in the web will result.

Experience and direct investigation have taught the stress analyst to beware of rapid changes in section. In the cross-section of a rail such rapid changes are to be observed at the points where the web meets the head and where it meets the base. The vertical stresses in the fillets at these points cannot easily be investigated by direct strain-gage measurements on a steel rail. The method used by the authors was that of measuring the stress in the web of an actual rail, after which photo-

elastic methods[16] were employed to find the relationship between the web stress and the fillet stress.

Concentric Vertical Load. A vertical load applied at the center of the head causes compression in the web. This vertical load, concentrated in a very small area at its point of application, spreads out along the rail as it progresses downward. In the case of a two-dimensional problem the pressure on a semi-cylindrical sec-

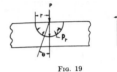

FIG. 19

tion of radius r and thickness b (see Fig. 19) produced by a load P is[17]

$$p_r = -\frac{2P \cos \theta}{\pi b r}$$

If we consider only the section of the rail directly under the load, then $\theta = 0$, $\cos \theta = 1$, and the compression in the web varies in inverse proportion to the thickness b of the web, and the distance r from the load. The applicability of this theory is demonstrated in a qualitative way by the test results shown in Fig. 20. Here, among other data, the vertical web stress produced by a centrally applied vertical load (A) is shown for different points along the height of the web. It will be observed that the stress near the bottom of the web is much less than that near the top.

Eccentric Vertical Load. When a vertical load is applied nearer one edge of the head than the other, it produces vertical bending in the web as well as compression. In Fig. 20 one of the curves shows the vertical web stress produced by an eccentric vertical load (B). Note that at the top of the web, on the side of the rail at which the load is applied, the stress produced by this type of loading is the highest of any found in the web. Fig. 21 shows the vertical web stress $3\frac{3}{4}$ in. above the base of a P. S. 130-lb. rail in actual track produced by centrally applied and eccentrically applied vertical loads. The maximum compression is somewhat higher than that shown in Fig. 20, probably due to the greater stiffness of the foundation ($k = 3000$ lb. per sq. in.).

Because it caused the most severe condition in the web, the eccentric vertical type of loading was investigated photoelastically. The photoelastic method was applied to thin celluloid models of rail sections.[18] A thin section to which only a single concentrated load is applied does not completely represent a rail because it takes no account of the spreading of the load in the longitudinal direction nor of the torsional rigidity of the head.

This torsional rigidity, in a full rail, opposes the rotation of the head at the section where the load is applied. In the loading arrangement used in the photoelastic tests (see Fig. 22) the force applied to the extension of the head at A acted in the same way

[16] See "Photoelasticity for Engineers," by E. G. Coker, *General Electric Review*, Nov. and Dec., 1920, and Jan., March, May, 1921.
[17] See Timoshenko, "Strength of Materials," vol. I, p. 147.
[18] The photoelastic tests described here were made by R. V. Baud of the Westinghouse Research Laboratories.

on the celluloid model. In the tests on steel rails it was found that the rotation of the head was $1/7$ of what it would have been if a section only 1 in. thick had been used. Therefore the force at A and its moment arm were adjusted so as to reduce by $6/7$ the twisting moment on the head produced by the main part of the eccentric load at B.

The spreading of the load along the length of the rail was taken into account by correcting the readings in accordance

FIG. 22   LOADING ARRANGEMENT USED IN PHOTOELASTIC TESTS

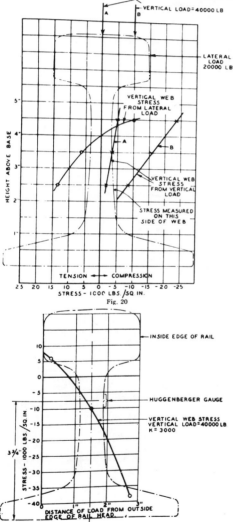

Fig. 20

Fig. 21

with the amount of spreading found in tests on steel rails. That is, the slope of the curve was adjusted to conform to the slope of curve B, Fig. 20.

Fig. 23 shows the results of photoelastic tests on a model representing the P. S. 130-lb. rail. The stress along the boundary of the cross-section was measured. It will be noted that the

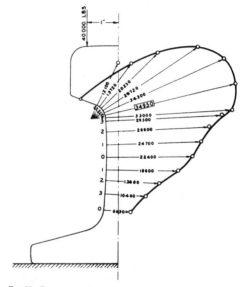

FIG. 23   RESULTS OF PHOTOELASTIC TEST. P. S. 130-LB. RAIL

highest stress occurs in the fillet under the head, and that the stresses near the bottom of the web are comparatively low because of the correction for the spreading of the load along the length of the rail. These results suggested that a more favorable stress distribution could be obtained if material were removed from the bottom of the web and placed nearer the tops. A model of such a rail was made and tested, with the result shown in Fig. 24. The redistribution of material in the web lowered the maximum stress by about 22 per cent.

The photoelastic results were not considered reliable in the

FIG. 20 (UPPER LEFT-HAND COLUMN) VERTICAL WEB STRESS PRODUCED BY VARIOUS TYPES OF LOADING. P. S. 131-LB. RAIL IN LABORATORY

FIG. 21 (LOWER LEFT-HAND COLUMN) VERTICAL WEB STRESS PRODUCED BY VARIOUS LOCATIONS OF VERTICAL LOAD. P. S. 130-LB. RAIL IN TRACK

region of the base and the fillet at the bottom of the web because the method of attachment of the base of the celluloid model was not similar to that of an actual rail. A few measure-

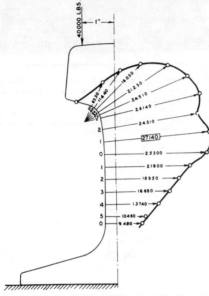

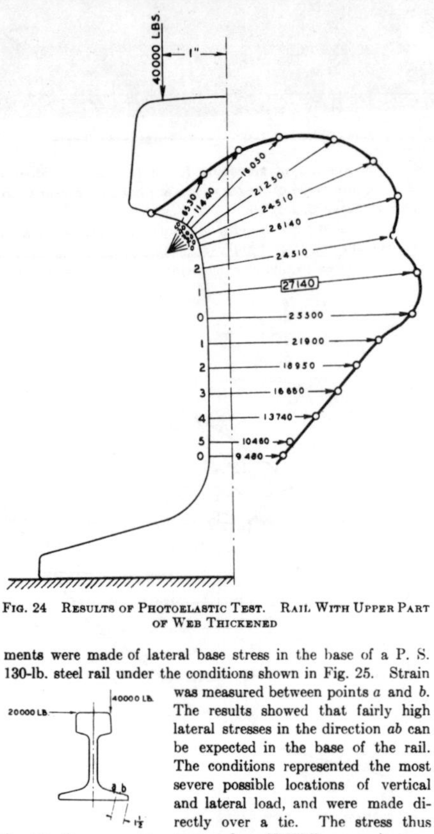

FIG. 24   RESULTS OF PHOTOELASTIC TEST. RAIL WITH UPPER PART OF WEB THICKENED

ments were made of lateral base stress in the base of a P. S. 130-lb. steel rail under the conditions shown in Fig. 25. Strain was measured between points a and b. The results showed that fairly high lateral stresses in the direction ab can be expected in the base of the rail. The conditions represented the most severe possible locations of vertical and lateral load, and were made directly over a tie. The stress thus measured was 28,000 lb. per sq. in. compression.

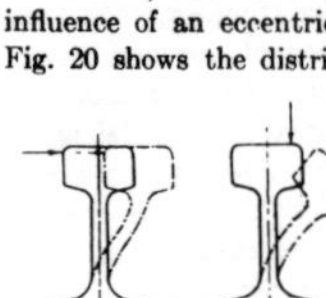

FIG. 25   CONDITIONS UNDER WHICH LATERAL BASE STRESS WAS MEASURED

Lateral Load. When a lateral load is applied to the head of a rail, the web bends, but not in the same manner as it does under the influence of an eccentric vertical load. One of the curves in Fig. 20 shows the distribution of vertical web stress produced by lateral load along the height of the web. The torsional rigidity of the head almost completely prevents rotation of the top of the web, and the curvature is of the type shown in Fig. 26 (*a*) instead of that shown in Fig. 26(*b*). Because of this reverse curvature, the stress in the fillet under the head is compression on the side near the lateral load

FIG. 26   NATURE OF DEFLECTION PRODUCED BY (*a*) LATERAL AND (*b*) ECCENTRIC VERTICAL LOAD

Summary. For the magnitudes of vertical and lateral load found in practice (see Section III) the highest vertical web stress is produced by a vertical load applied near one edge of the rail head. In most rails this maximum stress is located in the fillet under the head, and the stress in the lower part of the web is comparatively low. The vertical web stress produced by lateral load is usually not excessive. This stress is important because, for the most usual combination of high vertical and lateral load (vertical load applied eccentrically on the gage side of the head and lateral load directed away from the center of the track), the stresses from the two load components (vertical and lateral) are additive, both being compression.

The points brought out by these tests that are of value to the rail designer are that a more uniform stress distribution can be obtained by thickening the upper part of the web at the expense of the lower part, and that bringing the wheel load nearer the center of the rail will lower the stress in the fillet under the head.

3   LONGITUDINAL STRESSES NEAR THE POINT OF LOAD APPLICATION

At points within about 10 in. of the load, the longitudinal stresses are quite different from those that could be calculated from the ordinary bending theory, as may be seen from the experimental data plotted in Figs. 27 and 28. These show the distribution of head and base stress along the length of a P. S. 130-lb. rail in track. The base stress was measured 0.25 in. above the bottom of the rail and the head stress 1.2 in. below the top.

In order to account analytically for this distribution of stress near the load, it is necessary to add to the usual bending stress the effects due to four different phenomena:

(*a*)   Torsion (Produced by lateral or eccentric vertical load)
(*b*)   Bending of the head alone on the elastic foundation formed by the web (Produced by any type of vertical or lateral load)
(*c*)   Reverse bending due to the concentration of the load (Produced by any type of load)
(*d*)   Contact stress (Produced mostly by vertical load).

(*a*)   *Torsion.* In a rail in pure torsion a cross-section originally plane does not remain so after the twisting moment has been applied. A rail built into a track, however, may be considered as an infinitely long bar with a twisting moment applied at some section along its length. (See Section I, Article 5.) In this case, due to symmetry, the section at which the load is applied cannot deform. But since the cross-sections at a little distance from the load do deform, there must be longitudinal tensions and compressions set up in the rail. A rail twists when a lateral or an eccentric vertical load is applied to the head.

The differential equation for a rail in torsion has been given in Section I, Equation [14], and its solution in Equation [15]. The longitudinal stresses set up near the load are such as would be produced by the forces Q in Fig. 8. The lateral deflection of the head is $h_1\phi$. Therefore the bending moment in the head is

$$M_H = EI_1 h_1 \frac{d^2\phi}{dx^2}$$

Differentiating the expression already obtained for $d\phi/dx$ in Equation [15] with respect to x, we obtain

$$\frac{d^2\phi}{dx^2} = -\gamma \frac{M_t}{C} e^{-\gamma x} \dots\dots\dots\dots\dots [29]$$

At the load point, $x = 0$ and $e^{-\gamma x} = 1$, therefore,

$$M_{II} = -EI_1 h_1 \gamma \frac{M_t}{C} \quad \dots \dots \dots \quad [30]$$

and similarly, the bending moment in the base is

$$M_{II} = -EI_2 h_2 \gamma \frac{M_t}{C} \quad \dots \dots \dots \quad [31]$$

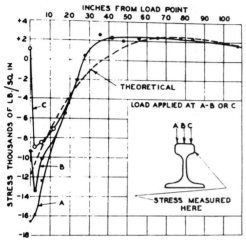

FIG. 27 LONGITUDINAL HEAD STRESS FROM 30,000 LB. VERTICAL LOAD. P. S. 130-LB. RAIL IN TRACK

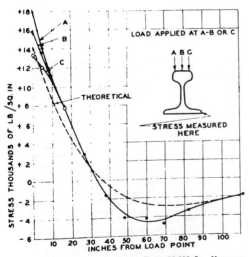

FIG. 28 LONGITUDINAL BASE STRESS FROM 30,000 LB. VERTICAL LOAD. P. S. 130-LB. RAIL IN TRACK

From these expressions and the dimensions of the head and base of the rail, the longitudinal stresses set up by the forces Q (Fig. 8) can be calculated.

(b) *Bending of the Head Alone.* If the base of a rail were rigidly supported and a vertical or lateral load applied in the usual way, there would still be bending stresses set up in the head. Since the head is much wider than the web, it may be

roughly considered as a beam bending on the elastic foundation formed by the web. The theory for this type of bending is similar to that already given for a rail bending on the elastic foundation formed by the ties, ballast, and ground. The only difference is in the calculation of the elasticity of the web foundation. The modulus of foundation, k, is by definition the load per unit length necessary to produce unit deflection at the union between the head and the web.

When the load is vertical, only the compression of the web need be considered. For vertical load, the modulus of foundation of the web is

$$k = \frac{tE}{d} \quad \dots \dots \dots \dots \quad [32]$$

where t = average web thickness,
d = web height, and
E = Young's modulus for rail material.

When the load is lateral the bending of the web must be taken into account. In the measurements of vertical web stress described above it was seen that the web bends, not as a cantilever, but in the manner shown in Fig. 26(a), without rotation of the top of the web. The deflection at the end of a cantilever, the end of which is prevented from rotating, is one-fourth that of a simple cantilever. Therefore, for lateral load, the modulus of foundation of the web is

$$k = \frac{Et^3}{d^3} \quad \dots \dots \dots \dots \quad [33]$$

(c) *Reverse Bending Due to Concentration of Load.* Consider a small hemispherical region concentric with the point of load application (see Fig. 29). The pressure on each element of the hemispherical surface has a component in the direction of the length of the rail. These components add together to form the forces F, which cause a bending moment in the rail as well as a uniform tension. The integration of these longitudinal components over the hemispherical area shows that $F = P/\pi$. The uniform tension produced by this effect is F/A, where A is the cross-sectional area of the rail. The bending moment that it produces is F times the distance of the point of application of the load from the neutral axis of the rail. The effect of the forces F should be considered for both vertical and lateral bending.

(d) *Contact Stress.* The contact pressure between the rail and the wheel is of importance in the study of the plastic flow of the rail head and the tire. The stress inside the head produced by contact pressure may also be a factor in hastening certain types of rail failure.

The solution for the pressure between the surfaces of two elastic bodies in contact was first given by Hertz, and can be found in most books on elasticity.[19] The solution for the state of stress inside a body produced by a concentrated load on its surface is also well known.[20] However, the calculation of the state of stress inside a body produced by a distributed load on its surface is exceedingly complicated, and is one that must be solved in each particular case of surfaces of contact for a complete, accurate study of the conditions in a rail. Two such solutions have been made independently, and are in perfect

[19] See "Strength of Materials," by S. Timoshenko. For the consideration of the tangential component of contact stress such as can be produced by tractive effort, see Fromm, "Schlupfberechnung beim Rollen Deformierbarer Schieben," *Zeitschrift für Angewandte Mathematik und Mechanik,* 1927, p. 27; also, R. Lorenz, "Schiene und Rad," Z.V.D.I., no. 6, 1928, p. 173.
[20] See A. E. H. Love, "Mathematical Theory of Elasticity," p. 190.

agreement. One was made by Prof. N. M. Belajef, Mechanical Laboratory, Institute of Ways of Communication, Leningrad, Russia. The solution best available to American readers is that of H. R. Thomas and V. A. Hoersch.[21] They have put their solution into a very usable form, and have also checked it experimentally by means of the Fry strain-etch method. The problem of the rail and the wheel is considered as that of two crossed cylinders.

The approximate formula given by Thomas and Hoersch for the maximum shear in two crossed cylinders in contact is

$$\text{Max. shearing stress} = \frac{11{,}750\ P^{1/3}}{(R_1/R_2)^{0.271}R_2^{2/3}} \dots \dots [34]$$

where P = load in pounds
R_1 = radius of larger cylinder in inches
R_2 = radius of smaller cylinder in inches
$1 < R_1/R_2 < 8$, and
Poisson's ratio = 0.25

The contact pressure between the two elastic bodies and the maximum shearing stress inside the bodies are functions of the load and the radii of curvature of the bodies. Thus a small wheel with a light load may produce just as much plastic flow in the rail head as a larger wheel with a heavier load. Thomas and Hoersch give the following two numerical examples to illustrate this point.

Wheel diam., in.	Radius of rail head, in.	Load, lb.	Depth to point of max. shear, in.	Area of contact, sq. in.	Max. shearing stress, lb. per sq. in.
33	14	25,000	0.121	0.215	56,500
80	14	60,000	0.179	0.502	59,800

Comparison Between Calculated and Experimental Results. The longitudinal stresses in the head and base produced by eccentric vertical load were calculated for the cross-section directly under the load and compared with experimental results from measurements on an actual track. (See Figs. 27 and 28.) The calculated stresses for concentric load were assumed, perforce, to be equal to the experimental values, since the modulus of foundation of the track could be determined only from the experiments themselves, and there was no purely theoretical method of calculating the stresses from simple bending.

The local stresses produced by eccentric vertical load were calculated according to the theories already outlined. The lateral bending due to twist was calculated from Equations [30] and [31], and modulus of foundation of the web from [32]. The forces F, Fig. 29, were considered to produce uniform tension and bending. The contact stress was calculated according to a theory in which it is assumed that the load is concentrated instead of distributed over a small area. The rail used was P. S. 130-lb.

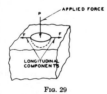

FIG. 29

Fig. 30 presents a comparison between the calculated and the experimental results. The very good experimental confirmation of the calculated stress values shows that the theories outlined above are well founded.

4 TRANSVERSE FISSURES

Transverse fissures are fatigue cracks which form inside the

[21] See "Stresses Due to the Pressure of One Elastic Solid Upon Another," Univ. of Ill., Engineering Experiment Station, Bulletin No. 212.

heads of rails in the transverse plane. They have become increasingly prevalent in America during the past score of years, and are particularly dangerous because they cannot be detected by the usual methods of inspection.

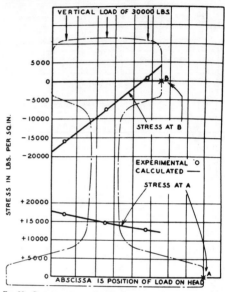

FIG. 30 COMPARISON OF CALCULATED LONGITUDINAL STRESSES WITH EXPERIMENTAL RESULTS

A long step toward the elimination of accidents from transverse fissures was made when E. A. Sperry introduced his fissure-detector car,[22] by means of which track can be inspected for the presence of such internal flaws. The method is an electrical one. A current is passed through the rail and used to detect changes in resistance such as occur when a transverse fissure is present. Cars of this type have already been used with good success on several railroads.

The detection of fissures in track is at best not a complete solution of the problem. What is really necessary is the determination of the cause of fissures and the development of a means for their prevention. The work of Freeman and others at the Bureau of Standards,[23] as well as the evidence of other observers, points to the conclusion that transverse fissures occur when, and only when, the rail head has internal cracks produced during the cooling period of manufacture. Freeman has studied the tensile properties of rail steels at elevated temperatures as well as the process of cooling of the rail. The study of tensile properties showed that some steels have, around 500 to 650 deg. cent., a ductility less than at normal atmospheric temperature. The study of the cooling process showed that tensile stresses are apt to be set up in the head at the time that the metal on the inside of the head is passing through this brittle range. If, then, we have the combination of a steel subject to brittleness

[22] See "Non-Destructive Detection of Flaws," by E. A. Sperry, *Iron Age*, vol. 122, no, 20, Nov. 15, 1928.
[23] See "Tensile Properties of Rail and Other Steels at Elevated Temperatures," by J. R. Freeman and G. W. Quick. Trans. A.I.M.E., Iron and Steel Division, 1930, p. 225.

at about 550 deg. cent. and a fairly rapid cooling of rails rolled from that steel, we are apt, according to Freeman, to find internal cracks in the head of the rail which will develop into transverse fissures under the action of wheel loads. There is some question as to whether the amount of the increase in brittleness found by Freeman is sufficient to account for the appearance of cracks during cooling. It may be that the cracks are due to the stresses on the inside of the head being tension in three dimensions (see Fig. 31), which is a very severe stress condition. It appears, then, that a complete solution of the problem may come with the development of an economical method for the slow cooling of rails.

FIG. 31

Attempts have been made to place the entire blame for transverse fissures on the stresses in the rail head produced by bending and contact pressure. There are, undoubtedly, high stresses in the head, and there is no question but that they cause a fissure to grow after it has once started. It seems unlikely, however, that these stresses ever start cracks in sound material, since fissures seldom, if ever, start where the bending and contact stresses are a maximum.

It is seen that transverse fissures are connected with the shape of the rail cross-section only in so far as the ratio between the volume and surface of the head affects the rate of cooling. The evidence now available indicates that the problem is one that can best be solved by the metallurgist and the manufacturer. A suggested line of attack would be the study of residual stresses and the effect upon them of different methods and rates of cooling.

III—FIELD TESTS

1 METHODS AND APPARATUS

The field tests made were primarily for the purpose of studying the action of various types of locomotive running gear on curved and tangent track. The results that were obtained are of major importance in the study of rail stresses because they tell what the forces are which can be exerted on rails in actual operation.

On the basis of the information obtained from the static tests (see Sections I and II), a method was devised whereby strain-gage measurements could be taken under dynamic conditions in such a way that they could be used to determine vertical and lateral wheel loads. This method is described in Section I.

At each test location a short static calibration was made to determine the relationship between vertical load and average base stress, and that between lateral load and web stress, for the particular spot where the tests were being made. The load was also applied at various distances from the gages to determine what correction should be made for the stress due to adjacent wheels. The apparatus used for these static calibrations was similar to that used in the static-stress studies. It consisted of a loaded car to which hydraulic jacks were rigidly attached, so that by moving the car the jacks could quickly be spotted over the point on the track where the calibration was to be made. Lateral loads were applied by means of a jack lying crosswise between the rails.

The calibration car was placed with the hydraulic jacks directly over the magnetic strain gages. Vertical and lateral loads were applied, and readings taken from all the gages. (Figs. 11, 12, and 13 show the location of the instruments.) The car was then moved to two or three locations, 3 to 10 ft. distant from the gages, and the procedure was repeated. At each location the car body was raised off the center pins with jacks in order to isolate the load applied at the center of the car as nearly as possible.

The deduction of wheel loads from stress data can best be explained by means of a simple example. Suppose we have a record of strain-gage measurements from a four-wheeled vehicle which has passed over the test spot, and wish to find the vertical loads. The axle spacing is 60 in. The static calibration has given us the two necessary curves, which are:

Curve No.	Abscissa	Ordinate
(1)	Distance from load	Average base stress from vertical load
(2)	Vertical load	Average base stress at load point

The peak base-stress readings on the north rail are:

	1st axle	2nd axle
Inner base	9,600	8,000
Outer base	10,800	6,000
Average	10,200	7,000

From curve (1) it is found that at 60 in. from the load the rail is in reverse bending and the base stress is −15 per cent of the base stress directly under the load.

Let A = maximum stress due to 1st wheel alone
B = maximum stress due to 2nd wheel alone

Then

$$10,200 = A - 0.15B$$

and

$$7000 = B - 0.15A$$

Solving for A and B,

$$A = 11,500, \text{ and } B = 8730$$

From curve (2) we can find the wheel loads corresponding to A and B, the corrected base stress values.

The method used for finding lateral loads is similar, with the web stress used in place of the average base stress. Ordinarily, due to the shorter wave length of the stress distribution from lateral load, no correction need be made for adjacent wheels, and curve (2) can be used directly.

For vehicles with more than two axles the calculations are more complicated, but the method is the same. When each stress reading has to be corrected for the effects of three or four adjacent wheel loads, it is best to solve the simultaneous equations by trial and successive approximations rather than by a direct method.

A typical oscillograph record of rail stress is shown in Fig. 32.

2 TESTS ON THE GREAT NORTHERN RAILWAY

Description of Locomotives and Operating Conditions. Field

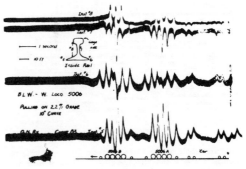

FIG. 32 TYPICAL OSCILLOGRAPH RECORD OF RAIL STRAIN

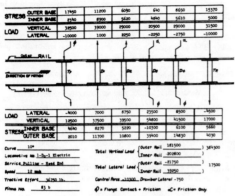

FIG. 33 WHEEL LOAD DIAGRAM

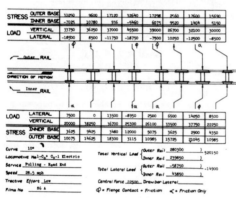

FIG. 34 WHEEL LOAD DIAGRAM

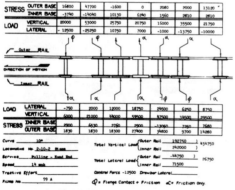

FIG. 35 WHEEL LOAD DIAGRAM

electrified portion of the Cascade Division, and for all types of locomotives operating over the Division, namely,

Electric, 1-D$_0$-1 (Mikado), G. N. Class Z-1
Electric, 1-C$_0$ + C$_0$-1 (Mallet), G. N. Class Y-1
Steam, 2-8-2 (Mikado), G. N. Class O-4
Steam, 2-10-2 (Santa Fe), G. N. Class Q-1
Steam, 2-6-0 + 0-8-0 (Mallet), G. N. Class M-2

The three test locations included a tangent, a 2-deg. 30-min. curve, and a 10-deg. curve, all on a 2.2 per cent grade. The

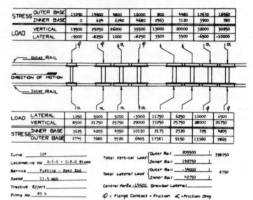

FIG. 36 WHEEL LOAD DIAGRAM

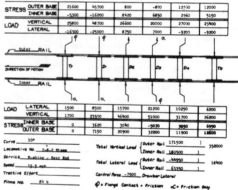

FIG. 37 WHEEL LOAD DIAGRAM

tangent and the 10-deg. curve had P. S. 130-lb. rail and the 2-deg. 30-min. curve had Great Northern 110-lb. rail. The speeds were mostly low, and never exceeded 30 m.p.h. As a consequence, the only severe conditions were found on the 10-deg. curve.

Results. Figs. 33–37 give the results from one representative test of each of the five locomotives on the 10-deg. curve. The directions of the arrows opposite the wheels indicate the directions of the lateral guiding forces exerted on the wheels, and so help to visualize the manner in which the locomotive is made to follow the curvature of the track against the resistance of friction and inertia. A minus sign preceding the value of lateral load indicates a force on the rail directed away from the center of curvature of the track.

tests were made on the Great Northern Railway during the months of August and September, 1929. Track stresses were measured at three locations between Merritt and Berne on the

Vertical Loads. Although the sum of all the vertical loads for any one test is always practically equal to the static weight of the locomotive, it will be observed that there is considerable non-uniformity in the loads on separate wheels. This non-uniformity is due to six different phenomena:

(1) Oscillations set up by unevenness in the track
(2) Rotation of counterbalance
(3) Angularity of connecting rod
(4) Longitudinal weight transfer. This is due to the height of the drawbar above the rail. The tractive effort at the level of the rail is resisted by the drawbar force, which produces a moment tending to lift the front of the locomotive into the air when it is pulling
(5) Centrifugal or superelevation force, when the locomotive is not traveling at the speed for which the curve is superelevated
(6) Lateral forces at the rims of the wheels, either flange pressures or friction. The lateral forces at the wheel rims are resisted at the wheel hubs, which causes a turning moment on each axle which can only be resisted by an unbalance in the vertical loads.

In low-speed operation, such as these tests represent, (5) and (6) are by far the most important effects, and they occur only on curves. The tests on the tangent stretch did show some irregularity in the vertical loads, but this may have been due largely to friction in the equalization system not allowing the wheel loads to readjust themselves after the active unbalancing forces

load is due to friction at the tread and how much to direct flange pressure? and (2) What is the angle between the vertical plane of the wheel and the vertical plane of the rail? (angle of incidence). In order to answer these questions it is necessary to make a detailed study of the action of the locomotive, which is beyond the scope of this paper. However, such a study has been made for a few of the test conditions used, and some of the results will be given. It can be shown that the amount of wear should be roughly proportional to the actual flange pressure and the angle of incidence of the wheel.[24] If we multiply these two values together we get a "wear factor" which can be used for a comparative study of the wear produced by various wheels. Table 1 presents a few typical results.

Table 1 shows that a high lateral load does not necessarily mean excessive flange and rail wear, since the wear depends so much on the actual flange pressure and the angle of incidence. In the first example given in the table the actual lateral load was quite low, but analysis showed that it was made up of a high flange pressure and a large friction force acting in opposite directions, and that the angle of incidence was large. It may be observed that the highest wear factors always occur on leading outer drivers. The last three examples in the table give the highest wear factors found on the locomotives to which they belong. It may be said that in general a high lateral force at the leading outer wheel of a multi-axled wheel base is indicative of excessive flange wear, whereas a high lateral force at one of the rear inner wheels is no cause for alarm.

Stresses. The only stresses which were measured directly

TABLE 1 WEAR FACTORS FOR VARIOUS LOCOMOTIVES

Locomotive	Service	Driver	Lateral load, lb. (exp.)	Wear factor
Electric, 1–D₀–1	1st of 2 cabs pulling	1st outer	1,000	971
Electric, 1–D₀–1	1st of 2 cabs pulling	3rd inner	23,500	72
Electric, 1–C₀ + C₀–1	1 cab pulling	3rd outer	21,250	495
Electric, 1–C₀ + C₀–1	1 cab pulling	4th outer	5,500	1870
Electric, 1–D₀–1	Regenerating at head end	1st outer	11,750	2540
Electric, 1–C₀ + C₀–1	Regenerating in train	4th outer	11,000	2640
Steam, 2–10–2	Pushing at rear end	1st outer	25,250	4800

had been removed. The effect of lateral force on vertical load distribution can be observed in Figs. 33–37 wherever the lateral forces are particularly high. See, for example, the third driving axle in Fig. 33, or the first driving axle in Fig. 35. On the third driver in Fig. 33 the total lateral force on the axle is 23,500–2250 or 21,250 lb. On a 56-in. driver this produces a turning moment of $28 \times 21,250 = 595,000$ in-lb. The vertical forces producing the resisting couple are 58 in. apart and so must be 59,500/58 or 10,250 lb. This would produce a difference between the vertical loads of 20,500 lb. Actually, there was a difference of 34,300 lb., the remainder of which must have been due to superelevation and other effects.

Lateral Loads. The tests showed that the lateral forces were negligible on the tangent location and fairly small on the 2-deg. 30-min. curve, as might be expected for low-speed operation. Figs. 33–37 show the lateral forces on the 10-deg. curve.

The importance of lateral wheel loads in the study of rail stress has already been made obvious in Sections I and II. However, when we come to study the action of the locomotive itself, two new factors present themselves which increase still more the importance of the lateral load. One is the sixth of the causes mentioned for non-uniformity in the vertical loads. A lateral load not only produces rail stress by itself, but it increases the accompanying vertical load with a consequent increase in stress. The other factor is that the magnitude of the lateral load, together with the manner in which it is applied, is a measure of flange wear and rail side wear.

The study of the manner of application of the lateral load involves answering two questions: (1) How much of the lateral

were those in a longitudinal direction in the base and in the web of the rail. The longitudinal web stresses were very small and were used only as a means of measuring lateral forces. The highest base stresses measured at the three locations were as follows:

Test location	Position	Stress, lb. per sq. in.
Tangent	Outer base	12,200
2° 30′ curve	Outer base, outer rail	19,400
10° curve	Outer base, inner rail	50,700

These results are typical of the general trend of the stresses found at the three locations and illustrate the importance of the lateral load as a stress producer.

After the forces and eccentricities were determined from the field tests, the head and web stresses were found by using the static-stress measurements described in Section II. The static-load tests showed that the longitudinal base stress is not apt to be the highest stress in the rail. It was found that a lateral flange pressure of 25,000 lb. would produce a stress of about 45,000 lb. per sq. in. compression on the gage side of the head. The maximum base stress found in the dynamic tests produced by a purely vertical load did not exceed 15,000 lb. per sq. in. The point of maximum bending stress on the head, which is the top of the gage side, is very nearly the same distance from the neutral axis as the point where the strain gage was located on the base in the dynamic tests, and so 15,000 lb. per sq. in.

[24] Based on the assumption that the wear between two surfaces is proportional to the pressure between the surfaces, the rubbing velocity, and the coefficient of friction.

can 'be used for the head also. Thus the compression on the gage side of the head due to bending may be said not to have exceeded 60,000 lb. per sq. in.

High stresses may also be expected in a vertical direction in the fillet under the head. The static tests showed that these stresses are produced mostly by vertical load and are affected quite considerably by the location of the vertical load on the head. This position of the vertical load was determined roughly in the dynamic tests by the use of a gage measuring vertical deflection of the head relative to the base. (See Section I, Art. 4.) It was found that this particular deflection was produced by vertical load much more than by lateral load, and was also affected by the position of the vertical load on the head. It could therefore be used as a rough measure of this position. A combination of the data obtained in the static tests, the photoelastic tests, and the dynamic tests led to the conclusion that for the maximum values of vertical and lateral load (60,000 lb. and 25,000 lb., respectively) and the most usual position of the vertical load ($^3/_4$ in. from the gage side of the head), the stress in the fillet under the head attains a value of 60,000 lb. per sq. in.

3 TESTS ON THE PENNSYLVANIA RAILROAD

Description of Locomotives and Operating Conditions. Field tests were made on the Pennsylvania Railroad during the months of September and October, 1930. The two test locations were both near Claymont, Del., on the Maryland Division.

Stresses were measured for three types of locomotives, which were:

Electric, 2–B$_0$–2 (4–4–4), P. R. R. Class O-1
Steam, 4–6–2 (Pacific), P. R. R. Class K-4s
Steam, 4–8–2 (Mountain), P. R. R. Class M-1a

The two test locations included a tangent and a 1-deg. curve, with practically no grade. The rail was P. S. 130-lb. Interest was centered chiefly on the high-speed tests, and maximum nominal speeds of 80, 90, and 100 miles per hour were attained with the Mountain, Pacific, and electric locomotives, respectively.

Results. The maximum stresses were found to be produced by dynamic effects at high speed, and were most severe at the tangent location.

It was observed that here, as in the tests on the Great Northern, the sum of the vertical wheel loads for a single test is about the same as the static weight of the locomotive, even though there was considerable non-uniformity in the loads on separate wheels. The non-uniformity was, however, due principally to oscillations and dynamic augments from the counterbalance.

The effect of oscillations on vertical loads is twofold. First of all, lateral oscillations produce lateral wheel loads at the rims which are resisted at the hubs and produce unbalance of the vertical loads as described earlier, in the discussion of the vertical loads found in the Great Northern tests. Secondly, slight unevennesses in the track can, at high speeds, start a rolling motion of the sprung weight of the locomotive, which results in a periodic shifting of the weight from one rail to the other. Studies of the vertical and lateral wheel loads on individual axles showed that the unbalance in the vertical loads could not all be due to the effect of lateral load, and consequently a considerable amount must have been due to rolling.

The tests showed that the highest lateral forces were produced, not by the guiding of the locomotives around the 1-deg. curve, but by lateral oscillations on the tangent.

The general importance of lateral loads has already been sufficiently discussed. From the point of view of rail study these tests serve to point out another cause of lateral wheel loads, that is, locomotive oscillations at high speeds. Flange

wear and rail side wear are not of importance in operation on tangent track and low-degree curves because of the small angles of incidence involved.

IV—CONCLUSIONS

1 PROPERTIES OF RAILS

In this paper an attempt has been made to point out some of the functions that a rail is called upon to perform, and to give what information is available on the factors which help it to perform those functions with a maximum of safety and economy. Let us consider for a moment some of the properties that a rail should possess.

Vertical Stiffness. The rigidity of a rail in the vertical plane is a very important factor. On it depends the pressure transmitted to individual ties, and hence it affects the amount of work necessary to maintain the track surface. The impact at the joints also depends partly on the vertical rigidity of the rail, but the problem of rail joints has not been dealt with in this paper.

Another factor which should be kept in mind when considering vertical rigidity is the damage to rolling stock caused by impact. As shown in Section I, Art. 5, the additional (dynamic) pressure due to a low spot on the rail or a flat spot on the wheel increases with the rigidity of the track.

Lateral Stiffness. Lateral stiffness is of importance in the study of locomotive oscillations at high speed as well as the study of operation on sharp curves at low speed. At high speed the problem is that of the lateral oscillations of the locomotive on the spring formed by the elasticity of the track and running gear. The problem is extremely complicated, and nothing definite can be said about the advantages or disadvantages of high lateral rigidity. In low-speed operation on sharp curves, the amount of lateral deflection of the rail will often affect the distribution of the flange pressures that guide the locomotive through the curve.

Soundness of Material. The recent prevalence of transverse fissures shows that there is a great deal of work to be done in improving the initial condition of rail steels. Manufacturers should study the cooling process with particular reference to the formation of residual stresses and internal flaws.

Hardness of Material. It is known that contact stresses produce plastic flow in the rail head, particularly at the joints. The very high axle loads used in America therefore make hard rail material a necessity. A large rail is given less mechanical work during the rolling process than a small one, which results in a coarser grain structure in the large rail. In order to have the same hardness as the small rail, it must have a higher carbon content. This tendency has resulted in carbon contents of 0.75 to 0.80 per cent in rails for main-line use, with consequent increase of brittleness. It is possible that the solution will be found in heat treatment, either of the whole rail or of the wearing surfaces.

Uniform Strength. There are several places in a rail where the stresses may be high. The optimum condition is to make all such places equally strong, and the experiments described in this paper give data which are helpful in designing a rail for uniform strength.

In considering the stress at any point of a rail, due thought should be given to whether the stress is of a cyclical and frequently repeated variety, or only occasional. If of the former the criterion of safety should be based on the fatigue limit of the material. If of the latter, the yield point can be used.

Studies in the fatigue of metals[13] have shown that the condi-

---

[13] See Soderberg, C. R., "Factor of Safety and Working Stress," Trans. A.S.M.E., APM-52-2 (1930).

tions of safety for repeated stress are well represented by a curve such as that shown in Fig. 38. In this diagram the abscissa represents "steady" stress and the ordinate, "alternating" stress. Any given stress cycle can be analyzed into a steady and an alternating component, much the same as is a fluctuating direct current in electrical theory. A stress cycle can therefore be represented by a point on the diagram, the coordinates of which are the steady and alternating components of the cycle. The limit of safety is determined by drawing a line from the yield point of the material on the steady-stress axis to the endurance limit on the alternating-stress axis. Points lying between this line and the axes represent safe conditions, and points lying outside the line represent unsafe conditions.[26]

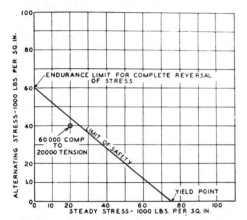

FIG. 38 DIAGRAM SHOWING LIMIT OF SAFETY OF STRESS CYCLES

As an example, take a stress range of 60,000 lb. per sq. in. compression to 20,000 lb. per sq. in. tension. The algebraic average of these two is 20,000, which is taken as the steady component. The variation from this point is plus and minus 40,000, which is the alternating component. Thus, for a steel with a yield point of 75,000 lb. per sq. in. and an endurance limit of 60,000 lb. per sq. in., such a stress is safe, but very near the border line, and slight defects in the material can easily cause failure.

Let us discuss some of the stresses mentioned in this paper from the viewpoint of their liability to cause failure. The values given are for 130-lb. rail.

Stresses Produced by Centrally Applied Vertical Load. This type of load produces vertical bending of the rail, compression of the web, and contact stress in the head. It is repeated often enough during the life of the rail to necessitate the consideration of fatigue.[27]

The stress due to vertical bending goes from tension to compression. The range is not apt to be more than from 15,000 lb. per sq. in. in one direction to 5000 lb. per sq. in. in the other.

The compression in the web directly under the load is produced by vertical bending of the head on the elastic foundation

<hr>

[26] Fatigue tests show that the true limit of safety is a curve and not a straight line. The line shown on the diagram is a convenient simplification of the actual data, and is known to err on the safe side.

[27] An exception must be made here for the augments of vertical load produced by some dynamic effects originating in the locomotive. For example, the augment produced by the rotation of the counterweight of a locomotive will not occur often enough at any one spot in a rail to produce fatigue.

formed by the web. Therefore it changes to tension a few inches away from the load, and the maximum tension is 20 per cent of the maximum compression (see Fig. 3). The wave length of this distribution is too short to allow the reversed stress between wheels to be more than 20 per cent of the maximum stress under one wheel. The highest compression that is apt to be found in the web due to centrally applied vertical load is 10,000 lb. per sq. in., so the stress range is from 10,000 lb. per sq. in. compression to 2000 lb. per sq. in. tension.

The contact stress produced by vertical load varies from zero to a maximum and is undoubtedly very high. However, it is also highly localized, and produces mostly plastic flow in the rail head.

Stresses Produced by Eccentrically Applied Vertical Load. This type of load produces all the stresses that are produced by centrally applied vertical load, with the addition of torsion, vertical bending stress in the web (see Section II, Art. 2), and lateral stress in the base (see Fig. 25). Its frequency of application is of the same order of magnitude as that of the centrally applied vertical load.

The torsion produced by this type of load is not severe, due to the shortness of the moment arm of the applied force. The lateral stress in the base is only high when the vertical load is eccentric on the outside of the head and accompanied by a high lateral flange pressure, which is an unusual condition.

The serious condition produced by eccentric vertical load is in the fillet under the head, and is due to bending of the web out of the vertical longitudinal plane. This stress goes from compression to tension, the same as the vertical web stress produced by centrally applied vertical load. Its maximum range is about 50,000 lb. per sq. in. compression to 10,000 lb. per sq. in. tension. When accompanied by a high lateral flange pressure, its maximum increases to about 60,000 lb. per sq. in. compression.

Stresses Produced by Lateral Load. Lateral load produces torsion, vertical stress in the web, lateral stress in the base, and lateral bending, principally in the head. The frequency of application of lateral load only approaches fatigue conditions on curves, where it is applied continuously during the passage of a locomotive. On tangent track the lateral forces are due to locomotive oscillations and they attain high values only occasionally.

The torsion is important only in that it produces lateral bending of the head and base [see Section II, Art. 3(a) and so can be considered along with the lateral bending. The vertical stress in the web produced by lateral load is not excessive, but is important because it must usually be added to the stress produced by eccentric vertical load.

The high stress produced by lateral load is that due to lateral bending of the head. This has a maximum of about 45,000 lb. per sq. in. and a reversal of 20 per cent of the maximum. On the gage side of the head, the maximum is compression and must be added to the stress produced by vertical load. Thus the maximum stress range in the head is about 60,000 lb. per sq. in. compression to about 15,000 lb. per sq. in. tension.

The work described in this paper shows that the weak points of present rails are the fillet under the head and the head itself.

2 ACKNOWLEDGMENTS

The authors wish to thank the officials of the Westinghouse Electric & Manufacturing Company for having sponsored and guided the development and application of the test methods that were used. The field tests were all made in cooperation with the Westinghouse Railway Engineering Department, represented by Mr. J. P. Shamberger.

Discussion

R. BERNARD.[28] Experiments similar to those described in the paper are being carried on in Germany, and a large number of stress measurements on rails have already been performed. For this purpose a carbon-pile instrument, analogous to that first used by the Bureau of Standards in Washington, has been further developed, and by means of it stresses, frequency of vibration, and modulus of foundation have been determined. Some experiments have also been made with magnetic strain gages similar to the one described in the paper.

For German "Reichsbahn" track it has been found that the stress fluctuates from 1200 kg. per cu. cm. to —900 kg. per cu. cm. and the frequencies from 6 to 400 per sec., and that the modulus of foundation is about 10 kg. per cu. cm.

If the different conditions, in America are taken into account, it can be concluded that the foregoing results obtained are in satisfactory agreement with those given in the paper.

C. B. BRONSON.[29] On page 3, and with reference to Fig. 5, the authors comment on the failure of splice bars, which they call fatigue cracks. Failure originates at the mid-distance of the top fishing or bearing surface and is induced by the notch effect from the sharp angle or edge of the rail head digging into the splice bar. Undercutting or filing of the rail-head bearing, rolling a notch or depression in the bar, and increasing the strength of the bar are all partially effective in overcoming this difficulty. Heat treatment of the splice bars has been very effective in reducing splice-bar failures.

In several places the authors call attention to the high stresses in the fillet joining head and web, and indicate that these are the most severe in the rail section. Rail failures, however, do not so indicate. In the Dudley rail sections, with fairly wide fillets joining head and web, failures of this type are practically unknown. Furthermore, with the greater and almost universal use and installation of canted tie plates, eccentric loading is being very much reduced, with more nearly center-bearing application.

In Section IV, under "Hardness of Material," the authors call attention to the fact that a large rail receives less work in rolling than a small one. While this is in part true, it must be remembered that the rail mills have faced the problem of heavier rail sections by rebuilding and modernizing their plants to keep pace with the changing conditions. As a result of this, much heavier mills are now in use, which produce very effective rolling pressures through the members of the heavy rail sections.

In particular, the New York Central Lines have continued the practice established by the late Dr. P. H. Dudley of using a broad, thin head on all of their rail sections, varying slightly from one weight to another. This has made it unnecessary to step up the carbon and other hardening elements in rolling the heavier rails, which the authors mention as being essential.

B. S. CAIN.[30] It may be of interest to compare some of the results of this valuable paper with results obtained in somewhat similar work done by the General Electric Company during several years' study of locomotive design and operation.

Equation [27] shows some theoretical basis for the observation made in practice that the vertical forces' due to balanced unsprung weight do not increase unduly with increase of speed on good track. In fact, at very high speed the weight does not

have time to drop into soft spots. Similar observations are made by the Special Committee on Stresses in Railroad Track.[31] Fig. 15 also shows that the maximum impacts do not occur at the center of the depression or at a joint, but some distance away.

The strain gages used by the General Electric Company were originally of the McCollum-Peters type[32] depending on the compression of carbon piles. Some good results have been obtained with these gages, but experience has led to the preference for an electromagnetic gage of the same general type as that described in this paper. The gage is a development of the electric micrometer,[33] is constructed for a 2-in. gage length, and operates on 2000-cycle current with compact and portable equipment.

When using track-stress measurements to calculate the lateral pressures of locomotive wheels, it has occasionally been found that the rail will slip on the tie plate and may be prevented by vertical load from immediately slipping back. This action must be watched for, as it does not correspond with the theory of lateral bending and, if not detected, may give incorrect values of lateral force. Track-stress measurements at one or two isolated points cannot be relied upon to yield maximum values of stress or load, the records being not even simultaneous on different wheels. With the object of obtaining records over a greater distance, the Pennsylvania Railroad equipped a special track with hardened balls and plates to support the rail and to register maximum forces by indentation of the plates.[34] An instrument which makes continuous records of both vertical and lateral pressures simultaneously on a number of ties has been constructed and used by the General Electric Company[35] and has given many valuable results, especially of vertical pressures on the rail. It has shown particularly the importance of oscillations of certain types of locomotives at high speed in producing high rail stresses, showing that the maximum stresses are indicated by rail-stress gages only if these happen to be located at the exact spots where the maximum stresses occur.

Another attack on the problem of continuously recording wheel pressures has been to mount gages on the locomotives or cars themselves so that the lateral pressures on axles are recorded, either the maximum by means of a hardened ball and plate, or continuously by an electromagnetic strain gage. Records of this sort have recently been obtained. It is to be hoped that these continuous records of forces will ultimately be correlated with the local stresses in the rail section which form the chief subject of this paper.

The authors use in Table 1 a so-called wear factor, based on the assumption that the .wear between two surfaces is proportional to the pressure between the surfaces, the rubbing velocity, and the coefficient of friction. Actually, it is also assumed that the coefficient of friction is the same for all cases. The writer does not believe that this factor is necessarily a good indication of wear, because rapid wear is often due to concentration of pressure on a small area, particularly in the familiar cases where incorrect contours are used, leading to cutting. In fact, the term "cutting" indicates a common source of rapid tire and rail wear which is not indicated by the so-called wear factor.

In the particular instance of the electric locomotives of the Great Northern Railway, as given in Table 1, there is a small

---

[28] Main Office of State Railway, Berlin, Germany.
[29] Assistant Inspecting Engineer, New York Central Lines, New York, N. Y.
[30] Locomotive Division, Transportation Engineering Department General Electric Co., Erie, Pa.

[31] Fourth Progress Report A.R.E.A. 1925, pp. 1167–1168.
[32] Proc. A.R.E.A., vol. 31, 1930, pp. 1556–1568. Also Technologic Paper of the Bureau of Standards no. 247.
[33] Jl. A.I.E.E., Sept., 1926, p. 820. Also Gen. Elec. Res., Nov., 1926, p. 815.
[34] Proc. A.R.E.A., vol. 19, 1918.
[35] Railway Age, Aug. 16, 1924, pp. 283–286. Also Gen. Elec. Res., Feb., 1924, p. 98.

difference between the maximum wear factors on different locomotives and considerable difference between individual wheels, even after averaging for both directions of motion. On the other hand, data obtained from the railway company covering tire wear on electric locomotives for the last two years, show that an even tire mileage is obtained on both classes of locomotives and "there is no measurable difference between tires wearing, regardless of position." It therefore appears that the "wear factor," while an interesting index of possible high wear in some cases, is not to be relied on as indicating relative performance, even qualitatively.

R. EKSERGIAN.[36] This paper is a very important and valuable contribution to the literature of stresses in rails. Very little study up to this time has been given as to the effect of lateral loads in producing stresses in the rail, and the authors' analysis of stress concentration in the rail is extremely interesting.

Some years ago the late Prof. G. Lanza made a critical analysis of the effect of the spacing of the ties as concentrated elastic reactions under vertical wheel loads, and came to the conclusion that, due to the long wave length of the elastic depression of the rail, the assumption of an elastic distributed reaction for the actual concentrated tie reactions was a sufficiently good first approximation. The writer believes that Professor Timoshenko himself had made a similar analysis and come to the same conclusion.

But now in the study of lateral loads on the rail, the authors themselves state that lateral bending and twist are of a localized character, and sufficiently localized so that the lateral pressures of adjacent drivers have no mutual effect. In such a case the writer would like to ask the authors to what degree the assumption of a continuous torsional and lateral elastic reaction given by Equations [17] and [18] is justified when compared with the actual spacing of the tie reactions.

If the vertical loading has no eccentricity it would appear the lateral and vertical loading stresses can be separated, so that, due to the localized condition of stress produced by lateral loadings, stresses can be calibrated for a unit lateral load so that we can quantitatively measure the lateral forces of a wheel base. On the other hand, the authors point out the importance of eccentric vertical loading in producing both torsion and additional bending in the rail. If the flange is bearing up against the head the eccentricity will differ from that when the flange is away from the head. A study of such eccentricities for different configurations of the wheelbase may possibly be of importance in order that we may differentiate experimentally for the obtaining of lateral forces separately. Or can the effect of eccentricity of vertical loading be neglected with reasonably large lateral loads?

The consideration of a distributed elastic torsional reaction at the base of a rail has suggested a torsional elastic track (per pair of rails) reaction in conjunction with unequal loadings for individual wheels per pair of wheels. Such conditions occur wherever lateral forces are exerted, as in the rolling of a locomotive, as seen from an analysis of the phase relations in the dynamic augment of steam locomotives. Any combination of these conditions resolves into a couple exerted on the axle and wheels, together with the total axle loading, which latter divides equally on both rails, and the couple augments the mean axle wheel loading on one side and decreases it on the other. The couple reaction on the track (i.e., per pair of rails) causes a distributed elastic torsion reaction of the roadbed, if we can assume the tie itself as rigid. Actually the flexibility of the tie itself with the assumption of a distributed elastic tie reaction

results in a more complicated torsional track elastic reaction. The mutual effect of tie reactions per pair of rails for unequal wheel loadings for the right rail as compared with the left rail, considering the distributed elastic reaction supporting the ties, would appear to be an interesting problem for study in connection with the vertical stresses in the rail.

The writer has made many calculations for the lateral forces exerted by various types of locomotives. A general discussion of the nature of these lateral forces is given in a paper by H. Uebelacker, and in the writer's "Static Adjustment of Trucks on Curves." It is interesting to note that with several pairs of drivers the largest lateral force for a locomotive with several pairs of drivers usually occurs on the next-to-the-rear driver, and the lateral reaction is exerted on the inner rail. Frequently the loadings may range from 20,000 to 30,000 lb. Such high loadings on the basis of the authors' analysis for stresses due to lateral forces must result in excessive rail stresses.

Such large lateral loadings are due to a considerable extent to the lateral guiding reactions of the front and rear trucks, and with swing-link trucks such loadings increase with the curvature. The authors' paper therefore reopens the question from another angle, i.e., that due to lateral rail stress limitations as to the type of truck-guiding apparatus such as a constant-resistance truck in preference to a swing-link truck and the use of an articulated wheelbase versus a completely rigid wheelbase.

In connection with vertical rail stress, the writer, in a paper on "The Balancing and Dynamic Rail Pressure of Locomotives," attempted to place the limitation of the counterbalance problem on the limiting rail stress. In connection with this the various phase angles of the dynamic augments for adjacent wheels were evaluated and the corresponding stresses estimated. The authors' paper has pointed out a further idea along this line, i.e., the estimating of the range of stress for the endurance or fatigue life of a rail. Using the master diagram of the bending moment, it is possible to construct an influence line for the passage of several drivers, and then, considering the phase relations of the dynamic augments of adjacent drivers, the complete variations of stress at a particular section can be estimated.

The relation of flange wear and angle of incidence have been recognized for some time. This relation has usually been stated by the equation, $W = kR\phi^n$, where W is the flange wear, R the lateral force, and ϕ the angle of incidence. It would be very interesting to establish experimentally the exponent n. The idea that flange wear depends essentially on the angle of incidence explains why the large lateral force of the next-to-the-last driver on the inner rail causes no appreciable flange wear.

F. M. GRAHAM.[37] The designer of improved rails for heavy steam or electric service is confronted by a serious lack of available theoretical and experimental knowledge from which to project a rail section of greater dimensions than previously used. He will desire to produce a rail of increased stiffness and with such proportions of dimensions as will insure lateral stability against overturning under maximum combinations of forces which may be exerted in the actual service for which the rail is intended. The section must lend itself to suitable joint connections and conform to necessary manufacturing processes to produce sound steel and also permit heat treatment, if desired. The shape of the head of the rail must conform to the necessary requirements of wheel contacts, and such contacts should be made with the lowest possible unit pressure.

As opposed to the foregoing requirements, the following conditions are known to exist:

---

[36] Consultant, Engineering Dept., E. I. du Pont de Nemours & Co., Wilmington, Del. Mem. A.S.M.E.

[37] Assistant Engineer of Standards, Pennsylvania Railroad, Altoona, Pa.

1   Speeds approaching 100 m.p.h. develop very large forces exerted on the rail which cannot be calculated and which have only been observed in very limited tests.

2   Hidden defects in rails raise stresses in service to the point where their frequent repetition results in ultimate failure.

3   The cost of rolling experimental, or trial, sections is prohibitive, and therefore dependence must be placed on experience and the limited theoretical and test data available.

4   Wheel pressures on rails develop unit compressive stresses entirely beyond the elastic capacity of ordinary rail steel, as is shown by the observed cold flow of rail tops throughout their length, and especially at rail ends.

5   The supporting character of subgrade ballast and ties varies continuously from point to point, and especially so as between wet and dry seasons and during the winter season when roadbed and ballast are deeply frozen so that the ties provide supports with widely varying spans and resultant stresses.

The paper under discussion will be helpful in solving some of the above-mentioned difficulties.

The writer disclaims ability to criticize the more difficult mathematical analyses included in the paper, but wishes to call attention to some of the bases of calculations and other practical considerations.

Referring to Section I, wherein the elastic constant k is involved in all longitudinal stress values, it is impractical to determine this value generally on account of the elaborate equipment required, the tedious measurements to be made, and necessary occupation of the track interfering with its use during a single determination. Very low values of k occur at different times and places, resulting in permanent deformation of rails, if actual failure does not occur.

In this section the suggestion is advanced that the weight of the rail should be directly proportioned to the axle loads, disregarding speed, counterweighting, and shape of rail section. In designing a stronger rail section, the height is increased to provide greater stiffness; however, in doing so the size of the head is not increased—it may be decreased. To provide equal stability against lateral forces, it is necessary to increase the width of the base, also its thickness, tending to retain a low position of the center of gravity and thus relatively increasing the distance between the neutral axis and the top of the rail. Calling this distance c, it is suggested that where two different rail sections are assumed to have the same extreme fiber stress, their relative strengths are as $I^{3/4}/c$ for each section.

From the above it can be noted that two rail sections properly designed are not of similar shape.

Referring to Fig. 5 and the accompanying text in regard to joint bars breaking at the center of their length and cracking from the top downward, and stating that this is due to the greater distance from neutral axis to top of bar compared to the distance from the neutral axis to the bottom of the bar, resulting in higher unit tensile stress at top of bar in reverse bending, this explanation seems hardly adequate in view of the relatively low value of the reverse bending moment as shown in Fig. 3. May not this type of failure be brought about by reverse bending stress combined with the large unit pressure of the head of rail on the joint bar at this point, and the resultant severe abrasion and cold working causing considerable distortion or cold movement of the metal?

In the last paragraph of Section II the existence of a couple is assumed which assists in preventing the rotation of the rail from external forces. This assumption is doubtless based on the holding-down capacity of the spikes on the base of the rail. This is an unsafe assumption as spikes are not usually in contact with the top of the base of the rail and a very considerable actual rotation of the base of the rail would be necessary to bring

them into action. Even if the spikes should act in this way, their effect would not be of a dependable elastic nature.

Similarly, in the first paragraph of Section III the resistance to lateral movement of the rail is assumed to be of an elastic character. Such movement is actually resisted by friction on the tie plates, which is of course not of an elastic nature, and also by contact of the rail base against spikes or shoulders of the tie plates. Such reactions are irregularly spaced and are of variable strength so that they do not provide a condition which can be properly included in a theoretical determination of rail stresses.

Referring to the tests on the Pennsylvania Railroad, the writer is not aware that simultaneous values of vertical and lateral forces exerted by each wheel have ever been measured. Such measurements have been made as the successive wheels arrive at a point of measurement, and it is probably not correct to assume that these are equal to simultaneous values.

The foregoing comments on some portions of the paper are only offered from a practical standpoint and are not of a constructive character.

The writer wishes to express his appreciation of this very interesting discussion of a difficult subject. It deals with stresses arising from the interaction of such diverse materials as dirt, stone, wood in various stages of decay, and steel when acted upon by modern locomotives at high speeds. The maximum forces often arise from accidental conditions which cannot be foreseen and which cannot be determined theoretically. Safe railroad operation is a question of maximums, not averages.

The writer suggests that the field work outlined by the authors be much extended to include the use of various types of modern locomotives (both steam and electric) at high speeds, using a large number of strain- and vibration-recording instruments so as to cover a considerable length of track instead of a single point. The track conditions should be varied so as to include all maintenance conditions which may be reasonably possible in actual service.

R. GRAMMEL.[38]   The authors' investigations provide a splendid example of fruitful cooperation between theory and experiment. The writer ventures to present some additional considerations which may perhaps be of use in furthering these investigations and in their practical application.

When the rail, as is usual, is attached to cross-ties which themselves are bedded on an elastic foundation, there obtains an interrelation between the vertical deflection [3] and the torsion ϕ. This is due to the fact that the loading of the tie near the two ends produces an upward bending of the tie in the middle, and hence a tendency of the ends to incline outward (except in the case when the parts of the tie under the rails themselves rest on some kind of a foundation but not in the middle). For an initial calculation we may assume that the moment of torsion which acts from the tie to the rail is proportional to the vertical deflection s of the rail and appears in Equation [21] as an additional member $k_s s$ on the right-hand side. Here k_s is a sort of coefficient of bedding, while s has the value given in [3]. A more exact calculation will take into consideration the connection between ϕ and s, and in addition the values of k_s must be expressed in terms of the coefficient of bedding k. This can be done approximately in the following way. Instead of an infinite number of ties let us assume a single elastically supported "plate" having a coefficient of bedding k, but no bending rigidity in the longitudinal direction of the rail. If we then measure x lengthwise to the rail, y crosswise to the rail horizontally (which means along the tie), and s vertically, we have then to load the "plate" lengthwise to the rail with the unknown forces $Z(x)$ and the unknown moment $M(x)$. In addition to

[38] Professor Dr.-Ing. Dr. R. Grammel, Stuttgart, Germany.

the known loads P (vertical) and H (horizontal) the rails then also carry the reactions $-Z(x)$ and $-M(x)$. In this way we obtain four linear differential equations, namely, for the deflection z' and inclination ϕ' of the "plate," for the vertical deflection z of the rail, for its torsion ϕ, and for its horizontal deflection y. These four equations are mutually interconnected by the magnitudes $Z(x)$ and $M(x)$, which may be omitted by the employment of an auxiliary condition to the effect that z and ϕ are the same as the values of z' and ϕ' at the locus of the rail. The actual calculation is rather complicated, but numerical results can be obtained. It would be of interest to compare them with results of actual measurements.

WALTER M. HAESSLER.[39] Regarding the lateral rail forces mentioned by the authors, the writer would like to ask how this factor varies according to the height of the center of gravity of the locomotive above the rail. He is cognizant of the fact that these quantities—the lateral rail forces and the height of the center of gravity—are roughly in inverse proportion to each other. Have any experiments been made to indicate in a quantitative manner the relationship existent between these two quantities?

J. J. KARPINSKI.[40] The tendency of rail design, as stated in the paper, has been toward increasing the vertical stiffness. This was effected by increasing the height of the cross-section and placing more material in the head or base, while making little or no change in the thickness of the web. Thus the 80-lb. Am. Soc. C.E. Standard rail has a web $^{35}/_{64}$ in. thick, while the 85-lb., 90-lb., 95-lb., and 100-lb. rails have the same thickness of web, namely, $^{9}/_{16}$ in. This is an indication that the rail designers have already felt that material in the web was not being properly utilized.

After thorough theoretical and experimental investigations the authors point out that a more favorable stress distribution could be obtained if material were removed from the bottom of the web and placed nearer the top.

It seems to the writer that it would be of interest to extend these investigations to a case of a rail having the web perforated at regular distances near the bottom. In this way it would be possible to form an idea whether it would be possible to treat the rail as a Vierendeel girder. In this case, if necessary, extra thickness could be given to the verticals representing the unperforated part of the web because of the economy of metal attained by punching the web. The stronger verticals would permit increasing the height of the rail cross-section without fear of excessive stresses resulting from an eccentric vertical load, and therefore they would make it possible to diminish the amount of metal in the head, thus facilitating the process of cooling and consequently diminishing the chances of transverse fissures occurring.

C. F. DENDY MARSHALL.[41] With regard to the question of longitudinal weight transfer when in "motion" which is due to what the writer calls "trim," the authors give as the reason the pull of the drawbar. There are in addition two other factors which they omit to mention, namely, the upward pressure on the slide bars, and the frontal air resistance (with regard to the latter it is true that they were only dealing in that part of their paper with moderate speeds). The slide-bar pressure is a very serious disturbing force. Imagine for a moment that the stroke was increased until it was nearly equal to the diameter of the

wheel. Suppose the crankpin to be at the bottom, brakes hard on, and steam admitted in front of the piston. It is obvious that there is a pressure downward on the rail under the driving wheels, and upward on the slide bars, tending to lift the front of the engine.

There is a point in connection with rail joints on which, though not touched on in the paper, the writer would like to lay his opinion before American engineers. In England they are set in line with one another; in the United States, he believes, they are usually alternated. Coming as they do at regular intervals, they are a potential danger if, at any attainable speed, their impacts can coincide, or harmonize, with the natural periods of the vehicles. With rails 45 ft. long, at 61 miles an hour a joint is met every second. The period of pitching, which is induced by parallel joints, is probably far quicker than this. But it has been found in England that the period of rolling (which alternate joints tend to produce) of a heavy tank engine is from 1 to $1^{1}/_{4}$ seconds, and rather less in the case of a tender engine. It would therefore appear that there is some risk about the alternative method, because the impulses, though small, are regular, and the writer is inclined to think that in this lies the explanation of the fact that elaborate and costly spring-compensating arrangements are found necessary in America, although not required in England: the reason being that they distribute the impulses and break up the rhythm.

S. MATSUNAWA.[42] In Japan, as well as in other countries, the study of stresses in railway track is regarded as of great importance from the economical viewpoint of railway operation, and the writer is very glad to have been afforded the opportunity of reporting some results of the investigations of similar subjects which were carried out by the Japanese Government Railways.

Statistical investigations of rail failures in 1929 covering a total operating track length of some 17,000 km. of the said railways have shown that 65 per cent of the total rail failures occurred within 1.6 meters from rail joints.

In view of this fact we think that investigations of rail stresses should be focused upon the effects of rail joints. In this connection the paper, "On the Strength, Design, and Maintenance of Rail Joints" by Mr. I. Horikoshi,[43] may be worth noting. Measurement of the stress in railway rails under moving loads is one of the most important tasks imposed upon those who are interested in scientific research on rail stresses, though it is attended with great difficulties. The electric telemeter as devised by Mr. H. Shibata, engineer, of the writer's office, may be numbered among the best apparatus for the purpose, and the attention of experts is called to the descriptions in his paper entitled "Measuring the Stress and Depression of Rails by Means of an Electric Telemeter."[44]

In this apparatus the amount of stress (that is, the strain within a given gage length) and of the depression of rails to be measured is read in terms of electric current which varies proportionally to the amount of stress or depression. The slidewire method is adopted, and the record is obtained by means of a portable six-element oscillograph designed for the purpose.

A chief advantage of the apparatus is that the stresses at four different points and the depressions at two different points can be recorded at the same time, and that the record can be easily magnified any number of times, as there is no considerable inertia mass of the recording part.

[39] 264 Palisade Ave., Union City, N. J.   Jun. A.S.M.E.
[40] Engineer, Bridge Department, Ministry of Public Works of Jugoslavia, Zemun, Jugoslavia.
[41] Guildford, England.   M.A., M.I. Loco. E.

[42] Engineer and Chief of the Research Office of the Japanese Government Railways, Tokyo, Japan.
[43] See Bulletin, Research Office, Japanese Government Railways, vol. 19, no. 21, May 25, 1931.
[44] Paper on file at A.S.M.E. Headquarters.

In Fig. 39, AB is a resistance wire, and a current from a battery E is adjusted by the rheostat R. A point C is soldered on AB, and D is a contact point which slides a distance in proportion to the strain or depression of the rail under rolling load. There is some potential difference between C and D according to the amount of current flowing through the resistance wire AB, and to the value of the resistance between C and D. The current

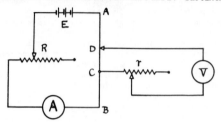

FIG. 39   ELECTRIC TELEMETER CIRCUITS

in the shunt circuit DVC will therefore vary with the amount of the strain or the depression. Thus, we can measure the strain or depression by recording the variation of this current by means of the oscillograph at any required magnification, which is made possible by adjusting the rheostats R and r.

Thus the longitudinal, lateral, and any other stresses in rail can be measured by applying a proper attachment which reduces different amounts of strain to proper variations of the electric current in the shunt circuit DVC.

H. F. MOORE.[44] The authors have given an interesting discussion of transverse fissures in rails, although their experimental methods are not such as to detect such fissures or to determine the complex stresses beneath the surface of a rail under a wheel load. They refer to Bulletin 212 of the University of Illinois Engineering Experiment Station. In that bulletin a mathematical analysis is developed for internal stresses, and it is found that theoretically there exist very high shearing stresses, which are a maximum beneath the surface of the rail. Whether these stresses are sufficiently great to start a fissure in sound rail steel is as yet a matter of uncertainty. Experiments are now in progress in the Materials Testing Laboratory of the University of Illinois, in connection with the Joint Investigation under the auspices of the American Railway Association, the Technical Committee of the Association of Steel Rail Manufacturers, and the University. Already a transverse fissure has been produced in the laboratory in a shatter-cracked rail which has never been in track service, and tests on specimens of sound rails are now under way. Until further experimental results have been obtained the writer does not believe that it can be safely assumed that it is unlikely that wheel-load stresses can ever start internal fissures in sound rail steel. Further tests may, or may not, show this to be the case.

A. ONO.[46] The calculation of stresses in rails and the experiments in the laboratory and field have so thoroughly and successfully been carried out by the authors that there appears nothing to be added except one thing relating to the rail joint. Some results given in or deduced from a note on the calculation of the joint[47] will be introduced here in the hope that they will

[44] Research Professor of Engineering Materials, University of Illinois. Mem. A.S.M.E.

[46] Professor, Institute of Strength of Materials, Kyushu Imperial University, Fukuoka, Japan.

[47] *Zeitschrift f. Angewandte Mathematik u. Mechanik*, Band 11, 1931, p. 165.

prove of interest to engineers interested in the present paper.

The joint is considered to consist of compound beams, and the relative displacement of the rail and fishplates, say, $y_1 - y_2$, is assumed to be represented by an equation such that $\mu = K_1 (y_1 - y_2)$, where μ is the intensity of pressure between the rail and fishplates induced by the action of load, and K_1 is the modulus of joint. In the calculation another constant α may be conveniently taken instead of K_1, viz.,

$$\alpha = \sqrt[4]{\frac{K_1}{4}\left(\frac{1}{E_1 J_1} + \frac{1}{E_2 J_2}\right)}$$

where $E_1 J_1$ and $E_2 J_2$ are the flexural rigidities of the rail and plates, respectively. As the modulus of elasticity of carbon steel is practically independent of the carbon content, E_1 and E_2 may be taken as equal. It is to be remarked that α plays a similar part to that of the constant β, which depends on the modulus of foundation as well as on the rigidity of rail.

The value of K_1 is unknown, but α may be determined by measuring the deflection of rails jointed together, and comparing this result with that observed on rails without joint. This was done in the laboratory of the Steel Works at Yawata, Japan, by taking specimens supported at both ends and loaded at the middle. Of course the value of α may vary greatly according to the tightness of the joint.

Now the greatest bending moment induced at the joint by a load P may be approximately found by the following equation:

$$M_b = \frac{P}{\beta\,(4 + q)}$$

where

$$q = \frac{4\beta J_1}{\alpha J_2}$$

The numerical value of q for a very tight joint was found to be 0.925 for 37-kg. rails (weight per meter) and 0.725 for a certain 50-kg. rail, used in Japan. Accordingly, the greatest bending moment in fishplates is a little less than that in rails without joints, while the stress in the former is very considerable as compared with that in the latter owing to the relatively small value of the section modulus.

Next the stress in rails may be considered by extending the calculation of the joint. For this purpose we find the positive and negative moments, and then the maximum and minimum values of the bending stress at a certain section of the rail. In this way we obtain the average stress and the alternating stress, as were also mentioned by the authors. Taking these stresses as factors determining the safety of material and assuming, e.g., a straight-line relation between these two for the fatigue limit, an equivalent alternating stress with the average stress zero may be found. Then the breaking section may be determined by finding a section in which the equivalent stress is a maximum.

Such calculation being performed, it can be shown that the fracture of a rail is likely to take place near a joint, so far as the bending stress is concerned, but when the joint is very tight, the straining action is only slightly greater than in long rails without joints. When the joint is so loose that it is quite unable to transmit force and moment, the calculation should be partly modified, as the magnitude of the negative moment is greatest when the load is at an end of the rail. In this case the straining action becomes much higher, say, some 33 per cent over that in long rails, and the distance between the breaking section and an end of a rail is some 76 cm. in 37-kg. rails and 88 cm. in 50-kg. rails. A report made by the research staff of the Steel Works at Yawata states that the transverse fissure of rails is rather localized in a region near an end. This seems to support the result of the calculation, although the writer does not mean to imply that the stress may be conclusively calculated by taking the bending only, as there are many other things to be considered, which were dealt with by the authors of the present paper.

C. Richardson.[48] It is interesting to note the effect of lateral forces on rail stresses. Eccentric loads also tend to increase the unit stresses. In canting one rail it is frequently found that the load is delivered on the outside of the head. In this case the lateral forces plus the vertical forces combine to produce an abnormally high unit stress.

The actual tests cover moderate speeds. It is hoped that further papers will disclose stresses involved at maximum speeds.

Continuation of the research work started should show whether a redesign of the rail is necessary to meet stresses actually incurred. Originally freight-car side frames were designed primarily for vertical stress. Investigation of failures showed that the lateral forces were the actual causes of failure. When the side frames were redesigned for both vertical and lateral forces, the life of side frames was increased to the point where they now outlive the car.

E. Schwerin.[49] This paper extraordinarily enriches our knowledge of the complicated stresses which arise in railroad tracks. The authors show that the probable stresses may be calculated with great accuracy, and that the weak points of the rails now used are the fillet under the head and the head itself; this last result seems to be extremely important for the development of new, more suitable forms of track.

With regard to this research the writer would like to know the opinion of the authors concerning the rise of grooves ("Riffelbildung") on the head of the rail. This phenomenon, which is especially observed at the entrance of stations, and which leads to quick destruction of the head of the rail, was much discussed some years ago. Has the Westinghouse Company already investigated this phenomenon, or are such experiments projected? As far as the writer knows, the cause of this phenomenon has not yet been fully explored, and he would be glad if the authors would express their opinion on this point.

Dr. Ing. Saller.[50] Some months ago the writer submitted an article entitled "Einheitliche Berechnung des Oberbaues" to the *Organ für die Fortschritte des Eisenbahnwesens* for publication, in which he gives simpler equations for the axle sequence than those offered by the authors. This article appeared in No. 2 of that journal for 1932.

Equation [5] of the present paper, as the writer sees it, is incorrect. The value of y in Equation [3] becomes zero when ($\cos \beta x + \sin \beta x$) equals zero, and this is the case when $\beta x = 3\pi/4$, and hence the total length $2 \times (3\pi/4\beta) = 1.5 \pi/\beta$.

Referring to Equation [9], the writer would say that it seems to him that here the longitudinal-tie-construction theory is applied to cross-tie construction. The longitudinal-tie construction employs no cross-ties. In the application of the longitudinal-tie theory to cross-tie road construction, the cross-tie and longitudinal-tie widths are often interchanged.

The writer has made a few tests with Thoma's electrical capacity extensometer at the rail base in straight sections, and has found that the influence of the lateral forces is not as great as the authors indicate. This work is still being continued.

A more specific reference to the table in Zimmermann's book (footnote 7) would be appreciated.

A. Spoliansky[51] and J. Lamoen.[52] The mathematical introduction to the paper gives as clear an insight into the stability of rail as may possibly be obtained when one restricts oneself to analytical methods. The theory used (of bending of bars continuously supported by an elastic foundation) has proved to be one of the most useful theories in applied mechanics, especially with reference to foundation problems. The most exhaustive work from this point of view is probably that written by Hayashi.[53] One of the present writers has also treated this question,[51] and has applied the theory to the computation of the horizontal reactions between piers and bridge in a weir consisting of a great number of slender piers supporting a bridge reaching from one abutment to the other.[55] The reactions of the piers on the bridge are in fact concentrated forces, but he has likened the bridge to a bar on an elastic foundation. The results of

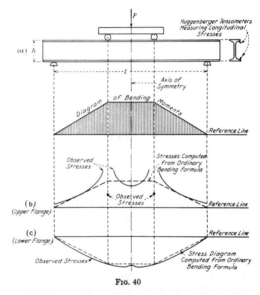

Fig. 40

the approximate computation, assuming continuous support, were 0.5 per cent higher than those obtained by the exact calculation, considering concentrated reactions. This fully corroborates the presumption that the rail of Fig. 17 of the paper is, practically speaking, continuously supported.

On page 3, second column, the authors say: "The inverse problem, i.e., of calculating the vertical pressures produced by locomotive wheels on the rail provided either the deflections or the stresses in the rail under the wheels have been determined by experiment, can also be solved without any difficulty." The

[48] Boston and Maine Railroad, Boston, Mass.

[49] Prof. Dr.-Ing. E. Schwerin, Berlin-Wilmersdorf, Germany.

[50] Director, German State Railways, Dechbettenerstrasse 32, Regensburg, Germany.

[51] C.E., E.E. Chief Engineer, Constructions Métalliques Enghien-St. Eloi, Enghien, Belgium.

[52] C.E. Laboratory, Institute of Civil Engineering, Liège University, Liège, Belgium.

[53] "Theorie des Trägers auf elastischer Unterlage und ihre Anwendung auf den Tiefbau," by Keiichi Hayashi, Professor at the Kyushu University, Japan. First edition, 1921, Julius Springer, Berlin.

[54] J. Lamoen, "La théorie de la poutre sur fondation élastique et ses applications," *Revue Universelle des Mines*, Nov., 1931.

[55] J. Lamoen, "Over de krachtsverdeeling in een stuw met groot aantal smalle pijlers." *Der Ingenieur*, Sept. 18, 1931.

writers quite agree as to the deflections, these being but feebly affected by the contact effects. But to make this method hold for stresses measured under the wheels, it would be necessary that the observed stresses—which are of course the existing stresses—be approximately equal to the stresses computed from the bending formula $M/\sigma = I/v$, M being measured on verticals passing through the wheel centers (see Fig. 4). But as the contact stress intervenes, these calculated stresses will be entirely different from the real stresses. (See Figs. 27 and 28.)

The writers are much interested in Figs. 27 and 28 showing the effect of contact stress. They have obtained similar results when experimenting with the arrangement shown in Fig. 40 (a). Their observations are roughly sketched at (b) for the compression in the upper flange, and at (c) for the extension in the lower flange. One might think that at a certain distance from the points of contact the computed and the observed stress diagrams would become identical. This is only true, however, for sufficiently great values of l/h, i.e., the transverse dimensions must be sufficiently small as compared with the longitudinal dimensions. When this condition is not satisfied, the ordinary theory of bending is contradictory to the theory of elasticity.

H. R. Thomas.[56] Referring to Fig. 30 and the accompanying text, the relative magnitude of the various local stresses might well have been indicated; and the method of calculating the contact stresses as well as the reason for assuming that the load makes contact at a point instead of over an area would be of interest.

The introduction of a discussion of transverse fissures into Section II—Local Stresses in Rails, does not seem warranted. The kind of repeated stress involved in the statement "Transverse fissures are fatigue cracks which form inside the heads of rails in the transverse plane," is not stated, nor are there any results presented which would indicate the presence of a repeated stress in the interior of the head sufficient in intensity to cause a fatigue crack to form and spread. Practically the whole of this discussion involves matters on which the evidence available (both in this paper and elsewhere) is not conclusive.

As suggested above, there does not seem to be anything in this paper which would warrant the paragraph on Soundness of Material.

Referring to Fig. 38, the use of the expression "Limit of Safety" is unfortunate, since any stress condition approaching this curve is certainly approaching the point of actual destruction.

In dismissing contact stresses as having only the effect of producing "mostly plastic flow in the rail head," the possibility that such cold working of the head may result in high internal residual stresses or may contribute to the start of surface cracks is being disregarded.

In presenting stress measurements and calculations, only locomotive-wheel loads seem to be considered. On account of the much greater frequency of application of car-wheel loads, it would seem that on the whole these loads might be even more important. This is especially the case if their effect in producing plastic flow and wear of the rail head is considered.

Hans Fromm.[57] The investigations which are discussed in the paper give important information regarding the magnitude of the stresses in rails, regarding the causes producing these stresses, and the calculation of the stresses. These investigations showed that it is possible, by using a simple theory, to calculate with sufficient accuracy stresses produced by vertical and lateral forces.

It is possible furthermore to obtain from a few suitably chosen strain measurements in the field the system of forces acting on the rail. Combining these two kinds of investigation it is possible to determine the static and dynamic forces acting between the wheels and the rail and to establish in this manner an important foundation (1) for the design of locomotives and cars, and (2) for the design of rail profiles and of railway track.

Especially interesting is the action of lateral forces, which in general consists of the pressure of the flanges and of the lateral friction forces. The lateral forces produce a very considerable increase of stresses in the rails (1) by direct action and (2) by producing changes in distribution of the vertical loads between the wheels.

The wear on the rail depends, in the writer's opinion, principally on the magnitude of the work of friction which is obtained as the product of the friction force and the corresponding magnitude of sliding (*Gleitschlupf*). We have to consider here (1) the wear between the flange and the rail, which is approximately proportional to the acting pressure of the flange, to the coefficient of friction, and to the height of the flange, and (2) the wear of the upper surface of the rail and of the surface of the wheel rim, for which not only lateral but also longitudinal friction forces must be considered. These longitudinal forces appear partially as the reaction against friction between the flange and the rail, but principally they represent the necessary circumferential forces acting on the driving wheels and the forces acting during braking. The work of friction can be calculated[58] in the case of a conical surface of the rim of the wheel as is usually the case in railways. It gives the friction losses due to sliding and also the lever of the rolling friction.

The longitudinal friction forces have only a negligible influence on stresses in the rail at a considerable distance from the point of contact of the wheel and of the rail. But at the surface of contact and near this surface the friction forces can have a considerable effect on the stresses. The calculations[59] in the case of a rim with the usual conical surface and a flat surface of the rail give an increase of the reduced stresses[60] up to 70 per cent. This increase depends on the dimensions, the magnitude of the load, and the coefficient of friction. In the case of a curved contact surface of the rail we have the case of contact of two cylinders with perpendicular axes, for which we have not yet a solution. We must expect here a similar increase in reduced stresses as for the above-mentioned case of a flat contact surface of the rail. Moreover, with continuous wear the contact surface of the rail approaches a flat surface. There exist also some profiles which have the flat surface from the very beginning.

So long as the reduced stress is far below the yield point the wear depends essentially upon the work of friction forces. When the reduced stress approaches the yield point, the hysteresis work becomes noticeable. This is shown by increase of rolling losses above the work of friction forces and on the other hand by the acceleration of wear due to fatigue. If the point of the maximum reduced stress is not on the contact surface but at a certain depth below the rolling surface of the rail, the well-known "pitting" phenomenon may occur.

---

[56] Dept. of Theoretical and Applied Mechanics, University of Illinois, Urbana, Ill.

[57] Technische Hochschule, Berlin, Germany.

[58] H. Fromm, "Zulässige Belastung von Reibungsgetrieben mit zylindrischen oder kegligen Rädern," *Z.V.D.I.*, vol. 73, 1929, p. 1031. The influence of the angle of incidence in the case of the angle between the plane of the wheel and the axis of the rail is discussed in *Zeitschrift für technische Physik*, 1928, p. 304.

[59] H. Fromm, *Z.V.D.I.*, vol. 73, 1929, pp. 957, 1029, and vol. 72, 1928, p. 1899.

[60] As reduced stress we take the expression

$$\sigma_{red.} = \sqrt{2(\tau_1^2 + \tau_2^2 + \tau_3^2)}$$

proposed by von Mises, in which τ_1, τ_2, and τ_3 are the principal shearing stresses.

AUTHORS' CLOSURE

S. TIMOSHENKO. In closing the discussion the present author will consider only questions concerning the introductory theoretical part of the paper and the general arrangement of field measurements. Those concerning field experiments and laboratory tests will be answered by Mr. Langer.

In the theoretical part of the paper the authors begin with the discussion of the action on the rail of vertical loads. A more detailed investigation of this problem has shown[61] that the isolated elastic supports can be replaced with sufficient accuracy by a continuous elastic foundation (see discussions by Dr. R. Eksergian and Dr. Saller). Although the actual support of the rails is very far from this ideal condition, the theory based on such an assumption proved a very useful one, and the authors were guided by this theory in planning their experiments. It was found also that by using this theory vertical loads could be calculated with sufficient accuracy from strain measurements if only the modulus of foundation k were determined by the preliminary calibration tests.

In investigating lateral bending and twisting of the rail, the authors applied the same assumption of continuous elastic support. Due to the simultaneous action of large vertical loads, it can be assumed that all clearances are taken up and that the rotation and lateral deflection of the rail are producing the corresponding elastic deformation of the ties (see discussion by F. M. Graham). The theory developed in this manner gives only a general picture of the deformation of the rail produced by lateral forces and by eccentric application of vertical loads. To obtain the numerical values of lateral forces and of eccentricities from their tests the authors did not use the theoretical equations but based their calculations on the results of the preliminary calibration of the track (see discussion by R. Eksergian) so that the defects of their theory do not affect the calculated values of lateral forces. The arrangement adopted for strain measurements makes it possible to measure the effect of lateral forces separately from the effect of eccentric application of vertical loads (see discussion by R. Eksergian).

The authors made their measurements only in two cross-sections, and in general they cannot be relied upon to yield maximum values of stress or load (see discussion by B. S. Cain and F. M. Graham), but their experiments showed that in the curves and at moderate speeds there is a steady distribution of vertical and lateral forces between the locomotive, wheels, and rails. Under such conditions, their measurements give a true picture of acting forces. In the case of a tangent track, it is necessary to take simultaneous readings in many cross-sections. The possibility of mounting the gages on the locomotive was also considered in this case.

The problem of stress conditions in joints was not investigated by the authors, and they mentioned the cracks in joint bars only because they show that there must be reverse bending stresses which can be explained if the rail be considered as a bar on an elastic foundation. The large local pressures of the head of the rail on the joint bar may also have an effect on the development of the above-mentioned fatigue cracks (see discussions by F. M. Graham and C. B. Bronson). The deformation of a joint depends greatly upon the tightness of the joint, and is affected also by friction. It would be very interesting to determine experimentally with what accuracy the bending moment acting in a rail joint can be calculated (see discussions by S. Matsunawa and A. Ono). In conclusion, the author would like to note that it was not suggested in the paper that the weight of the rail should be directly proportioned to the axle loads (see discussion by F. M. Graham). It is shown only that if the rail profiles are geometrically similar,

the maximum bending stress produced by an isolated force remains constant if the "weight of the rail per unit length is proportional to the load."

B. F. LANGER. Mr. Cain criticizes the use of the "wear factor" mentioned in Table 1 because it does not consider high concentrations of pressures due to incorrect contours. The wear factor is not intended to cover the whole subject of flange wear and rail side wear, but merely shows how this wear is affected by the layout of the wheelbase and the distribution of the guiding forces.[62] The fact that it does do this is demonstrated by the side wear of the outer instead of the inner rails on curves and the common practice of interchanging tires between end drivers and inner drivers to equalize the wear over the whole locomotive. A good article on flange wear, with particular reference to the shape of flange and rail contour, may be found in Heumann's "Spurkranz und Schienenkopf.[63]

Dr. Saller's method of finding the wave length of the deflection from Equation [3] is not correct, since he incorrectly assumes that the distance from the point where y is maximum to the point where y is zero is one-half of a wave length. The true wave length is found by putting the variable angle βx equal to 2π. This results in the value given in Equation [5].

Regarding Dr. Saller's criticism of Equation [9], the whole paper considers only cross-tie construction, and not longitudinal-tie construction. Equation [9] is correct for the former, but meaningless for the latter, since it does not consider the stiffness of the tie in bending.

The table referred to in Zimmerman's book (footnote 7) may be found on page 289 of the 2nd edition (1930).

The authors were very much interested in the information given by Messrs. Spoliansky and Lamoen on the effect of localized stress on stress distribution in beams. It was on account of this effect that they avoided the use of stresses in the head of the rail, near the point of contact, in calculating wheel loads. In the base and the web, the localized stresses are present, but do not introduce an error because the wheel loads are calculated from the experimental and not the purely theoretical relationship between stress and load.

Referring to Professor Thomas' discussion, the details of the calculations whose results are shown in Fig. 30 were not considered of sufficient importance to be included. The deformations from contact pressure were calculated from a formula given in A. E. H. Love's "Mathematical Theory of Elasticity," p. 192.

The appropriateness of a discussion of transverse fissures in this paper is apparently a matter of opinion. The authors felt that even though they had not done any original work themselves, it was a subject of such great importance that it could not be completely ignored, and therefore mentioned such work of other investigators which seemed to offer most hope of an ultimate solution. They will look forward with great interest to the completion of Professor Moore's work and its final answer to the question of whether or not fissures can be produced by wheel loads in sound rails. The evidence now available may not be conclusive, but it certainly indicates very strongly that the initial condition of the rail and not the loads imposed on it in service is the factor which determines whether or not it will develop fissures.[64]

In Fig. 38, the expression "Limit of Safety" should not be con-

---

[61] See author's paper in "Bulletins of the Institute of Engineers of Ways of Communication," St. Petersburg, 1915.

[62] See also, "Rail Stresses and Locomotive Tracking Characteristics Found in Tests on the Great Northern Railway," by J. P. Shamberger and B. F. Langer, A.R.E.A. Bulletin, vol. 33, no. 339, September, 1931.

[63] *Organ für die Fortschritte des Eisenbahnwesens*, Dec. 1 and 15, 1931.

[64] In addition to the work referred to in the paper, see also "Effect of Controlled Cooling and Temperature Equalization on Internal Fissures in Rails," by C. P., O. F. A., and N. P. P. Sandberg, *Metals and Alloys*, vol. 3, no. 4, April, 1932.

strued as meaning a safe working stress for design purposes. The well-known "factor of ignorance" should be applied.

The authors were very much interested in the strain gage mentioned by Dr. Matsunawa, and hope to be able to obtain a more detailed description of it. The mechanical construction must be quite ingenious to translate such small motions into electrical variations by the simple means of a slide-wire resistance.

Mr. Dendy Marshall mentions two causes of longitudinal weight transfer in addition to the pull of the drawbar. One is frontal air resistance, which was not considered in the paper, but which is negligible at moderate speed. The other he calls "slide-bar pressure," which is the same as the authors referred to as non-uniformity in vertical load due to angularity of the connecting rod. (See section on Vertical Loads, under III—Field Tests.)

Mr. Bronson mentions that the high stresses in the fillet joining the head to the web have been overcome by widening the fillet and canting the rail. This is quite in line with the authors' ideas on correct rail design, although they feel that the canting of the rail, while desirable, should not be relied on entirely to reduce the eccentricity of the vertical load. The fillet should be adequate to withstand the eccentric load in case it does occur.

The determination of the modulus of foundation, k, need not be as difficult as Mr. Graham thinks. If this one value is all that is required, it can be found with sufficient accuracy by measuring the deflections under the wheels of a locomotive of known axle loading by means of a surveyor's level.

Mr. Haessler asks how the height of the center of gravity affects the lateral rail forces. This is a subject on which opinions differ and no experimental work has been done, to the author's knowledge. The commonly accepted idea is that a high center of gravity introduces elasticity between the spring mass and the rail, and hence reduces the lateral forces. This is of importance only at the moment of entrance to a curve or else during severe lateral oscillations. If the motion is steady, the height of the center of gravity can have no effect on the lateral rail forces.

Professor Schwerin asks an opinion regarding the formation of grooves (*Riffelbildung*) across the head of the rail. The authors have not done any work on this subject and can offer no new suggestions as to their cause.

Mr. Graham criticizes the theory of torsion of the rail, since it assumes the existence of a couple which opposes the rotation of the rail. This assumption is not, as Mr. Graham supposes, based on the holding-down capacity of the spikes, but merely on the existence of a vertical load. If there is pressure between the base of the rail and a tie plate, then a resisting moment can take the form of a redistribution of this pressure, without any spikes being used at all.

It is not stated in the paper that simultaneous records of vertical and lateral load under all the wheels of a locomotive have already been made. In footnote 10, it is merely stated that this is contemplated.

The authors heartily welcome Mr. Graham's suggestion that the methods outlined here be extended to the use of more gages and a greater variety of operating conditions. A burning problem at the present time is that of oscillations at high speed. Theories and models can be and are being used, but the final proof of any theory will always depend on full-scale tests. The authors believe that such tests can best be made by developments of the method outlined in this paper. The Otheograph of the General Electric Co. is not satisfactory for the following reasons:

1   The recorded values of lateral load are unreliable since the mounting of the rail is such that purely vertical load can produce lateral deflection and hence record as lateral load. It makes no attempt to record lateral forces directed toward the center of the track.

2   The recorded values of vertical load are in error at high speed due to the inertia of the steel ties supporting the spring mechanism.

Effect of Flat Wheels on Track and Equipment

Abstract of a Report Prepared by the Joint Committee on Relation Between Track and Equipment of the Mechanical and Engineering Divisions, AAR*

Summary

Under present AAR rules governing the removal of flat wheels, flat spots are limited to 2½-in. length for one slid flat, and 2 in. each for adjoining spots on freight car wheels and 1 in. on passenger car wheels. These limitations were established from the experience and judgment of those concerned with the operation and maintenance of equipment and track. To date mathematical solutions to evaluate the impact effects from flat spots have not been adequate. Until recent years, instruments of sufficiently high frequency response to measure accurately the rapid stress changes have not been available.

Tests made on the New York, New Haven, and Hartford Railroad in 1942 established the characteristics required for reliable instrumentation. Suitable stress-measuring instruments were obtained and a comprehensive test program to determine the effects of flat spots on both the track and equipment was conducted on the Chicago & North Western Railway during the summer of•1947.

A special test train was used consisting of a locomotive, a passenger car carrying the measuring and recording instruments for the measurements on the test car, and a flat test car having a flat wheel and loaded with rails. A similar set of instruments was located in a test house along the track for the measurements on the rails. By varying the weight on the flat car, tests were made with wheel loads of 7600 lb., 16,400 lb., and 25,300 lb. Test runs were made at various speeds up to 90 mph. on track laid with 100 RA–A rail and 131-RE rail. Tests were made first with round wheels to provide a basis for comparison; then successively with a 2½-in., 3½-in., and 4½-in. flat spot on one wheel. After these were completed, a 4½-in. flat spot was provided on the opposite wheel of the axle, and finally both of these spots were rounded off at the ends to provide flat spots of 8½-in. length, but of no greater depth.

Impact effects on the track were evaluated principally from measurements of flexural stresses in the rail base. Vertical web stresses were also measured directly beneath the rail head to aid in determining the impact forces on the rail.

Impact effects on the car were evaluated from stress measurements on the wheel plate, axle, truck frame, and one coil spring, and from acceleration measurements on both the sprung and unsprung weights.

A complete description of the test procedure and a detailed presentation of the results are given in the report. The principal conclusions are as follows:

Effect of Speed

(1) Rail flexural stresses increased rapidly with speed, reached a maximum value at 17 to 23 mph., and were somewhat less at higher speeds up to the 90 mph. top speed in the tests.

(2) Wheel plate stresses increased rapidly with speed and reached their maximum values at the highest test speeds.

(3) Axle stresses increased moderately with speed to a maximum value at less than 20 mph., and generally were no higher thereafter.

---

* This abstract presents primarily only those phases of the investigation and stress measurements with respect to the track. Report to be published in full, in mimeograph form, by the AAR.

(4) Truck frame stresses increased with speed, but were sufficiently low throughout all test conditions to be of little concern.

(5) Spring stresses showed a slight release at low speed and no noticeable effect from the flat spot at higher speeds.

(6) The accelerometers on both the sprung and unsprung weight reflected a disturbance from the flat spot at all speeds, but this could not be evaluated because of insufficient damping of the instruments. Transmission of the impact effect to the sprung weight at high speed was evidently through the snubber used in the spring group.

Effect of Flat Spot Length

(1) The impact effect on the rail flexural stress was approximately proportional to the length of flat spot. The ratio of stress with a flat spot to the round wheel stress was approximately equal to the length of the flat spot in inches. There was some indication that greater lengths of flat spot than $4\frac{1}{2}$ in. might give greater relative stresses.

(2) The effect on wheel plate stress for different lengths of flat spot corresponds closely to that on the rail flexural stress.

(3) Axle stresses increased with the length of flat spot to a maximum effect of about 60 percent for the $4\frac{1}{2}$-in. length.

(4) The depth of a flat spot is a better criterion of its impact effect upon track and equipment than its length.

Effect of Wheel Load

(1) The impact effects on rail, wheel plate, and axle stresses increased almost in proportion to the increase in wheel load.

(2) Impact effects on rail flexural stress and wheel plate stress were only slightly greater with the $3\frac{1}{2}$-in. flat spot and half load, and no greater with the $4\frac{1}{2}$-in. flat spot and light load, than with the $2\frac{1}{2}$-in. flat spot and full load.

Impact Force from a Flat Spot

(1) It appears probable that the striking force with the 25,000-lb. wheel load was of the order of 50,000 lb. for the $2\frac{1}{2}$-in. flat spot, 70,000 lb. for the $3\frac{1}{2}$-in. flat spot, and 90,000 lb. for the $4\frac{1}{2}$-in. flat spot.

The following recommendations are presented for consideration:

Removal of Flat Wheels

(1) The depth of a flat spot rather than its length should be the basis for replacing flat wheels. Rounding the ends of a $4\frac{1}{2}$-in. flat spot to provide an $8\frac{1}{2}$-in. length and the same depth showed no change in impact effect.

(2) A suitable gage should be devised for measuring flat spot depth.

(3) A depth of 0.05 in. (corresponding to that for a chord of $2\frac{1}{2}$-in. length on the wheel circumference) is the maximum that should be permitted.

Operation of Flat Wheels to Terminals for Removal

(1) Cars with flat spots may be operated into terminals for wheel replacement without speed restriction if the flat spot depth and wheel load do not exceed the following amounts:

Wheel Load—Lb.	Flat Spot Depth—In.
25,000	0.05
20,000	0.075
15,000	0.100
10,000	0.150

(2) If the wheel load and flat spot depth exceed the above values, the car should be operated into the terminal at a speed not exceeding 10 mph. Operation at speeds of 17 to 23 mph. will produce maximum impact effects on the rail and wheel and should not be permitted. Operation above this critical range, although being somewhat less damaging, does not appear practical.

Introduction

1. Acknowledgment

These tests of flat wheels were carried on as a part of the research program of the Joint Committee on Relation between Track and Equipment of the Engineering and Mechanical Divisions of the Association of American Railroads. The work was under the general direction of G. M. Magee, research engineer and J. R. Jackson, mechanical engineer. Randon Ferguson, electrical engineer in charge of the tests was assisted by M. F. Smucker, assistant electrical engineer, and G. U. Moran, former assistant mechanical engineer. The report was prepared by Mr. Ferguson.

Some of the equipment and services required for the tests were furnished by the Chicago and North Western Railroad. These facilities were of great aid to the test program. E. C. Vandenburgh, chief engineer, and L. R. Lamport, engineer of maintenance, arranged all matters regarding the track, and J. E. Goodwin, executive vice-president, and G. W. Bohannon, chief mechanical officer, handled all arrangements regarding shop work and operating equipment. A passenger car to carry the test equipment and a freight car loaded with rails were assigned to the tests and the necessary shop work in preparing them was done in the railroad's shops. The cars were operated on the C.&N.W. track near Harvard, Ill., as a special test train during the summer of 1947. The work of loading and unloading the rails from the car and the preparation of the track at Harvard was done by the local maintenance of way department forces of the railroad.

2. Purpose of Tests

The test program was planned to develop sufficient information of the impact effects produced by slid flat spots on car wheels to permit review and revision, if found desirable, of the present AAR rules governing the removal of flat wheels. The AAR regulations regarding flat spots are given in the Code of Rules for the Interchange of Traffic, under Rule 68 for freight car wheels and P.C. 8 for passenger car wheels. Flat spots are limited to a 2½-in. length for 1 slid flat and 2 in. each for adjoining spots on freight car wheels, and 1 in. on passenger car wheels. The AAR Wheel and Axle manual refers to these rules and further states (paragraph 98, page 72) that the full length slid flat is not dangerous as far as its effect on the wheel is concerned, but that it makes a rough riding car, may damage the rail, and increases rolling resistance.

Thus it is evident that the aim of the tests was to measure such effects of flat wheels on track and equipment that limits of safe and economical operation might be established. A further objective of the tests was to determine how best to operate slid flat wheels into terminals where replacement facilities are available.

3. Previous Investigations and Analyses

There has been considerable interest in the effect of flat spots on wheels for many years. In spite of this, little experimental work could be done on the subject until the advent of electrical strain and vibration measuring and recording equipment. The severity of the impact caused by the flat spot and the high frequencies involved were beyond the capacities of any of the mechanical-type instruments to measure reliably. An attempt was made in 1920 by a test party of the AREA Committee on Stresses in Railroad Track to measure stresses in rail due to a flat wheel by means of stremmatographs. These instruments (1)* were mechanical-type strain recorders producing true scale records (no magnification) on smoked glass disks. The strains were read by a microscope. This attempt was entirely unsuccessful and was not reported because the severe impact set up such vibrations in the instrument that the recording needle lifted from the surface of the recording disk.

A second attempt was made by the same committee (2) in tests conducted on the Pennsylvania Railroad in 1937, using a flat spot length of about 4 in. and depth of 0.12 in. The speed was limited to 30 mph. for these tests because of the length and depth of the flat spot and the thinness of the wheel rim. Magnetic strain gages and oscillograph recording were used. For the first time records were obtained showing the pattern of stress and depression at a given point in the rail as a wheel with a flat spot rolled over it. (see Fig. 1)

One important finding from these tests was that the stresses in the rail due to a flat wheel were greatest at about 20 to 22 mph., with lesser values at lower and higher speeds. The same was true of the depressions, but the depression curve was not so sharply peaked. There was some indication that the values at the higher speeds had an upward trend, but the maximum speed of 32 mph. was not high enough to indicate this definitely. The maximum rail stresses under the flat wheel were 2.5 times those under the round wheel.

The above tests indicated some of the characteristics of the action of a flat wheel, but there was some doubt as to whether the response of the equipment used at that time was sufficient to indicate the peak values correctly. Magnetic strain gages and oscillographic recording were used and it was considered that this equipment would record stress changes up to 500 cps. with good accuracy. The stress frequency developed during flat wheel impact was not known, but it was suspected to be considerably in excess of this value. Also, measurements at much higher train speeds were obviously desirable.

Accordingly, a set of exploratory tests (3) was run by the AAR research staff on the New Haven Railroad in 1942 with the aid of Prof. A. C. Ruge of the Massachusetts Institute of Technology, using wire resistance gages and cathode-ray recording apparatus of high frequency response, a requisite sensitivity and high recording speed. These tests indicated that any apparatus whfch would respond with the required accuracy and sensitivity to stress variations of 1000 cps., would give reliable results. The shape of the stress variations in the rail were similar to those found in the tests on the Pennsylvania. Shown in Fig. 2 is a reproduction of records taken of stresses in the rail at various speeds in the New Haven tests. It may be seen that the effect of the flat spot reaches a maximum at 20 mph. and decreases slightly at the higher speeds. For the 2.5-in. flat spot used, the maximum rail stress was 2 times as great as with the round wheel. At the higher speeds, the rail stress decreased almost to zero directly under the flat spot, and then increased quite sharply during the period of impact.

Concurrently with the various investigations just described, consideration was given to analytical evaluations of the impact effects. Timoshenko published in 1925 an analysis of the effect of a flat spot on a wheel (or low spot in track) in his book Applied Elasticity (4). This analysis treated the mass of the wheel supported on the elastic track structure as a single degree of freedom vibration problem. Certain assumptions were made to simplify the calculations and the limitations of these assumptions were then pointed out. The analysis evaluated the impact effect as an addition to the static wheel load as determined by the added depression of the rail.

---

* Numbers in parentheses throughout this report refer to references in Appendix E, page 447.

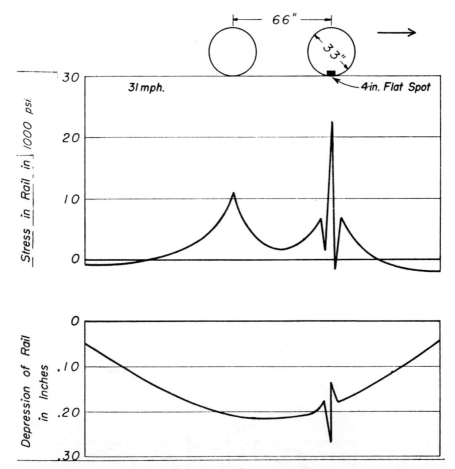

Fig. 1—Stress in Base of Rail and Depression of Rail with 4-in. Flat Spot on Wheel and Round Wheel—Pennsylvania R. R. Tests of 1937

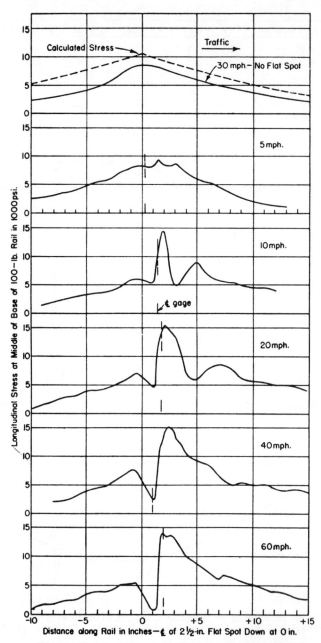

Fig. 2—Stress in Base of Rail at Various Speeds with a 2½-in. Flat Spot on a 33-in. Wheel—New Haven Tests of 1942.

One of the most important limitations in the analysis is undoubtedly the assumption that there is continuous contact between the flat spot and the rail for the full length of the flat spot. Consideration of the factors involved indicates that continuous contact can be maintained only at the lowest speeds.

The assumption is also made that the forces arising from the action of the flat spot produce the same effect as a static or slowly acting force. This, in effect, means neglecting the mass of the rail and other parts of the track affected in producing inertia resistance to added impact depression, and thereby modifying the shape of the flexural curve of the rail from the static form. Timoshenko recognized this factor when he stated that the mass of the support may be neglected if the time required for the flat spot to pass is long compared to the fundamental period of the rail. Since the fundamental period of the rail may be 0.02 to 0.03 sec., and a 4-in. flat spot will be crossed in 0.025 sec. at 10 mph., the validity of the assumptions is limited to a very low speed. The analysis also deals only with the unsprung mass of the wheel and does not consider the spring force on the wheel due to the sprung load.

As previously stated, the impact evaluation in the analysis is determined by the added deflection of the rail. In most of the tests, the impact evaluation has been based upon measurements of rail stress, and it is well known that slight variations in curvature, hardly detectable in the deflection curve, can make important variations in the stresses present. This was shown by R. N. Arnold (5) in impact tests where weights were dropped from various heights on a short length of rail supported at its ends, and the stresses measured with scratch gages at various locations. This was also shown in the Pennsylvania tests where rail stress and depression were both measured (Fig. 1). A significant point in these tests is that although the depression of the rail decreased only slightly when the flat spot lost contact, the stress in the rail decreased to almost zero. This could only occur as a result of a very localized change in the flexure of the rail, extending over an insufficient length to appreciably affect the general depression curve under the wheel load.

It is evident that the present analytical approach to the problem is far from satisfactory. No attempt is made in this report to develop a general mathematical analysis. From the measurements made it may be that enough information can be obtained regarding the forces present and their time rate of variation to make possible the analysis of the problem in the future by an analog computer or other similar method. However, the tests were planned to include sufficient variables in track and operating conditions to obtain from actual measurement the objectives of the investigation.

Description of Test and Test Apparatus

4a. The Track Structure

A location was selected for the tests on the single-track main line of the Chicago and North Western Railroad between Harvard, Ill., and Sharon, Wis. This track was suitable for high-speed running and was reasonably free of train movements during daylight hours. The test house was placed about halfway between these two towns, thus providing distance for accelerating and braking the test train before reaching Harvard.

The track was laid with 100 RA–A rail in 1936, on gravel ballast. In order to also include heavier rail in the tests, 5 new 39-ft., 131 RE rails were laid, 3 in the south rail and 2 directly opposite in the north rail, about 150 ft. east of the test house. The test rail was the middle one of the three in the south rail. The lift for the increased height of the 131-lb. rail was run out in about two rail lengths by tamping up the ties. A test rail for the 100-lb. section, having little play between the ties, tie plates and the rail, was selected about 150 ft. west of the test house. Tests of these two rail sections provided data on both the heaviest and lightest rails generally used in mainline track.

The tie plates for the 100-lb. rail were 7 in. by 12 in., single shoulder, with about ⅜ in. eccentricity. The plates for the 131-lb. rail were new double-shoulder, 8 in. by 14 in., with ⅜ in. eccentricity. Tie spacing was somewhat irregular, but the spacing at the gage application point was about 19 in.

4b. Location of the Track Gages

The location of the wire resistance strain gages on the rail is indicated in Fig. 3. The strain gages were limited to eight in all by the amplifier channels available. Four gages were located at 2-in. intervals on the middle of the base of the rail to measure mean longitudinal stress, and one was at 16 in. in the next tie space, as shown in Fig. 3. It was hoped from this arrangement to obtain the shape of the stress curve along the rail at the instant the flat spot struck, compared to that due to a slowly applied loading. Two gages were placed vertically at the fillet near the head of the rail on the inner and outer web of the rail. Previous tests (6) have determined that the average of these gages will give an indication of the load on the head of the rail. The eighth gage was placed longitudinally on the head of the rail to be as close to the point of impact as possible.

It was necessary to know immediately the place the flat spot hit the rail at the time each run was made in order that the run might be repeated if the contact was not close to one of the track gages. To ascertain the point of impact a hook was attached to the side of the rim of the wheel diametrically opposite the flat spot. The hook extended out about 2 in. beyond the edge of the rim. Alongside the track a trough was placed so the hook would dip into it and make a mark in modeling clay in the trough. The trough was about 30 in. long and the whole arrangement was displaced one-half the circumference of the wheel to clear the gages on the wheel, and also to permit taking moving pictures of the wheel position at the track gages as a check. The surface of the modeling clay was coated with a jelly-like mixture of graphite, tragacanth and water, the mixture possessing some electrical conductivity. The contact of the hook closed a circuit between the rail and trough through a galvanometer, which made an indication on the track oscillograph record. Of course, this indication was displaced on half of the circumference of the wheel to the time scale of the record.

5a. Instrument and Test Cars

A passenger-baggage combination car served as an instrument car and carried the testing equipment required to make the measurement on the test car.

The test car was a 70-ton C.&N.W. flat car with a cast steel frame, 6-in. by 11-in. journals, double-truss spring plankless trucks, and 33-in. diameter, one-wear wrought steel wheels. Each bolster end was supported by four double-coil springs and one Simplex snubber. The test car was placed at the rear of the test train, and the flat wheel was the last wheel on the car so that the stress was influenced by only the one adjacent wheel.

The test car was loaded with 70 tons of rails that were marked so that 35 tons could be removed to give one-half rated load, or all removed to give no load. The rails were tied down by cross members bolted to the sides of the car and were held longitudinally by a tie barricade. The weight of the car was 60,700 lb. light, 131,200 lb. with one-half load, and 202,100 lb. fully loaded. The rails were loaded and unloaded between series of runs by a section gang using a traveling crane. The two cars were pulled by a steam passenger locomotive capable of attaining the speeds desired.

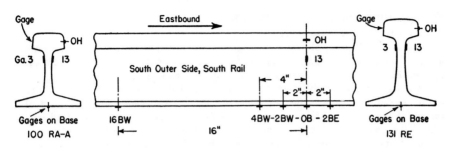

Fig. 3—Location of Strain Gages on Rails.

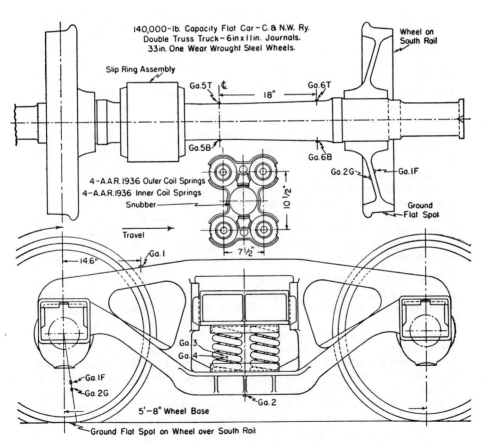

Fig. 4—Location of Slip Ring Assembly and Strain Gages on Rear Wheel
Plate and Axle and on Truck Frame and Spring.

A

5b. Measuring Equipment and Methods

(1) Gages and Accelerometers

The general location of the strain gages on the wheel, axle, and truck are shown in Fig. 4. These gages were placed to indicate most advantageously the effects from the flat spot impact. All strain gages were of the wire resistance type.

A series of gages was placed on the wheel plate on both sides, radially to the striking end of the flat spot. Prior to the test runs a static test was made in which the point of bearing of the wheel on the rail was varied across the width of the wheel tread, and two of the gages were chosen for the dynamic tests because they most nearly gave a constant numerical sum when the stresses were added. This procedure tended to eliminate the effect of eccentricity of bearing on the indicated wheel plate stress, and to make the indication proportional to the load or force on the wheel.

Gages were placed to measure the bending stress in the axle at mid-length, where the axle diameter was a minimum, and also at 18 in. from mid-length, which was as close to the flat wheel as practicable. These gages and the wheel gages were applied at the C.&N.W. shops before installing the assembly in the car.

In addition to the gages on the wheel and axle, there were gages (3 and 4, Fig. 4) to measure the load transmitted by the bolster spring group on the flat wheel side; also gages 1 and 2, to measure the stresses in the top and bottom of the truck frame at locations where the stresses had been found to be a maximum in other tests. The acceleration of the unsprung weight was indicated by an accelerometer placed on the journal of the flat wheel, and that of the sprung weight by an accelerometer placed on the car floor. The journal accelerometer was a 200 g Statham instrument with a natural frequency of about 1000 cps., and the other was of 10 g capacity with about 200 cps. natural frequency. Both were found to be insufficiently damped when the tests were started, but this could not be corrected without undue delay, and the records obtained from them are of little value at speeds above 5 mph. because of resonant vibration at their natural frequency.

(2) Slip-Ring Assembly

Because of the rotation of the wheels and axles, a slip-ring assembly mounted on the axle was required to transmit the signals from the wheel and axle gages to the recording equipment. The slip-ring assembly was installed before pressing the wheels on the axle. It was mounted near the wheel that had no flat spot to minimize the shock on the brushes from the impact. The wheel and slip-ring assembly is shown in Fig. 5. This assembly was designed and built by the Ruge–Deforest Company of Cambridge, Mass.

6. Recording and Amplifying Equipment

The recording of all stresses was done with one 12-element Hathaway magnetic oscillograph in the car and one in the test house. The amplifiers were the carrier-wave type designed and built by the Association research staff and previously described (7). Eight channels were available for the car and eight for the track. For the purpose of these tests a higher frequency response was desired, and a special lot of higher-frequency galvanometers was obtained. These galvanometers gave good response to 1000 cps., and were down about 10 percent at 1200 cps. The sensitivity of the galvanometers was considerably lower (about $\frac{1}{4}$ of the usual amount), so the operation of the amplifiers was modified to obtain the increased output current required. The discriminator normally used was switched out and an external rectifier and filter used to operate with a galvanometer offset in a manner similar to the method used for the magnetic gages. This mode of operation gave a usable sensitivity for all gages and provided the frequency response which the New Haven tests had shown to be necessary.

371

Fig. 5—View of the Slip-Ring Assembly in Place on the Axle
with Cover Removed.

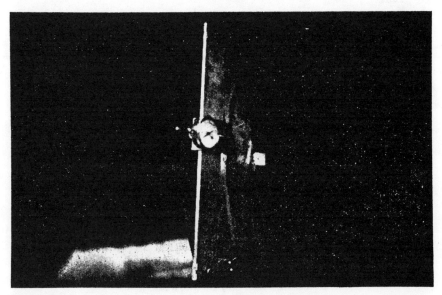

Fig. 6—View of Profile Gage in Place for Measurement of Flat Spot Contour.

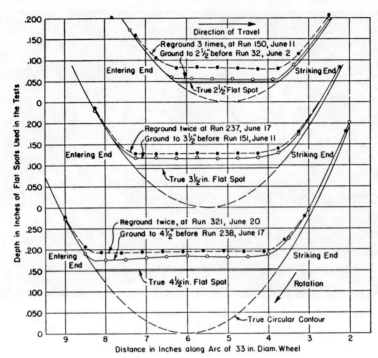

Fig. 7—Profiles of the Three Lengths of Ground Flat Spots on a 33-in. Wheel—Profiles shown are before and after test runs.

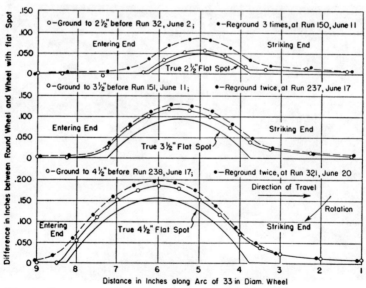

Fig. 8—Contours of the Three Lengths of Ground Flat Spots on a 33-in. Wheel—Contours shown are before and after test runs.

7. Test Program and Procedure

Two series of tests were first run with round wheels and fully loaded car on the 100-lb. and 131-lb. rail. These were followed by 18 series of tests, including full load, half load, and light car on both the 100-lb. and the 131-lb. rail, and with flat spots of 2½-in., 3½-in., and 4½-in. lengths. Nominal speeds were used for each test condition of 5, 10, 15, 20, 30, 40, 60, 70, 80, and 90 mph.

After completion of these tests, two additional series were run with the fully loaded car. In one series a 4½-in. flat spot was ground on the opposite wheel of the axle to determine the difference in impact effects compared to those with a flat spot on one wheel only. In the last series, the 4½-in. flat spots on the two wheels were rounded off at both ends, making a total length for each of 8½ in., but with no increase in their maximum depth.

The flat spot was made on the right rear wheel, at the proper location with respect to the gages, by a portable grinder. A straight chord of 2½ in. was ground across the wheel for the first test, and the striking end of the flat spot (the last point to contact the rail) was taken as the zero position of reference, and the strain gage location for the gages on the wheel and axle was along the same radial line. The maximum impact was found in previous tests to occur when this end of the flat spot struck the rail. Obviously, all tests with a given length of flat spot had to be made before grinding a larger spot unless the wheel was replaced, a rather impracticable undertaking in this case. Thus, the tests were made with a given car loading on the 100-lb. rail, and then the gage leads on the track gages were shifted to the 131-lb. rail. After testing the 131-lb. rail the load was then changed and the tests repeated on the two weights of rail. The load was changed again, and the tests again run with the same flat spot. Each series with a given condition took about a day. After the six test series with a given length of flat spot, the flat spot was increased 1 in. in length.

The contour of the flat spot was checked with a special contour measuring gage before and after each day's run, and sometimes during the day. At times the spot was reground because the corners had rounded off. A view of this instrument in place on the wheel is shown in Fig. 6. Representative profiles of the flat spots plotted with reference to the variation from a true circle are shown in Fig. 7 for the various lengths of spot. The same readings are also plotted in Fig. 8 as contours of the wheel, with the ordinates to an enlarged scale. The readings shown were taken after grinding and following a number of test runs. It may be noted that there was some rounding off, especially at the striking edge of the flat spot, after a number of runs. The depth of the 4½-in. flat spot was about 0.19 in. The flat spot of about 4-in. length previously tested on the Pennsylvania was 0.12 in. deep, the ends being rounded off some by running.

Since the number of channels available for the track measurements was limited to eight, this made the distance covered by the gages along the rail relatively short. Considerable difficulty was experienced in getting the flat spot to come down within this distance. It was desired to have the point of impact within 1 in. of a gage, preferably the one designated OB in Fig. 3. At the lower speeds the point of impact did not change very greatly and could be readily controlled. Of course, the distance traveled was not great in making the runs up to 30 mph. At the higher speeds the point of impact could not be predicted with any accuracy. At the extreme speeds of 80 or 90 mph. the running distance was 6 or 8 miles, and the location of the flat spot impact was quite variable. This is the principal reason for the small number of plotted points on the track records for the higher speeds. Also, it was difficult to attain the 90-mph. speed because a curve not far from the test section required a speed restriction of 80 mph., and the locomotives available could not readily accelerate to 90 mph. in the intervening distance.

When the flat spot struck beyond the range of the gage location, it was necessary to slip the wheel to bring it back to the desired location. This was done by placing hardwood wedges under the wheels and sliding the wheels the proper amount. Several trials were usually necessary to get it exactly to the desired position.

Results of the Tests on the Track

8. Discussion of Typical Records

All measurements on the rail were obtained at eight gage positions; five showed the flexural or bending stress along the centerline of the base; two, the stress in a vertical direction in the upper part of the rail web; and one, the vertical (and lateral, if present) bending stress along the outer side of the rail head (See Fig. 3). All eight gages were recorded simultaneously on one oscillograph.

Study of the stress records indicates several interesting characteristics of the flat spot impact. Typical records of rail stress in the 100-lb. rail at 10 mph. and 80 mph. for full load with round wheels are shown in Fig. 10 to illustrate the stress variation without the flat spot, and to provide a basis for comparison of the flat spot effects. Without the flat spot, the five traces of bending stress in the base (traces 16 BW, 4 BW, 2 BW, OB, and 2 BE) each show a peak tension stress directly under each passing wheel, with a smooth transition into compression between wheels. These traces are seen to be smooth and symmetrical, even at 80 mph., although at this speed the effect of the impact of the wheels on nearby rail joints is apparent. Traces 3 and 13 show vertical stress in the web, and it will be noted that these stresses show sharp peaks under each wheel load, and that there is little stress present except when the wheel is within a few inches of the stress gage. Trace OH is the longitudinal stress along the outer side of the rail head; the small reverse peak directly under the wheel load is the transverse tension component from the vertical bearing pressure under the wheel load.

The difference in the stress pattern due to a flat spot is illustrated in Fig. 11. This record is with the fully loaded car and a 4½-in. flat spot at speeds of 6 and 65 mph., also on the 100-lb. rail. The traces are in the same relative position as in Fig. 10. The flat spot struck between gages OB and 2 BW in the 6-mph. record, according to the indication made by the wheel marker. The sharp peak of stress and a double oscillation after the initial impact are similar in form and magnitude for gage lines OB and 2 BW. The frequency of the oscillation is approximately 65 cps. At this low speed there is little if any reduction of stress prior to the impact, because contact is probably maintained with the rail throughout.

The right side of Fig. 11 is at 65 mph. The flat spot in this case struck only ½ in. east from gage OB, the third trace from the bottom of the record. The traces were very faint at the instant of the impact due to the high rate of travel of the light beam, and the record has been reinforced so it will be visible in the reproduction. In this test the stress reduction due to the presumed loss of contact is seen to be quite definite, and the rail stress under the wheel actually becomes compressive for a short interval. This point is easily picked out by noting where the trace first suddenly departs from its usual form seen in the adjacent round wheel record, and becomes quickly compressive. A relatively high stress is produced at the gage OB, after the flat spot gets a revolution past the gage location, as shown by this record. This stress for the first revolution beyond is 10,000 psi. tension, and becomes progressively less for later revolutions. A careful examination of the sign of this stress at OB, compared to that at the same instant in the

375

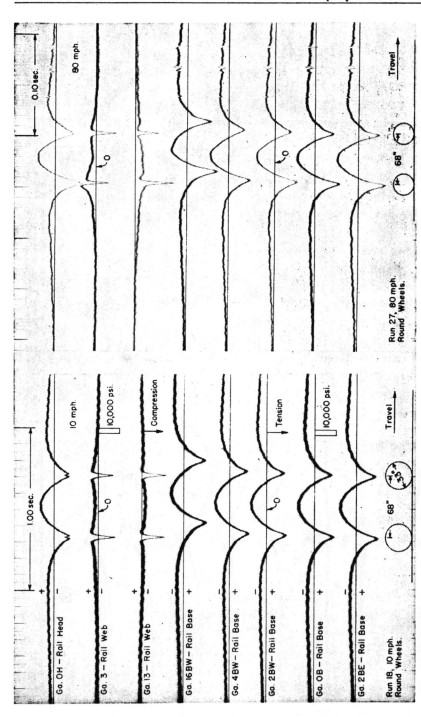

Fig. 10—Typical Records of Rail Stress at 10 and 80 mph. with Round Wheels—Full Load, 100-lb. Rail.

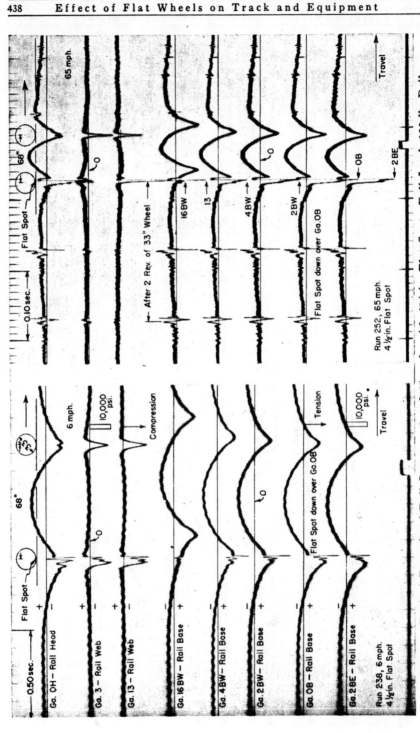

Fig. 11—Typical Records of Rail Stress at 6 and 65 mph. with 4½-in. Flat Spot—Full Load, 100-lb. Rail.

head of the rail, the top trace, indicates that the stress is caused by a flexure of the rail, rather than a longitudinal wave along the rail vibrating in the manner of a prismatic bar struck on the end. The effect appears to be a transverse wave induced by the impact that travels down the rail in a manner similar to the wave that travels down a rope when it is "flipped" at one end and the other is fixed. It is especially noticeable that this effect does not occur between the trucks of the car to nearly as great an extent as it does after the last truck has passed beyond the gage location. The load from the two trucks apparently restrains the whipping action of the rails between the trucks in the manner that transverse restraint of the rope tends to restrain a wave in the rope from traveling along its length.

To illustrate further the effect of the flat spot on the rail stress Fig. 12 is given. Here are presented the records of longitudinal stress in rail for the various speeds. The records are with the full load of 70 tons on the car, and with respect to the 100-lb. and 131-lb. rail. Certain characteristics of these records are significant. The appearance of the records for both weights of rail are similar at 5 and 10 mph., but due to the impact the shape of the stress curve changes above that speed. The amplitude is greatest at 20 mph. and smaller at higher and lower speeds. The record for the 131-lb. rail has a double peak above 40 mph., which is not present in the records for the 100-lb. rail. This double peak would indicate a double impact, as if the wheel "bounced" up enough after the first impact to hit again with force comparable to the first impact. This double impact effect was also present in the wheel plate stress and axle stress. A possible explanation of its occurrence in the 131-lb. rail and not the 100-lb. rail is that the greater stiffness and mass of the heavier rail give more tendency for the wheel to rebound. The wheel has the full force of the compressed car springs acting to force it quickly back down onto the rail whenever contact with the rail is lost.

The maximum impact stress at 20 mph. may readily be compared quantitatively with that under the round leading wheel.

9. Impact Effects

(a) Effect of Speed

The gages measuring bending stress along the centerline of the rail base provide the best means of analyzing the impact effects in these tests. Unfortunately, the test location on the 131-lb. rail was found to have considerable play between the rail, ties, and the ballast bed, possibly due to disturbance of the ballast in laying the heavier rail. This play had the effect of increasing the bending stresses in this rail by a constant amount at each gage location. This added stress tended to distort the relation between the impact stress and wheel load stress, and in order to correct for this, and also provide a better comparison with the 100-lb. rail location at which no play existed, calculations were made as explained in Appendix A* to bring the stress values into their proper relative magnitudes for the two weights of rail. These corrections are given in Table 1† for the several gage locations.

The readings of maximum bending stress in the rail base for the three load conditions are plotted with respect to train speed in Fig. 13 for both the 100-lb. and 131-lb. rail (after being adjusted to correct for play). Only readings from those runs in which the flat spot struck within 1 in. of a gage are included. Certain series, as mentioned previously, have a shortage of points at the higher speeds, but fortunately there are some points for the most severe conditions with the 4½-in. flat spot. For comparison, the

---

* Appendix A, as well as Appendices B, C, and D, referred to later, are not presented in this abstract.

† Table 1 is not presented in this abstract.

378

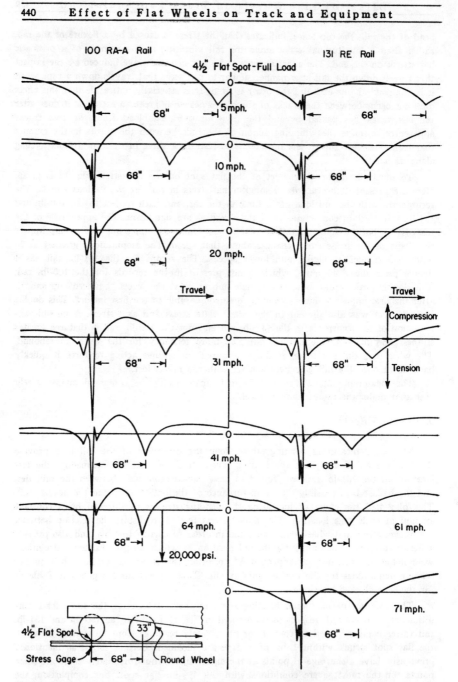

Fig. 12—Traced Records of Stress in Rail Base Due to 4½-in. Flat Spot at Various Speeds—Full Load, 100-lb. and 131-lb. Rails.

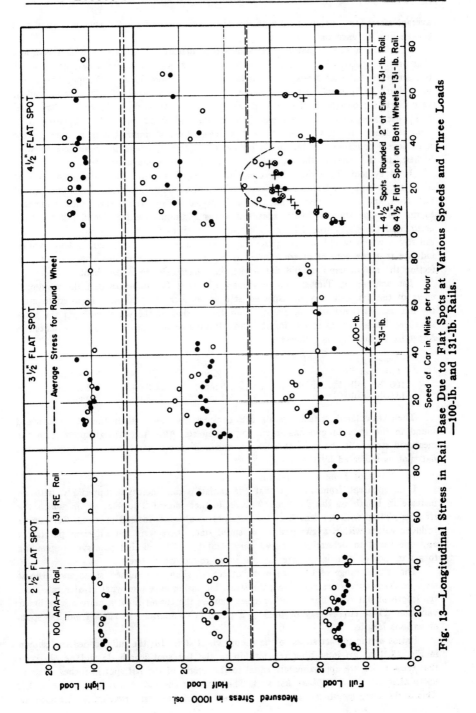

Fig. 13—Longitudinal Stress in Rail Base Due to Flat Spots at Various Speeds and Three Loads
—100-lb. and 131-lb. Rails.

average stress for runs up to 20 mph. for the wheel without the flat spot is plotted as a broken line for each test condition.

It will be observed that the flat spot stress increased quite rapidly with speed, and that only at speeds of 5 mph. or less was this stress near the round wheel stress. In all test series the flat spot stress reaches a peak value at approximately 20 mph. This is not very clearly defined in the tests with no load, but in the others it is clearly defined or very marked, especially in the tests on the 100-lb. rail. At 40 mph. the stresses have generally decreased to about the same amount as found at 10 mph. There appears to be some tendency for the flat spot stress to increase above 40 mph., but in no case for the most severe conditions of full load and longest flat spot, where the peak stresses were highest, did the stress at the top speeds reach the 20 mph. maximum stress.

It is evident, therefore, that the rather general practice of putting slow orders of 15 to 25 mph. on trains with flat wheels is disadvantageous from the standpoint of rail stress, and actually means that the flat spot will be run at the speed most damaging to the rail. Operation at higher speeds involves additional hazard should rail breakage occur, and the speed would have to be limited to below 10 mph. to effectively reduce rail stress, which would only be practical for movements of short distance. These values indicate that the control of train speed is not in general a very effective way of protecting the rail in handling slid flat wheels into terminals for replacement.

The analysis by Timoshenko previously discussed (4) indicates that the maximum effect of the flat spot may be expected at a speed such that the time required to cross the flat spot is two-thirds the natural vibration period of the wheel mass on the track structure. These critical speeds for the three lengths of flat spot have been calculated in Appendix B, and are as follows:

Length of Flat Spot	2½ in.	3½ in.	4½ in.
100-lb. rail	7.6 mph.	10.5 mph.	14.1 mph.
131-lb. rail	8.2 mph.	11.5 mph.	14.6 mph.

These calculated critical speeds are considerably lower than the 20-mph. speed found in the tests to give maximum impact effects. Also, the critical speed from the measured stresses is the same throughout, and does not increase with the length of the flat spot as indicated by the analysis.

(b) Effect of Length of Flat Spot

It is apparent from Fig. 13 that the impact stress increases appreciably with an increase in length of the flat spot. This is further indicated in Fig. 14, in which the stress is plotted with the length of the flat spot as abscissa, instead of speed. Each curve includes values within a given range of speed since there were not sufficient points for any one speed to determine a curve very definitely. The plotted points corresponding to a flat spot of zero length are the measured round wheel stresses.

The critical range of 17 to 23 mph., of course, shows the highest stress and steepest slope, and the curves are not linear, the stress increasing at a somewhat greater rate than the length of flat spot. For the other speed ranges, the curves show a more nearly linear variation. These curves may be used as a guide in comparing the effect from flat spots of various lengths.

Ratios of the impact stress to the round wheel stress for the fully loaded car, shown in Fig. 15, bear an interesting relationship to the flat spot length. It will be observed that these ratios are approximately equal to the length of the flat spot in inches, ranging up to almost 5 for the 4½-in. flat spot. The ratio for the 2½-in. flat spot was 2 to 2.5. This is the same length flat spot used in the New Haven tests, previously discussed, in

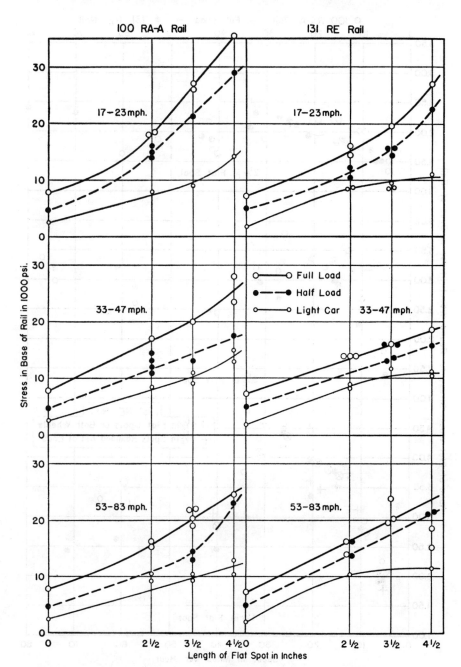

Fig. 14—Longitudinal Stress in Rail Base Due to Flat Spots at Three Ranges of Speed and Three Loads—100-lb. and 131-lb. Rails.

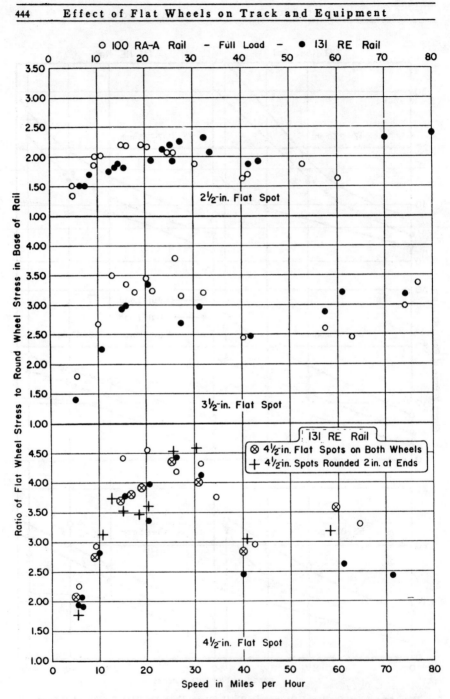

Fig. 15—Ratio of Flat Wheel Stress to Round Wheel Stress in Base of Rail
at Various Speeds—Fully Loaded Car, 100-lb. and 131-lb. Rails.

which the stresses due to the flat spot were found to be about 2 times the stresses with a round wheel, a good agreement with the present data. The corresponding ratio for the Pennsylvania Railroad tests was about 2.5 for a 4-in. flat spot. However, the ends were rounded somewhat, so its depth actually corresponded to a flat spot of less length. Also, there is the previously mentioned question as to whether the frequency response of the instruments used in the Pennsylvania tests was sufficiently high to record the true maximum value of the impacts.

Reference has been made to the length of flat spot without regard to depth because in the tests the flat spot was cut squarely across the wheel as a chord on the arc of a circle, and the depth would vary as the length. Flat spots encountered in service are often rolled out to a considerable length, but are not of comparable depth. In the final series of tests the 4½-in. flat spot was rounded off 2 in. at both ends to form a flat spot 8½ in. long without increasing the depth. The results of these tests, included in the lower right-hand corner of Fig. 13, show that the rail stresses were no higher with the 8½-in. flat spot than with the 4½-in. flat spot of the same depth. This indicates clearly that the depth of the flat spot determines the impact effect rather than the length, and that the length should only be used as a guide to the extent that it is representative of the depth.

(c) Effect of Wheel Load

Fig. 13 shows that the impact stress, as well as the round wheel stress, increases with increasing wheel load. This was not anticipated from the theoretical analysis, which indicates that the impact effect (as determined by additional rail depression) is only influenced by the depth of the flat spot and the mass of the unsprung weight. It seems logical to expect, however, that when the wheel loses contact with the rail, a circumstance not considered in the analysis, the greater spring force produced by the greater weight will accelerate the wheel downward more rapidly. Also, the rail, being depressed farther by the heavier wheel loads, will tend to spring upward more quickly. With both the mass of the wheel and the mass of the rail moving more rapidly toward each other at the time of impact, it would seem logical with the heavier loads that the rail would tend to "wrap" itself farther around the wheel and produce the higher bending stresses actually measured.

In the tests the impact stress was little greater with a 3½-in. flat spot and one-half load, and no greater with a 4½-in. flat spot and light load, than with a 2½-in. flat spot and a fully loaded car. Consideration might well be given to this in handling slid flat wheels into terminals. As a temporary measure, wheels with flat spots longer than 2½ in. could be operated into terminals if the car was not heavily loaded. On passenger cars with relatively moderate wheel loads, the inconvenience to passengers of transference to another car might be avoided for flat spots not exceeding 3½ in. in length. With flat spots of 4½-in. length or slightly longer, the unloading of freight cars might be desirable in some cases to permit movement into terminals and avoid changing wheels at outlying points.

10. Conclusions

The preceding data support a number of conclusions in regard to the effect of flat spots on the rail:

(a) The rail stress due to a flat spot increases rapidly with speed, reaching a maximum at 20 mph. irrespective of flat spot length, wheel load, or weight of rail. It decreases somewhat to 40 mph., then tends to increase at higher speeds, but does not again reach the 20 mph. maximum stress up to 90 mph.

(b) Reduction of train speed to protect the rail from flat spot damage is only effective if limited to below 10 mph.

(c) Rail stress increases with the length of flat spot. For a fully loaded car the bending stress in the rail is increased by a ratio approximately equal to the length of the flat spot in inches.

(d) The rail stress with the 2½-in. maximum length of flat spot now permitted is not excessive. However, since the impact effect is from 100 to 150 percent additional, it would not seem wise to increase the permissible length beyond this amount because of possible rail breakage in cold weather.

(e) Rail stress increases with increasing wheel load. Maximum rail stress was only slightly greater with a 3½-in. flat spot and one-half load, and no greater with a 4½-in. flat spot and light load, than with a 2½-in. flat spot and full load.

(f) The depth of the flat spot, rather than the length, determines the impact effect upon the rail.

Results of Tests on the Car

[The following articles in the report, which deal primarily with stress measurements in equipment, are not presented in this abstract:

11. Discussion of Typical Records
12a. Static Stresses in the Wheel Plate
12b. Dynamic Stresses in the Wheel Plate
13. Stresses in the Car Axle
14. Stresses in the Car Spring
15. Stresses in the Truck Frame
16. Accelerometer Measurements on the Car Body and Journal Box.]

17. Impact Force Between Rail and Wheel Due to a Flat Spot

Measurements of the flexural stresses in the rail base have been presented as the best criterion of the damaging effect of a flat spot on the rail. However, it has been pointed out that at the higher speeds the inertia of the rail, no doubt, affects the flexural stresses developed, so these stresses could not be considered a very reliable index of the actual force due to the flat spot impact. Gages 3 and 13, placed to measure the vertical stress in the web immediately under the rail head, have been found in previous tests to be a reliable indication of wheel load under ordinary conditions. It seems probable that this is the best measure of the impact force from the flat spot that can be obtained from measurements on the rail. It also seems likely that this will constitute a fairly reliable measure, and that the stress at this location will not be too much affected by the inertia of the rail.

Accordingly, in Appendix D a comprehensive analysis is given of the evaluation of the impact force between rail and wheel as determined from these rail web stress measurements. A similar evaluation is also made to determine the impact force from the wheel plate stresses. Since the impact force with which the wheel strikes the rail is the same as that with which the rail strikes the wheel, the two evaluations, if each is correct, should give equal results.

Examination of the two evaluations shows that this is only partially true. At speeds of about 15 to 30 mph., the impact forces so evaluated agree reasonably well, particularly for the fully loaded car. For this condition, it appears that the total wheel load, including the impact effect, is on the order of 50,000 lb. for the 2½-in. flat spot, 70,000 lb. for the 3½-in. flat spot, and 90,000 lb. for the 4½-in. flat spot.

385

At higher speeds the impact forces evaluated from the wheel plate stresses show a well defined increase. A similar relative increase was noted in the maximum values of wheel plate stresses for round wheels, attributed largely to the bouncing and rolling action of the car body on the springs.

Evaluation of the striking force on the rail at high speeds is not possible from the measured rail stresses. On only a few of the high-speed runs did the flat spot strike sufficiently near the one set of web stress gages to make this measurement of value. For these few measurements it is not likely that the spring pressure was at or near its maximum amount.

Probably the general values given above for maximum total wheel load, including impact at speeds of 15 to 30 mph., would be increased on the order of 50 percent at the highest speeds.

18. Conclusions

From the preceding data, the following may be concluded regarding the effect of flat spot impact on the components of the car:

(1) Wheel plate stresses increase with speed, wheel load, and length of flat spot. The increase due to impact effect is as much as 200 percent for a 2½-in. flat spot and fully loaded car. Reduction of speed to 10 mph. or less will effectively reduce wheel plate impact stress. The impact effect is no greater with a 3½-in. flat spot and half load, or with a 4½-in. flat spot and light load, than with a 2½-in. flat spot and full load.

(2) Total axle stresses, including the flat spot impact effect for a 2½-in. flat spot and full load, are but little under the lower values for endurance limit of axles. However, these stresses are not so greatly increased with longer lengths of flat spots, so axle stress does not appear to be a factor of major concern in limiting flat spot length.

(3) Car spring stresses are somewhat reduced by the impact effect at slow speed, and are not influenced at all at high speed.

(4) Truck frame stresses were found to be low, even for the 4½-in. flat spot and full load. Maximum truck frame stress for full load and round wheels was approximately 4000 psi. at low speed and 6000 psi. at high speed. Although the impact effect of the 4½-in. flat spot increased this to 10,000 psi., this is still a stress well within that permissible.

(5) There was some transmission of the impact effect to the car body (sprung weight) by the snubbers used in these tests. It was not possible to evaluate the extent of the disturbance to the car body with the equipment used.

Appendix E*—List of References

(1) First Progress Report—Special Committee on Stresses in Railroad Track, Vol. 19, 1918, page 873, Proceedings of the American Railway Engineering Association, and Vol. 82, 1918, of the Transactions of the American Society of Civil Engineers.

(2) Seventh Progress Report—Committee on Stresses in Railroad Track, Vol. 42, 1941, page 139, Monograph section, Proceedings of the American Railway Engineering Association.

(3) Investigation of the Impact Effect of Flat Wheels—Preliminary Report, by G. M. Magee and E. E. Cress. Vol. 45, 1944, page 9 of Monographs, Proceedings, American Railway Engineering Association.

(4) Applied Elasticity—(page 334)—by S. Timoshenko.

* Appendices A, B, C, and D are not presented in this abstract.

(5) Impact Stresses in a Freely Supported Beam, by R. N. Arnold—Vol. 137, page 217, Transactions of The Institution of Mechanical Engineers.

(6) Static Stress Measurements on Five Test Rails in Special Tangent Track under Controlled Loading Conditions—Vol. 46, 1945, page 684, and Vol. 48, 1947, page 785, Proceedings, American Railway Engineering Association.

(7) Design of and Stresses in Tie Plates—Vol. 47, 1946, page 507, Proceedings, American Railway Engineering Association.

(8) Fourth Progress Report, April 1, 1940, Table A, and Seventh Progress Report, page 3, April 12, 1948, Passenger Car Axle Tests, Mechanical Division, Association of American Railroads; also Fatigue Strength of Machined Forgings 6 in. to 7 in. in Diameter, Proceedings, American Society for Testing Materials, 1939, pages 723 to 737, incl.

(9) The Effect on Wheel Loads of Irregularities of Wheels and Track, by H. R. Thomas and N. H. Roy—Vol. 39, 1938, page 843, Proceedings, American Railway Engineering Association.

Altoona, Pa. 12-15-47. CJC/ld

Mr. J. L. Gressitt,
    Chief Engineer.

        Final report on Test 405, Rail Design, and Test 416, Service
Measurement of Rail Web Stresses Outside of Joint.

I. Introduction
        Test 405 was verbally authorized in July 1944 and had its
inception in investigation of split web failures in 131 RE rail. Test 416
was authorized by your letter of January 29, 1945.

        Between the years 1940 and 1943 web failures in 112 RE
rail had been reported by the D. & R. G. W. Railroad, and some work had
been done in investigating the cause of these failures by the Research
Engineer, Association of American Railroads. In May 1943 Mr. L. Yeager
wrote to membership of the Rail Committee, suggesting that the Committee
should undertake to investigate the desirability of improving the rail
sections generally in use on American railroads, with particular reference
to the 112 lb. RE section. This matter was discussed at a meeting of the
Rail Committee, A.R.E.A., on May 11, 1943, and a resolution was adopted to
investigate recent developments as affecting rail design. Subcommittee 12
under the Chairmanship of Mr. C. B. Bronson was appointed to carry out
this investigation. On July 13, 1943, Mr. C. H. Magee, in a report to this
Subcommittee, stated that rail web failures are not at the present time of
such extent as to cause apprehension.

        Up to this time there had been no mention of any difficulty
with the 131 RE section, and our own correspondence at this time refers to
scarcity of web failures on the Pennsylvania Railroad.

        In October 1943 Mr. Raymond Swenk, Chief Engineer M. W.,
Central Region, sent to the laboratory a piece of rail of 131 RE section
from Lilly, Pittsburgh Division, with crack in the upper web fillet, for
examination. While there was a dark streak in the web of this rail at the
time it was received, laboratory examination failed to reveal any evidence
of crack.

        On February 10, 1944, Mr. Swenk wrote the Chief Engineer,
suggesting that a limit on head wear of 131 RE rail be imposed in connection
with transposing. On February 28, 1944, Mr. Swenk sent in for examination
rails from South Fork, Pittsburgh Division, with web cracks, in connection
with the same question of transposing.

        Between February and July, 1944, we examined a number of
rails at the laboratory and investigated a number of locations in the field
where split web failures of the 131 RE section were developing. In all
cases examined up to this time the rails in which failure was experienced
showed a considerable amount of head wear, generally in the neighborhood of
1/4" of vertical wear, and in a large percentage of cases had been transposed.

On July 26, 1944, we recommended that 131 RE rail with 1/4" vertical head wear be considered as badly worn and treated accordingly.

On April 20, 1944, we ordered an instrument for measuring strains under static conditions with SR-4 wire resistance strain gauges (strain indicator) and by the 1st of August, 1944, had received this instrument and sufficient auxiliary equipment to permit us to begin laboratory measurement of web stresses in rail sections.

The first laboratory work was done on 131 RE rails with varying degrees of wear, in an effort to establish the relationship between head wear and stress in the rail web. These tests showed a definite relationship between web stress and head wear. The web stress increases materially as the rail head becomes thinner.

This observation coincided with service experience. Split web failures, even in the 130 lb. section, had long been recognized as accompanying extremely heavy head wear in rails on the low side of curves. The 130 lb. rail with its 2" thick head had considerably greater resistance to this sort of difficulty than the 131 RE section with a 1-3/4" head (measured from the line of intersection of the fishing surfaces).

Following the initial tests of 131 RE rail with various amounts of head wear, work was begun on redesign of the 131 RE section with the thought in mind of reducing the stress in the rail web and increasing the life of the rail, first by adding metal to the rail head, and second by thickening the web so that its strength after several years of wear would be equal to or greater than the strength of the existing sections when new.

In an Altoona Laboratory report dated December 6, 1944, recognition was given to heavy corrosion as a factor in connection with a web failure which occurred in Carnegie 1932 rail, 131 RE, on November 11, 1944, in the vicinity of mile post 264, Pittsburgh Division. In February 1945 we reported that corrosion may be a greater or less factor in this type of failure, and where corrosion is heavy, failure may result in spite of what may be considered as moderate head wear.

At this time, failures of the split web type in 131 RE rail were definitely on the increase and had become a major problem.

II. Laboratory Tests
1. Method
(a) Rail Support

In making these tests in the laboratory it was recognized that there would be a difference in the deflection of the rail and the normal bending stresses on rigid laboratory supports as compared with support on ties in the track. It was anticipated that the effect of this on web stress would be small. A spacing of the supports of 48", with a centrally applied load, was adopted with the thought in mind that this would give a relationship between concentrated load and bending moment somewhat similar to that obtained in track. Comparison of the results first obtained on 131 RE rail with results obtained by the Research Engineer, Association of American

Photo, T35221
140-K Rail in Testing Machine
Method of Applying Eccentric Load

Railroads in static tests in track at Proviso Yard, showed such close agreement that it was concluded that the method of support was satisfactory, and this method was used throughout the tests.

(b) Load Application

Initially, strain gauges were placed in the center of the upper web fillet, at the point of minimum section in the web, and at the center of the bottom web fillet. These gauges were placed around the cross section of the rail with their center lines in a vertical plane, perpendicular to the length of the rail, and the load was applied directly over them, using a bearing block machined to represent a 33" wheel. Tests were made with the load on the center line of the rail and with 3/4" eccentricity toward each side. Initially, the rail was canted to represent the canting of the rail in track, but this procedure was later dropped and the rail tested in a vertical position, canting the loading block to such degree as was necessary to obtain flat contact between the loading block and the rail. See photograph T-35281.

Difficulty was experienced in locating the load exactly 3/4" from the longitudinal center line of the rail, and the procedure was adopted of applying the load through a 5/8" annealed steel disk intended to approximate the area of contact between wheel and rail. This disk could be placed with reasonable precision.

(c) Location of Maximum Stress. Stresscoat Tests.

After the initial tests, it was suspected that the longitudinal center line of the upper web fillet might not be the location of maximum stress and Stresscoat tests were carried out in order to determine the location of maximum stress. The maximum stress in the rail web is compression, and in order to reveal this stress by the use of Stresscoat it was necessary to use a reverse method of loading. The procedure adopted was to coat the rail specimen with Stresscoat the afternoon before it was desired to make tests, hold it over night under a load of 60,000 to 80,000 lb., then on the morning of the test to remove this load in increments, observing the surface of the rail web, until cracks showed up in the Stresscoat. The amount of load removed was taken as representing the applied test load, and the tensile stress induced due to the removal of this load was taken as representing the compressive stress due to an equal applied load. Photographs Nos. T-34423 and T-36359, attached, show the appearance of the Stresscoat patterns for typical cases. A sample Stresscoat data sheet may be of interest and is attached.

These Stresscoat tests showed that the maximum web stress was near the bottom of the upper web fillet. The procedure was adopted, whenever a new rail section was to be tested, of first making a Stresscoat test to locate the point of maximum stress and then applying a gauge at the location of maximum stress, other gauges being distributed up and down the rail web so that a curve could be plotted showing in detail the distribution of the web stress.

2. Test Specimens

The first means adopted of increasing the strength of the 131 RE section was by adding 1/4" to the thickness of the head. A specimen

-3-

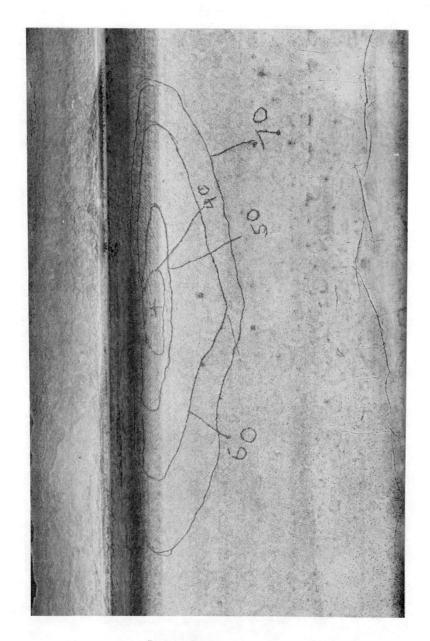

Photo. T34423
131 lb. RE Rail
Stresscoat Test under Eccentric Loading

392

Photo. T36359
139 lb. TR Rail
Stresscoat Test under Eccentric Loading

TABLE NO. 1
TEST RESULTS
STRESS IN RAIL WEB
COMPRESSIVE STRESS IN VERTICAL PLANE
CENTER OF 48" SPAN

-oOo-

Rail Section	Upper Web Fillet Location of Maximum Stress				Minimum Section			
	20,000# Load		40,000# Load		20,000# Load		40,000# Load	
	On Center Line	3/4" Off Center Line	On Center Line	3/4" Off Center Line	On Center Line	3/4" Off Center Line	On Center Line	3/4" Off Center Line
130 PS	6,600	13,200	13,400	27,000	3,500	7,100	7,400	14,700
131 RE	7,000	16,600	14,400	33,100	4,000	10,600	8,400	21,300
131 RE Planed 3/16"	8,900	19,800	16,500	39,800	5,000	11,800	9,500	23,000
131 PSM	6,700	16,500	12,800	31,500	4,200	10,600	7,900	19,900
132 AAR	5,300	13,300	11,800	26,200	3,400	10,000	7,400	18,200
134.6 (133A)	4,800	11,900	10,100	23,000	3,500	7,900	6,800	14,700
136 LVH	6,000	16,400	12,100	32,100	3,300	7,200	6,300	15,000
137 Welded	6,500	14,200	11,200	27,700	4,200	9,700	7,900	18,600
140 C	4,600	12,200	9,500	25,300	3,200	6,900	6,100	13,800
140 J	4,900	11,700	8,700	24,400	3,000	6,100	5,100	12,200
140 K	4,800	12,000	10,300	24,000	3,700	9,600	7,900	19,400
140 R	4,300	10,900	8,000	21,300	3,100	6,900	5,900	14,200
140 PS	4,500	10,400	9,000	20,700	3,000	6,600	5,900	14,400
152 PS	5,800	13,800	12,300	27,600	4,200	9,800	8,300	19,500
152 PSM	6,200	15,700	12,100	30,100	3,100	7,500	6,200	13,900
155 PS	4,500	10,600	9,700	21,400	2,730	6,400	5,900	13,000
155 PS Planed 1/4"	5,400	13,500	10,900	26,800	3,150	7,875	6,330	15,570

Altoona, Pa.
4-18-47.

was prepared by adding weld metal somewhat greater than the desired thickness to a 6 ft. section of rail, the metal then being machined down to the desired contour. This rail weighed about 137 lbs. to the yard and was designated as 137-W. It showed a material decrease in the web stress, but not as much as was desired. Next, a specimen was prepared by machining out of a solid billet of axle steel of similar physical properties to rail steel. The specimen was prepared at Chambersburg Reclamation Plant. This section included an increase in the thickness of the head to 2-1/16", a change in the fishing angle from 1 in 4 to 1 in 3, thickening of the web from 31/32" to 3/4" at its minimum section and to 1" at the bottom of the upper fillet, and using a 7/16" fillet radius. This section, designated on 140-C, showed some improvement over the 137-W section, but not as much as was expected, and this precipitated an investigation into the question of stress concentration at the upper web fillet. This feature will be discussed later.

Altogether, eight experimental rail sections were tested, including seven of our own and one of A.A.R. design. Six existing standard sections were tested, including both the standard and modified head contour sections of the 131 RE and 152 PS, known as 131 RSM and 152 PSM. Tests have been run on "as rolled" sections of the new 140 PS and 155 PS, but to date the 133 RE has not been tested "as rolled". Tests were also run on 131 RE planed 3/16", and on 155 PS planed 1/4" to represent wear. Attached table No. 1 shows results on 17 laboratory tests of web stress in various rail sections. Charts are also attached (Appendix A) showing the web stress distribution under 20,000 lb. load with 3/4" eccentricity for these sections.

It will be noted that the 150 PS section of 1916 shows about 20% lower stress than the 131 RE under eccentric loading, confirming service observation as to its greater web strength. Two charts are included in Appendix A showing relationship between web stress and eccentricity of load.

III. Mathematical Theory

At the same time that our tests were being carried out, the Research Engineer, Association of American Railroads, was developing a new 112 lb. section. He reported results of tests on a rail with longer head-web fillet radius, indicating that improved results might be obtained by simply increasing this radius with an accompanying slight increase in the thickness of the web at this point. He then applied this procedure to the 131 lb. section and developed his 132 lb. section, of which he sent us a sample for test. While this section had higher web stresses than our 140-C, J or K sections, it had no increase in thickness of head, yet showed a material reduction in stress under the 131 RE.

The theory of stress concentration in a fillet joining a thick and a thin section, when subjected to direct and bending stresses, as set forth by Timoshenko in his "Strength of Materials", was studied for its application to this problem.

We had concluded that increased thickness of the head improved the stress situation in the web due to the effect of simple beam strength in the head distributing direct stresses over a greater length of rail web. We had also concluded that a similar improvement in web bending

-4-

stress under eccentric load resulted from an increase in torsional rigidity of the head, the thicker more rigid head distributing the bending stress over a greater length of web. Curves were plotted attempting to develop a definite relationship between the direct web stress, the thickness of the web and the moment of inertia of the head about a horizontal axis. Further curves were plotted, using experimental data as to bending stress in the rail web and attempting to coordinate this with the section modulus of the rail web in bending and the torsional rigidity of the head. Application of published factors of stress concentration in connection with these curves showed some improvement, but it was not until we turned away from published factors of stress concentration and developed stress concentration factors based on our own experimental data that we were able to plot satisfactory curves.

At this point it may be well to note that the principles of stress concentration in fillets joining a thinner and a thicker section are thoroughly explained by S. Timoshenko in his "Strength of Materials". Also, in a paper presented before the American Society of Mechanical Engineers in November 1931, Timoshenko and Langer described in a general way the effect of torsional rigidity of the rail head in reducing the vertical bending of the rail web immediately under an eccentric load.

A fairly good agreement was found between the distribution of direct stress in the web as determined by laboratory tests and the theory of distribution of stress in an infinitely large plate due to a concentrated vertical force acting on a straight boundary."

The stress in the web is inversely proportional to the depth, or the distance away from the applied force (approximately), and the maximum stress is in the direction of a radius drawn from the point of force application. Stresscoat stress lines at right angles to this direction illustrate this point which has also been confirmed by strain rosette measurements. Allowance had to be made for the strength of the head. When the average direct stress in the upper web fillet for various sections was plotted against the moment of inertia of the head, most of the points fell on a reasonably smooth curve, but for some sections of rail the points deviated from the line by a considerable amount.

Similarly, when the bending stress in the web was plotted against the torsional rigidity of the head, a fairly good line was plotted for certain sections but others deviated by a large amount.

It was noted in both cases that the sections deviating from the line were those where there was a considerable change in the ratio of the fillet radius to the thickness of the web, from that in the conventional sections.

By assuming a stress concentration factor for those sections having a more or less uniform ratio of fillet radius to thickness of web, it was possible to derive from the plotted curves of web stress against strength of head, approximate concentration factors for those sections which deviated from the plotted lines. In this way, by a series of three or four

* Timoshenko - Theory of Elasticity, pages 82 to 88.

-5-

approximations, a set of four curves was derived which are shown in Appendix B attached, entitled "A Method of Calculating Maximum Stress in Web of Rail due to an Eccentric Vertical Load".

Based on the results thus obtained it was concluded that it would be necessary to use a longer head web fillet radius than we had previously contemplated. The Research Engineer, Association of American Railroads, had in redesigning the 112 lb. and 131 lb. sections adopted the device of a compound fillet radius, with a longer radius adjoining the web and a shorter radius adjoining the head. This made it possible to retain a reasonable width of fishing surface under the head. With his permission we adopted this device, which it had been found was not patentable, and went to an 11/16"- 7/16" compound in our 140-R section, and finally to a 3/4" - 7/16" combination in the 140-S section, which eventually became the 140 PS section adopted.

The material contained in Appendix B relative to method of calculating maximum stress in the web of rail was published as a monograph in Bulletin 461 of the American Railway Engineering Association, September-October 1946, and is protected by A.R.E.A. copyright. This monograph is also published in Vol. 48 of the Proceedings, American Railway Engineering Association, 1947.

In addition to conferring frequently with Mr. G. M. Magee, Research Engineer, Association of American Railroads, in connection with this work, we had the benefit of several conferences with Prof. H. F. Moore, Research Professor of Engineering-Materials, University of Illinois.

IV.   Application of Theory to Design of 133 lb. and 155 lb. Sections

Upon conclusion of development of the 140 PS section, it was decided to apply the knowledge obtained to strengthening the 152 PS section, and also to develop a lighter rail section more nearly the same weight as the 131 RE for use in portions of the railroad where the use of a section as heavy as the 140 PS was not necessary or desirable. With the benefit of the theory already developed in connection with 140 lb. section, it was a comparatively simple matter to modify the 152 lb., and it became the 155 PS. The 133-A section developed as shown in tables and charts in this report was eventually found to weigh somewhat over 134 lbs. per yard, and was further modified to the 133-C section, which eventually became the 133 RE, being adopted by the American Railway Engineering Association as an alternative section to its 132 RE, in addition to being adopted by the Pennsylvania Railroad.

The 140 PS and 155 PS sections were designed to have no less girder strength than the 131 RE and 152 PS which they replaced, and also to have sufficient web strength to resist the most severe conditions of head wear and web stress known to be encountered on the railroad, while sacrificing little or nothing in the matter of fishing height, essential to a good design of joint bar.

The 133 RE section has greater web strength and greater thickness of head than the 132 RE section, and was, hence, considered more desirable for use on the Pennsylvania Railroad, under our particular conditions of traffic and curvature.

The 129 lb. torsion resisting rail developed by Mr. George Burkhart of the Chicago, Burlington & Quincy Railroad and patented by him, was given full consideration in connection with recommending sections for adoption on the Pennsylvania Railroad. It was concluded that the narrow head of the 139 TR section (2-5/8" as against 3" for the 131 RE, 152 RE, and the new Pennsylvania sections) rendered it unsuitable for use on the Pennsylvania Railroad, where flange wear on curves is so frequently an important factor. Comparison of the strength of this section with that of the sections adopted is shown in tables and charts attached.

V.   Service Measurement of Stresses
    1. Field Measurement with Static Load

Until December 1944 we had been working more or less in the dark as to the magnitude of stresses to which the rail might be subjected in track. In December 1944 we made some stress measurements under static conditions on No. 1 track, No. 7 curve, Middle Division, near Union Furnace, Pa., using wire resistance strain gauges and the SR-4 strain indicator. These measurements indicated the possibility of extremely high web stresses in 131 RE rail under eccentric loading with locomotive wheels. In a way this merely confirmed the expectation based on laboratory test and also based on results obtained on other railroads by the Research Engineer, Association of American Railroads.

    2. A.A.R. Tests

The A.A.R. field work had been done at locations where no rail failures were developing. The rapidity with which rail failures were developing on the Pennsylvania Railroad lead us to believe that the rail in some of our curves was being subjected to higher stresses or to a greater frequency of high stresses than any results reported by the Research Engineer, A.A.R.

The tests made at Lathrop, Missouri, in 1944 by the A.A.R. gave indirect information concerning the probability of high stresses in 131 RE rail, but they gave no direct information inasmuch as these tests were all made on 112 lb. section or modified section approaching 112 lbs. in weight.

Preliminary results of A.A.R. stress measurements on 131 RE rail in service on 6 deg. curves on the Norfolk & Western were available to us in August 1945. These showed occasional stresses as high as 80,000 lbs. per sq. in., but stresses of this magnitude did not seem to be of sufficiently frequent occurrence to indicate more than the remote possibility of fatigue failure.

    3. Equipment for Dynamic Stress Measurement

In September 1944 an order was placed with the General Electric Company for a Model PM10B2 oscillograph with six double galvanometers; also for amplifiers for use with wire resistance strain gauges, providing 12 channels, that is, permitting simultaneous measurements under dynamic conditions with 12 strain gauges. The first stress measurements under service conditions with this equipment were made at Petersburg, Middle Division, September 24 to November 23, 1945. This work was more or less a trial run for the equipment as there had been no rail failures at this point, and no high stresses were anticipated. measurements at this point are shown in tabular form on two sheets

Late in December 1945 an automotive trailer was received for housing oscillograph and amplifier equipment. The equipment was mounted in the trailer and service stress measurements in the vicinity of mile posts 10 and 11, Panhandle Division, west of Carnegie, Pa. were started in March 1946.

4. Location of Service Tests

Measurement of service stresses in the web of 131 RE rail has been made on No. 2 track, Panhandle Division, Slag Dump Curve west of Carnegie; No. 1 track, Panhandle Division, mile post 10 curve west of Carnegie; Nos. 1 and 2 tracks, mile post 80 curve, Panhandle Division, east of Bowerston, Ohio, and No. 10 curve No. 3 track, Middle Division, east of Birmingham, Pa. in addition to the original work on Petersburg curve, Middle Division.

For each location a tabular statement has been prepared, based on the service stress measurements and a traffic study, to show the number of cycles of stress of various magnitudes to which the rail is subjected in one year's time. These tables are included in Appendix C.

5. Results of Service Tests

Table No. 2 attached shows a summary of these stresses for all locations except No. 1 track, mile post 10 curve, Panhandle Division. Results of this location have been omitted because at this location, while rail failures had been experienced, the strain gauges were not so placed as to measure the maximum stresses. In this table have been included columns showing number of cycles equated to an equivalent number of cycles of 90,000 lbs. per sq. in. stress. Details of this will be discussed more thoroughly under the section on fatigue tests; however, it will be noted that according to this table, failure of rail may be expected after approximately 6,000 to 13,000 cycles of stress equated to 90,000 lbs. per sq. in.

At Slag Dump Curve, Panhandle Division, after completion of stress measurements in 131 RE rail, new rail of the adapted 140 PS section was laid, and stress measurements were made on this rail.

It may be stated briefly that the improvement in service stresses with the new design of rail approximately equals that which was anticipated, based on laboratory tests. Table No. 3 is attached showing comparison of the stresses in the 131 RE worn 3/16", and the 140 PS new, as measured on Slag Dump Curve for various classes of locomotives. This is also shown by Charts 57, 58, and 59, Appendix D.

-8-

Photo. 635
Gauges on Outside of Low Rail
and on Temperature Compensating Piece
No. 1 Track, "OB" Curve, M.P.80
Panhandle Div.

Table No. 2

Corroded Fatigue Life of Rail Web Steel

Maximum Stress in Rail Web in Vertical Plane outside of Joints
131 RE Rail

Cycles of Stress above Endurance Limit
Equated to No. of Cycles at 90,000 #/in.2
Based on Measurement of Stresses in Track 1945, 1946, & 1947

		Panhandle Division						Middle Division			
		Slag Dump Curve No. 2 Track		M.P.80 Curve No. 2 Track		M.P.80 Curve No. 1 Track		No. 10 Curve No. 3 Track		Petersburg Curve No. 1 Track	
Stress Lbs. per Sq. In.	Factor Rate (1)	No. Cycles 1 Yr.	Equiv. at 90,000	No. Cycles 1 Yr.	Equiv. at 90,000	No. Cycles 1 Yr.	Equiv. at 90,000	No. Cycles 1 Yr.	Equiv. at 90,000	No. Cycles 1 Yr.	Equiv. at 90,000
100,000	2.56	781	1843					303	475		
95,000	1.59	781	781	637	637	224	535	308	480		
90,000	1.00			294	188	224	139	402	249		
85,000	.62	1562	595	1254	477	220	85	605	229		
80,000	.38	781	180	459	106	444	102	1175	271	350	90
75,000	.25	391	58	505	70	385	45	598	84	1407	169
70,000	.16	1378	124	1090	98	2193	197	1711	154	390	55
65,000	.09	1378	69	1495	75	2072	105	3966	198	817	41
60,000	.05	2096	63	2750	83	335	10	2390	117	7416	222
55,000	.03	2654	29	3585	37	1696	19	4937	54	3585	57
50,000	.011										
Total Equivalent Cycles at 90,000 #/in.2 in 1 Yr.		3133		2290		1055		2611		994	
Life of Rail		2 Yrs.		3 Yrs.		15 Yrs. Note (2)		5 Yrs.		8 Yrs.	
Cycles during Life		6165 Failed		6870 Failed		Failed		13,055 Failed		4752 No Failure	

Note (1) – Factor derived from Laboratory S-N Curve for rail web steel subjected to a combination of cyclic stress and corrosion, and assuming that relative damage due to each magnitude of stress is in inverse proportion to fatigue life at that stress.

"   (2) – There was a change to a heavier type of locomotive (J1) about 4 yrs. before failure so that cycles per year in this case cannot be assumed to be average for life of rail.

Altoona, Pa.
9-30-47. CJu/LA

TABLE NO. 3

Comparison of Recorded Stresses
131 R.E. Worn 1/8" Vs. 140 P.S. New.
Various Classes of Locomotives

**Stresses at Various Speeds Taken from
Charted Curves of Stress.**

Slag Dump Curve, P.H. Division

Class of Loco.		Stress in 1000 #/in.²			
		15 M.P.H.	20 M.P.H.	25 M.P.H.	30 M.P.H.
I1	131 R.E.	53.5	49.0	45.5	40.5
	140 P.S.	35.0	31.5	28.0	25.0
	% Reduction	34.5	35.8	38.5	38.5
M1	131 R.E.	61.0	53.0	46.0	38.5
	140 P.S.	31.0	28.0	25.5	23.0
	% Reduction	49.0	47.2	44.5	40.3
J1	131 R.E.	80.0	73.0	65.0	57.0
	140 P.S.	47.5	45.0	40.5	33.5
	% Reduction	40.6	38.3	37.8	41.2

	Maximum Recorded Stress for each Class.		
	131 R.E.*	140 P.S.	% Reduction
I1	66,000	45,000	32%
M1	70,000	37,000	47%
J1	96,000	56,000	48%

* – Runs 551 to 1128.

When the stress measurements were started at Slag Dump Curve, there was some indication that the rail was canting outward due to wear of the tie plate into the ties, and it was believed that this might be a contributing factor toward the high stresses experienced. Consequently, after a reasonable number of stress measurements had been made, the track forces were requested to adz the ties so as to restore the rail and tie plate to normal bearing. At the same time it was necessary to surface the track in order to correct irregularities in surface and superelevation, aggravated by the adzing of the ties. The result was a decrease in average stress of approximately 10 per cent, and the tables and charts included in Appendixes C and D showing stresses before and after adzing indicate a material reduction in the number of cycles of high stress.

At the locations where rail failures are being experienced, compressive stresses of the order of 90,000 lbs. per sq. in. are experienced quite frequently. These stresses are always under locomotive driving wheels and the maximum stress under a locomotive under the conditions of these tests can generally be found under the rear or the next to the rear driver. With the J1 locomotive having a 2-10-4 wheel arrangement, maximum stress was nearly always under the No. 4 driver, that is, the next to the rear driver. With the M1 locomotive having a 4-8-2 wheel arrangement, the maximum stress was generally under the No. 4 or rear driver.

Split web failures on the Pennsylvania Railroad have almost without exception been on the low rail of curves, and also almost without exception on the gauge side of the low rail. Apparently the condition which leads to a high stress is the operation of a locomotive on a heavily super-elevated curve at less than the speed for which the curve is superelevated. This condition results not only in more than half the weight of the loco-motive being carried on the low rail, but also in a crowding of the low rail by the rear driving wheels so that the weight of the wheel on the low rail is carried at the throat of the flange and, consequently, near the gauge edge of the rail. This results in the combination of a heavy wheel load and high eccentricity of the load which gives extremely high stress.

A study was made of the relationship between speed and stress for various classes of locomotives at Slag Dump Curve and Mile Post 80 Curve, Panhandle Division, and No. 10 Curve, Middle Division. Generally speaking, the stress increases as the speed decreases. Appendix D includes a series of charts showing this relationship. Charts must be considered as applicable only at the location where the stresses were measured. Varia-tion in results under apparently similar conditions of alignment and curvature have so far rendered it impossible to coordinate the results between different locations.

While high stresses under certain classes of freight cars were at first anticipated, in no case have we measured stresses under cars higher than 55,000 lbs. per sq. in. The highest car stresses were measured at Petersburg, Middle Division.

At Slag Dump Curve experiments were carried out to determine the effect of changing the cant of the tie plate. Aside from the effect of adzing the ties to restore even bearing, which was accompanied by surfacing the track, no appreciable change was effected by changing the cant of the tie plate between the limits of 0 and 1 in 20.

VI. Fatigue Tests
1. Tests at University of Illinois

In December 1945 Prof. R. S. Jensen of the University of Illinois reported results of fatigue tests on rail web steel on a special T shaped specimen, so designed that the failure could be made to occur on the narrow face of the specimen. The type of specimen is illustrated by the drawing, Fig. 1 attached. The specimen was loaded in a vibratory type fatigue machine so that the specimen was stressed in repeating bending, and the machine was so adjusted that the stress on the narrow face of the specimen alternated from a heavy compression stress to a tensile stress 20 per cent as great. These results are reported in A.R.E.A. Bulletin No. 458, and included in A.R.E.A. proceedings, Vol. 47, page 464.

Mr. Jensen presented two curves, one for unstamped specimens and one for stamped specimens, that is, specimens with heat number impressions on them, the idea having been obtained from earlier failures on some of the western railroads that the heat number stamps might be responsible for the failures.

No heat number stamps were involved in any of our failures so that it was necessary to refer to the curve for unstamped specimens, or to assume that due to a condition of corrosion, the service results might conform more nearly to the results on the stamped specimen. The endurance limit for unstamped specimens was shown as 59,000 lbs. per sq. in., and for stamped specimens 51,000 lbs. per sq.in.

These figures were made use of in designing the 140 lb. rail section, our efforts in reduction in stress in this section being pointed toward the ultimate goal of obtaining a rail which would not have a stress of more than 51,000 lbs. per sq. in. under the most severe conditions of loading on a worn section. The design load assumed was 80,000 lbs. applied 3/4" from the center of the rail head. For the 140 PS rail worn 1/4", the stress under this loading is approximately 52,000 lbs. per sq. in. so that the goal was not completely attained; however, as will be shown later, the results of service stress measurements and further fatigue studies indicate that no fear need be felt for the adequacy of the 140 PS design.

Using Prof. Jensen's chart of December 1, 1945 for stamped specimens, failure might be expected to occur at 5,000,000 cycles of stress of 52,000 lbs. per sq. in. compression combined with reversal to a tensile stress 20 per cent as great.

Service stress measurements on Slag Dump Curve at Carnegie showed that stresses of a magnitude of 90,000 lbs. per sq. in. compression were of reasonably frequent occurrence.

However, according to Prof. Jensen's chart, 50,000 cycles of such stress were required on a stamped specimen, and over 100,000 cycles

-10-

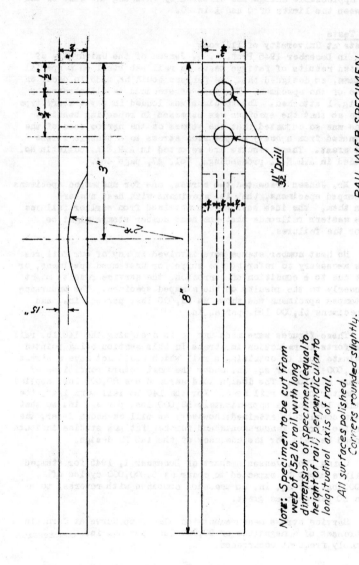

on an unstamped specimen to cause failure, that is, the development of a crack.

2. Tests at Altoona

In May 1946 we began making our own fatigue tests on rail web steel. The first results with these tests were merely to confirm the results obtained by Prof. Jensen. With rail web specimens cut from 152 RE rail, long dimension of the specimen vertical in the web, and retaining the original as rolled surface at the critical point of the specimen, we obtained failures at approximately 72,000 cycles of stress reversed from 90,000 lbs. per sq. in. compression to 15,000 lbs. per sq. in. tension, using a 6 to 1 ratio between compression and tension.

Further analysis of the results on Slag Dump Curve at Carnegie where 131 RE rail laid new had failed in two years indicated that this rail had suffered not more than 5,000 cycles of this magnitude in its life. The rail of course was subjected to a variety of stresses, varying from 20,000 lbs. per sq. in. tension to 95,000 lbs. per sq. in. compression. Any of these stresses above the endurance limit of the material might be considered as damaging stresses and contributing to its ultimate failure.

Evidence in the field and from laboratory examination of failed specimens indicated that corrosion might be an important factor in these failures and might result in failure at a considerably lower number of cycles of stress than indicated by laboratory tests so far available.

3. Corrosion Fatigue Tests at Altoona

A specimen was accordingly arranged with a piece of wet waste attached to it at the critical section, and this specimen was subjected to a series of stress cycles intended to represent the stress undergone in two years of service life. The stresses and number of cycles applied were as follows: 5600 compression to 5600 tension, 5,000,000 cycles; 35,000 compression to 5600 tension, 60,000 cycles; 60,000 compression to 10,000 tension, 16,000 cycles. The specimen was then run at 90,000 compression to 15,000 tension until a crack developed.

Following the above described procedure, and running the specimen full time at the normal speed of the machine or 1750 cycles per minute, failure was developed at 51,000 cycles of 90,000 lb. stress. The machine was shut down over one week-end and the total duration of the test was approximately 10 days. The amount of corrosion developed was small.

The Krouse vibratory fatigue machine was then moved to a location where water could be continuously applied in a small stream to the test specimen, and a Telechron clock was connected in the circuit leading to the machine so that the machine could be operated 5 minutes out of each hour automatically.

The new specimen was then subjected to the same series of stress cycles described above, but with continuous stream of tap water, and with the machine operated only 5 minutes out of every hour so that the total duration of the test was prolonged to approximately 25 days. With

T. 3582G

Photo. T35826
Corrosion Fatigue Specimen
Rail Web Steel
(Magnified 2-1/2 Times)

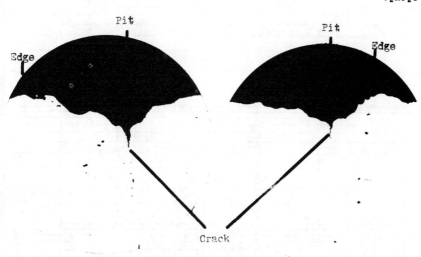

M. P. *399*
2M 6-19-46
7½x9½C

M **23352**
Magnification **100** Diameters.
Etched with **Unetched**

M **23353**
Magnification **100** Diameters.
Etched with **Unetched**

PHOTOMICROGRAPHS Altoona, Pa.,

Material **Vibration - Corrosion pitting**
Longitudinal sections
Average structures

Remarks:
Specimen #5   **Specimen #6**

One of the very numerous pits along the surface with a crack extending
from the root of a pit toward the interior, the pits being the result
of corrosion and the cracks being produced by vibration.

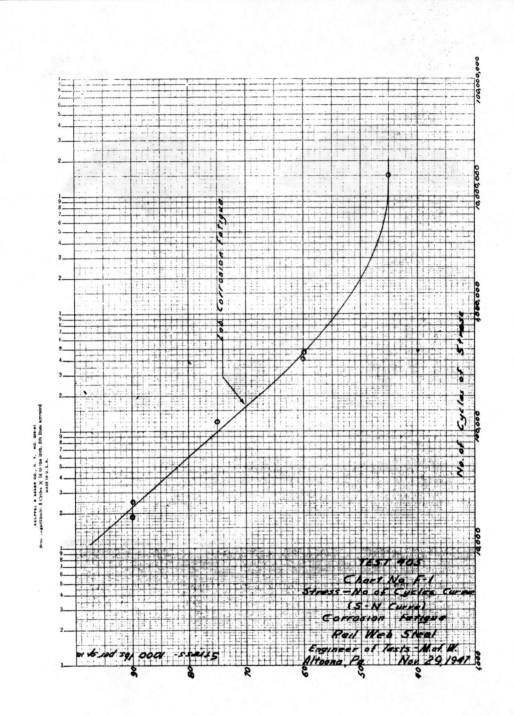

Lab corrosion fatigue

No. of Cycles of Stress

STRESS - 1000 lbs. per in

TEST 403
Chart No. F-1
Stress - No. of Cycles Curve
(S - N Curve)
Corrosion Fatigue
Rail Web Steel
Engineer of Tests - Mat. W.
Altoona, Pa.   Nov. 29, 1941

this procedure heavy corrosion was experienced, pronounced stress corrosion pitting was observed in the specimen at the critical section, and the failure was obviously a corrosion fatigue type of failure, that is, a failure resulting from a combination of corrosion and fatigue. Failure took place at approximately 20,000 cycles of 90,000 lbs. per sq. in. stress.

The character of failure developed is illustrated in photograph No. T-85826 and photomicrographs M-23352 and M-23353, attached. Incidentally, the appearance of the failure is very similar to that experienced in track.

A series of tests was then run following the above described procedure, but using various final stresses from 90,000 lbs. per sq. in. to 45,000 lbs. per sq. in. The results are shown on the SN curve (Stress-number of cycles curve) attached (Chart No. F-1).

4. Correlation with Service Failures

This procedure served to reduce considerably the wide margin between the number of cycles of stress experienced in a rail failure in track and the number of cycles required to produce a failure in the laboratory.

In February 1947, upon completion of these tests, we conferred with Dr. D. J. McAdam in the Bureau of Standards, Washington, D. C., described our testing procedure, showed him the results of our tests and advised him of the information obtained from field testing. He indicated that such a margin as we now found between laboratory results and service results was not at all surprising to him, particularly since the duration of the test in the laboratory was so much shorter and the speed of the test machine so much more rapid than the rate at which stresses are applied in the field.

A study of the record of stresses in the field will indicate that it is a practical impossibility to run a laboratory test which will completely duplicate the cycling of the specimen in the field. The stresses in service are applied in random order which would require resetting of the deflection of the fatigue machine every few cycles. Some further slowing down of the testing procedure is, of course, practical and a Krouse vibratory fatigue machine has been ordered with variable speeds so that the specimens may be tested at rates down to 50 cycles per minute. It is anticipated that, using this machine at a slow rate of testing and possibly a somewhat greater mixing up of the order in which the cycles of stress are applied, may result in failure at a number of cycles even more closely approximating service results.

In order to arrive more definitely at the fatigue life of a rail in service, studies of service stresses have been made at a number of locations where service failures have been experienced as described in a previous section of this report.

In order to coordinate these results, we have attempted to reduce the wide variety of stresses experienced for varying numbers of cycles to an equivalent number of cycles at a given stress. Because we have, in discussion of the subject, so frequently referred to the number of cycles at a stress of 90,000 lbs. per sq. in., the number of cycles at this stress was chosen as unity in preparing the equating factor. The factor used was derived by determining from the laboratory fatigue curve the ratio between the number of cycles for failure at each stress to the number of cycles for failure at 90,000 lbs. per sq. in. This was taken in increments of 5,000 lbs. per sq. in. from 50,000 to 100,000 lbs. per sq. in. The factors shown in the table are the number of cycles at 90,000 lbs. per sq. in. divided by the number of cycles at the given stress, and these factors have been used to multiply the number of cycles of stress at each magnitude experienced in the field, in order to determine an equivalent number of cycles at 90,000.

In table No. 2 attached these figures are shown for five locations. They are totaled to show total equivalent cycles at 90,000 lbs. per sq. in. in one year, then multiplied by the life of the rail to show the total number of cycles experienced during the life of the rail.

For No. 2 track, Slag Dump Curve, and No. 2 track, Mile Post 80 Curve, Panhandle Division, the figures are quite consistent, the number of cycles during life being 6166 for Slag Dump Curve, and 6770 for Mile Post 80 Curve.

For No. 1 track, Mile Post 80 Curve, the number of cycles per year was 1055, and the rail was in track 13 years. However, the rail was subjected to the heavy stress developed by the J1 locomotive only during the last four years of its life, so that one cannot multiply 1055 by 13 to determine the number of cycles during life.

For No. 10 Curve, No. 3 track, Middle Division, the number of cycles during life is 13055, failure resulting in five years. We do not feel that this discrepancy between the number of cycles to failure on the Panhandle Division and the number of cycles to failure on the Middle Division represents a break-down of our method, but that it rather shows a difference in conditions on the two Divisions. There may be a further discrepancy due to the difference in the condition of the track as to surface, and bearing on the ties, on No. 10 curve during its early life, and its condition at the time when stress measurements were taken which was just before renewals were carried out. Any adverse condition of surface and tie bearing undoubtedly adds considerable to the magnitude of the stresses experienced.

Based on this method of evaluating the magnitude and number of cycles of stress experienced in track, we have then a comparison of service life of 6100 to 13,000 cycles at 90,000 lbs. per sq. in., as against a laboratory life of 20,000 cycles at 90,000 lbs. per sq. in. This seems to us to constitute a reasonably close check, all factors being considered.

On the rail in No. 1 track, Petersburg Curve, Middle Division, which was in service eight years and experienced a total of 4752 cycles, there was no evidence of incipient failure when the rail was removed from track, indicating that it probably would not have failed at 6,000 cycles, but probably would have lasted 13,000 cycles.

Various investigators have reported studies to establish a relationship giving the damage done to a fatigue specimen by stressing it for a given number of cycles less than its fatigue life in terms of its remaining life at another magnitude of stress.

Prof. J. B. Kommers, of the University of Wisconsin, in a paper delivered at the annual meeting of the American Society for Testing Materials in 1945, entitled "The Effect of Over Stress in Fatigue on the Endurance Life of Steel", has demonstrated that "in general when a high over-stress has produced a percentage of damage to endurance life, a subsequent lower over-stress will show a greater percentage of damage. This damage to endurance life may be four times greater at the final stress than at the initial stress."

"On the other hand when a low over-stress is followed by a higher over-stress, the damage to endurance life is less at the final stress than at the initial. When the initial over-stress is low and the number of cycles not too large, the effect of the initial over-stress is to increase the endurance life at the final stress. This increase of life may be over 100 per cent."

According to Prof. Kommers' conclusion, the procedure which we have adopted in equating the cycles of stress is inaccurate. However, the variety of magnitude and frequency of service stresses is such that we have been unable to apply with any exactitude the results of studies similar to that of Prof. Kommers to the current problem. It is felt that while the procedure adopted in equating cycles of stress is probably subject to many inaccuracies, it serves a reasonable purpose from a practical point of view in showing the relationship between the fatigue life of rail in track and the fatigue life of a specimen of rail steel subjected to a laboratory fatigue test.

VII. Estimated Life of 140 Lb. Rail

Referring in Appendix C to the tabulation of estimated number of cycles of stress in one year for 140 PS rail on the westward track, Slag Dump Curve, it will be observed that the highest stresses are 459 cycles at 55,000, 306 cycles at 50,000, and 889 cycles at 45,000. If these stresses are increased 20 per cent to allow for the difference between new 140 PS rail and 140 PS rail worn 1/4", these stresses and numbers of cycles become 459 cycles at 65,000, 306 cycles at 60,000, 889 cycles at 55,000 and 2817 cycles at 50,000. Applying to these the factors shown on table No. 2 to get equated number of cycles at 90,000 lbs. per sq. in., we get a total number of equated cycles per year of 111. Since the steel seems to be good for not less than 6,000 of such cycles in its life, it would appear that 140 PS rail had a possible life of approximately 60 years under the conditions as found at Slag Dump Curve after adzing ties and surfacing track and with an average assumed wear of 1/4". If we add another 10 per cent to these stresses to allow for the condition of the track prior to adzing ties and surfacing track, we get 256 equated cycles, or an estimated life of

23 years. Of course, the rail will be removed for other causes long before it has attained any such life, and it is also probable that if the life were so extended, corrosion over the longer period of time would have a greater effect, so that the actual life at this location would be somewhat less than 23 years if it were not necessary to remove the rail earlier for other causes.

In any event, the indications are that no difficulty should be experienced with split web failures due to corrosion fatigue with the 140 PS section under the conditions found on the westward track at Slag Dump Curve where 131 RE rail failed in two years.

It was stated above that adzing the ties and surfacing the track on Slag Dump Curve reduced the stress in 131 RE rail approximately 10 per cent. If the same line of reasoning as above is applied to the table of cycles of stress in 131 RE rail after adzing and surfacing track, it will be found that, in theory at least, the life of the 131 RE rail could have been considerably extended if it had been possible to maintain it in the optimum condition as to surface and correct bearing of tie plates throughout its life.

VIII. Possibilities of Protection Against Corrosion

Comparing our laboratory SN curve for corrosion fatigue of rail web steel with Prof. Jensen's curve for unstamped, uncorroded specimens, it will be found that the ratio of life in the range of stress from 60,000 to 80,000 lbs. per sq. in. is between 3 to 1 and 5 to 1. In other words, the uncorroded specimen can be expected to last somewhere between three and five times as long as the corroded specimen. This seems to indicate the possibility of extending the life of rail subjected to corrosion fatigue materially by protecting it against corrosion. This possibility is under field investigation in M. W. test No. 468.

IX. Stress Effect of Various Classes of Locomotives

Under article V, Service Measurement of Stresses, we mentioned briefly the charts included in Appendix D showing relationship between web stress and speed for various classes of locomotives.

There are 58 of these charts numbered 18 to 80 inclusive, with certain numbers omitted which it was not thought advisable to include in this report.

On the Panhandle Division both at Slag Dump Curve and at Bowerston the high stresses were associated almost exclusively with the J1 locomotive. With Q2 locomotive No. 6198 light, extremely high stresses were measured, but these were not repeated under the Q2 hauling trains. Other than this, the stresses measured under the Q2, T1, I1, M1 and M1a, K4, and L1 were all moderate as compared with those measured under the J1.

The operating speeds at Slag Dump Curve were generally so low that the question of dynamic augment was hardly an important factor in the high stresses and the heavy wheel loads. It is thought that the extremely high individual wheel loads which are associated with some of

the high stresses were due principally to a combination of unbalance due
to superelevation of the track, and shifting of weight through the spring
and equalization system of the locomotive. Irregularities in rail surface
which were known to exist undoubtedly exercised an important influence
on this. Profiles are included in Appendix X for the Slag Dump Curve after
surfacing, for both tracks at Bowerston and for No. 3 track on No. 10
curve, Middle Division.

Mr. Magee has expressed a theory to the effect that vertical
wheel loads are increased where there is heavy lateral thrust due to the
reaction required to overcome the moment of the lateral thrust. This is
explained in detail on page 88 of A.R.E.A. Proceedings, Vol. 48, in connection with report on stress measurements on the Norfolk and Western. We
see no reason to doubt the correctness of this theory, and it probably
accounts to a considerable extent for the high vertical loads.

Maximum stress under a locomotive is generally associated
not with the maximum vertical load, but with a relatively high vertical
load and a high eccentricity.

Based on laboratory calibration of a rail as to amount and
eccentricity of vertical load, it is possible to calculate with reasonable accuracy the amount and eccentricity of a vertical load in the
track. The vertical load is proportional to the average stress in two
gauges located on opposite faces of the rail at the top fillet. In other
words, it is proportional to the direct stress on the rail web, while
the eccentricity is proportional to the bending stress shown by these two
gauges divided by the direct stress. It will be seen that this is
proportional to the moment arm of the load, hence the eccentricity.

This procedure has been applied in studying the stresses
measured under locomotives in this test. The sum of the wheel loads thus
calculated for the low and the high rail at a given point equals the
published weight of the locomotive within plus or minus 10 per cent in
a large majority of cases, and often with a much smaller tolerance. The
tracking characteristics of a locomotive may be studied from the wheel
load eccentricities thus calculated.

The eccentricities thus calculated are not entirely
accurate, probably due to the effect of lateral thrust, but they are useful for comparative purposes.

On Slag Dump Curve, Panhandle Division, in the late fall
of 1946, a calibration car was used loaded with rail, and equipped with
hydraulic jacks capable of exerting both horizontal and vertical forces
on the track, to determine the relationship between lateral thrust and
bending stress at the bottom fillet of the rail. This was done on 140 lb.
rail and the results were then used to calculate the lateral thrust on
the track due to various locomotives. The results are not reported herein
as they are scarcely within the scope of this report.

On No. 10 curve, Middle Division, M1 and M1a locomotives
were found to give web stresses as high as the J1 gave on Slag Dump Curve,

-16-

Panhandle Division, and the curve of stresses for the Ml locomotive at this location lies considerably higher than the corresponding curve for the Ml at Slag Dump Curve. Superelevation is the same for the two locations. Curvature was slightly less at No. 10 curve, six degrees, as compared with six degrees thirty minutes. This would tend to throw slightly more weight on the low rail for like speeds. It is thought that the higher stresses measured under the Ml locomotive at this location must be due principally to local conditions as to line and surface, with some possible effect of the working of the locomotive on the heavier grade.

On No. 1 eastward track, Bowerston, the track gauge was 4'-9" as found, and was later adjusted to 4'-8-1/2". This did not make much difference in the magnitude of the stresses, the equated number of cycles in a year being slightly higher after the track was gauged.

X.   Summary

1.   By a series of laboratory tests, using Stresscoat (brittle lacquer) to determine location of maximum web stress, and SR-4 wire resistance strain gauges to determine magnitude of stress, the web stresses in 131 RE rail under eccentric loading have been studied. Studies of a number of other existing standard rail sections have been included.

2.   Based on practical experience and application of mathematical theory, a series of modified rail sections have been devised and samples manufactured and subjected to the same laboratory testing procedure. As a culmination of this cut and try process the 140 PS section has been developed, tested, adopted, and manufactured. Companion sections, the 133 RE and 155 PS have been developed, applying the knowledge gained in development of the 140 lb. and these have been adopted.

3.   Laboratory fatigue tests have been conducted in order to determine the life of rail web steel when subjected to stresses of various magnitudes, when stress is reversed from heavy compression to a tensile stress one-sixth as great, a ratio of stress similar to that experienced in track. The effect of corrosion has been studied.

4.   Service measurement has been made of rail web stresses in track at six locations in order to determine the magnitude and frequency of stress to which rail is subjected in track, principally at locations where failure of the 131 RE section has developed.

5.   The new 140 PS section has been laid in track at a location where rapid failure of the 131 RE section was experienced, and where service stress measurements had previously been made on 131 RE rail. Service stress measurements have been made on the 140 PS section at this point.

6.   A method has been developed for computing equated cycles of stress of a given magnitude so that the service life of a rail at any location may be expressed as so many equated cycles at 90,000 lbs. per sq. in., rather than as a series or schedule of stresses at various

-17-

magnitudes. By this means a comparison has been made of the life of rail to failure at various locations, and the life of rail web steel subjected to laboratory corrosion fatigue test. The results are consistent.

7. The failure of 131 RE rail by split web, sometimes called head and web separation, has been explained in terms of stress and corrosion, in other words, corrosion fatigue. A large number of laboratory samples of failed rail examined have borne out this conclusion.

8. The service stress measurements bear out the conclusion based on laboratory tests that 140 PS rail has been adequately designed to withstand the conditions under which 131 RE failed, and that it may be expected to have greatly extended life as compared with 131 RE. As corollary conclusions, it may be expected that 133 RE will also have extended life as compared with 131 RE although to less degree, and 155 lb. will have extended life as compared with 152 PS.

9. Curves have been plotted showing the relationship between web stress and speed for various locomotives at three of the locations where service stress measurements have been conducted. These are principally of value in showing the difference in the effect of locomotives of various classes, and the extremely high stresses induced in the rail by certain locomotives at low speed on sharp, heavily elevated curves. The charts developed at one location do not apply at another, and the differences have not been completely explained. Differences in track surface, grade, alinement, and train resistance all undoubtedly have their effect.

Individual locomotive wheel loads have been calculated for a large number of cases. The data are not presented herewith, but it may be stated that individual wheel loads equal to the entire axle load are not at all uncommon on the low rail of curves, and isolated cases of wheel loads up to 89,000 lbs. have been noted.

10. Further work remains to be done. The 133 RE as rolled will be subjected to laboratory test and should be subjected to service stress measurement. More research is desirable on corrosion fatigue. However, it is thought advisable to submit a final report at this time, further work to be covered by supplementary reports.

11. Service performance of the new rail sections is being followed in Test 461, and the effect of corrosion protection in Test 468.

XI. Conclusions

1. The cause of split web failures (head and web separations) in 131 RE rail has been found to be corrosion fatigue. Laboratory and service stress measurements have demonstrated that this section develops high stresses in the upper web fillet gauge side, on the low rail of sharp curves.

2. Based on practical experience, mathematical theory, and laboratory and service tests using modern strain measuring equipment, the 140 PS rail section has been developed to retain all the desirable

characteristics of the 131 RE section and eliminate its weaknesses. Companion sections, the 133 RE for somewhat less severe service conditions, and the 155 RS for conditions requiring the maximum girder strength have been developed using the same principles. These sections have been adopted.

3. The 140 RS section has been tested in track and the anticipated improvement in web stresses has been realized. Based on these stress measurements, and the theory of fatigue failures, it is anticipated that this section should have approximately ten times the life of the 131 RE, as far as web failure outside the joint is concerned, under like conditions.

C. J. Code,
Engineer of Tests, M. of W.

-19-

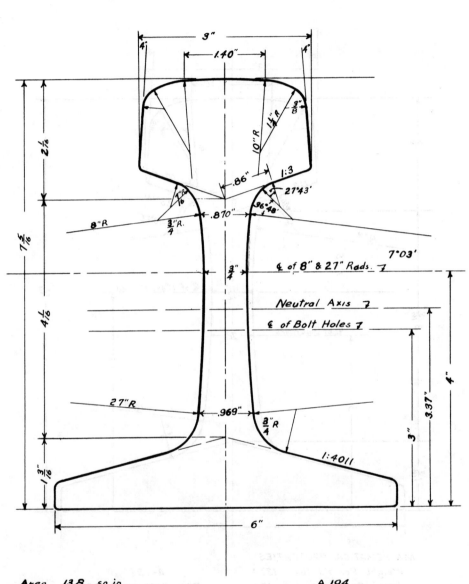

Area 13.8 sq. in.
Wt. per Yd. 140.6 lbs.
Moment of Inertia 97
Sec. Mod. Above N.A. 25
Sec. Mod. Below N.A. 29

A 194
140 lb. Rail, Sec. S
Engineer of Tests, M. of W.
Altoona, Pa.   May 24, 1946.

(140 PS)

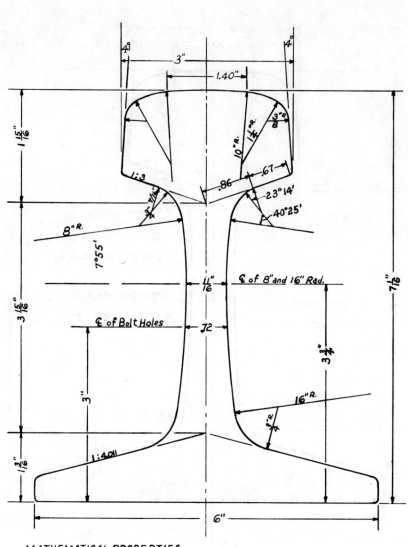

MATHEMATICAL PROPERTIES

Weight Per Yd. lbs.	133.4
Area - Sq. Inches	13.1
Moment of Inertia	86.3
Sec. Mod. Above N.A.	22.3
Sec. Mod. Below N.A.	26.9

A-196

RAIL SECTION-C 133 LB.

ENGINEER of TESTS M.W.

ALTOONA, PA. JUNE 24, 1946

(133 RE)

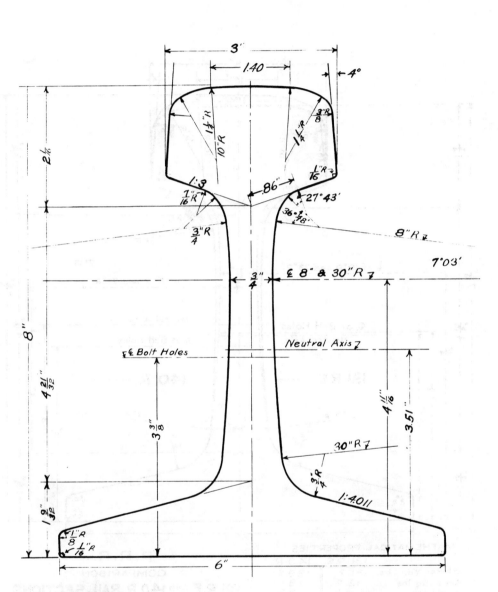

Area **15.2** sq.in.
Wt. **155.5** lb.per yd.
Moment of Inertia **129**
Sec. Mod. above N.A. **29**
Sec. Mod. below N.A. **37**.

A 195
155 lb. Rail   Sec.B
Engineer of Tests, M. of W.
Altoona, Pa.   May 29, 1946
(155 PS)

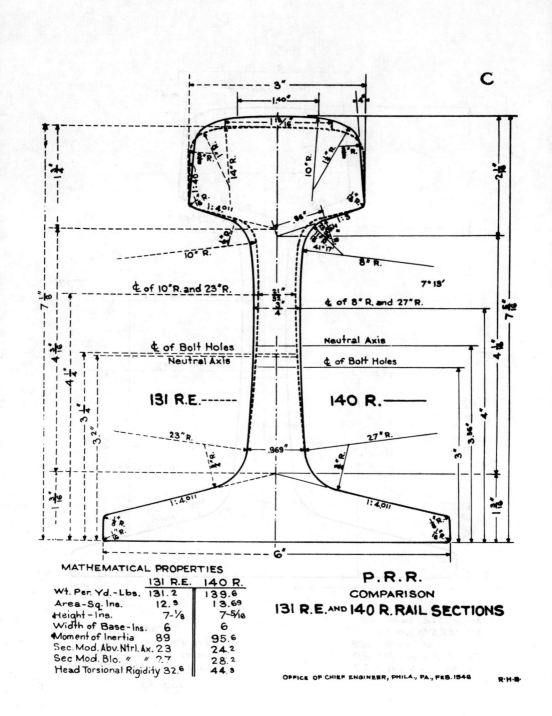

C

MATHEMATICAL PROPERTIES

	131 R.E.	140 R.
Wt. Per. Yd.-Lbs.	131.2	139.6
Area-Sq. Ins.	12.9	13.69
Height-Ins.	7-1/8	7-5/16
Width of Base-Ins.	6	6
Moment of Inertia	89	95.6
Sec. Mod. Abv. Ntrl. Ax.	23	24.2
Sec. Mod. Blo. " "	27	28.2
Head Torsional Rigidity	32.6	44.3

P. R. R.

COMPARISON

131 R.E. AND 140 R. RAIL SECTIONS

OFFICE OF CHIEF ENGINEER, PHILA., PA., FEB. 1946

R·H·B·

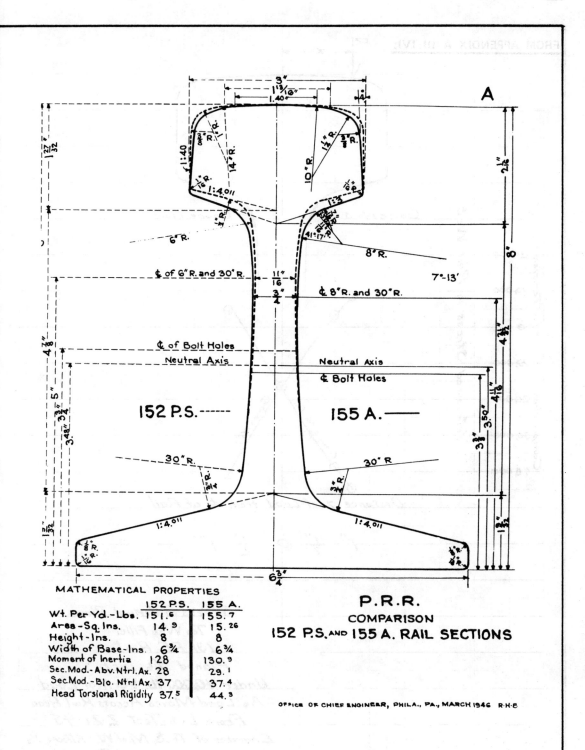

MATHEMATICAL PROPERTIES

	152 P.S.	155 A.
Wt. Per Yd.-Lbs.	151.6	155.7
Area-Sq. Ins.	14.9	15.26
Height-Ins.	8	8
Width of Base-Ins.	6¾	6¾
Moment of Inertia	128	130.9
Sec. Mod.-Abv. Ntrl.Ax.	28	29.1
Sec. Mod.-Blo. Ntrl.Ax.	37	37.4
Head Torsional Rigidity	37.5	44.3

P.R.R.
COMPARISON
152 P.S. AND 155 A. RAIL SECTIONS

OFFICE OF CHIEF ENGINEER, PHILA., PA., MARCH 1946 R·H·E

422

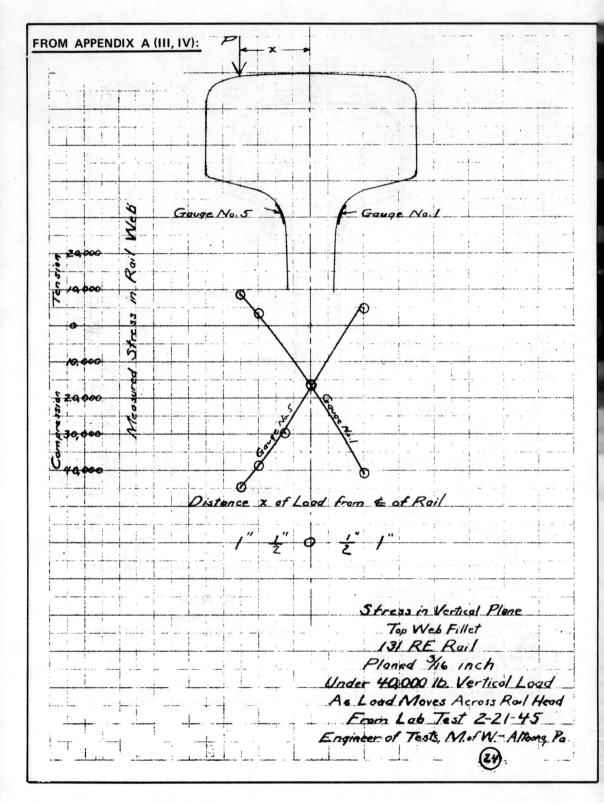

Stress in Vertical Plane
Top Web Fillet
131 RE Rail
Planed 3/16 inch
Under 40,000 lb. Vertical Load
As Load Moves Across Rail Head
From Lab Test 2-21-45
Engineer of Tests, M. of W. - Altoona, Pa.

24

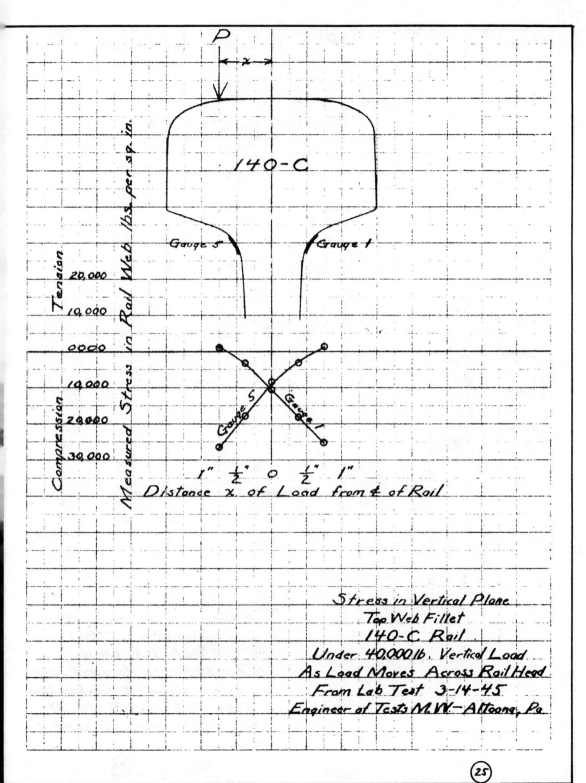

P

x

140-C

Gauge 5   Gauge 1

Tension.
20,000
10,000
0000
10,000
20,000
30,000
Compression.

Measured Stress in Rail Web lbs. per sq. in.

Gauge 5   Gauge 1

1"   ½"   0   ½"   1"
Distance x of Load from ₵ of Rail

Stress in Vertical Plane
Top Web Fillet
140-C Rail
Under 40,000 lb. Vertical Load
As Load Moves Across Rail Head
From Lab Test 3-14-45
Engineer of Tests M.W.—Altoona, Pa

25

424

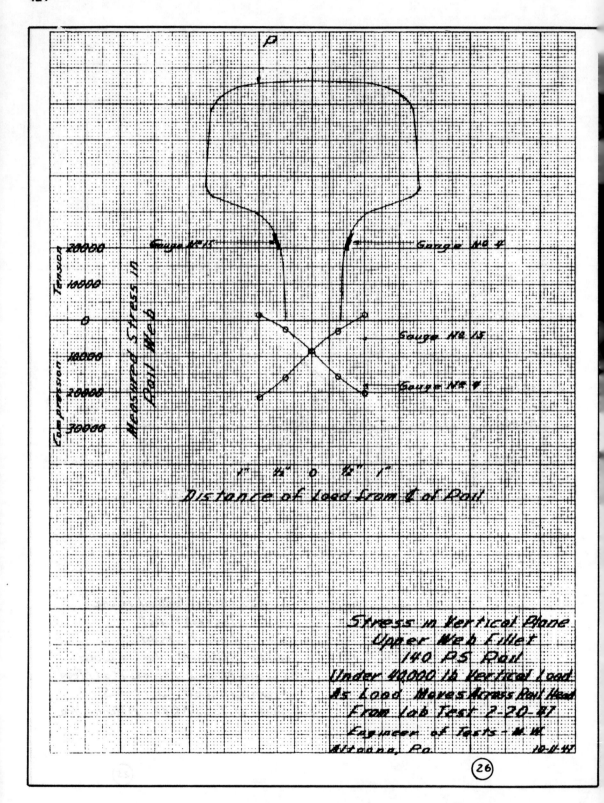

Stress in Vertical Plane
Upper Web Fillet
140 PS Rail
Under 40000 lb Vertical Load
As Load Moves Across Rail Head
From Lab Test 2-20-27
Engineer of Tests - M. W.
Altoona, Pa.

26

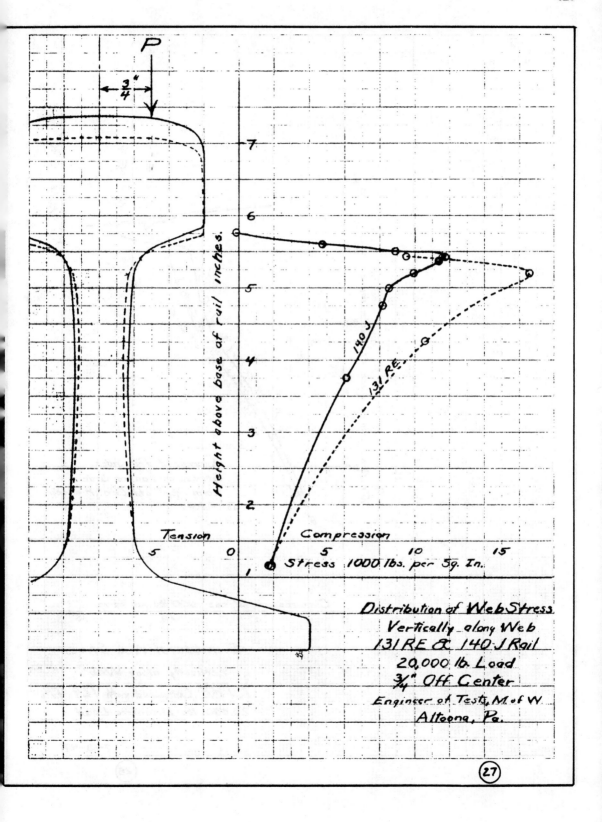

P

3/4"

Height above base of rail inches.

7

6

140 J

131 RE.

5

4

3

2

Tension   Compression

5   0   5   10   15

Stress 1000 lbs. per Sq. In.

1

Distribution of Web Stress
Vertically along Web
131 RE & 140 J Rail
20,000 lb. Load
3/4" Off Center
Engineer of Tests, M of W
Altoona, Pa.

27

426

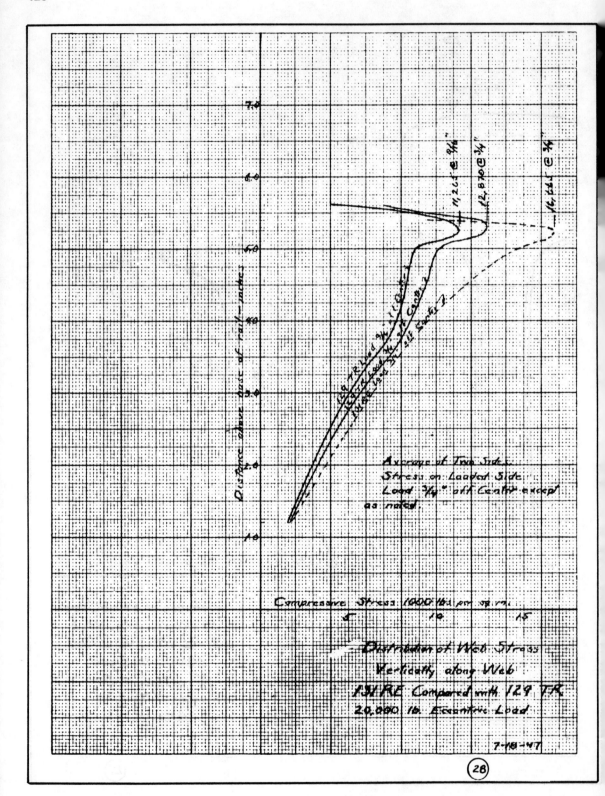

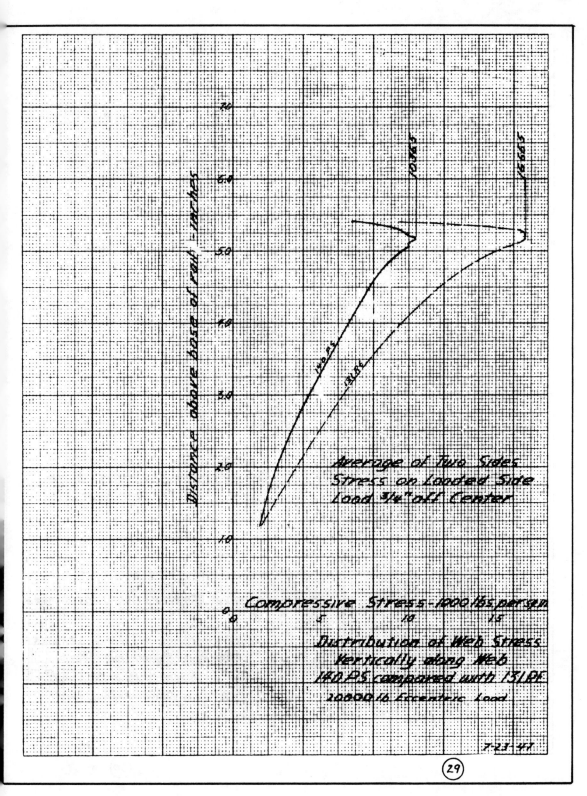

Average of Two Sides
Stress on Loaded Side
Load 3/4" off Center

Compressive Stress - 1000 lbs per sq in

Distribution of Web Stress
Vertically along Web
160 P.S. compared with 131 P.E.
20000 lb Eccentric Load

7-23-47

29

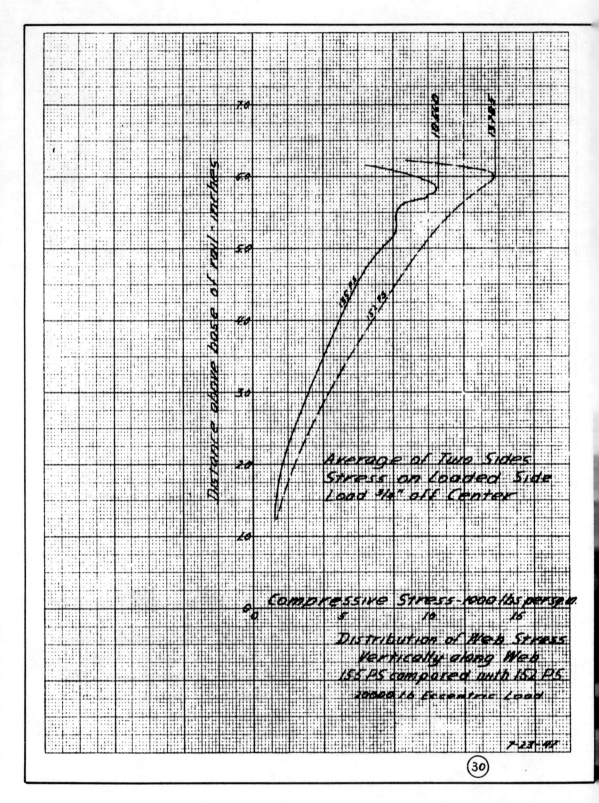

FROM APPENDIX B:

A METHOD OF CALCULATING THE MAXIMUM STRESS IN THE WEB OF RAIL DUE TO AN ECCENTRIC VERTICAL LOAD.

I. **Basis of Method:**

This method of calculating maximum web stress in a vertical plane in railroad T rails due to a vertical eccentric load is principally empirical, and is based on a series of tests conducted at the Altoona Laboratories, Pennsylvania Railroad, using Stresscoat to determine location of maximum stress, and wire resistance strain gauges to determine magnitude of stress.

The stress referred to is actually the measured strain, multiplied by the modulus of elasticity, and is not the true stress which would have been obtained by a rosette measurement and calculation. In other words a uni-axial stress is assumed, and the discrepancy due to the vertical component of strain attributable to the longitudinal stress at this point is neglected. The error is small, as shown by rosette measurements, and is of little importance, assuming the maximum strain theory of failure. This theory seems to be justified in this case, since failures seem to be due to compressive stresses or strains, beyond the yield point of the material. The line of failure is definitely perpendicular to the line of maximum compressive strain.

The method of calculation gives the stress due to a 20,000 lb. load applied in a direction parallel with the vertical axis of the rail at a point 3/4 in. from the longitudinal center line of the rail. Stresses were measured at the middle of a simple 48 inch span, but field measurements show stresses determined in this manner to be in good agreement with actual stresses in track due to a wheel load with the same eccentricity. The calculated stresses may be adjusted to other magnitudes of loading by simple proportion, and to other eccentricities of load by adjusting that part of the stress due to bending in proportion to the relative eccentricity of the applied load.

Stress measurements show that the web of the rail is subjected to a column type of loading, that is to a combination of axial compression and bending. The stresses are affected to a marked extent by concentration factors connected with the relationship between the fillet radius at the top of the web and the thickness of the web. They are also affected by the thickness and torsional rigidity of the rail head.

If the geometrical properties of the rail web, that is, thickness, radius of curvature, and fillet radius, are held constant, the stress is reduced by giving the rail a thicker head and increased by giving the rail a thinner head. This had been observed in maintenance experience, as rails with the head worn thin have been particularly subject to web failure.

The maximum stress is always found near the bottom of the top fillet curve, and is compressive, being a combination of direct compressive stress and bending stress.

Holding the geometrical properties of the head constant, the stress is not inversely proportional to the thickness of the web, as might be expected. Attempts to reduce the stress in the web by thickening of the web have not been successful, unless the thickening of the web has been accompanied by an increase in the fillet radius, so that the ratio of fillet radius to web thickness is held relatively constant.

Existing tables and charts of stress concentration factors such as those given in Vol. II, Timoshenko, Strength of Materials, page 339, for bending of a flat plate with fillets, do not fully meet the needs of this problem. New curves of concentration factors based on experimental results serve to iron out otherwise unexplainable discrepancies in the test results, and make it possible to present a method of calculation which meets the needs of the problem and coincides with the results of experimental measurements with a maximum error of approximately five percent.

Four curves are presented, two for use in calculating bending stress and two for calculating direct stress.

For calculating bending stress one curve gives stress concentration factors plotted against ratios of fillet radius to web thickness. One curve gives bending moment in a one inch thick section of the rail immediately below the load plotted against the torsional rigidity of the head.

For calculating direct stress, one curve gives stress concentration factors, and one curve gives total load on a one inch section of the rail web, plotted against the moment of inertia of the rail head.

In order to apply the method it is first necessary to prepare an accurate full scale drawing of the rail section under consideration, and from this drawing to determine the dimensions and properties of the rail.

II. Method of Calculating Stress:
A. Bending Stress
1. By mechanical integrator or other convenient method determine:
   (a) Moment of inertia of head about horizontal axis.
   (b) Moment of inertia of head about vertical axis.
   (c) Area of head.

The sum of (a) and (b) gives the polar moment of inertia of the head, and from this figure and the area, the torsional rigidity of the head may be calculated by the approximate method given in Timoshenko, Vol. II, Strength of Materials, pages 265 and 266. (See also Vol. I page 270).

$$\frac{Mt}{\theta} = C = \frac{A^4 G}{4\pi^2 Ip} \quad \text{taking } G = 12,000,000 \text{ for steel.}$$

2.(a) On an accurate drawing of the section, draw a line from the center of the upper web fillet circle to the point of intersection of the lines representing the top fishing surfaces. Where this line intersects the outline of the rail is assumed to be the critical section. Measure accurately or compute the web thickness at this point.

(b) Ratio of the fillet radius to the thickness at the critical section gives the ratio $\frac{r}{d}$ which determines the concentration factor.

3. From chart No. 3 determine the bending moment in the web corresponding to the torsional rigidity "C". Multiply this by the concentration factor

-3-

from chart No. 1, corresponding to the ratio $\frac{r}{d}$ determined under 2(b) on preceding page.

    4. From the drawing, or by calculation, determine the thickness of the web at the bottom of the upper web fillet. Using this as "d", calculate the section modulus of a one inch section of the web from the formula $\frac{bd^2}{6}$ using b = 1 in.

    5. Divide the bending moment multiplied by concentration factor by the section modulus to get the bending stress at the critical section.

B. <u>Direct Stress</u>

    1.(a) Using the moment of inertia of the head about a horizontal axis, obtain from chart No. 4 the corresponding direct load on a one inch section of the web.

    (b) Determine from chart No. 2 the concentration factor corresponding to the ratio $\frac{}{d}$ previously determined.

    (c) Divide the direct load by the thickness of the web <u>at the critical section</u> and multiply by the concentration factor to get the direct stress.

C. <u>Total Stress</u>

    The sum of the bending stress plus the direct stress gives the total vertical compressive stress at the point of maximum stress on the side of the web nearest the load, under a 20,000 lb. load with 3/4" eccentricity.

    For other loads the stress can be determined by applying direct proportion to the stress under 20,000 lb. load.

    For eccentricities other than 3/4 in., apply direct proportion to the bending stress only.

    The results may be expected to be within 5 percent of the true stress (strain x 30,000,000) as obtained by test.

C. J. Code,
Altoona, Pa.,
March 1, 1946.
Rev. Aug. 19, 1946.

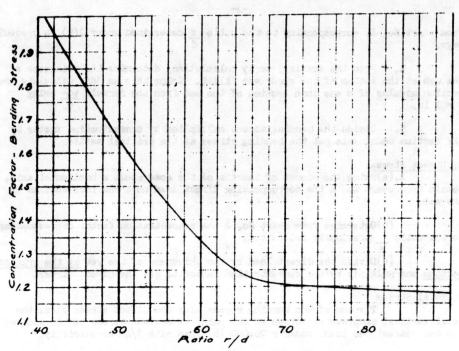

Chart No.1. Concentration Factors for Bending Stress
in upper web fillet of rail.

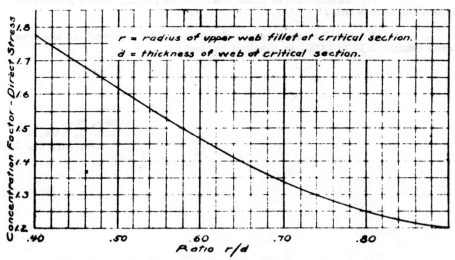

r = radius of upper web fillet at critical section.
d = thickness of web at critical section.

Chart No.2. Concentration Factors for Direct Stress
in upper web fillet of rail.

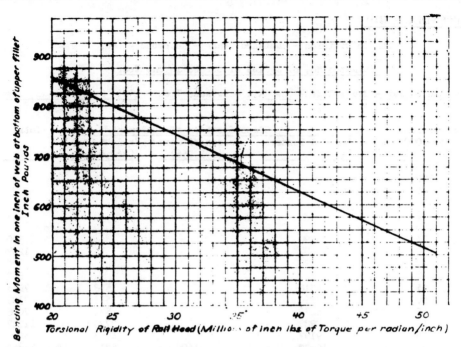

Chart No.3. Bending Moment Top Web Fillet
20,000 lb. Load 3/4 inch off center.

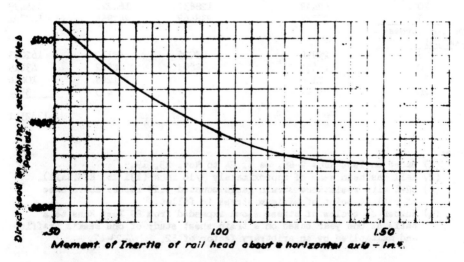

Chart No.4. Direct Load on One Inch Section of Rail Web
20,000 lb. Load

FROM APPENDIX C (II):

Middle Division - Eastward Track - Petersburg, Pa.

Estimated No. of Cycles of Stress in One Year

Top Web Fillet - Gauge Side - Low Rail - Between Ties - 2°45' Curve - 6 in. Elev.

Compression Stress-1000 psi	Classification of Equipment			Total
	Loco. & Tenders	Passenger Cars (191,256)	Freight Cars (262,028)	
100				
95				
90				
85				
80				
75	390			390
70	1207			1207
65	390			390
60	817			817
55	5818		1598	7416
50	2850		533	3383
45	6472		533	7005
40	7989		3728	11717
35	9197		4793	13990
30	10438	1600	6814	18852
25	14112	4801	10431	29344
20	20427	18405	44261	83093
15	21705	53615	65975	141295
10	42438	128837	164224	335499
5	27397	238469	242855	508721
Tension Stress-1000 psi				
5	25956	88025	48112	162093
10	25654	8803	8562	43019
15	9178		1268	10446
20	3441		423	3864
				1382541

Note:
    (1) Based on Test Runs 2-88, Sept. 24 to Nov. 23, 1945.
    (2) Rail has head wear of approximately 3/16 inch (131 lb. R.E.Rail).
    (3) SR-4 wire resistance strain gauge mounted 5.19 inches above base
         of rail at point of maximum stress in fillet.
    (4) Number of cycles of stress shown expanded from 89 Test Runs to a
         basis of one year based on a train sheet study of one week's traffic
         and multiplied by an aribtrary factor of 52.   4-23-47.

10.

PanHandle Division - Eastward Track - M.P.10 Curve

Estimated No. of Cycles of Stress in One Year

Top Web Fillet - Gauge Side - Low Rail - Opposite Joint - 4° Curve - 5-1/2 in. Elev.

Compression Stress-1000 psi	Classification of Equipment			Total
	Loco. & Tenders	Passenger Cars	Freight Cars	
100				
95				
90				
85	593			593
80	251			251
75				
70	502			502
65	1027			1027
60	3165			3165
55	2625			2625
50	5942			5942
45	8193	340		8533
40	11283	1361		12644
35	13761	5443		19204
30	14257	10886		25143
25	11307	23814		35121
20	21854	87772	5478	115104
15	28262	216367	27391	272020
10	36536	392251	77693	506480
5	13485	352107	64774	430366
Tension Stress-1000 psi				
5	31184	187450	85163	303797
10	27681	59195	15937	102813
15	8853			8853
20	3173			3173
25	647			647
30	548			548
				1858551

Note:
  (1) Based on Test Runs 100-165, March 5, 1946 to March 13, 1946.
  (2) Rail had head wear of approximately 1/16 inch (131 lb. R.E.Rail).
  (3) Previous rail had failed in one year.
  (4) SR-4 wire resistance strain gauge mounted 5.19 inches above base of rail at point of maximum stress in fillet.
  (5) Number of cycles of stress shown expanded from 66 Test Runs to a basis of one year, based on a train sheet study of one week's traffic and an additional factor based on comparison of this week's traffic with the year's traffic.   4-18-47.

435

PANHANDLE DIVISION - WESTWARD TRACK - SLAG DUMP CURVE-
ESTIMATED NO. OF CYCLES OF STRESS
IN ONE YEAR

TOP WEB FILLET - GAUGE SIDE - LOW RAIL - 6° 30' CURVE - 6 IN. ELEVATION

BEFORE ADZING OF TIES & RESURFACING TRACK

	Classification of Equipment			
Compression Stress - 1000 p.s.i.	Loco. & Tenders (23274)	Passenger Cars (98609)	Freight Cars (445662)	Total
100				
95	781			781
90	781			781
85				
80	1562			1562
75	781			781
70	391			391
65	1378			1378
60	1378			1378
55	2096			2096
50	2654			2654
45	1825			1825
40	4802			4802
35	6616			6616
30	7725			7725
25	9672			9672
20	13968	3147	1762	18877
15	13576	1049	12331	16956
10	22642	15735	91598	129975
5	19147	37765	216665	273577
Tension Stress - 1000 p.s.i.				
5	53486	110148	170866	334500
10	37106	6294	26423	69823
15	18779			18779
20	2255			2255
				907204

Note:
(1) Based on Test Runs 200 to 232 April 4, 5, 8, 10, 11, 1946.
(2) Rail has head wear of approximately 1/8 inch (131 lb. R. E. Rail).
(3) Rail laid new in 1942 in this curve was removed because of web
    failure in 1945 (131 lb. R. E. Rail).
(4) SR-4 wire resistance strain gauge mounted 5.19 inches above
    base of rail at point of maximum stress in fillet.
(5) Number of cycles of stress shown expanded from 33 Test Runs to
    a basis of one year, based on a train sheet study of one week's
    traffic and an additional factor based on comparison of this
    week's traffic with the year's traffic.

4-10-47.

PANHANDLE DIVISION - WESTWARD TRACK @ OS CURVE
Estimated No. of Cycles of Stress in One Year
Top Web Fillet - Gauge Side - Low Rail - 3° 00' Curve - 6 In. Elev.

Compression Stress-1000 p.s.i.	Classification of Equipment			
	Loco. & Tenders	Freight Cars (407561)	Pass. Cars (92504)	Total
100	209			209
95				
90	627			627
85	294			294
80	1254			1254
75	499			499
70	503			503
65	1090			1090
60	1495			1495
55	2730			2730
50	3385			3385
45	4599	161		4760
40	5907			5907
35	8117	322		8439
30	13906	805		14711
25	14470	1770	242	16482
20	15394	2735	242	18371
15	18442	7723	483	26648
10	42716	56637	14249	113602
5	45193	232018	72692	349903
Tension Stress-1000 p.s.i.				
5	27815	21239	64481	113535
10	9226	483	966	10675
Over 10	165			165

Note:
(1) Based on Test Runs 1493-1774, May 14 to 27, 1947.
(2) Rail has head wear of approximately 1/8 inch (131 lb. RE Rail).
(3) SR4 wire resistance strain gauge mounted 5.19 inches above base of rail at
    point of maximum stress in fillet.
(4) Number of cycles of stress shown expanded from 282 Test Runs to a basis of
    one year based on a train sheet study of one week's traffic and an
    additional factor based on comparison of this week's traffic with the
    year's traffic.

7-12-47.

PANHANDLE DIVISION - EASTWARD TRACK - ON CURVE
Estimated No. of Cycles of Stress in One Year
Top Web Fillet - Gauge Side - Low Rail - 3° 00' Curve - 6 In. Elev.
Track Gauge 4' 9"

Compression Stress-1000 p.s.i.	Classification of Equipment			
	Loco. & Tenders	Freight Cars (405165)	Pass. Cars (78917)	Total
100				
95	224			224
90				
85	224			224
80	220			220
75	444			444
70	325			325
65	2192			2192
60	2072			2072
55	325			325
50	1696	139		1835
45	5795			5795
40	5012	279		5291
35	7252	418		7670
30	8026	1255	281	9562
25	6848	1952	1124	9924
20	11537	5158	5055	21750
15	13295	16589	26957	56841
10	18606	141909	41559	202074
5	20579	323826	118498	462903
Tension Stress-1000 p.s.i.				
5	28704	217882	19937	266523
10	44061	14219		58280
Over 10	6203			6203

Note:
(1) Based on Test Runs 1493-1680, May 14 to 22, 1947.
(2) Rail has head wear of approximately 1/8 inch   (131 lb. RE Rail).
(3) SR4 wire resistance strain gauge mounted 5.19 inches above base of rail at
    point of maximum stress in fillet.
(4) Number of cycles of stress shown expanded from 188 Test Runs to a basis of
    one year based on a train sheet study of one week's traffic and an
    additional factor based on comparison of this week's traffic with the
    year's traffic.

7-12-47.

PANHANDLE DIVISION - EASTWARD TRACK - ON CURVE
Estimated No. of Cycles of Stress in One Year
Top Web Fillet - Gauge Side - Low Rail - 3° 00' Curve - 6 In. Elev.
Track Gauge 4' 8-1/2"

Compression Stress-1000 p.s.i.	Classification of Equipment			
	Loco. & Tenders	Freight Cars (405165)	Pass. Cars (78917)	Total
100				
95				
90	628			628
85				
80				
75	440			440
70	1256			1256
65	2952			2952
60	1812			1812
55	2485			2485
50	4165			4165
45	10577			10577
40	7171			7171
35	5456			5456
30	11274	209		11483
25	9063	1461	357	10881
20	15853	3339		19192
15	19614	16279	2857	38750
10	18752	113116	29639	161507
5	14695	166751	24997	206443
Tension Stress-1000 p.s.i.				
5	30898	299485	123914	454297
10	23251	19409	17498	60158
Over 10	2583			2583

Note:
(1) Based on Test Runs 1681-1790, May 22, 23, 26, 27, 28, 1947.
(2) Rail has head wear of approximately 1/8 inch (131 lb. RE Rail).
(3) SR4 wire resistance strain gauge mounted 5.19 inches above base of rail at point of maximum stress in fillet.
(4) Number of cycles of stress shown expanded from 110 Test Runs to a basis of one year based on a train sheet study of one week's traffic and an additional factor based on comparison of this week's traffic with the year's traffic.

7-12-47.

MIDDLE DIVISION - NO. 3 TRACK WESTWARD - NO. 10 CURVE
Estimated No. of Cycles of Stress in One Year
Top Web Fillet - Gauge Side - Low Rail - 6° 00' Curve - 6 in. Elev.

Comp. Stress 1000 Lbs./Sq.In.	Classification of Equipment			Totals
	Loco. & Tenders	Freight Cars (335972)	Pass. Cars (187564)	
100	302			302
95	302			302
90				
85	402			402
80	603			603
75	1175			1175
70	598			598
65	1711			1711
60	3966			3966
55	3890			3890
50	4937			4937
45	6995			6995
40	6293	449		6742
35	9477	1346		10823
30	13313	2467	457	16237
25	14762	6953	2516	24231
20	18061	21531	7320	46912
15	26769	53154	36598	116521
10	36876	211496	173842	422214
5	33617	377688	208840	620145

Tension Stress 1000 Lbs./Sq.In.				
5	17754	19512	141390	178656
10	8747	1121	39343	49211
15	2469		229	2698
20	541			541
25	101			101

Note:-
   (1) Based on Test Runs 1800 - 1970, Aug. 7-27, 1947.
   (2) Rail has head wear of approximately 1/16 inch (131 lb. RE Rail).
   (3) SR-4 wire resistance strain gauges mounted 5.19 inches above base of rail at point of maximum stress in fillet.
   (4) Number of cycles of stress shown expanded from 171 test runs to a basis of one week's traffic, (Traffic Study for the week of Oct. 15-21, 1946) and multiplied by an arbitrary factor of 52.

Altoona, Pa.
9-11-47.

FROM APPENDIX D:

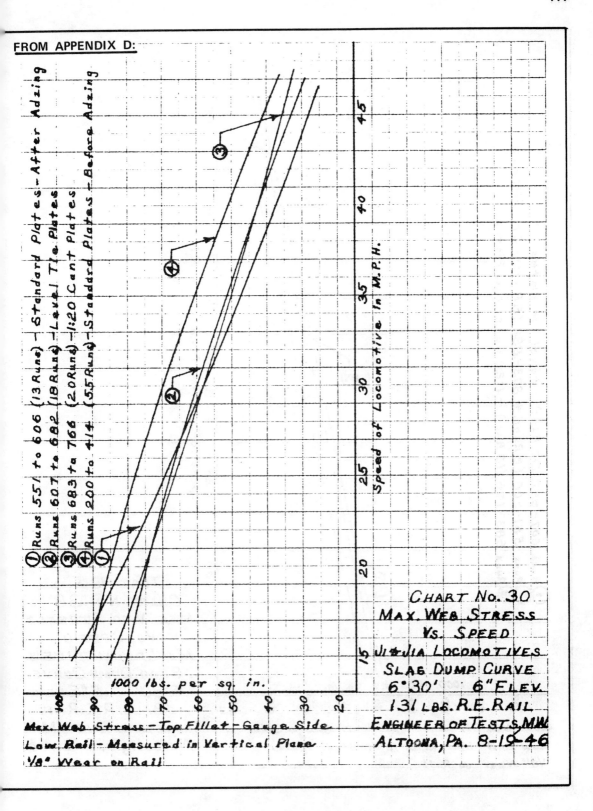

CHART No. 30
MAX. WEB STRESS
VS. SPEED
J1 & J1A LOCOMOTIVES
SLAB DUMP CURVE
6°30'   6" ELEV.
131 LBS. R.E. RAIL
ENGINEER OF TESTS, M.W.
ALTOONA, PA. 8-19-46

442

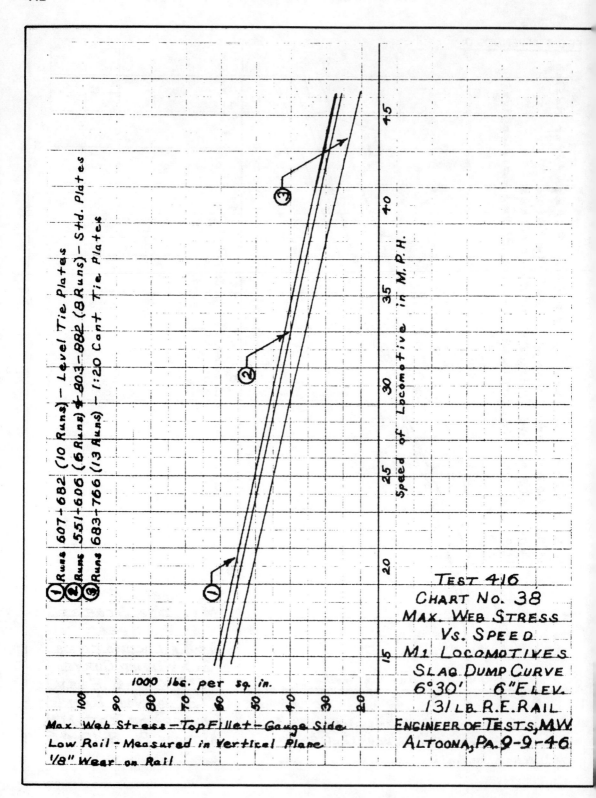

Runs 607-682 (10 Runs) — Level Tie Plates
Runs 551-606 (6 Runs) + 803-882 (8 Runs) — Std. Plates
Runs 683-766 (13 Runs) — 1:20 Cant Tie Plates

① Runs 607-682 (10 Runs) — Level Tie Plates
② Runs 551-606 (6 Runs) + 803-882 (8 Runs) — Std. Plates
③ Runs 683-766 (13 Runs) — 1:20 Cant Tie Plates

1000 lbs. per sq. in.

100 90 80 70 60 50 40 30 20

Max. Web Stress — Top Fillet — Gauge Side
Low Rail — Measured in Vertical Plane
1/8" Wear on Rail

Speed of Locomotive in M.P.H.

15   20   25   30   35   40   45

TEST 416
CHART No. 38
MAX. WEB STRESS
VS. SPEED
M1 LOCOMOTIVES
SLAG DUMP CURVE
6°30'   6" ELEV.
131 LB. R.E. RAIL
ENGINEER OF TESTS, M.W.
ALTOONA, PA. 9-9-46

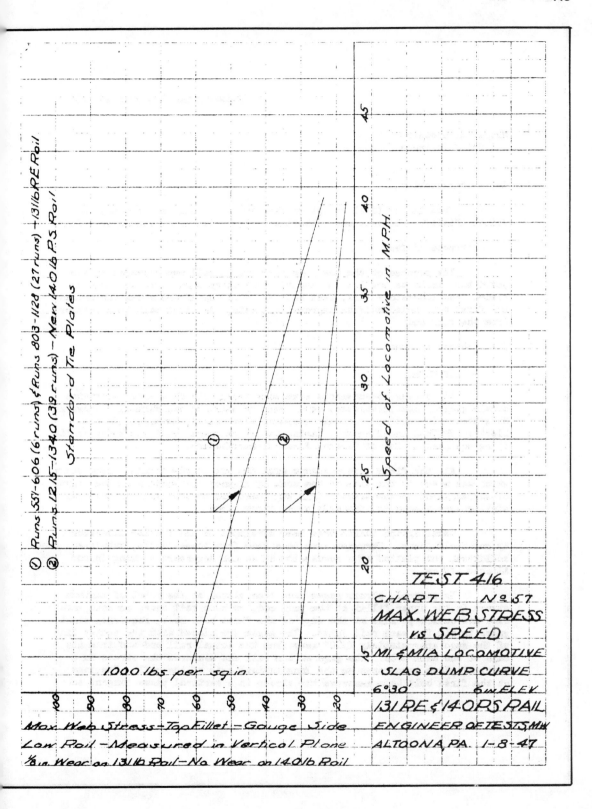

① Runs 557-606 (6 runs) ¢ Runs 803-1128 (27 runs) +131 lb RE Rail

② Runs 1215-1340 (39 runs) – New 140 lb P.S. Rail

Standard Tie Plates

Speed of Locomotive in M.P.H.

1000 lbs per sq in

TEST 416

CHART   N° 57

MAX. WEB STRESS
vs SPEED

MI ¢ MIA LOCOMOTIVE
SLAG DUMP CURVE

6°30′   6 in ELEV.

131 RE ¢ 140 PS RAIL

ENGINEER OF TESTS.M.W.

ALTOONA, PA. 1-8-47

Max. Web Stress–Top Fillet – Gouge Side
Low Rail – Measured in Vertical Plane
⅛ in. Wear on 131 lb Rail – No Wear on 140 lb Rail

TEXT 29

Philadelphia, November 19, 1951.

Mr. J. L. Gressitt
  Chief Engineer.

I - Introduction.

   This is the final report on Test No. 417, Rail Web Stresses in
Joints (Field). The test was authorized by your letter of January 29, 1945.

II - Purpose of Test.

   The purpose of the test was research in rail web stresses within
joint bar limits to confirm and amplify laboratory work. It had been concluded from laboratory work, Test No. 391, that the stress situation around
the first bolt hole could be improved by moving the first bolt hole farther
from the rail end.

III - Method of Test.

   1. General.

   All stress measurements were made using 1/4" SR-4 wire resistance
strain gages. Static stresses were read by means of two Baldwin Southwark
SR-4 Strain Indicators. Dynamic stresses were read by means of General
Electric PM10B-2 Oscillograph, having twelve channels, with necessary ampli-
fying equipment, also of General Electric manufacture.

   All the field work was done with the aid of the "trailer laboratory"
which was moved to the site of the work by highway and spotted on the right-
of-way adjacent to the track. This equipment has been in use for this and
similar work almost continuously since March, 1946.

   Oscillograph charts have been developed in the trailer laboratory
by our field force. Stresses have been read from those charts, tabulated, consolidated, and plotted by a succession of Junior Engineers working in our
Altoona office.

   In general, strain gages have been placed at the point of maximum
stress in the upper fillet at the rail end, on both rail ends, on both gage
side and outside; also at the edge of the first bolt hole, requiring eight
gages in all for each rail joint. The gages are placed with the center line
of the gage approximately 1/10" away from the actual rail end and from the
edge of the bolt hole. The gage at the rail end measures the stress in a
vertical plane transverse to the longitudinal axis of the rail. The gage
at the first bolt hole measures the stress in a vertical plane tangent to

the bolt hole. Stresscoat tests and previous tests with SR-4 gages
have shown these to be the locations of maximum stress.

It has been found by laboratory test that the stress in a gage
fastened on the curved inner surface of the bolt hole is about 50% higher
than that with gage in position above described. In the table of equivalent stresses, Nos. 69 to 73, inclusive, the measured stresses have been
increased by 50% to allow for this. In the service tests it was not
practicable to place the gages on the inside surface of the bolt holes
because of clearance difficulties.

After tabulating the number of cycles of stress of each magnitude in increments of 5,000 pounds for a representative number of units
of each class of equipment from the oscillograph charts, the number of
cycles counted has been converted to the basis of one year's traffic by
applying factors determined from a traffic study of Middle Division train
sheets.

2. Stress Measurements at Forge - 131-lb. R.E.Rail.

Stresses were first measured in 131-lb. new rail at Forge, #3
track, on tangent track, within the limits of the interlocking, during
the summer and fall of 1947. Blind end rails and blind joint bars were
obtained from Steelton and these were drilled at Chambersburg with the
special bolt spacing required. The rails were first installed as received
from the mill with hot sawed ends, but it was found that the pinch at the
rail ends caused such erratic stresses as to eliminate any possibility of
comparison of stresses between the various drillings and the rails were
subsequently cold sawed to eliminate the hot sawed ends and were redrilled.
The manner in which this was accomplished, together with the spacing of
the bolt holes for the special drilling, is shown on print attached, dated
February 20, 1948. These rails with the cold sawed ends were installed at
the same location and the test with these rails was continued during the
spring, summer, and fall of 1948.

Photographs illustrating the appearance of the standard joint,
and joints A, B, and C, Nos. G-114, G-115, G-142, and G-143, are attached.
It will be noted from an appearance point of view the four-hole spacing of
bolts in the 36" joints is not out of proportion.

3. Stress Measurements at No. 7 Curve.

Early in 1949 it was found necessary, due to web failures in the
joint, to renew with 140-lb. P.S. rail a long stretch of 131-lb. R.E. rail
laid in 1942 between Spruce and Forge. Advantage was taken of this fact
to get some stress measurements on the 131-lb. R.E. rail before it was

446

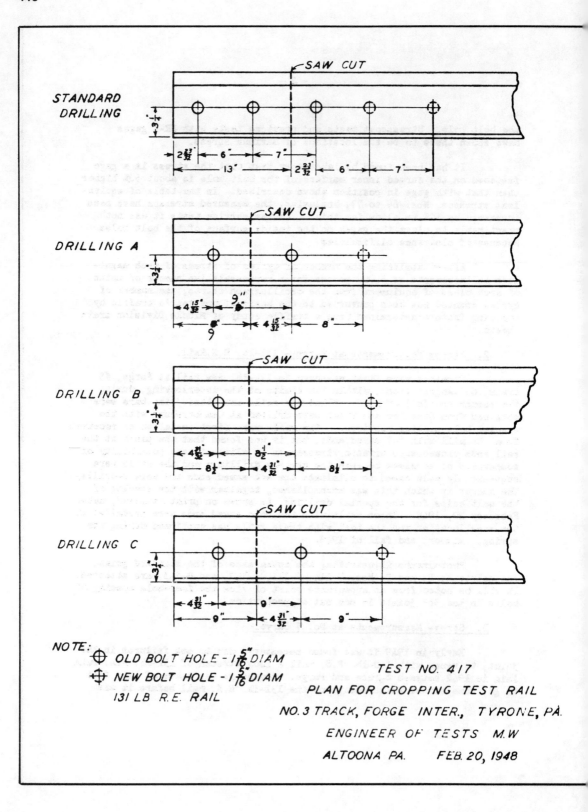

NOTE:
⊕ OLD BOLT HOLE - 1 5/16" DIAM
⊕ NEW BOLT HOLE - 1 5/16" DIAM
131 LB R.E. RAIL

TEST NO. 417
PLAN FOR CROPPING TEST RAIL
NO. 3 TRACK, FORGE INTER., TYRONE, PA.
ENGINEER OF TESTS M.W
ALTOONA PA.   FEB. 20, 1948

PHOTO G142
131 R.E. RAIL   DRILLING B

PHOTO G143
131 R.E. RAIL   DRILLING C

removed and on the 140-lb. P.S. rail immediately after it was installed.
Tables of these stresses are included in the report. This was done on the
low side of a six degree curve, with six inches superelevation.

4. Stress Measurements at Forge - 140-lb. P.S. Rail.

During the summer and fall of 1949, stress measurements were made
in 140-lb. P.S. rail on tangent track at Forge Interlocking, #3 track, at
the same location where stresses were previously measured in the 131-lb.
R.E. rail. After a brief analysis of the results with the 131-lb. R.E.
rail, drilling C was eliminated, and in the 140-lb. P.S. rail test, drillings
A and B were tested in comparison with A.R.E.A. drilling and P.R.R. standard
6-hole drilling. These rails were also cut to give cold sawed ends,
eliminating the variable of the pinch at the rail end. Photographs Nos. 326,
327, and 328 are included showing the appearance of the 140-lb. P.S. joints.
Prints attached, dated 7-18-49, show the bolt hole spacing.

5. Measurements of Joint Bar and Bolt Stress.

In order to check on the possibility that reduction in the number
of bolts from 6 to 4 might weaken the joint to the extent of causing higher
stresses in the joint bars themselves, a supplementary test was conducted on
the 140-lb. P.S. rail and joint bars.

On each bar of a pair, a gage was placed near the top of the bar
and one near the bottom of the bar at its center. From the stresses measured
in these bars, and from their known positions, the maximum stress in the
extreme fiber top and bottom of each bar was calculated by the methods
described in the 5th Progress Report of the Special Committee on Stresses in
Track - A.R.E.A.

Similarly to determine the effect on the stress in the bolts of a
reduction in the number of bolts, gages were placed on both sides of each
bolt in a 4-hole joint with "A" drilling and in a standard 6-hole joint and
the stresses measured under a number of trains.

These stress measurements in bolts and joint bars have not been
completely analyzed, but the results are referred to briefly below.

6. Fatigue Tests.

During the progress of this field work, laboratory tests were run
at Altoona on the Krouse variable speed repeated bend test machine to determine the corrosion fatigue characteristics of rail web steel for complete
reversal and for a stress cycle from zero to maximum tension. Similar tests
were run without corrosion. S-N curves, Figures A and B, are included showing
the results.

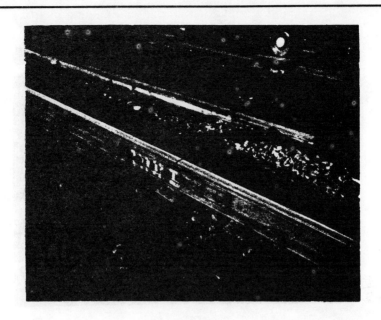

PHOTO G326
140 P.S. RAIL   DRILLING A.R.E.A.

PHOTO G328
140 P.S. RAIL   DRILLING A

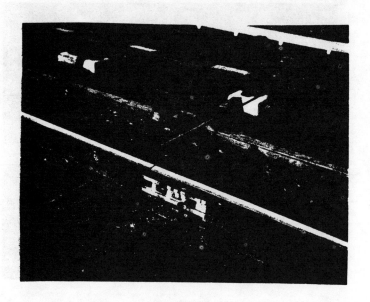

PHOTO G327
140 P.S. RAIL   DRILLING B

PHOTO G114
131 R.E. RAIL   DRILLING STANDARD

PHOTO G115
131 R.E. RAIL   DRILLING A

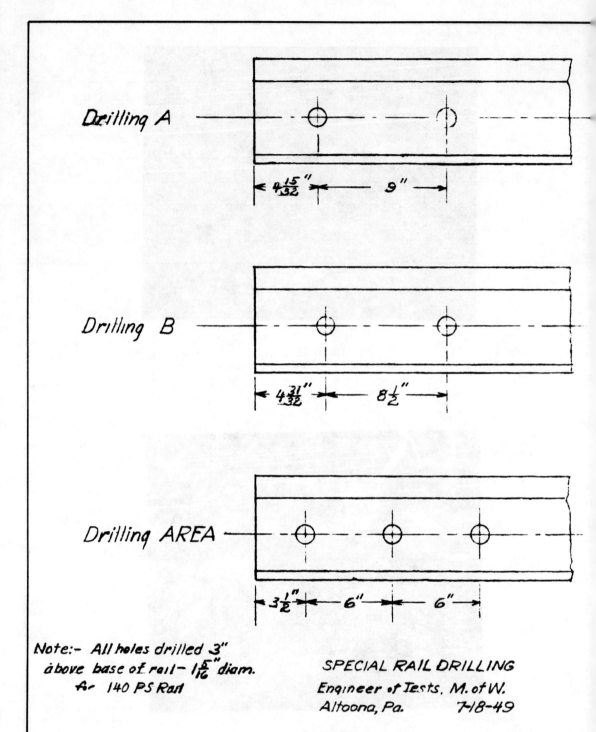

Drilling A

$4\frac{15}{32}"$ 9"

Drilling B

$4\frac{31}{32}"$ $8\frac{1}{2}"$

Drilling AREA

$3\frac{1}{2}"$ 6"   6"

Note:- All holes drilled 3"
  above base of rail— $1\frac{5}{16}"$ diam.
    for 140 PS Rail

SPECIAL RAIL DRILLING
Engineer of Tests. M. of W.
Altoona, Pa.   7-18-49

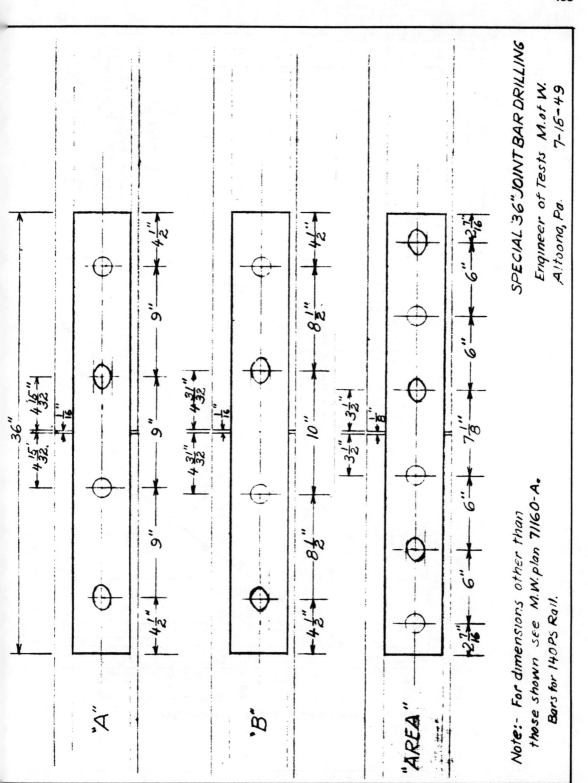

"A"

"B"

"AREA"

SPECIAL 36" JOINT BAR DRILLING

Engineer of Tests   M. of W.

Altoona, Pa.   7-16-49

Note:- For dimensions other than those shown see M.W. plan 71160-A. Bars for 140Ps Rail.

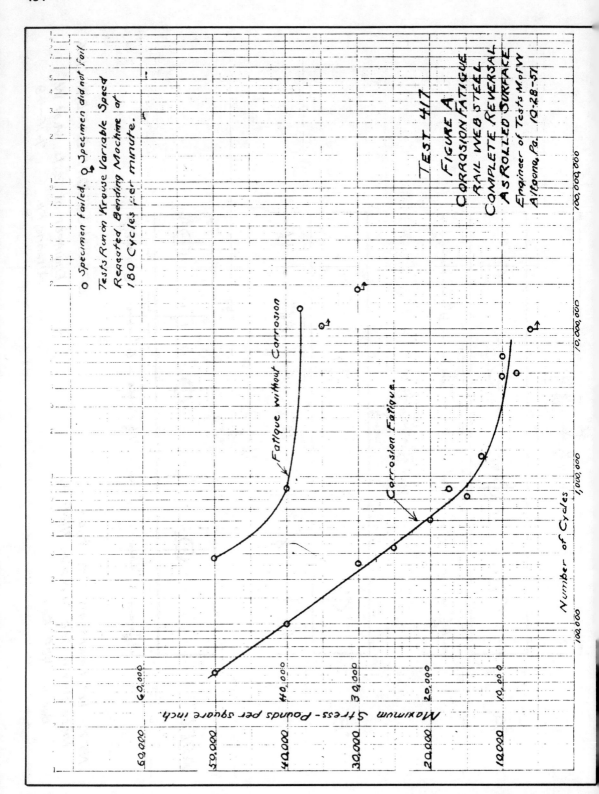

TEST 417

FIGURE A

CORROSION FATIGUE

RAIL WEB STEEL

COMPLETE REVERSAL

AS ROLLED SURFACE

Engineer of Tests M of W
Altoona, Pa. 10-28-51

o Specimen failed. ⦶ Specimen did not fail

Tests Run on Krouse Variable Speed
Repeated Bending Machine at
180 Cycles per minute.

Fatigue without Corrosion

Corrosion Fatigue.

Number of Cycles

Maximum Stress - Pounds per square inch.

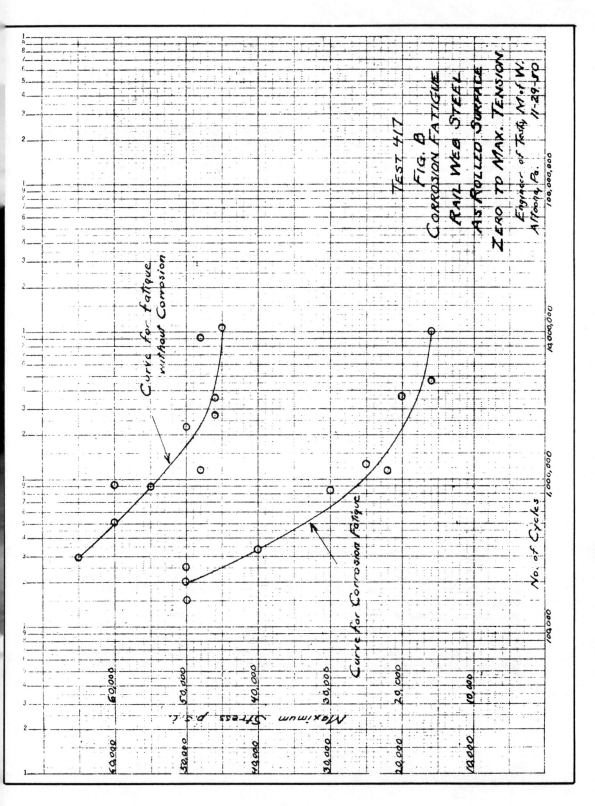

TEST 417
FIG. B
CORROSION FATIGUE
RAIL WEB STEEL
AS ROLLED SURFACE
ZERO TO MAX. TENSION

Engineer of Testy M. of W.
Altoona, Pa.   11-29-50

Curve for Fatigue
without Corrosion

Curve for Corrosion Fatigue

No. of Cycles

Maximum Stress p.s.i.

- 4 -

These tests were run in a slightly different manner than the previous tests in connection with web failures outside the joint. In the present series of tests the specimen was run at the same stress throughout its life. The machine was operated at 180 cycles per minute eight hours a day during the first five days of the test, and where failure at this rate of testing in less than five days was anticipated the number of minutes the machine was run per hour was adjusted to prolong the test so that no test lasted less than five days. This was considered necessary in order to get sufficient effect of corrosion.

After the first five days the specimen was run continuously eight hours a day. Where the fatigue life reached a million cycles or more, the test was then continued at twenty-four hours per day until failure. Failure in each case was taken as the time at which a definitely observable crack was developed, positive indication of which was taken as the pumping or bubbling of water in and out of the crack during flexing. It was frequently necessary to remove loose scale from the specimen with a penknife in order to definitely determine the presence of a crack.

The similarity between the type of failure obtained in these specimens and the type of failure found in rail ends in track is illustrated in Photographs Nos. T36015-T37317, attached. Photograph T37400 illustrates further the development of this type of failure in the upper fillet of a rail end, and T37284 illustrates the development at a bolt hole.

Similar failures have also been observed in the mitred ends of rails in heat treated crossings.

These fatigue tests were previously reported in part in the report of the Rail Committee, A.R.E.A., for 1950 - Bulletin 486, Page 620, and Proceedings for 1950, Vol. 51, Page 620.

IV - Results.

1. Tables of Stresses Measured.

Tables 1 to 16, inclusive, show the results obtained on new 131-lb. R.E. rail on tangent track at Forge. There are eight sets of two tables each, one set or pair for each gage position. The first table for each gage position shows number of cycles of stress of each range per year for each of the joint types. The second shows the average maximum stress for each range.

Tables 17 to 20 show the same information for 131-lb. R.E. rail on the low rail of No. 7 curve, there being but four tables, as there were only two gage positions.

[Note: Tables 1-67 are not included in this reprint.]

PHOTO T37317
LABORATORY CORROSION FATIGUE SPECIMEN
ENLARGED THREE TIMES COMPARED WITH
RAIL SPECIMEN FROM SERVICE, SHOWING
SIMILARITY OF CORROSION FATIGUE CRACKS

PHOTO T37400
CORROSION FATIGUE IN UPPER FILLET

PHOTO T37284
CORROSION FATIGUE AT FIRST BOLT HOLE

Tables 21 to 36, inclusive, show similar information for 140-lb. P.S. rail on the low side of No. 7 curve. There are again eight sets of two tables each, representing the eight gage positions.

Tables 37 to 52 cover the same information for 140-lb. P.S. rail at Forge on tangent track.

Tables 53 to 68 repeat the information for 140-lb. P.S. rail on tangent track at Forge with bolts loose, the previous tables representing normal bolt tension.

These 68 tables represent a mass of data which is of value in comparing the service life of rails with the results of fatigue tests, the first table in each pair giving the number and amplitude of the various stress cycles to which the material has been subjected and the second fixing the position of this stress cycle on the stress diagram.

The volume of data and its complex character are such that comparisons are difficult. In order to facilitate comparison a further set of tables and a set of charts have been prepared.

2. Tables of Equivalent Numbers of Cycles.

The additional tables Nos. 69 to 73 represent a condensation of the data presented in the previous 68 tables. Position of the cycle of stress on the stress diagram has been disregarded; in other language, mean stress has been disregarded. Based on fatigue test curve for completely reversed stress, a table of factors was prepared and applied to the original data in such a way as to produce an equivalent number of cycles at a range of 30,000 psi to take the place of the tabulation of cycles of stress at various ranges.

The derivation of these factors is shown in table No. 74, attached.

This condensation permits showing a comparison on one page of all the data obtained in one series of tests. While there are grounds for criticism of this method of condensing fatigue data, it gives in our opinion a reasonable comparison of the various gage positions and joint bar combinations included in the test.

According to our fatigue tests, with corrosion, the life of rail steel at a range of 30,000 psi with complete reversal is 880,000 cycles. With the same range running from zero to a maximum in tension, the life is somewhat less, 660,000 cycles. These figures will vary greatly with the relative degree of corrosion. Without corrosion, the fatigue life at this range of stress is infinite. For a cycle varying from low tension to high compression the life at this stress with corrosion is also infinite.

- 6 -

3. Estimated Life of Rail.

A comparison of these figures with numbers of equivalent cycles of stress shown in tables 69 to 73 gives some interesting information as to the probable length of time in which fatigue cracks may be expected to develop under various conditions where corrosion is present.

Several samples follow:

	Equivalent Cycles per Year	Estimated Life in Years
Tangent at Forge		
131-lb. RE Upper Fillet Gage Side, Receiving, Joint C.	524,684	1.7
131-lb. " " " " " ", " , Worn Std. Jt.	738,794	1.2
131-lb. " " " " Outside , " , Worn Std.	1,304,537	# 0.7
131-lb. " 1st Bolt Hole Outside, Receiving , Std.	327,198	# 2.7
131-lb. " " " " Gage Side, Receiving, Worn Std.	189,472	4.6
131-lb. " " " " " " ", " , Std. Loose Bolts	189,886	# 4.6
131-lb. " " " " Outside , " , " " "	215,805	4.1
Low Side No. 7 Curve (Worn Rail and Bars)		
131-lb. RE Upper Fillet Gage Side, Receiving, Jt. #4	136,678	# 6.4
131-lb. " " " " " " , Jt. #3	79,661	#11.1
140-lb. PS " " " " " , Jt. #1	112,370	# 7.8
140-lb. " " " " " " , Jt. #2	133,888	# 6.5
140-lb. " " " " " " , Jt. #4	81,827	#10.8
Tangent at Forge		
140-lb. PS Upper Fillet Gage Side, Receiving, A.R.E.A.	80,860	10.9
140-lb. " " " " " " , Jt. B	185,323	# 4.8
140-lb. " " " Outside, " , A.R.E.A.	40,819	21.6
Tangent at Forge - Bolts Loose		
140-lb. PS Upper Fillet Gage Side, Receiving, Jt. B	100,210	8.8
140-lb. " " " " " " , Jt. A	113,475	7.8
140-lb. " " " " " " , Std.	33,960	25.9

Joints so marked stresses show more or less complete reversal.

In examining the tabulation above, it must be borne in mind that in only those cases marked with (#) does the stress cycle approximate complete reversal. In other cases the predominant stress is on the compression side, and the probable life is considerably greater than that shown.

4. Charts of Measured Stress.

The charts show the complete stress picture more clearly. In these charts, Nos. 1 to 35, inclusive, the number of cycles is represented as the abscissa, with the stress shown as the ordinate. The cycle of stress is plotted in its true position with respect to zero stress, taking into account both the static stress and the superimposed dynamic stress. A certain number of cycles at a given range thus appears as a rectangle whose vertical dimension represents range of stress, horizontal dimension the number of cycles, and its position above or below the zero line shows whether the stress was tension or compression. Cycles above the zero line are more damaging than those below.

In this connection, it must be noted that the position of the stress cycle above or below the zero line is very much dependent on the fit of the individual bars and rails. Any pinching or extremely tight fitting of the bar in the fishing space, especially if the tight fit is confined to a short space at the end of the rail will result in high static tension stress, so that a superimposed compressive stress will give a cycle of stress completely above, or perhaps above and below the zero line. Uniformly close fitting bars will give the minimum static tensile stress.

On the other hand, loosely fitting bars may show a relatively high superimposed dynamic tensile stress due to a prying action as the wheel load passes over the ends of the bars.

The relatively low estimated life in years in the tabulation above calls attention to the importance of avoiding unfavorable conditions of rapid corrosion and the necessity for providing protection against corrosion. This applies not only to the 131-lb. R.E. but also to the 140-lb. P.S. section.

V - Discussion.

A general review of the charts and tables develops the following:

1. In 131-lb. R.E. rail the stresses at the first bolt hole are definitely reduced by moving the bolt hole back to 4-1/2" and eliminating the intermediate bolt.

2. In 131-lb. R.E. rail the stresses in the upper fillet are not improved in the proposed 4-hole design, and are made greater on the average with the possible exception of the B design, where the difference is small.

3. In 140-lb. P.S. rail the stresses at the first bolt hole as measured in this test are so small as to be negligible, regardless of bolt hole spacing.

- 8 -

4. In 140-lb. P.S. rail the stresses at the upper fillet are, on the average, higher for the A and B designs of 4-hole 36-inch joint than for either the A.R.E.A. drilling or the standard drilling of 6-hole 36-inch joints.

5. At best, it can be said as a result of this test only that there is no advantage in stress distribution in the rail web of 140-lb. P.S. rail in changing to a 4-hole drilling with the 36-inch bar. The A.R.E.A. 6-hole drilling furthermore shows no advantage over the P.R.R. 6-hole drilling.

6. The rail joint with its two bars, two rails, 4 or 6 bolts, 4 or 6 nuts, and 4 or 6 lock washers, all varying in dimension in greater or less degree, is a very complex structure. No two assemblies are exactly alike and no two assemblies give the same stress distribution even though of the same design. Even the same pair of bars and the same rails never fit together twice the same way and there is a variation in the stress distribution every time the joint is disassembled and reassembled. In this connection, attention is directed to the difference in stresses in the four presumably similar joints of 131-lb. A.E. and 140-lb. P.S. rail tested in No. 7 curve.

For the reasons above outlined, too much reliance can not be placed on these tests as a comparison of the joint bar and rail drillings. Differences in fit of the bars may account for fully as much change of stress as the difference in bolt spacing.

7. Stresses in bolts are definitely higher with the 4-bolt 36-inch joint than with the 6-bolt joint. It is doubtful, however, that these stresses are significant, as the maximum dynamic bolt stress measured was only 6,000 to 7,000 pounds per square inch for the 4-hole joint and 3,000 to 4,000 pounds per square inch for the 6-hole.

8. Stresses in the joint bars themselves tended to be slightly higher with the 6-hole bar with A.R.E.A. drilling than with the standard drilling, or with the 4-hole bars. The resisting moment developed in the bar with A.R.E.A. drilling was proportionately higher. There seems to be no reason to associate this with the drilling, and it was probably due to some other local condition. As between the bars with P.R.R. Standard 6-hole drilling and the 4-hole drilling, there is no significant difference in the joint bar stresses.

VI - Conclusion and Recommendation.

While no advantage of the 4-hole drilling other than reduction
of bolt hole stresses in the 131-lb. section has been demonstrated, no
disadvantage has been found except slightly higher bolt stresses. In
view of the very considerable economy in bolts and nutlocks that would
result, it is recommended that a mile of track of each of our three
standard rail sections be laid with 4-hole drilling "B", in order to
determine by service of a large number of joints whether or not there is
any disadvantage in the reduced number of bolts. A comparative mile
should be laid with Standard 6-hole drilling and a further comparative
mile with A.R.E.A. 6-hole drilling.

C. J. Code
Engineer of Tests, M.W.

TABLE NO. 69

M. of W. TEST 417

STRESS IN RAIL WEB WITHIN JOINT BAR LIMITS
TRACK No. 3 (TANGENT) FORGE INTERLOCKING, EAST OF TYRONE, PA.
TOTAL EQUIVALENT CYCLES PER YEAR AT RANGE OF 30,000 PSI
COMPLETE REVERSAL
(DISREGARDING MEAN STRESS)
131 RE NEW RAIL

Gauge Location		Std.	A	B	C	Worn Std. (No K4's)	Std. Bolts Loose
Upper Fillet	Gage Side	12,049	63,210	1,211	12,089	2,987	6,262
Leaving	Outside	2,960	119,678	39,973	5,414	16,693	12,492
Upper Fillet	Gage Side	-	22,043	74,331	524,684	738,794	120,102
Receiving	Outside	95,463	227,923	50,511	84,473	1,304,537	76,787
1st. Bolt Hole	Gage Side	-	-	-	-	-	38,663
Leaving	Outside	-	-	27,249	-	24	65,827
1st. Bolt Hole	Gage Side	36,168	375	-	-	189,472	189,886
Receiving	Outside	327,198	564	780	-	641	215,805

TABLE NO. 70

M. of W. TEST 417

STRESS IN RAIL WEB WITHIN JOINT BAR LIMITS
No. 7 CURVE, EAST OF TYRONE, PA.
TOTAL EQUIVALENT CYCLES PER YEAR AT RANGE OF 30,000 PSI
. COMPLETE REVERSAL
(DISREGARDING MEAN STRESS)
131 RE RAIL

Gauge Location		#1 Std.	#2 Std.	#3 Std.	#4 Std.
Upper Fillet Receiving	Gage Side	Gage loosened by Joint Bar.		79,661	136,678
1st. Bolt Hole Receiving	Gage Side	43,430	5,550	31	47,370

TABLE NO. 71

M. OF W. TEST 417

STRESS IN RAIL WEB WITHIN JOINT BAR LIMITS
NO. 7 CURVE, EAST OF TYRONE, PA.
TOTAL EQUIVALENT CYCLES PER YEAR AT RANGE OF 30,000 PSI
COMPLETE REVERSAL
(DISREGARDING MEAN STRESS)
140 PS NEW RAIL & BARS

Gage Location		#1 Std.	#2 Std.	#3 Std.	#4 Std.
Upper Fillet	Gage Side	3,752	2,310	14,524	2,087
Leaving	Outside	8,168	9,158	688	1,786
Upper Fillet	Gage Side	112,370	133,888	45,614	81,827
Receiving	Outside	13,823	3,405	89,600	2,371
1st. Bolt Hole	Gage Side	-	-	-	-
Leaving	Outside	61	122	1,061	813
1st. Bolt Hole	Gage Side	-	-	-	-
Receiving	Outside	-	43	-	-

TABLE NO. 72

M. OF W. TEST 417

STRESS IN RAIL WEB WITHIN JOINT BAR LIMITS
TRACK NO. 3 (TANGENT) NORTH RAIL, FORGE, EAST OF TYRONE, PA.
TOTAL EQUIVALENT CYCLES PER YEAR AT RANGE OF 30,000 PSI
COMPLETE REVERSAL
(DISREGARDING MEAN STRESS)
140 PS NEW RAIL

Gage Location		Area	B	A	Std.
Upper Fillet	Gage Side	37	1,769	407	1,114
Leaving	Outside	429	67	538	393
Upper Fillet	Gage Side	80,860	185,323	15,820	10,480
Receiving	Outside	40,819	12,580	8,790	8,030
1st.Bolt Hole	Gage Side	-	-	-	1,058
Leaving	Outside	-	-	-	-
1st.Bolt Hole	Gage Side	-	-	24	18
Receiving	Outside	-	-	-	-

TABLE NO. 73

M. OF W. TEST 417

STRESS IN RAIL WEB WITHIN JOINT BAR LIMITS
TRACK NO. 3 (TANGENT) NORTH RAIL, FORGE, EAST OF TYRONE, PA.
TOTAL EQUIVALENT CYCLES PER YEAR AT RANGE OF 30,000 PSI
COMPLETE REVERSAL
(DISREGARDING MEAN STRESS)
140 PS NEW RAIL

BOLTS LOOSE

Gage Location		Area	B	A	Std.
Upper Fillet	Gage Side	138	19,609	2,247	426
Leaving	Outside	571	1,821	10,187	1,463
Upper Fillet	Gage Side	25,908	100,210	113,475	33,960
Receiving	Outside	12,937	13,347	22,361	13,450
1st.Bolt Hole	Gage Side	2,626	374	480	801
Leaving	Outside	-	158	-	306
1st.Bolt Hole	Gage Side	2,051	1,738	20,006	116
Receiving	Outside	3,910	5,085	24,136	-

TABLE NO. 74

CONVERSION FACTORS USED
IN CALCULATING TABLES OF EQUIVALENT CYCLES

Maximum Stress	Range of Stress	Cycles of Failure from S-N Curve	Conversion Factor (to equivalent cycles at 30,000 range)
40,000	80,000	103,000	8.54
35,000	70,000	155,000	5.68
30,000	60,000	230,000	3.83
25,000	50,000	350,000	2.52
22,500	45,000	440,000	2.00
20,000	40,000	530,000	1.66
17,500	35,000	660,000	1.33
15,000	30,000	880,000	1.00
12,500	25,000	1,350,000	0.65
10,000	20,000	# 8,000,000	0.11
7,500	15,000	-	0.00

Since preparing these tables a few additional specimens have
been run which indicate a somewhat shorter life at the low
stresses.   The figure marked above does not, therefore, coincide with the S-N curve, Figure A, presented herewith. While
this will affect the tables of equivalent stress to a certain
degree it has not been thought necessary to revise them in
view of very considerable variation in the life of corrosion
fatigue specimens at low stress and consequent uncertainty as
to correct position of the line on the chart.

STRESS AT MAXIMUM STRESS POINT AND AT FIRST BOLT HOLE IN

100-LB. PS RAIL – MEASURED AT 60" SPAN WITH A-7 1/4" SR 4 GAGES

NO. 1, 3, 6 AND 8 MAXIMUM STRESS POINT – 3.86" ABOVE BASE (UPPER FILLET)
NO. 2, 4, 7 AND 9 FIRST BOLT HOLE 2.484" ABOVE BASE

Distance From R. End	Stress – East Rail						Stress – West Rail					
	No. 1	No. 3	Ave.	No. 2	No. 4	Ave.	No. 6	No. 8	Ave.	No. 7	No. 9	Ave.
30,000 LB. – LOAD ON CENTER												
Stress From Bolt Tension	2,100	-3,600	-750	6,900	4,200	5,550	1,200	900	1,050	2,400	-1,800	800
W. R. 5"	15,600	23,400	19,500	12,600	11,400	12,000	21,900	57,000	39,950	46,500	9,600	28,050
W. R. 2"	18,300	26,400	22,350	13,200	12,000	12,600	15,000	53,700	34,350	46,800	2,400	21,600
W. R. 5/16"	25,500	33,600	29,550	15,300	12,900	14,100	21,300	30,900	26,100	39,000	8,100	23,550
E. R. 5/16"	7,200	18,600	12,900	17,700	13,800	15,750	37,100	37,800	27,450	32,100	7,200	14,550
E. R. 2"	27,600	41,400	34,500	10,200	9,000	9,600	15,600	34,500	25,050	27,300	6,900	17,100
E. R. 5"	28,800	44,100	36,450	17,100	15,600	16,350	15,000	30,600	22,800	22,500	5,700	14,100
Finish B. T.	2,100	3,000	2,550	3,000	-6,900	4,950	1,190	1,560	1,325	1,260	910	1,085
Start & Finish	-600	1,200	300	-600	-6,300	-3,450	-2,700	-3,900	-2,850	2,100	4,800	3,450
30,000 LB. – LOAD 3/4" NORTH OF CENTER LINE												
3/4" N-WR 5"	13,200	16,800	15,000	7,500	11,700	9,600	35,700	15,000	25,350	40,500	11,700	26,100
3/4" N-WR 2"	15,600	24,000	19,800	14,400	14,400	14,400	4,800	39,900	22,350	41,700	9,300	25,500
3/4" N-WR 5/16"	16,500	25,200	20,850	8,100	15,000	11,550	8,100	23,700	15,900	4,200	15,000	9,600
3/4" N-ER 5/16"	-14,400	23,700	4,650	6,300	23,400	14,850	9,900	26,400	18,150	17,700	9,900	13,800
3/4" N-ER 2"	21,900	35,100	28,500	-900	19,500	9,300	9,000	21,300	15,150	13,200	8,700	10,950
3/4" N-ER 5"	33,300	43,200	38,250	10,800	22,800	16,800	10,200	19,800	15,000	14,400	7,500	10,950
30,000 LB. – LOAD 3/4" SOUTH OF CENTER LINE												
3/4" S-WR 5"	6,000	17,700	11,850	9,000	12,300	10,650	19,200	44,700	31,950	27,900	6,900	17,400
3/4" S-WR 2"	13,200	24,300	18,750	12,000	17,600	14,800	18,900	49,500	34,700	34,500	-3,900	15,300
3/4" S-WR 5/16"	13,800	14,000	13,900	12,900	12,600	12,750	23,400	3,900	13,650	23,700	-600	11,550
3/4" S-ER 5/16"	8,100	-7,800	150	21,000	9,000	15,000	17,400	22,800	20,100	20,700	3,000	11,850
3/4" S-ER 2"	26,700	43,800	35,250	16,200	3,000	9,600	16,800	25,800	17,700	21,600	4,200	12,900
3/4" S-ER 5"	22,800	12,600	17,700	17,100	12,900	15,000	13,800	18,600	16,200	11,700	4,200	7,950

Dimensions: 30" — 25" — 25" — 60"

$M = 437{,}500$ inch lbs. to $450{,}000$ inch lbs.

TEXT 30

LENGTH OF SPIRAL TRANSITION CURVE ANALYSIS AND RUNNING TESTS

I. Acknowledgement

The test program was carried out under an assignment of the Joint Committee on Relation Between Track and Equipment and of Committee 5 - Track of the American Railway Engineering Association as a part of the research activities of the Research Center, Association of American Railroads, W. M. Keller, vice president-research. The work was under the general direction of G. M. Magee, director of engineering research. Randon Ferguson, electrical engineer, was in direct charge of the program assisted by Ralph Schinke, stress analyst; the instrumentation was developed and operated by H. H. Remington and R. L. Laskowski, electronic assistants. The report and analyses were prepared by Mr. Ferguson and Mr. Schinke.

The running tests were made possible through the cooperation of the Pennsylvania Railroad, arranged by C. J. Code, asst. chief engineer-staff, by furnishing a locomotive, a passenger coach and other facilities. S. H. Poore, chairman Committee 5 - Track and L. H. Jentoft, chairman subcommittee 9, directed the work for the Track Committee and Mr. Code, chairman, represented the Joint Committee. Assistance in the preparation for the tests and running arrangements were directed for the railroad by D. N. Worfel, asst. engineer of tests, M of W, assisted by various members of the test, track and mechanical departments of the railroad.

II. Purposes and Objectives

The introduction of the diesel locomotive and modern passenger equipment promoted a trend to faster schedules and focused attention on ride comfort. Many of the railroads had extensive programs of lengthening spiral transition or easement curves and improving the general alignment of the track with better riding the objective at that time. Tests made in 1954 by the AAR research staff on the "Passenger Ride Comfort on Curved Track"[1] gave information on the importance of various factors in track and equipment and established criteria for calculating performance and judging results. Information from the records of those tests indicated the need for more data on the fundamental factors related to the design of the spiral easement curves and the levels of acceleration suitable for the requisite comfort. The tests here reported are for that purpose and are intended to establish a basis for recommendations for the AREA Manual. Of course, the volume of passenger travel has diminished greatly since the inception of the project, but freight equipment is getting heavier and larger and being run at increasing speeds. Much of the information in the report is also applicable to the problems of freight operations. There has also been some recent thought and studies on possible increases in scheduled passenger train speeds to compete with air line schedules over moderate distances where there is a large amount of passenger travel and the travel time to and from airports is comparable to the train schedule.

---

1. All references are listed on pages 20-21.

III. Previous Work and History

It has long been recognized that one of the requirements for smooth, comfortable riding around curves, especially at high speeds, is a suitable transition spiral to ease the change from no curvature to a given constant curvature. The most logical method of doing this is to have a uniform change of curvature and elevation until the curvature and elevation of the circular curve are attained. The principal question is how long a period is needed to accomplish this with safety and suitable comfort or freedom from damage to lading and without the introduction of forces detrimental to the track and equipment.

A discussion given by Jenkins[2] in the 1909 Proceedings of the AREA Track Committee quotes a report presented by W. H. Short before the Institution of Civil Engineers in London that gives a very logical description of the purpose of the transition spiral and even recommends a rate of change of acceleration of 1 ft. per sec.[2] for each second of time as a suitable value to be "unnoticed" as follows.

"The true purpose of a transition curve is, therefore, to enable the centrifugal force to be applied gradually and so obviate the swing produced by its sudden action------. In the author's experience the maximum rate of gain or loss of acceleration that will pass unnoticed is 1 ft. per sec. per sec. in a sec.--------"

A rate of 0.03g per sec. selected from the British tests reported in "Passenger Ride Comfort on Curved Track"[3] is 0.966 ft. per sec. per sec. in a second a quantitative value that corresponds almost exactly to the 1 ft. per sec. per sec. in a second suggested almost 50 years previously. The existence of this paper was not known at the time the curve test report was made. Mr. Jenkins was a member of the Joint Committee on Stresses in Railroad Track and also recommended in the same discussion that the formula for equilibrium elevation be changed to take account of the fact that a track level measured approximately between the centers of the rail rather than the gage corners. This change was made following the report on curve tests where the revised formula was used.

The formula for the "desirable" length of spiral as presently given in the Manual

$$L_{(min)} = 1.17 EV$$

where L is desirable length of spiral in feet, E the elevation of outer rail in inches and V the maximum train speed in miles per hours, first appeared in the Proceedings[4] in 1941 as

$$L = \frac{88}{75} ES \text{ (S is speed in miles per hour)}$$

with the statement that this formula provides a "runoff" of elevation of 1 1/4 in. per second. The same equation is now stated in the Manual as

$$L_{(min)} = 1.17\,EV$$

and still stands as recommended practice for "desirable" spiral length.

The earliest index reference to transition curves given in the AREA Proceedings is in 1901 by Camp.[5] Reference to this article is made by Landon[6] in a report where it is stated "Transition curves enable the elevation to rise uniformly as the curvature increases." This states in our opinion the most desirable form of the transition curve. A later reference 1909,[7] reports the results from a questionnaire in which three questions concerned the rate of runoff for various conditions. It is stated that the average of the replies indicated a runoff of elevation of 1 1/6 in. per sec. was satisfactory for various speeds. This information was used by Carter[8] to develop a formula for length of spiral for 1 1/4 in. and 1 1/2 in. rise per second and is probably the source of the 1 1/4 in. rise per sec. in the present Manual formula.

A discussion and analysis was written for the Track Committee in 1958 but not published. In this report the ride comfort approach to the determination of minimum length was presented and discussed and other possible factors or limitations analyzed that might limit the application of the ride comfort formula in certain ranges. It was not considered possible to decide on some of these factors by analysis only and approval was given for running tests that would give information on them. For various reasons the tests were delayed until June 1962 and this report presents the results with recommendations for the Manual.

IV. Analysis of the Problem

As discussed in the preceding chapter the need and desirable characteristics of easement curves were established many years previously. Much was written at that time on the methods of laying them out with requisite accuracy and ease and articles are still appearing on that subject. However, this report is not concerned with that phase of the problem with the exception perhaps of the "sinous" spiral proposed by Kamiya[9]. Schramm[10] has also proposed a "flattened S ramp" with a smaller rate of change of elevation at the ends of easement curves. The basis of these proposals is the elimination of the theoretical vertical discontinuities at the ends of the easement curves (Figs. 8 and 9). However, examination of the various test recordings which were run at speeds to 100 mph did not indicate any noticeable disturbances at the ends of the transition except in cases where the cross level or curvature records indicated variations of alignment or curvature. Theoretically the vertical discontinuity at the ends of the spiral will cause an instantaneous change from zero of the vertical acceleration at the ends of the spiral, but the vertical stiffness of the rails in use is large enough that such a theoretical discontinuity will be smoothed out and not actually appear for the usual spiral slopes and speeds. The equipment also has considerable length relative to the spiral which will also tend to smooth out effects of discontinuities. Requirements for measurements closer than 1/8 in. in track alignment or surface are impractical and not of sufficient importance to justify extra expense.

The tests of ride comfort on curves established a comfortable level as being a maximum of 0.10g for the constant lateral acceleration on the circular portion of the curve. This constant acceleration is attained during the time the car is in the transition curve and changes from zero on the tangent to the 0.10g in the transition curve. Many workers in the field of the effects of vibrations on persons have established the ranges of acceleration amplitude and frequency that cause various degrees of discomfort. In the lower range, 1 to 6 cps, it has been found that the rate of change of the acceleration, d^3y/dt^3, is more directly related to the effect on people than the acceleration. The results of various workers on this is well presented by Janeway[11]. However, the type of acceleration developed in the spiral is not truly vibratory in the sense usually considered and it was deemed desirable to rely on actual tests involving personal observations.

At the time of making the report on ride comfort on circular curves a set of tests made by Loach & Maycock[12] which included passenger ride tests on spirals was available. A plot of some of these tests as given in the AAR report is reproduced here as Fig. 12. The value of 0.03g per sec. as recommended previously was obtained from these tests as a conservative figure allowing for some irregularities for obtaining minimum spiral length on the basis of ride comfort. If the allowable maximum of terminal acceleration in the circular curve is 0.10g and the rate of attainment is 0.03g per sec., the time in the spiral must be

$$\frac{0.10g}{0.03g/sec.} = 3.33 \text{ sec.}$$

This time can be related to L, the mininum length of spiral in feet, E_u, the unbalanced elevation in inches on the circular curve, and V, the speed in miles per hour. The unbalanced elevation acting on the passenger is greater than the track unbalance because of the decrease in the effective elevation of the track due to the roll of the car body on its springs. The passenger senses this as an increase in unbalanced lateral acceleration over that of the track. This total unbalance, including E_u of the track and the roll of the car, is given by the expression

$$\frac{E_u + 60 \sin \Theta}{60},$$

where Θ is the car body roll angle with respect to the track for the E_u value of the track and the distance between the rail centers is 60 inches.

The minimum length of the spiral for a 0.03g per sec. rate of change of unbalanced lateral acceleration will then be

$$L = \frac{E_u + 60 \sin \Theta}{60 \times 0.03} \times \frac{5280}{3600} V \tag{1}$$

If the spiral is to be designed to accommodate a specific type of passenger equipment, a static lean test may be made as described in reference 1 to obtain the appropriate value of Θ to be used in equation 1. However, for passenger cars having an average roll tendency, it has been found that 60 sin Θ is approximately equal to E_u and for this type equipment the above formula becomes

$$L = \frac{2 E_u}{60 \times 0.03} \times \frac{5280}{3600} V$$

$$L = 1.63 E_u V \tag{2}$$

If a lower level of comfort is acceptable, larger values of the rate of change of acceleration than the above 0.03g can be used.

Application of this formula to the usual ranges of conditions encountered on railroads and analyses of some of the forces involved indicated that use of this formula alone is not satisfactory and other criteria must be applied to obtain safe and comfortable conditions. The greatest lack of applicability is found where unbalanced elevation is small or zero or at low speeds where the equation gives spirals too short for reasons other than ride comfort. The short spirals will also develop high lateral turning forces.

The spiral must be long enough so that the force required to accelerate the car or locomotive up to the constant angular rotation of the circular curve is not excessive and long enough relative to the length of the equipment so that there is not excessive racking of the equipment or racking forces which may tend to produce derailments. Since 31 ft. stations are commonly used for string lining, a slope of 1/2 in. in 31 ft. has been selected as the limiting factor in this latter respect and may be expressed by the equation

$$L = 62 E_a , \tag{3}$$

where E_a is the actual elevation in inches at the end of the spiral. This equation should be used whenever it gives a length greater than Equation 2. This slope will give about one inch difference in the height of diagonal corners of 85 ft. cars at the truck center lines. This seems a reasonable value and is undoubtedly satisfactory for most speeds as based on experience. However, no experimental data are available on the effect of high speed on this action and in cases of extreme speed it may be good judgment to use a little flatter slope. Examples of the use of these equations are given in Tables 1, 2 and 3 which use a rate of change of acceleration of 0.03g per sec. and 3, 2 and 0 in. of unbalance; Tables 4 and 5 are also for 3 and 2 in. of unbalance but use 0.04g per sec. rate of change. Table 6 uses the AREA formula, $L = 1.17 E_a V$, for 3 in. unbalanced elevation.

The tables also give values of the angular acceleration forces and total (angular + centrifugal) forces for significant cases. The development of equations for these forces is shown in the Appendix.

It will be informative to report some typical examples to illustrate the proposed method for comparison with the AREA formula results.

Assume a one degree curve with 3 in. unbalance (76 mph) and 1 in. elevation

(AREA) L = 1.17 x 1 x 76 = 89 ft.

(Proposed) L = 1.63 x 3 x 76 = 371 ft.

The 89 ft. at 76 mph is covered in 0.80 sec. which is a short time to attain 0.10 g or 0.125 g per sec. instead of 0.03 or 0.04 g per sec. The calculated force given in the tables is 11,300 lb. for the AREA formula and 9850 lb. for the proposed formula, all of the increase being due to the larger force required for angular acceleration on the shorter spiral. The railroads have long recognized this area of deficiency in the AREA formula and devised various empirical methods of getting a more suitable result.

Assume a 3° curve with 3 in. elevation and the same 3 in. unbalance (54 mph)

(AREA) L = 1.17 x 3 x 54 = 190 ft.

(Proposed) L = 1.63 x 3 x 54 = 264 ft.

This AREA result is still short for comfort, but not so greatly deficient.

Assume a 5° curve with 6 in. elevation and the same 3 in. unbalance at 51 mph.

(AREA) L = 1.17 x 6 x 51 = 358 ft.

(Proposed) L = 62 x 6 = 372 ft.

The two results are comparable here, the proposed length coming in the slope limitation region which also helps keep the lateral forces within reasonable magnitude.

Assume a 10° curve with 3 in. elevation, 3 in. unbalance and 29 mph.

(AREA) L = 1.17 x 3 x 29 = 102 ft.

(Proposed) L = 62 x 3 = 186 ft.

The lateral forces for the AREA result are about 1200 lb. larger.

It is seen that the proposed methods are based on several logical and calculable factors and give reasonable results for all cases encountered in practice. The basic logic behind the AREA formula seems to be that there is a relation between the steepness of the slope and the speed, probably a comfort factor related to vertical acceleration, since it is seen from the examples that some of the results do not come within what now seems a desirable slope limitation based on relative length of equipment and the length of spiral. Fig. 8 from the "Passenger Ride Comfort on Curved Track" report is reproduced again here to illustrate some of the relations of various quantities with time. It is seen that in Fig. 8b that y, the vertical displacement, varies at a uniform rate in the spiral. In Fig. 8c, dy/dt, the vertical velocity is zero on the tangent and instanteously becomes a constant value on entering the spiral. This relation makes $\frac{d^2y}{dt^2}$ the theoretical acceleration (Fig. 8d) instantaneously infinite and then zero where the vertical velocity is constant. Thus there is no vertical acceleration in the spiral except

478

perhaps at the ends of the spiral which as discussed previously is smoothed out by the natural stiffness of the rail resisting the introduction of sharp corners which smooth out dynamic end effects. No noticeable indications of such effects are evident in the test records.

Fig. 9 diagrams the angular motion and forces on a car as it traverses a spiral. The discontinuities in the angular acceleration and the resulting vertical forces as shown for the transverse plane are similar to those diagramed in Fig. 8. However, it should be emphasized that a spiral of conventional design does not suffer from any such discontinuities with regard to the angular acceleration of the equipment in the hor- izontal plane or the resulting lateral forces, as shown in the figure, and this is the primary function of a transition spiral. The fact that the angular acceleration and the lateral forces acting at the trucks which produce this acceleration are approximately constant is proven in the Appendix. The main advantage of the "sinous" spiral pre- viously mentioned is, therefore, only the removal of the vertical discontinuities at the ends of the spiral, and these are not troublesome for the spiral slopes and speeds usually used in North American practice. The use of smaller rates of change of curvature and elevation at the ends of a sinous spiral requires greater rates of change between the ends.

V.   Test Procedure and Instrumentation

The British ride tests on spirals had given good correlation with passenger sensations and the results were used in the analyses prior to our tests, but the British cars and track are considerably different than those in this country and it was considered important to repeat that type of program in connection with any in- strumental readings. Accordingly, the committees involved were invited to take active part in the tests as well as others working in the field or familiar with the problem. About twenty people were present on each of the two days running. Views of the group are shown in Fig. 3. A high speed, 100 mph maximum, round trip and a scheduled speed round trip were made from Harrisburg, Pa. to Philadelphia, Pa. the first day and a maximum speed round trip from Harrisburg to Baltimore, Md. the second day.

A thorough advance study was made of the track in both stretches and a schedule of maximum speeds was made to insure the highest possible speeds with due regard for safety. About 30 curves were selected in each of the two territories to pro- vide a proper variety of spirals. A detailed listing of the curves is given in Tables 7 and 8. The curves were specially measured by the railroad to give accurate data for calculations and correlation with the tests. Each of the curves was listed in a table giving its location and other data and four columns were available for a check mark as to the observers' impression of the ride on both entering and leaving spirals. A column was also available for special remarks.

It was decided from examination of previous test records that the best way to call the spirals was to watch the records for cross level and curvature rather than using wayside markers which may be missed at times. An address system was placed in the car for announcements and indication of the spirals. After announcing the approach of a particular spiral an audible tone was sounded on the address system while the car was in the entering and leaving spirals. This system worked well and eliminated the difficulty of checking markers other than mileposts and the identity of the curve. Oscillograph records were taken for most of the test run as well as on the test curves.

Two six channel pen writing oscillographs and twelve amplifiers of the proper types were used for several reasons; (Views of these instruments are shown in Fig. 2) the pen writing records are visible as taken, response required is relatively low in frequency, the output of the accelerometers can be filtered to remove the effects of unimportant small displacement, high frequency vibrations which give high amplitude accelerations and troubles in the equipment can be more quickly spotted.

A P85H coach from the Congressional fleet (Fig. 1) was used for the passengers and instruments, the latter being placed in the smoking compartment end on special tables. An Onan propane engine generator was in the vestibule for an independent supply of power for the instruments. However, an amplidyne motor generator set on the car normally supplied the power. The single unit EMD diesel electric locomotive (Class EP22) shown in Fig. 1 of 335,000 lb. weight, 70 ft. 3 in. coupled length and with six wheel trucks to obtain the maximum force effects was used. The diesel was preferred even in electrified territory because the EMD axle load cells could be applied to it but not to the electric locomotives.

One oscillograph recorded (Figs. 17 and 19) the resultant forces on each of the three axles on the front truck (which was assumed to be the most important for turning forces), the lateral acceleration on the locomotive, the lateral acceleration at the center of the car and the vertical acceleration also at the center of the car. The second oscillograph recorded (Figs. 16 and 18) the vertical gyro on the locomotive, the vertical gyro on the car (Fig. 4), the extensometer (Fig. 6) record of the actual car body roll with respect to the track, the cross level from the algebraic sum of car angle with the vertical (vertical gyro) and car body roll, the speed, and the rate of turn signal from the rate of turn gyro (Fig. 4) which gave a record proportional to the rate at which the car body was traversing the central angle of the curve. A simplified schematic diagram of the track cross level and car body roll angle circuits is shown in Fig. 15. The rate of turn gyro also switched off the erection system of the vertical gyros whenever the rate of turn was more than 0.4^{o} per sec.

The centrifugal acceleration due to the curvature would cause the gyro to drift from true vertical at the rate the erection system acts to erect it. The inherent drift rate is much slower so the error will be minimized by this method. This means that the switch would operate at about 30 mph on a 1° curve or any similar rate of turn. An electromechanical servo-divider has since been devised that divides the signal of the rate of turn gyro by the speed signal so that the quotient output of the divider will be directly proportional to curvature. However, the record as it was obtained has been found valuable in showing whether curvature is irregular or not (See Ronks curve Fig. 18). This irregularity in the record checked with measurements made on the curve after the tests (Fig. 20.)

The strain gage load cells on the locomotive axles (Fig. 7) were borrowed from the Electro Motive Division of General Motors Corp. and replaced the regular thrust bearings at the end of the axle. The electrical outputs of the two cells on an axle were summed algebraically to give the resultant for the whole axle with respect to the track as a whole.

VI. Passenger Ride Comfort Results

The results of the observers ride sensations are plotted in Figs. 10 and 11. For each test curve the sensations recorded by all 15 to 20 observers were weighted to obtain an average value (collective comfort opinion) on the ride index scale for both entering and leaving spirals. The corresponding rate of change of unbalanced lateral acceleration in g per second for each spiral was obtained by reading off the slope of the recording from the lateral accelerometer mounted on the floor of the observers coach. The average lines on the plotted graphs were fitted by the theory of least squares. The width of the band of variation as shown by the dashed lines was taken as plus or minus two times the standard deviation of the error of estimate so as to include 95 percent of the possible points. While there is considerable scatter to the plotted points, they do show a correlation between ride comfort and rate of change of unbalanced acceleration in the spirals. This rate of change of unbalanced acceleration will, of course, be inversely proportional to the length of spiral for a given circular curve, elevation and speed. The observers recorded very few sensations above perceptible on any of the curves and consequently very few values above 2.0 on the ride index scale were obtained. This was the result of the relatively long spirals on the test curves and the small roll of the observers coach giving low g per second values in spite of the higher than regular schedule speeds of up to 100 mph.

The above results are very similar to those reported by Loach and Maycock[13]. They also had considerable scatter in their observer sensations versus g per second plots of their first tests with the curves in an "as is" condition. After lining and surfacing the test curves the results shown in Fig. 12 were obtained showing excellent correlation. Taking their average sensation number of 3.2 equal to our ride index of 2.0 (at the margin of our perceptible and strongly noticeable regions), their results show a rate of change of unbalanced lateral acceleration of .04 g per second at the left hand edge of the variation band corresponding to this ride index value. The value of

0.03 g per second previously selected is more conservative to provide a greater degree of comfort and allow for effect of variations in track condition. Figures 10 and 11 give comparable values of 0.019 to 0.047 g per second. These results thus give similar values to those obtained in the British tests and confirm quantitatively the coefficient of the basic ride comfort equation $L = 1.63 E_u V$.

VII. Lateral Forces on Leading Locomotive Truck

The Appendix gives the analytical basis for calculating the lateral force on the leading truck of a locomotive in a spiral and shows that it consists of an angular acceleration component and an unbalanced centrifugal force component. The angular acceleration component is required to accelerate the locomotive angularly in a horizontal plane to attain the constant angular velocity it will have in the circular part of a curve. Application of the formulas in the Appendix shows that for the usual spiral lengths the angular acceleration component is less than 15 percent of the total lateral force for high speeds with large amounts of unbalance. This is shown by the lateral force values in Tables 1 to 5.

As a check on the approximate theory of the Appendix the locomotive axle end thrusts which were recorded from the axle load cells were averaged and summed to obtain the total lateral force on the front truck of the locomotive. These recordings showed that the maximum lateral force occurred at the junction of the spiral with the circular part of the curve as was expected from the approximate theory. These maximum values were plotted versus unbalanced elevation in Fig. 13. The line is the theoretical relation between unbalance elevation and unbalanced centrifugal force. These plots show that the total lateral force on the front truck of a locomotive is not significantly larger than the unbalanced centrifugal force predicted by the approximate theory. It may be noted that the predicted centrifugal lateral force for a 3.0 in. unbalance is a little over 8000 lb. which is, of course, the amount for the whole truck. The variations from the centrifugal force are mostly above the line and represent the additional amount due to the angular acceleration force and the dynamic action of the locomotive as affected by its own dynamic characteristics and track irregularities. These values are averages of the rather irregular variations occurring from instant to instant for a given wheel.

The distribution of the lateral loads among the wheels was not uniform, though the first axle generally had the greatest load values being as much as 15,300 lb. instantaneously. However, the rear axle also often showed large values at the same time or by itself.

VIII. Effects of Track Variations

Oscillograph recordings of some of the most noticeable track irregularities are reproduced in Figs. 16 to 19. The new circuit for track cross level measurement and the new rate of turn gyro for track curvature measurement performed quite well. The accuracy of these new devices was evaluated by comparing their recorded values with field measurements of a number of the test curves. Sets of these field measurements for two curves are reproduced in Fig. 20 and may be compared with oscillograph records of the same quantities in Figs. 16 and 18. This comparison shows the faithful recording of variations in track cross level and curvature on the oscillograms. Since the rate gyro's electrical output is proportional to speed, the actual magnitude of the curvature must be obtained by means of the formula shown on the oscillogram. Apparently the yawing (nosing) of the test coach, to which the rate gyro responds, follows the variations in line of the track very closely.

It is interesting to note some of the track irregularities which can be recognized in the oscillograms. The Bradford Hills Curve in Fig. 16 shows some irregularities in the cross level channel. Also, comparison of the cross level and curvature channels shows that the elevation is run out on to the tangent for a considerable distance on both ends of this curve. This results in an inward car body roll (Fig. 16) and an inward lateral acceleration (Fig. 17) as shown on their respective channels. The somewhat irregular line of Ronk Curve shows up in the curvature channel in Fig. 18. This curve indicates elevation has run out on to the tangent of its entering spiral but not on its leaving spiral. It is believed that these new devices could find important applications for track inspection and relating car performance to track variability for both passenger and freight equipment, particularly "piggyback" and high center of gravity cars.

Figure 14 shows the relation between the car body roll angle and unbalanced elevation. The car body roll angle data were obtained from extensometers mounted on each side of a truck of the car between car body and the midpoint of the equalizer bars and connected in a circuit so as to give the algebraic difference between their deflections. The figure shows the car has a small ratio of roll to unbalance as compared with some passenger cars previously tested[14]. The average roll angle at 3.0 in. unbalance is about 1.4° which compares with 2.4° for some other passenger cars tested. The figure also shows that the track curvature data as measured with the rate of turn gyro was at least as good as the tabular values of curvature supplied by the railroad as evidenced by the nearly identical slope and variation in the upper and lower plots. The elevation values for computation of the unbalanced elevation were also obtained from the oscillograph records for both the upper and lower diagrams. The slope of the average lines and the width of the band of variation were obtained by a modified method of least squares. The correlation of the plotted points is greatly improved over that obtained in some previous tests where nominal values from track charts were used.

IX. Discussion and Recommendations

The reported results have approximately confirmed the British ride comfort results though there is more scatter in the plots than in the second set of British tests shown in Fig. 12. The British found a similar or greater scatter in their first set of tests made with the track in an "as is" condition, but a good correlation was obtained after aligning the test curves. The AAR ride comfort results were for the track in an "as is" condition. The results would have been more conclusive if higher values of ride index had been obtained to extend the range of the points. The low values obtained even at the high speeds are mainly attributable to the relatively long spirals and the low value of the car body roll of 1.4^0 with 3 in. unbalanced elevation. Many cars will roll almost twice as much at the same unbalance. The roll counteracts the beneficial effect of the outer rail elevation at speeds greater than equilibrium and the greater the roll the less the effectiveness of the elevation.

The original idea that there would be a large initial lateral force to accelerate the locomotive in angular rotation as the locomotive entered the spiral that would be a criterion of spiral length has been disproven by the revised analysis and the test results. The angular acceleration force is calculated to be a maximum of 15 percent of the total force at the end of the spiral and of a constant value in the spiral. The points plotted from the load cell records fall near the line for the calculated centrifugal forces in Fig. 13.

It is believed the previously stated purpose of the tests to get data on fundamental factors related to the design of spiral easement curves has been demonstrated by the preceding results to a reasonable degree and that a logical basis for spiral design may be proposed. The rate of change of acceleration selected from the British tests of 0.03g per sec. has been found to be a quite conservative value and is proposed for use in new construction or cases where long spirals are not excessively expensive. This "desirable" length, L, will be given by the formula

$$L = 1.63 \, E_u V \, , \qquad\qquad (2)$$

where E_u is the unbalanced elevation in the circular curve and V is the speed in miles per hour. This formula is equivalent to a 0.03g per sec. rate of change of unbalanced lateral acceleration acting on a passenger for a car with an average roll tendency which approximately doubles the acceleration on the passenger.

Due to the length of the car relative to the spiral and possible racking and torsional forces as discussed in Section IV, it was considered desirable to establish a slope limitation in addition to the above formula which would limit the racking of the car to approximately 1 in. at diagonal corners for an 85 ft. car with the usual truck spacing of about 60 ft. Since 31 ft. stations are commonly used for string lining, this limiting slope is taken as 1/2 in. in 31 ft. and the length of spiral for such a slope is given by

$$L = 62 \, E_a \qquad (1/744 \text{ maximum slope}) \qquad (3)$$

The longer of the two lengths given by Formulas 2 (or 1 if preferred) and 3 should be used. The application of the above formulas to curves of various degrees and speeds corresponding to 3, 2 and 0 in. unbalance is illustrated in Tables 1 to 3. Lengths of spirals for curvatures, elevations and speeds not listed in these tables may be easily calculated directly from the formulas. As shown in Table 1, the ride comfort formula applies for most cases except in the lower right hand region where the maximum slope formula is used. A heavy line outlines this region which becomes larger with lower unbalances and comprises the whole of Table 3 where the unbalanced elevation is zero and the slope formula was used for all cases.

It is recognized that many instances of spiral design will be on established track where the conservative values of Equation 2 may result in expensive line revision. It is believed that use of a value of 0.04g per sec. rate of change of unbalanced acceleration will give a comfortable ride especially where the track is well maintained. Substituting 0.04 for 0.03 in equation 2 gives the following:

$$L = \frac{2\ E_u}{60 \times 0.04} \times \frac{5280}{3600}\ V$$

$$L = 1.22\ E_u V \tag{4}$$

The ride resulting from the lengths given by all the formulas would be further improved if the equipment has less roll than assumed, as was the case with the test car which had almost half the assumed roll. Use of Equation 1 previously given will indicate the effect of the roll on the spiral length. For example the P85H coach used in our tests had a 1.35^o car body roll angle for E_u equal to 3 inches; then 60 sin Θ is 1.44 which is equivalent to 0.48 E_u, and equation 1 can be written

$$L = \frac{E_u + 0.48\ E_u}{60 \times 0.03} \times \frac{5280}{3600}\ V$$

or $L = 1.20\ E_u V$

The same maximum slope formula 3 should be retained for use with either ride comfort formula 1, 2 or 4 as a minimum value. There is a lack of data on the effect of speed on the action of cars where the slope is changing so as to produce a twisting of the car, and it may be well to use a little flatter slope in cases where speeds are above 80 mph.

Application of the above formulas 2 (or 1), 3 and 4 to the spirals between compound curves will present no difficulties in calculation. The differences of the unbalanced elevations and actual elevations for the circular portions of a compound curve are simply substituted in these equations to obtain the proper spiral length.

The spiral lengths obtained with the present AREA Manual formula, $L = 1.17\ E_a V$ for 3 in. of unbalance are illustrated in Table 6. Comparison of these lengths with those of Tables 1 and 4 obtained from the recommended formulas show the present Manual formula gives lengths which are too short for a good many cases, especially for curves with small elevations, and which are longer than necessary for light curves with large elevations at high speeds.

It is of interest to make the following comparison of the above recommended spiral length formulas with foreign practice.

Great Britain

Expressing the recommended limiting values of Loach and Maycock[15] in formula form,

$$L = 0.65\ E_a V \qquad\qquad \text{(2 1/4 in. change of elevation per sec.)}$$

$$L = 0.65\ E_u V \qquad\qquad \text{(ride comfort formula)}$$

$$L = 25\ E_a \qquad\qquad \text{(1/300 maximum slope)}$$

The largest of the values given by the three formulas is used.

Japan

Matsubara[16] gives the following formulas for spiral lengths on their new high speed line where maximum speeds are 200 km. per hour (124 mph).

$$L = 6.2\ C_m V$$

$$L = 7.5\ C_d V$$

where lengths are in meters and V is in kilometers per hour. Converting these formulas to English units gives,

$$L = 0.83\ E_a V \qquad\qquad \text{(1.76 in. change of elevation per sec.)}$$

$$L = 1.01\ E_u V \qquad\qquad \text{(ride comfort formula)}$$

One difference between the above foreign practice and our recommended formulas is their limitation on the maximum rate of change of elevation per unit time (inches per second) while this report recommends no such restriction although a restriction of 1-1/4 in. change of elevation per second is the basis of the present AREA formula. This would result in the foreign roads using a longer spiral than with our recommended formulas in a few cases where the speed is above 95 mph for the British formula and 75 mph for the Japanese formula. It is believed that a limitation of rate of change of elevation per unit time is not needed except possibly in cases of extremely high speed. Tests to give information in regard to effect of speed in this respect would be helpful if schedules are to be increased above 100 mph.

The British ride comfort formula, $L = 0.65\ E_u V$, which limits the rate of change of unbalanced lateral acceleration (g per second) in spirals, gives a spiral length considerably shorter than either our $L = 1.63\ E_u V$ or $L = 1.22\ E_u V$ formulas, because it is applicable to equipment with very little roll tendency due to its stiff springing. This British formula is based on a rate of change of unbalanced lateral acceleration in a spiral of 0.047g per sec. acting on a passenger, or $\frac{0.047}{1.25} = 0.038g$ per sec. not including effect of car body roll. The 0.047 rate is comparable with our 0.03 and 0.04g per sec. rates. Comparable g per sec. rates for the Japanese ride comfort formula have not been calculated, because data for the roll tendency of their equipment is not available.

The English formula limiting the maximum slope to prevent undue twisting or racking of the cars permits a much steeper slope than our equation 3. Presumably this is due to the relatively short length of their equipment. The Japanese formulas are for the high speed New Tokaido Line and for the conditions of this line no slope limitation would be needed because of the change of elevation per unit time limitation.

486

Excellent summaries of foreign practice are given by Matsurbara[17] and Thille[18]. Our recommended formulas are of similar form to much of this practice, with the exception of our not placing a limitation on maximum rate of change of elevation per unit time.

5869.18

Appendix

Lateral Forces on a Locomotive in a Transition Spiral

While traversing a spiral transition curve a locomotive (or car) is accelerated angularly in a horizontal plane to attain gradually the constant angular velocity it will have through the circular part of a curve. An expression for this angular acceleration may be obtained in the following manner for a spiral of conventional design. The basic equation of such a spiral[19] is

$$\Delta = 1/2 \frac{1}{100} a L^2,$$

where Δ is the angle in degrees a tangent to the spiral curve makes with the tangent track at any point, a is the degree of curvature change per foot and L is the distance to the point along the spiral in feet. L may be expressed in terms of v the velocity in ft. per sec. and t the time in sec.,

$$L = vt$$

$$\Delta = 1/2 \frac{1}{100} a v^2 t^2$$

The angular acceleration α will be,

$$\alpha = \frac{d^2 \Delta}{dt^2} = \frac{d}{dt} \frac{a v^2 t}{100} = \frac{a v^2}{100}$$

This is the angular acceleration in a horizontal plane of a tangent to a moving point on a spiral. While the motion of a locomotive would be somewhat different because it contacts the track at its front and rear trucks, the above expression for α is sufficiently accurate for a locomotive for our purposes. The above shows that the angular acceleration α of a locomotive is approximately constant while traversing a spiral.

The angular acceleration of a locomotive in a horizontal plane when traversing a spiral requires lateral forces to be developed between the locomotive and track. These forces may be analyzed by the following inertia force method. Considering forces parallel to the plane of the track at any point on a spiral,

5869.19

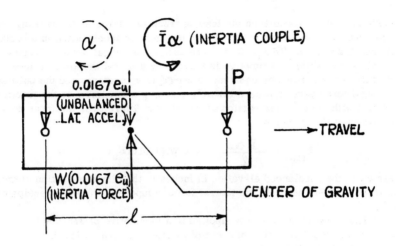

where, P is the lateral force in lb. on the leading truck

$0.0167\ e_u$ is the unbalanced lateral acceleration in g

e_u is the unbalanced elevation in inches at any instant

$W\ (0.0167\ e_u)$ is the inertia force in lb.

W is the weight of locomotive in lb.

α is the angular acceleration in radians per sec.

$\bar{I}\alpha$ is the inertia couple in the lb. ft.

$\bar{I}$ is the polar moment of inertia of the locomotive about a vertical axis through its center of gravity in lb. sec.^{2} ft.

ℓ is the spacing of the truck centers in ft.

Taking moments,

$$P\ell = \bar{I}\,\alpha + W\,(0.0167\,e_u)\,1/2$$

$$P = \frac{\bar{I}\alpha}{\ell} + 1/2\,W\,(0.0167\,e_u)$$

This shows that the force P on the leading truck (the force on the trailing truck is smaller than P) consists of $\frac{\bar{I}\,\alpha}{\ell}$ due to the angular acceleration in a horizontal plane and $1/2\,W/g\,(0.0167\,e_u)$ due to unbalanced centrifugal force. These expressions show that while a locomotive is traversing a spiral the angular acceleration part of the force P remains constant, since α is a constant, and the unbalanced centrifugal force part increases linearly reaching a maximum at the junction of the spiral with the circular portion of the curve. Therefore, the force P reaches a maximum at this junction.

$$P_{max} = \frac{\bar{I}\,\alpha}{\ell} + 1/2\,W\,(0.0167E_u)$$

where E_u is the unbalanced elevation in inches in the circular portion of the curve. The above analysis neglects the lateral force component of coupled equipment.

The above formula can be applied to a locomotive of 375,000 lb. weight, 3,260,000 lb. sec.^{2} ft. polar moment of inertia and 41.5 ft. truck centers (Fairbanks-Morse H24-66) as follows:

Angular Acceleration Part

Since $\alpha = \frac{Dv^2}{100\,L}$, where D is the curvature of circular portion of a curve in degrees and L is the length of spiral in ft.,

$$\frac{\bar{I}\,\alpha}{\ell} = \frac{\bar{I}}{\ell}\,\frac{Dv^2}{100L}\left(\frac{\pi}{180}\right)$$

Combining constants and using V the velocity in mph,

$$\frac{\bar{I}\alpha}{\ell} = \frac{1}{2650}\,\frac{\bar{I}}{\ell}\,\frac{DV^2}{L}$$

Since $E_r = 0.00070\,DV^2$, where E_r is the equilibrium elevation in the circular portion of the curve in inches,

$$\frac{\bar{I}\alpha}{\ell} = 0.539\,\frac{\bar{I}\,E_r}{\ell\,L}$$

Substituting I and ℓ for this particular locomotive,

$$\frac{\bar{I}\alpha}{\ell} = (0.539)\left(\frac{3,260,000}{41.5}\right)\frac{E_r}{L} = 42,500\,\frac{E_r}{L}$$

5869.21

Centrifugal Force Part

$$1/2 \; W \; (0.0167 \; E_u) = 1/2 \; (375,000)(0.0167 \; E_u) = 3130 \; E_u$$

Therefore, the maximum lateral force on the trucks of this locomotive (375,000 lb. weight, 3,260,000 lb. sec.^{2} ft. polar moment of inertia and 41.5 ft. truck centers) as it traverses a spiral curve is,

$$P_{max} = 42,500 \; \frac{E_r}{L} \; + 3130 \; E_u$$

Where E_r and E_u are the equilibrium and unbalanced elevations in inches, respectively, on the circular portion of the curve and L is the length of spiral in ft.

5869.22

List of References

1. Passenger Ride Comfort on Curved Track, AREA Proc., 1955, pp. 125-214.

2. J. B. Jenkins, Discussion, AREA Proc., 1910, p. 481.

3. Reference 1, p. 150.

4. Spirals for High Speed Operation, AREA Proc., 1941, p. 637.

5. W. M. Camp, Curve Elevation, AREA Proc., 1901, p. 266.

6. H. C. Landon, Maintenance of Line, AREA Proc., 1901, p.

7. The Use of Spirals----------, AREA Proc., 1909, p. 420.

8. F. H. Carter, Selection of Length of Transition Spiral, AREA Proc., 1911, pp. 439-446.

9. S. Kamiya, Transition Sine Curve Decreased and Transition of Compound and Reverse Curve, Permanent Way (Tokyo), Dec. 1959, pp. 1-24.

10. G. Schramm, Permanent Way Technique and Permanent Way Economy, Otto Elsner (Darmstadt), 1961, pp. 160-161.

11. R. N. Janeway, Vehicle Vibration Limits to Fit the Passenger, Journal SAE, Aug. 1948, pp. 48-49.

12. J. C. Loach and M. G. Maycock, Recent Developments in Railway Curve Design, Proc. The Institution of Civil Engineers (London), Oct. 1952, pp. 503-572.

13. Loach and Maycock, reference 12, pp. 516-517.

14. Reference 1, p. 166.

15. Loach and Maycock, reference 12, p. 522.

16. K. Matsubara, Track for the New Tokaido Trunk Line, Permanent Way (Tokyo) Dec. 1962, p. 7.

17. K. Matsubara, Adaption of Methods of Laying, Aligning and Maintaining the Permanent Way to Carry Traffic at Very High Speeds-----, Bull. IRCA (Brussels), English Edt., Dec. 1961, pp. 981-987.

5869.23

18. M. Thille, Adaption of the Methods of Laying, Aligning and Maintaining the Permanent Way to Carry Traffic at Very high Speeds----, Bull. IRCA (Brussels), English Edt., April 1962, pp. 527-537.

19. A. N. Talbot, The Railway Transition Spiral, McGraw Hill, 1927, p. 6.

20. J. C. Loach and M. G. Maycock, personal communication. The graphs on pages 516 and 517 of reference 12 were derived from this original data by subtracting out the effect of the roll of their test coach from the abscissa.

5869.

FIG. 1. EP22 Locomotive and P85H Coach used in test runs.

FIG. 2. Recording oscillographs and amplifiers in instrument room of coach.

5869.

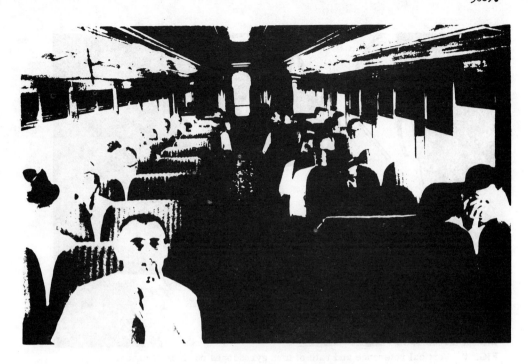

FIG. 3.   Observers recording impressions of ride entering and leaving curves.

494

FIG. 4. Vertical reference and rate of turn gyroscopes on floor of coach.

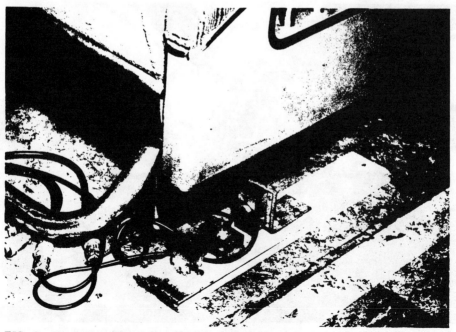

FIG. 5. Vertical and lateral accelerometers on floor of coach.

5869.

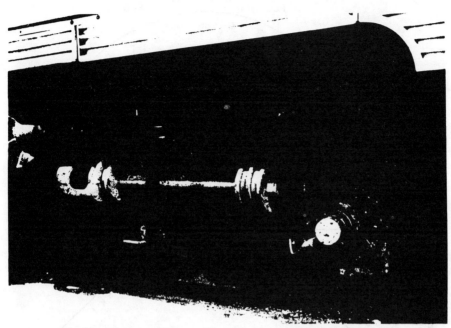

FIG. 6. One of two extensometers connected between coach body and equalizer bar for measuring coach body roll, and axle tachometer generator.

FIG. 7. Special locomotive journal cap incorporating strain gage load cell for measuring axle end thrust.

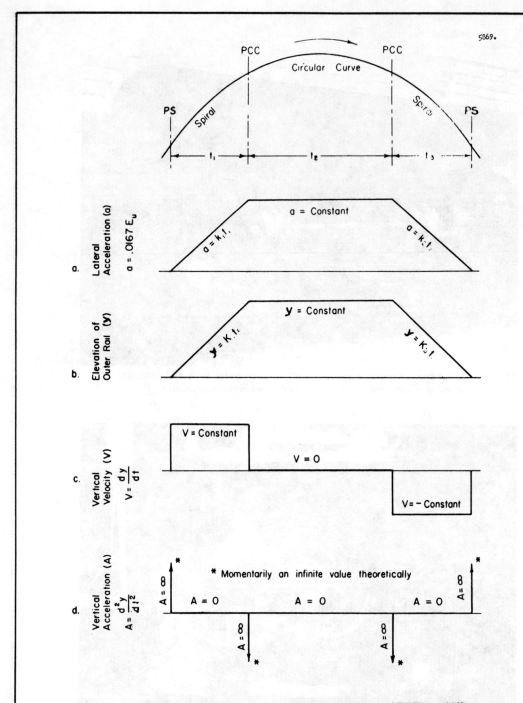

FIG. 8. DIAGRAM OF VERTICAL VELOCITY AND LATERAL AND VERTICAL ACCELERATIONS AS A CAR TRAVERSES A CURVE

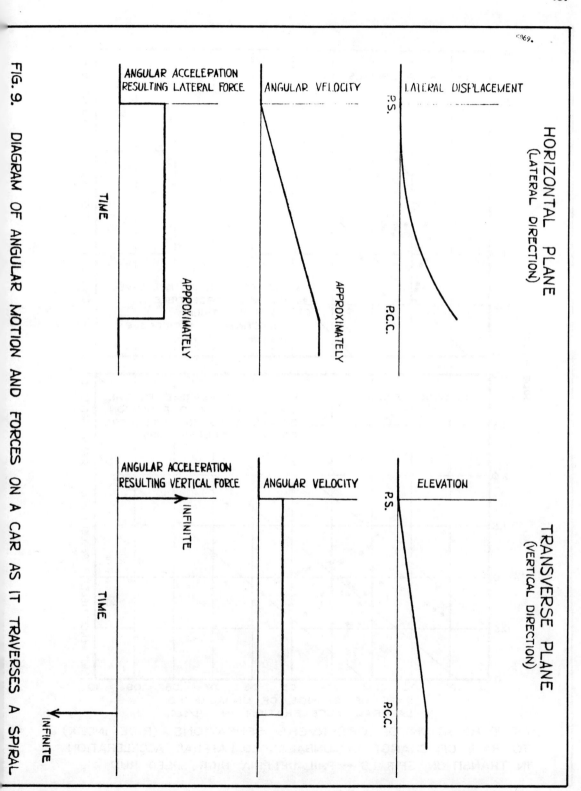

FIG. 9. DIAGRAM OF ANGULAR MOTION AND FORCES ON A CAR AS IT TRAVERSES A SPIRAL

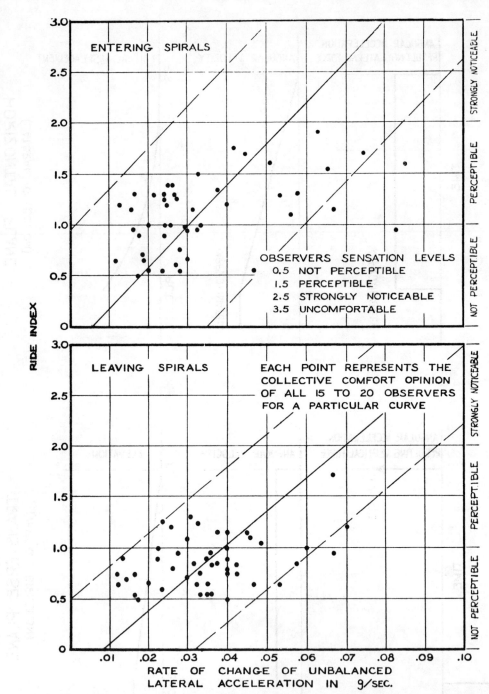

FIG. 10. RELATION OF OBSERVERS SENSATIONS (RIDE INDEX) TO RATE OF CHANGE OF UNBALANCED LATERAL ACCELERATION IN TRANSITION SPIRALS — PHILADELPHIA HIGH SPEED RUN

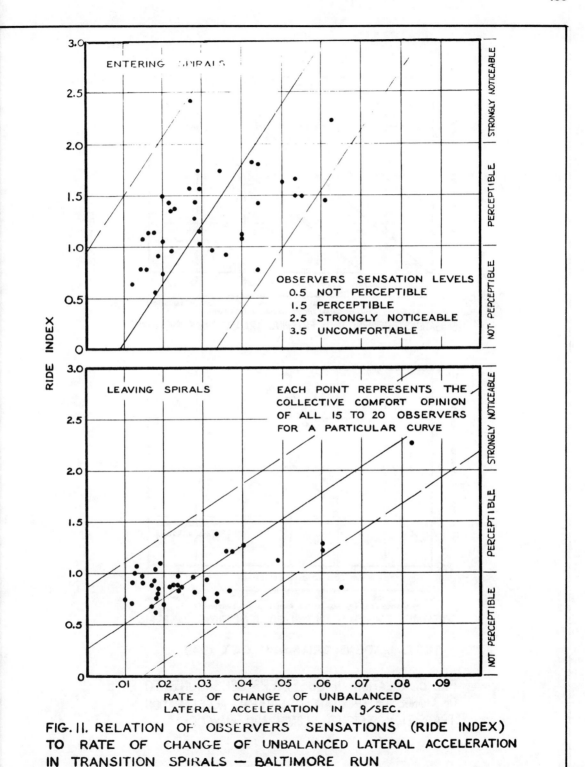

FIG. 11. RELATION OF OBSERVERS SENSATIONS (RIDE INDEX) TO RATE OF CHANGE OF UNBALANCED LATERAL ACCELERATION IN TRANSITION SPIRALS — BALTIMORE RUN

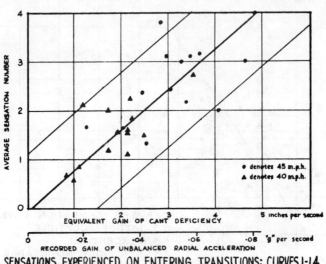

SENSATIONS EXPERIENCED ON ENTERING TRANSITIONS: CURVES 1-14

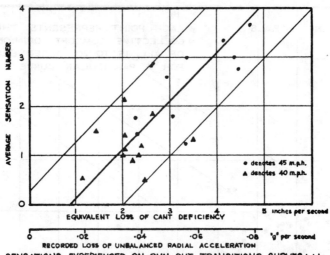

SENSATIONS EXPERIENCED ON RUN-OUT TRANSITIONS: CURVES 1-14

TESTS MADE IN BRITAIN: 11 OCT. 1949

FIG. 12. RELATION OF OBSERVERS SENSATIONS TO RATE OF CHANGE OF UNBALANCED LATERAL ACCELERATION IN TRANSITION SPIRALS, LOACH AND MAYCOCK[20]

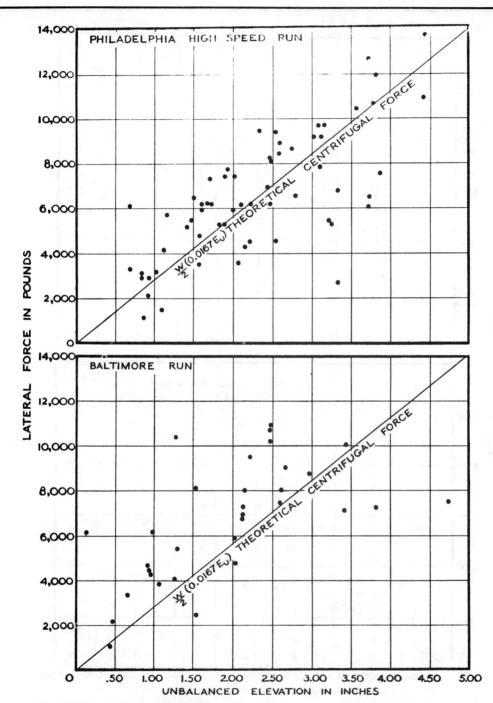

FIG. 13. RELATION OF LATERAL FORCE ON FRONT TRUCK OF LOCOMOTIVE TO UNBALANCED ELEVATION AT START OF CIRCULAR PORTION OF CURVES

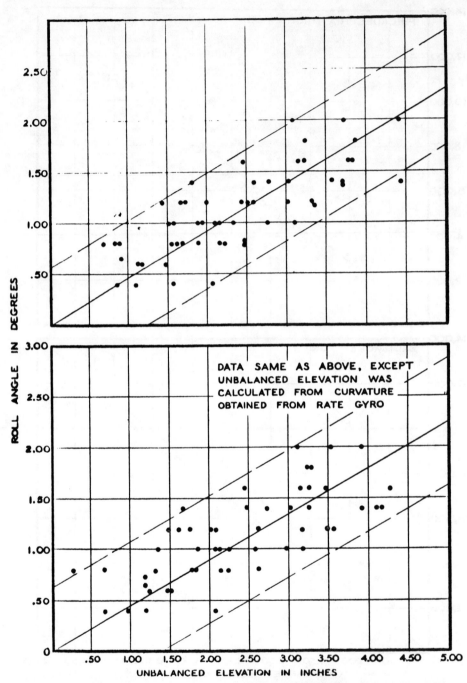

FIG. 14. RELATION OF CAR BODY ROLL ANGLE TO UNBALANCED
ELEVATION — PHILADELPHIA HIGH SPEED RUN

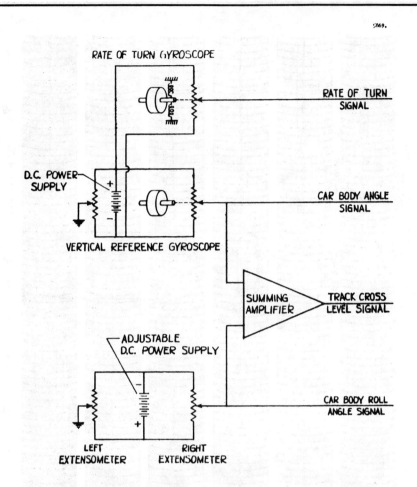

5069.

RATE OF TURN GYROSCOPE

RATE OF TURN
SIGNAL

D.C. POWER
SUPPLY

CAR BODY ANGLE
SIGNAL

VERTICAL REFERENCE GYROSCOPE

SUMMING
AMPLIFIER

TRACK CROSS
LEVEL SIGNAL

ADJUSTABLE
D.C. POWER SUPPLY

CAR BODY ROLL
ANGLE SIGNAL

LEFT
EXTENSOMETER

RIGHT
EXTENSOMETER

FIG. 15. DIAGRAM OF TRACK CROSS LEVEL AND CAR BODY
ROLL ANGLE ELECTRONIC CIRCUITS

504

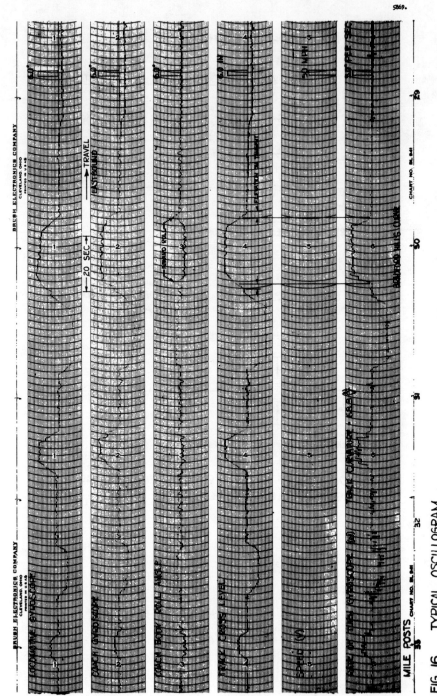

FIG. 16. TYPICAL OSCILLOGRAM

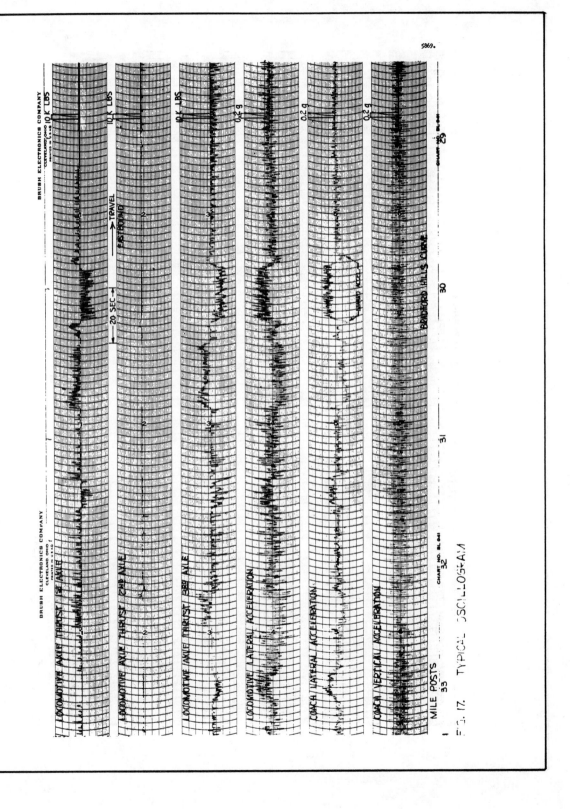

FIG. 17. TYPICAL OSCILLOGRAM

506

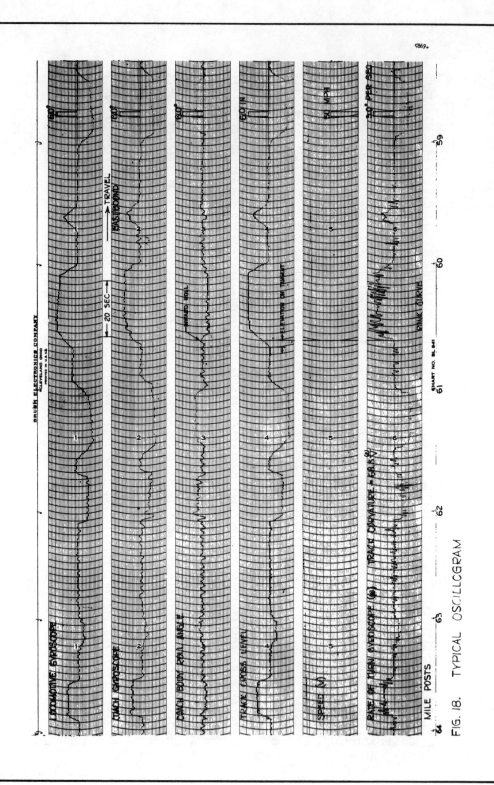

BRUSH ELECTRONICS COMPANY
CLEVELAND, OHIO
PRINTED IN U.S.A.

← 20 SEC →

→ TRAVEL
EASTBOUND

1 — LOCOMOTIVE GYROSCOPE

2 — COACH GYROSCOPE

3 — COACH BODY ROLL ANGLE — INBOARD ROLL

4 — TRACK CROSS LEVEL — 6.0 IN — ELEVATION ON TANGENT

5 — SPEED (V) — 50 MPH

6 — RATE OF TURN GYROSCOPE (φ) — 5.0° PER SEC — TRACK CURVATURE = 686.57 — PINK CURVE

MILE POSTS   64   63   62   61   60   59

SHART NO. BL 841

FIG. 18.   TYPICAL OSCILLOGRAM

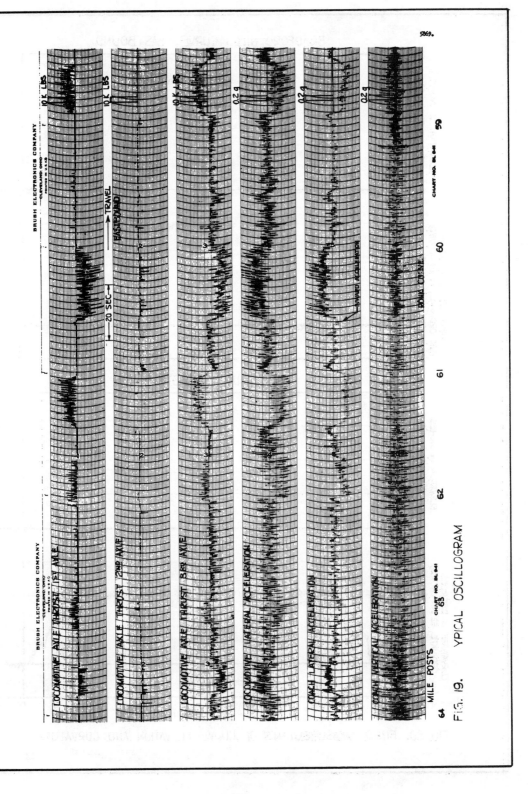

FIG. 19. TYPICAL OSCILLOGRAM

508

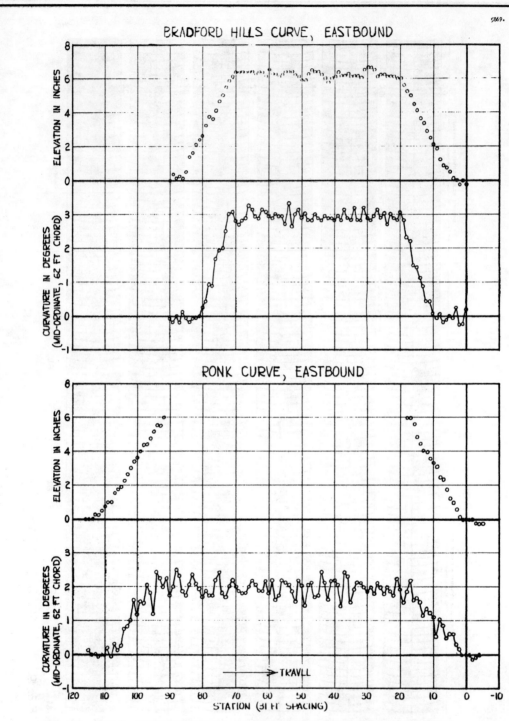

FIG. 20. FIELD MEASUREMENTS OF CURVE ELEVATION AND CURVATURE

5869.

TABLE I - DESIRABLE LENGTH OF TRANSITION SPIRAL

3 INCHES UNBALANCED ELEVATION
TABLE LISTS LARGEST OF FOLLOWING TWO VALUES
LENGTH = $1.63\,E_u V$ (RIDE COMFORT FORMULA, .03g PER SEC)
LENGTH = $62\,E_a$ (MAXIMUM SLOPE FORMULA, ONE INCH IN 62 FT)

Each cell lists LENGTH (ft) over SPEED (mph). The stepped bold line separates the RIDE COMFORT FORMULA region (upper right) from the MAXIMUM SLOPE FORMULA region (lower left). FORCE values given in the original (small 4‑digit figures) are largely illegible and are omitted here.

CURVA‑TURE		ELEVATION IN INCHES												
		0	½	1	1½	2	2½	3	3½	4	4½	5	5½	6
½°	LENGTH	450	489	523	553	587	612							
	SPEED	92	100	107	113	120	125							
1°	LENGTH	318	342	371	390	410	429	450	469	489	504	525	538	553
	SPEED	65	70	76	80	84	88	92	96	100	103	107	110	113
1½°	LENGTH	259	283	303	322	336	351	371	385	400	410	424	440	450
	SPEED	53	58	62	66	69	72	76	79	82	84	87	90	92
2°	LENGTH	225	244	264	287	293	307	322	335	347	356	371	381	390
	SPEED	46	50	54	57	60	63	66	68	71	73	76	78	80
2½°	LENGTH	200	215	234	249	259	275	283	297	307	318	332	342	372
	SPEED	41	44	48	51	53	56	58	61	63	65	68	70	72
3°	LENGTH	185	200	215	225	239	249	264	273	283	293	310	341	372
	SPEED	38	41	44	46	49	51	54	56	58	60	62	64	65
3½°	LENGTH	171	185	200	210	219	229	244	254	259	279	310	341	372
	SPEED	35	38	41	43	45	47	50	52	53	55	57	59	60
4°	LENGTH	161	171	185	195	205	215	225	234	248	279	310	341	372
	SPEED	35	35	38	40	42	44	46	48	50	52	54	55	57
4½°	LENGTH	156	161	176	185	195	205	215	225	248	279	310	341	372
	SPEED	32	33	36	38	40	42	44	46	47	49	51	52	54
5°	LENGTH	142	156	166	176	185	195	200	217	248	279	310	341	372
	SPEED	29	32	34	36	38	40	41	45	45	46	48	49	51
6°	LENGTH	132	142	151	161	166	176	186	217	248	279	310	341	372
	SPEED	27	29	31	33	34	36	38	39	41	42	44	45	46
7°	LENGTH	122	132	142	147	156	166	186	217	248	279	310	341	372
	SPEED	25	27	29	30	32	34	35	37	38	39	42	42	43
8°	LENGTH	112	122	132	137	147	155	186	217	248	279	310	341	372
	SPEED	23	25	27	28	30	31	33	34	35	37	38	39	40
9°	LENGTH	107	117	122	132	137	155	186	217	248	279	310	341	372
	SPEED	22	24	25	27	28	29	31	32	33	35	36	37	38
10°	LENGTH	102	107	117	127	132	155	186	217	248	279	310	341	372
	SPEED	21	22	24	26	27	28	29	31	32	33	34	35	36

LENGTH IN FT (L)
SPEED IN MPH (V)
FORCE IN LBS, LOWER VALUE = $42{,}500\,E_r/L + 3130\,E_u$ (TOTAL LATERAL FORCE ON LEADING TRUCK OF LOCOMOTIVE)
UPPER VALUE = $42{,}500\,E_r/L$ (ANGULAR ACCELERATING FORCE ONLY)
FOR LOCOMOTIVE OF 375,000 LB WEIGHT, 3,260,000 LB SEC² FT POLAR MOMENT OF INERTIA AND 41.5 FT TRUCK CENTERS

WHERE E_u, E_a AND E_r ARE UNBALANCED, ACTUAL AND EQUILIBRIUM ELEVATIONS IN INCHES, RESPECTIVELY

TABLE 2 - DESIRABLE LENGTH OF TRANSITION SPIRAL

2 INCHES UNBALANCED ELEVATION

TABLE LISTS LARGEST OF FOLLOWING TWO VALUES

LENGTH = $1.63\,E_u V$ (RIDE COMFORT FORMULA, .03g PER SEC)

LENGTH = $62\,E_a$ (MAXIMUM SLOPE FORMULA, ONE INCH IN 62 FT)

5869.

CURVATURE		0	½	1	1½	2	2¼	2½	3	3¼	3½	4	4½	5	5½	6
½°	LENGTH	244	274	300	326	349	368		391	408						
	SPEED	75	84	92	100	107	113		120	125						
	FORCE															
1°	LENGTH	173	196	212	228	248	261		274		287	300	313	326	341	372
	SPEED	53	60	65	70	76	80		84		88	92	96	100	105	107
	FORCE															
1½°	LENGTH	140	160	173	189	202	215		225		235	248	279	310	341	372
	SPEED	43	49	53	58	62	66		69		72	76	79	82	84	87
	FORCE															
2°	LENGTH	124	137	150	163	176	186		196		217	248	279	310	341	372
	SPEED	38	42	46	50	54	57		60		63	66	68	71	73	75
	FORCE															
2½°	LENGTH	111	124	134	143	156	166		186		217	248	279	310	341	372
	SPEED	34	38	41	44	48	51		53		56	58	61	63	65	68
	FORCE															
3°	LENGTH	101	111	124	134	143	155		186		217	248	279	310	341	372
	SPEED	31	34	38	41	44	46		45		51	54	56	58	60	60
	FORCE															
3½°	LENGTH	95	104	114	124	134	155		186		217	248	279	310	341	372
	SPEED	29	32	35	38	41	43		45		47	50	52	53	55	57
	FORCE															
4°	LENGTH	86	98	108	114	124	155		186		217	248	279	310	341	372
	SPEED	27	30	33	35	38	40		42		44	46	48	50	52	52
	FORCE															
4½°	LENGTH	82	91	101	108	124	155		186		217	248	279	310	341	372
	SPEED	25	28	31	33	36	38		40		42	44	46	47	49	51
	FORCE															
5°	LENGTH	78	88	95	104	124	155		186		217	248	279	310	341	372
	SPEED	24	27	29	32	34	36		38		40	41	43	45	46	46
	FORCE															
6°	LENGTH	72	78	88	95	124	155		186		217	248	279	310	341	372
	SPEED	22	24	27	29	32	33		34		36	38	39	41	42	44
	FORCE															
7°	LENGTH	65	75	82	93	124	155		186		217	248	279	310	341	372
	SPEED	20	23	25	27	29	30		32		34	35	37	38	39	40
	FORCE															
8°	LENGTH	62	68	75	93	124	155		186		217	248	279	310	341	372
	SPEED	19	21	23	25	27	28		30		31	33	34	35	37	38
	FORCE															
9°	LENGTH	59	65	72	93	124	155		186		217	248	279	310	341	372
	SPEED	18	20	22	24	25	27		28		29	30	32	33	35	36
	FORCE															
10°	LENGTH	55	62	68	93	124	155		186		217	248	279	310	341	372
	SPEED	17	19	21	22	24	26		27		28	29	31	32	33	34
	FORCE															

ELEVATION IN INCHES

RIDE COMFORT FORMULA — MAXIMUM SLOPE FORMULA

LENGTH IN FT (L)

SPEED IN MPH (V)

FORCE IN LBS, LOWER VALUE = $42,500\,E_T + 3130\,E_a$ (TOTAL LATERAL FORCE ON LEADING TRUCK OF LOCOMOTIVE)

UPPER VALUE = $42,500\,E_T$ (ANGULAR ACCELERATING FORCE ONLY)

FOR LOCOMOTIVE OF 375,000 LB WEIGHT, 3,260,000 LB SEC² FT POLAR MOMENT OF INERTIA AND 41.5 FT TRUCK CENTERS

WHERE E_u, E_a AND E_T ARE UNBALANCED, ACTUAL AND EQUILIBRIUM ELEVATIONS IN INCHES, RESPECTIVELY

5869.

TABLE 3 - MINIMUM LENGTH OF TRANSITION SPIRAL

O INCHES UNBALANCED ELEVATION, EQUILIBRIUM SPEED
TABLE LISTS LARGEST OF FOLLOWING TWO VALUES
LENGTH = $1.63 E_a V$ (RIDE COMFORT FORMULA, .03g PER SEC)
LENGTH = $62 E_a$ (MAXIMUM SLOPE FORMULA, ONE INCH IN 62 FT)

CURVA-TURE		0	½	1	1½	2	2½	3	3½	4	4½	5	5½	6
							←		ELEVATION IN INCHES — MAXIMUM SLOPE FORMULA →					
½°	LENGTH	0	31	62	93	124	155	186	217	248	279	310	341	372
	SPEED	0	39	53	65	75	84	92	100	107	113	120	125	
	FORCE													
1°	LENGTH	0	31	62	93	124	155	186	217	248	279	310	341	372
	SPEED	0	26	38	45	54	60	65	70	76	80	84	88	92
	FORCE			690/650		650/620		690/620		690/620		690/620		690/620
1½°	LENGTH	0	31	62	93	124	155	186	217	248	279	310	341	372
	SPEED	0	22	31	38	43	49	53	58	62	66	69	72	76
	FORCE													
2°	LENGTH	0	31	62	93	124	155	186	217	248	279	310	341	372
	SPEED	0	19	27	33	38	42	46	50	54	57	60	63	66
	FORCE			650/620		650/620		650/620		650/620		650/620		690/620
2½°	LENGTH	0	31	62	93	124	155	186	217	248	279	310	341	372
	SPEED	0	17	24	29	34	38	41	44	48	51	53	56	58
	FORCE													
3°	LENGTH	0	31	62	93	124	155	186	217	248	279	310	341	372
	SPEED	0	15	22	26	31	34	38	41	44	46	49	51	54
	FORCE			650/690		650/690		650/690		650/690		650/690		650/690
3½°	LENGTH	0	31	62	93	124	155	186	217	248	279	310	341	372
	SPEED	0	14	20	25	29	32	35	38	41	43	45	47	50
	FORCE													
4°	LENGTH	0	31	62	93	124	155	186	217	248	279	310	341	372
	SPEED	0	13	19	23	27	30	33	35	38	40	42	44	46
	FORCE			690/620		690/620		690/620		690/620		690/620		690/620
4½°	LENGTH	0	31	62	93	124	155	186	217	248	279	310	341	372
	SPEED	0	12	18	22	25	28	31	33	36	38	40	42	44
	FORCE													
5°	LENGTH	0	31	62	93	124	155	186	217	248	279	310	341	372
	SPEED	0	12	17	21	24	27	29	32	34	36	38	40	41
	FORCE			690/690		690/690		690/690		690/690		690/690		690/690
6°	LENGTH	0	31	62	93	124	155	186	217	248	279	310	341	372
	SPEED	0	11	15	19	22	24	27	29	31	33	34	36	38
	FORCE			690/620		690/620		690/620		690/620		690/620		690/620
7°	LENGTH	0	31	62	93	124	155	186	217	248	279	310	341	372
	SPEED	0	10	14	17	20	23	25	27	29	31	32	34	35
	FORCE			690/650		690/650		690/650		690/650		690/650		690/650
8°	LENGTH	0	31	62	93	124	155	186	217	248	279	310	341	372
	SPEED	0	9	13	16	19	21	23	25	27	28	30	31	33
	FORCE			690/650		690/650		690/650		690/650		690/650		690/650
9°	LENGTH	0	31	62	93	124	155	186	217	248	279	310	341	372
	SPEED	0	9	12	15	17	20	22	24	25	27	28	29	31
	FORCE			690/620		690/620		690/620		690/620		690/620		690/620
10°	LENGTH	0	31	62	93	124	155	186	217	248	279	310	341	372
	SPEED	0	8	12	14	17	19	22	24	25	27	28	29	
	FORCE			620/690		620/690		620/690		650/690		650/690		650/690

LENGTH IN FT (L)
SPEED IN MPH (V)
FORCE IN LBS, LOWER VALUE = $42\,500\,E_T/L + 3130\,E_u$ (TOTAL LATERAL FORCE ON LEADING TRUCK OF LOCOMOTIVE)
                UPPER VALUE = $42\,500\,E_T/L$ (ANGULAR ACCELERATING FORCE ONLY)
FOR LOCOMOTIVE OF 375 000 LB WEIGHT, 3 260 000 LB SEC² FT POLAR MOMENT OF INERTIA AND 44.5 FT TRUCK CENTERS

WHERE E_u, E_a AND E_T ARE UNBALANCED, ACTUAL AND EQUILIBRIUM ELEVATIONS IN INCHES, RESPECTIVELY

5169.

TABLE 4 – MINIMUM LENGTH OF TRANSITION SPIRAL

3 INCHES UNBALANCED ELEVATION

TABLE LISTS LARGEST OF FOLLOWING TWO VALUES

$\text{LENGTH} = 1.22\, E_u V$ (RIDE COMFORT FORMULA, .04 g PER SEC)

$\text{LENGTH} = 62\, E_a$ (MAXIMUM SLOPE FORMULA, ONE INCH IN 62 FT)

Each cell lists **LENGTH** (ft, top) / **SPEED** (mph, bottom). Columns to the right of the stepped boundary use the MAXIMUM SLOPE FORMULA; columns to the left use the RIDE COMFORT FORMULA.

CURVA-TURE	\(E_a=0\)	½	1	1½	2	2½	3	3½	4	4½	5	5½	6
½°	337/92	366/100	392/107	414/113	439/120	467/125							
1°	238/65	256/70	278/76	293/80	307/84	322/88	337/92	351/96	366/100	377/103	392/107	403/110	414/113
1½°	194/53	212/58	227/62	242/66	253/69	263/72	278/76	289/79	300/82	307/84	318/87	341/90	372/92
2°	168/46	183/50	198/54	208/57	219/60	231/63	242/66	249/68	260/71	279/73	310/76	341/78	372/80
2½°	150/41	161/44	176/48	187/51	194/53	205/56	212/58	223/61	248/63	279/65	310/68	341/70	372/72
3°	139/38	150/41	161/44	168/46	179/49	187/51	198/54	217/56	248/58	279/60	310/62	341/64	372/66
3½°	126/35	139/38	150/41	157/43	165/45	172/47	186/50	217/52	248/53	279/55	310/57	341/59	372/60
4°	121/33	128/35	139/38	146/40	154/42	161/44	186/46	217/48	248/50	279/52	310/54	341/55	372/57
4½°	113/31	121/33	132/36	139/38	146/40	155/42	186/44	217/46	248/47	279/49	310/51	341/52	372/54
5°	106/29	117/32	124/34	132/36	139/38	155/40	186/41	217/43	248/45	279/46	310/48	341/49	372/51
6°	99/27	106/29	113/31	121/33	124/34	155/36	186/38	217/39	248/41	279/42	310/44	341/45	372/48
7°	92/25	99/27	106/29	110/30	124/32	155/34	186/35	217/37	248/38	279/39	310/40	341/42	372/45
8°	84/23	92/25	99/27	102/28	124/30	155/31	186/33	217/34	248/35	279/37	310/38	341/39	372/40
9°	81/22	88/24	92/25	99/27	124/28	155/29	186/31	217/32	248/33	279/35	310/36	341/37	372/38
10°	77/21	81/22	88/24 (1930/1320)	95/26 (1230/1100)	124/27	155/28	186/29	217/31	248/32	279/33	310/34	341/35	372/36

ELEVATION IN INCHES

← RIDE COMFORT FORMULA —→ ←— MAXIMUM SLOPE FORMULA —→

LENGTH IN FT (L)

SPEED IN MPH (V)

FORCE IN LBS, LOWER VALUE $= 42\,500\, E_u/L + 3130\, E_u$ (TOTAL LATERAL FORCE ON LEADING TRUCK OF LOCOMOTIVE)

UPPER VALUE $= 42\,500\, E_r/L$ (ANGULAR ACCELERATING FORCE ONLY)

FOR LOCOMOTIVE OF 375,000 LB WEIGHT, 3,260,000 LB SEC² FT POLAR MOMENT OF INERTIA AND 44.5 FT TRUCK CENTERS

WHERE E_u, E_a AND E_r ARE UNBALANCED, ACTUAL AND EQUILIBRIUM ELEVATIONS IN INCHES, RESPECTIVELY

TABLE 5 - MINIMUM LENGTH OF TRANSITION SPIRAL

2 INCHES UNBALANCED ELEVATION

TABLE LISTS LARGEST OF FOLLOWING TWO VALUES
LENGTH = 1.22 E_u V (RIDE COMFORT FORMULA, .04g PER SEC)
LENGTH = 62 E_a (MAXIMUM SLOPE FORMULA, ONE INCH IN 62 FT)

5069.

ELEVATION IN INCHES — each cell shows LENGTH (top) / SPEED (bottom)

CURVATURE		0	½	1	1½	2	2½	3	3½	4	4½	5	5½	6
½°	LENGTH	183	205	224	244	261	276	293	305					
	SPEED	75	84	92	100	107	113	120	125					
1°	LENGTH	129	146	159	171	185	195	205	217	248	279	310	341	372
	SPEED	53	60	65	70	76	80	84	88	92	96	100	103	107
1½°	LENGTH	105	120	129	142	151	161	186	217	248	279	310	341	372
	SPEED	43	49	53	58	62	66	69	72	76	79	82	84	87
2°	LENGTH	93	102	112	122	132	155	186	217	248	279	310	341	372
	SPEED	38	42	46	50	54	57	60	63	66	68	71	73	76
2½°	LENGTH	85	93	100	107	124	155	186	217	248	279	310	341	372
	SPEED	34	38	41	44	48	51	53	56	58	61	63	65	68
3°	LENGTH	76	83	93	100	124	156	186	217	248	279	310	341	372
	SPEED	31	34	38	41	44	46	49	51	54	56	58	60	62
3½°	LENGTH	71	78	85	93	124	155	186	217	248	279	310	341	372
	SPEED	29	32	35	38	41	43	45	47	50	52	53	55	57
4°	LENGTH	66	73	81	93	124	155	186	217	248	279	310	341	372
	SPEED	27	30	33	35	38	40	42	44	46	48	50	52	54
4½°	LENGTH	61	68	76	93	124	155	186	217	248	279	310	341	372
	SPEED	25	28	31	33	36	38	40	42	44	46	47	49	51
5°	LENGTH	59	66	71	93	124	155	186	217	248	279	310	341	372
	SPEED	24	27	29	32	34	36	38	40	41	43	45	46	48
6°	LENGTH	54	59	66	93	124	155	186	217	248	279	310	341	372
	SPEED	22	24	27	29	31	33	34	36	38	39	41	42	44
7°	LENGTH	49	56	62	93	124	155	186	217	248	279	310	341	372
	SPEED	20	23	26	27	29	30	32	34	35	37	38	39	40
8°	LENGTH	46	51	62	93	124	155	186	217	248	279	310	341	372
	SPEED	19	21	23	25	27	28	30	31	33	34	35	37	38
9°	LENGTH	44	49	62	93	124	155	186	217	248	279	310	341	372
	SPEED	18	20	22	24	25	27	28	29	31	32	33	35	36
10°	LENGTH	41	46	62	93	124	155	186	217	248	279	310	341	372
	SPEED	17	19	21	22	24	26	27	28	29	31	32	33	34

Table regions labeled: RIDE COMFORT FORMULA and MAXIMUM SLOPE FORMULA (stepped boundary).

LENGTH IN FT (L)
SPEED IN MPH (V)
FORCE IN LBS, LOWER VALUE = 42 500 E_r/L + 3130 E_u (TOTAL LATERAL FORCE ON LEADING TRUCK OF LOCOMOTIVE)
UPPER VALUE = 42 500 E_r/L (ANGULAR ACCELERATING FORCE ONLY)
FOR LOCOMOTIVE OF 375 000 LB WEIGHT, 3 260 000 LB SEC² FT POLAR MOMENT OF INERTIA AND 41.5 FT TRUCK CENTERS

WHERE E_u, E_a AND E_r ARE UNBALANCED, ACTUAL AND EQUILIBRIUM ELEVATIONS IN INCHES, RESPECTIVELY

TABLE 6 - DESIRABLE LENGTH OF TRANSITION SPIRAL
3 INCHES UNBALANCED ELEVATION
PRESENT AREA 'MANUAL FORMULA, LENGTH = $1.17\,E_aV$

5869.

CURVATURE		0	½	1	1½	2	2½	3	3½	4	4½	5	5½	6
½°	LENGTH	0	58	125	198	281	366							
	SPEED	92	100	107	113	120	125							
	FORCE	INFINITE												
1°	LENGTH	0	41	89	141	197	258	323	394	468	542	626	708	793
	SPEED	65	70	76	80	84	88	92	96	100	103	107	110	113
	FORCE	INFINITE	3670 13020	11300		10410		10080		10250		9840		9870
1½°	LENGTH	0	34	73	116	161	211	267	324	384	442	509	579	646
	SPEED	53	58	62	66	69	72	76	79	82	84	87	90	92
	FORCE	INFINITE												
2°	LENGTH	0	29	63	100	140	185	232	279	332	384	445	502	562
	SPEED	46	50	54	57	60	63	66	68	71	73	76	78	80
	FORCE	INFINITE		2080						900 10290		10150		10110
2½°	LENGTH	0	26	56	90	124	164	203	250	295	342	398	451	505
	SPEED	41	44	48	51	53	56	58	61	63	65	68	70	72
	FORCE	INFINITE												
3°	LENGTH	0	24	51	81	115	149	190	230	272	316	363	412	463
	SPEED	38	41	44	46	49	51	54	56	58	60	62	64	66
	FORCE	INFINITE		2320										
3½°	LENGTH	0	22	48	76	105	138	175	213	248	290	334	380	451
	SPEED	35	38	41	43	46	47	50	52	53	55	57	59	60
	FORCE	INFINITE		14110										
4°	LENGTH	0	20	44	70	98	129	162	197	234	274	316	354	405
	SPEED	33	35	38	40	42	44	46	48	50	52	54	55	57
	FORCE	INFINITE		3860										
4½°	LENGTH	0	19	42	67	94	123	154	189	220	258	298	335	379
	SPEED	31	33	36	38	40	42	44	46	47	49	51	52	54
	FORCE	INFINITE												
5°	LENGTH	0	19	40	63	89	117	144	176	211	242	281	315	355
	SPEED	29	32	34	36	38	40	41	43	45	46	48	49	51
	FORCE	INFINITE		4250 15440										
6°	LENGTH	0	17	36	58	80	105	133	160	192	211	257	290	323
	SPEED	27	29	31	33	34	36	38	39	41	42	44	45	46
	FORCE	INFINITE		4720 14110										
7°	LENGTH	0	16	34	53	75	100	123	152	178	205	234	270	302
	SPEED	25	27	29	30	32	34	35	37	38	39	40	42	43
	FORCE	INFINITE		5070 14390										
8°	LENGTH	0	15	32	49	70	91	116	139	164	195	223	251	281
	SPEED	23	25	27	28	30	31	33	34	35	37	38	39	40
	FORCE	INFINITE		5700										
9°	LENGTH	0	14	29	48	66	86	109	131	154	184	211	238	267
	SPEED	22	24	25	27	28	29	31	32	33	35	36	37	38
	FORCE	INFINITE		5850										
10°	LENGTH	0	13	28	46	63	82	102	127	150	174	199	225	253
	SPEED	21	22	24	26	27	28	29	31	32	33	34	35	36
	FORCE	INFINITE	12480 29790	6070 15460		13760 12760		11690		11370		11100		1510 10900

LENGTH IN FT (L)
SPEED IN MPH (V)
FORCE IN LBS, LOWER VALUE = $42500\,E_u/L + 3130\,E_a$ (TOTAL LATERAL FORCE ON LEADING TRUCK OF LOCOMOTIVE)
UPPER VALUE = $42500\,E_f/L$ (ANGULAR ACCELERATING FORCE ONLY)
FOR LOCOMOTIVE OF 375,000 LB WEIGHT, 3,260,000 LB SEC² FT POLAR MOMENT OF INERTIA AND 41.5 FT TRUCK CENTERS

WHERE E_u, E_a AND E_f ARE UNBALANCED, ACTUAL AND EQUILIBRIUM ELEVATIONS IN INCHES, RESPECTIVELY

TABLE 7 - TEST CURVES
Philadelphia High Speed Run

5869.

Curve	Mile Post	WESTBOUND					EASTBOUND				
		Curvature Nominal degrees	Elevation Nominal inches	Spiral Length feet East	West	Test Speed mph	Curvature Nominal degrees	Elevation Nominal inches	Spiral Length feet East	West	Test Speed mph
Whitford	28.2 29.2	0°09'	1	128	154	90	0°09'	1	256	253	80
Bradford Hills	29.8 30.3	3°07'	6	495	526	68	3°07'	6	503	504	67
Quarry	30.3 30.8	2°30'	6	505	515	74	2°30'	6	504	496	70
Chestnut Street	31.3 31.5	1°45'	6	506	507	83	1°45'	6	501	502	83
Downingtown	32.2 32.5	1°	3	376	378	91	1°	3 1/2	441	442	88
Pans	32.9 33.1	0°52'	3	376	372	92	0°52'	2 3/4	343	342	97
E.of MP 34	33.5 34.0	0°17'	1	201	204	94	0°52'	3	-	455	101
W.of MP 34	34.2 34.6	0°20'	1	203	131	96	1°	3 1/2	314	-	102
Thorndale	34.8 35.2	-	-	-	-	-	0°30'	1 3/4	444	-	102
MP 35	35.0 35.2	0°45'	1 3/4	221	220	97	-	-	-	-	-
Caln	36.8 37.3	1°	3 1/2	444	440	98	1°	3 1/2	438	436	103
E.of MP 38	37.4 37.9	1°	3 1/2	439	435	100	1°	3 1/2	439	439	102
High Bridge	38.4 39.1	0°30'	1 3/4	187	188	101	0°30'	1 3/4	351	349	101
Bone Mill	39.4 39.9	0°45'	2 3/4	346	348	100	0°45'	2 1/2	511	507	102
MP 41	40.8 41.1	0°46'	2 3/4	344	344	99	0°46'	2 1/2	314	314	102
Hopes	41.3 41.6	0°43'	2 1/2	319	320	99	0°43'	2 1/2	313	314	102
E.of Parkesburg	43.5 43.7	0°23'	1	124	126	98	0°23'	3/4	403	203	101
Parkesburg	43.9 44.0	-	-	-	-	-	0°30'	1 1/4	160	159	100
Bridge 44.70	44.6 44.9	-	-	-	-	-	0°30'	1	200	132	93
MP 45	45.2 45.3	0°30'	1	200	204	101	0°30'	1	212	199	92
E.of Atglen	46.7 46.9	0°30'	1	200	201	102	0°30'	1	201	203	88
North Bend	47.4 48.2	2°	6	502	497	87	2°	6	497	498	84
Christiana	48.3 48.7	1°	3 1/2	442	439	86	1°	3 1/2	434	426	85
MP 49	48.8 49.2	1°	3 1/2	439	434	87	1°	3 1/2	435	438	85
MP 50	49.8 50.1	1°	3 1/2	437	438	84	1°	3 1/2	460	465	78
E.of Gap	50.2 50.6	2°07'	5	438	438	68	2°07'	5	436	432	67
Gap	50.8 51.6	4°	6	446	406	56	4°	6	-	409	54
Eby's	52.0 52.4	4°	6	470	474	56	4°	6	405	408	56
K.I. - MP 53	52.8 53.2	2°07'	6	500	501	73	2°07'	6	498	502	77
Kinser	53.7 54.0	0°30'	1 3/4	403	401	87	0°30'	2	400	400	97
Vintage	54.4 54.6	0°30'	1 1/2	186	187	95	0°30'	1 3/4	221	220	99
Leaman Place	55.8 56.7	1°	4	492	499	102	1°	4	498	500	100
E.of Gordonville	57.4 57.7	0°40'	2 1/4	280	277	101	0°40'	2	248	246	100
E.of MP 59	58.4 59.0	1°30'	5 1/4	439	432	95	1°30'	5 1/2	687	684	93
E.of Ronk	59.5 59.7	1°16'	4	500	501	92	1°16'	5	356	357	86
Ronk	60.0 60.6	2°07'	6	501	493	84	2°07'	6	747	535	85
Bird-In-Hand	61.0 61.5	2°	6	490	744	85	2°	6	742	745	83
Mill Creek	61.6 62.0	1°	3 3/4	473	467	88	1°	3 3/4	315	316	95
MP 63	63.0 63.5	0°30'	1	122	120	93	0°30'	1 3/4	339	336	96
E.of MP 64	63.5 63.9	1°	3	376	375	97	1°	3 1/2	313	315	93
MP 65	64.8 65.6	0°20'	1/2	186	186	99	0°20'	1	186	186	90

Test speeds are the average of the east and west spiral speeds.

TABLE 8 - TEST CURVES
Baltimore Run
Single Track

5869.

Curve	Mile Post	Curvature Nominal degrees	Elevation Nominal inches	Spiral Length feet		Westbound Test Speed mph	Eastbound Test Speed mph
				East	West		
Mystic Quarry Rev.	18.7 19.0	6°45'	3 1/4	277	-	34	37
Mystic Quarry Rev.	19.0 19.2	4°38'	1 1/2	-	187	42	34
W. End Rev. MP 20 to Glencoe	20.1 20.4	6°	3	124	-	40	40
Corbett	22.0 22.3	3°	4	249	261	54	60
E. of Monkton	22.6 22.8	1°	1	218	153	52	54
2nd. W. of Monkton	23.3 23.8	6°	6	375	-	46	44
W. of Bluemont	25.0 25.3	4°30'	4 1/2	-	309	49	50
MP 26	25.9 26.2	2°	3 1/2	218	245	59	61
Graystone	27.0 27.2	8°	5	437	-	32	36
Spencer Cut	29.5 29.8	5°	-	-	-	44	46
2nd. W. of Walker	30.5 30.8	6°	-	-	-	40	41
E. of Bentley Springs	31.1 31.3	7°	6	493	434	40	40
W. of Bentley Springs	31.4 31.5	0°30'	1	125	124	39	37
E. of MP 32	31.5 31.8	6°	-	-	-	39	34
Rev. W. of Freeland	34.5 34.7	2°	2	250	249	53	56
Rev. W. of Freeland	34.7 35.0	2°	2	250	249	58	58
Shrewsbury	38.5 38.7	6°	6	377	407	44	42
Signal 398 Rev.	39.6 39.7	4°	3	189	186	50	45
Signal 398 Rev.	39.7 39.8	4°	3 1/2	190	245	49	45
MP 40	40.0 40.2	5°	-	-	-	48	45
Bridge 40.39	40.4 40.6	4°	3 1/2	223	216	49	49
1st. E. of Seitzland	40.7 40.8	1°	1 1/2	185	186	45	49
MP 45	44.9 45.2	4°	6	399	493	44	44
Rev. E. of MP 48	47.6 47.7	2°	2	187	188	45	44
Rev. E. of MP 48	47.7 47.9	2°30'	2 1/2	216	214	45	46
Glatfelter	48.4 49.0	3°30'	5 1/2	464	-	54	53
E. of Howard Tunnel	50.3 50.6	4°30'	-	-	-	40	38
W. Rev. W. of Howard	51.0 51.2	6°	4 1/2	280	280	39	40
Brilhart	52.2 52.6	4°	-	-	-	40	39
W. of MP 54	54.0 54.6	4°	5 1/2	339	-	39	40

Test speeds are the average of the east and west spiral speeds.

Appendix 8–b

Report on Pennsylvania Railroad M. of W. Test No. 591, Determination of Plastic Flow in Rail Head

1. Purpose of Test

The purpose of the test was to determine the amount of plastic flow which takes place in the gage corner of a rail on the high side of a curve under conditions which produce shelling. For this purpose three rails were to be placed in the high side of a sharp curve in three-track territory on the Middle Division.

2. Method

Brass pins 5/64 in by ¾ in were inserted in holes drilled in the rail head. The rails were prepared in the machine shop of the Altoona laboratory. It was found difficult accurately to drill holes of such small diameter in the high-carbon rail steel. Therefore, a special jig was prepared for this purpose.

In addition to the jig used for guiding the drill, it was necessary to obtain high speed drills, 5/64 in diameter, and a speed-control clutch for use with the drill.

The accompanying drawing, dated June 1951, shows the layout of the holes with respect to the cross section of the rail. The general object was to place the pins at right angles to the surface of the rail head at various locations in the vicinity of the gage corner.

It will be noted that four locations, "a", "b", "c" and "d" were chosen, beginning with location "a" at the center of the ⅜-in fillet at the corner of the rail head, "b" at the junction of the ⅜-in fillet with 1¼-in fillet, "c" at the mid-point of the 1¼-in fillet, and "d" at the junction of the 1¼-in fillet with the 10-in head radius. These four locations were repeated twice in the length of the rail.

518

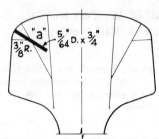

"a" Thru center of ⅜" radius at angle of 30° with horizontal

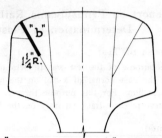

"b" Thru center of 1¼" radius at angle of 60° with horizontal

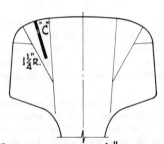

"c" Thru center of 1¼" radius midway between "b" and "d" 73° with horizontal

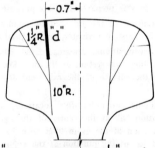

"d" Thru center of 1¼" radius 0.7" from ₵ of top of rail 4° from vertical

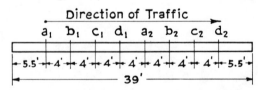

Direction of Traffic

a₁ b₁ c₁ d₁ a₂ b₂ c₂ d₂

5.5'—4'—4'—4'—4'—4'—4'—4'—5.5'

39'

PLASTIC FLOW IN 140 RE RAIL HEAD
LOCATION OF 5/64" DIA. BRASS PINS

OFFICE OF CHIEF ENGINEER, P.R.R.
PHILA., PA.- JUNE, 1951

The rails were eventually laid on the Pittsburgh Division, No. 1 Track, Bolivar Curve, M.P. 295.3. At this location the track was laid with 140-lb, 1948 rail, which in August 1953, was showing flaking and light shelling.

This is a 4-deg curve with 4 in superelevation, authorized speed 45 mph, and carries moderate to heavy eastward freight traffic. Records kept in connection with another test indicate a tonnage of approximately 29,000,000 gross tons annually.

The three test rails were installed August 17, 1953.

3. Results

Throughout the life of the test, inspections were made at frequent intervals in order to determine if any type of defect was developing in the rail at the location of the pins, there being some concern that detail fractures might develop from the drilled holes. There was no such development. Inspections were made by means of Magnaflux powder. The only defect discovered was an indication of light flaking at the location of the pins in a few cases.

In July 1956, Rail P8, which showed the most definite indication of flaking, was removed from track and sent to the laboratory for examination. This rail was sectioned at the center line of each of the pins. Mr. Pinney's report No. 9398, included herein, dated December 5, 1956, covers examination of this rail and includes photographs showing the position of the pins. The letter designation on each photograph indicates the position of the pin.

In October 1956, a derailment damaged the remaining rails in this curve, and Rails P3 and P6 were turned into the laboratory for similar examination. Mr. Pinney's two reports, Nos. 9409 P–3 and 9409 P–6, also presented herein, dated April 19, 1957, cover the examination of these remaining rails and include photographs showing the distortion of the pins.

Only representative photographs are included with this report.

Table No. 1 shows measurements taken from the various photographic cross sections to show the deformation of the pins. The measurements were not made on all photographs, but only on those which showed the pin fairly clearly throughout its length. It will be noted that there was some longitudinal movement of the pin, as well as a lateral movement, so that generally speaking neither a section taken at right angles to the length of the rail, nor one parallel to the length of the rail shows the complete alinement of the pin.

The exact amount of the deformation is probably not of great importance, although the direction of the relative movement at various parts of the rail head may have some significance. It will be noted that pins "b", "c" and "d", which were located at either end and in the center of the 1¼-in radius arc, show a lateral movement at the end of the pin of 0.05 to 0.08 in, the average being about 0.07 in. Pins "a", on the other hand, which were located at the center of the ⅜-in radius arc at an angle of 30 deg from horizontal, show a movement of 0.02 to 0.06 in, the average being 0.04 in. It would, therefore, seem that the principal flow of metal is roughly parallel to the tread of the wheel; that is, the head metal tends to flow toward the gage corner and to be worn off when it reaches that corner.

It is also of interest to note that the maximum depth of visible movement is 0.20 to 0.40 in, so that in general it may be said that the flow of metal extends ¼ in to ⅜ in below the surface of the rail head. It will be noted that this is the depth at which the metal separation in a shelly spot is generally observed.

(Text Continued on page 975)

THE PENNSYLVANIA RAILROAD

M. W. 34 F
11-1-17   1M   8x10½

LABORATORY REPORT

Report No. 9398

CHEMICAL AND PHYSICAL EXAMINATION OF RAIL AND OTHER TRACK MATERIAL

T.D. 4638   Altoona, Pa., December 5, 1956

Sample No. 253755-57, representing 140-lb., P.S., Steelton, Bethlehem Steel Company rail, rolled 1951, heat No. 81131-A7, which was removed from track containing MW Test No. 591, Plastic flow in rail head.

Referred to in CJC to MAP dated 7-27-56.

CHEMICAL ANALYSIS

LOCATION OF BORINGS	C.	Mn.	P. Below	Si.	S.
0	.83	.80	.030	.15	.030
M	1.01				
C	1.01				

PHYSICAL TESTS

Mill Drop Test Permanent Set-Inches	Tensile Strength Lbs. per Sq. In.	Elastic Limit Lbs. per Sq. In.	Elongation Per Cent. in 2 Ins.	Reduction of Area—% of Original Sec.	Character of Fracture
	136,150	105,800	10.0	15.0	

NOTE: The word "Borings" refers also to Chippings and other kinds of test fragments.

LOCATION	1	2	3	4	5	6	7	AVERAGE
Brinell	285	285	277	302	282	302	302	291
Rockwell								

Chem. Analysis O M C
Tensile Tests O M
Location of Brinell and Scleroscope Hardness Numbers

ACCOMPANYING THIS REPORT ARE:—
Photograph of Original Fracture
Photograph of Sulphur Print — X
Photograph of Etching / Photomicrographs
Photographs of Etching—Longitudinal
Photograph of Deep Etching—Sawed End

Classification of Failure— M.W. Test No. 591 - "Plastic Flow"

REMARKS:— The following photographs are attached:
T-41380, 41381, 41382 and 41383 - showing 3/4" long brass pins inserted at various angles on the gage-side of the head. See attached drawing, Plan 275, dated June, 1951. All sections were cut vertical-transverse except the bottom one, C-7, shown on print T-41383. This section was cut vertical-longitudinally.
T-41427 - Sulfur print. Segregation is indicated in the web center (black streak).
The analysis of standard location "O" drillings shows 0.83% carbon and "M" and "C" location drillings 1.01% carbon, indicating 21.6% carbon segregation, which is excessive. The analysis is in line with the sulfur print, the Brinell hardness tests and the physical properties.
The brass pins were inserted every four feet in the rail, as described in the attached Plan 275, dated June, 1951, and "plastic flow" should be indicated in each pin. The photographs show a slight deformation of the brass pins and on this basis some plastic flow may be present.

APPROVED:—

M. A. Pinney

ENGINEER OF TESTS

966   R a i l

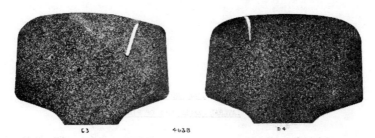

T. 41381

Plastic flow in rail head. (Each hole ¾ in deep). C3—Through center of 1¼-in radius, midway between (b) and (d). D4—Through center of 1¼-in radius, 0.7 in from center line of top of rail, 4 deg from vertical.

T. 41382

Plastic flow in rail head. (Each hole ¾ in deep). A5—Through center of ¾-in radius at angle of 30 deg with horizontal. B6—Through center of 1¼-in radius at angle of 60 deg with horizontal.

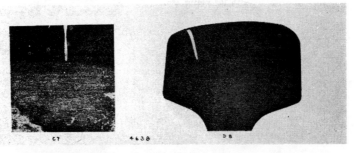

T. 41383

Plastic flow in rail head. (Each hole ¾ in deep). C7—Through center of 1¼-in radius midway between (b) and (d). Note section cut longitudinally. D8—Through center of 1¼-in radius 0.7 in from center line of top of rail, 4 deg from vertical.

TABLE NO. 1

LATERAL DEFORMATION OF PINS

Photo No.	Original Angle with Horizontal	Position	Maximum Lateral Movement	Radius of Pin Curvature	Max. Depth of Visible Flow	Rail No.
T41382 A-5	30°	Middle of 3/8" radius corner fillet arc.	.04"	.78"	.25"	P-8
T41380 A-1	30°	Middle of 3/8" radius corner fillet arc.	.06"	1.03"	.40"	P-8
T41554 A-2	30°	Middle of 3/8" radius corner fillet arc.	.02"	1.82"	.27"	P-6
T41552 A-1	30°	Middle of 3/8" radius corner fillet arc.	.04"	1.72"	.37"	P-6
T41382 B-6	60°	Junction of 3/8" radius arc with 1-1/4" radius arc.	.08"	.46"	.27"	P-8
T41554 B-2	60°	Junction of 3/8" radius arc with 1-1/4" radius arc.	.07"	.83"	.34"	P-6
T41552 B-1	60°	Junction of 3/8" radius arc with 1-1/4" radius arc.	.05"	.73"	.27"	P-6
T41555 C-2	73°	Middle of 1-1/4" radius arc.	.08"	.77"	.35"	P-6
T41383 D-8	96°	Junction of 1-1/4" radius arc with 10" radius arc.	.06"	.47"	.28"	P-8
T41381 D-4	96°	Junction of 1-1/4" radius arc with 10" radius arc.	.06"	.33"	.20"	P-8

THE PENNSYLVANIA RAILROAD

M W 34 F
1-4-56   1M   8×10½

LABORATORY REPORT

Report No. **9409**

CHEMICAL AND PHYSICAL EXAMINATION OF RAIL AND OTHER TRACK MATERIAL

T.D. 4638   Altoona, Pa.,   April 19,   19 57

Sample No. **254834-836**, representing **140 lb. Carnegie rail, designated 3-P,
1950, 6 months, with heat and ingot number 07E-890-F15, which was removed
from track containing M.W. Test No. 591, Plastic Flow in Rail Head.**

Referred to in **C.J.C. memo. to M.A.P. 12-10-56**

CHEMICAL ANALYSIS

LOCATION OF BORINGS	C.	Mn.	P.	Si.	S.		
O	.750	.82	.012	.158	.031		
M	.750						
C							
HEAT ANALYSIS							

NOTE: The word "Borings" refers also to Chippings and other kinds of test fragments.

PHYSICAL TESTS

Mill Drop Test Permanent Set-Inches	Tensile Strength Lbs. per Sq. In.	Elastic Limit Lbs. per Sq. In.	Elongation Per Cent. in 2 Ins.	Reduction of Area—% of Original Sec.	Character of Fracture

	LOCATION	1	2	3	4	5	6	7	AVERAGE
HARDNESS NUMBER	Brinell	262	262	273	273	262	262	262	266
	Rockwell								

Chem. Analysis
O M C
Location of Brinell and Scleroscope Hardness Numbers
Tensile Tests
O M

ACCOMPANYING THIS REPORT ARE:—	YES	NO		YES	NO		YES	NO
Photograph of Original Fracture						Photographs of Etching—Longitudinal		
Photograph of Sulphur Print			Photomicrographs			Photograph of Deep Etching—Sawed End		

Classification of Failure—

REMARKS:—   Rail - P-3 - The following photographs are attached:
       T-41548 - Locations A-1 & B-1, Vertical-transverse.
       T-41549 -   "   B-1 & C-1,   "   "
       T-41550 -   "   A2 & B-2,   "   "
       T-41551 -   "   C-2 & D-2,   "   "
       T-41596 -   "   C-2 & D-2, Vertical-Longitudinal
     For location and angle of pin insertion see attached drawing No.275, marked
"Test 591 - Plastic Flow of Rail Head".
     Prints are enlarged approximately 1-1/3 diameters. The upper portion of the
originally straight pins showed curvature, caused by cold working of the upper
gage side head metal in service.
     The analysis of drillings taken at standard location "O" meets the chemical
requirements of Spec.C.E.35(e). Those taken at location "M" show negligible
carbon segregation. The analysis and Brinell hardness tests are in agreement.
     Our conclusion is the same as that originally reported on 10-5-56, report
9398. On the basis of pin curvature, some "plastic flow" is indicated.

APPROVED:—

ENGINEER OF TESTS

524

P3-A2

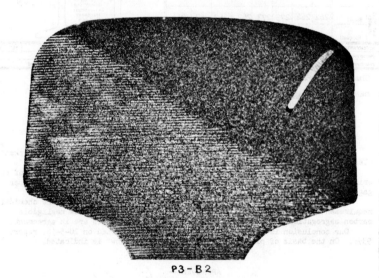

P3-B2

T. 41550

Plastic flow of rail head, rail P3 enlarged 1.3 diameters. (Each hole ¾ in deep). A2—Through center of ¾-in radius at an angle of 30 deg with horizontal. B2—Through center of 1¼-in radius at an angle of 60 deg with horizontal.

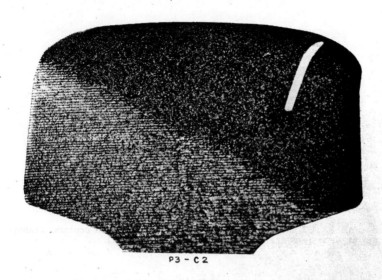

P3 – C 2

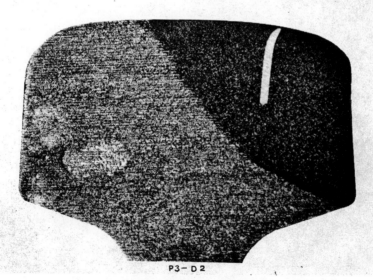

P3 – D 2

T. 41551

Plastic flow of rail head, rail P3 enlarged 1.3 diameters. (Each hole ¾ in deep). C2—Through center of 1¼-in radius, midway between (b) and (d). D2—Through center of 1¼-in radius, 0.7 in from center line of top of rail, 4 deg from vertical.

526

T. 41596

Rail P3. C2 and D2—Longitudinal cuts through pin centers. Transverse cuts of these pins are shown on photograph T. 41551.

972   Rail

THE PENNSYLVANIA RAILROAD

LABORATORY REPORT

Report No. 9409

CHEMICAL AND PHYSICAL EXAMINATION OF RAIL AND OTHER TRACK MATERIAL

T.D. 4638   Altoona, Pa.,   April 19,   19 57

Sample No. 254834-836, representing 140 lb. Carnegie rail, designated 6-P, 1950, 6 months, with heat and ingot numbers 06E-592-B4, which was removed from t track containing M.W. Test No. 591, Plastic Flow in Rail Head

Referred to in C.J.C. memo. to M.A.P. 12-10-56

CHEMICAL ANALYSIS							PHYSICAL TESTS					
LOCATION OF BORINGS	C.	Mn.	P.	Si.	S.		Mill Drop Test Permanent Set-Inches	Tensile Strength Lbs. per Sq. In.	Elastic Limit Lbs. per Sq. In.	Elongation Per Cent in 2 In.	Reduction of Area—% of Original Sec.	Character of Fracture
0	.812	.83	.011	.17	.033							
M	.831											
C												
HEAT ANALYSIS												

NOTE: The word "Borings" refers also to Chippings and other kinds of test fragments.

LOCATION		1	2	3	4	5	6	7	AVERAGE
HARDNESS NUMBER	Brinell	273	273	255	262	262	262	262	264
	Rockwell								

Chem. Analysis
O M C
Tensile Tests
O M

Location of Brinell and Scleroscope Hardness Numbers

ACCOMPANYING THIS REPORT ARE:—	YES	NO		YES	NO		YES	NO
Photograph of Original Fracture			Photograph of Etching			Photographs of Etching—Longitudinal		
Photograph of Sulphur Print			Photomicrographs			Photograph of Deep Etching—Sawed End		

Classification of Failure—

REMARKS:—Rail - 6-P - The following photographs are attached:
                    T-41552 - Location A-1 & B-1
                    T-41553 -   "   C-1 & D-1
                    T-41554 -   "   A-2 & B-2
                    T-41555 -   "   C-2 & D-2
    Prints are enlarged approximately 1-1/3 diameters. Upper portions of the originally straight pins show a slight curvature.
    For location and angle of pin insertion, see attaching drawing No. 275, marked "Test 591 - Plastic Flow of Rail Head".
    The analysis of drillings taken at standard location "0", meet the chemical requirements of Spec.C.E.35(e). Those taken at "M" show negligible carbon segregation and the analysis and the Brinell hardness are in agreement.
    Our conclusion is the same as that originally reported in report 9398, dated 3-5-56. On the basis of pin curvature, some plastic flow is indicated.

APPROVED:—

ENGINEER OF TESTS

528

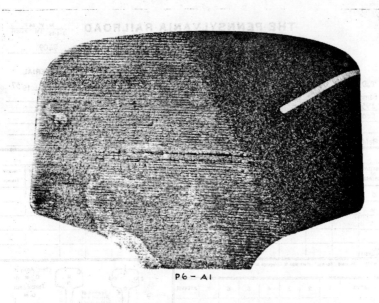

P6 - A1

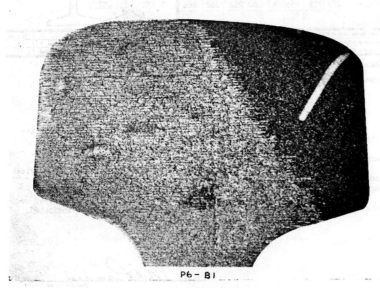

P6 - B1

T. 41552

Plastic flow of rail head, rail P6 enlarged 1.3 diameters. (Each hole ¾ in deep). A1—Through center of ¾-in radius at angle of 30 deg with horizontal. B1—Through center of 1¼-in radius at angle of 60 deg with horizontal.

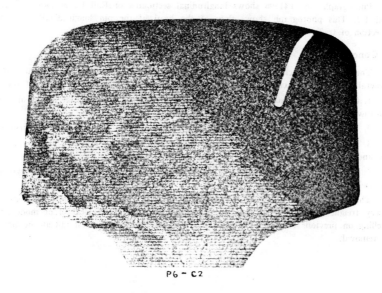

P6 – C2

P6 – D2

T. 41555

Plastic flow of rail head, rail P6 enlarged 1.3 diameters. (Each hole ¾ in deep). C2—Through center of 1¼-in radius midway between (b) and (d). D2—Through center of 1¼-in radius 0.7 in from center line of top of rail, 4 deg from vertical.

Photograph No. T41596 shows longitudinal sectioning of Rail P3 at locations C2 and D2. This photograph shows flow of the head of the pin longitudinally in the direction of traffic.

4. Conclusions

The following conclusions of a general nature can be reached as a result of this test. Generally they verify conclusions reached from previous examinations of failed rails.

1. On the high rail of curves there is a flow of metal at the top gage corner of the rail toward the gage side.

2. This flow of metal extends to a depth of $\frac{1}{4}$ in to $\frac{3}{8}$ in below the rail surface.

3. The flow of metal toward the gage side extends back to the edge of the center arc and beyond, probably to the center of the rail head.

4. The magnitude of deformation is positive evidence of shear stresses well beyond the yield point of the steel.

This condition was demonstrated on the high rail of a 4-deg curve under moderately heavy freight traffic after 75,000,000 gross tons. This was at a location of moderate shelling on previous rail. Only light flaking had developed in the test rail at the time of removal.

Chapter 3

Ties,
Ballast,
and Subgrade

TEXT 32

Part 1

(a) Roadbed. Load Capacity. Relation to Ballast. Allowable Pressure

Fifth Progress Report on Soil Pressure Cells—1953

Synopsis

This is the fifth progress report on the measurement and study of soil pressures under normal rail traffic by means of soil pressure cells. The test installation, which consists of 12 cells, is described in detail in the "Third Progress Report on Soil Pressure Cells", which can be found in the Proceedings, Vol. 52, 1951, page 482. The pressure cells were installed on July 7, 1950. Readings were taken that year for 42 runs, 20 before grouting and 22 after grouting. In 1951 readings were taken for 27 runs, and in 1952 for 31 additional runs.

The present report includes an analysis of the data obtained in 1950, 1951, and 1952, and a comparison of the 1952 results with those of 1950 and 1951. In previous reports comparisons have been made between theoretical pressures and shears and recorded pressures and shears, and the apparent effect of pressure grouting on recorded pressures has been noted.

The pressure cells all functioned well in 1950, but at the time of the 1951 readings pressure cell 7, for measuring horizontal pressures on vertical planes 4 ft to the left of the track center line, and pressure cell 12, for measuring vertical pressures on horizontal planes 8 ft to the left of the center line, were out of order and consequently did not register. The reason for failure was thought to be somewhere in the electrical circuits, but cannot be definitely ascertained until the cells are removed from the ground.

Introduction

This is the fifth progress report on the measurement of subgrade soil pressures from rail traffic by means of pressure cells. The work was conducted with committee sponsorship under the general direction of G. M. Magee, director of engineering research of the Engineering Division, AAR, and under the guidance of Rockwell Smith, research engineer roadway, AAR, by G. L. Hinueber, assistant research engineer roadway, and M. F. Smucker, assistant electrical engineer, both members of the AAR Engineering Division research staff. The test installation is described in detail in the Proceedings, Vol. 52, 1951, page 485.

The pressure cell provides a means of determining directly the stress distribution within the earth structure which constitutes the roadbed subgrade of a railroad. This function is important because it furnishes a check on the theories of stress distribution. These theories require certain general assumptions as to the conditions which prevail in a soil mass. The actual conditions found in nature generally will vary from the assumed conditions to a greater or lesser degree, and the extent of errors introduced by these variations is usually unknown.

The data for this year's report were obtained between June 8 and June 17, 1952. Records were taken for 42 runs, 31 of which were usable.

As mentioned previously, pressure cell 7 and pressure cell 12 failed in 1951, and consequently did not register on either the 1951 or 1952 records. It has been the practice in previous reports to use average values from two cells for all pressures at the 4-ft off track center line and 8-ft off-center line positions since the pressure cell clusters at these positions, both to the left and to the right of the center line of the track, are duplicates. However, pressure cells 7 and 12 are not in working order, hence the values for horizontal pressures on vertical planes 4 ft off the track center line and vertical pressures on horizontal planes 8 ft off center line for 1951 and 1952 runs are of necessity not average values, but only the readings of single cells.

Discussion

As in previous reports, the theoretical pressures were determined from Newmark charts (Influence Charts for the Computation of Stresses in Elastic Foundations, Nathan M. Newmark, Bulletin Series 338, University of Illinois Engineering Experiment Station) for the tie loads involved. The theoretical and recorded vertical pressures were integrated graphically for the 16-ft width of the pressure cell installation, thus obtaining the average values of the equivalent vertical pressure. Curves of equivalent vertical pressure vs tie loads on five ties for theoretical pressures and recorded pressures for 1950 runs before and after grouting, 1951 runs, and 1952 runs, are shown in Fig. 1. The curve for 1952 runs appears as a dotted line. It can be seen that the 1951 and 1952 curves are in close agreement, the reduction of pressure brought about by grouting still being evident, although not as great as immediately after treatment in 1950.

Curves of lateral horizontal pressure vs tie loads on five ties for theoretical pressures and for recorded pressures for 1950, 1951, and 1952 runs are shown in Fig. 2. The 1952 curve appears as a dotted line. The 1951 and 1952 curves for recorded lateral horizontal pressures 8 ft off the track center line are almost identical, the decrease in pressure after grouting still being in evidence, although not to quite the extent as immediately after treatment.

The 1952 curve for lateral horizontal pressures 4 ft off the center line shows a decrease in pressures for corresponding tie loads over the corresponding curve for 1951. This brings the curve for recorded pressures somewhat closer to the theoretical curve. However, it must be kept in mind that the pressure cell recording horizontal pressures on vertical planes 4 ft to the left of the track center line was not in working order. The plotted values are, therefore, not an average of two cells, but rather representative of only one cell. Furthermore, in the 1952 runs the tie plates on the right hand side of the ties generally took a lesser portion of the load than did those on the left hand side, probably due to uneven tamping of the ties. Consequently, the pressure cells to the right of the track center line took a smaller portion of the total load than those on the left. This would offer a reasonable explanation for the decrease in recorded horizontal pressures for corresponding tie loads 4 ft off the center line of the track in 1952.

Fig. 3 shows curves of longitudinal horizontal pressure vs tie loads on five ties for 1950, 1951 and 1952 runs. The 1952 curve, which appears as a dotted line, indicates a slight decrease in pressure for corresponding tie loads from 1951 results. The deviation between theoretical and recorded pressure is still in evidence.

Figs. 4, 5, 6 and 7 show the distribution of vertical pressure over the 16-ft wide pressure cell installation for individual runs. Recorded pressures are indicated by solid lines and theoretical by broken lines. The pressure distribution for the 1952 runs is very similar to that of the 1951 runs. Close agreement exists for the most part between theoretical and recorded.vertical pressures. The recorded vertical pressures at the position 8 ft to the left of the track center line are omitted for both the 1951 and 1952 runs because of the failure of the pressure cell recording vertical pressures at this position.

Figs. 8, 9, 10 and 11 show the distribution of lateral horizontal pressures over the 16-ft wide pressure cell installation for individual runs. The curves for 1952 runs are very similar to the 1951 curves. Because the pressure cell recording lateral horizontal pressures 4 ft to the left of the track center line was not functioning, the reading of the pressure cell located 4 ft to the right of the center line for measuring horizontal pressure on vertical planes was used in plotting the recorded pressure for both positions. Since there is no cell for recording lateral horizontal pressure on the center line, a straight line was used to connect the readings 4 ft to the left and 4 ft to the right of the center line.

Fig. 12 shows curves of theoretical and recorded maximum shears vs tie loads on five ties for 1950, 1951, and 1952 runs. Readings from the clusters of 3 cells 4 ft to the right and 4 ft to the left of the track center line supplied sufficient information from which the maximum shears at these positions could be computed. Theoretical maximum shear values 8 ft off the track center line are considerably less than theoretical maximum shears 4 ft off the center line. The pressure cell clusters 8 ft to the left and right of the track center line are not complete enough to permit the calculation of shears from pressure cell readings at these positions. Theoretical maximum shears were computed using the elastic theory with a Poisson's ratio of 0.5. The 1951 and 1952 results were again quite similar. A wide variation between theoretical maximum shears and shears computed from pressure cell readings still exists.

Summary of Conclusions

The results of the 1952 readings are in very close accord with the 1951 results. Recorded vertical pressures are in fairly close agreement with theoretical vertical pressures, but considerable divergence exists between theoretical maximum shear values and recorded maximum shear values.

From a complete analysis of all the data on this pressure cell installation it appears that the elastic theory can be used satisfactorily for computing vertical stresses. It would appear, however, that the elastic theory does not give sufficient accuracy for predicting lateral pressure intensities and shearing stresses in earth masses.

The 1952 readings give additional evidence that steam powered locomotives produce higher pressure intensities than diesel locomotives produce, and that the pressure increase is in greater proportion than the corresponding increase in axle loads. As further evidence of the above, reports have been received that some troublesome sections of roadbed have shown appreciable improvement when diesel power was substituted for steam.

Grout stabilization decreases the subgrade pressure intensities somewhat, but this effect seems to be most pronounced immediately after treatment. The amount of decrease is relatively small and does not appear to explain the excellent results attributed to pressure grouting. Other hypotheses, such as increase of internal friction along potential sliding planes, sealing of shrinkage cracks, waterproofing action, and increase of density, would seem to be of greater consequence.

Apparently the pressure cells are registering pressures and variation in pressure faithfully, showing impact and vibratory effects of traffic in detail.

This will be the last report on this particular pressure cell installation. Another more extensive and more complete installation is proposed for the near future.

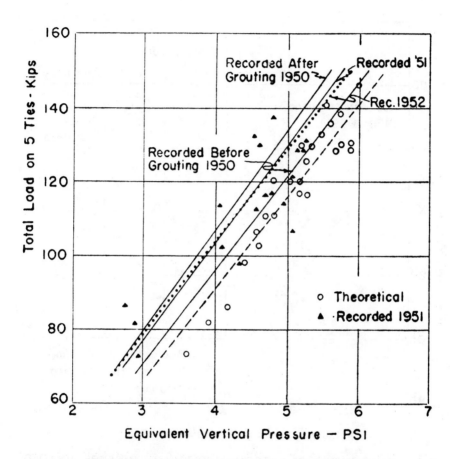

FIG. I — RELATIONSHIP OF VERTICAL PRESSURE TO LOAD

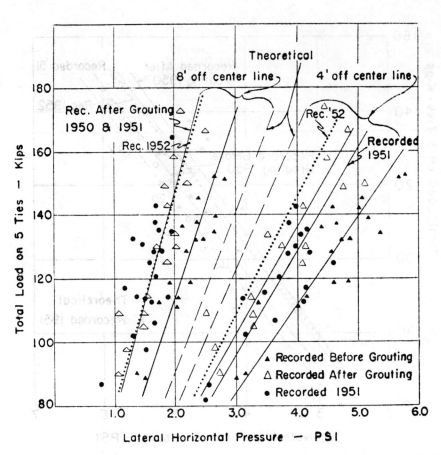

FIG.2 - RELATIONSHIP OF LATERAL HORIZONTAL PRESSURE TO LOAD

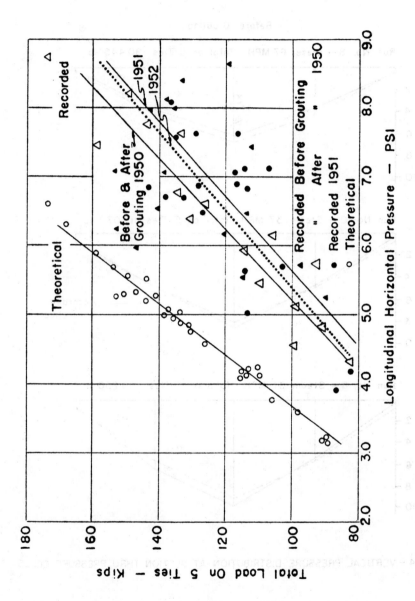

FIG. 3 – RELATIONSHIP OF LONGITUDINAL HORIZONTAL PRESSURE TO LOAD

Before Grouting

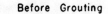

Run No. 8 — Diesel 67 MPH Total on 5 Ties 90 445 lb

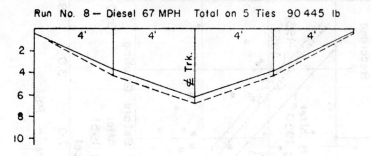

Run No. 10 — Steam 37 MPH Total on 5 Ties 113 070 lb

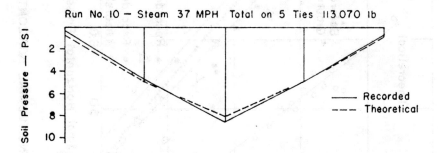

Run No. 6 — Steam 31 MPH Total on 5 Ties 133 250 lb

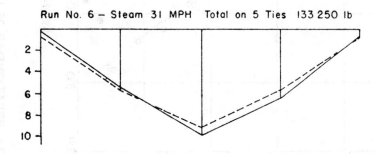

FIG. 4 – VERTICAL PRESSURE DISTRIBUTION AT SECTION THRU PRESSURE CELLS

After Grouting

Run No. 29 — Diesel 70 MPH Total on 5 Ties 81920 lb

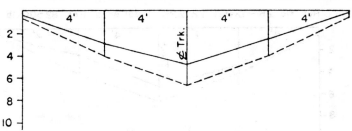

Run No. 32 — Steam 28 MPH Total on 5 Ties 113520 lb

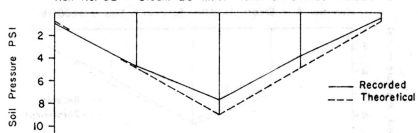

Run No. 36 — Steam 67 MPH Total on 5 Ties 143270 lb

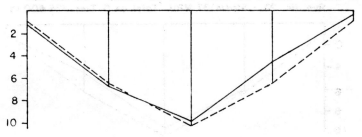

FIG.5 - VERTICAL PRESSURE DISTRIBUTION AT SECTION THRU PRESSURE CELLS

540

1951 RUNS

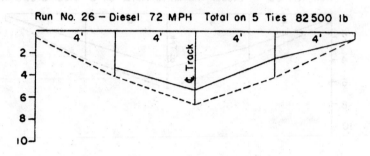

Run No. 26 — Diesel 72 MPH Total on 5 Ties 82 500 lb

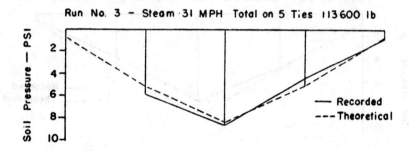

Run No. 3 — Steam 31 MPH Total on 5 Ties 113 600 lb

— Recorded
-- Theoretical

Soil Pressure — PSI

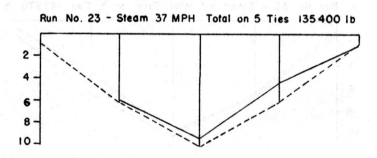

Run No. 23 — Steam 37 MPH Total on 5 Ties 135 400 lb

FIG. 6 — VERTICAL PRESSURE DISTRIBUTION AT SECTION THRU PRESSURE CELLS

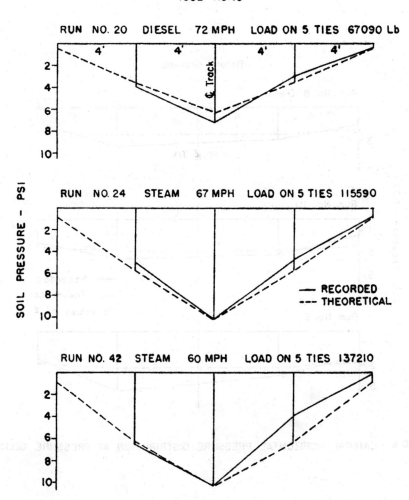

FIG.7 -VERTICAL PRESSURE DISTRIBUTION AT SECTION THRU PRESSURE CELLS

542

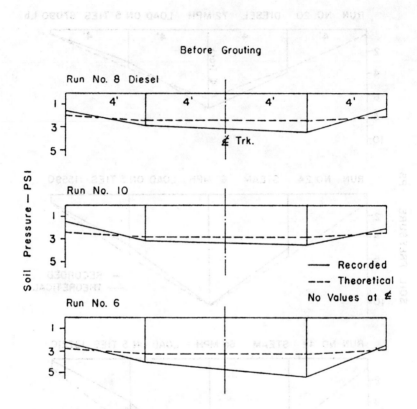

FIG. 8 – LATERAL HORIZONTAL PRESSURE DISTRIBUTION AT PRESSURE CELLS

543

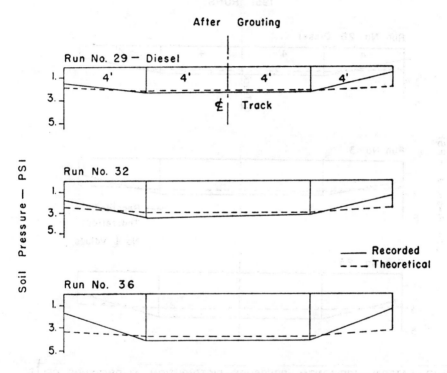

FIG. 9 - LATERAL HORIZONTAL PRESSURE DISTRIBUTION AT PRESSURE CELLS

544

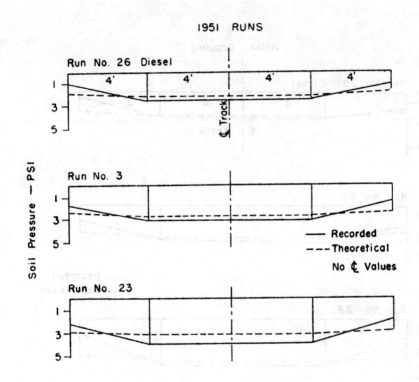

FIG.10 - LATERAL HORIZONTAL PRESSURE DISTRIBUTION AT PRESSURE CELLS

545

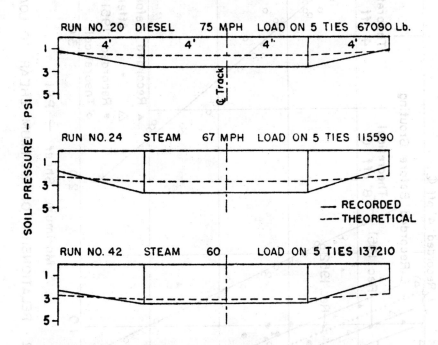

1952 RUNS

RUN NO. 20 DIESEL 75 MPH LOAD ON 5 TIES 67090 Lb.

RUN NO. 24 STEAM 67 MPH LOAD ON 5 TIES 115590

—— RECORDED
--- THEORETICAL

RUN NO. 42 STEAM 60 LOAD ON 5 TIES 137210

SOIL PRESSURE – PSI

FIG.11- LATERAL HORIZONTAL PRESSURE DISTRIBUTION AT PRESSURE CELLS

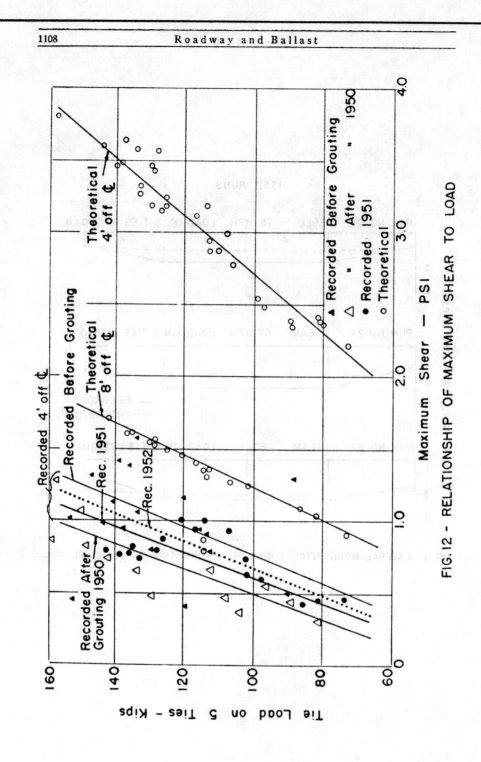

FIG. 12 - RELATIONSHIP OF MAXIMUM SHEAR TO LOAD

Report on Assignment 6

Roadway: Formation and Protection

B. H. Crosland (chairman. subcommittee), J. C. DeJarnette, Jr., R. A. Gravelle, F. W. Hillman, G. W. Payne, C. S. Robinson, F. H. Simpson, C. E. Webb, W. L. Young.

Your committee has been given three subassignments under the general assignment of Roadway formation and protection, namely: 6 (a) Roadbed stabilization; 6 (b) Construction and protection of roadbed across reservoir areas; specifications; and 6 (c) Chemical eradication of vegetation.

Each of the above assignments is studied by a special section of the subcommittee with its own section chairman, and reports on two of them are presented below. Comments and suggestions are particularly invited. It is requested that such comments be addressed to the section chairman.

Report on Assignment 6 (a)

Roadbed Stabilization

F. H. Simpson (chairman section (a)). F. W. Hillman, W. L. Young.

The following report presented as information was prepared by the Engineering Division research staff and is divided into three parts. Part I covers field studies, results and maintenance data for roadbed stabilization. Part II gives the recommended procedures for various types of stabilization and Part III is the report on the laboratory study of stabilization conducted by the University of Illinois.

A few general remarks on Parts I and II follow:

For pressure grouting the results are fully documented by records of savings, that are directly attributable to the treatment, for the years since stabilization. The amount and duration of these savings are usually sufficient to amortize the original cost within four years. These results are sufficiently favorable to place stabilization by grouting beyond the experimental state and in the category of recommended practice.

The first roadbed grouting on railroads was over a short section of the Pennsylvania Railroad near North Point, Md., where a water pocket was stabilized in 1936. This section is now 13 years old and the railroad has reported continued benefits. Limited stabilization by grouting was done on the Pennsylvania and other roads in succeeding years, and in 1941 the New York Central Railroad and the Atchison, Topeka & Santa Fe Railway started extended programs that have continued to the present time. More than 55 roads have used pressure grouting for roadbed stabilization. Each year additional roads use the method for certain of their subgrade problems.

Other methods of stabilization have also been very effective, but to evaluate the results definitely a service record and a knowledge of costs and maintenance savings must be built up. Tie and pole driving has been in use for many years and has generally given good results. However, not all installations have been successful, due to insufficient planning, and further investigation and maintenance cost data are necessary before definite conclusions as to the efficacy of this treatment under various conditions can be established. The records now available to the committee cover a range of conditions that is rather narrow both in geographical and pedological extent, but they do indicate that favorable results are usually obtained by the method over low fills on wet ground.

The sand pile and sand-filled blast hole methods are relatively new in their application to railroad subgrades, and more time and data are necessary for complete evaluation of their efficacy.

It is the hope of the committee that the merits of the various methods of stabilization will ultimately be evaluated so that the most effective and most economical means at a given site can be determined from a survey of fixed conditions.

The report on laboratory tests in Part III is highly interesting. Ballast pockets have been developed under laboratory conditions that bear very close resemblance to those occurring in roadbeds. Further, this report begins to explain the manner in which stabilization by pressure grouting produces results. A continuation of this work may lead to a more complete understanding of the factors involved in stabilization and thus permit many refinements in methods.

Part I. 1950 Report of the Investigation of Roadbed Stabilization

This is the fifth progress report on the investigation of methods and results of stabilization of railroad roadbeds, and has been conducted under sponsorship of Committee 1—Roadway and Ballast, by the Engineering Division research staff in cooperation with the Engineering Experiment Station of the University of Illinois. G. M. Magee, resarch engineer of the Engineering Division, AAR, and Dr. R. B. Peck, research professor of soil mechanics of the university staff, directed the work. Rockwell Smith, roadway engineer, research staff, performed the field work and prepared this portion of the report. Laboratory tests and research and the report on these activities were under the direction of Dr. Peck, assisted by Dr. T. H. Thornburn and H. O. Ireland. also of the university staff.

A.T.& S.F. GROUT TEST SECTIONS
WATER POCKETS AND SOFT TRACK

Location	Date Grouted	Length Section Miles	Mixtures	Cu.Ft. Grout per Lin.Ft. Track	Cost per Tr.Ft.
Thatcher, Colo. MP 595-603 4 locations	5/42 to 9/42	3.4	1/8-1/40	1.42	0.535
Maxwell, N.M. MP 684-685	12/42 to 8/43	1.0	1/4-1/8	1.26	0.68
Dermott, Tex. MP 748-749	2/43	1.0	1/8	1.45	0.56
Maxwell, N.M. MP 682-683	7/43	1.0	1/8	1.05	0.65
Edgerton, Kas. Curve 47	11/43	0.218	1/6	3.17	1.46
Taiban, N.M. MP 704-709	5/44 to 7/44	5.0	1/10	2.18	0.50
Onava-Azul, N.M. MP 761-762	7/45	1.0	1/16	3.95	1.58
Texico, N.M. MP 649-651 Double Trk.	12/45 to 7/46	4.0	1/16	6.21	2.43
#Snyder, Tex. MP 775-776	7/46	1.0	1/32	2.5	0.52

Average of water pocket test sections.................................

Location	Date Grouted	Length Section Miles	Mixtures	Cu.Ft. Grout per Lin.Ft. Track	Cost per Tr.Ft.
#Brenham, Tex. MP 126 plus Sliding embankment	9/46 to 3/47	0.354	1/16	35.14	8.89

#A.R.E.A. designated test sections.
*Includes spotting behind out-of-face resurfacing.

Location	Date Grouted	Length Section Miles	Mixtures	Cu.Ft. Grout per Lin.Ft. Track	Cost per Tr.Ft.
Monroe, Mich.	1941	0.362	1/1	1.25	0.65
Port Clinton, O.	1942	0.555	1/1	1.50	0.90
Canada Division	1943	0.827	1/1	2.77	1.60
(" ") (Welland, Ontario)	1945	1.482	1/1	5.75	2.78
Hillsboro, Ill.	1945	0.615	1/1	4.54	1.07
Corunna, Ind.	1946	0.488	1/1	5.62	2.95

Average of water pocket sections - - - - - - - - - - - - - - - - - -

Location	Date Grouted	Length Section Miles	Mixtures	Cu.Ft. Grout per Lin.Ft. Track	Cost per Tr.Ft.
Bridge 222 Guilford, Ind.	1945	233 feet	1/1	31.8	18.06
M.P. 33.16 Near Weisburg, Ind.	1947	400 feet Double tr.	1/1	15.0	9.60

MAINTENANCE SPOTTING TRACK

Before Grouting Man Hours Per Year Per Mile	After Grouting - Man Hours Per Yr. Per Mi.							Avge Saving Man Hours Per Mile Per Year
	1st year	2nd year	3rd year	4th year	5th year	6th year	Avge.	
7359	4463	2544	3742	2860	2670	2652	3155	4204
3614	1803	1424	846	1169	1218		1292	2322
2952	731	1443	2015	1718	304		1242	1710
2743	2927	1746	555	216	856		1260	1483
6595	1464	2840	3574	2935	2546		2672	3923
1813	321	606	630	798			589	1224
6750	2544	1415	1813				1923	4827
2535	1581	629					1105	1430
806	622	328					475	331
3927	1828	1422	1882	1616	1519		1524	2403

- - - - - - - - -

Sliding Fill

6215	424						424	5791

NEW YORK CENTRAL - GROUT TEST SECTIONS
WATER POCKETS & SOFT TRACK

Dollars per year per mile	Dollars per year per mile							Dollars
7800	245	212	1675	1570	314	311	754	7046
14600	288	862	829	304	0.0	0.0	380	14220
10500	1038	1410	1760	922	1320		1290	9210
6354	994	418	275				562	5792
13365	5760	160	660				2193	11172
5450	0.0	211	0.0				70	5380
9678	1387	546	900	932	545	156	875	8803

Sliding Fills
$ Per year for section grouted

2859.72	31.20	0.0	12.96				14.72	2845
228	0.0	0.0					0.0	228

Railroad and Location	Year	Length of Section Reported Feet	Grout Acceptance cu.ft. per tr. ft.	Cement	Sand	Fly-Ash	Gal. Asphalt
TABLE NO. 2 -- GROUTING AND MAINTENANCE DATA				Grout Mixture Cu. Ft.			
AT&SF - Santa Fe							
See Table No. 1							
Baltimore & Ohio							
Baltimore E.E. & Toledo Divs.	1946	13,191	5.92	1	14	-	-
				1	10		
					14	1	1,240 ft.
Baltimore E.E. Akron,St.L. Divs.	1947	31,619	4.40	1	7,8,14	-	-
" " " " " "	1948	23,204	4.98	1	7,12,16	Used on some portions.	
Canadian National							
Stevensville, Ont.	1945	(1,232)	2.01	1	1.5	-	-
		(520)	1.67	1	1	-	-
M.P. 58.7 Cayuga Subdivn.	1949	2,142	4.4	1	2	-	-
				1	7	1	-
CB&Q - Burlington							
M.P. 123.19 Beardstown, Ill.	1946	269	14.58	1	7	1/2	2/3
Alliance Div. M.P.438-439.2	1946	6,336	7.85	1	7	1/2	2/3
" " " 458.8-459.05	1947	1,320	5.76	1	7	1/2	2/3
St. Joseph " 129.5-130.04	1947	2,884	5.23	1	4		
Chicago & North Western							
Near Mondamin, Ia.	1945	10,560	4.2	1	7	-	1
" Council Bluffs, Ia.	1946	12,500	4.1	1	7	-	1
" Clinton, Ia.	1946	325	27.9	1	3	-	0.5
" Salix, Ia.	1947	6,500	4.0	1	7	-	1.5
CMStP&P - Milwaukee							
Near Owega, Ia.	1945	16,297	1.65	1	4	-	-
Delaware & Hudson							
Whitehall, N.Y.	1947	(524)	2.00	1	1 1/2	-	-
		(335)	4.78	1	1 1/2	-	-
Smith's Basin, N.Y.	1948	2,841	3.60	1	1 1/3	-	-
Great Northern							
Near Glasgow, Mont.	1946-47	8,012	4.51	1	6	-	1
" Fargo, N. Dak.	1947	10,545	5.36	1	5		1
" Wahpeton, N. Dak.	1947	19,701	2.65	1	5		2
" " " "	1948	10,880	4.34	1	5		2
" Noyes, Minn.	1948	815	45.88	1	5		1 1/2
Illinois Central							
Robb, Ill. Tunnel No. 2	1945	3,215	1.90	Cement only			-
Chicago Terminal	1944	80	13.90	1	4	1	-
Carbondale, Ill., Yard	1946	3,577	1.48	1	7	1	-
Near Bluford, Ill.	1947	1,521	23.30	1	7	1	-
Louisville & Nashville							
Duckers, Ky. M.P. 74	1947	400	3.6	1	2	-	-
" " " "	1948	600	6.03	1	2	-	-
Ravenna, Ky. M.P. 232	1948	1,156	3.76	1	2 1/2	-	-
Pennsylvania							
North Point, Md.	1936	75	Av. for Western Region	-	-	Pulv. Limestone	
Ft. Wayne, Ind. Div.	1945	137	1.29	1	-	2	-
Toledo, Ohio Div.	1945	7,300	1.29	1	-	2	-
Chicago Terminal	1945	2,388	1.29	1	-	2	-
Bedford, Ohio	1946-47	6,416	5.02	1	1	2	-
Wheeling & Lake Erie							
Near Baltic, Ohio M.P. 100	1948	600	38.48	1	2	-	-
" " " M.P. 99.56	1949	429	42.69	1	2	-	-
" " " M.P. 99.31	1949	147	12.27	1	2	-	-
New York Central System							
See Table 1.							
MStP&SSM - Soo Line							
Near Borea, Wis.	1946	4313	2.01	1	5.2	-	-
	1947	11468	1.92	1	6.7	-	-
	1948	24006	1.08	1	5.8	-	-
Virginian - Westgate, Va.	1949	540	26.8	1	4	-	-

Character of Track Ballast Type & Type Instability Max Cut & Fill	Dollar Total	Cost of tr.ft.	Grouting cu.ft.
Crushed stone, soft track, unstable fills. Cinders, squeezes, ballast pockets.	35,491	2.69	0.455
Crushed stone, slag, soft track. Unstable fills.	59,472	1.88	0.426
" " " " " "	61,375	2.64	0.531
Crushed stone & gravel. 10' max fill.	2,895		(1.14)
	1,118		(1.29)
Crushed rock - side slips.	6,030	2.82	0.64
4' to 12' fill.			
Cinders - 50' sliding fill.	1,662	6.18	0.42
Crushed rock. Unstable low fill,heavy clay	13,939	2.20	0.28
" " " " " "	3,379	2.56	0.44
Chatt - Unstable low fill, heavy clay.	7,441	2.58	0.49
Cinders - Unstable 7' fill.	16,790	1.59	0.39
Cr. stone, gravel, cinders. Unstable 10' fill	23,625	1.99	0.46
Cr. stone & cinders. Sliding 30' fill.	5,206	16.02	0.43
Cinders, soft track, unstable 4' fills.	-	-	-
Gravel, cinders - pocketed Tr. 6' fill.	22,164	1.36	0.83
Stone ballast on timber mat on wet clay.	1,593	3.04	(1.52)
" " " " " " "	2,312	6.93	(1.45)
" " ,pockets, 6' cut to 10' fill.	9,517	3.35	0.93
Gravel, pockets & splitting 10' fills.	13,561	1.73	0.44
" , soft track, 4' fills.	19,824	1.88	0.35
" " " " "	22,065	1.12	0.36
" " " " "	13,056	1.20	0.28
" , pockets & slipping 12' fill.	14,662	17.99	0.39
Crushed rock, tunnel, mud boils	13,085	4.07	2.13
" " soft track dbl.slip switch.	674	8.42	0.61
Cinders, squeezes, soft track.	1,359	0.36	0.26
Crushed slag, cinders, sliding fill.	12,442	8.18	0.35
Limestone	1,292	3.23	0.90
"	3,348	5.58	0.92
Cinders	2,682	2.32	0.62
Water pocket.	700	9.33	-
		Average for Western Region	
Crushed stone, settlement.	166	1.36	1.044
Gravel "	9,928	1.36	1.044
" "	3,248	1.36	1.044
Crushed stone, soft track, 20' cut.	15,938	2.64	0.53
Slag on cinders, sliding 40'-50' fill.	13,512	22.52	0.586
" " " " 30'-40' "	9,592	22.36	0.524
" " " " 5'-10' "	989	6.73	0.548
Pit run gravel 10' unstable fill.	3321	0.77	0.39
" " " 8-10' " "	7798	0.68	0.36
" " " 2-12' " "	12723	0.53	0.49
Cinders, cr.stone. Sliding 65' fill.	8,040	14.89	0.555

Maintenance Data Before Grouting Man Hrs. per Year	After	Savings Man Hrs. Per Year	Percent	Period of Record Yrs. Before	After	Remarks Grouting Equipment & Type of Work
11,042	5,160	5,882	53	1	1	Hydraulic, track & fill.
38,910	12,672	26,238	68	1	1	" " "
-	-	-	-	-	-	" " "
3,440	541	2,899	84	1	4	Pneumatic, track only.
Eliminates shims						
4,800	Est.600	4,200	87	5	3 mos.	" track & fill.
$2,107.28	$ 5.75	$2,101.53	99	1	2	Hydraulic, track & fill.
$2,366.00	$ 16.76	$2,349.24	99	1	2	" " "
$2,867.80	0.0	$2,867.80	100	1	2	" " "
$2,671.44	0.0	$2,671.44	100	1	2	Pneumatic, track only.
5,608	1,456	4,152	74	1	4	Hydraulic, track only.
2,085	448	1,637	78	6 mos.	3	Hydraulic & pneu.track only.Welded rail.
2,545	290	2,255	88	1	3	Hydraulic, track & fill.
3,360	1,805	1,555	46	1	2	" " "
$2,370.	$632.	$1,738	73	1	3	Contract pneumatic, track only.
1,129	0.0	1,129	100	1	2	Pneumatic over mat.
						" under "
2,366	0.0	2,366	100	1	1	" track only.
11,930	364	11,566	97	1	2	Pneumatic track & fill.
1570 c.y. bal. None						
15,015	3,350	8,315	55	1	2	" track only.
800 c.y. bal. 25 c.y.bal.						
15,128	2,188	11,052	72	1	2	" " "
5800 c.y. bal. None						
10,680	1,280	9,400	88	1	1	" " "
1500 c.y. bal. None						
3,448	0.0	3,448	100	1	1	" track & fill.
350 c.y. bal. None						
6,192	446	5,746	93	1	4 1/2	Hydraulic on track equipment.
100	20	80	80	1	5	Pneumatic, track only, fill ground.
2,178	120	2,058	94	1	3	Hydraulic on track equipment.
1,248	120	1,128	90	1	2	" track & fill.
$1,136.	$ 11.00	$1,125	99	1	2	Hydraulic.
$4,543.	$ 33.33	$4,510	99	1	1 1/2	"
$1,762.	$184.00	$1,578	89	1	1 1/4	
		1,400	-	1	13	
1,415	410	1,005	71	2 1/6	2 1/6	Hydraulic
12,350	715	11,635	94	2 1/4	2 1/4	"
4,410	779	3,631	82	2	2	"
2,431	416	2,015	83	1	3	
$3,000.	0.0	$3,000	100	1	1	Pneumatic fill grouting.
-	-	-	-	-	-	" " "
-	-	-	-	-	-	
$1169	$325	$844	72	8 mos.	3	Pneumatic, track only.
$2478	$656	$1822	73	2	2	" " "
$2779	$710	$2069	74	3	1	
8,500	-	-				Pneumatic, track & fill.

Field Studies and Results of Roadbed Stabilization

General

The investigation in 1949 included a study of the different methods and the costs of roadbed stabilization now in use, namely pressure grouting, tie and pole driving, sand piles and sand-filled blast holes. Grouting and maintenance costs prior to and following such stabilization have been tabulated and appear in Tables 1 and 2. These will be discussed in a following section.

Similar cost data for the other methods have not been obtained but arrangements have been made to secure some information of this type in 1950.

In the field work this year, considerable attention has been given to analyzing the underlying causes of instability in order to prescribe the most effective and most economical treatment. However until maintenance data for methods other than grouting have accumulated only general terms can be used in evaluating the conditions best suited for a particular type of stabilization. Part II of this report describes typical procedure for all the methods in current use and indicates those physical features of unstable track most likely to react favorably to a particular procedure.

Cost Data

The cost data in Table 1 for the Santa Fe and the New York Central show the results obtained for periods up to six years after grouting. There is no apparent trend toward increased maintenance cost with increased years of service. The results are very favorable, the savings in yearly maintenance are as a rule over 70 percent, and the cost of the work is generally amortized within a four year period.

Table 2 shows the record of grouting projects up to 4½ years old on 12 railroads. The lowest saving in percentage of the pregrouting maintenance cost is 46. Many of these projects return the cost of stabilization within 3 years. This is especially true of water pocket and soft track stabilization.

Sliding fills as a rule show a much greater acceptance of grout and a corresponding increase of original cost. Several, however, such as the Great Northern fill near Noyes, Minn., and the Wheeling & Lake Erie fill near Baltic, Ohio, both with very high acceptance, show sufficient maintenance savings to amortize the cost within five years.

It is difficult to conceive of any other maintenance expenditure that will yield returns equal to those of the dollar spent in judicious stabilization.

Permanence of the stabilization still deserves consideration, but records of 4, 6 and, in one case on the Pennsylvania, 13 years indicate that such stabilization is of long duration. The only known project that has ceased to remain stable is on the Pennsylvania, near Fort Wayne, Ind. This project was reported last year as showing continued savings for 10 years. This year it was reported as failing and the section was regrouted. The original cost was $1000 and the annual saving was 360 man-hours.

Fill Stabilization

In this report only two specific projects with several unusual features will be discussed. They are the grouting of a fill at Westgate, Va., on the Virginian Railway and the sand filled blast holes on the Southern Railway near Centralia, Ill.

The Virginian

In 1949 the Virginian stabilized a fill on its lines near Westgate, Va., approximately 20 miles east of Roanoke, that differed from previous fill stabilization in the character of the soils involved. Most of this type of work that has come to the attention of this investigation has been in clay soils of medium to high plasticity. The soils in the Westgate fill, on the basis of grain size, would be classified as silty sands, but their action under load is unusual.

Along the slopes of the Appalachian mountains and auxiliary ranges, the soils have largely been developed from decomposed schists and granites. Subsequent weathering has produced a reddish soil consisting of a sandy topsoil and a second horizon clay of low plasticity. The subsoil, however, is a light, fluffy, highly micaceous material. It is slightly plastic to nonplastic, but is very elastic so that it rebounds upon removal of loads. Compaction of the material is difficult, and the compacted material has a tendency to swell.

The Westgate fill, a section of high maintenance costs for years, was constructed of material of this type. The fill ¼ mile to the west, of comparable height and slope, was construction from the upper horizons of slightly plastic clay and has shown no indication of instability such as has been recorded for the Westgate fill.

The fill, about 40 years old, is approximately 65 ft. in height and runs across a narrow valley for about 400 ft. The valley floor has a slope to the north, of three to four percent, and especially in wet weather the track would go out of cross level, and maintenance was required two or three times weekly. The instability was further evidenced by bulging slopes. A speed restriction of 12 mph. was in effect.

The grouting procedure was typical for fills of these characteristics. Injections along each slope with holes on a gridwork about 10 ft. apart were followed by injections from the top of the grade. Pneumatic pressure with a mix of 1 part cement to 4 parts sand was used. Acceptance, costs and estimated savings are listed in Table 2. Fig. 1 shows a view during grouting.

Experience in the six months since grouting has indicated excellent results. Eight inches of rain in one week in mid-July produced no reaction in the fill, whereas records for previous years, showed that continual maintenance was required during and after such wet periods. In addition to the direct and assessable savings in maintenance costs

Fig. 1.—Grouting Operation on the Westgate Fill.

there is an appreciable saving in operational costs by the removal of speed restrictions from a track carrying 16 million gross tons annually. Fig. 2 shows the completed fill.

The Southern

Between M. P. 69 and M. P. 77 near Centralia, Ill., on the Louisville–St. Louis division, the Southern Railway has stabilized approximately 5000 track feet this year by means of sand filled blast holes. This work was done on short sections of track where pushes and squeezes were common, usually in cuts but on some fills less than four feet in height. A general description of the method is given in Part II of this report. Fig. 3 shows a view of typical conditions.

The line through this territory is a single track over rolling country with alternate cuts and fills. The soils are clay tills of medium to high plasticity susceptible to the development of pockets in the subgrade. The ballast is fine chatt. Ballast pockets have a depth of three to four feet and contain free water.

For one section observed the filling required an average of 11 cu. ft. of dry loose sand per hole. Where both sides of the track are treated, this is equivalent to 16.5 cu. ft. of sand per track foot. This amount of sand introduced into a clay subgrade should be of considerable benefit and the service record to date so indicates.

There is no evidence at present that this sand becomes an intimate mixture with the clay. Samples of the clay taken before sand filling and within 9 in. of a sand filled hole had almost identical gradation. The field moisture was, however, somewhat lower after the filling. This may be a result of the blasting and is, of course, of value in producing increased stability. No knowledge of the disposal of the excess moisture has been obtained, but it is possibly dispersed into the subgrade and ballast by concussion.

The stabilization in this territory has cost approximately $3 per track foot where both sides of the track were treated. No record is as yet available as to the amount of maintenance savings, but supervisory officials are unanimous in declaring that the stabilization has corrected soft track and squeezes for the sections treated.

In 1947 to 1949, incl., the Southern also treated with the sand blast method considerable trackage between Alexandria and Culpepper, Va., in double-track territory. This work has usually been performed on low fills, although one fill 15 ft. high and part of one cut 18 ft. deep were included.

The procedure in this area was very similar to that described in Part II of this report, but it varied in several respects. A two-inch pipe spud was driven with air hammers replacing the earth auger. On the higher fills, after the first blast a second charge of dynamite was placed and the hole filled with sand. This charge was then set off and the hole again filled. Also, on fill work, an additional hole was blasted near the shoulder every 15 to 20 ft. where it would form an opening for drainage to the side. This, of course, was not possible in cuts and reliance was placed on vertical drainage.

The soils in this area consist of a sandy topsoil underlain by a shaly red clay which tends to retard downward percolation of water. The fills are composed principally of clay of medium to high plasticity. Apparently the shaly clay stratum is lubricated and weakened by ground water and the fills are moving in this zone. In treatment the blasts are made below or, in this layer, to roughen it and key the fill to the ground. The results have been very satisfactory, although as yet no definite figures are available as to the amount of maintenance savings. The cost of the work is about $3 to $3.50 per embankment foot where both sides of the tracks are treated.

Fig. 2.—Appearance of the Fill After Completion of the Grouting.

Fig. 3.—Track of Southern Railway Near Centralia, Ill.

Part II. Suggested Procedure For Roadbed Stabilization

General

The following discussion may serve as a general guide to the primary considerations and practices involved in roadbed stabilization. It is not intended to replace the practices evolved by various roads in the light of their experience. It is rather a résumé of the various procedures which have been successful. These procedures include pressure grouting, tie and pole driving, sand-filled spud holes and sand-filled blast holes.

Preliminary Investigation

Before stabilization is undertaken, it is essential to make an investigation of the conditions involved. Instability can be caused by a number of different factors, singly or in combination, and may be evidenced in a variety of ways. The purpose of the investigation or survey is to determine the type and depth of the instability, the soil and moisture conditions, and from these the most effective and economical method of correction. A tabulation of the more common types of instability and a brief discussion of each follow:

1. *Water or Ballast Pockets.*—These are indicated by squeezes or push-ups beyond the ends of the tie. They result in soft track, requiring excessive expenditures to maintain line and surface. Ballast pockets occur in the more plastic soils. They may attain a depth of over 10 ft. and on fills may develop into slope failures. Their presence and character are well known to all maintenance men. The investigation should include the determination of the extent and depth of the pockets, the type of soil in the subgrade, and the amount of water present.

2. *Slides.*—For this purpose slides may be classified into three general categories:

(a) *Slope failures resulting from a failure of the soil in shear.* In perfectly homogenous clays the sliding occurs along a nearly circular path (Fig. 4.). Since few railroad embankments are even approximately uniform in strength or composition, most slope failures have only a rough similarity to the ideal type shown in the figure.

(b) *Sliding failure along a lubricated surface.* Fig. 5 shows a diagrammatic sketch of an actual condition illustrating this type of failure. This condition is most often encountered on side hill fills or cut and fill sections. The plane of sliding is often lubricated by seepage or water from the fill. This type of failure is often combined with slope failures.

(c) *Foundation failures.* Where the weight of the fill overstresses the foundation this type of failure occurs. It is manifested in several ways. The least serious is a more or less vertical subsidence due to the consolidation of the underlying foundation by the weight of the fill. The movement is slow and is not a problem in embankments of railroads in service for a number of years. A more serious condition is encountered where the underlying material is displaced laterally. This can occur steadily or intermittently over many years. It is manifested by heaving of the ground surface beyond the toes of the fill. Fig. 6 is an idealized sketch of a foundation failure. Such failures are most common in swamps but soft clay can cause a similar condition. and for this material the instability is often of long duration. The slope, height, depth of weak subsoil, and of fill and subsoil are the principal determining factors in speed and duration of movements.

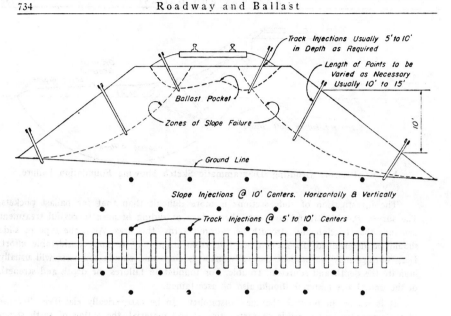

Fig. 4.—Pressure Grouting. Typical Injection Plan for Fill Slope Failures.

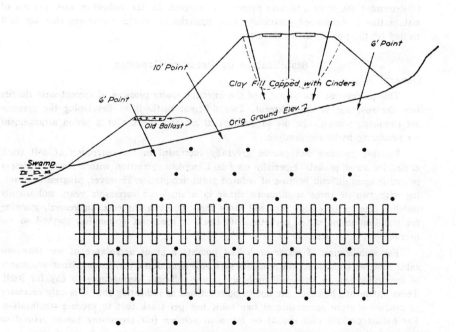

Fig. 5.—Pressure Grouting. Fill Sliding on Foundation and Typical Injection Plan.

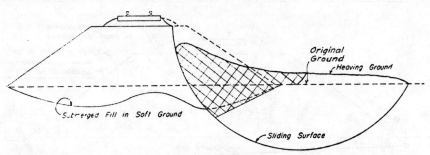

Fig. 6.—Pressure Grouting. Diagrammatic Sketch Showing Foundation Failure.

The investigation of slide sections is more difficult than that for ballast pockets. The survey should attempt to locate the surface of sliding because successful treatment demands that friction and strength be restored across this area. Also, the type of slide should be determined. In some cases full exploration may require considerable effort. Deep borings may be needed. Carefully made borings and simple soil tests will usually indicate the depth and source of trouble. For foundation failures the depth and strength of the underlying material should also be ascertained.

It is seldom in practice that any instability can be categorically classified. Because of the uncertain and variable characteristics of soil material, the action of earth structures does not conform to ideal analyses based on perfectly plastic material, having uniform characteristics.

The above discussion applies for any method of stabilization proposed. It may help to determine the most adequate process to be used. In the following, each process of stabilization is considered separately, with remarks as to the conditions that are best treated by the process under discussion.

Stabilization by Pressure Grouting

General

This process consists basically of the injection under pressure of cement-sand slurries into the subgrade or embankment. Two different methods of developing the pressure are common; namely, the use of compressed air and the use of a piston arrangement for producing hydraulic pressure.

Pressure grouting has proved generally successful in the correction of soft track caused by water pockets, especially on fills. Complete correction with a single treatment in cuts is more difficult because of reduced grout acceptance. However, progressive grouting with two or three applications either in a single or successive years will usually stabilize cuts to an extent that will more than amortize the cost. In general, grouting for stabilization of water pocketed soft track is the most economical method so far devised.

For stabilization of water or ballast pockets a grout acceptance of less than one cubic foot per track foot will probably give only temporary correction. Grout acceptance of two cubic feet or over will probably insure sufficient permanence to pay for itself. These statements, however, are not to be construed as indicating that it is only necessary to produce a grout acceptance of two cubic feet per track foot to procure stabilization. For ballast pockets care should be taken to achieve full acceptance before refusal or breakout.

Ballast Pockets

1. *Equipment.*—Basic equipment required for pneumatic grouting consists of a mixer and an injector pressure tank or combination thereof. The tank should be equipped with agitator paddles attached to a power-driven shaft, even if used only for injection purposes, to reduce separation of the grout materials. The tank can be shop fabricated or commercially produced. The usual capacity is approximately five cubic feet of dry material.

For hydraulic pressure grouting, a mud-jack or other machine must be provided to mix the slurry mechanically and supply it to the grout line under pressure through direct piston action.

Injection points of varied lengths, 5 ft. to 10 ft., are adequate for most ballast pocket stabilization. These can be purchased commercially or made in the shops. Heavy duty pipe equipped with couplings to provide variable length can be used. All points must be equipped with suitable heads to withstand driving. The points may be open ended or pointed with openings cut above the point.

Grout line hose is usually 1¼ in. inside diameter of heavy duty quality. Lines and points may be equipped with glad-hand couplings for speed in handling. A length of 200 ft. of hose is usually sufficient.

An air compressor of 105 cu. ft. capacity will be adequate to supply one injector tank and the air hammers. The air hammers should be provided with a special chuck to fit the driving head on the injection points or pipes. Where it is necessary to drive points through coarse ballast, a hammer weighing 50 lb. or more is advisable.

Other tools should include point pullers, wrenches as required and standard small tools. Unless the sand is absolutely free of all oversize particles or lumps, a sand screen is necessary to minimize plugging in the grout lines. This screen may be constructed of ¼-in. mesh screen cloth or slotted cloth. A screen is usually included in hydraulic equipment.

2. *Materials.*—Best results are obtained by the use of a rather fine rounded sand such as dune or beach sand. If possible 100 percent should pass the No. 20 mesh sieve and more than 80 percent the No. 40 sieve. As much as 20 percent passing the No. 200 sieve is permissible if the material is of such character as not to ball up in the mixer. Many local sources of suitable sand are available and the gradation, other than the maximum size, is relatively unimportant. This consideration permits the use of a sand that will be relatively inexpensive. Many roads have developed their own sources. Rather coarse sands can also be used but difficulties with line plugs, etc., tend to develop more readily. Finer gradations will permit the use of less cement if desired. See the Proceedings, Vol. 48, 1947.

Standard portland cement (Type I) is usually used, although good results have been obtained with air entraining cement of similar characteristics (Type IA). It has been reported that the air entraining cement reduces friction and line plugs to some extent. The air entraining qualities are not of value in the grout after injection.

3. *Mixtures.*—The usual mixtures for pneumatic grouting vary from one part cement with one part sand to one part cement with seven parts sand. For hydraulic grouting, mixtures up to one part cement with 32 parts sand have been used. The type and gradation of sand will determine to a large extent the amount of sand that can be used without operational difficulties. Water requirements vary from 3 to 6 gal. per cu. ft. of loose material depending on the amount of moisture in the sand. Fly-ash is often used to supply additional fines to the sand and reduce cement requirements. It is a by-product of steam power plants burning powdered coal and is collected on the electrical precipitators. Pulverized limestone will also serve this purpose.

The proportions of the mix are determined to a large extent by the policy of the road and the purpose and type of grouting. Labor costs are by far the greatest factors in this type of stabilization and savings in cement costs by the use of lean harsh mixtures may be nullified by line plugs or by failure to procure adequate penetration. Where it is desired to penetrate the coarse ballast in the bottom of a deep pocket the richer mixes are often used. Where the pockets are relatively shallow, less than five feet, mixtures of the order of one to four may be more desirable to avoid setting the ties and producing too much cementing strength in the upper ballast. Where acceptance is high, the cement content of the mixture may be reduced without apparent effect on the results obtained.

Certain conditions may arise where a cement-water mixture only is indicated, such as tunnel floors on rock or shale, or in roadbeds where acceptance is low and grout penetration difficult to obtain.

Asphalt emulsion is often used as a lubricant to produce better flow of the grout through the lines and appears to be of considerable value in reducing wear in hydraulic equipment. When asphalt emulsion is used, the amount applied ranges from 0.1 to 0.2 gal. per cu. ft. of dry ingredients.

Note: It has been suggested that the gradation of the solid particles in a grouting slurry should conform to the formula: $p = \dfrac{d}{D}$ where p is the percentage smaller than any grain size d, and D is the maximum size. In grouting slurries where the maximum size corresponds to the No. 20 sieve, (grain size 0.84mm.) this formula requires 71 percent to pass the No. 60 sieve (0.25mm.), 42 percent the No. 100 sieve (0.149mm.), and 30 percent the No. 200 sieve (0.074mm.). This refinement in gradation is not required, but slurries for which the gradation curve approaches that given by the formula are very satisfactory for injection and appear to segregate less readily. For a discussion on slurry mixtures see the Procedings, Vol. 48, 1947, page 492.

4. *Procedure.*—The results of the preliminary investigation will determine the depth of the pockets and the severity of the moisture conditions in the pockets. Injections should be placed accordingly. Common practice is to space injections at 5 to 10 ft., staggered, along each side of the track. The closer spacing is used if there are indications of considerable variation in the depth of the ballast. Fig. 7 shows a typical layout of injection holes diagrammatically.

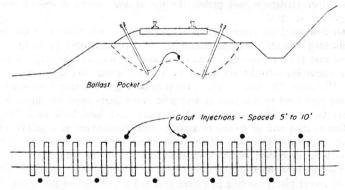

Ballast Pocket

Grout Injections - Spaced 5' to 10'

Fig. 7.—Pressure Grouting. Typical Injection Plan for Ballast Pockets.

Injection points may be driven either vertically between ties and close to the rail or on an inward slope from near the end of the tie so that the injection end is approximately under the rail. In either case care should be taken that the grout will flow out of the point and into the pocket. The point should penetrate through the pocket and a few inches into the subgrade material. A change in driving resistance will usually determine the correct depth if this has not been previously determined for all locations. Pneumatic hammers are used almost exclusively for driving points, although at times the points have been sledge driven. Bull points are sometimes used in ballast sections prior to the insertion of the injection points.

Where open-end points are used the open end should be plugged with a rivet or track bolt held in place with paper wrapping. Prior to grouting, this plug must be rodded out and the point pulled up a few inches. Where closed-end points are used it is necessary to circulate grout or water through the point during driving. Water is usually used as this opens channels for the grout. It is often advisable to inject water through the open-end points after driving, and in cinders and sand it is necessary. Usually 10 to 15 gal. are sufficient to insure grout acceptance.

The grout is mixed in the desired proportions, the line is attached to the injection point and pressure applied. Most compressors are governed at 85 to 100 psi. This pressure is required for efficient operation of the air hammers, but it is too high for most pneumatic grout injection. Some equipment has a reduction valve controlling this pressure at 60 psi. or below. In practice, however, the pressure can be controlled by hand operation of the air intake on the injector sufficiently to eliminate the bad features of too much pressure. In most cases the flow of the grout and the sweep of the agitator paddles in the tank keep the pressure at the injection point actually below that in the compressor storage tank. High pressures tend to segregate the slurry constituents and to hump the track before grout penetration is complete. In all cases, however, the air should be shut off before it penetrates into the hole. The completion of injection for a batch can be determined by holding the hose at its union with the injection point. The flow of the last of the slurry followed by air will cause a considerable jump in the hose apparent to the touch of the hand.

The pressure for hydraulic grouting is a function of the equipment. It is pulsating and may be much higher than in pneumatic grouting. Other details of procedure are identical for the pneumatic and hydraulic processes.

Injection is continued in any one hole until the grout breaks out or the track is raised objectionably, possibly $\frac{1}{2}$ in. or less. The hose line is moved to an adjacent point and the process repeated. In pneumatic equipment an arrangement of two tanks, one above the other with gravity flow between, controlled by suitable valves, permits mixing to proceed simultaneously with injection. This arrangement eliminates most of the delay between batches and the addition of one or two men to the crew will raise daily production by approximately 50 percent. In hydraulic equipment, mixing and injections can usually proceed simultaneously.

Injection joints should be pulled soon after they have been used. All equipment should be washed thoroughly at the end of the day's work and at any interruption at any time. It is also advisable to provide fittings so that the grout hose can be attached directly to the air supply. This will facilitate cleaning if the line becomes plugged.

In grouting a section of soft track the injections should be continued at least one rail length beyond the confines of the unstable section. Confining the stabilization to the exact limits will often cause a soft section to develop at the end. Even with very little grout acceptance the length extended will serve as a run-off or transition zone. After grouting, the track usually requires a clean-up to eliminate grout in the top ballast, and a general spotting to smooth out any irregularities produced by the grout under pressure.

Fills

1. *Equipment.*—Same as for ballast pockets.

2. *Sand.*—Same as for ballast pockets.

3. *Mixtures.*—Considerations set forth for slurries for ballast pocket injections apply also for fill stabilization.

4. *Procedure.*—It is the usual practice on sliding fills to grout the slopes, starting at the bottom or part way up the slope, so that the first injections will occur in the vicinity of original ground or in the area that the preliminary investigation has shown is the surface of failure. The length of injection points is adjusted to reach the desired depth. In this scheme of stabilization, 15-ft. points are usually the longest required, and often 10 or 12 ft. will be sufficient. Injections spaced at 10-ft. intervals longitudinally and at 10 ft. vertically in a grid pattern will usually be sufficient but if needed, additional injections may be made. Figs. 4 and 5 show suggested layouts diagrammatically. Most sliding fills are weaker on one side and where this is apparent, injections on the more stable slope can be reduced below the normal pattern. Injections along the track are usually made last. It is often possible to reach the failure zone or zones from the top of the roadbed by the use of sectionalized injection pipes driven to the required depth, and in some cases this may be the best method. However, it appears that 20 ft. is about the practical and economical limit, beyond which the cost and uncertainty of driving and pulling will favor slope injections on most projects.

In driving injection points through the ballast bull points are sometimes used to a depth up to five feet. The point then is pulled and the injection point inserted and driven by the air hammer to the required depth. Water or grout is forced through the points during driving if pointed-end pipes are used. Bolt or rivet-plugged, open-end pipes must be rodded out prior to injection. In fill stabilization, driving the points while forcing grout or water through them has much to recommend it. Areas of acceptance can be detected in which it is of value to permit grout penetration even if not at the predetermined depth. As mentioned previously, injection of water prior to grout is a requirement where the point penetrates cinders or fine sand.

Grouting is continued through a point until it breaks or until it raises the track, except where acceptance is extremely high and there is reason to suspect that the grout is escaping unseen. In these areas an arbitrary limit such as 150 cu. ft. may be placed on the acceptance. After this limit has been reached, injection is stopped and grouting transferred to another point. After a suitable interval of one day or longer, grouting may again be tried at the location of high acceptance.

There are no data to show how much of the grout pumped into a fill is of value in the stabilization. There are some indications that complete and full acceptance is not required. These indications have been obtained from sections where the acceptance has been limited to a given amount short of break-out. They apply only to areas of very high requirements, such as fills of broken rock, etc. Where acceptance averages five percent or less of the theoretical volume of the fill, it is doubtful if limitation of grout acceptance should be specified except for individual injections. Thickening of the slurry may also be advisable in areas of high acceptance.

Piling

See Manual, pages 66.081–66.084.

Pole Driving

General

What is known as tie and pole driving consists of the driving ties or poles 8 to 20 ft. in length vertically along the track closely adjacent to the ends of the cross ties. Cull or unusable second-hand ties are often driven where 8 ft. lengths are indicated. See Fig. 8.

This method has been used extensively and with good results in the southwest on low fills over wet or swampy ground. In general, a height of fill of 6 ft. is the practical limit for this treatment, but some success has been attained in fills up to 10 ft. in height. Water pockets in cuts will also usually yield to correction by this method. Five-foot poles or ties have been used in cuts, but the results from the few installations observed have not been satisfactory. A general rule of thumb somewhat borne out by observations is to provide sufficient length of tie or pole so that at least 50 percent of the length will penetrate below the zone or zones of instability.

The factors tending to increase stability in this method probably include the additional strength of the soil structure accompanying the increase in density due to the driving, the containing influence of the poles, the direct support provided by the members acting as piles, and possibly vertical drainage. Preliminary investigation should disclose the conditions of instability, and the treatment should be designed as far as possible to take advantage of the above factors.

Savings effected by the pole treatment have not in general been a matter of record so there are no means of direct assessment of the value of the treatment. For one project, however, the costs of pole driving and of grouting on very similar sections were practically the same and the results were equivalent.

2. *Equipment.*—The principal item of equipment is a pole driver. Regular on-track pile drivers may be used, but for any extensive work with lengths up to 15 ft. a tractor equipped with suitable leads and a drop hammer will prove profitable. Small on-track drivers may also be used and a special on-track machine equipped with two leads has been used but is not commercially available.

3. *Materials.*—Cull ties may be used, as may be reclaimed ties if they retain sufficient strength to stand driving. Where available unpeeled poles of six inches minimum diameter are often economical.

4. *Procedure.*—The poles and ties are driven at about one foot beyond the end of each cross tie and to a depth approximately six inches below the top of the cross tie. See Fig. 8. Some raising of the track may result from the driving, and adequate run offs or a general surfacing must be made. Conditions of the section to be treated and preliminary investigations will determine if vertical ties or poles are needed on one or both sides of the track.

Sand-Filled Spud Holes

1. *General.*—This method of stabilization embraces the driving of a spud into the subgrade adjacent to and between the rails, removing the spud, and filling the hole with sand. See Fig. 9. The depth of treatment is limited to the depth from which the spud can be readily extracted, up to 10 ft. but usually less than 6 ft. This type of stabilization can be called sand piles. The success of the treatment apparently depends on the supporting power of the piles, plus the additional soil strength obtained through the consolidation of the subgrade and, in some cases, through vertical drainage. There may also be some modification of the soil characteristics by combination with the sand, but this has not as yet been established.

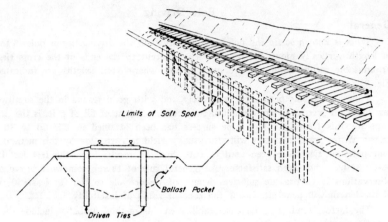

Fig. 8.—Tie and Pole Driving. Typical Treatment for Soft Track.

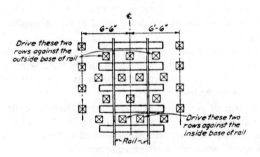

20 PERCENT MIXTURE

☒ = Holes shown thus – 12" x 12" bridge timber used in driving holes.

Fig. 9.—Sand Piles. Typical Treatment for Soft Track.

2. *Equipment.*—An on-track pile driver has been used commonly, but off-track or light weight on-track equipment could be developed for extensive work. Provision must be made for the stability against overturning required in pulling the spud. The spuds are usually butt ends of piles with diameters of 12 in. or greater, or 12-in. by 12-in. bridge timbers.

3. *Sand.*—The sand should be clean and sharp. Engine sand or concrete sand is usually suitable.

4. *Procedure.*—Preliminary investigations will disclose the depth of the pockets and these pockets must be penetrated by the spud hole. The severity of the instability will determine the degree of treatment. Fig. 9 shows the plan of the spud holes for what is called the 20-percent treatment. This treatment is usually sufficient for most soft track conditions caused by water pockets.

The spud is driven to the required depth and retracted. It is common practice to drive the spud to the depth from which it can be extracted by a direct pull on the line. This depth soon becomes apparent in the field. The holes are immediately filled with

567

Roadway and Ballast

Fig. 10.—An Earth Auger in Operation.

sand by hand with shovels or buckets. By staggering the order of driving, both driving and filling can be done at the same time. At times the spud has been used to compact the sand in the hole after filling.

The sand-pile treatment will raise the track, possibly up to four inches. Provision must be made for run-offs and adequate protection for traffic at all times.

Sand-Filled Blast Holes

1. *General.*—A recent modification of the sand-pile method is the sand-filled blast hole. In this process a two or three-inch spud or auger hole replaces the large spud. A charge of dynamite then blasts a cavity which is filled with sand forced in by compressed air. Each hole is blasted and filled before the next one has been blown. This method has been successful in cut sections and on fills up to 15 ft. in height where the slippage has occurred on a stratum below original ground. The performance record, although very good, is limited to one railroad. Until further investigation, use of the method should be limited to water pockets in cuts and low fills and to failures or slips on the foundation of higher fills. It should be used cautiously if at all on fills founded on slopes. There is also some question as to whether its use in areas of deep frost penetration will prove sufficiently permanent to amortize the cost. Sections now in service, however, have been very successful over a two-year period. The process gives promise of yielding good results for certain conditions of instability.

2. *Equipment.*—A metal spud of approximately three inches in diameter may be driven to produce the hole for blasting. However, a power earth auger mounted on wheels and with a frame support to permit drilling at any angle will prove economical.

Fig. 11.—A Sand-Filled Blast Hole Gang at Work. The fogged appearance at the sand tank is due to the dust cloud caused by a blast.

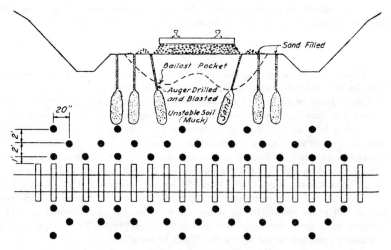

Fig. 12.—Sand-Filled Blast Holes. Typical Treatment for Soft Track in Cuts.

The auger should be equipped with detachable bits of convenient length to permit any depth of drilling. Such equipment is a variation of a quarry wagon drill and is available commercially. Fig. 10 is a view of the earth auger used on one project.

In addition to the auger, a compressor is required to blow the sand into the holes. If the auger is powered by compressed air a compressor capacity greater than 105 cu. ft. per min. will be required for simultaneous operation of the drill and the sand blast. Other equipment required will include a sand blast tank, hoses, a sand drier and blasting apparatus. A sand tank is shown in Fig. 11.

3. *Materials.*—The sand should be coarse and sharp. To flow satisfactorily from the tank through the hose into the cavity it must be completely dried. About 1½ sticks of standard 40-percent dynamite are commonly used, with blasting caps and an electric detonator.

4. *Procedure.*—The severity of the instability will determine the degree of treatment. Fig. 12 shows a typical layout of the blast holes where both sides of the track are treated. For stabilizing water pockets the blast holes should penetrate through the water pocket at least three feet. For the treatment of fills sliding along an underground stratum, the holes should penetrate the stratum by at least one foot. Fig. 11 is a reproduction of a photograph taken during a blast and shows that the surface disturbance is small.

MECHANICAL WEAR OF TIES*

By Hermann von Schrenk

(I) INTRODUCTION

Cross-ties form one of the large expenditures in the construction and maintenance of railway track. In the early days of railway construction and operation, when cross-ties were exceedingly plentiful and cheap, with correspondingly cheap labor, short length of life was not so material a factor as it has become at the present time with high initial cost for the cross-ties, together with high labor costs. Thirty-two years ago in a Government report (Report on the Use of Metal Railroad Ties, etc., by E. E. Russell Tratman, U. S. Department of Agriculture, Division of Forestry, Bulletin 9, page 250, 1894), the average price for cross-ties is given as 30 cents and the cost of laying 10 cents per tie. Compare this with an average price of cross-ties at the present time of $1.50–$2.00 and the cost of laying of 50 cents or more. In those days the early removal of ties was due to three causes:

(1) Decay of the wood,
(2) Mechanical disintegration of the wood fibers under the rail,
(3) Mechanical injuries, due to spiking or to checking, splitting and derailments.

Of these three factors, decay of the wood fiber was the principal one which made a tie unfit for further service. This decay took place principally under the rail and around the fastening, although frequently, of course, the tie as a whole was destroyed by decay. In those days, decay was an important factor in what was then called mechanical wear or mechanical destruction. Destruction of the wood fiber under the rail was almost invariably followed by decay except in such naturally long-lived species of wood as cypress, cedar and redwood.

With the advent of chemically preserved ties, decay, as a factor in causing early removal of ties, became a secondary factor—in other words, the chemical preservation of ties made them far more decay resistant. The degree of protection against decay varied with the preservative used. In late years with the increasing use of creosoted ties, decay has bcome a secondary factor in tie removal, particularly in those cases where ties are treated so as to give maximum penetration with sufficient quantities of a high grade creosote and where such ties have been adzed and bored before treatment.† With the increased efficiency in the inspection of ties before treatment, careful seasoning, adzing and boring, and good treatment, it can probably

---

*Submitted, October 1927.
†The figures for tie removals on the D. L. & W. show this in a striking manner. Since 1910, 5,321,116 creosoted ties have been laid, and up to the end of 1926, 132,200 had been removed. The causes of removal are divided as follows:
Decay or other physical defects............................ 1,987
Mechanical destruction 86.460
Wrecks, derailments and other causes...................... 43,753

be stated without fear of contradiction that instead of the former six to eight year life, we may now reasonably anticipate twenty years or more.

The full life realization, due to efficient decay protection is, however, not yet possible because the factors of checking and splitting, mechanical destruction around the fastening and above all, the so-called mechanical wear, are factors which have been only partially reduced because of the preservative process. Properly creosoted ties when removed from track as no longer serviceable now come out largely because of mechanical destruction at or near the rail, and secondarily, because of splitting or checking. Ties treated with water soluble salts are still frequently removed because of decay at or near the rail, due to the disappearance of the protective chemical.

The present discussion deals with a study of the mechanical wear of creosoted ties and possible methods for reducing or preventing such wear. Much of the following will also apply to ties made of naturally long-lived woods like cedar, cypress and redwood. It should, however, be thoroughly understood that none of the following discussions in any way apply to untreated ties or to ties treated with more or less water soluble preservatives.

(II) HISTORICAL

In considering the subject of mechanical wear, it is of interest to present a brief historical review. At the outset, the term "mechanical wear" as herein used should be defined. By this I mean the destruction of the wood fiber under rails or tie plates, which results in the rail or tie plate apparently sinking into the wood. This is sometimes spoken of as rail cutting. It excludes, as stated in the introduction, any reference to decay.

(a) **First Uses of Tie Plates.**—When railroads were first built by using longitudinal rails laid on wooden cross-ties, fastened with two or more cut spikes or for that matter, screw spikes, it was the general experience that the narrow base rail more or less rapidly "cut" into the tie. As a result of this experience, very early in railway history, both in Europe and in the United States, a piece of metal was laid between the base of the rail and the tie as a protective device. These pieces were called tie plates or bearing plates or wear plates. At first, these were very thin flat plates whose bearing area on the tie was only slightly larger, if at all, than the base of the rail. Very soon after their introduction, these early tie plates, although they were held in position by the spikes, became loose and rattled. "As soon as this occurred the plate would pound the tie, and the tie would be cut almost as much as if the plates were not used." (Maintenance of Way and Structures, by William C. Willard, 1915, page 170.) These early tie plates were smooth on both sides. Before they had been used very long it was realized that the plates had to be attached in some way to the tie to reduce the rattling and incident wear. As a result of this, a number of plates were designed in which prongs, flanges, or corrugations were added to the bottom of the plate. The fundamental idea underlying these changes was that by this addition the plate could be more securely imbedded in the wood and thus afford additional protection. This gave rise to such early tie plates as the Servis, Goldie, C. A. C., Wolhaupter, Glendon, Q. & W., Oliver, and many others. The prongs or flanges in some of these tie plates were sharp projections, which sometimes extended one inch or more into the tie. The plates were usually laid on the ties and became seated by the traffic. In the early part of this century, these types of tie plates were universally used. The Southern Pacific Company, using the Harriman plate, and the Pennsylvania Railroad, using the Richards plate, were two lines using types of practically flat bottom plates. An excellent account of the tie plate development on the Pennsylvania Railroad, from a flange plate (Servis 1890-98) to a flat plate (1899) is given by Robert Trimble in Proceedings American Railway Engineering Association, 18:528; 1917. In 1903 and 1904, a rather voluminous discussion developed apropos prongs, flanges and other projections because it was claimed by many that while plates provided with such appendages undoubtedly seated themselves in the wood and assisted in maintaining gage, the prongs and flanges, particularly under increasing loads and traffic, destroyed the wood fibers and resulted in premature renewal of cross-ties. In 1904, in discussing tie plates and rail fastenings, I called attention to the doubtful value of projections or flanges on the bottom of tie plates as a gage holding factor, and recommended the use of flat bottom tie plates (U. S. Department of Agriculture, Bureau of Forestry, Bulletin 50, 1904). Since 1904 there has been a gradual reduction in the depth of the projections and at the present time the bottom of most tie plates is either entirely flat or practically flat, or when provided with projections, these are rarely very deep nor are they very sharp. Plates of the type known as the Sellers, Compression-bottom plates, or those standard on the New York Central Lines are typical examples of the change which has come about in the design of tie plates in the last twenty years.

(b) **Early Ideas as to Function of Tie Plates.**—The principal idea regarding the use of the tie plates in the early days undoubtedly was to reduce what I herein call mechanical wear. It is interesting to note, however, that the function of the tie plate in the early days was variously interpreted. The reasons for using tie plates were of course connected with the ideas then held as to why the rail sank into the tie, or why the wood was apparently destroyed under the rail. Speaking of durability of white cedar ties, Dr. P. H. Dudley in 1887 said, "The rings do not separate so freely as those of the yellow pine, and the cutting down of the fibers is due largely to abrasion; the spikes draw, and from the looseness of the rails, together with the sand and grit between them and the ties, the fibers are crushed by the passing of every train. Could the rails be kept tightly spiked, the cutting would not proceed so rapidly." (Bulletin No. 1, Department of Agriculture, Forestry Division, 1887, page 44.)

It appears from the above that Dr. Dudley had the idea that the mechanical destruction was due to abrasion as distinguished from load.

In 1894 Mr. Tratman (U. S. Forest Service, Bulletin No. 9, page 249) made the following statement, "With wooden ties the rails usually give considerable trouble by cutting the ties at the rail seats, thus decreasing the hold of the spikes, allowing the rails to tilt on curves, and rendering the tie unserviceable. Direct pressure of the rail on the tie would have no effect beyond a very slight compression of the wood, but the cutting and wearing is due to the slight motion of the rail, grinding and abrading the fibers, and so greatly facilitating local rot and a softening which hastens the cutting effect."

Quoting from some of the latest authorities, Mr. Tratman (Railway Track and Maintenance, 1926, page 50) has recently reiterated his viewpoint as to the purpose of tie plates, stating, "As unprotected wood ties soon begin to deteriorate at the rail seats, owing to the abrasion and cutting which result from the continual motion of the rails, with consequent entrance of moisture to aid decay, there has been an extensive introduction of metal tie plates which are placed between the rail and tie in order to distribute the load over a larger area of the tie and to protect the wood from wear by the motion of the rails. In this way and at small expense, the life of ties of durable but soft timber (treated or untreated) is increased materially, with consequent reduction in maintenance work and in disturbance of track for renewals. Where unprotected ties have had to be renewed in three years on account of rail cutting, ties of the same kind but fitted with tie plates have lasted six to nine years." It should be noted that his earlier statement in 1886 is somewhat more definite as to the cause of the abrasion or cutting.

Sellew (Railway Maintenance Engineering, 1915, page 163) says as follows, "Plates were formerly made with the idea of being anchored to the tie so as to prevent the communication of the motion of the rail to the plate."

Willard (Maintenance of Way and Structures, 1915), in speaking of the proper design of tie plates (page 170) says, "In designing a tie plate or adopting a certain plate for use on a railway, it should be borne in mind that the purposes for which tie plates are used, in order of importance, are first: (a) to distribute the direct pressure from the rail over a larger surface of the tie and to prevent pounding or cutting of the tie; (b) to assist the spikes in preventing the rails from splitting and overturning."

Camp (Notes on Track, 1903, page 135) makes the following statement: "Tie plates, or 'wear plates,' as they are known in Europe, are metal bearing plates placed on the tie to protect them from being cut by the rails. Rails cut into the ties by crushing down and abrading the fiber. The crushing action is due to direct pressures or impact and the abrasion takes place by the infinitesimal creep or sawing action of the rail in its wave motion under the traffic. The presence of grit on the ties, where it can work in upon the rail seat, as on grades or in yards where sand is used freely, augments the rasping or cutting action of the rail. Some students of the question ascribe the principal cause to the abrasion, while others go so far as to claim that it is the sole cause of rail-cut ties. The symptoms, however, clearly indicate that rail pressure has considerable effect in cutting the ties; otherwise a thin sheet of metal would suffice for their protection. The fact that tie plates ¼ inch thick buckle in service disproves any assumption which ignores the effect of rail pressure. It is further to be noticed that the rail cutting of ties is most rapid at the joints where the rail is weakest and *rail* pressure the most intense. The point is sometimes raised that tie plates do not greatly increase the surface over which rail pressure is distributed, and at first consideration this fact would seem to nullify the importance of rail pressure. It should be understood, however, that the ribs or under-projections of tie plates assist materially in the support of the plate. It is a matter of common observation that the plates placed upon the ties without being seated resist the pressure of the traffic for some time before they become fully settled into the timber."

In 1905 at the Seventh Session of the International Railway Congress (Bulletin of the International Railway Congress, Report No. 2, page 754, 1905) G. E. Louth, of the Great Western Railway of England, made this statement, "But it would be interesting to know what is the cause of mechanical wear. That is one question. Further, in what form is the mechanical wear chiefly?" At this same session, M. Descubes, of the French Eastern Railway of France, explains mechanical wear as follows, "Wear is due to the hammering of the rail on the sleeper; this hammering disintegrates the wood and, the adzed surface splitting, there is no longer perfect adhesion between the sleeper and the rail."

I have given the above quotations from standard books dealing with railway construction largely because such authorities are liable to more or less accurately reflect the feeling of the time entirely independent of the personal viewpoint of the author. In looking through the files of engineering publications, it is rather surprising to note how few references to the problem of the function and design of tie plates occur. This is another reason for quoting the standard reference books as given above.

One additional quotation may be given to show the opinion of a very experienced authority on track. In his very interesting paper on "Conservation of Cross-Ties by Means of Protection from Mechanical Wear" (Proceedings of the American Railway Engineering Association, *11*: 589, 1910), J. W. Kendrick, after discussing the enormous drain on our American forests, due to the necessity for frequent tie renewal, and as an introduction to the discussion on mechanical protection, says, "Some eighteen or twenty years ago the subject of the protection of ties against rail cutting was actively introduced, and as the weight of locomotives and cars was increased, and the necessity for tie protection became apparent, tie plates were gradually adopted. Then, as now, and as it will be in the future, the element of first cost in connection with a new and untried device of unknown merit was a matter of prime consideration.

"It is well-known to everyone that the tie plates of eighteen or twenty years ago were entirely inadequate. They shriveled under the weight imposed upon them as the green leaf does under the influence of frost. Like the leaf, they disintegrated. The finely spun theories about the plate becoming part of the tie because its ribs, or flanges, were forced into the grain of the wood, were dissipated by the inexorable demonstrations of practical experience. The wood composing the tie invariably developed a cross check coincident with the penetration of the ribs or flanges, and the rail rested upon a bent, buckled, or broken sheet of pressed or cast metal, which in turn rested unstably upon a disintegrated mass of wood fiber, and into the cavity thus formed water entered, decay spores followed and the days of the cross-ties so armored were practically numbered. The lessons of experience are only learned at great cost." A little further on, he says "The tie plate as used in the United States has in many cases been a destructive rather than a protective agent." In his final recommendations dealing with the subject of cross-ties so as to obtain the longest life are given as follows: "Tie plates of adequate length, width and thickness should be used in order to properly distribute the maximum pressure transmitted through the base of the rails to the upper surface of the ties." Mr. Kendrick concludes his paper with the following paragraph, "The purpose of this paper is to direct attention to the magnitude of the problem, to its vastness. Some better and cheaper method of accomplishing the ends herein referred to may be discovered, but none has been, and the writer presents the problem to the American Railway Engineering and Maintenance of Way Association for consideration, with the hope that its study will result in the invention of expedients and methods superior to those suggested."

Since 1914 the Tie Committee of the A.R.E.A. has repeatedly reported on matters dealing with the design of tie plates and methods of fastening. In the 1913 Proceedings, Vol. 14, pages 728 to 741, they give the reports received from 61 railroads as to the standard tie plates used. It is interesting to note that most of the roads reporting, used tie plates with flanges, pronged or corrugated bottoms. In 1916, the Committee (Vol. 17, page 233) reported, "The fact is that the methods of properly protecting the ties are going through rapid changes." The Committee calls attention to the fact that "The primary purpose or function of the tie plate is to protect the tie from mechanical wear and all other functions should be subordinated to this. Assuming that the tie plate will be of sufficient area to properly distribute the load imposed, and that it is of sufficient thickness so that it will not buckle, it is necessary that the movement between the plate and the tie be reduced to a minimum or eliminated, if possible. If this is not done, this movement will defeat the purpose of the plate." The Committee then calls attention to several different methods which have been used or suggested, namely; first, by using cut spikes independent of those that secure the rail; second, by using screw spikes or lag screws independent of the fastening securing the rail; and third, by using a flat plate bolted through the tie.

The Committee also stated, "The general tendency at the present time seems to be towards a flat bottom plate, or at least plates that have no deep ribs or projections on the bottom."

In the 1921 Proceedings (Vol. 22, page 692) the Committee on Track gives a list of 47 roads, showing in this table the types of bottoms for different kinds of tie plates. Of 43 answers, it is notable that only seven used flat bottom plates.

In 1922 (Vol. 23, page 259) the Tie Committee presents a discussion entitled "Effect of Design of Tie Plates and Track Spikes on the Durability of Cross-Ties, and Results of Improperly Protecting Ties from Mechanical Wear." After a brief resumé of the work to date, the Committee under the heading of "Effect of Design" gives three requirements which are so fundamental that they are herewith reprinted in full.

"The following features should be provided for to ensure a minimum of damage to the tie:

"(a) Adequate strength and area to prevent buckling and excessive settlement in the tie. The required bearing area and thickness will be governed by the kind of wood and character and amount of traffic. The distances the plate extends beyond either side of the rail base should be so proportioned as to prevent uneven settlement of the plate into the tie and consequent rolling of the rail. Allowance should be made for the deterioration of the tie plate which will normally take place, particularly near salt water or where there are brine drippings.

"(b) It is important that the tie plate have a shoulder to maintain gage, so that the thrust from the rail is transmitted to the tie through the bearing area of the tie plate and the spikes as a unit, instead of being directly resisted by any spike.

"(c) There should be no movement between the tie plate and the tie. The effect of any looseness is to make a "track which rattles," causing damage to the plate bearing area of the tie and enlargement of the spike holes. This close connection between tie plate and tie can best be accomplished by the use of separate fastenings which do not touch the rail and whose only function is holding down the plate. The ordinary means is to provide projections on the bottom of the tie plate; these should be deep enough to provide the required bond and to do their part in strengthening the tie plate, but so shaped and of a depth to do as little damage as possible to the tie, and it is believed that the depth of such projections should not exceed $\frac{7}{8}$ inch, and be so shaped as not to cut the fiber of the wood. When screw spikes are used, a rest shoulder should be provided on which the screw spike bears when driven home, leaving a freeway between the rail base and the under side of the spike head; this aids in making the bond between tie plate and tie. The freeway between the underside of the spike head and the rail base is of great importance and should be from $\frac{7}{8}$ inch to $\frac{3}{8}$ inch, depending on character of the subgrade."

The foregoing review clearly shows that in spite of the frequent references to the necessity for more careful design, there has actually been very little accomplished towards that end. I have given this rather extensive historical review to better emphasize what follows.

Discussions as to the function of the tie plate from the very earliest times have included statements to the effect that one of the functions of the tie plate, in addition to reducing mechanical wear, was to assist in holding track to gage. The introduction of the projections or flanges on the bottom of the tie plate so urgently recommended in the earlier period, particularly when they were to be used on softwood ties, was urged largely on account of the suggested gage holding value of such projections or flanges. As I have already indicated, as time went on, the gage holding value of the tie plate has come to be recognized to be due more to the assistance of the inner spike or spikes in holding the rail in place rather than upon the projections on the lower side of the tie plate. In fact there have been a good many railways of the first class with heavy power and heavy traffic, which for years have used flat bottom plates with the greatest success. In the following, therefore, I am going to assume that the gage holding value of the tie plate depends less upon projections or flanges from the base than it does on the additional holding power given by spikes or screws. That this assumption is not unwarranted is indicated by the fact that present-day tie plates in the majority of cases are practically flat-bottomed and as indicated by Mr. Kendrick in the quotation above given, the original idea as to the gage holding value of these projections has largely been abandoned.

In looking over the past forty years of experience with tie plates, one cannot help but be struck by the contrast in the earlier and later viewpoints. In the early days attempts were made to design plates which would become more or less integral parts of the ties. The early designers believed that the so-called mechanical destruction as distinguished from decay or as a forerunner of decay, was due to the motion of the plate, aided by the finely divided ballast; that they thought little of load distribution was indicated by the fact that most of the early tie plates hardly, if at all, exceeded the area of the rail base in contact with the tie. The size of the plate, to be sure, was fundamentally affected by considerations of economy, but it never-theless is a striking fact that load distribution had very little to do with the early ideas as to tie plate design. The flanges or spines or projections of different types were put onto the plates with the idea that the plate should become solidly attached to the wood. (See also A.R.E.A. Proceed-ings 23:259, 1922.)

As time went on increasing experience indicated that these projections did not function for more than a brief number of years, and one finds the idea of load distribution coming into more and more favor. The result has been that in recent years, particularly on those railways which could afford the expense, tie plates have increased in their bearing area and correspond-ingly in thickness. This has taken place in spite of the fact that because of increased weight of the rail and correspondingly increased stiffness, a better load distribution has been possible. With the exception of only two roads, the standard tie plate of the American railways to-day is essentially the same as it was at the beginning, a flat piece of metal with or without projections on the bottom with one or more shoulders, laid between the rail and the tie and held in position by one or more cut spikes. The chief differ-ence in the early designs and the later ones is that the present tie plates have a larger bearing area, are correspondingly thicker and have fewer bottom projections than did the old type. In spite of this increase in size, modern tie plates "still sink" into the wood. The rate at which this sinking takes place differs with the kind of wood used, the type of ballast, the type of tie plate and rail and the traffic. One is, however, likely to find just as much sinking of the plate into the tie with large plates as with small ones. As a result of many years of study of this problem, I am convinced that the proper design of tie plate to prevent mechanical wear, as above defined, has not yet been developed (except in two instances), and that in spite of extensive study, we cannot hope to obtain the full decay protection life of creosoted ties unless some change is made which will give better mechanical protection than is obtained at the present time.

(III) THE CAUSE OF MECHANICAL WEAR

It appeared to me many years ago that an absolute pre-requisite to a properly designed method for mechanical protection of ties was a definite answer to the question (so well put by Mr. Louth in 1905), "What is the cause of mechanical wear?" To date, so far as I can find, there have been simply expressions of opinion. Omitting all those references which deal with mechanical wear in connection with decay, there have been, as pointed out above, two "opinions"; one, that mechanical wear was due to the movement of the plate, and the other, that it was due to the compression of the wood because of excessive loading. It occurred to me that a critical examination of the wood under the tie plates which had been forced into the tie might enable one to answer the question as to what mechanical wear really was due to. A large number of ties were accordingly collected which showed typical mechanical wear phenomena. Many extreme cases were picked for detailed study. All of the ties selected were such as had been removed from track because tie plates and rail had sunk into the tie to a sufficient extent to require removal. All of the ties examined with the exception of several white oak, cypress and redwood ties were creosoted ties. In all cases, a critical examination was made of the character of the surface of the tie immediately under the tie plate and rail. Careful comparisons were made at the surface of the tie immediately outside of the rail bearing. The ties were then cut longitudinally and across the bearing area and a macroscopic examination was made of the wood fibers immediately below the tie plate seat and at some point in the tie immediately adjacent to the tie plate seat. Typical pieces of wood from the tie plate area as well as from the area immediately outside of the tie plate were then subjected to microscopic study. Through the courtesy and with the assistance of the Forest Products Laboratory of the U. S. Forest Service, a series of microphotographs were prepared which served as a further basis for study. In the following pages a number of photographs of typical ties are reproduced showing the top view of the tie plate bearing area and in many cases a side view of the same tie, longitudinal views along the median line of the ties and microphotographs of the region immediately under the tie plate and from the middle of that same tie. The results of this investigation are briefly summarized herewith.

(1) Gross Appearance of Mechanically Worn Ties

Mechanical wear manifests itself by the apparent sinking in of the tie plate or rail into the tie so that sooner or later the tie plates look as if they had sunk into a pocket. In some cases this pocket is deep enough so that the top surface of the tie plate is lower than the edge of the original top of the tie and the rail has then begun to sink into the edges of the tie. These pockets are generally almost the size of the tie plate. The word, "almost," is used advisedly, meaning thereby that the fit of the plate in the hole is almost snug. In most cases, however, the pocket is just a little larger. It was extremely difficult to obtain any exact measurements because of the nature of the walls of the pocket and the disintegration of the wood at the edges of the tie plates. It may be said, however, that frequently the difference in size between the pocket and the tie plate does not exceed $\frac{1}{16}$ inch, although often it is considerably more. The harder the wood, the closer fit there is.

In general, this sinking in is most marked with the usual type of track construction using cut spikes as the fastening. This is well illustrated in Fig. 1 to 32, which show typical examples of various untreated long-lived woods like cypress and redwood and of creosoted red oak, pine, Douglas fir, etc. Where the tie plates are partially fastened to the tie as has been

FIG. 1.

K. C. S. Ry. Lowry creosoted red oak tie. Service 1912-1924, showing mechanical wear and checking.

the practice on the Delaware, Lackawanna & Western Railroad for some years, this sinking in of the plates is less marked. This is well shown in Fig. 8 to 10. It is still less noticeable on ties in which the tie plates have been fastened to the tie independent of the rail as shown in some typical examples from the Pittsburgh & Lake Erie Railroad. (See Fig. 11 to 13.)

Considering first of all the gross appearance of mechanically worn ties in which the rail is fastened by the use of cut spikes, it will be noted that in practically all cases, provided the plate has been in service for a sufficient length of time, the surface of the wood immediately under the tie plate is rough, fibrous or splintered. (See Fig. 7, 14, 25.) The extent of splintering or shattering differs with the types of tie plates used, the kind of wood, the type of ballast and the extent of traffic. The softwoods such as pine

and fir, cypress and redwood, usually silver and splinter, whereas the hardwoods such as red oak, beech, maple, etc., more frequently look fuzzy or
woolly. In most cases, both in pine and hardwoods, groups of wood cells
become separated from the body of the tie in larger or smaller groups and
it is comparatively easy to tear off splinters or even chips. This splintering
or breaking away of masses of wood fiber immediately under the tie plate
is very evident when longitudinal sections of the rail bearing are made.
Note in this connection, Fig. 18, showing lodgepole pine tie No. 267; Fig. 35,
showing Douglas fir tie No. 34; Fig. 37, showing untreated cypress tie, and
Fig. 34, showing untreated redwood ties. A study of these ties shows that
this splintering goes to various depths; in some cases it is confined to the

FIG. 2.
C. C. C. & St. L. Ry. Upper tie, creosoted ash 1910-1924. Lower tie, creosoted red oak
1909-1924. Both ties with 6 in. × 9 in. tie plates with two cross ribs on the bottom.

immediate surface (see Fig 54, showing section of creosoted red oak), in
other cases it may extend into the tie for ½ inch or more. (See Fig. 55,
showing section of badly shattered creosoted red oak tie.) In the majority
of cases, however, the breaking up of the fibers is more or less a surface
matter. Numerous microscopic examinations made of these chips or splinters
have shown that invariably they were sound wood fibers, that is, not decayed,
and in most cases, the fibers were considerably broken.

Coming now to the partially fastened and independently fastened tie
plates, Fig. 8, 9 and 10, showing a partially fastened tie plate on the
Lackawanna, indicate that the surface immediately under the tie plate is
very much smoother than is the case under loosely fastened plates where
cut spikes are used. Sections of such ties show that the splintering, for

instance, such as shown in Fig. 19, of a creosoted pine tie, 11 years in track, is confined more or less to the surface. In speaking of these partially fastened plates, particular attention is called to the round knobs of wood which project through unused holes in the tie plate. These show very plainly in Fig. 9 and 10. Further reference to these will be made further on.

Fig. 12 and 13 show two hardwood ties on the Pittsburgh & Lake Erie Railroad in which the plate had been firmly fastened. Note particularly

FIG. 3.

B. & O. R. R. Untreated white oak tie, badly mechanically-worn, under 7 in. × 9 in. tie plate with two longitudinal flanges.

FIG. 4.

C. C. C. & St. L. Ry. Three 1905 creosoted ties. Top and bottom ties, red oak; middle tie, ash. Plates 6 in. × 9 in., with two cross ribs on the bottom.

the smooth character of the surface immediately under the tie plate after 12 years of service, and in conjunction therewith, note the slight sinking in of the plate.

A further interesting condition of more or less firmly seated bearing is illustrated in Fig. 124 and 125, showing both ends of three Baltic pine

Fig. 5.

N. Y., N. H. & H. R. R. Steam-seasoned creosoted pine ties. N. Y. Division—service 1912-1924. Wolhaupter tie plates 5 in. × 8¾ in.

Fig. 6.

N. Y. C. R. R. Untreated white oak tie showing shattered wood fibers under tie plate. Tie plate had two longitudinal flanges.

Fig. 7.

Untreated redwood ties from main line Southern Pacific Company. For side view of these ties see Fig. 15.

ties after 20 and 22 years of service on the London, Midland and Scottish Railway. These three ties represented the most severe bedding which I was able to find among a large number of ties removed from track in the course of the usual removal practice of the British railways. A felt cushion had been in service between the chair and the tie. The interesting point in connection with these ties is the fact that the surface of the bearing is perfectly smooth and free from any splintered or fuzzy condition.

Longitudinal and Cross-Sections.—In order to determine the condition of the wood fiber under tie plate seats, a large number of longitudinal and cross-sections were made of ties in which very considerable mechanical wear was evident. As has already been stated, severe cases were selected,

FIG. 8.

Creosoted yellow pine tie, D. L. & W. R. R., service 1910-1925. Flat bottom tie plate 10½ in. × 6 in. Rail fastened with two screw spikes. Note smooth surface and knobs of wood projecting through unused holes in the tie plate.

believing that these would show the most extreme conditions. Fig. 33 to 62 represent sections of a wide range of species of wood from the hardest to the softest. With the exception of the cypress, white oak and redwood, all are creosoted ties, and in the case of the former, the ties were all perfectly sound with no decay whatever. In these sections, the annual growth rings are cut in such a manner that they appear as longitudinal lines in the photographs of the longitudinal sections, and as circles in the cross-sections. In the coniferous woods, pine, fir and cypress, the distinction between the hard dark summerwood and the softer springwood is clearly evident. In the hardwoods, this distinction is less clear but the differentiation between the individual annual rings is frequently noticeable in the oaks where the large vessels show as longitudinal lines. Taking up some of the individual cases, Fig. 54 shows a section of the tie shown in Fig. 14. This is a typical mechanically worn creosoted red·oak tie which had been in service for 12 years in a chat ballasted track. The maximum locomotive axle load operating over this track (Mallet compound) is 63,000 lb. and the extent of traffic may be gaged by the fact that in 1926 approximately 5,000,000 tons passed over this particular tie. A study of the photographs shows that there is no evidence of any compression of wood fibers under the tie plate. The lines of fibers extend in a perfectly straight line from the part outside of the tie plate to the part under the tie plate seat. In other words, there is no compression or bending. Fig. 34, 35, 38, 41, 42, 43, 45 and Fig. 47 to 53, inclusive (Douglas fir 34; lodgepole pine No. 267; shortleaf pine, Santa Fe; Douglas fir, Santa Fe No. 302; Douglas fir,

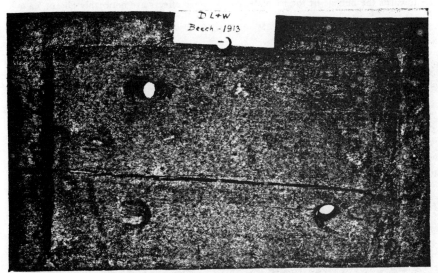

FIG. 9.

Creosoted beech tie, D. L. & W. R. R.; service 1913-1925. Tie plate 10½ in. × 6 in. Note smooth surface and knobs of wood projecting through unused holes in the tie plate.

Santa Fe; redwood, Southern Pacific, etc.), are all sections of coniferous ties with varying lengths of service and various traffic conditions. Under each photograph the details of tonnage, axle loads, etc., are given. As in the case of the oak just referred to, it will be noted that the direction of the wood fibers under the tie plate is practically unchanged. The splintering above referred to is very evident in all of these cases and they also show to what extent the splintering extends down into the tie. The examples illustrated herein are simply a few cases from a great many which have been carefully examined. A large percentage of these badly rail worn or mechanically worn ties show no evidences of compression as indicated by the direction of the wood fibers when comparing the regions under the tie plate and immediately outside of the tie plate area.

In the course of these investigations, however, a number of cases were found which showed some deflection. Fig. 37 (untreated cypress tie) is a photograph of an untreated cypress tie 22 years in the track. In this tie a slight deflection of the fibers is noted towards the edge of the tie plate. This, however, is very largely due to the broken condition of the fibers at the spike hole. With a softwood like cypress, under the action of the rail (there was no tie plate on this tie), compression of the wood fiber would have been far more marked had this been the cause of mechanical compression. Another instance of partial apparent shifting has been noted in a number of loblolly pine ties under very small tie plates. Fig. 36 shows such a tie under a four flange 5 inch by 8¾ inch tie plate with maximum axle loads of 56,100 lb., and a gross tonnage of 50,000 tons per day. It is certainly remarkable that while there is a slight bending of the wood fibers towards the outside of the tie plate, compressive effects are noticeably absent.

Fig. 10.

Creosoted pine tie, D. L. & W. R. R., service 1913-1925. Flat bottom tie plate, 10½ in. × 6 in. Rail fastened with two screw spikes.

Fig. 47, 48, 49, 51, 52 and 53 are examples of ties in which there is an evident deflection under the tie plate area. This is most noticeable in Fig. 51, 52 and 53, and less so in 48. In all of these cases a careful study of the photograph will show a separation of the annual rings in the springwood portion. These examples also show a bending down of the annual rings in the immediate center of the tie plate area. Little if any deviation from the parallel lines is noticeable towards the edges of the tie plate area. Immediately under the tie plate the fibers show the typical shattering which has already been referred to. Specific reference is made to Fig. 52. This is a very coarse-grained loblolly pine, zinc-treated, which has begun to decay. In studying these photographs, the top views of some of these ties should be consulted. (See Fig. 20, 23, 27, 28 and 30.) The most aberrant tie of all was a creosoted Douglas fir tie, No. 328 (see Fig. 17 and 56), 21 years

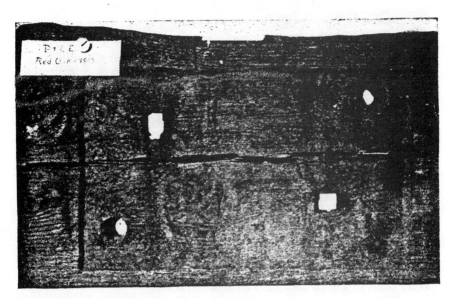

FIG. 11.

Creosoted red oak tie, P. & L. E. R. R., service 1913-1925. Rail fastened with two cut spikes; tie plates with two screw spikes. Note smooth surface of tie plate bearing.

FIG. 12.

Creosoted maple tie, P. & L. E. R. R., service 1913-1925. Tie plate held to tie with two screw spikes independent of the rail; two cut spikes held rail. Note smooth surface.

588

Fig. 13.

Creosoted red oak tie, P. & L. E. R. R., service 1913-1925. Tie plate 6½ in. ×
11 in., held to tie with two screw spikes independent of the rail.

Fig. 14.

K. C. S. Ry. creosoted red oak tie; service 1914-1926. Tie plate compression bottom,
6½ in. × 8½ in.; maximum locomotive axle load 63,000 lb. Tonnage 1926—519,399,037 ton-
miles or 4,965,705 tons over this tie in 1926. For section of this tie see Fig. 54.

in track with a tie plate 6 inches by 8½ inches. The tonnage over this particular track is estimated at about 8,000,000 tons per year with maximum axle loads of 50,666 lb. Fig. 17 shows the two rail bearings of this tie, and Fig. 2 a close view of the bearing after the removal of the tie plate. Fig. 56 shows longitudinal sections through these two bearings. In the center of the bearing (and this will be seen by a close study of Fig. 56), distinct bowl-shaped chips occur which are very evident in the sectional views. In this particular case the fibers are bent to a low point in the very center of the bearing. At both bearings the ties have apparently failed by shearing. Particular attention is called to the fact that this appears to be a compression failure and that the failure is greatest in the center of the tie plate.

FIG. 15.

Untreated redwood ties, Southern Pacific Company, with 8 in. × 8¼ in. tie plates; service, No. 1, 1913-1926; No. 2, 1910-1926; No. 3, 1906-1926. All with gravel ballast. Maximum axle load 63,000 lb.

This apparent compression may be due to various causes. Physically, the compression is doubtless due to the giving way of the springwood fibers which have failed by shear, as will be shown subsequently in a discussion dealing with the microscopic appearance of wood under tie plates. When the springwood shifted laterally it resulted in a reduced volume, and this naturally allowed the stronger summerwood section to be let down, as it were, with the resultant appearance of bent lines of annual rings. It is rather striking that practically all of the cases where bending down of the annual rings was found were in ties which had a preponderant amount of springwood. The exact explanation as to why the wood in these ties failed as it did is a rather difficult matter. Practically all show the maximum

590

FIG. 16.

Creosoted Lodgepole pine and Douglas fir ties from test track C. B. & Q. R. R., Elsberry, Mo., service 1905-1926, showing heavy mechanical wear.

NOTE—These ties although badly worn were left in this track between new ties wherever possible, as this was a test made to show what the maximum *decay* protection life might be. As a rule they were considerably over-size.

FIG. 17.
Creosoted Douglas fir tie (Nos. 328 and 328-B) from test track C. B. & Q. R. R., Elsberry, Mo., showing mechanical wear; service 1905-1926.
NOTE—These ties were carefully kept in track to determine maximum decay resistant life.

Cause of Mechanical Wear 25

Fig. 18.
Creosoted lodgepole pine (No. 267) tie from test track C. B. & Q. R. R., Elsberry, Mo., showing mechanical wear; service 1905-1926.
Note—This tie was carefully kept in track to determine maximum decay resistant life.

Fig. 19.
Creosoted pine tie, D. L. & W. R. R., service 1913-1924. Flat bottom tie plate. Note surface more or less broken, and knobs of wood projecting into unused holes in the tie plate.

compression near the center of the tie plate. This is particularly evident in Fig. 51, 53 and 56. This compression near the center of the plate is probably due to the resultant of a number of factors. It is conceivable that with an uneven bearing these particular tie plates were subjected to concentrated loads of locomotives and cars. Doubtless, also, there may have been a premature compression of the wood near the edges of the tie

Fig. 20.

N. Y. C. R. R. Tie sections Nos. 31 and 31-A. The two rail-bearing areas of a Lowry creosoted pine tie, service 1910-1926. Tie plates 7 in. × 9¾ in., with two longitudinal bottom flanges.

plate due to the rocking action of the latter. This would then gradually concentrate the load into the median area of the plate, which would, of course, result in increasing concentration of load. The striking fact about this slight compression, however, is that the edges of the tie plate area are unaffected, excepting Fig. 52, where decay has set in and where one would naturally expect a failure of this type.

594

Fig. 22.

N. Y. C. R. R. Tie sections Nos. 33 and 33-A. The two rail-bearing areas of a Lowry creosoted pine tie, service 1910-1926. Tie plates 7 in. × 9 in., with two longitudinal bottom flanges.

Fig. 21.

N. Y. C. R. R. Tie sections Nos. 35 and 35-A. The two rail-bearing areas of a Lowry creosoted pine tie, service 1910-1926. Tie plates 7 in. × 9 in., with two longitudinal bottom flanges.

In presenting this explanation I do so with considerable reservation, because in the absence of definite knowledge as to the exact motions which the tie plate develops under passing loads, any explanation can at best be only speculative. These cases are presented, however, because they should lead to further investigation as to the probable cause for this central compression.

One now and then finds deformation in the vicinity of driven spike holes. Fig. 55 shows a striking instance of this kind. This represents a

FIG. 23.

N. Y. C. R. R. Tie sections Nos. 36 and 36-A. The two rail-bearing areas of a Lowry creosoted pine tie, service 1911-1926. Tie plates 7 in. × 9 in., with two longitudinal bottom flanges.

section through a creosoted red oak tie laid in 1914, removed in 1926. The maximum locomotive axle load over this track was 63,000 lb. This is a particularly striking case of shattering or column failure induced by the breaking of the fibers when the spikes were driven.

It was thought that further data might be obtained from a study of cross-sections of ties made through the center of the tie plate bearing area. Photographs of ties NYC-101, 93-A, 93, 90, and P&LE-100 (Fig. 61, 60, 58 and 59) represent such cross sections. (See also Fig. 40 and 62.) It is very evident from a study of these photographs that there is practically no evidence of compression of the rings. If there had been much compression, the circular form of the annual rings would have been much distorted. The ties represented in photographs of ties NYC-93 and 93-A (Fig. 58 and 60) show a slight flattening of the circles immediately under the tie plate. This, however, is very small. What the photographs do show is that the one to two inches of wood which originally filled the cavity finally occupied by the tie plate have disappeared. The significant point is that they have disappeared entirely. The wood has, in other words, not been compressed under the tie plate during its years of service, because if it had been, this compressed wood would still be evident, particularly when viewed in cross-section.

Fig. 24.

NYC-90, NYC-90A: N. Y. C. R. R.—creosoted pine tie from Tarrytown, N. Y. Service 1910-1927. Tie plates 7 in. × 9¼ in., with two longitudinal ribs.

Of the extensive series of ties investigated only one was found in which there was a distinct breakage of the annual rings, together with compression. This is represented in Fig. 57. This was one of a lot of pine ties taken from the main line of the New York, New Haven & Hartford Railroad, inserted in 1909 and removed in 1924, on the New York Division (see Fig. 5). This particular lot of ties was heavily steamed during treatment. The probability is that this steaming very materially weakened the wood fibers. Furthermore, these ties were subjected to intensely concentrated loads due to the small tie plates used (5 inches by 8¾ inches). The direct compression, therefore, in this case, was no doubt due to concentrated loads on the already weakened wood. A great many of these ties failed about the same time. They were all very badly mechanically worn (see in this connection Fig. 66 in the discussion on microscopic studies), and doubtless there were others than the one referred to which were similarly compressed. I believe that the steaming, together with the small plate used, amply accounts for this exceptional appearance.

Summing up the foregoing, the indications found by detailed examination of the sections of ties through the badly mechanically worn areas show

Fig. 25.
SF-72 and SF-75: Two Santa Fe creosoted Douglas fir ties from Barstow, California. Service 1910-1927. Tie plates 7 in. × 9 in., with two longitudinal ribs.

little evidence of compression or deformation. There are, undoubtedly, ties, for instance, Douglas fir tie No. 328 (Fig. 56), which have been stressed beyond the elastic limit, but they are apparently the exception and not the rule. The conclusion which I have drawn from this macroscopic study, both of surface and longitudinal and cross-sections, is that there is little evidence of extensive compression of wood fibers. The volume of the wood fiber removed, that is, the wood fiber which formerly was there instead of the hole or pocket formed by the tie plate, would be plainly visible when viewed in cross-section had it disappeared into the tie because of com-

598

pression (so, for instance, as it actually did appear in tie No. 328, Fig. 56). In most cases there is no such extra volume evident and I conclude, therefore, that the wood fiber which formerly occupied the pocket in which the rail or tie plate has become seated must have disappeared in some other way.

(2) Microscopic Appearance of Mechanically Worn Ties

As indicated above, a number of typical mechanically worn ties were selected for a microscopic study. In each case, a typical area on the tie plate seat and a similar area in the region outside of the tie plate seat

FIG. 26.

MP-50 and MP-55: Two Missouri Pacific zinc-treated pine ties from Leavenworth, Kansas. Service 1923-1927. Sellers tie plates 6 in. × 9 in.

were selected. The succeeding photographs, Fig. 63 to 93, should be studied in groups of two; one representing the normal structure of the wood as it may be called, taken from the outside of the tie plate bearing area, and the second, the structure of the wood from the tie plate bearing area. In each case, the top of the photograph is the top surface of the tie. In looking at these photographs, it should be remembered that these are end views. Wood is composed of a number of tubes having varying thicknesses of cell walls. In the conifers, the darker layers represent the summerwood; the lighter lines, the springwood. The size of the openings in the wood fibers will be larger in the so-called springwood than in the summerwood.

In the oak, the very large holes represent the vessels which occur in greater number in the spring growth. The denser portion represents the fibers. The curious mass shown in some of the large ducts in Fig. 77 are tyloses, characteristic of white oak. Some of the microphotographs of the wood under the tie plates are somewhat broken, due to shattering of the fiber and to pieces torn from the wood in making the sections. It should be remembered that wood from worn ties is full of dirt and is very difficult to section. The remarkable results obtained by the technical men of the Forest Products Laboratory deserve every commendation.

Fig. 27.

MP-86 and MP-87: Two Missouri Pacific zinc-treated pine ties from Monroe, La. Service 1924-1927. Tie plates—none used.

In making these microscopic studies, the ties selected were taken from three groups; first, typical ties in which the rail was fastened with two cut spikes; second, typical ties from the Lackawanna Railroad in which the rail was fastened with two screw spikes which at the same time held the tie plate more or less firmly to the tie; and third, typical ties from the Pittsburgh & Lake Erie Railroad in which two cut spikes held the rail and two screw spikes held the tie plate entirely independent of the rail. Taking up these cases in detail, first, ties with two cut spikes; Fig. 69 represents a pine tie (No. 3) four years in track under a compression bottom tie plate. Fig. 70 is a view of the wood taken from the middle of the tie (note that cracks and torn places are due to sectioning). It will be noted

600

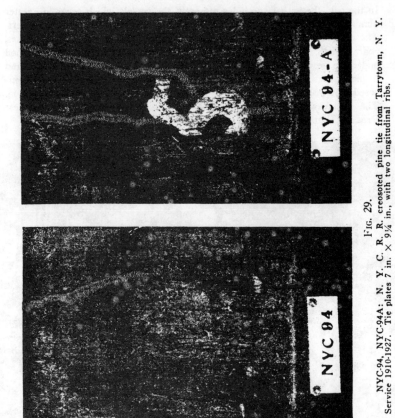

Fig. 29.

NYC-94, NYC-94A: N. Y. C. R. R. creosoted pine tie from Tarrytown, N. Y. Service 1910-1927. Tie plates 7 in. × 9¼ in., with two longitudinal ribs.

Fig. 28.

SF-77 and SF-85: Two Santa Fe untreated Douglas fir ties from Needles, Calif. Service 1910-1927. Tie plates 7 in. × 9 in., with two cross ribs.

that the wood fibers are arranged in radial lines. Furthermore, that in this tie, these lines are almost at a 45 deg. angle to the top of the tie. Fig. 71 represents a section of the wood immediately under the tie plate. At this particular point, the radial lines were at almost right angles to the tie plate. A study of this figure shows that in the first and second rings immediately under the plate, there has been a slight shifting of the radial lines in the springwood. It will be noted also that the lumen of the holes in the wood fibers is plainly visible.

Fig. 66 represents a loblolly pine tie (No. 2) with a Wolhaupter tie plate under extremely heavy traffic, in service fifteen years. Fig. 67 represents

Fig. 30.

MP-54 and MP-52: Two Missouri Pacific zinc-treated pine ties from Leavenworth, Kansas. Service 1923-1927. Tie plates 6 in. × 8½ in. flat bottom.

the wood in the middle of the tie. Here again the radial lines are at an angle of about 45 deg. to the top. Fig. 68 shows a section under the tie plate. In this section the lateral shifting of the radial lines in the springwood is much more evident than in the first case. These cells look black, due to infiltration of foreign matter. A careful examination with a lens will show that the lumen of the cells is plainly visible.

Fig. 84 is another one of the ties (No. 7) from the same lot as Fig. 66. Fig. 86 is a small piece of wood immediately under the tie plate. This again shows the lateral shifting in the springwood, the perfect visibility of the lumen of the cells and it also shows how individual groups of fibers are breaking apart, some in small groups and some in larger groups.

Fig. 76 shows an untreated white oak tie. The view taken from the section outside of the tie plate shows the same type of radial lines as in the pine. Fig. 78 representing a section from the tie plate bearing area indicates that these radial lines were practically perpendicular to the tie plate. In this very interesting photograph, the lateral shifting of the different annual rings is very plainly evident. It is to be particularly noted that the large vessels show no indication of compression or diminution in size. They have simply broken and the rings have moved laterally. Fig. 79 is

FIG. 31.

NYC-93, NYC-93A: N. Y. C. R. R. creosoted pine tie from Tarrytown, N. Y. Service 1910-1927. Tie plates 7 in. × 9¼ in., with two longitudinal ribs.

another view from the tie plate bearing area showing how portions of the wood have been torn and are spreading from the main mass in groups of fibers.

We now come to a second series. The foregoing were all ties in which the rail was fastened to the tie by means of two cut spikes. Believing that certain valuable information might be obtained from ties fastened with screw spikes, a number of photographs were made of ties which were removed from the main track of the Delaware, Lackawanna & Western Railroad. Fig. 64 is a view showing wood not under the plate and Fig. 65 of wood under the plate of Delaware, Lackawanna & Western Railroad Tie No.

1, Fig. 63. Here again a decided lateral shifting of the radial lines is noticeable, although not by any means as extreme as in the cases first referred to. It will also be noted that there is a smaller tendency towards the breaking away of individual groups of fibers. No. 4 and 6 (Fig. 72 and 80) represent similar ties taken from the Boston & Albany and Lackawanna roads; both of them show the lateral shifting, and in No. 4 (Fig. 72) there is considerable breaking away of the top groups of wood fibers. By comparing Fig. 72 and 80 it will be readily seen that the surface of No. 4 tie (Fig. 72) shows very much more fuzziness than does No. 6 (Fig. 80). By referring to photographs 4 and 6 (Fig. 72 and 80) it will

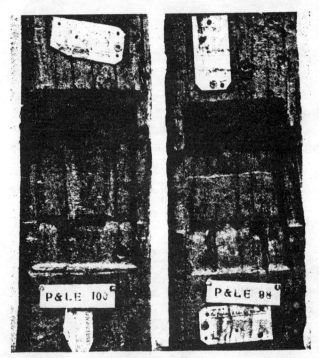

FIG. 32.

(Left) P&LE-100: P. & L. E. R. R. creosoted pine tie from Milepost 406. Service 1914-1927. Tie plates 6½ in. × 11 in., with two cross ribs. (Right) P&LE-98: P. & L. E. R. R. creosoted white oak tie from Milepost 378. Same service and tie plate.

be noted that in the case of No. 4, there are two knobs of wood—in the case of No. 6, three such knobs plainly visible. I call these knobs because they consist of circular pieces of wood which have projected up through holes in the tie plate which had not been used. They are particularly clear in photograph No. 6 (Fig. 80). In view of the fact that these knobs had been subjected to only a small load, it was considered of interest to section the wood from these knobs. Fig. 75 and 83 are sections through these knobs. Here again the curious shifting in the springwood is plainly visible just as it was in the wood under load.

A third series is taken from a tie in service of the Pittsburgh & Lake Erie Railroad for twelve years. (See Fig. 87.) This particular tie is a pine tie in which the tie plate was fastened to the tie with two lag screws independent of the rail. A comparison of the two photographs taken from this tie, one from the section not under the tie plate (Fig. 88), the other from the section under the tie plate (Fig. 89), shows that the two are practically indistinguishable. In other words, in this lag-fastened plate no deformation of the wood fibers is evident. There is a slight breaking away

Fig. 33.

Untreated 7 in. × 10 in. redwood tie, Southern Pacific; service 1913-1926; flat bottom tie plate, 8 in. × 8¼ in. Maximum axle loads 63,000 lb. Average tonnage per year 7,882,900 tons.

Fig. 34.

Untreated 7 in. × 10 in. redwood tie, Southern Pacific; service 1913-1926; flat bottom tie plate, 8 in. × 8¼ in. Maximum axle loads 63,000 lb. Average tonnage per year 7,882,900 tons. This is a section of tie shown in Fig. 33.

of the fibers at the top, but this may very well have been caused by the microscopic manipulation, because the same is also evident in the photograph of the section not under load. Fig. 90 and 91 represent two photographs of a creosoted Baltic pine tie from the London, Midland & Scottish Railway (Fig. 125, Tie A1), twenty years under heavy traffic. This is one of a group of ties which I selected recently at the re-conditioning yard at Bletchley, England. It was one of three ties selected from thousands of this particular lot. Most of the ties from this renewal group showed practically no evidence of mechanical wear. The three ties which I selected (Fig. 124 and 125) showed the most evident signs of mechanical wear and they were the worst of the lot, speaking from the standpoint of compression of the chair or seating of the chair. The two microphotographs

FIG. 35.

C. B. & Q. R. R. Creosoted Douglas fir tie No. 34. Service 1905-1926. Section at rail bearing under tie plate. Four longitudinal flange tie plates 6 in. × 8½ in.— 90-lb. rail. 8,000,000 gross tons traffic per year. Rail changed 1916. Maximum locomotive axle load 50,666 lb. (6 driver R-5 freight engine).

NOTE—This is one of the experimental ties at Elsberry, Mo., to test decay resistance.

FIG. 36.

N. Y., N. H. & H. R. R. Steam-seasoned creosoted loblolly pine laid 1909, removed 1924. Gross tonnage 50,000 tons per day. Maximum locomotive axle load 56,100 lb. Four longitudinal flange tie plates 5 in. × 8¾ in.

show practically the same condition although not quite so extreme as indicated in the photograph of American pine ties. There is a slight lateral shifting in the springwood, noticeable in the upper two rings and to a very slight degree in the third. In other respects, these microphotographs are very similar to those for the Delaware, Lackawanna & Western ties.

The most aberrant of all ties examined was the Douglas fir tie No. 328 (see Fig. 17 and 56), to which reference has already been made. A series of microscopic studies were made of this tie. Fig. 92 and 93 represent two microphotographs, one of the appearance of the wood immediately outside of the tie plate area, and the other immediately under the tie plate. It will be noted that the springwood section of each annual ring for a very

Fig. 37.

Untreated cypress tie, Santa Fe Ry. 85-lb. A. S. C. E. rail. Base of rail $5\frac{3}{16}$ in. wide. Service 22 years.

Fig. 38.

C. B. & Q. R. R., Elsberry, Mo. Creosoted lodgepole pine tie No. 267, Longitudinal section through tie plate area. Service 1905-1926. Four flange tie plates 6 in. × 8½ in. 8,000,000 tons gross traffic per year. Rail 90-lb. changed in 1916. (See Fig. 18.)

considerable distance down has shifted laterally, and the cell lumen has in many places practically disappeared. This is not only evidence of rolling shear, but direct compression. We have, in other words, a picture very much like the one obtained under the testing machine. As has been indicated in the previous discussion with reference to this tie, this direct compression is doubtless due to peculiar causes, the principal one of which is probably concentrated loading.

A careful microscopic study of the structure of these badly rail worn ties can lead to only one conclusion. The wood under the tie plates even in the worst cases is practically normal as to the condition of the wood

Fig. 39.

Section of pine tie at the edge of the pocket formed by the rail. Note the parallel annual rings.

fiber. The changes evident are a lateral shifting of the uppermost layers. This shifting may extend down into the tie for three or four rings. It is rarely more than 45 deg. and frequently not as much as that. It is evident in oaks as well as pine. In addition to this shifting, there is a breaking

608

away of groups of wood fiber immediately under the tie plate. These groups consist of fibers which are practically unchanged as to form.

These photographs also show that the most evident shifting and breaking of the wood fibers takes place in those ties in which the most motion was possible between the plate and the wood. There is far less evidence of this shifting and shattering in the Lackawanna tie plates, which are partially fastened, and practically no shifting in the case of ties from the Pittsburgh & Lake Erie Railroad in which the tie plates were independently

FIG. 40.

Pine tie shown in Fig. 39 looking at the end of a section through the middle of the tie plate bearing area. Note absence of compression.

fastened. The most striking result in my opinion is the finding of the shifting in the knobs of wood projecting through the tie plate in the case of the Lackawanna ties. As has been stated, these knobs were subjected to only a small compression but they were subjected to lateral stresses. If direct loading were responsible for the shifting in the direction of the wood fibers, there should have been no change of position in these knobs. The fact that the fibers were shifted indicates that other forces were at work.

These studies certainly indicate one thing and that in a very striking manner; namely, that the fibers are not compressed. They confirm the macroscopic examination and indicate that the phenomenon of the sinking in of the tie plate into the tie—in other words, what I call mechanical wear —is certainly not due to compression.

Compression Studies.—The question which naturally arises after looking at these photographs is what do wood fibers which are really compressed look like. It therefore occurred to me to actually compress some wood fibers and make some microscopic studies to determine what compressed wood fibers would show. Again through the courtesy of the Forest

FIG. 41.

Two Douglas fir ties from Beaumont Division, Santa Fe Ry., used without tie plates; service 1910-1926. For longitudinal sections of these ties see Fig. 42 and Fig. 43. 85-lb. A. S. C. E. rail, base 5$\frac{1}{8}$ in. Width of tie 8 inches. Maximum locomotive axle load 62,000 lb. Tonnage (1924) 3,805,274 tons.

Products Laboratory, we made two tests, one with a dry Douglas fir tie and one with a red oak tie, both new and untreated. These ties were placed under the testing machine. An old type New York Central tie plate, 7 in. by 9 in., with two longitudinal flanges was placed as the actual rail bearing, and a piece of steel to simulate the rail was put on the tie plate. Pressure was then gradually applied and was kept continuously on the rail until the tie plate had become seated in the tie approximately 1½ inches. It is a matter of incidental interest to note that in the case of

610

FIG. 42.

Douglas fir tie No. 302 from Beaumont Division, Texas, Santa Fe Ry.; service 1910-1926. No tie plate. 85-lb. A. S. C. E. rail. Rail base 5¾ in. Width of tie 8 in. Tonnage (1924) 3,805,274 tons. Maximum locomotive axle load 62,000 lb.

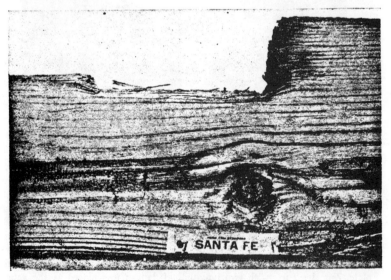

FIG. 43.

Douglas fir tie, Santa Fe Ry., Beaumont Division, Texas; service 1910-1926. Tonnage 3,805,274 tons during 1924. No tie plate. 85-lb. A. S. C. E. rail. Rail base 5¾ in. wide; width of tie 8 in.

FIG. 44.

Longitudinal section of D. L. & W. R. R. creosoted longleaf pine tie. Service 1910-1924. Screw fastening of rail. Note knob of wood extending into unused hole in tie plate.

FIG. 45.

Shortleaf pine tie, Santa Fe Ry. 85-lb. A.S.C.E. rail. Rail base 5¾ in.

FIG. 46.

RI-69: Rock Island creosoted red oak tie from Chickasha, Okla. Tie plate 6½ in. × 8¾ in., with four longitudinal ribs.

red oak, the pressure exerted was 4440 lb. per square inch; in the case of Douglas fir, 3000 lb. per square inch. As quickly as possible after the test, the ties were photographed and then cut longitudinally. Fig. 94 shows the appearance of these two pieces immediately after the test. Microscopic sections were then made of both woods, and Fig. 104 to 106 represent the microphotographs for the red oak tie, and Fig. 96 to 102 microphotographs for the Douglas fir tie. Referring to Fig. 103 and 95 representing the longitudinal view of oak and fir, respectively, it will be noted that the

FIG. 47.

NYC-33 and NYC-34: N. Y. C. R. R. creosoted pine ties from Batavia, N. Y. Service 1910-1926. Tie plates 7 in. × 9 in., with two longitudinal ribs.

FIG. 48.

NYC-36A: N. Y. C. creosoted pine tie from Batavia, N. Y. Service 1911-1926. Tie plate 7 in. × 9 in., with two longitudinal ribs.

FIG. 49.

NYC-31: N. Y. C. creosoted pine tie from Batavia, N. Y. Service 1910-1926.
Tie plate 7 in. × 9¾ in., with two longitudinal ribs.

FIG. 50.

P&LE-96: P. & L. E. creosoted shortleaf pine tie from Milepost 401. Service
1914-1927. Tie plate 6½ in. × 11 in.

FIG. 51.

MP-52: Missouri Pacific zinc-treated pine tie from Leavenworth, Kansas. Service
1923-1927. Tie plate 6 in. × 8½ in. flat bottom.

FIG. 52.

MP-86: Missouri Pacific zinc-treated pine tie from Monroe, La. Service 1924-1927. Tie plate—none used.

FIG. 53.

SF-77: Santa Fe untreated Douglas fir tie from Needles, Calif. Service 1910-1927. Tie plate 7 in. X 9 in. with two cross ribs.

FIG. 54.

K. C. S. Ry. creosoted red oak tie, service 1914-1926. Compression bottom 6½ in. X 8½ in. tie plate. Maximum locomotive axle load 63,000 lb. This is a section of tie shown in Fig. 14.

longitudinal lines representing the annual rings shows a distinct bending down in both cases. In the case of the oak this was visible for about two inches under the tie plate, while in the case of the fir, it was visible for over four inches under the tie plate. By looking at the surface at an angle, a distinct compression area was easily discernible. The most striking part of this test is indicated at the edges of the plate. Note how the fibers were bent down and eventually broken. This is very evident in both cases. Referring to Fig. 104 to 106 which represent the microscopic studies, Fig. 104 is a view of the red oak taken at point 9 as shown on Fig. 103, that is, from a section not under compression. Note again the radial parallel lines of arrangement with large spring vessels and smaller lumened wood fibers. Fig. 105 is a view in region 7 immediately under the plate. Fig. 106 is a microphotograph from region 8, one inch below the tie plate. Note how in these two compression photographs the vessels have become compressed and distorted. Fig. 96 is a view at point 5 (Fig. 95) in the Douglas fir

FIG. 55.

K. C. S. Ry. creosoted red oak tie laid in 1914, removed 1926, showing extensive column fracture under tie plate beginning at the spike hole. Maximum locomotive axle load 63,000 lb.

tie showing the normal structure of Douglas fir. The succeeding figures, numbers 97 to 100, represent sections at points 1 to 4, representing, respectively, 1, 2, 3 and 4 inches under the tie plate. Each of these views shows the typical crinkling effect of compression which is noticeable beyond the fourth inch.

Fig. 101 and 102 represent microphotographs in which the wood fibers are reproduced magnified 250 times. Fig. 101 is taken from the Douglas fir tie just described, from the layer of wood immediately under the tie plate at a point marked "A" in Fig. 97. Fig. 102 is taken from the same piece of wood, and represents the sixth annual ring below the tie plate; in other words, the section marked "B" in Fig. 97. These enlarged views show how under the effect of direct pressure the cell walls buckled, crinkled and shifted. This is particularly evident in the wood immediately under the tie plate, but it also is evident in the sixth annual ring. Note particularly in the latter how marked the lateral shifting is, in the youngest cells of the springwood. Note also how the summerwood is practically unaffected. In other words, these microphotographs show a distinct volume reduction as distinguished from mere change in position. By comparing these photographs with those taken of the wood from ties under track service, it will be noted that there is a striking difference. In no case do any of the track ties show the phenomena indicated in the compression photographs.

Fig. 56.

C. B. & Q. R. R. creosoted Douglas fir tie No. 328. Service 1905-1926. Section at both rail bearings under tie plate. Tie plate 6 in. × 8½ in. Tonnage 8,000,000 tons per year. 90-lb. rail changed in 1916. Maximum axle load 50,666 lb. This is one of the experimental ties inserted in 1904 to test the decay protection life of the treatment.

A second series of tests involving the compression of tie plates into wood was undertaken at the testing laboratories of Washington University, using shortleaf pine ties. The plates used were 6 in. by 7.1 in. They were compressed into the ties for 1½ in., and pressure was then released. The pressures used were approximately 2000 lb. per square inch. Sections were cut immediately after compression, but in this case the sections were made across the tie through the middle of the tie plate area. Fig. 107 shows two

typical cases of shortleaf pine ties after machine compression. By cutting
the ties transversely the effect of compression at the edges of the tie,
that is, at the long dimension of the tie plate, becomes far more evident
than when the ties were cut longitudinally. In every case the rings of
wood showed a distinct flattening on the upper side of the tie where
pressure had been applied. The dark summerwood of each annual ring
formed a series of almost perfect concentric circles. Tie No. 2 (Fig. 107)
shows the marked flattening at the tops of these rings in a very striking
manner.

Fig. 57.

N. Y. N. H. & H. R. R. steam-seasoned creosoted pine tie; 1909-1924—section through
plate-bearing area showing distortion of annual rings.

The most striking manifestation, however, is the actual breaking of
the wood at the two edges of the tie plate, which shows up as a distinct
fracture. In both of the photographs the definite compression of the immediate wood fiber under the tie plate is plainly visible by tracing the rings of
wood outside of the compression area and noting how the normal position
of the wood has been distorted in the section immediately under the tie
plate. Compare these photographs with Fig. 58 to 61, representing sections
of badly rail-worn ties under heavy traffic. No sign of bending of the
rings or fracture at the edge of the tie plate is manifest in any of these
cases. Of the large number of ties examined, there was only one, a
loblolly pine tie, which had been steam creosoted, which showed any sign
of lateral breakage.

The photographs of the second series of compression tests are in many
respects more illustrative of what actually happens when wood is actually

618

compressed under a heavy load, than are the photographs of the longitudinal sections of the first series. In this connection, attention is called to
the X-ray studies of these same ties which I discuss in detail below.

Fig. 58.

NYC-90, NYC-93: N. Y. C. R. R. creosoted pine ties from
Tarrytown, N. Y. Service 1910-1927. Tie plates 7 in. × 9¼
in. with two longitudinal ribs.

The results of these compression tests, therefore, corroborates the
statement above made, after a study of the tie sections, that whatever may
be the actual cause of mechanical wear, it is certainly not solely due to
direct compression of the fibers.

(3) Strength of Wood Under Tie Plates

As has been indicated, the surface of the wood immediately under the
tie plate in mechanically worn ties in the majority of cases looks rough
and splintered. Realizing the fact that continuous impacts on the wood
transmitted through the rail and tie plate might in some way affect the
strength of the wood fiber, it was decided to make a series of preliminary
tests to ascertain, if possible, what, if any, strength changes had taken

place in the wood immediately under the tie plate. Incidentally, it was thought that we might find some indication as to so-called fatigue. Tests of the timber under long continued strains while interesting have hitherto yielded very little definite information because it was impossible to com-

Fig. 59.

P&LE-100: P. & L. E. R. R. creosoted pine tie from Mile-post 406. Service 1914-1927. Tie plate 6½ in. × 11 in. with two cross ribs.

Fig. 60.

NYC-93A: N. Y. C. R. R. creosoted pine tie from Tarry-town, N. Y. Service 1910-1927. Tie plate 7 in. × 9¼ in. with two longitudinal ribs.

pare the results obtained with the strength of the same timber at the outset.* With this point in view, two ties were removed from the main line of the New York Central Railroad which had been under constant traffic for 13

---

*Proceedings A. R. E. A. *24*:755; 1923.

years. One of these was a creosoted, rather rapid growth loblolly pine tie, the other was an untreated longleaf pine tie. Tests were made with pieces five-eighths of an inch square taken directly under the tie plates and some pieces taken from the center of the tie near the top surface. I am indebted to J. A. Newlin, in Charge of the Section of Timber Mechanics of the Forest Products Laboratory, for the following report with reference to these tests: "In both ties the material under the tie plate showed greater toughness than that from the center of the tie. Their strength in compression across the grain was slightly lower for the material under the tie plate. In compression parallel to the grain, the material under the tie plate in the treated tie showed only 55 per cent of the strength of the material in the center of the tie, and in the longleaf pine tie, the material under the tie plates showed 73 per cent of the strength of that in the center.

FIG. 61.

NYC-101: N. Y. C. R. R. creosoted pine tie from Greystone, N. Y. Service 1910-1925.

"The increased toughness appears to be due to a breaking point of the springwood fibers which permitted the specimen to fail in shear between the rings. (In this connection see discussion below on the relative strength of springwood and summerwood.) This breaking down of the fibers would be expected to have little influence on the compression-perpendicular strength which the tests showed to be correct. In compression parallel to the grain, the lack of strength of the fibers in adjacent rings would permit the specimen to fail more or less as independent columns, and the strength would be reduced. Photographs taken by Mr. Koehler on other ties seem to show this same phenomenon. The separation or weakness between the rings seemed to be more pronounced adjacent to the points where the spikes had been inserted. One of these ties had been respiked at least three times, and the other at least four times. This breaking down of the springwood appears to allow the material immediately under the tie plate to become macerated and lose all of its efficiency, other than the cushioning. There is a possibility that were the tie plate held firmly to the tie at all times, this breaking down of the springwood would be materially reduced. It also appears to be very desirable to avoid respiking from the standpoint of rail cutting as well as decay."

In view of the finding that ties into which cut spikes had been driven showed a reduction in the column strength of the wood immediately under the tie plate, it was thought advisable to repeat this type of test with ties taken from track in which holes had been bored previous to the insertion of the fastening. Accordingly two ties, taken from the Delaware, Lackawanna & Western Railroad, were tested. These were creosoted pine ties laid in 1912. The total tonnage over these ties was 265,645,000 tons. The gross traffic in 1924 was 19,749,756 tons and for 1925, 18,399,874 tons. The maximum locomotive axle load for 2200 class engines was 69,500 lb., for 2100 class engines, 69,100 lb. The tie plates were 7 in. x 10 in. x ⅝ in., flat bottom. Two screw spikes held the rail. These were inserted in holes

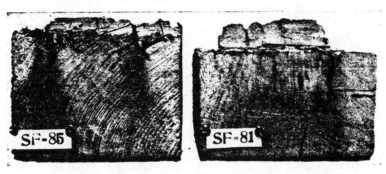

FIG. 62.

Sections of two untreated Douglas fir ties, Santa Fe Railway, from track near Needles, Calif. Service 1910-1927. These ties had 7 in. × 9 in. tie plates with two transverse flanges on the bottom. Tie SF-85 shows the splintering immediately under the tie plate. Tie SF-81 showed the same splintering, but the splinters were torn off in sawing. Note the absence of distortion in the annual rings.

bored before treatment. These two ties were tested in the same manner as the New York Central ties. Mr. Newlin reports as follows: "So far as the tests go, an analysis of the data does not show any weakening due to mechanical action of the loads. The tie plates had been held down with screw spikes and but very little separation of the rings had apparently taken place due to the action of the spike. This is in marked contrast to the separation which had occurred in the other ties where the plates had been apparently spiked down with cut spikes."

While this test should be regarded in the nature of a preliminary determination, it is of interest to note that the compression strength of the wood had not been materially reduced and that the high strength reduction on longitudinal column strength was due to a separation of the fibers, apparently by shear.

Strength of Wood.—At this point brief reference should be made to the strength of wood. As has been indicated, the first visual impression which one gets of a mechanically worn tie is that the wood fibers under the plate have been torn and broken Farther on data will be given to show the actual loads to which wooden ties are subjected under various types of locomotives. For the sake of ready reference, the actual strength in compression perpendicular to the grain and of side hardness, both for green and air-dry wood, is given for various species of wood commonly used for tie purposes.

I am indebted to the Forest Products Laboratory of the U.S. Forest Service for these figures which represent the latest revisions obtained by the Forest Service from their large number of strength studies.

TABLE I

STRENGTH OF VARIOUS WOODS USED FOR TIES

| | Compression Perpendicular to Grain | | Side Hardness | |
	Green lb.	Air Dry 12% moisture lb.	Green lb.	Air Dry 12% moisture lb.
Longleaf Pine	600	1410	590	910
Shortleaf Pine	470	1170	560	790
Loblolly Pine	550	1220	450	710
White Oak	830	1320	1060	1360
Red Oak	760	1260	1000	1290
Beech	670	1260	850	1300
Birch (yellow)	530	1180	780	1260
Hard Maple	800	1780	960	1470
Cedar (white)	290	380	230	320
Gum (black)	600	1180	640	810
Gum (tupelo)	590	1110	710	890
Gum (red)	460	870	520	700
Douglas Fir	510	920	480	670

FIG. 63.

Tie No. 1. D. L. & W. R. R. creosoted pine tie; service 1912-1925, with flat tie plate 6½ in. × 10½ in., two screw spikes holding the rail.

The compression figures just given represent the strength of the wood as a whole. For instance, the compression strength of air dry longleaf pine is 1410 lb. The Pines and Douglas Fir, two very important tie woods, consist of two very distinct types of wood fibers, commonly called spring-wood and summerwood. It is commonly recognized that springwood is by no means as strong as summerwood. Actual data as to the relative strength of the wood fibers of these two distinct types have, however, been lacking. Realizing that the structural changes manifest in the wood under tie plates of mechanically worn ties might be explained by some difference in the strength of the summerwood and springwood fibers, or stating it in

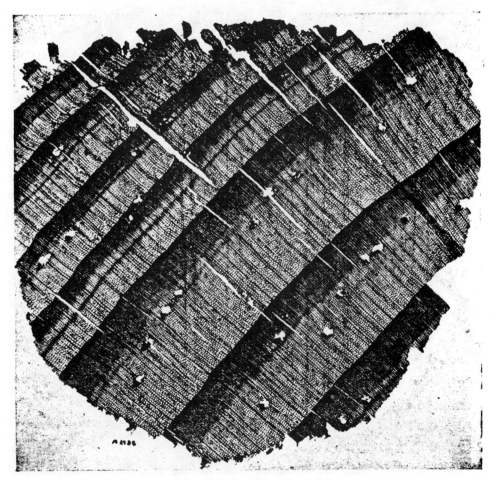

FIG. 64.

Microphotograph of a section of creosoted pine tie No. 1 (see Fig. 63), from wood not under the tie plate. Magnification fourteen times.

624

a better form, the summerwood and springwood regions, I made some preliminary tests by carving out small sticks of springwood and summerwood from the same rings. These sticks were subjected to cross-breaking tests. The individual stick had cross-sections of approximately 20 to 25 square mm. The following table gives the results of 24 determinations consisting of three groups of springwood and summerwood, respectively.

FIG. 55.

Microphotograph of a section of creosoted pine tie No. 1 (see Fig. 63), immediately under the tie plate. Magnification fourteen times.

Fig. 66.

Tie No. 2. N. Y. N. H. & H. R. R. steam-seasoned creosoted pine tie, service 1909-1924. Four longitudinal flange tie plates 5 in. × 8¾ in. Tonnage 50,000 tons per day. Maximum locomotive axle load 56,100 lb.

Table II

Comparative Strength of Summerwood and Springwood in Southern Pine

Wood Sample:	Summerwood	Maximum Fiber Stress Lb. per Sq. In. Average	Springwood	Average
I	12,440		4,720	
	10,880		4,510	
	8,385		5,100	
	9,460		5,230	
		10,291		4,890
II	10,230		3,800	
	9,340		4,150	
	9,070		5,220	
	9,210		9,450	
	.....		5,190	
		9,462		4,662
III	12,450		7,800	
	9,930		9,540	
	11,020		5,400	
	.....		10,980	
		11,133		8,430

Note.—The individual pieces of springwood and summerwood tested from each wood sample, i. e., I, II and III, were cut from the same annual ring in each case, but are not necessarily immediately adjacent to each other.

It will be noted that in general the summerwood is approximately twice as strong as the springwood. All of the figures refer to loading perpendicular to the grain.

626

X-Ray Studies.—While both the macroscopic as well as the microscopic examinations of ties, both for those in which tie plates had been forced into the ties under the testing machine as well as badly worn ties from the track, showed many interesting phenomena, it was thought that possibly X-ray studies might present features not readily visible when the necessarily small pieces of wood for both macroscopic and microscopic studies were examined. A number of trials were accordingly made at the X-Ray Laboratories of Washington University, using both old and new ties. I wish at this point to express my very sincere appreciation for the enthusiastic interest and extensive assistance given me by Dr. Sherwood Moore, head of the X-Ray Department of Washington University. The photo-

FIG. 67.

Microphotograph of a section of wood from creosoted pine tie No. 2 (see Fig. 66), not under the tie plate. Magnification fourteen times.

graphs illustrating this particular chapter were all taken by him and his assistants, and they speak for themselves.

The first X-ray studies were made of new ties into which tie plates had been artificially forced (see page 63). The long section of the Douglas fir tie shown in Fig. 95 was first X-rayed. Fig. 108 represents the result. This is an X-ray through approximately 5 inches of wood. Immediately under the tie plate area extending for a considerable distance into the tie, a very much darker area will be noted which is sharply limited from the

FIG. 68.

Microphotograph of a section of wood from creosoted pine tie No. 2 (see Fig. 66), immediately under the tie plate. Magnification fourteen times.

628

surrounding wood (the irregular dark lines near the bottom of the photograph represent defects in the film). The darkly shaded portion coincides in extent with that portion of the tie in which the wood cells had become distinctly compressed, as indicated in the microphotographs already described for pieces taken from this particular tie. (See Fig. 97 to 102.) The X-ray, in other words, records the denser portion of this tie. It also shows how the annual rings are bent down at the very edge of the tie plate. Almost in the center of the photograph one will note that the downward slanting rings seem to cross perfectly horizontal lines. This is due to the stereoscopic effect of the X-ray, which projects the bent rings immediately under the tie plate on top of the unbent rings beyond the tie plate at the edge of the tie.

FIG. 69.

Tie No. 3. Nickel Plate Lines, creosoted pine tie; service 1921-1925, with compression bottom tie plate 6¾ in. × 10 in.

The next photograph taken (Fig. 109) was of a Douglas fir tie which had been in service on the Chicago, Burlington & Quincy Railroad from 1905 to 1926, that is, for 21 years, with a tie plate 6 in. x 8½ in., under engines of maximum axle load of 50,666 lb. (For median section of this tie see Fig. 35.) In this X-ray photograph the perfect parallelism of the annual rings outside of the tie plate and under the tie plate are again manifest, and incidentally, the downward thrusting of the rings wherever the cut spikes penetrated into the wood. The most interesting part of this picture, however, is the fact that there is no such sharply defined compression diagram as in the Douglas fir tie, in which the plate had been actually compressed into the tie under the testing machine. Some of the dark spots in the photograph of the tie under traffic are doubtless accumulations of dirt and iron rust. The comparison between Fig. 108 and 109 brings out in a very striking manner that the disappearance of the wood under the tie plate is apparently not a compression phenomenon.

Fig. 110 is an X-ray photograph of a red oak tie into which a New York Central tie plate was pressed under the testing machine. (See Fig. 103.) Fig. 111 is a similar X-ray photograph of the tie illustrated in Fig. 14 and 54—a creosoted red oak tie from the Kansas City Southern Railway Company, in track twelve years. While the contrast between these two is not as striking as in the coniferous wood, nevertheless the machine-compressed tie shows the dark shadow at the edges of the tie plate and to a lesser extent under the tie plate, whereas the rail-worn tie shows no such shadow. The difference between the two is more marked in the original negative than can be brought out in a reproduction.

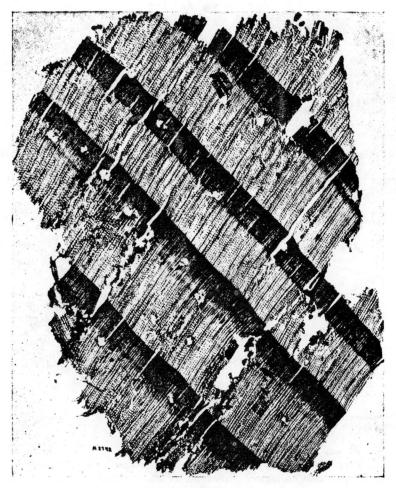

FIG. 70.

Microphotograph of a section of wood from tie No. 3 (see Fig. 69), not under tie plate. Magnification fourteen times.

In order to still further study the behavior of what I call compressed wood, as compared with mechanically worn wood, a series of X-ray studies was made of cross-sections of ties under compression. Fig. 112 represents a shortleaf pine tie (similar to the one shown in Fig. 107). In this instance a thin section only was photographed (approximately 2 in. thick) to show the effect of the compression on the rings themselves in the region immediately under the plate. In order to get sharper contrasts, this and the subsequent tie sections were soaked in a strong alcoholic solution of corrosive sublimate, and after complete penetration had been secured the

FIG. 71.

Microphotograph of a section of wood from tie No. 3 (see Fig. 69), immediately under the tie plate. Magnification fourteen times.

alcohol was allowed to evaporate. (The advantage of using alcohol as compared with water is that alcohol does not produce any swelling of the wood fiber with consequent disturbance of the structure as would be the case with water). The X-ray photograph again brings out the distortion of the rings immediately under the plate already referred to above. Another series of negatives was then made in which the tie was cut transversely, as follows: The first cut was made at about the middle of the tie plate bearing area, and the second cut was made outside of the tie plate bearing area towards the end of the tie for an equal distance. This gave a block of wood about 8 inches in length, half of which contained the volume compressed by the testing machine, while the other half consisted of the uncompressed end. The X-ray photograph was then taken endwise. Fig. 113 and 114 give two views of the same tie, one with the compressed end nearest the X-ray negative, the other with the uncompressed end nearest the X-ray negative.

Fig. 115 is another negative of a third tie compressed under the testing machine. In looking at these photographs one must think of the wood as if it were a piece of glass, in which the front portion is projected upon the back portion. Each of these three photographs shows a set of double rings in the top half. One set of these rings is almost circular, while the

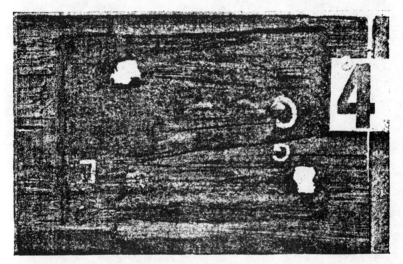

Fic. 72.

Boston & Albany R. R. creosoted pine tie; service 1914-1924. Flat bottom tie plate 6 in. × 9 in.; two cut spikes.

other set is very much flattened at the top. In Fig. 113, 114 and 115 the manner in which the rings split into two are particularly evident. This, of course, means that the X-ray shows the flattened rings (see Fig. 107 of actual photograph) of the compressed portion of the tie plotted over the same rings in the uncompressed portion of the tie. Attention is called, however, to the fact that there are also certain cross-rings near the bottom of the ties, particularly in Fig. 115. It took quite a while to find out where these apparent cross-rings came from, and it was finally discovered that this was due to the fact that in a perfectly grown tree the individual annual rings form perfect cylinders of which one might conceive the summerwood region to be the walls. In such a perfectly grown tree the walls of these concentric cylinders would be perfectly parallel, so that when

632

FIG. 73.

Microphotograph of a section of creosoted pine tie No. 4 (see Fig. 72), cut under the tie plate. Magnification fourteen times.

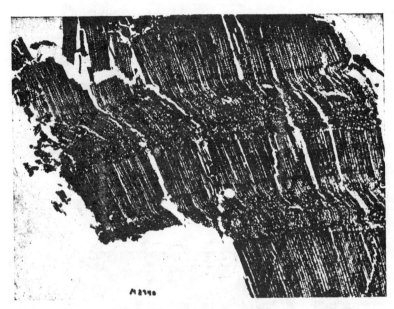

FIG. 74.

Microphotograph of a section of creosoted pine tie No. 4 (see Fig. 72), immediately under the tie plate. Magnification fourteen times.

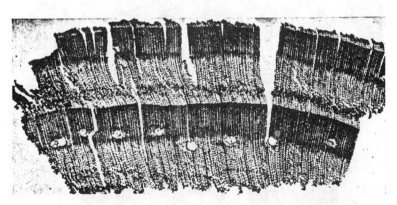

FIG. 75.

Microphotograph of a section of creosoted pine tie No. 4 (see Fig. 72), through knob protruding through unused hole in tie plate. Magnification fourteen times.

FIG. 76.

Tie No. 5, M. P. R. R. Untreated white oak tie used without tie plate, exact age unknown. Rail base 5 in. wide. Note torn condition of wood fibers under the rail.

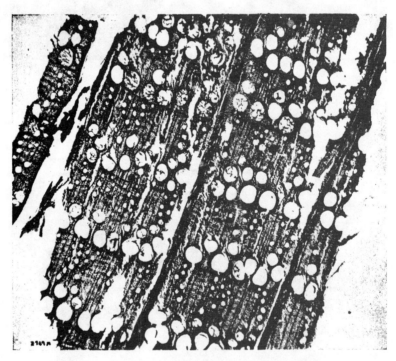

FIG. 77.

Microphotograph of a section of white oak tie No. 5 (see Fig. 76) not under the rail. Magnification fourteen times.

looked at from the end one would see a series of concentric circles. Such perfect trees are, however, very rare. In the ordinary tree these walls are not perfectly parallel. In the X-ray photographs a portion of the walls is accordingly visible, which gives this apparent crossing. A careful study of the photographs, however, will show that this crossing is very different from the splitting in the annual rings manifested under the tie plate area. Having determined from a number of studies of the wood under actual compression that one gets, first of all, a darkened area where there is compressed wood, and what appears to be more significant, a manifestation of

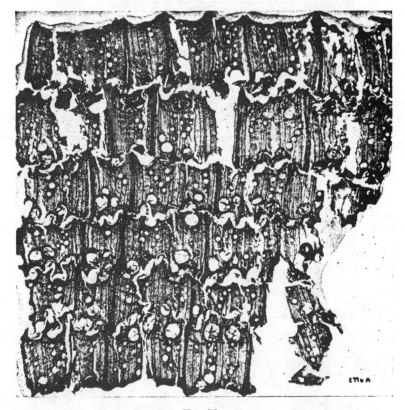

FIG. 78.

Microphotograph of a section of white oak tie No. 5 (see Fig. 76), immediately under the rail. Magnification fourteen times.

crossed rings under the tie plate area visible in cross-sections, it was believed that a means had been found for definitely diagnosing whether mechanically worn ties were compressed under the tie plate area or not. There has been time for only a comparatively few studies; in fact, this type of work has just begun. Only a few cases, therefore, are presented at this time. It is hoped that this phase of the subject may be developed more fully in a subsequent paper.

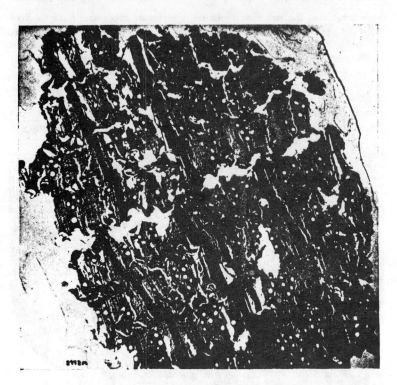

Fig. 79.

Microphotograph of a section of white oak tie No. 5 (see Fig. 76), immediately under the rail. Magnification fourteen times.

FIG. 80.

D. L. & W. R. R. creosoted pine tie (No. 6); service 1912-1924,
flat bottom plate 6 in. × 10½ in.

FIG. 81.

Microphotograph of a cross-section of creosoted pine tie No. 6 (see Fig. 80) not
under the tie plate. Magnification fourteen times.

638

The following three pictures illustrate early trials with badly worn ties. Fig. 116 represents an X-ray picture of a mechanically worn redwood tie. There is no evidence of any darkening under the tie plate, nor of any compression. Redwood does not lend itself very well to X-ray photography, probably because of its extremely uniform texture. Fig. 117 is an X-ray photograph of a Douglas fir tie from the Beaumont Division of the Santa Fe, and Fig. 118 represents a similar creosoted pine tie, badly worn, in service 1909-1924, taken from the New York, New Haven & Hartford Railroad. In both of these cases the X-ray photograph was taken endwise; that is, with half of the tie below the tie plate area and half of the tie outside of the tie plate area. In both of these photographs the area beyond the tie plate is shown at the top of the picture. The extent of mechanical wear is likewise very evident. The point of particular interest in both of these pictures is that the direction of the annual rings is exactly the same under the tie plate area as it is outside of the tie plate area; in fact, they match absolutely where the rings under the tie plate meet the rings outside of the tie plate.

FIG. 82.

Microphotograph of a section of creosoted pine tie No. 6 (see Fig. 80), immediately under the tie plate. Magnification fourteen times.

These preliminary X-ray studies confirm the macroscopic and microscopic studies already presented, and seem to indicate most conclusively that the disappearance of the wood in mechanically worn ties is not due to compression as the sole factor.

Track Evidences.—Some twenty-three years ago, I was very much struck by the practice of the French Eastern Railway (see Bureau of Forestry, Bulletin No. 50; page 62: 1904). The creosoted ties, chiefly

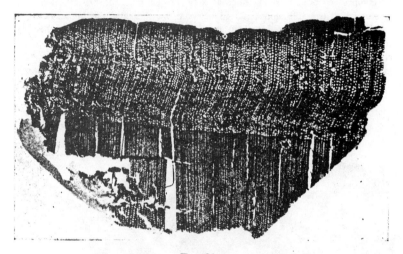

FIG. 83.

Microphotograph of a cross-section through knob projecting in the tie plate of creosoted pine tie No. 6 (see Fig. 80). Magnification fourteen times.

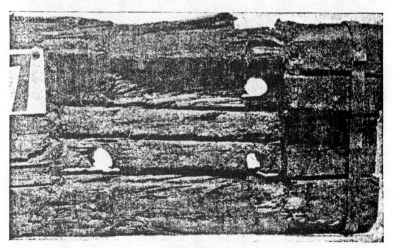

FIG. 84.

N. Y., N. H. & H. R. R. creosoted pine tie No. 7, service 1909-1924. Four longitudinal flange tie plates, 5 in. × 8¾ in. Tonnage 50,000 tons per day. Maximum locomotive axle load 56,100 lb.

beech, gave an average life of 30 years or more. The most striking fact in connection with this long life was the observation that there was as little if any mechanical wear. When compared with the results on other continental European railroads, this absence of mechanical wear was most striking. The engineers of this company claimed that these remarkable results were due to the fact that they had discarded or practically never used any type of metal tie plate. Instead of metal tie plates they were using compressed poplar wood shims as a tie protection. In 1879 this company started to use felt shims, placed between the rail and the tie. These felt shims were compressed and in many cases, creosoted. At first they were used exclusively, and they continued to use some of them until 1895. Early in 1893 an experimental installation on the divisions in the neighborhood of Paris was constructed with poplar wood shims without compression and from 1895 to 1903 the uncompressed poplar shim was used on the entire system. The poplar shims were substituted for the felt because the latter were more expensive and furthermore, because they were found not to have the necessary qualifications. In 1903, with the invention of the

Fig. 85.

Microphotograph of a section of wood from creosoted pine tie No. 7 (see Fig. 84), not under the tie plate. Magnification fourteen times.

compressed poplar shim, an experimental section was put in on the Paris Division and by 1910 the compressed poplar tie plate was used on the entire system, concurrently with the non-compressed poplar shim. By the end of 1913, the compressed poplar shim was made standard on the whole system and it is still so used. A specification for these shims as purchased at the present time is attached hereto. (See page 115.)

The shims are 4 mm. in thickness, of a width corresponding to the base of the rail used (97 to 132 mm.) and 240 mm. long. They are made of carefully selected wood and are compressed one-half. Fig. 128 shows the method of use.

As a matter of interest, Fig. 129 is a photograph showing a portion of the French Eastern main line in southeastern France. The two ties with white squares are creosoted beech ties inserted in 1871 as indicated by the dating nails. They showed no evidence of any mechanical wear. The shims are simply laid on pre-adzed ties and are held in position by the pressure exerted on the rail by the two screw spikes. (See Fig. 128.)

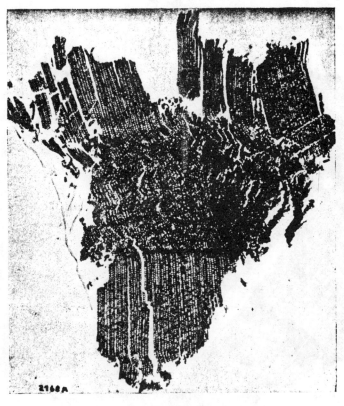

FIG. 86.

Microphotograph of a section of wood from creosoted pine tie No. 7 (see Fig. 84), immediately under the tie plate. Magnification fourteen times.

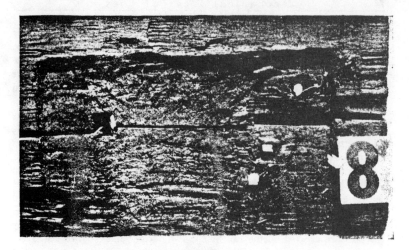

FIG. 87.

Tie No. 8. P. & L. E. R. R. creosoted pine tie, service 1913-1925; using two screw spikes for holding tie plate.

FIG. 88.

Microphotograph of a section of creosoted pine tie No. 8 (see Fig. 87) not under tie plate. Magnification fourteen times.

The life of these shims varies with circumstances and may be from one
year to many years.   On the recent inspection referred to, I took out
some from the very heavy traffic yard tracks near Paris which had been
in service five years or more.   These shims were somewhat splintered but
were still functioning.

The most striking feature of the employment of these shims is that
there is practically no mechanical wear on the ties. A great many of the
older ties were examined with care and the surface of the wood under
these shims was perfectly smooth and showed no evidences of splintering or

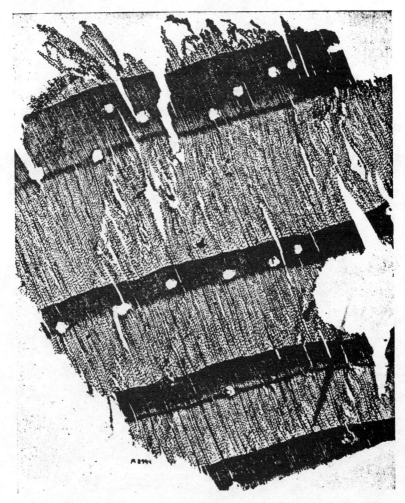

FIG. 89.

Microphotograph of a section of creosoted pine tie No. 8 (see Fig. 87), immediately under tie plate. Magnification fourteen times.

FIG. 90.

Microphotograph of a section of wood from London, Midland & Scottish Railway, England; creosoted pine tie, 20 years' service. (See Fig. 125-A1.) View taken from section not under the chair. Magnification fourteen times.

FIG. 90.

Microphotograph of a section of wood from London, Midland & Scottish Railway, England; creosoted ne tie, 20 years' service. (See Fig. 125-A1.) View taken from section not under the chair. Magnification urteen times.

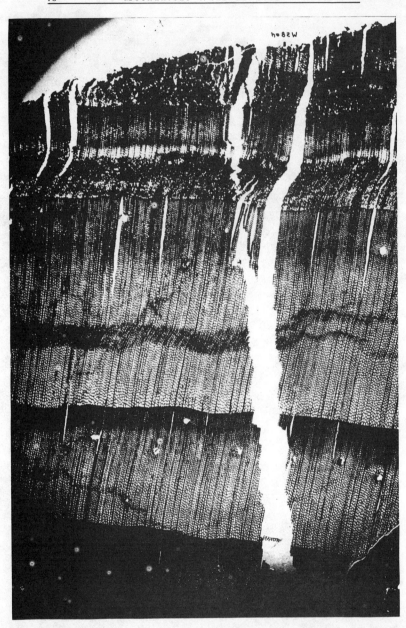

Fig. 91.

Microphotograph of a section of wood from London, Midland & Scottish Railway, England; creosoted pine tie, 20 years' service. (See Fig. 125-A1.) View taken from section immediately under the chair. Magnification fourteen times.

Cause of Mechanical Wear

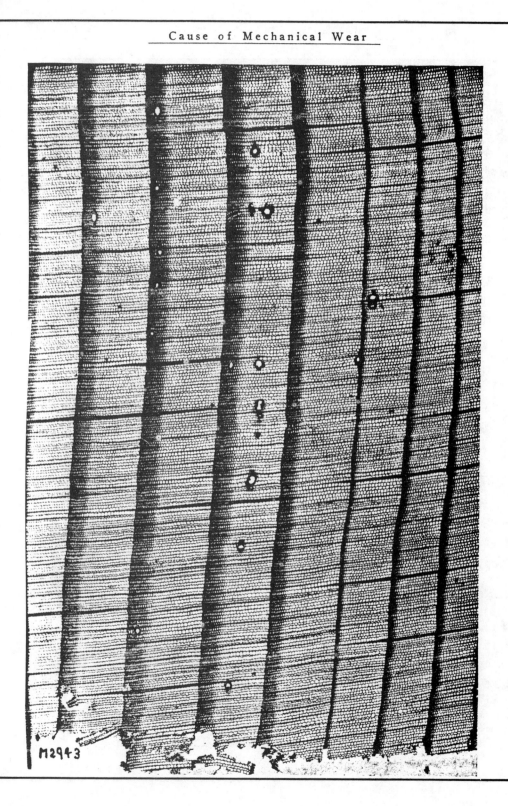

M2943

Fig. 92.

Microphotograph of a section from C. B. & Q. R. R. Douglas fir tie No. 328 (see Fig. 56). Not under tie plate. Magnification fourteen times. (Compare with Fig. 93.)

Fig. 94.

Compression test on oak and Douglas fir ties, using New York Central tie plate.
(A) Douglas fir with tie plate after compression; (B) Douglas fir tie, plate removed
immediately after compression; (C) Red oak tie with tie plate immediately after compression; (D) Red oak tie, tie plate removed after compression. Pressure on fir tie,
3000 lb. per sq. in.; on oak tie, 4440 lb. per sq. in.

Fig. 95.

Longitudinal section of Douglas fir tie in compression test. Numerals 1 to 6 indicate position at which microscopic sections were made. Note the manner in which the annual rings are crushed down under the plate seat.

FIG. 96.

Section of wood from Douglas fir tie used in compression test, taken from region *outside* of tie plate at point 5, in Fig. 95. Magnification eleven times.

wear. The French Eastern engineers are absolutely positive in their viewpoint that the extremely long life (incidentally longer than on any other European railroad) which they obtained from their ties is due to the wooden shim protection. It is certainly remarkable to note that there is a possibility of obtaining 50 years or more mechanical life, to say nothing of decay resistance for that period. As will be indicated further on, the railroads in Belgium, Germany, Austria and other continental European countries have the same difficulty with the sinking in of tie plates and rail—in other words, mechanical destruction of their ties, as we do. Contrasting with this general experience is that of the French Eastern. As will be indicated further on, the axle load of locomotives and cars is practically the same

Fig. 97.

Section of wood from Douglas fir tie used in compression test, taken immediately under the tie plate, point 1 in Fig. 95. Magnification eleven times. (For more highly magnified photographs of Regions A and B see Figs. 101 and 102.)

for the French Eastern as for the other continental railroads. There is some factor then connected with the use of these wooden shims which has a very significant bearing on the general question of mechanical wear.

American Tests.—On my return from Europe in 1903, I felt very much impressed with this experience and in the discussion printed in 1904 (see U.S. Forest Service Bulletin 50) I made the following statement: "The theory upon which the use of this wooden plate is used may be briefly stated. The principal function of the plate has been said to consist of preventing the wear of the fibers of the tie immediately under the rail base. This wear consists in the actual breakage of the wood fibers under a grinding and tearing action rather than in crushing them.

FIG. 98.

Section of wood from Douglas fir tie used in compression test, taken one inch below tie plate, point 2 in Fig. 95. Magnification eleven times.

"In considering the function of the tie plate we have three bodies to deal with—the tie, the tie plate, and the rail. Motion might conceivably take place either between the rail and the tie plate or between the tie plate and the tie. When a metal tie plate is used on the hardwood tie, and is successfully anchored in it, the tie plate and the tie act as one body, over which the rail moves back and forth. As soon as the tie plate loses its holding power, however, the chances are that when the rail moves across the tie the tie plate will oscillate back and forth in unison with the rail. This results in breaking the wood fibers underneath the plate. Where a

Fig. 99.

Section of wood from Douglas fir tie used in compression test taken two inches below tie plate, point 3 in Fig. 95. Magnification eleven times.

wooden plate is used it adheres so closely to the wood that when the rail moves across the tie the wooden plate and the wooden tie are liable to act as one, even though the tie plate is not anchored to the tie.

"This means that any wear will probably be at the expense of the plate instead of the tie. The wooden plate is cheap, and can be replaced at no great cost. By its use the wear caused by the steel plate in the softer woods is practically entirely avoided. Ties which have been in position with these wooden plates for many years on the French roads show a most remarkable absence of wear of any sort. The wooden plates have the further advantage that they are quickly and easily applied, and that they are ex-

FIG. 100.

Section of wood from Douglas fir tie used in compression test taken three inches below tie plate, point 4 in Fig. 95. Magnification eleven times.

tremely cheap. They can, however, be used only under a fastening which holds the base of the rail strictly against the tie, such as the screw spike."

Some years after the appearance of this publication, a number of trial pieces of track were put in, notably on the Big Four, Santa Fe, Rock Island, Frisco and Northern Pacific Railways, using the French wooden shim idea. These shims were placed on new ties, none of which, however, were adzed. In view of the fact that we had no screw spikes, these shims were nailed to the ties with small galvanized nails. Fig. 119 shows a new tie on the Santa Fe inserted with wooden shims, and Fig. 119 and 120 show some of the shims in position. (See also Mr. Kendrick's reference to this experiment, Proceedings A.R.E.A., *11*:589; 1910.) Many of the shims splintered and broke very badly after traffic started over that particular section where they had been installed. Some of them remained in position, however (Fig. 121). The chief impression gained, however, was that they

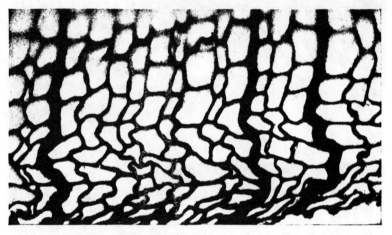

FIG. 101.

Cross-section of Douglas fir springwood immediately under compression plate (see A in Fig. 97 at lower magnification). Magnification 145 times.

were unsuited to our American conditions. The nails would not hold them; they splintered and broke, probably largely because of the uneven surface upon which they were applied; they moved out from under the rail and there was no way of putting new ones back. The general conclusion, therefore, was that they could not be used. And so far as I know there was no further attempt made to experiment with this idea.

During the past year, however, stimulated by my renewed observations on the French Eastern Railway recently, a thorough investigation of the workings of these old wooden shims on our American railroads was made. Much to our surprise we found some of them still in service on the Big Four Railway. The shims on the Big Four were made of beech and were nailed with two nails. They, as in other cases, were applied to ties both sawed and hewn.

FIG. 102.

Cross-section of Douglas fir tie in sixth annual ring below compression plate. (See B in Fig. 97 at lower magnification.)   Magnification 145 times.

658

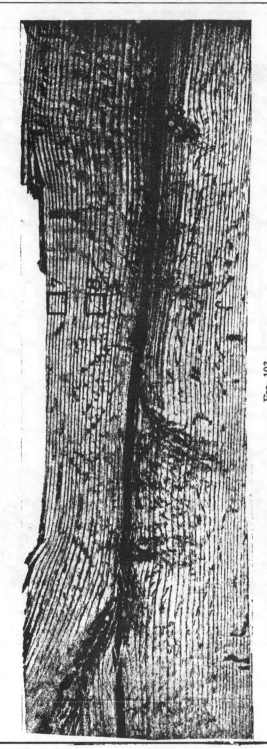

Fig. 103.

Longitudinal section of wood from oak in compression test. Numerals 7, 8 and 9 indicate positions at which microscopic sections were made. Note the manner in which the annual rings curve down under the plate seat.

Fig. 122 shows a 1906 creosoted red oak tie on which one of these beech shims was placed in 1908. This tie was taken out in 1926. Fig. 122 also shows the red oak tie immediately adjacent to the tie just described, which had no shim on it when taken out. Fig. 122 likewise shows a view of these two ties from the side. Fig. 123 shows another tie (No. 2) from which the shim dropped off when the tie was removed. Tie marked 3 in this same photograph is a creosoted red oak tie which evidently had a shim in the early days, as indicated by the two nails, but which had none at the time of removal. Fig. 123 also shows a side view of these same two ties. At-

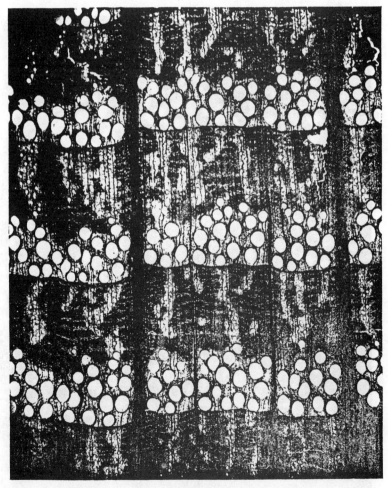

Fig. 104.

Section of wood from red oak tie used in compression test. View from region outside of tie plate at point 9 in Fig. 103. Magnification eleven times.

tention is called first to the fact that these ties had been in position two years before the application of the shims; hence they showed some mechanical wear. The next point of interest is to note that these two ties with the shims show no further evidence of mechanical wear after twenty years in track, whereas the ties immediately adjacent show not only mechanical wear but the characteristic roughened, splintered surface so well known when ties are worn mechanically. In distinction thereto, note the smooth, undisturbed surface of the ties in Fig. 123, tie No. 2 from which the shim has been removed.

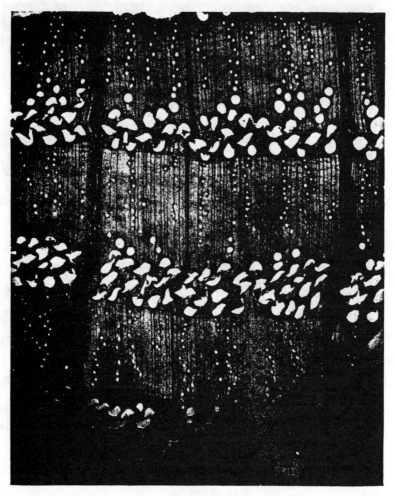

Fig. 105.

Section of wood from red oak tie used in compression test. View taken at point 7 in Fig. 103, immediately under tie plate. Magnification eleven times.

The report from the roadmaster in charge of this particular section is furthermore illuminating. He states that the ties which were protected by the wooden shims showed no signs of mechanical wear.

The above-reference to these wooden shims is made at this place because it should be taken in connection with the preceding description of mechanically worn ties, both macroscopic and microscopic. A further reference to these wooden shims will be made in a later part of this discussion.

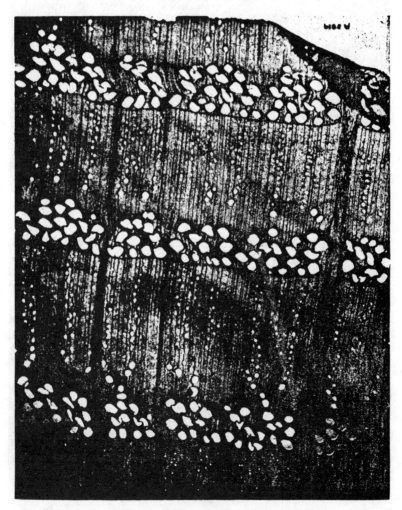

FIG. 106.

Section of wood from red oak tie used in compression test. View taken at point 8 in Fig. 103, one inch below tie plate. Magnification eleven times.

662

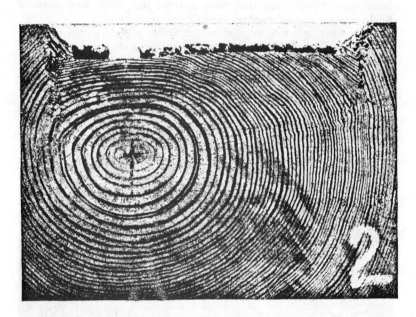

Fig. 107.

Two sections of shortleaf pine ties into which a tie plate was pressed 1½ inches under testing machine, under a load of 2,000 lb. per sq. in. Section through the middle of tie plate area. Note distortion of rings and breakage of wood fibers.

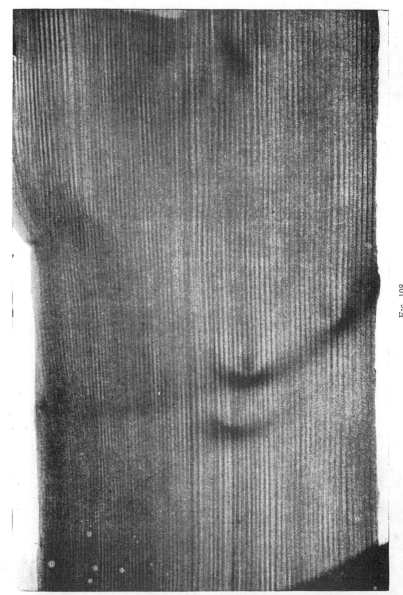

Fig. 108.

X-Ray photograph of a Douglas fir tie into which a N. Y. C. tie plate was pressed, using 150,000 lb. under testing machine. Note the well-defined shadow showing compression under the tie plate. (The very black marks are the result of defects in the plate.)

Fig. 109.

EUROPEAN PRACTICE*

Introduction.—The subject of mechanical destruction of cross-ties has naturally engaged the attention of European railway engineers as much as it has our own. While their conditions of traffic, weight of locomotives and trains are different from ours, there are fundamental considerations with reference to track construction which are significant and worthy of study. Accordingly, during the summer of 1925 I spent several months on various railways in England, France, Holland, Belgium, Germany, Austria, Switzerland and Italy, in an endeavor to see how they were meeting

---

*As indicated above, the data which follow reference European practice were obtained in the latter part of 1925 and all costs are as given at that time. They doubtless have changed somewhat since then. The standard practice, so far as the writer is advised, is the same in all countries, with the exception of Germany, where, according to latest advices, the use of a modified track plan as shown in Fig. 132, i. e., what has been called herein a modified Austrian chair tie plate, has been adopted as standard early in 1928 (see p. 179).

Fig. 110.

X-Ray photograph of a red oak tie into which a N. Y. C. tie plate was pressed under testing machine. Note shadow under the plate area.

the problem of mechanical wear. It was interesting to note that in all of these countries, this was a subject uppermost in the mind of those responsible for track construction and maintenance. I found this to be particularly true in Germany and Austria. Believing that their practice and investigations may have some bearing on our own problems, a brief statement of present practice follows herewith.

Types of European Tie Protection and Rail Fastening

There are at present in use various types of protection and fastening which for the sake of convenience may be briefly classified as follows:

First. Tie plates with cut spikes—this system is still in use in some parts of Germany, Austria, and Italy.

Second. Modified form of tie plate with clips, using either spikes or more frequently screw spikes. This type of fastening is standard in Germany, Belgium, Holland, Austria, and Italy.

FIG. 111.

X-Ray photograph of a K. C. S. Ry. red oak tie—1914-1926 (see Figs. 14 and 54). Note absence of shadow.

Third. Chair tie plates in which the plate is attached to the tie independently of the rail with screw spikes and the rail is held to the tie plate by means of bolts. This system is used on some of the Austrian railways.

Fourth. Chair fastening—this consists in the use of a large cast iron chair firmly bolted or screwed to the tie. The rail is held in a socket in the chair by means of wooden plugs. This system is standard practice on all the English railways and is used to some extent in France.

Fifth. Wooden shim and screw spike fastening. This system consists of placing a ~~ ressed poplar wood shim between the rail and the tie, and the rail is ~~ned to the tie by means of screw spikes. This is the system employed by the French Eastern Railway and in an experimental manner on the German Railway System.

For a proper understanding of these different types more or less detailed description of tie practice, plate protection and fastening for each country follow herewith, together with incidental information obtained as to weight of rail, axle load of locomotives, cost factors, etc. This information has been arranged by countries for the sake of convenience.

FIG. 112.

X-Ray photograph of shortleaf pine tie into which tie plate was forced by testing machine. Tie treated with 0.5 per cent HgCl₂ alcoholic solution and then dried.

668

England.—The English railways use Baltic pine ties (very much like our shortleaf pine) 8 ft. 6 in. long, 10 in. wide and 5 in. thick. These ties are laid 2112 to the mile. All ties after careful seasoning, adzing and boring are thoroughly creosoted. The cast iron chairs, weighing 46 lb., with a bearing area of 115 sq. in. are then fastened to the ties by means of lag screws. On the Great Western Railway the chairs are firmly seated by means of a hydraulic press exerting a pressure of approximately 11 tons. A felt cushion is placed between the tie and the chair. The chairing machine which I saw operated by the Great Western Railway operated eight hours a day and had a capacity of about 528 ties per day. Newly creosoted and chaired ties are distributed to the track in specially

X-Ray photograph of a Douglas fir tie (Fig. 107-2), into which a tie plate was forced by testing machine. View taken through 6 inches of tie, including 3 inches of tie plate area and 3 inches outside of the tie plate area. Tie plate area next to negative. In the original negative the part of the tie outside of the tie plate was very dim, and in order to bring same out in the print, a sharper line of demarcation was necessary than in the original negative. Compare, in this connection, with Fig. 114, which is an exact print of the original negative, but which does not show the uncompressed portion of the tie. This double printing was carried out in order to show the continuity of the uncompressed rings beyond the tie plate area as compared with the flattened rings under the tie plate area. Note, also, in this connection, the denser shadow under the immediate compression area, particularly at the edge.

constructed cars and are laid out of face. They remain in track from 15 to 20 years after which all ties are removed out of face, loaded on cars and shipped to a central storage yard (see Fig. 126). At the storage yard the chairs are removed and all ties are carefully inspected and classified into three grades:

No. 1—Ties which are without any defects whatever and which are serviceable for another term of years.

No. 2—Ties in which slight defects are visible. These ties are sawed into 4 x 4 fence posts and fencing slats. At the storage yard of the London Midland and Scottish Railway the No. 2 ties are invoiced on the books at 5 shillings ($1.25). After sawing the bar posts are invoiced at 62 cents a piece to the Maintenance Department, the rails and stick at 15 cents each and larger end posts at $2.50 each. One tie will make one post, two prick posts or two rails, or six rails, or six prick posts. It is of interest to note that the sawdust obtained from the mill is also sold for hog bedding. Truly an interesting chapter in conservation.

No. 3.—Ties which are decayed (usually in the untreated heartwood) for which no future service may be expected, are used for fuel.

Fig. 114.

X-Ray photograph of Douglas fir tie (Fig. 107-2), into which a tie plate was forced by testing machine. Views taken through 6 inches of tie, including 3 inches of tie plate area and 3 inches outside of the tie plate area. Uncompressed part next to negative.

In 1924 the classification of ties removed after twenty years of service was as follows:

No. 1	20 per cent
No. 2	75 per cent
No. 3	5 per cent

A careful study was made of the mechanical action of the chair on the tie. A great many of the 20-year old ties were carefully measured as the chairs were being removed. The attached photographs (Fig. 124 and 125) show some of the chairs in position and the appearance of the chair seat after removal of the chair. It was rather remarkable to note that in the majority of cases there was apparently little or no compression of the wood. The deepest compression was found in some water trough ties in which the compression amounted to ½ in. on the outside. (See Fig. 127.) The felt cushions under these old chairs were still intact. The screws were

Fig. 115.

X-Ray photograph of sawed pine tie into which tie plate was compressed by testing machine. This piece was treated with one-tenth per cent HgCl₂ alcoholic solution. Note the crossed rings under the tie plate.

bright and close examination showed that they had all been galvanized. Samples of the chair bearing were secured for detailed microscopic study of the wood fiber structure which is now in progress.

Conclusions as to British Railway Practice

The results of my investigations clearly indicate that the chair fastening undoubtedly prevents what we call mechanical destruction of ties—in fact, the British engineers do not recognize any such classification. The failures in their ties are due almost wholly to decay and that in the untreated heartwood (no evidences of decay of the creosoted ring were noted anywhere). The loads which are carried by the ties are smaller than is the practice in the United States. The maximum axle load on their engines is about 22 U.S. tons and the heaviest cars about 12½ tons to the axle. The actual bearing area of the chairs

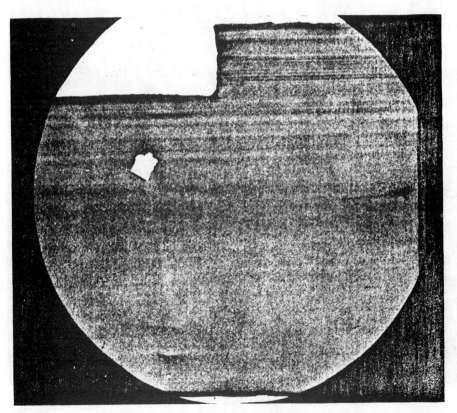

FIG. 116.

X-Ray photograph of Redwood tie, Southern Pacific Company; service 13 years. (See Figs. 33 and 34.) Note absence of shadow under the tie plate.

(115 sq. in.) as contrasted with, for instance the New York Central 11 in. x 7 in. plate (77 sq. in.) gives them approximately the same bearing area per mile as is the case with 11 in. x 7 in. tie plates in the United States (see attached table of bearings). The absence of mechanical destruction is, in my opinion, due largely to the fact that the chairs are securely anchored to the ties and that there is very little, if any, motion between the base of the chair and the top of the tie. It is this factor rather than larger distribution which undoubtedly accounts for the small amount of tie wear. The following tabulation gives details as to the various parts of track for the London Midland and Scottish Railway and for the Great Western Railway.

FIG. 117.

X-Ray photograph of a Rueping-treated Douglas fir tie—Santa Fe, Beaumont Division, treated with HgCl₂. Tie plate section was next to negative. Piece 8 in. thick including half of the tie plate section, and an equal volume of tie outside the tie plate area. The lighter part at the top is the region beyond the tie plate area.

London, Midland & Scottish Railway

Rail

95 lb.—60-foot lengths.
Service main line—18-20 years.
Tunnel clearances—2'9".

Ties

Size—8½' x 10¼" x 5" (formerly 9' length).
24 to 60' Rail—2112 to mile.
General spacing 2'7½"—joints closer.
Cost: Baltic pine 14/3 = $3.56.
       Douglas fir 17/6 = $4.37.
Chairs: Area 7¾" x 14⅜" = 111 sq. in. (old) weight 45 lb.
       No pressure applied on new chairs.

Locomotives

Max. axle load—20 tons = 22.04 U. S. tons.

FIG. 118.

X-Ray photograph of a creosoted pine tie 1909-1924—N. Y., N. H. & H. R. R. (See Fig. 5.) Note the pocket caused by the tie plate, also the lighter-colored rings of wood of the tie beyond the tie plate pocket. The rings of the two portions coincide perfectly.

GREAT WESTERN RAILWAY

Ties

Size—8'6" x 10" x 5".
18 to 45' Rail = 2112 per mile.
24 to 60' Rail = 2112 per mile.
Chairs—New standard: Area 115 sq. in.
                  Weight 46 lb.
                  Cost £7 a ton = per chair $0.80.
Average spacing 2'7" to centers, i.e., space between sleepers = 1'9".
Their actual bearing = 21,120 lin. in.
  (Ave. 3200 ties = 28,800 in.)

Locomotives

Max. axle load engines: 20 tons = 22.04 U. S. tons.
Cars: 4-5 tons per axle, car weight 20 tons = 22.04 U. S. tons.

FIG. 119.
New cypress ties—Santa Fe Ry., with new cypress shims applied.

FIG. 120.
Cypress tie—Santa Fe Ry., rail-worn, with new cypress shim placed in depression.

France.—In France my studies were confined to the French Eastern Railway. Installation, using wooden shims has already been referred to (see Fig. 128). The French Eastern system of tie protection differs from our own and that of almost all other railways in that there is no attempt at load distribution. In other words, our tie plate design is based largely on the idea that in order to protect the ties from mechanical destruction a plate should be used which will distribute the loads over a greater area of the tie. In the French Eastern plant the wooden shim has the

Fig. 121.

Cypress ties—Santa Fe Ry., with cypress shims removed to show absence of wear. Service 3 years.

exact area of the rail and the French argue that it is not load distribution which they desire to attain but what they are after is to take up any mechanical abrasion and have such abrasion act on the cheap easily replaceable shim, thereby protecting and saving the valuable tie. While their loads (19.8 U. S. tons per locomotive axle) are very much lighter than our own, they also have a very much lighter rail so that the total number of square inches of bearing on the tie per mile is very much smaller than on our

676

Fig. 122.

Springfield Division, C. C. C. & St. L. Ry. Creosoted red oak ties, service 1906 to 1926; wood shims were applied in 1908. No. 1 showing position of beech shim (5 in. × 8 in. × ¼ in.), applied 1908; No. 4, tie next to No. 1 which had no shim. Heaviest present weight on drivers 210,000-240,000 lb. (four axles). Gross ton-miles 440,432 (1913) to 737,258 (1925).

Fig. 123.

Springfield Division, C. C. C. & St. L. Ry. Top and side views of creosoted beech and red oak ties; service 1906-1926. No. 2 creosoted beech which had wooden shim placed two years after insertion. No. 3 creosoted red oak tie adjacent to No. 2 which also had wooden shim. In this case, however, the wooden shim was destroyed. Gross ton-miles, 440,432 (1913) to 737,258 (1925). Maximum weight on drivers (4 axles) at present is 210,000-240,000 lb.

678

standard railways, for instance, the actual figures being 161,381 sq. in. for the French Eastern, and 246,400 sq. in. for the New York Central. The chief difference in my mind between the French Eastern plan and our own is that in the former the movement of the rail is taken up by the shim, while in our own case it is transmitted through the tie plate to the tie. In the first case the shim wears out, and in our case the tie is worn out.

The mechanical life of the creosoted beech tie, as used by the French Eastern, is always astonishing to an American. Fig. 129 shows a piece of main line track in which there were many ties which had been in service fifty years or longer. The two ties marked with square white markers were laid in 1871. The photograph was taken in 1925; in other words, these ties had been in continuous service for 54 years.

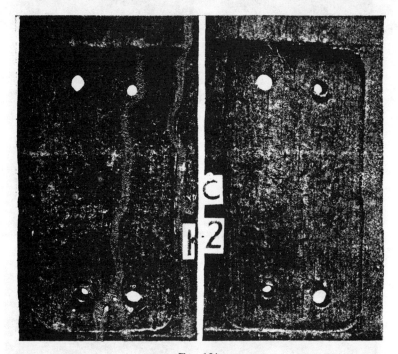

Fig. 124.

London, Midland & Scottish Railway, England. Tie "C" removed from track near Cheddington after 22 years' service, showing bearing area of chairs. Approximate traffic 550,000,000 tons.

The shims which are being used at the present time are compressed creosoted poplar, 9½ in. long, 6 in. wide, and approximately ¼ in. in thickness between the rail and the tie. The longitudinal fiber of the shim runs parallel with the rail and is at right angles to the fiber of the tie. The shim is the exact width of the base of the rail. It is held in position by the pressure of the two screw spikes as shown in attached Fig. 128.

The history of the wooden shim is of interest, and the following gives a detailed statement of its development:

679

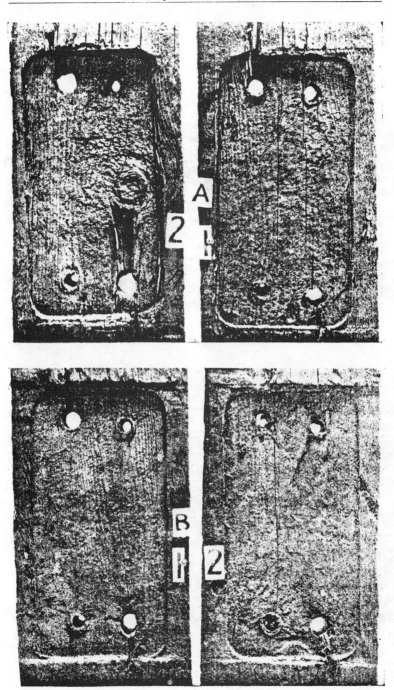

FIG. 125.

London, Midland & Scottish Railway, England. Views showing bearing area of chairs. Ties "A" and "B" removed from track near Tring after 20 years' service. Approximate traffic 500,000,000 tons.

FIG. 126.

Typical track, Great Western Railway, England, showing relation of ties and chairs. In the upper photograph note ties at the side, recently removed out of face after 15 years' service, from adjacent track. These old ties are now about to be classified and many will go back into service.

FIG. 127.

London, Midland & Scottish Railway, England. Three chairs on creosoted Baltic
pine ties after 20 years' service in track. Note method of fastening; also how little
the chairs have become seated in the wood. Maximum axle load 22 tons.

The French Eastern Railway has used some kind of shim since 1879. The following gives a detailed history of the various phases:

From 1879 to 1895—Felt shims were used which were compressed and creosoted.

From 1893 to 1895—Experimental installation of poplar shims used without compression on the divisions in the neighborhood of Paris.

From 1895 to 1903—General use of uncompressed poplar shims on the entire system. The poplar shims were used instead of the felt shims because the latter cost too much and were found not to have the necessary qualifications.

In 1903   —Invention of the compressed poplar tie plate which was put in experimental sections in the Paris Division.

In 1910   —A compressed poplar tie plate was used on the entire system concurrently with the non-compressed poplar tie plate.

End of 1913   —Exclusive use on the whole system of the compressed poplar tie plate.

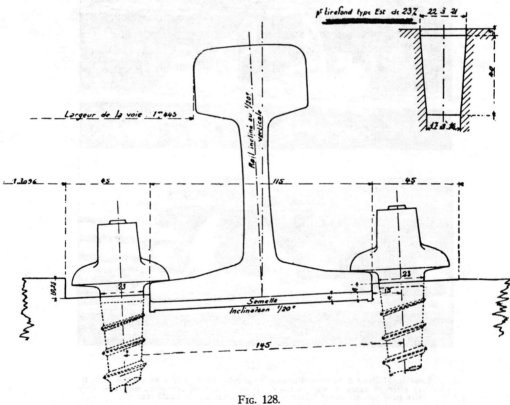

Fig. 128.

Standard Construction, French Eastern Railway. Note the wooden shim (Semelle) under the rail.

There is attached hereto a specification for the poplar shim. At the present time the creosoted compressed poplar tie plate is universally used. The life of these shims varies with circumstances and may be from one year to many years. I took out some from the very heavy traffic yard tracks near Paris which had been in service 5 years or more. These were somewhat splintered but were still functioning.

The specifications used by the French Eastern for the purchase of poplar shims are as follows:

Type of Shims

The Company uses two kinds of shims, one, ordinary shims compressed, and second, canted shims which are not compressed. The shims should have the following dimensions:

ORDINARY

Before Compression

Weight of Rail	Length	Width	Thickness
72.8 lb.	240 mm.	92- 93 mm.	7-8 mm.
101.4 lb.	240 mm.	121-122 mm.	7-8 mm.
79.4 lb.	240 mm.	107-108 mm.	7-8 mm.
101.4 lb.	240 mm.	125-126 mm.	7-8 mm.

After Compression

Width	Length	Width	Thickness
72.8 lb.	240 mm.	97- 98 mm.	4 mm.
101.4 lb.	240 mm.	127-128 mm.	4 mm. 5
79.4 lb.	240 mm.	112-113 mm.	4 mm.
101.4 lb.	240 mm.	131-132 mm.	4 mm. 5

Fig. 129.

French Eastern Railway with creosoted beech ties. The two marked with white squares were inserted in 1871—photographed 1925; 54 years' service. Both had wooden shims between the rail and tie.

CANTED

Without Compression

Weight of Rail	Length	Width	Thickness
72.8 lb.	240 mm.	96- 97 mm.	$\frac{3+6}{2}$
101 4 lb.	240 mm.	125-126 mm.	$\frac{3+6}{2}$
79.4 lb.	240 mm.	111-112 mm.	$\frac{3+6}{2}$
101.4 lb.	240 mm.	130-131 mm.	$\frac{3+6}{2}$

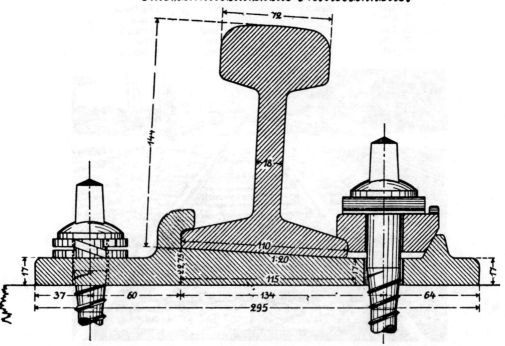

Querschnitt durch die Mittelschwelle.

FIG. 130.

German Government Railways. Tie plate design used in 1911. Note lock washer between screw head and tie plate.

Quality

The shims should be of poplar wood including the one known as gris-sard, Dutch, Swiss or Canadian poplar, but not including Italian poplar. The wood must be of the best quality, free from heartwood, perfectly sound and without any traces of fermentation, entirely free from knots, worn holes, checks, splits or other defects. They must be manufactured from the trunk of the tree, that is, wood from the branches should not be used. The flat faces must be parallel. Ordinary shims must have exact thickness as above specified. The cross-section of the canted shims must conform to the design.

Before fabrication, the contractor must furnish the Company samples of each type of shim. After acceptance of these pieces, they will serve as types for future delivery. The shims should be piled before acceptance in such a manner as to avoid any trace of moulding or fermentation.

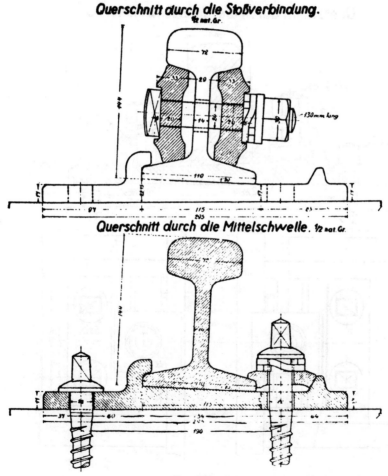

Querschnitt durch die Stoßverbindung.

Querschnitt durch die Mittelschwelle. ½ nat. Gr.

FIG. 131.

Standard construction for wood ties, German Railway Co. Joint and intermediate sections.

Acceptance and Compression

Before compression, the plates will be examined individually at the works of the contractor by a representative of the Railway. After acceptance, they are to be packed in packages of 100 firmly secured by means of two wire circlets. The trademark of the contractor should be applied to each shim so as to be readily visible. All packages should carry the acceptance number of the Railway representative.

After individual compression the shims should be placed in packages of 25 or 50 with at least two tie wires having a diameter of 2 mm.

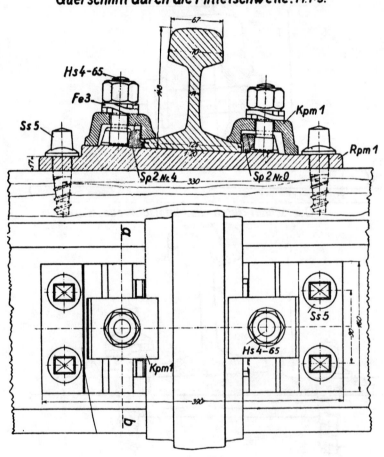

Oberbauform K49m

Querschnitt durch die Mittelschwelle. M.1:3.

FIG. 132.

Experimental design, German Railway Co.—using a type of chair tie plate similar to the Austrian standard (for curves).

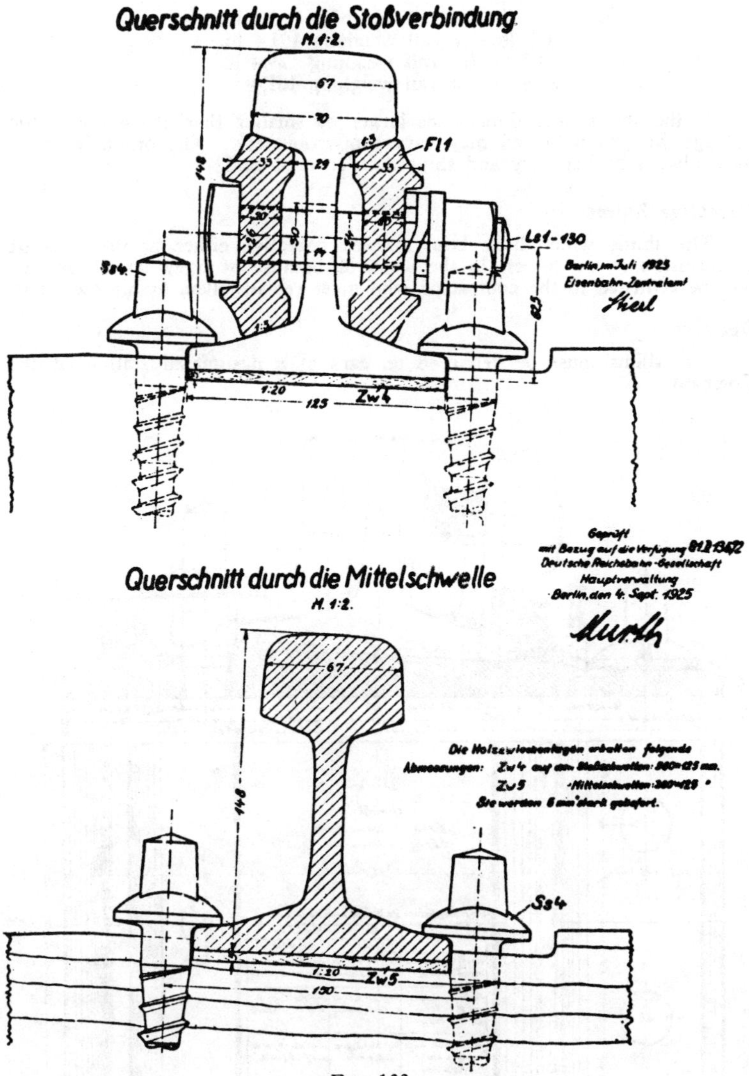

687

FIG. 133.

German Railway Co. Experimental construction using the French Eastern wood shim design. Joint and intermediate sections.

Drying

The canted shims must be furnished green. The ordinary shims may be furnished dry before compression. The weight of the ordinary shims in an air dry condition must be in the neighborhood of 26.5 lb. per cu. ft., which corresponds for 100 shims of the average dimension to the following weights:

    15.8 lb. for rail weighing 72.8 lb.
    20.7 lb. for rail weighing 101.4 lb.
    18.3 lb. for rail weighing 79.4 lb.
    21.4 lb. for rail weighing 101.4 lb.

If the shims have dimensions larger or smaller than the average, the average weights indicated may vary proportionately. The ordinary shims must always be kept dry and shipped in covered cars.

Defective Shims

The shims which have been marked defective either at the time of compression or of defects in the wood or because of irregular dimensions will be returned to the contractor who must replace them at his own cost.

Delivery

The shims must be delivered on cars at a designated station of the Company.

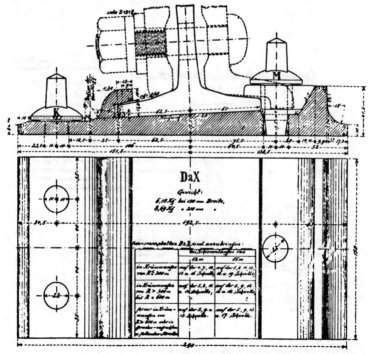

Fig. 134.

German Railway Co., Bavarian Division. Joint tie plate.

The following gives the various details of the French Eastern practice:

French Eastern

Rail

46 k and 55 k meter = 93 to 111 lb. to yard in tunnels.
55 k per M = 111 lb. to yard.
Length 24 metres = 78 ft.

Ties

Cost beech 17 f = $0.80.
Size 2.6 M x 24 x 14 cm. = 8'6" x 9.45" x 5.5".
Treatment cost = 15 F = $0.71.
Total cost = 32 f = $1.51.
Creosote 525 f. per 1000 k. = $.10379 per gallon.
Ties per mile, 2500-2833.
Replacements 1924 = 25-28 per kilometer.
$\qquad$ = 42-46 per mile.
Wooden shim size 9½" x 6".
Tie renewals: 250-300,000 per year for 9200 k. = 5700 miles or 52 ties
$\qquad$ to mile.
Elevation: Max. 12-15 mm. to meter.

Locomotives

Weight per axle: 18 tons (metric).
$\qquad$ 19.8 tons (U. S.).
Total weight of engine and tender—50 tons (metric).
$\qquad$ 65 tons (U. S.).

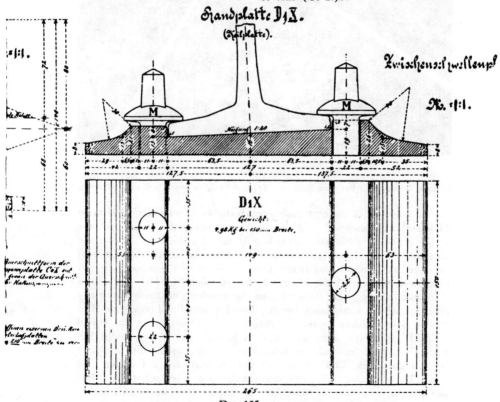

FIG. 135.
German Railway Co., Bavarian Division.   Intermediate tie plate.

690

Germany.—Up to the end of the war, there were a number of separate divisions of the German Railway Administration, each of which had different standards of maintenance. Since the war, the German Railways have been turned over to a private corporation and a general process of standardization for all phases of railway operation is in progress. This includes maintenance of way factors and I found that in no country visited were so many studies being made with reference to track as there were in Germany.

Two types of ties are still in use, namely, steel ties and creosoted wooden ties. The actual percentage is about 25 to 27 per cent steel ties and 73 to 75 per cent wooden ties actually in track. Renewals are divided about equally between steel and wooden ties. The continued

Fig. 136.

German Railway Co., Bavarian Division. Track showing tie plates and rail fastenings.

use of steel ties in spite of their comparatively shorter life (maximum 15 years) as against 22 to 25 years for the creosoted ties is still due to the economic conditions prevailing in the steel industry. From the cost sheet which follows, it will be noted that the comparative price of the steel and wooden ties is still much in favor of the wooden tie. A new steel tie costs $2.60, a new creosoted pine tie $1.87 and a new creosoted oak tie $2.37. Referring to the wooden ties, these are chiefly pine, oak, and in some cases, beech. Ties are adzed and bored and then treated with creosote by the Rueping process. During the war period a small percentage were treated with fluoride salt combinations but since peace was declared, creosote alone is again used. On first-class heavy traffic track, 2360 intermediate ties are used and 214 double joint ties. These double joint ties are simply two intermediate ties laid one immediately next to the other to support the joint. This makes a total of 2574 ties to the mile. The largest sized ties are 8.5 ft. long, 10.23 in. wide and 6.3 in. in thickness. On all main lines, wooden ties are universally protected by tie plates. In this brief abstract it is impossible to give all of the designs of tie plates which I found in use in Germany and reference is made only to the significant variables. The last edition of the German Book of Standards, published in 1911, shows tie plates which are flat on the bottom (see Fig. 130) generally, with a hook on the outside and three screw spikes; two of these hold the tie plate to the tie on the outside of the hook shoulder, and one screw spike placed in the center line of the plate holds the rail and the tie plate by means of a clip. The 1911 design of the intermediate plate is shown in the attached photograph, Fig. 130. It is 11.6 in. x 6.29 in.

The new standard design (see Fig. 131) differs but very little from the old one except that there has been a reversal of the spring washer. The new standard has the same dimensions, namely, 11.6 in. x 6.29 in., but has a slightly different type of clip. There are three screw spikes as in the old plate. This new plate is being generally applied all over the German railways.

Intensive studies made during the last few years led the German railway engineers to the conclusion that some change would have to be made, however, in the method of fastening, and I was very much interested in discovering that they had come almost to the same conclusion to which I had come, namely, that the mechanical destruction from which their ties are suffering was probably due to the motion of rail and plates causing abrasive action of the tie plate aided by sand and dirt from the ballast, and that it would be necessary to fasten the plates in some way. I found that the Germans had been making extensive investigations in England and France, and that as a result they had worked out two experimental designs with each of which they have laid a good many kilometers of track. The two drawings attached hereto marked "Experimental Plates" (Fig. 132 and 133) were issued, one in August, 1925, and the other on the 4th of September, 1925. The first experimental construction (Fig. 133), it will be noted, is identical with the French Eastern type, namely, the use of the wooden shims of the exact width of the base of the rail, held in position (as well as the rail) by three lag screws alternating two on the outside and one on the inside, and the next tie, one on the outside and two on the inside. The Germans were very enthusiastic about this plan and it speaks well for the French Eastern pattern to have the Germans not only discuss the same but actually build several hundred miles of track. The other experimental plate (Fig. 132) is apparently modeled somewhat after the design of the Austrian chair plate which will be referred to herein later on. The rail is held to the tie plate by means of two complicated looking clips which are held in position by two bolts. Each bolt has an enlarged base, imbedded in the tie plate. The tie plate itself is held in position by four screw spikes. These plates measure 15.35 in. in length x 6.29 in. in width. The idea of this type of design seems to be to hold the tie plate more firmly to the tie than is the case with their present standard.*

*NOTE: Since the above was written the German Railways have adopted the Geo plate as standard (see p. 179 and Fig. 178).

In Bavaria, in which an independent system had been used for years, the present standard is illustrated in the two drawings attached (Fig. 134 and 135), one of which is, as will be noted, similar to the new German standard. The second plate is one in which no clips are used. It is a double shouldered plate in which the rail as well as the plate are anchored by means of three screw spikes. Note also photograph of Bavarian track (Fig. 136).

General Conclusions as to German Results

The impression gained all over Germany was that the destruction of ties is largely due to mechanical reasons, that the screw fastening had not given as great a mechanical protection as was the case in either England or France. They realize just as we do that something better must be designed. They feel it impossible to go to the English system on account of the expense involved and they lean towards the French idea, or possibly towards an even firmer fastening of the plate independent of the rail. Of all the countries visited, the future developments of Germany will probably be of most interest to us. Herewith follows a table giving various details of cost, etc., on the German Railways.

GERMANY

1 Mark = $0.25

Rail

    45-49 kilo per M — 91-100 lb. to yard
    Service 10 yr. — 15 yr. then turned get 20 years more
    Length 12 M — 18 M = 40.3 feet — 59 feet

Tie Plates (Hook plate)

    29.5 cm. x 16 cm. x 17 mm. x 22.5 mm. = 11.61 in. x 6.29 in. x .669 in. x .89 in.
    Weight 16.33 lb.

Ties Iron

    Cost—130 M per ton = $32.50 per ton (metric) = $35.82 per U.S. ton
    Each tie 80 K = 176 lb. = 10M40Pf = $2.60

Wooden Ties

    1467 intermediate and 67 double joint ties per kilometer =
        2360 intermediate ties
        214 double joint ties

        ——
        2574
    Total 2574 to 1 mile (heavy track) 1st class

26 x 16 cm. = 10.23 in. x 6. 3 in.

	Pine	*Oak*
Cost of tie................	M 5.50 = $1.37	M 7.50 = $1.87
Treatment	2.00 .50	2.00 .50
Total	M 7.50 = $1.87	M 9.50 = $2.37

Tie Spacing

    Av. dist. between centers = 600 mm. = 26.77 in.
    Av. dist. at R joint = Om = 0 inches, i. e., 2 ties laid close together
        i. e., 2360 intermediate ties and 214 double ties per mile.

Locomotives

    7920 Kilo per axle   8 tons = 8.8 U.S. Tons   Sw. engine
      20 Tons per axle   = 22 U.S. Tons   heaviest type

Holland.—The Netherlands Railways since 1912 have been using 46 kg. (101.2 lb.) rail attached to the ties with cast iron chairs. These chairs have a base dimension of 360 mm. x 175 mm. (14.17 in. x 6.89 in.), equivalent to 96.75 sq. in. of bearing surface on the tie. It will be noted that this is a little less than the bearing area of the English chair.

These chairs are fastened on the ties with screws independently of the rail. (See Fig. 137, 138 and 139.) The rail is fastened on the chairs with separate bolts and clips, as shown in these figures. Usually 1333 ties are laid per kilometer, equivalent to 2147 ties per mile. The distance between two ties is 78 cm., equal to 30.7 in. For main lines with great density of traffic, and also for main lines on soft, boggy sub-soil, the number of ties is increased to 1666 ties per kilometer, equal to 2683 ties per mile.

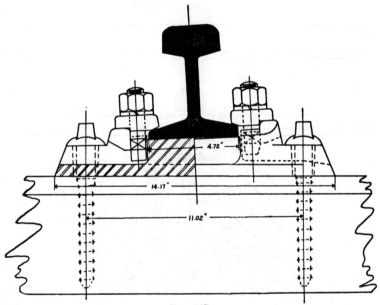

FIG. 137.
Netherland Railways. End view of chair plate.

The distance between two ties in this case is 60 cm., equal to 23.6 in. Before the adoption of these cast iron chairs, the Netherlands Railways used a flat tie plate using two cut spikes for the rail fastening.

The maximum axle load of their locomotives at the present time is 18,000 kg., equivalent to 39,600 lb. However, the present 46 kg. (101.2 lb.) rail is fit for axle loads of 44,000 lb.

In 1907 the Netherlands Railways began the application of compressed poplar shims (as used by the French Eastern). The first applications were in the nature of a trial, but since 1922 this construction has been used generally for the 42 kg. (92.4 lb.) rail. (Fig. 140.) The number of ties per mile and their spacing for the 92 lb. rail is the same as for the 101-lb. rail. Attention is called to the fact that the wooden shims are used with lag

694

screw fastening, that is, the rail is laid directly on the shim as in the case of the French Eastern.

Austria.—Both steel and wooden ties are in use in Austria, but by far the greater percentage are creosoted wooden ties. These are either beech, oak, or larch, with some pine. On the Austrian Government Railways all ties are adzed and bored and usually treated with creosote. Owing to the more or less impoverished condition of the railroad, however, many of the ties are treated with zinc chloride or zinc chloride and creosote, and it has also happened that other preservatives had to be used, and in some cases they had to be left untreated. Incidentally, there is probably no country in which more preservatives have been tried during the last thirty years; due, as stated, to varying economic conditions. As was stated by

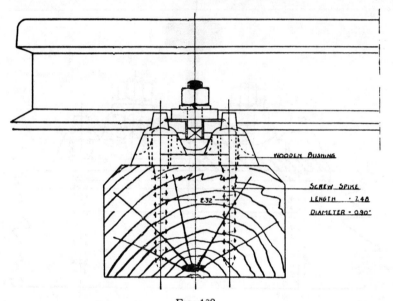

FIG. 138.
Netherland Railways. Side view of chair plate.

the leading expert on this subject, however, "The only thing to treat ties with is straight coal-tar creosote of the best grade obtainable. If it should occur that such is not available in sufficient quantities or if it becomes too expensive, it will prove economical (rather than to leave the ties untreated) to use various substitutes such as zinc chloride, corrosive sublimate, fluorides, etc., but . . . . . in case you do use these inferior compounds, never forget one thing, always add a little creosote."

The following notes reference the practice on the Austrian Government Railways practically include most of the lines in Austria proper. Ties are 8.2 ft. in length, 5.9 in. in thickness, minimum top width 6.9 in., base width 9.8 in. For the main tracks a maximum of 2468 ties to the mile are laid, running down to 2032 ties on lesser lines. Practically all ties are tie plated.

Two types of plates are in use, one the so-called intermediate plate (Fig. 143) and the other, which for want of a better term, I call a chair tie plate (Fig. 141 and 142). The intermediate plate is 8.26 in. x 5.5 in., weighing 7 lb. The so-called joint or chair tie plates are used on every third tie and on the two joint ties (joints are opposite and suspended). In other words, they lay 19 ties to a 49-ft. rail, and for these they use 24 intermediate plates and 14 chair plates. The intermediate plates (see attached drawings, Fig. 141, 142 and 143) are very much like some of the German plates, that is, a flat bottom plate with three screws holding the rail in position. Note that the outer edge of the head of the screw is not supported. The chair

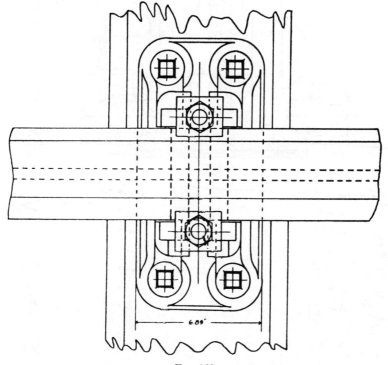

FIG. 139.
Netherland Railways. Top view of chair plate.

tie plate is a development of the old plate used on the Kaiser Ferdinand Nord Railway, and as will be noted, is probably the basis of the experimental tie plates with which the Germans are working at the present time. Two bolts fastened into the bottom of the plate hold two clips which in turn support the rail, and the plate itself is held in position by three screws which have no relation to the rail. The three drawings attached hereto (Fig. 141, 142 and 143) show the plan of the chair plate and the intermediate plate. The Austrians are very well satisfied with this arrangement and advise that by means of this plate they have succeeded very well in reducing the mechanical destruction of their ties. Their engines are light, having a maximum axle load of 20.16 U.S. tons. The design of their track is for a 22.4 ton loading and they run with speeds of 60 miles an hour. As a whole I should say that the tracks are not as well kept up as in Germany, France or England, due largely to the lack of money. The

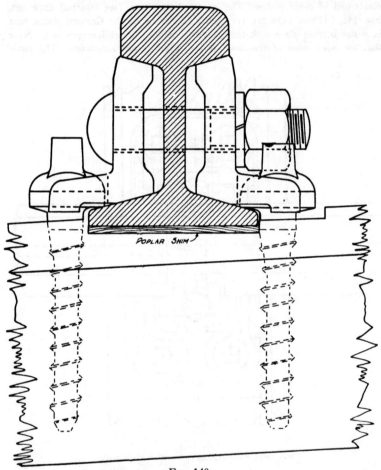

Fig. 140.
Netherland Railways. Section of chair plate.

chair plate is undoubtedly something which should be followed with careful study. The criticism to be made is that it is very complicated and it has too many pieces, which makes it difficult to maintain the fastenings in proper condition. For us it would be altogether out of the question. The following table gives details reference various factors on the Austrian Government Railways.

AUSTRIA

Rail

Length 15 M = 49.2 feet
Weight 44.35 kg. per meter = 89.2 lb. per yard

Tie Plate—Intermediate plate:

Weight 3.2 kg. = 7 lb. 210 x 140 mm. = 8.26 in. x 5.5 in.
Cant 1:20
Joint plate: 354 x 140 mm. = 13.93 in. x 5.5 in.
Weight = 5.82 kg. = 12.9 lb.

Tie Dimensions

Length 2.5 M = 8.2 ft.
Thickness 150 mm. = 5.9 inches.
Top width min. 180 mm. = 6.9 inches. Base 250 mm. = 9.8 inches.

Ties

For heaviest rail per rail length
   = 23 per 15 M rail (49.2 ft.).
   = 2468 per mile.
Minimum = 2032 per mile.

Engines

15 tons = 16.8 tons (U.S.), next year 18 tons = 20.16 tons (U.S.).
Design of track 20 tons = 22.4 tons (U.S.). Speed 100 km. = 60 miles.

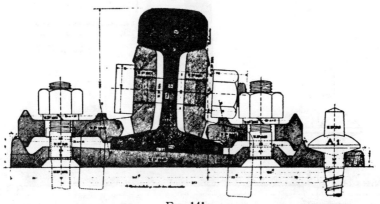

FIG. 141.
Chair tie plate, Austrian Government Railways.

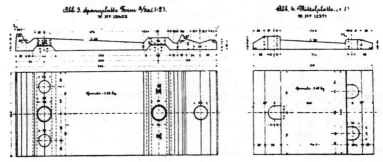

FIG. 142.
Austrian Government Railways. Plan of "chair tie plate" and intermediate tie plate.
Bul. 306

698

Belgium.—The Belgian State Railways use creosoted beech and oak, a great many of them the so-called half-round ties 5 in. thick with 11½ in. bearing on the ballast. All ties are adzed and bored before treatment and are thoroughly creosoted. 2326 ties are laid per mile. All ties are provided with tie plates which on the heavier lines are 11.21 in. long and 5.11 in. wide, weighing approximately 10.54 lb. Stone or slag ballast is used and the tracks are well maintained. The type of tie plate and fastening are illustrated in attached photograph showing the 1:20 canted plate and a flat plate (Fig. 144). The tie plates are of the hook shoulder type and are fastened by means of three screw spikes, one screw spike on the hook side of the plate located on the center axis of the plate and the other

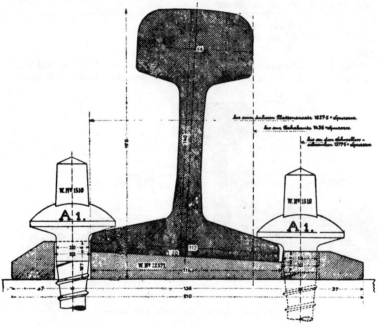

Fig. 143.

Austrian Government Railways. Intermediate tie plate.

two screw spikes on the inside of the rail. The outer screw spike holds the tie plate on the outside, while the two inner screw spikes are in contact with the base of the rail and stand slightly above a raised shoulder on the inside of the plate (see drawing, Fig. 144). The appended photographs also illustrate some of these tie plates in track (Fig. 145). Incidentally, the Belgian railways have had an interesting experience with reference to canting of rail. From 1835 to 1887 they used 1:20 cant. From 1887 to 1925 they used a horizontal plate, and at the beginning of 1925, they went back to the 1:20 cant.

The life of ties on the Belgium railways is very good. We saw some creosoted oaks which were being taken out of main line track with dating nails 1880, that is, 45 years in track. These ties were being relaid in a side track. Failure is due both to decay and to mechanical wear. In fact, all of the ties taken out of track which I looked at showed unmistakable

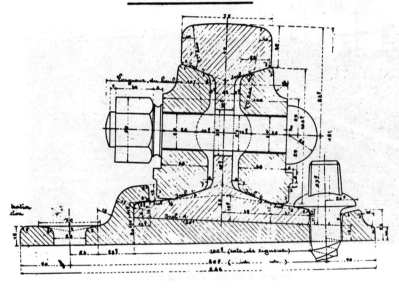

Coupe transversale des éclisses et de la plaque inclinée (voie courante)

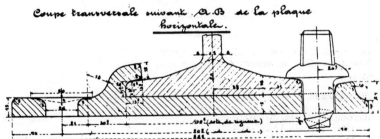

Coupe transversale suivant A B de la plaque horizontale.

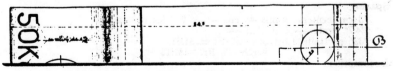

Vue en plan

Fig. 144.

Belgian State Railway. Standard design for joint and intermediate sections.

signs of wear under the plate. Many of the ties renewed came out because of decay or wearing away of the wood fiber around the screws. Loads on the Belgian railways are comparatively light. Their maximum axle load is 22 tons with comparatively light car equipment. Derailments during the past year were only two for the whole system. Following herewith is a table showing details for various factors on the Belgium railways.

Fig. 145.

Belgian Railways. Note lug plate.

BELGIAN RAILWAYS

1 Fr. = $.0435

Rail

Old type—52 k to meter = 115 lb. to yard.
New type—50 k to meter = 110 lb. to yard.

Tie Plates

285 x 130 mm. = 11.21″ x 5.11″—weight 4.79 k = 10.54 lb.
cost 4.75 Fr. = $.207.
Bearing of ties on ballast:
Half round—11.02″-11.42″.
Squared—10.2″-10.63″.

Ties

Most used size = .28 x .14M = 11½ x 5″—half round.

Spacing

73 cm. centers—joints 46 cm. = i.e., 26 ties per rail =
2′4.7″ centers—joint 1′6.1″ =
2326 per mile. Cost oak—30 Fr. = $1.31.
beech—26 Fr. = $1.13.

Locomotives

Heaviest type—20 tons (metric) axle load = 22 U.S. tons.
Cars—heaviest type (loaded) = 19 tons per axle.

Conclusions as to European Practice.—In the following table a summarized statement is given showing the bearing areas and maximum axle loads of various European railway systems.

TABLE III—TIE PLATE DIMENSIONS AND BEARING AREAS

Railroad	Tie Plate Dimensions, Inches	Area Sq. In.	Ties per Mile	Tie Width on Ballast, Inches	Area		Max. Axle Loads, Tons
					Ties × Plate per Mile Sq. In.	Tie Bearing on Ballast, Lin. In.	
England							
L. M. S. Ry............		111	2112	10	234,432	21,120	22
G. W.		115	2112	10	234,432	21,120	
Germany	11.61 x 6.29	73.03	2360 intermediate	10.23	187,979	26,332	22
			214 double				
			2574				
Belgium	11.21 x 5.11	57.28	2326	11.5	133,233	26,749	22
Austria	8.26 x 5.5	45.43	2468	9.8	112,121	24,186	20
France							
Fr. Eastern	9.5 x 6	57.0	2833	11.8	161,481	33,429	19.8
Italy	9.4 x 5.5	51.7	2414	9.4	124,803	22,692	20
Holland	14.17 x 6.89	96.75	2147	9.76	207,722	20,954	19.8

My chief reason for dwelling at such length on European practice is that they all have more or less the same loading and speeds of operation. They all use more or less the same woods and have similar types of track. It is, therefore, significant that two outstanding systems have been developed which show marked results in the way of reduction of mechanical wear, namely, the English system with the chair and the French Eastern system with the compressed poplar wood shim. I would like to have it thoroughly understood that there is herein no advocacy whatever of either system for use on American railroads except as indicating a principle of design. The English secure this long service from what we are accustomed to call a very soft wood (Baltic Pine) by securing an anchoring of the rail chair to the tie, and, incidentally, by using a very large bearing area. The French obtain

Fig. 146.

Typical Belgian track, showing tie plates and rail fastening.

the same results by wearing out a cheap cushion instead of a valuable tie. In neither case does the load factor, that is, the possible compression of the wood fibers, play much part. In both cases, the result is obtained because of reduced abrasive action between the rail, chair and tie.

American Track Experiences.—As far back as 1904, I called attention to the possibility of using a wooden cushion between the rail or tie plate and the tie. In 1908 some actual track experiments were conducted with this system of tie protection as described above. These early experiments on the Big Four and other lines were unfortunately never followed up. After several additional trips to Europe for the purpose of studying this question, I became convinced in 1907 that some system of tie plate fastening would be absolutely essential to reduce the mechanical wear of creosoted ties. At that time, realizing that the wooden shim would possibly not do, I had in mind a modification of the so-called chair tie plate of the Austrian railways (see Fig. 142). The difficulty with that plate, however, was that the motion of the rail was transmitted through the tie plate to the screw fastening which held the tie plate to the tie. While this was better than the ordinary cut spike with no fastening at the tie plate, it nevertheless showed mechanical wear even under the lighter loads on the Austrian railways. After considerable investigation, J. A. Atwood, then Chief Engineer of the Pittsburgh & Lake Erie Railroad, decided to adopt my suggestion of a fastened plate. Accordingly in 1910, the first extensive use of plates independently fastened was started.

I am indebted to A. R. Raymer, Assistant Vice-President and Chief Engineer of the Pittsburgh & Lake Erie Railroad Company, for the following statement with reference to the Pittsburgh & Lake Erie Railroad Company practice:

"The Pittsburgh & Lake Erie Railroad has a track alinement in which tangent length and curvature length are about equal in mileage, with many curves of 5 deg. and upward.. The rapid increase in weight of locomotives and of cars and the increased length of trains, beginning with 1898, made serious trouble on sharp curves by forcing the rails into the ties and widening the gage of track. To remedy this, malleable iron rail braces were first used on the outside of the outer rails and on the inside of the inner rails on curves, from 1898 to 1903, inclusive. In 1903 the first Goldie tie plates, 6 in. x 8 in., were installed for 71-lb., 80-lb. and 90-lb. rail. In 1908, the year that the installation of 100-lb. rail began, the Goldie tie plate was increased to 6½ in. x 9 in. for 100-lb. rail, as illustrated in Chart No. I, Fig. 1, using two cut spikes. In addition to the Goldie tie plates used in the period from 1908 to 1910, several different types of tie plates for 100-lb. rail were also used, among which were the following: Sellers, Single Rib, Glendon Cushion and Canted 3 Rib. All of these tie plates were unsatisfactory in counteracting the effect of rapidly increasing axle loads and it became imperative to have a larger tie plate held rigidly in place on the tie to prevent tie destruction under the tie plates. It was found that the claws of the Goldie tie plates and the ribs on the other tie plates by movement were cutting the ties lengthwise of the ties, thus making pockets which collected moisture, which caused decay of ties under the tie plates. To prevent damage to the ties on the portions under the tie plates, it was obvious that all claws and ribs must be eliminated to avoid pockets in the ties under the plates, and it was also obvious that a larger size tie plate must be provided for distribution of load. In 1910 a totally different type of tie plate was designed and applied, as shown by Chart No. I, Fig. 2. This was a 6½ in. x 11 in. tie plate, ⅝ in. in thickness with double shoulder and flat on bottom, except two cross thickenings as shown in drawing. The 1910 tie plate was provided with two holes for cut spikes and two holes for screw spikes. As indicated in Fig. 2, these were punched at an angle of 10 deg. The screw spikes fasten the tie plate securely to the tie and prevent tie damage under the tie plate and prevent any change in gage of rails. The rail is held in place by the two shoulders of the tie plate and by the two cut spikes. The first tie plates of this type had two recesses in the top for the purpose of saving metal. These recesses were eliminated in 1917 because tie plates were breaking at the

FIG. 147.
Standard track, P. & L. E. R. R.

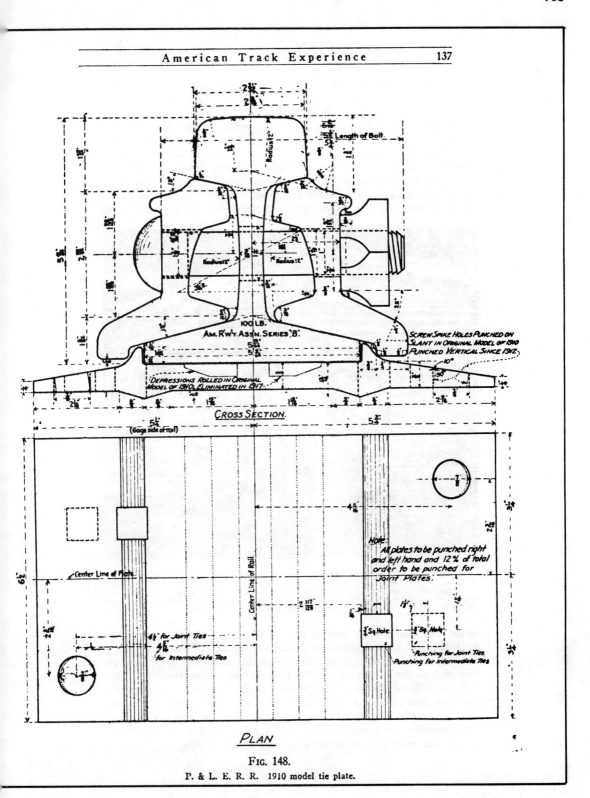

CROSS SECTION.

PLAN

FIG. 148.

P. & L. E. R. R. 1910 model tie plate.

recesses. In 1921 the size of the tie plate was increased by 6½ in. x 11 in. to 7 in. x 11 in., as shown by Chart No. I, Fig. 3. This size tie plate has continued to be standard from 1921 to the present time.

"In 1910 and 1911 the holes for the two screw spikes and for the two cut spikes were bored by hand augers and the two screw spikes were driven by hand wrenches of the Greenlee type. In 1910 and 1911 the tie plates were applied on unadzed ties, both sawed and hewed, without hand adzing and with the thought that the tie plates would be properly seated on the ties by train loads on rails. It was found that on hewed ties the seating of the tie plates by this method was such that the tie plates were not all

FIG. 149.

Experimental section of screw fastened tie plates, C. C. C. & St. L. Ry., Cincinnati Division, after eight years' service. Note heads of screws standing away from top of tie plates. Screws were not tightened after first application.

in the same plane, which resulted in some tie plates not bearing uniformly under the rail. In 1912 a Greenlee Adzing and Boring Machine was installed for adzing and boring ties, including the cutting of two grooves to fit the thickened portion of the tie plate lying immediately under the edge of the rail base. Since the installation of this adzing and boring machine, the ties have been adzed and bored by this machine and prior to the time the ties are treated. In 1915 a machine was constructed to apply the tie plates under pressure to the ties, but this work was abandoned after a short time because the machine was neither powerful nor rapid enough.

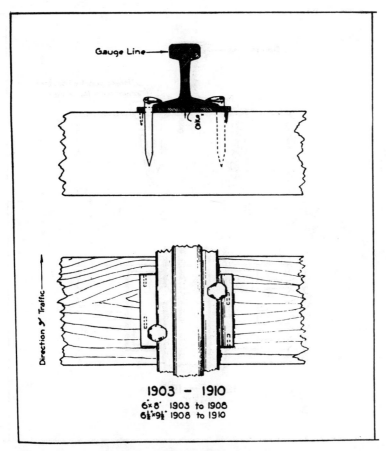

FIG. 1.

Standard practice 1903 to 1910 using Goldie tie plates
with 2 cut spikes; tie plates 1903-1908, 6 in. x 8 in.;
1908-1910, 6½ in. x 9½ in.

708

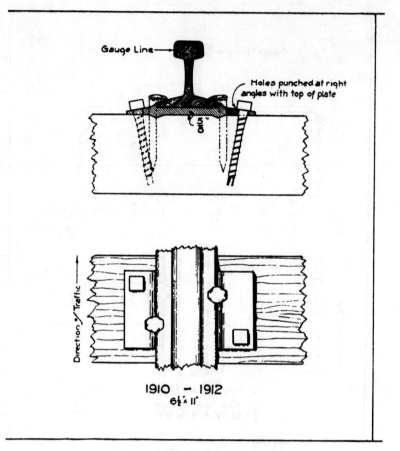

Fig. 2.

Form of tie plate used 1910-1912—6½ in. x 11 in. x
⅝ in. with double shoulder and flat bottom, except two
cross thickenings as shown in drawing. Two cut spikes
for holding the rail, and 2 screw spikes independent of
the rail were used.

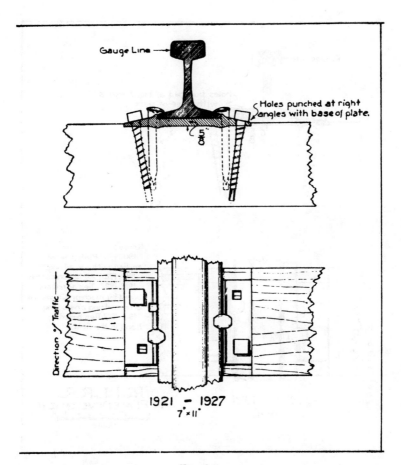

Fig. 3.

Tie plates as applied 1921-1927, 7 in. x 11 in. x ⅝ in.
This tie plate differs from the previous one only in size.

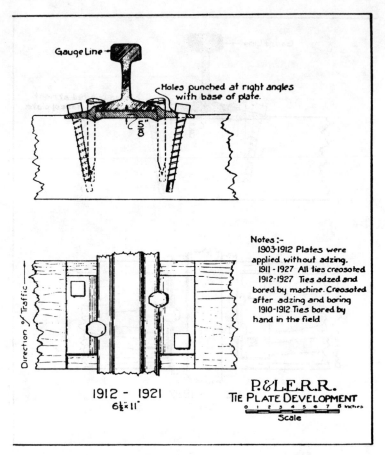

FIG. 4.

Tie plate as used 1912-1921, 6½ in. x 11 in. x ⅝ in.
This tie plate differs from the one in previous use only
in the fact that two recesses in the top of the older tie
plate for the purpose of saving metal were eliminated
in 1917, because the tie plates were breaking at the
recesses.

"The driving of the screw spikes was continued to be done by hand with the Greenlee type wrenches until the end of 1915. In 1916 pneumatic tie tamping machines were equipped with wrenches for driving screw spikes, and these tie tamping machines with screw spike wrenches have been used to date for screw spike driving.

"Tie plates are applied on every tie in all main tracks and all of the tie plates are as shown by Chart No. I, Fig. 3, for 115-lb. rail, except a very few where there still remains a small amount of 100-lb. rail, where the 6½ in. x 11 in. tie plates are applied.

"There was a period, from June 1, 1919, to August 1, 1921, during which time no screw spikes were installed in tie plates on tangents and on curves flatter than 2 deg. curvature, but it was found that abrasion was taking place on tops of the ties underneath the tie plates, and all of the screw spikes that were omitted were soon afterwards installed.

"Switch ties and bridge ties which are too long to be bored in the adzing and boring machine, are bored in field by tools attached to pneumatic tie tamping machines.

"In 1911, the treating of ties began on the Pittsburgh & Lake Erie Railroad and has continued without interruption to the present time, with the Rueping process and using creosote oil."

The experience of the Pittsburgh & Lake Erie Railroad has shown in a very striking manner that independently fastened plates reduce mechanical wear. While this has been generally true, a considerable number of ties do show mechanical wear in spite of the independent fastening. (See Fig 32, 50 and 59.) This result was doubtless due to the fact that the heads of the screws were very frequently not in contact with the top of the tie plate; in order words, the plates were loose. Fig. 149 shows a piece of track on the Big Four installed with the Pittsburgh & Lake Erie plates and fastenings, in which the heads of the screws stand out above the tie plate. Wherever this takes place because of lack of proper maintenance, mechanical wear will doubtless occur to a greater or less extent.

Practice on the Delaware, Lackawanna & Western Railroad.—About the same time as the discussions were going on on the Pittsburgh & Lake Erie Railroad, the same type of study was being made on the Delaware, Lackawanna & Western Railroad. Believing that the idea of fastening the plate could be accomplished by changing from a cut spike (Chart II, Fig. 1) to a screw spike fastening, the Lackawanna designed a tie plate using two screw spikes in place of the two cut spikes theretofore used. In the first installation (1910) the head of the screw spike when firmly seated was in contact with the rail base on one side and with the tie plate on the other, giving a very rigid fastening. (Chart II, Fig. 2.) It was soon found that this idea had to be changed, and accordingly a tie plate was designed (Chart II, Fig. 3) in which the head of the screw when firmly seated stood ¼ in. above the base of the rail and on the other side was in contact with a knob projecting from the upper surface of the tie plate. In other words, the screw spike held the tie plate firmly to the tie by permitting a play between the top of the base of the rail and the lower side of the head of the screw spike. With slight modification, this has been the standard practice on the Lackawanna system until recently. For a full

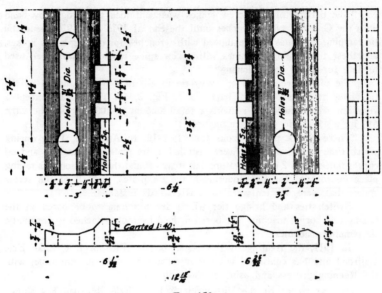

Fig. 150.
Standard D. L. & W. tie plate.

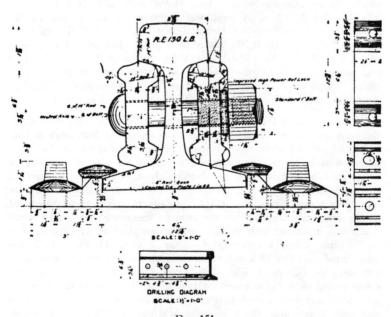

Fig. 151.
Standard D. L. & W. tie plate.

account of the installation and early experiences with the screw spike fastening, the reader is referred to an exhaustive statement by George J. Ray, Chief Engineer, entitled, "Results with Five Years' Use of Screw Spikes in Both Construction and Maintenance," Proceedings A.R.E.A. *16*:301 to 364; 1915. In 1924 the Lackawanna redesigned their tie plate, changing same to a tie plate fastened entirely independent of the rail by means of two screw spikes, at the same time using two cut spikes to hold the rail. The present Lackawanna tie plate is illustrated in Fig. 150 and 151. Fig. 152 and 153 show the present Lackawanna track construction.

I am indebted to George J. Ray, Chief Engineer, and to A. J. Neafie, Principal Assistant Engineer, for the following statement reference the Lackawanna practice:

"The Lackawanna Railroad first commenced to creosote cross-ties in the year of 1910. During the year of 1910 and since that time all main and side-track tie renewals have been made with creosoted ties, excepting such chestnut ties as were available along the line of railroad. Chestnut ties were, however, only used in side-tracks and on minor branches. During the past five or six years very few chestnut ties have been utilized. We are utilizing no chestnut ties at this time.

"Prior to 1910 it was the practice to use flanged tie plates as per tie plate No. 1 (7 in. x 9⅝ in. x ½ in.) on the print furnished you (Chart II), cut spike. It was found after years' experience that much damage was done to the tie by the use of flanged plates. It was, therefore, concluded in 1910 (at which time we started treatment for maintenance and construction work) that the use of such a plate should not be further considered. Therefore, after a careful investigation of all available data on screw and other spikes, bolts, etc., it was concluded to adopt screw spikes with a flat bottom plate as per plate No. 2, Chart II. The plate in question was 7 in. x 10 in. x ⅝ in. thick, with raised lugs to support the heads of the screw spikes on the outside, while the one or two screw spikes on the inside were seated on the contour of the rail base.

"This construction was quickly changed during the year 1910 to No. 3, Chart II (size 7 in. x 10⅝ in. x ⅝ in.), increasing the thickness of the plate to ⅝ in., with shoulders on both sides, arranging a free-way between the base of the rail and the head of the spike. Joint tie plates were also provided for this particular construction.

"In 1911 careful consideration was given to the question of the spike. We increased the diameter of the head and arranged templates for a uniformly manufactured spike to eliminate the variation in the thread of the spike. This to prevent the destroying of the threads formed in the wood.

"In the first few years all screw spikes were set by hand. In 1911 we purchased adzing and boring machines from Greenlee Brothers and installed the same at our creosoting plant. All adzing and boring was handled at that point. In 1913 we installed two machines, which are operating at the present time. The machines in question turn out approximately 5,000 ties per day.

"Exhibit No. 4, Chart II, covers a hook shoulder tie plate (7 in. x 11½ in. x ¾ in.) that was carefully considered to replace tie plate No. 3 in case of mechanical destruction in connection with the screw spikes as

FIG. 152.
New standard track, D. L. & W. R. R.

FIG. 153.
New standard track, D. L. & W. R. R.

715

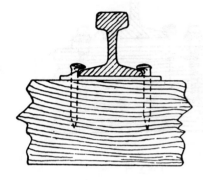

No.1

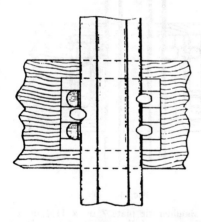

FIG. 1.

A flange tie plate used prior to 1910 with three cut spikes as the rail fastening.
Size 7 in. x 9⅝ in. x ½ in.

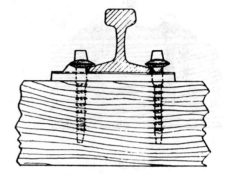

No.2

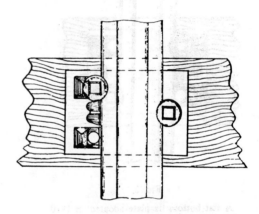

FIG. 2.

A flat bottom tie plate adopted 1910, 7 in. x 10 in. x ⅝ in. thickness with two raised lugs to support the heads of the screw spikes on the outside. The lugs were just high enough so that the bottom of the head of the screw spike fit tight against the rail base.

716

No. 3

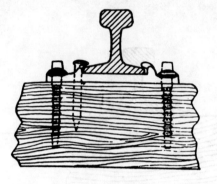

No. 4

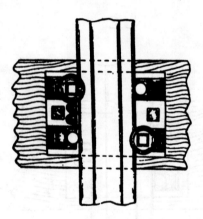

FIG. 3.

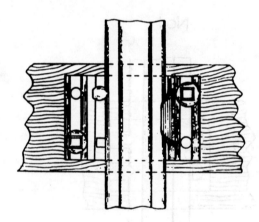

FIG. 4.

A flat bottom tie plate adopted in 1910 after it was found that the direct contact between screw and rail base was not desirable. This tie plate was 7 in. x 10⅝ in. x ⅝ in. with two shoulders and lugs on both sides, so arranged to allow a free-way between the base of the rail and the head of the screw spike, amounting to a minimum of ⅛ in. and a maximum of ₁₆ in. Joint tie plates were also provided for this particular construction. Prior to 1911 all screw spikes were set by hand in holes bored on the track. After 1911 all ties were adzed and bored by machinery.

A hook shoulder tie plate 7 in. x 11½ in. x ¾ in. which was carefully considered to replace tie plate as shown in Fig. 3, in case of mechanical destruction in connection with the screw spikes as placed; that is, the destruction of the hole thread lines in the timber holding the plate. The lugs provided a freeway between the head of the screw spike and the base of the rail of a minimum of ⅛ in. and a maximum of ₁₆ in.

D. L. & W. R. R. TIE-PLATE DEVELOPMENT

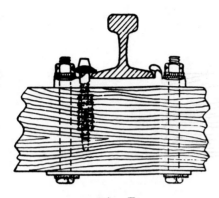

No. 5

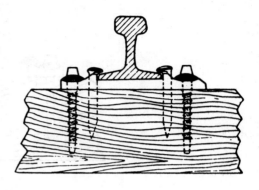

No. 6

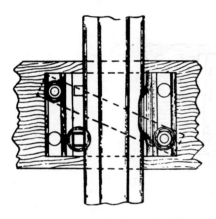

Fig. 5.

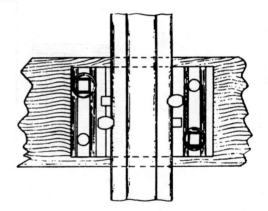

Fig. 6.

Construction in which a hook shoulder tie plate, as in Fig. 4, 7 in. x 11½ in. x ¾ in., was fastened to the tie with bolts with a metallic insert. These inserts were also utilized in connection with plates as in Fig. 3 for testing purposes. These, however, were abandoned about 1918. Plates as per Fig. 5 were inserted about 1915. The lugs provided a freeway between the head of the screw spike and the base of the rail of a minimum of ⅛ in. and a maximum of ₁₆ in.

About a mile or more of this bolted construction has been in service for about ten years and is working out very satisfactorily.

In 1920 a tie plate 7½ in. x 12¼ in. x ¾ in. as per this figure was adopted to take the place of the tie plate shown in Fig. 5, and also to replace plate as in Fig. 3, when the mechanical destruction had reduced the holding power of the screw spikes in question to such an extent that it was necessary to replace the spikes. On heavy curve lines plate as per Fig. 3 was simply removed, the holes were plugged, new holes were bored in new timber location, and cut spikes and screw spikes applied as in Fig. 6. The cut spikes served simply to hold the rail in position, while the screw spikes held the tie plate. This particular plate had a double shoulder, and the plate functions as an anti-

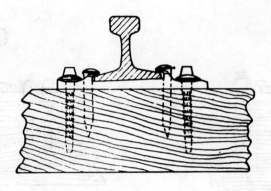

No. 7

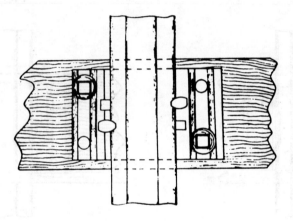

creeper, as well as a tie plate, on account of the shoulder in question.

The lugs provided a freeway between the head of the screw spike and the base of the rail of a minimum of ⅛ in. and a maximum of 3/16 in.

Fig. 7.

This plate was adopted in 1924, and is the present standard. It is 7½ in. wide, 12 13/16 in. long and ¾ in. thick; it is a canted plate 1 in 40. The lugs provide a freeway between the head of the screw spike and the base of the rail of a minimum of ⅛ in. and a maximum of 3/16 in.

placed; that is, the destruction of the hole thread lines in the timber holding the plate intact. We also placed, on or about 1915, plate shown in exhibit No. 5, Chart II, with bolted construction with a metallic insert (7 in. x 11½ in. x ¾ in.). These inserts were also utilized in connection with plate No. 3 for testing purposes. These, however, were abandoned about 1918.

"In 1920 we adopted plate No. 6, Chart II (size 7½ in. x 12¾ in. x ¾ in.) to take the place of plate 5 and also to replace plate 3 when mechanical destruction had reduced the holding power of the spikes in question to such an extent that it was necessary to replace the spikes. On heavy curve lines we simply removed plate No. 3, plugged the holes, bored new holes in new timber locations and applied screw spikes and cut spikes, the cut spikes simply to hold the rail in position in the plate in question. This particular plate has a double shoulder and the plate functions as an anti-creeper as well as a tie plate on account of the shoulder in question.

"Plate No. 7, Chart II, is a plate 7½ in. wide, 12$\frac{7}{8}$ in. long, ¾ in. thick, 1 in 40 cant, the same as Exhibit 6, excepting it is a canted tie plate. This plate was adopted in 1924. All tie plates 3, 4, 5, 6 and 7 were manufactured to provide free-way, with a minimum of ⅛ in. and a maximum of $\frac{7}{8}$ in.

"In the year of 1915 we adopted the present type of screw spike; this spike with a uniform thread line and with a pilot and a cutter as per blue print herewith attached. We found that the large percentage of screw spikes as manufactured had a distorted thread line and were not uniform to size, and it was necessary to drive them in the holes as provided to enable the machines to start the spikes, thereby destroying a part of the hole. We, therefore, had designed and had manufactured a screw spike with a pilot. This screw spike is uniform in every dimension, standard thread line throughout and uniform in root. The root is ⅝ in. and the maximum size under the neck is ⅞ in. All of these measurements are uniform.

"We have plate No. 3 placed in 1911 in service on our cutoff, 16 years. Not any of these plates have been removed excepting where we have applied 130-lb. rail with the canted plate and the renewals as made were necessary on account of the size of the rail and the number of years the same was in service. The average life of the rail was 12.72 years. A lighter section (91-lb.) showed a ten-year life, while the 101-lb. rail showed an average life of 13.72 years and a maximum life of 15.28 years.

"In this particular cutoff as laid in 1910 and 1911 we have a mileage of 57.06 miles of main track; side-track and main line mileage of 71.47. We have a total number of ties in track of 214,929. We have removed to date 22,526 ties, 20,687 on account of mechanical destruction, 1671 account of wrecks and 168 account of decay and physical defects. We have removed to date, that is, December 31, 1926, 10.52 per cent of the total installation. As stated, the original ties, tie plates and screw spikes still remain intact on this cutoff line excepting in the location where we have laid the 130-lb. rail with its 7½ in. plate canted. This change was made necessary on account of the wider base and 60 per cent of the tie plates taken out were again used and about 80 per cent of the screw spikes re-applied in plate No. 7, Chart II.

"Exhibit 5, Chart II, bolted construction. We have approximately a mile or more of this construction about ten years old, which is working out very satisfactorily.

"Prior to Exhibit No. 1 we utilized a similar tie plate excepting it had no shoulder and was utilized with cut spikes. All of these plates, both No. 1 and the similar tie plates used prior to 1910, had flanges and it was found after years' experience that much damage was done to the tie by the use of a flanged plate, and we, therefore, substituted the flat bottom plate in 1910 which is being used successfully to date."

Fig. 152 and 153 are photographs of the new tie plate installation and well illustrate the principle of this design. Specific attention is called

FIG. 154.

K. C. S. Ry., Saginaw, Mo. Lifted rail with tie plate removed showing pockets formed by tie plates.

to the fact that we have here a plate which theoretically should not move at all, because it is independent of the rail except as the rail acts on the shoulders and spikes of the plate. Most of the motion, however, usually in plates which are not thus fastened, has been eliminated by this new plate. These plates have been in service for only a comparatively short number of years but there is no evidence to date of any tie plate seating.

Tie Plates as Load Distributing Factors.—In the foregoing I have discussed the actual physical appearance of mechanically-worn ties. At this point it seems desirable to add a brief discussion as to the loads which ties are required to withstand under present-day conditions of traffic. This is of particular significance because many still believe that the direct loads of locomotives and cars are solely responsible for the mechanical wear of ties. This viewpoint is brought forward with particular force whenever the track experience of the European railroads is mentioned. It is frequently stated that there can be no correlation between their experience and ours because their locomotives and cars are so much lighter, and it would only be reasonable to expect less destruction under the rail or tie plate under their conditions than under ours.

The pressure exerted by a moving train is distributed for a considerable distance through the rail and ties to the ballast. Until recently very little was known as to the actual character of this distribution. The work of the Special Committee on Track Stresses of this Association has thrown very considerable light upon this much-mooted question. It is not my purpose to discuss this problem except as it applies directly to the pressure exerted on the tie plate, and from the tie plate to the wood. For obvious reasons, a discussion as to load distribution must be more or less general, and in what follows it should be distinctly understood that the considerations herein discussed should be taken as applying only to the specific cases referred to. In other words, the figures given for specific pressures on various railroads will probably apply only to ideal track and for conditions as specified in the general formula. The data to be presented will at least give one an approximation and are, therefore, useful to a discussion of the problem of mechanical wear.

I am indebted to Professor A. N. Talbot, Chairman of the Committee on Track Stresses, for the following succinct statement as to what load distribution may be expected under ideal track conditions:

"The analysis of the action of track shows that for, say, 100 to 130-lb. rail on a substantial roadbed for a single axle not close to another the reaction or load taken by a tie immediately under the axle equals approximately $1/80 \, Ps$ (one-eightieth the axle load times the tie spacing in inches center to center). For ties 20 in. center to center this is $0.25 \, P$ and for ties 30 in. center to center it is $0.37 \, P$. Reactions or loads carried by adjacent ties will be less than this amount, gradually diminishing so that for the 20-in. spacing the load will be spread over eight or more ties. For two axles spaced 5 ft. 6 in. apart, the amount on one tie immediately under one of the axles will be approximately $0.30 \, P$ for 20-in. tie spacing and $0.45 \, P$ for 30-in. spacing, the amount for the intermediate ties being nearly the same as for the tie under an axle, gradually diminishing for the ties on each side of the axles. For three or four or more wheels, say 5 ft. 6 in. apart, as in the case of drivers, the load taken by the more heavily loaded ties runs nearly $\frac{1}{3} \, P$ for 20-in. spacing and nearly $\frac{1}{2} \, P$ for 30-in. spacing.

"Tests on good track show values corresponding rather closely to those given above for a spacing of 20 in. Tests have not been made by us for the 30-in. spacing, but doubtless the values will correspond to those given above.

"For track under ordinarily good condition, an occasional tie might be expected to take possibly as much as 50 per cent more load than the values given above. It seems possible that a tie near a poorly maintained joint possibly might take 100 per cent more load, or double the values first given. This is merely an estimate to get at the range of values.

"It must be kept in mind, of course, that the bearing on the tie plate
will not be uniformly distributed over the tie. Lateral forces and eccentric
loading will thus increase the intensity of stress on the tie. It should also
be noted that the bearing resistance of ties (their yield point, so to speak)
is relatively low."

Using Professor Talbot's formula, I have developed the probable loads
in pounds per square inch transmitted by the tie plate to the tie. I have
done this for various European railroads and a number of railroads in
the United States. The American railroads included are those from which
ties in track have been specifically studied. All figures are based on an
assumed spacing for 2 and 3 axles of 5 ft. 6 in. between axles. Referring
to the American railways, the axle loads and plate areas represent the
practice at the time the ties studied and specifically referred to herein were
in service; in other words, they are not necessarily the present practice,
except the figures for the New York Central, the Pittsburgh & Lake Erie,
the new Lackawanna standard, and the Southern Pacific. Axle loads of
75,000 lb. may, however, be regarded as among the highest now in use
in the United States.

FIG. 155.

K. C. S. Ry., Saginaw, Mo., showing track after wooden shims were placed in
tie plate pockets. Tie plates and rail replaced.

A study of the number of pounds per square inch shows some rather
interesting results. One of these is that there is no such tremendous difference between the loads which the European ties are required to withstand
compared with similar ties in the United States, as is frequently supposed.
This is due largely to the wider tie spacing prevalent on European roads.
Personally, I am particularly interested in the comparison between our loads
and those of the French Eastern, because as has already been indicated,
it is on this road that the least mechanical destruction for any European
road is evident. While the number of pounds per square inch of bearing
is lower than our own, it is not sufficiently far below our own to account
for the great difference in the behavior of the ties under the rail.

A further point of interest is a comparison between the strength in
compression perpendicular to the grain of various woods with the loads
which these woods are required to carry. Note in this connection the table

of strength values on page 55. It will be noted that with the exception of very soft woods like cedar, all of the tie woods have strength values, both green and dry, far higher than any of the loads shown for locomotives in Table IV. It should, of course, be pointed out that such a comparison must be made with some caution. The compression values of the various species of wood are averages. There will be many pieces in which the compression strength will be far below that given in the table, and doubtless the low values for such pieces will come close to the values given in the table of axle loads.

It should furthermore be remembered (as indicated by Professor Talbot) that ties practically never take equal loads, even in good track. There is a most unequal load distribution—instead of the neighboring ties bearing their proportion, one or more ties may take the whole load, or as stated by Professor Talbot, "it seems possible that a tie near a poorly maintained joint possibly might take 100 per cent more load."

Fig. 156.

K. C. S. Ry., Bunch, Okla. Rail being relayed. The old tie plates were removed; ties were then adzed for the larger plates, and the cut area was coated with creosote. Note mechanical wear.

Another factor which is particularly significant for all coniferous woods is the different strength of the spring and summerwood. (See page 58.) While the wood as a whole may have a high resistance to compression, the weaker springwood will fail under loads far less than those which the wood as a whole seems to be able to stand. That this is frequently the case has already been pointed out, particularly where any one tie is called upon to bear an unequal share of the load.

Even with all of these reservations, it is nevertheless significant that most of the tie woods are strong enough to resist the ordinary vertical compression caused by locomotives and cars.

724

Table IV—Axle Loads in Europe and the United States

	Ties Spacing. In.	Axle Load Lb.	Plate Area Sq. In.	1 Axle Factor	1 Axle Lb.*	2 Axles Factor	2 Axles Lb.*	3 Axles† Factor	3 Axles† Lb.*
EUROPE									
LMS	30	44,000	111	.37	73	.45	90	.50	100
Germany	25.2	44,000	73.03	.315	95	.378	114	.42	130
Belgium	27.5	44,000	57.28	.343	132	.412	158	.458	174
Austria	26	40,000	45.43	.325	145	.39	172	.431	192
French Eastern	22.8	39,600	57	.285	99	.342	119	.38	132
Italy	26.5	40,000	51.7	.331	128	.397	153	.44	172
Holland	30.7	39,600	97.65	.384	78	.460	93	.511	104
UNITED STATES									
N. Y. C.	20	64,000	77	.25	104	.30	125	.331	140
N. Y. C., Electric	20	48,000	77	.25	...	.30	225	.50	104
Big Four (old)	20	60,000	40	.25	187	.30	225	.33	250
New Haven	20	56,100	43.75	.25	160	.30	192	.33	214
P. & L. E.	20	75,000	77	.25	122	.30	146	.33	161
C. B. & Q.	20	50,666	51	.25	124	.30	149	.33	164
D. L. & W. (old)	20	69,000	74.75	.25	115	.30	138	.33	152
D. & L. W. (new)	20	69,000	96.31	.25	90	.30	108	.33	118
S. P.	20	63,000	70	.25	113	.30	135	.33	149
Santa Fe	20	62,000	41.5	.25	186	.30	224	.33	246
Missouri Pacific	20	59,200	51	.25	145	.30	174	.33	191
Rock Island	20	66,000	57	.25	145	.30	174	.33	191

*Lb. in these columns means load per square inch of tie plate. †Spaced 5 ft. 6 in. apart.

Conclusions as to the Cause of Mechanical Wear.—Taking all of the results of the investigations described, I am of the opinion that they all point more or less to the fact that mechanical wear is due to the motion of the track parts, specifically of the rail, tie plate and tie, and that load is not the only factor. Of course, high pressures and impacts may materially assist and increase the mechanical wear of the tie. Where a tie plate sinks into the wood for two inches or more, a large volume of wood has naturally disappeared. If it had disappeared because of simple compression, that would be plainly indicated, if not in gross, certainly in microscopic sections. We would have pictures such as were obtained by actual compression. As has been shown there is no evidence in the mechanically worn ties of any material compression of the fiber. However, the fibers are badly torn on the surface immediately under the tie plate. The wood is more or less physically worn, abraded and what might be called powdered. This disintegration occurs between the rail and the wood where no tie plate is used. It occurs with all forms of tie plates and it occurs with tie plate having large bearing areas as well as with smaller bearing areas. The manner in which this physical destruction of the wood fibers takes place may be roughly compared to a sand papering or rasping action. Under passing loads, tie plates move. This motion is a very complex one because it is the resultant of a number of motions. The one which is most readily visible to the human eye is an up and down movement. There is, however, in addition to this, a movement parallel to the longitudinal axis of the tie, a movement at right angles to the longitudinal axis of the tie and in addition, a rocking movement. What the final resultant of all of these movements actually is I have been unable to tell because this movement takes place so fast that the human eye is incapable of registering same. Plans are now under way for making more specific determinations by means of motion pictures to be subsequently studied with the slow motion effect.

I visualize the action of the tie plate under actual traffic briefly as follows: After a shorter or longer period after insertion, particles of sand, dirt, or stone creep in between the bottom of the tie plate and the wood. This foreign matter probably acts as the abrading agent. The motion across the track and parallel to the track is probably very small. I have measured a considerable number of tie plate seats, particularly those in which the knobs of wood stuck up through the holes in the tie plate not used for spikes or screws, and find that in many of them there is a freedom of play between the knob and the edge of the hole of not more than ⅛ in., and often not as much as that. When it is remembered, however, that the diameter of vessels and wood fibers is extremely small (the average diameter in red oak wood of vessels is 0.0142 in. and of fibers 0.0005 in.; for longleaf pine the average diameter of tracheids in the springwood in 0.00184 in. and in the summerwood 0.00106 in.) it will readily be seen that it takes only an infinitesimal amount of movement to extend over a considerable group of wood fibers. As a matter of reference the following tables (5 and 6) give some detailed dimensions of the lumen or opening in vessels and wood fibers in red oak and longleaf pine, and thickness of cell walls in terms of millimeters and inches.

TABLE V—RED OAK

Diameter of Lumina of Large Vessels

	Average		Maximum		Minimum	
	mm.	Inches	mm.	Inches	mm.	Inches
Tangential 0.279		.0109	0.380	.0148	0.164	0.0064
Radial 0.356		.0139	0.490	.0191	0.208	0.00811

Diameter of Lumina of Wood Fibers

Average		Maximum		Minimum	
mm.	Inches	mm.	Inches	mm.	Inches
0.00411	0.00016	0.00669	0.00026	0.00209	0.000078

Thickness of Double Walls of Wood Fibers

Average		Maximum		Minimum	
mm.	Inches	mm.	Inches	mm.	Inches
0.00873	0.00034	0.01355	0.00050	0.00565	0.00022

Thickness of Combined Walls of Vessels and Surrounding Cells (Parenchyma)

Average		Maximum		Minimum	
mm.	Inches	mm.	Inches	mm.	Inches
0.00717	0.00027	0.0117	0.00046	0.00334	0.00013

Shortest Distance Between Two Large Vessels

Average		Maximum		Minimum	
mm.	Inches	mm.	Inches	mm.	Inches
0.0683	0.0026	0.1905	0.0071	0.0157	0.0058

Average Diameter of Vessels and Fibers (Wall and Lumen)

Vessels		Fibers	
mm.	Inches	mm.	Inches
0.3647	0.0142	0.0128	0.00050

TABLE VI—LONGLEAF PINE

Diameter of Lumina of Tracheids

	Chiefly		Range	
	mm.	Inches	mm.	Inches
Springwood ...0.040 -0.045		0.0015 -0.00175	0.0362-0.0479	0.00140-0.00186
Summerwood .0.0105- .014		0.00041-0.00055	0.0092-0.0161	0.00036-0.00062

Thickness of Double Walls of Tracheids

	Chiefly		Range	
	mm.	Inches	mm.	Inches
Springwood ...0.0052-0.0056		0.00020-0.00021	0.0044-0.0061	0.00017-0.00024
Summerwood .0.0146-0.0156		0.00057-0.00061	0.0134-0.0168	0.00052-0.00065

Average Diameter of Tracheids

	mm.	Inches
Springwood 0.0474		0.00184
Summerwood 0.0273		0.00106

I further visualize this action as very similar to the polishing action of any material using a rubber of some sort. For instance, in the polishing of marble, the operator holds a piece of stone in his hand, which is rubbed on the marble surface with an intermediate abrading substance. The extent of the abrasion of the surface will depend upon the number of movements back and forth and the pressure exerted; the larger the number of movements, the greater the abrasion, and the greater the pressure, the greater the abrasion. In addition to the abrading action of the rail or plate manifesting itself in the pulverization of the uppermost fibers of the wood, there is a certain amount of shear, which, for want of a better term, may be called "rolling shear." That there is such a lateral pull is evident from the microphotographs which show the axial shifting of the rows of wood fibers. This axial shifting is due to lateral forces frequently repeated which push and pull groups of wood fibers back and forth. In all of the microphotographs it is evident that this type of shear extends down into the wood under the tie plate for a number of annual rings. The extent of the shifting will at first be slight, but will increase with time as the number of impacts of the locomotives and cars successively pass over the tie plate. Under pressure, certain groups of wood fibers act as a unit and the axial shifting or breakage will naturally take place in the weakest section. That this actually happens only in the springwood portion of the wood has, I believe, been well illustrated in the various microphotographs. There is probably some relation between these impacts and the ultimate disappearance of the wood fibers. Repeated impacts may be responsible for the giving way of the weaker elements of the annual rings, as shown in the various microphotographs. After certain portions of the rings have been thus weakened, it is easy to understand how the wood immediately under the tie plate could be split, rasped or powdered, and ultimately disappear. These weakened fibers have, in other words, become predisposed to easy splitting, rasping or powdering. This will be particularly true for woods in which there is a distinct difference between the strength of the wood fibers in different portions of the ring; that is, the coniferous woods like pine, Douglas fir, cypress, redwood, and cedar. It has already been shown (see Fig. 7, 20, 37, 38, 51 and 62) that one of the characteristic appearances of mechanically destroyed ties, particularly in the softwoods, is the checking and splintering immediately under the tie plate. This is not so striking in the case of the hardwoods. All of the cleavage lines between adjacent splinters are in the springwood section, that is, the weakest portion of the ring. This is particularly evident in Fig. 42, 43 and 51, where the fine black lines, denoting a separation of wood fibers, occur in the early springwood. This may be the explanation as to why the softwood ties, as a whole, usually suffer more from mechanical wear than do hardwood ties. As has already been pointed out, the impact factor is probably one of great significance, and its relation to the changes under the tie plate will form a fruitful field for extensive further investigations.

A third factor is the destruction caused by the interaction of the broken wood columns, due to the driving of cut spikes and shear effect when

FIG. 157.

K. C. S. Ry., Bunch, Okla.   After adzing, creosoted shims and new tie plates being applied.

FIG. 158.

K. C. S. Ry., Bunch, Okla.   New rail, tie plates and wooden shims after completion of work.

loads pass over the ties (Fig. 53). This manifests itself in the splintering and shattering of the wood into the large number of small columns.

It looks, therefore, as if the complex motion of the tie plate aided by abrading materials between the plate and the wood acting under heavy pressure is bound to destroy the wood fibers in exactly the manner in which we find them in mechanically worn ties. The broken masses immediately under the tie plate involving separation between the rings, the broken and pulverized wood fibers between the plate and the tie all point to this conclusion. Moreover, the absence of material compression finally indicates that pressure of moving loads alone is not the direct cause of mechanical wear. This is very clearly shown by the appearance of wooden shims both in France and in this country. The rate at which this abrasion takes place will naturally depend upon a number of factors:

(1) The number and amount of impacts;
(2) The amount and kind of dirt or abrading material present;
(3) The loads exerted;
(4) The kind of wood;
(5) The type of the bottom of the tie plate; and
(6) The general character and upkeep of the track.

That all of these factors enter into the problem is plainly indicated by observations not only of my own but of others. Note, for instance, Fig. 14 showing a red oak creosoted tie after ten years' service. This is a particularly striking case of abrasion, made possible by the high percentage of abrading material from the chat ballast. Similar excessive abrasion is a matter of common observation in sand ballasted track. In stone ballasted track, this abrasion is less noticeable and takes longer. Taking all of these considerations together, I believe the assumption warranted that the looseness of the plate is the principal cause of mechanical wear.

In presenting these conclusions, I would like to reprint the comments made by Professor Talbot after my preliminary presentation at the March meeting of the A.R.E.A.,* because they so clearly express the viewpoint of our leading authority on track stresses.

"Observations on the wear of ties under loose tie plates and under tie plates held firmly to the tie, made at the time of our track tests, apparently have a bearing on the matter presented by Dr. von Schrenk. What has been observed seems to explain, in part at least, the way the wood acts and the effect upon the wood of the two conditions of the tie plates. First, loose tie plates, those which are not held down in some way independently of the rail, produce abrasive action on the tie, as has been observed by all. It appears that much of the movement of the tie plate comes when the rail is lifted from the tie at points between the groups of wheels, as occurs when the middle of a car is over the tie. When the wheel load is over the tie the movement of the tie plate is probably slight. It seems to me, however, that the breaking down of what we may call the particles of the wood by lateral forces which have an effect for some distance below the surface, as shown by the slides, is an important feature of it all. In a lateral direction the

*Proceedings A.R.E.A., Vol. 28, 1927, pp. 1284 and 1285.

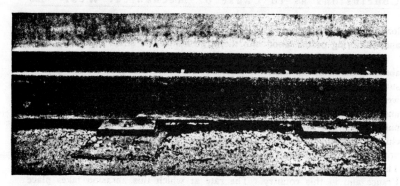

FIG. 159.

K. C. S. Ry., Bunch, Okla.   Wooden shims under tie plates after about one year's service.

FIG. 160.

K. C. S. Ry., Bunch, Okla.   Wooden shims under tie plates after about one year's service.

FIG. 161.

Screw spike fastened tie plates, K. C. S. Ry. test track at M.P. 256¼.   Note wooden shim under tie plate.   Photographed after 9 months' service.

wood, of course, has little resistance. That brings the thought that under such circumstances this failure or breakdown under heavy loading comes from the separation of particles, first by lateral movement at the weakest point, and then by the spreading of this separation under repetition of pressure from zero load to maximum applied by each group of wheels of a train. This repetition of application of load from zero to maximum may be expected to form an important element in the deteriorating process. The failure, then, is in the nature of a fatigue failure, which, of course, implies many applications of load and inferentially many repetitions or cycles of stress from small to maximum. It would follow, then, that if a tie plate is fastened to the tie in such a way as to produce and maintain a state of high compression in the wood at the top of the tie, this wood would not be subjected to violent changes in stress from small to large and therefore the wood so held under compression would be freed to a considerable extent from the high variations in stress that contribute to fatigue failure. The conditions that produce this result may be described as follows: When two screw spikes are put through the tie plate independently of the rail and screwed down tight, there will be produced a compression in the wood in the neighborhood of as great an amount as that produced in the tie by the loaded rail. That is not exact—it may be more or less, according to the way the motor-driven wrench may work. In large part this compression will afterward be maintained in the tie, though, of course, it will vary more or less as time goes on. Now with this high initial compression existing in the wood, the application of the wheel load on the rail will tend to relieve the tension in the screw spike, but it will not add to the compression in the wood at the upper left part of the tie, or at least it may be expected to modify but little the amount the wood is compressed. There is thus little or no variation in the compression of the wood fiber at and near the bearing surface. Now, continuous compression of the wood will have very little deteriorating effect as compared with the repetition from zero to maximum, and thus the fatigue effect on the wood will be greatly reduced.

"The reduction in wear and in the deterioration of the wood in track having the tie plates securely fastened to the tie and independently of the rail is apparent in our examination of track where the two methods of holding the tie plate are used.

"I wish to add that I believe that there are other important effects on track maintenance resulting from the fastening of the tie plate securely to the tie and that they are shown by our track tests. I need not go into that now."

Recent Experimental Track Installations.—While the foregoing appears to indicate rather clearly that loose tie plates are directly responsible for mechanical wear, it is evident that no final conclusion can be drawn until after more or less extensive actual experience in track construction. I accordingly suggested that a number of experimental track sections be built to try out these conclusions. In designating these test sections the mechanical relations between rail, tie plate and tie were kept uppermost in mind. All of the sections so far laid involve,

First. A piece of track with the present standard construction; that is, steel tie plates and cut spikes to hold the rail in position.

Second. Wooden shims placed directly under the railbase after the manner of the French Eastern Railroad. Some of these shims were placed with the grain running parallel with the longitudinal axis of the rail, others with the wood fibers at right angles to the longitudinal axis of the rail. In this section the shims were made the exact width of the base of the rail, and as long as the top face of the tie. They were held in position by means of short nails.

Third. A section in which wooden shims were placed under steel tie plates; cut spikes were used to hold the rail. The wooden shims had the exact dimensions as to width and length of the tie plates. They were bored in the same manner as the tie plates. All shims were creosoted.

Fourth. A section using steel tie plates with the usual punching for cut spikes. In addition holes were punched outside of the cut spike holes, and the tie plates were attached to the tie by means of screw spikes which held the tie plates without any contact with the rail.

Fifth. A section similar to the last, but in this section creosoted wooden shims, having dimensions as to width and length of the tie plates, were placed under the steel tie plate.

To date, three such sets of sections are completed, namely, on the Kansas City Southern, the Wabash, and the Missouri-Kansas-Texas. The following gives a brief description of these sections.

Kansas City Southern Experiment.—(See Chart III.) The experiment on the Kansas City Southern consists of two sections with wooden shims and one section with plates fastened with screw spikes. The experiment is being conducted on three separate sections of line. The first is on a section of track near Saginaw, Missouri. This track was completed out of face in 1914. The track was originally laid with creosoted 6 in. x 8 in. x 8 ft. red oak ties, grade No. 3, ballasted with chats. It now has 85 lb. rail. All ties have been tie plated with 6 in. x 8½ in. x 5/16 in. Railroad Supply Company three-hole tie plates. Since its original construction this track has been subject to extremely heavy traffic. After 12 years the tie plates had sunk into the ties so that in many cases the rail was cutting the edges of the tie. In June, 1926, this section of track was relaid with new rail. Believing that further tie plate cutting might be prevented or at least retarded, creosoted cottonwood shims having the exact dimensions of the tie plates, that is, 6 in. x 8½ in. x 5/16 in. in thickness, were laid in the depressions caused by the tie plates and the tie plates were then replaced on top of these wooden shims. The shims were bored with holes corresponding to those in the tie plate. The shims are held in position not only by the two spikes which go through the tie plate and the shim but also by the edges of the depression caused by the tie plates during the past years. Most of the shims were so made that the fiber runs parallel to the longitudinal axis of the ties. The shims were treated with 10 lb. of creosote per cu. ft. and cost $0.017 a piece. There are about 4 miles of this track. On this section experiments are also being made with shims of other materials.

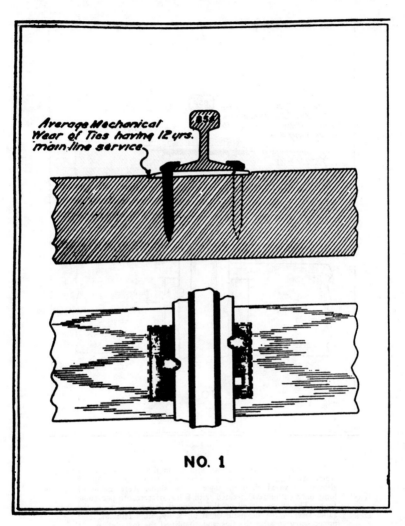

Average Mechanical Wear of Ties having 12 yrs. main line service

NO. 1

Fig. No. 1.

This figure shows a typical section of rail, tie plate and tie on the 3.7 miles of Saginaw line change south of Joplin as existed before the shims were installed. This section of track was laid new in 1914 with 85 lb. rail on treated red oak ties fully plated. The grading of the road bed was completed in 1912. The track was fully ballasted with chat. The ties were 6 in. x 8 in. x 8 ft., and the tie plates used were 6 in. x 8½ in. These plates have two small cross ribs and five small lens shape projections on the bottom of each plate. The track has been subjected to comparatively heavy traffic since its installation and something like 95% of the original ties still remain in place.

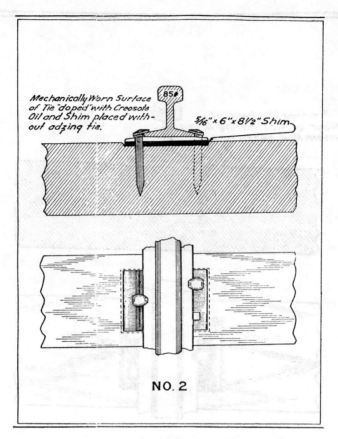

FIG. No. 2.

This shows a section of rail and tie in the same section of track as Fig. 1, the only difference being that Fig. 2 shows the wood shim in place. The shims were made of long fibre cottonwood treated with 8 lbs. of creosote per cubic foot. The shims placed on the Saginaw line change were the same size as the tie plate or 6 in. x 8½ in. This made it unnecessary to adze the ties and simplified the installation. It was only necessary to draw the spikes, raise the rail, plug the spike holes, and slip the shim under the plate. The shim being the same size as the plate, no adzing was necessary. All shims placed in this section of track were bored to conform to the punching of the plates.

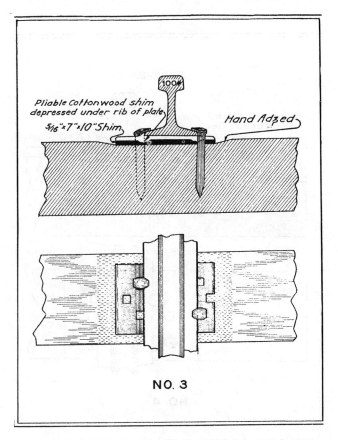

FIG. No. 3.

This figure shows the typical installation of wood shims under 37 miles of 100-lb. rail laid in 1926, Mile 248 to 285. The 100-lb. rail on this section of track replaced 85-lb. rail on various kinds of ties, but consisted mostly of white oak and treated red oak. Only a portion of these were plated and the pllates in place were of various sizes. In laying the 100-lb. rail all ties were plated with ¾ in. x 7 in. x 10 in. plates. This made it necessary to adze those ties which were cut by rail or tie plates. The shims used were $\frac{5}{16}$ in. in thickness and the same size as tie plates, or 7 in. x 10 in.

They were also treated with 8 lbs. of creosote and were bored to conform with the punching of the tie plates. 90% of them were bored with only four holes and the remaining 10% had six holes, making them adaptable for use under joints. Shims ¼ in. in thickness were first tried but were not found to be substantial enough in that they warped or cupped badly before they could be applied. The thickness was then changed to $\frac{5}{16}$ in. and this trouble was practically eliminated. Less than one mile of track was equipped with ¼ in. shims.

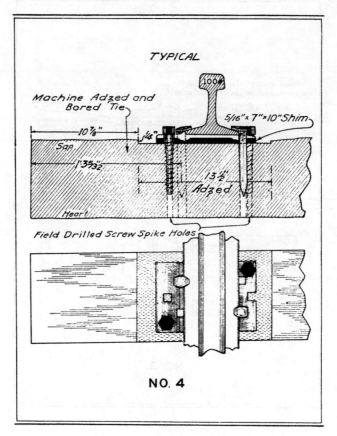

Fig. No. 4.

On one mile (M.P. 256-¼ to 257-¼) of the track mentioned in Fig. No. 3, the tie plates and shims were secured to the ties by screw spikes. The installation was the same as described in Fig. 3 with the exception that each plate was fastened down by two ¾ in. x 6 in. screw spikes. The tie plates and shims were drilled at the shops, and the ties drilled in the field. The cross tie indicated in Figure 4 shows the way in which our treated ties are now being adzed and bored.

GENERAL NOTES

All Tie Shims to be made of Long Fiber Cottonwood and treated with 6 lbs. of Creosote per cubic foot.

Surface of adzed portion of old ties are "doped" with creosote oil when shims are installed.

Ties as shown on Plate No. 1 & 2 are 6"x8"-8' Treated Red Oak, treated with 2½ gal. of creosote each. Plate No. 3 shows various treated and untreated ties, while No. 4 shows 7"x9"-8' T.R.O. tie having 3 gal. creosote each.

Tie Plates in Plate No. 1 & 2 have Cant of 1:40 and plates in No. 3 & 4 have 1:20 Cant under rail.

THE KANSAS CITY SOUTHERN RY. CO.

TIE SHIM

EXPERIMENTS

0" 1" 2" 3" 4" 5"

OFFICE OF CHIEF ENGINEER

KANSAS CITY, MO.

FEB. 8, 1927   DRAWING NO. 475-19

The second section is located near Bunch, Oklahoma, beginning with line post 275. This is an older piece of track in which untreated white oak ties and creosoted red oak ties are mixed. All of the creosoted ties had 6½ in. x 8½ in. compression bottom tie plates. In addition to these there is a large number of other types of tie plates scattered along the entire section. This piece of track approximately 37 miles long was relaid in June, 1926, with 100-lb. rail and 7 x 10 in. compression bottom tie plates. The rail laying procedure was briefly as follows: the old rail was taken up, the old ties removed, creosoted tie plugs were inserted in the spike holes and driven; the surface was then hand adzed where necessary and all freshly cut surfaces were given a thorough coating of hot creosote. On the new surfaces creosoted cottonwood shims 7 in. x 9 in. x 5/16 in. bored

FIG. 162.

Screw spike fastened tie plates, K. C. S. Ry. test track at M.P. 256¼. Note wooden shim under tie plate. Photographed after 9 months' service.

with four holes for intermediate, and five holes for joint ties were placed, and on top of these shims, the new tie plates were placed. The rail was then put in position and spiked through the steel and wooden plates. The section has chat ballast. These larger shims cost approximately $0.022 a piece. Fig. 154 to 160 show operations at both Saginaw and Bunch during June, 1926, and Fig. 161 and 162 those of more recent date.

The third section, one mile in length, was completed during December, 1926. This section is located from mile post 256¼ to 257¼. In this mile standard compression bottom tie plates of the Railroad Supply Company's pattern 7 in. x 10 in. x ¾ in. were used. These plates were punched for four cut spike holes in the usual position, and two round holes for screw

Fig. 163.

Wabash Ry. experimental track near Sand Creek, Mich. (Upper) Standard track construction; flat bottom 7½ in. × 10½ in. tie plates and two cut spikes. (Lower) 7½ in. × 10½ in. tie plate, two cut spikes, creosoted wooden shim between tie and tie plate.

spikes located at opposite corners of the tie plate but outside of the cut spike holes. (See Fig. 4, Chart III). Cottonwood shims were first laid on the dapped portion of the tie. The tie plates then were placed on the wooden shims and fastened with two screw spikes ¾ in. x 6 in. The tie plates weighed 9.88 lb. each. Two cut spikes were applied for holding the rail. Fig. 161 and 162 show typical sections of this track several months after installation.

I am indebted to C. E. Johnston, President, for the following expression of opinion concerning the service which this track has so far given.

"On the Kansas City Southern, a large majority of our cross-ties in the main tracks are creosoted, and in that way we have been able to greatly increase their life. We are, however, confronted with the serious problem of protecting these ties from mechanical wear, in order that we may get the full life available from treatment.

"During the early spring of 1926 we concluded to make an experiment with wooden shims laid on top the tie and under the tie plates. These shims were made from cottonwood timber and treated, the dimensions being the same as to length and width as the tie plate (7 in. x 10 in.) and 5/16 in thick. These shims were laid under 100-lb. rail and 37 track miles are included in the test.

"At the same time we also applied approximately four miles of 5/16 in. treated cottonwood shims in a similar manner in a stretch of track laid in 1914. At the time this stretch of track was constructed all the material, including rail, ties and ballast, was new. The construction consists of 85-lb. rail laid on treated red oak ties fully tie plated and with chat ballast. During the twelve years of service the plates had imbedded themselves in the ties an average of approximately one-quarter inch, the plates being 6 in. x 8 in. x 5/16 in., and in order to improve the situation it was necessary to either adze the ties and reset the rail or raise the rail and plates on shims.

"The test was made by applying shims the exact size of the tie plates under the plates and in the depression created by mechanical wear during the twelve years of service. This brought the base of the tie plate to the general level of the original top of tie, and enabled us to straighten up the rail without seriously injuring the ties by adzing.

"May also state that in the application of these wooden shims our track forces were very careful to clean out the depression and apply creosote oil before inserting the shim.

"In both cases, that of new 100-lb. rail and the twelve-year-old 85-lb. rail, all ties are plated and the wooden shims were punched to correspond with the punching of the tie plates.

"As to the axle load operating over both stretches of track. The heaviest is our main driving axles on our Mallet locomotives of approximately 63,000 lb.

"The tie plates under the 100-lb. rail are the Railway Supply Company's pattern compression bottom, having a dimension of 7 in. x 10 in. x ¾ in.

"In the application the majority of the ties were not adzed or bored when laid originally, and in order to properly install the wood shims it was necessary to hand adze the ties to secure a uniform bearing surface. When the hand adzing did not give an absolute uniform bearing surface some of the shims split as soon as the load was applied. Since that time, due to the track wave under load, a large number of the shims have split, but in most cases are still functioning.

"The track spikes used are ⅝ in. x 6 in. with two to the tie plate on tangent track and three to the plate on curves; the extra spike being applied on the outside of the curve.

"A test section of one mile of ¾ in. x 6 in. screw spikes was installed and in this track two screw spikes were placed in each tie plate, and in addition, two track spikes. The screw spikes are of the Illinois Steel Company design.

"No trouble has been experienced with spikes bending under the head on curves due to the longer arm between top of tie and bearing of rail flange against head of spike. Also, no trouble has been noted with spikes expanding the spike hole near the surface of the tie.

"To date the results to be obtained from the application of wood shims as indicated are not definitely known. There is, however, indication that the use of screw spikes without wood shims is more effective than wood shims without screw spikes. In other words, there is evidence that the positive anchoring of the plate to the tie has advantages over the other methods.

"We are satisfied that properly treated cross-ties have an increased life over the untreated tie sufficient to warrant the cost of treatment, and with that fact before us a way must be found to protect against mechanical wear, since it does not appear that the tie plate applied in the usual manner will protect against mechanical wear.

"What we have done in way of testing the use of wood shims, while not showing all the results desired, seems to point to an ultimate satisfactory solution, and contains much promise of real progress in the elimination of mechanical wear on our cross-ties."

Wabash Experiment.—(See Chart IV.) The test track on the Wabash is located near Sand Creek, Mich., and is part of a new piece of double track. The experiment here included five pieces, each one-half mile in length, as follows: one-half mile of standard present type construction using adzed and bored creosoted red oak ties 7½ in. x 10½ in. tie plates and two cut spikes. (Chart IV, Fig. 1; also Fig. 163.) Second, one-half mile of ties adzed the exact width of the base of the rail, bored for cut spikes, creosoted black gum shims 5½ in. x 8 in. x 5/16 in. (Chart IV, Fig. 2; also Fig. 163.) These shims were so made that the grain runs parallel with the longitudinal axis of the tie. Third, creosoted red oak ties bored and adzed, standard flat bottom Wabash tie plates 10½ in. x 7½ in. (Chart IV, Fig. 3.) In this section wooden shims were placed between the tie plate and the tie. All of these shims were bored with four holes corresponding to the spike

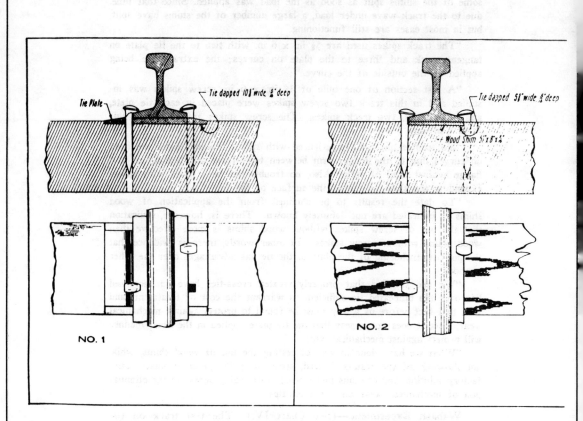

FIG. 1.

Present standard tie plate, 7½ in. x 10½ in., using two cut spikes to hold the rail in position. In this first section creosoted adzed and bored red oak ties were used. 110-lb. rail.

FIG. 2.

Second experimental section using wooden shims 5½ in. x 8 in. x ⅞ in., of the exact width of the base of the rail, nailed to the tie. 110-lb. rail used.

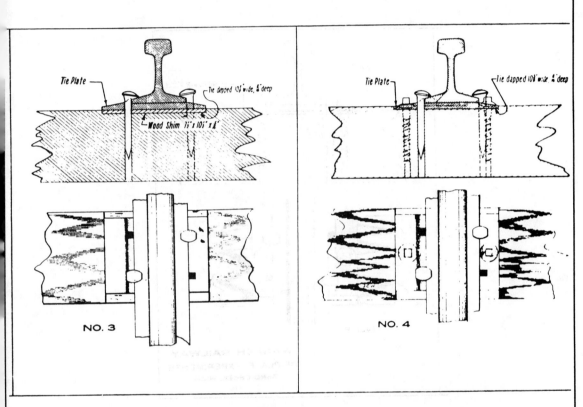

Fig. 3.

Third experimental section using the present standard tie plate (as in Fig. 1) with a wooden shim placed below the tie plate. The wood shim is 7½ in. x 10½ in. x ⅞ in. 110-lb. rail used, and two cut spikes to hold the rail.

Fig. 4.

In the fourth experimental section special flat bottom tie plates 10½ in. x 7½ in. were used. 110-lb. rail held in place by two cut spikes. The tie plates were held in position by two screw spikes on the median center line of the tie plate. Ties were creosoted red oak, adzed and bored for all holes before treatment.

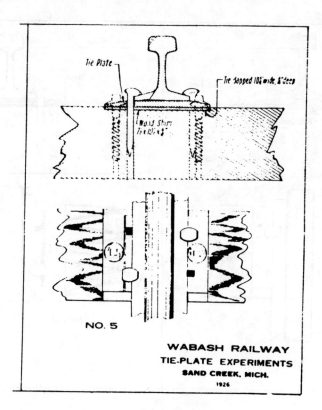

FIG. 5.

The fifth experimental section is exactly the same as the fourth, except that a wooden shim of the exact dimensions of the tie plate, that is, 7½ in. x 10½ in., ⅛ in. thick, was placed under the steel plate. The plate was independently fastened with two screw spikes, and two cut spikes were used to hold the rail. All ties were creosoted red oak adzed and bored for all holes before treatment. Rail used, 110-lb.

Fig. 164.

Wabash Ry. experimental track near Sand Creek, Mich. (Upper) 7½ in. × 10½ in. tie plate, two cut spikes, creosoted wooden shim between tie and tie plate. (Lower) Standard 7½ in. × 10½ in. tie plate using two cut spikes and two screw spikes for holding tie plate. Wooden shim between tie plate and tie.

holes in the standard tie plate. 1300 ties were applied with black gum shims in which the fibers ran parallel with the rail, and 105 ties with black gum shims in which the fibers ran at right angles to the rail. In addition to this, 130 ties were equipped with cottonwood shims in which the fibers ran parallel to the rail, and 130 ties with creosoted tupelo shims of the same type. Cut spikes were used as the fastening. Fourth, in this section, Wabash standard flat bottom tie plates 10½ in. x 7½ ih. were used, but in these plates two additional holes were bored outside of the spike holes. (Chart IV, Fig. 4; see also Fig. 164.) The tie plates were fastened to the creosoted red oak ties, adzed and bored before treatment with two screw spikes, while the rail was held in position by two cut spikes. Fifth, this section was identical with the fourth except that wooden shims were placed between the screw spike fastened tie plates and the tie. (Chart IV, Fig. 5; also Fig. 164.) On this section 1300 ties had black gum shims whose fibers ran at right angles to the rail, and 105 ties were provided with creosoted black gum shims whose fibers ran parallel to the rail. In addition there were 130 ties each provided with cottonwood shims whose fibers ran at right angles to the rail, and 130 ties provided with tupelo shims with fibers running at right angles to the rail. 110-lb. rail was used throughout. The attached figures show these different installations diagrammatically.

Missouri-Kansas-Texas Experiments.—In November, 1926, the M.-K.-T. Lines completed a five-mile section of test track located in the south-bound track north of Atoka, Oklahoma. (See Fig. 165-171.) I am indebted to Frank Ringer, Chief Engineer of the M.-K.-T. Lines, for the following details concerning the construction of this test track.

"In the construction of these experimental sections the track as it existed at the time of installation was used. Rail was removed and tie plates and shims were inserted on the existing ties. These were of all kinds and conditions, and included untreated, zinc chloride treated, and creosoted ties (both pine and oak). They included ties in all conditions of mechanical wear from newly sawed ties with approximately flat surfaces, to ties which had been in track many years. This installation, therefore, differed from the Wabash installation which was laid on adzed and bored ties, all of them new and placed out of face. The rail used was 90-lb. rail. The maximum locomotive axle operating over this track is 60,726 lb."

Five one-mile sections were installed, as follows:

Test No. 1.—Standard Construction. This mile is located at M.P. 608.2-609.2. There are 0.52 mile of tangent and 0.48 mile of 0 deg. 40 min. curve. Type "G" tie plates were used, size 7½ in. x 10 in. x ⅝ in., with two shallow transverse ribs on the bottom at the edge of the rail base. The rail was held in position by two cut spikes 5½ in. x 9/16 in. (See Fig. 165.)

Test No. 2—Wooden Shim. This mile is located at M.P. 607.1-608.1 —all tangent track. Creosoted black gum shims 5⅛ in. x 8½ in. x 5/16 in. (that is, the exact width of the base of the rail and length of the top of the tie) treated by the Rueping process with 6 lb. of creosote per cubic foot, were fastened to the tie by means of two 3d nails. The grain of the

FIG. 165.

M.-K.-T. Tie Plate Installation, showing standard track with 7½ in. × 10 in. × ⅝ in. transverse ribbed tie plates held in position by two cut spikes.

FIG. 166.

M.-K.-T. Tie Plate Installation, showing ties adzed 5½ in. wide to exact width of base of rail. Into the adzed section creosoted shims were applied fastened with small screws.

wood shims was laid so that the fibers ran at right angles to the longitudinal axis of the rail; two cut spikes 5½ in. x 9½ in. hold the rail in position.

In addition to the wooden shims laid in 1926, 39 new adzed and bored ties were laid out of face on August 15, 1927. These ties were adzed to the exact width of the rail base, that is, 5⅛ in. The creosoted wooden shims were then placed in the adzed section, and were fastened by means of small screws. (See Fig. 166.)

Test No. 3—Wooden Shims and Steel Plates—Spike Fastened. This mile is located at M.P. 606.1-607.1 consisting of 0.87 mile of tangent, and 0.13 mile of 1 deg. 00 min. curve. In this test wooden shims of the exact dimensions of the tie plate, namely, 7½ in. x 10 in. x 5/16 in., creosoted by the Rueping process with 6 lb. per cubic foot, were laid on the ties, and type "G" tie plates, 7½ in. x 10½ in. x ⅝ in. were placed on the shims. (Fig. 167 and 168.) The shims were bored for 4 spike holes corresponding to the tie plate. In this mile 4926 black gum shims, 472 tupelo gum, and 461 cottonwood shims were laid, all with the grain at right angles to the longitudinal axis of the rail. In addition, 411 black gum shims were laid with the grain running parallel to the longitudinal axis of the rail.

Test No. 4—Screw Spike Fastened Steel Plates. This mile is located at M.P. 604.1-605.1, consisting of 0.49 mile of tangent and 0.51 mile 1 deg. 00 min. curve. Two type "G" tie plates (see Fig. 169) were applied, each with two screw spikes, 5½ in. x ¾ in. Two 5½ in. x 9/16 in. cut spikes were used to hold the rail in place. Plate "G" is the standard M.-K.-T. tie plate, which was punched specially for the two screw spikes as per the drawing in Fig. 171. The two holes are staggered, the center of the hole being ¾ in. from the center line of the tie plate.

Test No. 5—Screw Fastened Steel Plate and Wooden Shim. This mile is located at M.P. 605.1-606.1, consisting of 0.75 mile of tangent, and 0.25 mile of 1 deg. 00 min. curve. This installation was exactly like test No. 4, except that creosoted wooden shims were laid between the tie plates and the ties (see Fig. 170). In this test 4609 black gum, 474 tupelo gum, and 498 cottonwood shims were laid with the grain at right angles to the longitudinal axis of the rail; also 400 black gum shims were laid with the grain parallel to the longitudinal axis of the rail. Holes for the screw spikes were bored through the wooden shims in the field by hand.

Other Tests.—In addition to the experimental sections just described, similar sections are under way and will be completed early in 1928 on the New York Central Railroad (see Chart V); Michigan Central Railroad; New York, New Haven & Hartford Railroad; the Nickel Plate Railroad, the Big Four* and the Missouri Pacific Railroad. The idea underlying the construction of these tracks is that practical experience alone will enable one to approach a solution of the mechanical wear problem. Included in these experimental sections are a number of variables. It has already been found that fastening wooden shims with nails as in the case of the Missouri-Kansas-Texas (and this was also found on the Big Four, Santa Fe and others in the early experiments in 1906 and thereabouts) is probably not workable with hardwoods

*The Big Four test track was completed in February, 1928.

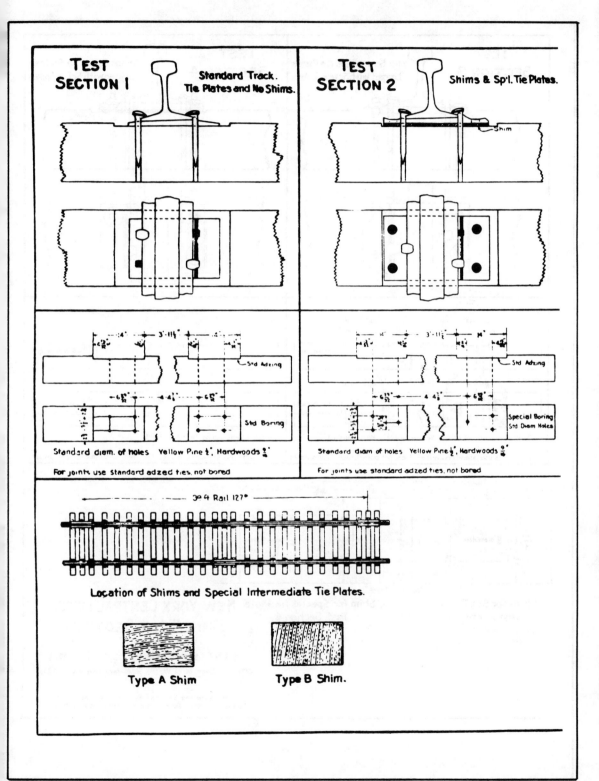

TEST SECTION 1 — Standard Track. Tie Plates and No Shims.

TEST SECTION 2 — Shims & Sp'l. Tie Plates.

Std Adzing

Std Boring

Special Boring
Std Diam Holes

Standard diam. of holes   Yellow Pine $\frac{1}{2}$", Hardwoods $\frac{9}{16}$"

For joints use standard adzed ties, not bored

Standard diam of holes   Yellow Pine $\frac{1}{2}$", Hardwoods $\frac{9}{16}$"

For joints use standard adzed ties, not bored

Location of Shims and Special Intermediate Tie Plates.

Type A Shim   Type B Shim.

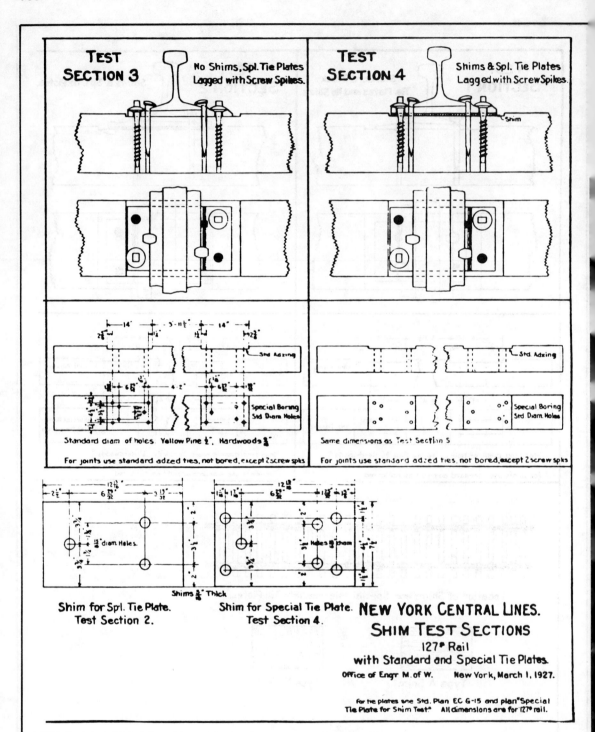

TEST SECTION 3 — No Shims, Spl. Tie Plates Lagged with Screw Spikes.

TEST SECTION 4 — Shims & Spl. Tie Plates Lagged with Screw Spikes.

Std. Adzing

Special Boring Std. Diam. Holes

Standard diam. of holes. Yellow Pine ½". Hardwoods ⅜".

For joints use standard adzed ties, not bored, except 2 screw spks.

Same dimensions as Test Section 3

For joints use standard adzed ties, not bored, except 2 screw spks.

Shims ⅜" Thick

Shim for Spl. Tie Plate. Test Section 2.

Shim for Special Tie Plate. Test Section 4.

NEW YORK CENTRAL LINES.
SHIM TEST SECTIONS
127° Rail
with Standard and Special Tie Plates.

Office of Engr M. of W.   New York, March 1, 1927.

For the plates use Std. Plan EC G-15 and plan "Special Tie Plate for Shim Test." All dimensions are for 127° rail.

FIG. 167.

M.-K.-T. Tie Plate Installation — ties with wooden shims under tie plates with two cut spikes (in service since November, 1926).

FIG. 168.

M.-K.-T. Tie Plate Installation — ties with wooden shims under tie plates with two cut spikes (in service since November, 1926). This illustrates two old ties with uneven bearing. In such a situation the shims will probably be of comparatively little service unless ties are carefully adzed before the application of the shim.

like beech and the gums. It may prove that the cottonwood shims are more satisfactory than the hardwoods. In all of these experiments I discarded the felt cushion because of the experience of the French that they are unsuitable. It should also be noted that in all of the independently fastened plates, screw spikes have been used. It will be desirable in addition to the screw spikes to try other methods of fastening. Some such experiments are already under way by the Delaware, Lackawanna & Western, who not long ago bolted a good many tie plates through the tie. Recently a device has been patented using a bolt extending clear through the tie and the tie plate which is held in position by means of a wedge-shaped key. This may have the possible advantage over the screw in that it will be easier to keep this fastened absolutely tight.

Other Protective Devices Against Mechanical Wear.—In the foregoing, reference has been made to the use of compressed poplar wood shims by the French Eastern Railways, placed between the rail and tie. Previous to the use of the wooden shim, felt pads had been used but had been found unsatisfactory. The English railways have for years been using felt pads placed between the chair and the wooden tie. In Austria fiber composition pads were used as far back as 1906 but so far as I can learn, these have never given as satisfactory service as the wooden shims used by the French Eastern.

From time to time various devices have been invented and patented for strengthening the rail bearing so as to reduce mechanical wear. In the bulletin of the International Railway Congress for 1913, page 267, M. Matthaei of the German Railways published a paper on "Hardwood Pads for Railway Sleepers." This invention (German patent 231,326) consisted of a hardwood pad fastened to the tie at the rail bearing. This device was "based on the principle that the different methods of pickling attempted do not readily fulfill the object if the sleeper has to be renewed in consequence of mechanical destruction when it otherwise would still have a good life." Fig. 172 shows varying forms of suggested pads. The pads are made of oak, hornbeam or beech. They are rotated into position after dipping in a tarry mass and are held by the oblique mortise in the upper surface of the tie. Tie plates of various designs are then placed on top of the pad and the rail secured in the usual manner.

So far as I have been able to learn, these pads were never used to any extent.

Based very much upon the same principle, but intended for the rehabilitation of mechanically worn ties, is the so-called Rambacher plate. Fig. 173 shows a plan and section of this device. A year ago I saw a great many thousand of ties equipped in accordance with this plan in actual service on the Bavarian Railways. I am indebted to the Bavarian Railways for the following brief statement.

"In the District of Bavaria, softwood ties which have been badly worn mechanically after 12 to 16 years' service in the track are provided with Rambacher plates, provided they show no organic signs of destruction (that is, decay) and after the application, they are inserted into main lines just as new ties are inserted. The application of this device differs from other

FIG. 169.

M.-K.-T. Tie Plate Installation, showing tie plates held in place by two independent screw spikes (in service since November, 1926).

FIG. 170.

M.-K.-T. Tie Plate Installation, showing ties with wooden shims under the tie plates, the latter held in position by two independent screw spikes (in service since November, 1926).

processes of similar character in that only such ties are provided with wooden blocks as have proven after a long period of service that they are very resistant to decay. These carefully selected ties after insertion of the wooden blocks give us an additional 12 to 15 years' life. Our experience with these rejuvenated ties is entirely satisfactory. Formerly we used to put the blocks in with hand labor, but in the last few years this has to a certain extent been done by means of machinery."

The following figures as to costs were recently submitted by the Bavarian Section of the Germany Railways:

(a) **Cost of Inserting 2 Rambacher Plates:**

1. Adzing of old tie...........................$ .025
2. Two plates, i. e., 6 wedges.....................400
3. Placing of wedges, including freight, on old ties to reconditioning plant 200
4. Total cost for 2 Rambacher plates..............625
5. Value of old ties...............................375
6. Final value of old tie with 2 Rambacher plates in place 1.00

(b) **Other Costs:**

7. Cost of adzing ties in track.......................075
8. Labor removing old tie and placing a new one... .250
9. Cost of new untreated tie........................ 1.50
10. Cost of new creosoted tie........................ 2.00

As is indicated in the drawings in Fig. 173 the Rambacher plate consists of three wedge-shaped blocks of wood of which the center one, marked B in the drawing, is the key block. The rail worn tie is adzed until sound wood is reached and the three blocks are then driven into the space thus provided. Two small wooden pins are then inserted so as to prevent the blocks from becoming loose. Fig. 174 shows a badly worn but otherwise sound creosoted pine tie taken from the main line track on the New York Central Railroad and the same tie after preparation according to the Rambacher plan.

Objections have been made to this process, due to the necessity for cutting so deeply into the tie at a point where the greatest strength is required. I personally looked over a great number of ties so prepared in the Bavarian tracks and found no evidence anywhere of breakage under the rail. I believe the plan to be one which deserves some consideration, at least many ties now doubtless impaired because of mechanical wear which are otherwise sound, might be reconditioned, if not for main line service, for service in secondary lines or industrial tracks. Trials are now being made to determine the cost of application of these blocks by hand.

The Plate Adhesive.—On the assumption that mechanical wear is due to the motion of the tie plate, and consequently that it might be considerably reduced or even entirely prevented, if the tie plate was stopped from moving, it was suggested last fall that one might glue the tie plates to the tie in some manner. While at first this appeared somewhat extraordinary, subsequent thought and investigations showed that this might be possible. The original suggestion and the development of the work so far accom-

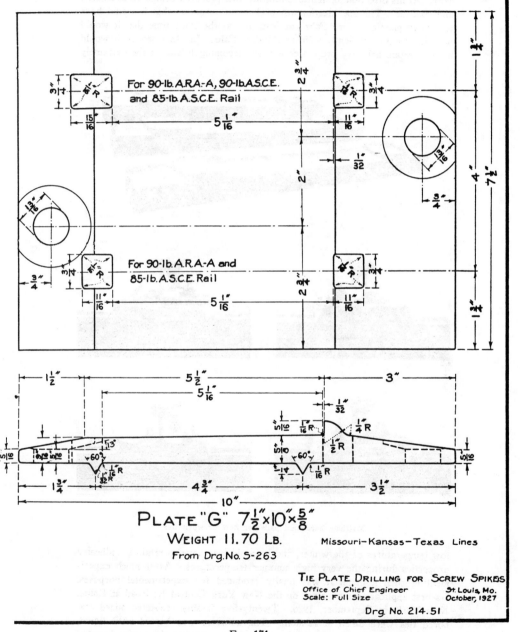

PLATE "G" 7½"×10"×⅝"
WEIGHT 11.70 LB.
From Drg. No. 5-263

Missouri—Kansas—Texas Lines

TIE PLATE DRILLING FOR SCREW SPIKES
Office of Chief Engineer   St. Louis, Mo.
Scale: Full Size   October, 1927

Drg. No. 214.51

FIG. 171.
M.-K.-T. Lines. Special tie plate for mechanical wear test track.

plished are due to A. L. Kuehn, President of the American Creosoting Company. At his direction an adhesive mixture was prepared composed as asphalt and coal-tar. The specification for such a mixture was that it would have to remain plastic at zero Fahr., or less, and at the same time that it would have to remain sufficiently solid at 160 deg. Fahr. In other words, it would have to retain adhesive properties without becoming brittle at the extremely

Fig. 172.

Matthaei hardwood pads for new or worn ties.

low temperatures of the winter, and it would also have to retain its adhesive properties during the very high summer temperatures. After much experimenting such a material was finally produced for experimental purposes. Its first application took place on the New York Central Railroad at Rome, New York, in September, 1926. Twenty-five freshly creosoted adzed and bored ties were taken at random. The adhesive was heated until liquid, and was then applied to the tie plate area. Two wooden plugs were inserted

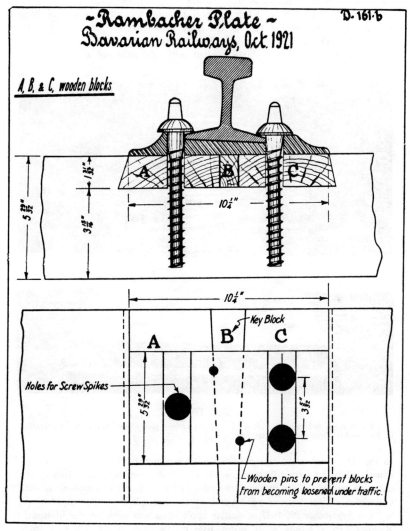

FIG. 173.

Rambacher tie cushion for worn ties.   German Railway Co., Bavarian Section.

in two of the bored holes, and the tie plates were slipped over these guides and pressed onto the ties. After a few minutes the adhesive cooled enough so that the wooden plugs could be withdrawn. In this experiment the tie plates used were standard New York Central Railroad plates, from which the two shallow cross ribs had been removed by planing. In other words, the bottom of the plate was flat. These ties, together with 25 ties upon which the standard New York Central tie plate with the ribs had been applied, were laid out of face in the main eastbound freight track east of Rome, New York. They have now been in service for over a year. At the last inspection all of the plates applied with the adhesive adhered firmly

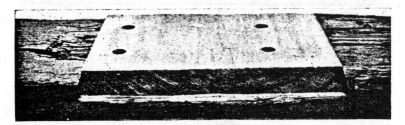

FIG. 174.

Worn creosoted pine tie, N. Y. C. R. R., before and after adzing and application of Rambacher three-piece tie cushion.

to the tie. Each plate was pounded with a hammer and gave forth a dull sound indicating firm adherence, while all of the control plates without the adhesive rattled. This rather extraordinary result has led to making similar experimental installations on several other railroads.

On September 20, 1927, a similar application was made on the Missouri-Kansas-Texas Lines at a point five miles east of St. Charles, Mo. In this case compression bottom tie plates were used. Thirty pine ties were laid with the tie plate adhesive, and thirty control ties of the same type without the adhesive. In both of these experiments the usual construction with two cut spikes was used. Similar applications have been made on the

Erie, New Haven, Missouri Pacific, Wabash, Cotton Belt, Kansas City Southern and Nickel Plate.

It is, of course, too early to tell what this manner of applying tie plates will ultimately amount to. It is, however, an extremely interesting suggestion, and the behavior of these plates will be carefully observed. The details of the composition will possibly have to be changed, and further work will have to be done as to the method of application and the most economical handling of the adhesive at the time of application.

Conclusions and Recommendations.—In concluding this study on the subject of mechanical wear of treated ties, certain conclusions and recommendations appear appropriate. The reduction of mechanical wear can be accomplished only by observing a number of factors.

In presenting these conclusions and recommendations it is assumed that the track as a whole is of high standard, that is, with good ballast, good ties, properly tamped ties, and that the track has good line and surface. Changes in the character of the tie plate or its method of attachment alone will not suffice, because as has already been indicated, the factors of the general type of track, the character and amount of traffic will have much to do with the success or failure of the tie plate phase of the matter. Provided the best conditions are maintained, an observance of the following recommendations will do much to reduce mechanical wear.

(1) ADZED AND BORED TIES.—In all first-class track only ties which have been adzed and bored before treatment should be used. The adzing gives a smooth seating for the tie plate, and to that extent reduces any irregular motion such as undoubtedly takes place in ties which have not been adzed. Boring the ties before treatment not only gives a better distribution of the preservative, but is a very vital factor in maintaining the strength of the wood fibers, not only in the immediate vicinity of the fastening, but under the whole tie plate area. Adzed and bored ties have been used long enough both in Europe and in this country to amply demonstrate the truth of this recommendation.

(2) CANTED AND CAMBERED TIE PLATES.—The use of canted and cambered tie plates will undoubtedly help in reducing the motion of the plate. With a properly designed camber and cant there is a better load distribution. This applies at all times during which the tie plate functions, namely, with the approach of the load application, and with the receding of the load application. As indicated before, the vital effect of the load application is probably not when it is immediately over the tie plate, but when it is approaching and receding. Anything, therefore, which will tend to reduce an unequal application of load will correspondingly reduce the rolling shear action of the tie plate.

(3) FLAT BOTTOM TIE PLATE.—It must be obvious from the foregoing that the best results will be obtained where the bottom of the tie plate is free from projections, flanges or other irregularities.

(4) SIZE OF TIE PLATE.—The size of the tie plate is a very vital factor. The tie plate must, under all circumstances, be large enough to give the best load distribution under any given set of circumstances. Under

heavy traffic no tie plate should be less than 7½ in. in width, and the length and thickness should be proportioned to the traffic demands. The larger the tie plate the more its motion will be reduced. There is, unfortunately, an insufficient amount of information as yet available to give a definite formula as to size in relation to traffic. This is one of the problems which should, I believe, receive increased attention and study. It is significant, however, that the present tendency to increase sizes of tie plates is in the right direction.

(5) INDEPENDENTLY FASTENED TIE PLATES.—The most promising factor in reducing mechanical wear is doubtless connected with the fastening of the tie plate to the tie independent of the rail. An independently fastened plate will restrict the motion of the plate, and will consequently do away with most of the rolling shear effect and impact of passing loads, and most certainly with much of the mechanical rasping so prevalent with plates not fastened. Many details will doubtless have to be worked out to develop an ideal fastening. This ideal fastening should be simple, easily applied, easily repaired in case of accidents or wrecks, and above all, demand low maintenance expenditure. The screw spike so extensively used at the present time may not be the final answer. There have been failures with screw fastened plates, due to the fact that the screws were not kept tight on the rail. The Germans believe that by the use of proper lock-washers (Fig. 130 and 131), an intimate, constant contact between the head of the screw and the tie plate can be secured. It may be that some form of bolt of the type used by the Lackawanna, or the experimental bolts referred to above, may prove to be more effective than the screws. It furthermore may prove that some sort of adhesive will suffice, which, of course, would mean that bolts, screws or other fastenings may be unnecessary. The best results will doubtless be obtained in case either screws or bolts are used if the tie plates are permanently attached to the tie at the creosoting plant, preferably under pressure, in the manner practiced by the Great Western Railroad of England in applying their chairs. This would mean that ties would be shipped to the track from the creosoting plant with the tie plates already applied. Problems of distribution due to different weights of rail would, of course, arise, but I do not regard such problems as insuperable.

(6) REPLACEMENT OF PLATES.—At the present time whenever rail changes are made, and particularly when new plates are laid, either of different design or of larger size, it is customary to adze ties by hand. This adzing results in much waste of wood, and frequent exposure of untreated wood, with consequent loss of decay protection. That this type of adzing frequently hastens mechanical wear by leaving pockets for water to stand, causing more rapid disintegration of the wood fibers, can hardly be questioned. One of the most practicable remedies for this matter has been the recent development of the Neafie Tie Scoring Machine (see Fig. 175, 176 and 177; see also Railway Engineering and Maintenance Journal, May, 1927, page 211). This machine mechanically saws an even cut without waste of wood, and enables the track operator to secure a smooth, even tie plate bearing. It is one of the most effective machines yet developed and it should be generally used.

FIG. 175.
Neafie Tie Scoring Machine.

FIG. 176.
Ties scored by Neafie Tie Scoring Machine, tie plugs inserted and ties ready for adzing.

(7) WOODEN SHIMS.—When first introduced the wooden shim was regarded as a possible substitute for the metal tie plate. This has given rise to much misconception. In France and Germany where the screw spike is used as a standard rail fastening, it is possible to insert wooden shims and to replace broken or otherwise destroyed shims with ease and rapidity. The pressure of the screw holds the shim in position. American experience has shown that with the cut spike fastening, where there is contact between the head of the spike and the rail for only a limited period, the wooden shims can be held under the rail only with difficulty. This is true even where they are nailed. It is probable therefore, that with our present cut spike fastening, the wooden shim alone will serve only as a temporary expedient, if at all, in reducing mechanical wear. The cut spike fastening,

FIG. 177.

Ties scored by Neafie Tie Scoring Machine; ties adzed and tie plates placed upon the ties.

furthermore, does not permit easy renewal of the shims where they creep out or are destroyed. An efficient method of fastening the shims to the tie, possibly with a material like the tie plate adhesive, might make the shims more serviceable. Some shims will doubtless remain in position and to that extent protect the ties, but the number is probably too small to warrant the additional expense for all ties. The wooden shim, I believe, however, has a place. Where ties have been partially abraded, forming pockets, as in the case described for the Kansas City Southern, the wooden shims will fill such pockets and will provide a cushion for the steel plate which will materially reduce further mechanical destruction of the tie. In such cases the shims are held on all four edges. They may break, to be sure, but the pieces cannot get away, and even in their broken condition they will serve. The wooden shims, furthermore, may prove to be a valuable factor when placed between an independently fastened tie plate and a tie. Experience alone will enable one to determine this definitely. From the experimental sections already established, and to be established, data should be forthcoming within a comparatively short time which will enable one to answer this question definitely. The Dutch have already found them of service under their plates. The use of the wooden shim for application on partially destroyed ties, is, I believe, good practice and should be more widely tried.

There are many problems connected with the development of the wooden shim, particularly as to the kind of wood to be used, and the direction of grain. Experience has already shown that various softwoods like cottonwood are probably superior to hardwoods like beech or gum, because they do not split so readily. It will also be desirable to further develop the idea of a possible compression of the wooden shim such as is practiced by the French. Materials other than wood, made into shim form are under test in various test sections.

(8) FUTURE DEVELOPMENTS.—In the foregoing paragraphs references have already been made as to future developments. It should be understood that the matters discussed in this investigation are largely of a fundamental nature. If it is once understood what it is that must be solved, a better point of attack is presented. It is felt that if the motion of the tie plate is responsible for the destruction of the ties, this gives a basis for further study and development. It is believed that with the track experiments already initiated, and with others still to be developed, that the mechanical life of creosoted ties may be considerably extended, with a consequent large saving.

This presentation is in the nature of a general report of progress, and it is expected that results of the different test tracks herein described will be reported on in detail from time to time.

Acknowledgments.—I am indebted to many railroad officials in Europe and America and to others for information and assistance in the preparation of this report. Without their cordial interest and cooperation the results herein described would have been impossible. I take great pleasure in acknowledging this interest and assistance, particularly to:

E. F. C. Trench, Chief Engineer, London, Midland & Scottish Railway;
J. C. Lloyd, Chief Engineer, Great Western Railway;
M. Geesteranus, Chief Engineer, Dutch Railways;
M. Descubes, Chief Engineer, Chemin de Fer de l'Est;
Georges Patte, Principal Assistant Engineer, Chemin de Fer de l'Est;
Reg. Baurat Frankenburg, German Railways;
Ing. Hunsdorfer, Chief Engineer, German Railways, Bavarian Section;
Oberbaurat Weidinger, German Railways, Bavarian Section;
Hofrat Fritz Hromatka, Austrian Railways;
Ministerialrat Ing. Josef Hiller, Austrian Railways;
Reichsbahn Oberbaurat Kröh, German Railways;
Jules Willem, Inspecteur General, Belgian Railways;

M. Gilson, Belgian Railways;

M. Barbieri, Italian Railways;

Comm. Ing. Fr. Salvini, Italian Railways;

Hadley Baldwin, Chief Engineer, C. C. C. & St. L. Railway;

J. J. Baxter, Assistant Chief Engineer, Wabash Railway;

R. S. Belcher, Manager Treating Plants, A. T. & S. F. Railway;

E. W. Boots, Engineer Maintenance of Way, P. & L. E. Railroad;

C. E. Denney, Vice-Prest., Erie Railroad;

R. C. Dixon, Roadmaster, C. B. & Q. Railroad;

C. F. Ford, Supervisor Tie and Timber Dept., Rock Island Lines;

E. A. Hadley, Chief Engineer, Missouri Pacific Railroad;

Paul Hamilton, Assistant Chief Engineer, C. C. C. & St. L. Railway;

A. C. Harvey, Chief Engineer, Nickel Plate Road;

R. H. Howard, Chief Engineer, Wabash Railway;

C. E. Johnston, President, Kansas City Southern Railway;

Arthur Koehler, Forest Products Laboratory, Madison, Wisconsin;

W. H. Kirkbride, Engineer Maintenance of Way and Structures, Southern Pacific Co.;

A. L. Kuehn, President, American Creosoting Company;

Dr. Sherwood Moore, Washington University, St. Louis;

A. A. Miller, Engineer Maintenance of Way, Missouri Pacific Railroad;

W. A. Murray, Engineer of Track, New York Central (East);

A. J. Neafie, Principal Assistant Engineer, D. L. & W. Railroad;

J. V. Neubert, Chief Engineer Maintenance of Way, New York Central Railroad;

J. A. Newlin, Forest Products Laboratory, Madison, Wisconsin;

A. W. Newton, Chief Engineer, C. B. & Q. Railroad;

E. J. Pearson, President, N. Y., N. H. & H. Railroad;

R. L. Pearson, Engineer Maintenance of Way, N. Y., N. H. & H. Railroad;

G. J. Ray, Chief Engineer, D. L. & W. Railroad;

A. R. Raymer, Assistant Vice-Prest. and Chief Engineer, P. & L. E. Railroad;

A. N. Reece, Chief Engineer, Kansas City Southern Railway;

Frank Ringer, Chief Engineer, Missouri-Kansas-Texas Lines;

R. O. Rote, Chief Engineer, New York Central Railroad (West);

W. J. Smith, Tie and Timber Agent, M.-K.-T. Lines;

Prof. E. O. Sweetser, Washington University, St. Louis;

Prof. A. N. Talbot, University of Illinois;

J. H. Waterman, C. B. & Q. Railroad.

And finally, I wish also to acknowledge the constant assistance and cooperation of my associate, Dr. A. L. Kammerer, and during the past year of Mr. Trifon von Schrenk, in the preparation of material and manuscript.

Appendix*

Since the preparation of the preceding the German Railways have adopted (early in 1928) a new type of tie plate. The design of this plate is shown in Fig. 178. This plate is the invention of Dr. Buchholz and is known as the Geo plate. This plate in its essentials is similar to the one shown in Fig. 132, page 118, but has certain important modifications. The base lugs of the older design have been omitted. The most important change consists in the addition of a compressed creosoted poplar wood shim, 4⅛ in. by 7⅞ in., between the base of the rail and the tie plate. These shims originally are 6 mm. in thickness, but after several weeks under traffic they compress to about 4.5 mm. thickness. They cost 12-14 pfenning (3-3½ cents) per piece. Since Oct., 1925, the German Railways have laid about 7,500 kilometers (4,500 miles or more) of track with this new plate. Experimental sections have also been laid in Sweden, Norway, Serbia, France, Japan, and arrangements are now being made for experimental sections on various American railways.

I am indebted to Dr. Buchholz for the following brief statements reference the advantages of his plate and construction:

"The fastening of the rail with the plate is separate and distinct from the fastening of the plate to the tie. The fastening of the rail to the plate is elastic, because the rail lies on softwood shims and the bolts which hold the rail are supplied with spring washers. The motion of the rail can on that account cause no movement of the screw spikes which hold the plate to the tie, and on that account the tie plates cannot sink into the tie. The wooden shim conforms to the changing position of the rail, as the latter alters its shape under moving loads. A flat top plate can accordingly be used because the shim does away with the necessity for using a cantered plate.

The poplar shims are prevented from moving out from under the tie plate longitudinally because very shortly after they have been inserted two ridges will form at the edges of the steel plate due to the compression of the wood immediately under the rail. These two edges will effectively hold the wooden shim from moving longitudinally.

*Date of Appendix, May 22, 1928.

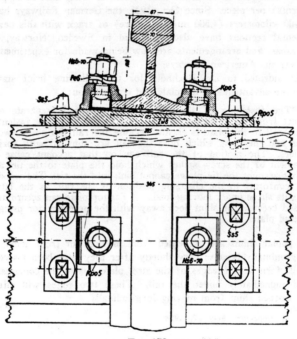

FIG. 178.

Present standard tie plate, German Railway Co.

The Railway Gazette   December 16, 1966

Recording in progress on the specially constructed test siding near Paddington

STRESSES BENEATH A RAILWAY TRACK

Load cell tests have confirmed the validity of stress calculations for common road bed materials

by D. L. HEATH and M. COTTRAM, British Railways Research Department, Derby

IN ITS ESSENCE a railway track consists of two parallel beams, supported at regular intervals by concrete or wooden strip footings, which in turn rest on and are held in position by a prepared bed of broken rock. This concept is simple, and has proved so effective that no basic change has been necessary for over a hundred years; nevertheless, the structure requires attention at regular intervals.

Although the introduction of continuously welded rail together with the associated elimination of joints has greatly reduced the need for attention, and modern maintenance machines have greatly reduced maintenance costs, the advent of modernisation and rationalisation has further accentuated the problem by concentrating very intensive flows of traffic—with axle loads greater than ever before—on to a restricted portion of the system. It is appropriate, therefore, that there should be fundamental research in the field of track stability, and the preliminary results of one facet of such an investigation are described.

The track structure may be considered as being in two parts: the sleepers and rails above, and the ballast and soil below. Great efforts have been made to quantify the response of the various elements at and above sleeper level to the dynamic loadings imposed by passing traffic. On the other hand comparatively little work has been done upon the behaviour of the track ballast and formation[1].

This research commenced with consideration of the more limited aspect of the failure of the formation to withstand the dynamic traffic loads. The remedy of this problem was costing British Railways well over £1 million annually, yet the remedial measures used were very much based on empirical design methods. To ensure that the maximum value was being obtained for the money spent, and in an attempt to obtain a scientific design method for the remedial measures,

a small programme of research was initiated.

Typical examples of formation failures are depicted; the surface manifestations of the erosion failure (pumping track) and the strength failure (cess heave) are clearly visible in the illustrations below and overleaf.

The cause of the erosion failure is breakdown of the formation soil by the abrasive action of the ballast. The very fine abraded particles have gone into suspension and formed a slurry, which has then worked its way up through the ballast and flowed into the cess where poor drainage has allowed it to accumulate.

In the example of the strength failure a deep drain has been forced to the surface by movement of a wedge of soil along the line outlined by the matchsticks placed in the wall of the trench. This movement has occurred because the applied stresses exceeded the residual strength of the soil along this plane.

Fortunately these failures do not directly effect the inherent safety of the track structure, but they greatly increase the maintenance requirement. Ideally modern track should need no maintenance for periods of more than a year between mechanised rehabilitations, and this requires complete elimination of such phenomena.

Soil types

In the British Isles there are seven main types of soils which as formations are particularly prone to these failures. All are to the south of the Tees-Exe line and cover a greater part of the surface of this region. The soils concerned together with the percentage proportion of the miles of those routes selected for further development in the Trunk Route Development Plan are:—

Keuper Marl	17
London Clay	6
Lias	6
Oxford Clay	3
Weald	2
Gault	1
Kimeridge Clay	1

Consideration of the number of track-miles—as opposed to route-miles—raises the figure for London Clay to the

Cess heave at Hullavington

1002

The Railway Gazette   December 16, 1966

Erosion failure causing flooding due to poor drainage

same magnitude as that for Keuper Marl, because of the long stretches of routes lying on London Clay with four or more tracks.

Although this research work was initiated by the Chief Civil Engineer of British Railways, it very quickly obtained international sponsorship through the O.R.E. Bureau of U.I.C. The adoption in 1963 of the proposed research programme by the newly formed D.71 Specialist Committee (which has a remit to study the complete permanent way system) ensured that the research programme would be cf value to all railway administrations.

The overall aim of the complete investigation is to evolve a comprehensive design method for track foundations. This design method will be backed by suitable theoretical calculations which

Application of too great a stress causes strength failure

have been verified by practical measurements. It will take into account the magnitudes of axle loadings and their frequency of application, and will be applicable both to standard and future track forms.

It will be applicable to the design of new works, the rehabilitation of existing lines, assessing in particular the load carrying potential of any routes selected for future intensive development, and the design of remedial measures for track foundation failures.

Investigations

Investigations currently in hand fall into three basic parts. Theoretically, calculation methods are being evolved which will account for the various phenomena observed in the field and the laboratory, and the start of this work is described first. The field studies are concerned with ascertaining the level of stresses induced in the layers beneath the sleeper (these are described later in this article) while laboratory tests are investigating the action of repeated loading on the seven major soil types mentioned above.

Little work has been done using theoretical methods to find the stresses in the formation beneath a railway track. The American Railway Engineering Association[2] has used Newmark's work[3] to calculate stresses, based on the assumptions that the baseplate loads are transmitted uniformly over the sleeper foundation interface, and that the foundation is uniform, elastic and semi-infinite in extent. R. C. A. Collins, in a B.R. Southern Region Report published in 1962, described some calculations of stresses at points in the formation, based on the assumption that the formation was an isotropic, elastic,

semi-infinite continuum, and that the baseplate loads on the sleeper were transmitted uniformly over a narrow infinite strip.

The actual physical system is considerably more complex than this as the foundation consists of two or three layers: ballast, frequently a blanket layer, and a semi-infinite lower layer of clay or rock, and the load consists of a non-uniform pressure distributed over the finite area of contact between the sleeper and the ballast.

The complexity of any mathematical model chosen to represent this system is limited by the theory available, and the complexity of any numerical analysis is, in addition, restricted by the amount of time that can be spent on carrying out the calculations which lead to a solution ot the problem. If the analysis is to be carried out with the aid of a digital computer, then the limiting factors are its size and speed.

At the time of this investigation the Research Department was equipped with an Elliott 402F digital computer, which was seven years old and, although versatile and easy to use, was comparatively small and slow. It was in fact necessary to split the problem in two: to find the pressure distribution over the contact area between a sleeper and the ballast first, and then to calculate the stresses in the formation.

Interface pressure distribution

M. Hétènyi[4] gives an analytical solution to the problem of an elastic beam with loads on its upper face, resting on a uniform Winkler foundation. A second approach[5] is due to L. Barden.

A peculiarity of the problem of a beam on a foundation as far as a railway is concerned is that the ballast is packed beneath the sleepers in the areas under and near the rails. More support is given to the sleepers in these areas than elsewhere, and it is essential that any method of solution takes account of this fact. It was necessary therefore to use a method of solution similar to that of Barden, to assume a Winkler foundation (that the sleeper was effectively resting on springs) and also that the springs were stiffer in the region of packing than elsewhere. It was also assumed that the packing area had vertical boundaries.

The system considered is shown in Fig. 1 where k is the foundation stiffness in the packing area, and A, the packing ratio, is the ratio of the stiffness in the packing area to the stiffness elsewhere.

Determination of the pressure distribution along the contact area between the sleeper and ballast is carried out as follows. The sleeper is assumed to be divided along its length into N equal parts which will be called cells. The pressure over each cell is assumed to be uniform and, in general, unequal to the pressures on adjacent cells. (See Fig. 1 where a_r is the distance from the end of the sleeper to the centre of the baseplate.)

By considering the equilibrium of the sleeper, its displacement at the mid-point of each cell is expressed as a linear function of the unknown pressures acting over the cells. The displacements at corresponding points of the foundation surface are also expressed in terms of the unknown pressures. By equating the displacements of the sleeper and displacements of the foundation surface at corresponding points, a set of simultaneous linear equations is obtained.

These equations can be solved by a standard computer programme to give an approximation to the pressure distribution along the contact area.

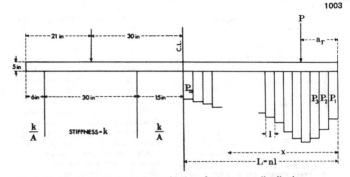

Fig. 1. Idealised model used to determine interface pressure distribution

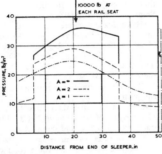

Fig. 2. Pressure distribution between a wood sleeper and ballast ($EI = 1·458 \times 10^8$ lb-in²). Overall stiffness, K_C, is (left) 125 ton/in and (right) 65 ton/in

For the calculations carried out on the 402F digital computer, the sleeper was divided into 68 cells each $1\frac{1}{2}$ in long. A special programme was written to calculate the coefficients in the linear equations which give the pressures, and to punch them on to paper tape ready for input to the programme which obtains the solution. The resulting pressures form part of the input to the programme which calculates the stresses at points in the foundation.

The problem considered under this heading is that of finding the stresses at a general point in the foundation due to the distributed pressure exerted on the surface by one sleeper; the effects of several sleepers can then be obtained by superposition.

As already stated the foundation in practice consists of several different layers. The only solutions which exist for such a system are for axially symmetrical loads, and these are expressed in terms of infinite integrals which are difficult to evaluate and would require further integration over the areas of contact between the sleeper and the foundation.

In view of the large amount of computer time required to evaluate these solutions, it was necessary to treat the foundation as a uniform, elastic semi-infinite continuum. J. Boussinesq[6] de-

rived expressions for the stress components at an interior point of a semi-infinite elastic solid due to a point load on its surface. These expressions have been integrated over a rectangular area carrying a uniform pressure to give the six co-ordinate stresses at a general point due to such a load.

A special computer sub-routine was written to evaluate these stresses, and this sub-routine was used in another programme which evaluated and summed the stresses due to all rectangles of uniform pressure which made up the load. This programme computed the stresses due to pressure distributions corresponding to several sleepers with different baseplate loads, but with all pressure distributions being of one type.

The variable parameters in the calculation of the interface pressure distribution were the overall track stiffness K_0 (the load per unit deflection measured at the baseplates), the packing ratio A, and the material of the sleeper. The values considered are:

Case	Overall track stiffness Kc (ton/in)	Packing ratio A	Material of sleeper
1	125	1	Timber
2	125	2	Timber
3	125	∞	Timber
4	65	1	Timber
5	65	2	Timber
6	65	∞	Timber
7	125	∞	Concrete
8	65	1	Concrete

The values of the parameters were chosen to ascertain the effects of different

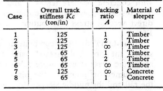

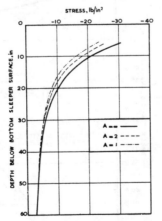

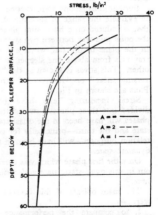

Fig. 3. Direct vertical component of stress (Z_Z) at points below the middle sleeper and under the rail due to three wood sleepers, with baseplate reactions of 2·5, 5·0 and 2·5 tons respectively. $EI = 1·458 \times 10^8$ lb-in², and $K_C =$ (left) 125 ton/in or (right) 65 ton/in

1004

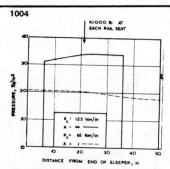

Fig. 4. Pressure distribution between a concrete sleeper (EI = 5·20⁸ × 10⁸ lb-in²) and the ballast

assumptions. Pressure distributions were evaluated first of all for timber sleepers, and the results are shown graphically in Fig. 2. Stresses were then evaluated at points in the foundation below the point of intersection of the rail and the middle sleeper of a group of three sleepers carrying baseplate loads of 2·5, 5·0 and 2·5 tons. The direct vertical component of stress is shown plotted against depth for each of cases 1 to 6 in Fig. 3.

Examination of these results shows that the greatest and least direct vertical stresses occur in cases 3 and 4 respectively. For this reason the same two support conditions only were considered with concrete sleepers (cases 7 and 8). The resulting pressure distributions and direct vertical stress distribution are in Fig. 4.

In addition the six components of stress, the principal stresses, and the maximum shear stresses were calculated at a number of points in the planes of the rail and the middle sleeper, but only for the four cases which produced the extremes of stress on the axis below the rail/middle sleeper intersection, that is cases 3, 4, 7 and 8.

Further calculations were carried out to evaluate the range of shearing stress that is induced on a horizontal plane at the point mid-way between two sleepers, in the plane of the rail, when a wheel traverses from above one sleeper to the other. This stress is known as the "reversing shear" or "revershear" stress. Plots are shown in Fig. 6.

Stress measuring tests have been divided into three phases: two of these phases will have been in the quasi-static state and the third—principally for correlation purposes—will have been in the dynamic state.

Only the first phase which was carried out in this quasi-static state is described here.

The main objects of this first phase were:—

1. to compare the performance of different designs of pressure cell
2. to assess the level of scatter in results arising from nominally

indentical installations of pressure cells
3. to compare two different types of ballast and blanket
4. to obtain realistic values of stress levels for use in the laboratory repeated stressing programme
5. to consider the validity of theoretical calculations.

The test site is situated 1¼ miles from Paddington on the up side of the line at Mousehole Sidings. The test siding was constructed, after removing the overburden, on a formation of weathered, fissured, stiff London Clay. Sectional elevations are shown in Fig. 7.

Pressure measuring transducers were installed in the top of the formation and in the first layer of the overlying blanket material. Each sub-site was constructed to give a track to a regional specification: sub-site one to that of the Southern Region (Meldon stone ballast overlying Meldon stone dust), and sub-site two to that of the Eastern Region (Appleby Frodingham slag ballast overlying Newark sharp sand). Three designs of pressure cell were considered: the Z, Y and SR series (see Fig. 8).

The test siding was constructed by compacting three 15-cm layers of blanket material and then three further 15-cm layers of ballast as in Fig. 6. The track was then laid and compacted.

A set of tests was carried out at each thickness of construction for a total of six thicknesses. At the completion of a series of tests the test siding was removed panel by panel, the top 15 cm of foundation material was dug away, the surface was reprofiled and the track

The Railway Gazette December 16, 1966

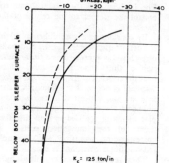

Fig. 5. Direct vertical component of stress (Z_z) at points below the middle sleeper and under the rail due to three concrete sleepers with baseplate reactions 2·5, 5·0 and 2·5 tons

replaced. After compaction by a locomotive the next set of tests began.

At each decrement of thickness the procedure was to winch a wagon to and fro across the test site for a total of five conditions of axle loading; the test wagon had two axles with a wheel base of approximately 8 m. The ratios of axle loadings enabled a full range of maximum baseplate reactions to be obtained from 5 to 10 tonnes (axleloads ranging from 18 tonnes to 36 tonnes).

The loading condition was altered by changing the position on the vehicle of scrap rails to give five ratios of loadings

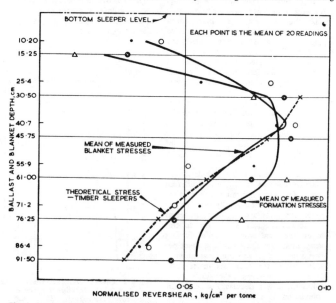

Fig. 6. Reversing shear stress

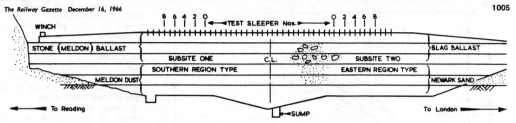

The Railway Gazette December 16, 1966

LONGITUDINAL SECTIONAL ELEVATION FACING NORTH

varying from 1:1·60 to 1:1. To relate all transducer signals to baseplate signals the test vehicle made a total of seven return passes across the test site for each ratio of axle loading.

Results

Presentation of the results is conveniently considered in two parts. The first part demonstrates the validity of the technique used in accommodating the differences in axle loading and sleeper support conditions for comparative purposes. It further demonstrates the magnitude of scatter that arises between nominally identical installations, and also between successive loading cycles in the same loading condition. The

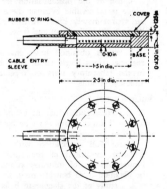

Fig. 8. Z-series pressure cell

second part considers the summaries of the various results.

Considering Fig. 9, this shows the relationship through the loading and unloading parts of a cycle between a baseplate reaction and the corresponding vertical stress for three different thicknesses. This figure shows that there is an approximately linear relationship between cell signal and baseplate signal. The existence of this approximately linear relationship is used in the process known as "normalisation" in which all recorded peak values of stress are divided by the corresponding baseplate reactions to produce stresses in terms of unit baseplate reaction.

Scatter is portrayed visually in Fig. 10. There are two distinct types of scatter: that arising between nominally identical

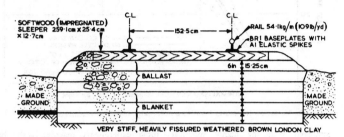

Fig. 7. Sections through the test track

installations, and that occurring within the relationship between any one pressure cell and its corresponding baseplate reaction at a given thickness of construction.

Degree of scatter

The degree of scatter is of the same order of magnitude in results from all three series of pressure cells. Figs. 11 and 12 compare the summary cases of vertical stresses measured in the formations with Z and Y series cells with the S.R. series cells, and the Y series with the S.R. series in the two blanket materials.

At the greater thicknesses of construction the cells of all three designs record more or less equivalent stresses, but as the construction becomes shallower so the vertical stresses recorded by the S.R. series cells become smaller than those from the Y and Z series cells until at 15 cm thickness the difference is of the

order of 50 per cent in the formation and 40 per cent in the blanket layer.

Basically the explanation for this is that that the small sized Y and Z series cells will measure the peak stresses in areas of high stress gradients whereas the S.R. series cells average the stress over their whole working diameter.

Levels of stresses

The magnitudes of the vertical stresses in the formation and the blanket are shown in Figs. 11 and 12 respectively. Fig. 11 clearly illustrates the very close agreement between the theoretically calculated values and those measured by the Z and Y series cells. Fig. 12 shows that the vertical stresses in the Meldon dust are larger than those in the Newark sand. This is probably due to the differences in the sleeper support condition for the two cases, the angular Meldon dust particles enabling more concentrated loads to be carried

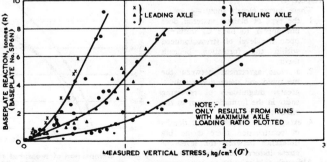

Fig. 9. Measured vertical stress (cell SC6V)

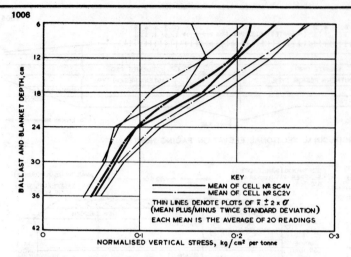

1008

KEY
—— MEAN OF CELL № SC4V
—·— MEAN OF CELL № SC2V
THIN LINES DENOTE PLOTS OF x̄ ± 2 x σ
(MEAN PLUS/MINUS TWICE STANDARD DEVIATION)
EACH MEAN IS THE AVERAGE OF 20 READINGS

NORMALISED VERTICAL STRESS, kg/cm² per tonne

Fig. 10. Variation in results from two nominally identical installations

compared with the highly spherical Newark sand particles which readily flowed to give a more uniform sleeper support condition and, hence, slightly lower stress levels.

This figure also shows good agreement with the theoretical values obtained from Fig. 3 (A=∞).

The remaining two diagrams show plots of two types of shear stresses (Figs. 5 and 13). The "direct shear stress" or the maximum semidifference of the principal stresses induced beneath a sleeper are plotted in Fig. 13. The revershear, or the total range of reversing shear stress which occurs on a horizontal plane at a point midway between two adjacent sleepers as the load passes from one to the other, is plotted in Fig. 5. These two types of shear stresses are completely different in that the former pulsates while the latter exhibits a true reversal.

Theoretical curves

On each diagram the appropriate theoretical curves are plotted, together with the mean curves for each of those stresses occurring in both the blanket and the formation on each sub-site respectively.

These curves clearly show:—
1. the type of blanket material does not appear to have an influence upon the level of stress induced within the formation beneath them
2. a close agreement between the measured and theoretical results
3. greater magnitudes of reversing shear in the formation than in the blanket layer
4. excepting at the shallowest depths of construction there is no big difference between the levels of stress induced on either sub-site. Although only at quite an early stage,

these experiments together with the theoretical method developed have enabled several major conclusions to be drawn and this has resulted in the drawing up of a set of clear objectives for the future work of the second and third phases.

These conclusions are strictly valid only for the range of conditions in which the experiments were carried out. The track structure consisted of B.R. standard (jointed) plain line supported on two types of blanket and ballast materials both of which were supported on a formation of over-consolidated clay. All the tests were carried out in the quasi-static state with very heavy axle loads.

Positive information

Positive information derived from the tests:—

1. comparison between the various designs of pressure cell clearly shows that smaller sized ones (Y and Z

The Railway Gazette December 16, 1966

series) are most suited for use in areas of high stress gradients and may be arranged in clusters

2. scatter between nominally identical installations of pressure cells is large; it is normally distributed and its magnitude is such that it tends to mask the differences between the two types of track construction

3. overall mean values of vertical stresses on the axis of the rail/sleeper intersection are in close agreement with theoretically calculated stresses based on the assumption of single layer elastic behaviour. This confirms the findings of earlier work at Kegworth, but differences between the horizontal stresses in the blanket and the clay point to multi-layer behaviour

4. equilibrium checks using Mohr's representation demonstrate that the vertical and horizontal stresses are principal ones except at the shallowest thickness

5. values of revershear between the sleeper are greater than those of the maximum shear stress on a plane through the axis of the rail/sleeper reaction, except at the two shallowest thicknesses

6. use of the normalisation technique is admissible because there is an approximately linear relationship between the cell output and baseplate reading

7. results obtained have enabled realistic stress levels to be adopted in the laboratory tests of repeated stressing of soils

Future work

It is recommended that in planning future work these points must be borne in mind:—

1. for full correlation with the dynamic conditions of the track a limited amount of information must be obtained from beneath main lines

2. a study of the sleeper to ballast

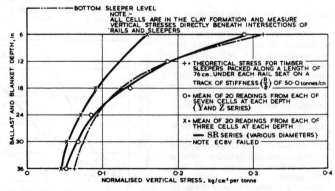

Fig. 11. Comparison of measured and theoretical values of vertical stress. Mean results of seven Z series and four SR series cells

The Railway Gazette   December 16, 1966

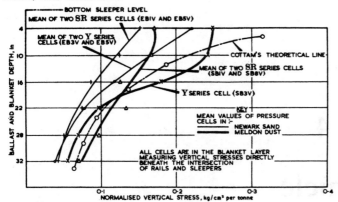

Fig. 12. Comparison of measured and theoretical vertical stress in the blanket

interrelated effects. The selection of a particular solution will be greatly influenced by local conditions, such as the need for very high speed or minimal interference to medium speed heavy axle loaded block trains.

The interrelated effects are:—

1. deformation of the formation
2. deformation of the ballast
3. decay of the sleeper support
4. loss of alignment
5. traffic pattern (axle loads and speed)
6. twist.

Providing the future traffic pattern, axle loadings' magnitude and frequency, the geology of the route in question and the fatigue characteristics of the relevant soils and ballast types are known, the track foundation may be designed accurately for any required life. Currently the fatigue characteristics of the relevant soils and ballasts are being obtained.

The authors wish to thank Mr. S. F. Smith, Director of Research, for permission to publish this article, Mr. F. R. L. Barnwell, C.C.E., W.R., for some of the photographs, and Dr. R. W. Sparrow, Messrs. P. J. Coates and J. M. Waters of the Research Department, Mr. C. W. Edwards of the C.C.E's Department, L.M.R., and Messrs. A. H. Toms and R. C. A. Collins of the C.C.E's Department, S.R., for their support and interest in this project over many months.

contact pressure distribution is required to assess the validity of the assumptions made in the theory, and effect a correlation with the corresponding blanket to formation interface stress distribution.

3. the effect of changes in the main track variables (sleeper spacing, sleeper rigidity, sleeper support conditions, ballast, blanket, formation conditions) must be considered.

Conclusions

In so far as the quasi-static conditions pertaining to the measurements described above are the limiting factors, then the theoretical method developed is basically accurate and representative of the stress systems observed beneath a railway track. If these conditions are also satisfied for the dynamic state then a theory has been evolved which is of sufficient generality for use in the solution of all track foundation problems. It will enable a big reduction to be made in the scope of future field investigations—their status may be contracted from the basic enquiry to that of a simple verification.

The results obtained from the field measurements have permitted the confirmation of the theoretical method. They have enabled the adoption of accurate and realistic levels of stresses in the pulsating loading (repeated stressing or fatigue testing) of cohesive soils programme. Together with the results obtained from this programme they form the basis of a tentative design method for track foundations.

The proposed design method will be such that it should be possible to assess the interaction of several major track parameters and compute the optimum set of values for any selected criteria. This represents a powerful facility for analysing, in a reasonably scientific manner, the factors which are relevant for determining the initial form of the track construction and when maintenance should be carried out.

In a simplified outline the basis of the method is the evaluation of the optimum set of conditions from the

References

1. E. W. Clarke " Track Loading Fundamentals: Parts 1-7." Pages 45, 103, 157, 220, 274, 335 and 479. Vol. 106 (Jan.-June 1957). Railway Gazette.
2. Proc. A.R.E.A. Vols. 46-55 (1945-1954). Reports of the Committee on Physical Properties of Earth Materials.
3. N.M. Newmark, Influence Charts for the Computation of Stresses in Elastic Foundations. Bulletin Series 338, University of Illinois Engineering Experiment Station, 1942.
4. M. Hétènyi "Beams on Elastic Foundation." 1958.
5. Barden. Géotechnique .Vol. XIII, No. 3, September 1962.
6. J. Boussinesq " Application des potentiels à l'étude de L'équilibre et du mouvement des solides élastique," Paris, 1885.

LOCOMOTIVE WORKS TO BECOME SUBWAY DEPOT

THE CITY OF FRANKFURT AM MAIN is to take over the German Federal Railway locomotive repair works at Frankfurt-Nied, which will be closed on the withdrawal of steam traction in the area. It will become a depot and main workshop for the city transport undertaking, serving both the new subway line and the street tramways.

A similar take-over occurred in the Ruhr four years ago when the town of Mülheim bought the locomotive overhaul works at Mülheim-Speldorf and converted it to serve as a tramway depot.

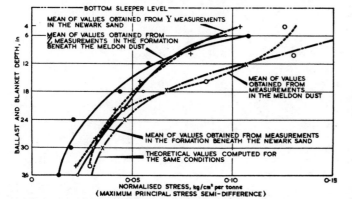

Fig. 13. Direct shear stresses

Chapter 4

Vehicle
and Track
Interaction

Wheel and Rail Loadings from Diesel Locomotives
72–633–3

By L. F. KOCI

Chief Locomotive Engineer
Electro-Motive Division, General Motors Corporation

We, at Electro-Motive, understandably deal primarily with the railroad Mechanical Departments. In recent years as axle loads, the number of axles commonly used on a locomotive, locomotive weights, and operating conditions moved in the direction of representing more demanding applications, we found it necessary to be certain of just what the wheel–rail loadings were not only from the standpoint of locomotive equipment but also from the standpoint of the effect on the rail, since the "tracking" capability of the locomotive is one of our concerns. Over the last dozen years or so we have become involved in a number of tests run by our customers or cooperative tests between particular railroads and Electro-Motive. Consequently, the data presented in parts of this review, will certainly be recognized by people on the various railroads on which the tests have taken place.

The following report represents a brief review of some of the data accumulated in these various tests. It is certainly not all inclusive nor is all of it new. It is clear, however, that when studying the tracking of railroad vehicles and such aspects as derailments, it is impossible to separate the effect of the Mechanical, Engineering, or Operating functions of a railroad operation. The following information does try to "bring together" some of the information developed in each of these various areas.

This review is divided into the following six areas:

1. Sample Derailment Data
2. Basic Curve Negotiation Mechanics
3. Experimentally Determined Wheel-to-Rail Forces
4. Rail Profile Data
5. The Effect of Dynamic Brake Levels
6. Mechanical Considerations

Following these there is a brief summary.

Note—Discussion open until October 15, 1971

I. SAMPLE DERAILMENT DATA

In preparing for one of the cooperative tests run with one of our major railroad customers, a brief summary was made of ten derailments the railroad had experienced which either reflected no clear cause, or for which the cause seemed questionable. This would include such things as a rail break in which there did not appear to be sufficient old break to explain the derailment entirely. In examining this summary we were looking for guidance to the types of things which should be investigated to provide most meaningful results. Figs. 1 and 2 summarize this information. It should be made clear that there was additional, detailed data available in many cases, including crew comments; however, what is summarized in these figures is the rail weight, curve condition, locomotive consist, and the location of derailment. For example, in the first situation listed the locomotive consist consisted of an SD-45 (one of EMD's 6-axle locomotives), a second SD-45, a GP-35 (which is an EMD 4-axle unit), and a U-25B (which is a competitive 4-axle unit). The x's in the illustration indicate what units or cars were derailed in the incident. The data represented as well as some of the details not indicated in the illustrations may be summarized as follows:

1. Either by crew comment, spectator comment, or locomotive speed tapes, change in train speed was indicated in almost all cases. In many cases locomotive braking was indicated. In one particular case the crew comment indicated that the train was being switched to a siding and the locomotive dynamic brakes were applied immediately after the locomotive consist crossed over the switch. As discussed in more detail later, this situation, in which the cars immediately behind the locomotive (which do not have the vertical load always present which a locomotive does) are subjected to the maximum buff loads available in locomotive braking while crossing over a switch or crossover or on curved track, can carry with it the risk of derailment. The application of heavy buff coupler loads can result in substantial lateral wheel-to-rail reaction. The lighter the vertical wheel load present, the more "unstable" the condition may be. As noted, this is discussed further later. In most of the situations summarized the speeds were in the range of 35 to 50 mph.

2. The curve size involved was generally about 3 to 4 deg. As will also be discussed later, the basic curve negotiation forces present on curves of this size are far lower than they are on tighter curves, such as those of 8 to 10 deg.

3. Transient drawbar conditions were indicated throughout the train. An example of this is the fourth situation noted in which three different groups of cars ended up derailed in various locations in the train.

4. In some cases empty "TTX" type cars were placed immediately next to the locomotive consist in operation involving locomotive braking. Placing any empty cars adjacent to the locomotive in heavy locomotive braking conditions involves the risk of developing unsatisfactory wheel-to-rail conditions. However, the long-overhang-type cars such as the TTX cars are particularly vulnerable to this, and this type of operation if combined with a chance occurrence of a low joint, or bad track alignment, or train handling giving substantial dynamic buff "run-in", increases the risk of a problem.

502   Special Features

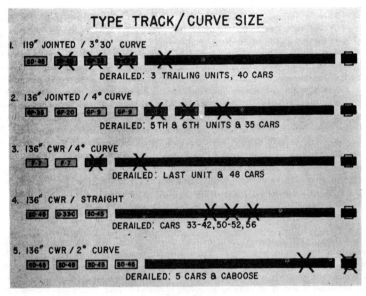

Fig. 1

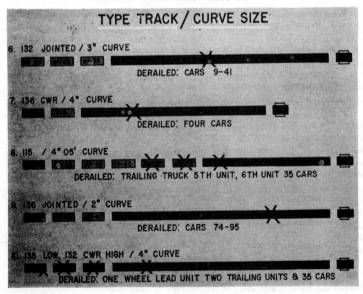

Fig. 2

5. In a number of cases the crew comment indicated that buckled rail occurred, sometimes ahead of the locomotive. The comments pointed to the possibility of track thermal strains perhaps being a factor. While considerable investigation of the effect of thermal strains on track stability has taken place, little seems to be known about how thermal strains below the threshold of instability themselves affect the ability of the track to withstand the not insignificant service loads applied to it during operation on curves. In other words, if occasionally the track thermal strains become great enough to be of concern from their own account, how is the ability of the track to withstand lateral loads in the area of 10,000 to 15,000 lb reduced when those thermal strains are half as high or ¾ as high?

6. Of the ten derailments noted:
    a. Five occurred within the train only, involving no locomotives
    b. Two involved EMD 6-axle locomotives
    c. One involved a competitive 6-axle locomotive
    d. Three involved 4-axle locomotives.

Although this summary involves one particular railroad, a number of similar summaries have been made on other railroads and in many ways they are not unlike. Similarities are particularly common from the standpoints of involving curve sizes in which lateral loads are not as high as elsewhere; involving braking conditions; and involving a variety of vehicles including cars and both 4- and 6-axle locomotives.

II. BASIC CURVE NEGOTIATION MECHANICS

What is intended here is a brief review of what may be termed the "basic" lateral loading which occurs due to normal curve negotiation of a railway vehicle truck around a curve. The forces resulting from this normal negotiation are among the predominant forces involved, at least in the tighter curves. To fully understand how some of the lateral loads developed by various operating, track, and mechanical conditions discussed later combine, it is necessary to appreciate what causes the basic curve-negotiation forces. The following is a brief review of this; for further explanation, ASME paper No. 65-WA/RR-4 may be helpful.

These curve-negotiation forces are not related in any manner to centrifugal force. They are the forces which would be present if the operating speed involved were exactly balanced by the superelevation of the track. Perhaps the best way to make this clear is to state that these are the forces which would occur if the locomotive or railroad car were standing still and the track were on a giant turntable moving around underneath it.

It should also be noted that these forces are the forces present with no driving or braking taking place. They result strictly from the frictional forces between wheel and rail and are the result of the fact that all wheels of the truck do not line up perfectly tangent to the rail, nor do they have a differential which would allow the inner and outer wheels to roll the different distances involved on the inner and outer rail of the curve.

Fig. 3 illustrates schematically a 3-axle truck position while traveling around a curve. This position is typical in that the truck assumes an "angle of attack" between the leading axle and the rail, tending to skew within the clearances allowed between wheel flanges and rail. The curve size and the clearances involved were

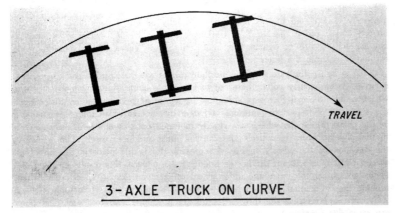

3-AXLE TRUCK ON CURVE

Fig. 3

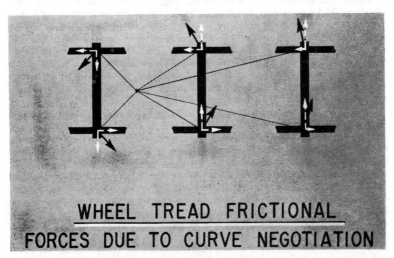

WHEEL TREAD FRICTIONAL
FORCES DUE TO CURVE NEGOTIATION

Fig. 4

obviously exaggerated in this illustration; actually on curve sizes down to approximately 300 ft radius the No. 3 or trailing axle of an EMD 6-wheel truck tends to be disposed toward or against the inner rail of the curve with the middle axle further away from the inner rail.

Fig. 4 helps illustrate why this position results when a railroad truck negotiates a curve. As previously noted there are two separate circumstances which cause the wheel-to-rail frictional forces resulting in this curve negotiation action. First of all, the outer rail of the curve represents a longer distance to travel than the inner rail of the curve. Since the wheels are rigidly mounted on a common axle some longitudinal slip between the wheels and the rail must and does result. The arrows in the direction of the wheels on Fig. 4 represent slip taking place in this direction; as can be shown, without driving or braking taking place, this results in equal and opposite slips on the inner and outer wheels of a given axle. (Wheel taper cannot provide the differential required both because it would be correct for only a given size curve and because the three axles do not position themselves such that taper can serve this function.)

Secondly, since all three axles are held parallel to one another within the truck, it is clear that all three of them cannot be "aligned" with the track such that the wheels would be tangent to the direction of the rail at the point of contact rather than at an angle making it necessary to slip sideways. Since all three axles cannot be aligned with the rail, at least two of them must be at an angle either "running into or away" from the rail and, therefore, "dragging sideways" resulting in lateral slip between wheel and rail. In truth the equilibrium position which finally occurs results in neither of the three axles being aligned with the rail; the arrows shown on Fig. 4 at right angles to the wheels reflect the lateral slip which takes place at the point of contact between wheel and rail.

These two slip components at right angles to one another combine to give a resultant direction of slip between wheel and rail as shown in the diagonal arrows on Fig. 4. With this relative motion or slip present, of course, frictional force from rail onto wheel results in the direction of the arrows shown. (These slip magnitudes are small and generally referred to as "creep" or microslip; however, for the purposes of this discussion it can be considered as slip or relative movement between rail and wheel.) As the truck passes through the curve these forces represented by the diagonal arrows cause the truck to turn or skew within the rails until flange forces at the leading outer wheel and sometimes at wheels of the second and third axle, balance these frictional forces and an equilibrium position results. The next illustration, Fig. 5, shows these frictional tread forces balanced by the one or more flange forces which may be present. With the lateral clearances within the axles and the truck available on an SD-type 3-axle truck the equilibrium position attained for curve sizes down to approximately 2100 ft radius, consists of the leading outer wheel obtaining a flange reaction from the outer rail, the trailing axle disposed toward the inner rail but without the flange contacting, and the second axle, dependent on curve size, sometimes against the outer rail or between rails. On curves between 2100 ft radius and down to extremely tight curves (approximately 280 ft radius) with sufficient lateral clearance designed into the truck between axles and truck frame, the trailing axle is actually against the inner rail. This is a desirable operating mode since it tends to reduce or limit the amount of angle of attack and related forces which may be present otherwise. It should be noted that consequently, additional gauge widening between the rails merely allows the truck

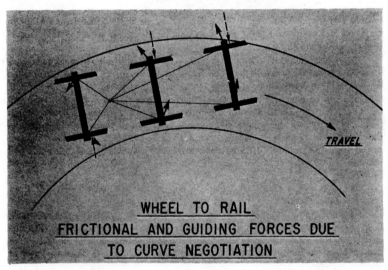

Fig. 5

to skew or cock to a greater extent and increases the angle present between wheels and rail. It also increases the resultant lateral forces. Therefore, if there is sufficient lateral within a truck for curve negotiation without demanding that the axles "bind" in the rail (that is, with the center axle against the inner rail), unnecessary gauge widening is undesirable. Similarly, placing the wheel flanges closer together to provide more wheel-to-rail clearance can have an undesirable effect, although this is a much smaller factor merely because of the dimensions involved generally in gauge widening.

There are a number of specific factors associated with curve negotiation which may be considered important from the standpoint of tracking or wheel–rail operating conditions. The flange reaction itself is important from the standpoint of wheel and rail wear since it represents the force pressing the flange surface and the inside rail surface together while they have relative sliding taking place; and it is also of interest from the standpoint of contact stresses and local forces on the wheel flange and the rail. The angle between the leading outer wheel and the rail is commonly referred to as the angle of attack. This is important not only because the greater the angle the greater the resultant lateral creep and frictional forces, but also because the greater the angle the more "scuffing" there is between wheel flange and rail and, therefore, the increased amount of wear. Generally, it is accepted that wheel flange-rail wear is a function of the flange force and the angle of attack, although the manner in which they combine is not clearly defined.

The "net lateral load" between wheel and rail at any given wheel is the difference between the flange force and the lateral component of the tread frictional force. This net lateral load is what is important from the standpoint of tracking; that

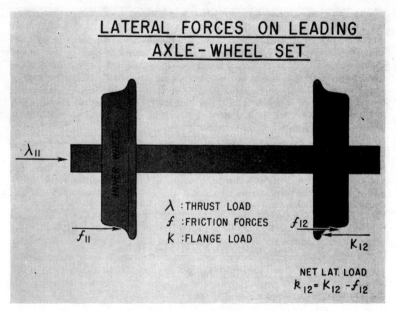

Fig. 6

is, the likelihood of either wheel climbing the rail or the rail rolling over depends on the level of this net lateral load. In following discussion where lateral load or the ratio of lateral load to vertical load is involved, it is this net lateral load that is referred to. This load is also of interest from the standpoint of wheel stress or axle stress resulting or lateral bending stresses produced in the rail. The net lateral load at the entire axle instead of at a particular wheel is the result, or difference between, the flange force at one wheel of the axle and the two lateral components of the tread frictional force at both wheels of the axle. This then represents the total net lateral load on both rails at a given axle location and is primarily of interest from the standpoint of shifting the entire track structure within the ballast.

Fig. 6 helps to clarify these forces as they act on the leading wheel axle set of a truck in passing through a curve.

The important relations and limits of these various forces considered from the standpoint of the effect on the rail and influence on possible derailments are generally as follows:

1. Wheel Climbing the Rail: Lateral-to-vertical wheel load ratio, L/V, equal to or greater than 0.9 at the leading outer wheel.

2. Rail Rollover: L/V for one side of an entire truck $\left(\dfrac{L_1 + L_2 + L_3}{V_1 + V_2 + V_3}\right)$ equal to or greater than 0.5

3. Track Shifting: Net lateral axle load equal to or greater than 40% of the vertical axle load on poor track conditions

The L/V limit of 0.9 is a value which is considered a minimum or lower limit for the possibility of wheel climbing to be considered likely. Most analytical or experimental work which has been done would tend to indicate this is probably in most cases required to be over 1.0, and with the flange configuration used in the United States as high as 1.5 before actual wheel climbing will occur. Also, in many specific operations it is known that ratios of approximately 0.9 do occur not uncommonly without derailment. However, because of the number of variables which can be and are involved in any derailment situation, the 0.9 figure seems a reasonable one to consider for the lower limit and for an indication of those load combinations at which this should start being of concern.

The ratio of 0.5 for total lateral load on one side of a truck to total vertical load on that side of the truck for rail rollover is merely the ratio of loads required to cause the resultant load on rail to fall outside of the edge of the rail base. On many common United States sections this occurs at a ratio of approximately 0.5 to 0.55. Obviously, this ratio can be exceeded at a single wheel without rollover occurring because the adjacent wheels provide vertical load which "holds" the rail down. The choice here of using the total for one side of a truck, whether it be a locomotive or a freight car truck, assumes no tiedowns or effective spikes, and a rail joint between the rail under that truck and the rail under adjacent trucks which provides no torsional restraint whatsoever.

The limit of 40% indicated for the entire axle relative to shifting of the track structure is taken from work performed in France some years ago indicating that this was the lowest value on poor track which could cause this to occur.

III. EXPERIMENTALLY DETERMINED WHEEL-TO-RAIL FORCES

A number of tests have been run in recent years determining the actual lateral wheel-to-rail reactions which occur in operation on U. S. railroads. This data is discussed below as related to four general areas of interest: due to basic curve-negotiation mechanics, as influenced by speed, as influenced by sanding, and as influenced by coupler reaction.

A few years ago, EMD manufactured its first road locomotives using 4-axle trucks. While a considerable amount of analytical and laboratory work had been done previous to this time related to lateral wheel-to-rail reaction during curve negotiation, it was felt necessary with the first use of a 4-axle truck (with all four axles in a common frame) to determine experimentally specifically what wheel-to-rail loads existed in actual operating conditions and how the wheel-to-rail loads which would occur with the 4-axle truck would compare to them. Loads had been measured under certain specific conditions, as with the use of instrumented rail sections and roller bearing tie plates. This, however, had the disadvantage of measuring only one condition at one specific location and not reflecting the types of dynamic loading typical with normally found track irregularities.

Shortly prior to that time, tests had been run in Europe in which the wheel plates of a wheel-axle set were instrumented to provide a measure of lateral load on a continuous basis. Fig. 7 shows the three EMD road locomotive trucks including the 2 and 3-axle in service and the 4-axle which was being tested at that time. Since all used a common wheel-axle-traction motor assembly, the use of an instrumented wheel-axle set would provide the opportunity to place it in three different trucks of widely varying wheel bases to obtain a good measure of what was desired.

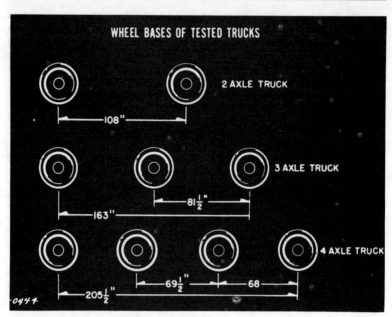

Fig. 7

Therefore, it was decided to develop an instrumented wheel-axle set providing a continuous record of net lateral load between wheel and rail. While this instrumentation gave a continuous record of lateral wheel-to-rail reaction it was also applied such to give an indication of vertical load once per revolution.

The experimental results are summarized in Fig. 8. These curves show the net lateral load in thousands of pounds along the bottom scale versus the radius of curvature along the vertical scale. Degrees of curvature are shown for reference. The three curves indicate the loads measured for the 2-axle, 3-axle, and 4-axle truck noted previously. It should be noted this data is based on coasting conditions; that is, there is no significant tractive effort or braking taking place, and little or no centrifugal force not balanced by track elevation. In other words this data reflects that loading occurring strictly from the curve-negotiation mechanics and the wheel tread frictional forces discussed previously. Also, these curves reflect the net lateral load between the leading outer wheel in the curve and the outer rail; the flange force itself would be higher.

There are a number of factors of interest apparent in examining these curves. For one, the loads are substantial, reflecting, for example, approximately 10,000 lb, 14,000 lb, and 16,000 lb for a 10-deg curve with the 2-axle, 3-axle, and 4-axle truck, respectively. As would be expected the loads increase substantially with curvature; however, the loads at the 3- and 4-deg curve size area, where most of the

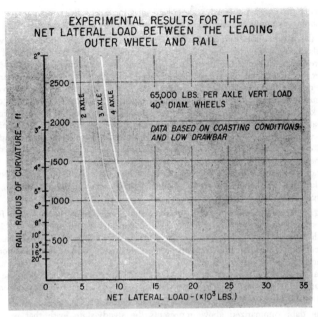

Fig. 8

WHEEL-RAIL LOADS

ON EMD TWO, THREE, AND FOUR AXLE TRUCKS

DUE TO CURVE NEGOTIATION

TRACK CURVE	2-AXLE TRUCK	3-AXLE TRUCK	4-AXLE TRUCK
19° (305' R)	14,000 LBS.	18,500 LBS.	19,500 LBS.
13° (440' R)	11,500	16,000	17,500
10° (573' R)	10,000	14,000	16,000
6° (955' R)	6,500	10,000	12,000
4° (1430' R)	5,500	8,000	10,000
2° (2860' R)	4,000	6,000	8,000

Fig. 9

derailments discussed previously take place, are far lower than they are on other tighter but commonly found curves.

As the curves show, the same basic phenomena and same relationship of wheel-rail loads occur with either the 2, 3, or 4-axle truck, although the "degree" of loading increases as the number of axles or the amount of tractive weight supported increases. As mentioned, these are the reactions from the wheel tread-to-rail friction and, therefore, the size of these forces depends on the adhesion conditions involved. These curves represent the average of many data points over a great deal of operation picked to represent average dry rail conditions. Under conditions which involve wet weather the adhesion and consequently the forces are lower, while under conditions which increase adhesion, such as sanding, the frictional loads and correspondingly the lateral reactions are higher. These forces are always present during curve negotiation due merely to negotiating the curve, and other factors which affect rail reactions add over-and-above this. These would include such things as centerplate reaction resulting from a high coupler force acting at an angle, or centrifugal force.

Fig. 9 is a table showing some of the values taken from the curves in Fig. 8. It shows, for example, that a 2-axle truck has a net lateral load reaction on a 10-deg curve the same as a 3-axle truck has on a 6-deg curve or a 4-axle truck has on a 4-deg curve. In making this comparison and evaluating different applications for different types of service, it should be remembered that to pull a certain trainload a similar number of axles must be involved. In other words, providing the same operation could be considered to require either six 2-axle trucks under a locomotive consist, or four 3-axle trucks.

The data summarized above represents the steady-state load; that is, it does not reflect the dynamic forces which occur at rail irregularities or at rail joints. Since the wheel and rail are being forced together with substantial loads, whenever a rail joint occurs it represents a change in path and dynamic loading over and above the base loads discussed occurs. The dynamic loads measured in typical operation are summarized in Fig. 10. The sample lateral-load trace shown across the bottom of the illustration is typical, with the lateral reaction increasing as the vehicle travels through the spiralling into the curve, developing a "more-or-less" steady state level throughout the curve, and then decreasing in passing from the curve to tangent track. As is apparent, the dynamic loads occur fairly continuously over and above the steady-state load. On curves these dynamic impacts are commonly 6,000 to 8,000 lb additional load occasionally reaching 12,000 to 15,000 lb. On tangent track, as indicated, they are somewhat higher at the test speeds of 65 mph. These dynamic loads are very short in duration, mostly below 0.1 second long. Therefore, while they are of interest from the standpoint of rail "batter" and shock loads locally affecting the wheel and the rail, they are not of primary interest from the standpoint of tracking or derailments since they are not long-lived enough for any significant displacement or change in location to take place.

It is also of interest to note that the dynamic loads measured were quite similar with either the 2-axle, 3-axle, or 4-axle trucks, thus indicating that they are primarily the result of the unsprung mass dynamics and represent too small a displacement to depend on the truck frame or the length of truck involved.

The next six illustrations show the effect of some other external loadings on these wheel-to-rail forces. Fig. 11 shows the same curve previously shown for the 6-wheel truck indicating net lateral load versus degree of curvature. In addition

512   Special Features

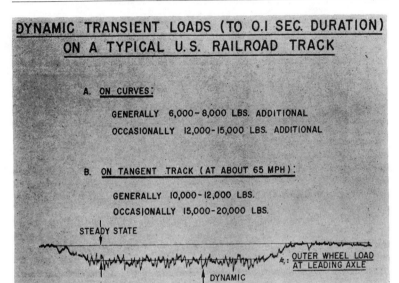

Fig. 10

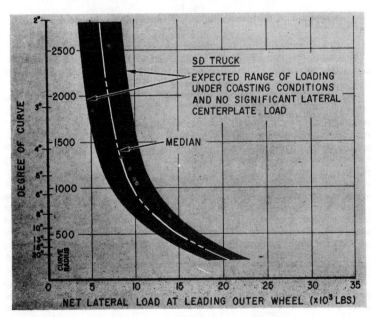

Fig. 11

788

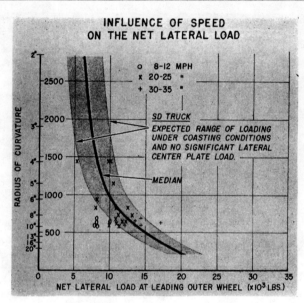

Fig. 12

to showing the average values, it also shows in the shaded area the range of loadings found under the considerable variables which exist in day-in and day-out operating practice. The following illustrations show the effect of speed, sanding, and different levels of coupler reaction upon these load levels.

Fig. 12 illustrates the effect of speed in a given group of curves. The same median curve and range previously discussed are shown. In addition to that, actual data points are shown, obtained while operating at three different speed ranges over a given series of curves. The x's indicate values obtained while operating at approximately the speed to balance track superelevation; therefore, there is little or no effect of centrifugal force in these data points. The small circles represent data obtained while operating at about 10 to 15 mph under the balanced condition. As may be noted on this group of curves, the net lateral loading is reduced slightly but not to a major extent. Similarly, the crosses reflect data obtained while operating at 10 to 15 mph over the balanced condition and again, while these show a slight increase, it is not a major change in the load levels present. Speed, then, does not make a major change in the load levels which occur. Traveling at reduced speeds over restricted areas or temporary track does, of course, reduce the risk involved if a derailment occurs but does not substantially reduce the load to which the track is subjected.

As noted previously the lateral reactions result from the frictional forces between rail tread and rail and, therefore, are a function of the amount of friction present. Fig. 13 shows some representative data points and a shaded range of data obtained on various size curves while continuous sanding was taking place on the

514   Special Features

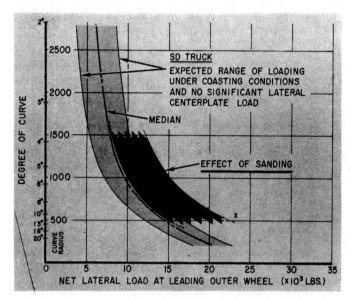

Fig. 13

locomotive. As might be expected the increased friction level resulting from sanding increases the lateral reaction substantially. For example, it increases from a value of approximately 14,000 lb to one of about 18,000 lb for a 10-deg curve. In general, the actual friction coefficient measured under conditions of continuous sanding, was found to be approximately 0.40, although it should be remembered that not all of this available frictional force goes into either driving or lateral reactions but a combination of both.

The next three illustrations illustrate the added effect of varying coupler buff reactions applied to the locomotive through the angle involved when curves are negotiated. This particular data is taken from tests run in a "pusher" operation; however, the reactions resulting would be present if this coupler reaction occurred due to braking or train "run-in" also. Fig. 14 shows some data points and the range of data measured under conditions of moderate buff load (approximately 100,000 lb) while operating over the curve sizes indicated. This data also included continuous sanding and, therefore, shows the increased effect of the coupler reaction. Fig. 15 is similar except the buff load coming through the coupler is still higher (in the range of 250,000 to 300,000 lb) and correspondingly the net lateral wheel-to-rail loads are seen to increase. Fig. 16 shows all these variables superimposed on the same curve. The cumulative effect of these external loads acting over and above the basic curving forces is apparent. It may be noted that lateral loads in the range of 25,000 to 27,000 lb for a wheel with average static loading of 32,000 lb occur here regularly. Under these particular conditions wheel and rail wear are quite high.

790

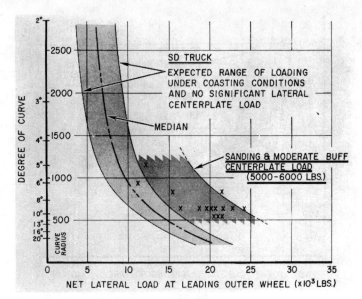

Fig. 14

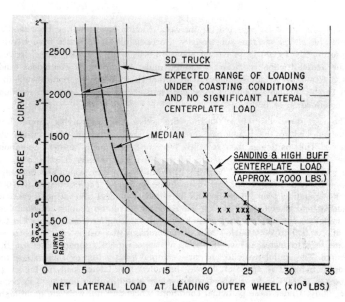

Fig. 15

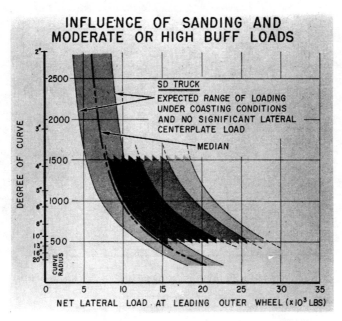

Fig. 16

In many of the tests which have been run, freight car wheel-axle sets on the cars immediately adjacent to the locomotive have also been instrumented. Primarily because of less vertical load available to "stabilize" the wheel and rail, it is generally found that the most vulnerable area for tracking difficulties or derailment is on the cars immediately adjacent to the locomotive. This is particularly so with some of the newer long-overhang cars.

Because the side frames of most freight car trucks are independent (that is, they are not held rigidly relative to one another) the basic frictional forces which occur in curve negotiation also tend to skew the freight car truck side frames, producing a greater angle of attack than would be present for a truck of similar wheel base otherwise. Consequently, the wheel-axle position that develops is as shown in Fig. 17. The axles shift relative to one another and after the trailing axle comes against the outer rail, the remaining frictional moment shifts the side frames and allows the axles to skew further, attaining a higher angle of attack and correspondingly somewhat increased lateral forces and reactions. Fig. 18 shows what the predicted net lateral load on rail would be at the leading outer wheel of a freight car truck with 65,000 lb vertical axle load. This illustration shows this curve overlayed on the 2-axle, 3-axle, and 4-axle locomotive truck data discussed previously. In addition, the circles and x's represent actual data points measured in railroad tests.

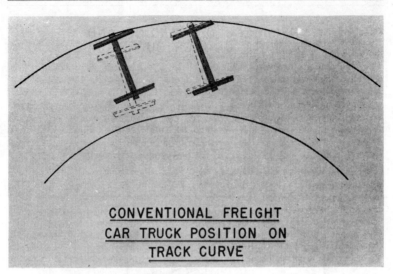

CONVENTIONAL FREIGHT
CAR TRUCK POSITION ON
TRACK CURVE

Fig. 17

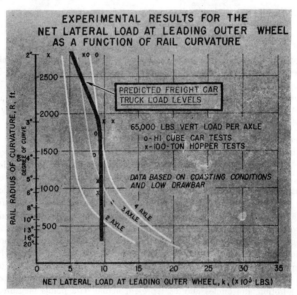

Fig. 18

IV. RAIL PROFILE DATA

Since it is the ratio of lateral to vertical load present between a wheel and the rail which is of interest, the vertical load present at any given time is important. This vertical load changes continuously as the wheel follows rail irregularities. To determine what vertical load was present during operation, it was considered mandatory to determine what rail profile the wheel followed in operation. That is, it was important to know what the "loaded" profile of the rail was when the wheel load was upon it, not what position the rail was in when there was no load present. The loaded profile can be and is substantially different from the unloaded shape of the rail. The instrumentation developed to obtain this, sample profiles obtained on U. S. railroads, and a summary of the data is discussed below.

Fig. 19 illustrates the change in wheel load which results when the particular wheels indicated are subjected to a track irregularity of the size indicated. This track irregularity is defined as vertical rail profile which is intended to represent the change in profile from the middle of a particular rail length (that is, approximately halfway between the rail joints) to the lowest point encountered at the joint. This will be more clear after viewing the subsequent illustrations. As can be seen, the changes in wheel load which occur are substantial. A not unusual rail profile of 1½ inches can cause a change in wheel load of approximately 10,000 lb out of total nominal static wheel load of about 32,000 lb. The effect on adhesion is obvious as well as the effect on wheel-rail stresses; also apparent should be the effect on tracking performance and possibility of derailments. Since this can be such a major factor, it must be taken into account in considering the relationship of lateral-to-vertical loads present and what type of tracking condition is involved.

To determine the loaded rail profile, new instrumentation was developed which did not depend on relative displacements between different points of the rail but rather gave an indication of the absolute path "in space" the wheel has to follow in passing over the rail. General Motors Research had developed such instrumentation for use on highways in 1962; it was first used in conjunction with locomotives and railroad track in 1965. The following four illustrations show some typical traces of rail profile which have been accumulated in recent years.

The first sample trace, Fig. 20, shows a typical main line section on one railroad. What is reproduced here is the exact profile that the wheel follows in passing over the rail, or correspondingly, the exact shape of the rail when the wheel load is applied to it except for the scale changes. The horizontal scale is condensed as shown by the 39-ft distances shown in Fig. 20 representing adjacent rail joints; the vertical scale is expanded relatively, as indicated by the 2.1-inch peak-to-valley displacement shown. The uniform rail joint pattern is apparent, and it is of interest that compared to the commonly considered unloaded rail profile, the irregularities under the condition shown are substantial.

Fig. 21 is a similar trace taken on a section of yard track. It is labelled "through" track to distinguish it from such facility tracks as sanding tracks or fueling tracks; that is, this represents track on which trains are made up and started, where demand for adhesion is often greatest. As can be seen and as may be expected, the uniformity of the rail joint pattern is not present because of the variations in rail pieces involved in the yard. Also of interest are the areas of immediate mismatch where adjacent rail sections were placed without shimming. For comparison purposes a 6-wheel SD truck is shown to the same scales, indicating that in

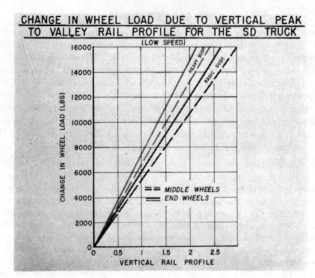

Fig. 19

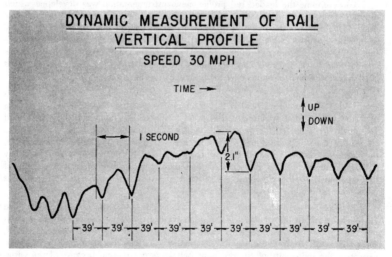

Fig. 20

520   Special Features

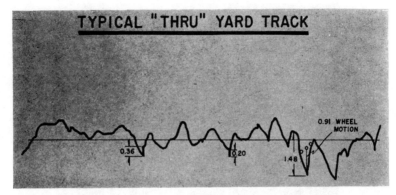

Fig. 21

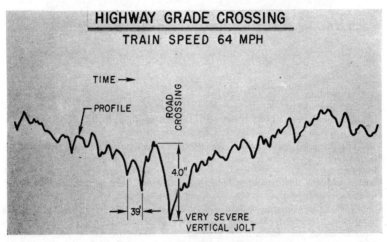

Fig. 22

796

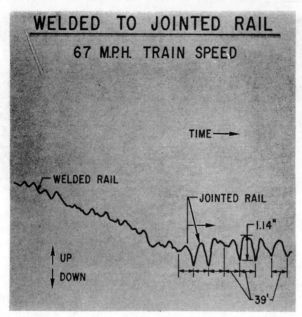

Fig. 23

passing over the rail lengths with 1.48-inch peak-to-valley displacements, the middle axle of the truck "feels" 0.91 inches of that displacement.

Fig. 22 shows an additional sample taken on main-line track at 64 mph. Because of the higher speed the horizontal scale is "squeezed down" somewhat further, as indicated by the 39-ft dimension shown. Again, the rail joint pattern is apparent, but in addition this sample includes passage over a highway grade crossing and reflects a 4-inch displacement within about a 20-ft length.

The last sample trace indicated, Fig. 23, shows passage from welded rail onto jointed rail. As may be expected, the welded rail irregularities are far smaller than those found on the jointed track; however, it is interesting that to some extent the 39-ft pattern is still present. This appears to be the result of the "memory" of the ballast and substructure due to the "pounding out" which took place when the joints were present.

As a summary of some of the rail profile data which has been accumulated, Fig. 24 shows the peak-to-peak vertical displacement plotted against the number of times a displacement of that level occurs per thousand miles of operation. Data accumulated on four different railroads is shown. For example, on Railroad D a 1½-inch peak-to-peak irregularity would occur 3500 times per thousand miles or about 3½ times every mile. The rather substantial difference between data obtained on different railroads (or sometimes between different areas of a railroad) is apparent.

797

522   Special Features

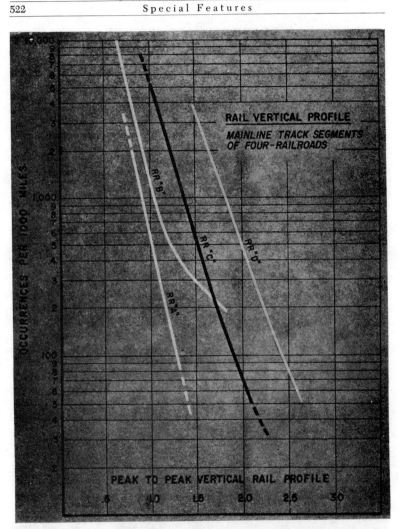

Fig. 24

V. THE EFFECT OF DYNAMIC BRAKE LEVELS

There are indications that locomotive braking practice and, in particular, dynamic braking, often may be involved in some of the tracking problems which have been investigated. In some cases it appears that personnel may not realize how "potent" a tool the dynamic brake level available to them today is. There are two aspects to this: the steady-state dynamic brake level available, and the dynamic reactions (run-ins) which can often be involved in locomotive braking practice.

Fig. 25 summarizes the braking effort available in pounds in dynamic braking a 4-unit consist of 6-axle units. The lower curve shows the braking available from four SD-7 units which are 6-axle units of approximately 1954 vintage. Use of the same number of axles, 24, in dynamic brake provides an increase as shown by the lighter intermediate shaded area on four units produced subsequently; the top curve shows the amount of braking effort available from the same 24 axles in dynamic brake on current locomotive units. This illustration reflects the significant increase in braking level available, an increase not apparent when the operator considers only the number of axles involved. In addition, the current models have available what is referred to as "extended range" dynamic brake which makes available the maximum level of braking down through the lower speeds which are normally involved in traveling over such areas as turnouts, crossovers, tight curvature, or temporary or poor track conditions.

In addition to these two factors (the approximate 40% increase in braking effort available with the same number of axles, and the availability of the extended range braking), changes in the electrical control of the dynamic brake also make it possible to obtain increasing braking levels from what was available in the past

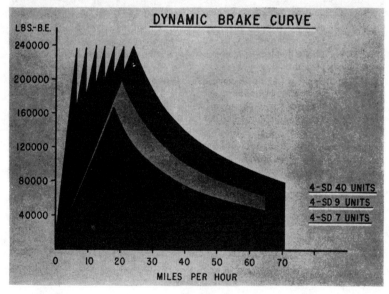

Fig. 25

when multiple-unit consists of more than four units are used. Initially, what is referred to as a "field loop" type control was used with which it was unable to provide increased braking effort if more than four units were used in multiple; the "potential trainline" type of control available today makes it possible that multiple units beyond four in number will add directly. On a 6-unit consist, this alone can represent a 14% increase in the amount of braking available for the same number of axles. For all these reasons, it is possible, as mentioned earlier, that this does represent a greater "tool" than is realized by some operating personnel.

In regard to the dynamic aspects, the following points are of importance:

1. Relatively high run-ins can be commonly measured, in the range of 250,000 to 300,000 lb, in locomotive braking practice today, and there is little or no reaction felt in the lead cab where the crew is located. The reason for this is that a 6-unit consist can represent almost 2½ million pounds of mass, and the 300,000-lb buff or run-in occurring between the trailing locomotive and the first cars in the train do not give much reaction to the lead cab when acting through that much mass and the 11 intermediate locomotive draft gears. Thus, it is impossible to determine whether braking practice is satisfactory by the "feel" in the lead cab.

2. It has not been possible to develop a universal dynamic brake handling procedure which would always be best. This is because it depends on the train makeup involved, and the terrain being travelled over. There are some procedures, however, which are very undesirable:

   a. It has been found that some personnel fail to provide the recommended 10-second delay in switching the selector handle from power to brake. If this switch is made rapidly, the residual magnetism in the generator can serve to give a high peak dynamic braking level immediately without any throttle motion made by the operating personnel. This has been confirmed in tests with substantial run-ins measured.

   b. Rapid buildup of the brake or "wiping out" of the handle can give high run-ins.

   c. Applying or maintaining high braking levels at turnouts, curves or crossovers where there is reason to consider conditions may be less than desirable can result in unsatisfactory conditions.

3. In almost all tests, the worst conditions have consistently been found to be on cars near the locomotive consist. This is particularly so with empty cars, and it is further exaggerated when the long-overhang TTX-type cars are placed adjacent to the locomotive. This is because cars in this position are subjected to the maximum drawbar values, often without having the substantial vertical load of the locomotive present helping to stabilize the wheel on the rail or the rail on the tie.

VI. MECHANICAL CONSIDERATIONS

There are a number of mechanical areas involved in the locomotive which can and do affect the wheel-rail loading. Among these (although there are many others) are: the alignment control draft gear, matching wheel sizes, and maintenance of truck bolster stops where necessary.

A number of years ago, when multiple-unit consist operation first became used, it was found that under conditions of significant locomotive buff, either braking or pushing, a phenomena occurred referred to as "jackknifing." This is simply the condition in which the locomotives skew relative to one another within the clearances available between the locomotive carbody and the track. This includes wheel-rail clearances, axle clearances, and the lateral clearances between the truck bolster and the truck frame. As a result of this the couplers between adjacent units are at an angle to the unit and, therefore, the buff load develops a lateral force component reacted at the truck centerplate and subsequently at the rail. At that time the best manner determined to control this jackknifing effect was to substantially reduce the lateral clearance between truck frame and truck bolster from the approximate 2¼ inch per side dimension present on the 4-axle trucks involved, to ½ inch per side by applying what is referred to as "bolster stops." By reducing the amount of shifting and skewing possible, these stops reduced the lateral component which could be developed and successfully limited the jackknifing forces involved, although they can increase the roughness of the ride laterally in higher speed operation.

In more recent years a coupler arrangement known as the "alignment control" draft gear has been used on road locomotives. This coupler arrangement provides a resistance to coupler angling in heavy buff conditions, which more successfully combats the jackknifing effect which can occur in heavy buff whether on tangent or curved track. Under common operating conditions today, the use of the alignment control draft gear, maintained in satisfactory operating condition, is mandatory to prevent significant lateral rail reactions. Fig. 26 illustrates a locomotive consist and the first two cars of a train actually involved in a derailment which was investigated. The consist is three 6-axle locomotives and three 4-axle loco-

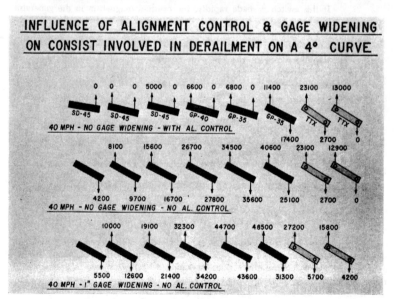

Fig. 26

526   Special Features

motives with TTX cars immediately behind the locomotive. The numbers indicated in the illustration are the lateral reactions resulting at the truck centerplate due to the skewing effect which takes place under the buff loading involved in this particular derailment. This centerplate loading combines with the curve negotiation loads to effect the wheel-to-rail reaction. In this particular consist and on this size curve, the unit with the highest centerplate reaction is the trailing locomotive unit, and of primary interest is the fact that this maximum loading increases from 17,400 lb at the point of maximum load to a value of 40,600 lb if alignment control were either not present or not maintained to engage properly. Also of interest is the fact, as illustrated in the bottom portion of the illustration, that 1 inch of gage widening allows this maximum load to additionally increase approximately 20%.

As noted previously, prior to the use of alignment control draft gears, it was necessary to apply bolster stops to 4-wheel locomotive trucks used in multiple-unit locomotive braking conditions. Fig. 27 illustrates another actual derailment condition which was investigated. In this case the three leading units were equipped with alignment control draft gear and the three trailing units, of older vintage, were not. The top portion of the illustration shows what centerplate reactions would be expected if all three of the trailing 4-axle units were equipped with bolster stops limiting the clearance to ½ inch per side. As may be noted the maximum reaction involved is approximately 30,000 lb. After the derailment occurred, actual measurements of the bolster lateral clearances present were made, and it was found that the fifth unit in the consist did not have bolster stops applied while the fourth and sixth units did have bolster stops; but these had become worn over the intervening years since application and resulted in lateral clearances per side of up to about 1⅜ inch instead of ½ inch. The result of these actual lateral clearances involved was sufficient to increase centerplate reactions to 67,000 lb, certainly

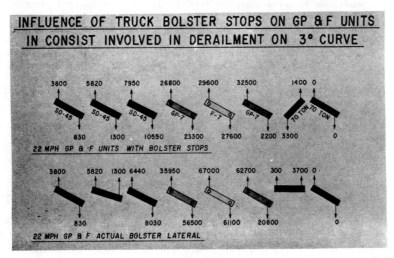

Fig. 27

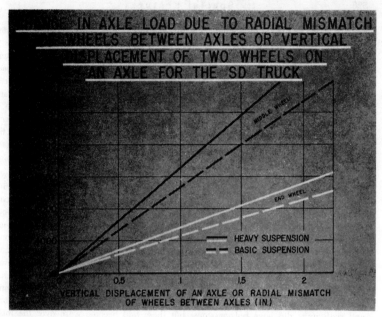

Fig. 28

sufficient to be of concern as a possible cause for the derailment. Two additional points may be noted about this situation: The three trailing units were being shipped "dead" in the train and there was some misunderstanding that they therefore did not require the same consideration as if powered. However, as long as they are subjected to the locomotive braking buff loads developed by the leading powered units, whether the units in question are dead or powered, does not affect the center bearing reactions. Secondly, because some railroads have understandably chosen to keep 4-wheel trucks interchangeable under locomotives of different vintages, it has been found that in some cases trucks without bolster stops from units with alignment control have become applied to older units without alignment control without the bolster stops being added.

Wheel size matching within a truck and within the locomotive can be very important, as illustrated in Fig. 28. It is not uncommon to find 6-axle locomotives operating today in which wheel sizes within one of the trucks are mismatched well beyond recommended limits. This can and does make substantial change in the wheel loads present affecting the locomotive tracking conditions. Fig. 28, for example, indicates that wheels mismatched by 1 inch in radius or 2 inches in diameter on the middle axle can cause a change in axle load of approximately 12,000 lb. In addition, this mismatch affects motor tractive effort distribution and axle load distribution, both of which influence attainable tractive effort the locomotive can develop. It seems largely since the advent of wheel truing machines that difficulties in wheel size measurement and matching have become common and that this area deserves greater attention.

CONCLUSION

It is difficult to summarize all the factors discussed above. Considering what areas seem to deserve the most attention would indicate the following:

1. Locomotive Braking Practice:
   a. Delay in power-to-brake transfer.
   b. Gradual buildup of braking level.
   c. Control of braking level over conditions such as crossovers, turnouts, and curves.

2. Track:
   a. Gage widening not excessive.
   b. Level of rail irregularities.
   c. Possible thermal strain investigations.

3. Mechanical:
   a. A 6-wheel locomotive truck supporting 195,000 lb adhesive weight has lateral loads 40 to 45% higher than a 4-wheel truck supporting 130,000 lb.
   b. Freight truck forces measured due to curving are of similar magnitude to a 6-wheel locomotive truck.
   c. Proper alignment control in draft gears.
   d. Proper bolster stops on units without alignment control.
   e. Long-overhang cars, especially empty cars, should not be near the locomotive consist in braking operation.
   f. Wheel size matching.

Measurement and Analysis of Wheel-Rail Forces

L. A. PETERSON   **W. H. FREEMAN**   **J. M. WANDRISCO**

INTRODUCTION

There are compelling reasons for wanting to know what occurs at the wheel-rail interface as a railroad freight car moves along a track. These reasons assume a more <u>practical</u> than <u>theoretical</u> importance when a railroad is plagued with specific maintenance or operating problems, such as severe and accelerated rail deterioration or a relatively high ratio of derailments. The desire to initiate remedies for such problems invariably provokes many "why" questions which cannot be acceptably answered through mutual experience comparisons or surveys. The dynamic responses between the wheels of a car and the rails on which they ride is a function of many variables or degrees of freedom associated not only with track characteristics and car design, but also greatly influenced by operating methods.

The relentless and continuing quest to achieve higher speeds, to carry heavier loads, and to reduce derailments while decreasing car and track maintenance costs is creating problems which can best be solved by a scientific, factual and "systems" approach. As an example, the ability to set "track standards" for a given unit train hauling operation or for a defined high-speed passenger run is highly dependent upon knowledge of the dynamic response of the component cars which, in turn, is significantly affected by such things as the dimensional relationships and characteristics of the bearings, springing, and snubbing in the suspension system of the cars.

Continuous measurement of the vertical and lateral wheel-rail forces of a moving railroad car is a fundamental starting point in understanding the dynamic relationships between various components of the car and the track structure. By changing or modifying individual components of the system in small degrees, while holding the other variables constant, maximum cause-effect information can be extracted.

BACKGROUND

Practical considerations prompted the initiation of this study in 1968. Severe rail corrugations, head checking, spalling, and excessive wear were regularly occurring on curves of the Quebec Cartier Mining Company Railroad, which is a high volume ore hauling railroad with unit train operations. This paper deals with the findings of field tests conducted in 1968 on the QCM and continued during 1969 and 1970 on the Bessemer and Lake Erie Railroad.

Beginning as an investigation of the cause of rail defects, the study necessarily evolved to include consideration and performance testing of the more comprehensive car-track system. Since the significance of tight lateral constraints in standard roller bearing cars was an unknown factor which could conceivably influence wheel-rail reactions, cars equipped with modifications to give different degrees and quality of lateral movement were tested.

During the analysis of these tests, the intimate interaction between the wheel and the rail under dynamic conditions was quantified.

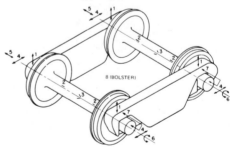

NOTATION	INSTRUMENT	LOCATION	MEASUREMENT
1	Load Cells	Between Bearing Cap & Side Frames	Vertical Force at Bearing
2	Strain Gages	Two Points On Each Axle	Axle Bending Moments
3	Strain Gages	Center of Each Axle	Axle Torque
4	Accelerometer	End of Each Axle	Longitudinal Accelerations
5	Accelerometer	End of Each Axle	Lateral Accelerations
6	Torsiographs	End of Each Axle	Torsional Velocity
7	Displacement Transducers	Between End of Each Axle & Side Frame	Relative Lateral Displacement
8	Strain Gages	On Bolster at Two Locations	Bolster Bending Strains

Note : The Strain Gage Channels were Wired into Chevron Bridge Connections with the Lead Wires Passing thru Drilled Holes and Terminated at Slip Rings on the End of each Axle

Fig. 1   Truck instrumentation

2

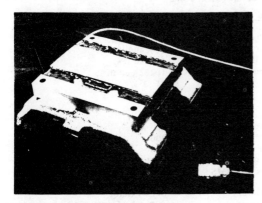

Fig. 2 Bearing reaction load cell for roller bearing car

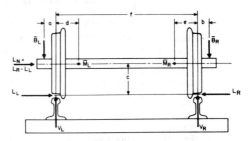

Fig. 3 Free body diagram of axle

METHOD OF INSTRUMENTATION AND MEASUREMENT

Car Instrumentation

Two basic cars, with five different car-truck configurations, were instrumented during the tests. Each truck tested was instrumented as shown in Fig. 1.

Track Instrumentation

Trackside instruments were located on a 6- and a 5-deg curve. The instrumentation consisted of linear variable differential transformers (LVDT's) attached to the field side of the heads of both the high and low rails at the same longitudinal locations to measure lateral movement of the rail head (both outward and inward). A photoelectric switch and light source at the same location were used to indicate the passage of each wheel, and a telemetry system transmitted the data onto magnetic tape in the recording car of the test train.

Lateral and Vertical Wheel Force Measurements

The means of determining the lateral and vertical force reactions at each wheel is a particularly critical part of the measurement. The vertical force transmitted from the car to the axle at each bearing was directly obtained by installation of specially made[1] bearing reaction load cells (Fig. 2). But, because of obvious direct measurement difficulties, determination of the vertical and lateral forces at the wheel-rail contact area was handled by an indirect procedure which relies upon the application and calibration

---

[1] Designed and assembled to specifications by Brewer Engineering Laboratories, Marion, Mass.

of pairs of strain gages at known locations on the axle to measure instantaneous axle bending moments.

Continuous measurement of the bending moment at any one point in a revolving axle is difficult. Oppositely placed (180 deg) strain gages in a single plane will yield a sine curve output as the point undergoes maximum tension at the top of the axle and maximum compression at the bottom with zero points at the two mid points between these extremes. Of course, this output is due to gage position and is not a direct measure of bending moment, except at the extreme points (twice per revolution). More accurate intermediate axle bending moment measures can be secured through installation of additional pairs of strain gages in rotative planes at the location. In addition, true intermediate bending moment values can be computed by trigonometric relationships involving the angle of revolution determined from the number of evenly spaced finite samples taken in each 90 deg of axle revolution.

Once appropriate axle bending moments are determined, they can be introduced as known values in free-body based equations of the wheel and axle unit using the forces and moment arms of Fig. 3.

Pertinent equations for equilibrium conditions are:

$$\bar{M}_L = L_L c + \bar{B}_L (a + d) - V_L d \qquad (1)$$

$$\bar{M}_R = L_L c + \bar{B}_L (a + (f - e)) - V_L (f - e) \qquad (2)$$

and

$$\bar{M}_R = L_R c + \bar{B}_R (b + e) - V_R e \qquad (3)$$

$$\bar{M}_L = L_R c + \bar{B}_R (b + (f - d)) - V_R (f - d) \qquad (4)$$

where $\bar{M}_L$, $\bar{M}_R$, $\bar{B}_L$, and $\bar{B}_R$ are known measured quantities and a, b, c, d, e, and f are physical dimensions.

These equations can be solved simultaneously.

3

Table 1 Test Car Features and Dimensions

Item	B. & L. E	Q. C. M.
Capacity	200,000 lbs.	199,000 lbs.
Load Limit	209,600 lbs.	199,400 lbs.
Lightweight	53,400 lbs.	51,500 lbs.
Cubic Capacity	2,775 cu. ft.	1,282 cu. ft.
Length over Strikers	41' 8''	31' 3 1/2''
Truck Centers	31' 8''	20' 6''
Wheel Base	68''	70''
Height Above Rail	10' 8 3/8''	8' 7''
Wheel Type	33'' MW	36'' MW
Test Wheel Tape Size	165	200
Test Wheel Circ.	104 5/8''	109''
Test Wheel Contours	Full Flange	Full Flange
Axles	6 1/2'' x 12'' RWS	6 1/2'' x 12'' RB
Axle Bearings	Plain	Roller
Spring Clusters	8-D-2 Outer	8-D-3 Outer
	6-D-2 Inner	4-D-3 Inner
Spring Cluster Travel	1 5/8''	2 1/2''
Ride Control	None	Yes
Bolster Gib Clearance	1 3/4'' Total	1/4'' Total
Nominal Static Wheel Load	32,000 lbs.	32,000 lbs.

in pairs, to give expressions for calculating the desired V_L, V_R, L_L, and L_R values. The equations so derived are:

$$V_L = \frac{\bar{M}_L - \bar{M}_R}{f - d - e} + \bar{B}_L \qquad (5)$$

$$V_R = \frac{\bar{M}_R - \bar{M}_L}{f - d - e} + \bar{B}_R \qquad (6)$$

$$L_L = \frac{\bar{M}_L - \bar{M}_R}{f - d - e}\left(\frac{f - e}{c}\right) + \frac{\bar{M}_R}{c} - \bar{B}_L\left(\frac{a}{c}\right) \qquad (7)$$

$$L_R = \frac{\bar{M}_R - \bar{M}_L}{f - d - e}\left(\frac{f - d}{c}\right) + \frac{\bar{M}_L}{c} - \bar{B}_R\left(\frac{b}{c}\right) \qquad (8)$$

and since $L_N + L_R = 0$, then

$$L_N = L_R - L_L \qquad (9)$$

The desired lateral and vertical force values are obtained by substituting the known dimensions and measured quantities for the appropriate terms. A resultant computed value having a negative sign indicates that the force vector is in the opposite direction to that shown in Fig. 3.

Although the physical dimensions, a, b, c, d, e, and f, represent known pre-measured constants, it is recognized that force application loci, such as the vertical rail-wheel locations, actually do shift on the wheel tread as the car rolls on the rails and that the force vectors, in general, are not always oriented or acting in as simple a manner as illustrated in the diagram.

However, the magnitude of error introduced by treating the moment arms as constants, appears to be well within acceptable limits. There was close agreement with measurements obtained by using an alternate method, similar to that described by Olson and Johnsson,[2] for determining lateral forces.

It is immediately apparent that the calculations as outlined in equations (5) through (9) could not be manually performed for even relatively small amounts of collected data. Consequently, all calibration and measurement data were recorded onto magnetic tape in analog form. This not only allowed immediate generation of strip chart displays, but also provided a mechanized way of Analogue to Digital (A to D) conversion of the data — achieving digital output on magnetic tape. These digital tapes were subsequently processed by computer where solution of the equations and comprehensive analysis were accomplished.

TEST PROCEDURES

The series of test runs were made over a 15-mile section of track which included six miles of tangent, curves from 1 to 8 deg, and grades up to 0.8 percent. The test track structure included welded 140-lb rail, and jointed 155- and 131-lb AREA rail sections laid on wooden ties, well bal-

---

[2] Olson, P. E., and Johnsson, S., "Lateral Forces Between Wheels and Rails," ASME-AIEE Railroad Conference, ASME Paper No. 60-RR-6, Pittsburgh, Pa., April 1960.

Table 2 Frequency Distributions for Selected Measurements
Modified R. B. Car on Tangent Track
1st Axle, Trailing Truck
35 MPH, Welded Rail

Freq. Dist.	Measurement	-51 To -75	-26 To -50	-0 To -25	0 To 25	26 To 50	51 To 75	76 To 100	Average (100 Lbs.)	Std. Dev. (σ) (100 Lbs.)
					Force Level Ranges (100 LBS.)					
1	Dynamic Part Of Vert. Force (V'_L)		6%	41%	48%	5%			-1	17
2	Dynamic Part Of Vert. Force (V'_R)		6	45	46	3			1	17
3	Dynamic Total Axle Force	1	15	33	36	13	2		0	25
4	Dynamic Axle Rock ($Rock_R$)		4	31	59	7			3	17
5	Lateral Force (L_L)				9	75	16		39	13
6	Lateral Force (L_R)				21	53	25	1	39	17
7	Net Axle Lateral Force (L_N)		2	47	46	5			1	17

		0 To .25	.26 To .50	Average	Std. Dev. (σ)
		L/V Ratios			
8	L_L/V_L Ratio	91%	9%	.16	.07
9	L_R/V_R Ratio	79	21	.18	.10

lasted with blast furnace slag.

Most test runs were made at a constant speed of either 20 or 35 mph, with several short runs being made over portions of the same section of track at 20, 25, 30, 35, 40, and 45 mph.

The usual consist of the test train included eight 100-ton hopper cars loaded to capacity with ore. The instrumented cars were centrally located. Comparative dimensions and components of the two cars tested as normally operated are listed in Table 1.

All the instruments were calibrated prior to the tests and checked after each test run. The output signals of all instruments, as well as a signal marking the passage of each milepost, were simultaneously recorded on magnetic tape by two 14-channel FM tape recorders. Synchronization of the two tapes was accomplished by simultaneously recording the milepost interrupt signals on both.

Test runs were made in both northbound and southbound directions, and data were obtained with the instrumented trucks in both the leading and trailing positions.

The QCM car, normally equipped with trucks having tapered roller bearings, was tested in four different configurations:

    1 Standard ride-control trucks
    2 Lateral pad equipped trucks

    3 Lateral pad equipped trucks with cylindrical roller bearings
    4 Standard ride-control trucks with cylindrical roller bearings.

During all the tests, limited data were simultaneously recorded for the P&LE car equipped with plain bearings for control purposes. This relationship was reversed during tests when measurement of the performance of the B&LE car was the prime objective.

One special series of runs was made with flat spots on the wheels, this condition having been simulated by intentional grinding of $1^1/2$- to 2-in. flat surfaces on each wheel of one axle.

In the duration of the tests, 28 channels of simultaneous data were recorded for over 500 miles of test train travel.

ANALYSIS

Vast amounts of detailed data were generated. Preliminary data reduction efforts pointed out the shortcomings of attempting to make conclusions based solely upon strip chart measurements or on simple averages and/or maximum values. The analytical machinery developed and used was able to examine dynamic actions sequentially, to distrib-

808

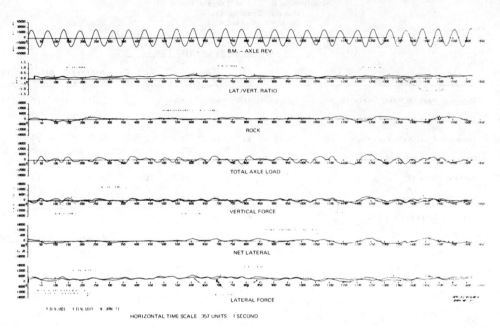

Fig. 4 Computer produced graphs of selected
forces on welded tangent track

ute instantaneous force measurements or ratios
into various range groupings, to determine the
percent of time the forces were within these
designated intervals, and to calculate various
other statistical measures, such as standard
deviations.

The recording of all data onto magnetic tape
in analog form provided versatility and flexibility. Strip chart displays were produced as desired. Representative portions of the total data
were selected for detailed analysis and converted
to 800-bpi digital tape at a 357 sample per second
rate and 11-bit resolution on each channel.

Conversational Fortran computer programs
were written and a DEC PDP-10 time-shared computer
utilized in analysis. The responsive man-computer
interaction afforded by this arrangement proved
invaluable and averted the problems and pitfalls
inherently present in historic transactions between
the analyzing scientist, a programmer "middleman,"
and a batch type computer processor.

The computer application described not only
provided an accurate quantified print-out of the
instantaneous lateral and vertical forces at each
wheel, but also allowed many other types of in-

stantaneous comparisons. Through appropriate
combinations and calculations, simultaneous values,
referred to as "rock," total axle load ("bounce"),
and lateral to vertical force ratios (L/V), were
determined for each 0.003 of a second. Numerous
graphical representations of each of these quantities as they varied with time were also output
from the computer. Two typical examples are illustrated in Figs. 4 and 5, for the case of welded
tangent track and jointed curved track, respectively. The vertical bearing forces, total axle
load, and "rock" traces are shown in reference to
deviations from static.

Table 2 is an example of the result of a
further step in processing of the data. In this
procedure, each instantaneous value is allocated
to a particular "cell" which represents a force
level range which envelopes it. The number of
times in which individual data points are allocated to each of these cells is counted. In this
way, a "frequency distribution" is produced.

DISCUSSION OF RESULTS

A good portion of the findings from this

6

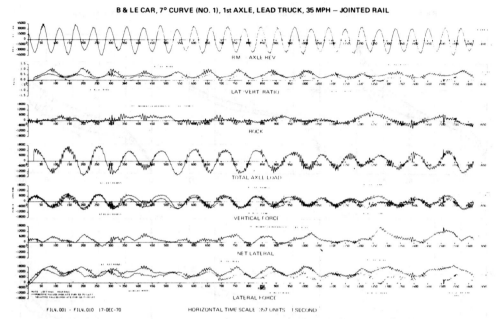

Fig. 5   Computer produced graphs of selected
forces on jointed rail in a 7-deg curve

study were expressed in the form of recommendations for alleviating specific problems. Viewed in a more general context, the results supply a surprisingly wide variety of information in several subject areas, many of which have been previously studied.

The more salient conclusions can be discussed by considering three of the car types tested:

1   B&LE plain bearing car — Std. P.B. car
2   QCM roller bearing car — Std. R.B. car
3   QCM roller bearing car with lateral pads — modified R.B. car.

Signatures

Relatively minor modifications in car components did produce different patterns of wheel-rail interaction, yet each remained reproducible (and thus predictable) under identical test conditions. The terms, "signature" and "fingerprint," carry with them qualitative connotations which include: (a) uniqueness, (b) reproducibility, and (c) utility. It turns out that under adequately defined conditions, these are appropriate descriptions for the frequency distributions produced from allocation of measured values into cells (defined ranges) on curves over 3 deg, and apply equally well to

distribution of the 357 sample per second values of the lateral forces at each wheel, the net lateral on the axle, the vertical force on each bearing and at each wheel, the lateral to vertical force (L/V) ratio at each wheel, the dynamic load shift from one side of the axle to the other (rock), and the total axle dynamic load (bounce). Sample signatures for several of these measurements, via cumulative frequency graphs, are displayed in Figs. 6 through 9.

Lateral track deflections, as measured from the trackside LVDT's, also satisfied signature requirements. Fig. 10 is an example of representative rail displacement signatures, for selected individual cars, obtained from track instrumentation at a fixed location in a 6-deg curve on jointed track. Fig. 11 has similar information for both travel directions from a 5-deg curve location on welded rail.

The potential implications of the establishment of a well-defined quality control type signature or fingerprint system are far reaching. Objective evaluation of car design changes, track inspection through measurements obtained from a "standard" car, and automated inspection of cars in a moving train from trackside instrumentation are suggested.

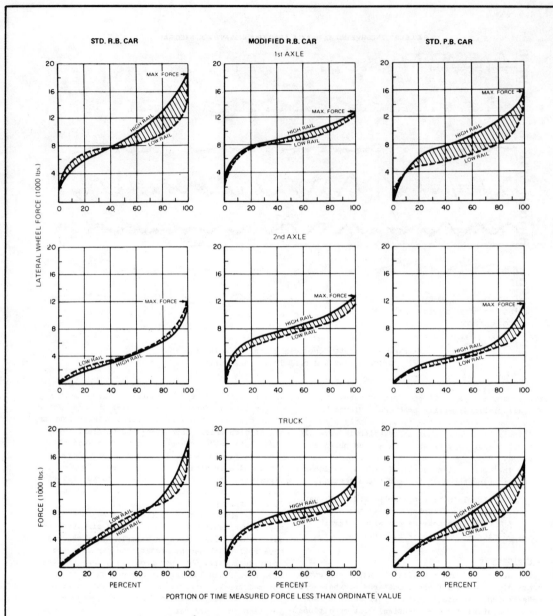

STD. R.B. CAR　　MODIFIED R.B. CAR　　STD. P.B. CAR

1st AXLE

2nd AXLE

TRUCK

PORTION OF TIME MEASURED FORCE LESS THAN ORDINATE VALUE

Fig. 6　Lateral wheel force comulative frequency
distribution signatures for three different car
designs at 35 mph on a welded rail 5-deg curve

Curved Versus Tangent Track

Due to differences in suspension, there are
definite differences in car performance in respect
to lateral and vertical reactions on curved and
tangent track.

Fig. 12 shows typical net lateral axle (L_N)
relationships at 35 mph for the force level one
standard deviation (1 σ) above the mean. The
points plotted are values corresponding to the
axle on the truck with the highest 1 σ value.

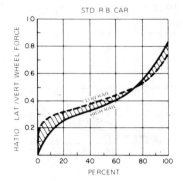 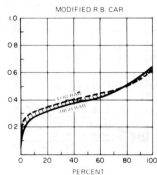 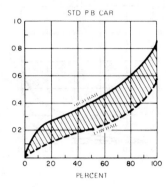

PORTION OF TIME MEASURED RATIO LESS THAN ORDINATE VALUE

Fig. 7 L/V first axle wheel ratio cumulative
frequency distribution signatures for three
different car designs at 35 mph on a welded
rail 5-deg curve

STD. P.B. CAR

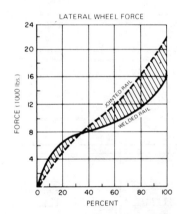 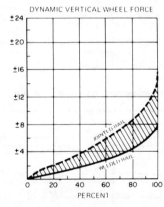 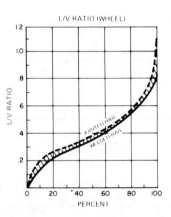

PORTION OF TIME MEASURED VALUE LESS THAN ORDINATE VALUE

Fig. 8 Selected cumulative frequency distribution
signatures for high rail side of first axle of the
standard plain bearing car at 35 mph on 5-deg
curves of jointed and welded rail

Table 3 Vertical Axle Loading (Thousands of Pounds)

Car	Range of Total Axle Load During Long Term Bounce Cycles		Characteristic Dynamic Peak To Peak "Shocks"	
	Tangent	5° Curve	Tangent	5° Curve
Standard Plain Bearing	44 - 84	56 - 72	5	5
Standard Roller Bearing	58 - 70	59 - 69	15	5
Modified Roller Bearing	58 - 70	60 - 68	10	3

9

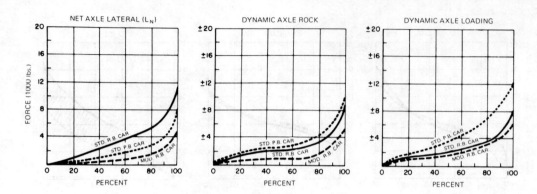

PORTION OF TIME MEASURED FORCE LESS THAN ORDINATE VALUE

Fig. 9 Comparison of cumulative frequency distribution signatures for lead axles of three different car designs at 35 mph on a welded rail 5-deg curve

JOINTED RAIL AT RENFREW (155 lbs.)

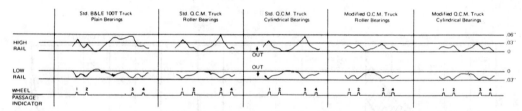

FROM SOUTHBOUND TEST TRAIN AT 20 M.P.H.

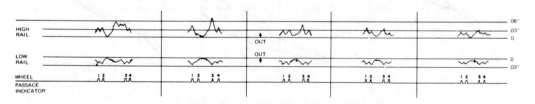

FROM SOUTHBOUND TEST TRAIN AT 35 M.P.H.

Fig. 10 Representative lateral rail displacement fingerprints for five different car designs at a location in a 6-deg jointed rail curve

The graph in Fig. 13 illustrates the similarly defined differences in fluctuating vertical total axle load force (bounce) for the three car types at a constant 35-mph-speed.

Note the increase in lateral force with curvature and the decrease in vertical bounce for the Standard Plain Bearing car with increasing curvature. (This truck is equipped with an unsnubbed D-2 spring grouping.)

Lateral Force Comparisons

The Standard Roller Bearing car, as used in normal everyday service, is typical of cars equipped with roller bearings allowing little lateral

Table 4 Comparison of Maximum Values for Various
Measurements Jointed Versus Welded Rail
(Standard Plain Bearing Car on 5-deg Curves at 35 mph)

Measurement	Rail Jointed	Welded	% Reduction
1. Vertical Dynamic Wheel-Rail Force (1000 lbs.)	14	8	43
2. Lateral Wheel-Rail Force (1000 lbs.)	21	16	24
3. Net Lateral Force Per Axle (1000 lbs.)	16	8	50
4. Rock Per Axle (1000 lbs.)	15	8	47
5. L/V Force Ratio per Wheel	1.10	.85	23
6. Axle Bending Moment (1000 lb.-ft.)	46	38	17

WELDED RAIL AT BULL CREEK (140 lbs.)

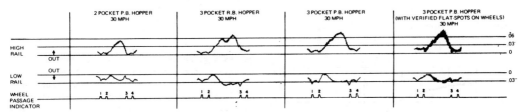

FROM SOUTHBOUND TRAINS

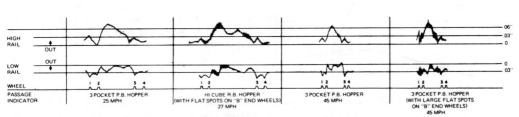

FROM NORTHBOUND TRAINS

Fig. 11 Selected lateral rail displacement
fingerprints from a location on welded rail
in a 5-deg curve

movement between the side frames and the axles, and only a small amount of lateral movement between the bolster and the side frames. Such trucks may be termed "rigid" as opposed to more "flexible" plain bearing cars.

On curves, cars with rigid trucks produce a characteristic type of rotative action about the lead, high rail wheel of the truck. This action is substantially diminished when the car is modified to allow lateral movement between the side frames and axles by the insertion of lateral springs (flexible rubber-steel sandwiches called lateral pads).

As Fig. 12 illustrates, lateral force levels are reduced in the modified roller bearing car case and are also less for the plain bearing car in comparison to the standard roller bearing car. In addition, dynamic lateral force frequencies (vibrations) corresponding to the peak-to-peak distance (7 to 12 in.) between corrugations on the

11

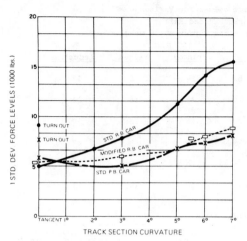

Fig. 12 1 σ level net lateral axle (L_N) forces on representative jointed rail track sections

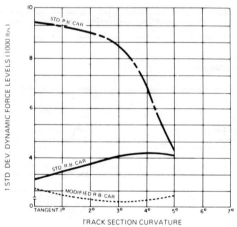

Fig. 13 1 σ level dynamic variations in total axle load ("bounce") on representative welded rail track sections

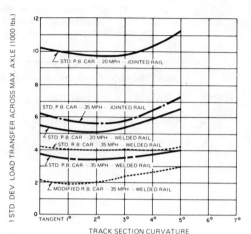

Fig. 14 1 σ level rock comparisons for selected car designs, speeds, and rail types

CM rail were much more pronounced in the standard roller bearing car measurements than on the other truck designs tested.

Vertical Force Comparisons

Transmittal of the load vertically to the axle bearings and eventually to the wheel-rail contact area is a much more complex occurrence when a car is moving (dynamic force) as compared to when it is standing still (static force). The dynamic pattern of load transmittal as a car tra-

verses a given section of track is determined chiefly by the suspension system of the truck (bolsters, springs, bearings, wedges, snubbers, etc.), and, as Fig. 13 depicts, the magnitude may vary significantly depending upon the characteristics and clearance between these components.

Rock is a method of viewing the transmittal of vertical force. The dynamic transfer of vertical load from one side of an axle to the other is termed "rock" in this paper. The traces in Figs. 4 and 5 each contain a labeled time-varying graphical interpretation of this quality as defined by:

$$\text{Rock}_R = \bar{B}'_R - \bar{B}'_L \qquad (10)$$

where each B' term is the "dynamic" portion (deviation from static) of the bearing load measurement at a given instant of time. Each B' term will assume a negative value when it is less than the static condition.

Repetitive car rocking was observed on jointed track, but only at widely separated locations on welded rail. The nature of the rocking on jointed rail is dependent upon the car design and the speed. Maximum rocking amplitudes on jointed track consistently corresponded to joint half intervals of $19\frac{1}{2}$ ft during speed ranges of 18 to 25 mph. Above 25 mph, rail joint input produces very short duration "shock" or impact effects of as much as 10,000 to 12,000 lb in 0.003 sec — rather than the longer term resonant reactions at lower speeds. Characteristic car actions associated with curving responses tend to make

B & LE CAR, TANGENT (NO. 2), 2nd AXLE, LEAD TRUCK, 35 MPH — WELDED RAIL

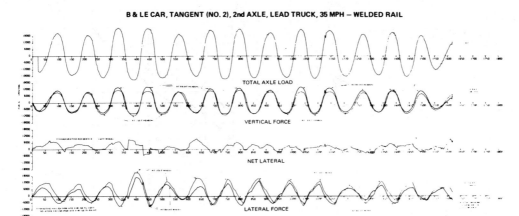

TOTAL AXLE LOAD

VERTICAL FORCE

NET LATERAL

LATERAL FORCE

HORIZONTAL TIME SCALE: 357 UNITS = 1 SECOND

Fig. 15 Characteristic axle loading and lateral
force effects of standard plain bearing car in
bounce mode on tangent track

joint-excited rock less discernible on curves.

Dynamic lateral·track profile reaction differences can be thought of as changes in track
lateral resistance sensed by a car in passage over
the track. The joint itself is a prime example
of a discontinuity in lateral track resistance with
the joint bar, bolts, etc. changing the lateral
resistance. Such lateral "input" to a moving car,
as well as the widely recognized vertical errors
at the rail joints, can be a trigger in causing
dynamic vertical load shifts ("rocking").

The modified roller bearing car exhibited a
higher capability for reducing resonant speed
activated rock and of absorbing shocks received at
higher speeds in accordance with Fig. 14 which
also illustrates overall speed effects.

Bounce is defined as a pattern of dynamic
total axle loading characterized by simultaneous
and synchronous loading of all bearings of trucks
of a car. An axle exhibits prominent bounce characteristics when the bearings on each end load and
unload together Time correlated axle loadings on
tangent track for the standard plain bearing car
are shown in Fig. 15. The values for the total
axle load trace shown in this exhibit and in other
similar figures represent deviations from static
conditions. They were arrived at by:

$$\text{Total dynamic axle load} = \bar{B}'_R + \bar{B}'_L \qquad (11)$$

Certain sections of tangent track caused the exhibited exaggerated bouncing of the plain bearing
car during each passage.

The standard roller bearing car was equipped

with friction snubbing in the spring group, while
the standard plain bearing car had an unsnubbed or
"free" spring travel system. This helps to account
for the very evident differences in behavior when
comparing this car to the friction snubbed roller
bearing car, such as in Fig. 4. There are definite
trade-offs. Friction snubbing generally reduces
the amplitude of vertical force fluctuations but
apparently initiates high-frequency vertical vibrations (60 to 80 Hz) which are also translated
into lateral vibrations corresponding to the wavelength of rail corrugations.

Table 3 is a simple quantified comparison
summary for the conditions of welded rail and 35-
mph car speeds.

In-depth examination of the dynamic vertical
forces in relationship to the simultaneous lateral
forces measured in this study proved that the outboard bearings on axles, as present in freight
cars, transform pure vertical force input at the
bearing into well-defined lateral as well as vertical force elements at the wheel▪rail contact
area. In fact, bounce-type vertical loading and
unloading of the axle will produce a reciprocating
lateral reaction at the rail tending to force the
rail inward and outward, respectively, as exag-
geratively depicted in Fig. 16. (The axle does
not bend in the reverse direction as shown in the
lower portion of the sketch.)

Outboard Bearing Effect

Railroad freight cars normally have outboard
bearings; i.e., the load is applied to the axle
outside the wheels. The study called attention to

13

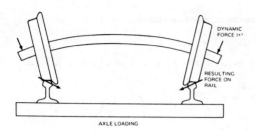

AXLE LOADING

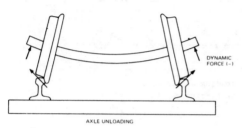

AXLE UNLOADING

Fig. 16 Grossly exaggerated depiction of fluctuating force on rails due to alternate axle loading
and unloading in bounce mode

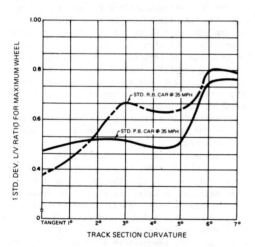

Fig. 17 1 σ comparisons of maximum wheel L/V
ratios for standard plain and roller bearing
cars on jointed rail

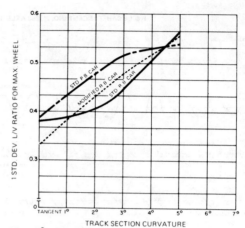

Fig. 18 1 σ comparisons of maximum wheel L/V
ratios on welded rail at 35 mph

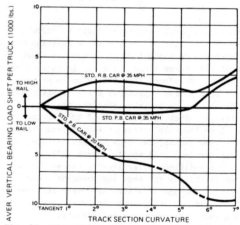

Fig. 19 Comparisons of average vertical bearing
load shifts across lead truck on given curves at
constant speeds of 20 and 35 mph

the fact that for either outboard or inboard bearings, the "offset" point of loading causes what
might be intuitively visualized as a characteristic flexing of the axle as it unloads and loads
in a bounce mode. Since the wheels are an inte-

gral right angle extension of the axle, the bouncing action produces not only vertical wheel-rail
forces, but also significant and corresponding
lateral wheel-rail forces.

Both trackside instrumentation and car instrumentation show that reactions resulting in an
inward force on the rail are incurred. The amount
of inward force is limited by the coefficient of
friction between the wheel and the rail, since
slipping will occur if the resisting frictional
force is exceeded. While frictional coefficients
as high as 0.6 were evidently reached in this

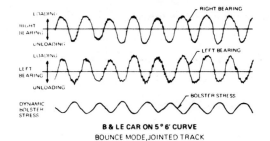

B & LE CAR ON 5° 6' CURVE
BOUNCE MODE, JOINTED TRACK

Fig. 20 Dynamic bolster stresses resulting from bounce mode of standard plain bearing car

study, no coefficient values in excess of 0.3 were found when the rail was being forced inward, even though such inward forces, which are limited by the coefficient of friction, infrequently reached as high as 12,000 lb per wheel. The reason for this is that the vertical force on the wheel at these peak lateral force periods was always in excess of 40,000 lb (maximum inward lateral always occurring at very heavy axle loadings). Thus, relatively high wheel-rail lateral forces were reached in these tests within the bounds of commonly accepted values of frictional coefficients.

This relationship of direct variation of lateral force with varying vertical loading has not been recognized to any extent in the industry, which may help to explain why many conflicting reports on lateral force levels and action are found. The importance of this finding, as applied to rail wear, is that vertical force dynamics alone can produce lateral stresses which could, under certain conceivable conditions, cause a type of lateral rail yielding at the wheel-rail contact area.

Wheel Plate Stresses

Past research papers[3] have stated that wheel plate failures would be more prevalent if forces applied in a direction away from the wheel flange actually occur, because these stresses would be additive to residual stresses that are inherently developed in the wheel heat treatment process. Present wheel design practice assumes wheel forces applied toward or against the flange as being the rule, and these are "subtractive." This study indicates that outward forces on the wheel can occur with a higher degree of regularity, due to

---

[3] Bruner, Levy, Jones, and Wandrisco, "Effect of Design Variation on Service Stresses in Railroad Wheels," ASME Paper No. 67-WA/RR-6, Pittsburgh, Pa., Nov. 1967.

prominent car bouncing on certain long tangent track sections, than could be expected from exposure to retarders, etc. — which can also produce wheel stresses away from the flange.

Fatigue failures of this type result from the accumulation of repetitive cycles of a critical force level which may take place over varying lengths of time. Even though industry-wide wheel plate failures are rare, this study suggests that certain specific conditions involving consistent operations of "bounce-prone" cars over "bounce-exciting" track sections could result in a relatively higher frequency of failure. In these low-speed tests, lateral force application cycles with a component away from the wheel flange exceeding 4000 lb were recorded on certain long tangent track sections at the rate of 150 per mile.

Unit Train Hazard

In addition to all other considerations concerning track, operating conditions and car design, there is a clear and definite hazard of incurring cyclic type rail deterioration due chiefly to the passage of identical consists of loaded cars with heavy wheel loads within consistent speed ranges.

The study has very conclusively shown that on curves over 3 deg, a selected point on the track will behave in an identical manner during each passage of a given consist of cars at a given **speed in a given direction; i.e., the entire** trace of the deflections of the selected point on the track will be the same each time the given consist passes that point at that speed. Also, each car will tend to behave in a characteristic repetitive manner in traveling over a particular section of track on a curve; i.e., it will bounce or rock at the same point, etc. Another point selected on the track at a different location in the curve will have a different overall trace, but will exhibit the same consistency upon repetitive passages of identical consists. This means that if nominal axle loads are near the critical threshold, each dynamic impact will cause an excessive **force to occur repeatedly in the same places.**

Tangent track does not, to as high a degree, produce this repetitive type action. It appears that the reason for this difference between curves and tangent is the "following" or guiding action of the wheel of the lead axle on the high side of the curve as opposed to a more random "hunting" action on tangent track. Another way of saying this is that the lead wheel on the high side of curves follows or conforms to the lateral profile of the rail, imparting a predetermined pattern of car action much like the role of a stylus on a template. The necessity to conform to any one rail is usually lacking on tangent track, and

818

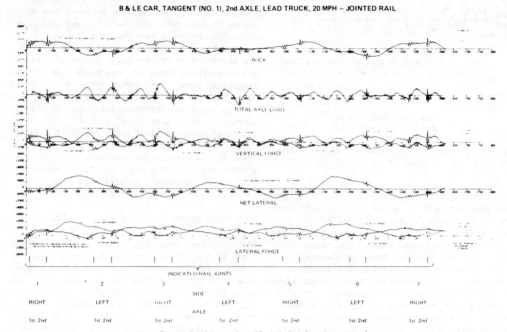

B & LE CAR, TANGENT (NO. 1), 2nd AXLE, LEAD TRUCK, 20 MPH — JOINTED RAIL

Fig. 21 Detection of rail joints from measured
car performance values on tangent track at 20 mph

there is no significant travel distance differential requirement between the opposite wheels of an axle as there is on curves. As a result, the action of trucks in curves, where wheel coning cannot overcome rolling distance differentials, is not only repetitive in nature but, in addition, tends to produce relatively higher dynamic (vibrational) wheel-rail force levels than tangent track.

Regardless of the reason for the difference between tangent and curves, the basis for a definite wear pattern is established on curves; i.e., a high lateral force (with the same repetitive motion) will always occur at the same point on the track each time an identical train consist traverses that section of the curve.

The case in which loaded cars travel in both directions over single track may actually be better than when loaded cars consistently travel in one direction and empty cars in the other. The reason for this is that "uneven" wear is more of a problem than a somewhat greater rate of "uniform" wear. Empty cars do not generate anywhere near as high vertical and lateral forces as loaded cars and, therefore, are less likely to have any noticeable offsetting effect on the wear pattern established by the loaded cars. Conversely, in

the case of loaded cars traveling in both directions, the loaded car pattern in one direction might offset a different wear pattern incurred in the opposite direction. Differences in wear patterns by direction occur because of track and operating condition variations; i.e., train action will be considerably different on an ascending versus a descending grade. The study did show differences because of direction, but no thorough analysis was made to determine whether the effects would usually tend to be offsetting — producing a more even overall rail wear pattern.

Consistent heavy wheel loads and consistent higher speeds will accentuate the problem because the force levels increase with speed and load. Cars with less dimensional clearance between truck components in their design and manufacture will also tend to provide undesired consistency in operating behavior in this respect. And, as on the QCM, cars of the same age, having been subjected to the same operations over a period of time, tend to wear in a similar manner and, in turn, will then react to a more consistent pattern on curves.

Paradoxically, though, it is not necessary that each car in the consist be identical with

16

B & LE CAR, TANGENT (T.O.), 1st AXLE, LEAD TRUCK, 35 MPH — JOINTED RAIL

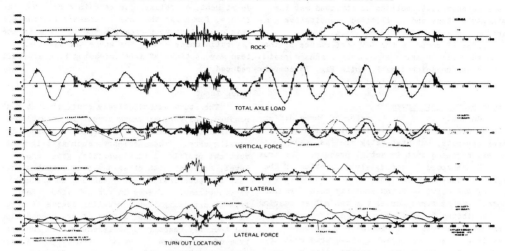

ROCK

TOTAL AXLE LOAD

VERTICAL FORCE

NET LATERAL

TURN OUT LOCATION   LATERAL FORCE

Fig. 22 Relative effects of turnout negotiation
by the standard plain bearing car at 35 mph

each of the other cars for a repetitive pattern to be established. Even with different types of cars, the total force and dynamic action sequence for the given consist will be the same for each passage of the train — under the conditions described. Thus, the hazard is present whenever the same cars remain coupled together for successive trips.

There seems to be no practical way of completely eliminating the hazard of patterned rail damage on railroads having a predominance of unit train operations, such as the QCM. Hopefully, car design changes, which reduce the level of wheel-rail forces and modify undesirable repetitive car actions on curves, will significantly prolong the period of acceptable operation before the rail damage becomes intolerable. Specific actions which would: (a) minimize unsprung weights of cars, (b) make vehicle suspension "softer," (c) vary car design characteristics which might influence natural periods of oscillation, (d) reduce static and dynamic axle loading, (e) adjust track parameters to better match operations, or (f) decrease the frequency and level of lateral wheel-rail forces in curves, are examples of appropriate objectives.

Jointed Versus Welded Rail

Marked positive advantages of welded over jointed rail were confirmed. Results indicate that car components, as well as track structure members, should last longer and that derailments

should be reduced, upon conversion from jointed to welded rail.

Fig. 8 illustrates comparisons concerning the lateral, vertical, and L/V ratio values for a particular case of the standard plain bearing car at 35 mph.

Other comparative <u>maximum</u> values incurred by the same car on similar 5-deg curves are shown in Table 4.

L/V Ratios

The obvious intent of this ratio is to provide an index comprehending the relationship between the force tending to drive the wheel, axle, truck, or car off the rail versus the force trying to keep the wheel, axle, truck, or car seated on the rail. The instantaneous ratio of the lateral force to the simultaneous vertical force at each wheel was determined for each fraction of a second and displayed during the analysis of the tests. Similar instantaneous ratios comprehending the net lateral (L_N) on each axle to vertical axle force and total net truck lateral to total truck vertical force were also computed. The degree of applicability or usefulness of these ratios is debatable, but they are of value in making relative performance comparisons in conjunction with other information. The short-term magnitude of such ratios is certainly not by itself an absolute indicator for forecasting derailments.

Great differences in L/V were found between curves and tangents, jointed and welded rail, speed ranges, and the various car designs tested. The frequency distributions constructed met the "signature" test and facilitated quantitative comparisons in all the mentioned areas.

Fig. 17 compares the L/V performance of the standard roller bearing car to the standard plain bearing car on jointed rail, while Fig. 18 compares the three car types on welded rail.

Superelevation of Curves

An analysis of the behavior of three different car designs, when traveling at 35 mph over three separate, but statically similar, 5-deg curves, revealed that in actual practice, the true equilibrium speed is not solely a function of the degree of curvature and the amount of superelevation of the curve — which commonly used formulas state. On the first curve, the two roller bearing cars exhibited lateral and vertical force behavioral measurements which indicated they were traveling at a speed somewhat above true equilibrium. On the second curve, the modified roller bearing car appeared to be at equilibrium speed and the other two car types below. All of the cars seemed to be below equilibrium speed on the third curve. This points out that there is a difference between static, no-load measured superelevation and the elevation sensed by a moving loaded car. Effective superelevation (under dynamic load) of the different curves and the dynamic response of the individual car designs affect equilibrium behavior. Cars with high centers of gravity are more sensitive to superelevation errors in respect to corresponding amounts of deviation from equilibrium behavior.

The evaluation of when a car is or is not at equilibrium speed, in itself, is difficult — even when all of the vertical and lateral force reactions are known, as they were in this analysis. Defined criteria for vertical and lateral force characteristics may be met on the first axle of the truck but not on the second (frequently the case with standard roller bearing car).

Fig. 19 is a graphical example of comparing equilibrium behavior based on average vertical truck load shifts between the high and low rails on selected curves at constant speeds of 20 and 35 mph. Differences between the standard roller bearing and plain bearing cars at 35 mph can be seen.

In practice, many railroad M of W Departments periodically adjust superelevation based upon the track wear pattern evolving under operations, thus deviating from purely calculated elevations. This tends to match the amount of elevation to predominant wheel loads and car speeds. Of course, optimizing track wear by continuing to reduce the superelevation past a certain level could produce an uneconomical risk of high rail derailment, especially for certain cars. For instance, for a car that has a tendency to bounce, this is equivalent to increasing the "L" term in the L/V ratio under conditions where the vertical (V) load may at times of axle unloading be drastically reduced.

Track Input

The study quantitatively confirms that rail, roadbed, and general track structure conditions act as stimuli for inducing various reactions in passing cars. Track geometry, such as alignment, vertical profile, lateral profile, gage, cross level, together with other qualities, such as ballast characteristics, etc., can and do produce very noticeable effects in car behavior. Each type of car design has a peculiar degree of sensitivity to certain combinations of track conditions and thus may react very differently from another type of car design. However, each car has a characteristic "carprint" or signature of action which is reproducible upon repetitive passage over a given section of track. When track conditions change, the measured car reactions also change.

Lower lateral wheel-rail forces are produced when the individual wheel and axle sets of the car can independently absorb lateral track irregularities. Cars having either plain bearings or lateral pad equipped axles possess this ability of independent accommodation to a greater degree than cars with common unmodified roller bearing axles.

It is important to realize that statically measured track dimensions do not necessarily yield an accurate index as to what the car will sense under moving (or dynamic) conditions. Historic track maintenance determinants relying heavily upon physical measurements of gage, cross level, alignment, etc., under no-load conditions do not always reliably appraise the acceptability of the track under normal operating conditions. Some factors, such as roadbed resiliency, are not even susceptible to historic methods of measurements. Dynamic track geometry measurements correlated with the type of car performance measurements described in this paper would provide a powerful combination in dealing with the problem of "setting track standards."

This study did show that the frozen roadbed, encountered in operations of the QCM Railroad during the winter season, does decrease track resiliency and that resulting dynamic loads during this time are higher by as much as 30 percent than under unfrozen roadbed conditions. Once track profile irregularities, such as corrugations, have begun, they act to trigger dynamic actions in the car, and the frozen track with a higher spring constant will consequently produce higher impact forces. Thus, further deterioration of the rail will proceed at a faster pace on railroads with the roadbed frozen for extended periods.

Car Design Implications

Theoretically, captive cars operating constantly over the same track could be designed in accordance with measured stresses and car behavior to achieve lower costs and better performance. For example, railroad cars operating strictly on welded rail and with a small percent of curves over 3 deg and none over 4 deg could be of a more economical design (smaller axles, etc.) than on a similar railroad with higher curvatures. This is true because bending moments, torsion in the axles, and stresses in other car components are greater on curves of higher curvature. Data, such as produced in this study, could be used to assist in designing cars to fit individual situations of this kind.

The study showed that the bolsters on the 100-ton standard plain bearing car tested were being subjected to flexing stresses of up to ±5000 psi to give a total stress of greater than 20,000 psi as the axles loaded and unloaded in the characteristic bounce mode of the car. Such bouncing, interestingly enough, took place to a greater extent on certain sections of tangent track than on curves. The quantitative force and frequency of occurrence measurements obtained can serve as a basis for design modification in the bolsters to reduce fatigue failures.

Fig. 20 is typical of truck bolster stress action in relation to bounce or bearing loading on each end of an axle of the standard plain bearing car tested.

POTENTIALS FOR AUTOMATED QUALITY CONTROL

As an outgrowth of the various techniques developed and used in the study and in conjunction with pertinent findings, a mechanized and objective method of quality control to detect, by exception, departures of individually measured track sections and individually monitored cars from expected limits (signatures) is deemed highly feasible.

Locating and Describing Track Defects

Track conditions do act as stimuli inducing certain behavioral patterns into cars. The response of the car to this "input" is dependent upon its design, but is repetitive in nature; i.e., when the car is subjected to the same stimulus, it will behave similarly. The instrumentation used during these tests adequately measured and pinpointed the location of various track condition inputs.

For instance, individual joints and other physical track discontinuities, such as track turnouts, were accurately located in the tests by the characteristic action which they induced into the instrumented cars. Each of the five different car designs tested reacted in an individualistic manner when passing through a given turnout, and induced reactions can be ranked according to severity. Furthermore, the difference between trailing and facing movements was distinguishable. The standard roller bearing design car generally behaved in a more unstable manner when negotiating turnouts, as compared to the other car designs tested. Figs. 21 and 22 illustrate joint and turnout input effects on the measured forces of the standard plain bearing car.

As previously mentioned, certain locations on tangent track caused the plain bearing car to go into a particularly exaggerated bounce, and this occurred each time the car passed these points. While a cursory inspection of the track was not sufficient to isolate the track condition responsible for inciting this reaction, it is felt that a concentrated effort would generally succeed in uncovering the necessary cause-effect relationships to correlate car reactions to track conditions and that this information could be methodically accumulated.

One of the major hypotheses evolving from this investigation contends that periodic (say monthly) measuring runs with a standard car will be successful in detecting deviations from normal signature trends for a given segment of track (i.e., particular curve) which, when they become of a statistically significant magnitude, can be "flagged." Then a computerized follow-up process could isolate more exactly the location within the track section responsible for the "out of control" reaction and, through a correlation catalog amassed from past experience, suggest the probable cause.

For this purpose, a box car has been remodeled to house equipment for in-motion receiving and processing of data from instruments attached to a nearby car having known (standard) signatures. Equipment on-board the recording car, consisting of an FM recorder, an A to D converter, a mini computer, two magnetic digital tape drives, a CRT display, and a teleprinter, was installed to accomplish real-time analysis and evaluation of data with on-the-spot "exception" reporting, while still permitting more detailed "after-the-fact" analysis.

Detecting and Describing Car Behavioral Defects

Car behavior can be measured to varying degrees from instrumentation located on the car itself or by transducers located at trackside sites.

Instrumentation located on the car possesses the added utility of being able to assess track conditions.

The car-located instrumentation used during these tests measured the reactions of five different car designs over many variations in track conditions. Each of these designs generated an individual signature in response to various track inputs, and the quantified results showed surprising differences between the standard roller bearing car and the same car with the lateral pad modification, which is a relatively minor car component revision. The instrumentation used supplied enough information to evaluate the degree of improvement of one design over the other.

The implications for future utilization and application of such equipment are obvious, and these tests indicate that a "package" to accomplish the job, whenever car design evaluation appears beneficial, is practical and feasible.

Trackside instrumentation can also appraise the differences in reaction of various car designs, but only in respect to a single track location. It has the advantage over car-located instrumentation of being less costly and requires only a one-time installation expense, while car-located instrumentation may necessitate the application of appropriate measuring devices for each car design to be tested. Trackside instrumentation has the disadvantage of being stationary. However, knowing the predictable and repetitive behavior of all cars on curves over 3 deg, it was possible to precisely locate trackside measuring equipment to appraise the performance of the five car designs tested and produce results in substantial agreement with the car-located instrumentation. In fact, the trackside equipment was able to:

1 Detect the presence and direction of each train
2 Detect each axle of each passing vehicle
3 Pick out and distinguish between locomotives, cars, and cabooses
4 Differentiate between the different type of cars (two-pocket hoppers, three-pocket hoppers, roller bearing cars, high cube hoppers, etc.)
5 Determine the speed of each train
6 Detect abnormal behavior in any car and pinpoint the axle on the car producing the abnormal effect
7 Transmit all of the foregoing information via radio to a remote location where it was recorded on magnetic tape.

Figs. 10 and 11 are representative individual car extractions from longer train traces but illustrate some of the aforementioned capabilities.

Recently, the track instrumentation package has been refined and enlarged to simultaneously measure lateral deflections at each wheel-rail contact point of a car. Ways of automatically comparing "carprints" to standards and communicating "exceptions" to the train dispatcher are being tested.

CONCLUSIONS

1 The methods employed for measuring and analyzing lateral and vertical forces at the wheel-rail interface appeared to give generally acceptable and meaningful results, although there is room for refinement and improvement.

2 Results from this study allowed development of plausible hypotheses for explaining the phenomena responsible for specific wheel-rail problems and provided feasible directional guides for relief.

3 Experimentally designed collection of data of this type can raise pertinent questions and supply unusual insights into many other subject areas of the car-rail system.

4 Preliminary findings that various force measurements or relationships meet signature criteria under defined conditions encourage prospects of successful extension of techniques into mechanized track inspection, automatic monitoring and detection of abnormally behaving cars, and more immediate evaluation of the effect of car component changes.

There is a great need for additional and continuing work to secure experimentally controlled factual data which adequately describes the dynamics of the car-rail system under a wide range of conditions. Such "field" measurements, in addition to furnishing direct information, would contribute necessary support for verification of mathematical models, development of computer simulations, and design of test lab facilities.

ACKNOWLEDGMENTS

The authors make special acknowledgment of the competent work performed by Brewer Engineering Laboratories, Inc., in delivering the necessary transducer and measurement skills to fulfill the terms of a very exacting contract. Deep appreciation is extended to the respective managements of the QCM and B&LE railroads who have financially supported our efforts and in many other ways inspired and encouraged us. Finally, we thank the personnel of both railroads who participated in the actual tests and various representatives of other companies and universities who furnished component parts and/or valuable advice.

DISCUSSION

W. W. Hay, *University of Illinois, Urbana, Ill.* The opportunity to review and comment upon the paper "Measurement and Analysis of Wheel-Rail Forces" by Messrs. Peterson, Freeman, and Wandrisco is welcome because of the significance the findings have for railroad engineering. These studies constitute a long overdue effort to establish the actual loadings transmitted from car to rail during the various stages of its passage over a length of track. The study is noteworthy in its emphasis upon the relation between car and track. It stands as a much-to-be desired recognition of the car and track as constituting a system of interdependent elements and forces.

The concept of instrumenting the cars and track to obtain instantaneous values of the forces is admirable. This, and the way in which that data was secured, analyzed, and interpreted is a notable accomplishment on the part of all concerned with the project.

Before commenting upon the excellence and significance of the findings, a word or two might be in order concerning the basic theories and procedures. The free-body diagram of Fig. 3 must be recognized as a simplification of the several forces at work. The track experiences bending, deflections, and lateral stress which will change somewhat the vertical reactions V_L and V_R of Fig. 3 and Fig. 16. Rails may tilt inward or outward depending upon the position of the rail on the tie (acting through the tieplate) and the support under the ties. The ties also are subject to bending. The rail experiences lateral bending and torsion. Axle journal loadings may not be vertical as shown. Bending in the truck frames is not included nor is bending in the bolster. Center plate scoring, bending, and binding may also affect the way the loads are transmitted to the journal. Uneven cargo distribution within the car may also have an effect upon the loads recorded.

More data on the track and its reaction would have been a helpful addition to the study. A record of track deflection, bending stress in the rails (both lateral and vertical), and some representative values of the modulus of elasticity of the track support would have provided better understanding of the data. The rate of rail vibration could also have been included.

The data and analysis as presented are, neverthe- less, sufficiently close to reality to disclose important relations.

The report treats in rather full detail the effect on the various force elements of differences in car truck design. The following comments will be more concerned with the effects of those forces on the track.

The forces involved and the uniform repetitive track loading at any given point from the passage of unit trains may offer one rational explanation for the initial formation and growth of rail shells. The finite element analyses of residual stresses by Dr. G. C. Martin indicates lateral forces of the magnitude secured in these tests to be sufficient to set up plastic flow and residual stresses within the rail head.[1] This study indicates the frequent occurrence of loadings sufficiently high to account for the frequent occurrence of shelly formation under heavy wheel loads within the concepts of Dr. Martin's hypothesis. A further relating of these two studies would seem to be warranted.

The value of continuous welded rail (CWR) is clearly demonstrated both in the text discussion and in the comparisons of Table 4. These findings give the track engineer an additional quantitative argument for extending CWR installations at a rapid rate.

The study clearly points out the need to pay more attention to excellence in track geometry so as to reduce to a minimum the number of "triggering" situations encountered in the passage of a wheel, car, or train. One is constrained, in this connection, to make mention of the need to strive for the sometimes neglected attribute of quality in track maintenance rather than more production, i.e., a maximum number of track feet worked per day — regardless of weather, season of the year, or type of tie or ballast. This study also gives emphasis to the need to measure and evaluate track geometry in the loaded condition, a need that calls for more widespread use of track geometry measuring cars heavy enough to simulate the loadings of revenue equipment.

There is further indicated a possible need to revise the conventional approach to designing and maintain-

---

[1] "The Influence of Wheel-Rail Contact Forces on the Formation of Rail-Shells," by G. C. Martin and W. W. Hay, University of Illinois, Civil Engineering Studies, Transportation Series No. 5, December 1970.

ing superelevation. The design of a procedure that takes into account differences in wheel loads, height of center of gravity, truck design and spacing, in addition to the conventional terms – degree of curve and train speed – is a challenging problem.

The effect of degree of curvature in generally increasing the severity of dynamic response is clearly evident in the several graphs and tabulations. This relation suggests that extra energy and money devoted to curve reduction, especially in new line location and construction, may offer attractive economic benefits.

The instantaneous L/V ratio is shown as reaching rather high values. Just what constitutes a derailing ratio is a subject of current debate. Values as low as 1.10 or even lower have been held sufficient for derailment. The values recorded in these tests attain that magnitude or greater, and may provide an answer thereby to some unexplained instances of derailment.

The findings will be awaited with much interest of the data to be collected by the test car being designed to accomplish real-time analysis and evaluation of data with on-the-spot "exception" reporting.

D. J. Reynolds, The Buckeye Steel Castings Co., Columbus, Ohio. Railroading is traditionally and reasonably divided into mechanical departments, concerned with track and structures. This paper demonstrates that an occasional happy combination of these two interests, with the usual 90 percent perspiration, can lead to serendipity. As the authors point out, this type of research can supply unusual insights into several areas of the railroad system.

To summarize very briefly some of the figures and graphs of the text, it appears that maximum dynamic forces are around 40 percent lower on welded rail than on jointed rail. It is very reasonable to suppose that rail wear and wheel wear are correspondingly reduced. It is also possible that a higher reduction might occur at higher speeds than the 35 mph at which the bulk of the test program was executed.

Next, it seems that the roller-bearing car develops dynamic forces about 13 percent higher than the plain-bearing car. Third, the car modified with lateral pads seems to reduce maximum dynamic forces, both vertical and lateral, by 30 percent under the plain-bearing car, or 45 percent under the unmodified roller-bearing car.

Recent indications from two railroads confirm that this pleasing reduction in maximum force is translated into exactly the same reduction in wheel wear.

The paper draws attention to the direct relation between variations of vertical and lateral forces, and it appears from the test records that for momentary periods in the passage of a car, one or even both rails can be urged inward by the wheels resting on it.

This is one of those facts which, like Columbus and the egg, is rather obvious when explained. But until I heard Mr. Peterson's explanation, I would not have thought it possible.

I find it difficult to give warm approval to the use of the L/V ratio. The ratio of lateral to vertical force at a wheel has traditionally been a measure of derailment tendency; when the lateral exceeds 0.6 of vertical force, derailment has been considered imminent. But this paper clearly establishes that one wheel affects the other; even when one wheel loses all vertical load, the opposite wheel can still resist inward movement and thus oppose derailment. While maintaining a due regard for the wisdom of our ancestors, it seems to me that it would now be a step forward to measure and add the lateral force at both wheels and divide by the vertical force at the outer wheel. This concept of net lateral force per axle is illustrated in several of the authors' graphs.

Two areas which have not been commented on in the paper are the effect of braking conditions and the effect of track lubricators.

With present truck and brake design, when the brakes go on, wheels and axles are pressed to the limits of the side-frames, whatever these may be, and they have no opportunity to accommodate themselves radially to curves. Thus the truck is more-or-less dragged in jerks around a curve with consequent high wear. Test data on lateral curve forces with and without braking would be of real usefulness.

Regarding track oilers, there is some indication that a reasonable number of oilers on curves may extend wheel and rail life by a factor of the order of 30 percent, and I would appreciate the authors' comment.

To conclude, I quote the paper's beginning sentence: "There are compelling reasons for wanting to know what occurs at the wheel-rail interface..."

We can now see that reductions of at least 50 percent in dynamic vertical and lateral forces are possible. That is to say, we can see the possibility, on our technological horizon, of doubling the life of wheels and rails. And since all the energy for wear comes from the draw-bar, we may expect to reduce draw-bar pull and make great savings in fuel consumption and even in locomotive purchases.

These are indeed compelling reasons for following along on the lines of research that this paper has defined.

CLOSURE

The written commentaries of Dr. W. W. Hay and Mr. D. J. Reynolds are appreciated by the authors.

Several of the comments suggested expansion of the measurement system for various purposes. We wish to report that the special B. & L. E. car (number A283) with the A/D and mini-computer equipment mentioned in the paper has been fully implemented. It is being used regularly to inspect track and evaluate car performance under a variety of conditions.

In the process of track inspection, specific locations of track have been found where dynamic force measurements indicated that potentially hazardous conditions may exist. Figure C-1 is a compressed

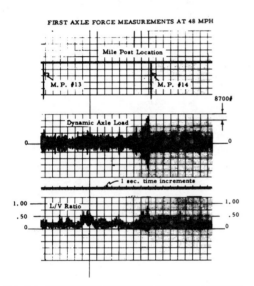

FIRST AXLE FORCE MEASUREMENTS AT 48 MPH

FIG. C-1 COMPRESSED COMPUTER PRODUCED GRAPHS OF SELECTED 1st AXLE REACTIONS AT A TYPICAL "BAD" SPOT

graphical example of the force traces for a small portion of a continuous main line measurement "run." Note the extreme axle loading just south of Milepost 14. Subsequent visual inspection of this exact location revealed the conditions depicted in the photograph of Fig. C-2. Other less obvious abnormalities have been detected at other locations and pertinent information furnished to the Maintenance of Way Department. In addition, the dynamic track geometry measurement capabilities of the existing D.O.T. car have been utilized through several trips over the B. & L. E. Railroad; and we are now attempting to correlate the simultaneously incurred dynamic force measurements with the dynamic track geometry — as Dr. Hay suggests.

FIG. C-2 PHOTOGRAPH OF EXACT "BAD" SPOT LOCATION OF FIGURE C-1

Since the paper was written, a host of additional car designs have been tested and evaluated. We have found that it is indeed practicable to rank such design modification in regard to the dynamic measurements made over a given section of track. Table C-1, representing only 12 of the over 30 design variations tested, is intended to illustrate that simplified summary "weighted" rankings can be generated for stipulated track sections. The weight assigned is dependent upon the investigator's appraisal of the relative importance of the individually measured parameters.

Mr. Reynolds makes some rather unqualified statements as to the benefits of lateral springing (pads). The authors wish to point out that only a very small portion of collected data was published in this paper and, in light of more comprehensive data, it is hazardous to make such specific quantified conclusions. The degree of benefit is dependent upon a number of factors, such as the statistical level at which evaluated, the speed, the degree of curvature, the other characteristics of the car, and the nature of the track section. Nevertheless, it is always rewarding to learn that practical experience supports our experimental findings, and a significant decrease in dynamic force levels *does* imply that wheel and rail wear should be reduced. Statistics associated with two years of in-service usage of a lateral pad equipped car versus otherwise identical cars on the QCM confirm that the life expectancy of the wheels for this case will be increased by about 20 percent. We are now attempting to determine if additional benefits can be derived by other modifications. Accordingly, we have tested the same car with increased lateral pad deflection, with a different pad material, with a capability of longitudinal springing, with differential axles, and with various designs of three axle trucks.

TABLE C-1

EXAMPLE OF A SIMPLE CAR DESIGN RANKING SCHEME

WEIGHTED RANKINGS

2 σ Level On 10° Curve At 30 MPH

	Weighting Factors:	4	5	6	2	3	1		
				Dynamic Forces					
Car Design		Wheel Lat.	Net Axle Lat.	L/V Ratio	Axle Vert.	Axle Rock	Wheel Vert.	Total	Overall Rank
QCM - Wide Adaptor - Natural Rubber Pad		4	20	6	10	15	4	59	1
QCM - Free Wheel		12	5	36	12	3	1	69	2
QCM - Wide Pedestal - Natural Rubber Pad		8	15	24	2	18	3	70	3
QCM - Barber - Natural Rubber Pad		16	10	42	6	6	5	85	4
QCM - Wide Adaptor - Butyl Rubber Pad		28	25	48	4	12	2	119	5
B&LE - With HS6 Snubbers		20	40	12	20	24	10	126	6
QCM - Barber		24	35	30	14	21	7	131	7
QCM - Barber - Butyl Rubber Pad		32	30	54	8	9	6	139	8
B&LE - Standard		40	45	18	24	30	11	168	9
QCM - 3 Axle - Metallastic		36	50	66	18	33	8	211	10
KCS - 3 Axle - Natural Rubber Pad		48	60	60	16	27	12	223	11
QCM - 3 Axle - Plate		44	55	72	22	36	9	238	12

At the present time, we are not in a position to report on the results of tests conducted to investigate the significance of braking in curves. Plans call for future tests to be aimed at evaluation of the effects of additional combinations of the variables in operating procedures, car designs, and wear-induced conditions for both the car and the track structure.

ERRATA TO PAPER 71-WA/RT-4

1. The equation following (8) on page 4 which now reads "and since $L_N + L_R = 0$, then" should read "and since $L_N + L_L - L_R = 0$, then"

2. "Cumulative" was misspelled in the caption of Fig. 6.

3. On page 11, there is a missing decimal place in "welded" column of Table 4, line 5. It should read .85 instead of 85.

4. The 4th line on the right-hand side of page 18 should begin "this is equivalent," instead of "this equivalent."

Chapter 5

Track
Materials

TEXT 38

Appendix 3–c

Specifications for Spring Washers for Use in Special Trackwork

This is the final report on this research project, submitted as information, and it consists of two parts: (1) The results of a five-year investigation of the causes of loss in tension in frog bolts leading to specifications for spring washers for frog bolts, and (2) suggested specifications for spring washers for use on frog bolts.

Part 1

Crossing Frog Bolt Tension Tests

Digest

This investigation was made for tne purpose of determining the reactive characteristics of spring washers required for the economical maintenance of adequate bolt tension in crossing and turnout frog bolts. Tests were conducted to determine the loss of bolt tension as related to the rate of wear of the crossing assembly during a five-year period under actual service conditions on six crossing frogs, including the bolted-rail, manganese insert, and solid manganese types, and one railbound manganese turnout frog. In addition, dynamic measurements were made of the change in bolt tension and impact ·or "shock" loads in the main bolts of a main track bolted rail crossing in high-speed territory. This is the first known thorough investigation of the loss in tension in frog bolts, and the causes thereof.

The service tests involved the measurement of bolt tension loss, pull-in or wear of the frog assembly, and nut back-off, all requiring specially designed gages. The test cycles included initial bolt tension of 40,000, 30,000 and 25,000 lb. Several kinds of single-coil washers, two designs of plate washers, and one shape of double-coil washer were tested with the 1⅜-in bolts in the main line crossing. The advantage of heat-treated nuts and hardened flat plate washers as bearing surfaces for the spring washers was investigated. Three designs of locknuts were included in the service tests.

Summary of Results

The more important results from these tests are summarized as follows:

1. In the bolted-rail and manganese insert types of crossings, the No. 1 position bolts (nearest to the flangeway intersection) lost, by far, the greatest amount of tension. This was attributed to a greater amount of wear of the crossing assembly at those bolts. The bolt tension measurements under traffic also indicated there were relatively large impact or shock loads on the No. 1 bolts of a bolted-rail crossing. This caused further dissipation of the tension by the spring washers imbedding into the nut and corner brace. Therefore, the chief causes of the loss in tension of frog bolts were found to be the wear of the crossing assembly and the imbedding and abrasion of the spring washers into the nuts and crossing braces, resulting from the larger shock loads on the bolts. Some of the larger shock loads increased the bolt tension from 40,000 lb (static) to 55,000 lb total. It was this excess load that caused indentation and abrasion on the small bearing areas of the spring washers. Bolt stretch and nut back-off were found to be unimportant as far as the dissipation of the bolt tension was concerned.

2. The use of hardened parts next to single-coil spring washers was beneficial in retarding the rate of loss in bolt tension for the medium reaction washers, but not for the high reaction washers. It is judged that more benefit would be derived if the corner braces in a crossing were heat treated, rather than adding a hardened flat plate washer next to the corner brace.

3. The double-coil spring washers tested held the tension in the No. 1 bolts above 20,000 lb twice as long as the single-coil spring washers. This increased efficiency was attributed to (1) the greater bearing areas provided by the double-coil type, and (2) the superior release curve.

4. The locknuts were found to be of no significant benefit in the retention of bolt tension. No locknuts backed off the bolts. None of the finger-free nuts backed off the bolts that had some remaining tension. These nuts did back off of some bolts with no tension, but in several instances such was not the case.

5. From the results of the service tests, it was found that (1) the initial tension should be 40,000 lb (plus or minus 5000 lb), and (2) the minimum tension should be 10,000 lb. The value of initial tension is the practical limit for manual wrenching, and the lower limit of 10,000 lb was determined from the service test measurements as that necessary to prevent excessive movement and wear between the parts of the crossing assembly.

Recommendation

The recommended test procedure and minimum reactive pressure for spring washers are as follows:

Place washer in the testing machine between steel plates having smoothly ground or machined surfaces and a Brinell hardness of not to exceed 150, which will provide bearing surfaces corresponding in hardness to the nuts and corner braces in crossings. Load assembly to 40,000 lb and take dial reading of the distance between platens of the testing machine. Increase load to 60,000 lb to include a simulated shock load of 20,000 lb. Release load to give the same dial reading as measured at 40,000 lb. From this point, release the platens 0.030 in additional, at which point the reactive load shall be not less than 10,000 lb.

Introduction

This investigation was initiated in 1948 for the purpose of determining the minimum reactive characteristics required of spring washers for economical and efficient maintenance of adequate bolt tension in crossing and turnout frog bolts. Because of the lack of information on the loss in tension in the main bolts of crossing frogs, a comprehensive series of field service tests was planned and executed. These service tests included seven crossing frogs of three types and one turnout frog. The field work involved the measurement of the loss in tension of the frog bolts, nut back-off, wear of the frog assembly, and observations of the effect of crushing of the nut and the side of the crossing arm by the several types of spring washers used. The causes for loss in bolt tension are: (1) wear of the assembled parts, (2) bolt stretch, (3) nut back-off, and (4) imbedding of the spring washers into the contact surfaces as a result of the shock loads. The field measurements gave complete information on the first three causes, but not for the fourth item because the imbedding effect could not be included in the out-to-out measurements of wear.

In the early stage of the field tests it was developed that bolts in certain positions lost a large amount of bolt tension, while others had only moderate reductions. Later, impact loads were measured in the main bolts of a bolted-rail crossing in high-speed territory. This test provided valuable information as to the cause of the variation in the loss in bolt tension with respect to bolt position and other practical aspects. The results of that test were published in the Proceedings, Vol. 54, 1953, pages 1002–1034. In the latter years of the field investigation, the primary objective was to determine how the dissipation of the bolt tension could be retarded by testing different types of spring washers and using hardened parts next to the washers. The first progress report covering the service tests was published in the Proceedings, Vol. 52, 1951, pages 532–553.

Test Procedure

In order to make the measurements on the frogs with long bolts, it was necessary to design a long caliper extensometer for measurement of the bolt tension, and an out-to-out gage to determine the wear of the parts of the crossing assemblies, and to revise the back-off gages for the large nuts. A second out-to-out gage was designed because consistent results could not be obtained with the original one which did not have a spring for holding it in place in order to eliminate the effect of variations in the technique of taking the readings. The bolt tension extensometer was similar to those used for track bolts and was entirely satisfactory.

Prior to beginning the service tests, a laboratory calibration of heat-treated $1\frac{1}{4}$-in and $1\frac{3}{8}$-in diameter frog bolts of lengths from 8 to 18 in was made in a compression-tension testing machine to determine the bolt tension constants per dial division (0.0002 in) of the extensometer for effective bolt lengths ranging from 7 to 17 in. For the purpose of the measurement of bolt tension the effective bolt length is the distance from working face of the bolt head to the mid-thickness of the nut. This length was determined in the field with outside calipers.

At first, all cycles of bolt tension loss were conducted with 40,000 lb initial tension. Later, supplementary information was obtained for 25,000 and 30,000 lb initial tension during the summer cycles. It was found in the crossings that were two to four years old when the tests were begun in 1948, that 2-man wrenching was required to tighten some of the $1\frac{3}{8}$ and $1\frac{1}{4}$-in diameter bolts to 40,000 lb, and later some bolts required 3 men. In the bolted-rail crossings carrying slow-speed traffic, it was necessary to renew some of the bolts because of battered threads which prevented wrenching them to 40,000 lb tension. At Warsaw, Ind., the test of the heat-treated bolted-rail crossing was started when the crossing was 14 months old. Most of the $1\frac{3}{8}$-in by 14-in bolts could be tightened to 40,000 lb by 1 man. However, later some of the bolts required 2 men. It, therefore, was assumed that 40,000 lb bolt tension was the limit of practicality, because most frog bolt wrenching in track is done manually.

Spring Washers, Hardened Parts and Locknuts Used

Several designs of single-coil spring washers, one of the double-coil type and two designs of plate washers, were included in the tests to cover a wide range of reactive spring pressures, variations in the characteristic bearing areas of the three types of washers, and to check the capacity of each for retention of bolt tension. Release curves for all of the spring washers tested with the $1\frac{3}{8}$-in and $1\frac{1}{4}$-in bolts are presented in Figs. 1* to 6, incl. Table 1* is included to give the dimensions and other physical properties of the washers. Initially, the Reliance Division, Eaton Manufacturing Company, furnished experimental single-coil spring washers for both sizes of bolts, but these are now included in their line of Improved Frog and Crossing Hy-Crome spring washers. These washers

---

* All figures and tables referred to in this report are represented at the end of the report.

are sometimes given the designation of wide bearing, because of their greater width. The same company, at the request of the AAR research staff, also furnished ¾-in square single-coil, high-reaction experimental spring washers for 1⅜-in bolts, known as "Heavy-Duty Hy-Crome". In addition, that company furnished a small lot of "Double Hy-Crome" washers for 1⅜-in bolts. These washers differ from the double-coil Thackeray in that the ends were bent inward. This feature provided two improvements over the Thackeray type, which was not included in the field tests: (1) a better release curve, and (2) less gouging of the bearing surfaces by the ends of the washer. Hubbard & Company furnished some experimental single-coil spring washers for 1⅜-in bolts, having a cross section larger than their Super Service line of washers. Erico Products, Inc., Cleveland, Ohio, furnished two designs of plate washers for 1⅜-in bolts—the type D-5 compression and the S-300 plate washers. Type D-5 consisted of five ⅛-in plates, cemented together and the S-300 was a single plate, 0.30-in thick. Each plate or ply was 3 in square and had a spherical shape. The Pennsylvania Railroad specifications for the 1⅜-in and 1¼-in spring washers tested stipulate a minimum reactive spring pressure of 300 lb when the washers are released from a load of 60,000 lb, 0.17 in and 0.15 in, respectively. The PRR washers have low reactive pressures.

During the first year of testing of the main line crossing, observations of the imbedding of the single-coil washers into the nuts and corner braces indicated that the medium and high-reaction washers imbedded deeper than the low-reaction washers. For the purpose of increasing the effectiveness of the spring washers by reducing the dissipation of bolt tension from imbedding, ASA heavy heat-treated medium-carbon nuts were obtained from the Oliver Iron and Steel Corporation, and heat-treated flat plate washers were specially made for use next to the corner braces. The hardened nuts had a Brinell hardness range from 250 to 300, and the flat plate washers had a hardness close to 400 Brinell. These hardened parts were tested in two corners of the eastward crossing at Warsaw, Ind. Before heat treatment the medium-carbon nuts ranged from 130 to 170 Brinell.

Locknuts were also tested on one of the manganese insert crossings and in the two bolted-rail crossings at Warsaw. Hexagon and square Elastic Stop Nuts, hexagon Security Nuts, and square MacLean–Fogg Unitary Nuts No. 3 were included in the field tests. All of the locknuts were made of low–carbon steel.

MAIN TRACK CROSSING AT WARSAW, IND.

Test Conditions

The crossing in which the bolt tension tests were conducted is in the eastward main of the double-track line of the Pennsylvania Railroad and a single-track branch line of the New York Central System, Warsaw, Ind. The PRR eastward main carried 18 million gross tons of traffic per annum, consisting of both passenger and freight trains operating at medium high speed. The NYC branch line had 2 million gross tons of freight traffic per annum which operated at speeds below 20 mph. In 1949, when the test was started, the PRR used both diesel and steam power, some of the latter being of the 4–4–6–4 type having four cylinders, divided drive and rigid frame. By 1953, when the field tests were concluded, little steam power was in use by the PRR. The NYC trains were hauled by moderate size steam locomotives, principally of the Mikado (2–8–2) type.

Both crossing frogs were of bolted construction, 3-rail design, with heat-treated 131 RE rail and flangeway fillers. Each crossing was supported on longitudinal timbers, consisting of three 7-in by 9-in creosoted oak ties bolted together, with a width of 21 in under the PRR rails, and stone ballast. The test included all of the 48 main or shoulder bolts, 1⅜ in by 14 in. At the beginning of the bolt tension test the eastward crossing had been in service 14 months. Fig. 7 is included to show the test conditions for the second cycle of loss in bolt tension. Figs. 8 and 9 show the special gages being used for measurement of bolt tension and pull-in of the eastward crossing at Warsaw.

Test Data

Tables 2 to 10, incl., give a summary of the measurements of bolt tension and pull-in of the crossing assembly and a description of spring washers, nuts, etc., used in each corner of the crossing for all of the nine cycles of loss in bolt tension conducted in the eastward crossing. In addition, most of the tables include information on the number of bolts having less than 20,000 and 10,000 lb final tension at the end of the test cycles. For good performance, a spring washer should first effect the minimum average loss in tension, and second, have the least number of bolts below a certain desired minimum bolt tension, which will be discussed later. Although these tests were conducted in one diamond which carried the same traffic, the condition of support of a corner, fit and state of wear of the assembled parts can affect the relative rate of loss in bolt tension in the four corners of a crossing. For the 4-year test period the total wear at the No. 1 bolts was the largest for the NE corner and the smallest for the SE corner.

Some data were taken for 25,000 and 30,000 lb initial bolt tension for comparison with 40,000 lb tension. In the first cycle (Table 2) the performance of the Type D-5 compression washers was the best, and the Hubbard washers were a little more effective in retaining the tension than the PRR low-reaction washers. In the second cycle (Table 3) the D-5 washers lost some of their effectiveness because at the end of the cycle, 9 out of 12 had one or more broken layers. The Hubbard and Heavy-Duty Hy-Chrome washers were about equal in performance. The PRR washers had the largest loss in tension. By this time it was quite well established that the bolts in the No. 1 position lost the greatest amount of tension, with the Nos. 2 and 3 following in the order named. The nuts and corner braces were examined for abrasion and imbedding. More imbedding was found at the No. 1 bolts than at the other positions. Likewise, more imbedding also occurred with the Hubbard and Heavy-Duty Hy-Crome spring washers than with the PRR washers. The Type D-5 washers provided a more favorable bearing area, and imbedding and abrasion were the least.

After this cycle, the latter washers were removed because of the excessive breakage and were replaced with the newly developed S-300 plate washers, 0.30 in thick. Also at the close of the second cycle, the locknut test was transferred from the eastward to the westward crossing. The locknuts were left in the SW corner of the eastward crossing because they were in better condition than the available used nuts. All of the locknuts were of low carbon, and it was desired to use medium carbon nuts in the bolt tension test to represent the practice of most of the Member Roads. The performance of the locknuts will be discussed in a separate section of this report. Because of the excessive nut imbedding by the Heavy-Duty Hy-Crome washers, ASA heavy M. C. nuts were placed on the SE corner, releasing the regular medium carbon nuts which were the PRR standard.

Table 4 gives a summary of the third cycle with the changes mentioned, but with 25,000 lb initial bolt tension. In this cycle the S-300 washers were best in performance and the high-reaction washers in the SE corner ranked second. The Hubbard and the PRR washers were equal as to tension lost in the No. 1 bolts, but the former were slightly better than the latter in the other two positions.

For the next cycle (Table 5) the nuts were changed for the experimental washers, as indicated in the table. This was for the purpose of increasing their effectiveness in holding up bolt tension, if possible. In this long cycle of 6.70 months with 40,000 lb initial tension, there was not much difference in the performance of the three kinds of single-coil washers. The S–300 washers were a little more effective in holding up bolt tension, particularly at the No. 1 bolts which had two washers nested normally. At the end of this cycle, 9 out of 16 of the S–300 washers were cracked. It was apparent that the heat-treated nuts did not increase the effectiveness of the Heavy-Duty Hy-Crome washers in the SE corner, because the washers had crushed the corner braces and dissipated about as much tension as in the second cycle, Table 3.

For the fifth cycle (Table 6), all of the crossing corners were provided with the ASA heavy medium carbon nuts, and in the SE corner they were heat treated. A second or improved lot of S–300 plate washers was furnished for the SW corner of the crossing. The improved S–300 washers were said to have improved metallurgy and heat treatment. In this cycle with 30,000 lb initial tension, the PRR washers were more effective than the Hubbard washers. There was no explanation for this other than the difference in support of the two corners, such as one corner swinging more than the other. The S–300 washers showed quite superior performance for the retention of the bolt tension for this 5-month cycle, and the Heavy-Duty Hy-Crome washers were the next best. No bolts in these two corners had less than 10,000 lb final tension. Two of the S–300 washers were cracked in this cycle.

Prior to starting the sixth cycle (Table 7), some hardened flat plate washers were made to use to eliminate the imbedding of the spring washers into the corner braces This was the simplest procedure for conducting the test, because of the complications of providing heat-treated corner braces. The Heavy-Duty Hy-Crome and Hubbard washers were provided with the hardened plate washers and heat-treated nuts, as indicated in the table. The hardened parts improved the performance of the Hubbard washers, but not that of the Heavy-Duty Hy-Crome washers. The performance of the S–300 washers was slightly better than that of the Hubbard washers. However, the SW corner had the advantage of two S–300 washers placed back to back on each of the No. 1 bolts. In this cycle of 6.93 months, only 2 of the bolts with S–300 plate washers had final tension of less than 20,000 lb, as compared with 4 of the Hubbard washers. All bolts had a final tension of more than 10,000 lb, except 2 with PRR washers. The improved lot of S–300 washers had much less breakage than the first lot. In two cycles, or approximately a year's service, the first lot had 9 out of 16 cracked, compared with 3 out of 16 of the improved lot.

For cycle 7 (Table 8), the Reliance Double Hy-Crome spring washers were substituted for the S–300 washers in the SW corner, and the construction in the other three corners remained the same as in cycle 6. Because of the severe imbedding of the medium and high-reaction single-coil spring washers having quite small contact areas, it was decided to investigate the double-coil design which has larger bearing areas against the nut and corner brace. No hardened parts were used with the PRR washers as it was desired to use that corner as the basis of comparison. During this 4.61-month cycle, with initial bolt tension of 30,000 lb, the PRR washers had a loss in bolt tension of 46 percent, compared with 25 percent for each of the other 3 kinds of test washers. The double-coil washers, without hardened parts, performed as well as the medium and high-reaction single-coil spring washers with heat-treated nuts and hardened flat plates. In addition to the double-coil washers providing larger bearing areas on the nuts and corner braces, they had the best release curve (Fig. 2) from zero to 0.037 in release from a load of 30,000 lb.

In cycle 8, the Reliance Heavy-Duty Hy-Crome single-coil washers were retired from the test to make room for new Reliance Frog and Crossing Hy-Crome washers with the same hardened parts. It was planned to compare the latter washers with the Hubbard washers, both with hardened parts. The Hubbard washers were replaced with new ones of the same design so that the comparison would be on an equal basis. In addition, it was decided to take data on the No. 1 bolts at approximately 3-month intervals, except those with the double-coil washers. Because this was the first cycle of 40,000 lb initial tension with the double-coil washers, the bolts were not disturbed until the end of the cycle. Table 9, consisting of four parts, covers cycle 8. Parts 1, 2 and 3 of the table give a summary of the 3-month cycles for each No. 1 bolt having single-coil washers. In the first 3-month cycle (Part 1), the Hubbard washers performed the best and the PRR washers showed the largest loss in tension. All of the washers performed better in the second 3-month cycle (Part 2), and only 1 bolt out of 12 (1–E with PRR washer) dropped below 20,000 lb tension. Part 3 is the average of the two 3-month cycles, which shows that the 2 medium-reaction spring washers with hardened parts held the bolt tension above 20,000 lb. The PRR washers had 2 bolts in 4 with tension less than 20,000 lb. Part 4 of Table 9 gives a summary of the 6½-month cycle for the double-coil washers, and only the Nos. 2 and 3 bolts for the other 3 corners of the crossing. It will be noted that all bolts having the double-coil washers had a final tension in excess of 20,000 lb. The effectiveness of the double-coil washers in the retention of bolt tension was far superior to that of any single-coil spring washer with or without hardened parts. The average remaining tension of the No. 1 bolts with double-coil spring washers after 6½ months was 26,500 lb. This value is about the same as shown in Part 3 of the table for the single-coil spring washers with hardened parts for only 3 months' service. Table 10 includes data for cycle 9 for all 4 corners of the crossing for a period of 2⅝ months. Crossing wear was not measured for this short cycle. In this cycle the Frog and Crossing Hy-Crome washers with hardened parts and the double-coil washers performed better than the other washers. There was only 1 bolt having less than 20,000 lb final tension in the corner with PRR washers, and 2 bolts in the corner with the Hubbard washers.

Table 11 is presented to give a summary of all cycles of bolt tension loss in which 40,000 lb initial tension was applied. This table, in addition to ranking the spring washers in the four columns on the right, also can be used for conveniently appraising the value of the several washers as to retaining bolt tension, and the benefits of the hardened parts. The best comparison as to cycles can be made from the even numbered cycles, which included a winter season. Prior to the fourth cycle, the PRR and the Hubbard washers were reversed as to corners to determine what effect the change in location would have on the loss in tension. The effect on all bolts with the PRR washer was to reduce the average tension loss from 62 to 51 percent. The average tension loss for all bolts with Hubbard washers increased from 50 to 53 percent. The benefits derived by adding the heat-treated nuts and hardened flat plates can be judged by comparing cycles 4 and 6. In the case of the Hubbard washers, tension loss in the No. 1 bolts dropped from 60 to 46 percent, or a reduction of 23 percent. For all bolts, the corresponding percentages were 53, 39, and 26 percent. The same comparison for the Reliance Heavy-Duty Hy-Crome washers for the No. 1 bolts was a drop from 65 to 56 percent, or a reduction of 14 percent. For all bolts there was no change in the percentage loss of bolt tension, this being 50 percent in both cycles. For the S–300 plate washers, cycles 4 and 6 showed for all bolts a drop in percentage loss from 46 to 36 percent, or a reduction of 22 percent, in favor of the second, or improved lot of washers. A part of this increased effectiveness may be attributed to the improvement in the manufacture of the washers, resulting in less breakage, and also because in cycle 6 the No. 1 bolts had two washers nested back-to-back, which was more effective in retaining bolt tension than with two washers nested normally as in the fourth cycle.

In the columns at the right of Table 11, the ranking percentages are based on the performance of the PRR washers without hardened parts. The performance of the double-coil washers for all bolts (last column) was outstanding in that the tension loss was less than one-half of that of the control washers. The next most effective washers were the S–300 with 77 percent, and type D–5 washers, 79 percent. Hubbard washers had a percentage of 87 and the Heavy-Duty Hy-Crome washers, 96 percent.

PENNSYLVANIA RAILROAD–GULF, MOBILE & OHIO. RAILROAD CROSSINGS AT CHICAGO

Test Conditions

These crossings are of construction similar to those at Warsaw, Ind., except the rail is the 130 PS section, and the main bolts did not have a drive fit such as was the case of the eastward crossing at Warsaw. The two diamonds selected for bolt tension tests (Fig. 10) are in the PRR eastward "Panhandle" track and the double-track main line of the GM&O, near 37th St. and Campbell Ave., Chicago. The PRR traffic, amounting to approximately 4 million gross tons per annum, was slow-speed yard freight movements between their 59th St. yard and various industries and interchange points. The GM&O traffic included passenger and yard freight movements. All movements over the crossings were hauled by diesel locomotives, except some steam power was operated by the PRR. Most of the traffic was operated at slow speed because all trains were required to stop at the crossings. The rear portion of some of the long GM&O passenger trains attained speeds up to 30 mph. In 1952 the GM&O estimated its annual gross tons of traffic at 4.2 and 4.8 million for their northward and southward tracks, respectively. The crossings were supported by longitudinal bolted creosoted oak timbers under the PRR rails, and stone ballast. These crossings were installed by the PRR in September 1944.

Test Data

In crossing "C" (Fig. 10), the PRR specification spring washers were compared with the Hubbard experimental washers like those tested at Warsaw. In crossing "D", the Reliance Frog and Crossing Hy-Crome washers were compared with the PRR washers. All tests were made with the ASA regular, medium-carbon nuts and 1⅜-in by 14-in bolts already in use in the crossings. Two cycles each of 40,000 lb and 25,000 lb initial bolt tension were conducted, and the results are summarized in Tables 12 to 15, incl. Cycle 1 (Table 12) covered four months' service with 40,000 lb initial tension, and cycle 2 (Table 13) was for a longer cycle to develop the capacity of the spring washers for retaining tension over a long period. In cycle 1, the special test washers were slightly more effective than the PRR washers. The medium weight washers were the most effective for the bolts in the No. 1 position. In crossing "C", the Hubbard washers had only 3 bolts with less than 20,000 lb final tension, compared with 7 for the PRR washers. In crossing "D", the PRR washers had only 1 bolt with less than 20,000 lb tension, compared with 4 for the Frog and Crossing Hy-Crome spring washers. Cycle 2 (Table 13) was too long for good maintenance of bolt tension, but it served the purpose of giving the washers a more severe test. The special washers averaged 53 percent tension loss, compared with 61–62 percent for the PRR spring washers. In each half of each crossing over one-half of the bolts dropped below 20,000 lb tension. In each crossing, the special washers permitted fewer bolts to drop below 10,000 lb tension. Cycles 3 and 4 (Tables

14 and 15) were made with 25,000 lb initial bolt tension to develop information on the use of low bolt tension. Initial tension of 25,000 lb was decidedly inadequate for these long test cycles in which many of the bolts dropped below both 20,000 and 10,000 lb tension. In crossing "C" (Table 14), the PRR washers lost 43 percent tension, compared with 46 percent for the Hubbard washers. In crossing "D", the Frog and Crossing Hy-Crome washers were more effective in retaining the bolt tension than the PRR washers. In Table 15 the Hubbard washers had the lowest percentage loss in tension.

CHICAGO AND WESTERN INDIANA RAILROAD AND INDIANA HARBOR BELT RAILROAD BELT LINE CROSSINGS AT CHICAGO

Test Conditions

The four crossings shown in Fig. 11 were installed by the IHB in October 1946 for the purpose of conducting service tests with the solid and reversible insert manganese types of frogs, supported by longitudinally framed timbers on stone ballast and integrally welded steel T-beam substructures on asphalt macadam ballast. Crossings "A", "C", and "D" were selected for conducting bolt tension tests. Crossing "A", with a steel substructure, was included for comparison with crossing "C" on timbers to determine if the difference in the crossing supports would influence the loss in tension of the main bolts in these insert crossings. The continuous timbers for crossings "C" and "D" were placed under the IHB rails. Solid manganese crossing "D" differed from AREA Plan 771 in that the castings were made so that the guard and running rails abutted the external arms in the same plane, instead of having an offset between the two junctions. The castings also had integrally extended bottom plates. All of the joint bars for the external and internal joints were of the machined type, and the outer bar for each external joint was sloped on top to serve as a riser for the wheels. The castings were 6 in high to match the 105-lb Dudley rail section, which was also used in the insert crossings. All of the main bolts in the two designs of crossings were 1¼ in diameter, except the internal bolts of the solid crossings were 1⅜ in diameter.

The traffic consisted largely of interchange freight movements, hauled by diesel and steam power at first, with a gradual conversion to diesels. Most of the traffic operated at moderately slow speeds, except some of the north and south movements ranged up to 30 to 35 mph. The tonnage on the two tracks of the IHB was said to be about equal, and the northward C&WI track (operated by the Belt Railway of Chicago) carried more tonnage than the southward track. Therefore, the two insert crossings carried about the same tonnage during the test period, and the two solid crossings had a greater tonnage.

During the first four cycles a test was made in crossing "A" with hexagon Elastic Stop Nuts in the west half of the crossing, with and without spring washers, as indicated in Fig. 11. However, for the fourth cycle, the washers were moved from the SW to the NW corner. These results will be discussed later. At the beginning of these tests all of the spring washers were second hand except in the west half of insert crossing "C". Through an error, 1⅜-in washers were furnished for the 1¼-in bolts. The washers were replaced with the correct size at the beginning of cycle 3. At the beginning of cycle 4, new Standard Hy-Crome spring washers were placed in the east half of crossing "C" to obtain a comparison between new spring washers of two weights. At the same time new nuts were placed on all bolts, and all of the beveled washers and headlocks on the bolts were spot welded to the corner braces to prevent them from twisting when wrenching the bolts (thereby fouling points for measurement of pull-in), and to reduce the eccentric load on the bolts which may have dissipated tension by the spring washers imbedding into the nuts and beveled washers.[1] No change was made in the spring washers in crossing "D" and in the east half of crossing "A", except to replace broken ones with used ones of the same design, as indicated in Fig. 11.

For the three crossings, a preliminary tension loss cycle was conducted from October 1948 to April 1949, before it was possible to secure reliable data on crossing wear or pull-in. A second gage with spring tension to hold it in place was developed and it proved satisfactory. The preliminary test was made with 40,000 lb initial bolt tension, and crossings "A" and "C" had the same loss in tension, or 56 percent. These data indicated the bolts in the insert crossings lost from 79 to 89 percent tension in the No. 1 position. The corresponding values for the Nos. 2 and 3 positions were 45 to 70 percent and 6 to 28 percent, respectively. As in the bolted-rail crossings, this indicated that the No. 1 bolts in the insert crossings lost the greatest tension and constituted the major problem in maintaining adequate bolt tension. In crossing "C" the average loss in tension of all bolts with the Frog and Crossing Hy-Crome washers was 52 percent, compared with 59 percent for the lighter weight used Standard Hy-Crome washers. In crossing "D", solid manganese on timbers, the exterior $1\frac{1}{4}$-in bolts lost 65 percent tension and the $1\frac{1}{8}$-in interior bolts lost 69 percent tension. In the external arms, the No. 1 bolts nearest to the flangeway intersection lost the largest amount of tension and the bolts in position 4 had the least loss in tension. In the 6-hole interior joints, the middle and intermediate bolts, Nos. 3 and 2, lost the most tension and the No. 1 bolts in the end position showed a smaller loss in tension.

The next cycle, designated as No. 1, was also conducted with 40,000 lb initial tension and extended from June to November 1949, or about 5 months. The average loss in tension for all bolts in the insert crossings was 31 percent for "A" on the steel substructure, and 26 percent for "C" on framed timbers. In crossing "C", all bolts with the used Standard Hy-Crome washers lost an average of 27 percent tension, compared with 25 percent for the Reliance Frog and Crossing washers. The latter washers were of the $1\frac{3}{8}$-in size on $1\frac{1}{4}$-in bolts, which probably detracted from their effectiveness because of the loss of bearing area next to the periphery of the bolt. Crossing "D", solid manganese on framed timbers, had an average loss in tension of 32 percent for all bolts and the same percentage also applied to both the exterior and interior bolts. The pattern of percentage loss in tension of the bolts by position was quite similar to that for the preliminary cycle. In both of the foregoing cycles, the tension loss was greater in the solid crossing than that of the insert crossing "C", both being supported on timbers. However, it cannot be concluded that the solid type of crossing dissipates bolt tension more than the insert type because the former carried more traffic by being in the northward track.

The results of cycle 2 (40,000 lb initial tension) for the three crossings were published in the Proceedings, Vol. 52, 1951, pages 546–551. The data indicated for this 8-month cycle an average loss in tension of 45 percent for the insert crossing on steel support, compared with 32 percent for the insert crossing on timber. In crossing "C", the Frog and Crossing Hy-Crome washers showed an average loss in tension of 26 percent, compared with 38 percent for the used Standard Hy-Crome washers, or a reduction of 32 percent loss by the former, which were for $1\frac{3}{8}$-in bolts. Crossing "D" had an average loss in tension of 40 percent for all bolts and 42 and 38 percent for the interior and exterior bolts, respectively. The tension loss pattern for the internal joints was similar to a 6-hole joint in that the middle bolts lost the most tension and the end bolts the

---

[1] In the insert-type crossing, only the Nos. 1 and 2 bolts had beveled washers and headlocks. Since the inception of this investigation, Ramapo Ajax has adopted the practice of forging in one piece the washers and headlocks for the Nos. 1 and 2 bolts.

least. In the case of the external joints the loss in tension decreased by bolt positions 1, 3, 2, and 4. In the last-mentioned reference to the Proceedings, graphs of final tension and pull-in were presented for the two insert crossings. The plotted points in these graphs were not in good agreement with the combined release curves for the spring washer used and the bolt. Later it was determined that (1) the spring washer release curve taken on simulated bolted-rail construction parts was well below that taken on hardened blocks, and (2) an appreciable amount of bolt tension was dissipated by the shock loads[1] on the bolts, which caused the spring washers to imbed into the nuts and the side of the crossing assembly. The effect of this imbedding was not included in the pull-in measurements because the wear measurements were made from out-to-out of corner braces or joint bars. Consequently, it was decided to discontinue the graphical presentation.

Tables 16 to 22, incl., are presented to cover the remainder of the field tests conducted on the three Belt Line crossings. Cycle 3, with 25,000 lb initial tension, was too long for good maintenance of the insert crossings, but it did give the washers a more severe test. Crossing "A" lost an average of 41½ percent tension and the corresponding figure for crossing "C" was 54½ percent, for a period of 9 months, ended April 1951. This was the first cycle in which the west half of crossing "C" had 1¼-in Frog and Crossing Hy-Crome washers, replacing those for 1⅜-in bolts. In the upper portion of Table 17, it will be noted that the latter washers dropped in effectiveness. Those bolts lost 53 percent tension, compared with 56 percent for the used Standard Hy-Crome washers. Upon inspection of the imbedding of the washers into the nuts, it was found that the previous 1⅜-in washers had worn a collar on the nut and the 1¼-in washers had imbedded into the collar, which increased the loss in tension. Crossing "D", for a 6-month cycle, lost an average tension of 34½ percent, or 37 and 32 percent for the interior and exterior bolts, respectively. With only 25,000 lb initial tension, the interior bolts in the 3 positions lost approximately the same percentage tension, which was a departure from the previous pattern similar to a 6-hole track joint.

In cycle 4, Tables 18 and 19, crossings "A" and "C" were tested with 30,000 lb initial tension for different lengths of test periods. The insert crossing on the steel support lost 41½ percent tension in 6.4 months, and the crossing on timber lost 28½ percent in 5 months. Prior to cycle 4 for crossing "C", new nuts were applied to all main bolts, new Standard Hy-Crome washers were applied to the east half of the crossing and all beveled washers and headlocks were spot welded to the corner braces for reasons previously stated. In this crossing, bolts with the Frog and Crossing washers lost 24 percent tension, compared with 33 percent for the new Standard Hy-Crome washers, or a reduction of 27 percent. The medium weight washers were most effective for holding up the bolt tension in the No. 1 position—the critical one. Solid manganese crossing "D", with initial tension of 25,000 lb (Table 19), had too many bolts below 20,000 and 10,000 lb final tension. The cycle was too long because the bolts in each group lost their normal loss in tension pattern and tended to equalize the tension loss in each group. After cycle 4, tests were discontinued with the insert crossing on steel support (Crossing "A").

In cycle 5 (Table 20), initial bolt tension of 40,000 lb was used in crossings "C" and "D" for periods of 6.7 and 7.6 months, respectively. Relative percentages of loss in tension were 34 and 62½, respectively. In crossing "C", the Frog and Crossing washers were slightly more effective in retaining the tension than the Standard Hy-Crome washers. This difference was entirely for the No. 1 bolts. Because of the long cycle the

---

[1] The report on the Measurement of Shock Loads in Crossing Frog Bolts was published in the Proceedings, Vol. 54, 1953, pp. 1002–1034.

two groups of bolts in crossing "D" departed from their normal pattern of loss in tension, although it was slightly evident for the interior bolts. Only 2 bolts in crossing "C" dropped below 10,000 lb tension, compared with 12 for crossing "D"

Cycle 6 (Table 21) was conducted with 30,000 lb initial tension for crossings "C" and "D", for a period of 4½ months. Crossing "C" lost only 16 percent tension compared with 40 percent for solid crossing "D". In crossing "C" the Frog and Crossing washers held the tension loss to 14 percent, compared with 18 percent for the Standard Hy-Crome washers, and the number of bolts having less than 20,000 lb final tension were 3 and 6, respectively. No bolts dropped below 10,000 lb. The pattern of loss in tension of the interior bolts of crossing "D" was in good agreement with that of a 6-hole track joint in that the loss in tension was greatest at the middle bolts (No. 3) and smallest at the end bolts. A much larger number of bolts in the solid crossing dropped below 20,000 lb tension than in the insert crossing on timbers.

Table 22 gives the results of cycle 7 for solid crossing "D" with 40,000 lb initial tension and a service period of 6½ months. In this cycle the exterior bolts lost more tension than the interior bolts. However, considering all test cycles, the average tension lost was about the same for each group. Eleven out of 24 internal bolts and 20 out of 32 external bolts dropped below 20,000 lb tension. One interior and 5 exterior bolts had final tension under 10,000 lb.

Bolt Tension Loss Patterns of Three Types of Crossings

It will be of interest to compare the patterns of tension loss of the three designs of crossings and the effect of operating conditions on two or more crossings of the same type. A typical cycle of loss in tension from 40,000 lb, including a winter season, was selected for each of the six crossings involved in the measurements of tension loss. This information is presented in Fig. 12. The numbers in the circles are the losses in tension expressed in percent of the initial tension of approximately 40,000 lb. At Warsaw the entire crossing lost 50 percent tension, with 61 and 39 percent loss in the PRR and NYC rails, respectively. The ratios indicate that the bolts in the PRR rails lost 56 percent more tension than in the NYC rails. The external bolts lost less than the internal bolts. At that location the PRR traffic was 9 times as heavy as the NYC, and the greater tension loss quite logically occurred in the PRR rails, although they were favored with the longitudinal timber support.

At the 37th St. location with the same type of crossing as at Warsaw, the tension loss patterns were quite different with respect to the support. The tonnage over each side of the two crossings was about equal. The tension loss in the GM&O rails was 26 percent greater than in the PRR rails, which were favored by having the supporting longitudinal timbers. The outstanding feature of these crossings was the heavy loss in tension of the GM&O external arms, being 45 to 58 percent greater than the values for the PRR external arms. Likewise, in the GM&O rails, the external bolts lost 46 to 51 percent more tension than the internal bolts. The external bolts in the GM&O rails had the greatest loss in tension of any of the arms. At that location equal support of the two sides of the crossings would be beneficial in reducing the tension loss in the GM&O rails, particularly in the external arms.

At the 55th St. location, the two manganese insert crossings had about the same amount of traffic, because both were in the southward track of the C&WI, and the two IHB tracks were said to have about the same tonnage. For both crossings, the ratios, IHB/C&WI rails, were close to unity, except the first and third listed ratios were greater for crossing "C" on a framed timber support. It is significant to note that the three ratios, external/internal bolts, for crossing "A" on the steel support, were close to unity, while those for crossing "C" on timber were approximately 1.50. Although the steel support was not beneficial in retarding the tension loss of all bolts, compared with that of crossing "C", the steel support did tend to equalize the tension loss in the external and internal arms of both tracks. In another cycle analyzed (30,000 lb initial tension), this beneficial equalization of the loss in the IHB rails was remarkable. The ratio of the tension loss, all external/internal bolts, was 1.92 in crossing "C" on timber, compared with 1.06 in crossing "A" on the steel support. In solid manganese crossing "D" the bolts in the C&WI rails lost 13 percent more tension, which difference was entirely due to the excess loss in the internal bolts. The percentage loss in all external bolts was about the same as the internal bolts.

Turnout Frog Bolt Tension Tests

A main line turnout frog was included in the bolt tension tests to develop some information on the rate of loss in bolt tension of this type of frog. The PRR very kindly permitted the AAR research staff to conduct tests on a No. 15, 25-ft railbound manganese frog with 140 PS rail in the westward main and crossover, immediately east of the crossings at Warsaw, Ind. This crossover was controlled by the interlocking plant at the crossing. The turnout was installed new in the spring of 1949, and the test was started in May 1950. This was a trailing turnout for westward movements, and the PRR traffic was similar to that previously described for the eastward test crossing.

All of the 18 bolts, 1⅜ in diameter, were included in the measurements. Thirteen of the bolts were replaced with longer ones, with extra threaded length, in order to reduce the number of lengths from nine to three for the purpose of simplifying the bolt tension measurements. In the railbound frog construction, the bolt heads were clamped against malleable iron beveled headlock washers shaped to fit the web of rail, and the spring washers were in contact with similar beveled washers without the headlock. All of the bolts had ASA regular medium-carbon nuts. The field measurements consisted of bolt tension loss, pull-in or wear of the frog assembly, and nut back-off, the same as for the crossing tests.

Three cycles of loss in bolt tension with 40,000 lb initial tension were conducted with two weights of washers for service periods ranging from 0.90 to 1.28 years. The first cycle was conducted with the PRR specification washers, and the other cycles included the Frog and Crossing Hy-Crome washers that had been in service for less than two years in one of the IHB–C&WI crossings being tested at the 55th St. location. The data for each test cycle are presented on a plan of the frog and in a table. Fig. 13 and Table 23 cover the first cycle of loss in tension, with an average loss of 23 percent for a period of 1.28 years. The second cycle was the first one in which the Frog and Crossing Hy-Crome spring washers were tested (Fig. 14, Table 24). The average tension loss for all bolts for a service period of 1 year was 29 percent, compared with 23 percent in the first cycle with the PRR specification washers. Cycle 3 (Fig. 15, Table 25) gave an average loss in tension of 22 percent with the medium weight washers for 0.90 year of service. The latter washers were not as effective in cycle 2 as in cycle 3, because of being placed against bearing surfaces which had been indented and abraded by the low-reaction washers having a much smaller width. In other instances the wide bearing washers dropped below expectations when first substituted for narrow washers on the crossing frogs.

In the three cycles, only bolt 9H in cycle 2 dropped below a final tension of 20,000 lb. This was influenced to some extent by not having the full 40,000 lb tension initially.

It will be observed from the figures and tables that bolts in certain positions lost more tension than the others. Taking the average tension loss of the three cycles, bolts 5T and 4T ahead of the frog point, and bolts 3H, 4H, and 6H behind the point lost the greater amounts of bolt tension in their respective groups. Bolts 5T and 4T are located near the toe end of the casting near the first bend in the rails from the toe of the frog. Bolts 3H and 4H are near the heel end of tread wings of the casting, near the receiving end of the casting tread for trailing main line movements (to the left in the figures). Bolt 6H was near the junctions between the running rails and the casting where its width was reduced to accommodate those rails. Bolts losing the next largest amount of tension were 2H, 5H, 8H, 9H, 11H, and 13H. Prior to these tests the PRR section foreman had indicated bolts 5T, 4T, 3H, 4H, 5H, 10H, and 11H had required the most wrenching in this design of frog.

The values of pull-in for the turnout frog tests had considerable scatter and some inconsistencies with respect to the amount of tension lost. It seems logical in this type of construction, where adjoining bolts lost widely different amounts of tension, that the horizontal flexure of the rails, caused by the irregularity of the final tension values, could partially offset some of the pull-in at points of the larger losses in tension, and possibly increase it at points of low losses in tension.

This test has indicated that with reasonably new frogs of this design and good maintenance, the problem of maintaining bolt tension is a minor one compared with that of crossing frogs under comparable service conditions. It is judged that maintaining adequate bolt tension in turnout frogs of bolted-rail construction, with or without high guards, in heavy-duty side tracks with a lower standard of maintenance, will require more frequent retightening of the frog bolts than in the test frog. Because of the slow rate of loss in bolt tension in the test frog, it seems logical to conclude that impacts imposed on the bolts by the traffic are much smaller than was measured in the No. 1 bolts of the westward crossing at Warsaw.

TESTS OF LOCKNUTS

Three types of locknuts were included in these tests to develop information on their utility and influence upon the maintenance of crossing frog bolt tension. All of the locknuts were made of low-carbon steel. Each had a different principle of providing thread friction for holding the nut in place. The Elastic Stop Nut was of the interference type in which the locking element was a compressed fiber collar insert locked in the crown side of the nut. As the nut was wrenched on the bolt, the threads on the bolt cut threads in the collar which provided thread friction. The Security locknut utilized an alloy steel threaded retainer in the crown of the nut which was made elliptical in shape to provide thread friction by having the retainer assume a round shape when the nut was wrenched on the bolt. The MacLean–Fogg Unitary Nut No. 3 had the top two or three threads deformed slightly out of a true helix to provide thread friction for locking itself in place.

Bolt Tension Tests

The first test conducted with locknuts was in the west half of crossing "A" (Fig. 11), which was the manganese insert crossing supported by the structural steel substructure and asphalt macadam ballast, at the 55th St. location. In the preliminary cycle and cycles 1, 2 and 3 (all with 40,000 lb initial tension, except No. 3, which had 25,000 lb), the northwest corner of the crossing had hexagon Elastic Stop Nuts for the 1¼-in bolts without spring washers and the southwest corner had the locknuts with used Hy-Pressure Hy-Crome spring washers. For cycle 4, with 30,000 lb initial tension, the spring washers were moved to the northwest corner of the crossing to determine if the service conditions were different in the two corners. In the preliminary cycle the corner with locknuts and without washers lost 47 percent tension, compared with 55 percent for the other corner with locknuts and spring washers. The corresponding figures for cycle 1 were 30 and 35 percent, and for cycle 2, 46 and 47 percent. Thus, a slight advantage was shown for the corner without spring washers at first, and this had practically disappeared in cycle 2. This small advantage of the locknuts without washers was influenced by the fact that there were no washers to imbed into the nuts and corner braces as a result of the shock loads, principally on the No. 1 bolts which lost the most tension. Also, the low-carbon locknuts were more easily indented by the spring washers than in the case of the medium-carbon nut generally used on frog bolts. The results for cycles 3 and 4 are given in Tables 16 and 18. In Table 16 for cycle 3,. with 25,000 lb initial tension, the corner with the locknuts and no spring washers lost 52 percent, compared with 39 percent in the southwest corner having the locknuts with spring washers. After moving the washers to the northwest corner for cycle 4, the percentages were 39 and 45, respectively, in favor of the northwest ·corner with the washers and locknuts. This test demonstrated that the locknuts remained in place with or without washers, but were of little value in retaining bolt tension throughout their service life.

The second bolt tension test with the three types of locknuts was made in cycles 1 and 2 of the eastward crossing at Warsaw, Ind. Fig. 7 shows the location of the locknuts in three corners of the crossing, all being used with the washers indicated in the figure. In each of these test cycles there was no significant difference in tension loss of the bolts with the locknuts and those with the medium carbon nuts. After completion of cycle 2, the three types of locknuts were placed in three corners of the westward crossing for further observations and to liminate the low-carbon nuts from the bolt tension test, because medium-carbon nuts were in general use on crossing frogs. In this test the bolt threads were oiled each time the tension was checked, and no trouble was experienced with the locknuts becoming frozen.

Service Test

This service test was started May 1, 1950, and terminated July 7, 1953. The bolts were retightened with the same frequency as in the eastward crossing. A record of the nut back-off was maintained. No measurements of bolt tension were taken in this test with locknuts. When the locknuts were first applied to the three-year old bolts, the bolt threads were not oiled. By August 1952, the bolts with the Security and Unitary No. 3 locknuts were very hard to wrench. To facilitate the bolt maintenance, the locknuts were removed and reapplied after oiling the bolt threads. Table 26 is included to give a record of the frictional torque required to wrench the nuts on the bolts twice. In the first application, several of the Security and Unitary No. 3 locknuts developed high friction torque because of damaged threads at the end of some of the bolts. All three types of locknuts lost a large proportion of their frictional torque in the reapplication with lubrication. A few of the nuts were finger free.

During the service tests it was difficult at times to wrench some of the Security and Unitary No. 3 locknuts. As a result of the large torque required, the headlock bars welded to the corner braces were damaged. With large frictional torques, it was difficult for two men to retighten the bolts. Some of the headlock bars on the corners having the two last-mentioned types of locknuts had been broken or bent. This made it necessary in retightening the bolts to use two wrenches, an additional one being required to hold the bolt head. All locknuts were removed and replaced with the PRR standard nut (ASA regular medium carbon) in July 1953. At that time it was difficult to remove some of the two last-mentioned types of locknuts.

There was no backing off of the locknuts in any of the tests. The locknuts were not beneficial for maintaining bolt tension, except that in one of the insert crossings where one type of locknut was tested with and without washers, there was a temporary advantage when no spring washers were used. A uniform bolt tension cannot be obtained with locknuts because of the wide variation in frictional torque.' Because of the large torque required to wrench some bolts with locknuts, adequate bolt tension cannot always be applied with two men on a wrench. It is possible for locknuts to conceal that frog bolts have lost all tension·and are no longer performing their primary function.

DISCUSSION OF TEST RESULTS

Accelerated Initial Loss of Bolt Tension

From the previous investigation of the loss in bolt tension in track joints, it was known that after tightening bolts, the loss in tension in the first few days was large as compared with 'the remainder of the service period. The crossing bolts were checked to ascertain the magnitude of this early loss in tension.

In crossing "C" (Fig. 10), at the 37th St. location, the loss in six bolts was checked for one day as follows:

	Initial Tension 40,000 lb	
	Percent Tension Lost	
Bolt Position	First Day	8 Months
SW Frog—PRR Specification Washers GM&O External Arm		
1W	28	100
2W	27	84
3W	32	63
Avg	29	82
SE Frog—Hubbard Exp. Washers GM&O External Arm		
1E	37	45
2E	30	74
3E	33	46
Avg	33	55

Bolts with PRR washers lost in one day a much smaller proportion of the 8-month total than the Hubbard washers with higher reaction. This was probably influenced by the shock loads causing a greater initial indentation in the case of the heavier washers. For the 8-month period, the Hubbard washers lost one-third less tension than the PRR washers. There was no back-off of the nut on bolt 1W, which lost all of its tension.

In the eastward crossing at Warsaw, an overnight check was made of the loss in tension of bolt 1E in the PRR external arm of the SE corner with a Reliance Heavy-Duty Hy-Crome washer (Fig. 7). The overnight loss in tension from 40,000 lb was 36 percent compared to 60 percent for the test cycle of 7 months.

From the results of the field measurements of the dynamic shock loads on the bolts and the laboratory imbedding tests with shock loads, it is evident the high initial loss in tension in track was caused by the larger of the shock loads occurring during the short period.

Tension Loss by Bolt Position

A review of the tension loss tables will reveal that bolts in certain positions of the three types of crossings lost more tension than in the other positions. The bolt tension loss patterns for the bolted-rail and manganese insert crossings were similar in that the No. 1 bolts, nearest to the flangeway intersection, lost the greatest amount of tension; the No. 2 bolts, next in magnitude; and the No. 3 bolts the least. It was found in the measurements of the shock loads in the bolted-rail crossing at Warsaw that the shock loads were relatively large at the No. 1 position and quite moderate at the Nos. 2 and 3 positions, the latter being of the magnitude comparable with the bolts in a track joint. Consequently, the major problem of maintaining the bolt tension is at the No. 1 position. However, in several instances some of the Nos. 2 and 3 bolts deviated from the foregoing pattern and actually lost a greater tension.

It was determined for the solid manganese type crossing tested that in the 6-hole internal joints the middle bolts lost the greatest amount of tension and the end bolts the least. In the case of the 4-hole external joints, the two bolts in the receiving end of the casting or rail lost slightly more tension. These patterns of tension loss for the solid type of crossing were not as pronounced as those for the other two designs tested, and it seems unnecessary to retighten the bolts that lost the larger amounts of tension more frequently than the others in this type of crossing.

Rate of Bolt Tension Loss Per Month

A comparison of the rate of tension loss per month in all of the main bolts of the three types of crossings was made by selecting two typical long cycles (40,000 lb initial tension), averaging six to seven months' duration. The rate of loss was 7.6 percent for the bolted-rail crossings at Warsaw and the 37th St. location. At the 55th St. location, the insert crossing on steel support lost 5.9 percent per month, compared with 4.6 percent for the same type of crossing on framed timbers. The solid crossing at the same location lost 5.7 percent tension per month.

The most significant finding from these values is that under comparable traffic and maintenance conditions, the bolted-rail type of crossing would dissipate the bolt tension more rapidly than the other types.

The comparison between the two insert crossings at the 55th St. location was reasonably good as to traffic conditions. However, the diamond on steel T-beams was handicapped as to the spring washers and the locknuts without washers. The crossing on timbers was favored with special washers in one-half of the diamond. From the results obtained, it seems justifiable to conclude that, for the test conditions, the structural steel substructure was not beneficial as to retarding the dissipation of tension in the main bolts. If it had been possible to keep the diamond rigidly fixed to the steel support, the downward flexure of the crossing under the passing wheels would have been reduced. This lesser flexure would decrease the severity of the shock loads on the main bolts, particularly in the No. 1 position, and reduce the attendant loss in tension.

Because the solid crossing at the 55th St. location carried more traffic than either of the two insert crossings, it cannot be said with certainty that under comparable conditions the solid crossing would have the higher rate of loss in tension. It seems probable, under identical conditions of traffic and maintenance, that the insert type on timbers would lose the greater tension for a given tonnage.

Using the same test cycles to determine the monthly tension loss for the No. 1 bolts only, the following percentage values were obtained: Bolted-rail crossings—Warsaw, 9.4, 37th St. location, 10.5; insert crossings on steel support, 9.4, and on timber 6.4. The corresponding percentages for the Nos. 2 and 3 bolts in the same cycles were, respectively, 6.6, 6.2, 3.8 and 3.5. The foregoing comparison demonstrates the relatively high rate of tension loss of the No. 1 bolts with respect to the other two positions in bolted-rail and insert types of crossings. The latter group of percentages shows that the rate of tension loss in bolts 2 and 3 of the two insert crossings was about the same. The excess loss in tension of the bolts in the insert crossing on the steel support was primarily in the No. 1 bolts. Apparently, the steel-supported crossing flexed more under wheel loads than the insert crossing on timber, and the shock loads were higher, causing more dissipation in the tension of the No. 1 bolts. It was developed in the shock load tests at Warsaw that when the crossing settled two days after a rain, the maximum shock loads on the No. 1 bolts suddenly increased from 13,000 to 17,000 lb (initial tension 40,000 lb), because of the greater downward flexure of the diamond.

Thus, it has been shown that the bolted-rail crossings were highest in the rate of loss in tension, and the No. 1 bolts in that type of crossing, as well as in the insert type, present the major problem of maintaining adequate bolt tension.

Pull-In or Wear of The Crossing Assembly

Values of pull-in or wear of the crossing assembly have been included in the tables covering the bolt tension loss cycles at the three locations. These values were concurrent with the drop in tension of the respective bolts. In other words, the amount of pull-in for each test cycle was the difference in the out-to-out readings taken for the initial and remaining values of measured bolt tension. During the early stage of the field tests, it was developed, in many instances, that the relation between the pull-in and final tension of the individual bolts, with respect to the release curve for the spring washer and bolt deformation, was not good. After measurement of the dynamic impacts in the main bolts of the westward crossing at Warsaw, it was determined, particularly for the No. 1 position bolts with relatively large shock loads, that the bolt tension was also dissipated by the shock loads causing the washers to imbed into the nuts and corner braces. For instance, if a bolt is torqued to 40,000 lb static tension, and a shock load is imposed by the traffic for a total tension of 55,000 lb, then the higher tension causes the washers to become imbedded deeper into the nut and corner brace and dissipate some of the initial static tension. Obviously, this effect was not included in the pull-in measurements, which were based on the change in out-to-out dimension of the corner braces or joint bars.

Considering the No. 1 bolts in only the 40,000 lb initial bolt tension cycles for the bolted-rail crossings, the rate of pull-in per month for the single-coil washers was approximately 0.002 in at Warsaw and 0.003 in at the 37th St. location. The higher values at the latter location may have been influenced by these crossings being four years older than the eastward crossing at Warsaw. The corresponding figure for the insert crossings at the 55th St. location was less than the value of 0.002 in for the Warsaw crossing. The larger average values in the solid crossing ranged up to 0.002 in per month. The rate of pull-in for the double-coil Hy-Crome washers at Warsaw was about the same as for the single-coil washers at that location. All of the foregoing values are based on the average length of bolt tension loss cycles of 6 to 7 months. Because of the many variables in traffic conditions as well as maintenance conditions and practices, it is apparent that the frequency of retightening crossing frog bolts to a certain standard will vary widely for the many sets of conditions.

Under the test conditions, it was not possible to determine accurately the relation between the rate of pull-in and the magnitude of the initial bolt tension. There were appreciable variations in the pull-in at the No. 1 bolts in the four corners of the same crossing. However, an analysis of the total wear at the No. 1 bolts of the crossing at Warsaw indicated the same rate per month for the cycles with 25,000, 30,000 and 40,000 lb initial tension. The total wear was determined from the change in the out-to-out dimensions taken before and after a test period when the bolts were set at their initial tension.

MISCELLANEOUS OBSERVATIONS

Broken Washers

All spring washer breakage which occurred in the four-year test of the eastward crossing at Warsaw was noted in Tables 2 to 10, incl. At that location there was no breakage of the following washers: Hubbard experimental, PRR specification, Reliance Heavy-Duty Hy-Crome, and Reliance Frog and Crossing Hy-Crome.

During the 3-year test of two bolted-rail crossings at the 37th St. location, 11 Hubbard experimental and 30 used PRR specification washers were broken. There were no Reliance Frog and Crossing Hy-Crome washers broken.

At the 55th St. location there was no breakage of the new spring washers tested. Three of the used washers, one 1¼-in Standard Hy-Crome, one 1¼-in Hy-Pressure Hy-Crome, and one 1⅜-in Hy-Pressure Hy-Crome were broken during the 5-year test of the three crossings.

Bolt Wrenching and Breakage

In the older crossings at the 37th St. and 55th St. locations, some of the bolts were difficult to tighten to 40,000 lb, because the threads had been battered by the washers when the bolts were loose. In a few instances the bolts could not be wrenched to 40,000 lb tension with 2 men. At the 37th St. location in 1951, when the test crossings were 7 years old, it was necessary to replace 10 bolts (of a total of 96) to facilitate the wrenching. Four 1¼-in bolts were replaced with new ones in the insert crossings at the 55th St. location in 1950. Some of the bolts in the older crossings required three-man wrenching. The foregoing difficulties can be avoided by lubricating the bolt threads with a grease known to have good weather-resisting qualities and by not permitting the nuts to become entirely loose, which will prevent the threads from becoming battered.

There was no breakage of any of the main bolts in the crossings in which bolt tension tests were conducted.

Stretching of Bolts

All of the main crossing and turnout bolts tested had been in service prior to the beginning of the bolt tension tests, and the extensometer readings indicated that none had been permanently elongated during these tests. Because of battered threads, 10 of the 1⅜-in main bolts in the crossings at the 37th St. location were replaced with new ones in 1951. Also, 4 of the 1¼-in No. 2 bolts in the insert crossings at the 55th St. location were renewed in 1950. None of the replacement bolts was found to be permanently elongated in the subsequent tension tests. Dissipation of bolt tension by permanently elongating the high-strength frog bolts is of little consequence.

Nut Back-Off

None of the nuts backed off of bolts that still had some tension left. A few of the nuts backed off in cases where the bolt tension became zero. In some instances, with no tension, the nut had not backed off. In one instance where a locknut without a washer was replaced with an ASA heavy medium-carbon nut on crossing "A" at the 55th St. location, the nut backed off of the bolt completely, but the bolt remained in place. Nut back-off did not dissipate bolt tension, as it occurred only after the bolts were loose. This deduction was based on the fact that nuts had not backed off of bolts with 1000 to 2000 lb tension, and did not always back off the bolts that had no remaining tension.

LABORATORY TESTS OF SIMULATED SHOCK LOADS ON CROSSING FROG BOLT ASSEMBLIES

During this five-year field investigation, careful observations were made of the indentation and abrasion of the nuts and corner braces of the crossings by all types of spring washers. Many specimens of nuts were examined in the laboratory by measuring the depth of the indentation. These measurements partially explained the lower efficiency of the medium and heavy weight single-coil spring washers. It was also determined that washers of the S–300 and D–5 compression types caused less indentation and resultant dissipation of the bolt tension. The imbedding of the double-coil washers was found to be much less than that of the single-coil washers, because of the greater bearing area on the nuts and corner braces. Because of the importance of this phase of the work, it was decided to conduct laboratory imbedding tests on $1\frac{3}{8}$-in bolts with the same nuts and corner brace material as encountered in the field. By this means, the imbedding characteristics of the several types of washers could be translated into reactive pressures and efficiency of the spring washers.

Preparation of Bolt Assemblies

All specimens were made to test spring washers for $1\frac{3}{8}$-in bolts. All nuts used were of the ASA heavy medium carbon steel, except one bolt was tested with a heat-treated nut and a hardened flat plate washer next to the corner brace block. After freezing a nut on a $1\frac{3}{8}$-in heat-treated bolt by wrenching it to the end of the threads, the excess threads were cut off and the top of the assembly was machined so that the compressive load applied to the threaded end of the bolt would be partially carried by the nut to avoid any movement of the nut with respect to the bolt. The bolt was then cut to a length of $4\frac{3}{8}$ in, the excess shank being used to guide the bolt in a dummy block below the corner brace. The Ramapo Ajax Division, American Brake Shoe Company, furnished three short pieces of corner brace material. The chemical analysis indicated the steel had 0.25 percent carbon and 0.55 percent manganese. The corner brace bars had a Brinell hardness of 136. The medium carbon nuts used had an average Brinell hardness reading of 138. The heat-treated medium-carbon nut had a hardness reading of 229, toward the lower end of the range. The hardened flat plate washers averaged 400 Brinell hardness. The corner brace bars were machined on top to provide a good surface for the spring washers. Likewise, the working face of the nut was machined.

Test Procedure

These tests were conducted in a Baldwin–Southwark hydraulic compression–tension testing machine. Each of the single-coil and S–300 spring washers was preloaded to 60,000 lb to avoid any perceptible permanent set during the tests. It was necessary to preload the double-coil washers with 75,000 lb to prevent permanent set during the test. The preloading was performed on special hardened blocks, the same as used for testing washers for their reactive properties. This test simulated a 40,000-lb static bolt tension and shock loads of 20,000 lb, or a total cyclic operating load of 60,000 lb. Each specimen was tested in exactly the same manner when assembled with a bolt and corner brace.

A

After preloading the washers, each was placed in a separate assembly of bolt, nut and corner brace block. The testing machine was set up for taking reactive pressure curves with an Ames dial indicator for measurement of the movement of the top platen. The specimen washer was first loaded to 40,000 lb, taking dial readings at 100 lb and 40,000 lb. A release curve to 0.060 in was then taken, which was plotted as curve 2 in Fig. 16. Then the load was increased to 60,000 lb and released to 40,000 lb five times. On the sixth release of the load from 60,000 lb, the platen was released to the same dial reading as was obtained for the first load of 40,000 lb. The load measured· was used for plotting curve 3 at zero release in Fig. 16. From that load, a release curve was taken to 0.060 in. Release curve 1 in the figure was taken on the hardened blocks prior to the shock load tests.

DISCUSSION OF TEST RESULTS

For convenient comparison of these tests with nine conditions, all of the graphs of the release curves have been included in Fig. 16. The loss in reactive pressure of the washers between curves 1 and 2 represents the effect of the relatively soft bearing surfaces prevalent in crossing frog construction. The spread between curves 2 and 3 is the effect of the six 20,000-lb shock loads. In practically all of the tests the dial readings remained constant for the 60,000-lb loads after the first application. Therefore in track, only one large shock load is all that is necessary to dissipate tension by imbedding due to shock loads. Because of the small scale used in Fig. 16, pertinent values of the reactive pressures have been shown as items a and b at a release of 0.030 in, which are defined in the legend.

It will be observed in the left portion of the first 6 graphs (except No. 4), Fig. 16, that the washers lost more of their effectiveness before application of the shock loads (difference between curves 1 and 2). In graph 4 the Heavy-Duty Hy-Crome washer lost most of its effectiveness after the shock loads. This finding contributed much to the explanation of the low effectiveness developed in the field by the last-mentioned washer when used without hardened parts. By comparing graphs 2 and 5, the advantage of the hardened parts is demonstrated. However, there was little difference in the release curves after the shock loads at the release point of 0.030 in. In the field tests, the hardened parts improved the efficiency of the medium reaction washers but not in the case of the Heavy-Duty Hy-Crome washer with a high reaction.

The drops in the release curves of the double-coil washers in graphs 7, 8 and 9, before and after the application of the shock loads, were about equal.

The improved lot of S–300 plate washers gave good performance in track. Graph 6 (Fig. 16) indicates that the shock loads had little effect on the efficiency of this washer. Likewise, the shock loads caused little drop in⸱the release curve for the washer with hardened parts in graph 5.

RECOMMENDATIONS

Specifications for Spring Washers

It is obvious from the test measurements that maintenance of a high bolt tension will be beneficial in keeping the various parts clamped tightly together so that the amount of relative movement between the parts and resultant wear will be minimized. In addition, a high bolt tension is beneficial in providing some stiffness of the crossing frog to resist deflection under wheel loads and thereby aid the supporting ties in maintaining a good surface over the crossing. The function of the spring washer is to aid in maintaining this bolt tension on a practical basis, so the labor cost for retightening, as required, will be minimized.

As previously discussed, 40,000 lb initial tension is about the practical limit of hand wrenching with the average condition of bolts. Therefore, it is recommended that the applied load in the specification test shall be 40,000 lb.

Because the No. 1 bolts in a bolted-rail crossing have the largest rate of bolt tension dissipation, emphasis should be placed on the requirements for those bolts. The value of the spring washer in maintaining bolt tension depends upon its ability to maintain a reactive force as wear occurs and the faces, which the bolt head and nut contact, come closer together, which is referred to in the report as "pull-in". In the test measurements which extended over a period of several years, it was found that the average amount of pull-in for the No. 1 bolts at the Warsaw crossing approximated 0.002 in per month; in the bolted-rail crossings at the 37th St. location, 0.003 in per month; in the manganese insert crossings at the 55th St. location, less than 0.002 in per month; in the solid manganese crossing at the latter location, up to 0.002 in per month. This would indicate that for the various types of crossings over a period of 1 year the pull-in would range from 0.024 to 0.036 in. Inasmuch as a pull-in value of 0.030 in has been used in specification requirements for spring washers for track joints, and since this pull-in value agrees reasonably well with the pull-in measurements on the crossings, it would seem desirable to use this same value of 0.030 in. in establishing the release distance for reactive pressure requirements of spring washers for crossing frogs.

With reference to the minimum bolt tension that is permissible before bolts should be retightened in order to maintain efficient functioning of the crossing frog assemblies, it is difficult to establish this value on any precise and definite basis. It is apparent, as previously stated, that the tighter the bolts the better. However, it does appear from the test measurements that the crossing frog functioned reasonably well and the rate of wear was not appreciably increased as long as the bolt tension was maintained above 10,000 lb. Accordingly, it is recommended that this value be used as the minimum bolt tension at the release point in the specification requirement.

In view of the fact that the investigation has shown the very great importance on the reactive characteristics of the imbedding action of spring washers into the relatively soft surfaces of the crossing brace and nuts, it seems necessary that this be included in the method of making the reaction test on the spring washers. Accordingly, it is recommended that the reaction test on the washers be made with the washer placed between steel plates in the testing machine, both above and below the washer, and that these steel plates shall have a Brinell hardness not to exceed 150, which is in conformity with th·hardness of the crossing brace and medium carbon nuts.

Also, since the measurements of impacts on the bolts under traffic at Warsaw showed that there was an increase in the bolt tension due to the flexural action of the crossing frog (termed shock load in this report), and since this will have an important influence on the reactive characteristics of the washer due to the imbedding action, it is necessary that provision for this be included in the reaction test. Study of the bolt tension measurements indicates that an increase in the applied load of 40,000 lb up to 60,000 lb will be adequate for maximum shock loads.

The recommendation, therefore, for the reaction test for spring washers for crossing frogs is as follows:

(a) Place the test washer in the testing machine between two steel plates not less than ½ in thick, having smoothly ground surfaces and a Brinell hardness not to exceed 150.

(b) Apply an initial load of 40,000 lb and record the dial reading for the position of the platens of the machine.

(c) Increase the test load to 60,000 lb.

(d) Release the load until the distance between platens is 0.030 in greater than that recorded in (b) above.

(e) The amount of load remaining in (d) shall be not less than 10,000 lb.

Observation of Fig. 16 shows that only one of the spring washers tested will meet this suggested specification requirement. That is the Reliance Double-Coil Hy-Crome spring washer shown in graph 7. However, it is believed that by giving consideration to minimizing the loss due to imbedding of the contact surfaces and using a sufficient cross sectional area, any manufacturer that so desires can meet these requirements.

Design of Spring Washers

It has been shown, both in the field tests and the laboratory tests of shock loads, that the imbedding of the washers in the bearing surfaces caused by the larger shock loads resulted in major losses in tension. It is possible that changes in the shape of coil washers may reduce the loss in tension attributed to the shock loads. Consideration should be given in the design of helical spring washers to provide more bearing area against the nut and corner brace when the washer goes solid and when it has opened slightly. Most of the spring washers are thicker at the inner periphery than at the outer one. The laboratory imbedding tests showed a concentration of the indentation on relatively small areas near the outer periphery of the bolt. A washer of uniform thickness should increase the width of the bearing areas and aid in reducing the depth of the indentation and abrasion, as well as the attendant dissipation of tension. Some washers are made of a cross section having sharp corners along the outer edges. When slightly open, in some instances these washers have only a line bearing on the edges diametrically opposite to the ends of the single coil. It is believed that the corners should have a little longer radius. Also, imbedding is concentrated at the heel of the ground deflection, or the chamfer at the ends of the washer, on a small area close to the inner periphery of the helical washers. Any improvement in spring washer designs that will enlarge the contact area and reduce the dissipation of bolt tension chargeable to the major shock loads will promote economy in maintaining bolt tension and simplify the problem of complying with the new specification.

Conclusions

The major loss of tension in frog bolts can be attributed primarily to wear of the crossing assembly, imbedding and abrasion from the shock loads, and possibly some corrosion. Stretching of the bolts and nut back-off were found to have a negligible effect on bolt tension dissipation.

The double-coil spring washers tested held the bolt tension above 20,000 lb twice as long as the single-coil washers.

The use of hardened nuts and hardened flat plate washers next to the corner braces increased the efficiency of the medium weight single-coil washers, but were of little benefit when used with the Heavy-Duty Hy-Crome washers.

The maintenance of bolt tension in the No. 15 railbound turnout frog was a minor problem as compared with the crossing frog bolts.

All types of the spring washers tested with the conventional construction lost some of their effectiveness because of the relatively soft bearing surfaces next to the washers.

Locknuts were not beneficial in the retention of bolt tension. No locknuts backed off of the bolts during these tests.

Nuts having the standard National Coarse thread did not back off as long as the bolt had some tension, and many of the nuts on bolts with zero tension did not back off.

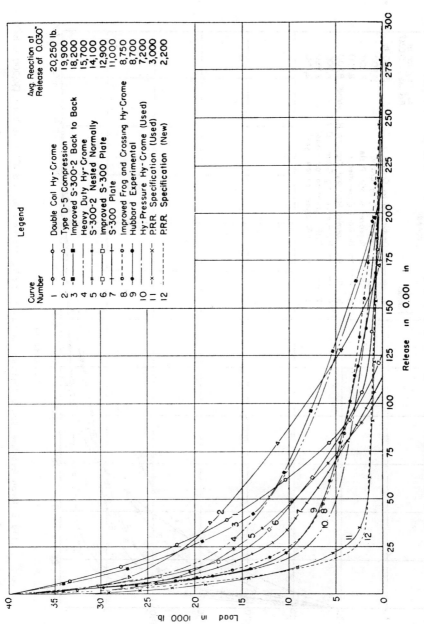

Fig. 1 Mean Reactive Spring Pressure Curves of Spring Washers for 1-3/8" Frog Bolts (40,000 lb load)

852

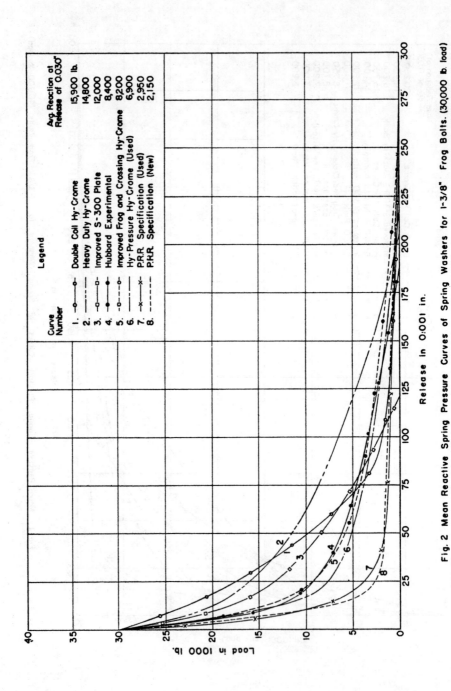

Fig. 2 Mean Reactive Spring Pressure Curves of Spring Washers for 1-3/8" Frog Bolts. (30,000 lb. load)

853

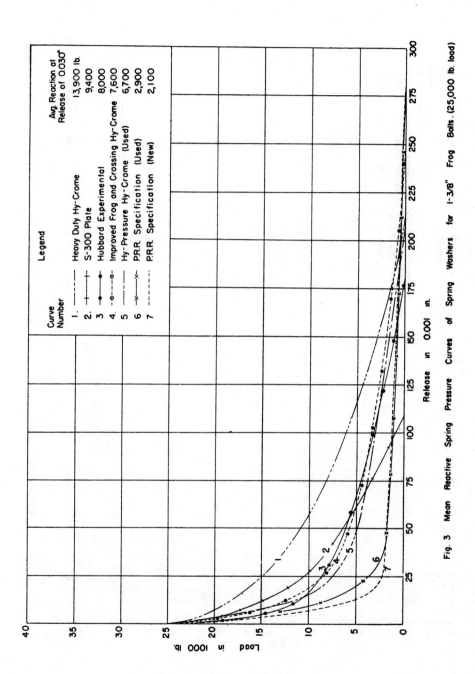

Fig. 3   Mean Reactive Spring Pressure Curves of Spring Washers for 1-3/8" Frog Bolts. (25,000 lb. load)

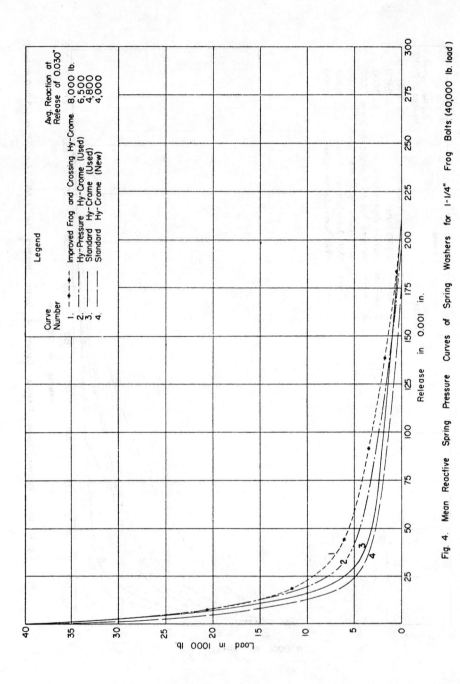

Fig. 4. Mean Reactive Spring Pressure Curves of Spring Washers for 1-1/4" Frog Bolts (40,000 lb. load)

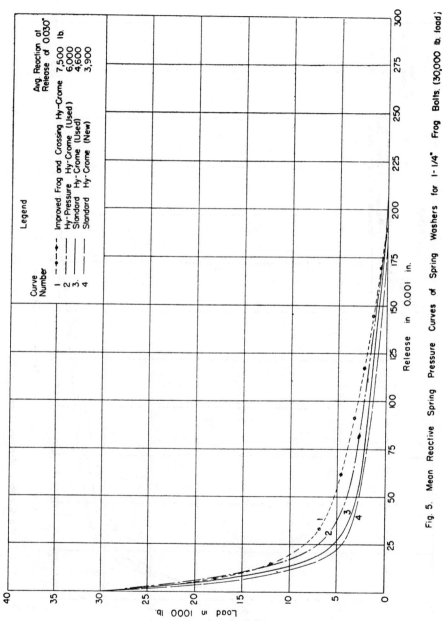

Fig. 5. Mean Reactive Spring Pressure Curves of Spring Washers for 1-1/4" Frog Bolts. (30,000 lb. load.)

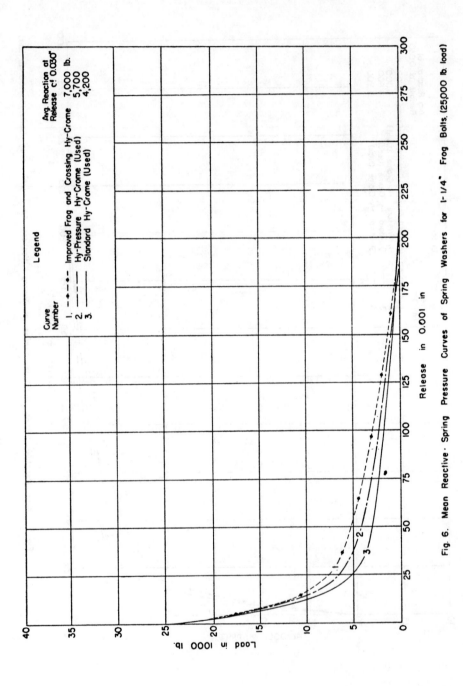

Fig. 6. Mean Reactive-Spring Pressure Curves of Spring Washers for 1-1/4" Frog Bolts. (25,000 lb. load)

857

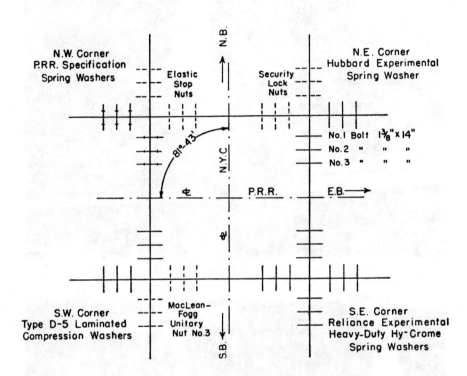

LEGEND

⊢—⊣ P.R.R. Standard Bolt, Nut and Spring Washer.
———— P.R.R. Standard Bolt and Nut with Washers as shown.
- - - - P.R.R. Standard Bolt, with Lock Nuts and Washers as shown.

Fig. 7. Plan of P.R.R.– N.Y.C. Crossing at Warsaw, Indiana, Showing Position and Description of Bolts, Washers and Lock Nuts for the Second Test Cycle.

Fig. 8. Extensometer Used for Determining The Loss in Frog Bolt Tension

Fig. 9. Out-to-Out Gage for Determining The Pull-In or Wear of Frog Assemblies

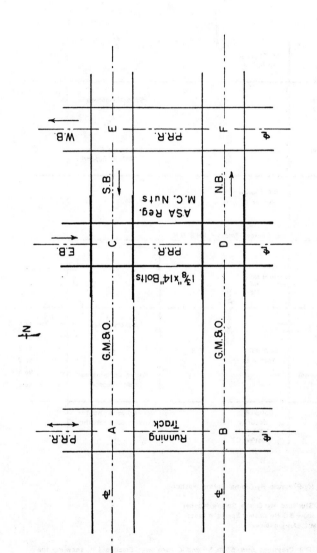

Note: Test Crossings are Crossings "C" and "D".
West Half of Both Test Crossings Contains Used P.R.R. Specification Spring Washers.
East Half of Crossing "C" Contains the Hubbard Experimental Spring Washers.
East Half of Crossing "D" Contains the Reliance Improved Frog and Crossing Hy-Crome Spring Washers.

Fig. 10. Plan of P.R.R.—G.M.&O. Crossings at 37th. St. and Campbell Ave., Chicago, Illinois, Showing Location of Test Crossings, Direction of Traffic and Construction for All Test Cycles

860

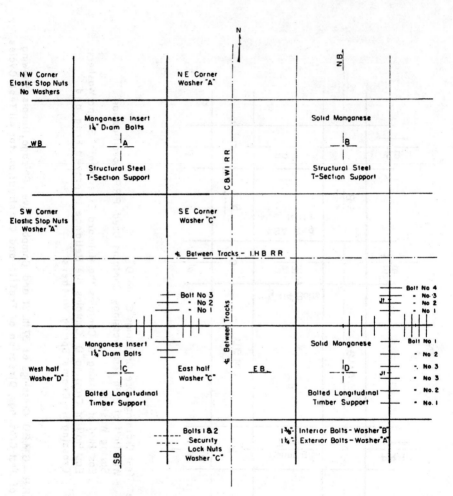

Note   Washer "A" Reliance Hy-Pressure Hy-Crome Spring Washer
       Washer "B" Reliance "   "   "   "   "   "
       Washer "C" Reliance Standard Hy-Crome Spring Washer
       Washer "D" Reliance Imp F&C. Hy-Crome Spring Washer
       All nuts are ASA Hvy. M.C. plus $\frac{1}{8}$ in thicker

Fig 11. Plan of IHB – C&WI RR Crossings near 55th St and Cicero Ave., Chicago, Ill, showing the
        location of bolts, washers and lock nuts, type of crossing and support, and direction of traffic
        for cycles 1 and 2

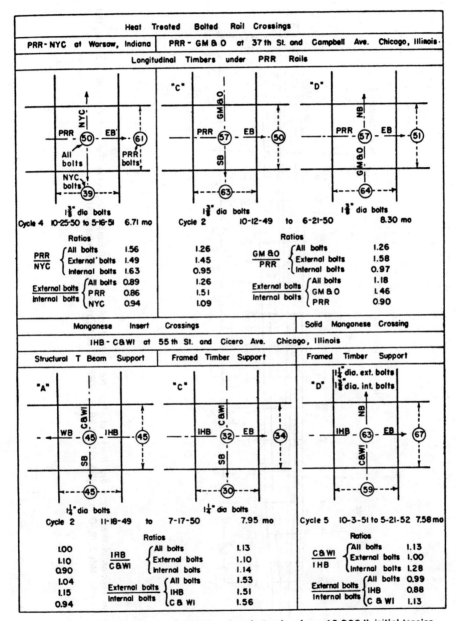

Figures in circles indicate percentage loss in tension from 40,000 lb initial tension.

Fig. 12. Typical Patterns and Ratios of Percentage Loss in Bolt Tension for Three Types of Crossings.

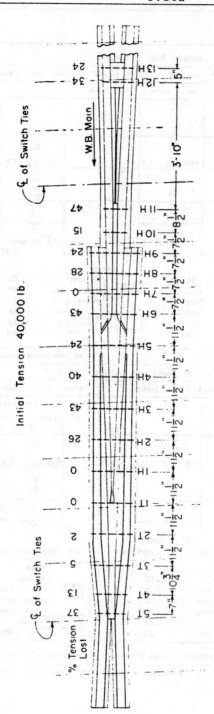

Fig 13. — Loss in Tension in the 1 3/8-in dia Bolts of The No.15-25-ft-140 P S Railbound Manganese Turnout Frog at Warsaw, Ind. (First cycle, May 3, 1950 to Aug.15, 1951- 1.28 yr, PRR Specification Spring Washers)

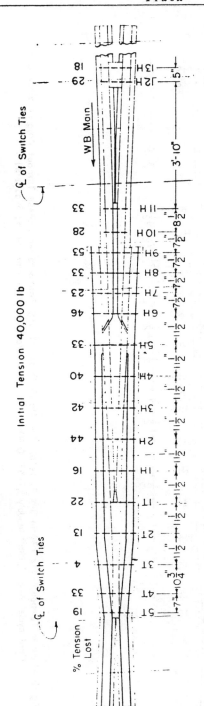

Fig. 14. — Loss in Tension in the $1\frac{3}{8}$-in dia Bolts of The No.15-25-ft-140 P S Railbound Manganese Turnout Frog at Warsaw, Ind. (Second cycle, Aug.15,1951 to Aug.14,1952 — 1.00 yr, Frog and Crossing Hy-Crome Spring Washers)

864

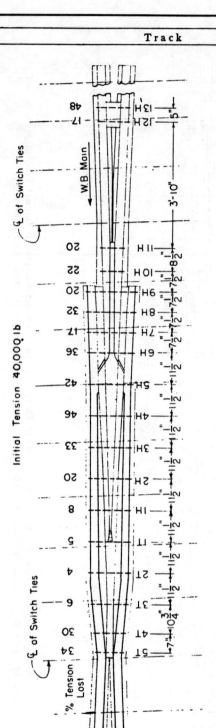

Fig 15.—Loss in Tension in the 1³⁄₈-in dia Bolts of The No.15-25-ft-140 P S Railbound Manganese Turnout Frog at Warsaw, Ind. (Third cycle, Aug. 14, 1952 to July 7, 1953–0.90 yr, Frog and Crossing Hy-Crome Spring Washers)

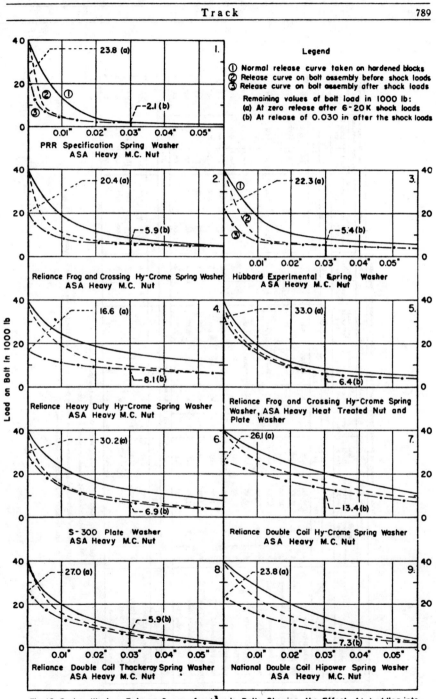

Legend

① Normal release curve taken on hardened blocks
② Release curve on bolt assembly before shock loads
③ Release curve on bolt assembly after shock loads

Remaining values of bolt load in 1000 lb:
(a) At zero release after 6-20K shock loads
(b) At release of 0.030 in after the shock loads

1. PRR Specification Spring Washer
ASA Heavy M.C. Nut

2. Reliance Frog and Crossing Hy-Crome Spring Washer
ASA Heavy M.C. Nut

3. Hubbard Experimental Spring Washer
ASA Heavy M.C. Nut

4. Reliance Heavy Duty Hy-Crome Spring Washer
ASA Heavy M.C. Nut

5. Reliance Frog and Crossing Hy-Crome Spring
Washer, ASA Heavy Heat Treated Nut and
Plate Washer

6. S-300 Plate Washer
ASA Heavy M.C. Nut

7. Reliance Double Coil Hy-Crome Spring Washer
ASA Heavy M.C. Nut

8. Reliance Double Coil Thackeray Spring Washer
ASA Heavy M.C. Nut

9. National Double Coil Hipower Spring Washer
ASA Heavy M.C. Nut

Fig. 16. Spring Washer Release Curves for $1\frac{1}{8}$-in Bolts Showing the Effect of Imbedding into the Crossing Frog Nuts and Corner Braces (Initial Bolt Load 40,000 lb and Six 20,000 lb Shock Loads)

866

Table 1. Summary of Several Physical Characteristics of Spring Washers for Frog Bolts

Designation of Spring Washer	Release from 10,000 lb				Release from 30,000 lb				Release from 25,000 lb				Nom. Dimensions of Cross Sections		Approximate Weight per 1000 pcs. (lb)
	Curve No.	No. of Washers Tested	(a) Average Reaction at 0.030"	(b) Total Deflection (in)	Curve No.	No. of Washers Tested	(c) Average Reaction at 0.030"	(b) Total Deflection (in)	Curve No.	No. of Washers Tested	(c) Average Reaction at 0.030"	(b) Total Deflection (in)	Width (in)	Thickness (in)	
Curve Reference	Fig. 1				Fig. 2				Fig. 3						
For 1 3/8" Diameter Bolts															
Double Coil Hy-Crome	1	4	20,250	0.26	1	4	15,900	0.25					3/4	13/32	1040
Type D-5 Compression	2	2	19,900	0.18									3 x 3	5/8(5 ply)	1800
Improved S-300 - 2 Back to Back	3	1 Pr.	18,200	0.21									3/4	3/4	1000
Heavy Duty Hy-Crome	4	4	15,700	0.22	2	*	14,800	0.21	1	4	13,900	0.21			
S-300 - 2 Nested Normally	5	1 Pr.	14,100	0.11											
Improved S-300 Plate	6	4	12,900	0.13	3	*	12,000	0.12					3 x 3	19/64	630
S-300 Plate	7	4	11,000	0.12									3 x 3	19/64	630
Improved Frog and Crossing Hy-Crome	8	4	8,750	0.16	5	*	8,200	0.15	2	1	9,100	0.15	7/8	15/32	725
Hubbard Experimental	9	4	8,700	0.19	4	*	8,100	0.18	4	4	7,600	0.18	17/32	21/32	665
Hy-Pressure Hy-Crome (Used)	10	4	7,200	0.22	6	*	6,900	0.22	3	4	8,000	0.18	9/16	1/2	105
P.R.R. Specification (Used)	11	4	3,000	0.29	7	*	2,950	0.28	5	*	6,700	0.21	1/2	3/8	290
P.R.R. Specification (New)	12	4	2,800	0.30	8	*	2,150	0.28	6	*	2,900	0.28	1/2	3/8	290
									7 *	4	2,100	0.28			
Curve Reference	Fig. 4				Fig. 5				Fig. 6						
For 1 1/2" Diameter Bolts															
Improved Frog and Crossing Hy-Crome	1	4	8,000	0.22	1	*	7,300	0.20	1	4	7,000	0.20	13/16	7/16	575
Hy-Pressure Hy-Crome (Used)	2	4	6,500	0.19	2	*	6,000	0.19	2	*	5,700	0.18	17/32	15/32	361
Standard Hy-Crome (Used)	3	4	4,800	0.21	3	*	4,600	0.20	3	*	4,200	0.20	1/2	7/16	295
Standard Hy-Crome (New)	4	4	4,000	0.18	4	4	3,900	0.18					1/2	7/16	295

(a) Average reactive spring pressure at fourth release from 10,000 lb.

(b) Deflections measured between indicated load and 100 lb.

(c) Average reactive spring pressure at first release from indicated load after four compressions to 10,000 lb.

* Data developed from 10,000 lb release curve.

TABLE 2. SUMMARY OF THE FIRST CYCLE OF LOSS IN TENSION IN THE MAIN BOLTS OF THE BOLTED RAIL CROSSING BETWEEN THE EASTWARD MAIN OF THE PENNSYLVANIA R. R. AND THE SINGLE TRACK BRANCH LINE OF THE NEW YORK CENTRAL SYSTEM AT WARSAW, INDIANA.

Location and Name of Spring Washers	Washer Reference Fig.No.	Curve Cv.No.	*Bolt Position	Avg. Bolt Tension (1000 lb) Initial	Final	Lost	Percent Tension Lost	Average Pull-in (in)	No. of Bolts with Final Tension less than 20 K	10 K	Remarks
N.W. Corner PRR Specification Spring Washers	1	12	1	42.5	18.0	24.5	58	0.013	2	0	ASA Heavy L.C. Elastic Stop Nuts on North & East Bolts. ASA Regular M. C. Nuts on South & West Bolts
	"	"	2	41.0	21.9	19.1	47	0.008	2	1	
	"	"	3	40.4	26.4	14.0	35	0.007	2	0	
			Avg.	41.3	22.1	19.2	46	0.009	6	1	
N.E. Corner Hubbard Experimental Spring Washers	1	9	1	39.9	17.9	22.0	55	0.023	3	0	ASA Regular Hex. L.C. Security Locknuts on North & West Bolts. ASA Regular M.C. Nuts on South & East Bolts
	"	"	2	38.5	21.9	16.6	43	0.016	1	0	
	"	"	3	40.5	27.6	12.9	32	0.012	1	0	
			Avg.	39.6	22.4	17.2	43	0.017	5	0	
S.E. Corner Used PRR Spec. Spring Washers	1	11	1	39.6	18.5	21.1	53	0.012	3	1	ASA Regular M. C. Nuts
	"	"	2	41.1	26.6	14.5	35	0.009	1	0	
	"	"	3	40.2	15.8	24.4	61	0.009	3	1	
			Avg.	40.3	20.3	20.0	50	0.010	7	2	
S.W. Corner Type D-5 Compression Washers	1	2	1	41.3	23.1	18.2	44	0.022	1	0	ASA Regular L.C. MacLean-Fogg Unitary No. 3 Locknuts on South & East Bolts. ASA Regular M.C. Nuts on North & West Bolts
	"	"	2	40.8	27.2	13.6	33	0.018	0	0	
	"	"	3	38.7	27.3	11.4	30	0.013	0	0	
			Avg.	40.3	25.9	14.4	36	0.018	1	0	

*Each corner of the crossing has twelve 1 3/8-in x 14-in main bolts. The No. 1 bolt position is the nearest one to the flangeway intersection in the four arms of a corner, the No. 2 position the next nearest one, and the No. 3 the farthest from the intersection.

These results cover the period from July 12, 1949 to November 9, 1949.

TABLE 3.   SUMMARY OF THE SECOND CYCLE OF LOSS IN TENSION IN THE MAIN BOLTS OF THE BOLTED RAIL CROSSING BETWEEN THE EASTWARD MAIN OF THE PENNSYLVANIA R.R. AND THE SINGLE TRACK BRANCH LINE OF THE NEW YORK CENTRAL SYSTEM AT WARSAW, INDIANA.

Location and Name of Spring Washers	Washer Curve Reference Fig. No.	Cv. No.	*Bolt Position	Avg. Bolt Tension (1000 lb) Initial	Final	Lost	Percent Tension Lost	Average Pull-in (in)	No. of Bolts with Final Tension less than 20 K	10 K	Remarks
N. W. Corner PRR Specification Spring Washers	1	12	1	40.8	10.5	30.3	74	0.011	4	2	ASA Heavy L.C. Elastic Stop Nuts on North & East Bolts. ASA Regular M.C. Nuts on South & West Bolts
	"	"	2	40.3	17.3	23.0	57	0.010	2	2	
	"	"	3	40.3	18.9	21.4	53	0.011	2	1	
			Avg.	40.5	15.5	25.0	62	0.011	8	5	
N. E. Corner Hubbard Experimental Spring Washers	1	9	1	39.1	14.2	24.9	64	0.019	4	0	ASA Regular Hex. L.C. Security Locknuts on North & West Bolts. ASA Regular M.C. Nuts on South & East Bolts
	"	"	2	39.1	18.9	20.2	52	0.015	3	0	
	"	"	3	38.5	24.9	13.6	35	0.009	1	0	
			Avg.	38.9	19.3	19.6	50	0.014	8	0	
S. E. Corner Reliance Heavy-Duty Hy-Crome Spring Washers	1	4	1	39.2	13.3	25.9	66	0.015	3	1	ASA Regular M.C. Nuts
	"	"	2	39.4	19.7	19.7	50	0.011	3	0	
	"	"	3	36.6	22.8	13.8	38	0.006	1	0	
			Avg.	38.4	18.6	19.8	52	0.011	7	1	
S. W. Corner Type D-6 Compression Washers	1	2	(a) 1(4)	40.8	18.3	22.5	55	0.012	2	0	ASA Regular L.C. MacLean-Fogg Unitary No. 3 Locknuts on South & East Bolts, ASA Regular M.C. Nuts on North & West Bolts
	"	"	2(2)	40.2	21.5	18.7	47	0.011	1	0	
	"	"	3(3)	40.3	24.5	15.8	39	0.006	1	0	
			Avg.	40.4	21.4	19.0	47	0.010	4	0	

*Each corner of the crossing has twelve 1 3/8-in x 14-in main bolts. The No. 1 bolt position is the nearest one to the flangeway intersection in the four arms of a corner, the No. 2 position the next nearest one, and the No. 3 the farthest from the intersection.

(a) Number of washers having one or more broken layers at end of test cycle.

These results cover the period from November 9, 1949 to June 5, 1950.

TABLE 4. SUMMARY OF THE THIRD CYCLE OF LOSS IN TENSION IN THE MAIN BOLTS OF THE BOLTED RAIL CROSSING BETWEEN THE EASTWARD MAIN OF THE PENNSYLVANIA R.R. AND THE SINGLE TRACK BRANCH LINE OF THE NEW YORK CENTRAL SYSTEM AT WARSAW, INDIANA.

Location and Name of Spring Washers	Washer Curve Reference		*Bolt Position	Avg. Bolt Tension (1000 lb)			Percent Tension Lost	Average Pull-in (in)	No. of Bolts with Final Tension less than		Remarks
	Fig. No.	Cv. No.		Initial	Final	Lost			20 K	10 K	
N. W. Corner PRR Specification Spring Washers	3	7	1	25.4	14.6	10.8	43	0.009	4	1	ASA Regular M. C. Nuts
	"	"	2	25.4	13.5	11.9	47	0.008	3	0	
	"	"	3	25.4	16.4	9.0	35	0.011	2	1	
			Avg.	25.4	14.9	10.5	41	0.009	9	2	
N. E. Corner Hubbard Experimental Spring Washers	3	3	1	25.4	14.6	10.9	43	0.006	4	0	ASA Regular M. C. Nuts
	"	"	2	24.7	15.2	9.5	38	0.007	3	0	
	"	"	3	25.4	17.1	8.3	33	0.006	2	1	
			Avg.	25.1	15.6	9.5	38	0.006	9	1	
S. E. Corner Reliance Heavy-Duty Hy-Crome Spring Washers	3	1	1	26.2	16.5	9.7	37	0.005	3	0	ASA Heavy M. C. Nuts
	"	"	2	24.6	17.8	6.8	28	0.004	3	0	
	"	"	3	24.9	19.6	5.3	21	0.004	2	0	
			Avg.	25.3	17.8	7.5	30	0.004	8	0	
S. W. Corner S-300 Plate Washers (First lot)	3	2	1	25.7	17.8	7.9	31	0.005	3	0	ASA Regular L.C. MacLean-Fogg Unitary No. 3 Locknuts on South & East Bolts. ASA Regular M.C. Nuts on North & West Bolts
	"	"	2	25.0	18.4	6.6	26	0.003	2	0	
	"	"	3	25.9	22.3	3.6	14	0.004	0	0	
			Avg.	25.6	19.6	6.0	23	0.004	5	0	

*Each corner of the crossing has twelve 1 3/8-in x 14-in main bolts. The No. 1 bolt position is the nearest one to the flangeway intersection in the four arms of a corner, the No. 2 position the next nearest one, and the No. 3 the farthest from the intersection.

These results cover the period from June 5, 1950 to October 25, 1950.

TABLE 5. SUMMARY OF THE FOURTH CYCLE OF LOSS IN TENSION IN THE MAIN BOLTS OF THE BOLTED RAIL CROSSING BETWEEN THE EASTWARD MAIN OF THE PENNSYLVANIA R.R. AND THE SINGLE TRACK BRANCH LINE OF THE NEW YORK CENTRAL SYSTEM AT WARSAW, INDIANA.

Location and Name of Spring Washers	Washer Curve Reference		* Bolt Position	Avg. Bolt Tension (1000 lb)			Percent Tension Lost	No. of Bolts with Final Tension less than		Remarks
	Fig.No.	Cv.No.		Initial	Final	Lost		20 K	10 K	
N. W. Corner Hubbard Experimental Spring Washers	1	9	1	41.3	16.5	24.8	60	2	0	ASA Heavy M. C. Nuts
	"	"	2	40.3	19.2	21.1	52	2	1	
	"	"	3	40.6	21.5	19.1	47	2	1	
			Avg.	40.7	19.1	21.6	53	6	2	
N. E. Corner PRR Specification Spring Washers	1	12	1	40.3	10.8	29.5	73	4	1	ASA Regular M. C. Nuts
	"	"	2	41.3	21.3	20.0	48	2	0	
	"	"	3	40.5	27.8	12.7	31	1	0	
			Avg.	40.7	20.0	20.7	51	7	1	
S. E. Corner Reliance Heavy–Duty Hy-Crome Spring Washers	1	4	1	41.0	14.4	26.6	65	4	0	ASA Heavy M. C. Heat Treated Nuts
	"	"	2	40.4	22.7	17.7	44	1	0	
	"	"	3	40.4	24.1	16.3	40	1	0	
			Avg.	40.6	20.4	20.2	50	6	0	
S. W. Corner S-300 Plate Washers (First Lot) (a)	1	5	1 } b	40.6	20.2	20.4	50	2	0	ASA Regular L.C. MacLean–Fogg Unitary No. 3 Locknuts on South & East Bolts. ASA Regular M. C. Nuts on North & West Bolts
	1	7	2 } b	41.0	18.6	22.4	55	2	0	
	"	"	3	40.5	27.3	13.2	33	1	0	
			Avg.	40.7	22.0	18.7	46	5	0	

*Each corner of the crossing has 12-1 3/8-in x 14-in main bolts. The No. 1 bolt position is the nearest one to the flangeway intersection in the four arms of a corner, the No. 2 position the next nearest one and the No. 3 the farthest from the intersection.

(a) Two new washers were nested normally on the No. 1 bolts only.
(b) Nine of 16 washers were cracked at the end of service period.
Pull-in measurements were omitted because of inconsistent results.

These results cover the period from October 25, 1950 to May 16, 1951.

TABLE 6. SUMMARY OF THE FIFTH CYCLE OF LOSS IN TENSION IN THE MAIN BOLTS OF THE BOLTED RAIL CROSSING BETWEEN THE EASTWARD MAIN OF THE PENNSYLVANIA R.R. AND THE SINGLE TRACK BRANCH LINE OF THE NEW YORK CENTRAL SYSTEM AT WARSAW, INDIANA.

Location and Name of Spring Washers	Washer Curve Reference		*Bolt Position	Avg. Bolt Tension (1000 lb)			Percent Tension Lost	Average Pull-in (in)	No. of Bolts with Final Tension less than		Remarks
	Fig.No.	Cv.No.		Initial	Final	Lost			20 K	10 K	
N.W. Corner Hubbard Experimental Spring Washers	2	4	1	30.9	11.1	19.8	64	0.009	4	2	ASA Heavy M. C. Nuts
	"	"	2	31.0	16.1	14.9	48	0.009	3	0	
	"	"	3	30.8	15.8	15.0	49	0.007	4	0	
			Avg.	30.9	14.3	16.6	54	0.008	11	2	
N.E. Corner PRR Specification Spring Washers	2	8	1	30.0	11.0	19.0	63	0.011	3	2	ASA Heavy M. C. Nuts
	"	"	2	31.0	18.1	12.9	42	0.010	2	1	
	"	"	3	30.5	21.5	9.0	30	0.010	1	0	
			Avg.	30.5	16.9	13.6	45	0.010	6	3	
S.E. Corner Reliance Heavy-Duty Hy-Crome Spring Washers	2	2	1	30.0	16.2	13.8	46	0.014	3	0	ASA Heavy M. C. Heat Treated Nuts
	"	"	2	30.0	21.3	8.7	29	0.010	1	0	
	"	"	3	29.4	23.3	6.1	21	0.009	0	0	
			Avg.	29.8	20.3	9.5	32	0.011	4	0	
S.W. Corner S-300 Plate Washers (Improved)	2	3	1(a)	31.1	24.5	6.7	21	0.012	0	0	ASA Heavy M. C. Nuts
	"	"	2	31.0	23.2	7.8	25	0.011	1	0	
	"	"	3	31.3	25.4	5.9	19	0.006	1	0	
			Avg.	31.1	24.4	6.7	22	0.010	2	0	

*Each corner of the crossing has 12-1 3/8-in x 14-in main bolts. The No. 1 bolt position is the nearest to the flangeway intersection in the four arms of a corner, the No. 2 position the next nearest one, and the No. 3 the farthest from the intersection.

(a) Two washers were cracked at the end of service period.

These results cover the period from May 16, 1951 to October 16, 1951.

TABLE 7. SUMMARY OF THE SIXTH CYCLE OF LOSS IN TENSION IN THE MAIN BOLTS OF THE BOLTED RAIL CROSSING BETWEEN THE EASTWARD MAIN OF THE PENNSYLVANIA R.R. AND THE SINGLE TRACK BRANCH LINE OF THE NEW YORK CENTRAL SYSTEM AT WARSAW, INDIANA.

Location and Name of Spring Washers	Washer Curve Reference		* Bolt Position	Avg. Bolt Tension (1000 lb)			Percent Tension Lost	Average Pull-in (in)	No. of Bolts with Final Tension less than		Remarks
	Fig.No.	Cv.No.		Initial	Final	Lost			20 K	10 K	
N.W. Corner Hubbard Experimental Spring Washers	1	9	1	40.7	22.1	18.6	46	0.010	2	0	ASA Heavy M. C. Heat Treated Nuts and Hardened, Flat Plate Washers
	"	"	2	40.2	25.2	15.0	37	0.011	2	0	
	"	"	3	39.7	26.2	13.5	34	0.008	0	0	
			Avg.	40.2	24.5	15.7	39	0.010	4	0	
N.E. Corner PRR Specification Spring Washers	1	12	1	39.9	14.2	25.7	64	0.003	4	1	ASA Heavy M. C. Nuts
	"	"	2	39.0	17.2	21.8	56	0.003	2	1	
	"	"	3	39.4	22.7	16.7	42	0.002	2	0	
			Avg.	39.4	18.0	21.4	54	0.003	8	2	
S. E. Corner Reliance Heavy-Duty Ey-Crome Spring Washers	1	4	1	39.8	17.6	22.2	56	0.011	3	0	ASA Heavy M. C. Heat Treated Nuts and Hardened, Flat Plate Washers
	"	"	2	40.4	21.7	18.7	46	0.008	2	0	
	"	"	3	39.8	20.7	19.1	48	0.009	1	0	
			Avg.	40.0	20.0	20.0	50	0.009	6	0	
S. W. Corner 8-300 Plate Washers (Improved) (a).	1	3	1	39.1	23.0	16.1	41	0.011	1	0	ASA Heavy M. C. Nuts
	1	6	2	40.0	23.4	16.6	*42	0.008	1	0	
	"	"	3(b)	40.5	29.7	10.8	27	0.004	0	0	
			Avg.	39.9	25.4	14.5	36	0.008	2	0	

*Each corner of the crossing has 12-1 3/8-in x 14-in main bolts. The No. 1 bolt position is the nearest one to the flangeway inter-section in the four arms of a corner, the No. 2 position the next nearest one, and the No. 3 the farthest from the intersection.

(a) Two new washers were placed back-to-back on the No. 1 bolts only.

(b) One of 16 washers was cracked at the end of service period.

These results cover the period from October 16, 1951 to May 14, 1952.

TABLE 8. SUMMARY OF THE SEVENTH CYCLE OF LOSS IN TENSION IN THE MAIN BOLTS OF THE BOLTED RAIL CROSSING BETWEEN THE EASTWARD MAIN OF THE PENNSYLVANIA R.R. AND THE SINGLE TRACK BRANCH LINE OF THE NEW YORK CENTRAL SYSTEM AT WARSAW, INDIANA.

Location and Name of Spring Washers	Washer Curve Reference		*Bolt Position	Avg. Bolt Tension (1000 lb)			Percent Tension Lost	Average Pull-in (in)	No. of Bolts with Final Tension less than		Remarks
	Fig.No.	Cv.No.		Initial	Final	Lost			20 K	10 K	
N.W. Corner Hubbard Experimental Spring Washers	2	4	1	29.7	21.0	8.7	29	0.007	1	0	ASA Heavy M. C. Heat Treated Nuts and Hardened, Flat Plate Washers
	''	''	2	29.1	22.8	6.3	22	0.006	1	0	
	''	''	3	30.0	23.2	6.8	23	0.008	1	0	
			Avg.	29.6	22.3	7.3	25	0.007	3	0	
N.E. Corner PRR Specification Spring Washers	2	8	1	30.0	14.2	15.8	53	0.007	4	1	ASA Heavy M. C. Nuts
	''	''	2	29.6	14.9	14.7	50	0.006	3	1	
	''	''	3	29.4	19.2	10.2	35	0.007	2	0	
			Avg.	29.7	16.1	13.6	46	0.007	9	2	
S.E. Corner Reliance Heavy-Duty Hy-Crome Spring Washers	2	2	1	29.4	20.2	9.2	31	0.007	2	0	ASA Heavy M. C. Heat Treated Nuts and Hardened, Flat Plate Washers
	''	''	2	30.7	24.9	5.8	19	0.007	1	0	
	''	''	3	29.5	22.0	7.5	25	0.008	1	0	
			Avg.	29.9	22.4	7.5	25	0.007	4	0	
S.W. Corner Reliance Double Coil Hy-Crome Spring Washers	2	1	1	29.7	20.0	9.7	33	0.007	2	0	ASA Heavy M. C. Nuts
	''	''	2	29.8	22.7	7.1	24	0.006	1	0	
	''	''	3(a)	30.0	24.5	5.5	18	0.005	1	0	
			Avg.	29.8	22.4	7.4	25	0.006	4	0	

*Each corner of the crossing has 12-1 3/8-in by 14-in main bolts. The No. 1 bolt position is the nearest on to the flangeway intersection in the four arms of a corner, the No. 2 position the next nearest one and the No. 3 the farthest from the intersection.

(a) One washer was broken at the end of service period.

These results cover the period from May 14, 1952 to October 2, 1952

TABLE 9. SUMMARY OF THE EIGHTH CYCLE OF LOSS IN TENSION IN THE MAIN BOLTS OF THE BOLTED RAIL CROSSING BETWEEN THE EASTWARD MAIN OF THE PENNSYLVANIA R.R. AND THE SINGLE TRACK BRANCH LINE OF THE NEW YORK CENTRAL SYSTEM AT WARSAW, INDIANA.

Part 1. Loss in Tension of the No. 1 Bolts in the N.W., N.E. and S.E. Corners for the Period from October 2, 1952 to January 13, 1953.

Location and Name of Spring Washers	Washer Curve-Reference		* Bolt Position	Average Bolt Tension (1000 lb)			Percent Tension Lost	Average Pull-in (in)	Remarks
	Fig. No.	Cv. No.		Initial	Final	Lost			
N.W. Corner Hubbard Experimental Spring Washers	1	9	1-N	41.6	31.6	10.0	24	0.002	ASA Heavy M.C. Heat Treated Nuts and Hardened, Flat Plate Washers
	"	"	1-S	38.8	29.5	9.3	24	0.007	
	"	"	1-W	38.1	22.0	16.1	42	0.004	
	"	"	1-E	38.1	17.0	21.1	55	0.007	
			Avg.	39.2	25.0	14.1	36	0.005	
N.E. Corner PRR Specification Spring Washers	1	12	1-N	37.8	21.4	16.4	43	0.002	ASA Heavy M.C. Nuts
	"	"	1-S	38.5	20.6	17.9	47	0.006	
	"	"	1-W	40.6	12.1	28.5	70	0.007	
	"	"	1-E	40.6	13.5	27.1	67	0.007	
			Avg.	39.4	16.9	22.5	57	0.006	
S.E. Corner Reliance Frog and Crossing Hy-Crome Spring Washers	1	8	1-N	39.5	24.3	15.2	39	0.004	ASA Heavy M.C. Heat Treated Nuts and Hardened, Flat Plate Washers
	"	"	1-S	38.8	26.5	12.3	32	0.002	
	"	"	1-W	40.2	19.7	20.5	51	0.006	
	"	"	1-E	40.2	13.4	26.8	67	0.004	
			Avg.	39.7	21.0	18.7	47	0.004	

*Each corner of the crossing has 12-1 3/8-in by 14-in main bolts. The No. 1 bolt position is the nearest one to the flangeway intersection in the four arms of a corner, the No. 2 position the next nearest one, and the No. 3 the farthest from the intersection.

TABLE 9.   SUMMARY OF THE EIGHTH CYCLE OF LOSS IN TENSION IN THE MAIN BOLTS OF THE BOLTED RAIL CROSSING BETWEEN THE EASTWARD MAIN OF THE PENNSYLVANIA R. R. AND THE SINGLE TRACK BRANCH LINE OF THE NEW YORK CENTRAL SYSTEM AT WARSAW, INDIANA.

Part 2.   Loss in Tension of the No. 1 Bolts in the N.W., N.E. and S.E. Corners for the Period from January 13, 1953 to April 17, 1953.

Location and Name of Spring Washers	Washer Curve Reference		*Bolt Position	Average Bolt Tension (1000 lb)			Percent Tension Lost	Average Pull-in (in)	Remarks
	Fig. No.	Cv. No.		Initial	Final	Lost			
N.W. Corner Hubbard Experimental Spring Washers	1	9	1-N	39.5	30.9	8.6	22	0.000	ASA Heavy M. C. Heat Treated Nuts and Hardened, Flat Plate Washers
	"	"	1-S	38.8	30.2	8.6	22	0.006	
	"	"	1-W	40.2	31.6	8.6	21	0.003	
	"	"	1-E	40.9	28.9	12.0	29	0.007	
			Avg.	39.8	30.4	9.4	24	0.004	
N. E. Corner PRR Specification Spring Washers	1	12	1-N	41.3	28.6	12.7	31	0.001	ASA Heavy M. C. Nuts
	"	"	1-S	42.0	31.1	10.9	26	0.004	
	"	"	1-W	38.5	20.0	18.5	48	0.004	
	"	"	1-E	39.3	19.2	20.1	51	0.001	
			Avg.	40.3	24.7	15.6	39	0.002	
S. E. Corner Reliance Frog and Crossing Hy-Crome Spring Washers	1	8	1-N	40.9	29.5	11.4	28	0.001	ASA Heavy M. C. Heat Treated Nuts and Hardened, Flat Plate Washers
	"	"	1-S	40.9	37.4	3.5	9	0.006	
	"	"	1-W	40.2	29.5	10.7	27	0.010	
	"	"	1-E	38.1	29.5	8.6	23	0.000	
			Avg.	40.0	31.5	8.6	22	0.004	

*Each corner of the crossing has 12-1 3/8-in by 14-in main bolts. The No. 1 bolt position is the nearest one to the flangeway intersection in the four arms of a corner, the No. 2 position the next nearest one, and the No. 3 the farthest from the intersection.

TABLE 9. SUMMARY OF THE EIGHTH CYCLE OF LOSS IN TENSION IN THE MAIN BOLTS OF THE BOLTED RAIL CROSSING BETWEEN THE EASTWARD MAIN OF THE PENNSYLVANIA R.R. AND THE SINGLE TRACK BRANCH LINE OF THE NEW YORK CENTRAL SYSTEM AT WARSAW, INDIANA.

Part 3. Average Loss in Tension of the No. 1 Bolts in the N.W., N.E. and S.E. Corners for the two 3-month periods from October 2, 1952 to January 13, 1953 and from January 13, 1953 to April 17, 1953.

Location and Name of Spring Washers	Washer Curve Reference		* Bolt Position	Average Bolt Tension (1000 lb)				Percent Tension Lost	Average Pull-in (in)	Remarks
	Fig. No.	Cv. No.		Initial	Final	Lost	Lost			
N.W. Corner Hubbard Experimental Spring Washers	1	9	1-N	40.6	31.2	9.4	23	0.001	ASA Heavy M.C. Heat Treated Nuts and Hardened, Flat Plate Washers
	"	"	1-S	38.8	29.8	9.0	23	0.006	
	"	"	1-W	39.2	26.8	12.4	32	0.004	
	"	"	1-E	39.5	23.0	16.5	42	0.007	
			Avg.	39.5	27.7	11.8	30	0.004	
N.E. Corner PRR Specification Spring Washers	1	12	1-N	39.6	25.0	14.6	37	0.002	ASA Heavy M.C. Nuts
	"	"	1-S	40.2	25.8	14.4	36	0.005	
	"	"	1-W	39.6	16.0	23.6	59	0.006	
	"	"	1-E	40.0	16.4	23.6	59	0.004	
			Avg.	39.8	20.8	19.0	48	0.004	
S.E. Corner Reliance Frog and Crossing Hy-Crome Spring Washers	1	8	1-N	40.2	26.9	13.3	33	0.002	ASA Heavy M.C. Heat Treated Nuts and Hardened, Flat Plate Washers
	"	"	1-S	39.9	32.0	7.9	20	0.004	
	"	"	1-W	40.2	24.6	15.6	39	0.008	
	"	"	1-E	39.2	21.4	17.7	45	0.002	
			Avg.	39.9	26.2	13.6	34	0.004	

*Each corner of the crossing has 12-1 3/8-in by 14-in main bolts. The No. 1 bolt position is the nearest one to the flangeway intersection in the four arms of a corner, the No. 2 position the next nearest one, and the No. 3 the farthest from the intersection.

TABLE 9. SUMMARY OF THE EIGHTH CYCLE OF LOSS IN TENSION IN THE MAIN BOLTS OF THE BOLTED RAIL CROSSING BETWEEN THE EASTWARD MAIN OF THE PENNSYLVANIA R.R. AND THE SINGLE TRACK BRANCH LINE OF THE NEW YORK CENTRAL SYSTEM AT WARSAW, INDIANA.

Part 4. Loss in Tension of the No. 2 and 3 Bolts in the N.W., N.E. and S.E. Corners and of the No. 1, 2 and 3 Bolts in the S.W. Corner for the Period from October 2, 1952 to April 17, 1953.

Location and Name of Spring Washers	Washer Curve Reference		*Bolt Position	Avg. Bolt Tension (1000 lb)			Percent Tension Lost	Average Pull-in (in)	No. of Bolts with Final Tension less than		Remarks
	Fig.No.	Cv.No.		Initial	Final	Lost			20 K	10 K	
N.W. Corner Hubbard Experimental Spring Washers	1	9	2	39.2	28.7	10.5	27	0.008	1	0	ASA Heavy M.C. Heat Treated Nuts and Hardened, Flat Plate Washers
	"	"	3	39.8	31.4	8.4	21	0.007	0	0	
			Avg.	39.5	30.0	9.5	24	0.008	1	0	
N.E. Corner PRR Specification Spring Washers	1	12	2	39.5	14.5	25.0	64	0.008	2	1	ASA Heavy M.C. Nuts
	"	"	3	40.8	25.3	15.5	38	0.008	0	0	
			Avg.	40.2	19.9	20.3	51	0.008	2	1	
S.E. Corner Reliance Frog and Crossing Hy-Crome Spring Washers	1	8	2	40.0	22.5	17.5	44	0.003	2	0	ASA Heavy M.C. Heat Treated Nuts and Hardened, Flat Plate Washers
	"	"	3	39.0	30.1	8.9	23	0.001	0	0	
			Avg.	39.5	26.3	13.2	33	0.002	2	0	
S.W. Corner Reliance Double Coil Hy-Crome Spring Washers	1	1	1	40.0	26.5	13.5	34	0.012	0	0	ASA Heavy M.C. Nuts
	"	"	2	40.0	33.4	6.6	16	0.009	0	0	
	"	"	3	38.7	30.5	8.2	21	0.008	0	0	
			Avg.	39.6	30.1	9.5	24	0.010	0	0	

*Each corner of the crossing has 12-1 3/8-in by 14-in main bolts. The No. 1 bolt position is the nearest one to the flangeway intersection in the four arms of a corner, the No. 2 position the next nearest one, and the No. 3 the farthest from the intersection.

TABLE 10   SUMMARY OF THE NINTH CYCLE OF LOSS IN TENSION IN THE NO. 1 BOLTS OF THE BOLTED RAIL CROSSING BETWEEN THE EASTWARD MAIN OF THE PENNSYLVANIA R.R. AND THE SINGLE TRACK BRANCH LINE OF THE NEW YORK CENTRAL SYSTEM AT WARSAW, INDIANA.

Location and Name of Spring Washers	Washer Curve Reference		*Bolt Position	Average Bolt Tension (1000 lb)			Percent Tension Lost	Remarks
	Fig. No.	Cv. No.		Initial	Final	Lost		
N.W. Corner Hubbard Experimental Spring Washers	1	9	1-N	40.2	28.9	11.3	28	ASA Heavy M.C. Heat Treated Nuts and Hardened, Flat Plate Washers
	"	"	1-S	41.6	31.6	10.0	24	
	"	"	1-W	41.6	19.7	21.9	53	
			1-E	38.8	19.0	19.8	51	
			Avg.	40.6	24.8	15.8	39	
N.E. Corner PRR Specification Spring Washers	1	12	1-N	40.0	26.6	13.4	34	ASA Heavy M.C. Nuts
	"	"	1-S	40.6	23.0	17.6	43	
	"	"	1-W	41.3	24.5	16.8	41	
			1-E	39.3	19.2	20.1	51	
			Avg.	40.3	23.3	17.0	42	
S.E. Corner Reliance Frog and Crossing Hy-Crome Spring Washers	1	8	1-N	38.8	28.9	9.9	26	ASA Heavy M.C. Heat Treated Nuts and Hardened, Flat Plate Washers
	"	"	1-S	40.2	30.9	9.3	23	
	"	"	1-W	40.9	25.8	15.1	37	
			1-E	40.2	32.3	7.9	19	
			Avg.	40.0	29.5	10.5	26	
S.W. Corner Reliance Double Coil Hy-Crome Spring Washers	1	1	1-N	41.4	30.0	11.4	28	ASA Heavy M.C. Nuts
	"	"	1-S	40.7	30.0	10.7	26	
	"	"	1-W	39.3	31.4	7.9	20	
			1-E	42.1	26.1	16.0	38	
			Avg.	40.9	29.4	11.5	28	

*Each corner of the crossing has 12-1 3/8-in by 14-in main bolts. The No. 1 bolt position is the nearest one to the flangeway intersection in the four arms of a corner, the No. 2 position the next nearest one, and the No. 3 the farthest from the intersection.

These results cover the period from April 27, 1953 to July 7, 1953.

TABLE 11.   Percent Tension Loss of 40,000 lb Initial Tension for the 1 3/8 in Main Bolts in the Eastward Crossing between the PRR and NYC at Warsaw, Indiana

Name of Washer	First Cycle 7-12-49 to 11-9-49	Second Cycle 11-9-49 to 6-6-50	Fourth Cycle 10-25-50 to 5-16-51	Sixth Cycle 10-16-51 to 5-14-52	Eighth Cycle 10-2-52 to 4-17-53	No. 1 Bolts Avg.	No. 1 Bolts Per-cent	All Bolts Avg.	All Bolts Per-cent
PRR Standard Spring Washers — Corner of Crossing No. 1 Bolts	NW 58	NW 74	NE 73	NE 64	Two 3-mo. cycles omitted	67	100		
All Bolts	46 See Note A	62 See Note A	51 ASA Reg. M. C. Nuts	54 ASA Heavy M. C. Nuts				53	100
Hubbard Experimental Spring Washers — Corner of Crossing No. 1 Bolts	NE 55	NE 64	NW 60	NW 46	Two 3-mo. cycles omitted	56	84		
All Bolts	43 See Note A	50 See Note A	53 ASA Heavy M. C. Nuts	39 ASA Heavy H.T. M.C. Nuts. Hardened plate washers next to corner braces				46	87
Reliance Heavy Duty Hy-Crome Spring Washers — Corner of Crossing No. 1 Bolts		SE 66	SE 65	SE 56		62	93		
All Bolts		52 ASA Reg. M. C. Nuts	50 ASA Heavy H.T. M.C. Nuts	50 ASA Heavy H.T. M.C. Nuts. Hardened plate washers next to corner braces				51	96
Type D-5 Compression Washers — Corner of Crossing No. 1 Bolts	SW 44	SW 55				50	75		
All Bolts	36 See Note A	47 See Note A						42	79
S-300 Plate Washers — Corner of Crossing No. 1 Bolts			SW 50	SW 41		46	69		
All Bolts			46 See Note A. Two first lot washers nested normally on No. 1 bolts	36 ASA Heavy M.C. Nuts. Two second lot washers back to back on No. 1 bolts only				41	77
Double Coil Hy-Crome Spring Washers — Corner of Crossing No. 1 Bolts					SW 34	34	51		
All Bolts					24 ASA Heavy M. C. Nuts. Double Coil Hy-Crome Washers after 5-14-52			24	45

Note A: Half L. C. Locknuts and half ASA Reg. M. C. Nuts   M. C. = medium carbon   H. T. = heat treated   L. C. = low carbon

A

TABLE 12. SUMMARY OF THE FIRST CYCLE OF LOSS IN TENSION IN THE MAIN BOLTS OF TWO BOLTED RAIL CROSSINGS BETWEEN THE EASTWARD TRACK OF THE PENNSYLVANIA R.R. AND THE DOUBLE TRACK MAIN OF THE G.M.&O.R.R., 37th STREET AND CAMPBELL AVE., CHICAGO, ILLINOIS.

Location and Name of Spring Washers	Washer Curve Reference		*Bolt Position	Avg. Bolt Tension (1000 lb)			Percent Tension Lost	Average Pull-in (in)	No. of Bolts with Final Tension less than		Remarks
	Fig.No.	Cv.No.		Initial	Final	Lost			20 K	10 K	
NORTHWEST CROSSING "C"											
East Half Hubbard Experimental Spring Washers	1	9	1	40.2	24.2	16.0	40	0.015	2	1	ASA Regular M. C. Nuts
	"	"	2	40.4	26.4	14.0	35	0.009	1	1	
	"	"	3	41.3	32.6	8.7	21	0.006	0	0	
			Avg.	40.6	27.7	12.4	33	0.010	3	2	
West Half Used PRR Spec. Spring Washers	1	11	1	41.9	17.0	24.9	59	0.011	5	2	ASA Regular M. C. Nuts
	"	"	2	44.9	31.9	13.0	29	0.006	2	0	
	"	"	3	39.5	32.9	6.6	17	0.004	0	0	
			Avg.	42.2	27.2	15.1	36	0.007	7	2	
SOUTHWEST CROSSING "D"											
East Half Improved Frog and Crossing Hy-Crome Spring Washers	1	8	1	38.7	21.1	17.6	45	0.017	3	1	ASA Regular M. C. Nuts
	"	"	2	42.8	29.5	13.3	31	0.011	1	0	
	"	"	3	41.9	33.1	8.8	21	0.008	0	0	
			Avg.	41.1	27.9	13.2	32	0.012	4	1	
West Half Used PRR Spec. Spring Washers	1	11	1	43.1	20.4	22.7	53	0.01b	1	1	ASA Regular M. C. Nuts
	"	"	2	41.3	28.1	13.2	32	0.013	0	0	
	"	"	3	40.2	30.1	10.1	25	0.009	0	0	
			Avg.	41.5	26.2	15.1	36	0.012	1	1	

*Each half of a crossing has 24-1 3/8-in x 14-in main bolts. The No. 1 bolt position is the nearest one to the flangeway intersection in the four arms of each corner, the No. 2 position the next nearest one, and the No. 3 the farthest from the intersection.

These results cover the period from June 15, 1949 to October 12, 1949.

TABLE 13 SUMMARY OF THE SECOND CYCLE OF LOSS IN TENSION IN THE MAIN BOLTS OF TWO BOLTED RAIL CROSSINGS BETWEEN THE EASTWARD TRACK OF THE PENNSYLVANIA R. R. AND THE DOUBLE TRACK MAIN OF THE G. M. &O. R. R., 37th STREET AND CAMPBELL AVE., CHICAGO, ILLINOIS.

Location and Name of Spring Washers	Washer Curve Reference		*Bolt Position	Avg. Bolt Tension (1000 lb)			Percent Tension Lost	Average Pull-in (in)	No. of Bolts with Final Tension less than		Remarks
	Fig.No.	Cv.No.		Initial	Final	Lost			20 K	10 K	
NORTHWEST CROSSING "C"											
East Half Hubbard Experimental Spring Washers	1	9	1	39.6	12.6	27.0	68	0.031	7	2	ASA Regular M. C. Nuts
	"	"	2	39.9	18.7	21.2	53	0.023	5	1	
	"	"	3	38.8	24.9	13.9	36	0.017	4	0	
			Avg.	39.4	18.7	20.7	53	0.024	16	3	
West Half Used PRR Spec. Spring Washers	1	11	1	39.3	10.1	29.2	74	0.022	8	3	ASA Regular M. C. Nuts
	"	"	2	39.8	19.9	19.9	50	0.021	4	2	
	"	"	3	41.0	17.2	23.8	58	0.021	2	1	
			Avg.	39.9	15.3	24.6	62	0.021	14	6	
SOUTHWEST CROSSING "D"											
East Half Improved Frog and Crossing Hy-Crome Spring Washers	1	8	1	37.5	11.8	25.7	69	0.019	6	4	ASA Regular M. C. Nuts
	"	"	2	37.6	20.5	17.1	46	0.013	4	2	
	"	"	3	38.2	20.9	17.3	45	0.012	3	1	
			Avg.	37.8	17.7	20.1	53	0.015	13	7	
West Half Used PRR Spec. Spring Washers	1	11	1	40.1	5.2	34.9	87	0.027	7	6	ASA Regular M. C. Nuts
	"	"	2	39.7	17.4	22.3	56	0.018	5	2	
	"	"	3	35.9	20.5	15.4	43	0.015	4	2	
			Avg.	38.6	14.9	23.7	61	0.019	16	10	

*Each half of a crossing has 24– 1 3/8–in x 14–in main bolts. The No. 1 bolt position is the nearest one to the flangeway intersection in the four arms of each corner, the No. 2 position the next nearest one, and the No. 3 the farthest from the intersection.

These results cover the period from October 12, 1949 to June 21, 1950.

TABLE 14. SUMMARY OF THE THIRD CYCLE OF LOSS IN TENSION IN THE MAIN BOLTS OF TWO BOLTED RAIL CROSSINGS BETWEEN THE EASTWARD TRACK OF THE PENNSYLVANIA R.R. AND THE DOUBLE TRACK MAIN OF THE G.M.&O.R.R., 37th STREET AND CAMPBELL AVE., CHICAGO, ILLINOIS.

Location and Name of Spring Washers	Washer Curve Reference Fig.No.	Cv.No.	*Bolt Position	Avg. Bolt Tension (1000 lb) Initial	Final	Lost	Percent Tension Lost	Average Pull-in (in)	No. of Bolts with Final Tension less than 20 K	10 K	Remarks
NORTHWEST CROSSING "C"											
East Half Hubbard Experimental Spring Washers	3	3	1	24.4	10.6	13.8	57	0.015	8	4	ASA Regular M. C. Nuts
	"	"	2	24.7	12.6	12.1	49	0.013	7	2	
	"	"	3	25.5	17.2	8.3	33	0.015	5	1	
			Avg.	24.8	13.3	11.5	46	0.014	20	7	
West Half Used PRR Spec. Spring Washers	3	6	1	23.4	12.2	11.2	48	0.015	8	3	ASA Regular M. C. Nuts
	"	"	2	24.4	14.9	9.5	39	0.011	3	2	
	"	"	3	24.8	14.7	10.1	41	0.020	4	2	
			Avg.	24.1	13.7	10.4	43	0.016	15	7	
SOUTHWEST CROSSING "D"											
East Half Improved Frog and Crossing Hy-Crome Spring Washers	3	4	1	24.5	9.9	14.6	60	0.017	8	3	ASA Regular M. C. Nuts
	"	"	2	24.9	13.9	11.0	44	0.023	6	3	
	"	"	3	25.3	17.9	7.4	29	0.027	4	1	
			Avg.	24.9	13.9	11.0	44	0.023	18	7	
West Half Used PRR Spec. Spring Washers	3	6	1	25.1	6.1	19.0	76	0.015	8	7	ASA Regular M. C. Nuts
	"	"	2	25.5	10.5	15.0	59	0.022	6	4	
	"	"	3	25.2	12.5	12.7	50	0.025	5	3	
			Avg.	25.3	9.6	15.7	62	0.021	19	14	

*Each half of the crossing had 24-1 3/8-in by 14-in main bolts. The No. 1 bolt position is the nearest one to the flangeway inter-section in the four arms of each corner, the No. 2 position the next nearest one, and the No. 3 the farthest from the intersection.

These results cover the period from June 21, 1950 to January 11, 1951.

TABLE 15 SUMMARY OF THE FOURTH CYCLE OF LOSS IN TENSION IN THE MAIN BOLTS OF TWO BOLTED RAIL CROSSINGS BETWEEN THE EASTWARD TRACK OF THE PENNSYLVANIA R.R. AND THE DOUBLE TRACK MAIN OF THE G.M.&O.R.R., 37th STREET AND CAMPBELL AVE., CHICAGO, ILLINOIS.

Location and Name of Spring Washers	Washer Curve Reference		*Bolt Position	Avg. Bolt Tension (1000 lb)			Percent Tension Lost	Average Pull-in (in)	No. of Bolts with Final Tension less than		Remarks
	Fig.No.	Cv.No.		Initial	Final	Lost			20 K	10 K	
NORTHWEST CROSSING "C"											
East Half Hubbard Experimental Spring Washers	3	3	1	25.1	13.4	11.7	47	0.013	8	0	ASA Regular M. C. Nuts
	"	"	2	24.6	11.7	12.9	52	0.020	7	3	
	"	"	3	25.1	13.7	11.4	45	0.018	6	2	
			Avg.	24.9	12.9	12.0	48	0.017	21	5	
West Half Used PRR Spec. Spring Washers	3	6	1	25.3	7.8	17.5	69	0.016	7	5	ASA Regular M. C. Nuts
	"	"	2	25.2	7.3	17.9	71	0.011	6	6	
	"	"	3	24.7	6.3	18.4	75	0.017	5	5	
			Avg.	25.1	7.2	17.9	71	0.015	18	16	
SOUTHWEST CROSSING "D"											
East Half Improved Frog and Crossing Hy-Crome Spring Washers	3	4	1	26.2	4.7	21.5	82	0.018	8	7	ASA Regular M. C. Nuts
	"	"	2	24.8	7.7	17.1	69	0.017	8	4	
	"	"	3	24.6	11.2	13.4	54	0.016	5	3	
			Avg.	25.2	7.7	17.5	69	0.017	21	14	
West Half Used PRR Spec. Spring Washers	3	6	1	24.8	4.8	20.0	81	0.012	7	7	ASA Regular M. C. Nuts
	"	"	2	25.4	6.3	19.1	75	0.013	8	6	
	"	"	3	24.5	9.7	14.8	61	0.016	7	5	
			Avg.	24.9	7.0	17.9	72	0.014	22	18	

*Each half of the crossing has 24-1 3/8-in by 14-in main bolts. The No. 1 bolt position is the nearest one to the flangeway intersection in the four arms of each corner, the No. 2 position the next nearest one, and the No. 3 the farthest from the intersection.

These results cover the period from January 11, 1951 to October 10, 1951.

TABLE 16. SUMMARY OF THE THIRD CYCLE OF LOSS IN TENSION IN THE MAIN BOLTS OF THE CROSSING BETWEEN THE SOUTHWARD TRACK OF THE C.&W.I.R.R. AND THE WESTWARD TRACK OF THE I.H.B.R.R., 55th STREET AND CICERO AVE., CHICAGO, ILLINOIS.

Location and Name of Spring Washers	Washer Curve Reference		*Bolt Position	Avg. Bolt Tension (1000 lb)			Percent Tension Lost	Average Pull-in (in)	No. of Bolts with Final Tension less than		Remarks
	Fig.No.	Cv.No.		Initial	Final	Lost			20 K	10 K	
NORTHWEST CROSSING "A" – Manganese Insert on T-Beam Support											
N.W. Corner No Spring Washers	-	-	1	26.0	2.2	23.8	92	0.010	4	4	ASA Regular Hex, L.C. Elastic Stop Nuts
	-	-	2	25.0	15.0	10.0	40	0.009	2	1	
	-	-	3	25.1	22.2	2.9	12	0.013	1	0	
			Avg.	25.4	12.3	13.1	52	0.010	7	5	
S.W. Corner Used Hy-Pressure Hy-Crome Spring Washers	6	2	1	25.3	6.7	18.6	74	0.017	4	3	ASA Regular Hex, L.C. Elastic Stop Nuts
	"	"	2	25.7	16.3	9.4	37	0.013	3	0	
	"	"	3	25.3	20.3	5.0	20	0.011	2	0	
			Avg.	25.4	14.4	10.0	39	0.014	9	3	
N.E. Corner Used Hy-Pressure Hy-Crome Spring Washers	6	2	1	25.3	8.4	16.9	67	0.016	4	3	ASA Heavy, 1/4-in extra thick M.C. Nuts
	"	"	2	25.6	22.4	3.2	12	0.015	1	0	
	"	"	3	25.6	20.5	5.1	20	0.012	2	1	
			Avg.	25.5	17.1	8.4	33	0.014	7	4	
S.E. Corner Used Standard Hy-Crome Spring Washers	6	3	1	25.2	10.0	15.2	60	0.014	4	2	ASA Heavy, 1/4-in extra thick M.C. Nuts
	"	"	2	25.2	16.7	8.5	34	0.013	3	1	
	"	"	3	25.3	17.9	7.4	29	0.015	2	0	
			Avg.	25.2	14.6	10.6	42	0.014	9	3	

*Each corner of the crossing has 12-1 1/4-in main bolts, 4 each of three lengths. The No. 1 bolt position is the one nearest the flangeway intersection in the four arms of a corner, the No. 2 position the next nearest one, and the No. 3 the farthest from the intersection.

These results cover the period from July 17, 1950 to April 20, 1951.

See Vol. 52, 1951, Page 547, Table 6 for second test cycle.

TABLE 17. SUMMARY OF THE THIRD CYCLE OF LOSS IN TENSION IN THE MAIN BOLTS OF THE CROSSING BETWEEN THE DOUBLE TRACK OF THE C.&W.I.R.R. AND THE EASTWARD TRACK OF THE I.H.B.R.R., 55th STREET AND CICERO AVE., CHICAGO, ILLINOIS.

Location and Name of Spring Washers	Washer Curve Reference		*Bolt Position	Avg. Bolt Tension (1000 lb)			Percent Tension Lost	Average Pull-in (in)	No. of Bolts with Final Tension less than		Remarks
	Fig.No.	Cv.No.		Initial	Final	Lost			20 K	10 K	
SOUTHWEST CROSSING "C" – Manganese Insert on Framed Timbers – 1 1/4-In Bolts											
East half Used Standard Hy-Crome Spring Washers	6 " "	3 " "	1 2 3	24.8 25.3 25.4	5.5 10.3 17.3	19.3 15.0 8.1	78 59 32	0.008 0.010 0.011	8 7 4	7 4 1	ASA Heavy, 1/4-in extra thick M. C. Nuts
Avg.				25.2	11.0	14.2	56	0.010	19	12	
West half New Improved Frog and Crossing Hy-Crome Spring Washers, replacing 1 3/8-in size	6 " "	1 " "	1 2 3	25.4 24.8 26.0	6.1 13.6 17.1	19.3 11.2 8.9	76 45 34	0.008 0.009 0.013	8 7 5	7 2 0	ASA Heavy, 1/4-in extra thick M. C. Nuts
Avg.				25.4	12.0	13.4	53	0.010	20	9	
SOUTHEAST CROSSING "D" – Solid Manganese on Framed Timbers											
1 3/8-in Interior Bolts Used Hy-Pressure Hy-Crome Spring Washers	3 " "	5 " "	1 2 3	24.2 24.9 25.0	15.2 15.6 15.6	9.0 9.3 9.4	37 37 38	0.011 0.010 0.008	5 5 7	1 1 1	ASA Heavy, 1/4-in extra thick M. C. Nuts
Avg.				24.7	15.5	9.2	37	0.010	17	3	
1 1/4-in Exterior Bolts Used Hy-Pressure Hy-Crome Spring Washers	6 " " "	2 " " "	1 2 3 4	25.0 25.4 25.7 26.0	15.4 20.0 15.8 18.4	9.6 5.4 9.9 7.6	38 21 38 29	0.010 0.005 0.010 0.011	5 2 7 3	0 1 1 1	ASA Heavy, 1/4-in extra thick M. C. Nuts
Avg.				25.5	17.4	8.1	32	0.010	17	3	

*Crossing "C" has the same arrangement of bolts as Crossing "A". New 1 1/4-in spring washers were placed on the west half of Crossing "C", July 17, 1950.

Crossing "D". – Each external arm has four main bolts for connecting the rails to the casting, and the bolts are numbered from flangeway intersection to the far end of the connecting joint. Each interior side of the crossing has a six-hole joint. Bolt position 3 includes the two middle bolts of the joint, position 2, the intermediate bolts, and position 1, the end bolts of the internal joints. These results cover the period from July 17, 1950 to April 20, 1951 for Crossing "C" and from July 17, 1950 to January 18, 1951 for Crossing "D".

See Vol. 52, 1951, Page 550. Table 7 for second test cycle.

TABLE 18   SUMMARY OF THE FOURTH CYCLE OF LOSS IN TENSION IN THE MAIN BOLTS OF THE CROSSING BETWEEN THE SOUTHWARD TRACK OF THE C.&W.I.R.R. AND THE WESTWARD TRACK OF THE I.H.B.R.R., 55th STREET AND CICERO AVE., CHICAGO, ILLINOIS.

Location and Name of Spring Washers	Washer Curve Reference		*Bolt Position	Avg. Bolt Tension (1000 lb)			Percent Tension Lost	No. of Bolts with Final Tension less than		Remarks
	Fig.No.	Cv.No.		Initial	Final	Lost		20 K	10 K	
NORTHWEST CROSSING "A" – Manganese Insert on T-Beam Support										
N.W. Corner Used Hy-Pressure Hy-Crome Spring Washers	5	2	1	31.3	13.8	17.5	56	4	1	ASA Regular Hex, L.C. Elastic Stop Nuts
	"	"	2	29.7	18.5	11.2	38	3	0	
	"	"	3	29.2	23.2	6.0	20	0	0	
			Avg.	30.1	18.5	11.6	39	7	1	
S.W. Corner No Spring Washers	–	–	1	30.2	8.1	22.1	73	3	2	ASA Regular Hex, L.C. Elastic Stop Nuts
	–	–	2	28.6	17.9	10.7	37	3	0	
	–	–	3	30.2	20.7	9.5	31	2	0	
			Avg.	29.6	16.2	13.4	45	8	2	
N.E. Corner Used Hy-Pressure Hy-Crome Spring Washers	5	2	1	30.0	15.2	14.8	49	3	0	ASA Heavy, 1/4-in extra thick M.C. Nuts
	"	"	2	30.4	17.2	13.2	43	4	0	
	"	"	3	30.3	28.2	2.1	7	0	0	
			Avg.	30.2	17.5	12.7	42	7	0	
S.E. Corner Used Standard Hy-Crome Spring Washers	5	3	1	30.1	12.2	17.9	60	4	1	ASA Heavy, 1/4-in extra thick M.C. Nuts
	"	"	2	30.7	15.8	14.9	49	3	1	
	"	"	3	32.3	30.8	1.5	5	0	0	
			Avg.	30.9	18.6	12.3	40	7	2	

*Each corner of the crossing has 12-1 1/4-in main bolts, 4 each of three lengths. The No. 1 bolt position is the one nearest the flange-way intersection in the four arms of a corner, the No. 2 position the next nearest, and the No. 3 the farthest from the intersection.

Pull-in measurements were omitted from tabulation because of inconsistent results.

These results cover the period from April 20, 1951 to November 1, 1951.

TABLE 19. SUMMARY OF THE FOURTH CYCLE OF LOSS IN TENSION IN THE MAIN BOLTS OF THE CROSSINGS BETWEEN THE DOUBLE TRACK LINE OF THE C.&W.I.R.R. AND THE EASTWARD TRACK OF THE I.H.B.R.R., 55th STREET AND CICERO AVE., CHICAGO, ILLINOIS.

Location and Name of Spring Washers	Washer Curve Reference		*Bolt Position	Avg.-Bolt Tension (1000 lb)			Percent Tension Lost	Average Pull-in (in)	No. of Bolts with Final Tension less than		Remarks
	Fig.No.	Cv.No.		Initial	Final	Lost			20 K	10 K	
SOUTHWEST CROSSING "C" - Manganese Insert on Framed Timbers - 1 1/4-in Bolts											
East Half New Standard Hy-Crome Spring Washers	5	4	1	29.9	15.9	14.0	47	0.010	7	2	New ASA Heavy, 1/4-in extra thick M. C. Nuts
	"	"	2	30.2	21.1	9.1	30	0.003	5	0	
	"	"	3	30.1	24.3	5.8	19	0.004	1	0	
			Avg.	30.1	20.1	10.0	33	0.006	13	2	
West Half Improved Frog and Crossing Hy-Crome Spring Washers	5	1	1	30.4	21.1	9.3	31	0.006	4	0	New ASA Heavy, 1/4-in extra thick M. C. Nuts
	"	"	2	30.0	22.8	7.2	24	0.002	1	0	
	"	"	3	30.2	26.0	4.2	14	0.006	1	0	
			Avg.	30.2	23.0	7.2	24	0.005	6	0	
SOUTHEAST CROSSING "D" - Solid Manganese on Framed Timbers											
1 3/8-in Interior Bolts Used Hy-Pressure Hy-Crome Spring Washers	3	5	1	25.5	11.3	14.2	56	0.023	5	4	ASA Heavy, 1/4-in extra thick M. C. Nuts
	"	"	2	24.5	10.5	14.0	57	0.011	8	4	
	"	"	3	25.7	11.0	14.7	57	0.008	8	3	
			Avg.	25.2	10.9	14.3	57	0.014	21	11	
1 1/4-in Exterior Bolts Used Hy-Pressure Hy-Crome Spring Washers	6	2	1	25.1	13.4	11.7	47	0.013	5	2	ASA Heavy, 1/4-in extra thick M. C. Nuts
	"	"	2	24.9	11.9	13.0	52	0.010	7	3	
	"	"	3	24.6	12.0	12.6	51	0.012	6	4	
	"	"	4	25.5	13.6	11.9	47	0.010	7	1	
			Avg.	25.0	12.7	12.3	49	0.011	25	10	

*Crossing "C" has the same arrangement of bolts as Crossing "A". The following changes were made to Crossing "C", June 1, 1951: (1) New nuts, faced, were applied to all main bolts, (2) all beveled washers and headlocks were welded to the corner braces, and (3) new spring washers were applied to the east half of the crossing.

Crossing "D". - Each external arm has four main bolts for connecting the rails to the casting, and the bolts are numbered from the flangeway intersection to the far end of the connecting joint. Each interior side of the crossing has a six-hole joint. Bolt position 3 includes the two middle bolts of the joint, position 2, the intermediate bolts, and position 1, the end bolts of the internal joints. These results cover the period from June 1, 1951 to November 1, 1951 for Crossing "C" and from January 19, 1951 to October 3, 1951 for Crossing "D".

TABLE 20. SUMMARY OF THE FIFTH CYCLE OF LOSS IN TENSION IN THE MAIN BOLTS OF THE CROSSINGS BETWEEN THE DOUBLE TRACK LINE OF THE C.&W.I.R.R. AND THE EASTWARD TRACK OF THE I.H.B.R.R. 55th STREET AND CICERO AVE., CHICAGO, ILLINOIS.

Location and Name of Spring Washers	Washer Curve Reference Fig.No.	Washer Curve Reference Cv.No.	* Bolt Position	Avg. Bolt Tension (1000 lb) Initial	Avg. Bolt Tension (1000 lb) Final	Avg. Bolt Tension (1000 lb) Lost	Percent Tension Lost	Average Pull-in (in)	No. of Bolts with Final Tension less than 1 1/4-in Bolts 20 K	No. of Bolts with Final Tension less than 1 1/4-in Bolts 10 K	Remarks
SOUTHWEST CROSSING "C" - Manganese Insert on Framed Timbers - 1 1/4-in Bolts											
East Half Standard Hy-Crome Spring Washers	4	4	1	40.1	15.3	24.8	62	0.010	5	2	ASA Heavy, 1/4-in extra thick M.C. Nuts
	"	"	2	39.9	29.0	10.9	27	0.009	0	0	
	"	"	3	39.5	33.0	6.5	16	0.012	0	0	
			Avg.	39.8	25.8	14.0	35	0.010	5	2	
West Half Improved Frog and Crossing Hy-Crome Spring Washers	4	1	1	40.7	20.1	20.6	51	0.006	4	0	ASA Heavy, 1/4-in extra thick M.C. Nuts
	"	"	2	40.7	28.7	12.0	30	0.008	0	0	
	"	"	3	39.8	32.6	7.2	18	0.010	0	0	
			Avg.	40.4	27.1	13.3	33	0.008	4	0	
SOUTHEAST CROSSING "D" - Solid Manganese on Framed Timbers											
1 3/8-in Interior Bolts Used Hy-Pressure Hy-Crome Spring Washers	1	10	1	40.3	17.0	23.3	58	0.014	6	2	ASA Heavy, 1/4-in extra thick M.C. Nuts
	"	"	2	39.4	13.8	25.6	65	0.010	7	1	
	"	"	3	39.7	13.2	26.5	67	0.005	7	2	
			Avg.	39.8	14.7	25.1	63	0.009	20	5	
1 1/4-in Exterior Bolts Used Hy-Pressure Hy-Crome Spring Washers	4	2	1	40.0	15.5	24.5	61	0.004	6	2	ASA Heavy, 1/4-in extra thick M.C. Nuts
	"	"	2	39.6	16.7	22.9	58	0.005	4	1	
	"	"	3	40.3	14.3	26.0	64	0.008	6	2	
	"	"	4	40.2	13.4	26.8	67	0.008	8	2	
			Avg.	40.2	15.0	25.0	62	0.006	24	7	

*Crossing "C" has the same arrangement of bolts as Crossing "A".

Crossing "D". - Each external arm has four main bolts for connecting the rails to the casting, and the bolts are numbered from the flangeway intersection to the far end of the connecting joint. Each interior side of the crossing has a six-hole joint. Bolt position 3 includes the two middle bolts of the joint, position 2, the intermediate bolts, and position 1, the end bolts of the internal joint.

These results cover the period from November 1, 1951 to May 21, 1952 for Crossing "C" and from October 3, 1951 to May 21, 1952 for Crossing "D".

TABLE 21. SUMMARY OF THE SIXTH CYCLE OF LOSS IN TENSION IN THE MAIN BOLTS OF THE CROSSINGS BETWEEN THE DOUBLE TRACK LINE OF THE C.&W.I.R.R. AND THE EASTWARD TRACK OF THE I.H.B.R.R., 55th STREET AND CICERO AVE., CHICAGO, ILLINOIS.

Location and Name of Spring Washers	Washer Curve Reference Fig.No.	Cv.No.	* Bolt Position	Avg. Bolt Tension (1000 lb) Initial	Final	Lost	Percent Tension Lost	Average Pull-in (in)	No. of Bolts with Final Tension less than 20 K	10 K	Remarks
SOUTHWEST CROSSING "C" - Manganese Insert on Framed Timbers - 1 1/4-in Bolts											
East Half Standard Hy-Crome Spring Washers	5	4	1	29.8	18.5	11.3	38	0.008	6	0	ASA Heavy, 1/4-in extra thick M.C. Nuts
	"	"	2	29.8	24.8	5.0	17	0.005	0	0	
	"	"	3	30.2	30.1	0.1	3	0.002	0	0	
			Avg.	29.9	24.5	5.4	18	0.005	6	0	
West Half Improved Frog and Crossing Hy-Crome Spring Washers	5	1	1	30.3	21.3	9.0	30	0.008	3	0	ASA Heavy, 1/4-in extra thick M.C. Nuts
	"	"	2	29.6	27.7	1.9	6	0.005	0	0	
	"	"	3	30.6	29.1	1.5	5	0.002	0	0	
			Avg.	30.2	26.0	4.2	14	0.005	3	0	
SOUTHEAST CROSSING "D" - Solid Manganese on Framed Timbers											
1 3/8-in Interior Bolts Used Hy-Pressure Hy-Crome Spring Washers	2	6	1	29.6	23.7	5.9	20	0.007	2	0	ASA Heavy, 1/4-in extra thick M.C. Nuts
	"	"	2	29.3	17.0	12.3	42	0.010	6	1	
	"	"	3	30.0	13.6	16.4	55	0.011	7	1	
			Avg.	29.6	18.1	11.5	39	0.009	15	2	
1 1/4-in Exterior Bolts Used Hy-Pressure Hy-Crome Spring Washers	5	2	1	29.7	22.9	5.8	20	0.012	7	3	ASA Heavy, 1/4-in extra thick M.C. Nuts
	"	"	2	29.7	15.8	13.9	47	0.010	5	1	
	"	"	3	29.7	16.5	13.2	44	0.010	7	2	
	"	"	4	29.3	13.6	15.7	54	0.010	2	1	
			Avg.	29.6	17.4	12.2	41	0.010	21	7	

*Crossing "C" has the same arrangement of bolts as Crossing "A".

Crossing "D". - Each external arm has four main bolts for connecting the rails to the casting, and the bolts are numbered from the flangeway intersection to the far end of the connecting joint. Each interior side of the crossing has a six-hole joint. Bolt position 3 includes the two middle bolts of the joint, position 2, the intermediate bolts, and position 1, the end bolts of the internal joint.

These results cover the period from May 21, 1952 to October 7, 1952.

TABLE 22. SUMMARY OF THE SEVENTH CYCLE OF LOSS IN TENSION IN THE MAIN BOLTS OF THE CROSSINGS BETWEEN THE DOUBLE TRACK LINE OF THE C.&W.I.R.R. AND THE EASTWARD TRACK OF THE I.H.B.R.R., 55th STREET AND CICERO AVE., CHICAGO, ILLINOIS.

Location and Name of Spring Washers	Washer Curve Reference Fig.No.	Washer Curve Reference Cv.No.	Bolt Position	Avg. Bolt Tension (1000 lb) Initial	Final	Lost	Percent Tension Lost	Average Pull-in (in)	No. of Bolts with Final Tension less than 20 K	10 K	Remarks
SOUTH EAST CROSSING "D" – Solid Manganese on Framed Timbers											
1 3/8-in Interior Bolts Used Hy-Pressure Hy-Crome Spring Washers	1	10	1	39.6	29.8	9.8	25	0.005	2	0	ASA Heavy, 1/4-in extra thick M. C. Nuts
	"	"	2	40.2	22.6	17.6	44	0.006	3	0	
	"	"	3	39.1	16.6	22.5	58	0.008	6	1	
			Avg.	39.6	23.0	16.6	42	0.006	11	1	
1 1/4-in Exterior Bolts Used Hy-Pressure Hy-Crome Spring Washers	4	2	1	39.9	19.1	20.8	52	0.005	4	1	ASA Heavy, 1/4-in extra thick M. C. Nuts
	"	"	2	39.6	16.2	23.4	59	0.007	6	1	
	"	"	3	39.7	13.4	26.3	66	0.012	6	3	
	"	"	4	40.1	19.6	20.5	51	0.014	4	0	
			Avg.	39.8	17.1	22.8	57	0.010	20	5	

Crossing "D". – Each external arm has four main bolts for connecting the rails to the casting, and the bolts are numbered from the flangeway intersection to the far end of the connecting joint. Each interior side of the crossing has a six-hole joint. Bolt position 3 includes the two middle bolts of the joint, position 2, the intermediate bolts, and position 1, the end bolts of the internal joint.

These results cover the period from October 7, 1952 to April 22, 1953.

TABLE 23. – SUMMARY OF THE FIRST CYCLE OF LOSS IN TENSION IN THE
1 3/8 IN DIA. BOLTS OF A NO. 15 – 25 FT – 140 PS RAILBOUND MANGANESE
TURNOUT FROG IN THE WESTWARD MAIN AND CROSSOVER OF THE PENNSYLVANIA
RAILROAD AT WARSAW, INDIANA.

Bolt No.	Nominal Length (in)	Bolt Tension in 1,000 lb			Percent Tension Lost	Average Pull-in (in)
		Initial	Final	Lost		
Bolts Ahead of Point of Frog						
5-T	11	40.0	25.2	14.8	37	0.014
4-T	11	40.6	35.1	5.5	14	0.001
3-T	14	41.0	38.8	2.2	5	0.001
2-T	15	39.8	39.1	0.7	2	0.004
1-T	15	41.3	41.3	0.0	0	0.001
Avg.		40.5	35.9	4.6	11	0.004
Bolts Behind Point of Frog						
1-H	15	41.8	41.8	0.0	0	0.001
2-H	18	41.3	30.6	10.7	26	0.002
3-H	18	41.3	23.6	17.7	43	0.004
4-H	18	42.0	25.0	17.0	40	0.006
5-H	18	40.0	30.5	9.5	24	0.006
6-H	18	41.5	23.5	18.0	43	0.002
7-H	18	40.6	40.6	0.0	0	0.000
8-H	18	40.4	29.1	11.3	28	0.002
9-H	18	39.5	30.0	9.5	24	0.007
10-H	9	39.8	34.0	5.8	15	0.007
11-H	9	40.0	21.3	18.7	47	0.016
12-H	11½	47.6	31.6	16.0	34	0.003
13-H	12	49.8	38.1	11.7	23	0.000
Avg.		41.9	30.7	11.2	27	0.004
Avg. All		41.6	32.2	9.4	23	0.004

The bolts are numbered each way from the actual point of frog
which is located between bolt Nos. 1-T and 1-H. All bolts have
PRR Specification Spring Washers.

These results cover the period from May 3, 1950 to August 15,
1951 (1.28 years).

TABLE 24. - SUMMARY OF THE SECOND CYCLE OF LOSS IN TENSION IN THE 1 3/8 IN DIA. BOLTS OF A NO. 15 - 25 FT - 140 PS RAILBOUND MANGANESE TURNOUT FROG IN THE WESTWARD MAIN AND CROSSOVER OF THE PENNSYLVANIA RAILROAD AT WARSAW, INDIANA.

Bolt No.	Nominal Length (in)	Bolt Tension in 1,000 lb			Percent Tension Lost	Average Pull-in (in)
		Initial	Final	Lost		
Bolts Ahead of Point of Frog						
5-T	11	37.2	30.2	7.0	19	0.001
4-T	11	40.8	27.3	13.5	33	0.003
3-T	14	40.4	38.8	1.6	4	0.002
2-T	15	40.3	34.9	5.4	13	0.002
1-T	15	38.6	30.0	8.6	22	0.002
Avg.		39.4	32.2	7.2	18	0.002
Bolts Behind Point of Frog						
1-H	15	41.8	35.1	6.7	16	0.000
2-H	18	41.2	23.2	18.0	44	0.001
3-H	18	39.9	23.3	16.6	42	0.002
4-H	18	41.8	25.0	16.8	40	0.005
5-H	18	39.4	26.2	13.2	33	0.001
6-H	18	39.1	21.2	17.9	46	0.004
7-H	18	41.1	31.8	9.3	23	0.002
8-H	18	39.3	26.2	13.1	33	0.001
9-H	18	38.7	18.3	20.4	53	0.002
10-H	9	40.4	28.9	11.5	28	0.007
11-H	9	41.2	27.4	13.8	33	0.004
12-H	11½	40.9	29.1	11.8	29	0.006
13-H	12	41.5	34.2	7.3	18	0.006
Avg.		40.5	26.9	13.6	34	0.003
Avg. All		40.2	28.4	11.8	29	0.003

The bolts are numbered each way from the actual point of frog which is located between bolt Nos. 1-T and 1-H. All bolts have Frog and Crossing Hy-Crome Spring Washers.

These results cover the period from August 15, 1951 to August 14, 1952 (1.00 year).

TABLE 25. – SUMMARY OF THE THIRD CYCLE OF LOSS IN TENSION IN THE
1 3/8 IN DIA. BOLTS OF A NO. 15 – 25 FT – 140 PS RAILBOUND MANGANESE
TURNOUT FROG IN THE WESTWARD MAIN AND CROSSOVER OF THE PENNSYLVANIA
RAILROAD AT WARSAW, INDIANA.

Bolt No.	Nominal Length (in)	Bolt Tension in 1,000 lb			Percent Tension Lost	Average Pull-in (in)
		Initial	Final	Lost		
Bolts Ahead of Point of Frog						
5-T	11	38.0	25.1	12.9	34	0.000
4-T	11	42.5	29.9	12.6	30	0.002
3-T	15	39.6	37.3	2.3	6	0.001
2-T	15	41.7	40.1	1.6	4	0.001
1-T	15	40.0	37.9	2.1	5	0.003
Avg.		40.4	34.1	6.3	16	0.001
Bolts Behind Point of Frog						
1-H	15	39.7	36.5	3.2	8	0.004
2-H	18	40.0	31.9	8.1	20	0.002
3-H	18	38.4	25.6	12.8	33	0.002
4-H	18	41.3	22.4	18.9	46	0.002
5-H	18	39.4	23.0	16.4	42	0.000
6-H	18	38.6	24.6	14.0	36	0.001
7-H	18	39.4	32.4	7.0	17	0.006
8-H	18	39.3	26.8	12.5	32	0.005
9-H	18	38.6	31.0	7.6	20	0.002
10-H	11	38.2	30.0	8.2	22	0.002
11-H	11	42.2	33.8	8.4	20	0.005
12-H	15	40.0	33.3	6.7	17	0.002
13-H	15	39.9	38.0	1.9	48	0.004
Avg.		39.6	29.9	9.7	24	0.003
Avg. All		39.8	31.1	8.7	22	0.002

The bolts are numbered each way from the actual point of frog
which is located between bolt Nos. 1-T and 1-H. All bolts have
the Frog and Crossing Hy-Crome Spring Washers.

These results cover the period from August 14, 1952 to July 7,
1953 (0.90 year).

TABLE 26. LOCKNUT TEST IN 1 3/8 IN MAIN BOLTS OF 131-LB HEAT TREATED BOLTED RAIL CROSSING BETWEEN THE WESTBOUND MAIN OF THE PRR AND THE NYC BRANCH TRACK AT WARSAW, IND.

(Values of Maximum Frictional Torque are shown in ft.-lb.)

Bolt Position	ASA Heavy Square Elastic Stop Nuts N.W. Corner		ASA Reg. Hex. Security Nuts N.E. Corner		ASA Reg. Square M.F. Unitary No. 3 Nuts S.W. Corner		
Date	5/50	8/52	5/50	8/52	5/50	8/52	
Col. -	(1)	(2)	(1)	(2)	(1)	(2)	Remarks
1-W	(a)	--	135	15	90	(e)	
2-W	135	20	(300)	25	(300)	(e)	
3-W	105	30	--	--	(c)	(e)	
1-N	(b)	--	*120	20	205	25	
2-N	120	10	*75	30	120	5	Averages
3-N	105	0	*75	(180)	180	5	exclude
1-E	165	(e)	90	45	195	0	values shown in
2-E	165	5	195	(d)	(315)	(d)	parentheses
3-E	135	0	135	(d)	(315)	(d)	
1-S	90	5	*(330)	0	240	0	
2-S	95	15	*105	(e)	180	0	
3-S	120	15	40	(e)	210	25	
Avg.	124	11	108	27	178	9	
(A)	90		135		265		One nut of each type

Col. (1). Frictional torque in ft.-lb. for first application of new nuts (except for the SH Security Nuts).

Col. (2). Frictional torque in ft.-lb. for reapplication of the same nuts, after cleaning and oiling the bolt threads.

(a) Omitted because of damaged threads at end of bolt which prevented application of Elastic Stop nuts without stripping them. (b) Omitted account of torque wrench fouled by another bolt. (c) Omitted account of first thread was battered which caused friction torque to exceed the 675 ft-lb capacity of the torque wrench. (d) Omitted account of bolt and nut had been damaged. (e) Bolt and nut replaced by maintenance forces.
* Second-hand nuts.

Values shown in parentheses are omitted from averages as these high values were caused by damaged threads at the end of the bolts. The locknuts were applied to the bolts May 1, 1950, without oiling the threads. The crossing was installed new in 1947. All locknuts were new, except six Security Nuts had been in service 11 mo. in the eastward crossing.

(A) Frictional torque values obtained for first application of new locknut on new bolt in laboratory, without lubrication.

Report on Assignment 5

Design of Tie Plates

Collaborating with Committees 3 and 4

L. A. Pelton (chairman, subcommittee), J. P. Barker, G. P. Chandler, J. W. Fulmer,
   A. B. Hillman, Jr., R. J. D. Kelly, C. N. King, S. H. Poore, J. M. Salmon, Jr.,
   R. D. Simpson, J. F. Smith, C. W. Wagner, G. S. Woodings, M. J. Zeeman.

This is a final report, offered as information, on the service test on the CNO&TP, in which seven designs of tie plates for the rail base of 6 in were subjected to 379 million gross tons of traffic.

The investigation was conducted by the AAR research staff under the general direction of G. M. Magee, director of engineering research, with direct supervision by H. E. Durham, research engineer track, aided by L. R. Lamport, assistant research engineer track.

Foreword

The test was installed in November 1944 on Mile 326 of the single-track main line of the Cincinnati, New Orleans & Texas Pacific Railway (Southern Railway System), approximately 12 miles north of Chattanooga, Tenn. The installation consisted of 7 designs of tie plates in 22 panels of track laid with new creosoted ties, stone ballast and 131 RE rail. Eight of the panels were on a short 6-deg curve having 6 in elevation, with the remaining 14 panels on tangent track and equaly divided between oak and pine ties. Stress measurements under traffic were made in 1945 and published in the Proceedings, Vol. 47, 1946, pages 491–514. The latest progress report was published in Vol. 59, 1958, pages 1028–1033.

The curve was relaid in December 1952 and subsequent regaging was done in March 1958 by lining the low rail only with a minimum of adzing on the gage side to permit shifting of the tie plates. Final test measurements were taken in May 1962 as the Southern was laying continuous welded 132 RE rail through the test area with heavy tie renewals and adzing of the remaining ties, thereby destroying the basis for further test data on tie wear, gage and rail wear. The tie plates were restored to their original position and it is hoped that at some later date some more tie plate deflection readings will be available for evaluation.

Gross tons of traffic during the last service period, June 1957 to May 1962, increased from 278 to 379 million. All trains have been hauled by diesel power since June 1953.

Tie Abrasion

A summary of tie plate cutting measurements for the 17.5-year service period, November 1944 to May 1962, is shown in Table 1. During the last test period of 4.92 years there has been an increase in rate of plate cutting on the 6-deg curve amounting to approximately 35 percent. On the oak tangent the rate of cutting decreased 11 percent and increased 13 percent on the pine tangent. There was little difference in the average rate of cutting for all panels in each section compared with the average of the four panels with 14-in plates. Acceleration of the plate cutting had not been apparent in prior test periods.

The size of tie plate does not appear to be a factor in the average plate cutting. Omitting Sec. 405–A with ribbed plates on the 6-deg curve, the average penetration of seven panels in each test section was practically identical to the average of the 14-in plates in the same section. This average cutting is probably not significant because of the limited number of panels involved and the fact that the variation in plate area is only about 15 percent.

On the inner rail of the 6-deg curve, it will be noted that the tie abrasion was nearly equallized under the 14¾-in plates in Sec. 831. This plate also gave the best performance on the outer rail. The average of the four 14-in plate sections and of the section with 13-in plates shows reasonably good results with the poorest performance in Sec. 405 with 12-in plates. On the tangent with oak ties there was generally good uniformity in plate cutting with the best results being obtained in the sections with 13-in and 14-in plates. On the pine ties all sections showed relatively heavy cutting on the gage end of the plates with the poorest performance being in the sections with 14¾-in and 12-in plates.

Tie Plate Bending

Field measurements of tie plate deflection were inconclusive in determining any appreciable tie plate bending, although a few plates indicated that some deflection had taken place. Eight such plates, three of which were from Sec. 831X of ¾ in thickness, were shipped to the laboratory for careful examination which failed to develop evidence of bending. As previously stated the test plates were left in track under the new rail and it is hoped that they may be checked again, but the performance under 379 million tons of traffic is considered very good.

Gage of Track

Figs. 1 and 2 are graphs of track gage for the curve since regaging in March 1958 and for the tangent sections since the beginning of the test, with all intervening years except 1957 omitted for clarity. The 6-deg curve had an average of 0.37 in wide gage, of which 0.08 in was due to wear on the high rail, when regaged in March 1958 by shifting the tie plates and lining the low rail. Since regaging, the average widening in 4.2 years was 0.20 in, of which 0.04 in was due to rail wear. The greatest change occurred in Sec. 405 with 12-in plates, with the minimum in Sec. 831 and 14¾-in plates.

TABLE 1. - SERVICE TEST OF MECHANICAL WEAR OF TIES WITH SEVEN DESIGNS OF TIE PLATES FOR 131 RE RAIL ON CNO&TP RAILWAY MILE 326 (SOUTHERN RAILWAY SYSTEM), NEAR CHATTANOOGA, TENN.

Tie Plate Design No.	Tie Plate Dimensions (in.)	Rail Seat	Tie Plate Penetration from Nov. 1944 to May 1962 in 0.001 in., 378 million gross tons of traffic						
			Inner or East Rail			Outer or West Rail			Both Rails
			Field End	Gage End	Avg.	Gage End	Field End	Avg.	Avg.
6° Curve – Creosoted Oak Ties									
831	7-1/2 x 14-3/4 x 31/32	Rolled Circular	266	274	270	274	416	345	308
831-Z	7-1/2 x 14 x 31/32	Rolled Circular	269	308	289	228	452	340	314
831-Y	7-1/2 x 14 x 7/8	Rolled Circular	295	299	297	255	445	350	323
831-X	7-1/2 x 14 x 3/4	Rolled Circular	306	317	311	225	418	320	316
420	7-3/4 x 14 x 7/8	Flat	220	294	257	216	460	338	298
Plan 5	7-3/4 x 13 x 27/32	Rolled Circular	282	341	312	267	453	360	336
405	8 x 12 x 3/4	Rolled Circular	225	355	290	193	455	324	307
*405-A	8 x 12 x 3/4	Rolled Circular	337	457	397	323	464	394	396
Tangent – Creosoted Oak Ties									
831	7-1/2 x 14-3/4 x 31/32	Rolled Circular	184	255	220	207	195	201	211
831-Z	7-1/2 x 14 x 31/32	Rolled Circular	184	214	199	200	209	204	202
831-Y	7-1/2 x 14 x 7/8	Rolled Circular	174	206	190	189	196	193	192
831-X	7-1/2 x 14 x 3/4	Rolled Circular	227	233	230	202	207	205	218
420	7-3/4 x 14 x 7/8	Flat	164	194	179	178	203	191	185
Plan 5	7-3/4 x 13 x 27/32	Rolled Circular	181	186	183	194	172	183	183
405	8 x 12 x 3/4	Rolled Circular	185	221	203	199	180	188	196
Tangent – Creosoted Pine Ties									
831	7-1/2 x 14-3/4 x 31/32	Rolled Circular	252	458	355	355	248	301	328
831-Z	7-1/2 x 14 x 31/32	Rolled Circular	198	430	314	395	225	310	312
831-Y	7-1/2 x 14 x 7/8	Rolled Circular	218	419	318	320	237	279	298
831-X	7-1/2 x 14 x 3/4	Rolled Circular	188	323	256	327	208	267	262
420	7-3/4 x 14 x 7/8	Flat	219	340	280	319	237	278	279
Plan 5	7-3/4 x 13 x 27/32	Rolled Circular	246	398	322	332	243	288	305
405	8 x 12 x 3/4	Rolled Circular	165	335	250	358	205	282	266

Note: All tie plates have 3/8 in. eccentricity, except design 831 has 1/2 in. and Plan 5, 1/4 in. All tie plates have flat bottom, except design 405-A has three transverse ribs. *Tie plates have flat bottom, except design *405-A has three transverse ribs. *Penetration measurements include cutting of the ribs into the ties. The 8-in x 12-in tie plates were not punched for anchor spikes.

898

It will be noted in Fig. 1 for the 6-deg curve that the sections divide at the joints in the outer rail and generally have wider gage at those points. This gage pattern on the curves prevailed in other service tests. As during previous test periods, Sec. 405–A with 12-in rib-bottom plates has resisted gage widening better than similar plates without ribs in Sec. 405, but the difference is due primarily to Sec. 405–A being on the spiral where the rail wear is practically nil.

On the two tangent sections there has been relatively little change in gage during the 17.5-year test period. The average reduction in gage is only 0.04 in for the oak tie section and 0.10 in for the pine tie section.

As a whole the gage has held reasonably well, including the section on the curve where the operating speeds are predominantly above the equilibrium speed of 38 mph.

Cant of Rail

In connection with the tie abrasion data presented in Table 1, an analysis has been made of the rail cant change from 1:40 because of the unequal plate cutting at the ends of the tie plates.

The following table includes the rail-cant data based on the initial 1:40 cant and the final tie wear measurements. It will be noted that, generally, the cant of the outer rail was appreciably smaller than 1:40. The 14¾-in plate with ½-in eccentricity retained a cant of 1:65. In general, the inner rail retained its initial cant or increased slightly. On tangent with pine ties the cant for the 12-in and 14¾-in tie plates increased on both rails. For the same two designs of tie plates on tangent with oak ties there was an increase in cant but slightly less than on the pine ties.

RAIL CANT AT END OF TEST

Plate Designation 1:40 Cant		East or Inner Rail	West or Outer Rail	Eccentricity
6-Deg Curve, Oak Ties				
405	12 in	1:31	1:310	
831	14¾ in	1:39	1:65	½ in
831–Z	14 in	1:36	1:110	⅜ in
402	14 in	1:38	1:130	⅜ in
Tangent, Pine Ties				
831	14¾ in	1:26	1:27	½ in
405	12 in	1:26	1:31	⅜ in
Tangent, Oak Ties				
831	14¾ in	1:33	1:39	½ in
405	12 in	1:35	1:32	⅜ in

Tie Renewals

The first tie renewals in the test sections were made during March 1958 after 13.3 years of service, when 11 were installed in the 6-deg curve, 7 in the oak tangent and 23 in the pine tangent. When test measurements were made on May 14, 1962, 39 additional ties had been renewed on the curve for a total of 50, or 28 percent of those in the 8 test panels. The heaviest renewals were in Sec. 405 where 14 of the 22 ties had been renewed. Many of the ties remaining in track in all test sections were found to be crushing in the plate area and others were splitting badly. New ties distributed indicated that the Southern Railway expected to make heavy renewals following the laying of the continuous welded rail.

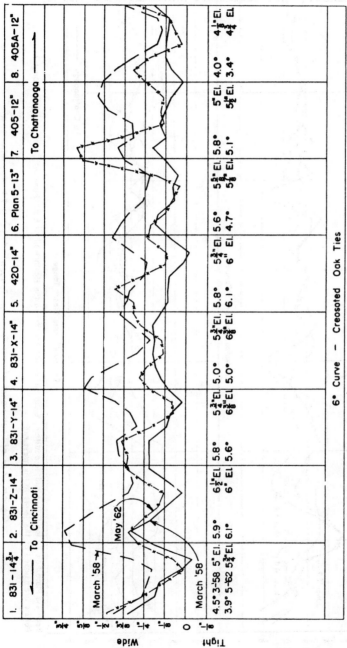

Fig. 1. - Gage, Curvature and Elevation of Each Panel of Test Track on the 6° Curve, C.N.O. & T.P. Ry., Mile 326

900

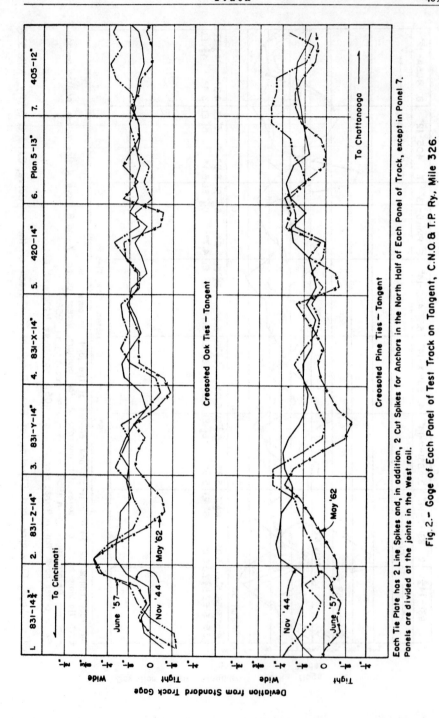

Each Tie Plate has 2 Line Spikes and, in addition, 2 Cut Spikes for Anchors in the North Half of Each Panel of Track, except in Panel 7. Panels are divided at the joints in the West rail.

Fig. 2.— Gage of Each Panel of Test Track on Tangent, C.N.O.& T.P. Ry., Mile 326.

Conclusions

The test results indicate good uniformity in plate cutting under the 14-in and 14¾-in plates on the inner rail of the 6-deg curve, but that the 14¾-in plates with ½-in eccentricity had the best performance on the outer rail. Better performance on the outer rail might be expected from the use of the special 16-in tie plates with 1¼-in eccentricity for use on curves per AREA Plan 21. The 14-in plate, AREA Plan 12, with ⅜-in eccentricity for 6-in rail base, should be adequate for the inner rail of the curve and also the tangent where it has performed well in the test. The 13-in plates have performed reasonably well and should be adequate, particularly under medium traffic or with 5½-in base rail. The 12-in plate is indicated to be inferior for heavy traffic, particularly on the curve and tangent with softwood ties.

The test results do not permit any conclusions regarding tie plate bending, but it is believed that the thickness of the various designs of plates in the AREA Manual are adequate to provide good service under all traffic conditions. No revisions to the tie plate designs in the AREA Manual are recommended.

This report supplements the conclusions in the final report on tie plates tested with the 5½-in rail base on the Illinois Central Railroad (See Vol. 56, page 824).

Acknowledgment

The Association gratefully extends its thanks to the Southern Railway for its cooperation and assistance which made possible the obtaining of field data for this report.

Report on Assignment 6

Hold-Down Fastenings for Tie Plates, Including Pads Under Plates—Their Effect on Tie Wear

Collaborating with Committee 3

N. C. Kieffer, Jr. (chairman, subcommittee), M. C. Bitner, E. W. Caruthers, E. D. Cowlin, F. W. Creedle, R. G. Garland, L. R. Hall, A. E. Hinson, R. J. Hollingsworth, L. H. Jentoft, C. H. Johnson, R. J. D. Kelly, E. J. Lisy, Jr., J. E. Martin, C. J. McConaughy, S. H. Poore, J. M. Salmon, Jr., R. N. Schmidt, T. R. Snodgrass, R. E. Tew, C. W. Wagner, Troy West, I. V. Wiley.

TESTS ON THE LOUISVILLE & NASHVILLE RAILROAD

This progress report, submitted as information, covers the committee's inspection of the AAR–L&N installations of tie pads, anchor spikes, etc., near London, Ky., on June 6, 1962.

Introduction

These tests were begun in 1947 for the purpose of developing information for determining the most effective and economical methods for increasing the service life of ties by minimizing plate cutting and reducing the frequency of regaging and readzing curves by the use of special hold-down fastenings, tie pads, etc. All of the test installations are located in the northbound track carrying loaded coal car tonnage near London, Ky.

The inspection was attended by 20 members and guests, including three representatives of the AAR research staff. Nine tie plates were removed to examine the condition of the pads, fastenings, etc. (See Figs. 1 to 9, incl.)

Change in Operation of the Existing Double-Track Main Line

The L&N plans to convert to single track CTC and will retain the southbound track. All of the test sections are located in the northward main. In view of these changes, it is planned to take readings in all of the test installations in 1963. The correlating tie wear machine tests of the installations on the L&N will be reported, as well as the other tests made with tie pads and two species of wood and two sizes of tie plates.

Acknowledgment

The Association is indebted to the L&N for their cooperation and assistance in making the inspection and furnishing transportation for the visitors.

Fig. 1—Control section 37 with 14-in tie plates and 2 each of cut line and anchor spikes, inner rail 5-deg curve. Plate cutting noted for 143 months of service, creosoted oak tie: field side 3/16 in, gage side 3/16 in, average 3/16 in. Inner rail plates were removed because the tie wear was greater than for the outer rail.

Fig. 2—North portion section 46, 14-in Racor tie pad, uncoated, 127 months of service, inner rail, joint tie. Some sand, dampness and wood compression were noted.

Fig. 3—South portion section 46, 14-in Racor tie pad, coated, 127 months of service, inner rail 5-deg curve. There was little difference in the conditions noted for the coated vs. the uncoated pad.

Fig. 4—Middle portion section 41, 14-in by ¼-in Fabco pad coated with asphalt on the bottom side, 131 months of service, inner rail 5-deg curve. Under-plate area was wet, with some sand present. Pad was in moderately good condition.

Fig. 5—South portion section 56, 14-in by ⅛-in Fabco pad, bottom coated, inner rail 5-deg curve, 32 months of service. This specimen was removed primarily to check the seal with the tie. The pad had a strong seal, most of the coating adhering to the wood.

444   Track

Fig. 6—Control section 9 with 13-in tie plates and 2 each of cut line and anchor spikes, outer rail long 4½-deg curve. Plate cutting measured for 178 months of service, creosoted oak tie: field side, ⅛ in, gage side 3/16 in, average 5/32 in. Outer rail plates were removed because of the larger tie wear under them.

Fig. 7—North portion section 28, 14-in by 3/16-in Konvex tie pad (tire carcass) coated both sides, outer rail long 4½-deg curve, 32 months of service. This pad had a strong seal and a clean area under it. In a previous inspection it was found that the seal with the tie plate was almost as strong as the seal with the tie. A sheet of polyethylene was placed next to the tie plate to avoid disturbing the seal with the wood.

906

Fig. 8—South portion section 28, 14-in by 3/16-in Konvex tie pad coated on both sides, outer rail long 4½-deg curve, 46 months of service. The bond with the tie was weaker than in the case of the pad shown in Fig. 7, but the under-plate area was clean.

Fig. 9—Section 5, Bird 7-ply 13-in duck-felt coated pad, outer rail long 4½-deg curve, 178 months of service. The pad had a strong bond with the tie, but a little wood compression was noted.

ASSOCIATION OF AMERICAN RAILROADS

RESEARCH DEPARTMENT

Engineering Research Division

REPORT NO. ER-77

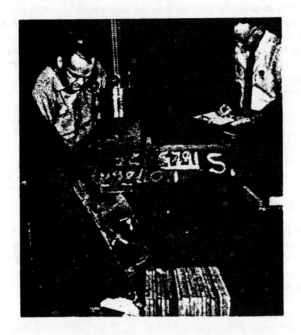

CAPABILITY OF FASTENERS TO

RESIST RAIL OVERTURNING

NOVEMBER 1967

39177.

RAIL OVERTURNING INVESTIGATION ON WOOD AND CONCRETE TIES

FOREWORD

The increased use of longer and heavier cars has created many problems and within recent years some railroads have experienced wheel lifting, rail climbing, derailments, loss of gage and rail over-turning on curves. Considerable research has been done by the AAR Research Center to determine the cause or causes of this trouble and several ER reports have been issued on the subject. In general, the test data indicate that the wheels of the car will exert lateral forces as large as 30,000 lb on the rail under certain operating conditions, but such forces are usually associated with high vertical forces on the rail. In addition, only about 50 percent of this load is carried by the tie directly under the wheel with the two adjacent ties carrying the other 50 percent of the wheel load.

The purpose of the investigation reported herein was to determine the overturning resistance of the rail fastened to either wood or pre-stressed concrete ties when subjected to various loading conditions. No effort was made to include the torsional resistance of the rail which would increase the overturning resistance by a considerable amount so the data obtained must be considered as conservative.

The investigation was conducted in the engineering laboratory of the Research Center as part of the research activity of the Research Department of which W. M. Keller is vice-president and G. M. Magee is director of engineering research. Funds for the investigation were provided by the AAR.

The investigation was under the direction of E. J. Ruble, executive research engineer, assisted by F. P. Drew, research engineer structures and K. W. Schoeneberg, research engineer track. Mr. I. A. Eaton, laboratory engineer, was in charge of the laboratory testing.

TEST PROCEDURE

The procedure used in testing the rail on the wood ties was accomplished by fastening a short piece of 136 lb rail and tie plate to a new treated oak tie by four spikes in pre-bored holes; two of the spikes were placed in the line position against the edges of the rail base and two were placed in the outer holes of the tie plate to hold the tie plate to the tie, as shown on Fig. 1. The rail on the prestressed concrete tie was fastened by two bolts and two AREA Specification clips with a 3/16 in polyethylene plastic pad between the rail and concrete.

39177.2

The rail and tie assembly was placed on the testing floor as shown on Figs. 1 and 2. The tie was positioned under the hydraulic Amsler jack so that the load was applied vertically to the head of the rail. The tie was installed at the proper angle or slope to secure the desired lateral and vertical components of load on the rail.

The lateral movements of the rail head and base produced by the lateral component of the load on the rail were determined by dial gages mounted as shown on Figs. 1 and 2. The one dial on the rail base shown on the pictures proved unsatisfactory due to the angle of the plunger rod and all subsequent tests were conducted with two dial gages on the rail; one on each side of the tie. The average of the two dial gage readings was used as the lateral movement of the rail.

In conducting the tests, the rail was loaded by small increments of load, taking dial gage readings for each load increment, until failure developed.

RESULTS

The relation between the load on rail and the lateral movement of the rail for various positions of the ties are tabulated on Tables 1 to 4, incl. for both the wood and prestressed concrete ties. For example, Table 1 shows the data for the tie in the vertical position so that the load on the rail has a lateral component only without any vertical component. For this position of the tie, the rail on the wood tie turned over under a lateral load of 6400 lb. The dial gages were removed after taking the readings for the 5500 lb load. Under a lateral load of 5500 lb the head of the rail moved 0.210 in while the base moved 0.031 in.

The rail fastened to the prestressed concrete tie failed under a lateral load of 10,850 lb with the head of the rail moving 0.325 in at the instant of failure. Time did not permit the reading of the dial gage on the base of rail, but a movement of 0.028 in was recorded under a lateral load of 10,500 lb. Failure resulted from a chipping of the concrete bearing area at the recess on the field side.

The data obtained with the tie on a slope of 2 to 1 or an angle of 63°-30' between the tie and the test floor, are shown on Table 2. It can be seen that the rail on the wood tie turned over under a rail load of 5100 lb. The rail load of 5100 lb produced a lateral component on the rail of 4600 lb and a vertical component of 2300 lb. Failure was caused by the spike on the gage side pulling out. It can be seen from Table 2 that

the rail on the prestressed concrete tie carried a total rail load of
22, 950 lb which produced a lateral component of 20, 500 lb on the rail
and a vertical component of 10, 200 lb. The head of the rail moved laterally
0. 755 in under a rail load of 22, 000 lb while the rail base moved 0. 220 in.
Overturning of the rail resulted from the stainless steel anchor on the gage
side pulling out but there was some slight chipping of the concrete bearing
area at the recess on the field side.

The data obtained with the wood and prestressed concrete ties on
a slope of 1 to 1 are shown on Table 3. The rail on the wood tie carried a
total rail load of 14, 000 lb which produced a lateral and vertical component
of 9900 lb each. The head of the rail moved laterally 0. 270 in and failure
resulted from the spike pulling out on the gage side. The rail on the prestressed concrete tie carried a total rail load of 25, 700 lb which produced
a lateral and vertical component of 18, 170 lb. The overturning of the rail
resulted from a tension failure in the concrete on a plane even with the
bottom of the stainless steel anchor on the gage side. The rail load for this
prestressed concrete tie was greater than that for the wood tie even though
the tie used for this particular test did not meet the requirements of the
tentative specification of AREA Committee 3 for prestressed concrete ties
and fastenings as the bottom of the stainless steel insert was only 1 3/4 in
from the top of the tie instead of the specified 2 3/4 in and no vertical
stirrups or ties were used in the rail seat area. A greater rail load can be
expected for the prestressed concrete ties when made in conformance with
the specifications.

The data with the wood tie on a slope of 1 to 2 are shown on
Table 4. The load on the rail was increased by increments to 40, 000 lb
and since there was no indication of rail lifting or impending failure, the
tests were discontinued. The data with the rail fastened to the prestressed
concrete ties under two conditions of bolt tension are shown on Table 4. The
first tests were conducted with the bolts tightened to a torque of 150 ft lb
as requied in the tentative specification. The load was increased by increments and failure resulted under a load of 60, 000 lb when the field side
shoulder on the recess failed by a chipping of the concrete. The second tests
were conducted with the bolts tightened to a torque of 75 ft lb as field experience
has shown that some bolt tension will be lost under traffic. The load was
increased by increments as shown on Table 4 to 92, 500 lb, the capacity of the
hydraulic jack, without failure of the shoulder on the recess.

The relation between the lateral load on the rail and the lateral
deflection of the rail head and base, as tabulated in Tables 1 to 4 incl.,
is shown on Figs. 3 to 10 incl. It can be seen that the rail on the prestressed concrete ties carried an appreciably greater lateral load than
the rail on the wood ties. The lateral deflection of the rail head and base
for the rails on the prestressed concrete ties was considerably greater
than that for the rails on the wood ties at failure, however, for the same
lateral load on the rail, the head and base deflections were lower for the
prestressed concrete ties.

39177.4.

SUMMARY

A summary of all test data as shown in Tables 1 to 4 incl. and Figs. 3 to 10 incl. are shown on Fig. 11 for the two types of fastenings and the four different angles or slopes of the ties. The lateral component of the rail load producing rail overturning or failure is plotted as the ordinate and the ratio of the vertical component to the lateral component of the rail load is plotted as the abscissa. It is quite evident that the rail on the prestressed concrete ties is capable of carrying considerably more lateral load than the rail fastened to wood ties with spikes.

An analytical study conducted at the Research Center indicate a definite relation between the wheel lifting off the rail, wheel climbing the rail and the lateral and vertical loads on the rail. For example, when the lateral component of the load on the rail is 82 percent of the vertical load or when P_V/P_L is equal to 1.22, there is impending wheel lift and this ratio is shown by the vertical dashed line. When the lateral component of the load on the rail is 1.29 times the vertical load component or when P_V/P_L is equal to 0.78, there is impending wheel climbing of the rail and this ratio is shown by the vertical dashed line.

The results of the analytical study shown on Fig. 11 indicate that all values of P_V/P_L smaller than 0.78 have no significance as the wheel will climb the rail and thus relieve the lateral load component on the rail. As previously mentioned, lateral wheel loads as large as 30,000 lb have been recorded and for this condition, the analytical study indicate the wheel will not climb the rail until the vertical component of the rail load is 23,400 lb or lower.

CONCLUSION

The method of fastening the rail to the prestressed concrete ties, as recommended in the Preliminary Specification for Design, Materials, Construction and Inspection of Prestressed Concrete Ties, is satisfactory for the imposed lateral forces.

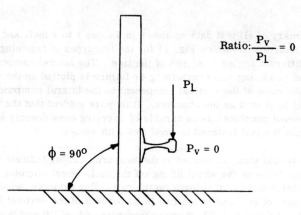

TABLE 1
RAIL OVERTURNING INVESTIGATION
Wood and Concrete Ties

39177

Ratio: $\dfrac{P_v}{P_L} = 0$

P_L

$P_v = 0$

$\phi = 90^\circ$

Type of Tie	Load P Lbs.	P_L Lbs.	P_v Lbs.	Rail Movement-In.	
				Head	Base
Wood	0	0	0	0	0
	2000	2000	0	0.030	0.020
	4000	4000	0	0.122	0.023
	5500(2)	5500	0	0.210	0.031
	6400	6400	0	-	-
Concrete (AREA Comm. 3 Spec.)	0	0	0	0	0
	1550	1550	0	0.020	0
	2360	2360	0	0.060	0.003
	3110	3110	0	0.100	0.006
	3840	3840	0	0.140	0.009
	4600	4600	0	0.180	0.013
	5450	5450	0	0.220	0.015
	7940	7940	0	0.260	0.019
	9710	9710	0	0.300	0.024
	10500	10500	0	0.320	0.028
	10850(1)	10850	0	0.325	-

(1)Failure by chipping of concrete at recess.
(2)Dial gages removed.

TABLE 2
RAIL OVERTURNING INVESTIGATION
Wood and Concrete Ties

39177

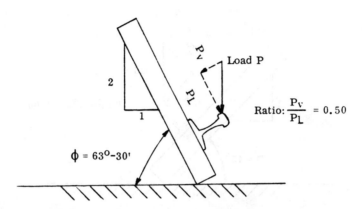

Ratio: $\dfrac{P_v}{P_L} = 0.50$

$\phi = 63^{\circ}\text{-}30'$

Type of Tie	Load P Lbs.	P_L Lbs.	P_v Lbs.	Rail Movement–In.	
				Head	Base
Wood (Oak)	0	0	0	0	0
	2000	1800	900	0.024	0.007
	4000[1]	3600	1800	0.068	0.018
	5100[2]	4600	2300		
Concrete (AREA Comm. 3 Spec.)	2000	1800	900	0.008	0
	4000	3600	1800	0.021	0.001
	6000	5400	2700	0.092	0.005
	8000[3]	7200	3600	0.285	0.016
	10000[4]	8900	4500	0.428	0.126
	12000	10800	5400	0.452	0.131
	14000	12500	6200	0.480	0.138
	16000	14400	7100	0.515	0.150
	18000	16100	8000	0.566	0.166
	20000	17800	8900	0.618	0.185
	22000	19800	9900	0.755	0.220
	22950[5]	20500	10200	–	–

[1]Rail lifting.
[2]Complete failure. Spike on gage side pulled out.
[3]Rail lifting.
[4]Slight chipping of concrete on field side.
[5]Complete failure. Stainless steel anchor on gage side pulled out.

TABLE 3
RAIL OVERTURNING INVESTIGATION
Wood and Concrete Ties

39177

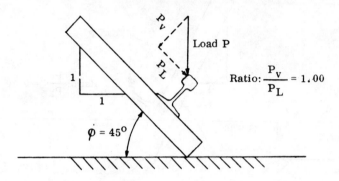

Load P

$$\text{Ratio:} \frac{P_V}{P_L} = 1.00$$

$\phi = 45°$

Type of Tie	Load P Lbs.	P_I Lbs.	P_V Lbs.	Rail Movement-In.	
				Head	Base
Wood (Oak)	0	0	0	0	0
	2000	1410	1410	0.015	0.001
	4000	2820	2820	0.040	0.003
	6000	4240	4240	0.064	0.007
	8000	5660	5660	0.088	0.012
	10000[1]	7070	7070	0.120	0.020
	12000	8480	8480	0.180	0.031
	14000[2]	9900	9900	0.270	-
Concrete Not AREA Comm. 3 Spec.	0	0	0	0	0
	2000	1410	1410	0.004	0.001
	4000	2820	2820	0.011	0.002
	6000	4240	4240	0.025	0.004
	8000	5660	5660	-	0.008
	10000[3]	7070	7070	0.120	0.015
	12000	8480	8480	0.180	0.021
	14000[4]	9900	9900	0.250	0.031
	16000	11300	11300	0.555	0.080
	18000	12700	12700	0.588	0.090
	20000	14140	14140	0.620	0.103
	22000	15600	15600	0.665	0.173
	24000	17000	17000	0.880	0.240
	25700[5]	18170	18170	0.900	-

[1]Rail lifting.
[2]Complete failure. Spike on gage side pulled out.
[3]Rail lifting.
[4]Slight chipping of concrete on field side.
[5]Complete failure. Tension failure of concrete on a plane with bottom of anchor.

TABLE 4
RAIL OVERTURNING INVESTIGATION
Wood and Concrete Ties

39177.

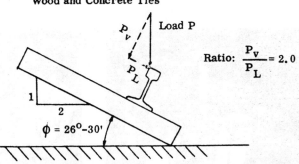

Ratio: $\dfrac{P_V}{P_L} = 2.0$

$\phi = 26^o\text{-}30'$

Type of Tie	Load P Lbs	P_L Lbs	P_V Lbs	Rail Movement-In.	
				Head	Base
	0	0	0	0	0
	4,000	1,800	3,600	0.032	0.020
	8,000	3,600	7,200	0.059	0.034
	12,000	5,400	10,800	0.076	0.045
	16.000	7,100	14,400	0.092	0.055
Wood	20,000	8,900	17,800	0.110	0.060
	24,000	10,700	21,400	0.128	0.080
	28,000	12,400	24,900	0.147	0.094
	32,000	14,300	28,600	0.167	0.109
	36,000	16,000	32,000	0.191	0.127
	40,000[1]	17,800	35,600	0.209	0.139
Concrete	0	0	0	0	0
Not	8,000	3.600	7,200	0.007	0.001
AREA	16,000	7.100	14,400	0.015	0.001
Com. 3	24,000	10,700	21,400	0.024	0.003
Spec.	32,000	14,300	28,600	0.034	0.005
150 ft lb	40,000	17,800	35,600	0.044	0.010
torque on	48,000	21,400	42,800	0.054	0.014
bolts as	56,000[2]	24,800	49,800	0.069	0.024
specified.	60,000[3]	26,700	53,400	-	-
	0	0	0	0	0
Concrete	8,000	3,600	7,200	0.010	0
Not	16,000	7,100	14,400	0.016	0.003
AREA	24,000[4]	10,700	21,400	0.032	0.015
Com. 3	32,000	14,300	28,600	0.058	0.033
Spec.	40,000	17,800	35,600	0.068	0.040
75 ft lb	48,000	21,400	42,800	0.081	0.046
torque	56,000	24,800	49,800	0.094	0.053
on bolts.	64,000	28,600	57,200	0.111	0.064
	72,000	32,000	64,000	0.124	0.071
	92,500[5]	41,100	82,200	-	-

[1] No failure and no lifting of rail.
[2] Slight chipping of concrete on field side.
[3] Failure by chipping of concrete on field side.
[4] Slight chipping of concrete on field side.
[5] No failure. Maximum capacity of jack.

916

FIG. 1
RAIL OVERTURNING INVESTIGATION

39177.

General view of wood tie and fastenings before testing.

FIG. 2
RAIL OVERTURNING INVESTIGATION

.39177.

General view of prestressed concrete tie and fastenings after failure of anchor.

918

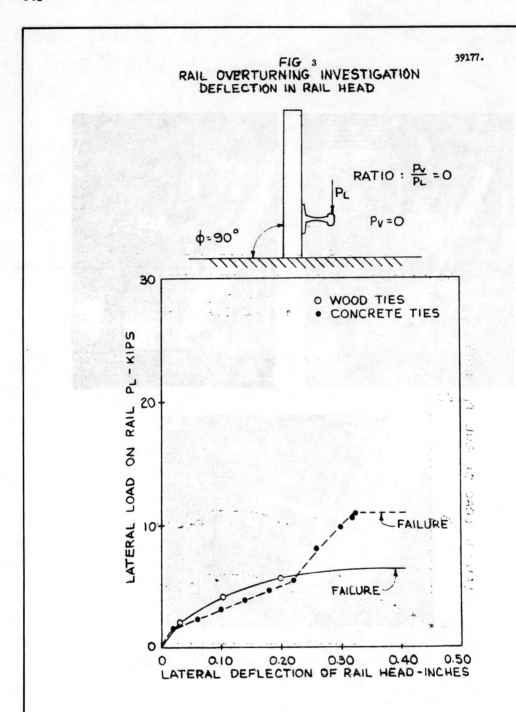

FIG 3
RAIL OVERTURNING INVESTIGATION
DEFLECTION IN RAIL HEAD

39177.

RATIO : $\dfrac{P_V}{P_L} = 0$

$P_V = 0$

$\phi = 90°$

o WOOD TIES
• CONCRETE TIES

FAILURE

FAILURE

LATERAL LOAD ON RAIL P_L - KIPS

LATERAL DEFLECTION OF RAIL HEAD - INCHES

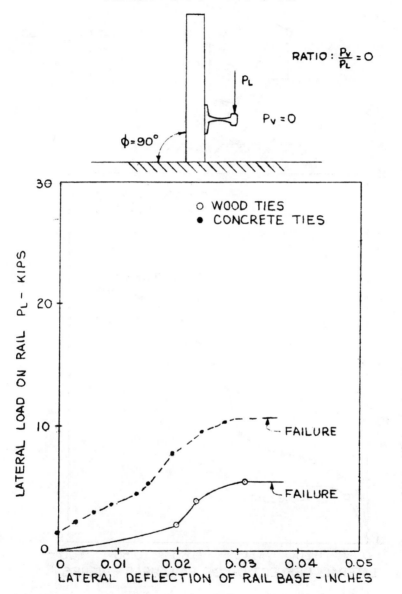

FIG. 4
RAIL OVERTURNING INVESTIGATION
DEFLECTION OF RAIL BASE

39177.

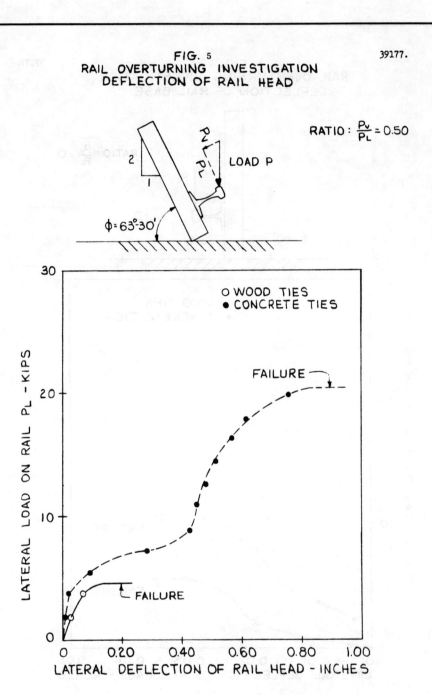

FIG. 5
RAIL OVERTURNING INVESTIGATION
DEFLECTION OF RAIL HEAD

39177.

RATIO : $\frac{P_V}{P_L} = 0.50$

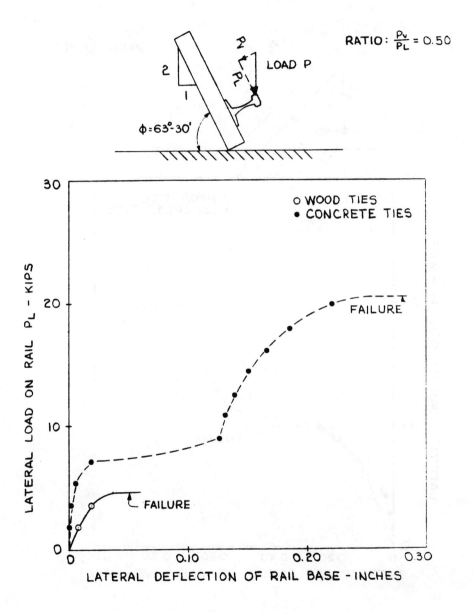

FIG. 6
RAIL OVERTURNING INVESTIGATION
DEFLECTION OF RAIL BASE

39177.

RATIO: $\frac{P_v}{P_L} = 0.50$

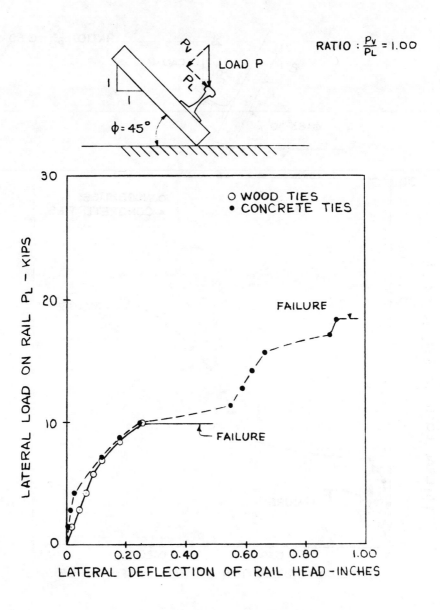

FIG. 7

39177.

RAIL OVERTURNING INVESTIGATION
DEFLECTION OF RAIL HEAD

RATIO : $\frac{P_V}{P_L} = 1.00$

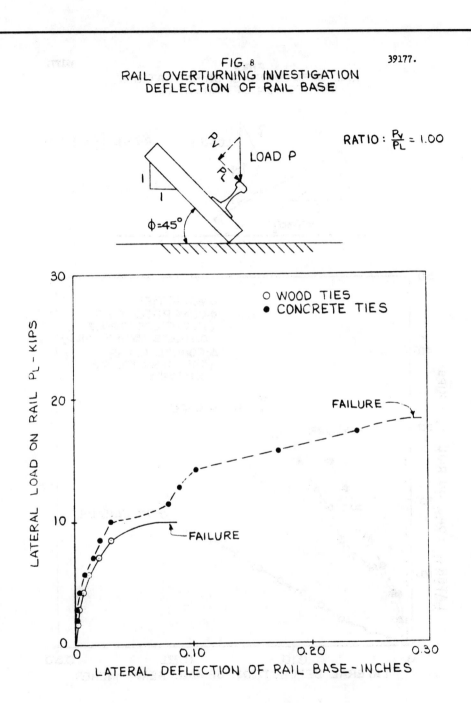

FIG. 8
RAIL OVERTURNING INVESTIGATION
DEFLECTION OF RAIL BASE

39177.

LOAD P

RATIO: $\frac{P_V}{P_L} = 1.00$

$\phi = 45°$

○ WOOD TIES
● CONCRETE TIES

FAILURE

FAILURE

LATERAL LOAD ON RAIL P_L – KIPS

LATERAL DEFLECTION OF RAIL BASE – INCHES

924

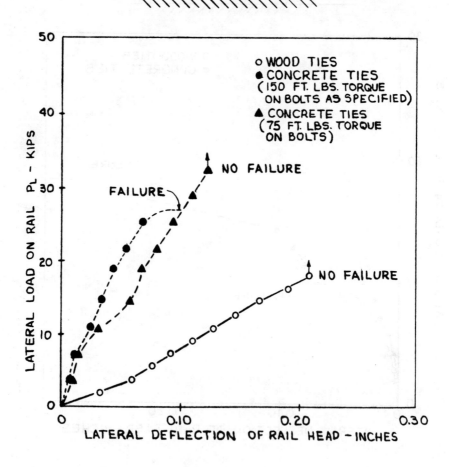

FIG. 9
RAIL OVERTURNING INVESTIGATION
DEFLECTION OF RAIL HEAD

39177.

R_V LOAD P   RATIO: $\dfrac{P_V}{P_L}$ = 2.00

P_L

1
2
$\phi = 26°-30'$

50

40

LATERAL LOAD ON RAIL P_L - KIPS

30

20

10

O WOOD TIES
● CONCRETE TIES
(150 FT. LBS. TORQUE
ON BOLTS AS SPECIFIED)
▲ CONCRETE TIES
(75 FT. LBS. TORQUE
ON BOLTS)

NO FAILURE

FAILURE

NO FAILURE

O   0.10   0.20   0.30
LATERAL DEFLECTION OF RAIL HEAD - INCHES

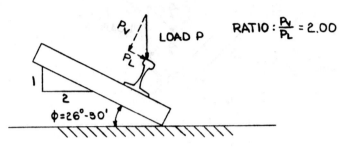

FIG. 10
RAIL OVERTURNING INVESTIGATION
DEFLECTION OF RAIL BASE

39177.

RATIO: $\dfrac{P_V}{P_L}$ = 2.00

LOAD P

$\phi = 26° \text{-} 50'$

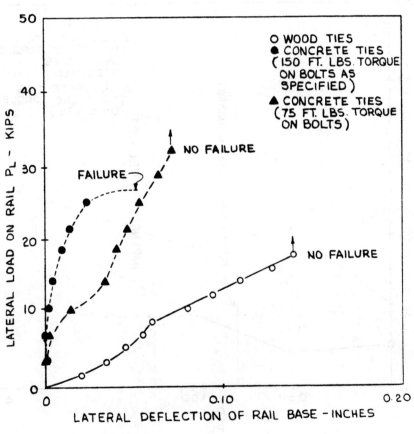

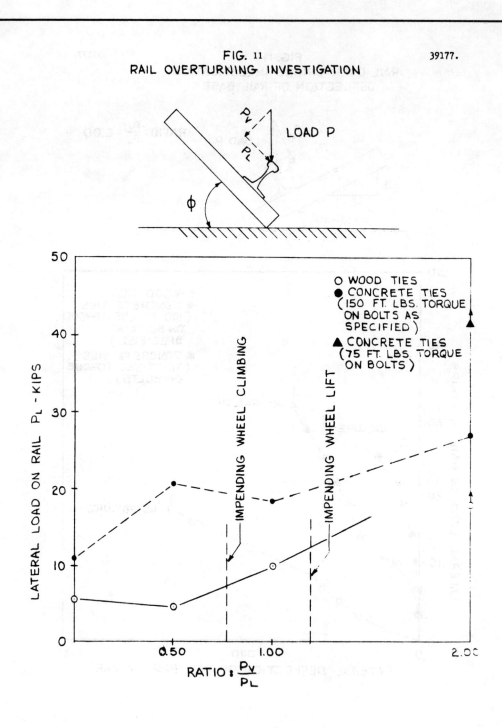

FIG. 11
RAIL OVERTURNING INVESTIGATION

36587.

RESEARCH CENTER REPORTS OF THE ENGINEERING RESEARCH DIVISION

ER-1   Investigation of 60 Ft. Glued Laminated Beams on the Weyerhaeuser Timber Company Railroad

ER-2   Investigation of Fatigue and Static Strength of 50-Year Old Timber Stringers from A.T.&S.F. Ry. Bridge near La Junta, Colorado

ER-3   Laboratory Investigation to Determine the Repeated Load Strength of Timber in Compression Perpendicular to the Grain

ER-4   Methods of Fireproofing Wood Bridges and Trestles

ER-5   The Lateral and Longitudinal Distribution of Loading on Steel Railway Bridges

ER-6   Test of Sustamid Joint Bars for 129 Lb. TR Rail

ER-7   Investigation of Special Joint Bars and Rail Plugs for Use in Joining Lengths of Continuous Welded Rail

ER-8   Physical Test Results of Oxy-Acetylene Pressure Butt Welds of Heat Treated Rails

ER-9   Insulated Rail Joint Development and Research

ER-10   Report on Asphalt Treatment of Ballast and Bridge Decks

ER-11   Field and Laboratory Investigation of Slope Failure of Railroad Cuts in Stiff Clay, Southwestern Iowa

ER-12   Second Progress Report on Performance of Filter Materials

ER-13   Rail Wear Tests on the St. Louis-San Francisco Railway

ER-14   Speed of Trains through Turnouts

ER-15   Engineering Aspects of Current Rail Sections

ER-16   Termite Control Investigation - Inspection of Specimens after 40 Months Exposure

ER-17   Running Tests of a Flat Car Trailer Carrier and a Three Level Auto Carrier on the Burlington Railroad

ER-18   Field Investigation of Santa Fe Railway Prestressed Concrete Girders

ER-19   Laboratory Tests of Jarrah Wood - A Product of Australia

ER-20   Prestressed Concrete Tie Investigation

ER-21   Field Investigation of Florida East Coast Prestressed Concrete Beams

ER-22   Rail Slippage Tests - Concrete Ties

ER-23   Termite Control Investigation - Inspection of Specimens after 52 Months Exposure

ER-24   Report on Open Hearth Slag for Railroad Ballast

ER-25   Field Investigation of Southern Pacific Company, Texas and Louisiana Lines Prestressed Concrete Girder Spans

ER-26   Laboratory Investigation to Determine Static and Repeated Load Strength of Full Size Douglas Fir Glued Laminated Stringers - First Progress Report

ER-27   Tracking Test of an Eighty Five Foot Flat Car Trailer Carrier on the Burlington Railroad

ER-28   Effect of Spring Travel, Height of Center of Gravity and Speed on Freight Car Clearance Requirements on Curved and Tangent Track

ER-29   Third Progress Report on Performance of Filter Materials

ER-30   1962 Condition Report on Asphalt Treatment of Ballast and Bridge Decks

ER-31   Comparison of Soil Density and Water Content Determinations with Conventional and Nuclear Equipment

ER-32   An Investigation of Various Welding Techniques for Building Up Battered Rail Ends

ER-33   Physical and Mechanical Test Results of Rails and Joint Bars Produced by the Basic Oxygen Steel Making Process

ER-34   Description of the Flame Hardening of Rail by Union Pacific Railroad and Physical and Metallurgical Test Results

928

36587.2

36587.3.

ER-71   Laboratory Investigation of Prestressed Lightweight Concrete Box Beams
ER-72   Flexural Behavior of Large Glued-Laminated Beams
ER-73   Termite Control Investigation Inspection of Specimens after 112 Months Exposure
ER-74   Report of Study on Weighing of Freight Cars, Two Draft, Coupled-in-Motion on the Tennessee Valley Authority Bull Run Steam Plant Electronic Scale Near Knoxville, Tennessee
ER-75   Use of Sonic Devices for Determining Internal Decay in Timber
ER-76   Laboratory Investigation to Determine Static and Repeated Load Strength of Full-Size Southern Pine Solid-Sawn Stringers
ER-77   Capability of Fasteners to Resist Rail Overturning

T. T. C. Hsu

N. W. Hanson

An Investigation of Rail-to-Concrete Fasteners*

By
T. T. C. Hsu, formerly Research Engineer,
and
Norman W. Hanson, Senior Research
Engineer
Structural Research Section
Research and Development Laboratories
Portland Cement Association

SYNOPSIS

Prestressed concrete railroad ties are being increasingly used. This investigation deals with the rail-to-concrete fasteners for concrete ties, bridge decks, and tunnel linings. For spring-clip fasteners in concrete ties, three methods of electrical insulation were studied. These fasteners were subjected to tie-wear tests, longitudinal-slip tests and electrical-resistance tests. The anchors used were also subjected to pullout tests. For fasteners in bridges and tunnels, three different fasteners were tested under repeated loading. In addition, the "second-cast" method of construction was studied.

KEY WORDS: anchors; concrete railroad ties; electrical insulation; electrical resistance; longitudinal slip; pullout tests; rail fasteners; railroad ties; repeated loads; testing

*The preparation of a part of this report has been financed through a mass transportation grant from the Department of Housing and Urban Development under the provisions of Section 6, Public Law 88-365, 88th Congress, as amended.

HIGHLIGHTS

The economy of concrete ties has improved in recent years. A 1966 study[1]** by the Chesapeake & Ohio and the Baltimore & Ohio Railroads showed that under many conditions it is more economical to install concrete than timber ties. Recent developments in mass transportation systems for large cities, such as San Francisco and Chicago, have also focused attention on the use of concrete ties. The San Francisco Bay Area Rapid Transit District (BARTD) surface tracks will be supported on 146,000 concrete ties (69 miles of track). Similarly, contracts for the surface extension lines of the Chicago Transit Authority call for concrete crossties.

Rail Fasteners for Ties

One of the technical problems of concrete ties has been development of suitable fasteners to connect the rail to the tie. Using rails to transmit electrical impulses that control modern signal systems severely limits the amount of electrical leakage that can be tolerated between the two rails of a track. One way to reduce this leakage is to use fasteners that insulate the rail from the concrete ties.

**Numbers in parentheses designate references at end of paper.

Static and repeated load tests were carried out on four spring-clip fastener assemblies to evaluate three ways of providing electrical insulation. In addition, electrical resistance tests and pullout tests were made both on the rail fastener assemblies and on individual anchors. The three ways of providing insulation are shown in Fig. 1. Plastic parts and coatings are used as insulating barriers between the rail and the concrete block representing the tie.

All fastener assemblies tested passed the severe "tie-wear test." This test requires that no sign of failure be visible after 2.5 million cycles of load have been applied alternately to the gage and field sides of the rail.

Longitudinal-slip tests revealed that a 200-lb-ft torque was required on *lubricated* anchor bolts to provide sufficient rail clamping for all fastener assemblies to pass the minimum specified slip load of 3.5 kips per fastener.[2]

After completion of the mechanical tests, electrical resistance measurements were made on the concrete tie blocks. Under conditions simulating dry weather, the measured resistance for three of the four specimens was greater than 100,000 ohms, which is more than adequate. However, drenching with water to represent rainy weather reduced the electrical resistance of all fasteners. The best fastener had an epoxy-coated anchor and an insulating plastic pad under both the rail and clip; it retained a resistance of about 10,000 ohms between the two rails. This resistance exceeds the 4000-ohm resistance needed to meet minimum requirements.

Pullout tests of fastener assemblies and anchors indicated that, although the individual anchor strength was as high as expected, the pullout strengths of the full assemblies were below the severe AREA Proposed Specifications[2] requirement of 18,000 lb.

Bridge and Tunnel Rail Fasteners

Three rail fasteners designed to provide the cushioning and electrical insulation

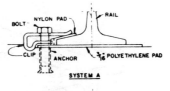

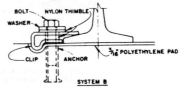

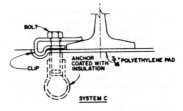

Fig. 1 — Insulating Systems for Rails Using Spring-Clip Fasteners.

necessary between rail and bridge decks (Fig. 2) or tunnel linings as required for use in the San Francisco BARTD[3] were tested under repeated loads. For one of the fasteners, the complete construction procedure was carried out by first casting a leveling course of concrete between a hardened concrete base and the rail fastener assemblies.[4] Tests were performed on the whole assembly. The three fasteners successfully withstood the stiffness and repeated load tests they were subjected to.

RAIL FASTENERS FOR CONCRETE TIES

Of the many rail fasteners used throughout the world, the one currently suggested for use in the United States is the spring clip described in the Draft Specifications proposed to the American Railway Engineering Association.[2] This fastener appears to be simple and economical. Since the clip is not proprietary, the present tests of methods to insulate the rail from the concrete tie were carried out on this type of fastener.

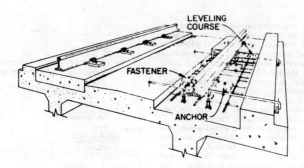

Fig. 2 — One Rail-Fastening System for Bridge Decks,
Utilizing a Second-Cast Method of Construction.

The test specimens were manufactured and tested at the Structural Laboratory of the PCA Research and Development Division. They were first subjected to the wear test and longitudinal-slip test required by the AREA Proposed Specifications[2] for rail-fastener assemblies. In addition, electrical resistance tests and pullout tests were made both on the rail fastener assemblies and on the individual anchors used in the test specimens.

Insulation Methods

Three ways of insulating the rail were considered for the spring-clip type of fastener. These are shown in Fig. 1.

System A was suggested in the AREA Proposed Specifications.[2] Here, one insulator (a $\frac{3}{16}$-in.-thick polyethylene pad) is placed under the rail, while a second insulator (a $\frac{3}{8}$-in.-thick nylon pad) is placed between the rail and the clips.

In System B, the polyethylene pad under the rail is extended under the clips. The other insulator (a $\frac{3}{16}$-in.-thick nylon thimble) is placed between the clip and the

bolt washer. The washer is needed to distribute the bolt force over the nylon thimble.

In System C, the polyethylene pad under the rail is again extended under the clips. With this system, the anchor is coated with an insulating material. Both polyethylene and epoxy were evaluated as insulating materials. BULLETIN 224[5]* reports electrical tests made on coated anchors embedded in saturated concrete and shows that these coatings greatly improve the electrical resistance.

Details regarding each specimen are given in Table 1.

Description of Specimen Parts

The spring clips used in the four specimens were made by hot-bending $\frac{1}{4}$ x 3-in. strip steel bar and then heat-treating to satisfy Section C5 of the AREA Proposed Specifications.[2] SAE 1095 steel was used rather than the SAE 1090 steel suggested by the Proposed Specifications. Although no clip tests as described in Section H3(a), (b), (c) and (d) of the AREA Proposed Specifications were made, the clips performed well during the mechanical tests of the fastener assemblies. No failure in the clips was observed. High-strength $\frac{3}{4}$-in.-diameter bolts satisfying Section C8 of the AREA Proposed Specifications were used in all specimens.

*PCA RESEARCH AND DEVELOPMENT DEPARTMENT BULLETINS will be identified in the text primarily by the BULLETIN number. BULLETINS are available on request in the United States and Canada.

TABLE 1 — FASTENER SPECIMENS TESTED

Fastener Specimen Designation	Insulating System ᵃ	Anchor Type ᵇ	Anchor Coating
I	A	I, 1⅛ in. long	Paint
II	B	I, 2⅛ in. long	Paint
III	C	II	Polyethylene
IV	C	II	Epoxy

ᵃ Fig. 1 shows configuration for each type of specimen.
ᵇFig. 3 shows the two types of anchors.

Two types of commercially available anchors were employed. The first type, shown in Fig. 3(a), is manufactured by bending a 3 or 2-in.-wide stainless steel plate to form a cylinder with a flared end. Threads are then cut inside the cylinder. The second type, shown in Fig. 3(b), consists of a 1⅛-in.-long closed cylinder that has a steel wire loop welded to it. This anchor is also internally threaded. Type I anchors 1⅞ and 2⅞ in. long were used in Specimens I and II, respectively. In Specimen III, the Type II anchors were covered with a 0.027-in.-thick polyethylene coating. This coating was very soft and could be indented with a fingernail. In Specimen IV, the Type II anchors were covered with a 0.023-in.-thick coating of a commercial epoxy protective resin called "Scotchkote." This coating was very hard.

Polyethylene pads that were ³⁄₁₆ in. thick and 7 in. wide were placed beneath the rails in the test specimens. These pads met both ASTM Specification D 1248,[6] Type II, Grade 3, Class B and Section C7 of the AREA Proposed Specifications.[2] The pads used with Specimens II, III and IV were shaped in the PCA Laboratories by pressing a flat sheet between a pair of hardwood molds and holding this in an oven at a temperature of 280 F for two hours. The contour of the hardwood mold was machined to fit the spring clips. The resulting molded pad is shown in Fig. 4.

The nylon pads in Specimen I and the nylon thimbles in Specimen II were made of Nylon 66 (Zytel 101). This material conforms to both ASTM Specification D 789,[7] Type I, Grade 4 and Section C6 of the AREA Proposed Specifications.[2] Both the pads and the thimble were machined from a single piece of material. The dimensions of the pads shown in Fig. 5, conform to Fig. 5A of the AREA Proposed Specifications.[2]

The concrete tie blocks were made with air-entrained concrete having a cylinder strength of about 7000 psi at 28 days. Dimensions and reinforcement details are shown in Fig. 6. The 7 x 9-in. cross section under the rail is roughly the same as for commercially available concrete ties. The contour of the upper surface, shown in Fig. 6, is designed to fit the spring clips and the polyethylene pads.

(a) Type I Anchor (2⅞ In. Long)

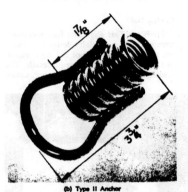

(b) Type II Anchor

Fig. 3 — Types of Anchors Used.

Fig. 4— Polyethylene Pad and Concrete Tie Block Used in Specimens II to IV.

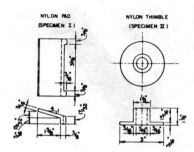

Fig. 5 — Nylon Pad and Nylon Thimble.

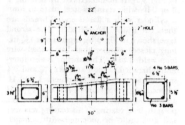

Fig. 6 — Concrete Tie Block.

Tie-Wear Test

Tie-Wear Test Rig. The four specimens were tested in a specially designed tie-wear test rig. A general view of the rig is shown in Fig. 7, while Fig. 8 shows its details. The loading scheme for the rail fastener, shown

Fig. 7 — General View of Tie-Wear Test Rig.

in Fig. 9, meets requirements of Section H4(a) of the AREA Proposed Specifications.[2]

Loads were applied alternately to the gage and field sides of the rail. These alternating loads were applied by two 25-ton Amsler rams described in BULLETIN D33.[8] The rams were attached to the cross member of a concrete frame which was prestressed to the laboratory floor by two 1⅝-in.-diameter high-strength rods. This test floor is described in BULLETIN D33.[8] The alternating loads were supplied by two separate pulsators connected 180 degrees out of phase by a mechanical coupling.

The hydraulic rams are designed to supply a load that varies sinusoidally with time. However, the tie-wear test requires the alternating load to be applied in such a manner that each load is completely released before the other load is applied. To obtain this loading, the combination of rams and springs shown in Fig. 8 was used. At each ram a square tube crosshead is attached. Each crosshead is connected by two steel rods to a spring assembly located on top of the concrete frame. Each spring assembly is made up of four springs sandwiched between two steel plates. The springs restrain the movement of the rams, thereby converting the sinusoidal load into a half-sinusoidal load.

The load from each ram is transmitted to the rail through a series of ball hinges, load cells, and a specially designed chair. Signals from the load cells are recorded on a Sanborn 67A continuous strip recorder as described in BULLETINS D33[8] and D91.[9] Representative output is shown in Fig. 10. It can be seen that the load-vs-time relationship is described by two half-sinusoidal curves 180 degrees out of phase.

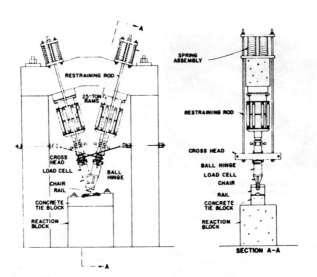

Fig. 8 — Details of Tie-Wear Test Rig.

Description of Test. A concrete reaction block was first prestressed securely to the laboratory floor, as in Fig. 8. Then the concrete tie block was grouted on top of the reaction block with the rail at its intended position. After the grout hardened, the concrete tie block was tied down to the reaction block by two $\frac{7}{8}$-in.-diameter rods. The tie block was then ready to receive the rail fastener assemblies.

After the rail clips were in place, the bolts in the assemblies were tightened down by a torque of 150 lb-ft as required by the AREA Proposed Specifications.[2] Application of loading alternately to the gage and field sides of the rail was then begun. The loads were applied at a rate of about 250 cycles per minute. In the early stages of the test, it was necessary to adjust the load frequently. The load was kept within ±10 percent of the intended value at all times.

Torque in the fastener hold-down bolts was checked periodically during the test. If the torque was found to be lower than 150 lb-ft, it was brought back up to this value.

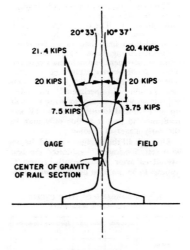

Fig. 9 — Loading Scheme.

Fig. 10 — Strip Recorder Showing Half-Sinusoidal
Load-vs-Time Relationships.

Test Results. The number of cycles applied to each specimen is listed in Table 2. All specimens withstood 2.5 million cycles of loading without visible sign of failure of any part of the fastener assembly. Consequently, each specimen satisfied the requirements of Section H4(a) of the AREA Proposed Specifications.[2] Although not considered serious, hairline cracks were observed around the inserts of the concrete tie block in Specimen III.

The bolt torque-vs-cycles of loading curves for Specimens I, II, and IV are shown in Fig. 11. The bolt torque in Specimen III was not checked. In Specimen I, the hold-down bolts had to be tightened frequently during the test. This may be the result of movement and deformation of the nylon pad between the clip and the rail. The torque stabilized after 1.9 million cycles of loading. In Specimen II, much less adjustment was necessary to bring the bolt up to the initial torque. Specimen IV was readjusted to proper torque only once in the early stages of loading.

Although all the specimens passed the tie-wear test, Specimen IV exhibited the best overall behavior. Consequently, system C appears to be the most desirable way to in-

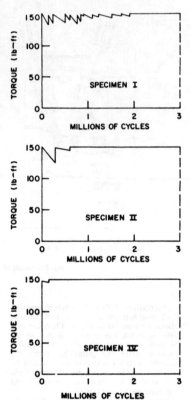

Fig. 11 — Torque in Bolts During Test.

sulate the rail so long as the coating on the anchor is sufficiently strong.

Longitudinal-Slip Test

Description of Test. Section H4(b) of the AREA Proposed Specifications[2] requires that "the end of the rail in the fastening assembly should be subjected to a longitudinal load of 3500 lb and the movement between the rail and the concrete tie recorded by dial gages reading to 0.001 in. The load of 3500 lb shall remain on the end of the rail for three minutes without

TABLE 2 — NUMBER OF LOAD CYCLES
ON FASTENER SPECIMENS

	Specimen I	Specimen II	Specimen III	Specimen IV
Total No. of Cycles Applied	3 175 000	3 617 000	3 356 000	3 356 000

any increase in the rail movement after the three-minute period."

After tie-wear tests were completed, each of the four specimens was subjected to a longitudinal-slip test as described above. A schematic view of the test setup is shown in Fig. 12. The concrete tie block was fastened to the laboratory floor by crossheads and rods. Horizontal load was supplied by a 10-ton hydraulic ram that acted against a reaction block. Load was applied to the centroid of the lower flange of the rail through a steel ball. The movement of the rail with respect to the concrete tie block was measured at each load stage by a dial gage after holding the load for three minutes.

Test Results. Two sets of longitudinal-slip tests were made. The first set was made without lubricating the hold-down bolts before they were tightened. The second set was made after each bolt had been coated with Molykote, a commercial lubricant, before the bolts were tightened down. A typical load-slip curve is shown in Fig. 13. Fig. 14 shows a plot of the load at which complete slipping occurred vs the torque on the hold-down bolts.

Fig. 14 shows that for the set of tests without lubricant the load at complete slipping is extremely erratic. In the process of tightening the hold-down bolts for these tests, the friction between the bolt and the clip or anchor is large. This friction takes up a large part of the applied torque and prevents achievement of the full tension intended in the bolts, and the intended holding force of the fastener. In the set of tests without lubricant, most of the specimens failed to sustain the 3500 lb of horizontal load specified in the Proposed Specifications.[2] This was true even when the torque on the bolts was increased to 300 lb-ft.

The resistance to slipping appeared to decrease with increasing torque on the nonlubricated hold-down bolts for Specimens I and II. Since the sequence of slip tests was made with increasing torque on the bolt, it appears that the friction between the polyethylene pad and the rail (or between the clip and the rail) decreased each time the test was repeated.

More consistent test results were obtained in the second set of longitudinal slip tests. For these, the hold-down bolts were lubricated before tightening. Fig. 14 shows that one out of four fasteners was able to sustain the 3500-lb horizontal load for

three minutes when the hold-down bolts were lubricated and tightened to 150 lb-ft. However, with the torque increased to 200 lb-ft, all four specimens meet requirements of Section H4(b) of the AREA Proposed Specifications.[2]

Electrical-Resistance Test on Individual Type II Anchors

Two types of electrical resistance tests were made on the Type II anchors shown in Fig. 3(b). The first group of tests was made on individual anchors, each coated with one of five types of insulating material. The coated anchor was embedded in a 4-in. cube of concrete. After the concrete had hardened, the cube was stored in a brine solution. Periodically, each cube was

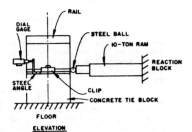

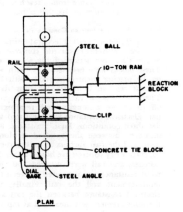

Fig. 12 — Setup for Longitudinal-Slip Test.

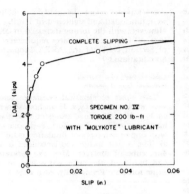

Fig. 13 — Typical Load-Slip Curve.

removed from the brine, the surface water was removed, and the electrical resistance was measured. The detailed description and the results of these tests are reported in BULLETIN 224.[5]

It was found that thin coatings of either nylon or teflon increased the electrical resistance only slightly. Coatings such as these should not be used for electrical insulation in saturated concrete. Coatings made with polyethylene, epoxy and vinylidene fluoride resins were found to improve the electrical resistance from a few hundred ohms to the order of 100,000 ohms.

Electrical-Resistance Tests on Concrete Tie Block

Description of Tests. Electrical-resistance tests were also made on the concrete tie blocks after completion of the wear tests. These blocks were first saturated with water by placing them in a room with 100 percent relative humidity for four days. Then one corner of each block was chipped off to expose a longitudinal reinforcing bar. Electrical resistance was measured under three conditions. First, resistance was measured between the exposed reinforcement and the two anchors in each saturated, surface-dry concrete tie block. Next, dry fasteners and rail were installed and electrical resistance was measured between the reinforcement and the rail. Finally, the electrical resistance between the rail and the reinforcement was measured as tap water was poured on the fastener and rail to simulate conditions during a heavy rain.

Alternating current of 1000 hertz (cycles per second) and four volts was applied. The electrical resistances measured under each condition are recorded in Table 3.

Test Results. Table 3 shows that the electrical resistance between anchors and reinforcement for Test Condition No. 1 varies from 100 ohms to 500 ohms for Specimens I and II. However, the coated anchors in Specimens III and IV had an electrical resistance between 12,000 and 1,000,000 ohms. These values compare very well with those obtained for individual anchors as reported in BULLETIN 224.[5] It must be mentioned, however, that the electrical resistance in Specimen III was lower than expected from tests of individual anchors. This may indicate that the polyethylene coating was damaged before the electrical tests were conducted.

When measurement was made between the rail and the reinforcement in the absence of surface water — Test Condition No. 2 — the electrical resistance exceeded 2,000,000 ohms (the maximum resistance which can be measured by the equipment) for Specimens I and II. This indicates that the nylon pad in Specimen I and the nylon thimble in Specimen II are extremely effective in improving the electrical resistance

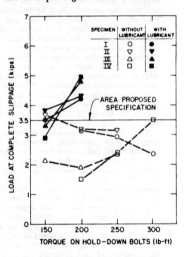

Fig. 14 — Load Required to Produce Total Slippage vs Torque on the Hold-Down Bolts.

TABLE 3 — ELECTRICAL RESISTANCE IN SATURATED CONCRETE TIES

Test Condition No.	Electrical Path and Surface Water Condition	Resistance, ohms			
		Specimen I	Specimen II	Specimen III	Specimen IV
1	Anchor to Reinforcement Without Surface Water	200 100	300 500	12 000 50 000	100 000 1 000 000
2	Rail to Reinforcement Without Surface Water *	>2 000 000	>2 000 000	10 000	150 000
3	Rail to Reinforcement With Surface Water *	1 000	3 000	4 000	5 000

*All values should be multiplied by 2 to obtain the electrical resistance between two rails on a tie.

of the dry fastener assembly. Under this similar condition, the electrical resistance for both Specimen III and Specimen IV was found to be adequate for practical application.

In Test Condition No. 3 the electrical measurement was made between the rail and the reinforcement with surface water present. The electrical resistance dropped to 1000 and 3000 ohms for Specimens I and II, respectively. Similarly, the electrical resistance for Specimens III and IV dropped to 4000 and 5000 ohms, respectively. It is obvious that the presence of surface water considerably reduces the electrical resistance. Since the electrical path through the surface water is longer for Specimens III and IV than for Specimens I and II, the electrical resistances of the former two specimens are better.

System C using an epoxy coating to insulate the Type II anchor from the concrete tie and using a pad to insulate the rail from the tie appears to have the best overall electrical resistance. Using this system, the electrical resistance between the two rails of a track is roughly 10,000 ohms even when surface water is present. This is considerably in excess of the 4000-ohm minimum resistance that is generally acceptable.[2]

Pullout Test of Individual Anchors

Description of Test. Both Type I and Type II anchors as shown in Fig. 3 were tested. The 1⅞-in.-long Type I anchors were embedded in concrete as received from the manufacturer. The outer surface was covered with a thin layer of paint. However, for the 2⅞-in.-long Type I anchors, two surface conditions were evaluated. In addition to a pair of anchors with painted surfaces, another pair was tested that had the paint removed from the outer

surface before they were cast into the concrete test blocks.

For Type II anchors, the surfaces of each pair of specimens were coated with one of the five insulating materials: epoxy, polyethylene, vinylidene fluoride, teflon, and nylon. In addition, two uncoated anchors were tested for comparison.

Pairs of identical anchors were cast in the bottom of a plain concrete block 10 in. deep, 18 in. wide and 48 in. long. The distance between each pair of anchors was 24 in. The average cylinder strength of the concrete was 6830 psi at the time of the pullout test.

The setup for pullout tests is shown in Fig. 15. A specially designed steel frame with a span of 20 in. was placed longitudinally on the concrete block. The center of the frame was lined up vertically with one of the anchors. A 30-ton center-hole ram and a 50-kip load cell were placed on the steel frame. A ¾-in.-diameter rod was passed through the ram and load cell and was threaded into the anchor. The rod was anchored on top of the load cell by a nut and a bearing plate. The pullout force on the anchor was supplied by the ram and was monitored by the load cell connected to a portable strain indicator using procedures described in BULLETIN D33.[8]

The vertical displacement of the anchor was measured by a dial gage reading to 0.0001 in. The dial gage was mounted on a light-gage steel bridge clamped securely to the sides of the concrete block and was fitted with a z-shaped needle that rested against the wall of the anchor.

Test Results for Type I Anchors. Results of the pullout tests of anchors are summarized in Table 4. For the 1⅞-in.-long Type I anchor, the pullout strength averaged 6.6 kips, for the 2⅞-in.-long Type I anchor 12.6 kips. No difference in pullout strength at-

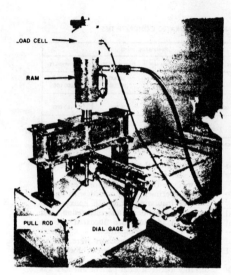

LOAD CELL

RAM

PULL ROD

DIAL GAGE

Fig. 15 — Pullout Tests of Individual Anchors.

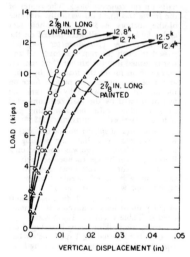

Fig. 16 — Load–Displacement Curves of Type I Anchors.

tributable to paint on the outer surface of the anchor was detected. However, the vertical displacement of the painted anchor was about twice that of the unpainted anchor at all load stages. This is shown by the load–displacement curves in Fig. 16. Apparently, the paint causes additional slipping due to reduced friction between the anchor and the surrounding concrete.

For 1⅞-in.-long painted anchors, failure occurred by pulling out a cone of concrete around the anchor. This cone has been turned upside down for photographing, and appears to the right of the crater from which it was removed in Fig. 17(a). For 2⅞-in.-long painted anchors, however, failure was caused by splitting of the concrete blocks as shown in Fig. 17(b). Finally, the failure of the 2⅞-in.-long unpainted anchors was caused by tearing off the top surface of the concrete block as shown in Fig. 17(c).

Test Results for Type II Anchors. For Type II anchors, Table 4 indicates that the variation in strength among anchors with epoxy, nylon, vinylidene fluoride, and teflon did not exceed ±10 percent. Consequently, the effect of these four coatings on pullout strength is considered insignificant.

Fig. 18 shows that the load–displacement curves for epoxy-coated and uncoated anchors are nearly identical. Similar load–displacement curves were recorded for anchors with vinylidene fluoride, nylon, and teflon coatings. Consequently, it can be concluded that these four coatings — epoxy, vinylidene fluoride, nylon and teflon — have no important effect on the load-vs-displacement relationship of Type II anchors.

In contrast, loads in Table 4 indicate that the polyethylene coating somewhat reduced the pullout strength. Fig. 18 shows that the displacement of the anchor with polyethylene coating is many times that of the uncoated anchor at all load stages. It is apparent that a soft and thick coating, such as polyethylene, will reduce the pullout strength and greatly increase the displacement.

According to the manufacturer's specifications, the Type II anchor is rated at 9600 lb, approximately the breaking strength of the wire loop. This value is very close to that obtained for polyethylene-coated anchors. It appears that the soft polyethylene coating does not contribute significantly to the pullout strength. The failure mode, shown in Fig. 19(a), indicates that the polyethylene-coated anchor slipped out of the concrete block with little resistance from the surrounding concrete.

Fig. 19(b) shows that when the epoxy-coated anchor was tested a cone of concrete surrounding the anchor was pulled out of the concrete block. The cone is pictured in an inverted position to the right of the re-

maining crater in the figure. This accounts for the pullout strengths of epoxy-coated anchors being significantly higher than the specified value of 9600 lb.

The coating of Type II anchors with a strong insulating material, such as epoxy, has no significant effect on either the pull-

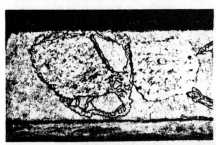

(a) Painted Anchor, 1⅞ In. Long

(b) Painted Anchor, 2⅞ In. Long

(c) Unpainted Anchor, 2⅞ In. Long

Fig. 17 — Pullout Failure of Type I Anchors.

TABLE 4 — PULLOUT STRENGTH OF ANCHORS

Type of Coating	Pullout Strength (kips)		
	Anchor Specimen No. 1	Anchor Specimen No. 2	Average
Type I Anchor, 1⅞ in. long [a]			
Painted	6.7	6.5	6.6
Type I Anchor, 2⅞ in. long [a]			
Painted	12.5	12.4	12.4
Unpainted	12.8	12.7	12.8
Type II Anchor [a]			
Uncoated	11.7	11.1	11.4
Epoxy	11.2	13.6	12.4
Polyethylene	9.8	9.9	9.8
Vinylidene Fluoride	11.4	10.7	11.1
Teflon	11.0	10.4	10.7
Nylon	12.7	12.5	12.6

[a] Anchors are shown in Fig. 3.

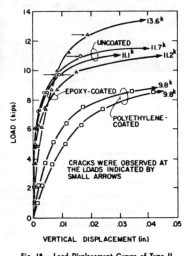

Fig. 18 — Load–Displacement Curves of Type II Anchors.

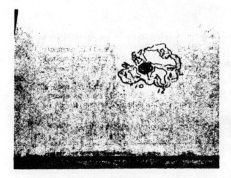

(a) Polyethylene-Coated Anchor

(b) Epoxy-Coated Anchor

Fig. 19 — Pullout Failure of Type II Anchors.

out strength or the displacement relationship. However, a soft coating does reduce the capacity and should be avoided.

Pullout Test of Anchors in Concrete Tie Blocks

Description of Test. Pullout tests of anchors in concrete tie blocks were made as described in Section H2(b) of the AREA Proposed Specifications.[2] A general view of the test setup is shown in Fig. 20. A rail two feet long was attached to the concrete tie block by the fastener assemblies. The two ends of the rail were supported by timber blocks so that the concrete tie block was suspended above the floor. A steel frame with a span of 20 in. was placed on the concrete tie block over the rail.

Load was applied to the frame through a system of crossheads, rams, and tie rods attached to the laboratory floor. The load was calculated from the oil pressure of the ram, taking into account the dead weight of the equipment. At the time of test the concrete strength of the blocks was somewhat greater than 7000 psi.

Test Results. The failure loads, P, in pounds, determined by pullout tests of anchors in concrete tie blocks are recorded in Table 5.

The force between the field clip and the rail base, R, and the force in the field bolt, Q, can be calculated from the pullout load, P, by equilibrium of forces using the lever systems illustrated in Fig. 21.

$$R = P \frac{2}{1.688 + 2} = 0.542 \, P$$

$$Q = R \frac{2.313 + 1.25}{1.25} = 2.85 \, R = 1.54 \, P$$

TABLE 5 — PULLOUT TESTS OF ANCHORS IN CONCRETE TIE BLOCKS

	Force or Load, lb			
	Specimen I	Specimen II	Specimen III	Specimen IV
Kind of Force or Load	Anchor Type I, 1⅞ in. Long	Anchor Type I, 2⅞ in. Long	Anchor Type II, Polyethylene-Coated	Anchor Type II, Epoxy-Coated
Total Pullout Load, P	3 930	16 800	6 110	9 980
Force Between Field Clip and Rail Base, R	2 140	9 120	3 320	5 420
Force in Field Bolt, Q	6 100	26 000	9 460	15 450
Pullout Strength of Individual Anchors (Table 4)	6 600	12 450	9 850	12 400

Fig. 20 — Pullout Test of Anchors in Concrete Tie Blocks.

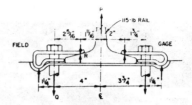

Fig. 21 — Arrangement of Rail, Clips and Bolts for 115-lb RE RAIL.

Calculated values of R and Q are also listed in Table 5.

For Specimens I, III, and IV the failure forces in the field bolt, Q, are reasonably close to the pullout strength of individual anchors as listed in Table 4 and also recorded in the last line of Table 5. The failure modes of anchors in these three specimens are also similar to those in corresponding pullout tests of individual anchors. The concrete tie blocks after the pullout tests were completed are shown in Fig. 22.

The failure force, Q = 26,000 lb, in Specimen II, Table 5, was about twice the average pullout strength of 12,450 lb of the individual Type I, 2⅞-in. anchor. The 2⅞-in. length of this anchor is enough to reach well beneath the top reinforcement of the concrete tie block. The individual pullout tests in plain concrete indicated that fail-

ure is caused by either splitting the block or tearing the top layer of concrete. Top reinforcement apparently helped prevent these two types of failure. Consequently, the pullout strength in the concrete tie block was higher than that of individual anchors in plain concrete.

Section H2(b) of the AREA Proposed Specifications requires that the total pullout strength of the rail fastening assembly shall be not less than 18,000 lb. Table 5 shows that none of the anchors satisfies this severe requirement. The AREA Proposed Specifications apply to prestressed concrete of slightly higher strength (8000 psi) than was used in these nonprestressed test specimens. Even so, the pullout strength of the assembly is much less than the sum of the strengths of the two anchors. This is because the forces on the anchors of a complete fastening assembly are magnified through the lever system described above so that the force on each bolt is much greater than one half the load on the rail.

Fig. 22 — Concrete Tie Blocks After Pullout Test.

Fig. 23 — Bonded-Elastomeric Fastener.

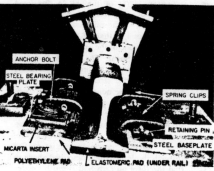

Fig. 24 — Spring-Clip Fastener.

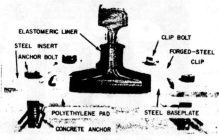

Fig. 25 — Forged-Clip Fastener.

RAIL FASTENERS FOR BRIDGES AND TUNNELS

On bridges and in tunnels, rails are sometimes connected directly to concrete decks. For the system used in the Bay Area Rapid Transit District (BARTD) in San Francisco, the requirements for such a fastener include cushioning of the rail against vibration in addition to electrical insulation, strength, and adjustability. In this rail system, the fastener is clamped to the rail, and the base of the fastener is bolted to anchors embedded in a "second-cast" leveling course of concrete as shown in Fig. 2. The concrete is leveled against the upper surface of the bridge or the tunnel lining.[4]

Three different types of fasteners were tested for this application. Two of the fasteners were subjected to the tie-wear test described earlier in this report while the third was subjected to a push–pull test to represent the "wave action" caused by wheel loading. For the third fastener the complete procedure of the proposed "second-cast" method of construction was also investigated.

Description of Fasteners

Bonded-Elastomeric Fastener. The bonded-elastomeric fastener shown in Fig. 23 consists of a permanent assembly of upper and lower steel plates spaced apart by a bonded, elastomeric pad. Steel clips bolted to the upper plate hold the rail in position. The bolting force holds the clip fulcrum in one of a series of surface indentations spaced $\frac{1}{8}$ in. apart in the top plate. The upper plate floats on the elastomeric cushion which is confined by the two bent-up edges of the lower plate. Two anchor bolts through the plate assembly connect the lower plate to anchors in the concrete base. Electrical insulation is provided by the elastomeric material that separates the upper and lower plates.

Spring-Clip Fastener. The spring-clip fastener shown in Fig. 24 consists of a steel baseplate, two spring clips with retaining pins, an elastomeric pad, a polyethylene pad and two Micarta (plastic) inserts with bearing plates and bolts. The rail rests on the elastomeric pad between shoulders formed in the steel baseplate. Two clips formed of spring steel bear against the top of the lower flange of the rail to restrain its movement. The spring clips are each installed over a short stud welded to the top surface of the plate.

Spring force is initially created by opening the throat of each spring with a specially designed hand tool. The pin is then inserted through holes in the studs. This permanently holds the spring force. Two anchor bolts pass through bearing plates and fitted Micarta inserts to the anchors in the concrete base. Electrical insulation is provided by the Micarta inserts and by the polyethylene pad between the plate and the concrete base. Various sizes of Micarta inserts can be used to provide adjustment of the rail position.

Forged-Clip Fastener. The forged-clip fastener shown in Fig. 25 consists of a steel baseplate, two forged-steel clips with bolts, two elastomeric liners, a polyethylene pad and two steel inserts. The elastomeric liner is composed of two identical rubber pieces molded to match the shape of half the lower part of the rail. This liner surrounds the lower 3½ in. of the rail over a 5-in. length.

Both liner and rail are held in place by a steel clip on each side of the rail and by the steel baseplate below. Clip bolts secure the clips to the steel baseplate. Two additional anchor bolts run through steel inserts in the baseplate and through the polyethylene pad to the anchors in the concrete base. Rail position can be adjusted by using various sizes of steel inserts. The rubber liner provides not only a cushion but also electrical insulation between the rail and the fastener.

Tie-Wear Test

The bonded-elastomeric and spring-clip fasteners were subjected to tie-wear tests similar to those described earlier in Figs. 7 to 10. Since the rail clips on each of these fasteners are not directly opposite one another, loading a rail segment on a single fastener could cause rotation of the rail that would not be possible in service. Therefore, pairs of rail fasteners placed 1 in. apart were tested. The test fasteners were attached to a precast concrete base representing the bridge or tunnel leveling course. Loads were applied to a 115-lb. RE rail at a point midway between the fasteners. Alternating loads producing a 30-kip resultant (15 kips per fastener) were applied to the test specimen.

Bonded-Elastomeric Fastener. Initial torque on the rail clip bolts was 300 lb-ft. Torque on the anchor bolts connecting the fastener pad to the concrete base was 200 lb-ft.

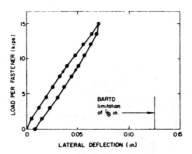

Fig. 26 — Load–Deflection Curve for Bonded-Elastomeric Fastener Before Application of Repeated Loads.

Before the repeated load test began, the fastener assemblies were placed in the tie-wear test rig and loaded statically on the gage side of the rail. The load–deflection curve obtained under the loading is shown in Fig. 26. Lateral deflection of the rail head under the maximum load of 30 kips (15 kips per fastener) was 0.071 in. This is well within the BARTD limitation of ⅛ in.[3]

After the deflection tests were completed, load was applied alternately to the gage and field sides of the fastener. The rate of loading was 250 cycles per minute. Considerable heat was generated during the repeated load portion of the test. The temperature on the surface of the steel reached 108 F, a value that should not be expected to influence the results of the tests.

After 310,000 cycles of repeated load, vertical cracks about ¼ in. long and 1/32 in. wide were observed in the rubber between the end of the top plate and the bent-up portion of the bottom plate. However, no change in behavior was observed.

After 1,137,000 cycles, the application of repeated loads was temporarily stopped so that lateral deflection of the rail head could be checked. Again static load was applied to the gage side of the rail. Lateral deflection under the maximum load was 0.089 in. The increased deflection shows that the lateral stiffness of the fastener decreased somewhat from the initial value. However, this lateral deflection is still well within the BARTD limitation. The torque on each bolt was checked and was found to have dropped about 10 to 30 lb-ft from the

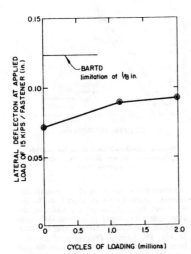

Fig. 27 — Lateral Deflection vs Cycles of Loading for Bonded-Elastomeric Fastener.

initial values. Before the test was resumed, these torques were brought back up to the initial values.

The test was stopped after 2 million cycles of loading. The lateral deflection under the maximum load of 30 kips (15 kips per fastener) was 0.092 in. A plot with the lateral deflection at an applied static load of 15 kips per fastener on the ordinate versus number of repetitions of load on the abscissa is shown in Fig. 27. This comparison indicates that the stiffness of the fastener was stabilizing as the test was completed.

After 2 million cycles of loading the crack in the rubber between the upper plate of the fastener and the bent-up portion of the lower plate was about 1 in. long. The maximum width of this crack under a static load of 15 kips per fastener applied on the gage side was somewhat more than $\frac{1}{16}$ in. It appears that the width of this crack accounts for most of the lateral movement of the rail. However, these cracks did not reduce the stiffness below that required in the BARTD Specifications.[8]

The fastener pads were subjected to an additional 10,000 cycles of repeated load, as described in Addenda 3 and 4 of the BARTD Specifications.[3] These Addenda require that this portion of the test be conducted with the anchor bolts connecting the fasteners to the concrete base on the gage side removed. No undesirable movements were observed under this loading.

The bonded-elastomeric fasteners met all requirements of the tie-wear tests as described in the BARTD Specifications.[3]

Spring-Clip Fastener. The initial torque in the anchor bolts connecting the fastener plate to the concrete base was 200 lb-ft.

Two million cycles of loading were applied to the fastener. During this part of the test, lateral deflection was checked. The maximum total lateral movement of the rail head was 0.039 in. This value is well within $\frac{5}{16}$ in. total movement implied by the BARTD Specifications.[3] No visible signs of distress were observed during this portion of the test.

The torque in the four anchor bolts connecting the baseplate to the concrete block was checked after 2 million cycles of loading. This check showed that torque in the bolts had dropped an average of 20 lb-ft from the initial value of 200 lb-ft.

After 2 million cycles of loading, indentations were found on the upper surface of the lower rail flange where the clips made contact with the rail. The maximum depth of the dents was measured to be 0.013 in.

The fasteners were subjected to an additional 11,500 cycles of loading according to Addenda 3 and 4 of the BARTD Specifications.[3] No undesirable movement was observed when repeated loads were applied with the bolts connecting the fasteners to the concrete base on the gage side removed.

The spring-clip fastener met all requirements of the tie-wear tests described in the BARTD Specifications.[8]

Second-Cast, and Wave-Action Test

The forged-clip fastener was subjected to a reversed load test intended to represent the "wave action" that occurs in tracks due to wheel loading. A construction sequence was also studied to determine the problems involved in casting a concrete leveling course under fasteners attached to a rail.

Manufacture of Test Base. As shown in Fig. 28 the base of the test specimen was a 9 x 48 x 96-in. concrete slab representing a portion of the deck of an elevated structure. The central trough, where the rail strip concrete was later cast, was formed by

30

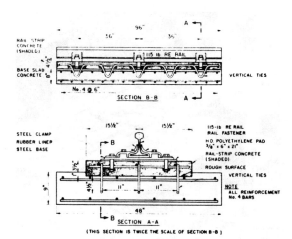

Fig. 28 —— Details of Test Specimen for Cyclic Loading.

scraping out the fresh concrete to the desired level 1 in. below the surface of the base slab. The surface of the trough was finished with a wood float, but was left slightly rough as shown in Fig. 29. The slab was cured and then stored for one month. After placing the additional reinforcement, an 8-ft length of a 115-lb RE rail with three fasteners attached was temporarily supported as shown in Fig. 30. The rail strip concrete was then cast beneath the rail. The concrete anchors were supported by the fastener while the concrete was being placed.

At 10 days from the date the concrete was placed, forms were removed to permit inspection of the finished specimen. The rail and fastener assembly was also removed to facilitate inspection of the concrete surface under the polyethylene pads. Fig. 31 shows both the concrete surface and the top surfaces of the polyethylene pads. It can be seen that mortar from the concrete had penetrated into the space between the polyethylene pads and the baseplates of the fasteners. These crescent-shaped pieces of mortar were about 0.10 in. thick.

The mortar did not adhere to the polyethylene pads. Consequently, it could not be expected to provide permanent load transfer between the fastener baseplate and the pad. Since this problem was the result of a construction procedure that could easily be changed the specimen was not remade. Loose mortar was removed and the space between the polyethylene pad and the rail strip concrete was filled with an epoxy filler (Araldite No. 502 with silica flour) mixed to the consistency of petroleum jelly. This filler served to hold the plastic pad in contact with the baseplate of the fastener. The rail assembly was then set in place. Riser holes in the plastic pads allowed the excess material to be forced out as the assembly settled into place. The riser

Fig. 29 — Trough for Rail-Strip Concrete.

Fig. 30 — Rail Positioned.

holes were plugged when firm support was reached at the bolts. Twenty-four hours later the anchor bolts were removed, cleaned, replaced, and tightened to the desired torque of 200 lb-ft. The clip bolts were tightened to a torque of 275 lb-ft.

Preparation for Cyclic Loading. Prior to the application of the cyclic loads, it was necessary to determine by application of static loads the distribution of forces to the three fasteners. In preparation for such static tests, the rail was instrumented and calibrated for both vertical and horizontal loads. Two strain gage bridges, each made up of four electrical resistance strain gages, were attached to the rail 10 in. to each side of its midlength. On each side of midlength, one bridge responded only to horizontal load, the other only to vertical. Horizontal and vertical bending tests for calibration were made with a central load applied to the bare rail. During the calibration, the rail was supported as a simple beam at the two end fastener locations. The load measuring bridges provided an accuracy of measurement of ±7 lb for horizontal load and ±26 lb for vertical load.

After calibration, the rail was placed in the fastener assembly. The entire test specimen was then placed in the test rig shown in Figs. 32 and 33, and static loads were applied. Distribution among the three fasteners was first determined for vertical down and up loads with the assembly horizontal under the load frame. Next, distribution of lateral load was determined with the specimen at an angle of 18.5 degrees from horizontal. The distribution of force to the center fastener was found to be 83, 67, and 88 percent for vertical-down, vertical-up, and horizontal load, respectively. After completion of the cyclic portion of the test, distributions were rechecked, and no change was noted.

To obtain the desired loads for the center fastener, the assembly was set at an angle of 24 degrees from the horizontal. From the geometry of loading at this angle, the component acting in the plane of symmetry of the rail was 91.3 percent of the applied load, the lateral component 40.7 percent. The components of the force on the center fastener acting in the rail symmetry plane were then 75.5 percent and 61.1 percent of the applied down and up loads, respectively. The maximum lateral force on the center fastener was 35.8 percent of the applied down load.

Cyclic-Load Test. A 50,000-lb capacity Amsler compression ram was used for the down-load portion of the cyclic loads applied to the rail assembly. The pulsator used with this ram provided a sinusoidal down-load at a rate of 500 cycles per minute. With this equipment, the maximum and minimum downward loads could be adjusted to any desired magnitude. However, for this test, an upward load was required for the "minimum." Since the Amsler rams are single-acting, this load could not be applied by the same ram. Consequently, it was necessary to use overhead springs, as shown in Figs. 32 and 33, to provide the up-load on the rail. The spring force was partially overcome at the ram minimum load and completely surpassed by the ram maximum load. Superposition of these forces gave a resultant load to the rail which varied sinusoidally.

The cyclic loading was carried out with the ram force varying from 22.2 kips to 2.0 kips, and with a spring force of 3.6 kips. The resultant total load acting on the rail in its plane of symmetry varied from 17.0 kips down to 1.5 kips up. The maximum lateral component was 7.6 kips at the rail centroid. Ten million cycles of this loading were applied at the rate of 500 cycles per minute.

The rail-clip-bolt and anchor-bolt torques were checked with a torque wrench at about every one million cycles. When a loss was noted, the bolt was tightened back to its original preload.

Test Results. No evidence of failure or damage was noted in any part of the specimen during the 10 million cycles of loading. Load–deflection curves obtained for the center fastener before and after the cyclic-load tests are shown in Fig. 34. During the first 2 million cycles, the bolts required periodic readjustment of torque. No loss of torque was noted thereafter.

At the conclusion of the test, inspection of the parts of the test specimen revealed that the only part visibly affected by the loading was the rubber liner at the center fastener. Scuffing and erosion were observed on the surfaces of this liner. Both halves of the liner showed minor damage where the rubber was in contact with the steel.

An indentation in the shape of the edge of the steel clip was visible in the rubber liners, as shown in Fig. 35. Cracking of the rubber occurred along this indentation in one of the liner halves. The crack was located on the outside surface of the liner at the lower flange of the rail. At this loca-

tion, there is a gap between the steel clip and the steel baseplate. The crack in the rubber followed the outline of the lower edge of the clip and turned upward along its sides for $\frac{1}{2}$ in. The depth of the crack varied from about 0.09 in. at the outer corners of the trace to a maximum of 0.13 in. at 0.5 in. from the corner. It decreased in depth to a slight indentation over the central 1 in. of the 3.8-in.-wide clip.

No cracks or other signs of distress were visible in the steel, polyethylene, or concrete.

(a) East Fastener

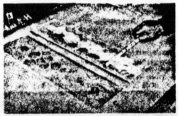

(b) Center Fastener

(c) West Fastener

Fig. 31 — Inspection of Rail-Strip Concrete Placement.

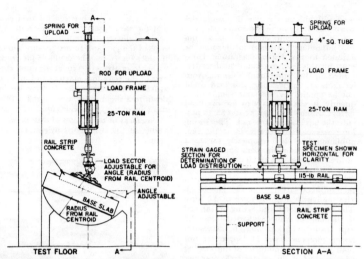

Fig. 32 — Details of Test Setup for Cyclic Loading.

CONCLUDING COMMENTS

Some fasteners for attaching rails to concrete crossties and to concrete bridge decks and tunnels provide adequate electrical insulation and have good mechanical properties. Major conclusions and recommendations have been discussed in the "Highlights" section at the beginning of this report.

ACKNOWLEDGMENT

This investigation was conducted in the Structural Research Laboratory, Portland Cement Association Research and Development Division under the direction of Dr. Eivind Hognestad, Director of Engineering Research, and Dr. W. G. Corley, Manager of the Structural Research Section. Preparation of the section of this report concerning fasteners for bridges and tunnels has

Fig. 33 — General View of Cyclic-Load Test Setup.

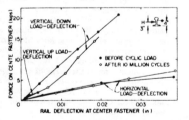

Fig. 34 — Rail Deflection.

Fig. 35 — Rubber Liner from Center Fastener After Test.

been financed in part through a mass transportation grant from the Department of Housing and Urban Development under the provisions of Section 6, Public Law 88-365, 88th Congress, as amended. This portion of the work was done to assist in development of the track system for the San Francisco Bay Area Rapid Transit District. It was carried out under contract with Parsons-Brinckerhoff-Tudor-Bechtel, general engineering consultants to SFBARTD. The authors wish to thank Messrs. B. W. Fullhart, O. A. Kurvits, R. K. Richter, W. C. Vix, B. J. Doepp, and S. Zintel, laboratory technicians, and R. G. Hoffman, photographer, for carrying out and recording the tests.

REFERENCES

1. "C&O-B&O Plan Concrete Tie Tests," *Modern Railroads*, **12**, No. 12, 91-92 (1966).
2. "AREA Proposed Specifications for Design, Materials, Construction and Inspection of Prestressed Concrete Ties." Proposal submitted to American Railway Engineering Association, private communication from Emerson J. Ruble, of American Association of Railroads, Chicago, Illinois. (Revised May 1, 1968).
3. Parsons-Brinckerhoff-Tudor-Bechtel, General Engineering Consultants for the San Francisco Bay Area Rapid Transit District, "Preliminary Technical Specifications for Rail Fasteners," No. 2Z4489 (1967).
4. Godfrey, K. A., Jr., "Rapid Transit Renaissance," *Civil Engineering*, **36**, No. 12, 28-33 (1966).
5. Monfore, G. E., "The Electrical Resistivity of Concrete," *Journal of the PCA Research and Development Laboratories*, **10**, No. 2, 35-48 (May 1968); *PCA Research Department Bulletin 224*.
6. ASTM Designation: D 1248-65T, "Tentative Specifications for Polyethylene Molding and Extrusion Materials," American Society for Testing and Materials, Philadelphia, Pennsylvania.
7. ASTM Designation: D 789-66, "Standard Specifications for Nylon Injection Molding and Extrusion Materials." As in Reference 6.
8. Hognestad, Eivind, Hanson, N. W., Kriz, Ladislav B., and Kurvits, Otto A., "Facilities and Test Methods of the PCA Structural Laboratory," papers under various titles in *Journal of the PCA Research and Development Laboratories*, **1**, No. 1, 12-20, 40-44 (January 1959); **1**, No. 2, 30-37 (May 1959); **1**, No. 3, 35-41 (September 1959); reprinted jointly as *PCA Development Department Bulletin D33*.
9. Hanson, N. W., Hsu, T. T. C., Kurvits, O. A., and Mattock, A. H., "Facilities and Test Methods of PCA Structural Laboratory — Improvements 1960-65," papers under various titles in *Journal of the PCA Research and Development Laboratories*, **3**, No. 2, 27-31 (May 1961); **7**, No. 1, 2-9 (January 1965); **7**, No. 2, 24-38 (May 1965); reprinted jointly as *PCA Development Department Bulletin D91*.

PCA.R&D.Ser.1381-3

Bulletins Published by the
Development Department
Research and Development Laboratories
of the
Portland Cement Association

D100—"Index of Development Department Bulletins D1-D99. Annotated List with Author and Subject Index."

Published by Portland Cement Association, Research and Development Laboratories, Skokie, Illinois (1967).

D101—"Rotational Capacity of Hinging Regions in Reinforced Concrete Beams," by ALAN H. MATTOCK.

Reprinted from FLEXURAL MECHANICS OF REINFORCED CONCRETE, Proceedings of the International Symposium, Miami, Fla. (November 1964) pages 143-181, joint sponsorship. Copyrighted 1965 by American Society of Civil Engineers.

D102—"Tests of Partially Prestressed Concrete Girders," by DONALD D. MAGURA and EIVIND HOGNESTAD.

Reprinted from the Journal of the Structural Division, Proceedings of the American Society of Civil Engineers, Proc. Paper 4685, 92, ST 1, 327-350 (February 1966).

D103—"Influence of Size and Shape of Member on the Shrinkage and Creep of Concrete," by TORBEN C. HANSEN and ALAN H. MATTOCK.

Reprinted from Journal of the American Concrete Institute (February 1966); Proceedings 63, 267-290 (1966).

D104—"Cast-in-Place Concrete Residences With Insulated Walls," by HARRY L. SCOGGIN.

Reprinted from Journal of the PCA Research and Development Laboratories, 8, No. 2, 21-29 (May 1966).

D105—"Tensile Testing of Concrete Block and Wall Elements," by RICHARD O. HEDSTROM.

Reprinted from Journal of the PCA Research and Development Laboratories, 8, No. 2, 42-52 (May 1966).

D106—"High Strength Bars as Concrete Reinforcement, Part 8. Similitude in Flexural Cracking of T-Beam Flanges," by PAUL H. KAAR.

Reprinted from Journal of the PCA Research and Development Laboratories, 8, No. 2, 2-12 (May 1966).

D107—"Seismic Resistance of Reinforced Concrete—A Laboratory Test Rig," by NORMAN W. HANSON and HAROLD W. CONNER.

Reprinted from Journal of the PCA Research and Development Laboratories, 8, No. 3, 2-9 (September 1966).

D108—"Rotational Capacity of Reinforced Concrete Beams," by W. GENE CORLEY.

Reprinted from Journal of the Structural Division, Proceedings of the American Society of Civil Engineers, Proc. Paper 4939, 92, ST5, 121-146 (October 1966).

D109—"Laboratory Studies of the Skid Resistance of Concrete," by G. G. BALMER and B. E. COLLEY.

Reprinted from ASTM Journal of Materials 1, No. 3, 536-559 (September 1966).

D110—"Connections in Precast Concrete Structures—Column Base Plates," by R. W. LaFRAUGH and D. D. MAGURA.

Reprinted from Journal of the Prestressed Concrete Institute, 11, No. 6, 18-39 (December 1966).

D111—"Laboratory Study of Shotcrete," by ALBERT LITVIN and JOSEPH J. SHIDELER.

Reprinted from Symposium on Shotcreting, American Concrete Institute, Paper No. 13 in Publication SP-14, 165-184 (1966).

D112—"Tests on Soil-Cement and Cement-Modified Bases in Minnesota," by TORBJORN J. LARSEN.

Reprinted from Journal of the PCA Research and Development Laboratories, 9, No. 1, 25-47 (January 1967).

D113—"Structural Model Testing—Reinforced and Prestressed Mortar Beams." by DONALD D. MAGURA.

Reprinted from *Journal of the PCA Research and Development Laboratories*, 9, No. 1, 2-24 (January 1967).

D114—"General Relation of Heat Flow Factors to the Unit Weight of Concrete," by HAROLD W. BREWER.

Reprinted from *Journal of the PCA Research and Development Laboratories*, 9, No. 1, 48-60 (January 1967).

D115—"Sand Replacement in Structural Lightweight Concrete—Sintering Grate Aggregates," by DONALD W. PFEIFER and J. A. HANSON.

Reprinted from *Journal of the American Concrete Institute* (March, 1967); *Proceedings* 64, 121-127 (1967).

D116—"Fatigue Tests of Reinforcing Bars—Tack Welding of Stirrups," by KENNETH T. BURTON and EIVIND HOGNESTAD.

Reprinted from *Journal of the American Concrete Institute* (May, 1967); *Proceedings* 64, 244-252 (1967).

D117—"Connections in Precast Concrete Structures—Effects of Restrained Creep and Shrinkage," by K. T. BURTON, W. G. CORLEY, and E. HOGNESTAD.

Reprinted from *Journal of the Prestressed Concrete Institute*, 12, No. 2, 18-37 (April, 1967).

D118—"Cast-in-Place Concrete Residences with Insulated Walls—Influence of Shear Connectors on Flexural Resistance," by HARRY L. SCOGGIN and DONALD W. PFEIFER.

Reprinted from *Journal of the PCA Research and Development Laboratories*, 9, No. 2, 2-7 (May 1967).

D119—"Fatigue of Soil-Cement," by T. J. LARSEN and P. J. NUSSBAUM.

Reprinted from *Journal of the PCA Research and Development Laboratories*, 9, No 2, 37-59 (May 1967).

D120—"Sand Replacement in Structural Lightweight Concrete—Splitting Tensile Strength," by DONALD W. PFEIFER.

Reprinted from *Journal of the American Concrete Institute* (July 1967); *Proceedings* 64, 384-392 (1967).

D121—"Seismic Resistance of Reinforced Concrete Beam-Column Joints," by NORMAN W. HANSON and HAROLD W. CONNER.

Reprinted from *Journal of the Structural Division, Proceedings of the American Society of Civil Engineers*, Proc. Paper 5537, 93, ST5, 533-560 (October 1967).

D122—"Precast Rigid Frame Buildings—Test of Scarf Connections," by PAUL H. KAAR and HAROLD W. CONNER.

Reprinted from *Journal of the PCA Research and Development Laboratories*, 9, No. 3, 34-42 (September 1967).

D123—"Precast Rigid Frame Buildings—Component Tests," by HAROLD W. CONNER and PAUL H. KAAR.

Reprinted from *Journal of the PCA Research and Development Laboratories*, 9, No. 3, 43-55 (September 1967).

D124—"Aggregate Interlock at Joints in Concrete Pavements," by B. E. COLLEY and H. A. HUMPHREY.

Reprinted from *Highway Research Record*, Number 189, 1-18 (1967).

D125—"Cement Treated Subbases for Concrete Pavements," by L. D. CHILDS.

Reprinted from *Highway Research Record*, Number 189, 19-43 (1967).

D126—"Sand Replacement in Structural Lightweight Concrete—Freezing and Thawing Tests," by DONALD W. PFEIFER.

Reprinted from *Journal of the American Concrete Institute* (November 1967); *Proceedings* 64, 735-744 (1967).

D127—"Ultimate Torque of Reinforced Rectangular Beams," by THOMAS T. C. HSU.

Reprinted from *Journal of the Structural Division, Proceedings of the American Society of Civil Engineers*, Proc. Paper 5814, 94, ST2, 485-510 (February 1968).

D128—"Sand Replacement in Structural Lightweight Concrete—Creep and Shrinkage Studies," by DONALD W. PFEIFER.

Reprinted from *Journal of the American Concrete Institute* (February 1968); *Proceedings*, 65, 131-140 (1968).

D129—"Shear and Moment Transfer Between Concrete Slabs and Columns," by NORMAN W. HANSON and JOHN M. HANSON.

Reprinted from *Journal of the PCA Research and Development Laboratories*, 10, No. 1, 2-16 (January 1968)

D130—"Trends in Consumer Demands for New Grades of Reinforcing Steel," by EIVIND HOGNESTAD.

Reprinted from *Proceedings*, Fall Business Meeting, Concrete Reinforcing Steel Institute, pages 22-32 (1967).

D131—"Influence of Mortar and Block Properties on Shrinkage Cracking of Masonry Walls," by RICHARD O. HEDSTROM, ALBERT LITVIN, and J. A. HANSON.

Reprinted from *Journal of the PCA Research and Development Laboratories*, 10, No. 1, 34-51 (January 1968).

D132—"Toward a Generalized Treatment of Delayed Elasticity in Concrete," by DOUGLAS McHENRY.

Reprinted from PUBLICATIONS, International Association for Bridge and Structural Engineering (Zurich), Vol 26, pages 269-283 (1966).

D133—"Torsion of Structural Concrete—A Summary of Pure Torsion," by THOMAS T. C. HSU.

Reprinted from TORSION OF STRUCTURAL CONCRETE, American Concrete Institute, Paper SP 18-6 in Publication SP-18, 165-178 (1968).

D134—"Torsion of Structural Concrete—Plain Concrete Rectangular Sections," by THOMAS T. C. HSU.

Reprinted from TORSION OF STRUCTURAL CONCRETE, American Concrete Institute, SP 18-8 in Publication SP-18, 203-238 (1968).

D135—"Torsion of Structural Concrete—Behavior of Reinforced Concrete Rectangular Members," by THOMAS T. C. HSU.

Reprinted from TORSION OF STRUCTURAL CONCRETE, American Concrete Institute, Paper SP 18-10 in Publication SP-18, 261-306 (1968).

D136—"Precast Rigid Frame Buildings—Summary of a Laboratory Investigation," by PAUL H. KAAR and HAROLD W. CONNER.

Reprinted from *Journal of the PCA Research and Development Laboratories*, 10, No. 2, 25-34 (May 1968).

D137—"Clear Coatings for Exposed Architectural Concrete," by ALBERT LITVIN.

Reprinted from *Journal of the PCA Research and Development Laboratories*, 10, No. 2, 49-57 (May 1968).

D138—"Torsion of Structural Concrete—Interaction Surface for Combined Torsion, Shear, and Bending in Beams Without Stirrups," by THOMAS T. C. HSU.

Reprinted from *Journal of the American Concrete Institute* (January 1968); *Proceedings*, 65, 51-60 (1968).

D139—"Influence of Aggregate Properties on Effectiveness of Interlock Joints in Concrete Pavements," by W. J. NOWLEN.

Reprinted from *Journal of the PCA Research and Development Laboratories*, 10, No. 2, 2-8 (May 1968).

D140—"Torsion of Structural Concrete—Uniformly Prestressed Rectangular Members Without Web Reinforcement," by THOMAS T. C. HSU.

Reprinted from *Journal of the Prestressed Concrete Institute*, 13, No. 2, 34-44 (April 1968).

D141—"Effects of Curing and Drying Environments on Splitting Tensile Strength of Concrete," by J. A. HANSON.

Reprinted from *American Concrete Institute* (July 1968); *Proceedings*, 65, 535-543 (1968).

D142—"Research on Thickness Design for Soil-Cement Pavements," by T. J. LARSEN, P. J. NUSSBAUM, and B. E. COLLEY.

Published by Portland Cement Association, Research and Development Laboratories, Skokie, Illinois (1969).

D143—"Fatigue Tests of Prestressed Concrete Pavements," by A. P. CHRISTENSEN and B. E. COLLEY.

Reprinted from *Highway Research Record*, Number 239, 175-196 (1968).

D144—"Shearhead Reinforcement for Slabs," by W. GENE CORLEY and NEIL M. HAWKINS.

Reprinted from *American Concrete Institute* (October 1968); *Proceedings*, 65, 811-824 (1968).

D145—"Fatigue Tests of Reinforcing Bars—Effect of Deformation Pattern," by J. M. HANSON, K. T. BURTON and E. HOGNESTAD.

Reprinted from *Journal of the PCA Research and Development Laboratories*, 10, No. 3, 2-13 (September 1968).

D146—"An Investigation of Rail-to-Concrete Fasteners," by T. T. C. HSU and N. W. HANSON.

Reprinted from *Journal of the PCA Research and Development Laboratories*, 10, No. 3, 14-35 (September 1968).

Chapter 6

Maintenance Methods

PART I:

The basics of track inspection—
Plus other helpful knowledge for those

In this installment, Blanchard first tells a new man how to get started on his territory. Next, the common rail defects are described and hints given on how to identify them. Problems encountered at joints are discussed and malfunctions of rail anchors are noted. Tie conditions to watch for are explained, and the need for maintaining a well-draining ballast section is emphasized. Finally, Blanchard tells about "split" fills and how to correct them.

By **Leo C. Blanchard**

(Part I of three parts)

● Let's assume that you have just recently been promoted to a position of responsibility in track maintenance. Let's assume further that your background of experience and training has been less than ideal and that you feel the need for a helping hand. That will be the supposition upon which this article is written.

The first thing on any new job is to get acquainted with the people with whom you will be working and to learn the limits of your new territory. Learning the territory may not be as simple as one might suppose. I once found an industry track ten years after I had assumed responsibility for it. Anytime you see a switch it has a track leading some place, although it may be covered with weeds and debris.

Never take for granted that a track won't be used because it shows no evidence of having been used recently. If the track is there, you can be sure it will be used and probably at a time most embarrassing to you. Therefore either make sure the track is serviceable or take it out of service by notifying the proper authority and then spike it or dismantle it so that it cannot be used.

The first time over our new territory will no doubt be by motorized equipment and that is fine as far as it goes, but the best way to get really acquainted is by walking. With territories as extended as they are, you can't just start out and walk it all at once. You will have to estimate the

total mileage and then program yourself accordingly. Suppose you set aside thirty minutes a day and inspect one mile of track. That would amount to 20 miles in one month. Not bad.

In making an intensive track inspection do not depend on your memory for details. Carry a note book and locate items for future attention by using a mile post number. For instance: "M.P. 271.3, a broken base rail should be angle barred". Another way would be to count the number of telegraph poles from the nearest mile post or perhaps from a culvert or bridge. In any case locate the item so you can return to it at a later date.

When you inspect track you must be sure you know what to look for. Let's review it item by item and let's start with rail.

A requirement for all track inspectors is a thorough knowledge of the FRA Track Safety Standards. If, at all possible you should have with you a copy when you are inspecting track. You should also be prepared to file written reports of your track inspections as required by the standards.

Common rail defects

Rail defects most common are transverse fissures; horizontal and vertical split heads; detail fractures from shelling; engineburn fractures; piped rails; end breaks through bolt holes; head-and-web separations; crushed heads; square and angular breaks; split ends; broken bases cor-

rugated rails; flowed heads; shelling and damaged or kinked rail.

No doubt your supervisor has a copy of a rail defect manual showing pictures and describing these defects in detail. You should make a point of studying these pictures and the explanation for each so that you can identify a defect when the occasion presents itself.

With the exception of the transverse fissure, most of these defects are visible to the experienced eye before final failure takes place. A transverse fissure is an internal defect that grows something like the rings of a tree. When it reaches the surface of the ball of the rail a fine crack will show. At that point it is extremely dangerous because it may signify a multi-fissure rail, and when it lets go the rail may break into several pieces and could cause a derailment.

Most railroad companies use electronic equipment to search out these hidden defects, but this is no excuse for not watching for those defects which are visible.

A horizontal split head is easily detected by noting a dark but fairly short streak on top of the ball of the rail. When you see it, drop down and sight along the under edge of the ball of the rail. If you note a slight drop or dip along this sight line, you have a bad one. Also, look for a hairline crack on one or both sides of the rail ball as the seam may have cracked out. Better get a pair of angle bars on the rail to support the weak spot until you can arrange to have the rail changed out.

Piped rails are a little different breed. They will have a similar dark streak on top of the rail, and the ball will appear to have settled slightly. By sighting underneath the ball you can see a settling, but also there will be a swelling of the web of the rail which indicates that the split has gone down through the web. Again you will want immediately to protect the rail with a pair of angle bars until you can arrange to have it changed.

When a fissured rail has been

958

with new responsibilities in track maintenance

found by a rail detector car, some railroads will allow it to be angle-barred and full-bolted until it can be changed out the next day. This is permissible if the detector car has determined that there is only one fissure in that rail. If more than one fissure is found, the rail should be changed out immediately. Likewise a rail which has cracked out and to the point where the crack is visible, but not found by the detector car, should be changed out immediately for the reason that there may be more than one fissure in that rail. If it is utterly impossible to change the rail immediately, then one should angle bar the cracked portion and put a slow order for trains over that rail until it can be changed. I once witnessed a multi-fissured rail that broke into thirteen pieces on the high side of a curve and under a passenger train. It is a miracle the train was not derailed, for that is how dangerous a fissured rail can be.

Joint bars, rail anchors

Joint bars have problems of their own. They crack, they break, they wear, they have bolts that break or stretch, leaving the bars less tight than they should be. Loose bars wear rapidly, then the ties start to pump and the track deteriorates. Cracked bars and missing bolts must be replaced. If in your judgment track bolts should be machine tightened, let your supervisor know about the condition.

Insulated joints require even more careful inspection and maintenance. The ties under insulated joints must be sound. Dirty ballast should be removed and clean ballast placed and well tamped. Make sure there is adequate drainage. Have a friendly chat with your signal maintainer about the care of insulated joints. Particularly you should know how to properly install insulation material in an emergency.

In bonded-track territory, the bonding wires are an important part of the total track structure. They carry the electric current past the joint

bars which are not very good conductors. It is important that all bonding wires be in place. For this reason you should report any which are broken or missing to the signal maintainer who has the equipment to re-install them.

Rail anchors are another important part of the track structure. As you walk the track, note the pattern that was established when they were first installed. Are any of the anchors missing? Are any loose or sliding on the rail? Are the anchors causing ties to bunch and twist out of shape? Incidently, when this happens the spiked ties can pull the gauge in to the point where it is as much as one-half inch tight and put a kink in the rail. If you find such conditions, report them to your supervisor.

Worrisome tie conditions

Crossties are a critical item of track maintenance and safety. Several broken, rotted or defective ties can be tolerated in a rail length provided the adjacent ties are sound. It becomes worrisome when two or more bad ties are next to each other, creating a soft spot that could surface bend the rail or allow the gauge to widen to the point of causing a derailment. If during your track inspection you should run across a nest of bad ties, make arrangements to have reinforcing ties installed. There can be no compromise with safety. Remember this: your job as a track inspector is to prevent derailments, accidents and injuries. When you see an unsafe condition, do something about it.

As soon as possible it would be a good idea to count the total number of unsound ties in each mile of main track and in each yard track. These should be the ties that could be expected to fail in the next two or three years.

Make a permanent record of the tie status because if your count of bad ties is reliable, it will hold up for three to five years and give you a basis from which to calculate your needs. You will also know in which

Over a period of some twenty years *RT&S* has published numerous articles by Leo Blanchard who retired several years ago as a roadmaster on the Milwaukee Road. These included two series of articles, one on "The art of track lining" and the other on "The art of track raising." Both of these series were reprinted in pamphlet form and also reproduced in the Eighth edition of the *Railway Track and Structures Cyclopedia*, published in 1956. His latest article, published in July and August 1973, was entitled "Lessons in supervision for track men." It was reprinted by a number of railroads for distribution among their employees.

From his writings it is obvious that Leo Blanchard combines a deep knowledge of track and track maintenance with the ability to put his knowledge and ideas into words. With him, track maintenance was more than a means to a livelihood; it is a field which brought out in him a desire to learn everything there was to learn and to impart that knowledge to other interested persons.

In his letter submitting this latest material Blanchard, recalled that in past years "a man was supposed to be seasoned by two or more years of experience in track work before he was promoted to a position of responsibility. Recently I have heard of men going from laborer to patrolman and foreman in less than six months of on-the-job experience.

"There is no question but what these men need help in knowing what to look for and how to evaluate what they see as they cover their territories. One cannot correct a defect that has not been noticed or understood.

"I would hope that this material could be used in a classroom setting for an organized discussion of track-inspection basics. Perhaps others who ride the rails can also benefit from the subject matter."

Blanchard's latest contribution will be published in three parts. The articles are recommended reading for all whose duties carry any responsibility for the integrity of railway tracks. *Editor.*

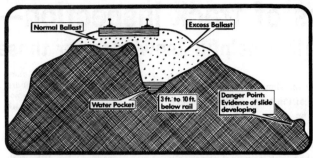

THIS CONDITION is called a "split" fill by Blanchard. He describes its causes and tells what to do if the signs indicate that a slide might occur.

miles to concentrate your heaviest tie renewals.

Your management will notify you of what you can expect in the way of a tie allotment for the coming season. Usually it will be less than you had hoped for and now you must use good judgment in how to use the ties allotted.

While making a tie count you may find one mile that will require around 300 ties and another mile that may need as many as 1200 ties over the next three years. Good judgment dictates that you use as few ties as possible in the first mile and as many as can be made available in the second mile. The object being to balance out the tie status over a period of time.

Under the pressure of a strictly limited allotment, you should not renew a tie just because it is a bad tie, as long as there are good ties on either side of it. A new tie should be installed to break up clusters of bad ties for gauge protection and for support under rail joints.

In years gone by many track foremen were more interested in getting a big daily count of ties renewed. They did not always use good placement judgment, with the result that we are now paying the penalty for this mistaken concept.

Ballast drainage essential

Ballast transmits the load from the rails and ties to the fill material which in turn transmits it to the solid earth. Whether ballast is of crushed stone, gravel, chats or other material, it must be able to drain water out of the ballast section. If it fails to do so, water will accumulate under the tie and with each passing train the tie will pump up and down, destroying

the solid bed under the tie.

Mud-splattered ties and ballast are the first indication that ballast has reached the end of its useful life. If no action is taken to get better drainage one can expect out-of-level track and low spots to develop, and they in turn will effect the line and gauge. Rock ballast should be cleaned. Gravel ballast should be renewed. Talk to your supervisor about which miles are most in need of attention.

Mud splattered ties are more likely to occur in cuts than on a fill. The reason is that the sides of cuts tend to slough off and fill the ditch on either side of the track. With the drainage obstructed the water accumulates under the ties and ruins the roadbed. If you have this condition talk to your supervisor about on-track or off-track equipment to clean out the ditches and restore the drainage. In more severe cases, such as a spring of water welling up in the cut, you may need to install drainage tile to lead the water away.

Troubles in fills

Fill material should be wide enough to properly support the ballast section. Fills that drop away quickly from the tie ends are too narrow for necessary support and should be widened.

Split fills is a subject not well understood by many trackmen. This condition is most likely to happen in clay or gumbo fills that have a tendency to develop water pockets. Cinder ballast is no longer available, but when it was, it tended to stabilize these spots because cinders would spread out and mix with the clay. Not so with gravel, which will not mix with the clay or gumbo, but will

continue to be a separate mass.

If a track has a tendency to get out of level on one side, it will often be raised and tamped, raised and tamped, over and over again. The final result will be that the tamped gravel will form a wedge directly beneath the rail that will drive deeper and deeper. These spots can be detected by the frequency with which the track must be raised and a noticeable swelling of the fill. Usually such spots will range from two to five rails in length.

On a high fill the final result will be a slide that drops down from the base of the rail and slides outward. Just before this happens there will be a wrinkle in the sod line at the base of the fill, which calls attention to an extremely dangerous condition. If you see the wrinkle, a slide is about to happen. Flag all trains and ease them over this spot until piling can be driven or some other action taken to make it safe.

Usually there is a water pocket at the bottom end of the gravel wedge which may go to anywhere from three feet to ten feet deep under the rail. Various methods have been tried to correct this condition such as drain tile, grouting and reconstruction of the fill, as well as driving piling.

I was once involved with a stretch of track about fifteen miles in length that had from one to several of these spots in each mile. Our solution was to have an on-track crane dig out the defective fill material and cast it aside. We then used dump cars and back-filled with sand taken from a nearby sand cut.

If you have such a condition on your territory, talk to your supervisor about it. Then, with an engineering aid present, dig a cross section between two ties. It will be easy to trace the outline of the ballast from which a drawing can be made to show to officers who can make a determination. ∎

Part II of this article, to be published in an early issue, will take up the inspection of line, surface and gauge and will discuss the significance of deviations in these parameters. Other matters discussed include the identification of problems at highway crossings, the need for being familiar with operating rules, and things to watch for at culverts and bridges.

PART II:

The basics of track inspection—
Plus other helpful knowledge for those

In this article, the second of three installments, Blanchard gives hints on how to check the condition of the track, especially gauge, discusses problems that can occur on curves in the presence of snow and ice, gives advice on inspection and maintenance of highway crossings, urges familiarity with operating and safety rules and discusses responsibilities in connection with communications, signals and bridges. The first installment was published in May.

By **Leo C. Blanchard**

● When walking or riding the track the best way to judge its condition is to observe the line. If the rails appear to be straight for long distances you can be reasonably sure that the track is in good level and probably in good gauge. Level, line and gauge are all dependent on each other. If one is affected the other two will soon show a corresponding effect. Usually the first to get out of kilter will be the track level, followed by the line and later the gauge.

If you notice that the alignment is poor you can be sure the level is not good and the gauge may have widened as a result of the track being out of level. You should check both the level and the gauge of the track with the proper instruments. If you cannot correct the condition you should report your findings to your supervisor.

For the purpose of a walking inspection I carry a pocket tape for checking gauge and clearances of switch points, guard rails, platforms, etc. I also carry a light inspection level board for measuring out-of-level spots in the track. This board has built-in markings to show the condition of the track gauge. In addition it has a scored groove at the center of the board through which to sight the tack head on a center stake. If you do not have such an instrument, you can convert a regular track level by filing in gauge marks and sawing in a sighting groove at the center line.

If either gauge or level is more

than one-half inch out of normal, trouble is brewing. Track that alternates out of level on first one side and then the other will cause freight cars to rock, and they have been known to rock right off the track. You should study the FRA Track Safety standards for their cross-level and track-gauge requirements until you are thoroughly familiar with them.

Never take for granted that your level board or track gauge is accurate. The way to test a level board is to check the track level, then reverse the board. If the bubble shows the same reading either way you can assume the board is accurate. On most level boards there is an adjusting screw for making a correction. If not, and your board is not accurate, order a different one. If you must use it for a time, check with a carpenter's level to see which way is the most accurate and then use the board in that direction until you can replace it.

Track gauges, too, have been known to be off as much as one-fourth inch or even more. To check your track gauge, measure the gauge of a track with a steel tape—not a cloth one. The inside balls of the running rails should be spaced exactly 4 ft 8½ in apart at a point ⅝ inch down on the balls; in other words 56½ inches part. When you find such a spot in your track, try the track gauge. It should set in just snugly. The track gauge is not adjustable, so if yours is not accurate replace it as soon as possible.

Track gauge is one of the most critical areas in track maintenance

and perhaps we should talk more about it. Let us assume that you are looking over a turnout and you notice the inside rail has a dark mark along the top of the rail. There is a good chance that this mark is caused by car wheels running on wide gauge, almost ready to fall in and tear up your track. The dark streak is caused by grease clinging to the outer edge of the car wheel, which is now wearing off because of the wide gauge.

Another sign of trouble

Suppose you are walking track in which snow is piled against the rail. Along the high rail of a curve you notice the snow has a chewed up appearance. You check the gauge with your tape and it appears within safe limits. Don't believe it: while the train is moving over it the rail moves in and out and the gauge may be dangerously wide. This is caused by loose rail fastenings allowing sideways movement. Clean the snow away from the base of the rail and examine it carefully. If the spikes are loose, plug and respike them. If sand or dirt is piled against the rail you can see movement in the same way as with snow.

I once found a condition on the low side of a curve where frozen soil and ice had lifted several 132-lb rails out of double-shoulder tie plates. The rail was sliding on the ice and bearing hard against the track spikes and bending them. An effective way to get the rail back into the tie plates would be to run a snow or weed burner back and forth to draw the frost, and then dig out from under the rail. During thawing weather salt could be used effectively, but I don't think your signal maintainer will like it. You can be sure we dug out from under the rail before the next winter arrived.

Problems at highway crossings

Highway crossings are another critical area in track maintenance. There are many methods of construction and we won't go into them

with new responsibilities in track maintenance

here. Rather we will try to identify what to look for as a track inspector. The first thing to go bad in a well-constructed highway crossing is the rail. Head-and-web separation is the most likely thing to happen, followed by a split head, pipe or fissure. Your company may use an electronic device to test these rails. In the absence of such a device use a hammer and tap along the top of the rail. If you hear a hollow sound or a different sound you had better investigate further. Any time you do major work on a highway crossing change the rail whether it appears to need it or not. The recovered rail can be used in a side track if it appears to have some service life left.

A good crossing requires a good bed of high-quality ballast, treated ties, welded rail and good water drainage. Your company has a standard· approved plan for highway crossings; ask for a copy.

Know your operating rules

Since safety is of the first importance in the discharge of duty, the one thing you should know without any question is how to stop or slow a train in accordance with the rules under any and all conditions. Your rule book provides specific rules for setting flags and signals for controlling trains. No doubt you have attended a rules class and have been certified. However, if you are like most of us, a rules class raises about as many questions as it answers.

Make a note of your questions in case you can't get a satisfactory answer from the rules examiner. When your supervisor is available ask him your questions. Make sure you understand exactly what is intended by a particular rule. When an emergency occurs there is no time to be uncertain as to how you should respond.

In addition to the Consolidated Code rules, you probably have another booklet entitled "Safety Rules." You can be sure that every rule in that book was written because someone made a mistake and was injured. If you repeat a mistake

enough times you can be sure you will be injured or you will be responsible for someone else's injury. Learn to form good safety habits in conformity to the rules; it will keep you out of trouble.

If you have unsafe equipment or a tool don't use it until it has been repaired or replaced. If you have a man in your crew that engages in unsafe practices, correct him. If he won't respond to your efforts, ask someone else in authority to talk to him. A railroad company can't afford to keep a man on the job who endangers his own and other persons' safety.

Use of slow orders

If you have a piece of track that in your judgment is not safe for scheduled speed and you are unable to make it safe, put a slow order on it. No doubt your supervisor will be out shortly to see about it. If you have used good judgment he will support your action. If not, you will get some heat, but you will still have a job. When you have an unsafe condition do something about it. If you drag your heels until something happens you will really be in trouble.

Push your supervisor, don't let him push you. You do it by having a plan. Ask for material and the help to use it. When the material arrives use it as soon as possible and then ask for more. Your supervisor may not be able to give you all you ask for, but he will respect you for trying. Remember, too, your supervisor can be your best friend. At times you may think he is pretty hard on you, but he has a vested interest in your success, because after all, your success is his success.

No article of this type can be all inclusive and fully comprehensive; the subject is just too big. I would hope that it will cause you to think about things you may have been overlooking. In addition to the things I have mentioned herein, there are other sources of information for trackmen. Among these would be a subscription to *Railway Track and*

Structures magazine. It is issued monthly and besides the feature articles there is a question-and-answer section that is of particular interest to trackmen.

I once had a supervisor who was a natural born teacher. He wanted to know why I didn't ask more questions about the track and track conditions. Being only seventeen at the time I told him I didn't know enough about it to ask intelligent questions. His reply was that the way to find out more is to ask questions. Then the more you know the more questions you will have.

Right-of-way fences, if you have them, are part of your responsibility and you should closely observe their condition. Good public relations are often dependent on well-maintained fences.

To a certain degree you are responsible for just about everything within the right-of-way limits. This includes communication lines, signals, culverts, bridges, roadway signs, public crossings, encroachments, etc. It is not that you maintain all of these, but as the person most often over the track it is your responsibility to report any condition that might effect the safe operation of trains.

Take culverts, for instance. Look through each culvert to make sure it is not leaking ballast. Inspect the receiving end to see that swirling water has not damaged it or cut its way through the fill, bringing on a washout. The discharge end should be clear so the water can get away. Does either end of the culvert need some riprap to protect it? If so, notify your supervisor.

Approaches to bridges are of direct concern to you since they are the weakest part of the track-fill structure. Too often there is a sudden drop-off at the ends of bridges. When a locomotive approaching a bridge strikes a low spot in the track just off the bridge, it puts a tremendous strain on the bridge and could severely damage it. Your problem is to keep enough ballast at the bridge ends to support the track on a level with the bridge. *(Continued)*

When you have an unsafe condition do something about it. If you drag your heels until something happens you will really be in trouble.

Sometimes bridges appear to be out of line with the track, or the track out of line with the bridge. In either case, notify your supervisor and have him inspect it. Check whether the guard rails on the bridge are fully spiked. If not, there is a standard plan that shows how these rails should be spiked.

Check under the bridge and note whether there is debris against the piling. If so, a heavy rain could cause the bridge to become unsafe. Notify your supervisor and, depending on the seriousness of the condition, take action accordingly. If you cannot clear it by hand, ask for an on-track crane to do the job.

Check whether riprap is in place and doing its job. If, while under a bridge, you notice anything that does not seem normal or right, notify the bridge supervisor so that he can send a qualified man to investigate.

Telephone lines, telegraph lines and signal wires will sometimes be found broken and down. Usually this happens during a storm. In any case, do not touch them because you could get hurt or even killed. Instead report the condition to the proper authority.

Just who is the proper authority? The answer, if the problem pertains to the movement of trains on a main track, is the chief train dispatcher. If it has to do with terminal yard tracks, the proper authority would be the yardmaster. All other matters, including those mentioned, should be handled with your immediate superior. Always keep your superior informed of actions you take with other persons in authority. ■

[The third and final installment of this series, to be published in an early issue, will be devoted entirely to the safety considerations to be kept in mind when inspecting switches and turnouts. Weak points and those subject to strain will be emphasized. Watch for this important installment.]

Congress considers track legislation

Legislation providing Federal grants for railroad property rehabilitation has cleared the Senate and is now under consideration in the House. However, the bill has some hurdles to overcome and may not get a welcome reception at the White House assuming it is passed by Congress.

The bill passed by the Senate, known as S1730, is a composite of bills proposed by several senators. Basically a make-work measure, the bill would authorize $600 million in Federal grants for paying labor engaged in rehabilitation projects. Another $100 million would be authorized for the purchase of materials and M/W equipment. The bill would also provide $100 million in loan guarantees for the purchase of materials and equipment. The bill cleared the senate by a vote of 67 to 10.

Up until the time that S1730 was approved by the Senate a comparable bill had not been considered by the House. However, hearings are slated to be held on this and similar bills by the House Subcommittee on Commerce and Transportation on June 23-24-25. Assuming a bill is cleared by the committee any differences between it and S1730 would have to be ironed out before further action by both houses.

An indication of the reception such a bill would receive at the White House is given by the fact that the Ford administration is on record as opposing the legislation. One reason is that too much time would be required in fighting unemployment caused by the recession. Another point is that giving the railroads money for making track repairs without attaching any strings might forestall mergers and other steps considered necessary in the interest of efficiency. In addition, the fear was expressed that the money might be spent in repairing unneeded tracks.

Meanwhile, the Ford administration has proposed legislation that would make $2 billion available on a loan basis for upgrading railroad tracks and equipment. This bill, it is understood, contains a provision that the government Federal Financing Bank could make the loans at low interest and that repayment could be deferred for the first five years of the loan if desired.

The administration bill is a new version of the Surface Transportation Act which was cleared by the House last year but killed by a Senate committee. A feature of the new bill is that railroads receiving government loans would be required to engage in merger or other agreements with other roads designed to promote efficiency.

The bill proposed by the administration would also relax regulation of the railroads by the Interstate Commerce Commission. The railroads would be permitted to raise or lower freight rates on individual items as much as 7% the first year, 12% the second year and 15% the third with less interference by the ICC.

The railroads would be free to raise any rates they can show are needed to meet their variable, or out-of-pocket costs. And the ICC wouldn't be allowed to hold rail rates at a high level to protect their competitors. Also, the railroads would be given more freedom to abandon branch lines that are being operated in the red.

With regard to mergers, the ICC, under certain conditions, would have only six months to approve or reject a merger plan, and with less freedom to decide on rejection than it now has.

Loans to railroads under this bill would be made at only 0.25 percentage point above the Treasury's lowest borrowing rate.

PART III

The basics of track inspection—

What to look for at switches

By Leo Blanchard

The vulnerable parts of switches are discussed in detail in this article, the third and last of a series. Parts I and II, which gave advice on other aspects of track inspection, as well as the responsibilities of new local maintenance officers, were printed in the May and June issues.

● Switches are the weakest and most critical part of the track structure. An entire book could be written about the construction, installation and maintenance of switches and a very great deal has been written and published.

For the purpose of this article I am going to limit myself to safety considerations. Let's start with the switch light and progress to the stand, to the switch points, turnout rails, frog and lead rails.

I presume there are still kerosene-burning switch lights in existence, although they are being phased out with reflector targets and electric light bulbs. In addition to proper filling and cleaning, it is very important that the flame centers with the bull's-eye in the lamp. Next the bull's-eye must be lined to hit the locomotive engineer in the eye while he is sitting in the cab of his locomotive. You should understand that the light beam from a switch lamp is very narrow, something like looking through a telescope. When properly lined and adjusted it will show like a full moon.

To make a quick check on whether a lamp is properly lined, step back about twelve feet from a high stand and six or seven feet out from the rail. You should see a wedge of light at exactly six o'clock. If you are looking down at a ground-throw stand, the wedge of light should show at twelve o'clock. If your eye is on a level with the bull's-eye of the lamp, the light should show dead center, and parallel with the track.

If the lamp does none of these things, what do you do now? First you center the flame with the bull's-eye in the lamp, then check to see that the light beam is parallel to the track by checking the wedge of light. If the wedge of light shows at three o'clock or nine o'clock the light beam is crosswise with the track.

There are three ways to line the target and switch lamp. First, there is a cog wheel that can be lifted and set over one notch. There is a jam key that can be lifted that will allow the staff to be turned a slight amount. Finally, if all else fails, use a pipe wrench to twist the staff until the target and lamp are in proper alignment with the track.

If, instead of a lamp, there is a painted or reflectorized target, make sure that it lines up properly. There is nothing worse than a cocked switch target that has an approaching locomotive engineer confused as to which way the switch is set. To line it, you use the same procedure outlined above.

Switches on main track, and certain other important switches, should be kept locked. Impatient switchmen have been known to throw these locks away, which result in a derailment and a torn-up switch. One remedy where this trouble exists is to buy a bull chain and have welder attach it to the lock and to the handle of the switch stand.

Weak point of switch stand

At the bottom end of the switch stand is a crankshaft and a clevis to the connecting rod. On some of the older stands this clevis was not too well designed since it depends on two small carriage bolts without cotter keys to hold the nuts in place. This is weakness that could lead to trouble, so watch it and make sure both bolts are in place and the nuts are holding.

Headblock ties should be sound. There is just too much at stake to allow these ties to become rotted and weak. The stand should be firmly secured to the headblock ties. If the switch stand is found to be loose on the headblock, an emergency action that can be taken is to lay a tie plate flat on the headblock against the base of the stand and spike it so that the switch points are snug against the stock rail. Be sure to check both points, because when you tighten one point you may loosen the other. The tie plate against the base of the stand will enable you to spike into solid wood. If you must resort to this

with safety the main consideration

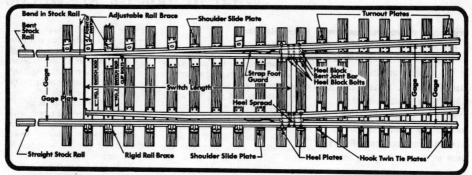

EVERY TRACKMAN should be thoroughly familiar with the construction of turnouts and the names of their parts.

practice, change out the headblock as soon as possible.

Connecting rods are subject to strain and vibration. They have been known to crack and break from crystallization. A visual examination is better than none, but a better way is to remove the rod and strike it sharply across a rail to open up any fissure-type crack that may be developing.

Both the bolt and the bolt hole where the connecting rod joins the switch rod can wear enough to become dangerous. Usually you can test the amount of wear by throwing the switch back and forth and observing any looseness. Sometimes you can see a shiny wear spot near the nut. But don't be too trusting: try putting a block in the switch point and then use the switch handle to put some strain on the bolt. This will positively show up any looseness. Make sure this important bolt has a cotter key in place to prevent the nut from coming off.

To the switch rod are attached clips that have bolts going through the switch point that must be carefully checked for a tight fit, and these too should have cotter keys to hold the nuts in place.

There is one thing often overlooked. It is that the switch rod and connecting rod should be in a relatively straight line when the switch is in its normal position. If there is a sharp bend where the connecting rod and the switch rod join, the switch stand should be moved until the two rods line up with each other. Double check to make sure there are cotter keys in all switch-rod bolts to make sure the nuts do not come off.

Good ties here are imperative

Switch points ride on slide or riser plates. There is more to this than just slide plates. They are riser plates also, and this means they are designed to lift the switch point a little higher than the stock rail so that car wheels will make the transfer by dropping down on to the stock rail. Otherwise the car wheel might catch against the side of the stock rail and force it out and overturn it. This has happened, so be aware of what is involved. It should go without saying that good ties under this critical area are imperative.

Switch-point heel fillers and bolts are subject to great strain and vibration. Thimbles wear, nuts vibrate loose, bolts break and disappear. Severe pounding of the wheels cause heel filler blocks to crack, rail ends to chip and the whole assembly to settle into a low spot in the track. When this happens, the pumping up and down of the switch-point heel causes the other end, the point end of the switch point, to flip up and down, creating a severe strain on the switch rods and clips. It is just asking for trouble not to correct this condition as soon as it starts. Should a switch point heel ever get loose from its fastenings it would be disastrous indeed, so watch it.

Stock rails wear out faster than other rails in a switch and have to be replaced more often. They are subject to split heads, head-and-web separation and all of the other defects mentioned under rail inspection. In addition, stock rails are subject to top-of-ball wear caused by the transfer of wheels from the switch point.

Switch points must fit firmly against the stock rail. They must not become badly chipped and worn lest a worn car wheel should climb the point and derail. As soon as chipping or excessive wear sets in a track welder should be called to build the point up to standard and grind it smooth. Don't wait too long to have this done. If a car wheel does not accept the wheel gauge, it would be literally impossible for such a wheel to split a switch and derail as long as the switch point and stock rail are properly fitted.

Derailments can occur from a split switch where the stock rail is loose enough in its fastenings to be pushed outward or tipped away from the switch point so as to cause a gap. Derailments can also occur where the point is loose against the stock rail, or where chipping provides a ladder for the wheel to climb on.

You must understand that worn

'You should be aware that the ties under the switch points have a tendency to settle more than the rest of the track.'

car wheels are caused when the wheel does not track straight. It is running crabwise and is trying hard to climb the rail at any point and is just looking for an excuse. Not only that, but such wheels are putting a severe pressure against the side of the rail trying to spread the rails. This is why stock rails must be solidly spiked and braced.

A car with perfect wheels, tracking perfectly, puts no strain on the track gauge. Such a car could probably cross over an unspiked rail without derailing, but don't try it.

"The best investment"

A track-welding crew is the best investment any railroad ever made for maintaining switch points, switch-point guards or protectors, frog points and other critical parts of the switch assembly. When an emergency condition develops that will not wait for the regular programmed schedule ask for the services of these people. They can build up a ragged point and grind both it and the stock rail to make a perfect fit.

Switch-point protectors are sometimes used at yard-track switches and other slow-track territory. They are of two kinds: one that fits outside of the rail and the other that fits against the running side of the rail. The outside kind will not be effective if the bolts and bracing are allowed to get loose. The inside kind can cause a derailment if not carefully installed. The rail should be ground off smooth and the protector must be precisely fitted. Both kinds can be restored to a condition like new by the welding crew. If you oil or graphite your switches, apply a little to these protectors.

You should be aware that the ties under the switch points have a tendency to settle more than the rest of the track. This puts an added strain on the switch-point layout. It is particularly important to lift and tamp these places before freezing weather sets in. At the same time try to provide adequate drainage from under the switch points. If nothing else, dig a sump for the water to drain into. Be sure you line it with an old cover and put a barrel cover over it for

safety's sake. If you dig a ditch, be sure you trim it so that no one will be caused a bad fall. Sometimes covered tile can be of help. Good drainage is most important.

Watch gauge closely

Turnout rails are subject to severe strain, especially when trains enter the turnout at too high a speed. It is well to watch the gauge closely. Notice whether the tie plates show any sign of movement on the ties. The curved lead rails beyond the frog are subject to the same severe strain, so watch the gauge there as well.

If the line through the main track of the switch is out of kilter the chances are good that the turnout rails are causing it. To properly line a switch, it is necessary to first loosen the turnout rails, then line the straight-through track. Next, respike the turnout rails in accordance with the measured curvature shown in your track standards for that turnout.

Fortunately, the spring-rail frog has been largely replaced by the manganese rigid frog or other types of rigid frogs which are less critical in their maintenance.

The spring-wing frog gave a smoother ride over the turnout and this was its main attraction. The danger lay in the free wing of the frog lifting enough for a car wheel to catch against the side of it, forcing it out and turning over the rail, causing a derailment. To avoid this trouble it is necessary, first, to maintain very good ties well tamped under the frog and second, to have the welders heat the wing caps and pound them down to where the frog wing can slide but not lift.

Rigid-type frog maintenance consists largely of proper guard-rail installation and maintenance. It is remarkable how many guard rails, particularly in yard tracks, have been improperly installed. Many are not properly located with respect to the frog point that they are designed to protect.

Guard-rail flangeways are often too wide due to wear or because the wrong spacing blocks were installed. Many trackmen do not understand

that the regular rules for track gauging have an exception when it comes to guard rails. It is the face of the guard rail that must be the proper distance from the frog point. Stated another way, if the guard-rail face has worn one-fourth inch, then the gauge should be spiked one-fourth inch wide to bring the guard rail the proper distance from the frog point. If the frog point is showing heavy wear you can be sure the guard rail is not doing its job.

In addition, the bolts in guard rails not only break and fall out, but they also stretch so that the nut becomes loose. It is essential that all bolts be in place. The bolts must be tight and the space or filler blocks must be in their proper location.

When frog points show considerable wear, the welders should be called to restore the point. Rigid frogs will have measurably longer life if they are supported by good ties and good ballast.

Perhaps one should emphasize again: A railroad car truck with full flanged wheels traveling true with the track would probably make it through a rigid frog without the guard rail. It is the badly worn flange traveling crabwise, which we mentioned in connection with switch points, that will try hard to get on the wrong side of the frog point.

You should ask your engineering department for copies of prints covering switches and frogs for the turnouts in your territory. You can then familiarize yourself with the various adjustments, clearances and location of the different units. These prints and drawings contain a lot of information with which a trackman should become familiar. You may think, for instance, that the center of a guard rail should be exactly opposite the the frog point. Not so. Look at your drawing. Do you know the proper opening between an open switch point and the stock rail? Do you know how and where to place the bend in a stock rail? Do you know what the approved flangeway opening is in a guard rail or a street crossing? All of these and many more are shown on your maintenance of way drawings. ■

TEXT 43

PART I

PANEL DISCUSSION ON TRACK RECORDER CARS

The Uses of Track Inspection Information in Railway Engineering

By G. H. WAY

Research Engineer Roadway

Chesapeake & Ohio Railway—Baltimore & Ohio Railroad

We have been told several times this afternoon that we are living in a world of rapid and dramatic change. It is difficult to comprehend the developments in technology alone much less keep pace with economics, sociology and politics. Like it or not, the world we live in today is a different world than yesterday's. Our rather narrow and specialized problems along with their solutions are changing, too. Ten years ago, we were developing cheaper ways to install ties. Now we are trying to find the ties themselves at a price we can afford. The simple art of inspecting a railroad track is no exception to the rule of change.

Track inspection has always been an essential part of good railway engineering maintenance. We find what is wrong with track by inspecting it. We program our maintenance work based on knowledge gained through inspection. And we insure that we've gotten our money's worth from any maintenance operation through inspection.

We admire the wisdom of experience in our profession. But experience is merely knowing what to expect from different possible ways of doing things. It cannot be gained without inspection—inspection before and after maintenance operations to learn their efficiency, inspection after traffic to learn of their durability.

"Knowledge of territory" is often used as a criterion for judging the competency of associates. And that knowledge of territory is gained only by repeated inspection.

But merger and consolidation tend to increase the geographic limits of individual responsibility and make complete and frequent surveillance a task of immense magnitude. The elimination of section gang maintenance in favor of highly mechanized regional specialty gangs curtails the intimate attention and knowledge of section foremen with their trackage. There are in some locations a shortage of the highly trained, experienced personnel capable of making the difficult subjective judgments required in track evaluation.

On one hand, these factors are reducing our track inspection capability, while on the other, increased train speed, greater wheel loadings and new car configurations are combining to increase the demands for both track quality and the inspection that can alone insure it. Lastly, there is the ever present problem of cost. When we face combined pressures to reduce expenditure and increase the quality and amount of output, we must consider automation. When we found it too costly to pick- or fork-tamp a tie, we developed machines to do it for us.

Track inspection machines, however, are not new ideas. In the late 20's a gage measuring device was developed in Austria which drew a graph of track gage vs. distance along a track. In 1936, the Chesapeake & Ohio Railway developed its RI-1 mechanical inspection car which measured rail surface, alignment and cross level.

Many years ago, the Pennsylvania Railroad measured track quality indirectly by determination of water spillage from a graduated container mounted in a railway office car. These are all examples of automation. Today, automated measurement of track geometry is both technically feasible and economically attractive.

We can purchase ready-made inspection vehicles, such as devices to be pushed along the track and which measure one aspect of quality, or complete inspection cars which measure many parameters while being moved in regular trains. Midway between these two in cost and size is a self-propelled track car, which while not as fast as the last named, measures the full gamut of track qualities and records them on a chart. Lastly, we can design a vehicle to our own needs, measuring what we want with the precision we desire.

Measurement devices can be classified into two groups. The first we call direct measuring. The Southern Railway's R1 car and the DOT inspection car which you will hear about later are examples, as are Track Fax and C&O RI-2. The second group are indirect measuring. Instead of directly measuring a physical dimension they measure effects and translate them into linear displacements. They rely on the mathematical principle that acceleration is the second derivative of distance with respect to time. Doubly integrating accelerometer outputs provides measurements of distance. The Canadian National car is of this type. Both systems work and they both have their place in track measurement.

Machines can be made to do some things very well but they tend to be stupid and lack initiative. A machine does not know when to inspect track, nor how accurately to measure or even what to measure. When inspection is done manually we rarely give much thought to these problems.

Each of us, depending on whether he is a track supervisor or a chief engineer, knows why he wants to make an inspection and, consequently, how thorough and precise he must be and of course when to make it. But, if we are going to consider using machines to do any part of the track inspection job, we must first decide what we want the machine to do. How are we going to use it? The alternative is to choose just any system without regard to its capabilities and limitations. Then after learning these characteristics through painful trial and error we would hopefully be in a position to put it to some intelligent use. But that isn't good engineering. I think it makes a good deal more sense to think carefully about what we really need, and then to design or select that which meets these needs.

A good place to start is to ask, "Why do we inspect track?" And then examine the reasons to see what bearing they have on how we should do it. To be very general for a moment, inspection covers all measurement, appraisal and evaluation of track. We use inspection to determine a best course of action, to make decisions. More specifically we use inspection information to decide how to spend our railroads' money. How much should we spend for labor, material and for machinery? Where should it be spent, and when, to achieve the most benefits.

In short, to make valid maintenance decisions management depends in large part on inspection information. But the kinds of information required by management differ widely. The same data isn't needed for every decision. Some choices depend on highly accurate specific measurement, others depend on more general information which can be less precise. For example, to judge which of several alternative rail sections is most economical for specific location demands one kind of data. To divide a maintenance budget among territories requires another. To decide if it is safe to run trains at scheduled speeds over a particular portion of track, still another.

I have divided these reasons for inspecting track, and consequently the kind of information we wish to develop, into 4 categories:

PURPOSES OF TRACK INSPECTION

1. Develop maintenance program.
2. Detect emergency track defects.
3. Evaluate methods, machines and material.
4. Control of work quality.

Each of these has its own set of requirements which determines how often and when we inspect, what we look at or measure and how accurately we measure or how closely we look. It matters little whether we employ sophisticated inspection devices or manual procedures. The reasons for inspection define how thorough and accurate it should be and when and how often the inspection should be made. Inspections on which we base annual maintenance programs must be comprehensive but not frequent or precise. Neither must inspections to insure safety of track be overly precise but they must also be comprehensive and should be frequent. Evaluation of techniques or materials does not require comprehension in inspection but it does require precision.

Of course, inspections can serve more than one purpose at a time. If a track supervisor counting bad ties to make up a detailed program finds a broken rail, he doesn't say, "I'm not patrolling track so I must ignore broken rails." Similarly mechanized inspection devices can have overlapping purposes. But it is important in designing, selecting and using these devices to have a clear understanding of their purpose.

When machines are employed to inspect track, they give no opinions. They are not subjective. We can't rely on their experience and judgment to tell us what they have found in terms familiar to us. This is, of course, an advantage too. If a machine can't give us an opinion, it can't give us a bad one. The machine can merely report back what it has found in very factual objective terms. We must form the opinions and make the judgments.

Most track measurement devices provide analog outputs. They produce a mechanical movement or voltage or some kind of signal proportional or analogous to a physical measurement of the track. It is then common practice to record this signal on paper, to produce a graph of how the measurement varies as the inspection device moves along a track. This is just fine for some kinds of inspection but not all. In looking for the cause of a known rough spot at a certain location, this kind of record is helpful. On the other hand, for attempting to compare the general geometric track quality of several divisions, the analog records of several measurements are not sufficiently concise. We would be almost as well off to go out and look at the track itself.

Reduction of measurement analogs has a great bearing on their usefulness. Appropriately presented, the same data is meaningful that when improperly shown is useless. As engineers, we have grown used to numbers. We feel comfortable with numerical comparisons of stress, weight, force, etc. Consequently, it is often desirable to convert analog data to digital data.

But when we do so we must exercise care. Track geometry is continuous while digital data is necessarily discrete. When we represent things by what they are not we run the risk of losing or distorting information.

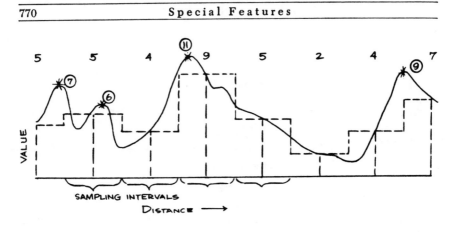

× PEAK VALUES MISSED

Fig. 1

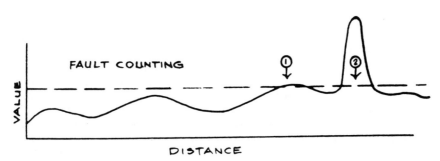

Fig. 2

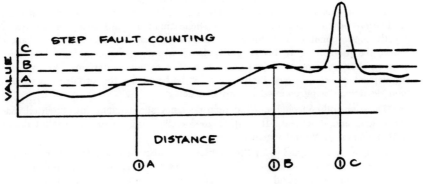

Fig. 3

970

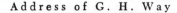
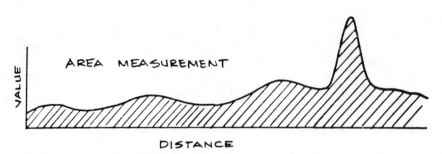

Fig. 4

Fig. 1 shows what can happen if we are careless in converting analog data to digital. In this case, the sampling rate is too low. Consequently, the system loses important data.

The conversion from analog to digital can be made in several ways. Some of them are shown in the following figures. Each of the systems has advantages and drawbacks. The first is simple fault counting (Fig. 2). It is excellent for locating emergency conditions, if the tolerance limit is appropriately set. It falls down on the job somewhat when it comes to more general evaluation. Because fault counting is simply a go—no go system, it is easily designed and interpreted. It is unfortunately insensitive to changes except those close to the tolerance limit and it can't discriminate at all between any value wholly above or below the tolerance.

The second system (Fig. 3) is a modification of the first. Fault counting with steps minimizes the problems associated with pure fault counting but its concept is the same. If there are sufficient steps it can be more useful. This system also permits use of weighting factors, so extreme faults can be further penalized.

Probably the most serious drawback to either of these systems is that they require arbitrary limit setting. The arbitrary limits introduce subjectivity to basically objective data. If the limits can be questioned, then so can the classification of data into them.

The third system or area measurement technique (Fig. 4) reminds us of elementary calculus. The integral of the function describing the analog trace is equal to the area under the curve. Like the other two systems it is good for some things but not for others. The area technique fortunately lends itself to what fault counting does not—making generalized evaluations. The area under the curve per mile or division or any distance limit is a single number. And that number can be directly proportional to the difference between standard and actual conditions. Of course, the problem with this system is that it averages, that it doesn't discriminate between short extreme variations and longer, less extreme variations. However, it is not dependent on arbitrary limits nor is it bothered by the problems of long or short deviations being counted as only one defect.

There are other techniques but time does not permit going into them all. Each has its long and short suits. It is up to good engineering judgment to select the one or combination of several which best does the job.

Completely entangled with the problem just discussed of information reduction are those of analysis and display. This is an area that relates to human engineering. We cannot afford to spend thousands of dollars to produce reams of reports and charts just to have them around to impress outsiders or, worse yet, to collect dust. Track inspections and their data must be used meaningfully if they are to be more than examples of good advertising. They must have the acceptance of management and of ground level supervision. Consequently, engineers must do more than design a device which will measure accurately. While we don't wish to minimize the importance of accurate measurement, it alone will not suffice. The data output of the measurement system must be interpreted. And this is probably more difficult. It is easy to use data for the wrong purposes. Nothing will limit the usefulness of inspection data more than inadvertent misapplication.

Today's track inspection systems are not as comprehensive as definition of inspection used earlier. They can't evaluate or appraise. They can't as yet tell us how many bad ties we have or even which ones are bad. They simply measure what we tell them to measure and report it, but they do this quickly and with considerable accuracy. So long as we expect no more, we will not be disappointed or misled. It is in making unjustified inferences from data or masking it by manipulation that danger lies. Both of these fallacies tend to occur when we try to serve too many needs with the same tool.

For example, data produced to pinpoint emergency defects, if used alone to establish general quality indices, can mislead.

If I find that mile 52 has six joints over ¼ inch low, while mile 101 has two such joints and decide that mile 52 is three times as bad, I have drawn an unwarranted conclusion. It may in reality contain very excellent track throughout much of its length, having one trouble area, while mile 101 could contain 269 joints ⅛ inch low.

Similarly, we must be careful of averages. The average temperature of a man with "his right foot in a bucket of ice water holding a red hot stove is warm, but he is probably not comfortable." A statement showing that the average depth of low joint on a division is very low tells us nothing about the possible extreme cases.

No measurement data should be manipulated or modified without a full understanding of why, how and when. It may be convenient to combine data to produce a priority or quality numbers or to multiply defects depending on their magnitude. Either of these operations can lead to disaster, especially if in doing so the raw data is lost or not shown as well. A clever technique for reduction of analog data to digital is electronic gating or filtering. We say we want to find all low joints more than ⅛ inch low. Our sensors produce a voltage proportional to lowness so it becomes a simple matter to screen out voltages or signals representing lowness less than ⅛ inch. Fig. 5 shows two gated signals so adjusted. They both show two defects. But what happened to the real original information produced by the sensors? If it had not been filtered this is what it had to say (Fig. 6). There is quite a difference. My point is that filtering to determine peaks should not destroy original data. If this original analog data had been recorded it could be subsequently processed or gated without destruction. We'd still be able to find the joints over ⅛ inch low—and a good deal more.

If through this kind of manipulation we overemphasize any particular measurement, so that the system is ultrasensitive to certain type defects, surface for example, while it ignores others, say line or gage, when determining general track quality, the result is invalid. People will quickly lose confidence in such a system and eventually ignore it. Even if the injustice is eventually corrected it will be a long time before confidence is restored.

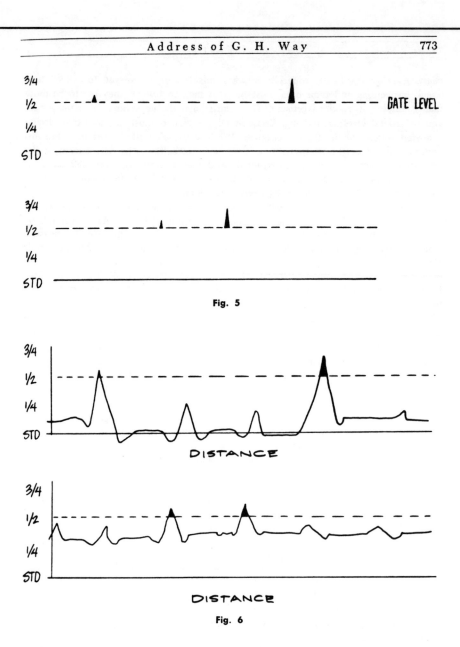

Fig. 5

DISTANCE

DISTANCE

Fig. 6

The problem then is that too much information is unacceptably bulky and un-manageable for convenient analysis, while if too condensed it may hide important details or mislead. Because some people need all the details and others cannot afford to have any, a compromise is not suitable. It would meet no one's need. What does seem appropriate is to tell each man what he needs to know, but not to make him sort this out of extraneous data. In other words, more than one report of information can be and should be obtained from the same raw data. Fortunately, computers make this quite feasible. They can be told to accept an overwhelming amount of raw data, remember it all and to selectively process the data and prepare reports appropriate to the use that will be made. We can ask for a report of only those defects which we have previously declared to be emergencies to be extracted. We can ask for simplified summaries of general conditions by miles, subdivisions or larger territories. We can even ask for comparisons after specified periods of time or traffic or before and after maintenance operations.

Computers can do more than sort information for us. They can help us analyze by simulating. We are learning, perhaps too slowly, that the interaction of equipment and track is complex. Perhaps a car will pass over a single low joint of considerable magnitude but if it encounters a certain succession of lesser low joints it will "rock" itself off the track. We can simulate the action of a car on a given track to determine its behavior at differing speeds with a computer. Why not then feed actual raw track data to a computer and simulate car behavior? When and if the computer senses wheel lift it could signal an emergency condition.

We must decide, if we intend to use them: should computers be on the inspection car operating in real time or should we merely record the data, on tape for example, and process it centrally at a later time? In the first case, we have the benefit of immediate output to balance against the possible loss of information due to breakdown. The central computer approach offers more economical processing, together with possibly more sophisticated programs but introduces delay. As we might expect, there are places for both. Obviously, we don't want to delay a report of conditions which could lead to derailments. These must be processed in real time, now. Other decisions, like test results and interpretation or budget consideration, can wait a day to take advantage of more sophisticated analysis at lower cost.

In conclusion, I would like to re-emphasize several points. Automated geometry measurement is available. It can be done in several ways and you will hear my associates describe a few very good ones. But data collection and its use are different things. Only after determining how it is to be used can we decide how to process it. Both general evaluation and location of extreme anomalies can be based on the same data but require separate analysis techniques, neither of which can be permitted to destroy the original information if we want the other. Because the amount of information we need and can collect is enormous, we are wise to rely on computers for assistance.

And let us avoid the trap of letting the system we design usurp good engineering judgment. It is a tool to help us, not replace us. For now, quality ratings, for example, should be used as information helpful in determining budget allocations. They should not dictate them.

Track measurement data can be helpful in many ways. It will help us find the most necessary places to spend our money. It will provide quantitative substantiation for budget requests. It will assist us in forecasting future maintenance requirements. And, it will relieve engineers of tedious repetitive work so that they may devote more time to the productive aspects of making sound judgments and the creativity so necessary to our continued meaningful contribution to society.

PART II:

Automated Track Inspection on the Southern Railway System

By L. S. CRANE

Vice President—Engineering, Southern Railway System

and CHARLES R. KAELIN

Analytical Engineer, Southern Railway System

INTRODUCTION

The purpose of this paper is to describe the track inspection system used on the Southern Railway System, the track rating index used in processing the data, and the benefits derived from automated track inspection. We on the Southern are proud of this program because: 1) it is a working program, with proven results; and 2) it has gained acceptance from all levels of management as a vital part of track maintenance and operating safety.

With today's heavy equipment making increased demands on track maintenance expenditures, it is a must to program maintenance on a priority basis. Specifically, a track index must be available to insure maintenance is performed where it is needed most.

In the past, the quality of track structure was gained by having supervisory personnel ride over track to assess ride quality, and later spot-check rough areas with manual measurement. The techniques had three major weaknesses:

1. The rating of ride quality was a subjective analysis and varied from one supervisor to another.
2. The spot-checks were made without the track being exposed to dynamic loading.
3. It was not practical to compile data over a sufficient period of time to study the behavior and maintenance needs of a particular segment of track.

Through automated track inspection and a track rating index, the following advantages can be realized:

1. Dangerous or priority maintenance conditions can be detected and corrected immediately.
2. Each mile of track can be assessed a numerical rating to indicate the relative quality of each mile within a division, or each division within the system.
3. Maintenance can be scheduled on a priority basis.
4. Qualitative assessment of surfacing work can be made.
5. Track behavior and rate of deteriorating can be correlated with speed and traffic density.

The track inspection vehicle presently used on the Southern Railway System provides continuous measurement of 7 parameters of track structure data. These parameters are twist or warp, surface of left and right rail, gage, superelevation, and alignment of left and right rail (Fig. 1). These traces are recorded continuously on a chart which also receives time and distance marks in event mark form. (Figs. 2 and 2A)

I would like now to briefly define each of the track parameters measured on the Southern's track inspection vehicle:

TRACK INSPECTION PARAMETERS

1.   TWIST OR WARP

2.   SURFACE - LEFT RAIL

3.   SURFACE - RIGHT RAIL

4.   GAUGE

5.   SUPERELEVATION

6.   ALIGNMENT - LEFT RAIL

7.   ALIGNMENT - RIGHT RAIL

Fig. 1

TWIST is the differential in cross level over a fixed measuring chord, which on our car is 11 ft. Thus, twist is a ratio. Any low joint will cause twist, assuming there is a cross level differential at the location of the joint.

SURFACE is defined as the vertical displacement of the middle axle of a 3-axle truck, with respect to the straight line chord connecting the end axles. This type measurement is designed to detect low joints and dips of less than 11 ft in longitude.

GAGE is measured by two contact feelers bearing against the gage side of the rail, at a point ⅝ inch below the head.

SUPERELEVATION is measured by means of a gyro-stabilized pendulum mounted in the center of the car body. In order to be correlated with the true superelevation taken at the top of the rail heads, compensations are made to correct for centrifugal force and spring deflection, which alter the position of the car body on a curve.

CURVATURE is measured over a 59.5-ft chord formed by the position of the center pins of the truck as the car negotiates a curve. Local alignment variations are measured by pairing two contact sensors on the same rail, 5½ ft apart. In accordance with the existing lever ratios, the readout is 1:1 for local variations and 0.1 inch = 1 degree for curvature.

The Southern Railway track inspection car was put into service in May of 1967 (Fig. 3). Even at that time, it was apparent that acceptability standards must be set, whereby the track could be rated on the basis of data obtained from the vehicle. For the first time, we were able to record vital statistics that would enable us to assess the quality of the track structure in a fully loaded state. Fully loaded in the case of our car is 275,000 lbs., which simulates the load of locomotives and 100-ton cars.

By September 1967, the framework had been set up for establishing a track index, which would enable us to interpret and utilize the large amount of data obtained from the car. The two objectives of this index were clear-cut:

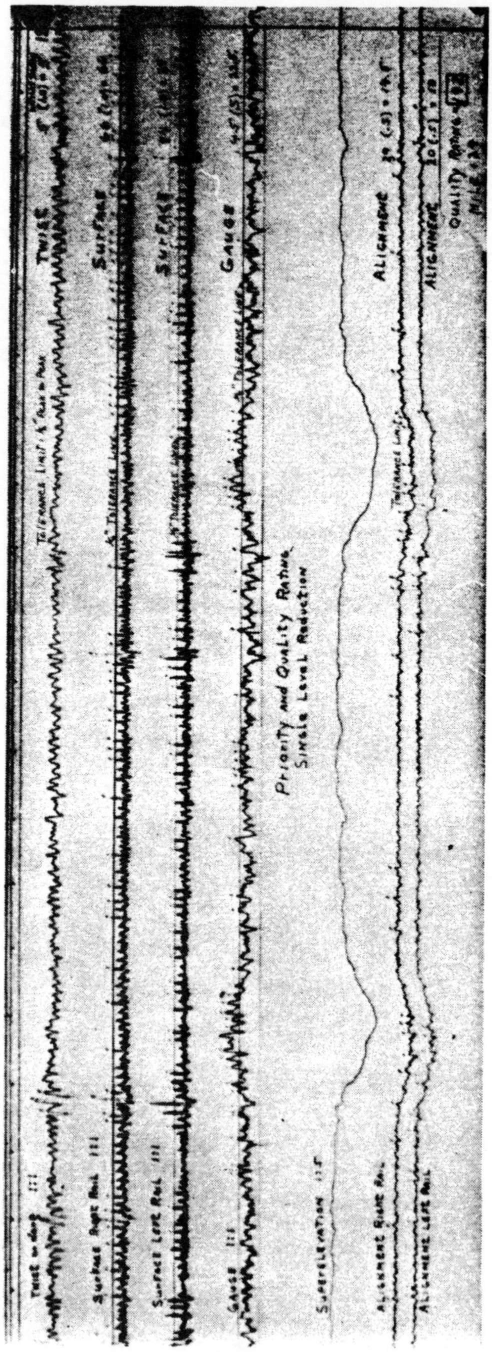
TWIST
SURFACE
SURFACE
GAUGE
Priority and Quality Rating
Single Level Reduction
SUPERELEVATION
ALIGNMENT
ALIGNMENT

Fig. 2

Fig. 2A

Fig. 3

1. Detect any condition which requires immediate attention to insure safe operation. This would be termed a "priority defect" and would be corrected as soon as possible.
2. Establish a numerical rating which would afford a comparison of the relative quality of each mile segment of track on the system. This number would be termed "P & Q Rating" and would be used for long-range scheduling of track maintenance.

In essence, the "priority defect" detection would be a safeguard to train operation, and would have precedence over any maintenance work scheduled. In order to expedite the correction of priority defects, the division engineer is present for the track inspection test, and notes the defects as they are recorded. On the other hand, the "P & Q Rating" would provide a statistical basis for programming track maintenance, comparing quality levels of division and making long-range studies of track behavior, and provide additional quality control of T & S Work. Certainly, management expects the "P & Q Rating" for a segment of track to improve significantly after surfacing work has been performed. Semi-annual, or annual checks on the "P & Q Rating" of the segment of track will also provide valuable insight toward correlating track deterioration with ton-miles or traffic density. In the final analysis, we will know more about our maintenance techniques and maintenance expenditures.

PRIORITY DEFECT LIMITS

Twist .... 1 inch peak to peak or 3 consecutive ¾ inch low joints.

Surface .... 1 inch low

Gage .... 1 inch open
¼ inch tight

Superelevation .... Maximum 1 inch change in 30 ft

Alignment .... 4° maximum change in 59.5 ft

P & Q RATING METHOD

The basic method of computing "P & Q Rating" includes assigning three level tolerance limits to each channel, and summating the tolerance deviations at each level for a mile segment of track. In order to stress magnitude as well as frequency of track irregularities, tolerance levels are exponentially weighted in parameter analysis.

TOLERANCE LEVEL WEIGHTING

.... level 3 weight factor 4
.... level 2 weight factor 2
.... level 1 weight factor 1
.... parameter zero line

In like manner, the individual parameter ratings are weighted in proportion to their bearing on ride quality, and summated to arrive at the "P & Q Rating" for the mile track segment.

The tolerance levels and weight factors were selected after combining much of the knowledge and research available on track measurement from European and American railroads and technical institutions.

The following table lists the tolerance limits and the parameter weight factors presently used in computing the "P & Q Rating."

Parameter Weight Factor	Parameter	Tolerance Limits	Level Weight Factor
20%	Twist	½″ peak to peak	1
		¾″ peak to peak	2
		1″ peak to peak	4
40%	Surface	¼″ low	1
		½″ low	2
		1″ low	4
20%	Gage	½″ open	1
		¾″ open	2
		1″ open	4
20%	Alignment	.15″ tangent	1
		.25″ tangent	2
		.4″ tangent	4

You will note that level 3 tolerance limits are the priority defect limits for each parameter.

DATA PROCESSING

In order to facilitate the interpretation of recorded data the decision was made to process the data in real time with an on-board digital computer. Since the original track recording equipment was a straight mechanical system, we had to adapt a mechanical to electrical interface and condition input signals for computer operation. More than six months were consumed constructing a mechanical to electrical interface, writing a program, and making actual test runs with a leased computer. The computer functioned properly in the rail car environment and the overall test was a success. Based on the results of the prototype system, we have placed an order for a computer to be used full-time on the car. Under the present computer program, track is sampled every 5 inches with a top operating speed of 80 mph. Priority defects are printed out as they occur and the defect marked in track by means of a paint sprayer located on the inspection car underframe and automatically controlled by the computer. "P & Q Ratings" are continuously tabulated and printed out at the end of each mile segment. The processor is cleared by the manual introduction of a milepost mark and the processing function restarted.

The computer printout (Fig. 4) lists the division and test date with all defects identified as to parameter, magnitude, and track location within 1/1000 mile.

PROGRAM OUTPUTS

The major benefits realized from the inspection program are in the form of reports to management summarizing the inspection results from each division, and in turn analyzing the results on a system basis. These reports include:

1. *List of All Priority Defects within a Division*
   This is taken from the computer printout and reported to the chief engineer for permanent record. The local division engineer receives the list at

```
SOUTHERN RAILWAY SYSTEM                    PAGE 001
TRACK INSPECTION DATA
SEGMENT CODE...I.4......
DIVISION..Knoxville.....
DATE..Oct.14......,19.69
```

A3=PRIORITY DEFECT, TWIST (1 IN.)

B3=PRIORITY DEFECT, SURFACE..EAST......RAIL (1 IN. LOW)

C3=PRIORITY DEFECT, SURFACE...West......RAIL (1 IN. LOW)

D3=PRIORITY DEFECT, GAGE (1 IN. OPEN)

E3=PRIORITY DEFECT, SUPERELEVATION

F3=PRIORITY DEFECT, ALIGNMENT..EAST......RAIL

G3=PRIORITY DEFECT, ALIGNMENT...West......RAIL

```
MP   0013.031           A3=1.772 IN.

MP   0013.961           D3=1.375 IN.

MP   0014       A1=0015,A2=0006,B1=0006,B2=0018,C1=0015,C2=0009,D1=0024,
                D2=0036,F1=0014,F2=0024,G1=0016,G2=0018,PQ=212

MP   0014.216           B3=2.010 IN.

MP   0014.571           F3=0.401 IN.

MP   0015       A1=0012,A2=0003,B1=0006,B2=0012,C1=0010,C2=0008,D1=0022,
                D2=0042,F1=0016,F2=0026,G1=0016,G2=0020,PQ=195
```

Fig. 4—Computer printout.

the time of inspection in order that he can proceed immediately with correcting the priority defects. Repetitive tests of divisions (quarterly) or comparative results between divisions, provide a statistical check for trends in priority defects. This information often guides the scheduling of major mainten.nce work.

2. *Graphical Displays of "P & Q Ratings" (Figs. 5 and 6)*

Such displays are generated on a division and territory basis to provide a comparison of overall track quality. The graphs provide a statistical analysis which aids management in planning T & S Work. Experience with our track rating index shows the best jointed rail will carry a "P & Q Rating" not exceeding 75. The best welded rail will have a rating less than 40.

CAR ROCKING PREDICTION

We on the Southern just as other railroads, know the problem of car rocking is real and demanding of correction. We feel the best solution lies in combatting the major cause of car rocking, which is vertical irregularities in track. Although we cannot afford the obvious solution of immediately laying our entire system with welded rail, we have had much success in policing selected sections of track with special tests designed to isolate and correct problem spots where rocking occurs. To this end we have been towing a loaded coal car at the critical speed of 18 mph, monitoring the lateral motion with a roll gyro, in order to protect the daily operation of 5 unit coal trains. These tests are made monthly, and resulted in the virtual elimination of derailments accountable to rocking on our unit coal train routes.

Since this task is slow and somewhat a problem to operations, we are currently engaged in a research project to enable the predictions of car rocking based on the measurements obtained from the track inspection car. The objective is to predict the critical speed rocking level without towing the car, while recording at speeds up to 80 mph. This basically entails constructing a mathematical model of a freight car and computing the roll action from the measured track inputs.

As a second approach, we have contracted with a research organization to design a similar roll prediction system which uses accelerometer inputs rather than track inspection car data as a basis for predicting roll. The advantage of this approach is that rocking tests could be run independent of the track inspection car. This equipment would basically consist of two axle-mounted accelerometers and a small analog computer package, and could be housed on any passenger car or office car.

We feel the roll angle data are important tools to the track maintenance officers, in that a dangerous condition can often be corrected at little expense and time. Since roll is affected by both magnitude and spacing of low joints, it is difficult to visually observe many locations which results in car rocking.

CONCLUSIONS

Since the outset of our track inspection program, our objective has been a utilitarian one. The program, as for any applied research program, could only be considered successful if: 1) it directly benefits the maintenance forces, and 2) the overall quality of our track is improved. The car does not negate the importance of track maintenance personnel, but rather places greater emphasis on their role.

Only these men can implement the maintenance procedures. Through applied research our objective was to provide a rapid inspection technique, an accurate picture of track quality, and a well defined list of track irregularities.

This type of information is vital to efficient track maintenance on a system basis. Management needs the data for planning and funding maintenance dollars; maintenance personnel need the information to evaluate track quality and expedite repairs.

982

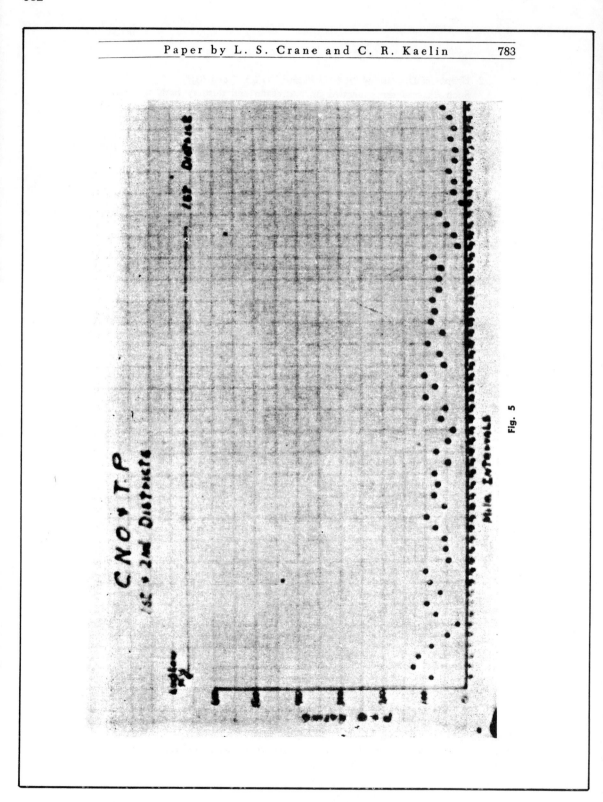

Fig. 5

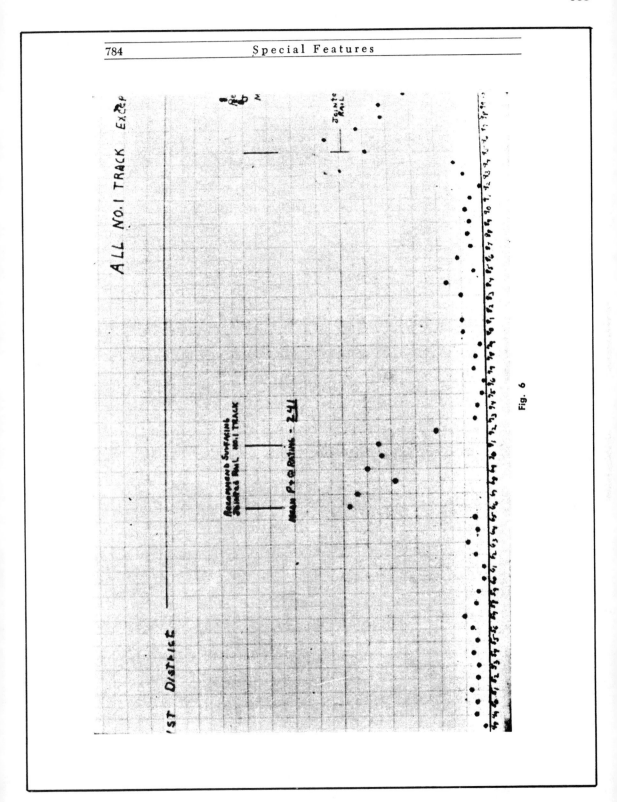

Fig. 6

While we are proud of our progress to date, the demands are greater than ever for the upgrading of the track structure and maintenance techniques. We have planned extensive tests for evaluating heavy-duty rail fasteners, concrete tie designs, and maintenance practices in 1970. The track inspection vehicle will play a vital role in monitoring the lateral and vertical stability of the test sections and effecting a relative comparison with control sections of conventional track. Through this qualitative assessment, we hope to identify and expedite structural requirements for a safe and efficient maintenance program.

PART III:

Special Features

Canadian National Recorder Car

By R. G. MAUGHAN
Assistant Chief Engineer—Maintenance
Canadian National Railways

In the time at my disposal, I would like to deal with two aspects of the total subject under discussion. Firstly, I will attempt to give you a general understanding of how the Canadian National car works. Secondly, and I suspect, of much greater interest to this group, I would like to speak about the form in which the data is produced by our car, and how we are using it.

First then, a few words on how the CN car works. As is obvious from Fig. 1, our car is a converted passenger coach and is suitably bi-lingual. It includes two bedrooms, kitchen, dining area, small workshop, observation area and instrument area. Fig. 1 is a view looking towards the front of the car; some of the recording instruments can be seen on the left. This is looking towards the observation deck at the rear. The second to last right side window is a bay to facilitate observation of mile posts and is equipped with a signal to mark them on the data sheets.

Fig. 2 is a view of the instrument area. The conversion of the car itself, the design of the measurement techniques, and installation of the equipment and instrumentation were all accomplished by CN personnel.

As much as we might like to think otherwise, no track is ever "perfect," but one basis for determining track quality is to compare its *actual* condition with the theoretical perfect condition.

The CN Track Recorder Car has been designed on that basis. Besides recording in graphical form the actual parameter being measured, it also compares that actual against perfection, and records the difference in the form of an index number.

As we are all aware, *surface roughness* is one of the important parameters influencing total track quality, and it is convenient to use this parameter to explain more fully how the CN car works. First though, it will be helpful to spend a moment or so to clarify what we mean by surface roughness.

Fig. 1—Exterior view of CN car.

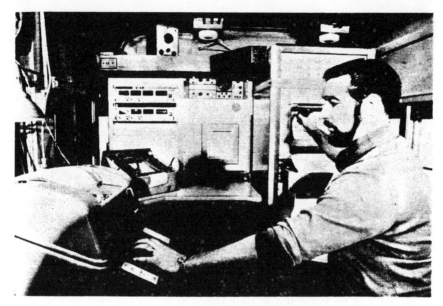

Fig. 2—Instrument panel.

Any irregularity in track surface is either a rise or a fall. Suppose, for the sake of simplicity, that the track profile takes the shape of a saw tooth, as shown in Fig. 3.

Because the changes in elevation of the track occur within relatively short horizontal distances, the wheel of the vehicle passing over such a profile would impart sharp forces to the vehicle body. On the other hand, if the same changes in elevation occurred in say ten times the horizontal distance shown, those same changes in elevation would impart greatly reduced forces to the vehicle body. Thus, from the standpoint of vehicle ride and therefore also from the track maintainer's viewpoint, it is the steepness of the slope at which the track rises or falls which is important.

For this reason, on the car a gradual rise in track elevation is filtered out by the equipment, but a sharp rise is measured and recorded. Since a sharp upward movement is just as harmful as a sharp downward movement, all slopes are averaged without reference to sign, and the average slope (either upward or downward) of the track over the distance being measured is its surface roughness index. These distances are usually quarter-mile lengths of track. Perhaps this shows more clearly in Fig. 4.

Thus, the index number for surface roughness is a measure of the average slope, up or down, of the rail over the distance measured. In fact, if the index number is 330, for example, the average slope of the irregularities would be equivalent to a 0.33% grade. The index number therefore has a real physical significance and relates directly to the track surface.

Now, how does the car succeed in making this measurement? The car measures surface irregularities as seen by a loaded wheel passing at varying operating speeds

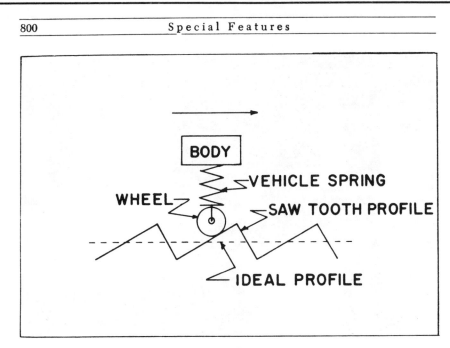

Fig. 3.

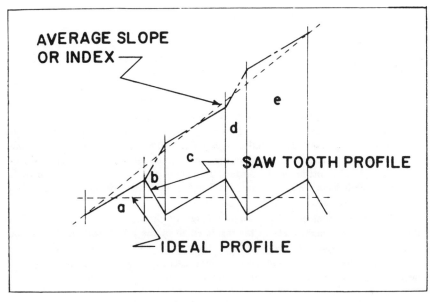

Fig. 4.

988

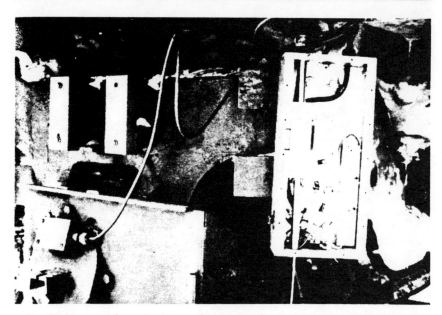

Fig. 5—Instrument box, showing accelerometer and transducer mounted on unsprung portion of car truck.

over the track. The process commences with an instrument box mounted on the side frame of the truck. By means of an accelerometer inside the box and a velocity probe connected between the side frame and the journal box, the vertical movement of the side frame as the car moves over the track is established. Fig. 5 shows the instrument box in place as just described. This permits measurement of the rail profile that the wheel of the loaded car sees as it passes over the track. These measurements are sent as an electrical signal to the processing unit within the car. The surface roughness measurements for each rail are averaged to give the surface roughness index for that quarter mile of track.

These same measurements are differenced to give the crosslevel error index for the same piece of track. These index numbers are computed and printed out immediately a section is traversed. At the same time a trace of the actual profile is made and a plot is also made of the surface roughness and crosslevel error indices for the whole subdivision. In a few moments I will go into more detail concerning these outputs and their use.

The measurement of gage is done by magnetic probes which are located a fixed distance apart and slightly above the inside edges of the rail. However, the methods of processing the data are very similar to those described for surface roughness.

I would like to point out that all measurements are made with non-contact devices, and this permits us to operate the car at speeds up to 100 mph, over switches and crossings, without taking any special precautions. Also it has the advantage of eliminating the problem of wear associated with contact devices, thereby simplifying the maintenance of the equipment and increasing its utilization.

802   Special Features

I hope that from the preceding very brief and non-technical outline, you have gained an appreciation of the basic principles behind the design of the CN Recorder Car, and I would like to move on now to speak about the use of the data which it produces. Again here, because of limited time, I will confine myself to discussion only of surface roughness.

Regardless of the parameter under discussion, we feel that data produced by the car must be in a form so that they are *immediately* useful to the track engineer, and must not require time-consuming interpretation to make them so. Furthermore, we want them to serve *all* requirements, and they must therefore fill the following needs:

1. To identify and locate, to the area forces, track conditions which require immediate corrective action.
2. To assist the area and regional engineering officers in intelligently planning short-range preventive and corrective work programs.
3. To assist system and regional engineering officers in planning long-range work programs and in making decisions relative to work priorities, work cycles and work methods through analysis of data to determine quality and rate of deterioration of work done by different methods or types of machines.

To permit this, the data are produced in several different ways.

In connection with surface roughness, the first of these is the teletype digital print-out of Index Numbers for longitudinal surface roughness and crosslevel for each quarter-mile section of track.

Fig. 6 is a close-up view of the teletype machine which produces the digital print-out, and Fig. 7 is a copy of a portion of the print-out of surface roughness and

Fig. 6—Teletype machine.

SAMPLE OF
<u>PRINT OUT</u>

<u>ENGINEERING TRACK RECORDER CAR</u>

GREAT LAKES REGION
SOUTHWESTERN ONTARIO AREA
OAKVILLE SUBDIVISION

WESTWARD 1/4 MILE SAMPLES - NOV. 16/69

SR (Surface) (Roughness)	CL (Cross) (Level)	SP (Speed)	Mile
			3
196	174	058	
191	163	058	
182	176	060	
183	167	060	
			4
176	181	063	
163	156	063	
191	151	066	
208	180	066	
			5
196	160	065	
205	161	066	
224	171	067	
208	150	067	
			6
288	260	067	
264	206	067	
209	163	068	
211	175	067	

Fig. 7—Typical print-out of surface roughness and cross level index numbers.

crosslevel indices for the Oakville Subdivision, westward track, as measured on November 16, 1969.

As may be seen, the surface and crosslevel readings are printed out four times for each mile. The data in line 1 for example, are the average readings between Miles 3.0 and 3.25.

The second form in which these surface roughness data are produced is referred to as the Dynamic Rail Profile. This is a continuous chart record of the profile of the top of each rail under dynamic load, produced to a horizontal scale of approximately 1 mile equals 15 inches, and to full scale vertically. Fig. 8 shows the 8-channel pen recorder on the car which produces the profile instantaneously.

The output from this instrument is illustrated in Figs. 9, 10 and 11. Fig. 9 shows a small portion of the data from a run made in November 1967 on our Thompson Subdivision, which is a branch line in northern Manitoba. As you can see, at that time the rail was old 80 lb and the ballast was pit run, which results in just about the kind of track (as far as surface is concerned), as might be expected. The vertical scale is shown by the dimension of 1 inch at the left of the slide. The lower trace of the profile is merely a continuation of the upper trace to enable a longer portion of the track to be shown. As you can see from the horizontal dimension of 39 ft shown in the upper left hand corner, the actual rail joints can be located on the trace. Some of the joints here were pretty bad under dynamic load and the track here has a surface roughness index of 550 and a crosslevel index of 550 also. Fig. 10 is somewhat better track—a portion of our Alderdale Subdivision in northern Ontario. Here the rail is 100 lb bolted, but ballast at the time of this run—November 1967—was still pit run. The track, as you can see from the trace, is obviously better than that shown on the previous slide. In fact, the surface roughness index was 305 at the time of this run, and the crosslevel index 328, which is quite acceptable track.

Fig. 11 shows part of a run, also made in November 1967, on our Rivers Subdivision, which is part of our transcontinental main route in the more southerly part of Manitoba. The rail at that time was only 4 years old and was 115 lb continuous welded and the ballast crushed rock. This is very good track, as confirmed both by the trace and the surface roughness index of 180.

A copy of the Continuous Dynamic Rail Profile and of the digital print-out is given to the supervisor as he leaves the car at the end of his territory, and with this information he is able to take immediate action to correct rough spots where necessary. This satisfies the first of the needs defined earlier, that is "to identify and locate for the area forces, track conditions which require immediate corrective action."

The second need, you will recall, was defined as "assist the area and regional engineering officers in intelligently planning short-range preventive and corrective work programs." For this purpose, the same output data are produced in a third different form. We call this form the "Mini-Chart" in keeping with today's vocabulary, developed to describe abbreviated items of interest. The "Mini-Chart" is a continuous plot of the index numbers for Surface Roughness and Crosslevel, and is also produced instantaneously on board the car.

As background to discussion of this form of the data it will help to look again at Fig. 7 showing the sample of the print-out from the Oakville Subdivision. As you can see, it tends to be a somewhat "Gee-Whiz" form of the data, especially when you find that you have a 5- or 6-ft length of paper filled with these numbers for every 100 miles of track.

992

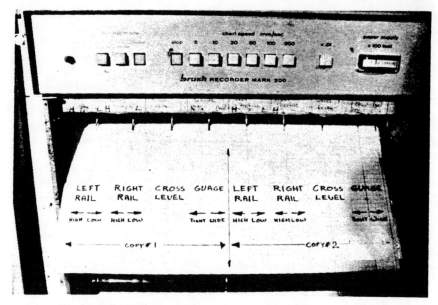

Fig. 8—Eight-channel pen recorder for producing Dynamic Rail Profile.

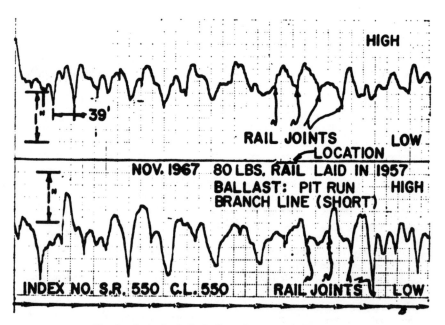

Fig. 9—Dynamic Rail Profile—Thompson Subdivision.

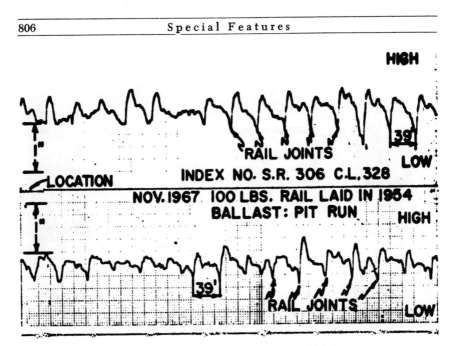

Fig. 10—Dynamic Rail Profile—Alderdale Subdivision.

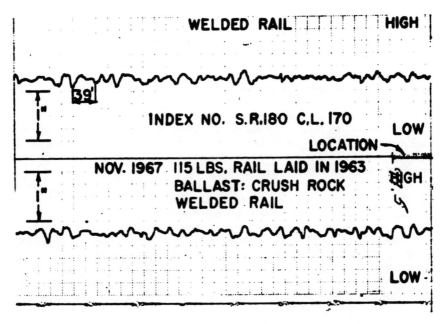

Fig. 11—Dynamic Rail Profile—Rivers Subdivision.

994

Fig. 12—Recorder for producing plot of surface roughness and cross level index numbers.

To make it more useful, our R. & D. were able to come up with a device which automatically plots the Surface Roughness and Crosslevel index number as they are produced on the car. Fig. 12 shows the recorder on the instrument panel which produces that plot and Fig. 13 shows a sample of that automatic plot. As I said, we call it the "Mini-Chart."

Despite the most vigorous attempts, we have not been able to produce a fully complete chart on board the car. The best we have been able to accomplish is the automatic *plotting* of the index numbers. To complete the chart, the plotted points must be joined by hand and appropriate identification added. However, the chart as it is produced by the car is given to the regional engineer's representative if he is on-board, or mailed to him if he is not. The finishing touches are made in the regional engineer's office and prints are made there and sent to the appropriate area engineer and to the system chief engineer.

You are looking at a portion of a completed chart, that is, the dots plotted by the recorder have been connected to show a continuous graph of the surface roughness and crosslevel indices. The appropriate labels have been added to assist in your interpretation, from which you can see that the lower graph is the surface roughness and the upper graph is the crosslevel. The scale is perhaps a little difficult to grasp. Horizontally, the distance between two of the heavy vertical lines represents 1⅓ miles. Thus, the portion of the chart on this slide covers about 30 miles.

There are two vertical scales, one for surface roughness and one for crosslevel. Zero for surface roughness is at the bottom of the chart; the first heavy horizontal line is an index of 100, the second heavy horizontal line is an index of 200, the third 300, and so on. Thus, the surface roughness here varies from approximately 300 on the left to approximately 200 on the right.

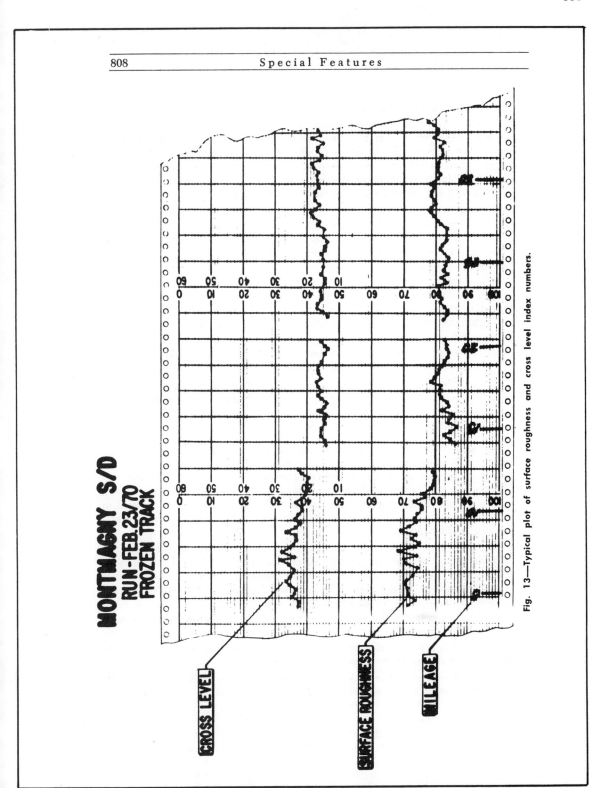

Fig. 13—Typical plot of surface roughness and cross level index numbers.

MONTMAGNY S/D
RUN–FEB.23/70
FROZEN TRACK

CROSS LEVEL

SURFACE ROUGHNESS

MILEAGE

For crosslevel, zero is the fourth horizontal line from the bottom which has been shaded to make it easier to pick out. Thus, the index number for the crosslevel plotted here is between 200 and 300 on the left and just under 200 on the right. This is fairly good track, although I must admit the run was made just last month at which time, of course, the track was frozen. This is the first year we have made extensive measurements during winter conditions and we are not yet sure how much difference there is between track quality when the track is frozen compared to not frozen. Roughly though, it seems that when the track is frozen, the index numbers are about 50 lower than for the same track when not frozen.

Examination of the completed "Mini-Chart" and comparison with charts made on previous runs of the car reveals to regional and area engineering officers variations in track quality resulting from work done between runs. It also enables them to observe if the track is deteriorating, and if so, to plan remedial spot or out-of-face surfacing. Furthermore, by comparison of charts, for different territories on his region, the regional engineer is able to gain a better understanding of relative needs and thereby do a better job of the establishment of regional priorities. With the identical information available also at system level, intelligent discussion of allocation of resources between the two administrative levels is possible.

Even this plot, however, does not present the data in quite the form required to facilitate answering many of the questions relative to longer term planning. This, you will recall, was stated in the third requirement as:

> "to assist system and regional engineering officers in planning long range work programs and making decisions relative to work priorities, work cycles and work methods through analysis of data to determine quality and rate of deterioration of work done by different methods or types of machines."

Meaningful comparison of a subdivision "before" and "after" certain work has been done is more than merely observing that the "after" profile is somewhat lower than the "before" profile. Some method of determining a percentage improvement is required to permit intelligent decisions regarding the real value of the work done; or to compare the output quality of two different machines each designed to do the same job; or to measure deterioration of track quality over a prolonged period by taking readings at regular intervals.

Well, we think we have the answer to that too. It consists of producing, on board the car, on an 8-level perforated tape, the record of S.R. and C.L. index numbers. This tape is subsequently fed into a computer at the R. & D. Research Center for automatic analysis. Depending on the program which is written, we can now produce the data in almost any form we wish.

Fig. 14 shows the format of the data produced by the computer on the basis of the present program.

I regret this is a trifle difficult to read. However, in order to explain the significance it was necessary to reproduce the entire sheet.

This is a copy of a sheet taken directly from the computer and is an analysis of the surface roughness index numbers for our Kingston Subdivision, between Miles 11 and 299 recorded on 5 September, 1969.

Included on the 8-level perforated tape which was the input data to the computer, was the information that the standard for this subdivision is a low limit of 200 and a high limit of 275. The computer repeats this information, and as you

KINGSTON SUB. A.S.   MILE 11-290
5 SEPTEMBER 1969
SURFACE ROUGHNESS
•
            DISTRIBUTION CURVE (HYSTOGRAM) OF TRACK INDEX NUMBERS

LOW LIMIT   : 290
HIGH LIMIT : 275

SMALLEST INDEX: 173   UNDER LOW LIMIT: 29
LARGEST INDEX: 635   OVER HIGH LIMIT: 643

AVERAGE VALUE : 297.   TOTAL 1/4 MILE : 1000
STD. DEVIATION: 65.

                        % OF OCCURRENCES

OC   %   CUM   0   5   10   15   18
                     •---•

 0   .0   0   10   •
 0   .0   0   11   •
 0   .0   0   12   •
 0   .0   0   13   •
 0   .0   0   14   •
 0   .0   0   15   •
 0   .0   0   16   •
 6   .6   0   17   ++•
 9   .9   1   18   +++•
 5   .5   2   19   ++•
26 2.6   4   20   ---------•
32 3.2   7   21   -----------•
23 2.3   10   22   --------•
28 2.8   12   23   ---------•
42 4.2   17   24   -------------•
65 6.5   23   25   ---------------------•
72 7.2   30   26   ------------------------•
91 9.1   39   27   ++++++++++++++++++++++++++++•
115 11.5 51   28   +++++++++++++++++++++++++++++++++++++•
117 11.7 63   29   +++++++++++++++++++++++++++++++++++++•
89 8.9   71   30   +++++++++++++++++++++++++++•
60 6.0   77   31   ++++++++++++++++++•
47 4.7   81   32   ++++++++++++++•
28 2.8   84   33   +++++++++•
21 2.1   86   34   ++++++•
22 2.2   88   35   +++++++•
22 2.2   91   36   +++++++•
14 1.4   92   37   ++++•
 9   .9   93   38   +++•
 9   .9   94   39   +++•
 8   .8   95   40   ++•
 4   .4   95   41   +•
 2   .2   95   42   +•
 3   .3   95   43   +•
 4   .4   96   44   +•
 2   .2   96   45   +•
 4   .4   96   46   +•
 4   .4   97   47   +•
 4   .4   97   48   +•
 2   .2   97   49   +•
 2   .2   98   50   +•
 0   .0   98   51   •
 0   .0   98   52   •

Fig. 14—Typical computer print-out of distribution curve (hystogram)
                    for surface roughness.

998

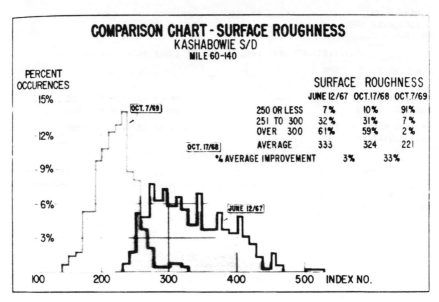

Fig. 15.

can see, also tells us that the smallest index found in that run was 173 and the largest 635. It also tells us that the average index for the entire 290 miles was 297 and that the standard deviation was 65. Furthermore, on the right hand side of the sheet, it tells us that there were 20 readings less than the minimum standard and 643 in excess of the maximum. Thus, insofar as surface roughness is considered, approximately 65% of the track is somewhat below standard.

The vertical columns on the left hand side of the sheet are the details of the number of occurrences and the fourth column from the left is a listing of index numbers starting at 100 at the top increasing to 520 at the bottom. For example, then, one can see that there were 6 occurrences with an index number of 170, 9 occurrences with an index number of 180 and so on. The occurrences of index numbers in steps of tens are plotted as a percentage of the total occurrences, and the resulting shape is the distribution curve or hystogram of the surface roughness index numbers.

Many uses can be made of these data, and very quickly and easily. Change in track quality can be readily observed merely by placing the sheets produced from data from consecutive runs side by side. Comparative movement of the center of gravity of the hystogram towards the top of the sheet means that the track has improved and movement downward means it has worsened. To illustrate this, Fig. 15 shows a manual plotting of the results from three separate runs on our Kashabowie Subdivision superimposed on one another. One outline is from a 1967 run and the shaded outline is from a 1968 run. There is very little difference in these two. However, the outline which is a plot of the 1969 run shows a significant improvement. This is further illustrated by the tabulations on the right which shows that the actual improvement in 1969 over 1968 was 33%.

RAIL GRINDING PROGRAM 1969

NAPADOGAN   SUBDIVISION
M. 16.88-31.84; 38.67-58.0; 115.0-127.57
155.76-160.71; 195.21-215.0

(71.60 MILES)

AVERAGE S.R. INDEX BEFORE GRINDING 217
AVERAGE S.R. INDEX AFTER GRINDING 203

AVERAGE IMPROVEMENT IN S.R. INDEX 6.4%

Fig. 16.

SURFACING PROGRAM   1969

NAPADOGAN SUBDIVISION
M. 59.09-87; 92-97; 106-109

(35.91 MILES)

AVERAGE S.R. INDEX BEFORE SURFACING 293
AVERAGE S.R. INDEX AFTER SURFACING 237

AVERAGE IMPROVEMENT IN S.R. INDEX 19%

Fig. 17.

Now as I said a moment ago, it is not necessary to plot these data as has been done here for illustration purposes. Very rapid comparison can be made by merely placing two sheets taken directly from the computer side by side. Somewhat more detailed analysis can be made by simple arithmetic using data from these output sheets. For example, Fig. 16 shows a comparison on the Napadogan Subdivision before and after rail grinding in 1969—an improvement of approximately 6 percent. The data on Fig. 17, also from the Napadogan Subdivision, is an example of the type of improvement achieved through a surfacing program. Similar comparisons can be made quickly following any work, and from them meaningful judgments can be made regarding benefits related to cost, comparative output of machinery or gangs or other factors of significance. Through this type of comparison of data obtained from runs of the car made in succeeding years, the rate of track quality deterioration can be established with consequent benefit to long-term planning and machinery evaluation procedures.

Well, that about concludes my presentation. I would like to close with this brief comment.

Throughout the railway industry we are faced with the tremendous, and I think, exciting challenge to continue to find ways and means to neutralize the alarming effects of continuing significant increases in labor and material costs.

Of all of the elements that go to make up the total roadway plant on our railways—bridges, culverts, buildings, signals, road crossings, etc., etc., track is far and away the most critical insofar as cost of maintenance and replacement is concerned. Up until now, our ability to successfully measure its condition across our many thousands of miles to establish meaningful long and short term plans, to improve our work methods and our standards, has been limited, and that limitation has been costing the industry money in many ways—non-essential work being done, essential work left undone, poor quality work unknowingly accepted, and in many other ways.

Through the Track Recorder Car we now have within our grasp an instrument to materially assist us in overcoming these liabilities and to achieve significant production improvement and cost reductions. We should use it.